W9-BSO-194

Population Density
Persons per Square Mile

Under 5
5 to 100
101 to 250
Over 250

Archangel

Dvina R.

L. Onega

Moscow

Kuibyshev

Smolensk

Uralsk

Volga R.

Saratov

Ural R.

Kursk

KAZAK S.S.R.

ARAL SEA

Volgograd
(Stalingrad)

Astrakhan

UZBEK S.S.R.

S O V I E T   U N I O N

Kiev

Kharkov

Don R.

UKRAINIAN S.S.R.

Dnepropetrovsk

Rostov

TURKMEN S.S.R.

AFGHANISTAN

LDAVIAN
S.S.R.

Dnieper R.

SEA OF
AZOV

C A U C A S I A

Grozny

CASPIAN SEA

Krasnovodsk

BIA

Odessa

CRIMEA

GEORGIAN
S.S.R.

Tiflis

AZERBAIJAN
S.S.R.

Baku

Sevastopol

Batum

ARMENIAN
S.S.R.

DOBRUJA

BLACK SEA

Ardahan

Yerevan

Varna

Sinop

Kars

Tabriz

Teheran

L. Van

L. Urmia

I R A N

Bosporus

Istanbul

Ankara

T   U   R   K   E   Y

Isfahan

Izmir

Tigris R.

Kirkuk

ardanelles

Adalia

Adana

Aleppo

Baghdad

Euphrates R.

SYRIA

I R A Q

Abadan

CYPRUS

Basra

Bushire

RETE (Greece)

Beirut

Damascus

KUWAIT

P E R S I A N   G U L F

LEBANON

GOLAN
HEIGHTS

Occupied by Israel

ISRAEL

WEST BANK

UNITED ARAB

Tel Aviv-Jaffa

Amman

BAHRAIN

EMIRATES

Jerusalem

Gaza

QATAR

OMAN

Alexandria

NILE DELTA

JORDAN

El Alamein

Nile R.

Suez Canal

SINAI
PENINSULA

Aqaba

S A U D I   A R A B I A

Cairo

GULF OF SUEZ

GULF OF AQABA

EGYPT

A History
of
the
Modern
World

sixth edition

A History
of
the
Modern
World

WITHDRAWN

R. R. PALMER
JOEL COLTON

Alfred A. Knopf
New York

THIS IS A BORZOI BOOK PUBLISHED BY ALFRED A. KNOPF, INC.

Copyright 1950, © 1956, 1965, 1971, 1978, 1984 by Alfred A. Knopf, Inc.

Library of Congress Cataloging in Publication Data

Palmer, Robert Roswell, 1909–
    A history of the modern world.

    Bibliography: p.
    Includes index.
    1. History, Modern.   I.   Colton, Joel G., 1918–
joint author.   II.   Title.
D209.P26   1984   909.08   83–47988
ISBN 0–394–33596–1 text
ISBN 0–394–53396–8

Published July 24, 1950. Reprinted seven times.

Second edition, revised, reset, and printed from new plates, with new maps, 1956. Reprinted fourteen times.

Third edition, revised, with new maps, 1965. Reprinted five times.

Fourth edition, revised, reset, and printed from new plates, with new maps and illustrations, 1971. Reprinted five times.

Fifth edition, revised, reset, and printed from new plates, with new maps and illustrations, 1978. Reprinted seven times.

Sixth edition, revised, reset, and printed from new plates, with new maps and illustrations, 1983.

Sixth Edition
9876

ACKNOWLEDGMENT IS HEREBY MADE FOR PERMISSION TO QUOTE FROM THE FOLLOWING WORKS:

The World's Food: A Study of the Interrelations of World Populations, National Diets and Food Potentials, by M. K. Bennett, 1954. Reprinted by permission of Harper & Row.

World Population, by A. N. Carr-Saunders. Clarendon Press, Oxford (1936).

British Economic Growth, 1688–1959: Trends and Structure, by Phyllis Deane and W. A. Cole (1962). Reprinted by permission of Cambridge University Press.

"The White Man's Burden" from The Five Nations by Rudyard Kipling. Reprinted by permission of The National Trust and Doubleday & Company, Inc.

European Historical Statistics: 1750–1970, by B. R. Mitchell, pp. 316 and 396. Copyright © 1975 by Columbia University Press.

Design: Levavi & Levavi

Manufactured in the United States of America by Kingsport Press, Kingsport, TN.

Preface

Once again we take pleasure in offering a new edition, now the sixth, of a work that continues to be well received. In structure, content, and coverage *A History of the Modern World* remains very much what it was in the fifth edition. Both of us, however, have carefully worked together over the whole volume in another effort to make it more useful and attractive.

The new features include a short geographical introduction, a new section on popular culture, more references to the role of women, a few revisions in treatment of the Enlightenment, more attention to Latin American independence, a new picture essay, and numerous smaller alterations in many places. Some of these changes are in response to comments made by readers, who may perhaps agree that the scale of the book, large as it is, allows too little to be said on many topics. The two concluding chapters on the years since the Second World War are as usual the most thoroughly revised, and have been brought abreast of contemporary developments. The bibliography has always been a special feature of the book. It has been reviewed and pruned but remains extensive; it has also been brought up to date and now may contain as many as four thousand titles, classified by subject according to the plan of the book as a whole. In general, we have done what we could to make so long and complex a volume more manageable and digestible. The whole structure of chapters, sections and subsections, the frequent cross-references, the chronological tables, and the detailed index are intended for this purpose. A student's Study Guide is also available for those who may wish to use it.

Since its first edition the book has been designed to set forth the modern history of Europe and European civilization as a unit, and in its later chapters it attempts to tell the story of an integrated, or at least interconnected, world. Emphasis falls on situations and movements of international scope, or on what Europeans and their descendants have done and faced in common. National histories are therefore somewhat subordinated, and in each national history the points of contact with a larger civilization are treated most fully. Historic regional differences within Europe, as between eastern and western Europe, are brought out, and the history of the Americas is woven into the story at various points, as are developments of the last century in Asia and Africa. A good deal of institutional history is included. Considerable space is given to the history of ideas, not only in special sections devoted to ideas, but throughout the book in close connection with the account of institutions and events. Social and economic development bulks rather large, as does the impact of wars and revolutions. Since our own age is one in which much depends on political decision, we think of this volume as political history in the broadest sense, in that matters of many kinds, such as religion, economics, social welfare, and international relations, have presented themselves as public questions requiring public action by responsible citizens or official persons. It seems to us that many subjects of current research interest, such as women's history, family history, the history of the laboring classes, the history of minorities, or demographic and quantitative studies, are best understood when seen within a wider framework such as this book attempts to provide.

We are again glad to thank all those who have helped with the book over the years, and in particular the half-dozen persons who have acted as consultants for this sixth edition. We are indebted to David Follmer, June Smith, and David Rothberg of Alfred A. Knopf, Inc., the former for his initiative in bringing this new edition into being, the latter two for their careful work on the manuscript. Since they have left the important decisions to us, and all the actual writing is ours, we assume all responsibility for errors, imperfections, questionable judgments, and other possible shortcomings. Esther Palmer and Shirley Colton have contributed in innumerable ways to the newest edition of this history, which can stand as some kind of continuing monument to marriage, friendship, and intellectual collaboration.

R. R. PALMER
JOEL COLTON

Contents

ILLUSTRATIONS

MAPS AND CHARTS

A History
of
the
Modern
World

A Few
Words on
Geography

istory is the experience of human beings in time, but it takes place also in space, on the planet Earth, so that geography always underlies it. It is the business of geography not merely to describe and map the earth and its various areas, but to study the changing relationships between human activities and the surrounding environment.

The earth is over four billion years old. The entire history of mankind since the Middle Stone Age has occupied less than a hundred-thousandth of the time in which the earthly habitat has been developed. Some minerals now put to human use were formed in the earliest ages of the planet, others such as coal and petroleum were not laid down until a few hundred million years ago, but none that are now being consumed in a flicker of geologic time can ever be replaced. Oceans and continents have moved about, changing in size, shape, and location with respect to one another and to the North and South Poles. There was a time when dinosaurs could walk from North America to Europe (as we now call them) on solid land in a warm climate. The continents as we now know them became fully distinct less than a hundred million years ago. It is only a few thousand years since the end of the most recent glacial age, which may not be the last. The melting back into the ocean of water frozen over a mile thick in Antarctica and in large parts of North America and Europe produced the coastlines, offshore islands, inland seas, straits, bays, and harbors that we see on a map today, as well as some of the largest river systems and lakes. It is only about three hundred years since the first French explorers saw Niagara Falls, which then looked quite different, because by eating away the underlying rock the falls have receded several hundred feet since that time.

3

At present, the oceans cover more than two-thirds of the surface of the globe. By no means is all the remaining third suited for occupation by human beings, or indeed by most other animal or vegetable organisms, for much of the land still lies under perpetual ice in Antarctica and Greenland, much is tundra, much is desert, and some is along the windswept ridges of high mountains. Like the oceans, these desolate regions have been important in human history, first in earlier times by acting as barriers. Man, as the anthropologists call him (and her), is now thought to have originated in Africa. He (and she) eventually spread to every continent except Antarctica. In doing so, human groups became isolated from each other for thousands of years, separated by oceans, deserts, or mountains, and so became differentiated into the modern races, though all are derived from the same source and belong to the same species. The same is true of cultures or civilizations over a time period measured in centuries rather than millennia. It is such separation that accounts for the historic cultural differences between Africa, pre-Columbian America, China, India, the Middle East, and Europe. On a smaller scale it explains the differences in languages and dialects.

Separation has also produced differences in flora and fauna, and hence in the plants and animals by which humans live. Wheat became the most usual cereal in the Middle East and Europe, millet and rice in East Asia, sorghum in tropical Africa, maize in pre-Columbian America. The horse, first domesticated in central Asia, was for centuries a mainstay of Europe for muscle power, transportation, and combat, while the less versatile camel was adopted later and more slowly in the Middle East, and America had no beasts of burden except the llama. Not until Europeans began to cross the oceans, taking plants and animals with them, and bringing others back, did these great differences begin to diminish.

The present book is concerned primarily with Europe, and with the last few hundred years. And as a traveler setting out on a journey may provide himself with a map, and carry its contents as much as possible in his head, so the reader is invited to examine the map of Europe on pages 6 and 7, and keep it in mind while reading the following history. The map shows the topographical features that have remained unchanged in historic times.

Europe is physically separated from Africa by the Mediterranean Sea, which however has been as much a passageway as a barrier. A more effective barrier was created when the Sahara Desert dried up only a few thousand years ago. The physical separation of Europe from Asia has always been less clear; the conventional boundary has long been the Ural Mountains in the Soviet Union, but the Soviet Union recognizes no such distinction. The Urals are in any case low and wide, and it can be argued that Europe is not a continent at all, but a cultural conception arising from felt differences from Asia and Africa. Europe, even with European Russia, contains hardly more than 6 percent of the land surface of the earth. It has about the same area as the United States including Alaska. It is a little larger than Australia, and a little smaller than Antarctica.

If we consider only its physical features Europe is indeed one of several peninsulas jutting off from Asia. It is altogether different, however, from the Arabian and Indian peninsulas, which also extend from the mass of Asia, as shown on the back endpaper of the present book. For one thing, the Mediterranean Sea is unique among the world's bodies of water. Closed in by the Strait of Gibraltar, which is only eight miles wide, it is more shielded than the Caribbean or East Asian seas from the open ocean. Hence it has very little tide, and is protected from the most violent ocean storms. Though over two thousand miles long, it is subdivided by islands and peninsulas into lesser seas with an identity of their own, such as the Aegean and the Adriatic, and it gives access also to the Black Sea. It is possible to travel for great distances without being far from land, so that navigation developed from early times, and one of the first civilizations appeared on the island of Crete. It is possible also to cross between Europe and Asia at the Bosporus and between Europe and Africa at Gibraltar, so that populations became mixed by early migrations, and various historic empires—Carthaginian, Roman, Byzantine, Arabic, Spanish, Venetian, and Turkish—have used the Mediterranean as an avenue between their component parts. After the Suez Canal was built the Mediterranean became a segment in the "lifeline of empire" for the British Empire in its heyday.

In southern Europe, north of the Mediterranean and running for its whole length, is a series of mountains, produced geologically by the pushing of the gigantic mass of Africa against this smaller Eurasian peninsula. The Pyrenees shut off Spain from the north, as the Alps do Italy; the Balkan Mountains have always been difficult to penetrate; and the only place where one can go at water level from the Mediterranean to the north is by the valley of the Rhone River, so that France, since it came together in the Middle Ages, is the only country that clearly belongs both to the Mediterranean and to northern Europe. North of the mountains is a great plain, with branches in England and Sweden, extending from western France through Germany and Poland into Russia and on into Asia, passing south of the Urals through what is called the Caspian Gate, north of the land-locked Caspian Sea. One might draw a straight line from Amsterdam eastward through the Caspian Gate as far as the borders of western China, and although this line would reach the distance from New York to a point five hundred miles west of San Francisco, one would never in traveling along it be higher above sea level than central Kansas. The continuity of this level plain has at various times opened Europe to Mongol and other invasions, enabled the Russians to move east and create a huge empire, and made Poland a troubled intermediary between Western Europe and what is now the Soviet Union.

The rivers as shown on the map are worth particular attention. Until quite recent times rivers offered an easier means of transportation than any form of carriage by land. The principal rivers also give access to the sea. Most are navigable, especially in the north European plains. With their valleys, whether in level country or confined between mountains, they provided areas where intensive local development could take place. Thus we see that some of the most important older cities of Europe are on rivers—London on the Thames, Paris on the Seine, Vienna and Budapest on the Danube, Warsaw on the Vistula. In northern Europe it was often possible to move goods from one river to another, and then in the eighteenth century to connect them by canals; and the networks of rivers and canals still carry much heavy traffic by barges. The importance of water is shown again by the location of Copenhagen, Stockholm, and Leningrad (formerly St. Petersburg) on the Baltic, which is a kind of inland lake, and of Amsterdam and Lisbon, which grew up after the ocean could be traversed by Europeans.

There are many important geographical conditions that a topographic map cannot show. One is climate, which depends on latitude, ocean currents, and winds that bring or withhold rainfall. In latitude Europe lies as far north as the northern United States and southern Canada, with Madrid and Rome in the lati-

tude of New York, and with Stockholm and Leningrad as far north as the middle
of Hudson Bay. All Europe thus is within what is called the temperate zone, somewhat misleadingly, since the temperate zone is by definition the region of pronounced difference between winter and summer. But the parts of Europe that are
near the sea have less extreme temperatures than the corresponding northerly
regions of America, and the Mediterranean countries have more sunshine and less
severe winters than either northern Europe or the northern United States. Everywhere, however, the winters are cold enough to keep out certain diseases by
which warmer countries are afflicted. They have also obliged the inhabitants to
expend more effort on clothing, housing, and heating. Warm summers with their
growing seasons have produced an annual cycle of agriculture, for which rainfall
has been adequate but not excessive. Although the Spanish plateau is arid, and
the Mediterranean shores are subject to seasonal variations of rainfall, Europe is
the only continent that has no actual desert. Thanks to a combination of causes,
including rainfall, ground water, deposits left by retreating glaciers, the character of the underlying rock, and the alternate freezing and thawing, Europe is also
for the most part a region of fertile soils. In short, since the end of the Ice Age, or
since humans learned how to survive the winters, Europe has been one of the
most favored places on the globe for human habitation. In recent times it has
been, as shown by the insets of the two endpaper maps in this book, one of the
few large regions, along with China and India, of very high density of population.

Climate itself can change. The Roman ruins in the interior of Morocco and Tunisia remind us that the climate there was once more favorable. Studies of tree
rings, fossil plants, and alpine glaciers show that average temperatures were
warmer from the end of the Ice Age throughout ancient and medieval times, and
then fell during what is called the "little Ice Age" from about 1400 to 1850, when
the winters lengthened and the growing season shortened, without drastic consequences for the people, who by that time could simply wear more wool, so that
sheep raising and the woolen trade became a main staple of European commerce.

There is no geographical determinism. Climate and the environment not only
set limits but provide opportunities for what human beings can do. What happens depends on the application of knowledge and abilities in any particular time
and place. A broad river is an obstruction and hence a good boundary under simple conditions; it is less so after bridges connect the two sides. The oceans that
long divided mankind became a highway for the Portuguese, Spanish, Dutch,
French, and English, and later for others. Distance, which any good map will
show by its scale, also varies in its effects according to the means of transportation; it must be remembered that for most of human history neither persons, information, nor commands could travel much more than thirty miles a day, so that
localism prevailed, and large organizations, in trade or government, were hard to
create and to maintain. For most of its history Europe was in fact made up of a
diversity of small local units, pockets of territory each having its own customs,
way of life, and manner of speech, each largely unknown to the others and looking inward upon itself, rather than of the blocks called "Germany" or "France"
that we take for granted on a map today. A "foreigner" might come from a thousand miles away, or from only ten.

What constitutes a natural resource varies with the state of technology and the
possibilities of exchange. The tin of Cornwall at the western tip of Britain became
an important resource as long ago as the early Bronze Age, when despite its

remoteness it gave rise to some of the first long-distance European trade. Deposits of coal lay little noticed and scarcely exploited until the nineteenth century, and petroleum was of no significance nor even known, until about a century ago. It is a big fact of human history, rather than of geologic history, that some of the world's greatest coal beds happened to be in northwestern Europe and the United States, which could the more readily industrialize because they had easy access to abundant fuel, over which they had control, an advantage that was lost as they became more dependent on natural gas and oil. If the future is like the past, it will see a similar conversion of natural materials into natural resources.

The Mediterranean coasts were more wooded three thousand years ago than they are today. It was not only the change of climate that changed their appearance. Many human generations spent in cutting timber, pasturing goats, and planting vines and olives brought about erosion and depletion of the soil. Europe north of the mountains was heavily forested before human intervention. Trees were cut down and burned there as in America centuries later, so that the landscape slowly became an orderly expanse of carefully tended fields, still interrupted by woodlands. The state of agriculture obviously depends on natural conditions. But it depends historically also on the invention and improvement of the plow, the finding of appropriate crops, the rotation of fields to prevent soil exhaustion, and the introduction of livestock from which manure can be obtained as a fertilizer. Socially, agriculture benefits from the existence of stable village communities, and is affected by demographic changes; if a population falls as a result of war or epidemics, some fields will be abandoned and return to "nature"; if population grows, new and less fertile or more distant areas will be brought under cultivation. Nor can agriculture be improved without the building of roads, a division of labor between town and country, and some degree of regional specialization, so that some areas may grow cereals, others raise livestock, and still others be devoted to orchards and vineyards. Basic to agriculture, as to other enterprises, is elementary security. Farming cannot proceed, nor food be stored over the winter, unless the men and women who work the fields can be protected from attack by marauders, brigands, barbarian invaders, warring chiefs, or hostile armies. Such protection, or what might be called the normalcy of peace, was for several centuries imposed by the Roman Empire, in more recent times (barring wars) by the national state, and in between by barons who at least protected the peasants who worked for them, and by kings attempting to pacify their kingdoms.

For maps with exact detail, or extensive coverage, it is best to consult a good historical atlas, of which several are listed in the bibliography at the end of this book. Over fifty maps are included in the present volume, but some are only diagrams rather than true maps; all are intended to supplement the written text, by showing the location and geographical spread of matters under discussion. Many of the maps are mainly designed to show political boundaries at particular dates. Readers in looking at them can use their imagination to fill in the mountains and rivers that these maps cannot show but which can be important for an understanding of the extent of political power. Readers can also, by using their imagination and consulting the scale, convert space into time, remembering that until the invention of the railroad both people and news traveled far more slowly than today, or that at a rate of thirty miles a day it would take three weeks to travel from London to Venice, and at least six weeks for an exchange of letters. In human terms Europe has not been such a small place after all.

I.
The Rise
of Europe

I t may seem strange for a history of the modern world to begin with the European Middle Ages, for Europe is not the world and the Middle Ages were not modern. But most of what is now meant by "modern" made its first appearance in Europe, and to understand modern Europe it is necessary to reach fairly far back in time. To understand the modern world it is likewise necessary to begin by looking at Europe.

Over the centuries Europe created the most powerful combination of political, military, economic, technological, and scientific apparatus that the world had ever seen. In doing so, Europe radically transformed itself, and also developed an overwhelming impact on other continents and other cultures in America, Africa, and Asia, sometimes destroying them, sometimes stimulating or enlivening them, and always presenting them with problems of resistance or adaptation. This European ascendancy became apparent about 300 years ago. It reached its zenith with the European colonial empires at the beginning of the twentieth century. Since then, the position of Europe has relatively declined, partly because of conflicts within Europe itself, but mainly because the apparatus which had made Europe so dominant can now be found in other countries. Some, like the United States, are essentially offshoots of Europe. Others have very different and ancient backgrounds. But whatever their backgrounds, and willingly or not, all peoples in the twentieth century are caught up in the process of modernization or "development," which usually turns out to mean acquiring some of the skills and powers first exhibited by Europeans.

Chapter Emblem: The symbolic Chi-Rho, or crossed X and P, standing for the first two letters of the Greek Khristos. From a Roman sarcophagus. "P" is the Greek letter rho, for small "r," so that the symbol stands for Christ.

There is thus in our time a kind of uniform modern civilization which overlies or penetrates the traditional cultures of the world. This civilization is an interlocking unity, in that conditions on one side of the globe have repercussions on the other. Communications are almost instantaneous and news travels everywhere. If the air is polluted in one country, neighboring countries are affected; if oil ceases to flow from the Middle East the life of Europe and North America may become very difficult. The modern world depends on elaborate means of transportation, on science, industry, and machines, on new sources of energy to meet insatiable demands, on scientific medicine, public hygiene, and methods of raising food. States and nations fight wars by advanced methods, and negotiate or maintain peace by diplomacy. There is an earth-encompassing network of finance and trade, loans and debts, investments and bank accounts, with resulting fluctuations in monetary exchanges and balances of payments. About 160 very unequal and disunited members compose the United Nations. The very concept of the nation, as represented in that body, is derived from Europe.

In most modern countries there have been pressures for increased democracy, and all modern governments, democratic or not, must seek to arouse the energies and support of their populations. In a modern society old customs loosen, and ancestral religions are questioned. There is a demand for individual liberation, and an expectation of a higher standard of living. Everywhere there is a drive for more equality in a bewildering variety of meanings—for more equality between sexes and races, between high and low incomes, between adherents of different religions, or between different parts of the same country. Movements for social change may be slow and gradual, or revolutionary and catastrophic, but movement of some kind is universal.

Such are a few of the indexes of modernity. Since they appeared first in the history of Europe, or of the European world in the extended sense in which the United States is included, the present book deals mainly with the growth of European society and civilization, with increasing attention, in the later chapters, to the earth as a whole. There have also been antimodern movements and protests; when they occur in Asia or Africa, as in the recent Islamic revival, they are called anti-Western, as if to show that Europe and the "West" have been at the heart of the problem.

If "modern" refers especially to a certain complicated way of living, it has also another sense, meaning merely what is recent or current. As a time span the word "modern" is purely relative. It depends on what we are talking about. A modern kitchen may be as much as 5 years old, modern physics is less than 100 years old, modern science over 300, the modern European languages about 1,000. Modern civilization, the current civilization in which we are living, and which may be passing, is in one sense a product of our own twentieth century, but in other senses it is much older. In general, it is agreed that modern times began in Europe about the year 1500. Modern times were preceded by a period of 1,000 years called the Middle Ages, which set in about A.D. 500, and which were in turn preceded by another 1,000 years of classical Greco-Roman civilization. Before that reached the long histories of Egypt and Mesopotamia, and, further east, of the Indus Valley and of China. All times prior to the European Middle Ages are commonly called "ancient." But the whole framework—ancient, medieval, and modern—is largely a matter of words and convention, without meaning except for Europe. We shall begin our history with a running start, and slow down the pace, surveying the scene more fully in proportion as the times grow more "modern."

1. ANCIENT TIMES: GREECE, ROME, AND CHRISTIANITY

Europeans were by no means the pioneers of human civilization. Half of recorded history had passed before anyone in Europe could read or write. The priests of Egypt began to keep written records between 4000 and 3000 B.C., but two thousand years later the poems of Homer were still being circulated in the Greek city-states by word of mouth. Shortly after 3000 B.C., while the pharaohs were building the pyramids, Europeans were laboriously setting up the huge, unwrought stones called megaliths, of which Stonehenge is the best-known example. In a word, until after 2000 B.C., Europe was in the Neolithic or New Stone Age. This was in truth a great age in human history, the age in which human beings learned to make and use sharp tools, weave cloth, build living quarters, domesticate animals, plant seeds, harvest crops, and sense the returning cycles of the months and years. But the Near East — Egypt, the Euphrates and Tigris valley, the island of Crete, and the shores of the Aegean Sea (which belonged more to Asia than to Europe) — had reached its Neolithic Age two thousand years before Europe. By about 4000 B.C. the Near East was already moving into the Bronze Age.

After about 2000 B.C., in the dim, dark continent that Europe then was, there began to be great changes that are now difficult to trace. Europeans, too, learned how to smelt and forge metals, with the Bronze Age setting in about 2000 B.C. and the Iron Age about 1000 B.C. There was also a steady infusion of new peoples into Europe. They spoke languages related to languages now spoken in India and Iran, to which similar peoples migrated at about the same time. All these languages (whose interconnection was not known until the nineteenth century) are now referred to as Indo-European, and the people who spoke them, merging with and imposing their speech upon older European stocks, became the ancestors both of the classical Greeks and Romans and of the Europeans of modern times. All European languages today are Indo-European with the exceptions of Basque, which is thought to be a survival from before the Indo-European invasion, and of Finnish and Hungarian, which were brought into Europe from Asia some centuries later. It was these invading Indo-Europeans who diffused over Europe the kind of speech from which the Latin, Greek, Germanic, Slavic, Celtic, and Baltic languages were later derived.[1]

The Greek World

The first Indo-Europeans to emerge into the clear light of history, in what is now Europe, were the Greeks. They filtered down through the Balkan peninsula to the shores of the Aegean Sea about 1900 B.C., undermining the older Cretan civilization, and occupying most of what has since been called Greece by 1300 B.C. Beginning about 1150 B.C., other Greek-speaking tribes invaded from the north in successive waves. The newcomers consisted of separate barbaric tribes and their coming ushered in several centuries of chaos and unrest before a gradual stabilization and revival began in the ninth century. The *Iliad* and the *Odyssey*, written

[1] Formerly the term "Aryan" was sometimes used to denote Indo-European. In Germany, under Adolf Hitler, much nonsense was written about an Aryan race, and the term Aryan was made in practice to mean simply non-Jewish. The grain of truth in all this was simply that Hebrew is not an Indo-European but a Semitic language, closely related to Arabic (which is also Semitic) and less closely to the language of the ancient Egyptians. There is no Indo-European (Aryan) or Semitic "race"; persons speaking these languages no more had to be of one physical descent than are persons who speak English today.

down about 800 B.C., but composed and recited much earlier, probably refer to wars between the Greeks and other centers of civilization, of which one was at Troy in Asia Minor. The siege of Troy is thought to have occurred about 1200 B.C.

The Greeks proved to be as gifted a people as mankind has ever produced, achieving supreme heights in thought and letters. They absorbed the knowledge of the, to them, mysterious East, the mathematical lore of the ancient Chaldeans, the arts and crafts that they found in Asia Minor and on voyages to Egypt. They added immediately to everything that they learned. It was the Greeks of the fifth and fourth centuries B.C. who first became fully conscious of the powers of the human mind, who formulated what the Western world long meant by the beautiful, and who first speculated on political freedom.

As they settled down, the Greeks formed tiny city-states, all independent and often at war with one another, each only a few miles across, and typically including a coastal city and its adjoining farmlands. Athens, Corinth, Sparta were such city-states. Many were democratic; all citizens (i.e., all grown men except slaves and "metics," or outsiders) congregated in the marketplace to elect officials and discuss their public business. Politics was turbulent in the small Greek states. Democracy alternated with aristocracy, oligarchy, despotism, and tyranny. From this rich fund of experience was born systematic political science as set forth in the unwritten speculations of Socrates and in the *Republic* of Plato and the *Politics* of Aristotle in the fourth century before Christ. The Greeks also were the first to write history as a subject distinct from myth and legend. Herodotus, "the Father of History," traveled throughout the Greek world and far beyond, ferreting out all he could learn of the past; and Thucydides, in his account of the wars between Athens and Sparta, presented history as a guide to enlightened citizenship and constructive statecraft.

Perhaps because they were a restless and vehement people, the Greeks came to prize the "classical" virtues, which they were the first to define. For them, the ideal lay in moderation, or a golden mean. They valued order, balance, symmetry, clarity, and control. Their statues revealed their conception of what man ought to be—a noble creature, dignified, poised, unterrified by life or death, master of himself and of his feelings. Their architecture, as in the Parthenon, made use of exactly measured angles and rows of columns. The classical "order," or set of carefully wrought pillars placed in a straight line at specified intervals, represented the firm impress of human reason on the brute materials of nature. The same sense of form was thrown over the torrent of human words. Written language became contrived, carefully planned, organized for effect. The epic poem, the lyric, the drama, the oration, along with history and the philosophic dialogue, each with its own rules and principles of composition, became the "forms" within which, in Western civilization, men long continued to express their thoughts.

Reflecting on the world about them, the Greeks concluded that something more fundamental existed beyond the world of appearances, that true reality was not what met the eye. With other peoples, and with the Greeks themselves in earlier times, this same realization had led to the formation of myths, dealing with invisible but mighty beings known as gods and with faraway places on the tops of mountains, beneath the earth, or in a world that followed death. Greek thinkers set to criticizing the web of myth. They looked for rational or natural explanations of what was at work behind the variety and confusion that they saw. Some, observing human sickness, said that disease was not a demonic possession, but a natural sequence of conditions in the body, which could be identified, understood, foreseen, and even treated in a natural way. Others, turning to physical nature, said that all matter was in reality composed of a very few things—of atoms or elements—which they usually designated as fire, water, earth, and air. Some said that change was a kind of illusion, all basic reality being uniform; some, that only change was real, and that the world was a flux. Some, like Pythagoras, found the enduring reality in "number," or mathematics. The Greeks, in short, laid the foundations for science. Studying also the way in which the mind worked, or ought to work if it was to reach truthful conclusions, they developed the science of logic. The great codifier of Greek thought on almost all subjects in the classical period was Aristotle, who lived in Athens from 384 to 322 B.C.

Greek influence spread widely and rapidly. Hardly were some of the city-states founded when their people, crowded within their narrow bounds, sent off some of their number with equipment and provisions to establish colonies. In this way Greek cities were very early established in south Italy, in Sicily, and even in the western Mediterranean, where Marseilles was founded about 600 B.C. Later the Greek city-states, unable to unite, succumbed to conquest by Philip of Macedon, who came from the relatively crude northern part of the Greek world, and whose son, Alexander the Great (356–323 B.C.), led a phenomenal and conquering march into Asia, across Persia, and on as far as India itself. Alexander's empire did not hold together, but Greek civilization, after having penetrated the raw world of the western Mediterranean, now began to revivify the ancient peoples of Egypt and the Near East. Greek thought, Greek art, and the Greek language spread far and wide. The most famous "Greeks" after the fourth century B.C. and on into the early centuries of the Christian era usually did not come from Greece but from the Hellenized Near East, and especially from Alexandria in Egypt. Among these later Greeks were the great summarizers or writers of encyclopedias in which ancient science was passed on to later generations—Strabo in geography, Galen in medicine, Ptolemy in astronomy. All three lived in the first and second centuries after Christ.

The Roman World

In 146 B.C. the Greeks of Greece were conquered by a new people, the Romans. The Romans, while keeping their own Latin language, rapidly absorbed what they could of the intellectual and artistic culture of the Greeks. Over a period of two or three centuries they assembled an empire in which the whole world of ancient civilization (west of Persia) was included. Egypt, Greece, Asia Minor, Syria all became Roman provinces, but in them the Romans had hardly any deep influence except in a political sense. In the West—in what are now Tunisia, Algeria, Morocco, Spain, Portugal, France, Switzerland, Belgium, and England—the Romans, though ruthless in their methods of conquest, in the long run acted as civilizing agents, transmitting to these hitherto backward countries the age-old achievements of the East and the more recent culture of Greece and of Rome itself. So thorough was the Romanization that in the West Latin even became the currently spoken language. It was later wiped out in Africa by Arabic but survives to this day, transformed by time, in the languages of France, Italy, Spain, Portugal, and Rumania.

In the Roman Empire, which lasted with many vicissitudes from about 31 B.C.

to the latter part of the fifth century A.D., virtually the entire civilized world of the ancient West was politically united and enjoyed generations of internal peace. Rome was the center, around which in all directions lay the "circle of lands," the *orbis terrarum*, the known world—that is, as known in the West, for the Han Empire at the same time in China was also a highly organized cultural and political entity. The Roman Empire consisted essentially of the coasts of the Mediterranean Sea, which provided the great artery of transport and communication, and from which no part of the empire, except northern Gaul (France), Britain, and the Rhineland, was more than a couple of hundred miles away. Civilization was uniform; there were no distinct nationalities; the only significant cultural difference was that east of Italy the predominant language was Greek, in Italy and west of it, Latin. Cities grew up everywhere, engaged in a busy commercial life and exchange of ideas with one another. They remained most numerous in the east, where most of the manufacturing crafts and the densest population were still concentrated, but they sprang up also in the west—indeed, most of the older cities of France, Spain, England, and western and southern Germany boast of some kind of origin under the Romans.

The distinctive aptitude of the Romans lay in organization, administration, government, and law. Never before had armies been so systematically formed, maintained over such long periods, dispatched at a word of command over such distances, or maneuvered so effectively on the field of battle. Never had so many peoples been governed from a single center. The Romans had at first possessed self-governing and republican institutions, but they lost them in the process of conquest, and the governing talents which they displayed in the days of the empire were of an authoritarian character—talents, not for self-government, but for managing, coordinating, and ruling the manifold and scattered parts of one enormous system. Locally, cities and city-states enjoyed a good deal of autonomy. But above them all rose a pyramid of imperial officials and provincial governors, culminating in the emperor at the top. The empire kept peace, the *pax Romana*, and even provided a certain justice as between its many peoples. Lawyers worked on the body of principles known ever afterward as Roman law.

Roman judges had somehow to settle disputes between persons of different regions, with conflicting local customs, for example, two merchants of Spain and Egypt. The Roman law came therefore to hold that no custom is necessarily right, that there is a higher or universal law by which fair decisions may be made, and that this higher, universal, or "natural" law, or "law of nature," will be understandable or acceptable to all men, since it arises from human nature and reason. Here the lawyers drew on Greek philosophy for support. They held also that law derives its force from being enacted by a proper authority (not merely from custom, usage, or former legal cases); this authority to make law they called *majestas*, or sovereign power, and they attributed it to the emperor. Thus the Romans emancipated the idea of law from mere custom on the one hand and mere caprice on the other; they regarded it as something to be formed by enlightened intelligence, consistently with reason and the nature of things; and they associated it with the solemn action of official power. It must be added that Roman law favored the state, or the public interest as seen by the government, rather than the interests or liberties of individual persons. These principles, together with more specific ideas on property, debt, marriage, wills, etc., were in later centuries to have a great effect in Europe.

The Coming of Christianity

The thousand years during which Greco-Roman civilization arose and flourished were notable in another way even more momentous for all the later history of mankind. It was in this period that the great world religions came into being. Within the time bracket 700 B.C.–A.D. 700 the lives of Confucius and Buddha, of the major Jewish prophets, and of Muhammad are all included. At the very midpoint (probably about 4 B.C.), in Palestine in the Roman Empire, was born a man named Jesus, believed by his followers to be the Son of God. The first Christians were Jews; but both under the impulse of its own doctrine, which held that all men were alike in spirit, and under the strong leadership of Paul, a man of Jewish birth, Roman citizenship, and Greek culture, Christianity began to make converts without regard to former belief. There were certainly a few Christians in Rome by the middle of the first century. Both Paul and the elder apostle, Peter, according to church tradition, died as martyrs at Rome in the time of the Emperor Nero about A.D. 67.

The Christian teaching spread at first among the poor, the people at the bottom of society, those whom Greek glories and Roman splendors had passed over or enslaved, and who had the least to delight in or to hope for in the existing world. Gradually it reached other classes; a few classically educated and well-to-do people became Christians; in the second century Christian bishops and writers were at work publicly in various parts of the empire. In the third century the Roman government, with the empire falling into turmoil, and blaming the social troubles on the Christians, subjected them to wholesale persecution. In the fourth century (possibly in A.D. 312) the Emperor Constantine was converted to Christianity. By the fifth century the entire Roman world was formally Christian; no other religion was officially tolerated; and the deepest thinkers were also Christians, men who combined Christian beliefs with the now thousand-year-old tradition of Greco-Roman thought and philosophy.

It is impossible to exaggerate the importance of the coming of Christianity. It brought with it, for one thing, an altogether new sense of human life. Where the Greeks had demonstrated the powers of the mind, the Christians explored the soul, and they taught that in the sight of God all souls were equal, that every human life was sacrosanct and inviolate, and that all worldly distinctions of greatness, beauty, and brilliancy were in the last analysis superficial. Where the Greeks had identified the beautiful and the good, had thought ugliness to be bad, and had shrunk from disease as an imperfection and from everything misshapen as horrible and repulsive, the Christians resolutely saw a spiritual beauty even in the plainest or most unpleasant exterior and sought out the diseased, the crippled, and the mutilated to give them help. Love, for the ancients, was never quite distinguished from Venus; for the Christians, who held that God was love, it took on deep overtones of sacrifice and compassion. Suffering itself was proclaimed by Christians to be in a way divine, since God himself had suffered on the Cross in human form. A new dignity was thus found for suffering that the world could not cure. At the same time the Christians worked to relieve suffering as none had worked before. They protested against the massacre of prisoners of war, against the mistreatment and degradation of slaves, against the sending of gladiators to kill each other in the arena for another's pleasure. In place of the Greek and pagan self-satisfaction with human accomplishments they taught humility in the face of an almighty Providence, and in place of proud distinctions between high and low, slave and free, civilized and barbarian, they held that all men were brothers because all were children of the same God.

On an intellectual level Christianity also marked a revolution. It was Christianity, not rational philosophy, that dispelled the swarm of greater and lesser gods and goddesses, the blood sacrifices and self-immolation, or the frantic resort to magic, fortune-telling, and divination. The Christians taught that since there was only one God, the pagan gods must be at best lesser demons, and even this idea was gradually given up. The pagan conception of local, tribal, or national gods disappeared. It was now held that for all the world there was only one God, one plan of Salvation, and one Providence, and that all mankind took its origin from one source. The idea of the world as one thing, a "universe," was thus affirmed with a new depth of meaning. The very intolerance of Christianity (which was new to the ancient world) came from this overwhelming sense of human unity, in which it was thought that all men should have, and deserved to have, the one true and saving religion.

It was for their political ideas that the Christians were most often denounced and persecuted. The Roman Empire was a world state; there was no other state but it; no living human being except the emperor was sovereign; no one anywhere on earth was his equal. Between gods and human beings, in the pagan view, there was moreover no clear distinction. Some gods behaved very humanly, and some human creatures were more like gods than others. The emperor was held to be veritably a god, *divus Caesar, semper Augustus.* A cult of Caesar was established, regarded as necessary to maintain the state, which was the world itself. All this the Christians firmly refused to accept. It was because they would not worship Caesar that the Roman officials regarded them as monstrous social incendiaries who must be persecuted and stamped out.

The Christian doctrine on this point went back to the saying gathered from Jesus, that one should render to Caesar the things that were Caesar's, and to God those that were God's. The same dualism was presented more systematically by St. Augustine about A.D. 420 in his *City of God.* Few books have been more influential in shaping the later development of Western civilization.

The "world," the world of Caesar, in the time of St. Augustine, was going to ruin. Rome itself was plundered in 410 by heathen barbarians. Augustine wrote the *City of God* with this event obsessing his imagination. He wrote to show that though the world itself perished there was yet another world that was more enduring and more important.

There were, he said, really two "cities," the earthly and the heavenly, the temporal and the eternal, the city of man and the City of God. The earthly city was the domain of state and empire, of political authority and political obedience. It was a good thing, as part of God's providential scheme for human life, but it had no inherently divine character of its own. The emperor was a man. The state was not absolute; it could be judged, amended, or corrected from sources outside itself. It was, for all its majesty and splendor, really subordinate in some way to a higher and spiritual power. This power lay in the City of God. By the City of God Augustine meant many things, and all sorts of meanings were found by readers in later ages. The heavenly city might mean heaven itself, the abode of God and of blessed spirits enjoying life after death. It might mean certain elect spirits of this world, the good people as opposed to the bad. It might, more theoretically, be a system of ideal values or ideal justice, as opposed to the crude approximations of the actual world. Or it was later thought, by some, to mean the organized church and its clergy.

In any case, with this Christian dualism the Western world escaped from what is called Caesaropapism, the holding by one man of the powers of ruler and of pontiff. Instead, the spiritual and the political power were held to be separate and independent. In later times popes and kings often quarreled with each other; the clergy often struggled for worldly power, and governments at various times (including the twentieth century with its totalitarian systems) have attempted to dictate what men should believe, or love, or hope for. But speaking in general of European history neither side has ever won out, and in the sharp distinction between the spiritual and the temporal has lain the germ of many liberties in the West. At the same time the idea that no ruler, no government, and no institution is too mighty to rise above moral criticism opened the way to a dynamic and progressive way of living in the West.

As for Augustine himself, he lived to see the world grow worse. He died in A.D. 430. In 429 the Roman province of Africa, where he had been a bishop, was pillaged by a wild Germanic tribe called the Vandals.

2. THE EARLY MIDDLE AGES: THE FORMATION OF EUROPE

There was really no Europe in ancient times. In the Roman Empire we may see a Mediterranean world, or even a West and an East in the Latin- and Greek-speaking portions. But the West included parts of Africa as well as of Europe, and Europe as we know it was divided by the Rhine-Danube frontier, south and west of which lay the civilized provinces of the empire, and north and east the "barbarians" of whom the civilized world knew almost nothing. To the Romans "Africa" meant Tunisia-Algeria, "Asia" meant the Asia Minor peninsula; and the word "Europe," since it meant little, was scarcely used by them at all. It was in the half-millennium from the fifth to the tenth centuries that Europe as such for the first time emerged with its peoples brought together in a life of their own, clearly set off from that of Asia or Africa.

The Disintegration of the Roman Empire

First of all the Roman Empire went to pieces, especially in the West. The Christianizing of the empire did nothing to impede its decline. The Emperor Constantine, who in embracing Christianity undoubtedly hoped to strengthen the imperial system, also took one other significant step. In A.D. 330 he founded a new capital at the old Greek city of Byzantium, which he renamed Constantinople. (It is now Istanbul.) Thereafter the Roman Empire had two capitals, Rome and Constantinople, and was administered in two halves. Increasingly the center of gravity moved eastward, as if returning to the more ancient centers in the Near East, as if the "modern" experiment of civilizing the West were to be given up as a failure.

Throughout its long life the empire had been surrounded on almost all sides by barbarians—wild Celts in Wales and Scotland, Germans in the heart of Europe, Persians or Parthians in the East ("barbarian" only in the ancient sense of speaking neither Greek nor Latin), and, in the southeast, the Arabs. (In the south the empire simply faded off into the Sahara.) These barbarians, always with the exception of Persia, had never been brought within the pale of ancient civilization. Somewhat like the Chinese, who about 200 B.C. built the Great Wall to solve the same problem, the Romans simply drew a line beyond which they themselves rarely ventured and would not allow the barbarians to pass. Nevertheless the barbarians filtered in. As early as the third century A.D. emperors and generals recruited bands of them to serve in the Roman armies. Their service over, they would receive farmlands, settle down, marry and mingle with the population. By the fourth and fifth centuries a good many individuals of barbarian birth were even reaching high positions of state. At the same time, in the West, for reasons that are not fully understood, the activity of the Roman cities began to falter, commerce began to decay, local governments became paralyzed, taxes became more ruinous, and free farmers were bound to the soil. The army seated and unseated emperors. Rival generals fought with each other. Gradually the West fell into decrepitude and an internal barbarization so that the old line between the Roman provinces and the barbarian world made less and less difference.

After some centuries of relative stability, the barbarians themselves, pressed by more distant peoples from Asia, rather suddenly began to move. Sometimes they first sought peaceable access to the empire, attracted by the warmer Mediterranean climate, or desiring to share in the advantages of Roman civilization. More often, tribes consisting of a few tens of thousands, men, women, and children, moved swiftly and by force, plundering, fighting, and killing as they went. At first most of the barbarians threatening the empire were Germanic, going under many names. The Angles and Saxons overran Britain about 450, the Franks invaded Gaul at the same time, the Vandals reached as far as Roman Africa in 429, the East Goths appeared in Asia Minor in 382 and in Italy in 493, the West Goths lunged toward Constantinople about 380, tore through Greece in 396, sacked Rome itself in 410, and reached Spain about the year 420. In 476 the last Roman emperor in the West was deposed by a barbarian chieftain. Sometimes in the general upheaval wild Turkman peoples fresh from Asia were intermixed. Of these the most famous were the Huns, who cut through central Europe and France about 450 under their leader Attila, the "scourge of God"—and then disappeared. Nor were these invasions all. Two centuries later new irruptions burst upon the Greco-Roman world on its opposite side, where hitherto outlying peoples poured in from the Arabian deserts. The Arabs, aroused by the new faith of Islam (Muhammad died in 632), fell as conquerors upon Syria, Mesopotamia, Persia, occupied Egypt about 640, the old Roman Africa about 700, and in 711 reached Spain, where they destroyed the Germanic kingdom set up there by the West Goths.

Beneath these blows the old unity of the Greco-Roman or Mediterranean world was broken. The "circle of lands" divided into three segments. Three types of civilization now confronted each other across the inland sea.

The Byzantine World, the Arabic World, and the West about A.D. 700

One was the Eastern Roman, Later Roman, Greek, or Byzantine Empire (all names for the same thing) with its capital at Constantinople, and now including only the Asia Minor peninsula, the Balkan peninsula, and parts of Italy. It represented the most direct continuation of the immemorial civilization of the Near

East. It was Christian in religion and Greek in culture and language. Its people felt themselves to be the truest heirs both of early Christianity and of the Greeks of the golden age. Art and architecture, trades and crafts, commerce and navigation, thought and writing, government and law, while not so creative or flexible as in the classical age, were still carried on actively in the eastern Empire, on much the same level as in the closing centuries of ancient times. For all Christians, and for heathen barbarians in Europe, the emperor of the East stood out as the world's supreme ruler, and Constantinople as the world's preeminent and almost fabulous city.

The second segment, and the most extensive, was the Arabic and Islamic. It reached from the neighborhood of the Pyrenees through Spain and all North Africa into Arabia, Syria, and the East. Arabic was its language; it became, and still remains, the common speech from Morocco to the Persian Gulf. Islam was its religion. It was organized in the caliphate in which all Muslims were included, and the caliph was regarded as the true religious and military successor to Muhammad himself. The Arabic world, like the Byzantine, built directly upon the heritage of the Greco-Romans. In religion, the early Muslims regarded themselves as successors to the Jewish and Christian traditions. They considered the line of Jewish prophets to be spokesmen of the true God, and they put Jesus in this line. But they added that Muhammad was the last and greatest of the prophets, that the Koran set forth a revelation replacing that of the Jewish Bible, that the New Testament of the Christians was mistaken because Christ was not divine, and that the Christian belief in a Trinity was erroneous because there was in the strictest and most rigid sense only One True God. To the Muslim Arabs, therefore, all Christians were contemptible infidels.

In mundane matters, the Arabs speedily took over the civilization of the lands they conquered. In the caliphate, as in the Byzantine Empire, the civilization of the ancient world went its way without serious interruption. Huge buildings and magnificent palaces were constructed; ships plied the Mediterranean; merchants ventured over the deserts and traversed the Indian Ocean; holy or learned men corresponded over thousands of miles; taxes were collected, laws were enforced, and provinces were kept in order. In the sciences the Arabs not only learned from but went beyond the Greeks. The Greek scientific literature was translated: some of it is known today only through these medieval Arabic versions. Arab geographers had a wider knowledge of the world than anyone had possessed up to their time. Arab mathematicians developed algebra so far beyond the Greeks as almost to be its creator ("algebra" is an Arabic word), and in introducing the "Arabic" numerals (through their contacts with India) they made arithmetic, which in Roman numerals had been a formidably difficult science, into something that every schoolchild can be taught.

The third segment was Latin Christendom, which about A.D. 700 did not look very promising. It was what was left over from the other two—what the Byzantines were unable to hold, and the Arabs unable to conquer. It included only Italy (shared in part with the Byzantines), France, Belgium, the Rhineland, and Britain. Barbarian kings were doing their best to rule small kingdoms, but in truth all government had fallen to pieces. Strange and uncouth peoples milled about. Usually the invading barbarians remained a minority, eventually to be absorbed. Only in England, and in the region immediately west of the Rhine, did the Germanic element supersede the older Celtic and Latin. But the presence of the

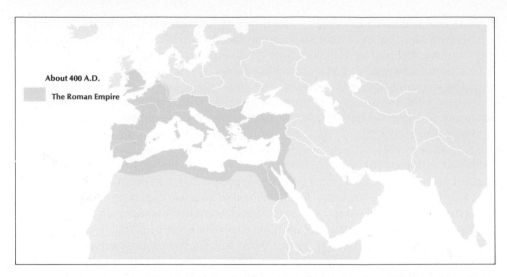

About 400 A.D.

The Roman Empire

About 800 A.D.

Latin Christians

Greek Christians

Muslims

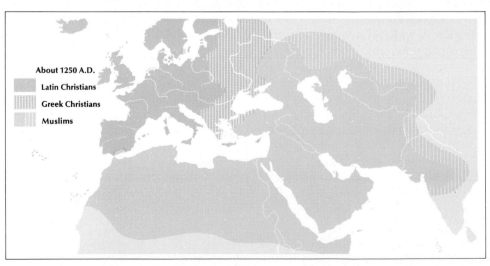

About 1250 A.D.

Latin Christians

Greek Christians

Muslims

invaders, armed and fierce amid peasants and city dwellers reduced to passivity by Roman rule, together with the disintegration of Roman institutions that had gone on even before the invasions, left this region in chaos.

The Western barbarians, as noted, were Germanic; and the Germanic influence was to be a distinctive contribution to the making of Europe. Some Germans were Christian by the fourth century, but most were still heathen when they burst into the Roman Empire. Their languages had not been written down, but they possessed an intricate folklore and religion, in which fighting and heroic valor were much esteemed. Though now in a migratory phase, they were an agricultural people who knew how to work iron, and they had a rudimentary knowledge of the crafts of the Romans. They were organized in small tribes, and had a strong sense of tribal kinship, which (as with many primitive peoples) dominated their ideas of leadership and law. They enjoyed more freedom in their affairs than did the citizens of the Roman Empire. Many of the tribes were roughly self-governing in that all free men, those entitled to bear arms, met in open fields to hold council; and often the tribe itself elected its leader or king. They had a strong sense of loyalty to persons, of fealty to the acknowledged king or chief; but they had no sense of loyalty to large or general institutions. They had no sense of the state—of any distant, impersonal, and continuing source of law and rule. Law they regarded as the inflexible custom of each tribe. In the absence of abstract jurisprudence or trained judges, they settled disputes by rough and ready methods. In the ordeal, for example, a person who obstinately floated when thrown into water was adjudged guilty. In trial by battle, the winner of a kind of ritualistic duel was regarded as innocent. The gods, it was thought, would not allow wrong to prevail.

The Germans who overran the old Roman provinces found it difficult to maintain any political organization at more than a local level. Security and civil order all but disappeared. Peasant communities were at the mercy of wandering bands of habitual fighters. Fighters often captured peasant villages, took them under their protection, guarded them from further marauders, and lived off their produce. Sometimes the same great fighting man came to possess many such villages, moving with his retinue of horsemen from one village to another to support himself throughout the year. Thus originated a new distinction between lord and servant, noble and commoner, martial and menial class. Life became local and self-sufficient. People ate, wore, used, and dwelled in only what they themselves and their neighbors could produce. Trade died down, the cities became depopulated, money went out of circulation, almost nothing was bought or sold. The

THE MEDITERRANEAN WORLD ABOUT A.D. 400, 800, AND 1250

Greco-Roman civilization, centered about the Mediterranean, was officially Christian and politically unified under the Roman Empire in A.D. 400, but broke apart into three segments in the early Middle Ages. Each segment developed its own type of life. Each segment also expanded beyond the limits of the ancient Mediterranean culture. By 1250 Latin Christendom reached to the Baltic and beyond, to include Iceland and even an outpost in Greenland. Greek Christendom penetrated north of the Black Sea, to include the Russians. The Muslim world spread into inner Asia and black Africa. In 1250, and until 1492, the Muslims, or Moors, still held the southern tip of Spain. There continued to be Greek, Armenian, and other Christians under Muslim rule in the eastern Mediterranean, and Jews in varying numbers in each of the three segments.

Roman roads fell into neglect; people often used them as quarries for ready-cut building blocks for their own crude purposes. The West not only broke up into localized villages, but also ceased to have habitual contacts across the Mediterranean. It became isolated from the eastern centers from which its former civilization had always been drawn. The West was reverting. From roughly A.D. 500 on, Europe was in the so-called Dark Ages.

The Church and the Rise of the Papacy

Only one organized institution maintained a tie with the civilized past. Only one institution, reaching over the whole West, could receive news or dispatch its agents over the whole area. This institution was the Christian church. Its framework still stood; its network of bishoprics, as built up in late Roman times, remained intact except in places like England where the barbarian conquest was complete.

In addition, a new type of religious institution was rapidly spreading with the growth of monasteries. The serious and the sensitive, both men and women (though not together, to be sure), rejected the savagery about them and retired into communities of their own. Usually they were left unmolested by rough neighbors who held them in religious awe. In a world of violence they formed islands of quiet and of peace. In a society of burly barbarians they lived the life of contemplation. Their prayers, it was believed, were of use to all the world, and their example might at the least arouse in obstreperous worldlings the pangs of shame. The monastic houses generally adopted the rule of St. Benedict (c. 480–543), and were generally governed by an abbot. Dedicated to the same ideals, they formed unifying filaments throughout the chaos of the Latin West.

Bishops, abbots, and monks looked with veneration to Rome as the spot where St. Peter, the first apostle, had been martyred. The bishop of Rome corresponded with other bishops, sent out missionaries (to England, for example), gave advice on doctrine when he could, and attempted to keep in mind the situation throughout the Latin world as a whole. Moreover, with no emperor any longer in Rome, the bishop took over the government and public affairs of the city. Thus the bishop of Rome, while claiming a primacy over all Christians, was not dominated by any secular power. In the East the great church functionaries, the patriarchs, fell under the influence of the emperor who continued to rule at Constantinople, so that a tradition of Caesaropapism grew up in the East; but in the West the independence of the bishop of Rome now confirmed in practice a principle always maintained by the great churchmen of the West—the independence of the spiritual power from the political or temporal.

In this way was built up the authority of the popes. It was fortified by various arguments. St. Peter, it was held, had imparted the spiritual authority given to him by Christ himself to the Roman bishops who were his successors. This doctrine of the "Petrine supremacy" was based on two verses in the Bible, according to which Christ designated Peter as the head of the church, giving him the "power of the keys," to open and close the doors of eternal salvation.[2] As for the

---

[2] "Thou art Peter, and upon this rock I will build my church; and the gates of hell shall not prevail against it. And I will give unto thee the keys of the kingdom of heaven, and whatsoever thou shalt bind on earth shall be bound in heaven; and whatsoever thou shalt loose on earth shall be loosed in heaven." Matthew xvi, 18–19. In Greek the name Peter meant a "rock"; a play upon words was involved. The pun is still evident in some modern languages, as in French, where *pierre*, a rock, is the same as *Pierre*, Peter.

pope's temporal rule in Rome, it was affirmed that the Emperor Constantine had endowed the bishop with the government of the city. This "Donation of Constantine" was accepted as historical fact from the eighth century to the fifteenth, when it was proved to be a forgery.

It was the church which incorporated the barbarians into a higher way of life, and when a barbarian embraced a more civilized way of living it was the church that he entered. As early as about A.D. 340, the church sent out Ulfilas to convert the Goths; his translation of the Bible represents the first writing down of any Germanic language. About 496 the king of the Franks, Clovis, was converted to Christianity. A hundred years later, in 597, the king of Kent in southeast England yielded to the persuasions of Augustine of Canterbury, a missionary dispatched from Rome, and the Christianization of the Anglo-Saxons gradually followed. Missionaries from Ireland also, to which Christians of the Roman Empire had fled before the heathen barbarians, now returned to both Britain and the Continent to spread the gospel. By some such year as A.D. 700, after three centuries of turmoil, the borders of Christianity in the West were again roughly what they had been in late Roman times. Then in 711, as we have seen, the Arabs conquered Spain. They crossed the Pyrenees and raced toward central Europe, but were stopped by a Christian and Frankish army in 732 at Tours on the river Loire. Islam was not destined to reach beyond Spain.

The Empire of Charlemagne, A.D. 800

Among the Franks, in what is now northern France and the German Rhineland, there had meanwhile arisen a line of capable rulers of whom the greatest was Charlemagne. The Frankish kings made it their policy to cooperate with the pope. The pope needed a protector against depredations by his barbarian neighbors and against the political claims of the Byzantine Empire upon the city of Rome. The Frankish kings, in return for protection thus offered, won papal support to their side. This made it easier for them to control their own bishops, who were more often seen on horseback than in the episcopal chair, and was of use in pacifying their own domains and in wars of conquest against the heathen. In the year 800, in Rome, the pope crowned Charlemagne as emperor of the West. Frankish king and Roman bishop both believed that if only the Roman Empire could be restored peace and order might once more reign. Church and empire, the spirit and the state, were to be as two mighty swords employed in the same holy cause.

Charlemagne crossed the Pyrenees and won back the northeastern corner of Spain to Christian rule. He overthrew and subordinated the barbarian kings who had set themselves up in Italy. He sent forces down the Danube, penetrated into Bohemia, and proceeded against some of the still heathen Germans (the Saxons) who lived along the river Elbe, and whom he either massacred or converted to Christianity. All these regions he brought within his new empire. Except for England and Ireland, which remained outside, the borders of his empire were coextensive with those of the Latin Christian world.

Once more, to a degree, the West was united. But a momentous change had occurred. Its capital was now not Rome and did not lie in the ancient world of the Mediterranean. Its capital was at Aix-la-Chapelle, or Aachen, near the mouth of the Rhine. Its ruler, Charlemagne, was a German of an ethnic group which ancient civilization had left outside. Its people were Germans, French, and Italians, or the ancestors from whom these nationalities were to be developed. In the Greco-Roman world the north had always been at best provincial. Now the north became a center in its own right. Charlemagne dispatched embassies to the emperor at Constantinople, and to Harun al-Rashid, the great caliph at Baghdad. In intellectual matters, too, the north now became a capital. Centuries of violence and confusion had left ignorance very widespread. Charlemagne himself, though he understood Latin, could barely read and never learned to write. He used his authority to revive the all but forgotten ancient learning and to spread education at least among the clergy. To his palace school came scholars from England, Germany, France, Italy, Spain. They wrote and spoke in Latin, the only Western language in which any complicated ideas could at the time be expressed. Disintegrating ancient manuscripts were copied and recopied to assure a more abundant supply for study—always by hand, but in a more rapid script than had before been used, the so-called Carolingian minuscule, from which come the small letters of the modern Western alphabet, only the capitals being Roman. Commerce also, which had virtually disappeared, Charlemagne undertook to foster. He created a new and more reliable coinage, which was based on silver, the gold coins of the Roman Empire having long since vanished. A pound of silver was divided into 20 *solidi* or 240 pennies. This scheme of values, though long used in many parts of Europe, survived longest in the country that remained outside Charlemagne's empire, namely, in England, the last country to replace it with a decimal currency, and then not until the twentieth century.

Ninth-Century Invasions; Europe by A.D. 1000

It is in Charlemagne's empire that we can first see the shape of Europe, as a unit of society and culture distinct from the Mediterranean world of antiquity. The empire did not last. The troubled era was not yet over. New hordes of barbarians assailed Western Christendom in the ninth century. The Magyars (called in Latin "Hungarians") terrified various parts of Europe until they settled down on the middle Danube about the year 900. New Germanic tribes uprooted themselves, coming this time from Scandinavia, and variously known as Norsemen, Vikings, or Danes. Bursting out in all directions, they reached Kiev in Russia in 864, discovered Iceland in 874, and even touched America in 1000. In the Christian world they assaulted the coasts and pushed up the rivers but settled in considerable numbers only in the Danelaw in England and in Normandy in France. Meanwhile the Arabs raided the shores of France and Italy and occupied Sicily. Nowhere was the power of government strong enough to ward off such attacks. Everywhere the harassed local population found its own means of defense or, that failing, was slaughtered, robbed, or carried off into slavery.

Gradually the second wave of barbarians was incorporated as the first had been, by the same process of conversion to Christianity. By the year 1000 the process was nearly complete. In 1001 the pope sent a golden crown to the Magyars to crown St. Stephen as their first king, thus bringing Hungary within the orbit of the Latin West. Poland, Bohemia, and the Scandinavian homelands of the Norsemen were being rapidly Christianized. In older Christian countries, such as France, the last remote and isolated rustics—the "heathen" who lived in the "heath"—were finally ferreted out by missionaries and brought within the Christian fold. In Christian countries Christianity now permeated to every corner, and the historic peoples of western Europe had come together within the spreading system of the Latin church.

Meanwhile West and East continued to drift apart. The refusal of Greek patriarchs at Constantinople to recognize the claims to primacy of the bishop of Rome, whom they regarded as a kind of Western barbarian, and the refusal of the Roman pontiff to acknowledge the political pretensions of the Byzantine Empire, led to the Great Schism of East and West. This schism, after developing for three centuries, became definite in 1054. It divided the Christian world into the Latin or Roman Catholic and the Greek Orthodox churches. It was from Constantinople that Christianity reached the peoples of Russia. The Russians, like the Balkan peoples, remained out of contact with the West during the centuries when spiritual and intellectual contacts were carried through the clergy. They believed, indeed, that the Latin West was evil, heretical, contumacious, and unholy. The Latin West, at the same time, by the schism, cut one more of its ties with antiquity and emerged the more clearly as an independent center of its own civilization.

By the year 1000, or soon thereafter, the entity that we call Europe had been brought into existence. From the turbulence that followed the collapse of the Greco-Roman civilization had issued the peoples and the countries of modern Europe. A kingdom of France was in being, adjoining the great ill-defined bulk of Germany to the east. There were small Christian kingdoms in northern Spain and a number of city-states in the Italian peninsula. In the north there were now a kingdom of England and a kingdom of Scotland; Denmark, Norway, and Sweden had also taken form. In the east rose the three great kingdoms of Poland, Bohemia, and Hungary, the first two predominantly Slavic, Hungary predominantly Magyar, but all Latin and Catholic in culture and religion, and Western in orientation. The east Slavs, or Russians, and the Slavs and other peoples of the Balkan peninsula also formed kingdoms of their own. Their way was diverging from the West. Christianized by Byzantine missionaries, they were Greek and Orthodox in culture and religion and oriented toward Constantinople.

The civilization of the West, in the year 1000, was still not much to boast of in the more polished circles of Byzantium or Baghdad. It might still seem that the West would suffer more than the East from their separation. But the West began at this time to experience a remarkable activity, ushering in the European civilization of the High Middle Ages.

3. THE HIGH MIDDLE AGES: SECULAR CIVILIZATION

Changes after A.D. 1000

Some historical periods are so dynamic that a person who lives to be fifty years old can remember sweeping changes that have come in his own lifetime. Such a time has been the last century of the modern age. Such a time, also, began in Europe in the eleventh century. People could see new towns rise and grow before their eyes. They could observe new undertakings in commerce or government. It is hardly too much to say that all the cities that Europe was to know before the modern industrial era sprang up between about 1050 and 1200. The population of western Europe, which had been sparse even in Roman days, and which was even more sparse after 500, suddenly began to grow more dense about the year

1000, and expanded steadily for two or three hundred years. The people of the High Middle Ages did not develop the conception of progress, because their minds were set upon timeless values and personal salvation in another world, but the period was nevertheless one of rapid progress in nonreligious or "secular" things. It was a period in which much was created that remained fundamental far into modern times.

The new era was made possible by the process of growth in population which went along with agricultural changes. After the Norse and Magyar inroads had stopped, Europe was spared the assaults of barbarians. There came to be more security of life and limb. A farmer could plant with more confidence that he would reap. A man could build a house and expect to live his life in it and pass it on to his children. Hence there was more planting and building. Sometime before the year 1000 a heavier plow had been invented, which cut a deeper furrow. Better methods of harnessing horses had been found than the ancients had ever known. The Romans had continued simply to throw a yoke over a horse's neck, so that the animal in pulling a weight easily choked. Europeans, before the year 1000, began to use a horse collar that rested on the animal's shoulders. The single horse could pull a greater load, or several horses could now for the first time be hitched in tandem. The amount of available animal power was thus multiplied, at a time when animals were the main source of power other than human muscle. Windmills also, unknown to the ancients, were developed in the Low Countries about this time. They too offered a new source of power. Thus at the very beginning of a specifically "European" history, one may detect a characteristic of European civilization—a faculty for invention, a quest for new sources of energy.

With such labor-saving devices people continued to work very hard, but they obtained more results by their efforts. Probably the use of such inventions, together with the influence of the Christian clergy, accounts for the gradual disappearance of slavery from Europe and its replacement by the less abject and less degrading status of serfdom. It is true that medieval Christians, when they could, continued to enslave whites as they were later to do with blacks. Usually such slaves were captives in war, taken from tribes not yet converted to Christianity, and sometimes exported as a form of merchandise to the Byzantine and Muslim worlds. As the successive European peoples became Christianized, the supply of slaves dried up. Medieval Christians did not enslave each other, nor was slavery essential to any important form of production.

Not only did population increase, and work become more productive, but groups of people became less isolated from one another. Communications improved. The roads remained poor or nonexistent, but bridges were built across the many European rivers, and settlers filled in the wildernesses that had formerly separated the inhabited areas. Trees were felled and land cleared, as they would be long afterward in the United States during the westward movement. But where the forest gave way in America to an agricultural world of detached individual farmsteads, in medieval Europe the rural population clustered in village communities. The "nucleated" village gave more security, more contact between families, and readier access to the blacksmith or the priest. It also made possible a communally organized agriculture.

Better ways of using land were introduced in the "three-field" system, which spread almost everywhere where cereal crops were the staple. In this "system" the peasant village divided its arable fields into three parts. In a given year one part was sown with one crop, such as wheat, a second part with another, such as barley, and the third was left to lie fallow. The three parts were rotated from year to year. Thus soil exhaustion was avoided at a time when fertilizers were unknown. Formerly half or less of the available fields had been cultivated at any one time. With the three-field system two-thirds of the land came into annual use. This fact, reinforced by better plowing and more effective employment of animals, led to a huge increase in the supply of food.

The peace and personal security necessary to agriculture were also advanced, in the absence of effective public authority, by the growth of institutions that we know as "feudalism." Feudalism was intricate and diverse, but in essence it was a means of carrying on some kind of government on a local basis where no organized state existed. After the collapse of Charlemagne's empire the real authority fell into the hands of persons who were most often called "counts." The count was the most important man of a region covering a few hundred square miles. To build up his own position, and strengthen himself for war against other counts, he tried to keep the peace and maintain control over the lesser lords in his county, those whose possessions extended over a few hundred or a few thousand acres. These lesser lords accepted or were forced to accept his protection. They became his vassals, and he became their "lord." The lord and vassal relation was one of reciprocal duties. The lord protected the vassal and assured him justice and firm tenure of his land. If two vassals of the same lord disputed the possession of the same village, the lord decided the case, sitting in council (or "court") with all his vassals assembled, and judging according to the common memory or customary law of the district. If a vassal died young, leaving only small children, the lord took the family under his "wardship" or guardianship, guaranteeing that the rightful heirs would inherit in due time. Correspondingly the vassal agreed to serve the lord as a fighting man for a certain number of days in the year. From other "unauthorized" fighting and squabbling the vassal was supposed to refrain. The vassal also owed it to the lord to attend and advise him, to sit in his court in the judging of disputes. Usually he owed no money or material payment; but if the lord had to be ransomed from captivity, or when his children married, the vassal paid a fee. The vassal also paid a fee on inheriting an estate, and the income of estates under wardship went to the lord. Thus the lord collected sporadic revenues with which to finance his somewhat primitive government.

This feudal scheme, which probably originated locally, gradually spread. Lords at the level of counts became in turn the vassals of dukes. In the year 987 the great lords of France chose Hugh Capet as their king, and became his vassals. The kings of France enjoyed little real power for another two hundred years, but the descendants of Hugh occupied their throne for eight centuries, until the French Revolution. Similarly the magnates of Germany elected a king in 911; in 962 the German king was crowned emperor, as Charlemagne had been before him; thus originated the Holy Roman Empire of which much will be heard in the following chapters.

To England, in these formative centuries, it was not given to choose a king by election. England was conquered in 1066 by the Duke of Normandy, William. The Normans (the old Norsemen reshaped by a century of Christian and French influence) imposed upon England a centralized and efficient type of feudalism which they had developed in Normandy. In England, from an early date, the king and his central officials therefore had considerable power. In England there was more civil peace and personal security than on the Continent. Within the framework of a strong monarchy self-governing institutions could eventually develop with a minimum of disorder.

The notable feature of feudalism was its mutual or reciprocal character. In this it differed from the old Roman imperial principle, by which the emperor had been a majestic and all-powerful sovereign. Under feudalism no one was sovereign. King and people, lord and vassal, were joined in a kind of contract. Each owed something to the other. If one defaulted, the obligation ceased. If a vassal refused his due services, the king had the right to enforce compliance. If the king violated the rights of the vassal, the vassals could join together against him. The king was supposed to act with the advice of the vassals, who formed his council or court. If the vassals believed the king to be exceeding his lawful powers, they could impose terms upon him. It was out of this mutual or contractual character of feudalism that ideas of constitutional government later developed.

Feudalism applied in the strict sense only to the military or noble class. Below the feudal world lay the vast mass of the peasantry. Here, in the village, the lowliest vassal of a higher noble was lord over his own subjects. The village, with its people and surrounding farmlands, constituted a "manor," the estate of a lord. In the eleventh century most people of the manor were serfs. They were "bound to the soil" in that they could not leave the manor without the lord's permission. Few wanted to leave anyway, at a time when the world beyond the village was unknown and dangerous, and filled at best only with other similar manors in which opportunities were no different. The lord, for his part, could not expropriate the villagers or drive them away. He owed them protection and the administration of justice. They in turn worked his fields and gave him part of the produce of their own. No money changed hands, because there was virtually no money in circulation. The manorial system was the agricultural base on which a ruling class was supported. It supported also the clergy, for the church held much land in the form of manors. It gave the protection from physical violence and the framework of communal living without which the peasants could not grow crops or tend livestock.

Many consequences flowed from the rise of agricultural productivity. Lords and even a few peasants could produce a surplus, which they might sell if only they could find a market. The country was able to produce enough food for a town population to live on. And since population grew with the increase of the food supply, and since not all the new people were needed in agriculture, a surplus of population also began to exist. Restless spirits among the peasants now wanted to get away from the manor. And many went off to the new towns.

The Rise of Towns and Commerce

We have seen how the ancient cities had decayed. In the ninth and tenth centuries, with few exceptions, there were none left in western Europe. Here and there one would find a cluster of population around the headquarters of a bishop, a great count, or a king. But there were no commercial centers. There was no merchant class. The simple crafts—weaving, metalworking, harness making—were carried on locally on the manors. Rarely, an itinerant trader might appear with such semiprecious goods as he could carry for long distances on donkeys—Eastern silks, or a few spices for the wealthy. Among these early traders Jews were often important, because Judaism, penetrating the Byzantine and Arabic worlds as well as the Western, offered one of the few channels of distant communication that were open.

Long-distance trading was the first to develop. The city of Venice was founded about A.D. 570 when refugees from the barbarians settled in its islands. The Venetians, as time went on, brought Eastern goods up the Adriatic and sold them to traders coming down from central Europe. In Flanders in the north, in what is now Belgium, there developed manufacturers of woolen cloth. Flemish woolens were of a unique quality, owing to peculiarities of the atmosphere and the skill of the weavers. They could not be duplicated elsewhere. Nor could Eastern goods be procured except through the Venetians—or the Genoese or Pisans. Such goods could not possibly be produced locally, yet they were in demand wherever they became known. Merchants traveled in increasing numbers to disseminate them. Money came back into more general circulation; where it came from is not quite clear, since there was little mining of gold or silver until the end of the Middle Ages. Merchants began to establish permanent headquarters, settling within the deserted walls of ghostly Roman towns or near the seat of a lord or ecclesiastic, whose throngs of retainers might become customers. Craftsmen moved from the overpopulated manors to these same growing centers, where they might produce wares that the lords or merchants would wish to buy. The process once started tended to snowball: the more people settled in such an agglomeration the more they needed food brought to them from the country, and the more craftsmen left the villages the more the country people, lords and serfs, had to obtain clothing and simple tools and utensils from the towns. Hence a busy local trade developed also.

By 1100, or not long thereafter, such centers existed all over Europe, from the Baltic to Italy, from England as far east as Bohemia. Usually there was one about every twenty or thirty miles. The smallest towns had only a few hundred inhabitants, the larger ones two or three thousand, or sometimes more. Each carried on a local exchange with its immediate countryside and purveyed goods of more distant origin to local consumers. But their importance was by no means merely economic. What made them "towns" in the full sense of the word was their acquisition of political rights.

The merchants and craftsmen who lived in the towns did not wish to remain, like the country people, subject to neighboring feudal lords. At worst, the feudal lords regarded merchants as fat possessors of ready money; they might hold them up on the road, plunder their mule trains, collect tolls at river crossings, or extort cash by offering "protection." At best, the most well-meaning feudal lord could not supervise the affairs of merchants, for the feudal and customary law knew nothing of commercial problems. The traders in the course of their business developed a "law merchant" of their own, having to do with money and money-changing, debt and bankruptcy, contracts, invoices, and bills of lading. They wished to have their own means of apprehending thieves, runaway debtors, or sellers of fraudulent goods. They strove, therefore, to get recognition for their own law, their own courts, their own judges and magistrates. They wished, too, to govern their towns themselves and to avoid payment of fees or taxes to nearby nobles.

Everywhere in Latin Christendom, along about 1100, the new towns struggled to free themselves from the encircling feudalism and to set themselves up as self-governing little republics. Where the towns were largest and closest together—along the highly urbanized arteries of the trade routes, in north Italy, on the upper Danube and Rhine rivers, in Flanders, or on the Baltic coast—they emancipated themselves the most fully. Venice, Genoa, Pisa, Florence, Milan became virtually independent city-states, each governing a substantial tract of its surrounding country. In Flanders also, towns like Bruges and Ghent dominated their localities. Along the upper Danube, the Rhine, the North Sea, the Baltic, many towns became imperial free cities within the Holy Roman Empire, each a kind of small republic owing allegiance to no one except the distant and usually ineffectual emperor. Nuremberg, Frankfurt, Augsburg, Strasbourg, Hamburg, and Lübeck were free cities of this kind. In France and England, where the towns in the twelfth century were somewhat less powerful, they obtained less independence but received charters of liberties from the king. By these charters they were assured the right to have their own town governments and officials, their own courts and law, and to pay their own kind of taxes to the king in lieu of ordinary feudal obligations.

Often towns formed leagues or urban federations, joining forces to repress banditry or piracy or to deal with ambitious monarchs or predatory nobles. The most famous such league was the Hanse; it was formed mainly of German towns, fought wars under its own banner, and dominated the commerce of the North Sea and the Baltic until after 1300. Similar tendencies of the towns to form political leagues, or to act independently in war and diplomacy, were suppressed by the kings in England, France, and Spain.

The fact that Italy, Germany, and the Netherlands were commercially more advanced than the Atlantic countries in the Middle Ages, and so had a more intensive town life, was to be one cause (out of many) preventing political unification. Not until 1860 or 1870 were nationwide states created in this region. In the west, where towns also grew up, but where more of a balance was kept between town and country, the towns were absorbed into nationwide monarchies that were arising under the kings. This difference between central and western Europe was to shape all the subsequent history of modern times.

The liberties won by the towns were corporate liberties. Each town was a collective thing. The townsman did not possess individual rights, but only the rights which followed from being a resident of a particular town. Among these were personal liberty; no townsman could be a serf, and fugitive serfs who lived over a year in a town were generally deemed to be free. But no townsman wanted individual liberty in the modern sense. The world was still too unsettled for the individual to act alone. The citizens wanted to join together in a compact body, and to protect themselves by all sorts of regulations and controls. The most obvious evidence of this communal solidarity was the wall within which most towns were enclosed. The citizens in time of trouble looked to their own defense. As the towns grew they built new walls farther out. Today, in Paris or Cologne, one may still see remains of different walls in use from the tenth to the thirteenth centuries.

Economic solidarity was of more day-to-day importance. The towns required neighboring peasants to sell foodstuffs only in the town marketplace. They thus protected their food supply against competition from other towns. Or they forbade the carrying on of certain trades in the country; this was to oblige peasants to make purchases in town, and protect the jobs and livelihood of the town craftsmen. They put up tariffs and tolls on the goods of other towns brought within their own walls. Or they levied special fees on merchants from outside who did business in the town. In Italy and Germany they often coined their own money; and the typical town fixed the rates at which various moneys should be exchanged. The medieval towns, in short, at the time of their greatest liberty, followed in a local way the same policies of protectionism and exclusiveness which national governments were often to follow in modern times.

Within each town merchants and craftsmen formed associations, or "guilds," for collective supervision of their affairs. Merchants formed a merchant guild. Stonemasons, carpenters, barbers, dyers, goldsmiths, coppersmiths, weavers, hatters, tailors, shoemakers, grocers, apothecaries, etc., formed craft guilds of their own. The guilds served a public purpose, for they provided that work should be done by reliable and experienced persons, and so protected people from the pitfalls of shoddy garments, clumsy barbers, poisonous drugs, or crooked and flimsy houses. They also provided a means of vocational education and marked out a career for young men. Typically a boy became an apprentice to some master, learned the trade, and lived with and was supported by the master's family for a term of years, such as seven. Then he became a journeyman, a qualified and recognized worker, who might work for any master at a stated wage. If lucky, he might become a master himself, open his own shop, hire journeymen, and take apprentices. So long as the towns were growing, a boy had some chance to become a master himself; but as early as 1300 many guilds were becoming frozen, and the masters were increasingly chary of admitting new persons to their own status. From the beginning, in any case, it was an important function of the guilds to protect their own members. The masters, assembled together, preserved their reputation by regulating the quality of their product. They divided work among themselves, fixed the terms of apprenticeship, the wages to be paid to journeymen, and the prices at which their goods must be sold. Or they took collective steps to meet or keep out the competition of the same trade in nearby towns.

Whether among individuals within the town itself, or as between town and country, or between town and town, the spirit of the medieval economy was to prevent competition. Risk, adventure, and speculation were not wanted. Almost no one thought it proper to work for monetary profit. The few who did, big merchants trading over large areas, met with suspicion and disapproval wherever they went.

The towns, although in many ways they tried to subject the peasants' interests to their own, nevertheless had an emancipating influence on the country. A rustic by settling in town might escape from serfdom. But the town influence was more widespread, and far out of proportion to the relatively small number of people who could become town dwellers. The growth of towns increased the demand for foods. Lords began to clear new lands. All western Europe set about developing a kind of internal frontier. Formerly villages had been separated by dark tracts of roadless woods, in which wolves roamed freely shadowed by the gnomes, elves, and fairies of popular folklore. Now pioneers with axes cleared farmlands and built villages in these immemorial forests. The lords who usually supervised such operations (since their serfs were not slaves, and could not be moved at will) offered freer terms to entice peasants to go and settle on the new lands. It was less easy for the lord of an old village to hold his people in serfdom when in an adjacent village, within a few hours' walk, the people were free. The peasants, moreover, were now able to obtain a little money by selling produce in town. The lords now wanted money because the towns were producing more articles which money could buy. It became very common for peasants to obtain personal freedom, holding their own lands, in return for an annual money payment to the lord for an indefinite period into the future. As early as the twelfth century serfdom began to disappear in northern France and southern England, and by the fifteenth century it had disappeared from most of western Europe. The peasant could now, in law, move freely about. But the manorial organization remained; the peasant owed dues and fees to the lord, and was still under his legal jurisdiction.

The Growth of National Monarchies

Meanwhile the kings were busy, each trying to build his kingdom into an organized monarchy that would outlast his life.[3] Monarchy became hereditary; the king inherited his position like any other feudal lord or possessor of an estate. Inheritance of the crown made for peace and order, for elections under conditions of the time were usually turbulent and disputed, and where the older Germanic principle of elective monarchy remained alive, as in the Holy Roman Empire, there was periodic commotion. The kings sent out executive officers to supervise their interests throughout their kingdoms. The kings of England, adopting an old Anglo-Saxon practice, had a sheriff in each of the forty shires; the kings of France created similar officers who were called bailiffs. The kings likewise instituted royal courts, under royal justices, to decide property disputes and repress crime. This assertion of legal jurisdiction, together with the military might necessary to enforce judgments upon obstinate nobles, became a main pillar of the royal power. In England especially, and in lesser degree elsewhere, the kings required local inhabitants to assist royal judges in the discovery of relevant facts in particular cases. They put men on oath to declare what they knew of events in their own neighborhood. It is from this enforced association of private persons with royal officers that the jury developed.

The kings needed money to pay for their governmental machinery or to carry on war with other kings. Taxation, as known in the Roman Empire, was quite unknown to the Germanic and feudal tradition. In the feudal scheme each person was responsible only for the customary fees which arose on stated occasions. The king, like other lords, was supposed to live on his own income—on the revenue of manors that he owned himself, the proceeds of estates temporarily under his wardship, or the occasional fees paid to him by his vassals. No king, even for the best of reasons, could simply decree a new tax and collect it. At the same time, as the use of money became more common, the kings had to assure themselves of a money income. In England, in the twelfth century, the customary obligation of the vassal to render military service to the king was being converted into a money payment, called "scutage" or shield money. As the towns grew up, with a new kind of wealth and a new source of money income, they agreed to make certain payments in return for their royal charters.

The royal demands for money, the royal claims to exercise jurisdiction, were regarded as innovations. They were constantly growing and sometimes were a source of abuse. They met with frequent resistance in all countries. A famous case historically (though somewhat commonplace in its own day) was that of Magna Carta in England in 1215, when a group of English lords and high churchmen,

[3] See pp. 29–30.

joined by representatives of the city of London, required King John to confirm and guarantee their historic liberties.

The king, as has been said, like any lord, was supposed to act in council or "court" with his vassals. The royal council became the egg out of which departments of government were hatched—such as the royal judiciary, exchequer, and military command. From it also was hatched the institution of parliaments. The kings had always, in a rough sort of way, held great parleys or "talks" (the Latin *parliamentum* meant simply a "talking") with their chief retainers. In the twelfth and thirteenth centuries the growth of towns added a new element to European life. To the lords and bishops was now added a burgher class, which, if of far inferior dignity, was too stubborn, free-spirited, and well furnished with money to be overlooked. When representatives of the towns began to be normally summoned to the king's great "talks," along with lords and clergy, parliaments may be said to have come into being.

Parliaments, in this sense, sprouted all over Europe in the thirteenth century. Nothing shows better the similarity of institutions in Latin Christendom, or the inadequacy of tracing the history of any one country by itself. The new assemblies were called *cortes* in Spain, diets in Germany, Estates General or provincial estates in France, parliaments in the British Isles. Usually they are referred to generically as "estates," the word "parliament" being reserved for Britain, but in origin they were all essentially the same.

The kings called these assemblies as a means of publicizing and strengthening the royal rule. They found it more convenient to explain their policies, or to ask for money, to a large gathering brought together for that purpose than to have a hundred officials make local explanations and strike local bargains in a hundred different places. The kings did not recognize, nor did the assemblies claim, any right of the parliament to dictate to the king and his government. But usually the king invited the parliament to state grievances; his action upon them was the beginning of parliamentary legislation.

The parliaments were considered to represent not the "nation" nor "people" nor yet the individual citizen, but the "estates of the realm," the great collective interests of the country. The first and highest estate was the clergy, the second the landed or noble class; to these older ruling groups were added, as a "third estate," the burghers of the chartered towns. Quite commonly these three types of people sat separately as three distinct chambers. But the pattern varied from country to country. In England, Poland, and Hungary the clergy as a whole ceased to be represented; only the bishops came, sitting with lay magnates in an upper house. Eventually the burghers dropped out in Poland, Bohemia, and Hungary, leaving the landed aristocracy in triumph in eastern Europe. In Castile and Württemberg, on the other hand, the noble estate eventually refused to attend parliament, leaving the townspeople and clergy in the assemblies. In some countries—in Scandinavia, Switzerland, and in the French Estates General—even peasants were allowed to have delegates.

In England the Parliament developed eventually in a distinctive way. After a long period of uncertainty there came to be two houses, known as the Lords and the Commons. The Lords, as in Hungary or Poland, included both great prelates and lay magnates. The House of Commons developed features not found on the Continent. Lesser landholders, the people who elsewhere counted as small nobles, sat in the same House of Commons with representatives of the towns. The

Commons was made up of "knights and burgesses," or gentry and townsmen together, a fact which greatly added to its strength, for the middle class of the towns long remained too weak to act alone. The mingling of classes in England, the willingness of townsmen to follow the leadership of the gentry, and of the gentry to respect the interests of townsmen, helped to root representative institutions in England more deeply than in other countries, in many of which the parliaments tended to die out in later times, in part because of class conflict. Moreover, England was a small country in the Middle Ages, even smaller than it looked on the map because the north was almost wild. There were no provincial or local parliamentary bodies (as in France, the Holy Roman Empire, or Poland) which might jealously cut into the powers of the central body or with which the king could make local arrangements without violating the principle of representative government. And finally, as a reason for the strength of Parliament in England, the elected members of the House of Commons very early obtained the power to *commit* their constituents. If they voted a tax, those who elected them had to pay it. The king, in order to get matters decided, insisted that the votes be binding. Constituents were not allowed to repudiate the vote of their deputy, nor to punish or harass him when he came home, as often happened in other countries. Parliament thus exercised power as well as rights.

In summary, the three centuries of the High Middle Ages laid foundations both for order and for freedom. Slavery was defunct and serfdom expiring. Politically, the multitude of free chartered towns, the growth of juries in some places, the rise of parliaments everywhere, provided means by which peoples could take some part in their governments. The ancient civilizations had never created a free political unit larger than the city-state. The Greeks had never carried democracy beyond the confines within which people could meet in person, nor had the Romans devised means by which, in a large state, the governed could share any responsibilities with an official bureaucracy. The ancients had never developed the idea of representative government, or of government by duly elected and authorized representatives acting at a distance from home. The idea is by no means as obvious or simple as it looks. It first appeared in the medieval monarchies of the West.

4. THE HIGH MIDDLE AGES: THE CHURCH

So far in our account of the High Middle Ages we have told the story of Hamlet without speaking of the Prince of Denmark, for we have left aside the church, except, indeed, when some mention of it could not be avoided. In the real life of the time the church was omnipresent. Religion permeated every pore. In feudalism the mutual duties of lord and vassal were confirmed by religious oaths, and bishops and abbots, as holders of lands, became feudal personages themselves. In the monarchies, the king was crowned by the chief churchman of his kingdom, adjured to rule with justice and piety, and anointed with holy oils. In the towns, guilds served as lay religious brotherhoods; each guild chose a patron saint and marched in the streets on holy days. For amusement the townspeople watched religious dramas, the morality and miracle plays in which religious themes were enacted. The rising town, if it harbored a bishop, took especial care to erect a new cathedral. Years of effort and of religious fervor produced the Gothic cathedrals which still stand as the best known memorials of medieval civilization.

The Development of the Medieval Church and Papacy

If, however, we turn back to the tenth century, the troubled years before 1000, we find the church in as dubious a condition as everything else. The church reflected the life about it. It was fragmented and localized. Every bishop went his own way. Though the clergy was the only literate class, many of the clergy themselves could not read and write. Christian belief was mixed with the old pagan magic and superstition. The monasteries were in decay. Priests often lived in a concubinage that was generally condoned. It was customary for them to marry, so that they had recognized children, to whom they intrigued to pass on their churchly position. Often rough laymen dominated their ecclesiastical neighbors, with the big lords appointing the bishops, and the little ones the parish priests. When people thought about Rome at all, they sensed a vague respect for something legendary and far away; but the bishop of Rome, or pope, had no influence and was treated in unseemly fashion in his own city. The popes of the tenth century were the creatures of the unruly Roman nobles. Marozia, daughter of a Roman "senator," became the mistress of one pope, by whom she had a son who became pope in turn, until she imprisoned him so that another son, by another father, could claim the papacy also.

The Roman Catholic church is in fact unrecognizable in the jumble of the tenth century. So far at least as human effort was concerned, it was virtually created in the eleventh century along with the other institutions of the High Middle Ages.

The impulse to reform came from many quarters. Sometimes a secular ruler undertook to correct conditions in his own domains. For this purpose he asserted a strict control over his clergy. In 962 the Holy Roman Empire was proclaimed. This Empire, like the Carolingian and Roman empires which it was supposed to continue, was in theory coterminous with Latin Christendom itself, and endowed with a special mission of preserving and extending the Christian faith. Neither in France nor in England (nor, when they became Christian states, in Spain, Hungary, Poland, or Scandinavia) was this claim of the Holy Roman Empire ever acknowledged. But the Empire did for a time embrace Italy as well as Germany. The first emperors, in the tenth and eleventh centuries, denouncing the outrageous conditions in Rome, strove to make the pope into their appointee.

At the same time a reform movement arose from spiritual sources. Serious Christians took matters into their own hands. They founded a new monastery at Cluny in France, which soon had many daughter houses. It was their purpose to purify monastic life and to set a higher Christian ideal to which all clergy and laity might look up. To rid themselves of immediate local pressures, the greed, narrowness, ignorance, family ambition, and self-satisfied inertia that were the main causes of corruption, the Cluniacs refused to recognize any authority except that of Rome itself. Thus, at the very time when conditions in Rome were at their worst, Christians throughout Europe built up the prestige of Rome, of the idea of Rome, as a means to raise all Latin Christendom from its depths.

As for the popes in Rome, those who preserved any independence of judgment or respect for their own office, it was their general plan to free themselves from the Roman mobs and aristocrats without falling into dependence upon the Holy Roman Emperor. In 1059 Pope Nicholas II issued a decree providing that future popes should be elected by the cardinals. The cardinals, at that time, were the priests of churches in the city of Rome or bishops of neighboring dioceses. By entrusting the choice of future popes to them, Pope Nicholas hoped to exclude all influence from outside the clergy itself. Popes have been elected by cardinals ever since, though not always without influence from outside.

One of the first popes so elected was Gregory VII, known also as Hildebrand, a dynamic and strong-willed man who was pope from 1073 to 1085. He had been in touch with the Cluniac reformers, and dreamed of a reformed and reinvigorated Europe under the universal guidance of the Roman pontiff.

To understand what followed, the reader must exert his imagination. In his mind's eye he must see a world in which all political barriers have dropped away. In this world people have no nationality. They do not live in the state, as in modern times; they live in the church. Society itself is a great religious community. Its leaders are the clergy, to which all educated persons belong. The public personage with whom people come into most frequent contact is the priest, and the most important public official is the bishop. The chief public buildings are churches, abbeys, and cathedrals. Secular interests, those of kings and dukes, of merchants and artisans, are earthbound and shortsighted. All persons, even kings, in addition to secular interests, have a higher concern. All are living in the religious community and preparing their souls for eternal life. The religious community, or church, reaches in principle as far as the borders of the known world. It is universal, for all men must be saved. At its head stands the bishop of Rome, the Vicar of Christ, the successor to Peter, the keeper of the keys, the *servus servorum Dei*, the servant of the servants of God.

Some such vision filled the mind of Gregory VII, and with it he founded the papal supremacy of the High Middle Ages. He believed that the church should stand apart from worldly society, that it should judge and guide all human actions, and that a pope could judge and punish kings and emperors if he deemed them sinful. His ideal was not a "world state," but its spiritual counterpart, a world church officered by a single-minded and disciplined clergy, centralized under a single authority. He began by insisting that the clergy free itself of worldly involvements. He required married priests to put aside their wives and families. Celibacy of the clergy, never generally established in the Greek Orthodox church, and later rejected by Protestants in the West, became and remained the rule for the Roman Catholic priesthood. Gregory insisted also that no ecclesiastic might receive office through appointment by a layman. In his view only clergy might institute or influence clergy, for the clergy must be independent and self-contained.

Gregory soon faced a battle with that other aspirant to universal supremacy and a sacred mission, the Holy Roman Emperor, who at this time was Henry IV. In Germany the bishops and abbots possessed a great deal of the land, which they held and governed under the emperor as feudal magnates in their own right. To the emperor it was vitally important to have his own men, as reliable vassals, in these great positions. Hence in Germany "lay investiture" had become very common. "Lay investiture" meant the practice by which a layman, the emperor, conferred upon the new bishop the signs of his spiritual authority, the ring and the staff. Gregory prohibited lay investiture. He supported the German bishops and nobles when they rebelled against Henry. Henry proving obstinate, Gregory excommunicated him, i.e., outlawed him from Christian society by forbidding any priest to give him the sacraments. Henry, baffled, sought out the pope at Canossa in Italy to do penance. "To go to Canossa" in later times became a byword for submission to the will of Rome.

In 1122, after both original contenders had died, a compromise on the matter of lay investiture was effected by which bishops recognized the emperor as their feudal head but looked to Rome for spiritual authority. But the struggle between popes and emperors went on unabated. The magnates of Germany, lay lords as well as bishops, often allied with the pope to preserve their own feudal liberties from the emperor. The emperor in Germany was never able to consolidate his domains as did the kings in England and France. In Italy, too, the popes and emperors quarreled, the foes of each commonly siding with the other. The unwillingness of lords and churchmen (and of towns also, as we have seen) to let the emperors build up an effectual government left its mark permanently upon Europe in two ways. It contributed to the centralization of Latin Christendom under Rome, while it blocked national unity in central Europe.

The height of the medieval papacy came with Innocent III, whose pontificate lasted from 1198 to 1216. Innocent virtually realized Gregory's dream of a unified Christian world. He intervened in politics everywhere. He was recognized as a supreme arbiter. At his word, a king of France took a wife, a king of England accepted an unwanted archbishop, a king of León put aside the cousin whom he had married, and a claimant to the crown of Hungary deferred to his rival. Innocent advised the kings of Bohemia, Poland, and Denmark on weighty matters, and the kings of England, Aragon, and Portugal acknowledged him as feudal overlord within their realms. Huge revenues now flowed to Rome from all over Latin Christendom, and an enormous bureaucracy worked there to dispatch the voluminous business of the papal court. As kings struggled to repress civil rebellion, so Innocent and his successors struggled to repress heresy, which, defined as doctrine at variance with that of the church at large, was becoming alarmingly common among the Albigensians of southern France.

In 1215 Innocent called a great church council, the greatest since antiquity, attended by 500 bishops and even by the patriarchs of Constantinople and Jerusalem. The council labored at the perplexing task of keeping the clergy from worldly temptations. By forbidding priests to officiate at ordeals or trials by battle, it virtually ended these survivals of barbarism. It attempted to regularize belief in the supernatural by controlling the superstitious traffic in relics. It declared the sacraments to be the channel of God's saving grace and defined them authoritatively.[4] In the chief sacrament, the Eucharist or Mass, it promulgated the dogma of transubstantiation, which held that, in the Mass, the priest converts the substance of bread and wine into the substance of Christ's body and blood. Except for heretics, who were suppressed, the acts of the Fourth Lateran Council were accepted with satisfaction throughout Latin Europe.

Intellectual Life: The Universities, Scholasticism

Under the auspices of the church, as rising governments gave more civil security, and as the economy of town and country became able to support men devoted to a life of thought, the intellectual horizon of Europeans began to open. The

---

[4] A sacrament is understood to be the outward sign of an inward grace. In Catholic doctrine the sacraments were and are seven in number: baptism, confirmation, penance, the Eucharist, extreme unction, marriage, and holy orders. Except for baptism, a sacrament may be administered only by a priest. A dogma is the common belief of the church, in which all the faithful share and must share so long as they are members of the church. Dogmas are regarded as implicitly the same in all ages; they cannot be invented or developed, but may from time to time be clarified, defined, promulgated, or proclaimed.

twelfth and thirteenth centuries saw the founding of the first universities. These originated in the natural and spontaneous coming together of teachers and pupils which had never wholly disappeared even in the Dark Ages. By 1200 there was a center of medical studies at Salerno in south Italy, of legal studies at Bologna in north Italy, of theological studies at Paris. Oxford was founded about 1200 by a secession of disgruntled students and professors from Paris, Cambridge shortly thereafter. By 1300 there were a dozen such universities in Latin Europe, by 1500 almost a hundred.

As the early agglomerations of traders developed into organized towns, so the informal concourses of students and teachers developed into organized institutions of learning, receiving the sharp corporate stamp that was characteristic of the High Middle Ages. It was in having this corporate identity that medieval universities resemble our own and differed from the schools of Athens or Alexandria in ancient times. A university, the early University of Paris, for example, was a body of men, young and old, interested in learning and endowed by law with a communal name and being. It possessed definite liberties under some kind of charter, regulated its own affairs through its own officials, and kept its own order among its often boisterous population. It gave, and even advertised, courses and lectures, and it decided collectively which professors were the best qualified to teach. It might consist of distinct schools or "faculties"—the combination of theology, law, and medicine, as at Paris, was the most usual. It held examinations and awarded degrees, whose meaning and value were recognized throughout the Latin West. The degree, which originated as a license to teach, admitted its holder to certain honors or privileges such as those of a craft guild. With it, a professor might readily move from one university to another. Students moved easily also, the language being everywhere Latin and the curriculum much the same. The university, moreover, though typically it began in poverty, was as a corporate body capable of holding property; and the benefactions of pious donors, as the years went on, often built up substantial endowments in lands and manors. So organized, free from outside control, and enjoying an income from property, the university lived on as an institution beyond the lifetime of all living men, through good times and bad.

The queen of the sciences was theology, the intellectual study of religion. Many in Europe, by the eleventh century, were beginning to reflect upon their beliefs. They continued to believe but could no longer believe with naïve or unthinking acceptance. It was accepted as a fact, for example, that the Son of God had been incarnated as a man in Jesus Christ. But in the eleventh century an Italian named Anselm, who became archbishop of Canterbury, wrote a treatise called *Cur Deus Homo?*—"Why Did God Become Man?"—giving reasoned explanations to show why God had taken this means to save mankind.[5] Soon afterward Abélard, who taught at Paris, wrote his *Sic et non*—"Yes and No" or "Pro and Con"—a collection of inconsistent statements made by St. Augustine and other Fathers of the Church. Abélard's purpose was to apply logic to the inherited mass of patristic writings, show wherein the truth of Christian doctrine really lay, and so make the faith consistent with reason and reflection.

---

[5] It may be useful to note that the Latin *homo* refers to all members of the human race, male and female, children and adults, the word for an adult male being *vir*. In English there is only the one word "man" to serve in both senses. Thus in modern biology and anthropology all members of the genus *homo*, of which *homo sapiens* is the only living species, are "man." In the present book the use of "man" in this generic sense will occur from time to time. In such contexts the pronouns "he," "his," and "him" are of indeterminate gender.

Meanwhile, in the twelfth century a great stream of new knowledge poured into Europe, bringing about a veritable intellectual revolution. It was derived from the Arabs, with whom Christians were in contact in Sicily and Spain. The Arabs, as has been seen, had taken over the ancient Greek science, translated Greek writings into Arabic, and in many ways added further refinements of their own. Bilingual Christians (assisted by numerous learned Jews who passed readily between the Christian and Muslim worlds) translated these works into Latin. Above all, they translated Aristotle, the great codifier of Greek knowledge who had lived and written in the fourth century B.C. The Europeans, barely emerging from barbarism, were overwhelmed by this sudden disclosure of an undreamed of universe of knowledge. Aristotle became The Philosopher, the unparalleled authority on all branches of knowledge other than religious.

The great problem for Europeans was how to digest the gigantic bulk of Aristotle, or, in more general terms, how to assimilate or reconcile the body of Greek and Arabic learning to the Christian faith. The universities, with their "scholastic" philosophers or "schoolmen," performed this useful social function. Most eminent of scholastics was Thomas Aquinas (1225–1274), the Angelic Doctor, known also to his own contemporaries as the Dumb Ox from the slow deliberation of his speech. His chief work, appropriately called the *Summa Theologica*, was a survey of all knowledge. The thought of Aquinas, as recently as 1879, was pronounced by Pope Leo XIII to be the foundation of official Catholic philosophy.

The chief accomplishment of Thomas Aquinas was his demonstration that faith and reason could not be in conflict. By reason he meant a severely logical method, with exact definition of words and concepts, deducing step by step what follows and must follow if certain premises are accepted. His philosophy is classified as a form of "realism." It holds, that is, that the general idea is more "real" than the particular—that "man" is more real than this or that man or woman, that "law" as such is more real and binding than this or that particular law. He derived his philosophy from what he took to be the nature of God, of man, of law, of reason, of beings in general. He taught a hierarchic view of the universe and of society, of which God was the apex, and in which all things and all men were subordinated to God in a descending order, each bound to fulfill the role set by its own place and nature. It was the emphasis on the superior reality of abstractions that enabled men in the Middle Ages to believe steadfastly in the church while freely attacking individual churchmen, to have faith in the papacy while denouncing the popes as scoundrels—or to accept without difficulty the mystery of transubstantiation, which declared that what admittedly looked and tasted like bread and wine was, in real inner substance, the body of Christ.

The scholastic philosophy, as perfected by Thomas Aquinas, was not very favorable to the growth of natural science, because, in its emphasis on an inner reality, it drew attention away from the actual details and behavior of concrete things. On the other hand, the scholastic philosophy laid foundations on which later European thought was to be reared. It habituated Europeans to great exactness, to careful distinctions, even to the splitting of hairs. It called for disciplined thinking. And it made the world safe for reason. If any historical generalization may be made safely, it may be safely said that any society that believes reason to threaten its foundations will suppress reason. In Thomas' time, there were some who said that Aristotle and the Arabs were infidels, dangerous influences that must be silenced. Any reasoning about the faith, they warned, was a form of weakness.

Thomas' doctrine that faith could not be endangered by reason gave a freedom to thinkers to go on thinking. Here Latin Christendom may be contrasted with the Muslim world. It was ruled, in about the time of Thomas Aquinas, that valid interpretation of the Koran had ended with the Four Great Doctors of early Islam. As Muslims said, the Gate was closed. Arabic thought, so brilliant for several centuries, went into decline.

The Crusades; New Invasions; Europe by 1300

Meanwhile, the West was expanding. Europe in the eleventh century took the offensive against Islam. All Latin Christendom went on the Crusades. War itself was subordinated to the purposes of religion.

The most ambitious, best remembered, and least successful of such expeditions were the Crusades to win back the Holy Land. The First Crusade was preached in 1095 by Pope Urban II, who hoped thereby to advance the Peace of God by draining off bellicose nobles to fight the infidels, and to build up the leadership of Rome, just asserted by Gregory VII, through raising a universal cause of which the pope might be the head. Crusades to the Holy Land, with varying success, and sometimes departing woefully from their religious aims, went on intermittently for two hundred years. It was the growth of Italian shipping in the Mediterranean, the rise of more orderly feudal monarchies, the increasing sense of a Europe-wide common purpose, that made possible the assembly and transport of considerable forces over a great distance. It is sometimes said that the Crusades, by bringing contacts with the East, stimulated the development of civilization in the West, but it seems more likely that, as Europe's counterthrust against Islam, the Crusades were the consequence of Europe's own growing strength. For a century the Latin Christians occupied parts of Palestine and Syria. But in the thirteenth century they had to withdraw, and the Muslims remained in possession.

THE MEETING OF ST. ANTHONY AND ST. PAUL
by Sassetta (Italian, 1392–1450)

Here we can see something of the medieval way of thinking. The picture tells a religious story. St. Anthony appears in three places, walking alone, converting a centaur, and meeting and embracing St. Paul. There is no attempt to present him as a unique individual person; his head and features disappear behind those of St. Paul in the principal scene. The picture gives the "idea" of the story. The two figures are typical saints, with the halos which conventionally designated sacred persons. The artist has painted the "idea" or "essence" of a forest, i.e., many trees; he has not shown the actual appearance of a particular forest, with underbrush, shadows, trees of different sizes, and foliage of different kinds. His hills are hills in general, i.e., mounds of earth; his cave is a cave in general, i.e., a dark hole. When the two saints embrace, their arms and legs are placed where the mind knows that they ought to be, not where the eye would see them concretely in any particular situation. The picture thus illustrates, on a simple level, what is meant by the abstractness or "realism" (the realism of ideas) of medieval thought. A child today, or an artistically untrained adult, draws in the same way, portraying the idea rather than the physical actuality. The idea of a forest is, after all, "many trees"; all else is special or incidental, not of the essence. Courtesy of the National Gallery of Art, Washington, D.C., Samuel H. Kress Collection.

CRUSADING ACTIVITY, 1100–1250

Medieval Christendom expanded geographically until about A.D. 1250. Darker regions are those Christianized shortly before and after A.D. 1000. Arrows indicate organized military-religious expeditions, which by 1250 had recovered most of Spain from Muslim control, but had failed to do so in the Holy Land. Dates are rounded and very rough.

Other crusades (for such they were) had more lasting results. A party of Normans won Sicily from the Arabs about 1100. Iberian Christians, descending from the mountains of northern Spain, carried on a *reconquista* of two centuries against the Moors. By 1250 they had staked out the Christian kingdoms of Portugal, León, Castile, Aragon, and Valencia, leaving the Muslims only Granada in the extreme south, which was conquered much later, in 1492. In southern France, an Albigensian crusade in the thirteenth century put down the heretics, those born in the faith but erring from it. Against remaining European heathen, those born in ignorance of the faith, of whom a few were still found along the Baltic coast, crusading expeditions were also launched. The Teutonic Order, a military-religious society of knights founded originally to fight in the Holy Land, transferred its operations to the north. Christianity, and with it the civilization of the Latin West, was brought by the sword to primitive Prussia and the east Baltic regions.

About the year 1250 there developed a new threat of invasion from Asia. As the

Huns had burst out of Asia in the fifth century, and the Magyars in the ninth, so now the Tartars appeared in the thirteenth century, to be followed in the fourteenth by the Ottoman Turks. We shall see how the Turks long continued to press upon central Europe. But, on the whole, by the thirteenth century, Europe was capable of resistance. Always until then it had lain open, an outlying, backward, thinly populated protuberance from the Eurasian land mass. It had lain open in the remote past to wandering Indo-Europeans, then to Roman imperial conquerors, to Germanic barbarians, to Huns, Magyars, and, in part, the Arabs. All these were assimilated. The blood of all flowed in European veins. In spirit all were assimilated by the Roman church, the Latin language, the common institutions of feudalism, monarchy, a free town life, parliamentary assemblies, and scholastic learning, which ran as an almost seamless web from England to Sicily and from Portugal to Poland.

By 1300 the "rise of Europe" was an accomplished fact. The third of the three segments into which the Greco-Roman world had divided, the one which in A.D. 700 had been the most barbarous, now some six hundred years later had a civilization of its own. It was still only one among the several great cultures of the world, such as the Islamic, Byzantine, Indian, and Chinese. It enjoyed no preeminence. The Chinese empire, for example, in the thirteenth century, had cities whose population reached into millions. It had an affluent merchant class, great textile manufactures, and an iron industry that produced over 100,000 tons a year. The arts and sciences were assiduously pursued. Government was centralized and complex; it issued paper money, and employed a civil service recruited by competitive examinations. Books on religious, technical, and agricultural subjects, including whole multivolume encyclopedias, were printed in enormous numbers, even though the lack of an alphabet and use of thousands of characters made it difficult for literacy to become widely spread. The Venetian Marco Polo was dazzled by the China that he lived in from 1275 to 1292.

Many have asked why China did not generate, as Europe did in these centuries, the forces that ultimately led to the modern scientific and industrial world. One answer is suggested by the fact that it was Europeans like Marco Polo who went to China, not Chinese who went to Europe. It was the Chinese who invented printing, but it was Europe that was revolutionized by printed books. The Chinese knew of gunpowder, but the Europeans invented guns. Chinese merchant vessels traded with India in the twelfth century, but did not pursue the advantage; Europeans did so three centuries later, and they also discovered America. Somehow Europe was more enterprising and restless. It was already on the alert for something new. In Europe there was no all-embracing empire as in China, but kings, lords, and towns that competed with each other. Conformity was not one of the primary virtues. With religion and the church kept distinct from the state, the questions of what one should do with one's life were less dependent on the political powers than in China. Europe was disorderly and full of conflict—rivalries and wars between kings, quarrels between kings and their barons, disputes between church and state, clashes between lords and their peasant workers. In such disorder there was also a kind of freedom, and a dynamism which promoted change.

II.
The Upheaval in Christendom, 1300-1560

I n the transition from a traditional to a more modern form of society all the old civilizations have had to reexamine their religious base. Today we can observe this process at work everywhere: the Chinese reconsider the age-old teachings of Confucius, the Muslims enter into wider activities than those known to the Koran, and the peoples of India attempt to found a society in which historic Hindu practices no longer form the dominant pattern. It is not necessarily that peoples reject their ancestral religion. They may even reaffirm it, but they try also to modernize it, to adapt it, to make room for new and nonreligious interests. The process of developing a variety of activities outside the sphere of religion is called "secularization."

Latin Christendom was the first of the world's major civilizations to become "secularized." In the very long run it was those aspects of European civilization that were least associated with Christianity, such as natural science and industrial technology, or military and economic power, that the "non-European" world from Islam to East Asia proved to be most willing to adopt. If in our own time there has come to be such a thing as a world civilization, it is because all the world's great traditional cultures have been increasingly secularized.

The Europe which by the thirteenth century was so triumphantly Christian soon entered upon a series of disasters. The Mongols after about 1240 held Russia in subjugation for two hundred years. The Ottoman Turks, who had originated in central Asia, penetrated the Byzantine Empire, crushed the medieval Serbian state in 1389, spread over the Balkans, and took Constantinople itself in 1453. Eastern Christianity continued to exist, but under alien political domination. Latin

Chapter Emblem: A medal struck in honor of Pico della Mirandola, Florentine humanist of the fifteenth century.

Christianity, reaching from Poland and Hungary to the Atlantic, remained independent but was beset with troubles. The authority of the papacy and of the Roman Catholic church was called into question. Eventually the Protestant churches emerged. The whole of medieval civilization was undermined. Yet new forces also asserted themselves, alongside or outside the religious tradition. Government, law, philosophy, science, the arts, material and economic activities were pursued with less regard for Christian values. Power, order, beauty, wealth, knowledge, and control of nature were regarded as desirable in themselves.

In this mixture of decline and revival, of religious revolution and secularization, medieval Christendom began to take on the outlines of modern Europe.

5. DISASTERS OF THE FOURTEENTH CENTURY

The Black Death and Its Consequences

During the fourteenth century, and quite abruptly, almost half the population of Europe was wiped out. Some died in sporadic local famines that began to appear after 1300. The great killer, however, was the bubonic plague, or Black Death, which first struck Europe in 1348. Since the plague recurred at irregular and unpredictable intervals, and killed off the young as well as the old, it disrupted marriage and family life and made it impossible for many years for Europe to regain the former level of population. In some places whole villages disappeared. Cultivated fields were abandoned for want of able-bodied men and women to work them. The towns were especially vulnerable, since the plague bacillus was carried by rats, which infested the dark houses crowded within town walls. Trade and exchange were obstructed; prices, wages, and incomes moved erratically; famine made its victims more susceptible to disease, and deaths from the plague contributed to famine. The living were preoccupied with the burial of the dead and with fears for their own future.

There were immediate social and political repercussions. For the survivors, at least, there were some advantages in that labor became scarce and so could expect higher wages. On the other hand, in the general disorganization, and with landowners and urban employers decimated also, many of the poor could find no work, or took to vagabondage and begging. The upper classes, acting through governments, attempted to control wages and prices, as in the English Statute of Laborers of 1351. Rebellions of workers broke out in various towns, especially in Flanders. There were massive insurrections of peasants in many parts of Europe. In France these were called "jacqueries" (from "Jacques," a nickname for a peasant), of which the first was in 1358. In England a similar large-scale uprising in 1381 came to be known as Wat Tyler's rebellion. Sometimes the spokesmen for these movements went beyond their immediate grievances to question the whole class structure, asking why some should be rich and others poor. It was in Wat Tyler's rebellion that the famous couplet was coined:

> *When Adam delved and Eve span*
> *Who was then a gentleman?*

Governments and the upper classes replied to this menace with ferocious repression. The peasants generally returned to their usual labors. Yet something was

MILLIONS
OF PERSONS

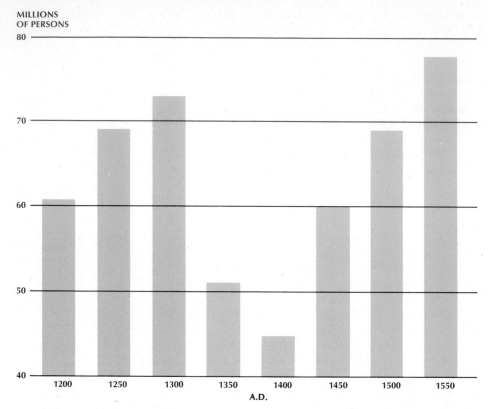

Source: M. K. Bennett, *The World's Food* (New York: Harper, 1954).

ESTIMATED POPULATION OF EUROPE, 1200–1550

The catastrophic drop shown between 1300 and 1400, unparalleled in the history of Europe, was due mainly to the bubonic plague or Black Death, which first appeared in 1348 and raged intermittently thereafter. It is thought that by about A.D. 600, after the collapse of the Roman Empire, the population of Europe may have gradually declined to about twenty million. Then with agricultural improvements, and the end of the Viking attacks and other raids, population grew rapidly, especially after A.D. 1000, reaching a high point in the early fourteenth century. Not until the early sixteenth century was the population of 1300 again attained.

gained for the rural workers, at least in the long run, as underlying economic and demographic forces continued to assert themselves. The landowners, or feudal class, in order to get the work done on their manors, and assure their own incomes, had to offer more favorable terms. These included, for example, the giving of lifetime tenures to peasant families, in return for fixed payment of sums of money. Over the years many of these peasant holdings became hereditary and the value of money decreased, so that payment of a shilling, for example, which in 1400 represented a significant amount, became much less burdensome for the rural worker by 1600. In effect, a class of small peasant property owners began to emerge in much of Europe.

The kings also, who had been building up their position against the church and the feudal lords since the eleventh century, found their problems complicated by the disasters of the fourteenth. They still had their governments to maintain, and their ambitions to satisfy, even if death removed large fractions of their subjects. They even had to increase their incomes, as it became usual for kings to employ royal armies of foot soldiers against the recurring possibility of feudal resistance. Various means of increasing the royal spending power were devised. Currency was debased; that is, the king ordered a given weight of gold or silver to be cut up into a larger number of monetary units. Thus he temporarily had more money, but the result was inflation and higher prices, that is, the declining value of money already mentioned. New taxes were introduced. About 1300 the kings of both England and France undertook to tax the clergy of their respective kingdoms, in both of which the clergy were substantial owners of land. The impact on the church was violent and dramatic, as will shortly be seen. The kings made increasing demands as well on great noble landholders and urban merchants. These demands were resisted, or made subject to bargains by the representative bodies whose origin was described in the last chapter, so that the fourteenth century, and still more the fifteenth, has been called the "golden age" of the medieval parliaments.

In 1337 the Hundred Years' War began between England and France. The battles all took place in France, which was internally divided, some parts, like Aquitaine, having long belonged to the English crown. France was ravaged by marauding bands of English soldiers and their French adherents, until it began to recover in the days of Joan of Arc, who was burned at Rouen in 1431. In England the effects of the long and intermittent war were less divisive. As English soldiers with their longbows defeated the mounted French knights, a kind of popular patriotism arose in England. Parliament widened its powers as the kings needed money for their campaigns. But the great barons also became more unruly. They deposed Richard II in 1399, then quarreled among themselves, in a confusion punctuated by invasion from Scotland and revolt in Wales. Disorder became worse in the fifteenth century. Dukes and earls and their followers formed private armies and fought with each other; they defied the royal law courts and intimidated juries, used Parliament and government for their own purposes, and exploited their peasants. In 1450 a movement known as Jack Cade's rebellion called for reform without success. From then until 1485 England was beset by the upper-class turmoil of the Wars of the Roses.

Troubles of the Medieval Church

Meanwhile similar calamities afflicted the church. In 1300, the church of the High Middle Ages, centralized in the papacy, stood at its zenith. But the church was weakened by its very successes. It faced the danger that besets every successful institution—a form of government or a university, to choose modern examples—the danger of believing that the institution exists for the benefit of those who conduct its affairs. The papacy, being at the top, was the most liable to this danger. It became "corrupt," set in its ways, out of touch with public opinion, and controlled by a self-perpetuating bureaucracy. It was unable to reform itself, and unwilling to let anyone else reform it.

Both Edward I of England and Philip the Fair of France, in the 1290s, assessed taxes on the landed estates belonging to the great abbeys, bishoprics, and other components of the church. The pope, Boniface VIII, prohibited the taxation of clergy by the civil ruler. In the ensuing altercation, in 1302, he issued the famous bull, *Unam Sanctam*, the most extreme of all assertions of papal supremacy, which declared that outside the Roman church there was no salvation, and that "every human creature" was "subject to the Roman pontiff."[1] The French king retorted by sending soldiers to arrest Boniface, who soon died. French influence in the College of Cardinals brought about the election of a pope who was subservient to Philip, and who took up his residence, with his court and officials, at Avignon on the lower Rhone river, on the then borders of France. Thus began the "Babylonian Captivity" of the church. The rest of Europe regarded the popes at Avignon throughout the century as tools of France. The prestige of the papacy as a universal institution was badly dimmed.

Attempts to correct the situation made matters worse. In 1378 the College of Cardinals, torn by French and anti-French factions within it, elected two popes. Both were equally legitimate, being chosen by cardinals, but one lived at Rome, one at Avignon, and neither would resign. The French and their supporters recognized the Avignon pope, England and most of Germany, the Roman. For forty years both lines were perpetuated. There were now two papacies, estranged by the Great Schism of the West.

Never had the papacy been so externally magnificent as in the days of the Captivity and the Schism. The papal court at Avignon surpassed the courts of kings in splendor. The papal officialdom grew in numbers, ignoring the deeper problems while busily transacting each day's business. Papal revenues mounted, and new papal taxes were devised, for example, the "annates," by which every bishop or abbot in Christendom had to transmit to Rome most of the first year's income of his office. In the continuing movement of funds from all over Europe to the papal court, from the thirteenth century on, a new class of international bankers rose and prospered.

But the papacy, never so sumptuous, had never since the tenth century rested on such shaky foundations. People pay willingly for institutions in which they believe, and admire magnificence in leaders whom they respect. But before 1378, with the pope submissive to France, and after 1378, with two popes and two papacies to support, there was growing complaint at the extravagance and worldliness of papal rule. It must be remembered that all this happened in a Europe traumatized by the plague, and with a declining number of people expected to bear increasing burdens. The most pious Christians were the most shocked. To them the behavior of the cardinals was disgraceful. Earnest souls were worried in conscience. They recognized the vital necessity of obtaining God's grace, but with two churches under two popes, each claiming to hold the keys of Peter, how could anyone be certain that his church gave true salvation? In a society that was still primarily a religious community, this sense of religious insecurity was a source of uneasiness and dread.

The old moorings were weakened, the wrath of God seemed to be raining upon mankind, and no one had the slightest notion of how the world was going to turn out. Symptoms of mass neurosis appeared. Some people sought refuge in a hectic merriment or luxury and self-indulgence. Others became preoccupied with grisly

---

[1] Bulls are known by their first one or two Latin words, which in this case mean "one holy (Catholic church)"; a "bull," while the most solemn form of papal edict, does not as such embody a dogma; and it is not Catholic practice today to affirm this policy of Boniface VIII.

subjects. Some frantically performed the Dance of Death in the cemeteries, while others furtively celebrated the Black Mass, parodying religion in a mad desire to appease the devil. The Order of Flagellants grew up; its members went through the streets, two by two, beating each other with chains and whips. It was at this time that the great witchcraft delusion, which was to reach its height in the fifteenth and sixteenth centuries, first became important.

Disaffection with the church, or the thought that it might not be the true or the only way to salvation, spread in all ranks of society. It was not only kings who disputed the claims of the clergy. Obscure parish priests, close to the distress of ordinary people, began to doubt the powers of their ecclesiastical superiors. One of these humble clerics was William Langland, who in his *Piers Plowman*, in the 1360s, contrasted the sufferings of the honest poor with the hypocrisy and corruption in high places. Such unsettling ideas spread very widely; in England those who held them were known as Lollards. Since the actual poor left no records, it is hard to say exactly what their ideas consisted of, but something like them was also expressed by John Wyclif, who taught at Oxford. About 1380, Wyclif was saying that the true church could do without elaborate possessions, and even that an organized church might not be necessary for salvation, since ordinary, devout persons could do without priests and obtain salvation by reading the Bible, which he translated into English. Similar ideas appeared in Bohemia in central Europe, with John Huss as their spokesman. Here they became a national movement, for the Hussites were both a religious party and at the same time a Slavic or Czech party protesting against the supremacy of the Germans who lived in Bohemia. The Hussite wars ravaged central Europe for decades in the fifteenth century. The ideas of the Lollards and of Huss and Wyclif were branded as heresy, or unacceptable deviations from the true doctrine of the church.

Influential and established persons did not yet turn to heresy, and still less to witchcraft or flagellation. Their answer to the needs of the day was to assemble a great Europe-wide or general council of the church, in which reforms could be pressed by the whole body of Christians upon the reluctant and rival popes.

The Conciliar Movement

In 1409 such a church council met at Pisa. All parts of the Latin West were represented. The council declared both reigning popes deposed, and obtained the due election of another, but since the first two refused to resign there were now three. In 1414 an even greater and more fully attended council met at Constance. Its aims were three: to end the now threefold schism, to extirpate heresy, and to reform the church "in head and members," or from top to bottom. Not much was accomplished in reform. To discourage heresy, John Huss was interrogated, condemned, and burned at the stake. The schism was ended. All three popes were at last persuaded or compelled to withdraw, and another, Martin V, was elected. The unity of the church, under the papacy, was at last restored.

The majority at the Council of Constance wished to make general councils part of the permanent apparatus of the church for all time in the future. They regarded the pope as, so to speak, a constitutional monarch, and the council as a representative body for all Christians. Martin V, however, no sooner elected pope, reaffirmed the prerogatives of the papal office. He dissolved the Council of

Constance, and repudiated its decrees. The next thirty years saw a continuing contest of wills between successive popes and successive councils.

In this battle for jurisdiction few reforms could be adopted, and fewer still enforced. Increasingly the life of the church was corrupted by money. No one believed in bribery; but everyone knew that many high churchmen (like many high civil officials of the day) could be bribed. To buy or sell a church office was a crime in the canon law, known as "simony," but it was a crime which in the fifteenth century could not be suppressed. For churchmen to live with mistresses was considered understandable, if unseemly; the standards of laymen in such matters were not high; but for a bishop or other ecclesiastic to give lucrative church positions to his own children (or other relatives) was the abuse known as nepotism, and it, too, could not be eradicated. To sell divine grace for money, all agreed, was not only wrong but impossible. But in 1300 Boniface VIII had given encouragement to the practice of "indulgences." A person, if properly confessed, absolved, and truly repentant, might, by obtaining an indulgence, be spared certain of the temporal punishments of purgatory. One obtained such an indulgence, almost always, in return for a donation of money. The practice proved to be a fatally easy method of fund raising, despite complaints against the sale of indulgences.

Gradually the popes prevailed over the councils. The conciliar movement was greatly weakened for Christendom as a whole when the powerful French element secured its aims by a local national arrangement. In the Pragmatic Sanction of Bourges, in 1438, the Gallican (or French) church affirmed the supremacy of councils over popes, declared its administrative independence from the Holy See, suppressed the payment of annates to Rome, and forbade papal intervention in the appointment of French prelates. The papacy thus lost influence in France, but the conciliarists themselves were divided. In 1449, with the dissolution of the Council of Basel, the conciliar movement came to an end. In 1450 a great Jubilee was held to celebrate the papal triumph.

The papacy, its prestige and freedom of action thus secured, now passed into the hands of a series of cultivated gentlemen, men of ┼he world, men of "modern" outlook in tune with their times—the famous popes of the Renaissance. Some, like Nicholas V (1447–1455) or Pius II (1458–1464), were accomplished scholars and connoisseurs of books. Some were like Innocent VIII (1484–1492), a pleasant man who was the first pope to dine in public with ladies. Alexander VI (1492–1503), of the Spanish Borgia family, exploited his office for the benefit of his relatives, trying to make his son Cesare Borgia the ruler of all Italy, while his daughter, Lucretia Borgia, gathered literary men and artists about her, and developed a perhaps exaggerated reputation for depravity. Alexander VI's successor, Julius II (1503–1513), was a capable general, and Leo X (1513–1521) was a superb patron of architects and painters. But we must now describe the Italian Renaissance, in which worthies of this kind were elevated to the Holy See.

6. THE RENAISSANCE IN ITALY

In Italy in the fifteenth century, and especially at Florence, we observe not merely a decay of medieval certainties but the appearance of a new and constructive attitude toward the world. The Renaissance, a French word meaning "rebirth," first received its name from those who thought of the Middle Ages as a dark time from which the human spirit had to be awakened. It was called a *rebirth* in the belief that men now, after a long interruption, took up and resumed a civilization like that of the Greco-Romans. Medieval people had thought of the times of Aristotle or Cicero as not sharply distinct from their own. In the Renaissance, with a new historical sense, arose the conception of "modern" and "ancient" times, separated by a long period with a different life style and appropriately called the Middle Ages.

A few useful distinctions can be made. The basic institutions of Europe, the very languages and nationalities, the great frameworks of collective action in law, government, and economic production, all originated in the Middle Ages. But the Renaissance marked a new era in thought and feeling, by which Europe and its institutions were in the long run to be transformed. The origins of modern natural science can be traced more to the medieval universities than to the Renaissance thinkers. But it was in the Italy of the Quattrocento (as Italians call the fifteenth century) that other fields of thought and expression were first cultivated. The Italian influence in other countries, in these respects, remained very strong for at least 200 years. It pertained to high culture, and hence to a limited number of persons, but extended over the whole area represented by literature and the arts—literature meaning all kinds of writing, and the arts including all products of human skill. The effects of the Italian Renaissance, though much modified with the passage of time, were evident in the books and art galleries of Europe and America, and in the architecture of their cities, until the revolution of "modern" art in the early twentieth century. They involved the whole area of culture which is neither theological nor scientific but concerns essentially moral and civic questions, asking what man ought to be or ought to do, and is reflected in matters of taste, style, propriety, decorum, personal character, and education. In particular, it was in Renaissance Italy that an almost purely secular attitude first appeared, in which life was no longer seen by leading thinkers as a brief preparation for the hereafter.

The Italian Cities and the New Conception of Man

The towns of Italy, so long as trade converged in the Mediterranean, were the biggest and most bustling of all the towns that rose in Europe in the Middle Ages. The crafts of Italy included many refined trades such as those of the goldsmith or stonecarver, which were so zealously pursued that artisanship turned into art, and a delight in the beautiful became common among all classes. Merchants made fortunes in commerce; they lent their money to popes or princes, and so made further fortunes as bankers. They bought the wares of the craftsmen-artists. They rejoiced, not so much in money or the making of money, as in the beautiful things and psychological satisfactions that money could buy; and if they forgot the things that money could not buy, this is only to say again that their outlook was "secular."

The towns were independent city-states. There was no king to build up a government for Italy as a whole, and for several generations the popes were either absent at Avignon or engaged in disputes arising from the Great Schism, so that the influence of Rome was unimportant. The merchant oligarchies, each in its own city, enjoyed an unhampered stage on which to pursue interests other than those of business. In some, as at Milan, they succumbed to or worked with a local prince or despot. In others, as at Florence, Venice, and Genoa, they continued to govern themselves as republics. They had the experience of contending for public office, of suppressing popular revolt or winning popular favor, of producing works of public munificence, of making alliances, hiring armies, outwitting rivals, and conducting affairs of state. In short, Italy offered an environment in which many facets of human personality could be developed.

All this was most especially true in Florence, the chief city of Tuscany. In the fifteenth century it had a population of about 60,000, which made it only moderately large as Italian cities went.[2] Yet, like ancient Athens, Florence produced an extraordinary sequence of gifted men in a short period. From the days of Dante, Petrarch, and Boccaccio, who all died before 1375, to those of Machiavelli, who lived until 1527, an amazing number of the leading figures of the Italian Renaissance were Florentines. Like Athens also, Florence lost its republican liberty as well as its creative powers. Its history can be summarized in that of the Medici family. The founder of the family fortunes was Giovanni (d. 1429), a merchant and banker of Florence. His son, Cosimo de' Medici (1389–1464), allying himself with the popular element against some of the leading families of the republic, soon became unofficial ruler himself. Cosimo's grandson, Lorenzo the Magnificent (1449–1492), also used his great wealth to govern but is chiefly remembered as a poet, connoisseur, and lavish benefactor of art and learning. In the next century Tuscany became a grand duchy, of which the Medici were hereditary grand dukes until the family died out in 1737. Thus established, they furnished numerous cardinals and two popes to the church, and two Medici women became queens of France.

What arose in Italy, in these surroundings, was no less than a new conception of man himself. The world was so exciting that another world need not be thought of. It seemed very doubtful whether a quiet, cloistered, or celibate life was on a higher plane than an active gregarious life, or family life, or even a life of promiscuity and adventure. It was hard to believe that clergy were any better than laity, or that life led to a stern divine judgment in the end. That man's will and intelligence might mislead him seemed a gloomy doctrine. That man was a frail creature, in need of God's grace and salvation, though perhaps said with the lips, was not felt in the heart. Instead, what captivated the Italians of the Renaissance was a sense of man's tremendous powers.

Formerly, the ideal had been seen in renunciation, in a certain disdain for the concerns of this world. Now a life of involvement was also prized. Formerly, poverty had been greatly respected, at least in Christian doctrine. Now voices were heard in praise of a proper enjoyment of wealth. In the past, men had admired a life of contemplation, or meditative withdrawal. Now the humanist Leonardo Bruni could write, in 1433, "The whole glory of man lies in activity." Often, to be sure, the two attitudes existed in the same person. Sometimes they divided different groups within the same city. As always, the old persisted along with the new. The result might be psychological stress and civil conflict.

The new esteem for human activity took both a social and an individualistic turn. In cities maintaining their republican forms, as at Florence in the early fifteenth century, a new civic consciousness or sense of public duty was expressed. For this purpose the writings of Cicero and other ancients were found to be

---

[2] See the picture essay, pp. 93–103.

highly relevant, since they provided an ethics independent of the Christian and medieval tradition. There was also a kind of cult of the great individual, hardly known to the ancients, and one which gave little attention to collective responsibility. Renaissance individualism put its emphasis on outstanding attainments. The great individual shaped his own destiny in a world governed by fortune. He had *virtù*, the quality of being a man (*vir*, "man"), and although women might also exhibit *virtù*, it was a quality which in the society of the day was more to be expected in the most aggressive adult males. It meant the successful demonstration of human powers. A man of *virtù*, in the arts, in war, or in statecraft, was a man who knew what he was doing, who, from resources within himself, made the best use of his opportunities, hewing his way through the world, and excelling in all that he did. For the arts, such a spirit is preserved in the autobiography of Benvenuto Cellini.

The growing preoccupation with things human can be traced in new forms of painting, sculpture, and architecture that arose in Italy at this time. These arts likewise reflected an increasing this-worldliness, a new sense of reality and a new sense of space, of a kind different from that of the Middle Ages, and which was to underlie European thinking almost to our own time. Space was no longer indeterminate, unknowable, or divine; it was a zone occupied by physical human beings, or one in which human beings might at least imagine themselves moving about. Reality meant visible and tangible persons or objects in this space, "objective" in the sense that they looked or felt the same to all normal persons who perceived them. It was a function of the arts to convey this reality, however idealized or suffused by the artist's individual feeling, in such a way that observers could recognize in the image the identity of the thing portrayed.

Architecture reflected the new tendencies. Though the Gothic cathedral at Milan was built as late as 1386, at Florence and elsewhere architects preferred to adapt Greco-Roman principles of design, such as symmetrical arrangements of doors and windows, the classical column, the arch and the dome. More public buildings of a nonreligious character were built, and more substantial town houses were put up by wealthy merchants, in styles meant to represent grandeur, or civic importance, or availability and convenience for human use. Gardens and terraces were added to many such buildings.

Sculpture, confined in the Middle Ages to the niches and portals of cathedrals, now emerged as an independent and free-standing art. Its favored subjects were human beings, now presented so that the viewer could walk around the object and see it from all directions, thus bringing it securely into his own world. The difference from the religious figures carved on medieval churches was very great. Like the architects, the sculptors in parting from the immediate past found much in the Greek and Roman tradition that was modern and useful to their purpose. They produced portrait busts of eminent contemporaries, or figures of great leaders sometimes on horseback, or statues depicting characters from Greco-Roman history and mythology. The use of the nude, in mythological or allegorical subjects, likewise showed a conception of humanity that was more in keeping with the Greek than with the Christian tradition.

Painting was less influenced by the ancients, since the little of ancient painting that had survived was unknown during the Renaissance. The invention of painting in oils opened new pathways for the art. Merchants, ecclesiastics, and princes provided a mounting demand. In subject matter painting remained conservative, dealing most often with religious themes. It was the conception and presentation that were new. The new feeling for space became evident. With the discovery of the mathematics of perspective, space was presented in exact relation to the beholder's eye. The viewer, in a sense, entered into the world of the painting. A three-dimensional effect was achieved, with careful representation of distance through variation of size, and techniques of shading or chiaroscuro added to the illusion of physical volume. Human figures were often placed in a setting of painted architecture, or against a background of landscape or scenery, showing castles or hills, which though supposedly far away yet closed in the composition with a knowable boundary. In such a painting everything was localized in place and time; a part of the real world was caught and put in the picture. The idea was not to suggest eternity, as in earlier religious painting, nor yet to express private fantasy or the workings of the unconscious, as sometimes in "postmodern" art, but to present a familiar theme in an understandable setting, often with a narrative content, that is, by the telling of a story.

Painters were able also, like the sculptors, by a close study of human anatomy, to show people in distinctive and living attitudes. Faces took on more expression; individual personality was depicted. Differences among men were shown, not merely abstract characteristics that all men or certain kinds of men, such as kings or saints, had in common. Painting became less symbolic, less an intimation of general truths, more a portrayal of concrete realities as they met the eye. In the portrait by Bellini of a *condottiere* the reader can see for himself, though who the man was is not known, how a strong, real, and vivid personality looks out from the canvas.[3] Similarly, the great religious paintings were peopled with human beings. In Leonardo da Vinci's *Last Supper* Christ and his disciples are seen as a group of men each with his own characteristics, Raphael's Madonnas seem to be young Italian women, and in the mighty figures of Michelangelo the attributes of humanity invade heaven itself.

There were always countercurrents that make such generalizations debatable. The main tone of the arts in Renaissance Italy was to take satisfaction in beauty, to present the world as desirable, to be clear-cut, lucid, and finite. But many Florentines were troubled by the worldliness and even paganism that had grown up about them. Their anxieties were expressed in a movement for religious reforms led by the priest Savonarola. As it ran its course it became involved in political questions, until Savonarola was tried and burned at the stake in 1498.

Humanism: The Birth of "Literature"

The literary movement in Renaissance Italy is called humanism because of the rising interest in humane letters, *litterae humaniores.* There had indeed been much writing in the later Middle Ages. Much of it had been of a technical character, as in theology, philosophy, or law; some of it had been meant to convey information, as in chronicles, histories, and cosmographical descriptions of the world. Great hymns had been composed, lively student songs had been heard at the universities, plays had been performed in cathedrals, the old legends of King Arthur and Roland had been written down, and occasionally a monk would try his hand at a long narrative poem. Yet it is hardly too much to say that literature, in the

[3] See p. 63.

modern sense, first appeared in the fourteenth and fifteenth centuries in Italy. There came to be a class of men who looked upon writing as their main life's work, who wrote for each other and for a somewhat larger public, and who used writing to deal with general questions, or to examine their own states of mind, or resolve their own difficulties, or used words to achieve artistic effects, or simply to please and amuse their readers.

The Italian humanists, like their predecessors, wrote a good deal in Latin. They differed from earlier literate persons in that they were not, for the most part, members of the clergy. They complained that Latin had become monkish, barbaric, and "scholastic," a jargon of the schools and universities, and they greatly preferred the classic style of a Cicero or a Livy. In all this there was much that was unfair, much that was merely literary, and something that anticipated the famous twentieth-century problem of the "two cultures," or failure of understanding between persons of humanistic interests and those of more scientific concerns. Medieval Latin was a vigorous living language that used words in new senses, many of which have passed into English and the Romance languages as perfectly normal expressions. Yet in the ancient writers the humanists found qualities that medieval writing did not have. They discovered a new range of interests, a new sensibility, discussion of political and civic questions, a world presented without the overarching framework of religious belief. In addition, the Greeks and Romans unquestionably had style—a sense of form, a taste for the elegant and the epigrammatic. They had often also written for practical ends, in dialogues, orations, or treatises that were designed for purposes of persuasion.

If the humanists therefore made a cult of antiquity it was because they saw kindred spirits in it. They sensed a relevancy for their own time. The classical influence, never wholly absent in the Middle Ages, now reentered as a main force in the higher civilization of Europe. The humanists polished their Latin, and increasingly they learned Greek. They made assiduous searches for classical texts hitherto unknown. Many were found; they had of course been copied and preserved by the monks of preceding times.

But while an especial dignity attached to writing in Latin, known throughout Europe, most of the humanists wrote in Italian also. Or rather, they used the mode of speech current in Florence. This had also been the language of Dante in the *Divine Comedy.* To this vast poem the humanists now added many writings in Florentine or Tuscan prose. The result was that Florentine became the standard form of modern Italian. It was the first time that a European vernacular—that is, the common spoken tongue as opposed to Latin—became thus standardized amid the variety of its dialects and adapted in structure and vocabulary to the more complex requirements of a written language. French and English soon followed, and most of the other European languages somewhat later.

The Florentine exile, Francesco Petrarca, or Petrarch, has been called the first man of letters. The son of a merchant, he spent his life in travel throughout France and Italy. Trained for the law, and ordained to the clergy, he became a somewhat rootless critic of these two esteemed professions, which he denounced for their "scholasticism." He lived in the generation after Dante, dying in 1374, and he anticipated the more fully developed humanism that was to come. His voluminous writings show him to have been the prey of contrary attitudes. He was attracted by life, love, beauty, travel, and connections with men of importance in church and state; he could also spurn all these things as ephemeral and deceptive. He loved Cicero for his common sense and his commitment to political liberty; indeed, he discovered a manuscript of Cicero's letters in 1345. He loved St. Augustine for his otherworldly vision of the City of God. But in Cicero's writings he also found a deep religious concern, and in St. Augustine he esteemed the active man who had been a bishop, a writer heavily engaged in the controversies of his time, and one who taught that for true Christians the world is not evil.

Petrarch wrote sonnets in Italian, an epic in Latin, an introspective study of himself, and a great many letters which he clearly meant to be literary productions. He aspired to literary fame. In all this we see a new kind of writer, who uses language not merely as a practical tool but as a medium of more subtle expression, to commune with himself, to convey moods of discouragement or satisfaction, to clarify doubts, to improve his own understanding of the choices and options that life affords. With Petrarch, in short, literature became a kind of calling, and also a consideration of moral philosophy, still related but no longer subordinate to religion. It was moral philosophy in the widest sense, raising questions of how human beings should adjust to the world, what a good life could be or ought to be, or where the genuine and ultimate rewards of living were to be found.

Petrarch was an indication of things to come. Boccaccio, his contemporary and also a Florentine, wrote the *Decameron* in Italian, a series of tales designed both to entertain and to impart a certain wisdom about human character and behavior. They were followed by the main group of humanists, far more numerous but less well remembered. Men of letters began to take part in public life, to gather pupils and found schools, to serve as secretaries to governing bodies or princes, and even to occupy office themselves. Thus the humanist Coluccio Salutati became chancellor of Florence in 1375. During the following decades Florence was threatened by the expansive ambitions of Milan, where the princely despotism of the Visconti family had established itself. Against such dangers a new and intense civic consciousness asserted itself. Salutati, in addition to the usual duties of chancellor, served the state with his pen, glorifying Florentine liberty, identifying it with the liberties of ancient republican Rome before they were undermined by the Caesars. He was succeeded as chancellor by two other humanists, Bruni and Poggio. Bruni wrote a history of Florence which marked a new achievement in historical writing, when compared with the annals and chronicles of the Middle Ages. He saw the past as clearly past, different from but relevant to the present; and he introduced a new division of historical periods. On the model of such ancient writers as Livy, he adopted a flowing narrative form. And he used history for a practical political purpose, to show that Florence had a long tradition of liberty and possessed values and attainments worth fighting for against menacing neighbors. History took on a utility that it had had for the Greeks and Romans and was to retain in the future in Europe and eventually America: the function of heightening a sentiment, not yet of nationalism, but of collective civic consciousness or group identity. It was meant to arouse men to a life of commitment and participation.

All this literary activity was of a scholarly type, in which authors broadened their understanding as much by reading as by personal experience of the world. And scholarly activity, the habit of attending closely to what a page really said, had consequences that went beyond either pure literature or local patriotism. A new critical attitude developed. Bruni, in his history, showed a new sense of the need for authentic sources. Lorenzo Valla became one of the founders of textual criticism. Gaining a historical sense for the Latin language, he observed that its characteristic words and expressions varied from one time to another. He put this knowledge to the service of the king of Naples in a dispute with the pope. Valla showed, by analysis of the language used in the document, that the Donation of Constantine, on which the papacy then based its temporal claims, could not have been written in Constantine's time in the fourth century, and so was a forgery. Pico della Mirandola and others looked for aspects of truth not revealed in the Christian Scriptures. As men of letters, they put their faith in books, but as men of the Renaissance they were receptive to anything written by men anywhere. A group at the Academy of Florence took a serious interest in the study of Plato. The enthusiastic and very learned young Pico, at the age of twenty-three, in 1486, offered to expatiate publicly on all human knowledge in 900 theses, to be drawn from "the Chaldaic, Arabic, Hebrew, Grecian, Egyptian and Latin sages."

Schooling and Manners

While Italian humanism thus contributed much to literature and scholarship, to classical learning, and to the formation of modern national languages, it also had tangible and lasting effects in education. Here its impact remained in all regions of European civilization until the twentieth century. The medieval universities were essentially places for professional training in theology, medicine, and law. Except in England this continued to be their primary function. What came to be known as secondary education, the preparation of young men either for the universities or for "life," owes more to the Renaissance. The organized education of women came much later.

Medieval schooling had been chaotic and repetitious. Youngsters of all ages sat together with a teacher, each absorbing from the confusion whatever he could of Latin rules and vocabulary. The Renaissance launched the idea of putting different age groups or levels of accomplishment into separate classes, in separate rooms, each with its own teacher, with periodic promotion of the pupil from one level to the next. Latin remained the principal subject, with Greek now added. But many new purposes were seen in the study of Latin. It was intended to give skill in the use of language, including the pupil's native tongue. Rhetoric was the art of using language to influence others. It heightened communication. Knowledge alone was not enough, said the historian and chancellor Bruni, who also wrote a short work on education—"to make effectual use of what we know we must add the power of expression." Nor was Latin merely the necessary professional tool for the priest, the physician, the lawyer, or the government servant. The student learned Latin (and Greek) in order to read the ancient writings—epics, lyrics, orations, letters, histories, dialogues, and philosophical treatises —and these writings, especially at a time when the modern literatures were undeveloped, opened his horizons in all directions. They had a practical application; and at least as late as the American and French revolutions men found useful lessons in the rise and decline of the Roman republic and the troubles of the Greek city-states. The classics were meant also to have a moral impact, to produce a balanced personality, and to form character. Not everyone could be important or gifted, said the humanist Vittorino, but we all face a life of "social duty," and "all are responsible for the personal influence which goes forth from us." These aims built themselves permanently into the educational system of modern Europe.

Young men were trained also for a more civilized deportment in everyday social living. Personal style in the upper classes became somewhat more studied.

Hitherto Europeans had generally acted like big children; they spat, belched, and blew their noses without inhibition, snatched at food with their fingers, bawled at each other when aroused, or sulked when their feelings were offended. It was Italians of the Renaissance who first taught more polite habits. Books of etiquette began to appear, of which the most successful was Castiglione's *Book of the Courtier.* The "courtier" was ancestor to the "gentleman"; "courtesy" was originally the kind of behavior suited to princely courts.

The "courtier," according to Castiglione, should be a man of good birth but is chiefly the product of training. His education in youth, and his efforts in mature years, should be directed toward mixing agreeably in the company of his equals. His clothes should be neat, his movements graceful, his approach to other people perfectly poised. He must converse with facility, be proficient in sports and arms, and know how to dance and appreciate music. He should know Latin and Greek. With literary and other subjects he should show a certain familiarity but never become too engrossed. For the well-bred man speaks with "a certain carelessness, to hide his art, and show that what he says or does comes from him without effort or deliberation." Pedantry and heaviness must yield to a certain air of effortless superiority, so that even if the "courtier" knows or does something seriously, he must treat it lightly as one of many accomplishments. At its best, the code taught a certain considerateness for the feelings of others, and incorporated some of the moral ideas of the humanists, aiming at a creditable life in active society. Castiglione's book was translated into numerous languages, and a hundred editions were printed before 1600. Its ideal was inculcated for centuries by private tutors and in the schools.

Politics and the Italian Renaissance

The Italian Renaissance, for all its accomplishments, produced no institution or great idea by which masses of men living in society could be held together. Indeed, the greatest of Europe's institutions, the Roman church, in which Europeans had lived for centuries, and without which they did not see how they could live at all, fell into sheer neglect under the Renaissance popes. Nor did Italy develop any effectual political institutions. Florence during the fifteenth century passed from a high-spirited republicanism to acceptance of one-man rule. Throughout the peninsula the merchants, bankers, connoisseurs, and courtly classes who controlled the city-states could not fight for themselves, nor arouse their citizens to fight for them. They therefore hired professional fighting men, *condottieri*, private leaders of armed bands, who contracted with the various city-states to carry on warfare, and often raised their price or changed sides during hostilities. Italian politics became a tangled web, a labyrinth of subterfuge and conspiracy, a platform on which great individuals might exhibit their *virtù.* "Italian cunning" became a byword throughout Europe. Dictators rose and fell. The Medici became dukes in Florence, the Sforza in Milan, while in Venice and Genoa, where the republics were kept, narrow oligarchies held the rule. These states, along with the states of the church, jockeyed about like pugilists in a ring, held within an intricate, shifting, and purely local balance of power.

Italy was the despair of its patriots, or of such few as remained. One of these was Niccolò Machiavelli, who, in *The Prince* (1513), wrote the most lasting work of the Italian Renaissance. He dreamed of the day when the citizens of his native

Florence, or indeed of all Italy, should behave like early Romans—show virility in their politics, fight in citizen armies for patriotic causes, and uphold their dignity before Europe. It was outside Italy, in kings Ferdinand of Aragon, Louis XI of France, and Henry VII of England, that Machiavelli was obliged to find his heroes. He admired them because they were successful builders of states. In *The Prince* he produced a handbook of statecraft which he hoped Italy might find useful. He produced also the first purely secular treatise on politics.

Medieval writings on politics, those of Thomas Aquinas or Marsiglio of Padua, for example, had always talked of God's will for the government of men, with such accompanying matters as justice and right, or divine and natural law. All this Machiavelli put aside. He "emancipated" politics from theology and moral philosophy. He undertook to describe simply what rulers actually did, and thus anticipated what was later called the scientific spirit, in which questions of good and bad are excluded, and the observer attempts to discover only what really happens. What really happens, said Machiavelli, is that effective rulers and governments act only in their own political interest. They keep faith or break it, observe treaties or repudiate them, are merciful or ruthless, forthright or sly, peaceable or aggressive, according to their estimates of their political needs. Machiavelli was prepared to admit that such behavior was bad; he only insisted that it was in this way, however regrettably, that successful rulers behaved. He was thought unduly cynical even in an age not characterized by political delicacy. He had nevertheless diagnosed the new era with considerable insight. It was an age when politics was in fact becoming more secular, breaking off from religion, with the building up of states and with state authority emerging as a goal requiring no other justification.

But the most successful states of the time, as Machiavelli saw, were not in Italy. They were what history knows as the New Monarchies, and they owed their strength to something more than princely craft, for they enjoyed a measure of spontaneous loyalty from their own peoples. Italy was politically helpless. Politics in Italy was not about anything vital; it was an affair of *virtù*; and the people of Italy lost interest in politics, as they did in war, becoming "effeminate" in the eyes of outsiders.

So Italy, the sunny land of balmy Mediterranean skies, rich in the busy life of its cities, its moneyed wealth, its gorgeous works of art, lay helplessly open to the depredations of less easygoing peoples, from Spain and the north, who possessed institutions in which men could act together in large numbers. In a new age of rising national monarchies the city-states of Italy were too small to compete. In 1494 a French army crossed the Alps. Italy became a bone of contention between France and Spain. In 1527 a horde of undisciplined Spanish and German mercenaries, joined by foot-loose Italians, fell upon Rome itself. Never, not even from the Goths of the fifth century, had Rome experienced anything so horrible and degrading. The city was sacked, thousands were killed, soldiers milled about for a week in an orgy of rape and loot, the pope was imprisoned, and cardinals were mockingly paraded through the streets facing backward on the backs of mules. By this time religious passions were aroused; we are encroaching on the story of the Reformation.

After the sack of Rome the Renaissance faded away. Politically, for over three hundred years, Italy remained divided, the passive object of the ambitions of outside powers. Meanwhile its culture permeated the rest of Europe.

7. THE RENAISSANCE OUTSIDE ITALY

Outside Italy people were much less conscious of any sudden break with the Middle Ages. Developments north of the Alps, and in Spain, were more an outgrowth of what had gone before. There was indeed a Renaissance in the Italian sense. In some of the innovations in painting the Flemish masters preceded those of Italy. In the north also, as in Italy a little sooner, writers favored a neoclassical Latin, but the modern written languages also began to develop.

But the northern Renaissance was more a blend of the old and the new. In it, above all, the religious element was stronger than in Italy. The most important northern humanists were men like Thomas More in England and the Dutch Erasmus. The French humanism that produced Rabelais also produced John Calvin.

Religious Scholarship and Science

It is customary to distinguish between the "pagan" humanism of Italy and the Christian humanism of the north. In the north, Christian humanists studied the Hebrew and Greek texts of the Bible and read the Church Fathers, both Latin and Greek, in order to deepen their understanding of Christianity and to restore its moral vitality. Among lesser people, too, without pretense to humanistic learning, religion remained a force. Medieval intellectual interests persisted. This is apparent from the continuing foundation of universities. The humanists generally regarded universities as centers of a pedantic, monkish, and "scholastic" learning. Concentrating upon theology, or upon medicine and law, the universities gave little encouragement to experimental science and still less to purely literary studies. In Italy in the fifteenth century no new universities were established. But in Spain, in France, in Scotland, in Scandinavia, and above all in Germany, new universities sprouted up. Between 1386 and 1506 no less than fourteen universities were established in Germany. At one of the newest, Wittenberg, founded in 1502, Martin Luther was to launch the Protestant Reformation.

Germany at this time, on the eve of the great religious upheaval, and before the shift of the commercial artery from central Europe to the Atlantic seaboard, was a main center of European life. Politically, the German-speaking world was an ill-defined and ill-organized region, composed of many diverse parts, from which the Netherlands and Switzerland were not yet differentiated. Parts of it were infested by robber knights, picturesque in legend, but unpleasant for those

PORTRAIT OF A CONDOTTIERE
by Giovanni Bellini (Italian, 1430–1516)

An emphatic portrayal of Renaissance individualism. Note the artist's ability to present a concrete human being, one who is not merely an abstract type. For the "condottieri" see p. 60. The name of this particular "condottiere" is not known. But the hard expression and set features, the firm lines about the mouth and chin, the bull neck and the unflinching gaze suggest an aggressive character of considerable "virtù." The face is thoughtful and intelligent but devoid of spirituality. The man is clearly in the habit of depending on himself alone. The artist has heightened the sense of his subject's independence and self-sufficiency by making him stand out from a dark and entirely vacant background. Courtesy of the National Gallery of Art, Washington, D.C., Samuel H. Kress Collection.

who had to live with them in reality. Economically, nevertheless, western and southern Germany enjoyed a lead; the towns traded busily, and German banking families, like the famous Fugger, controlled more capital than any others in Europe. Technical inventiveness was alive; mining was developing; and it was in the Rhineland, at Mainz, that Gutenberg, about 1450, produced the first books printed with movable type. In painting, the western fringe of the Germanic world produced the Flemish masters, and south Germany gave birth to Dürer and the Holbeins.

Intellectually, Germany shared in the Latin culture of Europe, a fact often obscured by the Latinizing of German names. Regiomontanus (the Latin name of Johann Müller) laid the foundations during his short lifetime (1436–1476) for a mathematical conception of the universe. He was probably the most influential scientific worker of the fifteenth century, especially since Leonardo da Vinci's scientific labors remained unknown. Nicholas of Cusa (1401?–1464), a Rhinelander, was a churchman whose mystical philosophy entered into the later development of mathematics and science. From such a background of mathematical interests came Copernicus (Niklas Koppernigk, 1473–1543), who believed that the earth moved about the sun; he was indeed a Pole, but he originated in the mixed German-Polish region of East Prussia. Fortified by the same mathematical interests, Europe's best-known cartographers were also Germans, such as Behaim and Schöner, whose world maps the reader may see on pages 292–293. Paracelsus (Latin for Hohenheim) undertook to revolutionize medicine at the University of Basel. His wild prophecies made him a mixture of scientist and charlatan; but, in truth, science was not yet clearly distinguished from the occult, with which it shared the idea of control over natural forces. A similar figure, remembered in literature and the arts, was the celebrated Dr. Faustus. In real life, Faust, or Faustus, was perhaps a learned German of the first part of the sixteenth century. He was rumored to have sold his soul to the devil in return for knowledge and power. The Faust story was dramatized in England as early as 1593 by Christopher Marlowe, and, much later, by Goethe in poetry and by Gounod in the opera. In the legend of Faust later generations were to see a symbol of the inordinate striving of modern man. Oswald Spengler published his *Decline of the West* in 1918. Needing a name for the European civilization whose doom he prophesied, he called it "Faustian."

The idea of man's powers to understand and control physical nature, as developed most especially north of the Alps, corresponded in many ways to the more purely Italian and humanistic idea of the infinite richness of human personality. Together, they constituted the new Renaissance spirit, for both emphasized the emancipation of humanity's limitless potentialities. The two ideas constantly interacted; in fact, most of the scientific workers just mentioned—Regiomontanus, Nicholas of Cusa, Copernicus—spent many years in Italy, receiving the stimulus of Italian thought.[4]

Mysticism and Lay Religion

In the north a genuine religious impulse, in addition to religious humanistic scholarship, also remained alive. Where in Italy the religious sense, if not extinct, seemed to pass into the aesthetic, into a joyous and public cult in which God was

[4] On da Vinci, Copernicus, and the rise of modern science in general, see Chapter VII.

glorified by works of art, in the north it took on a more mystical and a more so-
berly moral tone. Germany in the fourteenth century produced a series of mystics.
The mystic tendencies of Nicholas of Cusa have been mentioned. More typical
mystics were Meister Eckhart (d. 1327) and Thomas à Kempis (d. 1471), author
of the *Imitation of Christ*. The essence of mysticism lay in the belief, or experience, that the individual soul could in perfect solitude commune directly with
God. The mystic had no need of reason, nor of words, nor of joining with other
people in open worship, nor even of the sacraments administered by the priests—
nor even of the church. The mystics did not rebel against the church; they accepted its pattern of salvation; but at bottom they offered, to those who could follow, a deeper religion in which the church as a social institution had no place. All
social institutions, in fact, were transcended in mysticism by the individual soul;
and on this doctrine, both profound and socially disruptive, Martin Luther was
later to draw.

For the church, it was significant also that religion was felt deeply outside the
clergy. Persons stirred by religion, who in the Middle Ages would have taken holy
orders, now frequently remained laymen. In the past the church had often needed
reform. But in the past, in the bad times of the tenth century, for example, the
clergy had found reformers within their own ranks. The church had thus been repeatedly reformed and renewed without revolution. Now, in the fifteenth and
early sixteenth centuries an ominous line seemed to be increasingly drawn: between the clergy as an established interest, inert and set in its ways, merely living,
and living well, off the church; and groups of people outside the clergy—religious
laymen, religiously inclined humanists and writers, impatient and headstrong
rulers—who were more influential than ever before, and more critical of ecclesiastical abuses.

Lay religion was especially active in the Netherlands. A lay preacher, Gerard
Groote, attracted followers by his sermons on spiritual regeneration. In 1374 he
founded a religious sisterhood, which was followed by establishments for religiously minded men. They called themselves, respectively, the Sisters and the
Brothers of the Common Life, and they eventually received papal approval. They
lived communally, but not as monks and nuns, for they took no vows, wore ordinary clothing, and were free to leave at will. They worked at relieving the poor,
and in teaching. The schools of the Brothers, since some of them came to have as
many as a thousand boys, were the first to be organized in separate classes, each
with its own room and its own teacher, according to the pupil's age or level of advancement. The Sisters maintained similar though less elaborate schools for girls.
Reading and writing were of course taught, but the emphasis was on a Christian
ideal of character and conduct, to instil such qualities as humility, tolerance,
reverence, love of one's neighbor, and conscientiousness in the performance of
duty. This Modern Devotion, as it was called, spread widely in the Netherlands
and adjoining parts of Germany.

Erasmus of Rotterdam

In this atmosphere grew up the greatest of all the northern humanists, and indeed
the most notable figure of the entire humanist movement, Erasmus of Rotterdam
(1466–1536). Like all the humanists, Erasmus chose to write in a "purified" and
usually intricate Latin style. He regarded the Middle Ages as benighted, ridiculed

the scholastic philosophers, and studied deeply the classical writers of antiquity. He had the strength and the limitations of the pure man of letters. To the hard questions of serious philosophy he was largely indifferent; he feared the unenlightened excitability of the common people, and he was almost wholly unpolitical in his outlook. He rarely thought in terms of worldly power or advantage and made too little allowance for those who did. An exact contemporary to the most notorious of the worldly Renaissance popes, Erasmus was keenly aware of the need of a reform of the clergy. He put his faith in education, enlightened discussion, and gradual moral improvement. He led no burning crusade and counseled against all violence or fanaticism. He prepared new Greek and Latin editions of the New Testament. Urging also the reading of the New Testament in the vernacular languages, he hoped that with a better understanding of Christ's teaching people might turn from their evil ways. In his *Praise of Folly* he satirized all worldly pretensions and ambitions, those of the clergy most emphatically. In his *Handbook of a Christian Knight* he showed how a man might take part in the affairs of the world while remaining a devout Christian. Mildness, reasonableness, tolerance, restraint, scholarly understanding, a love of peace, a critical and reforming zeal which, hating nobody, worked through trying to make men think, a subdued and controlled tone from which shouting and bad temper were always excluded—such were the Erasmian virtues.

Erasmus achieved an international eminence such as no one of purely intellectual attainments has ever enjoyed. He corresponded with the great of Europe. He lectured at Cambridge and edited books for a publisher at Basel. The king of Spain named him a councilor, the king of France called him to Paris, Pope Leo X assisted him when he was in trouble. Theologians found fault with Erasmus' ideas (in which, indeed, the supernatural had little importance), but among the chief practical men of the church, the popes and prelates, he had many admirers. Erasmus, it must be noted, attacked only the abuses in the church, the ignorance or sloth of the clergy, the moral or financial corruption of their lives. The essence and principle of the Roman Catholic church he never called into question. Whether the Erasmian spirit, so widely diffused about 1520, would have sufficed to restore the church without the revolutionary impact of Protestantism is one of the many unanswerable questions of history.

8. THE NEW MONARCHIES

Meanwhile, in Europe outside Italy, kings were actively building up the institutions of the modern state. It was these states, more than any other single factor,

ERASMUS OF ROTTERDAM
by Hans Holbein, the Younger (German, 1497–1543)

The classic portrayal of humanism at its best. The portrait was painted in 1523, when Erasmus was fifty-six, and the Lutheran Reformation had already begun in Germany. Holbein has conveyed the mood of tight-lipped calm, or of saddened humanity, felt by a lifelong reforming writer who has lived to see violent revolution. The face, finely delineated, and highlighted against the deeper tones of the cap and cloak, is concentrated upon Erasmus' only weapon, the pen. The picture captures the life of thought; it is a picture of the human mind, as Bellini's "Condottiere" is a picture of the will. Courtesy of the Louvre (Giraudon).

that were to determine the course of the religious revolution. Whether a country turned Protestant, remained Catholic, or divided into separate religious communities was to depend very largely upon political considerations.

War, civil war, class war, feudal rebellion, and plain banditry afflicted a good deal of Europe in the middle of the fifteenth century. In this formless violence central governments had become very weak. Various rulers now tried to impose a kind of civil peace. They have been conveniently called the New Monarchs, but they were not really very new, because they resumed the interrupted labors of kings in the High Middle Ages.[5] They thus laid foundations for the national, or at least territorial, states.

The New Monarchs offered the institution of monarchy as a guarantee of law and order. Arousing latent sentiments of loyalty to the reigning dynasty, they proclaimed that hereditary monarchy was the legitimate form of public power, which all should accept without turmoil or resistance. They especially enlisted the support of middle-class people in the towns, who were tired of the private wars and marauding habits of the feudal nobles. Townspeople were willing to let parliaments be dominated or even ignored by the king, for parliaments had proved too often to be strongholds of unruly barons, or had merely accentuated class conflict. The king, receiving money in taxes, was able to organize armies with which to control the nobles. The use of the pike and the longbow, which enabled the foot soldier to stand against the horseman, was here of great potential value. The king, if only he could get his monarchy sufficiently organized, and his finances into reliable order, could hire large numbers of foot soldiers, who generally came from the endless ranks of plebeians, unlike the knightly horsemen. But to organize his monarchy, the king had to break down the mass of feudal, inherited, customary, or "common" law in which the rights of the feudal classes were entrenched. For this purpose, at least on the Continent, the New Monarch made use of Roman law, which was now actively studied in the universities.[6] He called himself a "sovereign"—it was at this time that kings began to be addressed as "majesty." The king, said the experts in Roman law, incorporated the will and welfare of the people in his own person—and they would cite the principle *salus populi suprema lex*, "the welfare of the people is the highest law." The king, they added, could *make* law, enact it by his own authority, regardless of previous custom or even of historic liberties—and they would quote, *quod principi placuit legis habet vigorem*, or "what pleases the prince has the force of law."

The New Monarchy in England, France, and Spain

The New Monarchy came to England with the dynasty of the Tudors (1485–1603), whose first king, Henry VII (1485–1509), after gaining the throne by force, put an end to the civil turbulence of the Wars of the Roses. In these wars the great English baronial families had seriously weakened each other, to the great convenience of the king and the bulk of the citizenry. Henry VII passed laws against "livery and maintenance," the practice by which great lords maintained private armies wearing their own livery or insignia. Since ordinary procedures had recently failed to give security, with witnesses afraid to testify and juries afraid to offend the mighty, Henry VII used his royal council as a new court

[5] See pp. 34–36.
[6] See p. 16.

to deal with property disputes and infractions of the public peace. It met in a room decorated with stars, whence its name, the Star Chamber. It represented the authority of the king and his council, and it dispensed with a jury. Later denounced as an instrument of despotism, it was popular enough at first, because it preserved order and rendered substantial justice. Henry VII, though miserly and unpleasant in person, was accepted as a good ruler. National feeling in England consolidated around the house of Tudor.

In France the New Monarchy was represented by Louis XI (1461–1483), of the Valois line, and his successors. In the five centuries since the first French king had been crowned, the royal domain had steadily expanded from its original small nucleus around Paris through a combination of inheritance, marriage, war, intrigue, and conquest. Louis XI continued to round out the French borders. Internally, he built up a royal army, suppressed brigands, and subdued rebellious nobles. He acquired far greater powers than the English Tudors to raise taxation without parliamentary consent. The Estates General of France met only once in his reign. On that occasion, remembering the anarchy of the past, they requested the king to govern without them in the future. The French monarchy also enlarged its powers over the clergy. We have seen how, by the Pragmatic Sanction of 1438, the Gallican church had won considerable national independence.[7] In 1516 King Francis I reached an agreement with Pope Leo X, the Concordat of Bologna. By this agreement the Pragmatic Sanction was rescinded; the pope received his "annates," or money income, from French ecclesiastics; the king appointed the bishops and abbots. The fact that, after 1516, the kings of France already controlled their own national clergy was one reason why, in later years, they were never tempted to turn Protestant.

Strictly speaking, there was no kingdom of Spain. Various Spanish kingdoms had combined into two, Aragon and Castile. To Aragon, which lay along the Mediterranean side of the peninsula, belonged the Balearic Islands, Sardinia, Sicily, and the south Italian kingdom of Naples. To Castile, after 1492, belonged the newly discovered Americas. The two were joined in a personal union by the marriage of Ferdinand of Aragon and Isabella of Castile in 1469. The union was personal only; that is, both kingdoms recognized the two monarchs, but they had no common political, judicial, or administrative institutions. There was little or no Spanish national feeling; indeed, the Catalans in northern Aragon spoke a language quite different from Castilian Spanish. The common feeling throughout Spain was the sense of belonging to the Spanish Catholic church. The common memory was the memory of the Christian crusade against the Moors. The one common institution, whose officials had equal authority and equal access to all the kingdoms, was a church court, the Inquisition. The church in Spain was in vigorous condition. Cardinal Ximenes, shortly before 1500, managed to rid it of the abuses and the inertia which debilitated the church in the rest of Europe. The *reconquista* was at last completed. In 1492 Granada, the southern tip of Spain, was conquered from the Moors. Its annexation added to the heterogeneous and undigested character of the Spanish dominions.

In these circumstances the New Monarchy in Spain followed a religious bent. Unification took place around the church. The rulers, though they made efforts at political centralization, worked largely through facilities offered by the church, notably the Inquisition. They insisted on religious conformity. National feeling

[7] See p. 52.

Habsburg Dominions

Church Lands

Boundary of Holy Roman Empire

SHETLAND I.

NORWAY

SWEDEN

FINLAND

THE HEBRIDES

ORKNEY I.

Bergen

Oslo

Helsingfors

Stockholm

ESTONIA

LIVONIA

SCOTLAND

Riga

Edinburgh

COURLAND

NORTH SEA

BALTIC SEA

IRELAND

DENMARK

Dublin

Copenhagen

Danzig

PRUSSIA

Vilna

York

Hamburg

WALES

ENGLAND

LITHUANI

DUTCH
NETHERLANDS

BRANDENBURG

Berlin

Vistula R.

London

Warsaw

Canterbury

Rhine

Münster

Antwerp

POLA

Calais
(England)

BELGIAN
NETH.

Brussels

Cologne

Wittenberg

POLAND

ATLANTIC OCEAN

SAXONY

Schmalkalden

SILESIA

Cracow

Rouen

LUX.

Trier

Prague

Breslau

Lemberg

St. Malo

PALA-
TINATE

Worms

BOHEMIA

GALICIA

Paris

Metz

MORAVIA

POD

Strasbourg

BAVARIA

F R A N C E

Ratisbon

Augsburg

CARPATH

Orléans

Munich

AUSTRIA

Vienna

MOL

Bourges

BURGUNDY

Basel

Danube R.

Angoulême

FR.
COMTÉ

SWISS
CONFEDERATION

Budapest

Bordeaux

Geneva

TYROL

H U N G A R Y

TRANSYLVANIA

SAVOY

Milan

Trent

Bayonne

PYRENEES

Avignon

DAUPHINE

Venice

Mohacs

NAVARRE

Parma

Belgrade

WALLACH

Marseilles

Genoa

Buchare

Burgos

Florence

BOSNIA

Oporto

Valladolid

ARAGON

CATALONIA

Barcelona

CORSICA
(Genoa)

PAPAL
STATES

DALMATIA

VENETIAN REPUBLIC

Danu

MONTENEGRO

PORTUGAL

S P A I N

Rome

ADRIATIC SEA

Sofia

Adriar

Lisbon

Escorial

Madrid

CASTILE

Toledo

Valencia

BALEARIC I.

SARDINIA
(Aragon)

NAPLES
(Aragon)

ALBANIA

Salonica

AEGEA
SEA

Seville

Granada

Naples

GREECE

Lepanto

G

Cadiz

GRANADA

MEDITERRANEAN

Palermo

IONIAN I.
(Venice)

MOREA

Melilla (Spain)

Algiers

SICILY
(Aragon)

SEA

(Venice)

SULTANATE
OF FEZ

SULTANATE OF ALGIERS

Tunis

SULTANATE
OF TUNIS

MALTA (Knights of St. John)

CR
(Ver

B A R B A R Y   S T A T E S

vgorod

Moscow

R U S S I A
(MUSCOVY)

v

YEDISAN   KHANATE OF THE CRIMEA

CRIMEA

BLACK SEA

Constantinople

E M P I R E

myrna

RHODES (Turkish)   CYPRUS
                          (Venice)

0   100   200   300 miles

EUROPE, 1526

The main feature of the political map of Europe about 1526 is the predominance of the house of Habsburg. Much of Europe was ruled by the Habsburg Emperor Charles V, who was at the same time King Charles I of Spain. As is explained in this and the following chapter, Charles left his possessions in Austria, Hungary, and Bohemia to his brother, those in Spain, the Netherlands, Italy, and America to his son. He thus established the Austrian and Spanish branches of the Habsburg dynasty. France was nearly encircled by Habsburg dominions and habitually formed alliances with various German princes and with Sweden, Poland, and Turkey. The Habsburgs remained the principal power in Europe until after the Thirty Years' War, which ended in 1648.

was church feeling; the sense of "Spanishness" was a sense of Catholicity. Formerly the Spanish had been among the most tolerant of Europeans; Christians, Muslims, and Jews had managed to live together. But in the wave of national (or religious) excitement that accompanied the conquest of Granada both the Jews and the Moors were expelled. The expulsion of the Jews by a decree of 1492 was actually a sign of former toleration in Spain, for the Jews had been similarly expelled from England in 1290 and from France in 1306. They were not again legally allowed in England until the mid-seventeenth century, nor in France (with great exceptions) until the French Revolution. It would appear that in the history of many European peoples the attainment of a certain degree of national consciousness brought a feeling against Jews as "outsiders."[8]

All persons in Spain were now supposed to be Christians. In fact, however, Spain was the one country in Europe where a person's Christianity could not be taken for granted, because many Spanish families had been Jewish or Muslim for centuries, and had only accepted Christianity to avoid expulsion. Hence arose a fear of false Christians, of an unassimilated element secretly hostile to the foundations of Spanish life. It was feared that Moriscos (Christians of Moorish background) and Marranos (Christians of Jewish background) retained a clandestine sympathy for the religion of their forebears. A distaste for eating pork, or an inclination not to work on Saturday, was enough to arouse suspicion. Thousands of such persons were haled before the Inquisition, where, as in the civil courts under Roman procedure, torture could be employed to extort confessions. Spanish life became rigidly and ostentatiously orthodox. It was safest to be profuse in one's external devotions. It was the way of proving oneself to be a good Spaniard. The national and the Catholic were fused.

The life of Spain remained a great crusade, a crusade within Spain against Moriscos and Marranos, a crusade carried against the Moors into Africa itself, which the Spanish invaded immediately after the conquest of Granada. The crusade crossed the ocean into the Americas, where the Spanish church set about gathering the Indians into the fold. And it was soon to spread to Europe also. Spain was ready, before Protestantism ever appeared, to play its role in the Reformation, to be the avenging angel to extirpate heresy, and the stern apostle demanding Catholic reform.

The Holy Roman Empire and the Habsburg Supremacy

Ideas of the New Monarchy were at work even in Germany, which is to say, in the Holy Roman Empire. There were three kinds of states in the Empire. There were the princely states—duchies, margraviates, etc.—each a little hereditary dynastic monarchy in itself, such as Saxony, Brandenburg, or Bavaria. There were ecclesiastical states—bishoprics, abbacies, etc.—in which the bishop or abbot, whose rule was of course not hereditary, conducted the government. A large portion of the area of the Empire consisted in these church-states, as may be seen from the map on pages 70–71. Third, there were the imperial free cities,

---

[8] The Jews who left Spain (the Sephardic Jews) went to North Africa and the Near East, and in smaller numbers to the Dutch Netherlands and even to southwestern France (one of the exceptions noted above). Those who left England two centuries earlier generally went to Germany, the great center of Ashkenazic Jewry in the Middle Ages. Driven from Germany in the fourteenth century they concentrated in Poland, which remained the great center of European Jewry until the Nazi massacres of the 1940s. See map, p. 819 below.

some fifty in number; their collective area was not large, but they dominated the commercial and financial life of the country. There was in truth also a fourth category, made up of some thousands of imperial knights, noblemen of minor consequence who possessed a few manors, but who belonged to no state, recognizing the supremacy of none but the emperor.

The states, over the centuries, had prevented the emperor from infringing upon their local liberties. They had taken care to keep the emperorship an elective office, so that with each election local liberties could be reaffirmed. After 1356 the right of electing an emperor was vested in seven electors—namely, four of the princely lords, the Count Palatine, Duke of Saxony, Margrave of Brandenburg, and King of Bohemia (the one king in the Empire), and in three ecclesiastical lords, the archbishops of Mainz, Trier, and Cologne. In 1452 the electors chose the Archduke of Austria to be emperor. His family name was Habsburg. The Habsburgs, by using the resources of their hereditary possessions in Austria (and later elsewhere) and by delicately balancing and bribing the numerous political forces within Germany, managed to get themselves consistently reelected to the Holy Roman Emperorship in every generation, with one exception, from 1452 until 1806.

The principles of New Monarchy were successful mainly in the hereditary princely states of reasonable size. Here the rulers went through the familiar process of quelling their own feudal subordinates, increasing their revenues, enforcing local peace, and letting their own parliamentary bodies fall into abeyance. Thus Brandenburg, Saxony, Bavaria, Württemberg, and a few others, though small, began to take on the semblance of modern states.

The Habsburg emperors also tried to introduce the centralizing principles of the New Monarchy in the Empire as a whole. Under Maximilian I (1493–1519) there seemed to be progress in this direction: the Empire was divided into administrative "circles," and an Imperial Chamber and Council were created, but they were all doomed to failure before the immovable obstacle of states' rights. Maximilian was the author of the Habsburg family fortunes in a quite different way. *Bella gerunt alii; tu, felix Austria, nubes*—"where others have to fight wars, you, fortunate Austria, marry!" Maximilian himself married the heiress of the dukes of Burgundy, who, over the past century, had acquired a number of provinces in the western extremities of the Empire—the Netherlands and the Free County of Burgundy, which bordered upon France. Maximilian by this marriage had a son Philip, whom he married to Joanna, heiress to Ferdinand and Isabella of Spain. Philip and Joanna produced a son Charles. Charles combined the inheritances of his four grandparents: Austria from Maximilian, the Netherlands and Free County from Mary of Burgundy, Castile and Spanish America from Isabella, Aragon and its Mediterranean and Italian possessions from Ferdinand. In addition, in 1519, he was elected Holy Roman Emperor and so became the symbolic head of all Germany.

Charles V of the Empire (he was known as Charles I in Spain) was thus beyond all comparison the most powerful ruler of his day. But still other fortunes awaited the house of Habsburg. The Turks, who had occupied Constantinople in 1453, were at this time pushing through Hungary and menacing central Europe. In 1526 they defeated the Hungarians at the battle of Mohacs. The parliaments of Hungary, and of the adjoining kingdom of Bohemia, hoping to gain allies in the face of the Turkish peril, thereupon elected Charles V's brother Ferdinand as their king. The Habsburg family was now entrenched in central Europe, in the Netherlands, in Spain, in the Mediterranean, in south Italy, in America. No one since Charlemagne had stood so far above all rivals. Contemporaries cried that Europe was threatened with "universal monarchy," with a kind of world-state in which no people could preserve its independence.

The reader who wishes to understand the religious revolution, and consequent emergence of Protestantism, to which we shall now turn, must bear in mind the extraordinarily intricate interplay of the factors that have now been outlined: the decline of the church, the growth of secular and humanistic feeling, the spread of lay religion outside the official clergy, the rise of monarchs who wished to control everything in their kingdoms, including the church, the resistance of feudal elements to these same monarchs, the lassitude of the popes and their fear of church councils, the atomistic division of Germany, the Turkish peril, the zeal of Spain, the preeminence of Charles V, and the fears felt in the rest of Europe, especially in France, of absorption or suffocation by the amazing empire of the Habsburgs.

9. THE PROTESTANT REFORMATION

Three streams contributed to the religious upheaval of the sixteenth century. First, among simple people, or the laboring poor, who might find their spokesmen among local priests, there was an endemic dissatisfaction with all the grand apparatus of the church, or a belief that its bishops and abbots were part of a wealthy and oppressive ruling class. For such people, religious ideas were mixed with protest against the whole social order. They found expression in the great peasant rebellion in Germany in the 1520s. The sects which emerged are known historically as Anabaptists, and the modern Baptists, Mennonites, and Moravian Brothers are among their descendants. Second, and forming a group generally more educated and with broader views of the world, were the middle classes of various European cities, especially of cities that were almost like autonomous little republics, as in Germany, Switzerland, and the Netherlands. They might wish to manage their own religious affairs as they did their other business, believing that the church hierarchy was too much embedded in a feudal, baronial, and monarchical system with which they had little in common. The modern churches of Calvinist origin came in large part from this stream. Third, there were the kings and ruling princes, who had long disputed with the church on matters of property, taxes, legal jurisdiction, and political influence. Each such ruler wanted to be master in his own territory. In the end it was the power of such rulers that determined which form of religion should officially prevail. The Lutheran and Anglican churches were in this tradition, and to some extent the Gallican church, as the French branch of the Roman Catholic church was called. As it turned out, by 1600, the second and third streams had won many successes, but the first was suppressed. Socio-religious radicalism was reduced to an undercurrent in countries where Anglican, Lutheran, Calvinist, or Roman Catholic churches were established.

Since northern Europe became Protestant while the south remained Catholic, it may look as if the north had broken off in a body from a once solid Roman church. The reality was not so simple. Let us for a moment put aside the term

"Protestant," and think of the adherents of the new religion as religious revolutionaries.[9] Their ideas were revolutionary because they held, not merely that "abuses" in the church must be corrected, but that the Roman church itself was wrong in principle. Even so, there were many who hoped, for years, that old and new ideas of the church might be combined. Many deplored the extremes but gradually in the heat of struggle had to choose one side or the other. The issues became drawn, and each side aspired to destroy its adversary. For over a century the revolutionaries maintained the hope that "popery" would everywhere fall. For over a century the upholders of the old order worked to annihilate or reconvert "heretics." Only slowly did Catholics and Protestants come to accept each other's existence as an established fact of European society. Though the religious frontier that was to prove permanent appeared as early as 1560, it was not generally accepted until after the Thirty Years' War, which closed in 1648.

Luther and Lutheranism

The first who successfully defied the older church authorities was Martin Luther. He was a monk, and an earnest one, until he was almost forty years old. A vehement and spiritually uneasy man, with many dark and introspective recesses in his personality, Luther was terrified by the thought of the awful omnipotence of God, distressed by his own littleness, apprehensive of the devil, and suffering from the chronic conviction that he was damned. The means offered by the church to allay such spiritual anguish—the sacraments, prayer, attendance at Mass—gave him no satisfaction. From a reading and pondering of St. Paul (Romans i, 17)—"the just shall live by faith"—there dawned upon him a new realization and sense of peace. He developed the doctrine of justification by faith alone. This held that what "justifies" a man is not what the church knew as "works" (prayer, alms, the sacraments, holy living) but "faith alone," an inward bent of spirit given to each soul directly by God. Good works, Luther thought, were the consequence and external evidence of this inner grace, but in no way its cause. A man did not "earn" grace by doing good; he did the good because he possessed the grace of God. With this idea Luther for some years lived content. Even years later some high-placed churchmen believed that in Luther's doctrine of justification by faith there was nothing contrary to the teachings of the Catholic church.

Luther, now a professor at Wittenberg, was brought out of seclusion by an incident of 1517. A friar named Tetzel was traveling through Germany distributing indulgences, authorized by the pope to finance the building of St. Peter's in Rome.[10] In return for them the faithful paid certain stipulated sums of money. Luther thought that people were being deluded, that no one could in this way obtain grace for himself, or ease the pains of relatives in purgatory, as was officially claimed. In the usual academic manner of the day, he posted ninety-five theses on the door of the castle church at Wittenberg. In them he reviewed the Catholic sacrament of penance. Luther held that, after confession, the sinner is freed of his burden not by the priest's absolution, but by inner grace and faith alone. Increas-

---

[9] The word "Protestant" arose as an incident in the struggle, at first denoting certain Lutherans who drew up a formal protest against an action of the diet of the Empire in 1529. Only very gradually did the various groups of anti-Roman reformers think of themselves as collectively Protestant.

[10] On indulgences see p. 52.

ingly, it seemed that the priesthood performed no necessary function in the relation between man and God.

Luther at first appealed to the pope, Leo X, to correct the abuse of indulgences in Germany. When the pope refused action Luther (like many before him) urged the assembly of a general church council as an authority higher even than the pope. He was obliged, however, to admit in public debate that even the decision of a general council might be mistaken. The Council of Constance, he said, had in fact erred in its condemnation of John Huss. But if neither the pope, nor yet a council, had authority to define true Christian belief, where was such authority to be found? Luther's answer was, in effect: There is no such authority. He held that each individual might read the Bible and freely make his own interpretation according to his own conscience. This idea was as revolutionary, for the church, as would be the assertion today that neither the Supreme Court nor any other body may authoritatively interpret or enforce the Constitution of the United States, since each citizen may interpret the Constitution in his own way.

From his first public appearance Luther won ardent supporters, for there was a good deal of resentment in Germany against Rome. In 1519 and 1520 he rallied public opinion in a series of tracts, setting forth his main beliefs. He declared that the claim of the clergy to be different from the laity was an imposture. He urged people to find Christian truth in the Bible for themselves, and in the Bible only. He denounced the reliance on fasts, pilgrimages, saints, and Masses. He rejected the belief in purgatory. He reduced the seven sacraments to two—baptism and the communion, as he called the Mass. In the latter he repudiated the new and "modern" doctrine of transubstantiation, while affirming that God was still somehow mysteriously present in the bread and wine.[11] He declared that the clergy should marry, upbraided the prelates for their luxury, and demanded that monasticism be eliminated. To drive through such reforms, while depriving the clergy of their pretensions, he called upon the temporal power, the princes of Germany. He thus issued an invitation to the state to assume control over religion, an invitation which, in the days of the New Monarchy, a good many rulers were enthusiastically willing to accept.

Threatened by a papal bull with excommunication unless he recanted, Luther solemnly and publicly burned the bull. Excommunication followed. To the emperor, Charles V, now fell the duty of apprehending the heretic and repressing the heresy. Luther was summoned to appear before a diet of the Empire, held at Worms in the Rhineland. He declared that he could be convinced only by Scripture or right reason; otherwise—"I neither can nor will recant anything, since it is neither right nor safe to act against conscience. God help me! Amen." He was placed under the ban of the Empire. But the Elector of Saxony and other north German princes took him under their protection. In safe seclusion, he began to translate the Bible into German.

Luther's excitable obstinacy, intemperate language, and sweeping repudiation of existing authorities antagonized many who had at first looked upon him with favor, and who still hoped for a reform of the church without revolution. Among these was Erasmus, who, as often happens to those who find themselves in the middle, was in his last years looked upon by both sides, Lutheran and Catholic, as a meddlesome friend of the opposition.

[11] See pp. 39, 41.

Lutheranism, or at least anti-Romanism, swept over Germany, assuming the proportions of a national upheaval. It became mixed with all sorts of political and social revolution. A league of imperial knights, adopting Lutheranism, attacked their neighbors, the church-states of the Rhineland, hoping by annexations to enlarge their own meager territories. In 1524 the peasants of a large part of Germany revolted. They were stirred by new religious ideas, worked upon by preachers who went beyond Luther in asserting that anyone could see for himself what was right. Their aims, however, were social and economic; they demanded a regulation of rents and security of common village rights and complained of exorbitant exactions and oppressive rule by their manorial overlords. Luther repudiated all connection with the peasants, called them filthy swine, and urged the princes to suppress them by the sword. The peasants were unmercifully put down, but popular unrest continued to stir the country, expressing itself, in a religious age, in various forms of extreme religious frenzy. Various leaders had various followings, known collectively as Anabaptists. Some said that all the world needed was love, some that Christ would soon come again, some that they were saints and could do no wrong, and some that infant baptism was useless, immersion of full-grown adults being required, as described in the Bible. The roads of Germany were alive with obscure zealots, of whom some tens of thousands converged in 1534 on the city of Münster. There they proclaimed the reign of the saints, abolished property, and introduced polygamy as authorized in the Old Testament. A Dutch tailor, John of Leyden, claimed authority from God himself, and, hemmed in by besieging armies, ruled Münster by a revolutionary terror. Luther advised his followers to join even with Catholics to repress such an appalling menace. After a full year Münster was relieved. The "saints" were pitilessly rooted out; John of Leyden died in torture.

Luther, horrified at the way in which religious revolution became confused with social revolution, defined his own position more conservatively. He restricted, while never denying, the right of private judgment in matters of conscience, and he made a larger place for an established clergy, Lutheranized, to be sure, but still established as teachers over the laity. Always well disposed to temporal rulers, having called upon the princes to act as religious reformers, he was thrown by the peasant and Anabaptist uprisings into an even closer alliance with them. Lutheranism took on a character of submissiveness to the state. Christian liberty, Luther insisted, was an internal freedom, purely spiritual, known only to God. In worldly matters, he said, the good Christian owed perfect obedience to established authority. Lutheranism, more than Catholicism and more than the Calvinism which soon arose, came to hold the state in a kind of religious awe as an institution almost sacred in its own right.

In the revolution that was rocking Germany it was not the uprising of imperial knights, nor that of peasants or tailors and journeymen, that was successful, but the rebellion of the higher orders of the Empire against the emperor. Charles V, as Holy Roman Emperor, was bound to uphold Catholicism because only in a Catholic world did the Holy Empire have any meaning. The states of the Empire, always fearing the loss of local liberty, saw in Charles' efforts to repress Luther a threat to their own freedom. Many imperial free cities, and most of the dynastic states of north Germany, now insisted on adding to their other rights and liberties the right, or liberty, to determine their own religion. The *ius reformandi*, they said, the right or power to reform, belonged to member states, not to the Empire itself. They became Lutheran, locally, introducing Lutheran bishops, doctrines, and forms of worship. Where a state turned Lutheran it usually "secularized" (i.e., confiscated) the church properties within its borders, a process which considerably enriched some of the Lutheran princes and gave them a strong material interest in the success of the Lutheran movement. In most of the church-states, since the Catholic archbishop or bishop was himself the government, Catholicism prevailed. But a few church-states turned Lutheran. A good example of the secularization of a church-state was afforded in East Prussia, just outside the Empire. This territory belonged to the Teutonic Order, a Catholic organization of which the grand commander, an elective official, was at this time Albert of Brandenburg. In 1525 Albert declared for Luther and converted East Prussia into a secular duchy, of which he and his descendants became hereditary dukes.

Against the emperor, a group of Lutheran princes and free cities formed the League of Schmalkald. The king of France, Francis I, though a Catholic in good standing, allied with and supported the League. Political interests overrode religious ones. Against the "universal monarchy" of the swollen Habsburgs the French found alliances where they could, allying with the Turks as with the Lutherans, building up a balance of power against their mighty foe. It became the studied policy of Catholic France to maintain the religious division of Germany.

Charles V strove to find some basis of agreement by which the permanent religious division of Germany could be avoided. He was at war with France over certain disputed territories and with the Turks, who in 1529 besieged Vienna itself. Though the Lutheran princes did render a little help at the last moment, it seemed on the whole that the infidels might overrun Germany before the German states would yield their liberties to their own emperor.

Charles appealed to the pope, urging him to assemble a Europe-wide council in which all disputed matters could be considered, the Protestants heard, compromises effected, and church unity and German unity (such as it was) restored. The king of France schemed at Rome to prevent the pope from calling any such council. The kings of both France and England urged national councils instead, in which religious questions could be settled on a national basis. Pope after pope delayed. The papacy feared that a council of all Latin Christendom might get out of control, since Catholics as much as Protestants demanded reform. At the very rumor of a council the price of salable offices in Rome abruptly fell. To the papacy, remembering the Council of Constance, nothing was more upsetting than the thought of a council, not even the Protestants, not even the Turks. So the popes procrastinated, no council met, years passed, and a new generation grew up in Lutheranism. Desperately, in 1548, Charles tried to settle matters himself, issuing the *Interim*, to guide religion in all Germany until a general church council could complete its work. The *Interim* upheld the main Catholic doctrines, but, to attract the Protestants, allowed marriage of the clergy and one or two other minor concessions. Neither side would accept it: Protestants found that it gave too little, and Catholics refused to have their religion tampered with by the temporal power.

Meanwhile the Schmalkaldic League, allied with France, had actually gone to war with the emperor in 1546. Germany fell into an anarchy of civil struggle between Catholic and Protestant states, the latter aided by France. The war was ended by the Peace of Augsburg of 1555.

The terms set at Augsburg signified a complete victory for the cause of Lutheranism and states' rights. Each state of the Empire received the liberty to be either

Lutheran or Catholic as it chose—*cuius regio eius religio*, "whose the region, his the religion." No individual freedom of religion was permitted; if a ruler or a free city decided for Lutheranism, then all persons had to be Lutheran. Similarly in Catholic states all had to be Catholic. The Peace of Augsburg provided also, by the so-called Ecclesiastical Reservation, that any Catholic bishop or other churchman who turned Lutheran in the future (or who had turned Lutheran as recently as 1552) should not carry his territory with him, but should turn Lutheran as an individual and move away, leaving his land and its inhabitants Catholic. Since the issues in Germany were still far from stabilized, this proviso was often disregarded in later years.

The Peace of Augsburg was thus, in religion, a great victory for Protestantism, and at the same time, in German politics and constitutional matters, a step in the disintegration of Germany into a mosaic of increasingly separate states. Lutheranism prevailed in the north, and in the south in the duchy of Württemberg and various detached islands formed by Lutheranized free cities. Catholicism prevailed in the south (except in Württemberg and certain cities), in the Rhine valley, and in the direct possessions of the house of Habsburg, which in 1555 reached as far north as the Netherlands. The Germans, because of conditions in the Holy Roman Empire, were the one large European people to emerge from the religious conflict almost evenly divided between Catholic and Protestant.

No rights were granted by the Peace of Augsburg to another group of religious revolutionaries which neither Lutherans nor Catholics were willing to tolerate, namely, the followers of John Calvin.

Lutheranism, it must be pointed out, was adopted by the kings of Denmark and Sweden as early as the 1520s. Since Denmark controlled Norway, and Sweden ruled Finland and the eastern Baltic, all Scandinavia and the Baltic regions became, like north Germany, Lutheran. Beyond this area Lutheranism failed to take root. Like Anglicanism in England (to be described shortly) Lutheranism was too closely associated with established states to spread easily as an international movement. The most successful international form of the Protestant movement was Calvinism.

Calvin and Calvinism

John Calvin was a Frenchman, born Jean Cauvin, who called himself Calvinus in Latin. Born in 1509, he was a full generation younger than Luther. He was trained both as a priest and as a lawyer, and had a humanist's knowledge of Latin and Greek, as well as Hebrew. At the age of twenty-four, experiencing a sudden conversion, or fresh insight into the meaning of Christianity, he joined forces with the religious revolutionaries of whom the best known was then Luther. Three years later, in 1536, he published, in the international language, Latin, his *Institutes of the Christian Religion*. Where Luther had aimed much of his writing either at the existing rulers of Germany, or at the German national feeling against Rome, Calvin addressed his *Institutes* to all the world. He seemed to appeal to human reason itself; he wrote in the severe, logical style of the trained lawyer; he dealt firmly, lucidly, and convincingly with the most basic issues. In the *Institutes* people in all countries, if dissatisfied with the existing Roman church, could find cogent expression of universal propositions, which they could apply to their own local circumstances as they required.

With Luther's criticisms of the Roman church, and with most of Luther's fundamental religious ideas, such as justification by faith and not by works, Calvin agreed. In what they retained of the Catholic Mass, the communion or Lord's Supper as they called it, Luther and Calvin developed certain doctrinal differences. Both rejected transubstantiation, but where Luther insisted that God was somehow actually present in the bread and wine used in the service ("consubstantiation"), Calvin and his followers tended more to regard it as a pious act of symbolic or commemorative character.

The chief differences between Calvin and Luther were two. Calvin made far more of the idea of predestination. Both, drawing heavily on St. Augustine, held that man by his own actions could earn no merit in the sight of divine justice, that any grace which anyone possessed came from the free action of God alone. God, being Almighty, knew and willed in advance all things that happened, including the way in which every life would turn out. He knew and willed, from all eternity, that some were saved and some were damned. Calvin, a severe critic of human nature, felt that those who had grace were relatively few. They were the "elect," the "godly," the little band chosen without merit of their own, from all eternity, for salvation. A person could feel in his own mind that he was among the saved, God's chosen few, if throughout all trials and temptations he persisted in a saintly life. Thus the idea of predestination, of God's omnipotence, instead of turning to fatalism and resignation, became a challenge to unrelenting effort, a sense of burning conviction, a conviction of being on the side of that Almighty Power which must in the end be everlastingly triumphant. It was the most resolute spirits that were attracted to Calvinism. Calvinists, in all countries, were militant, uncompromising, perfectionist—or Puritan, as they were called first in England and later in America.

The second way in which Calvinism differed from Lutheranism was in its attitude to society and to the state. Calvinists refused to recognize the subordination of church to state, or the right of any government—king, parliament, or civic magistracy—to lay down laws for religion. On the contrary, they insisted that true Christians, the elect or godly, should Christianize the state. They wished to remake society itself into the image of a religious community. They rejected the institution of bishops (which both the Lutheran and Anglican churches retained), and provided instead that the church should be governed by presbyteries, elected bodies made up of ministers and devout laymen. By thus bringing an element of lay control into church affairs, they broke the monopoly of priestly power and so promoted secularization. On the other hand, they were the reverse of secular, for they wished to Christianize all society.

Calvin, called in by earlier reformers who had driven out their bishop, was able to set up his model Christian community at Geneva in Switzerland. A body of ministers ruled the church; a consistory of ministers and elders ruled the town. The rule was strict; all loose, light, or frivolous living was suppressed; disaffected persons were driven into exile. The form of worship was severe, and favored the intellectual rather than the emotional or the aesthetic. The service was devoted largely to long sermons elucidating Christian doctrine, and all appeals to the senses—color, music, incense—were rigidly subdued. The black gown of Geneva replaced brighter clerical vestments. Images, representing the saints, Mary, or Christ, were taken down and destroyed. Candles went the way of incense. Chanting was replaced by the singing of hymns. Instrumental music was frowned upon, and many Calvinists thought even bells to be a survival of "popery." In all things Calvin undertook to regulate his church by the Bible. Nor was he more willing than Luther to countenance any doctrine more radical than his own. When a Spanish refugee, Michael Servetus, who denied the Trinity, i.e., the divinity of Christ, sought asylum at Geneva, Calvin pronounced him a heretic and burned him at the stake.

To Geneva flocked reformers of all nationalities, Englishmen, Scots, Frenchmen, Netherlanders, Germans, Poles, and Hungarians, to see and study a true scriptural community so that they might reproduce it in their own countries. Geneva became the Protestant Rome, the one great international center of Reformed doctrine. Everywhere Calvinists made their teachings heard (even in Spain and Italy in isolated cases), and everywhere, or almost everywhere, little groups which had locally and spontaneously broken with the old church found in Calvin's *Institutes* a reasoned statement of doctrine and a suggested method of organization. Thus Calvinism spread, or was adopted, very widely. In Hungary and Bohemia large elements turned Protestant, and usually Calvinist, partly as a way of opposing the Habsburg rule. In Poland there were many Calvinists, along with less organized Anabaptists and Unitarians, or Socinians, as those who denied the Trinity were then called. Calvinists spread in Germany, where, opposing both Lutheran and Catholic churches as ungodly impositions of worldly power, they were disliked equally by both. In France the Huguenots were Calvinist, as were the Protestants of the Netherlands. John Knox in the 1550s brought Calvinism to Scotland, where Presbyterianism became and remained the established religion. At the same time Calvinism began to penetrate England, from which it was later to reach British America, giving birth to the Presbyterian and Congregationalist churches of the United States.

Calvinism was far from democratic in any modern sense, being rather of an almost aristocratic outlook, in that those who sensed themselves to be God's chosen few felt free to dictate to the common run of mankind. Yet in many ways Calvinism entered into the development of what became democracy. For one thing, Calvinists never venerated the state; they always held that the sphere of the state and of public life was subject to moral judgment. For another, the Calvinist doctrine of the "calling" taught that a man's labor had a religious dignity, and that any form of honest work was pleasing in the sight of God. In the conduct of their own affairs Calvinists developed a type of self-government. They formed "covenants" with one another, and devised machinery for the election of presbyteries. They refused to believe that authority was transmitted downward through bishops or through kings. They were inclined also to a democratic outlook by the circumstance that in most countries they remained an unofficial minority. Only at Geneva, in the Dutch Netherlands, in Scotland, and in New England (and for a few years in England in the seventeenth century) were Calvinists ever able to prescribe the mode of life and religion of a whole country. In England, France, and Germany, Calvinists remained in opposition to the established authorities of church and state and hence were disposed to favor limitations upon established power. In Poland and Hungary many Calvinists were nobles who disliked royal authority.

The Reformation in England

England was peculiar in that its government broke with the Roman church before adopting any Protestant principles. Henry VIII (1509–1547) in fact prided himself on his orthodoxy. When a few obscure persons, about 1520, began to whisper Luther's ideas in England, Henry himself wrote a *Defense of the Seven Sacraments* in refutation, for which a grateful pope conferred upon him the title of "Defender of the Faith." But the king had no male heir. Recalling the anarchy from which the Tudor dynasty had extricated England, and determined as a New Monarch to build up a durable monarchy, he felt, or said, that before all else he must have a son. In order to remarry, he requested the pope to annul his existing marriage to Catherine of Aragon. Popes in the past had obliged monarchs similarly pressed. The pope now, however, was embarrassed by the fact that Catherine, who objected, was the aunt of the Emperor Charles V, whom the pope was in no position to offend. Henry, not a patient man, drove matters forward. He put in a new archbishop of Canterbury, repudiated the Roman connection, and married the youthful Anne Boleyn. The fact that only three years later he put to death the unfortunate Anne, and thereafter in quick succession married four more wives, for a total of six, threw considerable doubt on the original character of his motives.

Henry acted through Parliament, believing, as he said, that a king was never stronger than when united with representatives of his kingdom. In 1534 Parliament passed the Act of Supremacy, which declared the English king to be the "Protector and Only Supreme Head of the Church and Clergy of England." All subjects were required, if asked, to take the oath of supremacy acknowledging the religious headship of Henry and rejecting that of the pope. For refusing this oath Sir Thomas More, a statesman and humanist best known as the author of *Utopia*, was executed for treason. He received a somewhat delayed reward four centuries later when the Roman church pronounced him to be a saint. Henry, in the next few years, closed all the monasteries in England. The extensive monastic lands, accumulated by never-dying corporations from gifts made over the centuries, were seized by the king, who passed them out to numerous followers, thus strengthening and reconstituting a landed aristocracy which had been seriously weakened in the Wars of the Roses. The new landed gentry remained firm supporters of the house of Tudor and the English national church, whatever its doctrines.

It was Henry's intent not to change the doctrines at all. He simply wished to be the supreme head of an English Catholic church. On the one hand, in 1536, he forcibly suppressed a predominantly Catholic rebellion, and, on the other, in 1539, through the Six Articles, required everybody to believe in transubstantiation, the celibacy of the clergy, the need of confession, and a few other test items of Catholic faith and practice. But it proved impossible to maintain this position, for a great many people in England began to favor one or another of the ideas of Continental Reformers, and a small minority were willing to accept the entire Protestant position.

For three decades the government veered about. Henry died in 1547 and was succeeded by his ten-year-old son, Edward VI, under whom the Protestant party came to the fore. But Edward died in 1553 and was succeeded by his much older sister, Mary, the daughter of Catherine of Aragon and a devout Roman Catholic whose whole life had been embittered by the break with Rome. Mary tried to re-Catholicize England, but she actually made Catholicism more unpopular with the English. In 1554 she married Philip of Spain, who became king of England, though only nominally. The English did not like Philip, nor the Spanish, nor the intense Spanish Catholicism that Philip represented. Under Mary, moreover, some three hundred persons were burned at the stake, as heretics, in public mass executions. It was the first (and last) time that such a thing had happened in

England, and it set up a wave of horror. In any event, Mary did not live long. She was succeeded in 1558 by Henry's younger daughter, Elizabeth, the child of Anne Boleyn. Whatever Elizabeth's real views in religion might be (she concealed them successfully and was rumored to have none), she could not be a Roman Catholic. For Catholics she was illegitimate and so unable to be queen.

Under Elizabeth the English became Protestant, gradually and in their own way. The Church of England took on a form of its own. Organizationally, it resembled a Lutheran church. It was a state church, for its existence and doctrines were determined by the temporal power, in this case the monarch acting through Parliament. All English subjects were obliged to belong to it, and laws were passed against "recusants," a term used to cover both the Roman Catholics and the more advanced Calvinists who refused to acknowledge it. With the exception of monasteries and certain other church foundations, the Church of England retained the physical possessions, buildings, and internal organization of the medieval church —the bishops and the archbishops, who continued to sit in the House of Lords, the episcopal courts with their jurisdiction over marriage and wills, the tithes or church taxes paid by all landowners, the parish structure, the universities of Oxford and Cambridge. In religious practice, the Church of England was definitely Protestant: English replaced Latin as the language of the liturgy, there was no cult of the saints, and the clergy married, though Elizabeth confessed to some embarrassment at the thought of an archbishop having a wife. In doctrine, it was Elizabeth's policy to make the dogmas broad and ambiguous, so that persons of all shades of belief could be more readily accommodated. The Thirty-nine Articles (1563), composed by a committee of bishops, defined the creed of the Anglican church. In the light of the burning issues of the day many of the articles were evasive, though Protestant in tone. All but one of the Anglican bishops had been newly appointed by Elizabeth at her accession; many had lived in exile among Continental Protestants in the reign of Mary Tudor; and except on the matter of church government through bishops (known as episcopacy) a strong Calvinist impress was set upon Anglican belief in the time of Elizabeth. Anglicans, for a century or more, generally considered themselves closer to Geneva than to Rome, the seat of "popery," and regarded Lutherans as "semi-papist." There remained, however, a High Church element, emphasizing the Catholic rather than the Protestant character of Anglicanism.

The same ecclesiastical settlement was prescribed for Ireland, where English or rather Anglo-Norman conquerors had settled since the twelfth century, shortly after the Norman conquest of England. A replica of the Church of England was now established, called the Church of Ireland, which took over the properties and position of the Roman church in the lesser island. The native Irish remained almost solidly Roman Catholic. As in Hungary or Bohemia people who resented the Habsburgs were likely to turn Protestant rather than share in the ruler's religion, so in Ireland the fact that the ruling English were Protestant only confirmed the Irish in their attachment to the Roman church. The Catholic priests, deprived of status, income, and church buildings, and often in hiding, became national leaders of a discontented people.

The Religious Situation by 1560

Neither in England, nor in Germany, nor in a Europe at large penetrated by international Calvinism were the issues regarded as settled in 1560. Nor had the

Roman church accepted the new situation. But by 1560 the chief Protestant doctrines had been affirmed, and geographically Protestantism had made many conquests. The unity of Latin Christendom had been broken. Christendom was disintegrating into a purely intangible ideal. A world of separate states and nations was taking its place.

Protestants differed with one another, yet there was much that all had in common. All rejected the papal authority. None participated in any effective international organization; the ascendancy of Geneva was spiritual only and proved to be temporary. All Protestants rejected the special, sacerdotal, or supernatural character of the priesthood; indeed, the movement was perhaps most fundamentally a revolt against the medieval position of the clergy. Protestants generally called their clergy ministers, not priests. All Protestant clergy could marry. There were no Protestant monks, nuns, or friars. All Protestant churches replaced Latin

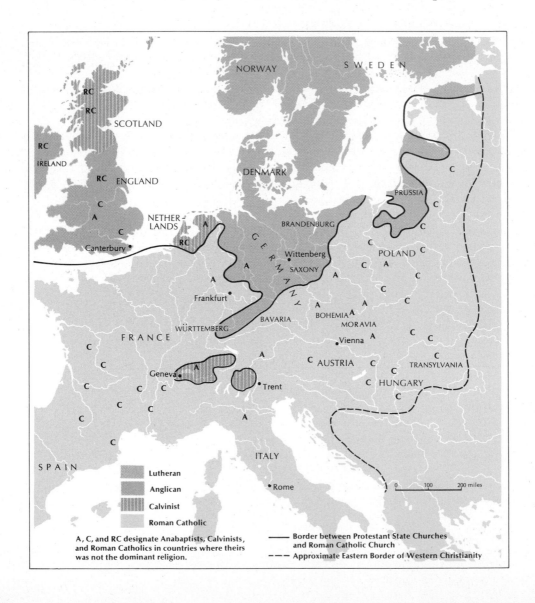

with the vernacular in religious services—English, French, German, Czech, as the case might be. All Protestants reduced the number of sacraments, usually to two or three; such sacraments as they retained they regarded more as symbols than as actual carriers of divine grace; all believed, in one way or another, in justification by faith. All denied transubstantiation, or the miracle of the Mass. All gave up the obligatory confessional, and with it priestly absolution. All gave up the idea of purgatory as a kind of temporal zone between heaven and hell and hence abandoned the practice of saying prayers and Masses for the dead. It need hardly be added that nothing like indulgences remained. All gave up the cult of the saints and of the Virgin Mary, whose intercession in heaven was no longer expected. All declared that the one true source of Christian belief was the Holy Scripture. And while all established Protestant churches, in the sixteenth century, insisted on conformity to their own doctrines, allowing no individual freedom, all Protestants still had some small spark of the spirit first ignited by Luther, so that none flatly repudiated the right of private judgment in matters of conscience.

It has sometimes been maintained that one of the motivations in Protestantism was economic—that a new acquisitive, aggressive, dynamic, progressive, capitalistic impulse shook off the restrictions imposed by medieval religion. The fact that Protestant England and Holland soon underwent a rapid capitalistic development gives added likelihood to this idea. The alacrity with which Protestant governments confiscated church lands shows a keen material interest; but in truth, both before and after the Reformation, governments confiscated church properties without breaking with the Roman church. That profound economic changes were occurring at the time will become apparent in the following chapter. Yet it seems that economic conditions were far less decisive than religious convictions and political circumstances. Calvinism won followers not only in cities, but in agrarian countries such as Scotland, Poland, and Hungary. Lutheranism spread more successfully in the economically retarded north Germany than in the busy south. The English were for years no more inclined to Protestantism than the French, and in France, while many lords and peasants turned Protestant, Paris

STATE RELIGIONS IN EUROPE ABOUT 1560

It is not possible to draw an accurate religious map of Europe during the Reformation, because in many countries persons of different religions were intermixed. What the map shows is the legally authorized, established or territorial churches about 1560. Many Catholics lived north of the heavy line, and many Protestants south of it. Most widely dispersed were the Calvinists and the more radical Protestants or Anabaptists. Calvinism was established in various Swiss cantons, the Dutch provinces, and Scotland, but there were many Calvinist congregations elsewhere, especially in southern France and in Poland and Hungary. Radical Protestants, who rejected the principle of the state church, could be found in both Protestant and Catholic countries; they were most numerous in parts of Germany and in Bohemia-Moravia, but included the American Pilgrim Fathers. In Germany, under the Holy Roman Empire, each principality and free city chose its own religion; hence, the Germans were the only large European nationality to emerge from the Reformation almost evenly divided between Catholics and Protestants. In other large countries in the century after 1560 one side or the other, Protestant or Catholic, was reduced to a small minority. Such minorities were either persecuted, barely tolerated, or at least out of favor with their respective governments until the French Revolution.

and many other towns remained as steadfastly Catholic. It is possible that Protestantism, by casting a glow of religious righteousness over a man's daily business and material prosperity, later contributed to the economic success of Protestant peoples, but it does not seem that economic forces were of any distinctive importance in the first stages of Protestantism.

10. CATHOLICISM REFORMED AND REORGANIZED

The Catholic movement corresponding to the rise of Protestantism is known as the Catholic Reformation or the Counter Reformation, the former term being preferred by Catholics, the latter by Protestants. Both are applicable. On the one hand the Catholic church underwent a genuine reform, which might have worked itself out in one way or another even if the stimulus of revolutionary Protestantism had been absent. On the other hand the character of the reform, the decisions made, and the measures adopted were shaped by the need of responding explicitly to the Protestant challenge; and certainly, also, there was a good deal of purely "counter" activity aimed at the elimination of Protestantism as such.

The demand for reform was as old as the abuses against which it was directed. Characteristically, it had expressed itself in the demand for a general or ecumenical church council. The conciliar movement, defeated by the popes about 1450, showed signs of revival after 1500.[12] But it was almost as hard, even then, to assemble a general council as it is today to create an international body possessing any effective authority.

Several years before Luther had been heard of, Europe's two most important secular rulers, the king of France and the Holy Roman Emperor, jointly convened on their own authority a council at Pisa in 1511. It was their purpose to force reforms upon Pope Julius II, and if necessary depose him. But no delegates from other countries attended; the five cardinals and handful of bishops who came to Pisa were regarded as minions of the two rulers who sent them. The council thus lacked moral authority, no one listened to it, and it accomplished nothing, never even attaining historically the name of a council. The pope, however, to ward off the danger of a council under secular auspices, himself assembled the Fifth Lateran Council at Rome in 1512. It was supposed to be general, ecumenical, Europe-wide, representing that "spiritual unity" sometimes imagined to have existed in Europe before Luther. In fact, few took it seriously, because it was composed mainly of Italian prelates, who began by denouncing the doctrines of the Council of Constance and ended by making a few tame resolutions on miscellaneous topics.

Then came the Lutheran upheaval, and the attempts of Charles V, in the interests of German unity, to persuade the pope to assemble a true and adequately empowered council, so that removal of abuses in the church, which no one really defended, would take away the grounds upon which many Germans were turning to Lutheranism. But meanwhile the king of France found reason to favor the pope and to oppose the emperor. The French king, Francis I (1515–1547), could support the pope because he had obtained from the papacy what he wanted, namely, control over the Gallican church, as acquired in the Concordat of

[12] On the conciliar movement see pp. 51–52.

Bologna of 1516.[13] And he had reason to oppose Charles V, because Charles V ruled not only in Germany but in the Netherlands, Spain, and much of Italy, thus encircling France and threatening Europe with what contemporaries called "universal monarchy." Francis I therefore actively encouraged the Protestants of Germany, as a means of maintaining dissension there, and used his influence at Rome against the calling of a council by which the troubles of the Catholic world might be relieved.

Gradually, in the curia, there arose a party of reforming cardinals who concluded that the need of reform was so urgent that all dangers of a council must be risked. The pope summoned a council to meet in 1537, but the wars between France and the Empire forced its abandonment. Then a council was called for 1542, but no one came except a few Italians so that it had to be suspended. Finally, in 1545, a council did assemble and begin operations. It met at Trent, on the Alpine borders of Germany and Italy. The Council of Trent, which shaped the destiny of modern Catholicism, sat at irregular intervals for almost twenty years—in 1545–1547, 1551–1552, and 1562–1563. It was not until the Second Vatican Council in the 1960s that some of the main decisions made at Trent were substantially modified.

The Council of Trent

The council was beset by difficulties of a political nature, which seemed to show that under troubled conditions an international council was no longer a suitable means of regulating Catholic affairs. For one thing, it was poorly attended. Whereas at the Fourth Lateran Council of 1215, and at Constance in 1415, some five hundred prelates had assembled, the attendance at Trent was never nearly so great; it sometimes fell as low as twenty or thirty, and the important decree on "justification," the prime issue raised by Luther, and one on which some good Catholics had until then believed a compromise to be possible, was passed at a session where only sixty prelates were present. The most regular in attendance were the Italians and Spanish; the French and Germans came erratically and in smaller numbers. Even with the small attendance, the old conciliar issue was raised. A party of bishops believed that the bishops of the Catholic church, when assembled in council from all parts of the Catholic world, collectively constituted an authority superior to that of the pope. To stave off this "episcopal" movement was one of the chief duties of the cardinal legates deputed by the pope to preside over the sessions.

The popes managed successfully to resist the idea of limiting the papal power. In the end they triumphed, through a final ruling, voted by the council, that no act of the council should be valid unless accepted by the Holy See. It is possible that had the conciliar theory won out, the Catholic church might have become as disunited in modern times as the Protestant. It was clear, at Trent, that the various bishops tended to see matters in a national way, in the light of their own problems at home, and to be frequently under strong influence from their respective secular monarchs. In any case, the papal party prevailed, which is to say that the centralizing element, not the national, triumphed. The Council of Trent in fact marked an important step in the movement which issued, three hundred

---

[13] See p. 69.

years later, in the promulgation of the infallibility of the pope when speaking *ex cathedra* on matters of faith and morals. After 1563 no council met at all until the Vatican Council of 1870 at which this papal infallibility was proclaimed.[14] The Council of Trent thus preserved the papacy as a center of unity for the Catholic church and helped prevent the very real threat of its dissolution into state churches. Even so, the council's success was not immediate, for in every important country the secular rulers at first accepted only what they chose of its work, and only gradually did its influence prevail.

Questions of national politics and of church politics apart, the Council of Trent addressed itself to two kinds of labors—to a statement of Catholic doctrine and to a reform of abuses in the church. When the council began to meet, in 1545, the Protestant movement had already gone so far that any reconciliation was probably impossible: Protestants, especially Calvinists, simply did not wish to belong to the church of Rome under any conditions. In any case, the Council of Trent made no concessions.

It declared justification to be by works and faith combined. It enumerated and defined the seven sacraments, which were held to be vehicles of grace independent of the spiritual state of those who received them.[15] The priesthood was declared to be a special estate set apart from the laity by the sacrament of holy orders. The procedures of the confessional and of absolution were clarified. Transubstantiation was reaffirmed. As sources of Catholic faith, the council put Scripture and tradition on an equal footing. It thus rejected the Protestant claim to find true faith in the Bible alone and reasserted the validity of church development since New Testament times. The Vulgate, a translation of the Bible into Latin made by St. Jerome in the fourth century, was declared to be the only version on which authoritative teaching could be based. The right of individuals to believe that their own interpretation of Scripture was more true than that of church authorities (private judgment) was denied. Latin, as against the national languages, was prescribed as the language of religious worship—a requirement abolished by the Second Vatican Council in the 1960s. Celibacy of the clergy was maintained. Monasticism was upheld. The existence of purgatory was reaffirmed. The theory and correct practice of indulgences were restated. The veneration of saints, the cult of the Virgin, and the use of images, relics, and pilgrimages were approved as spiritually useful and pious actions.

It was easier for a council to define doctrines than to reform abuses, since the latter consisted in the rooted habits of thousands and millions of people's lives. The council decreed, however, a drastic reform of the monastic orders. It acted against the abuse of indulgences while upholding the principle. It ruled that bishops should reside habitually in their dioceses and attend more carefully to their proper duties. It gave bishops more administrative control over clergy in their own dioceses, such as mendicant friars, who in the past had been exempt from episcopal jurisdiction, and whose presence had often caused disturbance, or indeed scandal, among the local people. The abuse by which one man had held numerous church offices at the same time (pluralism) was checked, and steps were taken to assure that church officials should be competent. To provide an educated clergy, the council ordered that a seminary should be set up in each diocese for the training of priests.

14 See p. 600.
15 See p. 39.

The Counter Crusade

As laws in general have little force unless sustained by opinion, so the reform decrees of the Council of Trent would have remained ineffectual had not a renewed sense of religious seriousness been growing at the same time. Herein lay the inner force of the Catholic Reform. In Italy, as the Renaissance became more undeniably pagan, and as the sack of Rome, in 1527, showed the depths of hatred felt even by Catholics toward the Roman clergy, the voices of severer moralists began to be heeded. The line of Renaissance popes was succeeded by a line of reforming popes, of whom the first was Paul III (1534–1549). The reforming popes insisted on the primacy of the papal office, but they regarded this office, unlike their predecessors, as a moral and religious force. In many dioceses the bishops began on their own initiative to be more strict. The new Catholic religious sense, more than the Protestant, centered in a reverence for the sacraments and a mystical awe for the church itself as a divine institution. Both men and women founded many new religious orders, of which the Jesuits became the most famous. Others were the Oratorians for men and the Ursulines for women. The new orders dedicated themselves to a variety of educational and philanthropic activities. Missionary fervor for a long time was more characteristic of Catholics than of Protestants. It reached into Asia and the Americas, and in Europe expressed itself as an intense desire for the reconversion of Protestants. It showed itself, too, in missions among the poor, as in the work of St. Vincent de Paul among the human wreckage of Paris, for which the established Protestant churches failed to produce anything comparable. In America, as colonies developed in the sixteenth and seventeenth centuries, the Protestant clergy tended to take the layman's view of the Indians, while Catholic clergy labored to convert and preserve them; and the Catholic church generally worked to mitigate the brutality of Negro slavery, to which the pastors in English and Dutch colonies, perhaps because they were more dependent upon the laity, remained largely indifferent.

We have seen how in Spain, where the Renaissance had never taken much hold, the very life of the country was a boundless Christian crusade.[16] It was in Spain that much of the new Catholic feeling first developed, and from Spain that much of the missionary spirit first went out. It was Spain that gave birth to St. Ignatius Loyola (1491–1556). A soldier in youth, he too, like Luther and Calvin, had a religious "experience" or "conversion," which occurred in 1521, before he had heard of Luther, and while Calvin was still a boy. Loyola resolved to become a soldier of the church, a militant crusader for the pope and the Holy See. On this principle he established the Society of Jesus, commonly known as the Jesuits. Authorized by Paul III in 1540, the Jesuits constituted a monastic order of a new type, less attached to the cloister, more directed toward active participation in the affairs of the world. Only men of proven strength of character and intellectual force were admitted. Each Jesuit had to undergo an arduous and even horrifying mystical training, set forth by Loyola in his *Spiritual Exercises*. The order was ruled by an iron discipline, which required each member to see in his immediate superior the infallibility of Holy Church. If, said Loyola, the church teaches to be black what the eye sees as white, the mind will believe it to be black. Aside from demanding absolute submission in matters of faith, the Jesuits generally favored rationality and a measure of liberty in the religious life. For two hundred

[16] See pp. 69–72.

years they were the most famous schoolmasters of Catholic Europe, eventually
conducting some five hundred schools for boys of the upper and middle classes. In
them they taught, besides the faith, the principles of gentlemanly deportment
(their teaching of dancing and dramatics became a scandal to more puritanical
Catholics), and they carried over the Renaissance and humanist idea of the Latin
classics as the main substance of adolescent education. The Jesuits made a specialty
of work among the ruling classes. They became confessors to kings and hence involved in political intrigue. In an age when Protestants subordinated the organized church either to the state or to the individual conscience, and when even
Catholics frequently thought of the church within a national framework, the Jesuits seemed almost to worship the church itself as a divine institution, the Church
Militant and the Church Universal, internationally organized and governed by
the Roman pontiff. All full-fledged Jesuits took a special vow of obedience to the
pope. Jesuits in the later sessions of the Council of Trent fought obstinately, and
successfully, to uphold the position of Rome against that of the national bishops.
The high papalism of the Jesuits (later called "ultramontanism") for centuries
made them as obnoxious to many Catholics as they were to the Protestants.

By 1560 the Catholic church, renewed by a deepening of its religious life, and
by an uncompromising restatement of its dogmas and discipline, had devised also
the practical machinery for a counteroffensive against Protestantism. The Jesuits
acted as an international missionary force. They recruited members from all
countries, including those in which the governments had turned Protestant. English Catholics, for example, trained as Jesuits on the Continent, returned to England to overthrow the heretic usurper, Elizabeth, seeing in the universal church a
higher cause than national independence in religion. Jesuits poured also into the
most hotly disputed regions where the issue still swayed in the balance—France,
Germany, Bohemia, Poland, Hungary. As after every great revolution, many
people after an initial burst of Protestantism were inclined to turn back to the old
order, especially as the more crying evils within the Catholic church were corrected. The Jesuits reconverted many who thus hesitated.

For the more recalcitrant other machinery was provided. All countries censored books; Protestant authorities labored to keep "papist" works from the eyes
of the faithful, and Catholic authorities took the same pains to suppress all
knowledge of "heretics." All bishops, Anglican, Lutheran, and Catholic, regulated reading matter within their dioceses. In the Catholic world, with the trend
toward centralization under the pope, a special importance attached to the list
published by the bishop of Rome, the papal Index of Prohibited Books. Only with
special permission, granted to reliable persons for special study, could Catholics
read books listed on the Index, on which most of the significant works written in
Europe since the Reformation have been included.

All countries, Protestant and Catholic, also set up judicial and police machinery to enforce conformity to the accepted church. In England, for example,
Elizabeth established the High Commission to bring "recusants" into the Church
of England. All bishops, Protestant and Catholic, likewise possessed machinery of
enforcement in their episcopal courts. But no court made itself so dreaded as the
Inquisition. In reality two distinct organizations went under this name, the word
itself being simply an old term of the Roman law, signifying a court of inquest or
inquiry. One was the Spanish Inquisition, established originally, about 1480, to
ferret out Jewish and Muslim survivals in Spain. It was then introduced into all

countries ruled by the Spanish crown and employed against Protestantism, particularly in the Spanish Netherlands, which was an important center of Calvinism. The other was the Roman or papal Inquisition, established at Rome in 1542 under a permanent committee of cardinals called the Holy Office; it was in a sense a revival of the famous medieval tribunal established in the thirteenth century for the detection and repression of heresy. Both the Spanish and the Roman Inquisition employed torture, for heresy was regarded as the supreme crime, and all persons charged with crime could be tortured, in civil as well as ecclesiastical courts, under the existing laws. In the use of torture, as in the imposition of the harshest sentence, burning alive, the Roman Inquisition was milder than the Spanish. With the growth of papal centralization the Roman Inquisition in principle offered a court to protect purity of faith in all parts of the Catholic world. But the national resistance of Catholic countries proved too strong; few Catholics wished the agents of Rome inquiring locally into their opinions; and the Roman Inquisition never functioned for any length of time outside of Italy. In France no form of the Inquisition was admitted either then or later.

In the "machinery" of enforcing religious belief, however, no engine was to be so powerful as the apparatus of state, of political sovereignty. Where Protestants won control of government, people became Protestant. Where Catholics retained control of governments, Protestants became in time small minorities. And it was in the clash of governments, which is to say in war, for about a century after 1560, that the fate of European religion was worked out. In 1560 the strongest powers of Europe—Spain, France, Austria—were all officially Catholic. The Protestant states were all small or at most middle-sized. The Lutheran states of Germany, like all German states, were individually of little weight. The Scandinavian monarchies were far away. England, the most considerable of Protestant kingdoms, was a country of only four million people, with an independent and hostile Scotland to the north, and with no sign of colonial empire yet in existence. In the precedence of monarchs, as arranged in the earlier part of the century, the king of England ranked just below the king of Portugal, and next above the king of Sicily. Clearly, had a great combined Catholic crusade ever developed, Protestantism could have been wiped out. To launch such a crusade was the dream of the king of Spain. It never succeeded; why, will be seen in the next chapter.

The Florence of the Renaissance

The supreme site of the Italian Renaissance, Florence was both a city lying on either side of the river Arno and an independent republic, with a territory extending, by 1500, for about fifty miles in most directions from Florence itself. The city had grown wealthy in the later Middle Ages from the production of woolens. It developed also an intense civic spirit in its conflicts with other Italian cities. It became a home of merchant princes, of whom the Medici were the most famous. Such families, enriched in earlier generations by the woolen trade, then passing into banking, emerged as an urban patriciate or governing class, the more easily because there was no royalty to overshadow them, and the feudal nobility in the surrounding country was very weak.

Patricians were sometimes opposed by the populace, and sometimes, like the early Medici, they had popular followings of their own. Outbursts of factionalism were therefore very common, compounded by the rivalry with other Italian cities, and by the increasing involvement of the Holy Roman Emperor, the king of France, and the pope. The Medici became dominant in the fifteenth century, were expelled in 1494, restored in 1512, expelled again in 1527, then again restored in 1530, this time permanently, since they remained as hereditary grand dukes of Tuscany until 1737. The following pages suggest something of the wealth, the civic life, and the political crises of Florence until the end of the republic in the 1530s.

More interesting to outsiders than the civil turmoil were Florentine literature and works of art. Writers of a new kind, the humanists, abounded in the city. Reflecting the new interests of the Renaissance, they rejected the church-centered and university-oriented learning of the Middle Ages, and they brought a new spirit to the study of the Latin and Greek classics, in which they found a keen significance for their own times. Of these writers, the best remembered is Machiavelli, who worked to strengthen Florentine republicanism during the period of the Medici exile from 1494 to 1512.

Also born in Florence, either in the city or in the republic, were Michelangelo, Leonardo da Vinci, Masaccio, Donatello, Brunelleschi, Botticelli, and Benvenuto Cellini, to name only the most eminent painters and sculptors, in addition to such lesser lights as the historian Guicciardini and the explorer Amerigo Vespucci, Latinized as Americus Vespucius, after whom America was named. Never since ancient Athens had so much talent appeared in so small a place within the short span of three or four generations. Patronage by the ruling elite was reinforced by a high degree of literacy in the general population; a chronicler reports that as early as 1338 there were 8,000 boys and girls in the schools. Such conditions promoted a degree of taste and understanding in which architecture, painting, sculpture, literature, and intellectual discussion could flourish.

This view of Florence shows the river Arno bisecting it and flowing on into the Tuscan plain. In the right center is the Duomo, or cathedral, dominating the city. The scene, painted by Vasari, shows the situation in 1530, when the city was besieged by the Holy Roman Emperor, Charles V. The defenses were strong, and Michelangelo himself served as one of nine citizens in charge of engineering and fortifications. The Imperial army, shown encamped outside the walls, eventually overcame the resistance and restored the exiled Medici to power.

   At the extreme left is the sign of the wool guild of Florence, in which a sheep is appropriately displayed. The near left shows the modest establishment of a fifteenth-century banker, engaged in the actual counting or changing of money.

Above, Lorenzo de' Medici, the "Magnificent," examines a model for a villa built for him about 1480 on the outskirts of the city. The Medici town house, or "palace," appears on the last page of the present essay.

At the left is a part of a huge fresco executed for the chapel of the Medici town house by Benozzo Gozzoli in 1469. It is called the Procession of the Three Kings to Bethlehem, but what it really represents is the important personages of Florence at their most resplendent. The presence of an African servant in Italy at this early date is to be noted. He wears his hair in African style and carries a bow. To the right of him is Cosimo de' Medici on a white horse, followed by a throng whose varied complexions and miscellaneous headgear, including the miter of a Greek patriarch, suggest the cosmopolitanism of the city.

97

The three figures at the left are from a painting by Domenico Ghirlandaio, done about 1490 for a chapel in memory of a woman who had died in childbirth. The theme is "Zacharias in the Temple," but the three heads are actually portraits of contemporary Florentine humanists. The painting thus illustrates, like the one by Gozzoli on the preceding pages, the use of religious themes to convey secular subjects, or of everyday observation to convey religious ideas.

Above, the governing council, or "signoria," deliberates on going to war against the neighboring city of Pisa, during the period of republican revival after expulsion of the Medici in 1494. A Nemesis floats over the councilors' heads.

Valse el c° della lana ags contanty 26 y 13 β 4 β di β

Upper left: Detail of the fall of Troy, enacted in Florentine costume in the streets of Florence. The building at the left is the Medici palace (see the next page). At the right, the African warrior wielding a large bow is Memnon, King of the Ethiopians, who according to an ancient legend fought at Troy on the side of the Trojans.

Lower left: Two wool merchants with their goods, from a book of 1492 on arithmetic. Arabic numerals are visible above, but the bags of wool are marked "CLX" or 160 in Roman numerals.

Above: The Piazza della Signoria showing the burning of Savonarola. The dome of the cathedral is half in view at the left. The arcade at the right is the "loggia dei lanzi," built about 1380 as an open but sheltered place for public assemblies. The "palazzo della signoria," or town hall, the large square building, very dark in this picture, dates from 1298 and so reflects the medieval fortress-like style, with small windows, crenelated roof lines, and high towers that characterized this part of Italy before the classicizing features of Renaissance architecture were adopted.

These are town houses, or "palazzi," of Florentine patricians. At the right is the Palazzo Medici, built for Cosimo de' Medici in the 1440s. At the left is the slightly later Palazzo Rucellai. Architects such as Brunelleschi transformed the old fortress-like dwellings of an earlier day into these massive and elegant residences. The new style is evident in the horizontal composition, the long rows of wide, closely spaced, identical windows, the pilasters, and the cornices under the over-hanging roof. The interiors were often even more classical, with arches and columns enclosing an open courtyard.

It was in the Medici Palace that Lorenzo the Magnificent received his following of artists and human-ists, and that Pope Leo X (born 1475; pope, 1513–1521) and Catherine de' Medici (born 1519; queen of France, 1547–1559; queen mother, 1559–1589) spent their youth.

III.
Economic Renewal and Wars of Religion, 1560-1648

I t is convenient to think of the period of about a century following 1560 as the age of the Wars of Religion, which may be said to have ended with the Peace of Westphalia in 1648. France, England, the Netherlands, and the Holy Roman Empire fell into internal struggles in which religion was the most burning issue, but in which political, constitutional, economic, and social questions were also involved. They, and other powers, also fought in international wars in which the conflict between Catholics and Protestants was a main source of contention but in which other interests were at work too. Often the ideological lines became blurred, as Catholics lent aid to Protestants, or vice versa, somewhat as ideological issues in our own day tend to be confused.

The time of the long, drawn-out Wars of Religion was also a time of economic renewal. From the beginning of the sixteenth century society was transformed by contacts with a newly discovered overseas world, by expanded trade routes, an emergent capitalism, and the formation of new social classes. The effects of these profound changes, however, were obscured and delayed by the politico-religious struggles. In the present chapter we must first examine the geographical discoveries, then survey the broad new economic and social developments under way, and

Chapter Emblem: A mariner's, or simplified, astrolabe that could be taken to sea and used in determination of latitude.

finally trace the impact of the religious wars on various parts of Europe. The wars, as we shall see, left Spain and Germany very much weakened, and opened the way for the English, Dutch, and French to profit from the economic changes and play leading roles in the drama of early modern times.

11. THE OPENING OF THE ATLANTIC

Always until about 1500 the Atlantic Ocean had been a barrier, an end. About 1500 it became a bridge, a starting place. In the Middle Ages, and even in Roman times, small craft had groped from port to port on Europe's Atlantic coast. Vikings settled Iceland in the ninth century, and even touched North America soon thereafter. In 1317 the Venetians established the Flanders galleys, commercial flotillas which regularly made the passage between the Adriatic and the North Sea. In the fifteenth century, with further improvements in shipbuilding, in the rigging and manipulation of sails, and with the adoption of the mariner's compass, it became feasible to sail in the open ocean out of sight of land. It was the Portuguese who first made use of this opportunity. They were perhaps mainly drawn by the simple lure of exploration, but they were certainly tempted, on the material level, by the thought of trading directly with Asia.

For centuries Asia had been a source for Europe of many highly valued commodities, partly manufactures in which Europe could not compete, such as silk and cotton fabrics, rugs, jewelry, porcelains, and fine steel, and partly raw or semimanufactured drugs and foodstuffs, such as sugar and above all spices. The latter—pepper, cinnamon, cloves, ginger, nutmeg, and many less common ones—were of more importance then than now. They were used in pharmacy and in the preservation of meat, as in the making of sausages. They added palatability to fresh meats and other foods, which easily spoiled in the absence of refrigeration. Europeans had never themselves gone to the sources of supply of Eastern goods. Somewhere, east of Suez, barely known to Europeans, was another world of other merchants, who moved the wares of China, India, and the East Indies Spice Islands by caravan over land and by boat through the Red Sea or Persian Gulf to the markets of the eastern Mediterranean. Traders of the two worlds met and did business at such thriving centers as Alexandria or Beirut or Constantinople.

The Portuguese in the East

For some time the Portuguese royal house had sponsored and encouraged exploration of the Atlantic. In 1498 the Portuguese navigator Vasco da Gama, having rounded Africa in the wake of other intrepid explorers, found himself in the midst of the unknown world of Arab commerce. He landed on the Malabar Coast (the southwest coast of India), where he found a busy commercial population of heterogeneous religious background. These people knew at least as much about Europe as Europeans did about India (one Jew was able to act as da Gama's interpreter) and they realized that the coming of the Portuguese would disturb their established channels of commerce. Da Gama, playing upon local rivalries, was able to load his ships with the coveted wares, but on his second voyage, in 1502, he came better prepared, bringing a fighting fleet of no less than twenty-one vessels. A ferocious war broke out between the Portuguese and Arab mer-

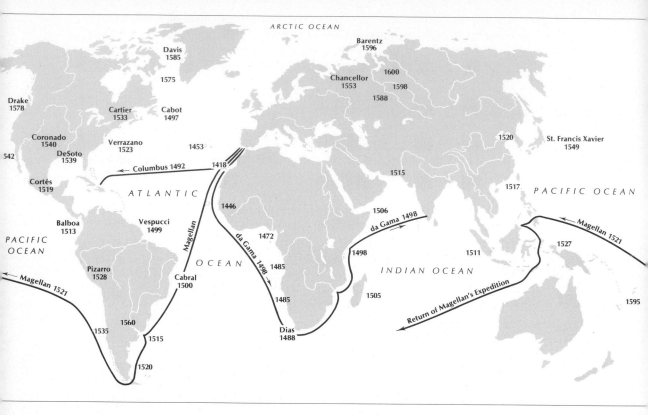

EUROPEAN DISCOVERIES, 1450–1600

Since very remote times the human race has occupied all the continents—except Antarctica —and most of the islands, and between A.D. 1000 and 1450 Norsemen reached Greenland and North America, various Europeans traveled overland to China, and Genoese sailors visited the Azores and the Canary Islands. "Discovery," however, means the bringing of newly found countries within the habitual knowledge of the society from which the discoverer comes. It was the Europeans who thus "discovered" the rest of the world between about 1450 and 1600. They did so by using maritime skills and geographical knowledge developed in the Mediterranean; hence many of the first discoverers—Columbus, Cabot, Vespucci, Verrazano—were Italians, though in the service respectively of Spain, England, Portugal, and France. Two of the greatest, however, da Gama and Magellan, were Portuguese. Dates on the map show the years of first significant European arrival at the points indicated. With a few exceptions, as for Coronado and the Russian penetration of Siberia, these dates mark the explorers' arrival by sea across the open ocean. Still unknown to Europeans in 1600 were most of the interior of both Americas and of Africa, northeastern Asia, and the very existence of Australia and New Zealand. (See also maps on pp. 292–293, and the picture essay, pp. 147–155.)

chants, the latter supported in one way or another by the Egyptians, the Turks, and even the distant Venetians, all of whom had an interest in maintaining the old routes of trade. For the Portuguese, trained like the Spaniards in long wars against the Moors at home, no atrocities were too horrible to commit against the infidel competitors whom they found at the end of their heroic quest. Cities were devastated, ships burned at their docks, prisoners butchered and their dismem-

bered hands, noses, and ears sent back as derisive trophies. One Brahmin, mutilated in this way, was left alive to bear them to his people. Such, unfortunately,
was India's introduction to the West.

In the following years, under the first governor general, Albuquerque, the Portuguese built permanent fortified stations at Goa on the Malabar Coast, at Aden
near the mouth of the Red Sea, at Ormuz near the mouth of the Persian Gulf, and
in East Africa. In 1509 they reached Malacca, near the modern Singapore, from
which they passed northward into China itself, and eastward to Amboina, the
heart of the Spice Islands, just west of New Guinea. Thus an empire was created,
the first of Europe's commercial-colonial empires, maintained by superiority of
firearms and sea power and with trade alternating with war and plunder. Albuquerque died in 1515, dreaming grandiose and preposterous dreams—to deflect
the course of the Nile and so destroy Egypt and Egyptian commerce, and to
capture Mecca and exchange it for the Holy Land. It should be added that bold
Jesuits soon arrived, led by St. Francis Xavier, who, by 1550, had baptized
thousands of souls in India, Indonesia, and even Japan.

By the new route the cost of Eastern goods for Europeans was much reduced,
for the old route had involved many transshipments, unloadings, and reloadings,
movements by sea and by land, through the hands of many merchants. In 1504
spices could be bought in Lisbon for only a fifth of the price demanded in Venice.
The Venetians (who in their desperation even talked of digging a Suez canal)
were hopelessly undersold; their trade thereafter was confined to products of the
Near East itself. As for the Portuguese, never was a commercial monopoly built so
fast. The lower prices added enormously to European demand and consumption.
Beginning in 1504, only five years after da Gama's first return, an average of
twelve ships a year left Lisbon for the East.

The Discovery of America

Meanwhile, as every American schoolchild can tell, the same quest for a route to
the East had led to the somewhat disappointing discovery of America. Like most
such discoveries, this was no chance hit of a queer or isolated genius. Behaim's
globe, constructed in 1492,[1] the very year of Columbus' first voyage, could hardly
fail to suggest the idea of sailing westward. Nevertheless, it was Christopher Columbus who had the persistence and daring to undertake the unprecedented
westward voyage. Before the invention of sufficiently accurate clocks (in the
eighteenth century) mariners had no way of determining longitude, i.e., their
east-west position, and learned geographers, as may be seen from Behaim's map,
greatly underestimated the probable distance from Europe westward to Asia.
When Columbus struck land, he naturally supposed it to be an outlying part of
the Indies. The people were soon called Indians, and the islands where Columbus
landed, the West Indies.

Columbus had sailed with the backing of Queen Isabella of Castile, and the
new lands became part of the composite dominions of the crown of Spain. The
Spaniards, hoping to beat the Portuguese to the East (which da Gama had not yet
reached), received Columbus' first reports with enthusiasm. For his second voyage they gave him 17 ships, filled with 1,500 workmen and artisans. Columbus

[1] See p. 292.

himself, until his death in 1506, kept probing about in the Caribbean, baffled and frustrated, hoping to find something that looked like the fabulous East. Others were more willing to accept the new land for what it was. Churchmen, powerful in Spain, regarded it as a new field for crusading and conversion. The government saw it as a source of gold and silver for the royal exchequer. Foot-loose gentry of warlike habits, left idle by the end of war with the Moors, turned to it to make their fortunes. The *conquistadores* fell upon the new lands. Cortés conquered the Aztecs in Mexico, Pizarro the Incas in Peru. They despoiled the native empires. Mines for precious metals were opened almost immediately. The Indians were put to forced labor, in which many died. The attempts of the church to protect its Indian converts, and restrictions set by the royal authorities on their exploitation, led almost immediately to the importation of African slaves, of whom, it was estimated, 100,000 had been brought to America by 1560.

Explorers began to feel their way along the vast dim bulk that barred them from Asia. A Spanish expedition, led by Magellan, found a southwestern passage in 1520, sailed from the Atlantic into the Pacific, crossed the Pacific, discovered the Philippine Islands, and fought its way through hostile Portuguese across the Indian Ocean back to Spain. The globe was thus circumnavigated for the first time, and an idea of the true size and interconnection of the oceans was brought back to Europe. Geographical experts immediately incorporated the new knowledge, as in the map drawn by Schöner in 1523.[2] Meanwhile others sailing for Spain, the Cabots sailing for England, Jacques Cartier for France, began the long and fruitless search for a northwest passage. An English expedition, looking for a northeast passage, discovered the White Sea in 1553. English merchants immediately began to take the ocean route to Russia. Archangel became an ocean port.

For a century it was only the Spanish and Portuguese who followed up the new ocean routes to America and the East. These two peoples, in a treaty of 1494, divided the globe between them. The Philippines, because of Magellan's discovery, went to Spain; Brazil, because it had been discovered by Cabral in 1500, to Portugal. Otherwise Spain received all America, and Portugal all rights of trade in Asia and the East Indies.

The Spanish Empire in America

In the populous and civilized East the Portuguese were never more than a handful of outsiders who could not impose their language, their religion, or their way of life. In America, after the first fiendishness of the *conquista*, the Spanish estab-

[2] See p. 292.

THE GEOGRAPHER
by Jan Vermeer (Dutch, 1632–1675)

The impact on Europe of the opening of the Atlantic may be seen in this painting and the following one. For the first time in human history it became possible to conceive, with some accuracy, of the relationships of the oceans and continents throughout the globe. The wonder aroused by the Age of Discovery is evident in this painting by Vermeer. By the seventeenth century the Dutch had built up a large ocean-going trade, and many of the leading instrument makers and cartographers lived in the Netherlands. For Vermeer and Dutch painting see below, p. 160. Courtesy of the Städelsches Kunstinstitut, Frankfurt.

lished their own civilization. In Protestant countries, and also in France, as the years went on there arose an extremely unfavorable idea of the Spanish regime in America, where, it was noted, the Inquisition was presently established and the native peoples were reduced to servitude by the conquerors. The Spanish themselves came to dismiss this grim picture as a Black Legend concocted by their rivals. The true character of the Spanish empire in America is not easy to portray. The Spanish government (like the home governments of all colonial empires until the American Revolution, and even later) regarded its empire as existing for the benefit of the mother country. The Indians were put into servitude, to work in mines or in agriculture. The government introduced the encomienda, a kind of distant analogue to the European manor. The "lord" of the encomienda controlled the labor of his Indians, but according to law he could not deprive Indians of their own parcels of land, and he must make Indians work for him no more than four days a week, leaving them two days to work on their parcels. Such conditions corresponded very closely to those in which the white masses of eastern Europe lived until the nineteenth century. How much the royal regulations were enforced in remote encomiendas is another question, on which answers vary. Negro slavery never assumed the importance in Spanish America that it later assumed in the Dutch, French, and English colonies. The white population remained small. Castilian Spaniards looked down on American-born whites, or creoles. Since few women emigrated from Spain, there arose a large class of mestizos, of mixed white and Indian descent.

The mestizos, along with many pure Indians, adopted to a considerable degree the Spanish language and the faith of the Spanish church. The Indians, while unfree, had usually been unfree under their own tribal chiefs; they were spared from tribal war; and the rigors of the Inquisition were mild compared with the sheer physical cruelty of the Aztecs or Incas. The printing press was brought to Mexico in 1544. By the middle of the sixteenth century Spanish America consisted of two great viceroyalties, those of Mexico and Peru, with twenty-two bishoprics, and with a university in each viceroyalty, the University of Lima established in 1551, that of Mexico in 1553. When Harvard College was founded in New England (in 1636) there were five universities on the European model in Spanish America.

In 1545 a great discovery was made, the prodigiously rich silver deposits at Potosí in Peru. (It is now in Bolivia.) Almost simultaneously, better methods of extracting silver from the ore by the use of mercury were developed. American

STUDY OF TWO BLACK HEADS
by Rembrandt van Rijn (Dutch, 1606–1669)

One consequence of the new intercontinental travel was the mass transportation to the Americas of black Africans as slaves. Some appeared also in Europe, where they attracted a great deal of personal curiosity and produced much speculation on the diversity of human races. Rembrandt, though he never traveled more than twenty miles from his native Leyden, painted all types of persons who streamed into the Netherlands. The greatest of the Dutch painters, and a profound observer of human beings, he was no doubt fascinated by the dark color tones, rugged features, and secret inner feelings of these two men in the strange world into which they had been cast. Courtesy of the Mauritshuis, The Hague (A. Dingjan).

production of precious metals shot up suddenly and portentously. For years, after the mid-century, half a million pounds of silver flowed annually from America to Spain, and ten thousand pounds of gold. The riches of Potosí financed the European projects of the king of Spain. Peruvian ores, Indian labor, and Spanish management combined to make possible the militant and anti-Protestant phase of the Counter Reformation.

The opening of the Atlantic reoriented Europe. In an age of oceanic communications Europe became a center from which America, Africa, and Asia could all be reached. In Europe itself, the Atlantic coast enjoyed great advantages over the center. No sooner did the Portuguese begin to bring spices from the East Indies than Antwerp began to flourish as the point of redistribution for northern Europe. But for a century after the great discoveries the northern peoples did not take to the oceans. French corsairs did indeed put out from Bayonne or Saint-Malo, and Dutch prowlers and English "sea dogs" followed at the close of the century, all bent upon plundering the Iberian treasure ships. Still the Spanish and Portuguese kept their monopoly. No organized effort, backed by governments, came from the north until about 1600. For it is by no means geography alone that determines economic development, and the English, Dutch, and French could not make use of the opportunities with which the opening of the Atlantic provided them until they had cleared up domestic troubles at home and survived the perils and hazards of the Wars of Religion.

12. THE COMMERCIAL REVOLUTION

In the great economic readjustment that was taking place in Europe, the opening of ocean trade routes was important, but it was by no means the only factor. Two others were the growth of population and a long, gradual rise in prices, or a slow inflation.

European population again grew rapidly, as in the High Middle Ages, reaching about 90 million in 1600, of which 20 million represented the growth during the sixteenth century. The increase took place in all countries, though it is well to remember that distribution was quite different from what we have known in more recent times. England in 1600 had no more than five million inhabitants. France had almost four times as many, and the German states altogether about as many as France. Italy and Spain had fewer than France, and distant Russia, within its then boundaries, may have had no more than ten million people. Some cities grew substantially, with London and Paris approaching 200,000; Antwerp, Lisbon, and Seville, thanks to the ocean trade, jumped to 100,000 by 1600. But smaller towns remained much the same; Europe as a whole was probably no more urbanized than in the later Middle Ages. Most of the population growth represented increasing density in the rural regions.[3]

The steady rise in prices, which is to say the steady decline in value of a given unit of money (such as a shilling), constituted a gradual inflation. It has been called a "price revolution," but it was so slow as to be hardly comparable to the kinds of inflation known in the twentieth century. One cause seems to have lain in the growth of population itself, which set up an increasing demand for food. This

---

[3] See Appendix III for estimates of population of certain cities and countries at various dates.

meant that new land was brought under cultivation, land that was less fertile, more inaccessible or more difficult to work than the fields that had been cultivated previously. With increasing costs of production, agricultural prices rose; in England, for example, they about quadrupled during the sixteenth century. Prices were also pushed upward by the increase in the volume of money. The royal habit of debasing the currency brought a larger amount of money into circulation, since larger numbers of florins, *reals*, or *livres* were obtained from the same amount of bullion. The flow of gold and silver from America also made money more plentiful, but the impact of Peruvian and Mexican mines can easily be exaggerated. Even before the discovery of America, the development of gold and silver mines had augmented the European money supply. In any case, an increase of money supply is inflationary only if it runs ahead of the volume of monetary transactions. The expansion of both population and commerce thus checked the inflationary forces. Nevertheless, the long trend of prices was upward. It affected all prices, including rents and other payments that were set in money values, but it seems that the price of hired labor, i.e., wages, rose the least. The price changes thus had different effects on the well-being of social classes.

Commercial undertakings were favored by rising prices and growing population. Merchants could count on increasing numbers of customers, new men could enter trade with hope of success, stocks of goods rose in value with the passage of time, and borrowed money could more easily be repaid. Governments benefited also, so far as kings could count on having more taxpayers and more soldiers.

The economic changes in Europe in the early modern period have been called the "Commercial Revolution," which in general signifies the rise of a capitalistic economy and the transition from a town-centered to a nation-centered economic system. This "revolution" was an exceptionally slow and protracted one, for it began at least as early as the fourteenth century and lasted until machine industry began to overshadow commerce.

Changes in Commerce and Production

In the Middle Ages the town and its adjoining country formed an economic unit.[4] Craftsmen, organized in guilds, produced common articles for local use. Peasants and lords sold their agricultural products to the local town, from which they bought what the craftsmen produced. The town protected itself by its own tariffs and regulations. In the workshop the master both owned his "capital"—his house, workbench, tools, and materials—and acted as a workman himself along with half a dozen journeymen and apprentices. The masters owned a modest capital, but they were hardly capitalists. They produced only upon order, or at least for customers whose tastes and number were known in advance. There was little profit, little risk of loss, and not much innovation.

All this changed with the widening of the trading area, or market. Even in the Middle Ages, as we have seen, there was a certain amount of long-distance trading in articles that could not be produced as well in one place as in another. Gradually more articles came within this category. Where goods were produced to be sold at some time in the future, in faraway places, to persons unknown, the local guildmaster could not manage the operation. He lacked the money (or "capital")

[4] See pp. 32–33.

to tie up in stocks of unsold wares; he lacked the knowledge of what distant customers wanted, or where, in what quantities, and at what price people would buy. In this type of business a new type of man developed. Economists call him the "enterpriser," or *entrepreneur.* He usually started out as a merchant working in an extensive market, and ended up as a banker. The Italian Medici family has been mentioned.[5] Equally typical were the German Fuggers.

The first of this family, Johann Fugger, a small-town weaver, came to Augsburg in 1368. He established a business in a new kind of cloth, called fustian, in which cotton was mixed, and which had certain advantages over the woolens and linens in which people then clothed themselves. He thus enjoyed a more than local market, and made trips to Venice to obtain the cotton imported from the Near East. Gradually the family began to deal also in spices, silks, and other Eastern goods obtained at Venice. They made large profits, which were invested in other enterprises, notably mining. They lent money to the Renaissance popes. They lent Charles V the money which he spent to obtain election as Holy Roman Emperor in 1519. They became bankers to the Habsburgs in both Germany and Spain. Together with other German and Flemish bankers, the Fuggers financed the Portuguese trade with Asia, either by outright loans or by providing in advance, on credit, the cargoes which the Portuguese traded for spices. The wealth of the Fuggers became proverbial and declined only through repeated Habsburg bankruptcies and with the general economic decline that beset Germany in the sixteenth century.

Other dealers in cloth, less spectacular than the first Fugger, broke away from the town-and-guild framework in other ways. England until the fifteenth century was an exporter of raw wool and an importer of finished woolens from Flanders. In the fifteenth century certain Englishmen began to develop the spinning, weaving, and dyeing of wool in England. To avoid the restrictive practices of the towns and guilds they "put out" the work to people in the country, providing them with looms and other equipment for the purpose, of which they generally retained the ownership themselves. This "putting out" or "domestic" system spread very widely. In France the cloth dealers of Rouen, feeling the competition of the new silk trade, developed a lighter, cheaper, and more simply made type of woolen cloth. Various guild regulations in Rouen, to protect the workers there, prohibited the manufacture of this cheaper cloth. The Rouen dealers, in 1496, took the industry into the country, installed looms in peasant cottages, and farmed out the work to the peasants.

Capital and Labor

This domestic system, or system of rural household industry, remained typical of production in many lines (cloth, hardware, etc.) in western Europe until the introduction of factories in the late eighteenth century. It signified a new divergence between capital and labor.[6] On the one hand were the workers, people who worked as the employer needed them, received wages for what they did, and had no interest in or knowledge of more than their own task. Living both by agriculture and by cottage industry, they formed an expansible labor force, available when labor was needed, left to live by farming or local charity when times were

[5] See pp. 54, 102.
[6] On capitalism, see also pp. 248–249, 259–263.

bad. On the other hand was the man who managed the whole affair. He had no personal acquaintance with the workers. Estimating how much of his product, let us say woolens, he could sell in a national or even international market, he purchased the needed raw materials, passed out wool to be spun by one group of peasants, took the yarn to another group for weaving, collected the cloth and took it still elsewhere to be dyed, paying wages on all sides for services rendered, while retaining ownership of the materials and the equipment and keeping the coordination and management of the whole enterprise in his own head. Much larger business enterprises could be established in this way than within the municipal framework of guild and town. Indeed, the very master weavers of the guilds often sank to the status of subcontractors, hardly different from wage employees, of the great "clothiers" and "drapers" by whom the business was dominated. The latter, with the widening market, became personages of national or even international repute. And, of course, the bigger the business the more of a capital investment it represented.

Certain other industries, new or virtually new in the fifteenth and sixteenth centuries, could by their nature never fit into a town-centered system and were capitalistic from the start, in that they required a large initial outlay before any income could be received. One such was mining. Another was printing and the book trade. Books had a national and even international market, being mainly in Latin; and no ordinary craftsman could afford the outlay required for a printing press, for fonts of type, supplies of paper, and stocks of books on hand. Printers therefore borrowed from capitalists, or shared with them an interest in business. Shipbuilding was so stimulated by the shift to the oceans as almost to be a new industry, and still another was the manufacture of cannons and muskets. For the latter the chief demand came from the state, from the New Monarchies which were organizing national armies. In the rise of capitalism the needs of the military were in fact fundamentally important. Armies, which started out by requiring thousands of weapons, in the seventeenth century required thousands of uniforms, and in the eighteenth century many solidly built barracks and fortifications. These were the first demands for mass production; and where governments themselves did not take the initiative, private organizers stepped in as middlemen between these huge requirements and the myriads of small handicraft workers by whom, before the industrial age, the actual product was still manufactured.

The new sea route to the East and the discovery of America brought a vast increase in trade not only of luxury items but of bulk commodities like rice, sugar, tea, and other consumer goods. Older commercial activities were transformed by the widening of markets. Spain increasingly drew cereals from Sicily. The Netherlands were fed from Poland, the French wine districts lived on food brought from northern France. With the growth of shipping, the timber, tar, pitch, and other "naval stores" of Russia and the Baltic came upon the commercial scene. There was thus an ever growing movement of heavy staple commodities, in which again only men controlling large funds of capital could normally take part.

Not all capital was invested; some was simply lent, either to the church, or to governments, or to impecunious nobles, or, though perhaps this was the least common type of lending in the sixteenth century, to persons engaged in trade and commerce. Bankers and others who lent money expected to receive back, after a time, a larger sum than that of the loan. They expected "interest"; and they sometimes received as much as 30 percent a year. In the Middle Ages the taking of interest had been frowned upon as usury, denounced as avarice, and forbidden in the canon law. It was still frowned upon in the sixteenth century by almost all but the lenders themselves. The Catholic church maintained its prohibitions. The theologians of the University of Paris ruled against it in 1530. Luther, who hated "Fuggerism," continued to preach against usury. Calvin made allowances, but as late as 1640, in capitalist Holland itself, the stricter Calvinist ministers still denounced lending at interest. Nothing could stop the practice. Borrowers compounded with lenders to evade prohibitions, and theologians of all churches began to distinguish between "usury" and a "legitimate return." Gradually, as interest rates fell, as banking became more established, and as loans were made for economically productive uses rather than to sustain ecclesiastics, princes, and nobles in their personal habits, the feeling against a "reasonable" interest died down, and interest became an accepted feature of capitalism. The Bank of Amsterdam, in the seventeenth century, because depositors knew that their money was safe and could be withdrawn at will, was able to attract deposits from all countries by offering a very low rate of interest, which enabled it in turn to make loans, at a low rate, to finance commercial activities.

The net effect of all these developments was a "commercialization of industry." The great man of business was the merchant. Industry, the actual processes of production, still in an essentially handicraft stage, was subordinate to the buyers and sellers. Producers—weavers, hatters, metalworkers, gunsmiths, glassworkers, etc.—worked to fill the orders of the merchants, and often with capital which the merchants supplied and owned. The man who knew where the article could be sold prevailed over the man who simply knew how to produce it. This commercial capitalism remained the typical form of capitalism until after 1800, when, with the introduction of power machinery, it yielded to industrial capitalism, and merchants became dependent on industrialists, who owned, understood, and organized the machines.

Mercantilism

There was still another aspect of the commercial revolution, namely, the various government policies that go historically under the name of "mercantilism." Rulers, as we have seen, were hard pressed for money, and needed more of it as it fell in value. The desire of kings and their advisers to force gold and silver to flow into their own kingdoms was one of the first impulses leading to mercantilist regulation. Gradually this "bullionist" idea was replaced by the more general idea of building up a strong and self-sufficient economy. The means adopted, in either case, was to "set the poor on work," as they said in England, to turn the country into a hive of industry, to discourage idleness, begging, vagabondage, and unemployment. New crafts and manufactures were introduced, and favors were given to merchants who provided work for "the poor" and who sold the country's products abroad. It was thought desirable to raise the export of finished goods and reduce the export of unprocessed raw materials, to curtail all imports except of needed raw materials, and thus obtain a "favorable" balance of trade so that other countries would have to pay their debts in bullion. Since all this was done by a royal or nationwide system of regulations, mercantilism became in the economic sphere what the state building of the New Monarchies was in the political, signifying the transition from town to national units of social living.[7]

Mercantilists frowned upon the localistic and conservative outlook of the guilds. In England the guilds ceased to have any importance. Parliament, in the time of Elizabeth, did on a national scale what guilds had once done locally when it enacted the Statute of Artificers of 1563, regulating the admission to apprenticeship and level of wages in various trades. In France the royal government kept the guilds in being, because they were convenient bodies to tax, but it deprived them of most of their old independence and used them as organizations through which royal control of industry could be enforced. In both countries the government assisted merchants who wished to set up domestic or cottage industry in the country, against the protests of the town guilds, which in their heyday had forbidden rural people to engage in crafts. Governments generally tried to suppress idleness. The famous English Poor Law of 1601 (which remained in effect, with amendments, until 1834) was designed both to force people to work and to relieve absolute destitution.

Governments likewise took steps to introduce new industries. The silk industry was brought from Italy to France under royal protection, to the dismay of French woolen and linen interests. The English government assisted in turning England from a producer of raw wool into a producer of finished woolens, supervising the immigration of skilled Flemish weavers, and even fetching from faraway Turkey, about 1582, two youths who understood the more advanced dyeing arts of the Near East. Generally, under mercantilism, governments fought to steal skilled workers from each other while prohibiting or discouraging the emigration of their own skilled workers, who might take their trade secrets and "mysteries" to foreign parts.

By such means governments helped to create a national market and an industrious nationwide labor supply for their great merchants. Without such government support the great merchants, such as the drapers or clothiers, could never have risen and prospered. The same help was given to merchants operating in foreign markets. Henry VII of England in 1496 negotiated a commercial treaty with Flanders, known as the Intercursus Magnus; and in the next century the kings of France signed a number of treaties with the Ottoman Empire by which French merchants obtained privileges in the Near East. A merchant backed by a national monarchy was in a much stronger position than one backed merely by a city, such as Augsburg or Venice. This backing on a national scale was again given when national governments subsidized exports, paying bounties for goods whose production they wished to encourage, or when they erected tariff barriers against imports to protect their own producers from competition. Thus a national tariff system was superimposed on the old network of provincial and municipal tariffs. These latter were now thought of as "internal tariffs," and mercantilists usually wished to abolish them, in order to create an area of free trade within the state as a whole. But local interests were so strong, and a sense of interprovincial and intertown unity was so slow to develop, that for centuries they were unable to get rid of local tariffs except in England.

In wild or distant parts of the world, or in exotic regions nearer home, such as

---

[7] On the New Monarchies, see pp. 66–74.

the Muslim Near East or Russia, it was not possible for individual merchants to act by merely private initiative. Merchants trading with such countries needed a good deal of capital, they often had to obtain special privileges and protection from native rulers, and they had to arm their ships against Barbary or Malay pirates or against hostile Europeans. Merchants and their respective governments came together to found official companies for the transocean trade. In England, soon after the English discovery of the White Sea in 1553, a Russia Company was established. A Turkey Company soon followed. Shortly after 1600 a great many such companies were operating out of England, Holland, and France. The most famous of all were the East India Companies, which the English founded in 1600, the Dutch in 1602, the French not until 1664. Each of these companies was a state-supported organization, with special rights. Each was a monopoly in that only merchants who belonged to the company could legally engage in trade in the region for which the company had a charter. Each was expected to find markets for the national manufactures, and most of them were expected to bring home gold or silver. With these companies the northern peoples began to encroach on the Spanish and Portuguese monopoly in America and the East. With them new commercial-colonial empires were to be launched. But, as has been already observed, before this could happen it was necessary for certain domestic and purely European conflicts and controversies to be settled.

13. CHANGING SOCIAL STRUCTURES

Social structure, for present purposes, refers to the composition, functions, and interrelationships of social classes. Because changes in social structure are slow, they are hard to identify with any particular period of time. In general, however, with the effects of the commercial revolution, population growth, and the falling value of money, the classes of Europe, broadly defined, took on forms that were to last until the industrial era of the nineteenth and twentieth centuries. These classes were the landed aristocracy, the peasantry or mass of agricultural workers, the miscellaneous middle classes, and the urban poor.

While all prices rose in the sixteenth century, it was agricultural prices that rose the most. Anyone who had agricultural products to sell was likely to benefit. Among such beneficiaries were peasants who held bits of land in return for payments to a manorial lord set in unchangeable sums of money, in the old values of the fourteenth or even thirteenth century. Such peasants in effect paid much less to the lord than in the past. Other rural workers, however, either held no land of their own or produced only at a subsistence level with nothing to sell in the market. Such peasants, and hired hands dependent on wages, found their situation worsened. Village life became less equalitarian than it had been in the Middle Ages. In England a class of small freeholders (the "yeomanry") developed between the landed gentry and the rural poor. On the Continent, at least in France, western Germany, and the Netherlands, some peasants acquired more secure property rights, resembling those of small freeholders in England. But both in England and on the Continent a large class of unpropertied rural workers remained in poverty.

Land rents went up as agricultural prices rose, and inflation and population growth drove up rentals for housing in the towns. Owners of real property (i.e., land and buildings) were favored by such changes, but within the former class of feudal lords the effects were mixed. If one's great-grandfather had let out land in earlier times in exchange for fixed sums of money, the income received had actually declined. But those who received payments in kind from their tenants, for example, in bushels of wheat or barley, or who managed their estates themselves, could sell their actual agricultural products at current prices and so increase their money income.

Basic Social Classes

The former feudal class, or nobles, thus turned into a more modern kind of aristocracy. If income from their estates declined, they sought service in the king's army or government or appointment to the more prestigious offices in the church. If landed income increased, they were more wealthy. In either case they became more concerned with civilian pursuits, and were likely to develop more refined tastes and pay more attention to the education of their children. Like the peasants, the landowning class became more heterogeneous, ranging from the small gentry to the great peers of England, and from small or impoverished nobles to the *grands seigneurs* of France. Some led a life of leisure; others were eager to work in the higher reaches of organized government. The most impoverished nobles sometimes had the longest pedigrees. As their social functions changed, and as persons of more recent family background competed for education, government employment, and even military service, there came to be an increasing importance set upon ancestry as a badge of status. Among the upper class, there was more insistence on high birth and distinguished forebears in the seventeenth and eighteenth centuries than there had been before.

Below the aristocracy were the "middle classes," or "bourgeoisie." *Bourgeois* was a French word, which, like the English "burgher," originally meant a person living in a chartered town or borough and enjoying its liberties. The bourgeoisie was the whole social class made up of individual bourgeois. In a much later sense of the word, derived from Karl Marx, the term "bourgeoisie" was applied to the class of owners of capital. This sense must be kept distinct from the earlier meaning, which is usually adopted in this book. In this latter sense, the word refers to the middle levels of society between the aristocracy on the one hand, which drew its income from land, and the laboring poor on the other, who depended on wages or charity, or who often went hungry. Class lines tended to blur as aristocratic families formed the habit of living in towns, and middle-class burghers began to buy land in the country. Some bourgeois thus came to live on landed rents, while some of the gentry and aristocracy, most notably in England, bought shares in the great overseas trading companies or engaged in other forms of business enterprise. Aristocrats possessing large agricultural estates, timberlands, or mines increasingly brought their products to market to be sold at a profit. But even when aristocrat and bourgeois became economically more alike, a consciousness of social difference between them remained.

The middle class became more numerous in the sixteenth century, and increasingly so thereafter. It was an indefinite category, since the countries of Europe were very different in the size and importance of their middle classes, in the kinds of persons that made them up, and in the types of occupations pursued. Near the top were the urban elites who governed the towns; they might draw their incomes from rural property, from commerce, or from the emoluments of government itself, and they sometimes intermarried with persons of noble status. Especially where the towns were strong or broad royal government was lacking, as in the Netherlands, the German free cities, or north Italy, such urban patriciates formed virtual aristocracies in themselves. But in a larger perspective the families of merchants, bankers, and shipowners were middle-class, as were those of the traditional learned professions, law and medicine. So in general were judges, tax officials, and other employees of governments, except in the highest ranks. In the professions and in government service the younger sons of the aristocracy might be found alongside the offspring of the middle classes, most commonly in England, less so in France, and even less as one moved into Germany or Spain. The clergy was drawn from all classes; there were poor parish priests, who might be the sons of peasants, and noblemen among the bishops and abbots; but the bulk of the clergy was recruited from middle-class families. In Protestant countries, where the clergy married, their sons and daughters became an important element in the middle class. Members of trade guilds were middle-class, though the guilds differed widely in social status, from those of the great wholesale merchants or the goldsmiths, down through the guilds of such humble occupations as the tanners and barrel makers. At the bottom the middle class faded into the world of small retail shopkeepers, innkeepers, owners of workshops in which ordinary articles were manufactured by hand, the lesser skilled tradespeople and their employees, journeymen, and apprentices.

The mass of the population in all countries was composed of the working poor. These included not only the unskilled wage laborers but the unemployed, unemployable, and paupers, with a large fringe that turned to vagabondage and begging. They were unable to read or write, and were often given to irregular habits which distressed both middle-class persons and government officials. The efforts of mercantilist governments to put the poor to work, or make them contribute to the wealth of the country, have already been mentioned. Charitable relief also developed toward the end of the sixteenth century, as shown in the English Poor Law of 1601 and in similar efforts on the Continent. The idea gained ground that begging was a public nuisance, and that the poor should be segregated in workhouses or hospices from the rest of society. Most of the poor were of course not recipients of such relief. They were the people who tilled the fields, tended the livestock, dug in the mines, went to sea as fishermen or common sailors, found work in the towns as casual laborers, porters, water carriers, or removers of excrement, or entered the domestic service of noble and upper middle-class families, whose rising standard of living required a growing number of chambermaids, washerwomen, footmen, lackeys, coachmen, and stable boys. It has already been remarked that wages rose less than prices in the sixteenth century. The poor, if not positively worse off than in former times, gained the least from the great developments with which much history is concerned. The very growth of social differentiation, the fact that the middle and upper classes made such advances, left the condition of the poor correspondingly worse.[8]

Social Roles of Education and Government

Education in the latter part of the sixteenth century took on an altogether new importance for the social system. One consequence of the Reformation, in both

Protestant and Catholic countries, was the attempt to put a serious and effective pastor in each parish. This set up a demand for a more educated clergy. The growth of commerce made it necessary to have literate clerks and agents. Governments wanted men from both the noble and middle classes who could cooperate in large organizations, be reliable, understand finance, keep records, and draft proposals. There was also a widespread need for lawyers.

The new demand for education was met by an outburst of philanthropy, which reached a high point in both England and France between about 1580 and 1640. Many endowed scholarships were established. At what would now be called a secondary level, hundreds of "grammar schools" were founded at this time in England. In France the *collèges* combined the work of the English grammar school with what corresponded to the first year or two of university work at Oxford or Cambridge. Of the 167 most important French colleges still existing at the time of the Revolution in 1789, only 36 had been founded in the centuries before 1560, and 92 were established in the years between 1560 and 1650. Provision for girls' schools was more sporadic, but the Ursuline sisters, for example, founded in Italy in 1535, by the year 1700 had about 350 convents in Catholic Europe and even in Canada, in most of which the education of girls was a principal occupation of the sisters. Mme. de Maintenon, the morganatic wife of Louis XIV, founded and closely supervised a school for the daughters of the French gentry and lesser nobility.

Dutch and Swiss Protestants founded the universities of Leyden and Geneva. New universities, both Protestant and Catholic, appeared in Germany. In Spain the multiplication of universities was phenomenal. Castile, with only two universities dating from the Middle Ages, had twenty by the early seventeenth century; Salamanca was enrolling over 5,000 students a year. Five universities also existed in Spanish America by 1600. In England, new colleges were founded at Oxford and Cambridge, and it was especially in these years that some of the Oxford and Cambridge colleges became very wealthy. Annual freshman admissions at Oxford, barely 100 in 1550, rose to over 500 in the 1630s, a figure not exceeded, or even equaled, during the following two hundred years. If this fivefold increase seems small, compared with figures for Spain or other countries, it must be remembered that England was not very populous, that English grammar schools did some of the teaching offered by universities elsewhere, and that the study of law, important in Continental universities, was carried on in England outside the universities, at the Inns of Court.

The schools, colleges, and universities drew their students from a wide range of social classes. For girls less organized schooling was offered, but an intelligent and lucky boy of poor family had perhaps a better chance for education than at any time in Europe until very recently. In Spain most of the students seem to have been nobles, or "hidalgos," aspiring to positions in the church or the royal government; but hidalgos were very numerous in Spain, overlapping with what might be called the middle class in other countries. The French colleges, including those operated by the Jesuits, recruited their students very widely, taking in the sons of nobles, merchants, shopkeepers, artisans, and even, more rarely, of peasants. English grammar schools did likewise; it was in later times that a few of them, like Eton and Harrow, became more exclusive Public Schools. As for universities, we have detailed knowledge for Oxford, which recorded the status of its students at matriculation, classifying them as "esquires," "gentlemen," "clergy," and "plebeians." From 1560 to 1660 about half of the Oxford students were "plebeians," which in the language of that time could embrace the whole middle class from big merchants down to quite modest levels. It seems certain that Oxford and Cambridge were more widely representative of the English people in 1660 than in 1900.

Social classes were formed not only by economic forces, and not only by education, but also by the action of governments. Government could inhibit economic growth, as in Spain, or promote it, as in England. Kings contributed to the rise of capitalism and a business class by granting monopolies, borrowing from bankers, and issuing charters to trading companies. In many countries, and notably in France, many families owed their middle-class position to the holding of government offices, some of which might become a form of inheritable property. It might also be the action of governments, as much as economic conditions, that kept alive a distinction between nobles and commoners, or "privileged" and "unprivileged" classes, of which more will be heard.[9] Where peasants suffered heavily from royal taxes, it was more from political than from economic causes. The king, by "making" nobles—that is, by conferring titles of nobility on persons who did not inherit them—could raise a few in the middle class to higher status. Tax exemption could be a sign of high social standing. The king was also the fountain of honor, at the top of "society" in the more frivolous sense of the word. The royal court formed the apex of a pyramid of social rank, in which each class looked up to or down upon the others. Those favored with the royal presence disdained the plain country nobility, who sniffed at the middle classes, who patronized or disparaged the hired servants, day laborers, and the poor. Looking upward, people were expected to show deference for their betters.

Eastern and Western Europe

One other remark may be made on social structure. It was in the sixteenth century that a great difference developed between eastern and western Europe. In the west, the commercial revolution and the declining value of money were advantageous to the middle class and to many of the peasantry for whom the old burdens of the manorial system were lightened. In eastern Europe, it was the lords who benefited from rising prices and the growing market for grain and forest products. Here too the institution of the manor existed; but the peasants' land tenures were more precarious than in the west, more dependent on accidents of death or on the wishes of the lord, and the lord worked a larger part of the manor with his own work force for his own use or profit.

The rise of prices and expansion of Baltic shipping gave the lord the incentive to increase his output. In northeast Germany (where such lords were called Junkers), in Poland, and as time went on in Russia, Bohemia, and Hungary, beginning in the sixteenth century and continuing into the eighteenth, a vast process set in by which the mass of the peasantry sank into serfdom. It was hastened in many regions by the violence and insecurity engendered by the religious wars. Typically, peasants lost their individual parcels of land, or received them back on condition that they render unpaid labor services to the lord. Usually peasants owed three or four days a week of such forced labor (called *robot* in Bohemia and adjoining territories), remaining free to work during the remainder of the week on their own parcels. Often the number of days of *robot* exacted by the lord was

[9] See pp. 182, 352, 357.

greater, since in eastern Europe, where central monarchy was weak and centralized legal systems almost unknown, the lord himself was the final court of appeal for his people. His people were in fact his "subjects." Serfdom in Germany was not called serfdom, an ill-sounding word, but "hereditary subjection." By whatever name they were known throughout eastern Europe, serfs, or hereditary subjects of the manorial lord, could not leave the manor, marry, or learn a trade without the lord's express permission. The lord, drawing on this large reserve of compulsory labor, using most of it for agriculture but teaching some quickminded youths the various handicrafts that were needed on the estate, worked the land as his own venture, sold the produce, and retained the profit.

Thus, in eastern Europe at the beginning of modern times, the rural masses lost personal freedom and lived in a poverty unknown among the peasants to the west, poor as the latter were. In western Europe there were peasants who were already on the way to becoming small proprietors. They were free people under the law. They could migrate, marry, and learn trades as opportunity offered. Those who held land could defend it in the royal courts, and raise crops and take part in the market economy on their own account. They owed the lord no forced labor—or virtually none, for the ten days a year of corvée still found in parts of France hardly compared with the almost full-time *robot* of the peasant of eastern Europe.

The landlord in the east, from the sixteenth century onward, was solidly entrenched in his own domain, monarch of all he surveyed, with no troublesome bourgeoisie to annoy him (for towns were few), and with kings and territorial rulers solicitous of his wishes. Travelers from the west were impressed with the lavishness of great Polish and Lithuanian magnates, with their palatial homes, private art galleries, well-stocked libraries, collections of jewels, swarms of servants, trains of dependent lesser gentry, gargantuan dinners, and barbaric hospitality. The Junkers of northeast Germany lived more modestly, but enjoyed the same kind of independence and social superiority. The importance of all this will become evident when, in later chapters, we turn to Prussia, Poland, Russia, and the Austrian lands.

But meanwhile, with all the economic growth and social development that has been sketched in the preceding pages, Europe was torn by the destructive ferocity of the Wars of Religion.

14. THE CRUSADE OF CATHOLIC SPAIN: THE DUTCH AND ENGLISH

The Ambitions of Philip II

Charles V, having tried in vain for thirty-five years to preserve religious unity in Germany, abdicated his many crowns and retired to a monastery in 1556, the year after the Peace of Augsburg.[10] He left Austria, Bohemia, and Hungary (or the small part of it not occupied by the Turks) to his brother Ferdinand, who was soon elected Holy Roman Emperor.[11] All his other possessions Charles left to his son Philip, who became Philip II of Spain. The Habsburg dynasty remained

[10] See p. 79.
[11] See map, pp. 70–71.

thereafter divided into two branches, the Austrian and the Spanish. The two cooperated in European affairs. The Spanish branch for a century was the more important. Philip II (1556–1598) not only possessed the Spanish kingdoms but in 1580 inherited Portugal, so that the whole Iberian peninsula was brought under his rule. He possessed the seventeen provinces of the Netherlands and the Free County of Burgundy, which were member states of the Holy Roman Empire, lying on its western border, adjacent to France. Milan in north Italy and Naples in the south belonged to Philip, and since he also held the chief islands, as well as Tunis, he enjoyed a naval ascendancy in the western Mediterranean which was threatened only by the Turks. For five years, until 1558, he was titular king of England, and in 1589, in the name of his daughter, he laid claim to the throne of France. All America belonged to Philip II, and after 1580 all the Portuguese empire as well, so that except for a few nautical daredevils all ships plying the open ocean were the Spanish king's.

Philip II therefore naturally regarded himself as an international figure, and the more so because he thought in terms not of nationality but of religion. Before all else he was a Catholic, fervid and fanatical, committed to upholding the sway of the universal church, within which all nations were no more than minorities and all heretics no more than rebels. A grave and sober man, of abstemious personal habits, sharing in the moral severity of the Catholic Reform, and in the dark, brooding, and tormented inner world of the Spanish mystics, he took upon himself the headship of a far-flung Catholic counteroffensive, into which he was willing to pour with grim persistence the blood and treasure of all his kingdoms. To economic and material interests he gave no thought, and in such matters Spanish society began to deteriorate in his reign; but for all material problems the wealth of Potosí provided a facile solution, and meanwhile Spain entered upon the Golden Age of its culture.

In this period, the *siglo de oro*, running in round dates from 1550 to 1650, Cervantes wrote his *Don Quixote* and Lope de Vega his seven hundred dramas, while El Greco, Murillo, and Velázquez painted their pictures, and the Jesuit Suarez composed works on philosophy and law that were read even in Protestant countries. But the essence of Spanish life was its peculiarly intensive Catholicism. The church was vitally present at every social level, from the archbishop of Toledo, who ranked above grandees and could address the king as an equal, down to a host of penniless and mendicant friars, who mixed with the poorest and most disinherited of the people. It is said that about 1600 a third of the population of Spain was in one way or another in the service of the church. Spain, whose whole history had been a crusade, was ideally suited to be Philip's instrument in the re-Catholicizing of Europe.[12]

Philip II built himself a new royal residence ("palace" is hardly the word), the Escorial, which well expressed in solid stone its creator's inner spirit. Madrid itself was a new town, merely a government center, far from the worldly distractions of Toledo or Valladolid. But it was thirty miles from Madrid, on the bleak arid plateau of central Castile, overlooked by the jagged Sierra, that Philip chose to erect the Escorial. He built it in honor of St. Lawrence, on whose feast day he had won a battle against the French. The great pile of connecting buildings was laid out in the shape of a grill, since, according to martyrologists, St. Lawrence,

[12] See pp. 69–72.

in the year 258, had been roasted alive on a grill over burning coals. Somber and vast, angular and unrelieved, made of blocks of granite meant to last forever, and with its highest spire rising three hundred feet from the ground, the Escorial was designed not only as a palace but as a monastery and a mausoleum. The monks moved in before the king, who, when he installed himself, brought with him eight coffins, those of his father, his dead wives, and his children, to remind him of his own. Here, in an atmosphere that could be painted only by El Greco, the king of Spain worked and lived, a slim figure dressed almost like a monk himself, always industrious, avid for detail, dispatching his couriers to Mexico, to Manila, to Vienna, to Milan, his troops and his bars of bullion to Italy and the Netherlands, his diplomats to all courts, and his spies to all countries, wholly and utterly absorbed in his one consuming project.

Let us try to see the events of the time internationally, for though it may be confusing to try to see all nations together, it is distorting to look at only one of them alone. The first years of Philip's reign were also the first years of Elizabeth's reign in England, where the religious issue was still in flux; they were years in which Calvinism agitated the Netherlands, and when France, ruled by teen-aged boys, fell apart into implacable civil war. Religious loyalties that knew no frontiers overlapped all political boundaries. Everywhere there were people who looked for guidance outside their own countries. Calvinists in England, France, and the Netherlands felt closer to one another than to their own monarchs or their own neighbors. Zealous Catholics, in all three countries, welcomed the support of international Catholic forces—the Jesuits, the king of Spain, the pope. National unity threatened to dissolve or was not yet formed. The sense of mutual trust between people who lived side by side was eaten away; and people who lived not only in the same country, but in the same town, on the same street, or even in the same house, turned against each other in the name of a higher cause.

For about five years, beginning in 1567, it seemed that the Catholic cause might prevail. The great crusade took the offensive on all fronts. In 1567 Philip sent a new and firmer governor general to the Netherlands, the Duke of Alva, with 20,000 Spanish soldiers; the duke proceeded to suppress religious and political dissidents by establishing a Council of Troubles. In 1569 Philip put down a revolt of the Moriscos in Spain. In the same year the Catholics of northern England, led by the Duke of Norfolk, and sewing the cross of crusaders on their garments, rose in armed rebellion against their heretic queen. In the next year, 1570, the pope excommunicated Elizabeth, and absolved her subjects from allegiance to her, so that English Catholics, if they wished, could henceforth in good conscience conspire to overthrow her. In 1571 the Spanish won a great naval battle against the Turks, at Lepanto off the coast of Greece; on their sails they wove the same cross that had been raised at the other corner of Europe, by the Duke of Norfolk in England; and they themselves believed that they were carrying on the crusades of the Middle Ages. In the next year, 1572, the Catholic leaders of France, with the advice of the pope and of Philip II, decided to make an end of the Huguenots, or French Protestants. Over three thousand were seized and put to death on the eve of St. Bartholomew's Day in Paris alone; and this massacre was followed by lesser liquidations throughout the provinces.

But none of these victories proved enduring. The Turkish power was not seriously damaged at Lepanto. In fact, the Turks took Tunis from Philip two years later. The Moriscos were not assimilated. The English Catholic rebellion was stamped out; eight hundred persons were put to death by Elizabeth's government. The revolt in the Netherlands remained very much alive, as did the French Huguenots. Twenty years later England was Protestant, the Dutch were winning independence, a Huguenot had become king of France, and the Spanish fleet had gone to ruin in northern waters. Let us see how these events came to pass.

The Revolt of the Netherlands

The Netherlands, or Low Countries (they had no other name), roughly comprised the area of the modern kingdoms of the Netherlands and Belgium and the grand duchy of Luxembourg. They consisted of seventeen provinces, which in the fifteenth century, one by one, had been inherited, purchased, or conquered by the dukes of Burgundy, from whom they were inherited by Charles V and his son, Philip II. In the mid-sixteenth century neither a Dutch nor a Belgian nationality yet existed. In the northern provinces the people spoke German dialects; in the southern provinces they spoke dialects of French; but neither here, nor elsewhere in Europe, was it felt that language boundaries had anything to do with political borders. The southern provinces had for centuries been busy commercial centers, and we have seen how Antwerp, having once flourished on trade with Venice, now flourished on trade with Lisbon. The northern provinces, or rather the two of them which were most open to the sea, the counties of Holland and Zeeland, had developed rapidly in the fifteenth century. They had a popular literature of their own, written in their own kind of German, which came to be called Dutch. The lay piety of the Brothers of the Common Life had originated in this region, and here Erasmus of Rotterdam had been born. The wealth of the northern provinces was drawn from deep-sea fishing. Amsterdam was said to be built on herring bones, and the Dutch, when they added trading to fishing, still lived by the sea.

The northern provinces felt no tie with each other and no sense of difference from the southern. Each of the seventeen provinces was a small state or country in itself. Each province enjoyed typical medieval liberties, privileges, and immunities, including the right to preserve its own law and consent to its own taxes. This constitution of the Netherlands, for such it was, went under the name of the *Joyeuse Entrée*, from the "joyous entry" made by the reigning duke into Brussels in 1355 after a solemn promise to recognize the liberties of the province of Brabant. The common bond of all seventeen provinces was simply that beginning with the dukes of Burgundy they had the same ruler; but since they had the same ruler they were called upon from time to time to send delegates to an estates general, and so developed an embryonic sense of federal collaboration. The feeling of Netherlandish identity was heightened with the accession of Philip II, for Philip, unlike his father, was thought of as foreign, a Spaniard who lived in Spain; and after 1560 Spanish governors general, Spanish officials, and Spanish troops were seen more frequently in the Netherlands. Moreover, since the Netherlands was the crossroads of Europe, with a tradition of earnestness in religion, Protestant ideas took root very early, and after 1560, when the religious wars began in France, a great many French Calvinists fled across the borders. At first, there were probably more Calvinists in the southern provinces than in the northern, more among the people that we now call Belgians than among those that we now call Dutch.

The revolt against Philip II was inextricably political and religious at the same time, and it became increasingly an economic struggle as the years went by. It

began in 1566, when some 200 nobles of the various provinces founded a league
to check the "foreign" or Spanish influence in the Netherlands. The league, to
which both Catholic and Protestant nobles belonged, petitioned Philip II not to
employ the Spanish Inquisition in the Netherlands. They feared the trouble it
would stir up; they feared it as a foreign court; they feared that in the enforcement of its rulings the liberties of their provinces would be crushed. Philip's
agents in the Netherlands refused the petition. A mass revolt now broke out.
Within a week fanatical Calvinists pillaged 400 churches, pulling down images,
breaking stained-glass windows, defacing paintings and tapestries, making off
with gold chalices, destroying with a fierce contempt the symbols of "popery" and
"idolatry." The fury spread from town to town, to Antwerp, to Amsterdam, to
Armentières (now in France, but then in the Netherlands); it was chiefly journeymen wage earners, numerous in the industrial Netherlands, and aroused by social
and economic grievances as well as religious belief, who formed the rank and file
for these anti-Catholic and anti-Spanish demonstrations. Before such vandalism
many of the petitioning nobles recoiled; the Catholics among them, as well as less
militant Protestants, unable to control their revolutionary followers, began to
look upon the Spanish authorities with less disfavor.

Philip II, appalled at the sacrilege, forthwith sent in the Inquisition, the Duke
of Alva, and reinforcements of Spanish troops. Alva's Council of Troubles, nick-
named the Council of Blood, sentenced some thousands to death, levied new taxes,
and confiscated the estates of a number of important nobles. These measures
united people of all classes in opposition. What might have been primarily a class
conflict took on the character of a national opposition. At its head emerged one of
the noblemen whose estates had been confiscated, William of Orange (called

THE LOW COUNTRIES, 1648

This group of towns and provinces,
along the lower reaches of the Rhine,
Meuse, and Scheldt rivers, originated in
the Middle Ages as part of the Holy
Roman Empire. The northern or Dutch
provinces were recognized as independent of the Empire in 1648. Early in the
seventeenth century a political frontier
emerged between the "Dutch" and
"Belgian" parts, but the word "Belgium" was not used until much later,
the southern or Habsburg provinces being called the Spanish Netherlands in
the seventeenth century and the Austrian Netherlands in the eighteenth.
The large bishopric of Liège remained
a separate church-state until the
French Revolution. The language frontier, then as now, ran roughly east and
west somewhat south of Brussels, with
French to the south and Flemish (a
form of Dutch, and hence Germanic)
to the north of the line.

William the Silent), Philip II's "stadholder" or lieutenant in the County of Holland. Beginning to claim the authority of a sovereign, he issued letters of marque, or authorizations to ship captains—Dutch, Danes, Scots, English—to make war at sea. Fishing crews, "sea dogs," and downright pirates began to raid the small port towns of the Netherlands and France, descending upon them without warning, desecrating the churches, looting, torturing, and killing, in a wild combination of religious rage, political hatred, and lust for booty. The Spanish reciprocated by renewing their confiscations, their inquisitorial tortures, and their burnings and hangings. The Netherlands was torn by anarchy, revolution, and civil war. No lines were clear, either political or religious. But in 1576 the anti-Spanish feeling prevailed over religious difference. Representatives of all seventeen provinces, putting aside the religious question, formed a union to drive out the Spanish at any cost.

The Involvement of England

But the Netherlands revolution, though it was a national revolution with political independence as its first aim, was only part of the international politico-religious struggle. All sorts of other interests became involved in it. Queen Elizabeth of England lent aid to the Netherlands, though for many years surreptitiously, not wishing to provoke a war with Spain, in which it was feared that English Catholics might side with the Spaniards. Elizabeth was troubled by having on her hands an unwanted guest, Mary Queen of Scots, a Catholic who had been queen of France until her husband's premature death, and queen of Scotland until driven out by irate Calvinist lords, and who—if the pope, the king of Spain, the Society of Jesus, and many English Catholics were to have their way—would also be queen of England instead of the usurper Elizabeth.[13] Elizabeth under these circumstances kept Mary Stuart imprisoned. Many intrigues were afoot to put Mary on the English throne, some with, and some without, Mary's knowledge.

In 1576 Don Juan, hero of Lepanto, and half-brother of Philip II, became governor general of the embattled Netherlands. It was his grandiose idea, formed after consultations in Rome, not merely to subdue the Netherlands but to use that country as a base for an invasion of England, and after overthrowing Elizabeth with Spanish troops, to put Mary Stuart on the throne, marry her himself, and so become king of a re-Catholicized England. Thus the security of Elizabethan and Protestant England was coming to depend on the outcome of fighting in the Netherlands. Elizabeth signed an alliance with the Netherlands patriots.

Don Juan died in 1578 and was succeeded as governor general of the Netherlands by the prince of Parma. A diplomat as well as a soldier, Parma broke the solid front of the seventeen provinces by a mixture of force and persuasion. He promised that the historic liberties of the *Joyeuse Entrée* would be respected, and he appealed not only to the more zealous Catholics but to moderates who were wearying of the struggle and repelled by mob violence and religious vandalism. On this basis he rallied the southernmost provinces to his side. The seven northern provinces, led by Holland and Zeeland, responded by forming the Union of Utrecht in 1579. In 1581 they formally declared their independence from the king of Spain, calling themselves the United Provinces of the Netherlands. Thus originated what was more commonly called the Dutch Republic, or simply "Holland"

---

[13] Mary Stuart, a great-granddaughter of Henry VII, was the next lawful heir to the English throne after Elizabeth, since Elizabeth had no children.

in view of the predominance of that county among the seven. The great Flemish towns—Antwerp, Ghent, and Bruges—at first sided with the Union.

Where formerly all had been turmoil, a geographical line was now drawn. The south rallying to Philip II now faced a still rebellious north. But neither side accepted any such partition. Parma still fought to reconquer the north, and the Dutch, led by William the Silent, still struggled to clear the Spanish out of all seventeen provinces. Meanwhile the two sides fought to capture the intermediate Flemish cities. When Parma moved upon Antwerp, still the leading port of the North Sea, and one from which an invasion of England could best be mounted, Elizabeth at last openly entered the war on the side of the rebels, sending 6,000 English troops to the Netherlands under the Earl of Leicester in 1585.

England was now clearly emerging as the chief bulwark of Protestantism and of anti-Spanish feeling in northwestern Europe. In England itself, the popular fears of Spain, the popular resentment against Catholic plots revolving about Mary Stuart, and the popular indignation at "foreign" and "outside" meddling in English matters produced an unprecedented sense of national solidarity. The country rallied to Protestantism and to Elizabeth, and even the Catholic minority for the most part disowned the conspiracies against her. The English were now openly and defiantly allied with the Protestant Dutch. Not only were they fighting together in the Netherlands, but both English and Dutch sea raiders fell upon Spanish shipping, captured the treasure ships, and even pillaged the Spanish Main, the mainland coast of northern South America. The Dutch were beginning to penetrate East Indian waters. Elizabeth was negotiating with Scotland, with German Calvinists and French Huguenots. At the Escorial it was said that the Netherlands could only be rewon by an invasion of England, that the queen of the heretics must be at last dethroned, that in any case it was cheaper to launch a gigantic attack upon England than to pay the cost of protecting Spanish galleons, year after year, against the depredations of piratical sea dogs.

Philip II therefore prepared to invade England. The English retorted with vigor. Mary Stuart, after almost twenty years' imprisonment, was executed in 1587; an aroused Parliament, more than Elizabeth herself, demanded her life on the eve of foreign attack. Sir Francis Drake, most spectacular of the sea dogs, sailed into the port of Cádiz and burnt the very ships assembling there to join the Armada. This was jocosely described as singeing the beard of the king of Spain.

The great Armada, the *armada católica*, was ready early in 1588. With crosses on the sails and banners bearing the image of the Holy Virgin, it went forth as to a new Lepanto against the Turks of the north. It consisted of 130 ships, weighing 58,000 tons, carrying 30,000 men and 2,400 pieces of artillery—the most prodigious assemblage of naval power that the world had ever seen. In Spain only the pessimistic observed that its commander was no seaman, that some of its ships were too cumbersome, and some too frail, to weather the gales of the north, that orders had to be issued to its crews in six languages, and the antagonisms of Portuguese, Catalans, Castilians, Irishmen, and émigré English Catholics somehow appeased. The plan was for the fleet to sail to the Netherlands, from which it was to escort the prince of Parma's army across the straits to the English coast. In the Channel the Armada was met by some two hundred English vessels, with Sir Francis Drake as vice-admiral under Lord Howard of Effingham. The English craft—lighter, smaller, and faster, though well furnished with guns—harried the lumbering mass of the Armada, broke up its formations, attacked its great vessels one by one. It found no refuge at Calais, where English fireships drove it out again to sea. Then arose a great storm, the famous "Protestant wind," which blew the broken Armada northward, into seas that to southerners seemed almost polar, around the tip of Scotland, the Orkneys, the Hebrides, and northern Ireland, forbidding coasts which the Spaniards had to skirt without charts or pilots, and which they strewed with their wreckage and their bones.

The Results of the Struggle

The war went on for several years. Philip died in 1598, after a long and horrible illness, a frustrated and broken man. In the wars with Spain the English had, above all else, assured their national independence. They had acquired an intense national spirit, a love of "this other Eden, demi-paradise," "this precious stone set in the silver sea," as Shakespeare wrote; and they had become more solidly Protestant, almost unanimously set against "popery." With the ruin of the Armada, they were more free to take to the sea; we have seen how the English East India Company was founded in 1600.[14]

In the Netherlands, the battle lines swayed back and forth until 1609. In that year a Twelve Years' Truce was agreed to. By this truce the Netherlands were partitioned. The line of partition ran somewhat farther north than it had in Parma's time, for the Spaniards had retaken Antwerp and other cities in the middle zone. The seven provinces north of the line, those that had formed the Union of Utrecht in 1579, were henceforth known as Dutch. The ten provinces south of the line were known as the Spanish Netherlands. Protestants in the south either became Catholics or fled to the north, so that the south (the modern Belgium) became solidly Catholic, while the number of Protestants in the north was increased. Even so, the Dutch were not a completely Protestant people, for probably as many as a third of them remained Catholic. Calvinism was the religion of most Dutch burghers and the religion favored by the state; but in the face of an exceptionally large religious minority the Dutch Netherlands adopted a policy of toleration. The southern Netherlands were ruined by almost forty years of war. The Dutch, moreover, occupied the mouth of the Scheldt and refused to allow ocean-going vessels to proceed upstream to Antwerp or to Ghent. The Scheldt remained "closed" for two centuries, and the Flemish cities never recovered their old position. Amsterdam became the commercial and financial center of northern Europe; it retained its commercial supremacy for a century and its financial supremacy for two centuries. For the Dutch, as for the English, the weakening of Spanish naval power opened the way to the sea. The Dutch East India Company was organized in 1602. Both Dutch and English began to found overseas colonies. The English settled in Virginia in 1607, the Dutch at New York in 1612.

As for Spain, while it remained the most formidable military power of Europe for another half-century, its internal decline had already begun. At the death of Philip II the monarchy was living from hand to mouth, habitually depending on the next arrival of treasure from the Indies. The productive forces of the country were weakened by inflation, by taxation, by emigration, by depopulation. At Seville, for example, only 400 looms were in operation in 1621, where there had been 16,000 a century earlier. Spain suffered from the very circumstances that made it great. The qualities most useful in leading the Counter Reformation were

---

[14] See above, p. 118.

not those on which a modern society could most easily be built. The generations of crusading against infidels, heathen, and heretics had produced an exceptionally large number of minor aristocrats, chevaliers, dons, and hidalgos, who as a class were contemptuous of work, and who were numerous enough and close enough to the common people to impress their haughty indifference upon the country as a whole. With the extreme concentration on religion the ablest men entered the church, and so great was the popular admiration for saints and mystics, missionaries and crusaders, theologians, archbishops, ascetics, and begging friars, that more secular activities offered little psychological satisfaction or reward.

The very unity accomplished under Ferdinand and Isabella threatened to dissolve. After more than a century of the Inquisition people were still afraid of false Christians and crypto-Muslims. The question of the Moriscos rose again in 1608.[13] The Moriscos included some of the best farmers and most skilled artisans in the country. They lived in almost all parts of Spain and were in no sense a "foreign" element, since they were simply the descendants of those Spaniards who, in the Muslim period, which had begun 900 years before, had adopted the Muslim religion and Arabic language and culture. They were now supposedly Christian, but the true and pure Christians accused them of preserving in secret the rites of Islam and of sympathy for the Barbary pirates. They were thought to be clannish, marrying among themselves; and they were so efficient, sober, and hard working that they outdistanced other Spaniards in competition. In 1609 some 150,000 Moriscos were driven out of Valencia; in 1610 some 64,000 were driven from Aragon; in 1611 an unknown number were expelled from Castile. All were simply put on boats and sent off with what they could carry. Spain, whose total population was rapidly falling in any case, thus lost one of the most socially valuable, if not religiously orthodox, of all its minorities.

Nor could the Christian kingdoms hold peaceably together. In 1640 Portugal, which had been joined to the Spanish crown since 1580 when its own ruling line had run out, reestablished its independence. That same year Catalonia rose in open rebellion. The Catalan war, in which the French streamed across the Pyrenees to aid the rebels, lasted for almost twenty years. Catalonia was at last reconquered, but it managed to preserve its old privileges and separate identity. Catalan and Castilian viewed each other with increased repugnance. The Spanish kingdoms were almost as disunited, in spirit and in institutions, as in the days of Isabella and Ferdinand. They suffered, too, during the seventeenth century from a line of kings whose mental peculiarities reached the point of positive imbecility. Meanwhile, however, the might of Spain was still to be felt in both Germany and France.

15. THE DISINTEGRATION AND RECONSTRUCTION OF FRANCE

Both France and Germany, in the so-called Wars of Religion, fell into an advanced state of decomposition, France in almost forty years of civil war between 1562 and 1598, Germany in a long period of civil troubles culminating in the Thirty Years' War between 1618 and 1648. From this decomposition France recovered in the seventeenth century, but Germany did not.

---

[15] See p. 72.

Political and Religious Disunity

The Wars of Religion in France, despite the religious savagery shown by partisans of both sides, were no more religious than they were political and were essentially a new form of the old phenomenon of feudal rebellion against a higher central authority. "Feudal," in this postmedieval sense, generally refers not to nobles only, but to all sorts of component groups having rights within the state, and so includes towns and provinces, and even craft guilds and courts of law, in addition to the church and the noble class. It remained to be seen whether all these elements could be welded into one body politic.

In France the New Monarchy, resuming the work of medieval kings, had imposed a certain unity on the country.[16] Normally, or apart from civil war, the country acted as a unit in foreign affairs. The king alone made treaties, and in war his subjects all fought on his side, if they fought at all. Internally, the royal centralization was largely administrative; that is, the king and those who worked for him dealt with subordinate bodies of all kinds, while these subordinate bodies remained in existence with their own functions and personnel. France by the ideas of the time was a very large country. It was three times as large as England and five times as populous. At a time when the traveler could move hardly thirty miles a day it took three weeks of steady plodding to cross the kingdom. Local influence was therefore very strong. Beneath the platform of royalty there was almost as little substantial unity in France as in the Holy Roman Empire. Where the Empire had three hundred "states," France had some three hundred areas with their own legal systems. Where the Empire had free cities, France had *bonnes villes*, the king's "good towns," each with its stubbornly defended corporate rights. Where the Empire had middle-sized states like Bavaria, France had provinces as great as some European kingdoms—Brittany, Burgundy, Provence, Languedoc—each ruled by the French king, to be sure, but each with its own identity, autonomy, laws, courts, tariffs, taxes, and parliament or provincial estates. To all this diversity, in France as in Germany, was now added diversity of religion. Calvin himself was by birth and upbringing a Frenchman. Calvinism spread in France very rapidly.

Nor was France much attached to a papal, Rome-centered, or international Catholicism. The French clergy had long struggled for its national or Gallican liberties; the French kings had dealt rudely with popes, ignored the Council of Trent, and allied for political reasons with both the Lutherans and the Turks. Since 1516 the king of France had the right to nominate the French bishops.[17] The fact that both the monarchy and the clergy felt already independent of Rome held them back from the revolutionary solutions of Protestantism. The Protestantism which did spread in France was of the most clear-cut and radical kind, namely, Calvinism, which preached at kings, attacked bishops, and smashed religious images and desecrated the churches. Even in countries that became Protestant—England, north Germany, even the Netherlands—this extreme Protestantism was the doctrine of a minority. In France there was no middle-of-the-road Protestantism, no broad and comfortable Anglicanism, no halfway Lutheranism inspired by governments, and in the long run, as will be seen, the middle of the road was occupied by Catholics.

[16] See p. 69.
[17] See above, pp. 52, 69, 91.

At first, however, the Huguenots, as the French Calvinists were called, though always a minority, were neither a small one nor modest in their demands. In a class analysis, it is clear that it was chiefly the nobility that was attracted to Protestantism, though of course it does not follow that most French Protestants were nobles, since the nobility was a small class. More than a third, and possibly almost a half, of the French nobility was Protestant in the 1560s or 1570s. Frequently the seigneur, or lord of one or more manors, believed that he should have the *ius reformandi*, or right to regulate religion on his own estates, as the princes of Germany decided the religion of their own territories. It thus happened that a lord might defy the local bishop, put a Calvinist minister in his village church, throw out the images, simplify the sacraments, and have the service conducted in French. In this way peasants also became Huguenots. Occasionally peasants turned Huguenot without encouragement by the lord. It was chiefly in southwestern France that Protestantism spread as a general movement affecting whole areas. But in all parts of the country, north as well as south, many towns converted to Protestantism. Usually this meant that the bourgeois oligarchy, into whose hands town government had generally fallen, went over to Calvinism and thereupon banned Catholic services, of which the sequel might be either that the journeymen wage earners followed along, or that, estranged by the class differences whose development has been described above, they remained attached to their old priests.[18] In general, the unskilled laboring mass probably remained the least touched of all classes by Calvinist doctrine.

Both Francis I and Henry II opposed the spread of Calvinism—as did Lutheran and Anglican rulers—for Calvinism, a kind of grassroots movement in religion, rising spontaneously among laity and reforming ministers, seemed to threaten not only the powers of monarchy but the very idea of a nationally established church. The fact that in France the nobility, a traditionally ungovernable class, figured prominently in the movement only made it look the more like political or feudal rebellion. Persecution of Huguenots, with burnings at the stake, began in the 1550s.

Then in 1559 King Henry II was accidentally killed in a tournament. He left three sons, of whom the eldest in 1559 was only fifteen. Their mother, Henry's widow, was Catherine de' Medici, an Italian woman who brought to France some of the polish of Renaissance Italy, along with some of its taste for political intrigue, with which she attempted to govern a distracted country for her royal sons. (Their names were Francis II, who died in 1560, Charles IX, who died in 1574, and Henry III, who lasted until 1589.) The trouble was that, with no firm hand in control of the monarchy, the country fell apart, and that in the ensuing chaos various powerful factions tried to get control of the youthful monarchs for their own purposes. Among these factions were both Huguenots and Catholics. The Huguenots, under persecution, were too strong a minority to go into hiding. Counting among their number a third or more of the professional warrior class, the nobles, they took naturally and aggressively to arms.

The Civil and Religious Wars

Exact history distinguishes no less than nine civil wars in the concluding four decades of the sixteenth century in France, but in this history they will be telescoped

---

[18] See pp. 118–123.

together. They were not civil wars of the kind where one region of a country takes up arms against another, each retaining some apparatus of government, as in the American Civil War or the civil wars of the seventeenth century in England. They were civil wars of the kind fought in the absence of government. Roving bands of armed men, without territorial base or regular means of subsistence, wandered about the country, fighting and plundering, joining or separating from other similar bands, in shifting hosts that were quickly formed or quickly dissolved. The underlying social conditions detached many people from their old routines and threw them into a life of adventure. The more prominent leaders could thus easily obtain followers, and at the coming of such cohorts the peasants usually took to the woods, while bourgeois would lock the gates of their cities. Or else peasants would form protective leagues, like vigilantes; and even small towns maintained diminutive armies.

The Huguenots were led by various personages of rank, such as Admiral de Coligny and Henry of Bourbon, king of Navarre, a small independent kingdom at the foot of the Pyrenees between Spain and France. A pronounced Catholic party arose under the Guise family, headed by the Duke of Guise and the Cardinal of Lorraine. Catherine de' Medici was left in the middle, opposed like all monarchs to Calvinism, but unwilling to fall under the domination of the Guises. While the Guises wished to extirpate heresy they wished even more to govern France. Among the Huguenots some fought for local liberties in religion, while the more ardent spirits hoped to drive "idolatry" and "popery" out of all France, and indeed out of the world itself. Catherine de' Medici for a time tried to play the two parties against each other. But in 1572, fearing the growing influence of Coligny over the king, and taking advantage of a great concourse of leading Huguenots in Paris to celebrate the marriage of Henry of Navarre, she decided to rid herself of the heads of the Huguenot party at a single blow. In the resulting massacre of St. Bartholomew's Day some thousands of Huguenots were dragged from their beds after midnight and unceremoniously murdered. Coligny was killed; Henry of Navarre escaped by temporarily changing his religion.

This outrage only aroused Huguenot fury and led to a renewal of civil war, with mounting atrocities committed by both sides. The armed bands slaughtered each other and terrorized noncombatants. Both parties hired companies of mercenary soldiers, mainly from Germany. Spanish troops invaded France at the invitation of the Guises. Protestant towns, like Rouen and La Rochelle, appealed to Elizabeth of England, reminding her that kings of England had once reigned over their parts of France, inviting English invasion and a renewal of the horrors of the Hundred Years' War; but Elizabeth was too preoccupied with her own problems to give more than very sporadic and insignificant assistance. Neither side could subdue the other, and hence there were numerous truces, during which fighting still flared up, since no one had the power to impose peace. The truces usually acknowledged the status quo, allowing Protestant worship locally in places where it was actually going on; but the Protestants felt no security in such terms, nor were Catholics satisfied at such recognition of heresy, so that each truce expired in further war.

Gradually, mainly among the more perfunctory Catholics, but also among moderate Protestants, there developed still another group, who thought of themselves as the "politicals" or *politiques*. The *politiques* were men who concluded that too much was being made of religion, that no doctrine was important enough to justify everlasting war, that perhaps after all there might be room for two churches, and that what the country needed above all else was civil order. Theirs was the secular not the religious view. They believed that men lived primarily in the state, not in the church. They were willing to overlook a man's ideas if only he would obey the king and go peaceably about his business. To escape anarchy they put their hopes in the institution of monarchy. Henry of Navarre, now again a Protestant, was at heart a *politique*. Another was the political philosopher Jean Bodin (1530–1596), the first thinker to develop the modern theory of sovereignty. He held that in every society there must be one power strong enough to give law to all others, with their consent if possible, without their consent if necessary. Thus from the disorders of the religious wars in France was germinated the idea of royal absolutism and of the sovereign state.

The End of the Wars: Reconstruction under Henry IV

In 1589 both Henry III, the reigning king, and Henry of Guise, the Catholic party chief who was trying to depose him, were assassinated, each by a partisan of the other. The throne now came by legal inheritance to the third of the three Henrys, Henry of Navarre, the Huguenot chieftain. He reigned as Henry IV. Most popular and most amiably remembered of all French kings, except for medieval St. Louis, he was the first of the Bourbon dynasty, which was to last until the French Revolution.

The civil wars did not end with the accession of Henry IV. The Catholic party refused to recognize him, set up a pretender against him, and called in the Spaniards. Henry, the *politique*, sensed that the majority of the French people were still Catholic, and that the Huguenots were not only a minority but after thirty years of civil strife an increasingly unpopular minority kept going as a political party by obstinate nobles. Paris especially, Catholic throughout the wars, refused to admit the heretic king within its gates. Supposedly remarking that "Paris is well worth a Mass," Henry IV in 1593 abjured the Calvinist faith, and subjected himself to the elaborate processes of papal absolution. Thereupon the *politiques* and less excitable Catholics consented to work with him. The Huguenots, at first elated that their leader should become king, were now not only outraged by Henry's abjuration but alarmed for their own safety. They demanded not only religious liberty, but positive guarantees.

Henry IV in 1598 responded by issuing the Edict of Nantes. The Edict granted to every seigneur, or noble who was also a manorial lord, the right to hold Protestant services in his own household. It allowed Protestantism in towns where it was in fact the prevailing form of worship, and in any case in one town of each *baillage* (a unit corresponding somewhat to the English shire) throughout the country; but it barred it from Catholic episcopal towns and from a zone surrounding and including the city of Paris. It promised that Protestants should enjoy the same civil rights as Catholics, the same chance for public office, and access to the Catholic universities. In certain of the superior law courts it created "mixed chambers" of both Protestants and Catholics—somewhat as if a stated minority representation were to be legally required in United States federal courts today. The Edict also gave Protestants their own means of defense, granting them about 100 fortified towns to be held by Protestant garrisons under Protestant command.

The Huguenot minority, reassured by the Edict of Nantes, became less of a rebellious element within the state. The majority of the French people viewed the Edict with suspicion. The parlements, or supreme law courts, of Paris, Bordeaux, Toulouse, Aix, and Rennes all refused to recognize it as the law of the land. It was the king who forced toleration upon the country. He silenced the parlements, and subdued Catholic opposition by doing favors for the Jesuits. France's chief minority was thus protected by the central government, not by popular wishes. Where in England the Catholic minority had no rights at all, and in Germany the religious question was settled only by cutting the country into small and hostile fragments, in France a compromise was effected, by which the Protestant minority had both individual and territorial rights. A considerable number of French statesmen, generals, and other important persons in the seventeenth century were Protestants.

Henry IV, having appeased the religious controversy, did everything that he could to let the country gradually recover, to replant, rebuild, transact business, and rediscover the arts of peace. His ideal, as he breezily put it, was a "chicken in the pot" for every Frenchman. He worked also to put the ruined government back together, to collect taxes, pay officials, discipline the army, and supervise the administration of justice. Roads and bridges were repaired and new manufactures were introduced under mercantilist principles. Never throughout his reign of twenty-one years did he summon the Estates General. A country that had just hacked itself to pieces in civil war was scarcely able to govern itself, and so, under Henry IV, the foundations of the later royal absolutism of the Bourbons were laid down.

Henry IV was assassinated in 1610 by a crazed fanatic who believed him a menace to the Catholic church. Under his widow, Marie de' Medici, the nobility and upper Catholic clergy again grew restless and forced the summoning of the Estates General, in which so many conflicting and mutually distrustful interests were represented that no program could be adopted, and Marie dismissed them in 1615 to the general relief of all concerned. No Estates General of the kingdom as a whole thereafter met until the French Revolution. National government was to be conducted by and through the king.

Cardinal Richelieu

In the name of Marie de' Medici and her young son, Louis XIII, the control of affairs gradually came into the hands of an ecclesiastic, Cardinal Richelieu. In the preceding generation Richelieu might have been called a *politique*. It was the state, not the church, whose interests he worked to further. He tried to strengthen the state economically by mercantilist edicts. He attempted to draw impoverished gentlemen into trade by allowing them to engage in maritime commerce without loss of noble status. For wholesale merchants, as an incentive, he made it possible to become nobles, in return for payments into the royal exchequer. He founded and supported many commercial companies on the Anglo-Dutch model.

For a time it seemed that civil war might break out again. Nobles still feuded with each other and evaded the royal jurisdiction. Richelieu prohibited private warfare and ordered the destruction of all fortified castles not manned and needed by the king himself. He even prohibited dueling, a custom much favored by the d'Artagnans of the day, but regarded by Richelieu as a mere remnant of private war. The Huguenots, too, with their own towns and their own armed forces under the Edict of Nantes, had become something of a state within the state. In 1627 the Duke of Rohan led a Huguenot rebellion, based on the city of La Rochelle, which received military support from the English. Richelieu after a year suppressed the rebellion, and in 1629, by the Peace of Alais, amended the Edict of Nantes. For this highly secularized cardinal of the Catholic church it was agreeable for the Protestants to keep their religion, but not for them to share in the instruments of political power. The Huguenots lost, in 1629, their fortified cities, their Protestant armies, and all their military and territorial rights, but in their religious and civil rights they were not officially molested for another fifty years.

The French monarchy no sooner reestablished itself after the civil wars than it began to recur to the old foreign policy of Francis I, who had opposed on every front the European supremacy of the house of Habsburg.[19] The Spanish power still encircled France at the Pyrenees, in the Mediterranean, in the Free County of Burgundy (the Franche-Comté), and in Belgium. The Austrian branch had pretensions to supremacy in Germany and all central Europe. Richelieu found his opportunity to assail the Habsburgs in the civil struggles which now began to afflict Germany.

16. THE THIRTY YEARS' WAR, 1618–1648: THE DISINTEGRATION OF GERMANY

The Holy Roman Empire extended from France on the west to Poland and Hungary on the east. It included the Czechs of Bohemia, and sizable French-speaking populations in what are now Belgium, Lorraine, eastern Burgundy, and western Switzerland; but with these exceptions the Empire was made up of Germans.[20] Language, however, was far less important than religion as the tie which people felt to be basic to a community; and in religion the Empire was almost evenly divided. Where in England, after stabilization set in, Roman Catholics sank to a minority of some 3 percent, and in France the Huguenots fell to not much over 5 percent, in Germany there was no true minority, and hence no majority, and religion gave no ground for national concentration. Possibly there were more Protestants than Catholics in the Empire in 1600, for not only was Protestantism the state religion in many of the 300 states, but individual Protestants were exceedingly numerous in the legally Catholic states of the Austrian Habsburgs. Bohemia had a Protestant majority, rooted in the Czech people, and even in Austria, in meetings of the estates, the Protestants sometimes prevailed. Farther east, outside the Holy Roman Empire, the Hungarian nobles were mainly Protestant, and Transylvania, in the elbow of the Carpathian Mountains, was an active center of Calvinism.

In 1500 Germany had led in the life of Europe, but in 1600 it showed evidences of backwardness and provincialism. Literature had declined, and the language itself became barbarized and ungainly. Where both Catholics and Calvinists recognized international affiliations and read with interest books written in other countries, Lutherans were suspicious of the world outside the Lutheran states of Germany and Scandinavia, and hence suffered from a cultural isolation. The German universities, both Lutheran and Catholic, attracted fewer students than

---

[19] See map, pp. 70–71; and p. 78.
[20] See maps, pp. 70–71, 142–143.

formerly, and their intellectual effort was consumed in combative dogmatics, each side demonstrating the truth of its own ideas. More witches were burned in Germany than in the west, the popular fairy tales were more gruesome, and the educated were more fascinated by astrology. The commerce of south Germany and the Rhineland was in decay, both because of the shift of trade to the Atlantic and because the Dutch controlled the mouth of the Rhine in their own interests. German bankers, such as the Fuggers, were of slight importance after 1600. It was now in the West that capital was being formed.

Background of the Thirty Years' War

The Peace of Augsburg in 1555, with its principle of *cuius regio eius religio*, had provided that in each state the government could prescribe the religion of its subjects.[21] In some states a bishop himself constituted the government. In these cases, whenever an incumbent died, there was a race to name his successor, to secure the territory as Lutheran or Catholic. In 1593 a small war was fought for the control of Aachen, in 1600 another for the control of Cologne. In general, in the decades following the Peace of Augsburg, the Lutherans made considerable gains, putting Lutheran administrators into the church states, or "secularizing" them and converting them into lay principalities. The Catholics did not accept this constant attrition, which violated the Ecclesiastical Reservation of the Peace of Augsburg. In addition, Calvinism spread into Germany. Though Calvinists had no rights under the Peace of Augsburg, a number of states became Calvinist. One of these was the Palatinate, important because it was strategically placed across the middle Rhine, and because its ruler, the Elector Palatine, was one of the seven persons who elected the Holy Roman Emperor. In 1608 the Protestant states, urged on by the Elector Palatine, formed a Protestant union to defend their gains. To obtain support, they negotiated with the Dutch, with the English, and with Henry IV of France. In 1609 a league of Catholic German states was organized by Bavaria. It looked for help from Spain.

The Germans were thus falling apart, or rather coming together, into two parties in anticipation of a religious war, and each party solicited foreign assistance against the other. Other issues were also maturing. The Twelve Years' Truce between Spain and the Dutch, signed in 1609, was due to expire in 1621. The Spanish (whose military power was still unaffected by internal decline) were again preparing to crush the Dutch Republic, or, at the very least, to open the mouth of the Scheldt and to get Dutch traders out of the East Indies. Since the Dutch insisted on independence, and were in any case unwilling to leave the Indies or to remove their stranglehold on the port of Antwerp, a renewal of the Dutch-Spanish war appeared to be inevitable. The Spanish also wished to consolidate the Habsburg position in central Europe. From Milan in north Italy they proposed to build up a fork of territory, one of whose prongs would lead through the easternmost of the Swiss cantons directly to Habsburg Austria, the other through the westernmost Swiss cantons to the valley of the Rhine. There, on and near the Rhine, if they could conquer a few states like the Calvinistic Palatinate, they might join the Netherlands and Franche-Comté (the Free County of Burgundy, ruled by Spain) into a large and continuous territorial block.[22] These Spanish

---

[21] See pp. 78–79.
[22] See map, pp. 142–143.

designs in the Rhineland and Switzerland naturally aroused the opposition of France. Moreover, the Austrian branch of the Habsburg family was slowly bestirring itself to eradicate Protestantism in its own domains and even to turn the Holy Roman Empire into a more modern and national type of state. The idea of a strong power in Germany was abhorrent to the French. France, through opposition to the Habsburgs, was again put in the position of chief protector of Protestantism. France, as we have observed, was a giant of Europe, five times as populous as England, over ten times as populous as Sweden or the Dutch Republic, incomparably more populous than any single German state. And France after 1600 was at last unified within—at least relatively. As a French writer has observed, speaking of these years, the appearance of the fleur-de-lis upon the Rhine would tumble to the ground the vast projects of the Counter Reformation.

The Thirty Years' War, resulting from all these pressures, was therefore exceedingly complex. It was a German civil war fought over the Catholic-Protestant issue. It was also a German civil war fought over constitutional issues, between the emperor striving to build up the central power of the Empire and the member states struggling to maintain independence. These two civil wars by no means coincided, for Catholic and Protestant states were alike in objecting to imperial control. It was also an international war, between France and the Habsburgs, between Spain and the Dutch, with the kings of Denmark and Sweden and the prince of Transylvania becoming involved, and with all these outsiders finding allies within Germany, on whose soil most of the battles were fought. The wars were further complicated by the fact that many of the generals were soldiers of fortune, who aspired to create principalities of their own, and who fought or refused to fight to suit their own convenience.

The Four Phases of the War

The fighting began in Bohemia. It is in fact customary to divide the war into four phases, the Bohemian (1618–1625), the Danish (1625–1629), the Swedish (1630–1635), and the Swedish-French (1635–1648).

In 1618 the Bohemians, or Czechs, fearing the loss of their Protestant liberties, dealt with two emissaries from the Habsburg Holy Roman Emperor, Matthias (who was also their king), by a method occasionally used in that country—throwing them out of the window. After this "defenestration of Prague" the king-emperor sent troops to restore his authority, whereupon the Bohemians deposed him and elected a new king. In order to obtain Protestant assistance, they chose the Calvinist Elector Palatine, the head of the Protestant Union. This young man proceeded to Bohemia, where he assumed the title of Frederick V. He brought aid to the Bohemians from the Protestant Union, the Dutch sent money, and the prince of Transylvania harried the Habsburg rear. The Emperor Ferdinand, Matthias' successor, assisted by money from the pope, Spanish troops sent up from Milan, and the forces of Catholic Bavaria, managed to overwhelm the Bohemians at the battle of the White Mountain in 1620. Frederick fled, jeered or pitied as the "winter king." His ancestral domains in the Palatinate were overrun by the Spaniards.

Two facts emerged in consequence of the Bohemian war. First, the Spaniards were entrenching themselves in the Rhineland, building up their position against the French and the Dutch. Second, Bohemia was reconquered and revolutionized by the Habsburgs. Ferdinand got himself elected again as king. He confiscated the estates of almost half the Bohemian nobles. He granted these lands as endowments for Catholic churches, orders, and monasteries, or gave them out to a swarm of adventurers of all nationalities who had entered his service, and who now became the new landed aristocracy of Bohemia. Jesuits streamed in, and through missions and schools, as well as court proceedings and executions, the re-Catholicization of Bohemia began. In Austria also, which had at first joined Bohemia in rebellion, Protestantism was stamped out.

With Protestant fortunes at a low ebb, and the Protestant Union itself dissolved in 1621, the lead in Protestant affairs was now taken by the king of Denmark, who was also Duke of Holstein, a state of the Holy Roman Empire. His aims were well mixed with politics, for he hoped by acquiring a few bishoprics in Germany to construct a kingdom for his younger son. With a little aid from the Dutch and English, and with promises from Richelieu, he entered the fray. Against him the Emperor Ferdinand raised another army, or, rather, commissioned Albert of Wallenstein to raise one on his own private initiative. Wallenstein assembled a force of professional fighters, of all nationalities, who lived by pillage rather than by pay. His army was his personal instrument, not the emperor's, and he therefore followed a policy of his own, which was so tortuous and well concealed that the name of Wallenstein has always remained an enigma. Possibly he dreamed of a united empire and a revived Germany from which foreigners should be expelled; certainly he dreamed of creating a sizable principality for himself. Wallenstein and other imperial generals soon defeated the king of Denmark, reached the Baltic coast, and even invaded the Danish peninsula.

The full tide of the Counter Reformation now flowed over Germany. Not only was Catholicism again seeping into the Palatinate, and again flooding Bohemia, but it rolled northward into the inner recesses of the Lutheran states. By the Edict of Restitution, in 1629, the emperor declared all church territories secularized since 1552 automatically restored to the Catholic church. Two archbishoprics, twelve bishoprics, and over a hundred small territories formerly belonging to monasteries and religious orders were involved. Some, like the bishopric of Lübeck, were as far north as the Baltic. Some had been Protestant since the oldest person could remember. Terror swept over Protestant Germany. It seemed that the whole Protestant Reformation, now a century old, might be undone.

Among those to be alarmed were the French and the Swedes. Richelieu, however, was still putting down fractious nobles and Huguenots. He had not yet consolidated France to his satisfaction and believed that France, without fighting itself, could counter the Habsburg ambitions through the use of allies. He sent diplomats to help extricate the king of Sweden from a war with Poland, and he promised him financial assistance, which soon rose to a million livres a year in return for the maintenance in Germany of 40,000 Swedish troops. The Dutch subsidized the Swedes with some 50,000 florins a month.

The king of Sweden was Gustavus Adolphus, a ruler of superlative ability, who had conciliated all parties in Sweden and thus created a base from which he could safely conduct overseas operations. He had extended Swedish holdings on the east shore of the Baltic. Using Dutch and other military experts, he had created the most modern army of the times, noted for its firm discipline, high courage, and mobile cannon. Himself a religious man, he had his troops march to battle singing Lutheran hymns. He was ideally suited to be the Protestant champion, a role he now willingly took up, landing in Germany in 1630. Richelieu, besides giving financial help, negotiated with the Catholic states of Germany, playing on their fears of imperial centralization and so sowing discord among German Catholics and isolating the emperor, against whom the Swedish war machine was now hurled.

The Swedes, with military aid from Saxony, won a number of spectacular victories, at Breitenfeld in 1631 and Lützen in 1632, where, however, Gustavus Adolphus was killed. His chancellor, Oxenstierna, carried on. The Swedish army penetrated into Bohemia, and as far south as the Danube. What those in the higher counsels of Sweden were aiming at is not clear. Perhaps they dreamed of a great federal Protestant empire, to include Scandinavia and north Germany, a Lutheran empire confronting a Catholic and Habsburg empire in the south. But the brilliant Swedish victories came to little. Both sides were weakened by disagreement. Wallenstein, who disliked the Spanish influence in Germany, virtually ceased to fight the Swedes and Saxons, with whom he even entered into private talks, hoping to create an independent position for himself. He was finally disgraced by the emperor and assassinated by one of his own staff. On the Swedish-Saxon side, the Saxons decided to make a separate peace. Saxony therefore signed with the emperor the Peace of Prague of 1635. The other German Protestant states concurred in it and withdrew their support from the Swedes. The emperor, by largely annulling the Edict of Restitution, allayed Protestant apprehensions. The Swedes were left isolated in Germany. It seemed that the German states were coming together, that the religious wars might be nearing an end. But, in fact, in 1635, the Thirty Years' War was only well begun. Neither France nor Spain wished peace or reconciliation in Germany.

Richelieu renewed his assurances to the Swedes, paid subsidies even to the wealthy Dutch, hired a German princeling, Bernard of Saxe-Weimar, to maintain an army of Germans in the French service, and, cardinal of the Roman church though he was, at last came out openly and plainly in favor of the German Protestants.

So the fleur-de-lis at last moved toward the Rhine, though not at first with the success for which Frenchmen or Protestants might hope. The Spanish, from their bases in Belgium and Franche-Comté, drove instead deep into France. Champagne and Burgundy were ravaged, and Paris itself was seized with panic. The Spanish also raided the south. The French had a taste of the plunder, murder, burnings, and stealing of cattle by which Germany had been afflicted. But the French soon turned the tables. When Portugal and Catalonia rebelled against Philip IV, France immediately recognized the independence of Portugal under the new royal house of Braganza—as did England, Holland, and Sweden with equal alacrity. French troops streamed over the Pyrenees into Catalonia, spreading the usual devastation. Richelieu even recognized a Catalan republic.

In Germany the last or Swedish-French phase of the war was not so much a civil war among Germans as an international struggle on German soil. Few German states now sided with the French and Swedes. A feeling of national resentment against foreign invasion even seemed to develop.

The Peace of Westphalia, 1648

Peace talks began in 1644 in Westphalia, at the two towns of Münster and Osnabrück. The German states were crying for peace, for a final religious settlement,

SHETLAND I.

ORKNEY I.

SCOTLAND
• Edinburgh

IRELAND
• Belfast

Dublin •   Liverpool •   ENGLAND
(COMMONWEALTH 1649-1660
UNITED KINGDOM 1707)

• Bristol

ATLANTIC OCEAN

ENGLISH CHANNEL

• Rennes
• Nantes

FRANCE

• Bordeaux

LaCoruña •

León •

NAVARRE

Oporto •

Valladolid •

PORTUGAL
(TO SPAIN
1580-1640)

SPAIN

Escorial • Madrid •
CASTILE

Lisbon •

Mérida •   Toledo •

ARAGON
CATALONIA

Saragossa •

Barcelona •

Cadiz •

Seville •

Malaga •

Murcia •

Tangier • Ceuta
(Portugal)

Valencia •

BALEARIC I.

MINORCA

MAJORCA

MEDITERRANEAN

Oran (Spain) •

Algiers •

FEZ AND MOROCCO

ALGERIA

TUNISIA

BARBARY   STATES

NORWAY
• Bergen

NORTH SEA

KINGDOM OF
DENMARK AND NORWAY

DENMARK
(TO SWEDEN 1658)
• Copenhagen

SCHLESWIG
HOLSTEIN

SWEDISH
POMERANIA

• Lübeck Stralsund

Hamburg •

Bremen •
Amsterdam •
Ryswick •
Utrecht •

UNITED
PROVINCES

Verden •
Osnabrück •
Münster •

HANOVER

SPANISH
NETH.

Brussels •

Cologne •

MINOR

GERMAN STATES

Mainz •
• Trier

Metz •

LORRAINE PALATINATE

ALSACE

Strassbourg •

FRANCHE-
COMTÉ

SWISS CANTONS

Lyons •

SAVOY

PIEDMONT

Milan •
Parma •

Genoa •

Florence •

TUSCANY

CORSICA
(Genoa)

SARDINIA

PAPAL
STATES

Rome •

Naples •

NAPLES

KINGDOM OF THE
TWO SICILIES

Palermo •

SICILY

Aquila •

Bari •

MALTA
(Knights of St. John)

SEA

Paris •

Rouen •

Montauban •

Avignon •

Marseilles •

PYRENEES

Tunis •

BALTIC SEA

Helsingfors •

Stockholm •

SWEDEN

FINLAN

ESTON

LIVC

• Riga

COURLAND

BRANDENBURG-PRUSSIA

• Danzig

DUCHY
OF
PRUSSIA

Stettin •

POMERANIA

Vistula R.

GREAT
POLAND

• Warsaw

Berlin •

BRANDENBURG

Magdeburg •

Leipzig •
SAXONY

Dresden •

Breslau •
SILESIA

Oder R.

LITTLE
POLAND

Prague •

BOHEMIA

MORAVIA

Cracow •

Lemberg •

GALICI.

CARPATI

AUSTRIA

Vienna •

BAVARIA

Augsburg •

KINGDOM OF HUNGARY

• Budapest

HUNGARY

OTTOM

TRA

SLAVONIA

BOSNIA

Belgrade •

SERBIA

REPUBLIC OF VENICE

Venice •

ADRIATIC SEA

Zara •

MONTENEGRO

ALBANIA

Salonica •

GREEC

IONIAN I.
(Venice)

Elbe

Rhine

Rhine R.

Austrian Habsburgs
Spanish Habsburgs
Swedish Dominions
Brandenburg-Prussia
Church Lands
Boundary of the Holy Roman Empire
0   100   200   300 miles

NGRIA

ask •

RUSSIA

• Moscow

U ANIA

AND

• Kiev

DLIA

MOLD AVIA   YEDISAN

IA   BESSARABIA   CRIMEA

IIA   DOBRUJA   BLACK SEA

arest •

u b e   R.

ARIA

IA   • Constantinople

E
 M
  P
   I
    R
     E

EAN
A   • Smyrna

ns

RHODES
(Turkish)   CYPRUS
(Turkish)

TE
ce)

EUROPE, 1648

The map shows the European states at the time of the Peace of
Westphalia. The main feature of the Peace of Westphalia was
that the threat of domination of Europe by the Catholic Habsburgs was averted. A plurality of independent sovereign states
was henceforth considered normal. The plurality of religions
was also henceforth taken for granted for Europe as a whole,
though each state continued to require, or at least to favor,
religious uniformity within its own borders. By weakening the
Habsburgs, and furthering the disintegration of Germany,
the Peace of Westphalia opened the way for the political
ascendancy of France.

and for "reform" of the Holy Roman Empire. France and Sweden insisted that the German states should individually take part in the negotiations, a disintegrating principle that the German princes eagerly welcomed and which the emperor vainly resisted. To Westphalia, therefore, hundreds of diplomats and negotiators now repaired, representing the Empire, its member states, Spain, France, Sweden, the Dutch, the Swiss, the Portuguese, the Venetians, many other Italians, and the pope. There had been no such European congress since the Council of Constance, and the fact that a European assemblage had in 1415 dealt with affairs of the church, and now in the 1640s dealt with affairs of state, war, and power, was a measure of the secularization that had come over Europe. The papal nuncio, it may be remarked, was barely listened to at Westphalia, and the pope never signed the treaties.

The negotiations dragged on, because the armies were still fighting, and after each battle one side or the other raised its terms. France and Spain refused to make peace with each other at all and in fact remained at war until 1659. But for the Holy Roman Empire a settlement was agreed to, incorporated in 1648 in the two treaties of Münster and Osnabrück, and commonly known as the Peace of Westphalia.

The Peace of Westphalia represented a general checkmate to the Counter Reformation in Germany. It not only renewed the terms of the Peace of Augsburg, granting each German state the right to determine its own religion, but it added Calvinism to Lutheranism and Catholicism as an acceptable faith. On the controversial issue of church territories secularized after 1552 the Protestants won a complete victory.

The dissolution of the Holy Roman Empire, which had been advanced by the drawing of internal religious frontiers in the days of Luther, was now confirmed in politics and international law. Borderlands of the Empire fell away. The Dutch and Swiss ceased to belong to it, both the United Provinces and Swiss cantons (or Helvetic Body) being recognized as sovereign and independent. The Dutch, in addition, were confirmed in their conquest of both banks of the lower Scheldt, the closure of that river to ocean-going vessels, and hence the commercial destruction of Antwerp. They likewise received, from Portugal, the right to have outposts in Brazil and Indonesia.

From the disintegrating western frontier of the Holy Empire the French cut off small pieces, receiving sovereignty over three Lorraine bishoprics, which they had occupied for a century, and certain rights in Alsace which were so confused that they later led to trouble. The king of Sweden received the bishoprics of Bremen and Verden and the western half of Pomerania, including the city of Stettin. Sweden thus added to its trans-Baltic possessions. The mouths of the German rivers were now controlled by non-Germans, the Oder, Elbe, and Weser by Sweden, the Rhine and the Scheldt by the Dutch. In the interior of the Empire Brandenburg received eastern Pomerania, the large archbishopric of Magdeburg, and two smaller bishoprics, while Bavaria also increased its stature, obtaining part of the Palatinate and a seat in the electoral college, so that the Empire now had eight electors.

It was in the new constitution of the Empire itself, not in territorial changes, that the greatest victory of the French and their Swedish and Dutch allies was to be found. The German states, over three hundred in number, became virtually sovereign. Each received the right to conduct diplomacy and make treaties with foreign powers. The Peace of Westphalia further stipulated that no laws could be made by the Empire, no taxes raised, no soldiers recruited, no war declared or peace terms ratified except with the consent of the imperial estates, the 300-odd princes, ecclesiastics, and free cities in the Reichstag assembled. Since it was well known that agreement on any such matters was impossible, the principle of self-government, or of medieval constitutional liberties, was used to destroy the Empire itself as an effective political entity. While most other European countries were consolidating under royal absolutism, Germany sank back into "feudal chaos."

Not only did the Peace of Westphalia block the Counter Reformation, and not only did it frustrate the Austrian Habsburgs and forestall for almost two centuries any movement toward German national unification, but it also marked the advent in international law of the modern European *Staatensystem*, or system of sovereign states. The diplomats who assembled at Westphalia represented independent powers which recognized no superior or common tie. No one any longer pretended that Europe had any significant unity, religious, political, or other. Statesmen delighted in the absence of any such unity, in which they sensed the menace of "universal monarchy." Europe was understood to consist in a large number of unconnected sovereignties, free and detached atoms, or states, which acted according to their own laws, following their own political interests, forming and dissolving alliances, exchanging embassies and legations, alternating between war and peace, shifting position with a shifting balance of power.

Physically Germany was wrecked by the Thirty Years' War. Cities were sacked by mercenary soldiers with a rapacity that their commanders could not control; or the commanders themselves, drawing no supplies from their home governments, systematically looted whole areas to maintain their armies. Magdeburg was besieged ten times, Leipzig five. In one woolen town of Bohemia, with a population of 6,000 before the wars, the citizens fled and disappeared, the houses collapsed, and eight years after the peace only 850 persons were found there. On the site of another small town Swedish cavalry found nothing but wolves. The peasants, murdered, put to flight, or tortured by soldiers to reveal their few valuables, ceased to give attention to farming; agriculture was ruined, so that starvation followed, and with it came pestilence. Even revised modern estimates allow that in many extensive parts of Germany as much as a third of the population may have perished. The effects of fire, disease, undernourishment, homelessness, and exposure in the seventeenth century were the more terrible because of the lack of means to combat them. The horrors of modern war are not wholly different from horrors that men and women have experienced in the past.

Germany as such, physically wrecked and politically cut into small pieces, ceased for a long time to play any part in European affairs. A kind of political and cultural vacuum existed in central Europe. On the one hand, the western or Atlantic peoples—French, English, Dutch—began in the seventeenth century to take the lead in European affairs. On the other hand, in eastern Germany, around Berlin and Vienna, new and only half-German power complexes began to form. These themes will be traced in the two following chapters.

With the close of the Thirty Years' War the Wars of Religion came to an end.

While in some later conflicts, as in Hungary or in Ireland and Scotland, religion remained an issue, it was never again an important issue in the political affairs of Europe as a whole. In general, by the close of the seventeenth century, the division between Protestant and Catholic had become stabilized. Neither side any longer expected to make territorial gains at the expense of the other. Both the Protestant and the Catholic reformations were accomplished facts.

The World Overseas

With the Age of Discovery, Europe entered into habitual communication with the "Indies," as Asia, Africa, and America were at first vaguely and collectively called.

Europeans found some peoples in these countries less civilized than themselves, and others whom they considered equally civilized or more so, as in India and China. From Asia, while the Europeans at first sought for spices, they soon imported manufactures of a more refined kind than Europe could then produce, such as Indian cottons and Chinese porcelains. In Asia, as in Africa, the Europeans were transients—traders, sailors, missionaries, and officials sent to govern small outposts. There was no settlement of European families except at the Cape of Good Hope. The interior of Africa remained unknown. The Mogul empire in India until after 1700, and the Ming empire in China, succeeded by the Ch'ing or Manchu empire about 1650, long commanded the awe and respect of Europeans. China exerted a special fascination. During the European Enlightenment, in the eighteenth century, China was admired as a huge empire that had no clergy, and was governed by an enlightened literary class, the mandarins, recruited by competitive examination rather than by noble birth.

The aboriginal Americans and the black Africans were regarded by the Europeans as savages, who in any case could not defend themselves against European organization and weapons. The American Indians were either killed off, subjugated or pushed aside. America was valuable to Europeans for its natural resources, whose exploitation required masses of labor which was supplied from Africa. In the ensuing slave trade, the number of Africans who were taken to America, including the two continents and the West Indies, was far greater than the number of Europeans who settled there before 1800. A few Spanish emigrated permanently to New Spain, and a few Portuguese to Brazil, but by the time of the American Revolution the most purely "European" region was the Atlantic coast of North America, where about two million whites lived with half a million blacks and a very few Indians.

Europe itself was transformed by these overseas ventures. A wealthy commercial class grew up in northwestern Europe. Naval power became decisive. The inflow of American gold and silver affected currency values and hence the relationship between social classes. Population grew with the adoption of the American potato. Men took increasing pride in their understanding of the world. There was much speculation on the diversity of human races and cultures, which sometimes led to a new kind of race consciousness on the part of Europeans, and sometimes to a cultural relativism in which European ways were seen as only one variant of human behavior as a whole.

Right: "Our Lady of the Navigators," painted about 1535 by Alejo Fernandez for the Casa de Contratacion, or Trade House, at Seville. The figures to whom the Virgin extends her protection, with their sharply individualized features, are thought to represent various actual explorers; the one to the left may be Columbus. The picture evokes the combination of religious spirit with adventure and gold-seeking that motivated the early expeditions.

The Spaniards stamped out much of the Indian religion as idolatrous, yet it is to Spanish priests that we owe the preservation of much of our knowledge of the pre-Conquest culture. The page at the above right is from a book in which a Spaniard wrote down the Aztec language in the Latin alphabet. A human sacrifice is also depicted.

At the above left is a page from a book published in England, translated from the Dutch. The author, Johannes Nieuhoff, spent three years in Java and nine in Brazil, where the Dutch had a settlement in the 1640s. He was thus well qualified to write on the "West and East Indies," whose wonders are suggested by palms, parasols, and elephants. The aerial creature is probably a "flying squirrel" of a kind that is common in Indonesia.

"An Episode in the Conquest of America," by Jan Mostaert of Haarlem in Holland. An early visualization of the New World by a painter who died in 1555. The multitude of busy small figures suggests the style of the Flemish Breughel, and the placid livestock is Dutch. The American Indians are seen as naked, helpless, and confused—and very different from Europeans.

151

Opposite, above: Europeans negotiate with an African chief and his council on the Guinea coast. The Europeans have guns, the Africans only spears, but the Africans, in contrast to the American Indians on the preceding page, are fully clothed and seated with dignity in an organized situation. They may be discussing the sale of slaves.

Above, center: Black slaves are stooped over in a diamond-processing operation in Brazil, while overseers watch with whips. The slaves seem to be sifting material in water made to flow through the little compartments.

Above, left: An early advertisement to attract European immigration to what eventually became the United States. This one was published in London two years after the founding of Jamestown, the first permanent English settlement in America. "Planting" meant settling in the seventeenth century.

Right: The headquarters of the Dutch East India Company in 1665 in Bengal, long before the British predominance there. It is wholly walled off from the Indian life around it, with offices, living quarters, and spacious gardens for the employees of the Company. A large Dutch flag flies at the corner of the enclosure, and others can be seen on the ships in the Hooghly River (in the Ganges delta); these ships kept the Dutch traders in continual touch with Holland, though the voyage took almost a year.

154

These two prints suggest some results of three centuries of European experience with the world overseas. In China, no Europeans had as yet any territorial foothold. China was seen by Europe as a kind of counterpart civilization to itself. Confucius is shown here in a library of suspiciously European appearance, but holding a book in which Chinese characters are represented. He symbolized for Europeans the great teacher of virtue and wisdom, of social harmony and civic duty, far removed from the theological bickering of European religions.

Meanwhile the settlement at Jamestown had grown into a string of populous colonies. Above, we see Boston Common in 1768. The town seems rural, but has substantial houses with fences and rows of planted trees. British troops have just moved in, because of rising political troubles. They have pitched their tents on the common, where they march and drill in full sight of the citizens. The first fighting of the American Revolution was soon to begin here.

IV.
The
Establishment of
West-European
Leadership

I f the reader were to take a map of Europe, set a compass on the city of Paris, and draw a circle with a radius of five hundred miles, a zone would be marked out from which much of modern or "Western" civilization has radiated since about 1650. It was within this zone that a secular society, modern natural science, a developed capitalism, the modern state, parliamentary government, democratic ideas, machine industry, and much else either originated or received their first full expression. The extreme western parts of Europe—Ireland, Portugal, and Spain—were mainly outside the circle. But within it were England, southern Scotland, France, the Low Countries, Switzerland, western and central Germany, and northern Italy. This area, for over two hundred years beginning in the seventeenth century, was the earth's principal center of what anthropologists might call cultural diffusion. Western Europe, as a dynamic cultural area, was to have a tremendous impact on the rest of Europe, the Americas, and ultimately the whole world.

This leadership of western Europe became established in the half-century following the Peace of Westphalia. The fading out of the Italian Renaissance, the subsiding of religious wars, the ruin of the Holy Roman Empire, and the decay of Spain all cleared the stage on which the Dutch, English, and French were to be the

Chapter Emblem: A commemorative medal, in which Louis XIV receives the homage of Tournai and Courtrai, Flemish towns temporarily annexed in 1667.

principal actors. But the Dutch were few in number, and the English during most of the seventeenth century were weakened by domestic discord. It was France that for a time played the most imposing role. The whole half-century following the Peace of Westphalia is in fact often called the Age of Louis XIV.

17. THE *GRAND MONARQUE* AND THE BALANCE OF POWER

This king of France inherited his throne in 1643 at the age of five, assumed the personal direction of affairs in 1661 at the age of twenty-three, and reigned for seventy-two years until his death in 1715. No one else in modern history has held so powerful a position for so long a time. Louis XIV was more than a figurehead. For over half a century, during his whole adult life, he was the actual and working head of the French government. Inheriting the achievement of Richelieu,[1] he made France the strongest country in Europe. Using French money, by bribes or other inducements, he built up a pro-French interest in virtually every country from England to Turkey. His policies and the counter-policies that others adopted against him set the pace of public events, and his methods of government and administration, war and diplomacy, became a model for other rulers to copy. During this time the French language, French thought and literature, French architecture and landscape gardens, French styles in clothes, cooking, and etiquette became the accepted standard for Europe. France seemed to be the land of light, and Louis XIV was called by his fascinated admirers Louis the Great, the *Grand Monarque*, and the Sun King. To the internal achievements of France we shall shortly return.

Internationally, the consuming political question of the last decades of the seventeenth century (at least in western Europe—eastern Europe we shall reserve for the next chapter) was the fate of the still vast possessions of the Spanish crown. Spain was what Turkey was later called, "the sick man of Europe." To its social and economic decline[2] was added hereditary physical deterioration of its rulers. In 1665 the Spanish throne was inherited by Charles II, an unfortunate afflicted by many ills of mind and body, impotent, even imbecile, the pitiable product of generations of inbreeding in the Habsburg house. His rule was irresolute and feeble. It was known from the moment of his accession that he could have no children, and that the Spanish branch of the Habsburg family would die out with his own death. The whole future not only of Spain but of the Spanish Netherlands, the Spanish holdings in Italy, and all Spanish America was therefore in question. Charles II dragged out his miserable days until 1700, the object of jealousy and outright assault during his lifetime, and precipitating a new European war by his death.

Louis XIV, who in his youth married a sister of Charles II, intended to benefit from the debility of his royal brother-in-law. His expansionist policies followed two main lines. One was to push the French borders eastward to the Rhine, annexing the Spanish Netherlands (or Belgium) and the Franche-Comté or Free County of Burgundy, a French-speaking region lying between ducal Burgundy and Switzerland.[3] Such a policy involved the further dismemberment of the Holy

[1] See pp. 136–137.
[2] See pp. 130–131.
[3] See map, pp. 142–143.

Roman Empire. The other line of Louis XIV's ambitions, increasingly clear as time went on, was his hope of obtaining the entire Spanish inheritance for himself. By combining the resources of France and Spain he would make France supreme in Europe, in America, and on the sea. To promote these ends Louis XIV intrigued with the smaller and middle-sized powers of Europe. He took various princes of Germany, and for a time a king of England, into his pay. He supported, with complete disregard of ideology, the republicans in Holland against their prince, and the royalists in England against the parliamentary opposition, knowing that in Holland it was the republicans, and in England the partisans of high monarchy, who were most dependent on foreign assistance.

Were Louis XIV to succeed in his aims, he would create the "universal monarchy" dreaded by diplomats, that is to say, a political situation in which one state might subordinate all others to its will. The technique used against universal monarchy was the balance of power. Universal monarchy had formerly been almost achieved by the Austro-Spanish Habsburgs. The Habsburg supremacy had been blocked mainly by a balance of power headed by France, of which the Thirty Years' War and the Peace of Westphalia were the outstanding triumphs. Now the danger of universal monarchy came from France, and it was against France that the balance of power was directed.

The Idea of the Balance of Power

It will be useful to explain what a balance of power was and was not meant to be. The phrase itself, which came into general use at this time, has been employed ever since in different though related senses. In one sense it refers to a condition of equilibrium, or of even balance, in which power is distributed among many separate states. The second sense arises when this equilibrium is disturbed. If one state preponderates, and if others then form a coalition against it, then the coalition itself may be called the "balance," though it is actually the counterweight by which balance or equilibrium is to be restored. In a third sense one speaks of "holding" or "controlling" the balance of power; here the balance refers to that decisive increment of weight or power which one state may bring to bear. Thus if a state is a vitally necessary member of a coalition, more needed by its allies than it is in need of them, it may be said to "hold" the balance. Or if it belongs to no coalition at all, but tries to keep all other states in a condition of equilibrium, so that its own intervention on one side or the other would be decisive, it may also be said to "hold" the balance, although strictly speaking not participating in the balance at all.

The aim of statesmen pursuing policies of balance of power in the seventeenth and eighteenth centuries was generally to preserve their own independence of action to the utmost. Hence the basic rule was to ally against any state threatening domination. If one state seemed to dictate too much, others would shun alliance with it unless they were willing (from ideological sympathy or other reasons) to become its puppets. They would seek alliance with the other weaker states instead. They would thus create a balance or counterweight, or "restore the balance," against the state whose ascendancy they feared. Another more subtle reason for preferring alliance with the weak rather than with the strong was that in such an alliance each member could feel his own contribution to be necessary and valued, hence could preserve his own dignity and prestige, and by threatening to withdraw his support could win consideration of his own policies. Indeed, the balance of power may be defined as a system in which each state tends to throw its weight where it is most needed, so that its own importance may be enhanced.

The purpose of balance-of-power politics was not to preserve peace, but to preserve the sovereignty and independence of the states of Europe, or the "liberties of Europe," as they were called, against potential aggressors. The system was effective as a means to this end in the seventeenth and eighteenth centuries. Combinations were intricate, and alliances were readily made and unmade to deal with emerging situations. One reason for the effectiveness of the system lay in the great number of states capable of pursuing an independent foreign policy. These included not only the greater and middle-sized states of Austria, Spain, France, England, Holland, Sweden, and Bavaria, but a great number of small independent states, such as Denmark, the German principalities, Portugal after 1640, and Savoy, Venice, Genoa, and Tuscany. States moved easily from one alliance to another, or from one side of the balance to another. They were held back by no ideologies or sympathies, especially after the religious wars subsided, but could freely choose or reject allies, aiming only to protect their own independence or enlarge their own interests. Moreover, owing to the military technology of the day, small states might count as important military partners in an alliance. By controlling a strategic location, like the king of Denmark, or by making a contribution of ships or money, like the Dutch Republic, they might add just enough strength to an alliance to balance and overbalance the opposing great power and its allies.

As the ambitions of Louis XIV became bolder, and as the capacity of Spain to resist them withered away, the prevention of universal monarchy under France depended increasingly on combining the states of Europe into a balance of power against him. The balance against Louis XIV was engineered mainly by the Dutch. The most tireless of his enemies, and the man who did more than any other to checkmate him, was the Dutchman William III, the prince of Orange, who in his later years was king of England and Scotland as well.

Let us, after first surveying the Dutch in the seventeenth century, turn to the British Isles, where a momentous conflict occurred between Parliament and king. We shall then examine the French absolute monarchy under Louis XIV and conclude the present chapter with the wars of Louis XIV, particularly the War of the Spanish Succession, in which the great international issues of the time conflicted and were resolved.

18. THE DUTCH REPUBLIC

Dutch Civilization and Government

The ambassadors of kings, strolling beside a canal at The Hague, might on occasion observe a number of burghers in plain black garments step out of a boat and proceed to make a meal of cheese and herring on the lawn, and they would recognize in these portly figures Their High Mightinesses the Estates General of the United Provinces, as the Dutch government was known in the diplomatic language of the day. Though noblemen lived in the country, the Dutch were the most bourgeois of all peoples. They were not the only republicans in Europe, since the Swiss cantons, Venice, Genoa, and even England for a few years were republics, but of all republics the United Provinces was by far the most wealthy, the most flourishing, and the most preeminently civilized.

The Dutch acquired a nationality of their own in the long struggle against Spain, and with it a pride in their own freedom and independence. In the later phases of the war with Spain, notably during the Thirty Years' War, they were able to rely more on their wealth, ready money, shipping, and diplomacy than on actual fighting, so that during the whole seventeenth century they enjoyed a degree of comfort, and of intellectual, artistic, and commercial achievement unexcelled in Europe. The classic Dutch poets and dramatists wrote at this time, making a literary language of what had formerly been a dialect of Low German. Hugo Grotius produced, in his *Law of War and Peace*, a pioneering treatise on international law. Baruch Spinoza, of a family of refugee Portuguese Jews, quietly turned out works of philosophy, examining the fundamentals of reality, of human conduct, and of church and state. Spinoza made his living by grinding lenses; there were many other lens grinders in Holland; some of them developed the microscope, and some of these, in turn—Leeuwenhoek, Swammerdam, and others —peering through their microscopes and beholding for the first time the world of microscopic life, became founders of modern biological science. The greatest Dutch scientist was Christian Huyghens (1629–1695), who worked mainly in physics and mathematics; he improved the telescope (a Dutch invention), made clocks move with pendulums, discovered the rings of Saturn, and launched the wave theory of light. A less famous writer, Balthasar Bekker, in his *World Bewitched* (1691) delivered a decisive blow against the expiring superstition of witchcraft.

But the most eternally fresh of the Dutch creations, suffering from no barrier of time or language, were the superb canvases of the painters. Frans Hals produced bluff portraits of the common people. Jan Vermeer threw a spell of magic and quiet dignity over men, and especially women, of the burgher class. Rembrandt conveyed the mystery of human consciousness itself. In Rembrandt's *Masters of the Cloth Hall* (see illustration) we face a group of men who seem about to speak from the canvas, inclined slightly forward, as intent on their business as judges on the proceedings in a courtroom; men of the kind who conducted the affairs of Holland, in both commerce and government; intelligent men, calculating but not cunning, honest but determined to drive a hard bargain, stern rather than mild; and the sober black cloaks, with the clean white collars, set against the carved woodwork and rich table covering of the Cloth Hall, seem to suggest that personal vanity must yield to collective undertakings, and personal simplicity be maintained in the midst of material opulence. And in Vermeer's *Geographer*, painted in 1669 (also reproduced in this book—see p. 109), there appears not only an immaculately scrubbed and dusted Dutch interior, but something of a symbol of the modern world in its youth—the pale northern sunlight streaming through the window, the globe and the map, the dividers in the scholar's right hand, instrument of science and mathematics, the tapestry flung over the table (or is it an Oriental rug brought from the East?), the head lifted in thought and eyes resting on an invisible world of fresh discoveries and opening horizons.

In religion, after initial disputes, the Dutch Republic adopted toleration. Early in the seventeenth century the Dutch Calvinists divided. One group favored a modification of Calvinism, with a toning down of the doctrine of absolute and unconditional predestination; it drew its main support from the comfortable

THE MASTERS OF THE CLOTH HALL
by Rembrandt van Rijn (Dutch, 1606–1669)

This painting was done on commission for the Cloth Hall of Amsterdam, that is, the guild
of "clothiers" or "drapers" such as are described on pp. 114–115 in connection with the
Commercial Revolution. The men shown are the heads of the guild. Over a period of forty
years Rembrandt produced some 600 paintings, in addition to etchings and drawings,
in which he conveyed all types of experience, from the commercial practicality of the
present group to the deeply mystical and religious. The vitality of Dutch culture in the
seventeenth century is shown also in the pictures on pp. 109, 111, and 282. Courtesy of the
Rijksmuseum, Amsterdam.

burghers and its doctrines from a theologian of Leyden named Arminius. To deal with this Arminian heresy a great international Calvinist synod met in 1618 at Dordrecht in Holland. Of the hundred delegates almost a third came from Scotland, England, Germany, Switzerland, and France. The orthodox party won out at the synod; one old man was put to death; the philosopher Grotius fled to France for safety. But beginning in 1632 the Arminians were tolerated. Rights were granted to the large Catholic minority. Jews had long been welcomed in the republic; and Christian sects despised everywhere else, such as the Mennonites, found a refuge in it. Although none of these people had as many political or economic rights as the Calvinists, the resulting mixture stimulated both the intellectual life and the commercial enterprise of the country.

The Dutch as early as 1600 had 10,000 ships, and throughout the seventeenth century they owned most of the shipping of northern Europe. They were the carriers between Spain, France, England, and the Baltic. Much coastwise shipping between ports of France was in Dutch hands. They settled in Bordeaux to buy wines, lent money to vintners, and soon owned many vineyards in France itself. They sailed on every sea. They explored the waters around Spitzbergen and almost monopolized Arctic whaling. They entered the Pacific by way of South America, where they rounded Cape Horn and named it after Hoorn in Holland. Organized in the East India Company of 1602, their merchants increasingly replaced the Portuguese in India and the Far East. In Java, in 1619, they founded the city of Batavia—the Latin name for Holland. (It is now called Jakarta.) Finding some Englishmen in 1623 at Amboina, in the midst of the Spice Islands, they tortured and killed them. The English did not return until the days of Napoleon. Not long after 1600 the Dutch reached Japan. But the Japanese, fearing the political consequences of Christian penetration, in 1641 expelled all other Europeans and confined the Dutch to limited operations on an island near Nagasaki. The Dutch remained for over two centuries the sole link of the West with Japan. In 1612 the Dutch founded their first settlement on Manhattan Island, and in 1621 they established a Dutch West India Company to exploit the loosely held riches of Spanish and Portuguese America. They founded colonies at Pernambuco and Bahia in Brazil (lost soon thereafter) and at Caracas, Curaçao, and in Guiana in the Caribbean. In 1652 the Dutch captured the Cape of Good Hope in South Africa from the Portuguese. Dutch settlers soon appeared—men, women, and children. From these settlers and from French Huguenots and others have come the modern Afrikaner people, whose language and religion still reflect their mainly Dutch origins.

In 1609 the Dutch founded the Bank of Amsterdam. European money was a chaos; coins were minted not only by great monarchs but by small states and cities in Germany and Italy, and even by private persons. In addition, under inflationary pressures, kings and others habitually debased their coins by adding more alloy, while leaving the old coins in circulation along with the new. Anyone handling money thus accumulated a miscellany of uncertain value. The Bank of Amsterdam accepted deposits of such mixed money from all persons and from all countries, assessed the gold and silver content, and, at rates of exchange fixed by itself, allowed depositors to withdraw equivalent values in gold florins minted by the Bank of Amsterdam. These were of known and unchanging weight and purity. They thus became an internationally sought money, an international measure of value, acceptable everywhere. Depositors were also allowed to draw checks against their accounts. These conveniences, plus a safety of deposits guaranteed by the Dutch government, attracted capital from all quarters and made possible loans for a wide range of purposes. Amsterdam remained the financial center of Europe until the French Revolution.

Under their republican government the Dutch enjoyed great freedom, but it can hardly be said that their form of government met all the requirements of a state. Their High Mightinesses (the *Hooge Moogende*), who made up the Estates General, were only delegates from their respective seven provinces and could act only as the estates of the provinces gave instructions. The seven provinces, like the states of the Holy Roman Empire in which they had originated, were jealous of their own independence. Each province had, as its executive, an elected stadholder, but there was no stadholder for the United Provinces as a whole. This difficulty was overcome by the fact that most of the various provinces usually elected the same man as stadholder. The stadholder in most provinces was usually the head of the house of Orange, which since the days of William the Silent and the wars for independence had enjoyed exceptional prestige in the republic. The prince of Orange, apart from being stadholder, was simply one of the feudal noblemen of the country. But the noble class had been outdistanced by the commercial, and affairs were generally managed by the burghers. The burghers, intent on making money and enjoying comfort, rarely worried over military questions and hated taxes.

Politics in the Dutch Republic was a seesaw between the burghers, pacifistic and absorbed with business, and the princes of Orange, to whom the country owed most of its military security. When foreigners threatened invasion, the power of the stadholder increased. When all was calm, the stadholder could do little. The Peace of Westphalia produced a mood of confidence in the burghers, followed by a constitutional crisis, in the course of which the stadholder William II died, in 1650. No new stadholder was elected for twenty-two years. The burgher, civilian, and decentralizing tendencies prevailed.

In 1650, eight days after his father's death, was born the third William of the house of Orange, seemingly fated never to be stadholder and to pass his life as a private nobleman on his own estates. William III grew up to be a grave and reserved young man, small and rather stocky, with thin compressed lips and a determined spirit. He learned to speak Dutch, German, English, and French with equal facility, and to understand Italian, Spanish, and Latin. He observed the requirements of his religion, which was Dutch Calvinism, with sober regularity. He had a strong dislike, Dutch and Calvinistic, for everything magnificent or pompous; he lived plainly, hated flattery, and took no pleasure in social conversation. In these respects he was the opposite of his life-long enemy the Sun King, whom he resembled only in his diligent preoccupation with affairs. In 1677 he married the king of England's niece, Mary.

Foreign Affairs: Conflict with the English and French

Meanwhile matters were not going favorably for the Dutch Republic. In 1651 the revolutionary government then ruling England passed a Navigation Act. This act may be considered the first of a long series of political measures by which the British colonial empire was built up. It was aimed against the Dutch carrying trade. It provided that goods imported into England and its dependencies must be brought in English ships, or in ships belonging to the country exporting the goods.

Since the Dutch were too small a people to be great producers and exporters themselves, and lived largely by carrying the goods of others, they saw in the new English policy a threat to their economic existence. The English likewise, claiming sovereignty of the "narrow seas," demanded that Dutch ships salute the English flag in the Channel. Three wars between the Dutch and English followed, running with interruptions from 1652 to 1674 and generally indecisive, though the English annexed New York.

While thus assaulted at sea by the English, the Dutch were menaced on land by the French. Louis XIV made his first aggressive move in 1667, claiming the Spanish Netherlands and Franche-Comté by alleging certain rights of his Spanish wife, and overrunning the Spanish Netherlands with his army. The Dutch, to whom the Spanish Netherlands were a buffer against France, set into motion the mechanism of the balance of power. Dropping temporarily their disputes with the English, they allied with them instead; and since they were able also to secure the adherence of Sweden, the resulting Triple Alliance was sufficient to give pause to Louis XIV, who withdrew from the Spanish Netherlands. But in 1672 Louis XIV again rapidly crossed the Spanish Netherlands, attacked with forces five times as large as the Dutch, and occupied three of the seven Dutch provinces.

A popular clamor now arose among the Dutch for William of Orange, demanding that the young prince, who was now twenty-two years of age, be installed in the old office of stadholder, in which his ancestors had defended them against Spain. He was duly elected stadholder in six provinces. In 1673 these six provinces voted to make the stadholderate hereditary in the house of Orange. William, during his whole tenure or "reign" in the Netherlands, attempted to centralize and consolidate his government, put down the feudal liberties of the provinces, and free himself from constitutional checks, moving generally in the direction of absolute monarchy, which by the tests of power and under French example was the successful form of government at the time. He was unable, however, to go far in this course, and the United Provinces remained a decentralized patrician republic until 1795. Meanwhile, to stave off the immediate menace of Louis XIV, William resorted to a new manipulation of the balance of power. He formed an alliance this time with the minor powers of Denmark and Brandenburg (the German margraviate around Berlin) and with the Austrian and Spanish Habsburgs. Nothing could indicate more clearly the new balance of power precipitated by the rise of France than this coming over of the Dutch to the Habsburg side. The alliance was successful to the extent at least of wearying Louis XIV of the war. Peace was signed in 1678 (treaty of Nimwegen), but only at the expense of Spain and the Holy Roman Empire, from which Louis XIV took the long coveted Franche-Comté, together with another batch of towns in Flanders. The Dutch preserved their territory intact.

In the next ten years came the great windfall of William's life. In 1689 he became king of England. He was now able to bring the British Isles into his perpetual combinations against France. Since the real impact of France was yet to be felt, and the real bid of Louis XIV for universal monarchy was yet to be made, and since the English at this time were rapidly gaining in strength, the entrance of England was a decisive addition to the balance formed against French expansion. In this way the constitutional troubles of England, by bringing a determined Dutchman to the English throne, entered into the general stream of European affairs and helped to assure that western Europe and its overseas offshoots should not be dominated totally by France.

19. BRITAIN: THE PURITAN REVOLUTION

After the defeat of the Spanish Armada and recession of the Spanish threat the English were for a time less closely involved with the affairs of the Continent. They played no significant part in the Thirty Years' War, and were almost the only European people, west of Poland, who were not represented at the Congress of Westphalia. At the time of the Westphalia negotiations in the 1640s they were in fact engaged in a civil war of their own. This English civil war was a milder variant of the Wars of Religion which desolated France, Germany, and the Netherlands. It was fought not between Protestants and Catholics as on the Continent, but between the more extreme or Calvinistic Protestants called Puritans and the more moderate Protestants, or Anglicans, adhering to the established Church of England. As in the wars on the Continent, religious differences were mixed indistinguishably with political and constitutional issues. As the Huguenots represented to some extent feudal rebelliousness against the French monarchy, as German Protestants fought for states' rights against imperial centralization, and the Calvinists of the Netherlands for provincial liberties against the king of Spain, so the Puritans asserted the rights of Parliament against the mounting claims of royalty in England.

The civil war in England was relatively so mild that England itself can be said to have escaped the horrors of the Wars of Religion. The same was not true of the British Isles as a whole. After 1603 the kingdoms of England and Scotland, while otherwise separate, were ruled by the same king; the kingdom of Ireland remained, as before, a dependency of the English crown. Between England and Presbyterian Scotland there was constant friction, but the worst trouble was between England and Catholic Ireland, which was the scene of religious warfare as savage as that on the Continent.

England in the Seventeenth Century

For the English the seventeenth century was an age of great achievement, during which they made their debut as one of the chief peoples of modern Europe. In 1600 only four or five million persons, in England and Lowland Scotland, spoke the English language. The number did not rise rapidly for another century and a half. But the population began to spread. Religious discontents, reinforced by economic pressures, led to considerable emigration. Twenty thousand Puritans settled in New England between 1630 and 1640, and about the same number went to Barbados and other West India islands during the same years. A third stream, again roughly of the same size, but made up mainly of Scottish Presbyterians, settled in northern Ireland under government auspices, driving away or expropriating the native Celts. English Catholics were allowed by the home government to settle in Maryland. A great many Anglicans went to Virginia in the mid-century, adding to the small settlement made at Jamestown in 1607. Except for the movement to northern Ireland, called the "plantation of Ulster," these migrations took place without much attention on the part of the government, through private initiative organized in commercial companies. After the middle of the century the government began deliberately to build an empire. New York was conquered from the Dutch, Jamaica from the Spanish, and Pennsylvania and the Carolinas were established. All the Thirteen Colonies except Georgia were founded before 1700, and there were at that time perhaps half a million people in

British North America. Relative to the home population, it was as if the United States should in three generations build up a distant colonial appendage with fifteen million inhabitants.

The English also, like the Dutch, French, and Spanish at the time, were creating their national culture. Throughout western Europe the national languages, encroaching upon international Latin on the one hand and local dialects on the other, were becoming adequate vehicles for the expression of thought and feeling. Shakespeare and Milton projected their mighty conceptions with overwhelming power of words, not since equaled in English or in any other tongue. The English classical literature, rugged in form but deep in content, vigorous yet subtle in insight, majestic, abundant, and sonorous in expression, was almost the reverse of French classical writing, with its virtues of order, economy, propriety, and graceful precision. The English could never thereafter quite yield to French standards, nor be dazzled or dumbfounded, as some peoples were, by the cultural glories of the Age of Louis XIV. There were no painters at all comparable to those on the Continent, but in music it was the age of Campion and Purcell, and in architecture the century closed with the great buildings of Christopher Wren.

Economically the English were enterprising and affluent, though in 1600 far outdistanced by the Dutch. They had a larger and more productive country than the Dutch, and were therefore not as limited to purely mercantile and seafaring occupations. Coal was mined around Newcastle, and was increasingly used, but was not yet a leading source of English wealth. The great industry was the growing of sheep and manufacture of woolens, which were the main export. Weaving was done to a large extent in the country, under the putting-out system, and organized by merchants according to the methods of commercial capitalism.[4] Since 1553 the English had traded with Russia by way of the White Sea; they were increasingly active in the Baltic and eastern Mediterranean; and with the founding of the East India Company, in 1600, they competed with the Dutch in assaulting the old Portuguese monopoly in India and the Far East. But profitable as such overseas operations were, the main wealth of England was still in the land. The richest men were not merchants but landlords, and the landed aristocracy formed the richest class.

Background to the Civil War: Parliament and the Stuart Kings

In England, as elsewhere in the seventeenth century, the kings clashed with their old medieval representative bodies. In England the old body, Parliament, won out against the king. But this was not the unique feature in the English development. In Germany the estates of the Holy Roman Empire triumphed against the emperor, and much the same thing, as will be seen, occurred in Poland. But on the Continent the triumph of the old representative bodies generally meant political dissolution or even anarchy. Successful governments were generally those in which kingly powers increased; this was the strong tendency of the time, evident even in the Dutch Republic after 1672 under William of Orange. The unique thing about England was that Parliament, in defeating the king, arrived at a workable form of government. Government remained strong but came under parliamentary control. This determined the character of modern England and launched into

[4] See p. 115.

the history of Europe and of the world the great movement of liberalism and representative institutions.

What happened was somewhat as follows. In 1603, on the death of Queen Elizabeth, the English crown was inherited by the son of Mary Stuart, James VI of Scotland, who became king of England also, taking there the title of James I. James was a philosopher of royal absolutism. He had even written a book on the subject, *The True Law of Free Monarchy.* By a "free" monarchy James meant a monarchy free from control by Parliament, churchmen, or laws and customs of the past. It was a monarchy in which the king, as father to his people, looked after their welfare as he saw fit, standing above all parties, private interests, and pressure groups. He even declared that kings drew their authority from God, and were responsible to God alone. The doctrine which he represented is known as the divine right of kings.[5]

Probably any ruler succeeding Elizabeth would have had trouble with Parliament, which had shown signs of restlessness in the last years of her reign, but had deferred to her as an aging woman and a national symbol. She had maintained peace within the country and fought off the Spaniards, but these very accomplishments persuaded many people that they could safely bring their grievances into the open. James I was a foreigner, a Scot, who lacked the touch for dealing with the English, and who was moreover a royal pedant, the "wisest fool in Christendom," as he was uncharitably called. Not content with the actualities of control, as Elizabeth had been, he read the Parliament tiresome lectures on the royal rights. He also was in constant need of money. The wars against Spain had left a considerable debt. James was far from economical, and, in any case, in an age of rising prices, he could not live within the fixed and customary revenues of the English crown. These were of a medieval character, increasingly quaint under the new conditions—rights of wardship and marriage, escheats, franc-fiefs and fees for the distraint of knighthood, together with "tunnage and poundage," or rights given to the king by Parliament at his accession (and normally unchanged during his reign) to collect specified duties on exports and imports, according to quantity, not value, and hence not rising in proportion to prices.

Neither to James I nor to his son Charles I, who succeeded him in 1625, would Parliament grant adequate revenue, because it distrusted them both. Many members of Parliament were Puritans, dissatisfied with the organization and doctrine of the Church of England.[6] Elizabeth had tried to hush up religious troubles, but James threatened to "harry the Puritans out of the land," and Charles supported the Anglican hierarchy which, under Archbishop Laud, sought to enforce religious conformity. Many members of Parliament were also lawyers, who feared that the common law of England, the historic or customary law, was in danger. They disliked the prerogative courts, the Star Chamber set up by Henry VII, the High Commission set up by Elizabeth.[7] They heard with trepidation the modern doctrine that the sovereign king could make laws and decide cases at his own discretion.[8] Last but not least, practically all members of Parliament were property owners. Landowners, supported by the merchants, feared that if the king suc-

[5] See p. 180.
[6] See pp. 79–81.
[7] See pp. 68–69, 90.
[8] See p. 68.

ceeded in raising taxes on his own authority their wealth would be insecure. Hence there were strong grounds for resistance.

In England the Parliament was so organized as to make resistance effective.[9] There was only one Parliament for the whole country. There were no provincial or local estates, as in the Dutch Republic, Spain, France, Germany, and Poland. Hence all parliamentary opposition was concentrated in one place. In this one place, the one and only Parliament, there were only two houses, the House of Lords and the House of Commons. The landed interest dominated in both houses, the noblemen in the Lords and the gentry in the Commons. In the Commons the gentry, who formed the bulk of the aristocracy, mixed with representatives of the merchants and the towns. Indeed the towns frequently chose country gentlemen to represent them. Hence the houses of Parliament did not accentuate, as did the estates on the Continent, the class division within the country. Nor was the church present in Parliament as a separate force. Before Henry VIII's break with Rome the bishops and abbots together had formed a large majority in the House of Lords. Now there were no abbots left, for there were no monasteries. The House of Lords was now predominantly secular; in the first Parliament of James I there were eighty-two lay peers and twenty-six bishops. The great landowners had captured the House of Lords. The smaller landowners of the Commons had been enriched by receiving former monastic lands and had prospered by raising wool. The merchants had likewise grown up under mercantilistic protection. Parliament was strong not only in organization but in the social interests and wealth that it represented. No king could long govern against its will.

In 1629 king and Parliament came to a deadlock. Charles I attempted to rule without Parliament, which could legally meet only at the royal summons. He intended to give England a good and efficient government. Had he succeeded, the course of English constitutional development would have paralleled that of France. But by certain reforms in Ireland he antagonized the English landlords who had interests in that country. By supporting the High Anglicans he made enemies of the Puritans. By attempting to modernize the navy with funds raised without parliamentary consent (called "ship money") he alarmed all property owners, whose opposition was typified in the famous lawsuit of a country gentleman, John Hampden, in 1637.

The ship-money case illustrates the best arguments of both sides. It was the old custom in England for coastal towns to provide ships for the king's service in time of war. More recently, these coastal towns had provided money instead. Charles I wished to maintain a navy in time of peace and to have ship money paid by the country as a whole, including the inland counties. In the old or medieval view it was the function of the towns which were directly affected to maintain a fleet. In the new view, sponsored by the king, the whole nation was the unit on which a navy should be based. The country gentlemen whom Parliament mainly represented, and most of whom lived in inland counties, had less interest in the navy, and in any case were unwilling to pay for it unless they could control the foreign policies for which a navy might be used. The parliamentary class represented the idea, derived from the Middle Ages, that taxes should be authorized by Parliament. The king represented the newer ideas of monarchy that were developing on the Continent. John Hampden lost his case in court, but he won the sympathy of

[9] See pp. 35–36.

the politically significant classes of the country. Until the king could govern with the confidence of Parliament, or until Parliament itself was willing, not merely to keep down taxes, but to assume the responsibilities of government under modern conditions, neither a navy nor any effectual government could be maintained.

The Scots were the first to rebel. In 1637 they rioted in Edinburgh against attempts to impose the Anglican religion in Scotland. Charles, to raise funds to put down the Scottish rebellion, convoked the English Parliament in 1640, for the first time in eleven years. When it proved hostile to him he dissolved it and called for new elections. The same men were returned. The resulting body, since it sat theoretically for twenty years without new elections, from 1640 to 1660, is known historically as the Long Parliament. Its principal leaders—men like John Hampden, John Pym, and Oliver Cromwell—were small or moderately well-to-do landowning gentry. The merchant class, while furnishing no leaders, lent its support.

The Long Parliament, far from assisting the king against the Scots, used the Scottish rebellion as a means of pressing its own demands. These were revolutionary from the outset. Parliament insisted that the chief royal advisers be not merely removed but impeached and put to death. It abolished the Star Chamber and the High Commission. The most extreme Calvinist element, the "root and branch" men or "radicals," drove through a bill for the abolition of bishops, revolutionizing the Anglican church. In 1642 Parliament and king came to open war, the king drawing followers mainly from the north and west, the Parliament from the commercially and agriculturally more advanced counties of the south and east. During the war, as the price of support from the Scottish army, Parliament adopted the Solemn League and Covenant. This prescribed that religion in England, Scotland, and Ireland should be made uniform "according to the word of God and the example of the best reformed churches." Thus Presbyterianism became the established legal religion of the three kingdoms.

The Emergence of Cromwell

The parliamentary forces, called Roundheads from the close haircuts favored by Puritans, gradually defeated the royalists. The wars brought a hitherto unknown gentleman named Oliver Cromwell to the foreground. A devout Puritan, he organized a new and more effective military force, the Ironsides, in which extreme Protestant exaltation provided the basis for morale, discipline, and the will to fight. Parliament had no sooner defeated the king than it fell out with its own army. The army, in which a more popular class was represented than in the Parliament, became the center of advanced democratic ideas. Many of the soldiers objected to Presbyterianism as much as to Anglicanism. They favored a free toleration for all "godly" forms of religion, with no superior church organization above local groups of like-minded spirits.

Cromwell concluded that the defeated king, Charles I, could not be trusted, that "ungodly" persons of all kinds put their hopes in him (what later ages would call counterrevolution), and that he must be put to death. Since Parliament hesitated, Cromwell with the support of the army broke Parliament up. The Long Parliament, having started in 1640 with some 500 members, had sunk by 1649 to about 150 (for this revolution, like others, was pushed through by a minority); of these Cromwell now drove out almost 100, leaving a Rump of 50 or 60. This operation was called Pride's Purge, after the Colonel Pride who commanded the soldiers by whom Parliament was intimidated; and in subsequent revolutions such excisions have been commonly known as purges, and the residues, sometimes, as rumps. The Rump put King Charles to death on the scaffold in 1649.

England, or rather the whole British Isles, was now declared a republic. It was named the Commonwealth. Cromwell tried to govern as best he could. Religious toleration was decreed except for Unitarians and atheists on the one hand, and except for Roman Catholics and the most obstinate Anglicans on the other—a considerable exception. Cromwell had to subdue both Scotland and Ireland by force. In Scotland the execution of the king, violating the ancient national Scottish monarchy of the Stuarts, had swung the country back into the royalist camp. Cromwell crushed the Scots in 1650. Meanwhile the Protestant and Calvinist fury swept over Ireland. A massacre of newly settled Protestants in Ulster in 1641 had left bitter memories which were now avenged. The Irish garrisons of Drogheda and Wexford were defeated and massacred. Thousands of Catholics were killed; priests were put to the sword, and women and small children dispatched in cold blood. Where formerly, in the "plantation" of Ulster, a whole Protestant population had been settled in northern Ireland, bodily replacing the native Irish, now Protestant landlords were scattered over the country as a whole, replacing the Catholic landlords and retaining the Catholic peasantry as their tenants. What now happened in Ireland was a close parallel to what had happened thirty years before in Bohemia, except that Protestant and Catholic roles were reversed.[10] For the Irish, as for the Czechs, the native religion and clergy were driven underground, a foreign and detested church was established, and a new and foreign landed aristocracy, originally recruited in large measure from military adventurers, was settled upon the country, in which, as soon as it assured the payment of its rents, it soon ceased to reside.

In England itself Cromwell ruled with great difficulty. In external affairs his regime was successful enough, for he not only completed the subjugation of Ireland, but in the Navigation Act of 1651[11] he opened the English attack on the Dutch maritime supremacy, and in a war with Spain, in which the English acquired Jamaica, he opened the English bidding for the inheritance of the Spanish Habsburgs. But he failed to gain the support of a majority of the English. The Puritan Revolution, like others, produced its extremists. It failed to satisfy the most ardent and could not win over the truly conservative, so that Cromwell found himself reluctantly more autocratic, and more alone.

A party arose called the Levellers, who were in fact what later times would call advanced political democrats. They were numerous in the Puritan army, though their chief spokesman, John Lilburne, was a civilian. Appealing to natural rights and to the rights of Englishmen, they asked for a nearly universal manhood suffrage, equality of representation, a written constitution, and subordination of Parliament to a reformed body of voters. They thus anticipated many ideas of the American and French revolutions over a century later. There were others in whom religious and social radicalism were indistinguishably mixed. George Fox, going beyond Calvinism or Presbyterianism, founded the Society of Friends, or "Quakers," who caused consternation by rejecting various social amenities in the name of the Spirit. A more ephemeral group, the "Diggers," proceeded to occupy and cultivate common lands, or lands privately owned, in a general repudiation

[10] See pp. 139–140, 218.
[11] See pp. 163–164.

of property. The Fifth Monarchy Men were a millennial group who felt that the end of the world was at hand. They were so called from their belief, as they read the Bible, that history had seen four empires, those of Assyria, Persia, Alexander, and Caesar; and that the existing world was still "Caesar's" but would soon give way to the fifth monarchy, of Christ, in which justice would at last rule.

Cromwell opposed such movements, by which all established persons in society felt threatened. As a regicide and a Puritan, however, he could not turn to the royalist and Anglican interests. Unable to agree even with the Rump, he abolished it also in 1653, and thereafter vainly attempted to govern, as Lord Protector, through representative bodies devised by himself and his followers, under a written constitution, the Instrument of Government. Actually, he was driven to place England under military rule, the regime of the "major generals." These officials, each in his district, repressed malcontents, vagabonds, and "bandits," closed ale houses, and prohibited cockfighting, in a mixture of moral puritanism and political dictatorship. Cromwell died in 1658; and his son was unable to maintain the Protectorate. Two years later, with all but universal assent, royalty was restored. Charles II, son of the dead Charles I, became king of England and of Scotland.

Cromwell, by beheading a king and keeping his successor off the throne for eleven years, had left a lesson which was not forgotten. Though he favored constitutional and parliamentary government and had granted a measure of religious toleration, he had in fact ruled as a dictator in behalf of a stern Puritan minority. The English people now began to blot from their memories the fact that they had ever had a real revolution. The fervid dream of a "godly" England was dissipated forever. What was remembered was a nightmare of standing armies and major generals, of grim Puritans and overwrought religious enthusiasts. The English lower classes ceased to have any political consciousness for over a century, except in sporadic rioting over food shortages or outbursts against the dangers of "popery." Democratic ideas were generally rejected as "levelling." They were generally abandoned in England after 1660 or were cherished by obscure individuals who could not make themselves heard. Such ideas, indeed, had a more continuous history in the English colonies in America, where some leaders of the discredited revolution took refuge.

20. BRITAIN: THE TRIUMPH OF PARLIAMENT

The Restoration, 1660–1688: The Later Stuarts

What was restored in 1660 was not only the monarchy, in the person of Charles II, but also the Church of England and the Parliament. Everything, legally, was supposed to be as it had been in 1640. The difference was that Charles II, knowing the fate of his father, was careful not to provoke Parliament to extremes, and that the classes represented in Parliament, frightened by the disturbances of the past twenty years, were for some time more warmly loyal to the king than they had been before 1640 and more willing to uphold the established church.

Parliament during the Restoration enacted some far-reaching legislation. It changed the legal basis of land tenure, abolishing certain old feudal payments owed by landholders to the king. The possession of land thus came to resemble private property of modern type, and the landowning class became more definitely a propertied aristocracy. In place of the feudal dues to the king, which had been automatically payable, Parliament arranged for the king to receive income in the form of taxation, which Parliament could raise or reduce in amount. This gave a new power to Parliament and a new flexibility to government. The aristocracy, in short, cleared their property of customary restrictions and obligations and at the same time undertook to support the state by imposing taxes on themselves. The English aristocracy proved more willing than the corresponding classes on the Continent to pay a large share of the expenses of government. Its reward was that, for a century and a half, it virtually ran the government to the exclusion of everyone else. Landowners in this period directed not only national affairs through Parliament, but also local affairs as justices of the peace. The justices, drawn from the gentry of each county, decided small lawsuits, punished misdemeanors, and supervised the parish officials charged with poor relief and care of the roads. The regime of the landlord-justices came to be called the "squirearchy."

Other classes drew less immediate advantage from the Restoration. The Navigation Act of 1651 was renewed and even added to, so that commercial, shipping, and manufacturing interests were well protected. But in other ways the landed classes now in power showed themselves unsympathetic to the business classes of the towns. Many people in the towns were Dissenters, of the element formerly called Puritan, and now refusing to accept the restored Church of England. Parliament excluded Dissenters from the town "corporations," or governing bodies, forbade any dissenting clergymen to teach school or come within five miles of an incorporated town, and prohibited all religious meetings, called "conventicles," not held according to the forms and by the authority of the Church of England. The effect was that many middle-class townspeople found it difficult or impossible to follow their preferred religion, to obtain an education for their children, either elementary or advanced (for Oxford and Cambridge were a part of the established church), to take part in local affairs through the town corporations, or to sit in the House of Commons, since the corporations in many cases chose the burgesses who represented the towns. The lowest classes, the very poor, were discouraged by the same laws from following sectarian and visionary preachers. Another enactment fell upon them alone, the Act of Settlement of 1662, which decentralized the administration of the Poor Law, making each parish responsible only for its own paupers. Poor people, who were very numerous, were condemned to remain in the parishes where they lived. A large section of the English population was immobilized.

But it was not long after the Restoration that Parliament and king were again at odds. The issue was again religion. There was at this time a tendency throughout Europe for Protestants to return voluntarily to Roman Catholicism, a tendency naturally dreaded by the Protestant churches. It was most conspicuously illustrated when the daughter of Gustavus Adolphus himself, Queen Christina of Sweden, to the consternation of the Protestant world, abdicated her throne and was received into the Roman church. In England the national feeling was excitedly anti-Catholic. No measures were more popular than those against "popery"; and the squires in Parliament, stiffly loyal to the Church of England, dreaded papists even more than Dissenters. The king, Charles II, was personally inclined to Catholicism. He admired the magnificent monarchy of Louis XIV, which he would have liked to duplicate, so far as possible, in England. At odds with his Parliament,

Charles II made overtures to Louis XIV. The secret treaty of Dover of 1670 was the outcome. Charles thereby agreed to join Louis XIV in his expected war against the Dutch; and Louis agreed to pay the king of England three million livres a year during the war. He hoped also that Charles II would soon find it opportune to rejoin the Roman church.

While these arrangements were unknown in detail in England, it was known that Charles II was well disposed to the French and to Roman Catholicism. England went to war again with the Dutch. The king's brother and heir, James, Duke of York, publicly announced his conversion to Rome. Charles II, in a "declaration of indulgence," announced the nonenforcement of laws against Dissenters. The king declared that he favored general toleration, but it was rightly feared that his real aim was to promote Roman Catholicism in England, and that his policy might be the opening wedge for the Counter Reformation, which had already swept Protestantism out of Bohemia and Poland and was at this very moment menacing it in France. Parliament retorted in 1673 by passing the Test Act, which required all officeholders to take communion in the Church of England. The Test Act renewed the legislation against Dissenters and also made it impossible for Catholics to serve in the government or in the army and navy. The Test Act remained on the statute books until 1828.

While Charles' pro-French and pro-Catholic policies were extremely unpopular, both among the country gentry who disliked Frenchmen from prejudice, and the merchants who found in them increasingly pressing competitors, still the situation might not have come to a head except for the avowed Catholicism and French orientation of Charles' brother James, due to be the next king since Charles had no legitimate children. A strong movement developed in Parliament to exclude James by law from the throne. The exclusionists—and those generally who were most suspicious of the king, Catholics, and Frenchmen—received the nickname of Whigs. The king's supporters were popularly called Tories. The Whigs, while backed by the middle class and merchants of London, drew their main strength from the upper aristocracy, especially certain great noblemen who might expect, if the king's power were weakened, to play a prominent part in ruling the country themselves. The Tories were the party of the lesser aristocracy and gentry, those who were suspicious of the "moneyed interest" of London, and felt a strong loyalty to church and king. These two parties became permanently established in English public life. But all the Whigs and Tories together, at this time, did not number more than a few thousand persons.

The Revolution of 1688

James II, despite Whig vexation, became king in 1685. He soon antagonized even the Tories. The Tories were strong Anglicans or Church of England men. As landowners they appointed most of the parish clergy, who imparted Tory sentiments to the rural population, and from their ranks were drawn the bishops, archdeacons, university functionaries, and other higher personnel of the church. The laws keeping Dissenters and Catholics from office had given Anglicans a monopoly in local and national government and in the army and navy. James II acted as if there were no Test Act, claiming the right to suspend its operation in individual cases, and appointed a good many Catholics to influential and lucrative positions. He offered a program, as his brother had done, of general religious toleration, to allow Protestant Dissenters as well as Roman Catholics to participate in public life. Such a program, whether frankly meant as a secularizing of politics or indirectly intended as favoritism to Catholics, was equally repugnant to the Church of England. Seven bishops refused to endorse it. They were prosecuted for disobedience to the king but were acquitted by the jury. James, by these actions, violated the liberties of the established church, threatened the Anglican monopoly of church and state, and aroused the popular terrors of "popery." He was also forced to take the position philosophically set forth by his grandfather James I, that a king of England could make and unmake the law by his own will. The Tories joined the Whigs in opposition. In 1688, a son was born to James II and baptized into the Catholic faith. The prospect now opened up of an indefinite line of Catholic rulers in England. Leading men of both parties thereupon abandoned James II. They offered the throne to his grown daughter Mary, born and brought up a Protestant before her father's conversion to Rome.

Mary was the wife of William of Orange. William, it will be recalled, had spent his adult life in blocking the ambitions of the king of France, who, it should be recalled likewise, threatened Europe with a "universal monarchy" by absorbing or inheriting the world of Spain. To William III it would be a mere distraction to be husband to a queen of England, or even to be king in his own name, unless England could be brought to serve his own purposes. He was immutably Dutch; his purpose was to save Holland and hence to ruin Louis XIV. His chief interest in England was to bring the English into his balance of power against France. Since the English were generally anti-French, and had chafed under the pro-French tendencies of their kings, William without difficulty reached an understanding with the discontented Whigs and Tories. Protected by a written invitation from prominent Englishmen, he invaded England with a considerable army. James II fled, and William was proclaimed co-ruler with Mary over England and Scotland. In the next year, 1690, at the Boyne River in Ireland, a motley army of Dutchmen, Germans, Scots, and French Huguenots under William III defeated a French and Irish force led by James II. Thus the liberties of England were saved. James II fled to France.

Louis XIV of course refused to recognize his inveterate enemy as ruler of England. He maintained James at the French court with all the honors due the English king. It was thereafter one of his principal war aims to restore the Catholic and Stuart dynasty across the Channel. The English, contrariwise, had added reason to fight the French. French victory would mean counterrevolution and royal absolutism in England. The whole Revolution of 1688 was at stake in the French wars.

In 1689, Parliament enacted a Bill of Rights, stipulating that no law could be suspended by the king (as the Test Act had been), no taxes raised or army maintained except by parliamentary consent, and no subject (however poor) arrested and detained without legal process. William III accepted these articles as conditions to receiving the crown. Thereafter the relation between king and people was a kind of contract. It was further provided, by the Act of Settlement of 1701, that no Catholic could be king of England; this excluded the descendants of James II, known in the following century as the Pretenders. Parliament also passed the Toleration Act of 1689, which allowed Protestant Dissenters to practice their religion but still excluded them from political life and public service. Since ways of evading these restrictions were soon found, and since even Catholics were not molested unless they supported the Pretenders, there was thereafter no serious trouble over religion in England and Lowland Scotland.

The English Parliament could make no laws for Scotland, and it was to be feared that James II might some day be restored in his northern kingdom. The securing of the parliamentary revolution in England, and of the island's defenses against France, required that the two kingdoms be organically joined. There was little sentiment in Scotland, however, for a merger with the English. The English tempted the Scots with economic advantages. The Scots still had no rights in the English East India Company, nor in the English colonies, nor within the English system of mercantilism and Navigation Acts. They obtained such rights by consenting to a union. In 1707 the United Kingdom of Great Britain was created. The Scots retained their own legal system and established Presbyterian church, but their government and parliament were merged with those of England. The term "British" came into use to refer to both English and Scots.

As for Ireland, it was now feared as a center of Stuart and French intrigue. The Revolution of 1688 marked the climax of a long record of trouble. Ireland had never been simply "conquered" by England, though certain English or rather Anglo-Norman families had carved out estates there since the twelfth century. By the end of the Middle Ages Ireland was organized as a separate kingdom with its own parliament, subordinate to the English crown. During the Reformation the Irish remained Catholic while England turned Protestant, but the monasteries were dissolved in Ireland as in England; and the organized church as such, the established Church of Ireland, with its apparatus of bishoprics, parishes, and tithes, became an Anglican communion in which the mass of native Irish had no interest. Next came the plantation of Ulster, already mentioned, in which a mass of newcomers, mainly Scottish and Presbyterian, settled in the northern part of the island.[12] Then in Cromwell's time, as just seen, English landlords spread through the rest of the country; or rather, a new Anglo-Irish upper class developed, in which English landowning families, residing most often in England, added the income from Irish estates to their miscellaneous revenues. Ireland therefore by the close of the seventeenth century was a very mixed country. Probably two-thirds of its population was Catholic, of generally Celtic ethnic background; perhaps a fifth was Presbyterian, with recent Scottish connections; the small remainder was made up of Anglicans, largely Anglo-Irish of recent or distant origin in England, who controlled most of the land, manned the official church, and were influential in the Irish parliament. It was essentially a landlord and peasant society, in which the Presbyterian as well as the Catholic mass was overwhelmingly agricultural; towns were small, and the middle class scarcely developed.

After the Revolution of 1688, in which the final overthrow of James II took place at the Boyne River, the English feared Ireland as a source of danger to the postrevolutionary arrangements in England. Resistance of the subjugated Catholics had also to be prevented. Hence to the burden of an alien church and absentee landlordism was now added the "penal code." Catholic clergy were banished, and Catholics were forbidden to vote or to sit in the Irish parliament. Catholic teachers were forbidden to teach, and Catholic parents were forbidden to send children overseas to be educated in Catholic schools. No Catholic could take a

[12] See pp. 83, 165, 170.

degree from Dublin University. Catholic Irishmen were forbidden to purchase land, to lease it for more than thirty-one years, to inherit it from a Protestant, or to own a horse worth more than £5. A Catholic whose son turned Protestant found his own property rights limited in his son's favor. Catholics were forbidden to be attorneys, to serve as constables, or, in most trades, to have more than two apprentices. Some disabilities fell on the Protestant Irish also. Thus Irish shipping was excluded from the British colonies, nor could the Irish import colonial goods except through England. Export of Irish woolens and glass manufactures was prohibited. No import tariff on English manufactures could be levied by the Irish parliament. About all that was left to the Irish, in international trade, was the export of agricultural produce; and the foreign exchange acquired in this way went very largely to pay the rents of absentee landlords.

The purpose of the penal code was in part strategic, to weaken Ireland as a potentially hostile country during a long period of wars with France. In part it was commercial, to favor English manufactures by removing Irish competition. And in part it was social, to confirm the position of the Anglican interest, or "ascendancy" as it came to be called. Parts of the code were removed piecemeal in the following decades, and a Catholic merchant class grew up in the eighteenth century; but much remained in effect for a long time, so that, for example, a Catholic could not vote for members of the Irish parliament until 1793, and even then could not be elected to it. In general, the Irish emerged from the seventeenth century as the most repressed people of western Europe.

England, immediately after the expulsion of James II, joined William III's coalition against France. To the alliance England brought a highly competent naval force, together with very considerable wealth. William's government, to finance the war, borrowed £1,200,000 from a syndicate of private lenders, who in return for holding government bonds were given the privilege of operating a bank. Thus originated, in 1694, both the Bank of England and the British national debt. Owners of liquid assets, merchants of London and Whig aristocrats with fat rent rolls, having lent their money to the new regime, had a compelling reason to defend it against the French and James II. And having at last a government whose policies they could control, they were willing to entrust it with money in large amounts. The national debt rapidly rose, while the credit of the government held consistently good; and for many years the Continent was astonished at the wealth that the British government could tap at will, and the quantities of money that it could pour into the wars of Europe.

The events of 1688 came to be known to the English as the Glorious Revolution. The Revolution was considered to have vindicated the principles of parliamentary government, the rule of law, and even the right of rebellion against tyranny. It has often been depicted as the climax in the growth of English constitutional self-government. Political writers like John Locke, shortly after the events, helped to give wide currency to these ideas.[13] There was in truth some justification for these views even though in more recent times some writers have "deglorified" the Revolution of 1688. They point out that it was a class movement, promoted and maintained by the landed aristocracy. The Parliament which boldly asserted itself against the king was at the same time closing itself to large segments of the people. Where in the Middle Ages members of the House of Commons had usually

---

[13] On John Locke and the philosophy of the Glorious Revolution see pp. 299–301.

received pay for their services, this custom disappeared in the seventeenth century, so that thereafter only men with independent incomes could sit. After the parliamentary triumph of 1688 this tendency became a matter of law. An act of 1710 required members of the House of Commons to possess private incomes at such a level that only a few thousand persons could legally qualify. This income had to come from the ownership of land. England from 1688 to 1832 was the best example in modern times of a true aristocracy, i.e., of a country in which the aristocratic landowning class not only enjoyed privileges but also conducted the government. But the landowning interest was then the only class sufficiently wealthy, numerous, educated, and self-conscious to stand on its own feet. The rule of the "gentlemen of England" was within its limits a regime of political liberty.

21. THE FRANCE OF LOUIS XIV, 1643–1715: THE TRIUMPH OF ABSOLUTISM

French Civilization in the Seventeenth Century

Having traveled in the outer orbits of the European political system, we come now to its radiant and mighty center, the domain of the Sun King himself, the France against which the rest of Europe felt obliged to combine, and on whose push and pull depended the course of the lesser bodies—the future of the Spanish possessions, the independence of Holland, the maintenance in England of the parliamentary revolution. The France of Louis XIV owed much of its ascendancy to the quantity and quality of its people. Population was stabilized or possibly even falling in the seventeenth century, the last century in which France was seriously disturbed by famine, pestilence, and peasant rebellion. With 19 million inhabitants in 1700 France was still over three times as populous as England and twice as populous as Spain. Its fertile soil, in an agricultural age, made it a wealthy country, though the wealth was very unevenly distributed. France was big enough to harbor many contradictions. Millions of its people lived in poverty, yet the number in comfortable or even luxurious circumstances was very large. There were both modest country nobles and cosmopolitan *grands seigneurs*. The middle class included an inordinate number of lawyers, officeholders, and bureaucrats, and the country was less commercial than Holland or England, yet in sheer numbers there may have been more merchants in France than in either of the other two countries. Protestants were a declining minority, yet in the mid-seventeenth century there were still more French Huguenots than Dutch Calvinists. It was a self-sufficient country, yet the French in this century began trading in India and Madagascar, founded Canada, penetrated the Great Lakes and the Mississippi valley, set up plantations in the West Indies, expanded their ancient commerce with the Levant, enlarged their mercantile marine, and for a time had the leading navy of Europe.

The dominance of France meant the dominance not merely of power, but of a people generally admitted to be in the forefront of civilization. They carried over the versatility of the Italy of the Renaissance. In Poussin and Claude Lorrain they produced a notable school of painters, their architecture was emulated throughout Europe, and they excelled in military fortification and general engineering. Much of their literature, though often written by bourgeois writers, was designed for an aristocratic and courtly audience, which had put aside the uncouth manners of an earlier day and prided itself on the refinement of its tastes and perceptions. Corneille and Racine wrote austere tragedies on the fundamental situations of human life. Molière, in his comedies, ridiculed bumbling doctors, new-rich bourgeois, and foppish aristocrats, making the word "marquis" almost a joke in the French language. La Fontaine gave the world his animal fables, and La Rochefoucauld, in his witty and sardonic maxims, a great nobleman's candid judgment on human nature. In Descartes the French produced a great mathematician and scientific thinker, in Pascal a scientist who was also a profound spokesman for Christianity, in Bayle the father of modern skeptics. It was French thought and the French language, not merely the armies of Louis XIV, which in the seventeenth century were sweeping the European world.

The Development of Absolutism in France

This ascendancy of French culture went along with a regime in which political liberties were at a discount. It was an embellishment to the absolute monarchy of Louis XIV. France had a tradition of political freedom in the feudal sense. It had the same kind of background of feudal liberties as did the other countries of Europe. It had an Estates General, which had not met since 1615 but was not legally abolished. In some regions Provincial Estates, still meeting frequently, retained a measure of self-government and of power over taxation. There were about a dozen bodies known as parlements,[14] which, unlike the English Parliament, had developed as courts of law, each being the supreme court for a certain area of the country. The parlements upheld certain "fundamental laws" which they said the king could not overstep, and they often refused to enforce royal edicts which they declared to be unconstitutional. We have already observed how France, beneath the surface, was almost as composite as Germany.[15] French towns had won charters of acknowledged rights, and many of the great provinces enjoyed liberties written into old agreements with the crown. These local liberties were the main reason for a good deal of institutional complication. There were some 300 "customs" or regional systems of law; it was observed that a traveler sometimes changed laws more often than he changed horses. Internal tariffs ran along the old provincial borders. Tolls were levied by manorial lords. The king's taxes fell less heavily on some regions than on others. Neither coinage nor weights and measures were uniform throughout the country. France was a bundle of territories held together by allegiance to the king.

This older kind of freedom discredited itself in France at the very time when by triumphing in Germany it pulled the Holy Roman Empire to pieces, and when in England it successfully made the transition to a more modern form of political liberty, embodied in the parliamentary though aristocratic state. In France the old medieval, feudal, or local type of liberty became associated with disorder. It has already been related how after the disorders of the sixteenth-century religious wars people had turned with relief to the monarchy and how Henry IV and then Richelieu had begun to make the monarchy strong.[16] The troubles of the Fronde provided additional incentive for absolutism in France.

---

[14] Spelled *parlements* in French, to distinguish from the English Parliament.
[15] See p. 132 and map, p. 183.
[16] See pp. 135–137.

The Fronde broke out immediately after the Peace of Westphalia, while Louis XIV was still a child, and was directed against Cardinal Mazarin, who was governing in his name. It was an abortive revolution, led by the same elements, the parlements and the nobility, which were to precipitate the great French Revolution in 1789. The parlements, especially the Parlement of Paris, insisted in 1648 on their right to pronounce certain edicts unconstitutional. Barricades were thrown up and street fighting broke out in Paris. The nobility rebelled, as it had often in the past. Leadership was assumed by certain prominent noblemen who, roughly like the great Whigs of England, had enough wealth and influence to believe that, if the king's power were kept down, they might govern the country themselves. The nobility demanded a calling of the Estates General, expecting to dominate over the bourgeoisie and the clergy in that body. Armed bands of soldiers, unemployed since the Peace of Westphalia and led by nobles, roamed about the country terrorizing the peasants. If the nobles had their way, it was probable that the manorial system would fall on the peasants more heavily, as in eastern Europe, where triumphant lords were at this very time exacting increased labor services from the peasants. Finally the rebellious nobles called in Spanish troops, though France was at war with Spain. By this time the bourgeoisie, represented in the parlements, had withdrawn support from the rebellious nobles. The agitation subsided in total failure, because bourgeoisie and aristocracy could not work together, because the nobles outraged the loyalty of many Frenchmen by joining with a power with which France was at war, and because the *frondeurs*, especially after the parlements deserted them, had no systematic or constructive program, aiming only at the overthrow of the unpopular Cardinal Mazarin and at obtaining offices and favors for themselves.

After the Fronde, as after the religious wars, the bourgeoisie and peasantry of France, to protect themselves against the claims of the aristocracy, were in a mood to welcome the exercise of strong power by the kings. And in the young Louis XIV they had a man more than willing to grasp all the power he could get. Louis, on Mazarin's death in 1661, announced that he would govern the country himself. He was the third king of the Bourbon line. It was the Bourbon tradition, established by Henry IV and by Richelieu, to draw the teeth from the feudal aristocrats, and this tradition Louis XIV followed. He was not a man of any transcendent abilities, though he had the capacity, often found among successful executives, of learning a good deal from conversation with experts. His education was not very good, having been made purposely easy; but he had the ability to see and stick to definite lines of policy, and he was extremely methodical and industrious in his daily habits, scrupulously loading himself with administrative business throughout his reign. He was extremely fond of himself and his position of kingship, with an insatiable appetite for admiration and flattery; he loved magnificent display and elaborate etiquette, though to some extent he simply adopted them as instruments of policy rather than as a personal whim.

With the reign of Louis XIV the "state" in its modern form took a long step forward. The state in the abstract has always seemed theoretical to the English-speaking world. Let us say, for simplicity, that the state represents a fusion of justice and power. A sovereign state possesses, within its territory, a monopoly over the administration of justice and the use of force. Private persons neither pass legal judgments on others nor control private armies of their own. For private and unauthorized persons to do so, in an orderly state, constitutes rebellion. This was in contrast to the older feudal practice, by which feudal lords maintained manorial courts and led their own followers into battle. Against these feudal practices Louis XIV energetically worked, though not with complete success, claiming to possess in his own person, as sovereign ruler, a monopoly over the lawmaking processes and the armed forces of the kingdom. This is the deeper meaning of his reputed boast, *L'état, c'est moi*—"the state is myself." In the France of the seventeenth century, divided by classes and by regions, there was in fact no means of consolidating the powers of state except in a single man.

The state, however, while representing law and order within its borders, has generally stood in a lawless and disorderly relation to other states, since no higher monopoly of law and force has existed. Louis XIV, personifying the French state, had no particular regard for the claims of other states or rulers. He was constantly either at war or preparing for war with his neighbors. The modern state, indeed, was created by the needs of peace at home and war abroad. Machinery of government, as devised by Louis XIV and others, was a means of giving order and security within the territory of the state, and of raising, supporting, and controlling armies for use against other states.

The idea that law and force within a country should be monopolized by the lawful king was the essence of the seventeenth-century doctrine of absolutism. Its principal theorist in the time of Louis XIV was Bishop Bossuet. Bossuet advanced the old Christian teaching that all power comes from God, and that all who hold power are responsible to God for the way they use it. He held that kings were God's representatives in the political affairs of earth. Royal power, according to Bossuet, was absolute but not arbitrary: not arbitrary because it must be reasonable and just, like the will of God which it reflected; absolute in that it was free from dictation by parlements, estates, or other subordinate elements within the country. Law, therefore, was the will of the sovereign king, so long as it conformed to the higher law which was the will of God. This doctrine, affirming the divine right of kings, was popularly held in France at the time and was taught in the churches. "Absolutism" and "absolute monarchy" became the prevailing forms of government on the European continent in the seventeenth and eighteenth centuries. It must be remembered, however, that these terms, if not historians' clichés, referred more to legal principle than to facts. A ruler was "absolute" because he was not legally bound by any other persons or institutions in the country. In reality he became dependent upon a host of advisers and bureaucrats, he often had to compromise with vested interests, and he could be thwarted by the sheer weight of local custom, or meet resistance from lawyers, ecclesiastics, nobles, grandees, hereditary officeholders, and miscellaneous dignitaries.

Government and Administration

Possibly the most fundamental step taken by Louis XIV was to assure himself of control of the army. Armed forces had formerly been almost a private enterprise. Specialists in fighting, leading their own troops, worked for governments more or less as they chose, either in return for money or to pursue political aims of their own. This was especially common in central Europe, but even in France great noblemen had strong private influence over the troops, and in times of disorder nobles led armed retainers about the country. Colonels were virtually on their own. Provided with a general commission and with funds by some government, they recruited, trained, and equipped their own regiments, and likewise fed and supplied them, often by preying upon bourgeois and peasants in the vicinity. In these circumstances it was often difficult to say on whose side soldiers were fighting. It was hard for governments to set armies into motion and equally hard to make them stop fighting, for commanders fought for their own interests and on their own momentum. War was not a "continuation of policy"; it was not an act of the state; it easily degenerated, as in the Thirty Years' War, into a kind of aimless and perpetual violence.

Louis XIV made war an activity of state. He saw to it that all armed persons in France fought only for him. This produced peace and order in France, while strengthening the fighting power of France against other states. Under the older conditions there was also little integration among different units and arms of the army. Infantry regiments and troops of horse went largely their own way, and the artillery was supplied by civilian technicians under contract. Louis XIV created a stronger unity of control, put the artillery organically into the army, systematized the military ranks and grades, and clarified the chain of command, placing himself at the top. The government supervised recruiting, required colonels to prove that they were maintaining the proper number of soldiers, and assumed most of the responsibility for equipping, provisioning, clothing, and housing the troops. Higher officers, thus becoming dependent on the government, could be subjected to discipline. The soldiers were put into uniforms, taught to march in step, and housed in barracks; thus they too became more susceptible to discipline and control. Armed forces became less of a terror to their own people and a more effective weapon in the hands of government. They were employed usually against other governments but sometimes to suppress rebellion at home. Louis XIV also increased the French army in size, raising it from about 100,000 to about 400,000. These changes, both in size and in degree of government control, were made possible by the growth of a large civilian administration. The heads of this administration under Louis XIV were civilians. They were in effect the first ministers of war, and their assistants, officials, inspectors, and clerks constituted the first organized war ministry.

Louis XIV was not only a vain man, but made it a political principle to overawe the country with his own grandeur. He built himself a whole new city at the old village of Versailles about ten miles from Paris. Where the Escorial had the atmosphere of a monastery, Versailles was a monument to worldly splendor. Tremendous in size alone, fitted out with polished mirrors, gleaming chandeliers, and magnificent tapestries, opening on to a formal park with fountains and shaded walks, the palace of Versailles was the marvel of Europe and the envy of lesser kings. It was virtually a public building, much of it used for government offices, and with nobles, churchmen, notable bourgeois, and servants milling about on the king's affairs. The more exclusive honors of the château were reserved for the higher aristocrats. The king surrounded his daily routine of rising, eating, and going to bed (known as the *lever, dîner,* and *coucher*) with an infinite series of ceremonial acts, so minute and so formalized that there were, for example, six different entries of persons at the *lever,* and a certain gentleman at a specified moment held the right sleeve of the king's nightshirt as he took it off. The most exalted persons thought themselves the greater for thus waiting on so august a being. In this way, and by more material favors, many great lords were induced to live habitually at court. Here, under the royal eye, they might engage in palace intrigue but were kept away from real political mischief. Versailles had a debilitating effect on the French aristocracy. The king himself was one of the few who could proceed through such rounds of elaborate living and still be able to attend regularly to public affairs. Neither the nobles whom he kept about him nor his own successors, Louis XV and Louis XVI, were able to carry the burden.

For positions in the government, as distinguished from his personal entourage, Louis XIV preferred to use men whose upper-class status was recent. Such men, unlike the greatest nobles, could aspire to no independent political influence of their own. He never called the Estates General, which in any case no one except some of the nobility wanted. Some of the Provincial Estates, because of local and aristocratic pressures, he allowed to remain functioning. He temporarily destroyed the independence of the parlements, commanding them to accept his orders, as Henry IV had commanded them to accept the Edict of Nantes.[17] He stifled the old liberties of the towns, turning their civic offices into empty and purchasable honors and likewise regulating the operation of the guilds. He developed a strong system of administrative coordination, centering in a number of councils of state, which he attended in person, and in "intendants" who represented these councils throughout the country. Councilors of state and intendants were generally of bourgeois origin or newly ennobled. Each intendant, within his district, embodied all aspects of the royal government, supervising the flow of taxes and recruiting of soldiers, keeping an eye on the local nobility, dealing with towns and guilds, controlling the more or less hereditary officeholders, stamping out bandits, smugglers, and wolves, policing the marketplaces, relieving famine, watching the local law courts, and often deciding cases himself. In this way a firm and uniform administration was superimposed upon the heterogeneous mass of the old France. In contrast to England, all local questions were handled by agents of the central government, usually honest and often efficient, but essentially bureaucrats constantly instructed by, and referring back to, their superiors at Versailles.

Economic and Financial Policies: Colbert

To support the reorganized and enlarged army, the panoply of Versailles, and the growing civil administration, the king needed a good deal of money. Finance was always the weak spot in the French monarchy. Methods of collecting taxes were costly and inefficient. Direct taxes passed through the hands of many intermediate officials; indirect taxes were collected by private concessionaries called tax farmers, who made a substantial profit. The state always received far less than what the taxpayers actually paid. But the main weakness arose from an old bargain between the French crown and nobility; the king might raise taxes without consent if only he refrained from taxing the nobles. Only the "unprivileged" classes paid direct taxes, and these came almost to mean the peasants only, since many bourgeois in one way or another obtained exemptions. The system was outrageously unjust in throwing the tax burden on the poor and helpless. It was ruinous to the government, since the government could never raise enough money, however hard it taxed the poor, being unable to tap the real source of ready wealth, namely, the wealthier people. It was ruinous also to the French nobility,

[17] See pp. 135–136.

who in paying no direct taxes lost their hold over the government, lacked incentive to interest themselves in public affairs, and were unable to assume leadership of the bulk of the population. Louis XIV was willing enough to tax the nobles but was unwilling to fall under their control, and only toward the close of his reign, under extreme stress of war, was he able, for the first time in French history, to impose direct taxes on the aristocratic elements of the population. This was a great step toward equality before the law and toward sound public finance, but so many concessions and exemptions were won by nobles and bourgeois that the reform lost much of its value.

Like his predecessors, Louis resorted to all manner of expedients to increase his revenues. He raised the tax rates, always with disappointing results. He devalued the currency. He sold patents of nobility to ambitious bourgeois. He sold government offices, judgeships, and commissions in the army and navy. For both financial and political reasons the king used his sovereign authority to annul the town charters, then sell back reduced rights at a price; this produced a little income but demoralized local government and civic spirit. The need for money, arising from the fundamental inability to tax the wealthy, which in turn reflected the weakness of absolutism, of a government which would not or could not share its rule with the propertied classes, corrupted much of the public life and political aptitude of the French people.

Louis XIV wished, if only for his own purposes, to make France economically powerful. His great minister Colbert worked for twenty years to do so. Colbert went beyond Richelieu in the application of mercantilism, aiming to make

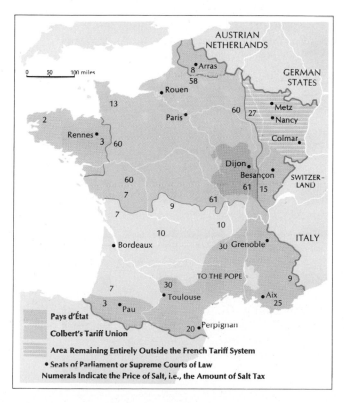

0   50   100 miles

AUSTRIAN
NETHERLANDS

• Arras
8
58

Rouen •

13

GERMAN
STATES

60   27

• Metz

• Nancy

Paris •

2

Rennes •
3
60

Colmar •

Dijon •
Besançon •
61   15

SWITZER-
LAND

60

7

61

9

7

10

10

• Bordeaux

30   Grenoble •

ITALY

TO THE POPE

9

7

30

3   • Pau

• Toulouse

• Aix
25

20 • Perpignan

Pays d'État

Colbert's Tariff Union

Area Remaining Entirely Outside the French Tariff System

• Seats of Parliament or Supreme Courts of Law

Numerals Indicate the Price of Salt, i.e., the Amount of Salt Tax

FRANCE FROM THE LAST YEARS OF LOUIS XIV TO THE REVOLUTION OF 1789

The map gives an idea of the diversity of law and administration before the Revolution. Dark areas are "pays d'état," provinces in which representative bodies ("estates") continued to meet. Cities named are the seats of what the French called parliaments (see p. 178). The key indicates Colbert's tariff union, the Five Great Farms (see p. 184). The area marked with hatching remained outside the French tariff system entirely; it continued to trade with the states of the Holy Roman Empire (from which it had been annexed) without interference by the French government. Numerals indicate the price of salt, i.e., the amount of the salt tax, in various regions. In general, it will be seen that regions farthest from Paris enjoyed the most "privileges" or "liberties," preserving their legal and judicial identity, Provincial Estates, local tariffs, and a favored position in national taxation.

France a self-sufficing economic unit and to increase the wealth from which taxes were drawn.[18] He managed to abolish local tariffs in a large part of central France, where he set up a tariff union oddly entitled the Five Great Farms (since the remaining tolls were collected by tax farmers); and although vested interests and provincial liberties remained too strong for him to do away with all internal tariffs, the area of the Five Great Farms was in itself one of the largest free-trade areas in Europe, being about the size of England. For the convenience of businessmen Colbert promulgated a Commercial Code, replacing much of the local customary law, and long a model of business practice and business regulation. He improved communications by building roads and canals, of which the most famous was one joining the Bay of Biscay with the Mediterranean. Working through the guilds, he required the handicraft manufacturers to produce goods of specified kind and quality, believing that foreigners, if assured of quality by the government, would purchase French products more freely. He gave subsidies, tax exemptions, and other privileges to expand the manufacture of silks, tapestries, glassware, and woolens. He helped to found colonies, built up the navy, and established the French East India Company. Export of some goods, notably food-stuffs, was forbidden, for the government wished to keep the populace quiet by holding down the price of bread. Export of other goods, mainly manufactures, was encouraged, partly as a means of bringing money into the country, where it could be funneled into the royal treasury. The growth of the army, and the fact that under Louis XIV the government clothed and equipped the soldiers, and hence placed unprecedentedly large orders for uniforms, overcoats, weapons, and ammunition, greatly stimulated the employment of weavers, tailors, and gun-smiths and advanced the commercial capitalism by which such labors were organized. In general, trade and manufacture developed in France under more direct government guidance than in England. They long gave the English an extremely brisk competition. Not until the age of iron and coal did France begin economically to lag.

Religion: The Revocation of the Edict of Nantes, 1685

The consolidation of France under Louis XIV reached its high point in his policies toward religion. Toward Rome Louis backed the old claims of the Gallican church to enjoy a certain national independence of policy. He repressed the movement known as Jansenism, a kind of Calvinism within the Catholic church, which persisted for almost two centuries. But it was the Protestants who suffered most.

France, in the early years of Louis XIV's reign, still allowed more religious toleration than any other large state in Europe. The Huguenots had lost their separate political status under Richelieu, but they continued to live in relative security and contentment, protected by the Edict of Nantes of 1598.[19] From the beginning, however, toleration had been a royal rather than a popular policy, and under Louis XIV the royal policy changed. The fate of Catholics at the hands of a triumphant Parliament in England suggests that the Protestants in France would have been no better off under more popular institutions.

Bending all else to his will, Louis XIV resented the presence of heretics among his subjects. He considered religious unity necessary to the strength and dignity of

[18] On mercantilism in general, see pp. 116–118.
[19] See pp. 135–137.

his rule. He perhaps envied the right claimed by most governments at the time, Protestant as well as Catholic, to determine the religion of their respective peoples. He fell under the influence of certain Catholic advisers, who, not content with the attrition by which some Protestants were turning back to Catholicism in any case, wished to hasten the process to the greater glory of themselves. Systematic conversion of Huguenots was begun. Life for Protestant families was gradually made unbearable. Finally they were literally "dragooned," mounted infantrymen being quartered in Huguenot homes to reinforce the persuasions of missionaries. In 1685 Louis revoked the Edict of Nantes. During the persecutions a good many Protestants left France, migrating to Holland, Germany, and America. Their loss was a blow to French economic life, for although Protestants were found in all levels of French society, those of the commercial and industrial classes were the most mobile. With the revocation of the Edict of Nantes France embarked on a century of official intolerance (slowly mitigated in practice), under which Protestants in France were in much the same position as Catholics in the British Isles. The fact that a hundred years later, when Protestants were again tolerated, many of them were found to be both commercially prosperous and politically loyal indicates that they fared far better than the Catholic Irish.

All things considered, the reign of Louis XIV brought considerable advantages to the French middle and lower classes. His most bitter critics, with the natural exception of Protestants, were disgruntled nobles such as the duke of Saint-Simon, who thought that he showed too many favors to persons of inferior social rank. Since Protestants were an unpopular minority, his repression of them won much approval. Colbert's system of economic regulation, and perpetuation of the guilds, meant that innovation and private enterprise developed less fully than in England, but France was economically stronger in 1700 than in 1650. Peasants were heavily taxed, but they did not sink into the serfdom that was rising in eastern Europe. Compared to later times, France was still a hodgepodge of competing jurisdictions, special privilege, and bureaucratic ineptitude. The king was in truth far from "absolute," but France was nevertheless the best organized of the large monarchies on the Continent. Louis XIV, in turning both high and low into dutiful subjects, put an end to civil war and even advanced the cause of civil equality. For a long time he was generally popular. What finally turned his people against him in his last years was the strain of his incessant wars.

22. THE WARS OF LOUIS XIV: THE PEACE OF UTRECHT, 1713

Before 1700

From the outset of his reign Louis pursued a vigorous foreign policy. The quarrel between the house of France and the house of Habsburg had gone on for more than a century. The Austrian branch of the Habsburgs had been checkmated at the Peace of Westphalia. With the Spanish branch the French remained at war for another decade, until the Peace of the Pyrenees in 1659. When, two years later, Louis XIV assumed his personal rule, Spanish territories still faced France on three sides, northeast, east, and south; but so weakened was Spain that this fact was no longer a menace to France so much as a temptation to French expansion. Louis XIV could count on popular national feeling to support him, for the dream of a frontier on the Rhine and the Alps was captivating to Frenchmen. He struck in 1667. (The war was called the "War of Devolution," from a legal term used in the preliminary demands.) He was blocked, as noted above, by a Triple Alliance engineered by the Dutch.[20] With strength renewed by reforms at home, and in alliance with Charles II of England, he struck again in 1672 (the "Dutch War"), invading the Dutch provinces on the lower Rhine, and this time raising up his great adversary and inveterate enemy, the prince of Orange.[21] William III, bringing the Austrian and Spanish Habsburgs, Brandenburg, and Denmark into alliance with the Dutch Republic, forced Louis to sign the treaty of Nimwegen in 1678. The French gave up their ambitions against Holland but took from Spain the rich province of Franche-Comté, which outflanked Alsace on the south, and brought French power to the borders of Switzerland.

In the very next year, 1679, Louis further infiltrated the dissolving frontier of the Holy Roman Empire, this time in Lorraine and Alsace. By the Peace of Westphalia the French king had rights in this region, but the terms of that treaty were so ambiguous, and the local feudal law so confusing, that claims could be made in contrary directions. Louis XIV now set up *chambres de réunion,* as he called them, law courts in which French judges examined the claims to various parcels of territory and pronounced in favor of the king of France. French troops thereupon moved in. In 1681 French troops occupied the city of Strasbourg, which, as a free city of the Holy Roman Empire, regarded itself as an independent little republic. A protest went up throughout Germany against this undeclared invasion. But Germany was not a political unity. Since 1648 each German state conducted its own foreign policy, and at this very moment, in 1681, Louis XIV had an ally in the Elector of Brandenburg (forerunner of the kings of Prussia); and the electors of the Rhineland church-states—the archbishops of Cologne, Trier, and Mainz— were on the French payroll, receiving "subsidies" from the French king. The diet of the Holy Roman Empire was divided between an anti-French and a pro-French party. The emperor, Leopold I, was distracted by developments in the East. The Hungarians, incited and financed by Louis XIV, were again rebelling against the Habsburgs. They appealed to the Turks, and the Turks in 1683 moved up the Danube and actually besieged Vienna—as in 1529. Louis XIV, if he did not on this occasion positively assist the Turks, ostentatiously declined to join the proposed crusade against them.

The emperor, with Polish assistance, succeeded in getting the Turkish host out of Austria.[22] Returning to western problems, observing the western border of the Empire constantly crumbling, Franche-Comté already lost, the Spanish Netherlands constantly threatened, Lorraine and Alsace absorbed bit by bit, and the Rhineland archbishops reduced to the status of French puppets, and not forgetting that Louis XIV had designs on the whole of Habsburg Spain, the Emperor Leopold gathered the Catholic powers into a combination against the French. The Protestant states at the same time, aroused by Louis' revocation of the Edict of Nantes in 1685 and by Huguenot émigrés who called down the wrath of God on the perfidious Sun King, began to ally the more readily with William of Orange. Catholic and Protestant enemies of Louis XIV came together in 1686 in the League of Augsburg, which comprised the Holy Roman Emperor, the kings of

[20] See p. 164.
[21] See pp. 164, 174.
[22] See pp. 215–216.

Spain and of Sweden, the electors of Bavaria, Saxony, and the Palatinate, and the Dutch Republic. In 1686 the king of England was still a protégé of France, but three years later, when William became king in England, that country too joined the League.

The War of the League of Augsburg broke out in 1688. The French armies won battles but could not drive so many enemies from the field. The French navy could not overpower the combined fleets of the Dutch and English. Louis XIV found himself badly strained (it was at this time that he first imposed direct taxes on the French nobles) and finally made peace at Ryswick in the Netherlands in 1697. The Peace of Ryswick, terminating the long "War of the League of Augsburg," left matters about where they had been when the war began.

In all the warring and negotiating, in the plans of the Augsburg allies and in the maneuvers of Louis XIV, the question had not been merely the fate of this or that piece of territory, nor even the French thrust to the east, but the eventual disposition of the whole empire of Spain. The Spanish king, Charles II, prematurely senile, momentarily expected to die, yet lived on year after year. He was still alive at the time of the Peace of Ryswick. The greatest diplomatic issue of the day was still unsettled.

The War of the Spanish Succession

The War of the Spanish Succession lasted eleven years, from 1702 to 1713. It was less destructive than the Thirty Years' War, for armies were now supplied in more orderly fashion, subject to more orderly discipline and command, and could be stopped from fighting at the will of their governments. Except for the effects of civil war in Spain and of starvation in France, the civilian populations were generally spared, and in this respect the war foreshadowed the typical warfare of the eighteenth century, fought by professional armies rather than by whole peoples. Among wars of the largest scale, the War of the Spanish Succession was the first in which religion counted for little, the first in which commerce and sea power were the principal stakes, the first in which English money was liberally used in Continental politics, and the first that can be called a "world war," because it involved the overseas world together with the leading powers of Europe.

The struggle had long been foreseen. The two main aspirants to the Spanish inheritance were the king of France and the Holy Roman Emperor, each of whom had married a sister of the perpetually moribund Charles II, and each of whom could hope to place a younger member of his family on the throne of Spain. During the last decades of the seventeenth century the powers had made various treaties agreeing to "partition" the Spanish possessions. The idea was, by dividing the Spanish heritage between the two claimants, to preserve the balance of power in Europe.[23] But when Charles II finally died, in 1700, it was found that he had made a will, in which he stipulated that the world of Spain should be kept intact, that all Spanish territories without exception should go to the grandson of Louis XIV, and that if Louis XIV refused to accept in the name of his seventeen-year-old grandson, the entire inheritance should pass to the son of the Habsburg emperor in Vienna. Louis XIV decided to accept. With Bourbons reigning in Versailles and Madrid, even if the two thrones were never united, French influence

[23] On the idea of the balance of power see pp. 158–159.

would run from Belgium to the Straits of Gibraltar, and from Milan to Mexico and Manila. At Versailles the word went out: "The Pyrenees exist no longer."

Never, at least in almost two centuries, had the political balance within Europe been so threatened. Never had the other states faced such a prospect of relegation to the sidelines. William III acted at once; he gathered the stunned or hesitant diplomats into the last of his coalitions, the Grand Alliance of 1701. He died the next year, before hostilities began, and with Louis XIV at the seeming apex of his grandeur, but he had in fact launched the engine that was to crush the Sun King. The Grand Alliance included England, Holland, and the emperor, supported by Brandenburg and eventually by Portugal and the Italian duchy of Savoy. Louis XIV could count on Spain, which was generally loyal to the late king's will. Otherwise his only ally was Bavaria, whose rivalry with Austria made it a habitual satellite of France. The Bavarian alliance gave the French armies an advanced position toward Vienna and maintained that internal division, balance of power, or cancellation of forces within Germany which was fundamental to the politics of the time, and of a long time to come.

The war was long, mainly because each side no sooner gained a temporary advantage than it raised its demands on the other. The English, though they sent relatively few troops to the Continent, produced in John Churchill, Duke of Marlborough, a preeminent military commander for the Allied forces. The Austrians were led by Prince Eugene of Savoy. The Allies won notable battles at Blenheim in Bavaria (1704), and at Ramillies (1706), Oudenarde (1708), and Malplaquet (1709) in the Spanish Netherlands. The French were routed; Louis XIV asked for peace but would not agree to it because the Allied terms were so enormous. Louis fought to hold the two crowns, to conquer Belgium, to get French merchants into Spanish America, and at the worst in self-defense. After minor successes in 1710 he again insisted on controlling the crown of Spain. The Spanish fought to uphold the will of the deceased king, the unity of the Spanish possessions, and even the integrity of Spain itself—for the English moved in at Gibraltar and made a menacing treaty with Portugal, while the Austrians landed at Barcelona and invaded Catalonia, which (as in 1640) again rose in rebellion, recognizing the Austrian claimant, so that all Spain fell into civil war.

The Austrians fought to keep Spain in the Habsburg family, to crush Bavaria, and to carry Austrian influence across the Alps into Italy. The Dutch fought as always for their security, to keep the French out of Belgium, and to close the river Scheldt. The English fought for these same reasons and also to keep the French-supported Catholic Stuarts out of England and preserve the Revolution of 1688. It was to be expected that the Stuarts, if they returned, would ruin the Bank of England and repudiate the National Debt. Both maritime powers, England and Holland, fought to keep French merchants out of Spanish America and to advance their own commercial position in America and the Mediterranean. These being the war aims, the Whigs were the implacable war party in England, the vaguely pro-Stuart and anticommercial Tories being quite willing to make peace at an early date. As for the minor allies, Brandenburg and Savoy, their rulers had simply entered the alliance to gain such advantages as might turn up.

The Peace of Utrecht

Peace was finally made at the treaties of Utrecht and Rastadt of 1713 and 1714. So fierce was the Whig war spirit in England that ratification of the treaty of

Utrecht incidentally marked a step in English constitutional history. The Whigs thought the treaty insufficiently favorable to England. The Tories, pledged to peace, had won the House of Commons in 1710, but the Whigs continued to control the House of Lords. Queen Anne, at the request of Tory leaders and in the interests of peace, raised twelve Tory commoners to the peerage, the number required to give a Tory majority in the Lords and hence to obtain ratification of the treaty. This established itself as a precedent; it became an unwritten article of the British constitution that when the Lords blocked the Commons on an issue of fundamental importance, enough new Lords of appropriate views would be created to make a majority in that House.[24]

The treaty of Utrecht, with its allied instruments, in fact partitioned the world of Spain. But it did not divide it between the two legal claimants only. The British remained at Gibraltar, to the great irritation of the Spaniards, and likewise annexed the island of Minorca. The Duke of Savoy was granted the former Spanish island of Sardinia in return for his contribution to the Allied cause.[25] The rest of the Spanish Mediterranean holdings—Milan, Naples, and Sicily—passed to the Austrian Habsburgs, as did the Spanish Netherlands (or Belgium), subsequently referred to as the Austrian Netherlands—except that the tiny region of Spanish Guelderland was handed over to the Elector of Brandenburg for his pains. In Spain itself, shorn of its European possessions but retaining America, the grandson of Louis XIV was confirmed as king (Philip V of Spain), on the understanding that the French and Spanish thrones should never be inherited by the same person. The Bourbons reigned in Spain, with interruptions, from Philip V to the republican revolution of 1931. French influence was strong in the eighteenth century, for a good many French courtiers, advisers, administrators, and businessmen crossed the Pyrenees with Philip V. They helped somewhat to revive the Spanish monarchy by applying the methods of Louis XIV, and they passed a swelling volume of French manufactures through Seville into Spanish America.

The old objective of William III, to prevent domination by France, was realized at last. The war itself was the main cause of French loss of strength. It produced poverty, misery, and depopulation, exposed Louis XIV to severe criticism at home, and led to a revival of aristocratic and parliamentary opposition. By the peace treaties the French abandoned, for the time being, their efforts to conquer Belgium. They ceased to recognize the Stuart pretender as king of Great Britain. They surrendered to the British two of their colonies, Newfoundland and Nova Scotia (called Acadia), and recognized British sovereignty in the disputed American northwest, known as the Hudson Bay territory. But the French were only checked, not downed. They retained the conquests of Louis XIV in Alsace and the Franche-Comté. Their influence was strong in Spain. Their deeper strength and capacity for recovery were soon evident in renewed economic expansion. Their language and civilization continued to spread throughout Europe.

The Dutch received guarantees of their security. They were granted the right to garrison the "Dutch Barrier," a string of forts in Belgium on the side toward

---

[24] The precedent was invoked in 1832 and 1911, but never since 1713 have the Lords allowed themselves to be swamped by newcomers. They have yielded at the threat.

[25] By the terms of 1713 Sardinia was awarded to Austria and Sicily to Savoy, but Sardinia and Sicily were exchanged in 1720. The kingdom of the Two Sicilies (Naples and Sicily) was thereby reconstituted. Savoy was originally a small region in the high Alps, whose ruler acquired the lowland area around Turin in the Middle Ages, with the title of Duke of Savoy. His domains were thereafter also called Piedmont because some of them lay at the foot of the Alps. After 1720 the Duke of Savoy became the King of Sardinia, because that island, though the least important of his possessions, provided a less controversial basis for a royal title. See the map on p. 317.

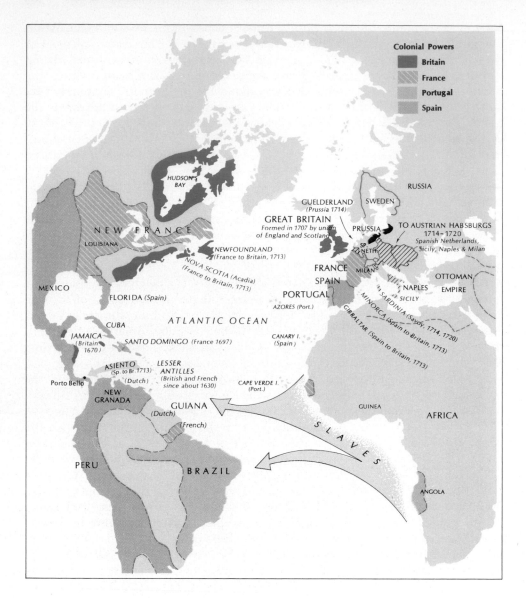

THE ATLANTIC WORLD AFTER THE PEACE OF UTRECHT, 1713

The map shows the partitioning of the Spanish empire and the rise of the British. Spain and its American possessions went to the Bourbon Philip V; the European possessions of Spain—the Netherlands, Milan, Naples, and Sicily—went to the Habsburgs. Britain meanwhile was strengthened by the union of England and Scotland, the acquisition of Minorca, Gibraltar, and the commercial privilege of the "asiento" from Spain, and of Newfoundland and Nova Scotia from France. (See also map, p. 317.)

France. With Belgium transferred to Austria, which was not expected to stimulate Belgian commerce, and with the closure of the river Scheldt reconfirmed at Utrecht, the Dutch could comfortably expect a minimum of competition from their southern neighbors. But the Dutch, strained by the war and outdistanced by England, never again played a primary role in European political affairs. Two other small states ascended over the diplomatic horizon, Savoy and Brandenburg. The rulers of both, for having sided with the victors, were recognized as "kings" by the treaty of Utrecht. Savoy came to be known as "Sardinia," and Brandenburg as "Prussia." More is said of Prussia in the next chapter.

The greatest winners were the British. Great Britain made its appearance as a great power. Union of England and Scotland had taken place during the war. Based at Gibraltar and Minorca, Britain was now a power in the Mediterranean. Belgium, the "pistol pointed at the heart of England," was in the innocuous hands of the Austrians. The Austrians had not especially wanted Belgium because it was too distant from Vienna and too likely to embroil them with France. They had taken it largely at the instigation of the maritime states, Britain and Holland, which saw in transfer to Austria a good solution to the problem. The British added to their American holdings at the expense of France. Far more valuable than Newfoundland or Nova Scotia, won from France, was the *asiento* extorted from Spain. The *asiento* granted the lucrative privilege (which the French had sought) of providing Spanish America with African slaves. Much of the wealth of Bristol and Liverpool in the following decades was to be built upon the slave trade. The *asiento*, by permitting one shipload of British goods to be brought each year to Porto Bello in Panama, also provided opportunities for illicit trade in nonhuman cargoes. The Spanish empire was pried open, and British merchants entered on an era of wholesale smuggling into Spanish America, competing strenuously with the French, who because of their favored position in Spain were usually able to go through more legal channels. Moreover, the British, by defeating France, assured themselves of a line of Protestant kings and of the maintenance of constitutional and parliamentary government. The landed aristocracy and their merchant allies could now govern as they saw fit. The result was a rapid increase of wealth in England, precipitating within a few generations a veritable Industrial Revolution.

Except for the addition of England, the same powers were parties to the treaty of Utrecht in 1713 as to the Peace of Westphalia in 1648, and they now confirmed the system of international relations established by Westphalia. The powers accepted each other as members of the European system, recognized each other as sovereign states connected only by free negotiation, war, and treaty, and adjusted their differences through rather facile exchanges of territory, made in the interests of a balance of power, and without regard to the nationality or presumed wishes of the peoples affected. With Germany still in its "feudal chaos," Italy negligible, and Spain subordinated to France, the treaty of Utrecht left France and Great Britain as the two most vigorous powers of Europe and as the two principal carriers and exporters of the type of civilization most characteristic of the modern world. In the next chapter we turn to central and eastern Europe, to see how these regions developed along lines of their own, though under strong influence from the West.

The Age of Grandeur

The seventeenth century was an age of high monarchy, or royal absolutism, of which the great exemplar was France. A style of life that developed first in Italy during the Renaissance, and which set high value on patronage of the arts, courtly manners, elaborate clothing, and elegant speech, was taken over in France (with some influence from the two Medici queens), and from France was diffused throughout much of Europe. It was especially suited to monarchies, since the kings, with their increasingly organized governments, could afford the necessary expense and even required a palatial atmosphere in which to impress their often unruly subjects. The same applies in a way to the papal monarchy of the church, and the new ideas came as much from papal Rome as from republican Florence. The result is best illustrated by architecture, to which the following pages are devoted.

It was an architecture derived from classical elements of design, but it soon went beyond the Greeks and Romans. The baroque, as it is called, delighted in arches and colonnades, domes and entablatures, and ornamented windows and cornices. Indoors and outdoors flowed together in complexes of façades, staircases, terraces, balustrades, gardens, fountains, and formal vistas. Statuary was distributed inside and out. Mirrors, paintings, and tapestries adorned the interiors. Great halls were built for state receptions, and paved courtyards for troops of soldiers, throngs of retainers, the arrival of coaches, or simply to provide open views.

Architecture passed over into city planning. Versailles was a new city; the plan of modern Paris also dates from Louis XIV; and Washington, D.C., planned by a Frenchman, with its diagonal streets and circles, punctuated by statues, still reflects these traditions of neoclassical monumentality. On the other hand it was the kings who initiated a movement to the suburbs. Versailles was built ten miles from Paris, away from the clamor and restlessness of the city, and where the king already owned enough land for a new spacious development. When other monarchs imitated Louis XIV they often did likewise. The Habsburgs built Schönbrunn outside Vienna, and the Hohenzollern Frederick II built Sans Souci at Potsdam about twenty miles from Berlin.

The Russian tsars, in their new city of St. Petersburg, and the kings of Sweden, in their new royal palace at Stockholm, joined the host of German princes in emulating the royal grandeur of France. It was different where royalty counted for less. The Dutch had no king and cared little for public magnificence. Sans Souci was hardly more than a wealthy gentleman's home. The English, with their antimonarchical revolutions, built no grandiose royal palaces at this time. But they built Blenheim Palace and presented it to John Churchill, the first Duke of Marlborough, as a reward for his services in the last great war against the *Grand Monarque.*

Above: The Emperor Constantine (d. 337) discusses with Pope Julius II (d. 1513) the building of a new church of St. Peter's in Rome. An older church, of which parts went back to Constantine's time, was torn down to make room for the new one.

The new St. Peter's, seen here in a seventeenth-century print, required a century and a half for completion. The great dome of the church is the work of Michelangelo. The pair of immense semicircular arcades, each four columns thick, was built about a hundred years later by Bernini, one of the great masters of the baroque.

The château of Versailles was mainly built by Louis XIV in the 1670s, on a site used by his predecessor as a hunting lodge. Thirty thousand workmen were employed at one time in the building operations, which are shown in a painting of the period at the left above. The painting below shows the château and its adjacent buildings about a hundred years later, shortly before the Revolution. The twin structures in the foreground, left and right of the vast court, were assigned to government offices. The château proper is in the middle distance, with the gardens invisible behind it, except that the long rectangular basin of the Grand Canal can be seen reaching to the horizon.

At Versailles, for thirty years, the Sun King received visitors from all countries in overwhelming splendor. The memorable arrival in 1684 of ambassadors from far-off Siam (now Thailand) is recorded in the print below.

Louis XIV gave sponsorship and subsidies to cultural activities of many kinds, usually organized as academies. At the left, he appears on a visit to the Academy of Sciences, founded in 1666. A scientific gentleman is explaining the "philosophical apparatus" to the king.

AMBASSADEURS DE SIAM

198

The opera developed as an art form in the seventeenth century and was characteristic of the baroque in its simultaneous use of different arts, its ostentation, and general staginess. At the left, below, Lully's "Alceste" is performed for Louis XIV in the courtyard of a lesser palace before the building of Versailles.

Left, above: Frederick the Great's Sans Souci. The young Frederick had been disciplined by his drill sergeant father for writing poetry and corresponding with Frenchmen, but after becoming king, in 1740, at the age of twenty-eight, he gave full rein to his French tastes, and after the first Silesian War built this residence, whose name means "carefree." Here he met with Voltaire and other intellectual companions.

Above: There were many buildings in St. Petersburg, now Leningrad, on the model of European palaces of the day, but here we have signs of the Western influences penetrating to Moscow. If the structures seem dreamy and evanescent, it is because they are only temporary pavilions set up in 1775 to celebrate the end of a victorious war with Turkey.

199

At the left: Schönbrunn Palace, near Vienna. The Habsburg monarchs, as the Turkish menace receded, planned this great edifice to compete with their Bourbon rivals. The plan was never completed, partly because the sensible Maria Theresa (1740–1780) thought that what is seen here was enough. It was here that the six-year-old Mozart astonished the court with his precocious virtuosity.

At the right: Blenheim Palace in Oxfordshire, presented to the Duke of Marlborough for his victories over Louis XIV. Built in the 1720s with funds voted by Parliament, a monument in a way to England's rising greatness, it has always been thought by the English to be a little exaggerated. The architect, Vanbrugh, left everyone dissatisfied. He sacrificed interiors to external splendor, putting the kitchen 400 yards from the dining room. Voltaire said that if only the rooms were as wide as the walls were thick, it would be a convenient little château.

These two buildings were built at the same time for the same purpose, as homes for old and retired soldiers. It was a sign of the growth of royal government to have professional standing armies, in which men might spend their whole lives apart from the civilian population.

At the left is Chelsea Royal Hospital, founded by Charles II; at the right, the Invalides, founded by Louis XIV. The much greater size and imposing dome of the French establishment contrast with the simplicity of the English, and reflect the far greater power of France at that time. The broad avenues radiating beyond the Invalides, then in open country, are now boulevards of central Paris.

203

V.
The Transformation of Eastern Europe, 1648-1740

I n Eastern Europe, in the century after the Peace of Westphalia of 1648, it became apparent that political systems that failed to become more "modern" might be in danger of going out of existence. In the mid-seventeenth century most parts of Eastern Europe belonged to one or another of three old-fashioned political organizations—the Holy Roman Empire, the Republic of Poland, and the empire of the Ottoman Turks.[1] All three were loose, sprawling, and increasingly ineffective. They were pushed aside and superseded by three new and stronger powers, Prussia, Austria, and Russia. These three, by overrunning the intermediate ground of Poland, came to adjoin one another and cover all Eastern Europe except the Balkans. It was in this same period that Russia expanded territorially, adopted some of the technical and administrative apparatus of Western Europe, and became an active participant in European affairs.

East and West are of course relative terms. For the Russians Germany and even Poland were "western." But for Europe as a whole a real though indefinite line ran along the Elbe and the Bohemian mountains to the head of the Adriatic Sea. East of this line towns were fewer than in the West, human labor less productive, the middle classes less strong. Above all, the peasants were governed by their landlords.[2] From the sixteenth to the eighteenth century, in eastern Europe in

---

[1] See maps, pp. 206 and 210.
[2] See pp. 122–123.

Chapter Emblem: A Russian medal commemorating the capture of Narva from the Swedes in 1704, and hence the establishment of Russian power on the Baltic.

contrast to what happened in the West, the peasant mass increasingly lost its freedom. The commercial revolution and widening of the market, which in the West raised up a strong merchant class and tended to turn working people into a legally free and mobile labor force, in eastern Europe strengthened the great landlords who produced for export, and who secured their labor force by the institutions of serfdom and "hereditary subjection." The main social unit was the agricultural estate, which the lord exploited with uncompensated compulsory labor (or *robot*) furnished by his people, who could neither migrate, marry, nor learn a trade except as he permitted, and who, until the eighteenth century, had no legal protector or court of appeal other than himself. In the East, therefore, the landlords were exceedingly powerful. They were the only significant political class. And the three new states that grew up—Prussia, Austria, Russia—were alike in being landlord states.

23. THREE AGING EMPIRES

In 1648 the whole mainland of Europe from the French border almost to Moscow was occupied by the three large and loosely built structures that have been mentioned—the Holy Roman Empire, the Republic of Poland, and the empire of the Ottoman Turks.[3] The Turkish power reached to about fifty miles from Vienna, extended over what is now Rumania, and prevailed over the Tartars on the north shore of the Black Sea. Even so, its European holdings were but a projection from the main mass in Asia and Africa. Poland extended roughly from a hundred miles east of Berlin to a hundred miles west of Moscow, and virtually from "sea to sea" in the old phrase of its patriots, from the Baltic around Riga almost to the Black Sea coast, which, however, was held by Tartar Khans under the overlordship of the Turkish sultan at Constantinople. The Holy Roman Empire extended from Poland and Hungary to the North Sea.

These three empires were by no means alike. The Holy Empire bore some of the oldest traditions of Christendom. Poland too had old connections with the West. Turkey was a Muslim power, strange to Europe and contemptuous of it. Yet in some ways the three resembled each other. In all of them central authority had become weak, consisting largely of understandings between a nominal head and outlying dignitaries or potentates. All lacked efficient systems of administration and government. All were being put out of date by newer types of state of which France was the leading example. All, but especially Poland and Turkey, were made up of diverse ethnic or language groups.[4] None of these peoples, nor any combination of them—neither the dominant Germans, Poles, and Turks, nor the submerged Lithuanians, White Russians, Ukrainians, Czechs, Slovaks, Rumanians, Croats, Magyars, Serbs, Bulgars, or Greeks—had been formed into a compact organization. The whole immense area was politically soft. It was malleable in the hands of whoever might become a little stronger than his neighbor. We must try to see in what this softness consisted, and then how newer and harder "state forms" (as the Germans would say) were created.

[3] For the origins of the Holy Roman and Ottoman Empires, see pp. 29 and 46.
[4] For language groups, see map in Chapter XI, section 53.

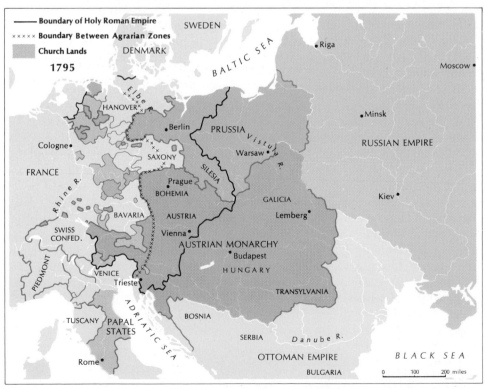

The Holy Roman Empire after 1648

With the Holy Roman Empire the reader is already familiar.[5] It was an empire, especially after the Peace of Westphalia, with next to no army, revenues, or working organs of government. Voltaire called it neither holy, Roman, nor an empire. As the seventeenth-century German jurist Pufendorf put it, it was somewhat of an abortion and a monstrosity. Created in the Middle Ages, it was Roman in that it was then believed to continue the imperial sway of the Rome of antiquity, and it was holy in being the secular counterpart to the spiritual empire of the pope. It had been ruined by the Reformation, which left the Germans divided almost evenly between Protestant and Catholic, with each side thereafter demanding special safeguards against the other. The Empire continued, however, to be universal in principle, having no relation to nationality, and theoretically being a form of government suitable to all peoples, although it had never made good this theoretical claim and had shown no expansionist tendency since the Middle Ages. In actuality, the Empire was very roughly coterminous with the German states and the region of the German language, except that it excluded after 1648 the Dutch and Swiss, who no longer considered themselves German; and it likewise excluded those Germans who since the fourteenth century had settled along the eastern shores of the Baltic.

Large parts of the Empire had suffered repeatedly from the Thirty Years' War. Yet the war, and the peace terms which followed it, only accentuated a situation which had long been unfavorable. Postwar revival was difficult; the breakup of commercial connections and the wartime losses of savings and capital were hard to overcome. Germany fell increasingly out of step with western Europe. The burgher class, its ambitions blocked, lost much of its old vitality. No overseas colonies could be founded, for want of strong enough government backing, as was shown when a colonial venture of Brandenburg came to nothing. There was no stock exchange in Germany until one was established at Vienna in 1771, half a century after those of London, Paris, and Amsterdam. Laws, tariffs, tolls, and coinage were more variegated than in France. Even the calendar varied. It varied, indeed, throughout Europe as a whole, since Protestant states long declined to accept the corrected calendar issued by Pope Gregory XIII in 1582, but in parts of divided Germany the holidays, the date of the month, and the day of the week changed every few miles. The arts and letters, flourishing in western Europe as never before, were at a low ebb in Germany in the seventeenth century. In science the Germans during and after the Thirty Years' War did less than the English, Dutch, French, or Italians, despite the great mathematician and philosopher

[5] See pp. 25, 29, 37, 72–74, 141–145.

CENTRAL AND EASTERN EUROPE, 1660–1795

This complex area is shown in simplified form on p. 210. The upper panel of the present map indicates boundaries as of 1660, the lower panel those of 1795. Both panels show the border between the eastern and western agrarian zones, running from the mouth of the Elbe River into central Germany and down to Trieste. East of this line, from the sixteenth to the eighteenth centuries, the mass of people sank into a kind of serfdom in which they rendered forced labor to their lords on large farms. West of the line the peasants owed little or no forced labor and tilled small farms which they owned or rented. This line is one of the most important sociological boundaries in the history of modern Europe.

Leibniz, one of the great minds of the age. Only in music, as in the work of the Bach family, did the Germans at this time excel. But music was not then much heard beyond the place of its origin. Germany for the rest of the world was a mute country, a byway in the higher civilization of Europe.

After the Thirty Years' War each German state had sovereign rights. These "states" numbered some 300 or 2,000, depending on how they were counted. The higher figure included the "knights of the Empire," found in south Germany and the Rhineland. They were persons who acknowledged no overlordship except that of the emperor himself. The knights had tiny estates of their own, averaging not over a hundred acres apiece, consisting of a castle and a manor or two, enclosed by the territory of a larger state but not forming a part of it. These free knights had arisen in various ways; in Württemberg, for example, the lords simply ceased to attend the diet, won exemption from the duke's jurisdiction, and retired to their own domains, leaving the surface of Württemberg pockmarked with small units politically independent of it. It was as if, in England, the peers had lost interest in the House of Lords and had set up independently, each on his own estates. Since the emperor, whom the knights regarded as their only superior, had in fact no authority, the knights were in effect private persons enjoying sovereign status—the last anomaly of bizarre neofeudalism and distorted freedom.

But even without the knights there were about three hundred states capable of some independence of action—free cities, abbots without subjects, archbishops and bishops ruling with temporal power, landgraves, margraves and dukes, and one king, the king of Bohemia. The highest ranking were called electors, who had the privilege of electing the emperor. By the Golden Bull of 1356 there were seven electors—three ecclesiastics (the archbishops of Cologne, Mainz, and Trier) and four laymen, the Count Palatine of the Rhine, the Duke of Saxony, the Margrave of Brandenburg, and the King of Bohemia. Bavaria was made an electorate at the Peace of Westphalia, and Hanover at the end of the century, so that finally there were nine electors. The fact that nearly half the electors were Protestants after the Reformation, whereas the Holy Empire had meaning only in a Catholic world, added to the internal confusion and general oddity of the system.

All these states were intent on preserving what were called the "Germanic liberties." They were gladly assisted by outside powers, notably but not exclusively France. The Germanic liberties meant freedom of the member states from control by emperor or Empire. The electors, at each election of an emperor, required the candidate to accept certain "capitulations," in which he promised to safeguard all the privileges and immunities of the states. The Habsburgs, though consistently elected after 1438, had none of the advantages of hereditary rulers, each having to bargain away in turn any gains made by his predecessor. The elective principle meant that imperial power could not be accumulated and transmitted from one generation to the next. It opened the doors to foreign intrigue, since the electors were willing to consider whichever candidate would promise them most. The French repeatedly supported a rival candidate to the Habsburgs. After 1648 they had a party in the electoral college, Bavaria and Cologne being the most consistently pro-French. Cardinal Mazarin in 1658 even entertained the thought of making the young Louis XIV Holy Roman Emperor. He had to accept election of a Habsburg, despite liberal use of French money, but the new emperor, Leopold I, undertook not to engage the Empire in any war supporting the Spanish Habsburgs against France. In 1742 the French obtained the elevation of their Bavarian ally to the imperial throne. The office of emperor became the political football of Germans and non-Germans working together.

Nor would the German states, after the Thirty Years' War, allow any authority to the imperial diet. The diet possessed the power to raise troops and taxes for the whole Empire, but the power remained unused. On matters affecting religion, after 1648, either Protestants or Catholics could demand the *ius eundi in partes*, or "right of sitting apart." Each religious group then constituted itself as a chamber, Protestant or Catholic, and since agreement of the two was required, each possessed a veto. The deliberations of the diet became notorious for their wordiness and futility. Many sessions were spent, for example, in attempts to fix for all Germany a common date for Easter, on which the whole calendar depended. In 1663 a diet met to consider measures against a new Turkish advance on the Danube. It was the last diet ever to be convoked, for it lasted "forever," i.e., until the end of the Holy Empire in 1806. It became the "perpetual diet" of Regensburg, never dismissed or renewed, unresponsive to events or issues, the states simply replacing their representatives individually, generation after generation, as at an endless congress of diplomats.

The states which insisted with such obstinacy on their liberties from the Empire gave few liberties to their subjects. The free cities were closed oligarchies, as indeed were most cities in other countries, but in Germany the burgher oligarchs of the free cities were virtually sovereign also. Most of the other states, large or small, developed in the direction of absolutism. Absolutism was checked for Germany as a whole, only to reappear in miniature in hundreds of different places. Each ruler thought himself a little Louis XIV, each court a small Versailles. Subjects became attached by ties of sentiment to their rulers, who almost always lived in the neighborhood and could be readily seen by passers-by. People liked the little courts, the toy armies, the gossipy politics, and the familiar officials of their tiny states.

The Empire, for all its faults, had the merit of holding this conglomeration of states in a lawful relation to one another. It was a kind of miniature league of nations. For a century and a half after the Peace of Westphalia infinitesimally small states existed alongside larger ones, or often totally enclosed within them, without serious fear for their security and without losing their independence. Only in power politics and in European or world affairs was the Empire a shadow. For the Germans it was a reality, a world in itself, which no one for a long time dreamed of violating or even reforming, for its existence assured a way of life which most Germans were glad to keep.

Yet there were many ambitious rulers in Germany after the Peace of Westphalia. They had won recognition of their sovereignty in 1648. They were busily building absolutist monarchies over their subjects. They aspired also to extend their dominions and cut a greater figure in the world. There were other ways of doing this than by devouring their smaller neighbors outright. One was by marriage and inheritance. The Empire in this respect was a paradise of fortune hunters; the variety of possible marriages was enormous because of the great number of ruling families. Another outlet for ambition lay in the high politics of the Empire. The Wittelsbach family, which ruled in Bavaria, managed to win an electorate in the Thirty Years' War; they consistently placed members of the family as archbishop of Cologne and in the other great Rhineland sees, and with the interest thus built up were able to sell their influence to France, which in turn backed them against the Habsburgs. The Guelph family, ruling in Hanover, schemed for years to obtain an electorate, which they finally extorted from the emperor in 1692; in 1714 they inherited the throne of Great Britain, preferred by the British as Protestants to their Catholic Stuart cousins. Two electors of Saxony in these years got themselves crowned king of Poland. The Hohenzollerns, electors of Brandenburg, were extremely fortunate in the seventeenth century in inheriting territories as far apart as the Rhine and the Vistula. The Habsburgs, hereditary rulers in Austria, a mere archduchy, were confirmed by the Peace of Westphalia as hereditary kings of Bohemia, where they had formerly depended on election.

The half-century after the Peace of Westphalia was a highly critical period in central Europe. The situation in Germany was fluid. No one could tell which, if any, of the half-dozen chief German states would emerge in the lead. Nothing was crystallized; anything might happen. Two states definitely came forward after 1700, built by the skill and persistence of their rulers—Austria and Prussia. It is a curious and revealing fact that neither really had a name of its own. They were for a long time known most commonly as "houses"—the house of Austria or Habsburg and the house of Brandenburg or Hohenzollern. Each house put together a certain combination of territories. Each would have been as willing to

AGING EMPIRES AND NEW POWERS

The left panel shows the "three aging empires" which occupied much of central and eastern Europe in the seventeenth century. (See pp. 205–214.) Though maintaining themselves with growing difficulty under modern conditions, the Polish Republic lasted until 1795, the Holy Roman Empire until 1806, the Ottoman Empire until 1923. Meanwhile, beginning in the seventeenth century, the political leadership in this area was assumed by three states of more modern type, organized around the institutions of monarchy, the standing army, and the professional bureaucracy or civil service—the reorganized Austrian Empire of the Habsburgs, the Hohenzollern kingdom of Prussia, and the Russian empire of the Romanovs. These are shown in the right panel. All three figured prominently in the affairs of Europe for over two hundred years; all perished in the First World War, 1914–1918.

possess any other combination had the course of events been different. By extension of meaning, one came to be called "Austria," which for centuries had been simply an archduchy on the upper Danube, and the other "Prussia," which for centuries had meant only a certain stretch of the Baltic coast. To the development of these two states we shall shortly turn.

The Republic of Poland about 1650

Running almost a thousand miles eastward from the Holy Roman Empire in the middle of the seventeenth century lay the vast tract of the Republic of Poland, called a republic because its king was elected, and because the political classes took pride in their constitutional liberties. Its vast size was one cause of its internal peculiarities. No administrative system could have kept up with the expansion of its frontiers, so that a large degree of freedom had always been left to outlying lords. In addition, the population was heterogeneous.

The Polish state was a far more recent and less substantial creation than the Holy Roman Empire. It was made up of two main parts, Poland proper in the west and the Grand Duchy of Lithuania in the east, the two having been joined by a union of their crowns.[6] Only in the extreme west, in the valley of the Vistula River, was there a mass of Polish population. The Duchy of Prussia, a fief of the Polish crown, was peopled by Germans. Further east a White Russian and Ukrainian peasantry was presided over by a scattering of Polish and Lithuanian landlords. Even in Poland itself the urban population was not generally Polish, the townspeople being largely Germans and Jews. The latter spoke Yiddish, a dialect basically German, and were very numerous because a king of Poland, in the later Middle Ages, had welcomed Jewish settlers fleeing from Germany.[7] The Jews did not adopt the Polish language. Tending at first to live in separate communities because of their religion, they were later confined to compulsory ghettos, islands of Orthodox Jewish life in the Gentile ocean. The Germans too held aloof, resisting assimilation to their less advanced surroundings. An unsurpassable barrier thus existed between town and country. There was no national middle class. The official and political language was Latin. Roman Catholicism was the leading religion.

Poland is interesting as the region in which the landed aristocracy won over all other groups in the country, neither allowing the consolidation of the state on absolutist lines, nor yet creating an effective constitutional or parliamentary government. The Polish aristocracy, or *szlachta*, made up some 8 percent of the population, a far higher proportion than the aristocracy of any country of western Europe. On this ground the old Polish kingdom has sometimes been considered, especially by later Polish nationalists, as the possessor of an early form of democracy. The aristocracy were sticklers for their liberties, called the "Polish liberties," which resembled the German liberties in consisting largely of a fierce suspicion of central authority and in being a perpetual invitation to foreign interference. As in the Holy Roman Empire, the monarchy was elective, and the king upon election had to accept certain contractual agreements, which, like the German "capitulations," made impossible the accumulation of authority by the crown. As in the Empire, the royal elections were a cockpit of foreign influence, bribery, and

[6] See maps, pp. 206 and 210.
[7] See p. 72, note.

intrigue. The Poles were too factious to accept one of their own number as king. They were divided into pro-French, pro-Swedish, pro-Russian, and other parties. From 1572 to the extinction of Poland over two centuries later there were only two native Polish kings who reigned for any length of time, and one of these was the discarded lover of a Russian empress. The other was the national hero John Sobieski, whose decisive action against the Turks is noted below.

As in Germany, also, the central diet was ineffective and the nuclei of political action were local. The aristocracy met in fifty or sixty regional diets, turbulent assemblages of warlike gentry, in which the great lords used the little ones for their own purposes. The central diet, from which the towns were excluded, was a periodic meeting of emissaries, under binding instructions, from the regional diets. It came to be recognized, as one of the liberties of the country, that the central diet could take no action to which any member objected. Any member, by stating his unalterable opposition, could oblige a diet to disband. This was the famous *liberum veto*, the free veto, and to use it to break up a diet was called "exploding" the diet. The first diet was exploded in 1652. Of fifty-five diets held from that year to 1764, forty-eight were exploded.

Government became a fiasco. The monopoly of law and force, characteristic of the modern state, failed to develop in Poland. The king of Poland had practically no army, no law courts, no officials, and no income. The nobility paid no taxes. By 1750 the revenues of the king of Poland were about one-thirteenth those of the tsar of Russia and one seventy-fifth those of the king of France. Armed force was in the hands of a dozen or so aristocratic leaders, who also conducted their own individual foreign policies, pursuing their own adventures against the Turks, or bringing in Russians, French, or Swedes to help them against other Poles. The landlords became local monarchs on their manorial estates, and the mass of the rural population fell deeper into a serfdom scarcely different from slavery, bound to compulsory labor on estates resembling plantations, with police and disciplinary powers in the hands of the lords, and with no outside legal or administrative system to set the limits of exploitation. Some Polish aristocrats, hiring architects or buying libraries from Germany and western Europe, traveling with trains of servants to Italy or France, masters of many languages and habitually associating with the great, became among the most accomplished and cosmopolitan people in Europe. A great Polish nobleman could boast of more territory and subjects, and of more international consideration, than many a sovereign princeling of Germany. But the mass of the aristocracy became an unruly body of decayed gentry, dependent on their connections with the powerful families, and indifferent to western Europe.

The huge expanse comprised under the name of Poland was, in short, a power vacuum, an area of low political pressure; and as centers of higher pressure developed, notably around Berlin and Moscow, the push against the Polish frontiers became steadily stronger. It was facilitated by the centrifugal habits of the Poles themselves. As early as 1660 the East Prussian fief became independent of the Polish crown. As early as 1667 the Muscovites reconquered Smolensk and Kiev. Already there was confidential talk of partitioning Poland, which, however, was deferred for a century. The history of the world would have been different had the Poland of the seventeenth century held together. There would have been no kingdom of Prussia and no Prussian influence in Germany; nor would Russia have become the chief Slavic power or reached so far into central Europe.

The Ottoman Empire about 1650

The Ottoman state, the third of the three empires which together spread over so much of Europe, was larger than either of the others, and in the seventeenth century was more solidly organized. In 1529 the Turks had attacked Vienna and seemed about to burst into Germany.[8] To the Christian world the Turks were a mystery as well as a terror. They were in truth among the rougher of the Muslim peoples, who had erupted from central Asia only a few centuries before and owed most of their higher civilization to the Arabs and the Persians. Their dominions extended, about 1650, from the Hungarian plain and the south Russian steppes as far as Algeria, the upper Nile, and the Persian Gulf. The empire was based to a large degree on military proficiency. Long before Europe the Turks had a standing army, of which the main striking force was the janissaries. The janissaries were originally recruited from Christian children taken from their families in early childhood, brought up as Muslims, reared in military surroundings, and forbidden to marry; without background or ties, interests, or ambition outside the military organization to which they belonged, they were an ideal fighting material in the hands of political leaders. The Turkish forces were long as well equipped as the Christian, being especially strong in heavy artillery. But by the mid-seventeenth century they were falling behind. They had changed little, or for the worse, since the days of Suleiman the Magnificent a century before, whereas in the better organized Christian states discipline and military administration had been improved, and firearms, land mines, and siegecraft had become more effective.

The Turks cared little about assimilating subject peoples to their language or institutions. Law was religious law derived from the Koran. Law courts and judges were hard to distinguish from religious authorities, for there was no separation between religious and secular spheres. The sultan was also the caliph, the commander of the faithful, and while on the one hand there was no clergy in the European sense, on the other hand religious influences affected all aspects of life. The Turks, for the most part, applied the Muslim law only to Muslims.

The Ottoman government left its non-Muslim subjects to settle their own affairs in their own way, not according to nationality, which was generally indistinguishable, but according to religious groupings. The Greek Orthodox church, to which most Christians in the empire belonged, thus became an almost autonomous intermediary between the sultan and a large fraction of its subjects. Armenian Christians and Jews formed other separate bodies. Except in the western Balkans (Albania and Bosnia) there was no general conversion of Christians to Islam during the Turkish rule, although there were many individual cases of Christians turning Muslim to obtain the privileges of the ruling faith. North of the Danube the Christian princes of Transylvania, Wallachia, and Moldavia (later combined in the modern Rumania) continued to rule over Christian subjects. They were kept in office for that purpose by the sultan, to whom they paid tribute. In general, since their subjects were more profitable to them as Christians, the Turks were not eager to proselytize for Islam.

The Ottoman Empire was therefore a relatively tolerant empire, far more so than the states of Europe. Christians in the Turkish empire fared better than Muslims would have fared in Christendom or than the Moors had in fact fared in

[8] See pp. 45, 73–74, and 78.

Spain. Christians were less disturbed in Turkey than were Protestants in France, after 1685, or Catholics in Ireland. The empire was tolerant because it was composite, an aggregation of peoples, religions, and laws, having no drive, as did the Western states, toward internal unity and complete legal sovereignty. The same was evident in the attitude toward foreign merchants.

The king of France had had treaty arrangements with Turkey since 1535, and many traders from Marseilles had spread over the port towns of the Near East. They were exempted by treaty from the laws of the Ottoman Empire and were liable to trial only by their own judges, who though residing in Turkey were appointed by the king of France. They were free to exercise their Roman Catholic religion, and if disputes with Muslims arose, they appeared in special courts where the word of an infidel received equal weight with that of a follower of the prophet. Similar rights in Turkey were obtained by other European states. Thus began "extraterritorial" privileges of the kind obtained by Europeans in later centuries in China and elsewhere, wherever the local laws were regarded as backward. To the Turks of the seventeenth century there was nothing exceptional about such arrangements. Only much later, under Western influence, did the Turks learn to resent these "capitulations" as impairments of their own sovereignty.

Yet the Turkish rule was oppressive, and the "terrible Turk" was with reason the nightmare of eastern Europe. Ottoman rule was oppressive to Christians if only because it relegated them to a despised position, and because everything they held holy was viewed by the Turks with violent contempt. But it was oppressive also in that it was arbitrary and brutal even by the none too sensitive standards of Europeans. It was worse in these respects in the seventeenth century than formerly, for the central authority of the sultans had become corrupt, and the outlying governors, or pashas, had a virtually free hand with their subjects.

Those parts of the Ottoman Empire which adjoined the Christian states were among the least firmly attached to Constantinople. The Tartar Khans of south Russia, like the Christian princes of the Danubian principalities, were simply protégés who paid tribute. Hungary was occupied but was more a battlefield than a province. These regions were disputed by Germans, Poles, and Russians. It seemed in the middle of the seventeenth century as if the grip of the Turks might be relaxing. But a dynasty of unusually capable grand viziers, the Kiuprilis, came to power and retained it contrary to Turkish customs for fifty years. Under them the empire again put forth a mighty effort. By 1663 the janissaries were again mobilizing in Hungary. Tartar horsemen were on the move. Central Europe again felt the old terror. The pope feared that the dreaded enemy might break into Italy. Throughout Germany by the emperor's order special "Turk bells" sounded the alarm. The states of the Empire assembled in 1663 as a diet at Regensburg. They voted to raise a small imperial army. The Holy Roman Empire, even in its senility, bestirred itself temporarily against the historic enemy of the Christians. But it was not the Empire, but the house of Austria, under whose auspices the Turks were to be repelled.

24. THE FORMATION OF AN AUSTRIAN MONARCHY

Having now surveyed the three very different empires whose occupancy of most of Europe from France to Muscovy kept the whole area politically malleable and soft, we turn to the three new states which consolidated themselves in this region, namely, Austria, Prussia, and Russia.

The Recovery and Growth of Habsburg Power, 1648–1740

The Austria which appeared by 1700 was in truth a new creation, though not as obviously so as the two others. The Austrian Habsburgs had long enjoyed an eminent role. Formerly their position had rested on their headship of the Holy Roman Empire and on their family connection with the more wealthy Habsburgs of Spain. In the seventeenth century these two supports collapsed. The hope for an effective Habsburg empire in Germany disappeared in the Thirty Years' War. The connection with Spain lost its value as Spain declined, and vanished when in 1700 Spain passed to the house of France. The Austrian family in the latter half of the seventeenth century stood at the great turning point of its fortunes. It successfully made a difficult transition, emerging from the husk of the Holy Empire and building an empire of its own. At the same time the Habsburgs continued to be Holy Roman Emperors and remained active in German affairs, using resources drawn from outside Germany to maintain their influence over the German princes. The relation of Austria to the rest of Germany became a political conundrum, forcibly solved by Bismarck in 1866 by the exclusion of Austria, only to be raised again by Adolf Hitler in the twentieth century.

The dominions considered by the house of Austria to be its own direct possessions were in three parts. The oldest were the "hereditary provinces"—Upper and Lower Austria, with the adjoining Tyrol, Styria, Carinthia, and Carniola. Second, there was the kingdom of Bohemia—Bohemia, Moravia, and Silesia joined under the crown of St. Wenceslas. Third, there was the kingdom of Hungary— Hungary, Transylvania, and Croatia joined under the crown of St. Stephen. Nothing held all these regions together except the fact that the Austrian Habsburg dynasty, in the seventeenth century, reaffirmed its grip upon them all. During the Thirty Years' War the dynasty rooted Protestantism and feudal rebelliousness out of Austria and the hereditary provinces, and reconquered and re-Catholicized Bohemia. And in the following decades it conquered Hungary also.

Since 1526 most of Hungary had been occupied by the Turks. For generations the Hungarian plain was a theater of intermittent warfare between the armies of Vienna and Constantinople. The struggle flared up again in 1663, when the Kiuprili vizier started Turkish armies moving up the Danube. A mixed force, assembled from the Empire and from all Christendom, obliged the Turks in 1664 to accept a twenty-year truce. But Louis XIV, who in these years was busily dismembering the western frontier of the Empire, stood to profit greatly from a diversion on the Danube. He incited the Turks (old allies of France through common hostility to the Habsburgs) to resume their assaults, which they did as the twenty-year truce came to a close.

In 1683 a vast Turkish host reached the city of Vienna and besieged it. The Turks again, as in 1529, peered into the very inner chambers of Europe. The garrison and people of Vienna, greatly outnumbered, held off the besiegers for two months, enough time for a defending force to arrive. Both sides showed the composite or "international" character of the conflict. The Turkish army included some Christians—Rumanian and Hungarian—the latter being in rebellion against Habsburg rule in Hungary. The Christian force was composed mainly of Poles, Austrian dynastic troops, and Germans from various states of the Empire. It was

THE GROWTH OF THE AUSTRIAN MONARCHY, 1521–1772

The map shows the main body of the Austrian monarchy as it came to be in the eighteenth century and continued until the collapse of the empire in 1918. There were three main parts: (1) a nucleus, composed of Austria and adjoining duchies, often called the "hereditary provinces"; (2) the lands of the Bohemian crown, which became Habsburg in 1526 and where the Habsburgs reasserted their power during the Bohemian phase of the Thirty Years' War; and (3) the lands of the Hungarian crown, where at first the Habsburgs held only the segment called Imperial Hungary, the rest remaining Turkish until reconquered by the Habsburgs in 1699. In the first partition of Poland the Habsburgs annexed Galicia. Silesia was lost to Prussia in 1740. Outlying parts of the empire in the eighteenth century, not shown on the map, were most of what is now Belgium (then the Austrian Netherlands) and the duchy of Milan in Italy. The Italian duchy of Tuscany, where the Medici family died out in 1737, was thereafter ruled as a separate state by a Habsburg archduke.

financed largely by Pope Innocent XI; it was commanded in the field by the Habsburg general, Duke Charles of Lorraine, who hoped to protect his inheritance from annexation by France; and its higher command was entrusted to John Sobieski, king of Poland. Sobieski contributed greatly to the relief of Vienna, and his bold action represented the last great military effort of the moribund Republic of Poland. When the Turks abandoned the siege, a general anti-Turkish counteroffensive developed. Forces of the pope, Poland, Russia, and the republic of Venice joined with the Habsburgs. It was in this war, in fighting between Turks and

Venetians, that the Parthenon at Athens, which had survived for two thousand years but was now used as an ammunition dump by the Turks, was blown to ruins.

The Habsburgs had the good fortune to obtain the services of a man of remarkable talent, Prince Eugene of Savoy. Eugene, like many other servants of the Austrian house, was not Austrian at all; he was in fact French by origin and education but like many of the aristocratic class of the time was an international personage. More than anyone else he was the founder of the modern Austrian state. Distinguished both as a military administrator and as a commander in the field, he reformed the supply, equipment, training, and command of the Habsburg forces, along lines laid out by Louis XIV, and in 1697 he won the battle of Zenta, driving the Turks out of Hungary. At the Peace of Karlowitz (1699) the Turks yielded most of Hungary, together with Transylvania and Croatia, to the Habsburg house.

The Habsburgs were now free to pursue their designs in the west. They entered the War of the Spanish Succession to win the Spanish crown, but although an Austrian archduke campaigned in Spain for years, assisted by the English, they had to content themselves at the treaty of Rastadt in 1714 with the annexation of the old Spanish Netherlands and with Milan and Naples. Prince Eugene, freed now in the west, again turned eastward. Never before or afterward were the Austrians so brilliantly successful. Eugene captured Belgrade and pushed through the Iron Gate into Wallachia. But the Turks were not yet helpless; and by the Peace of Belgrade (1739) a frontier was drawn which on the Austrian side remained unchanged until the twentieth century. The Turks continued to hold Rumania and the whole Balkan peninsula except Catholic Croatia, which, incorporated in the Habsburg empire, was again faced toward Europe. The Habsburg government, to open a window on the Mediterranean, developed a seaport at Trieste.

The Austrian Monarchy by 1740

Thus the house of Austria, in two or three generations after its humiliation at the Peace of Westphalia, acquired a new empire of very considerable proportions. Though installed in Belgium and Italy, it was essentially an empire of the middle Danube, with its headquarters at Vienna in Austria proper, but possessing the sizable kingdoms of Hungary and Bohemia, and so filling the basin enclosed by the Alpine, Bohemian, and Carpathian mountain systems. Though German influence was strong, the empire was international or nonnational. At the Habsburg court, and in the Habsburg government and army, the names of Czech, Hungarian, Croatian, and Italian noblemen were very common. It is hard today to see this empire as it was, because it is hard to see it except through the eyes of its enemies. It made enemies of all Protestants. Democrats came to hate it. When the nationalistic movement swept over Europe in the nineteenth century, the empire was denounced as tyrannical by Hungarians, Croats, Serbs, Rumanians, Czechs, Poles, Italians, and even some Germans, whose national ambitions were blocked by its existence. Later, disillusioned by nationalism in central and eastern Europe, some tended to romanticize unduly the old Danubian monarchy, noting that it had at least the merit of holding many discordant peoples together.

The empire was from the first international, based on a cosmopolitan aristocracy of landowners who felt closer to each other, despite difference of language, than to the laboring masses who worked on their estates. Not for many years, until after 1848, did the Habsburg government really touch these rural masses; it dealt with the landed class and with the relatively few cities, and left the landlords to control the peasants. The old diets remained in being in Bohemia, Hungary, and the Austrian provinces. No diet was created for the empire as a whole. The diets were essentially assemblages of landlords; and though they no longer enjoyed their medieval freedom, they retained certain powers over taxation and administration and a sense of constitutional liberty against the crown, like the Provincial Estates in France. So long as they produced taxes and soldiers as needed, and accepted the wars and foreign policy of the ruling house, no questions were asked at Vienna. The peasants remained in, or reverted to, serfdom.[9]

The Habsburgs were determined to make their new empire unmistakably hereditary and Catholic. The first to feel the blow had been Bohemia. The Czech rebellion had been crushed, as we have seen, at the battle of the White Mountain in 1620.[10] This ended, until 1918, the national independence of a people who had greatly prospered in the Middle Ages. The reigning Habsburg, Ferdinand II, abrogated the elective Bohemian monarchy and declared the kingdom hereditary. He poured Catholic missionaries into the country. He confiscated the estates of the rebel nobles and granted them to a host of adventurers of many nationalities, mostly colonels and generals of the Thirty Years' War. A few of these were Czechs, but most were ignorant of the languages and customs of the people, and they owed their position entirely to the Habsburgs. Bohemia remained an entirely separate kingdom. Its new aristocracy, while remaining apart from the native peasantry and the towns, soon developed a sense of Bohemian autonomy and a desire to be let alone by the central government at Vienna.

Somewhat the same happened in Hungary after its reconquest from the Turks in 1699. Protestantism was widespread in Hungary, where it formed part of the famous Hungarian liberties. Every Hungarian magnate, like princes of the Holy Roman Empire, possessed the *ius reformandi*, or right to reform religion on his own estates. There was thus religious disorder, and religion and politics were mixed. The Turks, during their occupation, favored the Protestants, knowing that Protestants would have no longing for a Catholic Habsburg king. In Hungary, therefore, as in Bohemia, the first step following the reconquest was to repress Protestantism, which was not only detested as heretical but feared as pro-Turkish. The elective monarchy was done away with; the crown of St. Stephen[11] became the hereditary possession of the Habsburgs. The Hungarian nobles lost their constitutional right of armed rebellion. German veterans were settled in the country, the Croats given privileges, and even Serbs imported from across the Danube, all to weaken the grip of the Magyar aristocracy; the effect was to scramble the nationalities in an already heterogeneous region. Hardly had Eugene's armies entered Turkish Hungary when a rebellion against the Habsburgs broke out in 1703, led by Prince Francis Rakoczy, who received help from Louis XIV but was finally crushed by 1711 and spent the rest of his life in France and Turkey. The Hungarians, proud and stubborn, became nationalistic before the era of nationalism. And for all that the Habsburgs could do, Hungary remained a distinct kingdom, and the magnates of Hungary remained the most free-handed aristocracy in Europe, except for the Poles.

[9] See pp. 122–123.
[10] See pp. 139–140.
[11] See p. 26.

Thus, despite the efforts of the Habsburgs, the Austrian monarchy remained a collection of territories held together by a personal union. Inhabitants of Austria proper considered their ruler as archduke, Bohemians saw in him the king of Bohemia, Magyars the apostolic king of Hungary. Each country retained its own law, diet, and political life. No feeling in the people held these regions together, and even the several aristocracies were joined only by common service to the house. For the empire to exist, all crowns had to be inherited by the same person.

After the reconquest of Hungary the king-archduke, Charles VI (1711–1740), devised a form of insurance to guarantee such an undivided succession. This took the form of a document called the Pragmatic Sanction, first issued in 1713. By it every diet in the empire and the various archdukes of the Habsburg family were to agree to regard the Habsburg territories as indivisible and to recognize only one specified line of heirs. The matter became urgent when it developed that Charles would have no children except a daughter, Maria Theresa, and that the direct male line of the Austrian Habsburgs, as of the Spanish a few years before, was about to become extinct. Charles VI gradually won acceptance of the Pragmatic Sanction by all parts of his empire and all members of his family. He then set about having foreign powers guarantee it, knowing that Bavaria, Prussia, or others might well put in claims for this or that part of the inheritance. This process took years, and was accomplished at the cost of many damaging concessions. Charles VI had attempted, for example, to revive Belgium commercially by founding an overseas trading company at Ostend. The British government, before agreeing to guarantee the Pragmatic Sanction, demanded and obtained the abandonment of this commercial project. Finally all powers signed. Charles VI died in 1740, having done all that could be done, by domestic law and international treaty, to assure the continuation of the Austrian empire.

He was scarcely dead when armed "heirs" presented themselves. A great war broke out to partition the Austrian empire, as the Spanish empire had been partitioned shortly before. Bohemia threw off its allegiance. Hungary almost did the same. But these events belong later in the story.[12] At the moment it is enough to know that by 1740 a populous empire, of great military strength, had been founded on the Danube.

25. THE FORMATION OF PRUSSIA

It was characteristic of the seventeenth century that very small states were able to play an influential part in European affairs, seemingly out of all proportion to their size. The main reason why small states could act as great powers was that armies were small and weapons simple. Difficulties of supply and communications, the poor state of the roads, the lack of maps, the absence of general staffs, together with many other administrative and technical difficulties, held down the number of soldiers who could be successfully managed in a campaign. The battles of the Thirty Years' War, on the average, were fought by armies of less than 20,000 men. And while Louis XIV, by the last years of his reign, built up a military establishment aggregating some 400,000, the actual field armies in the wars of Louis XIV did not exceed, on the average, 40,000. Armies of this size were well within the reach of smaller powers. If especially well trained, disciplined, and

---

[12] See pp. 264–275.

equipped, and if ably commanded and economically employed, the armies of small powers could defeat those of much larger neighbors. On this fact, fundamentally, the German state of Prussia was to be built. But Prussia was not the first to exploit the opportunity with spectacular consequences. The first, it may be said, was Sweden.

Sweden's Short-Lived Empire

Sweden almost, but not quite, formed an empire out of the malleable matter of central and eastern Europe in the seventeenth century. The population of Sweden at the time was not over a million; it was smaller than that of the Dutch Republic. But the Swedes produced a line of extraordinary rulers, ranging from genius in Gustavus Adolphus (1611–1632) through the brilliantly erratic Queen Christina (1632–1654) to the amazing military exploits of Charles XII (1697–1718). The elective Swedish kingship was made definitely hereditary, the royal power freed from control by the estates, craftsmen and experts brought from the west, notably Holland, war industries subsidized by the government, and an army created with many novel features in weapons, organization, and tactics.

With this army Gustavus Adolphus crossed the Baltic in the Thirty Years' War, made alliances with Protestant German princes, cut through the yielding mass of the Holy Roman Empire, and helped to ward off unification of Germany by the Habsburgs.[13] The Swedish crown, by the Peace of Westphalia, received certain coastal regions of Germany—western Pomerania, including the city of Stettin, and the former bishoprics of Bremen and Verden on the North Sea. Subsequently, in a confused series of wars, in which a Polish king claimed to be king of Sweden, and a Swedish king claimed to be king of Poland, the Swedes won control of virtually all the shores and cities of the Baltic. Only Denmark at the mouth of that sea and the territories of the house of Brandenburg, which had almost no ports, remained independent. For a time the Baltic was a Swedish lake. The Russians were shut off from it, and the Poles and even the Germans, who lived on its shores, could reach it only on Swedish terms.

The final Swedish effort was made by the meteoric Charles XII. As a young man he found his dominions attacked by Denmark, Poland, and Russia; he won victories over them but would not make peace; he then led an army back and forth across the East European plain, only to be ruined by the Russians, and spend more long years as a guest and protégé of the Turks.[14] With the death of Charles XII in 1718 the Swedish sphere contracted to Sweden itself, except that Finland and reduced holdings in northern Germany remained Swedish for a century more. The Swedes in time proved themselves exceptional among European peoples in not harping on their former greatness. They successfully and peaceably made the transition from the role of a great power to that of a small one.

The Territorial Growth of Brandenburg-Prussia

In the long run it was to be Prussia that dominated this part of Europe. Prussia also became famous for its "militarism," which may be said to exist when military

---

[13] See pp. 140–144.
[14] See p. 233.

needs and military values permeate all other spheres of life. Through its influence on Germany over a period of two centuries it played a momentous part in the modern world. The south coast of the Baltic, where Prussia was to arise, was an unpromising site for the creation of a strong political power. It was an uninviting country, thinly populated, with poor soil and without mineral resources, more backward than Saxony or Bohemia, not to mention the busy centers of south Germany and western Europe. It was a flat open plain, merging imperceptibly into Poland, without prominent physical features or natural frontiers.[15] The coastal region directly south from Sweden was known as Pomerania. Inland from it, shut off from the sea, was the electoral margraviate of Brandenburg, centering about Berlin. In 1415 the Hohenzollern family had come to rule Brandenburg, which was to be the nucleus of modern Prussia. Brandenburg had been founded in the Middle Ages as a "mark" or "march" of the Holy Roman Empire, to fight the battles of the Holy Empire against the then heathen Slavs. All Germany east of the Elbe represented a medieval conquest by the German-speaking peoples—the German *Drang nach Osten*, or drive to the East. From the Elbe to Poland, German conquerors and settlers had replaced the primitive Slavs, eliminating them or absorbing them by intermarriage.

Extending eastward from Brandenburg and Pomerania, and outside the Holy Roman Empire, stretched a region inhabited by Slavic peoples and known historically as Pomerelia. Next to the east came "Prussia," which eventually was to give its name to all territories of the Hohenzollern monarchy. This original Prussia formed part of the lands of the Teutonic Knights, a military crusading order which had conquered and Christianized the native peoples in the thirteenth century.[16] Except for its seacoast along the Baltic, the duchy of Prussia was totally enclosed by the Polish kingdom. To the north, along the Baltic, as far as the Gulf of Finland, German minorities lived among undeveloped Lithuanians, Latvians (or Letts), and Estonians. The towns were German, founded as German commercial colonies in the Middle Ages, and many of the landlords were German also, descendants of the Teutonic Knights, and later known as the "Baltic barons." These Germans at that time, since nationalist sentiment scarcely existed, felt no affiliation with the main block of Germans farther west, but they retained their German language and traditions.

Modern Prussia began to appear in the seventeenth century when a number of territories came together in the hands of the Hohenzollerns of Brandenburg, who, we have noted, had ruled in Brandenburg since 1415. In 1618 the Elector of Brandenburg inherited the duchy of Prussia. Another important development occurred when the old ruling line in Pomerania expired during the Thirty Years' War. Although the Swedes succeeded in taking the better part of Pomerania, including the city of Stettin, the Elector of Brandenburg received at the Peace of Westphalia eastern or Farther Pomerania. Barren, rural, and harborless though it was, it at least had the advantage of connecting Brandenburg with the Baltic. The Hohenzollerns no sooner obtained it than they began to dream of joining it to the duchy of Prussia, a task which required the absorption of the intermediate and predominantly Slavic Pomerelia, which was part of Poland. (This task was accomplished in 1772. The Hohenzollern administrators then called the old duchy "East Prussia" and the old Pomerelia "West Prussia"; but by that time, in a

---

[15] See maps, pp. 6–7, 142–143, 206, 210.
[16] See p. 44.

THE GROWTH OF PRUSSIA, 1415–1918

The maps shown here give a conspectus of Prussian history from the time when Brandenburg began to expand in the seventeenth century. One may see, by looking at all the panels
together, how Prussia was really an east-European state until 1815; its center of gravity
shifted westward, in significant degree, only in the nineteenth century. Panel 2 shows the
early formation of three unconnected masses; Panel 3, the huge bulk of Silesia relative to
the small kingdom that annexed it (pp. 265–268); Panel 4, the fruits of the partitions of
Poland (p. 328); Panel 5, Napoleon pared Prussia down (pp. 395–396). The main crisis at
the Congress of Vienna, and its resolution, are shown in Panels 6 and 7 (pp. 422–423). Bismarck's enlargement of Prussia appears in Panel 8 (pp. 523–524). The boundaries established by Bismarck remained unchanged until the fall of the Prussian monarchy in 1918.

general confusion of nomenclature, "Prussia" also referred to all the Hohenzollern
provinces taken together.)

Had the duchy of Prussia and Farther Pomerania been the only acquisitions of
the Hohenzollerns, their state would have been oriented almost exclusively
toward eastern Europe. But at the Peace of Westphalia they received, in addition
to Farther Pomerania, the large bishopric of Halberstadt and the still larger arch-

bishopric of Magdeburg, which lay on the west bank of the Elbe. Moreover, through the play of inheritance so common in the Holy Roman Empire, the Hohenzollerns had earlier fallen heir, in 1614, to the small state of Cleves on the Rhine at the Dutch border and a few other small territories also in western Germany. These were separated from the main mass around Brandenburg by many intermediate German principalities. But they gave the Hohenzollerns a direct contact with the more advanced regions of western Europe, and a base from which larger holdings in the Rhineland were eventually to be built up.

In the seventeenth century, meanwhile, the dominions of the house of Brandenburg were in three disconnected masses. The main mass was Brandenburg, with the adjoining Pomerania and Elbe bishoprics. There was a detached eastern mass in ducal Prussia and a small detached western mass on and near the Rhine. The middle and western masses were within the Holy Roman Empire. The eastern mass was outside the Empire, and until 1660, a fief of Poland. To connect and unify the three masses became the underlying long-range policy of the Brandenburg house.

In the midst of the Thirty Years' War, in 1640, a young man of twenty, named

Frederick William, succeeded to these diverse possessions. Known later as the Great Elector, he was the first of the men who made modern Prussia. He had grown up under trying conditions. Brandenburg was one of the parts of Germany to suffer most heavily from the war. Its location made it the stamping ground of Swedish and Habsburg armies. In 1640, in the twenty-two years since the beginning of the war, the population of Berlin had fallen from about 14,000 to about 6,000. Hundreds of villages had been wiped out. Wolves roamed over the countryside.

Frederick William concluded that in his position, ruling a small and open terri-tory, without natural frontiers or possibility of defense in depth, he must put his main reliance on a competent army. With an effective army, even if small, he could oblige the stronger states to take him into their calculations and so could enter with some hope of advantage into the politics of the balance of power. This long remained the program of the Brandenburgers—to have an army but not to use it, to conserve it with loving and even miserly care, to keep an "army in be-ing," and to gain their ends by diplomatic maneuver. They did so by siding with France against the Habsburgs, or with Sweden against Poland. They aspired also to the title not merely of margrave or elector, but king. The opportunity came in 1701, when the Habsburg emperor was preparing to enter the War of the Spanish Succession. He wanted the support of 8,000 Brandenburg troops. The elector named his price: recognition of himself, by the emperor, as king "in Prussia." The emperor yielded; the title, at first explicitly limited to the less honorable king *in* Prussia, soon became king *of* Prussia. Another rent was made in the old fabric of the Holy Empire. There was now a German king above all the other German princes.

The Prussian Military State

The preoccupation of Prussia with its army was unquestionably defensive in origin, arising from the horrors of the Thirty Years' War. But it outlasted its cause, and became the settled habit and character of the country. Prussia was not unique, in a world of Bourbons and Habsburgs, Swedes, Russians, Turks, and the growing British navy, in the attention it paid to its armed forces. The unique thing about Prussia was the disproportion between the size of the army and the size of the resources on which the army was based. The government, to maintain the army, had to direct and plan the life of the country for this purpose. Nor was Prussia the originator of the "standing" army, kept active in time of peace, and always preparing for war. Most governments imitated Louis XIV in establishing standing armies, not merely to promote foreign ambitions but to keep armed forces out of the hands of nobles and military adventurers, and under control by the state.

But Prussia was unique in that, more than in any other country, the army de-veloped a life of its own, almost independent of the life of the state. It was older than the Prussian state. In 1657 the Great Elector fought a great battle at War-saw with soldiers from all parts of his dominions. It was the first time that men from Cleves, Brandenburg, and ducal Prussia had ever done anything together. The army was the first "all Prussian" institution. Institutions of civilian govern-ment developed later and largely to meet the needs of the army. And in later gen-erations the army proved more durable than the state. When Prussia collapsed before Napoleon in 1806, the spirit and morale of the Prussian army carried on; and when the Hohenzollern empire finally crashed in 1918, the army still maintained its life and traditions on into the Republic, which again it survived.[17]

In all countries, to some extent, the machinery of the modern state developed as a means of supporting armed forces, but in Prussia the process was exceptionally clear and simple. In Prussia the rulers drew roughly half their income from the crown domain and only about half from taxes. The crown domain, consisting of manors and other productive enterprises owned directly by the ruler as lord, was in effect a kind of government property, for the Prussian rulers used their income almost entirely for state purposes, being personally men of simple and even Spartan habits. The rulers of Prussia, until a century after the accession of the Great Elector, were able to pay the whole cost of their civil government from their own income, the proceeds of the crown domain. But to maintain an army they had to make the domain more productive, and also find a new income derived from taxes. To develop the domain and account for and transfer the funds, they created a large body of civilian officials. The domain bulked so large that much of the economy of the country was not in private hands but consisted of enterprises owned and administered by the state. For additional income the Great Elector introduced taxes of the kind used in France, such as excise taxes on consumers' goods and a government monopoly on the sale of salt. These taxes, together with the old land tax, began to be collected during the disorders of the Thirty Years' War by war commissioners, later organized into a general commissariat. In effect, the army itself collected the taxes and determined the purposes for which the funds should be spent. All taxes, for a century after the accession of the Great Elector, were levied for the use of the army.

Economic life grew up under government sponsorship, rather than by the enterprise of a venturesome business class. This was because, for a rural country to maintain an organized army, productive and technical skills had to be imported, mainly from the West. The Great Elector in his youth spent a number of years in Holland, where he was impressed by the wealth and prosperity that he saw. After becoming elector he settled Swiss and Frisians in Brandenburg (the Frisians were almost Dutch); he welcomed Jews from Poland; and when Louis XIV began to persecute the French Protestants, he provided funds and special officials to assist the immigration of 20,000 Huguenots to Brandenburg. Frenchmen for a time formed a sixth of the population of Berlin and were the most advanced element of that comparatively primitive city. The government, as in France under Colbert, initiated and helped to finance various industries; but the importance of such government participation was greater than in France, because the amount of privately owned capital available for investment was incomparably less. Military needs, more than elsewhere, dominated the market for goods, because civilian demand, in so poor a country, was relatively low; so that the army, in its requirements for food, uniforms, and weapons, was a strong force in shaping the economic growth of the country.

The army had a profound effect also on the social development and class structure of Prussia. The civilian middle class remained submissive, and it became the policy of the rulers to absorb practically the whole landed aristocracy, the Junkers, into military service. They used the army, with conscious purpose, as a means

---

[17] See pp. 412–414, 682–683, 747.

of implanting an "all Prussian" psychology in the landed families of Cleves, Brandenburg, Pomerania, and the former dominions of the Teutonic Knights. The sense of service to the king or state was exalted as the supreme human virtue. The fact that Prussia was a very recent and artificial combination of territories, so that loyalty to it was not at first a natural sentiment, made it all the more necessary to instill it by obvious and martial means. Emphasis fell on duty, obedience, service, and sacrifice. That military virtues became characteristic of the whole Prussian aristocracy was also due, like so much else, to the small size of the population. In France, for example, with perhaps 50,000 male adult nobles, only a small minority served habitually as army officers. In Prussia there were few Junker families that did not have some of their members in uniform.

Moreover, the Great Elector and his successors, like all absolutist rulers, repressed the estates or parliamentary assemblages in which the landed aristocracy was the main element. To mollify the squires, the rulers promised commissions in the army to men of their class. They promised them also a free hand over their peasants. The Prussian monarchy was largely based on an understanding between the ruler and the landlord gentry—the latter agreed to accept the ruler's government and to serve in his army, in return for holding their own peasants in hereditary subjection. Serfdom spread in Prussia as elsewhere in eastern Europe.[18] In East Prussia the condition of the peasants became as deplorable as in Poland.

The Prussian rulers believed that the Junkers made better army officers because they were brought up in the habit of commanding their own peasants. Bourgeois officers, a minority in all armies, were of the utmost rarity in Prussia. To preserve the officer class, legislation forbade the sale of "noble" lands, i.e., manors, to persons not noble. In France, again by way of contrast, where manorial rights had become simply a form of property, bourgeois and even peasants could legally acquire manors and enjoy a lordly or "seigneurial" income. In Prussia this was not possible; classes were frozen by owning nonexchangeable forms of property. It was thus harder for middle-class persons to enter the aristocracy by setting up as landed gentry. The bourgeois class in any case had little spirit of independence. Few of the old towns of Germany were in Prussia. The Prussian middle class was not wealthy. It was not strong by the possession of private property. The typical middle-class man was an official, who worked for the government as an employee or leaseholder of the large crown domain, or in an enterprise subsidized by the state. The civil service in Prussia, from the days of the Great Elector, became notable for its honesty and efficiency. But the middle class, more than elsewhere, deferred to the nobles, served the state, and stood in awe of the army.

These peculiar features of Prussia developed especially under Frederick William I, who was king from 1713 to 1740. He was an earthy, uncouth man, who, were the matter less serious, might almost be regarded as a comical character. He disdained whatever savored of "culture," to which his father and grandfather (the Great Elector) and also his son (Frederick the Great) were all strongly attracted. He begrudged every penny not spent on the army. He cut the expense of the royal household by three-fourths. On his coronation journey to Königsberg he spent 2,547 thalers, where his father had spent five million. He ruled the country in a fatherly German way, supervising it like a private estate, prowling the streets of Berlin in an old seedy uniform, and disciplining negligent citizens with blows of

[18] See pp. 122-123, 204-205, 212, 218, 228.

his walking stick. He worked all the time, and expected everyone else to do like-wise. He loved the army, which all his policies were designed to serve. He was the first Prussian king to appear always in uniform. He rearranged the order of courtly precedence, pushing army officers up and civilians down. His love of tall soldiers is famous; he collected a special unit, men between six and seven feet high, from all over Europe, and indeed Peter the Great sent him some from Asia. He devised new forms of discipline and maneuver, founded a cadet corps to train the sons of the Junkers, and invented a new system of recruiting (the canton system, long the most effective in Europe), by which each regiment had a particular district or canton assigned to it as a source of soldiers. He raised the size of the army from 40,000 at his accession to 83,000 at his death. During his reign Berlin grew to be a city of 100,000, of whom 20,000 were soldiers, a proportion probably matched in no other city of Europe. He likewise left to his successor (for he fought practically no wars himself) a war chest of 7,000,000 thalers.

With this army and war chest Frederick II, later called the Great, who became king in 1740, startled Europe. Charles VI of Austria had just died. His daughter Maria Theresa entered upon her manifold inheritance. All Europe was hedging on its guarantee of the Pragmatic Sanction. While others waited, Frederick struck. Serving no notice, he moved his forces into Silesia, to which the Hohen-zollerns had an old though doubtful claim. Silesia was a part of the kingdom of Bohemia on the side toward Poland, lying in the upper valley of the Oder River, and adjoining Brandenburg on the north. The addition of Silesia to the king-dom of Prussia almost doubled the population and added valuable industries, so that Prussia now, with 6,000,000 people and an army which Frederick raised to 200,000, at last established itself as a great power. It must be added that, judged simply as a human accomplishment, Prussia was a remarkable creation, a state made on a shoestring, a triumph of work and duty.

26. THE "WESTERNIZING" OF RUSSIA

The affairs of central and eastern Europe, from Sweden to Turkey and from Ger-many to the Caspian Sea, were profoundly interconnected. The underlying theme of the present chapter, it may be recalled, is that this whole great area was fluid, occupied by the flabby bodies of the Holy Roman Empire, Poland, and Turkey, and that in this fluid area three harder masses developed—the modern Austrian monarchy, the kingdom of Prussia, and the Russian empire. All, too, in varying degree, were modernized by borrowings from the West.

In the century after 1650 the old tsardom of Muscovy turned into modern Rus-sia. Moving out from the region around Moscow, the Russians not only estab-lished themselves across northern Asia, reaching the Bering Sea about 1700, but also entered into closer relations with Europe, undergoing especially in the time of Tsar Peter the Great (1682–1725) a rapid process of Europeanization. To what extent Russia became truly European has always been an open question, disputed both by western Europeans and by Russians themselves. In some ways the Rus-sians have been European from as far back as Europe itself can be said to have existed, i.e., from the early Middle Ages. Ancient Russia had been colonized by Vikings, and the Russians had become Christians long before the Swedes, the Lithuanians, or the Finns. But Russia had not been part of the general development of Europe for a number of reasons. For one thing, Russia had been con-verted to the Greek Orthodox branch of Christianity; therefore, the religious and cultural influence of Constantinople, not of Rome, had predominated. Second, the Mongol invasions and conquest about 1240 had kept Russia under Asiatic domination for about two hundred and fifty years, until 1480 when a grand duke of Muscovy, Ivan III (1462–1505), was able to throw off the Mongol overlordship and cease payment of tribute.[19] Last, Russian geography, especially the lack of warm-water or ice-free seaports, had made commerce and communication with the West difficult. For these reasons Russia had not shared in the general Euro-pean development after about 1100, and the changes that took place in the seven-teenth and eighteenth centuries may accurately be called Europeanization, or at least a wholesale borrowing of the apparatus of civilization from the West. The Europeanizing or westernizing of Russia was by no means a unique thing. It was a step in the expansion of the European type of civilization and hence in the for-mation of the modern world as we have known it in the last three hundred years.

In some ways the new Russian empire resembled the new kingdom of Prussia. Both took form in the great plain which runs uninterruptedly from the North Sea into inner Asia. Both lacked natural frontiers and grew by addition of territories to an original nucleus. In both countries the state arose primarily as a means of supporting a modern army. In both the government developed autocratically, in conjunction with a landlord class which was impressed into state service and which in turn held the peasantry in serfdom. Neither Russia nor Prussia had a native commercial class of any political importance. In neither country could the modern state and army have been created without the importation of skills from western Europe. Yet Prussia, with its German connections, its Protestant religion, its universities, and its nearness to the busy commercial artery of the Baltic, was far more "European" than Russia, and the Europeanization of Russia may per-haps better be compared with the later westernization of Japan.[20] In the Russia of 1700, as in the Japan of 1870, the main purpose of the westernizers was to obtain scientific, technical, and military knowledge from the West, in part with a view to strengthening their own countries against penetration or conquest by Euro-peans. Yet here too the parallel must not be pushed too far. Russia became more fully Europeanized than did the peoples of Asia. In time, its upper classes inter-married with Europeans, and Russian music and literature became part of the culture of Europe. Russia developed a unique blend of European and non-European traits.

Russia before Peter the Great

The Russians in the seventeenth century, as today, were a medley of peoples dis-tinguished by their language, which was of the Slavic family, of the great Indo-European language group.[21] The Great Russians or Muscovites lived around Mos-cow. Moving out from that area, they had penetrated the northern forests and had also settled in the southern steppes and along the Volga, where they had as-similated various Asiatic peoples known as Tartars. After two centuries of expan-sion, from roughly 1450 to 1650, the Russians had almost but not quite reached

[19] See pp. 27, 45.
[20] See pp. 543–549.
[21] See p. 13, and the language map in Chapter XI, section 53.

the Baltic and the Black seas. The Baltic shore was held by Sweden. The Black Sea coast was still held by Tartar Khans under the protection of Turkey. In the rough borderlands between Tartar and Russian lived the semi-independent cowboy-like Cossacks, largely recruited from migratory Russians. West of Muscovy were the White Russians (or Byelorussians) and southwest of Muscovy the Little Russians (or Ruthenians or Ukrainians), both in the seventeenth century under the rule of Poland, which was then the leading Slavic power.

The energies of the Great Russians were directed principally eastward. They conquered the Volga Tartars in the sixteenth century, thus reaching the Ural Mountains, which they immediately crossed. Muscovite pioneers, settlers, and townbuilders streamed along the river systems of Siberia, felling timber and trading in furs as they went. In the 1630s, while the English founded Boston and the Dutch New York, the Russians were establishing towns in the vast Asiatic stretches of Siberia, reaching to the Pacific itself. A whole string of settlements, remote, small, and isolated—Tomsk and Tobolsk, Irkutsk and Yakutsk—extended for 5,000 miles across northern Asia.

It was toward the vast heartland of central Asia that Muscovy really faced, looking out upon Persia and China across the deserts. The bazaars of Moscow and Astrakhan were frequented by Persians, Afghans, Kirkhiz, Indians, and Chinese. The Caspian Sea, into which flowed the Volga, the greatest of Russian rivers, was better known than was the Baltic. Europe as sensed from Moscow was in the rear. During most of the seventeenth century even Smolensk and Kiev belonged to Poland. Yet the Russians were not totally shut off from Europe. In 1552, when Ivan the Terrible conquered Kazan from the Tartars, he had a German engineer in his army. In the next year, 1553, Richard Chancellor arrived in Moscow from England by the roundabout way of Archangel on the White Sea.[22] Thereafter trade between England and Muscovy was continuous. The tsars valued Archangel as their only inlet from the West, through which military materials could be imported. The English valued it as a means of reaching the wares of Persia.

Russia in the seventeenth century reflected its long estrangement from Europe and its long association with the peoples of Asia. Women of the upper classes were secluded and often wore veils. Men wore beards and skirted garments that seemed exotic to Europeans. Customs were crude, wild drunkenness and revelry alternating with spasms of repentance and religious prostration. Dwarfs and fools, no longer the fashion in the West, still amused the tsar and his retainers. Superstition infected the highest classes of church and state. Life counted for little; murder, kidnapping, torture, and elaborate physical cruelty were common. The Russian church supported no such educational or charitable institutions as did the Catholic and Protestant churches of Europe and had developed no such respect for learning or sentiments of humanity. Churchmen feared the incipient Western influences. "Abhorred of God," declared a Russian bishop, "is any who loves geometry; it is a spiritual sin." Even arithmetic was hardly understood in Russia. Arabic numerals were not used, and merchants computed with the abacus. The calendar was dated from the creation of the world. Ability to predict an eclipse seemed a form of magic. Clocks, brought in by Europeans, seemed as wonderful in Russia as they did in China, where they were brought in by Jesuits at about the same time.

[22] See p. 108.

Yet this great barbarous Russia, which fronted on inner Asia, was European in some of its fundamental social institutions. It possessed a variant of the manorial and feudal systems. It felt the same wave of constitutional crises that was sweeping over Europe at the same time. Russia had a duma or council of retainers and advisers to the tsar, and the rudiments of a national assembly corresponding to meetings of the estates in western Europe. In Russia as in Europe the question was whether power should remain in the hands of these bodies or become concentrated in the hands of the ruler. Ivan the Terrible, who ruled from 1533 to 1584 and was the first grand duke of Muscovy to assume the title of tsar,[23] was a shrewd observer of contemporary events in Poland. He saw the dissolution that was overtaking the Polish state and was determined to avoid it in Muscovy. His ferocity toward those who opposed him made him literally terrible, but though his methods were not used in Europe, his aims were the aims of his European contemporaries. Not long after his death Russia passed into a period known as the Time of Troubles (1604–1613), during which the Russian nobles elected a series of tsars and demanded certain assurances of their own liberties. But the country was racked by contending factions and civil war, like the religious wars in France or the Thirty Years' War in central Europe.

In 1613 a national assembly, hoping to settle the troubles, elected a seventeen-year-old boy as tsar, or emperor, believing him young enough to have no connection with any of the warring factions. The new boy tsar was Michael Romanov, of a gentry family, related by marriage to the old line of Ivan the Terrible. Thus was established, by vote of the political classes of the day, the Romanov dynasty which ruled in Russia until 1917. The early Romanovs, aware of the fate of elective monarchy in Poland and elsewhere, soon began to repress the representative institutions of Russia and set up as absolute monarchs. Here again, though they were more lawless and violent than any European king, they followed the general pattern of contemporary Europe.

Nor can it be said that the main social development of the seventeenth century in Russia, the sinking of the peasantry into an abyss of helpless serfdom, was exclusively a Russian phenomenon. The same generally took place in eastern Europe.[24] Serfdom had long been overtaking the older free peasantry of Russia. In Russia, as in the American colonies, land was abundant and labor scarce. The natural tendency of labor was to migrate over the great plain, to run off to the Cossacks, or to go to Siberia. In the Time of Troubles, especially, there was a good deal of moving about. The landlords wished to assure themselves of their labor force. To this end they obtained the support of the Romanov tsars. The manor, or what corresponded to it in Russia, came to resemble the slave plantation of the New World.[25] Laws against fugitive serfs were strengthened; lords won the right to recover fugitives up to fifteen years after their flight, and finally the time limit was abolished altogether. Peasants came to be so little regarded that a law of 1625 authorized anyone killing another man's peasant simply to give him another peasant in return. Lords exercised police and judicial powers. By a law of 1646 landowners were required to enter the names of all their peasants in government registers;

---

[23] The Slavic word *tsar*, like the German *Kaiser*, derives from *Caesar*, a title used as a synonym for *emperor* in the Roman, the Holy Roman, and the Byzantine (or Eastern Roman) empires. The spelling *czar*, also common in English, reveals the etymology and the current English-language pronunciation, *zar*.

[24] See pp. 122–123, 204–205, 226–227.

[25] See pp. 251–252.

peasants once so entered, together with their descendants, were regarded as attached to the estate on which they were registered. Thus the peasant lost the freedom to move at his own will. For a time he was supposed to have secure tenure of his land; but a law of 1675 allowed the lords to sell peasants without the land, and thus to move peasants like chattels at the will of the owner. This sale of serfs without land, which made their condition more like slavery as practiced in America, became indeed a distinctive feature of serfdom in Russia, since in Poland, Prussia, Bohemia, and other regions of serfdom, the serf was generally regarded as "bound to the soil," inseparable from the land.

Against the loss of their freedom the rural population of Russia protested as best it could, murdering landlords, fleeing to the Cossacks, taking refuge in a vagrant existence, countered by wholesale government-organized manhunts and by renewed and more stringent legislation. A tremendous uprising was led in 1667 by Stephen Razin, who gathered a host of fugitive serfs, Cossacks, and adventurers, outfitted a fleet on the Caspian Sea, plundered Russian vessels, defeated a Persian squadron, and invaded Persia itself. He then turned back, ascended the Volga, killing and burning as he went and proclaiming a war against landlords, nobles, and priests. Cities opened their gates to him; an army sent against him went over to his side. He was caught and put to death in 1671. The consequence of the rebellion, for over a century, was that serfdom was clamped on the country more firmly than ever.

Even from the church the increasingly wretched rural people drew little comfort. The Russian Orthodox church at this same time went through a great internal crisis, and ended up as hardly more than a department of the tsardom, useful to the government in instilling a superstitious reverence for Holy Russia. The Russian church had historically looked to the Patriarch of Constantinople as its head. But the conquest of Constantinople by the Turks made the head of the Greek Orthodox church a merely tolerated inferior to the Muslim sultan-caliph, so that the Russians in 1589 set up an independent Russian patriarch of their own. In the following generations the Russian patriarchate first became dependent on, then was destroyed by, the tsarist government.

In the 1650s the Russian patriarch undertook certain church reforms, mainly to correct mistranslations in Russian versions of the Bible and other sacred writings. The changes aroused the horror and indignation of the general body of believers. Superstitiously attached to the mere form of the written word, believing the faith itself to depend on the customary spelling of the name of Jesus, the malcontents saw in the reformers a band of cunning Greek scholars perpetrating the work of Antichrist and the devil. The patriarch and higher church officials forced through the reforms but only with the help of the government and the army. Those who rejected the reforms came to be called Old Believers. More ignorant and fanatical than the established church, agitated by visionary preachers, dividing into innumerable sects, the Old Believers became very numerous, especially among the peasants. Old Believers were active in Stephen Razin's rebellion and in all the sporadic peasant uprisings that followed. The peasants, already put by serfdom outside the protection of law, were also largely estranged from the established religion. A distrust of all organized authority settled over the Russian masses, to whom both church and government seemed mere engines of repression.

But while willing enough to modernize to the extent of correcting mistranslations from the Greek, the church officials resisted the kind of modernization that was coming in from western Europe. They therefore opposed Peter the Great at the end of the century. After 1700 no new patriarch was appointed. Peter put the church under a committee of bishops called the Holy Synod, and to the Synod he attached a civil official called the Procurator of the Holy Synod, who was not a churchman but head of a government bureau, and whose task was to see that the church did nothing displeasing to the tsar. Peter thus secularized the church, making himself in effect its head. But while the consequences were more extreme in Russia than elsewhere, it must again be noted that this action of Peter's followed the general pattern of Europe. Secular supervision of religion had become the rule almost everywhere, especially in Protestant countries. Indeed an Englishman of the time thought that Peter the Great, in doing away with the patriarchate and putting the church under his own control, was wisely imitating England, which he visited in his youth.

Peter the Great: Foreign Affairs and Territorial Expansion

The Russia in which Peter the Great became tsar, in 1682, was in short European in some ways and had in any case been in contact with Westerners for over a century. Without Peter, Russia would have developed its European connections more gradually. Peter, by his tempo and methods, made the process a social revolution.

Peter obtained his first knowledge of the West in Moscow itself, where a part of the city known as the German quarter was inhabited by Europeans of various nationalities, whom Peter often visited as a boy. Peter also in his early years mixed with Westerners at Archangel, still Russia's only port, for he was fascinated by the sea and took lessons in navigation on the White Sea from Dutch and English ship captains. Like the Great Elector of Brandenburg, Peter as a young man spent over a year in western Europe, especially Holland and England, where he was profoundly impressed with the backwardness of his own country. He had considerable talents as a mechanic and organizer. He labored with his own hands as a ship's carpenter in Amsterdam and talked with political and business leaders on means of introducing Western organization and technology into Russia. He visited workshops, mines, commercial offices, art galleries, hospitals, and forts. Europeans saw in him a barbarian of genius, a giant of a man standing a head above most others, bursting with physical vitality and plying all he met with interminable questions on their manner of working and living. He had neither the refinement nor the pretension of Western monarchs; he mixed easily with workmen and technical people, dressed cheaply and carelessly, loved horseplay and crude practical jokes, and dismayed his hosts by the squalid disorder in which he and his companions left the rooms put at their disposal. A man of acute practical mind, he was as little troubled by appearances as by moral scruples.

Peter on his visit to Europe in 1697–1698 recruited almost 1,000 experts for service in Russia, and many more followed later. He cared nothing for the civilization of Europe except as a means to an end, and this end was to create an army and a state which could stand against those of the West. His aim from the beginning was in part defensive, to ward off the Poles, Swedes, and Turks who had long pushed against Russia; and in part expansionist, to obtain seaports or "windows on the West," warm-water ports on the Baltic and Black seas, free from the shortcomings of Archangel, which was frozen a good part of the year and in any case offered only a roundabout route to Europe. For all but two years of his long reign Peter was at war.

The Poles were a receding danger. A Polish prince had indeed been elected tsar of Muscovy during the Time of Troubles, and for a while the Poles aspired to conquer and Catholicize the Great Russians, but in 1667 the Russians had regained Smolensk and Kiev, and the growing anarchy in Poland made that country no longer a menace, except as the Swedes or others might install themselves in it. The Turks and their feudatories the Tartars, though no longer expanding, were still obstinate foes. Peter before going to Europe managed in 1696 to capture Azov at the mouth of the Don, but he was unable to hold any of the Black Sea coast and learned in these campaigns to know the inferiority of the Russian army. The Swedes were the main enemy of Russia. Their army, for its size, was still probably the best in Europe. By occupying Finland, Karelia, and Livonia they controlled the whole eastern shore of the Baltic including the Gulf of Finland. In 1697, the Swedish king having died, Peter entered into an alliance with Poland and Denmark to partition the overseas possessions of the Swedish house.

The new king of Sweden, the youthful Charles XII, though descended from civilized enough forebears, was in some ways as crude as Peter (as an adolescent he had sheep driven into his rooms in the palace in order to enjoy the warlike pleasure of killing them), but he proved also to have remarkable aptitude as a general. In 1700, at the battle of Narva, with an army of 8,000 men, he routed Peter's 40,000 Russians. The tsar thus learned another lesson on the need of westernizing his state and army. Fortunately for the Russians Charles XII, instead of immediately pressing his advantage in Russia, spent the following years in furthering Swedish interests in Poland, where he forced the Poles to elect the Swedish candidate as their king. Peter meanwhile, with his imported officers and technicians, reformed the training, discipline, and weapons of the Russian army. Finally Charles XII invaded Russia with a large and well-prepared force. Peter used against him the strategy later used by the Russians against Napoleon and Adolf Hitler; he drew the Swedes into the endless plains, exposing them to the Russian winter, which happened to be an exceptionally severe one, and in 1709, at Poltava in south Russia, he met and overwhelmed the demoralized remainder. The entire Swedish army was destroyed at Poltava, only the king and a few hundred fugitives managing to escape across the Turkish frontier. Peter in the next years conquered Livonia and part of eastern Finland. He landed troops near Stockholm itself. He campaigned in Pomerania almost as far west as the Elbe. Never before had Russian influence reached so deeply into Europe. The imperial day of Sweden was now over, terminated by Russia. Peter had won for Russia a piece of the Baltic shore and with it warm-water outlets. These significant developments ending the great Northern War (1709–1721) were confirmed in the treaty of Nystadt in 1721.

War is surely not the father of all things, as has been sometimes claimed, but these wars did a good deal to father imperial Russia. The army was transformed from an Asiatic horde into a professional force of the kind maintained by Sweden, France, or Prussia. The elite of the old army had been the *streltsi*, a kind of Moscow guard, composed of nobles and constantly active in politics. A rebellion of the *streltsi* in 1698 had cut short Peter's tour of Europe; he had returned and quelled the mutiny by ferocious use of torture and execution, killing five of the rebels with his own hands. The *streltsi* were liquidated only two years before the

THE GROWTH OF RUSSIA IN THE WEST

At the accession of Peter the Great in 1682 the Russian empire, expanding from the old grand duchy of Muscovy, had almost but not quite reached the Black and Baltic seas. Most of Peter's conquests were in the Baltic region where he pushed back the Swedes and built St. Petersburg. Under Catherine the Great (1762–1796) Russia took part in the three partitions of Poland and also reached the Black Sea. Tsar Alexander I (1801–1825), thanks largely to the Napoleonic wars, was able to acquire still more of Poland and annex Finland and Bessarabia; he also made conquests in the Caucasus. In the nineteenth century the western boundary of Russia remained stabilized but additional gains were made in the Caucasus. Russia also spread over northern Asia in the seventeenth century, first reaching the Pacific as early as 1630. (See also map, pp. 720–721.)

great Russian defeat at Narva. Peter then rebuilt the army from the ground up. He employed European officers of many nationalities, paying them half again as much as native Russians of the same grades. He filled his ranks with soldiers supplied by districts on a territorial basis, somewhat as in Prussia. He put the troops into uniforms resembling those of the West and organized them in regiments of standardized composition. He armed them with muskets and artillery of the kind used in Europe and tried to create a service of supply. With this army he had not only driven the Swedes back into Sweden, but also dominated Russia itself. At the very time of the Swedish invasion large parts of the country were in rebellion, as in the days of Stephen Razin, for the whole middle and lower Volga, together with the Cossacks of the Don and Dnieper, rose against the tsar and rallied behind slogans of class war and hatred of the tsar's foreign experts. Peter crushed these disturbances with the usual ruthlessness. The Russian empire, loose and heterogeneous, was held together by military might.

While the war was still in progress, even before the decisive battle of Poltava, Peter laid the foundations of a wholly new city in territory conquered from the Swedes and inhabited not by Russians but by various Baltic peoples. This city is now called Leningrad. Peter named it St. Petersburg after himself and his patron saint. From the beginning it was more truly a city than Louis' spectacular creation at Versailles established at almost the same time. Standing at the head of the Gulf of Finland, it was Peter's chief window on the West. Here he established the offices of government, required noblemen to build town houses, and gave favorable terms to foreign merchants and craftsmen to settle. Peter meant to make St. Petersburg a symbol of the new Russia, a new city facing toward Europe and drawing the minds of the Russians westward, replacing the old capital, Moscow, which faced toward Asia and was the stronghold of opposition to his westernizing program. St. Petersburg soon became one of the leading cities of northern Europe. It remained the capital of Russia until the Revolution of 1917 when Moscow resumed its old place.

Internal Changes under Peter the Great

The new army, the new city, the new and expanding government offices all required money, which in Russia was very scarce. Taxes were imposed on an inconceivable variety of objects—on heads, as poll taxes; on land; on inns, mills, hats, leather, cellars, and coffins; on the right to marry, sell meat, wear a beard, or be an Old Believer. The tax burden fell mainly on the peasants; and to assure the payment of taxes the mobility of peasants was further restricted, and borderline individuals were classified as peasants in the government records, so that serfdom became both more onerous and more nearly universal. To raise government revenues and to stimulate production Peter adopted the mercantilist policies exemplified by Colbert in France. He encouraged exports, built a fleet on the Baltic, and developed mining, metallurgy, and textiles, which were indispensable to the army. He organized mixed groups of Russians and foreigners into commercial companies, provided them with capital from government funds (little private capital being available), and gave them a labor supply by assigning them the use of serfs in a given locality. Serfdom, in origin mainly an agricultural institution, began to spread in Russia as an industrial institution also. The fact that serf owners obtained the right to sell serfs without land, or to move them from landed estates into mines or towns, made it easier for industry in Russia to develop on the basis of unfree labor. Nor were the employers of serfs, in these government enterprises, free to modify or abandon their projects at will. They too were simply in the tsar's service. The economic system rested largely on impressment of both management and labor, not on private profit and wages as in the increasingly capitalistic West. In this way Peter's efforts to force Russia to a European level of material productivity widened the gap between Russia and western Europe.

To oversee and operate this system of tax collecting, recruiting, economic controls, serf hunting, and repression of internal rebellion Peter created a new administrative system. The old organs of local self-government wasted away. The duma and the national assembly, decadent anyway in that they could not function without disorder, disappeared. In their place Peter put a "senate" dependent on himself, and ten territorial areas called "governments," or *gubernii*—the very words were not Slavic but Latin and showed imitation of the West. The church he ruled through his Procurator of the Holy Synod.[26] At the top of the whole structure was himself, an absolute ruler, tsar, and autocrat of all the Russias. Before his death, dissatisfied with his son, he abolished the rule of hereditary succession to the tsardom, claiming the right for each tsar to name his own successor. Transmission of supreme power was thus put outside the domain of law, and in the following century the accession of tsars and tsarinas was marked by strife, conspiracy, and assassination. The whole system of centralized absolutism, while in form resembling that of the West, notably France, was in fact significantly different, for it lacked legal regularity, was handicapped by the insuperable ignorance of many officials, and was imposed on a turbulent and largely unwilling population. The empire of the Romanovs has been called a state without a people.

Peter, to assure the success of his westernizing program, developed what was called "state service," which had been begun by his predecessors. Virtually all landowning and serf-owning aristocrats were required to serve in the army or civil administration. Offices were multiplied to provide places for all. In the state service birth counted for nothing. Peter used men of all classes; Prince Dolgoruky was of the most ancient nobility, Prince Menshikov had been a cook, the tax administrator Kurbatov was an ex-serf, and many others were foreigners of unknown background. Status in Peter's Russia depended not on inherited rank

[26] See p. 232.

which Peter could not control, but on rank in his state service, civilian grades being equated with military, and all persons in the first eight grades being considered gentry. "History," wrote a Scot serving in Peter's army, "scarcely affords an example where so many people of low birth have been raised to such dignities as in tsar Peter's reign, or where so many of the highest birth and fortune have been leveled to the lowest ranks of life." In this respect especially, Peter's program resembled a true social revolution. It created a new governing element in place of the old, almost what in modern parlance would be called a party, a body of men working zealously for the new system with a personal interest in its preservation. These men, during Peter's lifetime and after his death, were the bulwarks against an anti-Western reaction, the main agents in making Peter's revolution stick. In time the new families became hereditary themselves. The priority of state service over personal position was abandoned a generation after Peter's death. Offices in the army and government were filled by men of property and birth. After Peter's revolution, as after some others, the new upper class became merged with the old.

Revolutionary also, suggesting the great French Revolution or the Russian Revolution of 1917, were Peter's unconcealed contempt for everything reminiscent of the old Russia and his zeal to reeducate his people in the new ways. He required all gentry to put their sons in school. He sent many abroad to study. He simplified the Russian alphabet. He edited the first newspaper to appear in Russia. He ordered the preparation of the first Russian book of etiquette, teaching his subjects not to spit on the floor, scratch themselves, or gnaw bones at dinner, to mix socially with women, take off their hats, converse pleasantly, and look at people while talking. The beard he took as a symbol of Muscovite backwardness; he forbade it in Russia, and himself shaved a number of men at his court. He forced people to attend evening parties to teach them manners. He had no respect for hereditary aristocracy, torturing or executing the highborn as readily as the peasants. As for religion, we are told that he was a pious man and enjoyed singing in church, but he was contemptuous of ecclesiastical dignity, and in one wild revel paraded publicly with drunken companions clothed in religious vestments and mocking the priests. Like most great revolutionists since his time he was aggressively secular.

The Results of Peter's Revolution

Peter's tactics provoked a strong reaction. Some adhered strictly to the old ways, others simply thought that Peter was moving too fast and too indiscriminately toward the new. Many Russians resented the inescapable presence of foreigners, who often looked down on Russians as savages, and who enjoyed special privileges such as the right of free exit from Russia and higher pay for similar employments. One center around which malcontents rallied was the church. Another was Peter's son Alexis, who declared that when he became tsar he would put a stop to the innovations and restore respect for the customs of old Russia. Peter, after some hesitation, finally put his own son to death. He ruled that each tsar should choose his own successor. He would stop at nothing to remake Russia in his own fashion.

Peter died in 1725, proclaimed "the Great" in his own lifetime by his admiring Senate. Few men in all history have exerted so strong an individual influence, which has indirectly become more far-reaching as the stature of Russia itself has grown. Though the years after Peter's death were years of turmoil and vacillation, his revolutionary changes held firm against those who would undo them. It is not simply that he Europeanized Russia and conquered a place on the Baltic; these developments might have come about in any case. It is by the methods he used, his impatient forcing of a new culture on Russia, that he set the future character of his empire. His methods fastened autocracy, serfdom, and bureaucracy more firmly upon the country. Yet he was able to reach only the upper classes. Many of these became more Europeanized than he could dream, habitually speaking French and living spiritually in France or in Italy. But as time went on many upper-class Russians, because of their very knowledge of Europe, became impatient of the stolid immovability of the peasants around them, sensed themselves as strangers in their own country, or were troubled by a guilty feeling that their position rested on the degradation and enslavement of human beings. Russian psychology, always mysterious to the West, could be explained in part by the violent paradoxes set up by rapid Europeanization. As for the peasant masses, they remained outside the system, egregiously exploited, estranged except by force of habit from their rulers and their social superiors, regarded by them as brutes or children, never sharing in any comparable way in their Europeanized civilization. These facts worked themselves out in later times. As for Peter's own time, Russia by his efforts came clearly out of its isolation, its vast bulk was now organized to play a part in international affairs, and its history thenceforward was a part of the history of Europe and increasingly of the world. Russia, like Prussia and the Austrian monarchy, was to be counted among the powers of Europe.

27. THE PARTITIONS OF POLAND

The fate of Poland in the eighteenth century reaches beyond the time limits of the present chapter, but it illustrates and brings together many of the strands traced in the preceding pages, so that a few words on it at this point may be useful. Poland in the eighteenth century, if Russia is considered non-European, was still by far the largest European state. It still reached from the Baltic almost to the Black Sea and extended eastward for 800 miles across the north-European plain. But it was the classic example, along with the Holy Roman Empire, of an older political structure which failed to develop modern organs of government.[27] It fell into ever deeper anarchy and confusion. Without army, revenues, or administration, internally divided among parties forever at cross-purposes, with many Poles more willing to bargain with foreigners than to work with each other, the country was a perpetual theater for diplomatic maneuvering and was finally absorbed by its growing neighbors.

   The Polish royal elections in the eighteenth century were as usual the subject of international interference. The election of 1733 precipitated a European war known as the War of the Polish Succession. Two Polish kings in these years were in fact Germans. Stanislas I, a native Pole, was twice dethroned, but since he was supported by France, and was in fact the father of Louis XV's wife, he was set up for his own lifetime as duke of Lorraine. The former duke of Lorraine, by the facile play of the balance of power, became grand duke of Tuscany and the husband

[27] See pp. 211–212, and maps, pp. 206 and 210.

of the Habsburg Maria Theresa. After these troubles of the 1730s a reforming movement began to gather strength in Poland. Polish patriots hoped to do away with the *liberum veto* and other elements in the constitution that made government impossible.[28] Their efforts were repeatedly frustrated by foreign influence, notably that of Catherine II, tsarina of Russia (1762–1796), who preferred a Poland in which she could intervene at will. In 1763 she strengthened her hold over the country by obtaining the election of another Russian puppet, a Polish nobleman named Stanislas Poniatowski, her former lover, as king. She declared herself protector of the Polish liberties. It was to the Russian advantage to maintain the existing state of affairs in Poland, which enabled Russian influence to pervade the whole country, rather than to divide the country with neighbors who might exclude Russian influence from their own spheres. The Prussians, however, long awaiting the day when they might join the old duchy of Prussia with Brandenburg-Pomerania in one continuous territory, were more willing to entertain the prospect of a partition of Poland.

The opportunity presented itself in 1772 in connection with a war between Russia and Turkey, which threw the whole situation in eastern Europe into question.[29] The Turkish empire was at last showing unmistakable signs of weakness. Russian victories were so overwhelming that both Austrians and Prussians feared for the balance of power in that part of Europe. The Prussians therefore came forward with a proposal. It was a proposal to prevent an Austro-Russian war and to preserve the balance in eastern Europe by leaving the Ottoman Empire more or less intact, while having all three European powers annex territory from Poland instead. The proposition was accepted by the three parties.

The Russians called off their war with Turkey and withdrew their armies. By the treaty of Kuchuk Kainarji, a village in Rumania, the sultan renounced his sovereignty over the Black Sea Tartars, admitted Russian shipping to the Black Sea and the Straits, and recognized the Russian government as the "protector" of Christian interests in Constantinople. The Russians soon used their advantage to absorb the north coast of the Black Sea, and to send Russian naval vessels into the Mediterranean for the first time.

Poland was meanwhile sacrificed.[30] By the first partition, in 1772, its outer territories were cut away. Russia took an eastern slice, around the city of Vitebsk. Austria took a southern slice, the region known as Galicia. Prussia took the Pomerelian borderland in West Prussia. The Prussians thus at last realized their old ambition. Prussia now reached continuously as a solid block from the Elbe to the borders of Lithuania.[31] The partition sobered the Poles, who renewed their efforts at a national revival, hoping to create an effective sovereignty which could secure the country against outsiders. But the Polish movement lacked deeper strength, for it was confined mainly to the nobles, who had themselves brought the country to ruin. The mass of the serf population, and the numerous Jews, did not care whether they were governed by Poles, Russians, or Germans. In addition, the Polish national revival was persistently blocked by the three neighboring powers. In 1792, when Europe was again at war in consequence of the great French Revolution, the three Eastern monarchies seized the opportunity to finish with Poland.

[28] See p. 212.
[29] See p. 327.
[30] For the partitions see map, p. 328.
[31] See map, panel 4, p. 222.

By the second and third partitions, in 1793 and 1795, they absorbed all the remaining Polish territory.

Russia, Prussia, and Austria thereby became contiguous, covering the whole of eastern Europe north of the Balkans; and they continued to do so, except for a few years in the time of Napoleon, until they all collapsed in the First World War, when Poland and the Baltic provinces of Russia reemerged.

VI.
The Struggle
for Wealth
and Empire

I n the preceding chapters we saw how western Europe, and especially England and France, by about the year 1700, came to occupy a position of leadership in Europe as a whole. We have traced the political history of western Europe through the War of the Spanish Succession, terminated in 1713–1714 by the treaties of Utrecht and Rastadt. Affairs of central Europe and Germany have been carried to 1740. In that year a new kingdom of Prussia and a new or renovated Austrian monarchy, each passing into the hands of a new ruler, stood on the eve of a struggle for ascendancy in central Europe. As for eastern Europe, we have observed the Europeanizing and expansion of the Russian empire, and seen how the vast area called Poland ceased to form an independent state.

More important in the long run than these political events, and going on through the seventeenth and eighteenth centuries, was the cumulative increase of all forms of knowledge, to which we turn in the two chapters that follow. Equally important was the growing wealth of Europe, or at least of the Atlantic region north of Spain. The new wealth, in the widest sense, meaning conveniences of every kind, resulted from new technical and scientific knowledge, which in turn it helped to produce; and the two together, more wealth and more knowledge, helped to form one of the most far-reaching ideas of modern times, the idea of progress, which retained its force well into the twentieth century.

The new wealth of Europe was not like the age-old wealth of the gorgeous East, said by Milton to "shower on her kings barbaric pearl and gold." It consisted of gold, to be sure, but even more of bank deposits and facilities for credit, of more and better devices for mining coal, casting iron, and spinning thread, more

Chapter Emblem: A Spanish doubloon or gold coin minted in 1790, showing Charles IV as King of Spain and the Indies.

productive agriculture, better and more comfortable houses, a wider variety of diet on the table, more and improved sailing ships, warehouses, and docks; more books, more newspapers, more medical instruments, more scientific equipment; greater government revenues, larger armies, and more numerous government employees. In the wealthy European countries, and because of the growing wealth, more people were freed from the necessity of toiling for food, clothing, and shelter, and were enabled to devote themselves to all sorts of specialized callings in government, management, finance, war, teaching, writing, inventing, exploring, and researching, and in producing the amenities rather than the barest necessities of life.

28. ELITE AND POPULAR CULTURES

The accumulation of wealth and knowledge was not evenly distributed among the various social classes.[1] There had always been differences between rich and poor, with many gradations between the extremes, but at the time we are now considering, as the seventeenth century turned into the eighteenth, there came to be a more obvious distinction between elite and popular cultures. The terms are hard to define. The elite culture was not exactly the culture of the rich and well-to-do, nor was the popular culture limited to the general run of the people. The word "elite" suggests a minority within a given range of interests; thus there are elites not only of wealth, but of social position and of power; elites of fashion, of patronage and connoisseurship in the arts, and of artists themselves; elites of education, of special training as in medicine and law, and of discovery and accomplishment in technology and the sciences. In general, persons taking part in an elite culture could share at will in the popular culture, by attending public amusements or simply by talking familiarly with their servants. But the relation was asymmetric. Those born in popular culture could not share in the culture of the elites, at least not without transforming themselves, through education or marriage, which could occur only in exceptional cases.

A main difference was simply one of language. At the popular level people generally used a local form of speech, varying from one place to another, with a distinctive accent, and full of words that had become obsolete elsewhere, or that might not be understood even a few miles away. In the Middle Ages this variety had been overcome by the use of Latin. Since the invention of printing and the rise of national literatures, and with the spreading influence of schools, of which we have seen that many were founded between 1550 and 1650, there came to be standard forms of English, French, Italian, and other languages employed by all educated persons. Grammar and spelling became regularized. Virtually all printing was in a national language when it was not in Latin. Since only a minority were able to get the necessary education, the mass of the people continued to speak as they did before. Their way of talking was now considered a dialect, a peasant language, or what was called *patois* in French or *Volkssprache* in German. And while it may be true, as some scientific philologists have said, that no form of speech is "better" than another, it is also true that facility in the national language was a sign of elite culture until the spread of universal elementary

[1] See pp. 119–122.

schooling in the nineteenth century. It gave access to at least certain segments of the elite culture, as it continues to do today.

The elite culture was transmitted largely by way of books, although acquired also by word of mouth within favored families and social circles. The popular culture was predominantly oral, although also expressed in cheaply printed almanacs, chapbooks, woodcuts, and broadsides. Since it was so largely oral, and left so few written records, popular culture is difficult for historians to reconstruct, although it made up the daily lives, interests, and activities of the great majority in all countries. It must always be remembered that what we read as history, in this as in most other books, is mostly an account of the work of minorities, either of power-wielders, decision-makers, and innovators whose actions nevertheless affected whole peoples, or of writers and thinkers whose ideas appealed to a limited audience. Persons who were illiterate or barely literate changed their ideas more slowly than the more mobile and more informed members of the elite. Great movements initiated by minorities spread slowly, generation after generation, to wider social classes, so that what was characteristic of popular culture at a given moment, such as a belief in magic, had often been common to all classes a century or two before.

The humanism of the Renaissance, being transmitted so largely through books and the study of Greek and Latin, remained limited to the elite culture. The strength of the Protestant Reformation lay in combining the efforts of highly educated persons, such as Luther and Calvin, with the anger, distress, disillusionment, and hopes of many very ordinary people. The rise of science and the ensuing Enlightenment, to be considered in the two following chapters, were originated by small numbers of experimenters and writers but slowly reshaped the thinking of others. The process of diffusion might be slow and uncertain. Astrology, for example, was in the Middle Ages a branch of scientific inquiry; in the seventeenth century astrologers were still consulted by emperors and kings; then divination by the stars was denounced by both the clergy and secular thinkers as a superstition, and astrology was expelled from astronomy, but horoscopes are still to be found in American and European newspapers in our own time.

The differences of wealth, if not wholly decisive, were of great importance. Culture in the broader or anthropologist's sense of the word includes material circumstances of food, drink, and shelter. In some respects the lot of the poor in the seventeenth century was worse than in the Middle Ages. Less meat was eaten in Europe, because as population grew there was less land available for the raising of livestock. With the growth of a market economy many peasants raised wheat, but ate bread made of rye, barley, or oats, or even looked for acorns and roots in times of famine. The consumption of bread by working people in France in the eighteenth century was about a pound per day per person, because little else except cabbages and beans was eaten on ordinary days; after 1750 the use of white bread became more usual. Meanwhile the rich, or the merely affluent, developed more delicate menus prepared by professional cooks, one of whom is said to have committed suicide when his soufflé fell.

In the towns the poor lived in crowded and unwholesome buildings, and in the country in dark and shabby cabins where stoves only gradually replaced holes in the roof for the escape of smoke. The poor had no glass in their windows, the middle classes had some, and the rich had glass windows and mirrors in profusion. In humble homes the dishes were wooden bowls, slowly replaced by pewter, while china plates began to appear on the tables of the more well-to-do. Table forks, with one for each diner, originating in Italy, were brought to France by Catherine de Medici along with other items of Italian culture, and soon spread among those able to afford them, though Louis XIV still preferred to use his fingers. Silver bowls and pitchers were ancient, but became more elaborate and more often seen in upper-class circles. The poor had no furniture, or only a few benches and a mat to sleep on; the middle classes had chairs and beds; the rich not only had substantial furniture but were becoming more conscious of style. Among persons of adequate income it became usual to have houses with specialized rooms, such as separate bedrooms, and a dining room. The prominent and the fashionable fitted out rooms for social receptions and entertainments, called salons in France, with walls of wood paneling, lighted by chandeliers reflected in mirrors, and provided with sofas and armchairs, which the invention of upholstery made more comfortable. The poor, after dark, huddled on chests or on the floor by a single candle.

In the use of beverages the seventeenth century saw progress, if that is the right word. Coffee and tea, along with sugar and tobacco, all imported from overseas, were exotic rarities in 1600, more widely enjoyed in 1700, and available to all but the very destitute by the time of the French Revolution. Coffee shops developed, and taverns multiplied. Cheap wines became more plentiful in southern Europe, as did beer in the north. The distillation of alcohol had been developed in the Middle Ages, when brandy, a distilled wine, was used as a medicine; by the seventeenth century it was a familiar drink. Whisky and gin also came into use at about this time. The taverns and coffee shops offered a place for neighborly gatherings for the middling and lower sorts of the population, but drunkenness also became more of a social problem, especially for the working classes that could not drink in domestic privacy, and so made themselves visible in the streets, as shown by Hogarth's pictures of "Gin Lane" in London about 1750. Arising from all this poverty and disorganization, especially in the large cities, was an increase in illegitimacy and abandonment of children. It was calculated that in Paris in 1780 there were 7,000 abandoned children for 30,000 births, but many of these infants were brought from the country to be deposited in the foundling hospitals of the city, which were overwhelmed.

There was much that persons of all classes and cultures shared. Most important, in principle, was religion. The refined and the rude, the learned and the untutored, heard the same sermons in church, were baptized, married, and buried by the same sacraments, often by the same priest, and were subject to religious and moral obligations that transcended the boundaries of social class. Such was most likely to be the case in small communities of unmixed religion, or where the lord and lady of the manor attended the same church as the villagers. Where different churches existed in fact, whether or not officially tolerated, religion played less of a role in social cohesion. In England, for example, the Nonconformists, who succeeded the old Puritans after the Stuart Restoration, developed a kind of middle-class culture that was noticeably different from the culture of the Anglican gentry. Rich families in both Protestant and Catholic countries might have their own private chaplains and build chapels of their own. In towns that were big enough for neighborhood diversification some churches became fashionable and others merely popular. In any case some people in the seventeenth century were not very good Christians at all; these would include those in inaccessible

rural areas as well as some of the poorest in the larger towns, who were often uprooted and homeless migrants from an overcrowded countryside. Reforming bishops, especially in France, undertook to ameliorate the situation, so that the seventeenth century was a great age of internal missionary work, and it may be that in
the following century, as skepticism began to pervade the elite culture, the popular culture was more Christianized than it had been in the past.

Rich and poor were also subject to the same diseases, the same dangers of
tainted food and polluted water, and the same smells and filth in noisy streets littered with horse droppings, puddles, and garbage. Not of course equally: in the
elite culture people called on the service of doctors, who had been trained in the
universities, while ordinary sufferers sought out popular healers, who were often
women; and it made a difference whether one rode through the streets in a coach,
as the affluent did, or picked one's way on foot with the common people. Conges-
tion was worst in rapidly growing cities, such as London, Paris, Amsterdam, and
Naples, where the differences between wealth and poverty were both more extreme and more shockingly visible. There were recurrent fears of shortage of
food, as crop failure or local famine struck this or that region, in which case some
starved and some ate less, while those able to do so simply paid higher prices. In
some towns charitable organizations developed, often on the initiative of upper-
class women, to finance and assist religious sisters in relief of the poor. Hunger
and the fear of hunger sometimes produced riots, which however had little political significance except insofar as upper-class people tried to make use of them for
their own purposes.

It was also in less material aspects that the elite and popular cultures increasingly diverged. The upper strata set a new importance on polite manners, in
which the French now set the tone, with much bowing, doffing of hats, and exchange of compliments, beside which the manners of ordinary people now seemed
uncouth.[2] The etiquette of princely courts became more formal, the court fools
and jesters disappeared, and royalty surrounded itself not with rough retainers
but with ladies and gentlemen. About 1600 the plays of Shakespeare were staged
in public theaters where all classes mixed and enjoyed the same performance, but
in the following century it became usual for the upper classes to have private
theaters, of the kind shown on p. 198 above. People of higher social position took
to stylish dancing, which their children had to learn from dancing teachers, while
plain people continued to cavort more spontaneously in country dances and jigs.
For evening parties, the polite world met in salons to engage in bright conversation, while working people, especially in the country, met in a neighbor's house
after the day's labors were over, and there, while the men mended their implements and the women mended the clothes, engaged in local gossip, or listened to
storytellers, or sat by while someone read aloud from one of the cheaply printed
books that were now widely circulated.

Enough of these books have survived, along with popular almanacs, to make it
possible to form some ideas of the mental horizons of the nonliterate and inartic-
ulate classes. They were often written by printers or their employees or by others
who were in effect intermediaries between the elite and popular cultures, and
who purposely addressed themselves to what they knew of popular interests. The
almanacs purveyed astrological observations, advice on the weather, proverbs,

---

[2] On etiquette see pp. 59–60 and 181–182.

and scraps of what had once been science but was now offered as occult wisdom. Other little books undertook to teach the ABCs, or told how to behave in church, how to approach persons of the other sex, how to show respect for superiors, or how to compose a proper letter of love, thanks, or condolence, or have such a letter written by the professional letter writers to whose services illiterate persons resorted. Still others put into print the stories that had long circulated in the oral tradition, fairy tales, saints' lives, or accounts of the doings of outlaws such as Robin Hood. Miracles, prodigies, witches, ogres, angels, and the devil figured prominently in such narratives. It is a curious fact that where educated persons were now schooled in Greek mythology and admired the heroes of ancient Rome, the plain people were still engrossed by tales of medieval chivalry, knights errant, and holy hermits that had once been avidly listened to in baronial halls. Memories of the times of King Arthur and Charlemagne lingered in the popular consciousness. There were many long and complex tales of the exploits of Roland and other paladins who had fought for Christianity against the infidels, all set in a world of faraway adventure without definite location in time or place. Saracens, Moors, Turks, and Muslims in general, along with Jews, were generally seen in such stories as a menace.

Belief in witchcraft and magic was to be found in 1600 in all social classes. The witches in *Macbeth* were perfectly believable to Shakespeare's audience. Learned books were still written on these subjects, and indeed it may be that learned writers, and the judges in law courts, had stirred up more anxiety about witches and magicians than ordinary people would otherwise have felt. By 1700 a great change was evident; witches, magicians, and miscellaneous enchantments were disappearing from the elite culture, but still figured in the popular mind. Unaffected as yet by either science or doubt, ordinary people inclined to think that there was something true about magic, which they distinguished as good and bad. Good magic unlocked the "secrets" of nature; popular writings on alchemy told of famous sages of the past who knew how to turn base metals into gold; there were special formulas that added to the efficacy of prayer; there were old women who had a secret knowledge of medicinal herbs, in which indeed there might be some pragmatic value, but which was blended with the mysterious and the occult. Bad magic was used to cause harm; it taught the black arts; it gave force to curses; it often involved a compact with the devil; it was what made witches so fearsome. By 1700 such ideas were subsiding. Judges no longer believed that such powers existed, and so would no longer preside at witchcraft trials. The same may be said of belief in prophecies and oracles; in the elite culture only those recorded in the Old Testament retained any credibility, but there was still a popular acceptance of recent prophecies and foretellings of the future.

Popular culture continued to express itself also in fairs and carnivals. For men and women who lived limited lives these were exciting events that occurred only at certain times of the year, and to which people flocked from miles around. At the fairs one could buy things that local shops and wandering peddlers could not supply. There would be puppet shows, jugglers, and acrobats. There were conjurers who refused to admit like modern magicians that they were using merely natural means. A mountebank was someone who mounted a platform (*banco* in Italian) where he sold questionable remedies for various ills, while keeping up a patter of jokes and stories, often accompanied by a clown. Blind singers and traveling musicians entertained the throngs, and for the tougher minded there were cockfights and bear baiting. In such a hubbub itinerant preachers might denounce the vanities of this world, or throw doubt on the wisdom of bishops and lawyers.

Carnival went on for several weeks preceding Lent. The word itself, from the Italian *carne vale*, meant "farewell to meat," from which good Christians were to abstain during the forty-day Lenten fast; in France it climaxed in the Mardi Gras ("fat Tuesday"). It persisted in Protestant countries also. It was a time for big eating and heavy drinking, and for general merrymaking and foolery. Comical processions marched through the streets. Farces were performed, and mock sermons delivered. Young men showed their strength in tugs-of-war, footraces, and a rough-and-tumble kind of football. A common theme was what was called in England "the world turned upside down." Men and women put on each other's clothing. Horses were made to move backward with the rider facing the tail. Little street dramas showed the servant giving orders to the master, the judge sitting in the stocks, the pupil beating the teacher, or the husband holding the baby while the wife clutched a gun. In general, the carnival was a time for defying custom and ridiculing authority. It is hard to know how much such outbursts were expressions of genuine resentments, and how much they were only a form of play. They could, indeed, be both.

In 1600 people of all classes took part in these festive activities. In the following century, as both the Protestant and the Catholic reformations extended their influences, the clergy undertook to purge such public events of what they considered excesses, and with the growth of the state the civil authorities began to frown on them as incitements to subversion. By 1700 the people of elite culture, the wealthy, the fashionable, and the educated, were more inclined to stay away, or attended only as spectators to be amused at the simple pleasures of the common people. In the eighteenth century, as the various elites took to more formal manners and to neoclassicism in literature and the arts, the gulf between the elite and popular cultures widened. The clergy campaigned against necromancy and tried to restrain the faithful in the matter of pilgrimages and veneration of dubious local saints. As the medical profession developed, the popular healers and venders of nostrums were seen as charlatans and quacks. As scientific and other knowledge increased, those who lacked it appeared simply as ignorant. It may be said both that the elites withdrew from the popular culture, and that the people as a whole had not yet been brought into the pale of higher civilization. In any case, class distinctions became sharper than ever. But nothing ever stands still, and before the year 1800 there were persons in the elite culture who were beginning to "rediscover" the people, to collect ballads and fairy tales, and lay a foundation for what in the nineteenth century was called "folklore."[3]

29. THE GLOBAL ECONOMY OF THE EIGHTEENTH CENTURY

The opening of the Atlantic in the sixteenth century, it will be recalled, had reoriented Europe. In an age of oceanic communications western Europe became a center from which America, Asia, and Africa could all be reached. A global economy had been created. The first to profit from it had been the Portuguese and Spanish, and they retained their monopoly through most of the sixteenth century,

[3] See pp. 410–411 and 440–442.

but the decline of the Portuguese and Spanish paved the way for the triumph of the British, the French, and the Dutch. In the eighteenth century the outstanding economic development was the expansion of the global economy and the fact that Europe became incomparably wealthier than any other part of the world.

Commerce and Industry in the Eighteenth Century

The increase of wealth was brought about by the methods of commercial capitalism and handicraft industry. Though the Industrial Revolution in England is usually dated from 1760 or 1780, it was not until the nineteenth century that the use of steam engines and power-driven machinery, and the growth of large factories and great manufacturing cities, brought about the conditions of modern industrialism. The economic system of the eighteenth century, while it contained within itself the seeds of later industrialism, represented the flowering of the older merchant capitalism, domestic industry, and mercantilist government policies which had grown up since the sixteenth century and which have been already described.[4]

Most people in the eighteenth century lived in the country. Agriculture was the greatest single industry and source of wealth. Cities remained small. London and Paris, the largest of Europe, each had a population of 600,000 or 700,000, but the next largest cities did not much exceed 200,000, and in all Europe at the time of the French Revolution (in 1789) there were only fifty cities with as many as 50,000 people. Urbanization, however, was no sign of economic advancement. Spain, Italy, and even the Balkan peninsula, according to an estimate made in the 1780s, each had more large cities (over 50,000) than did Great Britain. Urbanization did not equate with industry because most industry was carried on in the country, by peasants and part-time agricultural workers who worked for the merchant capitalists of the towns. Thus, while it is true to say that most people still lived in the country, it would be false to say that their lives and labors were devoted to agriculture exclusively. One English estimate, made in 1739, held that there were 4,250,000 persons "engaged in manufactures" in the British Isles, a figure that included women and children, and comprised almost half the entire population. These people worked characteristically in their own cottages, employed as wage earners by merchant capitalists under the "domestic" system.[5] Almost half of them, about 1,500,000, were engaged in the weaving and processing of woolens. Others were in the copper, iron, lead, and tin manufactures; others in leather goods; much smaller were the paper, glass, porcelain, silk, and linen trades; and smallest of all, in 1739, was the manufacture of cotton cloth, which accounted for only about 100,000 workers. The list suggests the importance of nonagricultural occupations in the preindustrial age.

England, even with half its population engaged at least part of the time in manufactures, was not yet the unrivaled manufacturing country that it was to become after 1800. England in the eighteenth century produced no more iron than Russia and no more manufactures than France. The population of England was still small; it began to grow rapidly about 1760, but as late as 1800 France was still twice as populous as England and Scotland together. France, though less

[4] See pp. 112–118.
[5] See p. 114.

intensively developed than England, with probably far less than half its people "engaged in manufactures," nevertheless, because of its greater size, remained the chief industrial center of Europe.

Although foreign and colonial trade grew rapidly in the eighteenth century, it is probable that, in both Great Britain and France, the domestic or internal trade was greater in volume and occupied more people. Great Britain, with no internal tariffs, with an insignificant guild system, and with no monopolies allowed within the country except to inventors, was the largest area of internal free trade in Europe. France, or at least Colbert's Five Great Farms,[6] offered a free-trading internal market hardly less great. A great deal of economic activity was therefore domestic, consisting of exchange between town and town or between region and region. The proportions between domestic and international trade cannot be known. But foreign trade was important in that the largest enterprises were active in it, the greatest commercial fortunes were made in it, and the most capital was accumulated from it. And it was the foreign trade that led to international rivalry and war.

The World Economy: The Dutch, British, and French

On the international economic scene a great part was still played by the Dutch. After the Peace of Utrecht the Dutch ceased to be a great political power, but their role in commerce, shipping, and finance remained undiminished, or diminished only relatively by the continuing commercial growth of France and Great Britain. They were still the middlemen and common carriers for other peoples. Their freight rates remained the lowest of Europe. They continued to grow rich on imports from the East Indies. To a large extent also, in the eighteenth century, the Dutch simply lived on their investments. The capital they had accumulated over two hundred years they now lent out to French or British or other entrepreneurs. Dutch capital was to be found in every large commercial venture of Europe and was lent to governments far and wide. A third of the capital of the Bank of England in the mid–eighteenth century belonged to Dutch shareholders. The Bank of Amsterdam remained the chief clearing house and financial center of Europe. Its supremacy ended only with the invasion of Holland by a French Revolutionary army in 1795.

The Atlantic trade routes, leading to America, to Africa, and to Asia, tempted the merchants of many nationalities in Europe. A great many East India companies were established—usually to do business in America as well as the East, for the "Indies" at the beginning of the eighteenth century was still a general term for the vast regions overseas. Both the English and the French East India companies were reorganized, with an increased investment of capital, shortly after 1700. A number of others were established—by the Scots, the Swedes, the Danes, the imperial free city of Hamburg, the republic of Venice, Prussia, and the Austrian monarchy. But, with the exception of the Danish company which lasted some sixty years, they all failed after only a few years, either for insufficiency of capital or because they lacked strong diplomatic, military, and naval support. Their failure showed that, in the transocean trade, unassisted business enterprise was not enough. Merchants to succeed in this sphere needed strong national backing. Nei-

[6] See p. 184.

ther free city, nor small kingdom, nor tiny republic, nor the amorphous Austrian empire provided a firm enough base.

It was the British and French who won out in the commercial rivalry of the eighteenth century. Britain and France were alike in having, besides a high level of industrial production at home, governments organized on a national scale and able to protect and advance, under mercantilist principles, the interests of their merchants in distant countries. For both peoples the eighteenth century—or the three-quarters of a century between the end of the War of the Spanish Succession in 1713 and the beginning of the French Revolution in 1789—was an age of spectacular enrichment and commercial expansion.

Although the trade figures are difficult to arrive at, French foreign and colonial trade may well have grown even more rapidly than the British in the years between the 1720s and the 1780s. In any event, by the 1780s, the two countries were about equal in their total foreign and colonial trade. The British in the 1780s enjoyed proportionately more of the trade with America and Asia, the French more of the trade with the rest of Europe and the Near East. The contest for markets played an important part in the colonial and commercial wars between Britain and France all through the eighteenth century and on into the final and climactic struggle, and British triumph, in the time of Napoleon.

Asia, America, and Africa in the Global Economy

In the expanding global economy of the eighteenth century each continent played its special part. The trade with Asia was subject to an ancient limitation. Asia was almost useless as a market for European manufactures. There was much that Europeans wanted from Asia, but almost nothing that Asians wanted from Europe. The peoples of Chinese, Indian, and Malay culture had elaborate civilizations with which they were content; they lacked the dynamic restlessness of Europeans, and the masses were so impoverished (more so even than in Europe) that they could buy nothing anyway. Europeans found that they could send little to Asia except gold. The drain of gold from Europe to Asia had gone on since ancient times and, accumulating over the centuries, was one source of the fabulous treasures of Oriental princes. To finance the swelling demand for Asian products it was necessary for Europeans constantly to replenish their stocks of gold. The British found an important new supply in Africa along the Gulf of Guinea, where one region (the present Ghana) was long called the Gold Coast. The word "guinea" became the name of a gold coin minted in England from 1663 to 1813 and long remained a fashionable way of saying twenty-one shillings.

What Europeans sought from Asia was still in part spices—pepper and ginger, cinnamon and cloves—now brought in mainly by the Dutch from their East India islands. But they wanted manufactured goods also. Asia was still in some lines superior to Europe in technical skill. It is enough to mention rugs, chinaware, and cotton cloth. The very names by which cotton fabrics are known in English and other European languages reveal the places from which they were thought to come. "Madras" and "calico" refer to the Indian cities of Madras and Calicut, "muslin" to the Arabic city of Mosul. "Gingham" comes from a Malay word meaning "striped"; "chintz" from a Hindustani word meaning "spotted." Most of the Eastern manufactures were increasingly imitated in the eighteenth century in Europe. Axminster and Aubusson carpets competed with Oriental rugs. In 1709 a

German named Boettcher discovered a formula for making a vitreous and translucent substance comparable to the porcelain of China; this European "china," made at Sèvres, Dresden, and in England, soon competed successfully with the imported original. Cotton fabrics were never produced in Europe at a price to compete with India until after the introduction of power machinery, which began in England about 1780. Before that date the demand for Indian cotton goods was so heavy that the woolen, linen, and silk interests became alarmed. They could produce nothing like the sheer muslins and bright calico prints which caught the public fancy, and many governments, to protect the jobs and capital involved in the old European textile industries, simply forbade the import of Indian cottons altogether. But it was a time of many laws and little enforcement, the forbidden fabrics continued to come in, and Daniel Defoe observed in 1708 that, despite the laws, cottons were not only sought as clothing by all classes, but "crept into our houses, our closets and bedchambers; curtains, cushions, chairs and at last beds themselves were nothing but calicoes or Indian stuffs." Gradually, in the face of tariff protection for "infant industries" in Europe, and the rapid growth of European cotton manufactures, import of cottons and other manufactures from Asia declined. After about 1770 most of the imports of the British East India Company consisted of tea, which was brought from China.

America in the eighteenth century bulked larger than Asia in the trade of western Europe. The American trade was based mainly on one commodity—sugar. Sugar had long been known in the East, and in the European Middle Ages little bits of it had trickled through to delight the palates of lords and prelates. About 1650 sugar cane was brought in quantities from the East and planted in the West Indies by Europeans. A whole new economic system arose in a few decades. It was based on the "plantation." A plantation was an economic unit consisting of a considerable tract of land, a sizable investment of capital, often owned by absentees in France or England, and a force of impressed labor, supplied by blacks brought from Africa as slaves. Sugar, produced in quantity with cheap labor at low cost, proved to have an inexhaustible market. The eighteenth century was the golden age, economically speaking, of the West Indies. From its own islands alone, during the eighty years from 1713 to 1792, Great Britain imported a total of £162,000,000 worth of goods, almost all sugar; imports from India and China, in the same eighty years, amounted to only £104,000,000. The little islands of Jamaica, Barbados, St. Kitts, and others, as suppliers of Europe, not only dwarfed the whole mainland of British America but the whole mainland of Asia as well. For France, less well established than Britain on the American mainland and in Asia, the same holds with greater force. The richest of all the sugar colonies, San Domingo, now called Haiti, belonged to France.

The plantation economy, first established in sugar, and later in cotton (after 1800), brought Africa into the foreground. Slaves had been obtained from Black Africa from time immemorial, both by the Roman Empire and by the Muslim world, both of which, however, enslaved blacks and whites indiscriminately. After the European discovery of America, blacks were taken across the Atlantic by the Spanish and Portuguese. Dutch traders landed them in Virginia in 1619, a year before the arrival of the Pilgrim Fathers in Massachusetts. But slavery in the Americas before 1650 may be described as occasional. With the rise of the plantation economy after 1650, and especially after 1700, it became a fundamental economic institution. Slavery now formed the labor supply of a very substantial and heavily capitalized branch of world production. About 610,000 blacks were landed from Africa in the island of Jamaica alone between 1700 and 1786. Total figures are hard to give, but it is certain that, until well after 1800, far more Africans than Europeans made the voyage to the Americas. The transatlantic slave trade in the eighteenth century was conducted mainly by English-speaking interests, principally in England but also in New England, followed as closely as they could manage it by the French. Yearly export of merchandise from Great Britain to Africa, used chiefly in exchange for slaves, increased tenfold between 1713 and 1792. As for merchandise coming into Britain from the British West Indies, virtually all produced by slaves, in 1790 it constituted almost a fourth of all British imports. If we add British imports from the American mainland, including what in 1776 became the United States, the importance of black labor to the British economic system will appear still greater, since a great part of exports from the mainland consisted of agricultural products, such as tobacco and indigo, produced partly by slaves. It can scarcely be denied that the phenomenal rise of British capitalism in the eighteenth century was based to a considerable extent on the enslavement of Africans. The town of Liverpool, an insignificant place on the Irish Sea in 1700, built itself up by the slave trade and the trade in slave-produced wares to a busy transatlantic commercial center, which in turn, as will be seen later, stimulated the "industrial revolution" in Manchester and other neighboring towns.[7]

The west-European merchants, British, French, and Dutch, sold the products of America and Asia to their own peoples and those of central and eastern Europe. Trade with Germany and Italy was fairly stable. With Russia it enormously increased. To cite the British record only, Britain imported fifteen times as much goods from Russia in 1790 as in 1700, and sold the Russians six times as much. The Russian landlords, as they became Europeanized, desired Western manufactures and the colonial products such as sugar, tobacco, and tea which could be purchased only from western Europeans. They had grain, timber, and naval stores to offer in return. Similarly, landlords of Poland and north Germany, in the seventeenth and eighteenth centuries, found themselves increasingly able to move their agricultural products out through the Baltic and hence increasingly able to buy the products of western Europe, America, and Asia in return. Landlords of eastern Europe thus had an incentive to make their estates more productive. "Big" agriculture spread, developing in eastern Europe a system not unlike the plantation economy of the New World. It had many effects. It contributed, along with political causes, to reducing the bulk of the east-European population to serfdom. It helped to civilize and refine, in a word to "Europeanize," the upper classes. And it helped to enrich the merchants of western Europe.[8]

The Wealth of Western Europe: Social Consequences

The wealth which accumulated along the Atlantic seaboard of Europe was, in short, by no means produced by the efforts of western Europeans only. All the world contributed to its formation. The natural resources of the Americas, the resources and skills of Asia, the gold and manpower of Africa, all alike went into producing the vastly increased volume of goods moving in world commerce.

[7] See p. 431.
[8] See pp. 122–123.

Europeans directed the movement. They supplied capital; they contributed technical and organizing abilities; and it was the demand of Europeans, at home in Europe and as traders abroad, that set increasing numbers of Indians to spinning cotton, Chinese to raising tea, Malays to gathering spices, and Africans to the tending of sugar cane. A few non-Europeans might benefit in the process—Indian or Chinese merchants "subsidized" by the East India companies, African chiefs who captured slaves from neighboring tribes and sold them to Europeans. But the profits of the world economy really went to Europe. The new wealth, over and above what was necessary to keep the far-flung and polyglot labor force in being, and to pay other expenses, piled up in Britain, Holland, and France.

Here it was owned by private persons. It accumulated within the system of private property and as part of the institutions of private enterprise or private capitalism. Governments were dependent on these private owners of property, for governments, in western Europe, had almost no source of revenue except loans and taxes derived from their peoples. When the wealth owners gave their support, the government was strong and successful, as in England. When they withdrew support, the government collapsed, as it was to collapse in France in the Revolution of 1789.

In a technical sense there were many "capitalists" in western Europe, persons who had a little savings which they used to buy a parcel of land or a loom or entrusted to some other person to invest at interest. And in a general sense the new wealth was widely distributed; the standard of living rose in western Europe in the eighteenth century. Tea, for example, which cost as much as £10 a pound when introduced into England about 1650, was an article of common consumption a hundred years later. But wealth used to produce more wealth, i.e., capital, was owned or controlled in significant amounts by relatively few persons. In the eighteenth century some people became unprecedentedly rich (including some who started quite poor, for it was a time of open opportunity); the great intermediate layers of society became noticeably more comfortable; and the people at the bottom, such as the serfs of eastern Europe, the Irish peasantry, the dispossessed farm workers in England, the poorest peasants and workmen of France, were worse off than they had been before. The poor continued to live in hovels. The prosperous created for themselves that pleasant world of the eighteenth century that is still admired, a world of well-ordered Georgian homes, closely cropped lawns and shrubs, furniture by Chippendale or à la Louis XV, coaches-and-four, family portraits, high chandeliers, books bound in morocco, and a staff of servants "below stairs."

Families enriched by commerce, and especially the daughters, mixed and intermarried with the old families which owned land. The merchant in England or France no sooner became prosperous than he bought himself a landed estate. In France he might also purchase a government office or patent of nobility. Contrariwise, the landowning gentleman, especially in England, no sooner increased his landed income than he invested the proceeds in commercial enterprise or government bonds. The two forms of property, bourgeois and aristocratic, tended to merge. Until toward the end of the century the various propertied interests worked harmoniously together, and the unpropertied classes, the vast majority, could influence the government only by riot and tumult. On the whole the period, though one of commercial expansion, was an age of considerable social stability in western Europe.

The foregoing might be illustrated from the lives of thousands of men and women. Two examples are enough, one English and one French. They show the working of the world economic system, the rise of the commercial class in western Europe, and the role of that class in the political life of the Western countries.

Thomas Pitt, called "Diamond" Pitt, was born in 1653, the son of a parish clergyman in the Church of England. He went to India in 1674. Here he operated as an "interloper," trading in defiance of the legal monopoly of the East India Company. Returning to England, he was prosecuted by the company and fined £400 but was rich enough to buy the manor of Stratford and with it the borough of Old Sarum, a rotten borough which gave him a seat in the House of Commons without the trouble of an election. He soon returned to India, again as an interloper, where he competed so successfully with the company that it finally took him into its own employment. He traded on his own account, as well as for the company, sent back some new chintzes to England, and defended Madras against the nawab of the Carnatic, buying off the nawab with money. In 1702, though his salary was only £300 a year, he purchased a 410-carat uncut diamond for £20,400. He bought it from an Indian merchant who had himself bought it from an English skipper, who in turn had stolen it from the slave who had found it in the mines and who had concealed it in a wound in his leg. Back in Europe, Pitt had his diamond cut at Amsterdam and sold it in 1717 to the regent of France for £135,000. The regent put it in the French crown; it was appraised at the time of the French Revolution at £480,000. A daughter of "Diamond" Pitt became the Countess of Stanhope, one of his sons the Earl of Londonderry. Another son became father to the William Pitt who guided Britain through the Seven Years' War with France, and who was raised to the peerage as the Earl of Chatham. After this Pitt the city of Pittsburgh was named, so that a fortune gained in the East gave its name to a frontier settlement in the interior of America. Chatham's younger son, the second William Pitt, became prime minister at twenty-four. The younger Pitt guided Britain through another and greater war with France, until his death in 1806 during the high tide of the Napoleonic empire.

Jean Joseph Laborde was born in 1724, of a bourgeois family of southern France. He went to work for an uncle who had a business at Bayonne trading with Spain and the East. From the profits he built up vast plantations and slaveholdings in San Domingo. His ships brought sugar to Europe, and returned with prefabricated building materials, each piece carefully numbered, for his plantations and refineries in the West Indies. He became one of the leading bankers in Paris. His daughter became the Countess de Noailles. He himself received the title of marquis, which he did not use. He bought a number of manors and châteaux near Paris. As a real estate operator he developed that part of Paris, then suburban, now called the Chaussée d'Antin. During the Seven Years' War he was sent by the French government to borrow money in Spain, where he was told that Spain would lend nothing to Louis XV, but would gladly lend him personally 20,000,000 reals. In the War of American Independence he raised 12,000,000 livres in gold for the government, to help pay the French army and navy, thus contributing to the success of the American Revolution. He acted as investment agent for Voltaire, gave 24,000 livres a year to charity, and subscribed 400,000 livres in 1788 toward building new hospitals in Paris. In July 1789 he helped to finance the insurrection which led to the fall of the Bastille and the Revolution. His son, in June 1789, took the Oath of the Tennis Court, swearing to write a constitution for France. He himself was guillotined in 1794. His children turned to scholarship and the arts.

30. WESTERN EUROPE AFTER UTRECHT, 1713–1740

The Peace of Utrecht registered the defeat of French ambitions in the wars of Louis XIV. The French move toward "universal monarchy" had been blocked. The European state system had been preserved. Europe was to consist of a number of independent and sovereign states, all legally free and equal, continuously entering or leaving alliances along the principles of the balance of power. More specifically, the peace settlement of 1713–1714 placed the Bourbon Philip V on the Spanish throne but partitioned the Spanish empire.[9] Spain itself, with Spanish America and the Philippines, went to Philip V. Of the remaining Spanish possessions, Belgium, Milan, and Naples-Sicily went to the Austrian Habsburgs, Sardinia ultimately to the Duke of Savoy, Minorca and Gibraltar to Great Britain. Britain likewise took from France Newfoundland, Nova Scotia, and the Hudson Bay region. Great Britain, consolidated during the wars as a combined kingdom of England and Scotland, installed as a naval power in the Mediterranean, winning territory from France and Spain, and receiving trading rights within the hitherto closed domain of Spanish America, emerged as the most dynamic of the Atlantic powers.

Men in authority turned to repairing the damages of war. Spain was somewhat rejuvenated by the French influence under its new Bourbon house. The drift and decadence that had set in under the last Habsburgs were at least halted. The Spanish monarchy was administratively strengthened. Its officials followed the absolutist government of Louis XIV as a model. The estates of the east-Spanish kingdoms, Aragon and Valencia, ceased to meet, going like the Estates General of France into the limbo of obsolete institutions. They had chosen the losing side in the Spanish civil war that accompanied the War of the Spanish Succession, and their disappearance in the reign of Philip V removed a source of the localism and cross-purposes which afflicted Spain. On the whole the French influence in eighteenth-century Spain was intangible. Nothing was changed in substance, but the old machinery functioned with more precision. Administrators were better trained and took a more constructive attitude toward government work; they became more aware of the world north of the Pyrenees, and recovered confidence in their country's future. They tried also to tighten up the administration of their American empire. More revenue officers and coast guards were introduced in the Caribbean, whose zeal led to repeated clashes with smugglers, mainly British. Friction on the Spanish Main, reinforced by Spanish dislike for British occupation of Gibraltar, kept Spain and Britain in a continual ferment of potential hostility.

The Dutch after Utrecht receded from the political stage, though their alliance was always sought because of the huge shipping and financial resources they controlled. The Swiss also became important in banking and financial circles. The Belgians founded an overseas trading company in 1723 on the authority of their new Austrian ruler; this "Ostend Company" sent out six voyages to China, which were highly profitable, but the commercial jealousy of the Dutch and British

[9] See pp. 189–191 and maps, pp. 190 and 317.

obliged the Austrian emperor to withdraw his support, so that the enterprise soon came to an end. The Scots began at about this time to play their remarkable role of energizing business affairs in many countries. Union with England gave them access to the British empire and to the numerous commercial advantages won by the English. John Law, the financial wizard of France, was a Scot, as was William Paterson, one of the chief founders of the Bank of England.

France and Britain after 1713

Our main attention falls on Britain and France. Though one was the victor and the other the vanquished in the wars ended in 1713, and though one stood for absolutism and the other for constitutionalism in government, their development in the years after Utrecht was in some ways surprisingly parallel. In both countries for some years the king was personally ineffective, and in both the various propertied interests therefore gained many advantages. Both enjoyed the commercial expansion described above. Both went through a short period of financial experimentation and frantic speculation in stocks, the bubble bursting in each case in 1720. Each was thereafter governed by a statesman, Cardinal Fleury in France and Robert Walpole in England, whose policy was to keep peace abroad and conciliate all interests at home. Fleury and Walpole held office for about two decades, toward the end of which the two countries again went to war. But the differences are at least as instructive as the parallels.

In France the new king was a child, Louis XV, the great-grandson of Louis XIV, and only five years old when he began to reign in 1715. The government was entrusted to a regent, the Duke of Orleans, an elder cousin of the young king. Orleans, lacking the authority of a monarch, had to admit the aristocracy to a share in power. Most of the nobles had never liked the absolutism of Louis XIV, and there was much dissatisfaction with absolutism among all classes, because of the ruin and suffering brought by Louis XIV's wars.

The higher nobles, ousted by Louis XIV, now reappeared in the government. For a time Orleans worked through committees of noblemen, roughly corresponding to ministries, a system lauded by its backers as a revival of political freedom; but the committees proved so incompetent that they were soon abandoned. The old parlements of France,[10] and especially the Parlement of Paris, which Louis XIV had reduced to silence, vigorously reasserted themselves after his death. The parlements were primarily law courts, originally composed of bourgeois judges; but Louis XIV and his predecessors, to raise money, had made the judgeships into salable offices, to which they attached titles of nobility to increase the price. Hence in the time of the Regency the judges of the parlements had bought or inherited their seats, and were almost all nobles. Because they had property rights in their offices, they could not be removed by the king. The Regent conceded much influence to the Parlement of Paris, utilizing it to modify the will of Louis XIV. The parlements broadened their position, claiming the right to assent to legislation and taxes, through refusing to enforce what they considered contrary to the unwritten constitution or fundamental laws of France. They managed to exercise this right, off and on, from the days of the Regency until the great Revolution of 1789. The eighteenth century, for France, was a period of absolutism checked and balanced by organized privileged groups. It was an age of aristo-

[10] See pp. 178–179, 182.

cratic resurgence, in which the nobles won back many powers of which Louis XIV had tried to deprive them.

In Great Britain the Parliament was very different from the French parlements, and the British aristocracy was more politically competent than the *noblesse* of France. Parliament proved an effective machine for the conduct of public business. The House of Lords was hereditary, with the large exception of the bishops, who were appointed by the government and made up about a quarter of the active members of the upper house. The House of Commons was not at all representative of the country according to modern ideas. Only the wealthy, or those patronized by the wealthy, could sit in it,[11] and they were chosen by diverse and eccentric methods, in counties and towns, almost without regard to the size or wishes of the population. Some boroughs were owned outright, like the Old Sarum of the Pitt family. But through the machinations of bosses, or purchase of seats, all kinds of interests managed to get representatives into the Commons. Some members spoke for the "landed interest," others for the "funded interest" (mainly government creditors), others for the "London interest," the "West India interest," the "East India interest," and others. All politically significant groups could expect to have their desires heeded in Parliament, and all therefore were willing to go through parliamentary channels. Parliament was corrupt, slow, and expensive, but it was effective. For Parliament was not only a roughly representative body; it could also act, having acquired, in practice, a sovereign power of legislation.

Queen Anne, the last reigning Stuart, died in 1714. She was succeeded by George I, Elector of Hanover, as provided for by Parliament in the Act of Settlement of 1701.[12] George I was the nearest relative of the Stuarts who was also a Protestant. A heavy middle-aged German who spoke no English, he continued to spend much of his time in Germany, and he brought with him to England a retinue of German ministers and favorites and two ungainly mistresses, dubbed in England the "Elephant and the Maypole." He was never popular in England, where he was regarded as at best a political convenience. He was in no position to play a strong hand in English public life, and during his reign Parliament gained much independence from the crown.

The main problem was still whether the principles of the Revolution of 1688 should be maintained.[13] The agreement of parties which had made that revolution relatively bloodless proved to be temporary. The Whigs, who considered the revolution as their work, long remained a minority made of a few great land-owning noblemen, wealthy London merchants, lesser business people, and Nonconformists in religion. The Whigs generally controlled the House of Lords, but the House of Commons was more uncertain; at the time of the Peace of Utrecht its majority was Tory. We have already noted the significance for English constitutional development of the conflict at that time between the prowar Whig majority in the House of Lords and the Tory majority in Commons, and how the conflict was resolved to help establish the primacy of the House of Commons.[14] After 1714 the two parties tended to dissolve, and the terms "Whig" and "Tory" ceased to have much definite meaning. In general the government, and the Angli-

[11] See pp. 176–177.
[12] See p. 174.
[13] See pp. 174–176.
[14] See p. 189.

can bishops who were close to the government, remained "Whig." Men who were remote from the central government, or suspicious of its activities, formed a kind of country party quite different from the earlier Tories. Gentry and yeomen of the shires and byways were easily aroused against the great noblemen and men of money who led the Whigs. In the established church the lesser clergy were sometimes critical of the Whig bishops. Outside the official church were a group of Anglican clergy who refused the oath of loyalty after 1688 and were called Non-Jurors; they kept alive a shadow church until 1805. In Scotland also, the ancestral home of the Stuarts, many were disaffected with the new regime.

Tories, Non-Jurors, and Scots made up a milieu after 1688 in which what would now be called counterrevolution might develop. Never enthusiastic for the "Whig wars" against France,[15] critical of the mounting national debt which the wars created, distrustful of the business and moneyed interests, they began to look wistfully to the exiled Stuarts. After 1701, when James II died in France, the Stuart claims devolved upon his son, who lived until 1766, scheming time and again to make himself king of England. His partisans were known as Jacobites, from *Jacobus*, the Latin for James; they regarded him as "James III," where others called him the Pretender. The Jacobites felt that if he would give up his Catholic religion, he should be accepted as Britain's rightful king. To strengthen his claims they kept agitating the theory of divine right.

The Whigs could not tolerate a return of the Stuarts. The restoration of "James III" and his divine-right partisans would undo the principles of the Glorious Revolution—limited monarchy, constitutionalism, parliamentary supremacy, the rule of law, the toleration of dissenting Protestants, in short all that was summarized and defended in the writings of John Locke.[16] Moreover, those who held stock in the Bank of England or who had lent their money to the government would be ruined, since "James III" would surely repudiate a debt contracted by his foes. The Whigs were bound to support the Hanoverian George I. And George I was bound to look for support in a strange country among the Whigs.

George lacked personal appeal even for his English friends. To his enemies he was ridiculous and repulsive. The successful establishment of his dynasty would ruin the hopes of Tories and Jacobites. In 1715 the Pretender landed in Scotland, gathered followers from the Highlands, and proclaimed a rebellion against George I. Civil war seemed to threaten. But the Jacobite leaders bungled, and many of their followers proved to be undecided. They were willing enough to toast the "king over the water" in protest against the Whigs but not willing in a showdown to see the Stuarts, with all that went with them, again in possession of the crown of England. The Fifteen, as the revolt came to be called, petered out. But thirty years later came the Forty-five. In 1745, during war with France, the Pretender's son, "Bonnie Prince Charlie" or the "Young Pretender," again landed in Scotland and again proclaimed rebellion. This time, though almost no one in England rallied, the uprising was more successful. A Scottish force penetrated to within eighty miles of London and was driven back and crushed with the help of Hanoverian regiments rushed over from Germany. The government set out to destroy Jacobitism in the Highlands. The social system of the Highlands was wiped out; the clans were broken up; McDuffs and McDougals were forcibly reorganized according to modern notions of property and of landlord and tenant.[17]

[15] See pp. 174, 176, 188–191.
[16] See pp. 173, 299–301.
[17] See pp. 338–339.

The Jacobite uprisings confirmed the old reputation of England in the eyes of Europe, namely, as Voltaire said, that its government was as stormy as the seas which surrounded it. To partisans of monarchy on the Continent they illustrated the weaknesses of parliamentary government. But their ignominious collapse actually strengthened the parliamentary regime in England. They left little permanent mark and soon passed into an atmosphere of romantic legend.

The "Bubbles"

Meanwhile, immediately after the Peace of Utrecht, the problem of dealing with a postwar economic situation had to be faced in both England and France. In both countries it meant finding a way to carry the greatly swollen government debt. Organized permanent public debt was new at the time. The possibilities and limitations of large-scale banking, paper money, and credit were not clearly seen. In France there was much amazement at the way in which England and Holland, though smaller and less wealthy than France, had been able to maximize their resources through banking and credit and even to finance the alliance which had eclipsed the Sun King. In addition there was much private demand for both lending and borrowing money. Private persons all over western Europe were looking for enterprises in which to invest their savings. And promoters and organizers, anticipating a profit in this or that line of business, were looking for capital with which to work. Out of this whole situation grew the "South Sea bubble" in England and the "Mississippi bubble" in France. Both bubbles broke in 1720, and both had important long-range effects.

A close tie between government finance and private enterprise was usual at the time, under mercantilist ideas of government guidance of trade. In England, for example, a good deal of the government debt was held by companies organized for that purpose. The government would charter a company, strengthen it with a monopoly in a given line of business, and then receive from the company, after the stockholders had bought up the shares, a large sum of cash as a loan. Much of the British debt, contracted in the wars from 1689 to 1713, was held in this way by the Bank of England, founded in 1694;[18] by the East India Company, reorganized in 1708 in such a way as to provide funds for the government; and by the South Sea Company, founded in 1711. The Bank enjoyed a legal monopoly over certain banking operations in London, the East India Company over trade with the East, the South Sea Company for exploiting the *asiento*[19] and other commercial privileges extorted from Spain. The companies were owned by private investors. Savings drawn from trade and agriculture, put into shares in these companies, became available both for economic reinvestment and for use of the government in defraying the costs of war.

In 1716 the Prince Regent of France was attracted to a Scottish financier, John Law, reputedly by Law's remarkable mathematical system in gambling at cards. Law founded a much needed French central bank. In the next year, 1717, he organized a *Compagnie d'Occident*, popularly called the Mississippi Company, which obtained a monopoly of trade with Louisiana, where it founded New Orleans in 1718. This company, under Law's management, soon absorbed the French East India, China, Senegal, and African companies. It now enjoyed a legal monopoly of all French colonial trade. Law then proposed, and was author-

18 See p. 176.
19 See p. 191.

ized by the Regent, to assume the entire government debt. The company received from individuals their certificates of royal indebtedness or "bonds," and gave them shares of company stock in return. It proposed to pay dividends on these shares and to extinguish the debt from profits in the colonial trade and from a monopoly over the collection of all indirect taxes in France. The project carried with it a plan for drastic reform of the whole taxation system, to make taxes both more fair to the taxpayer and more lucrative to the government. Shares in the Mississippi Company were gobbled up by the public. There was a frenzy of speculation, a wild fear of not buying soon enough. Quotations rose to 18,000 livres a share. But the company rested only on unrealized projects. Shareholders began to fear for their money. They began to unload. The market broke sharply. Many found their life savings gone. Others lost ancestral estates on which they had borrowed in the hope of getting rich. Those, however, who had owned shares in the company before the rise, and who had resisted the speculative fever, lost nothing by the bursting of inflated prices, and later enjoyed a gilt-edged commercial investment.

Much the same thing happened in England, where it was thought by many that Law was about to provide a panacea for France. The South Sea Company, outbidding the Bank of England, took over a large fraction of the public debt by receiving government "bonds" from their owners in return for shares of its stock. The size and speed of profits to be made in Spanish America were greatly exaggerated, and the market value of South Sea shares rose rapidly for a time, reaching £1,050 for a share of £100 par value. Other schemes abounded in the passion for easy money. Promoters organized mining and textile companies, as well as others of more fanciful or bolder design: a company to bring live fish to market in tanks, an insurance company to insure female chastity, a company "for an undertaking which shall in due time be revealed." Shares in such enterprises were snatched at mounting prices. But in September 1720 the South Sea stockholders began to sell, doubting whether operations would pay dividends commensurate to £1,000 a share. They dragged down the whole unstable structure. As in France, many people found that their savings or their inheritances had disappeared.

Indignation in both countries was extreme. Both governments were implicated in the scandal. John Law fled to Brussels. The Regent was discredited; he resigned in 1723, and French affairs were afterward conducted by Cardinal Fleury. In

M. BACHELIER, DIRECTOR OF THE LYONS FARMS
by Jean-Baptiste Oudry (French, 1686–1755)

The "farms" of which M. Bachelier was a director were the semiprivate syndicates to which the French monarchy delegated or "farmed" the collection of its indirect taxes. The government received a definite sum in advance from the farmers, who then engaged in the more uncertain but profitable business of actual collection. Tax farmers were generally hated, and many became very rich. Nothing is known of the man in this picture. He may have been one of the wealthy persons who advanced money to the government, or only one of their high-level employees. In any case, he is shown writing at a table as a man of business, but he is not looking at his work; and with his head turned toward the spectator, his huge wig, his lace cuffs, and his left hand politely extended, he typifies the ruling elite at the close of the reign of Louis XIV. Courtesy of the University of Michigan Museum of Art, Ann Arbor.

England there was a change of ministers. Robert Walpole, a country gentleman of Whig persuasion, who had long sat in the Commons, and who had warned against the South Sea scheme from the beginning, became the principal minister to George I.

Britain recovered from the crisis more successfully than France. Law's bank, a useful institution, was dissolved in the reaction against him. France lacked an adequate banking system during the rest of the century. French investors developed a morbid fear of paper securities and a marked preference for putting their savings into land. Commercial capitalism and the growth of credit institutions in France were retarded. In England the same fears were felt. Parliament passed the "Bubble Act," forbidding all companies except those specifically chartered by the government to raise capital by the sale of stock. In both countries the development of joint-stock financing along the lines of the modern corporation was slowed down for over a century. Business enterprises continued to be typically owned by individuals and partnerships, which expanded by reinvestment of their own profits, and so had another reason to keep profits up and wages down. But in England Walpole managed to save the South Sea Company, the East India Company, and the Bank, all of which were temporarily discredited in the eyes of the public. England continued to perfect its financial machinery.

The credit of the two governments was also shaken by the "bubbles." Much of the French war debt was repudiated in one way or another. Repudiation was in many cases morally justifiable, for many government creditors were unscrupulous war profiteers, but financially it was disastrous, for it discouraged honest people from lending their money to the state. Nor was much accomplished toward reform of the taxes. The nobles continued to evade the taxes imposed on them by Louis XIV, John Law's plans for taxation evaporated with the rest of his project, and when in 1726 a finance minister tried to levy a 2 percent tax on all property, the vested interests, led by the Parlement of Paris, annihilated this proposal also. Lacking an adequate revenue, and repudiating its debts, the French monarchy had little credit. The conception of public or national debt hardly developed in France in the eighteenth century. The debt was considered to be the king's debt, for which no one except a few ministers felt any responsibility. The Bourbon government in fact often borrowed through the church, the Provincial Estates, or the city of Paris, which lenders considered to be better financial risks than the king himself. The government was severely handicapped in its foreign policy and its wars. It could not fully tap the wealth of its own subjects.

In England none of the debt was repudiated. Walpole managed to launch and keep going the system of the sinking fund, by which the government regularly set aside the wherewithal to pay interest and principal on its obligations. The credit of the British government became absolutely firm. The debt was considered a national debt, for which the British people itself assumed the responsibility. Parliamentary government made this development possible. In France no one could tell what the king or his ministers might do, and hence everyone was reluctant to trust them with his money. In England the people who had the money could also, through Parliament, determine the policies of state, decide what the money should be spent for, and levy enough taxes to maintain confidence in the debt. Similarities to France there were; the landowners who controlled the British Parliament, like those who controlled the Parlement of Paris, resisted direct taxation, so that the British government drew two-thirds or more of its revenues from indirect taxes paid by the mass of the population. Yet landowners, even dukes, did pay important amounts of taxes. There were no exemptions by class or rank, as in France. All propertied interests had a stake in the government. The wealth of the country stood behind the national debt. The national credit seemed inexhaustible. This was the supreme trump card of the British in their wars with France from the founding of the Bank of England in 1694 to the fall of Napoleon 120 years later. And it was the political freedom of England that gave it its economic strength.

Fleury in France; Walpole in England

Fleury was seventy-three years old when he took office, and ninety when he left it. He was not one to initiate programs for the distant future. Louis XV, as he came of age, proved to be indolent and selfish. Public affairs drifted, while France grew privately more wealthy, especially the commercial and bourgeois classes. Walpole likewise kept out of controversies. His motto was *quieta non movere*, "let sleeping dogs lie." It was to win over the Tory squires to the Hanoverian and Whig regime that Walpole kept down the land taxes; this policy was successful, and Jacobitism quieted down. Walpole supported the Bank, the trading companies, and the financial interests, and they in turn supported him. It was a time of political calm, in which the lower classes were quiet and the upper classes not quarreling, favorable therefore to the development of parliamentary institutions.

Walpole has been called the first prime minister and the architect of cabinet government, a system in which the ministers, or executives, are also members of the legislative body. He saw to it, by careful rigging, that a majority in the Commons always supported him. He avoided issues on which his majority might be lost. He thus began to acknowledge the principle of cabinet responsibility to a majority in Parliament, which was to become an important characteristic of cabinet government. And by selecting colleagues who agreed with him, and getting rid of those who did not, he advanced the idea of the cabinet as a body of ministers bound to each other and to the prime minister, obligated to follow the same policies and to stand or fall as a group. Thus Parliament was not only a representative or deliberative body like the diets and estates on the Continent, but one that developed an effective executive organ, without which neither representative government nor any government could survive.

To assure peace and quiet in domestic politics the best means was to avoid raising taxes. And the best way to avoid taxes was to avoid war. Fleury and Walpole both tried to keep at peace. They were not in the long run successful. Fleury was drawn into the War of the Polish Succession in 1733. Walpole kept England out of war until 1739. He always had a war party to contend with, and the most bellicose were those interested in the American trade—the slave trade, the sugar plantations, and the illicit sale of goods in the Spanish empire. The British official figures show that while trade with Europe, in the eighteenth century, was always less in war than in peace, trade with America always increased during war, except, indeed, during the War of American Independence.

In the 1730s there were constant complaints of indignities suffered by sturdy Britons on the Spanish Main. The war party produced a Captain Jenkins, who carried with him a small box containing a withered ear, which he said had been cut from his head by the outrageous Spaniards. Testifying in the House of Commons, where he "commended his soul to God and his cause to his country," he stirred up a commotion which led to war. So in 1739, after twenty-five years of peace, England plunged with wild enthusiasm into the War of Jenkins' Ear. "They are ringing the bells now," said Walpole; "they will soon be wringing their hands." The war soon became merged in a conflict involving Europeans and others in all parts of the world.

31. THE GREAT WAR OF THE MID–EIGHTEENTH CENTURY: THE PEACE OF PARIS, 1763

The fighting lasted until 1763, with an uneasy interlude between 1748 and 1756. It went by many names. The opening hostilities between England and Spain were called, by the English, the War of Jenkins' Ear. The Prussians spoke of three "Silesian" wars. The struggle on the Continent in the 1740s was often known as the War of the Pragmatic Sanction. British colonials in America called the fighting of the 1740s King George's War, or used the term "French and Indian Wars," for the whole sporadic conflict. Disorganized and nameless struggles at the same time shook the peoples of India. The names finally adopted by history were the War of the Austrian Succession for operations between 1740 and 1748 and the Seven Years' War for those between 1756 and 1763. The two wars were really one. They involved the same two principal issues, the duel of Britain and France for colonies, trade, and sea power, and the duel of Prussia and Austria for territory and military power in central Europe.

Eighteenth-Century Warfare

Warfare at the time was in a kind of classical phase, which strongly affected the development of events. It was somewhat slow, formal, elaborate, and indecisive. The enlisted ranks of armies and navies were filled with men considered economically useless, picked up by recruiting officers among unwary loungers in taverns or on the wharves. All governments protected their productive population, peasants, mechanics, and bourgeois, preferring to keep them at home, at work, and paying taxes. Soldiers were a class apart, enlisted for long terms, paid wages, professional in their outlook, and highly trained. They lived in barracks or great forts, and were dressed in bright uniforms (like the British "redcoats"), which, since camouflage was unnecessary, they wore even in battle. Weapons were not destructive; infantry was predominant and was armed with the smooth-bore musket, to which the bayonet could be attached. In war the troops depended on great supply depots built up beforehand, which were practically immovable with the transportation available, so that armies, at least in central and western Europe, rarely operated more than a few days' march from their bases. Soldiers fought methodically for pay. Generals hesitated to risk their troops, which took years to train and equip, and were very expensive. Strategy took the form not of seeking out the enemy's main force to destroy it in battle, but of maneuvering for advantages of position, applying a cumulative and subtle pressure somewhat as in a game of chess.

There was little national feeling, or feeling of any kind. The Prussian army recruited half or more of its enlisted personnel outside Prussia; the British army was largely made up of Hanoverian or other German regiments; even the French army had German units incorporated in it. Deserters from one side were enlisted by the other. War was between governments, or between the oligarchies and aristocracies which governments represented, not between whole peoples. It was fought for power, prestige, or calculated practical interests, not for ideologies, moral principles, world conquest, national survival, or ways of life. Popular nationalism had developed farthest in England, where "Rule Britannia" and "God Save the King," both breathing a low opinion of foreigners, became popular songs during these mid–eighteenth-century wars.

Civilians were little affected, except in India or the American wilderness where European conditions did not prevail. In Europe, a government aspiring to conquer a neighboring province did not wish to ruin or antagonize it beforehand. The fact that the west-European struggle was largely naval kept it well outside civilian experience. Never had war been so harmless, certainly not in the religious wars of earlier times, or in the national wars initiated later. This was one reason why governments went to war so lightly. On the other hand governments also withdrew from war much more readily than in later times. Their treasuries might be exhausted, their trained soldiers used up; only practical or rational questions were at stake; there was no war hysteria or pressure of mass opinion; the enemy of today might be the ally of tomorrow. Peace was almost as easy to make as war. Peace treaties were negotiated, not imposed. So the eighteenth century saw a series of wars and treaties, more wars, treaties, and rearrangements of alliances, all arising over much the same issues, and with exactly the same powers present at the end as at the beginning.

The War of the Austrian Succession, 1740–1748

The War of the Austrian Succession was started by the king of Prussia. Frederick II, or the "Great," was a young man of twenty-eight when he became king in 1740. His youth had not been happy; he was temperamentally incompatible with his father. His tastes as a prince had run to playing the flute, corresponding with French men of letters, and writing prose and verse in the French language. His father, the sober Frederick William I,[20] thought him frivolous and effeminate, and dealt with him so clumsily that at the age of eighteen he tried to escape from the kingdom. Caught and brought back, he was forced to witness the execution, by his father's order, of the friend and companion who had shared in his attempted flight. Frederick changed as the years passed from a jaunty youth to an aged cynic, equally undeceived by himself, his friends, or his enemies, and seeing no reason to expect much from human nature. Though his greatest reputation was made as a soldier, he retained his literary interests all his life, became a historian of merit, and is perhaps of all modern monarchs the only one who would have a respectable standing if considered only as a writer. An unabashed freethinker, like many others of his day, he considered all religions ridiculous and laughed at the divine right of kings; but he would have no nonsense about the rights of the house of Brandenburg, and he took a solemn view of the majesty of the state.

Frederick, in 1740, lost no time in showing a boldness which his father would have surely dreaded. He decided to conquer Silesia,[21] and on December 16, 1740,

---

[20] See pp. 226–227.
[21] See map, p. 222, panel 3.

he invaded that province, a region adjoining Prussia, lying in the upper valley of the Oder, and belonging to the kingdom of Bohemia and hence to the Danubian empire of the Habsburgs. The Pragmatic Sanction, a general agreement signed by the European powers, including Prussia, had stipulated that all domains of the Austrian Habsburgs should be inherited integrally by the new heiress, Maria Theresa.[22] The issue was between law and force. Frederick in attacking Silesia could invoke nothing better than "reason of state," the welfare and expansion of the state of which he was ruler. But he was not mistaken in the belief that if he did not attack the Austrians someone else soon would.

The Pragmatic Sanction was universally disregarded. All turned against Maria Theresa. Bavaria and Saxony put in claims. Spain, still hoping to revise the Peace of Utrecht, saw another chance to win back former Spanish holdings in Italy. The decisive intervention was that of France. It was the fate of France to be torn between ambitions on the European continent and ambitions on the sea and beyond the seas. Economic and commercial advantage might dictate concentration on the impending struggle with Britain. But the French nobles were less interested than the British aristocrats in commercial considerations. They were influential because they furnished practically all the army officers and diplomats. They saw in Austria the traditional enemy, in Europe the traditional field of valor, and in Belgium, which now belonged to the Austrians, the traditional object for annexation to France. Cardinal Fleury, much against his will and judgment, found himself forced into war against the Habsburgs.

Maria Theresa was at this time a young woman of twenty-three. She proved to be one of the most capable rulers ever produced by the house of Habsburg. She bore ten children, and set a model of conscientious family living at a time of much indifference to such matters among the upper classes. She was as devout and as earnest as Frederick of Prussia was irreligious and seemingly flip. She dominated her husband and her grown sons as she did her kingdoms and her duchies. With a good deal of practical sense, she reconstructed her empire without having any doctrinaire program, and she accomplished more in her methodical way than more brilliant contemporaries with more spectacular projects of reform.

She was pregnant when Frederick invaded Silesia, giving birth to her first son, the future emperor Joseph II, in March 1741. She was preoccupied at the same time by the political crisis. Her dominions were assailed by half a dozen outside powers, and were also quaking within, for her two kingdoms of Hungary and Bohemia (both of which had accepted the Pragmatic Sanction) were slow to see which way their advantage lay. She betook herself to Hungary to be crowned with the crown of St. Stephen—and to rally support. The Hungarians were still in a grumbling frame of mind, as in the days of the Rakoczy rebellion forty years before.[23] She made a carefully arranged and dramatic appearance before them, implored them to defend her, and swore to uphold the liberties of the Hungarian nobles and the separate constitution of the kingdom of Hungary. All Europe told how the beautiful young queen, by raising aloft the infant Joseph at a session of the Hungarian parliament, had thrown the dour Magyars into paroxysms of chivalrous resolve. The story was not quite true, but it is true that she made an eloquent address to the Magyars, and that she took her baby with her and proudly exhibited him. The Hungarian magnates pledged their "blood and life," and delivered a hundred thousand soldiers.

[22] See p. 219.
[23] See pp. 218–219.

The war, as it worked out in Europe, was reminiscent of the struggles of the time of Louis XIV, or even of the Thirty Years' War now a century in the past. It was, again, a kind of civil struggle within the Holy Roman Empire, in which a league of German princes banded together against the monarchy of Vienna. This time they included the new kingdom of Prussia. It was, again, a collision of Bourbons and Habsburgs, in which the French pursued their old policy of maintaining division in Germany, by supporting the German princes against the Habsburgs. The basic aim of French policy, according to instructions given by the French foreign office to its ambassador in Vienna in 1725, was to keep the Empire divided by the principles of the Peace of Westphalia,[24] preventing the union of German powers into "one and the same body, which would in fact become formidable to all the other powers of Europe." This time the Bourbons had Spain on their side. Maria Theresa was supported only by Britain and Holland, which subsidized her financially, but which had inadequate land forces. The Franco-German-Spanish combination was highly successful. In 1742 Maria Theresa, hard pressed, accepted the proposals of Frederick for a separate peace. She temporarily granted him Silesia, and he temporarily slipped out of the war which he had been the first to enter. The French and Bavarians moved into Bohemia and almost organized a puppet kingdom with the aid of Bohemian nobles. The French obtained the election of their Bavarian satellite as Holy Roman Emperor, Charles VII. In 1745 the French won the battle of Fontenoy in Belgium, the greatest battle of the war; they dominated Belgium, which neither the Dutch nor British were able to defend. In the same year they fomented the Jacobite rebellion in Scotland.

But the situation overseas offset the situation in Europe. It was America that tilted the balance. The French fortress of Louisburg on Cape Breton Island was captured by an expedition of New Englanders in conjunction with the British navy. British warships drove French and Spanish shipping from the seas. The French West Indies were blockaded. The French government, in danger of losing the wealth and taxes drawn from the sugar and slave trades, announced its willingness to negotiate.

Peace was made at Aix-la-Chapelle in 1748. It was based on an Anglo-French agreement in which Maria Theresa was obliged to concur. Britain and France arranged their differences by a return to the *status quo ante bellum.* The British returned Louisburg despite the protests of the Americans and relaxed their stranglehold on the Caribbean. The French returned Madras, which they had captured, and gave up their hold on Belgium. The Atlantic powers recognized Frederick's annexation of Silesia and required Maria Theresa to cede some Italian duchies— Parma and Piacenza—to a Spanish Bourbon. Belgium was returned to Maria Theresa at the especial insistence of Britain and the Dutch. She and her ministers were very dissatisfied. They would infinitely have preferred to lose Belgium and keep Silesia. They were required, in the interest of a European or even intercontinental balance of power, to give up Silesia and to hold Belgium for the benefit of the Dutch against the French.

The war had been more decisive than the few readjustments of the map seemed to show. It proved the weakness of the French position, straddled as it was between Europe and the overseas world. Maintaining a huge army for use in Europe, the French could not, like Britain, concentrate upon the sea. On the other hand, because vulnerable on the sea, they could not hold their gains in Europe or

[24] See pp. 141–146.

conquer Belgium. The Austrians, though bitter, had reason for satisfaction. The war had been a war to partition the Habsburg empire. The Habsburg empire still stood. Hungary had thrown in its lot with Vienna, a fact of much subsequent importance. Bohemia was won back. In 1745, when Charles VII died, Maria Theresa got her husband elected Holy Roman Emperor, a position for which she could not qualify because she was a woman. But the loss of Silesia was momentous. Silesia was as populous as the Dutch Republic, heavily German, and industrially the most advanced region east of the Elbe. Prussia by acquiring it doubled its population and more than doubled its resources. Prussia with Silesia was unquestionably a great power. Since Austria was still a great power there were henceforth two great powers in the vague world known as "Germany," a situation which came to be known as the German dualism. But the transfer of Silesia, which doubled the number of Germans ruled by the king of Prussia, made the Habsburg empire less German, more Slavic and Hungarian, more Danubian and international. Silesia was the keystone of Germany. Frederick was determined to hold it, and Maria Theresa to win it back. A new war was therefore foreseeable in central Europe. As for Britain and France, the peace of Aix-la-Chapelle was clearly only a truce.

The next years passed in a busy diplomacy, leading to what is known as the "reversal of alliances" and Diplomatic Revolution of 1756. The Austrians set themselves to nipping off the growth of Prussia. Maria Theresa's foreign minister, Count Kaunitz, perhaps the most artful diplomat of the century, concluded that the time had come to abandon ideas that were centuries old. The rise of Prussia had revolutionized the balance of power. Kaunitz, reversing traditional policy, proposed an alliance between Austria and France—between the Habsburgs and the Bourbons. He encouraged French aspirations for Belgium in return for French support in the destruction of Prussia. The overtures between Austria and France obliged Britain, Austria's former ally, to reconsider its position in Europe; the British had Hanover to protect, and were favorably impressed by the Prussian army. An alliance of Great Britain and Prussia was concluded in January 1756. Meanwhile Kaunitz consummated his alliance with France. One consequence was to marry the future Louis XVI to one of Maria Theresa's daughters, Marie Antoinette, the "Austrian woman" of Revolutionary fame. The Austrian alliance was never popular in France. Some Frenchmen thought that the ruin of Prussia would only enhance the Austrian control of Germany and so undo the fundamental "Westphalia system." The French progressive thinkers, known as "philosophes," believed Austria to be priest-ridden and backward, and were for ideological reasons admirers of the freethinking Frederick II. Dissatisfaction with its foreign policy was one reason for the growth of a revolutionary attitude toward the Bourbon government.

In any case, when the Seven Years' War broke out in 1756, though it was a continuation of the preceding war in that Prussia fought Austria, and Britain France, the belligerents had all changed partners. Great Britain and Prussia were now allies, as were, more remarkably, the Habsburgs and the Bourbons. In addition, Austria had concluded a treaty with the Russian empire for the annihilation of Prussia.

The Seven Years' War, 1756–1763: In Europe and America

The Seven Years' War began in America. Let us turn, however, to Europe first. Here the war was another war of "partition." As a league of powers had but recently attempted to partition the empire of Maria Theresa, and a generation before had in fact partitioned the empires of Sweden and Spain, so now Austria, Russia, and France set out to partition the newly created kingdom of Prussia. Their aim was to relegate the Hohenzollerns to the margraviate of Brandenburg. Prussia, even with Silesia, had less than 6,000,000 people; each of its three principal enemies had 20,000,000 or more. But war was less an affair of peoples than of states and standing armies, and the Prussian state and Prussian army were the most efficient in Europe. Frederick fought brilliant campaigns, won victories as at Rossbach in 1757, moved rapidly along interior lines, eluded, surprised, and reattacked the badly coordinated armies opposed to him. He proved himself the great military genius of his day. But genius was scarcely enough. Against three such powers, reinforced by Sweden and the German states, and with no ally except Great Britain (and Hanover) whose aid was almost entirely financial, the kingdom of Prussia by any reasonable estimate had no chance of survival. There were times when Frederick believed all to be lost, yet he went on fighting, and his strength of character in these years of adversity, as much as his ultimate triumph, later made him a hero and symbol for the Germans. His subjects, Junkers and even serfs, advanced in patriotic spirit under pressure. The coalition tended to fall apart. The French lacked enthusiasm; they were fighting Britain, the Austrian alliance was unpopular, and Kaunitz would not plainly promise them Belgium. The Russians found that the more they moved westward the more they alarmed their Austrian allies. Frederick was left to deal only with the implacable Austrians, for whom he was more than a match. By the peace of Hubertusburg in 1763 not only did he lose nothing; he retained Silesia.

For the rest, the Seven Years' War was a phase in the long dispute between France and Great Britain. Its stakes were supremacy in the growing world economy, control of colonies, and command of the sea. The two empires had been left unchanged in 1748 by the peace of Aix-la-Chapelle. Both held possessions in India, in the West Indies, and on the American mainland.[25] In India both British and French possessed only disconnected commercial establishments on the coast, infinitesimal specks on the giant body of India. Both also traded with China at Canton. Both occupied way stations on the route to Asia, the British in St. Helena and Ascension Island in the south Atlantic, the French in the much better islands of Mauritius and Reunion in the Indian Ocean. Frenchmen were active also on the coasts of Madagascar. The greatest way station, the Cape of Good Hope, belonged to the Dutch. In the West Indies the British plantations were mainly in Jamaica, Barbados, and some of the Leeward Islands; the French in San Domingo, Guadeloupe, and Martinique. All were supported by the booming slave trade in Africa.

On the American mainland the French had more territory, the British more people. In the British colonies from Georgia to Nova Scotia lived perhaps two million whites, predominantly English but with strong infusions of Scots-Irish, Dutch, Germans, French, and Swedes. Philadelphia, with some 40,000 people, was as large as any city in England except London. The colonies, in population, bulked about a quarter as large as the mother country. But they were provincial, locally minded, incapable of concerted action. In 1754 the British government called a congress at Albany in New York, hoping that the colonies would assume some collective responsibility for the coming war. The congress adopted an

[25] See maps, pp. 190, 274.

"Albany plan of union" drawn up by Benjamin Franklin, but the colonial legislatures declined to accept it, through fear of losing their independence. The colonials were willing, in a politically immature way, to rely on Britain for military action against France.

The French were still in possession of Louisburg on Cape Breton Island, a stronghold begun by Louis XIV, located in the Gulf of St. Lawrence. It was designed for naval domination of the American side of the north Atlantic, and to control access to the St. Lawrence River, the Great Lakes, and the vast region now called the Middle West. Through all this tract of country Frenchmen constantly came and went, but there were sizable French settlements only around New Orleans in the south and Quebec in the north. One source of French strength was that the French were more successful than the British in gaining the support of the Indians. This was probably because the French, being few in numbers, did not threaten to expropriate the Indians from their lands, and also because Catholics at this time were incomparably more active than Protestants in Christian missions among non-European peoples.

Both empires, French and British, were held together by mercantilist regulations framed mainly in the interest of the home countries. In some ways the British empire was more liberal than the French; it allowed local self-government and permitted immigration from all parts of Europe. In other ways the British system was more strict. British subjects, for example, were required by the Navigation Acts to use empire ships and seamen—English, Scottish, or colonial—whereas the French were more free to use the carrying services of other nations. British sugar planters had to ship raw sugar to the home country, there to be refined and sold to Europe, whereas French planters were free to refine their sugar in the islands. The mainland British colonials were forbidden to manufacture ironware and numerous other articles for sale; they were expected to buy such objects from England. Since the British sold little to the West Indies, where the slave population had no income with which to buy, the mainland colonies, though less valued as a source of wealth, were a far more important market for British goods. The colonials, though they had prospered under the restrictive system, were beginning to find much of it irksome at the time of the Seven Years' War, and indeed evaded it when they could.

Fighting was endemic even in the years of peace in Europe. Nova Scotia was a trouble spot. French in population, it had been annexed by Britain at the Peace of Utrecht. Its proximity to Louisburg made it a scene of perpetual agitation. The British government in 1755, foreseeing war with France, bodily removed about 7,000 of its people, who called themselves Acadians, scattering them in small numbers through the other mainland colonies. But the great disputed area was the Alleghenies. British colonials were beginning to feel their way westward through the mountains. French traders, soldiers, and empire builders were moving eastward toward the same mountains from points on the Mississippi and the Great Lakes. In 1749, at the request of Virginia and London capitalists, the British government chartered a land-exploitation company, the Ohio Company, to operate in territory claimed also by the French. The French threw up a fort at the point where the Ohio River is formed by the junction of two smaller rivers—Fort Duquesne, later called Pittsburgh. A force of colonials and British regular troops, under General Braddock, started through the wilderness to dislodge the French. It was defeated in July 1755, perhaps through its commander's unwillingness to take advice from the colonial officers, of whom one was George Washington.

A year later France and Britain declared war. The British were brilliantly led by William Pitt, subsequently the Earl of Chatham, a man of wide vision and superb confidence. "I know that I can save the country," he said, "and I know that no one else can." He concentrated British effort on the navy and colonies, while subsidizing Frederick of Prussia to fight in Europe, so that England, as he put it, might win an empire on the plains of Germany. Only the enormous credit of the British government made such a policy feasible. In 1758 British forces successfully took Fort Duquesne. Louisburg fell again in the same year. Gaining entry to the St. Lawrence, the British moved upstream to Quebec, and in 1759 a force under General Wolfe, stealthily scaling the heights, appeared by surprise on the Plains of Abraham outside the fortress, forcing the garrison to accept a battle, which the British won. With the fall of Quebec no further French resistance was possible on the American mainland. The British also, with superior naval power, occupied Guadeloupe and Martinique and the French slave stations in Africa.

The Seven Years' War, 1756–1763: In India

Both British and French interests were meanwhile profiting from disturbed conditions in India. As large as Europe without Russia, India was a congested country of impoverished masses, speaking hundreds of languages and following many religions and subreligions, the two greatest being the Hindu and the Muslim. Waves of invasion through the northwest frontier since the Christian year A.D. 1001 had produced a Muslim empire, whose capital was at Delhi and which for a short time held jurisdiction over most of the country. These Muslim emperors were known as Great Moguls. The greatest was Akbar, who ruled from 1556 to 1605, built roads, reformed the taxes, patronized the arts, and attempted to minimize religious differences among his peoples. The Muslim artistic culture flourished for a time after Akbar. One of his successors, Shah Jehan (1628–1658), built the beautiful Taj Mahal near Agra, and at Delhi the delicately carved alabaster palace of the Moguls, in which he placed the Peacock Throne, made of solid gold and studded with gems.

But meanwhile there was restlessness among the Hindus. The Sikhs, who had originated in the fifteenth century as a reform movement in Hinduism, went to war with the Mogul emperor in the seventeenth century. They became one of the most ferociously warlike of Indian peoples. Hindu princes in central India formed a "Mahratta confederacy" against the Muslim emperor at Delhi. Matters were made worse when Aurungzeb, the last significant Mogul emperor (1658–1707), adopted repressive measures against the Hindus. After Aurungzeb, India fell into political dissolution. Many of the modern princely states originated or became autonomous at this time. Hindu princes rebelled against the Mogul. Muslims, beginning as governors or commanders under the Mogul, set up as rulers in their own right. Thus originated Hyderabad, which included the fabulous diamond mines of Golconda, and whose ruler long was called the wealthiest man in the world. Princes and would-be princes fought with each other and with the emperor. New Muslim invaders also poured across the northwest frontier. In 1739 a Persian force occupied Delhi, slaughtered thirty thousand people and departed with the Peacock Throne. Between 1747 and 1761 came a series of forays from Afghanistan, which again resulted in the looting of Delhi and the massacre of uncounted thousands.

The situation in India resembled, on a larger and more frightful scale, what had happened in Europe in the Holy Roman Empire, where also irreconcilable religious differences (of Catholics and Protestants) had torn the country asunder, ambitious princes and city-states had won a chaotic independence, and foreign armies appeared repeatedly as invaders. India, like central Europe, suffered chronically from war, intrigue, and rival pretensions to territory; and in India, as in the Holy Roman Empire, outsiders and ambitious insiders benefited together.

The half-unknown horrors in the interior had repercussions on the coasts. Here handfuls of Europeans were established in the coastal cities. By the troubles in the interior the Indian authorities along the coasts were reduced, so to speak, to a size with which the Europeans could deal. The Europeans—British and French—were agents of their respective East India companies. The companies built forts, maintained soldiers, coined money, and entered into treaties with surrounding Indian powers, under charter of their home governments, and with no one in India to deny them the exercise of such sovereign rights. Agents of the companies, like Indians themselves, ignored or respected the Mogul emperor as suited their own purpose. They were, at first, only one of the many elements in the flux and reflux of Indian affairs.

Neither the British nor the French government, during the Seven Years' War, had any intention of territorial conquest in India, their policy in this respect differing radically from policy toward America. Nor were the two companies imperialistic. The company directors, in London and Paris, disapproved of fantastic schemes of intervention in Indian politics, insisted that their agents should attend to business only, and resented every penny and every sou not spent to bring in commercial profit. But it took a year or more to exchange messages between Europe and India, and company representatives in India, caught up in the Indian vortex, and overcome by the chance to make personal fortunes or by dreams of empire, acted very much on their own, committing their home offices without compunction. Involvement in Indian affairs was not exactly new. We have seen how "Diamond" Pitt, in 1702, purchased the good will of the nawab of the Carnatic, when the nawab threatened, by military force, to reduce the English traders at Madras to submission.[26] But the first European to exploit the possibilities of the situation was the Frenchman Dupleix. Dupleix felt that the funds sent out by the company in Paris, to finance trade in India, were insufficient. His idea seems to have been not empire-building, but to make the company into a local territorial power, in order that, from taxes and other political revenues, it might have more capital for its commercial operations. In any case, during the years of peace in Europe after 1748, Dupleix found himself with about 2,000 French troops in the Carnatic, the east coast around Madras. He lent them out to neighboring native rulers in return for territorial concessions. The first to drill native Indians by European methods, he was the originator of the "sepoys." Following a program of backing claimants to various Indian thrones, he built up a clientele of native rulers under obligation to himself. He was very successful, for a few European troops or sepoys could overcome hordes of purely Indian forces in pitched battle. But he was recalled to France in 1754, after the company became apprehensive of war with Britain and other trouble; and he died in disgrace.

When war came in 1756, British interests in India were advanced chiefly by

[26] See p. 254.

Robert Clive. He had come out many years before as a clerk for the company but had shown military talents and an ability to comprehend Indian politics. He had maneuvered, with little success, against Dupleix in the Carnatic in the 1740s. In 1756, on hearing the news of war in Europe, he shifted his attention to Bengal, hoping to drive the French from their trading stations there. The French were favored in Bengal by the local Muslim ruler, Suraja Dowla, who proceeded to anticipate Clive's arrival by expelling the British from Calcutta. Capturing the city, he shut up 146 Englishmen in a small room without windows (soon known as the "Black Hole of Calcutta") and kept them there all night, during which most of them died of suffocation. Clive, soon appearing with a small force of British and sepoys, routed Suraja Dowla at the battle of Plassey in 1757. He put his own puppet on the Bengal throne and extorted huge reparations both for the company and for himself. Back in England he was received with mixed feelings, and again, in India, strove to purify the almost incredible corruption of company employees there, men normal enough but demoralized by irresistible chances for easy riches. Finally he committed suicide in 1774.

It was British sea power, more fundamentally than Clive's tactics, that assured the triumph of British over French ambitions in the East. The British government still had no intention of conquest in India, but it could not see its East India Company forced out by agents of the French company in collaboration with Indian princes. Naval forces were therefore dispatched to the Indian Ocean, and they not only allowed Clive to shift from Madras to Calcutta at will, but gradually cut off the French posts in India from Europe and from each other. By the end of the war all the French establishments in India, as in Africa and America, were at the mercy of the British. The French overseas lay prostrate, and France itself was again detached from the overseas world on which much of its economy rested. In 1761 France made an alliance with Spain, which was alarmed for the safety of its own American empire after the British victories at Quebec and in the Caribbean. But the British also defeated Spain.

The Peace Settlement of 1763

The British armed forces had been spectacularly successful. Yet the peace treaty, signed at Paris in February 1763, five days before the Austro-Prussian peace of Hubertusburg, was by no means unfavorable to the defeated. The French Duke of Choiseul was a skillful and single-minded negotiator. The British, Pitt having fallen from office in 1761, were represented by a confused group of parliamentary favorites of the new king, George III. France ceded to Britain all French territory on the North American mainland east of the Mississippi. Canada thereby became British, and the colonials of the Thirteen Colonies were relieved of the French presence beyond the Alleghenies. To Spain, in return for aid in the last days of the war, France ceded all holdings west of the Mississippi and at its mouth. France thereby abandoned the North American continent. But these almost empty regions were of minor commercial importance, and the French, in return for surrendering them, retained many economically more valuable establishments elsewhere. In the West Indies the British planters, and in England the powerful "West India interest," feared competition from the French sugar islands, which produced more cheaply, and wanted them left outside the protected economic system of the British empire. France therefore received back Guadeloupe and

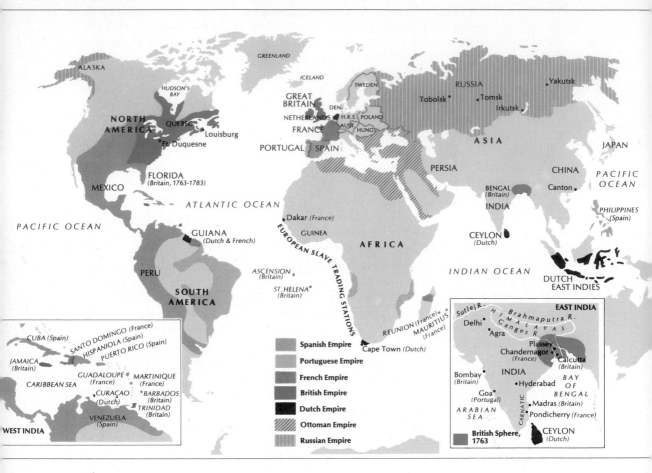

THE WORLD IN 1763

At the Peace of Paris of 1763 the British overseas empire triumphed over the French. The French ceded their holdings on the North American mainland east of the Mississippi to Britain, those west of the Mississippi to Spain. Britain also took Florida from Spain in 1763, but lost it, returning it to Spain in 1783, at the close of the War of American Independence. The French retained their sugar islands in the West Indies and their trading stations in India; they were stopped from empire-building but did not greatly suffer commercially from the Seven Years' War. The British proceeded to build their empire in India. (See also map, p. 317.)

Martinique, as well as most of its slave stations in Africa. In India, the French remained in possession of their commercial installations—offices, warehouses, and docks—at Pondicherry and other towns. They were forbidden to erect fortifications or pursue political ambitions among Indian princes—a practice which neither the French nor the British government had hitherto much favored in any case.

The treaties of Paris and Hubertusburg, closing the prolonged war of the midcentury, made the year 1763 a memorable turning point. Prussia was to continue in being. The dualism of Germany was to be lasting; Austria and Prussia eyed each other as rivals. Frederick's aggression of 1740 was legalized and even moralized by the heroic defense that had proved necessary to retain the plunder. Frederick himself, from 1763 until his death in 1786, was a man of peace, philosophical and even benign. But the German crucible had boiled, and out of it had come a Prussia harder and more metallic than ever, more disposed, by its escape from annihilation, to glorify its army as the steel framework of its life.

The Anglo-French settlement was far-reaching and rather curious. Although the war was won overwhelmingly by the British, it resulted in no commercial calamity to the French. French trade with America and the East grew as rapidly after the Seven Years' War as before it, and in 1785 was double what it had been in 1755. For England the war opened up new commercial channels. British trade with America and the East probably tripled between 1755 and 1785.[27] But the outstanding British gains were imperial and strategic. The European balance of power was preserved, the French had been kept out of Belgium, British subjects in North America seemed secure, and Britain had again vindicated its command of the sea. British sea power implied, in turn, that British seaborne commerce was safe in peace or war, while the seaborne commerce of the French, or of any others, depended ultimately on the political requirements of the British. But the French still had a few cards to play, and were to play them in the American and French Revolutions.

For America and India the peace of 1763 was decisive. America north of Mexico was to become part of an English-speaking world. In India the British government was drawn increasingly into a policy of territorial occupation; a British "paramount power" eventually emerged in place of the empire of the Moguls. British political rule in India stimulated British business there, until in the greatest days of British prosperity India was one of the main pillars of the British economic system, and the road to India became in a real sense the lifeline of the British empire. But in 1763 this state of affairs was still in the future and was to be reached by many intermediate steps.

[27] See pp. 250–252.

VII.
The Scientific
View of
the World

T he seventeenth century has been called the century of genius. One reason is that it was the age when science became "modern." It was the great age of Galileo and Sir Isaac Newton, whose combined lifetimes spanned the century, with Galileo dying and Newton being born in the same year, 1642. When Galileo was young those who probed into the secrets of nature still labored largely in the dark, isolated from one another and from the general public, working oftentimes by methods of trial and error, not altogether clear on what they were trying to do, with their thinking still complicated by ideas not nowadays considered scientific. They had nevertheless accomplished a good deal. Discoveries had been made, and ideas developed, without which the intellectual revolution of the seventeenth century would not have occurred. But in a way all scientific investigators before Galileo seem to be precursors, patient workers destined never to enter into the world toward which they labored. In 1727, when Newton died, all was changed. Scientific men were in continual touch with one another, and science was recognized as one of the principal enterprises of European society. Scientific methods of inquiry had been defined. The store of factual knowledge had become very large. The first modern scientific synthesis, or coherent theory of the physical universe, had been presented by Newton. Scientific knowledge was applied increasingly to navigation, mining, agriculture, and many branches of manufacture. Science and invention were joining hands. Science was accepted as the main force in the advancement of civilization and progress. And science was becoming popularized; many people who were not themselves scien-

Chapter Emblem: A Copernican globe designed by Kepler in 1596 to illustrate movement of the planets about the sun.

tists "believed" in science and attempted to apply scientific habits of thought to diverse problems of man and society.

The history of science is too great a story to be told in this book, but there are a few ideas about it which even a book of this kind must attempt to make clear. First, science, purely as a form of thought, is one of the supreme achievements of the human mind, and to have a humanistic understanding of man's powers one must sense the importance of science, as of philosophy, literature, or the arts. Second, science has increasingly affected practical affairs, entering into the health, wealth, and happiness of humankind. It has changed the size of populations and the use of raw materials, revolutionized methods of production, transport, business, and war, and so helped to relieve some human problems while aggravating others. This is especially true of modern civilization since the seventeenth century. Third, in the modern world ideas have had a way of passing over from science into other domains of thought. Many people today, for example, in their notions of themselves, their neighbors, or the meaning of life, are influenced by ideas which they believe to be those of Freud or Einstein—they talk of repressions or relativity without necessarily knowing much about them. Ideas derived from biology and from Darwin—such as evolution and the struggle for existence—have likewise spread far and wide. Similarly the scientific revolution of the seventeenth century had repercussions far beyond the realm of pure science. It changed ideas of religion and of God and man. And it helped to spread certain very deep-seated beliefs, such as that the physical universe in which man finds himself is essentially orderly and harmonious, that the human reason is capable of understanding and dealing with it, and that man can conduct his own affairs by methods of peaceable exchange of ideas and rational agreement. Thus was laid a foundation for belief in free and democratic institutions.

The purpose of this chapter is to sketch the rise of modern science in the seventeenth century and the emergence of the scientific view of the world and of human affairs. The chapter that follows will describe the popularization and application of these ideas in the eighteenth century, in the era generally known as the Age of Enlightenment.

32. PROPHETS OF A SCIENTIFIC CIVILIZATION: BACON AND DESCARTES

Science before the Seventeenth Century

The scientific view became characteristic of European society about the middle of the seventeenth century. There had, indeed, been a few in earlier times who caught glimpses of a whole civilization reared upon science. To us today the most famous of these is Leonardo da Vinci (1452–1519), the universal genius of the Italian Renaissance, who had been artist, engineer, and scientific thinker all in one. Leonardo, by actual dissection of dead bodies, had obtained an accurate knowledge of human anatomy; he had conceived of the circulation of the blood and the movement of the earth about the sun; and he had drawn designs for submarines and airplanes and speculated on the use of parachutes and poison gases. But Leonardo had not published his scientific ideas. He was known almost exclusively as an artist. His work in science remained outside the stream of scientific thought, without influence on its course. It was not even known until the discovery of his private notebooks in recent years. Leonardo thus figures in the history of science as an isolated genius, a man of brilliant insights and audacious theories, which died with their author's death, whereas science depends on a transmission of ideas in which investigators build upon one another's discoveries, test one another's experiments, and fill in the gaps in one another's knowledge.

A century after the death of Leonardo da Vinci educated Europeans were by no means scientifically minded. Among thoughtful persons many currents were stirring. On the one hand there was a great deal of skepticism, a constantly doubting frame of mind, which held that no certain knowledge is possible for human beings at all, that all beliefs are essentially only customs, that some people believe one thing and some another, and that there is no sound way of choosing between them. This attitude was best expressed by the French essayist Montaigne (1533–1592), whose thought distilled itself into an eternal question, *Que sais-je?* "What do I know?" with the always implied answer, "Nothing." Montaigne's philosophy led to a tolerant, humane, and broad-minded outlook; but as a system of thought it was not otherwise very constructive. On the other hand, there was also a tendency to over-belief, arising from the same inability to distinguish between true and false. There was no accepted line between chemistry and alchemy, or between astronomy and astrology; all alike were regarded as ways of penetrating the "secrets" of nature. The sixteenth century had been a great age of charlatans, such as Nostradamus and Paracelsus, some of whom, notably Paracelsus, mixed magic and valid science in a way hardly understandable to us today.[1] As late as the seventeenth century, especially in central Europe where the Thirty Years' War produced chaos and terror, kings and generals kept private astrologers to divine the future. The two centuries from about 1450 to about 1650 were also the period when fear of witches was at its height. The witchcraft panic lasted longest in Germany and central Europe, probably kept alive by the insecurities engendered by the Thirty Years' War. But about twenty persons were hanged as witches in Massachusetts as late as 1692, for the English colonies, as a remote and outlying part of the European world, were among the last to feel some of the waves originating in Europe. It was in Scotland, another outlying region of Europe, that the last known execution for witchcraft took place, in 1722.

It was by no means clear, in the early part of the seventeenth century, which way Europe was going to develop. It might conceivably have fallen into a kind of chaos, as India did at about this time. We have seen that much of Europe was racked by chronic and marauding violence, to which an end was put by the consolidation of the modern state and the conversion of armed bands into organized and disciplined armies. Similarly, in things of the mind, there was no settled order. Doubt went with superstition, indifference with persecution. Science in time provided Europe with a new faith in itself. The rise of science in the seventeenth century possibly saved European civilization from petering out in a long post-medieval afterglow, or from wandering off into the diverse paths of a genial skepticism, ineffectual philosophizing, desultory magic, or mad fear of the unknown.

Bacon and Descartes

Two men stand out as prophets of a world reconstructed by science. One was the Englishman Francis Bacon (1561–1626), the other the Frenchman René Descartes

[1] See p. 64.

(1596–1650). Both published their most influential books between 1620 and 1640. Both addressed themselves to the problem of knowledge. Both asked themselves how it is possible for human beings to know anything with certainty or to have a reliable, truthful, and usable knowledge of the world of nature. Both shared in the doubts of their day. They branded virtually all beliefs of preceding generations (outside religion) as worthless. Both ridiculed the tendency to put faith in ancient books, to cite the writings of Aristotle or others, on questions having to do with the workings of nature. Both attacked earlier methods of seeking knowledge; they rejected the methods of the "schoolmen" or "scholastics," the thinkers in the academic tradition of the universities founded in the Middle Ages. On the whole, medieval philosophy had been rationalistic and deductive.[2] That is, its characteristic procedure was to start with definitions and general propositions and then discover what further knowledge could be logically deduced from the definitions thus accepted. Or it proceeded by affirming the nature of an object to be such-and-such (e.g., that "man is a political animal") and then describing how objects of such a nature do or should behave. These methods, which owed much to Aristotle and other ancient codifiers of human thought, had generally ceased to be fruitful in discovery of knowledge of nature. Bacon and Descartes held that the medieval (or Aristotelian) methods were backward. They held that truth is not something that we postulate at the beginning and then explore in all its ramifications, but that it is something which we find at the end, after a long process of investigation, experiment, or intermediate thought.

Bacon and Descartes thus went beyond mere doubt. They offered a constructive program, and though their programs were different, they both became heralds or philosophers of a scientific view. They maintained that there was a true and reliable method of knowledge. And they maintained in addition that once this true method was known and practiced, once the real workings of nature were understood, men would be able to use this knowledge for their own purposes, control nature in their own interests, make undreamed of useful inventions, improve their mechanical arts, and add generally to their wealth and comfort. Bacon and Descartes thus announced the advent of a scientific civilization.

Francis Bacon planned a great work in many volumes, to be known as the *Instauratio Magna* or "Great Renewal," calling for a complete new start in science and civilization. He completed only two parts. One, published in 1620, was the *Novum Organum* or new method of acquiring knowledge. Here he insisted on *inductive* method. In the inductive method we proceed from the particular to the general, from the concrete to the abstract. For example, in the study of leaves, if we examine millions of actual leaves, of all sizes and shapes, and if we assemble, observe, and compare them with minute scrutiny, we are using an *inductive* method in the sense meant by Bacon; if successful, we may arrive at a knowledge, based on observed facts, of the general nature of a leaf as such. If, on the other hand, we begin with a general idea of what we think all leaves are like, i.e., all leaves have stems, and then proceed to describe an individual leaf on that basis, we are following the *deductive* method; we draw logical implications from what we already know, but we learn no more of the nature of a leaf than what we knew or thought we knew at the beginning. Bacon advised men to put aside all traditional ideas, to rid themselves of prejudices and preconceptions, to look at the world with fresh eyes, to observe and study the innumerable things that are

[2] See pp. 39–43.

actually perceived by the senses. Men before Bacon used the inductive method, but he formalized it as a method and became a leading philosopher of empiricism. This philosophy, the founding of knowledge on observation and experience, has always proved a useful safeguard against fitting facts into preconceived patterns. It demands that we let the patterns of our thought be shaped by actual facts as we observe them.

The other completed part of Bacon's great work, published in 1623, was called in its English translation *The Advancement of Learning.* Here Bacon developed the same ideas and especially insisted that true knowledge was useful knowledge. In *The New Atlantis* (1627), he portrayed a scientific utopia in which men enjoyed a perfect society through their knowledge and command of nature. The usefulness of knowledge became the other main element in the Baconian tradition. In this view there was no sharp difference between pure science and applied science or between the work of the purely scientific investigator and that of the mechanic or inventor who in his own way probed into nature and devised instruments or machines for putting natural forces to work. The fact that knowledge could be used for practical purposes became a sign or proof that it was true knowledge. For example, the fact that men could aim their cannon and hit their targets more accurately in the seventeenth century became a proof of the theory of ballistics which had been scientifically worked out. Enthusiastic Baconians believed that knowledge was power. True knowledge could be put to work, if not immediately at least in the long run, after more knowledge was discovered. It was useful to mankind, unlike the "delicate learning" of the misguided scholastics. In this coming together of knowledge and power arose the far-reaching modern idea of progress. And in it arose many of the problems of modern men, since the power given by scientific knowledge can be either bad or good.

But Bacon, though a force in redirecting the European mind, never had much influence on the development of actual science. Kept busy as Lord Chancellor of England and in other government duties, he was not even fully abreast of the most advanced scientific thought of his day. Like the public generally of his lifetime, he was undisturbed by the new theories of astronomers who held that the earth moved about the sun. Bacon's greatest weakness was his failure to understand the role of mathematics. Mathematics, dealing with pure abstractions and proceeding deductively from axioms to theorems, was not an empirical or inductive method of thought such as Bacon demanded. Yet science in the seventeenth century went forward most successfully in subjects where mathematics could be applied. Even today the degree to which a subject is truly scientific depends on the degree to which it can be made mathematical. We have pure science where we have formulas and equations, and the scientific method itself is both inductive and deductive.

Descartes was a great mathematician in his own right. He is considered the inventor of coordinate geometry. He showed that by use of coordinates (or graph paper, in simple language) any algebraic formula could be plotted as a curve in space, and contrariwise that any curve in space, however complex, could be converted into algebraic terms and thus dealt with by methods of calculation. And one effect of his general philosophy was to create belief in a vast world of nature that could be reduced to mathematical form.

Descartes set forth his ideas in his *Discourse on Method,* in 1637, and in many more technical writings. He advanced the principle of systematic doubt. He began by trying to doubt everything that could reasonably be doubted, thus sweeping away past ideas and clearing the ground for his own "great renewal," to use Bacon's phrase. He held that he could not doubt his own existence as a thinking and doubting being (*cogito ergo sum*, "I think, therefore I exist"); he then deduced, by systematic reasoning, the existence of God and much else. He arrived at a philosophy of dualism, the famous "Cartesian dualism," which held that God has created two kinds of fundamental reality in the universe. One was "thinking substance"—mind, spirit, consciousness, subjective experience. The other was "extended substance"—everything outside the mind and hence objective. Of everything except the mind itself the most fundamental and universal quality was that it occupied a portion of space, minute or vast. Space itself was conceived as infinite, and everywhere geometric.

This philosophy had profound and long-lasting effects. For one thing, the seemingly most real elements in human experience, color and sound, joy and grief, seemed somehow to be shadowy and unreal, or at least illusive, with no existence outside the mind itself. But all else was quantitative, measurable, reducible to formulas or equations. Over all else, over the whole universe or half-universe of "extended substance," the most powerful instrument available to the human understanding, namely, mathematics, reigned supreme. "Give me motion and extension," said Descartes, "and I will build you the world."

Descartes also, with French genius, expressed the Baconian idea. Instead of the "speculative philosophy of the schools," he wrote in the *Discourse on Method*, men might discover a "practical philosophy by which, understanding the forces and action of fire, water, air, the stars and heavens and all other bodies that surround us, as distinctly as we understand the mechanical arts of our craftsmen, we can use these forces in the same way for all purposes for which they are appropriate, and so make ourselves the masters and possessors of nature. And this is desirable not only for the invention of innumerable devices by which we may enjoy without trouble the fruits of the earth and the conveniences it affords, but mainly also for the preservation of health, which is undoubtedly the principal good and foundation of all other good things in this life."

33. THE ROAD TO NEWTON: THE LAW OF UNIVERSAL GRAVITATION

Scientific Advances

Meanwhile actual scientific discovery was advancing on many fronts. It did not advance on all with equal speed. Some of the sciences were, and long remained, dependent mainly on the collection of specimens. Botany was one of these; Europe's knowledge of plants expanded enormously with the explorations overseas, and botanical gardens and herb collections in Europe became far more extensive than ever before, bringing important enlargements in the stock of medicinal drugs. Other sciences drew their impetus from intensive and open-minded observation. The Flemish Vesalius, by a book published in 1543, *The Structure of the Human Body*, renewed and modernized the study of anatomy. Formerly anatomists had generally held that the writings of Galen, dating from the second century A.D., contained an authoritative description of all human muscles and tissues. They had indeed dissected cadavers but had dismissed those not conforming

to Galen's description as somehow abnormal or not typical. Vesalius put Galen behind him and based his general description of the human frame on actual bodies as he found them. In physiology also, dealing with the functioning rather than the structure of living bodies, there was considerable progress. Here the method of laboratory experiment could be profitably used. William Harvey, after years of laboratory work, including the vivisection of animals, published in 1628 a book *On the Movement of the Heart and Blood*. Here he set forth the doctrine, confirmed by evidence, of the continual circulation of the blood through arteries and veins. The Italian Malpighi, using the newly invented microscope, confirmed Harvey's findings by the discovery of capillaries in 1661. The Dutch Leeuwenhoek, also by use of the microscope, was the first to see blood corpuscles, spermatozoa, and bacteria, of which he left published drawings.

These sciences, and also chemistry, although work in them went continually on, did not come fully into their own until after 1800. They were long overshadowed by astronomy and physics. Here mathematics could be most fully applied, and mathematics underwent a rapid development in the seventeenth century. Decimals came into use to express fractions, the symbols used in algebra were improved and standardized, and in 1614 logarithms were invented by the Scot John Napier. Coordinate geometry was mapped out by Descartes, the theory of probabilities developed by Pascal, and calculus invented simultaneously in England by Newton and in Germany by Leibniz. These advances made it more generally possible to think about nature in purely quantitative terms, to measure with greater precision, and to perform complex and laborious computations. Physics and astronomy were remarkably stimulated, and it was in this field that the most astonishing scientific revolution of the seventeenth century took place.

The Scientific Revolution: Copernicus to Galileo

From time immemorial, since the Greek Ptolemy had codified ancient astronomy in the second century A.D.,[3] educated Europeans had held a conception of the cosmos which we call Ptolemaic. The cosmos in this view was a group of concentric spheres, a series of balls within balls each having the same center. The innermost ball was the earth, made up of hard, solid, earthy substance such as men were familiar with underfoot. The other spheres, encompassing the earth in series, were all transparent. They were the "crystalline spheres" made known to us by the

[3] See p. 15.

A SCHOLAR HOLDING A THESIS ON BOTANY
by Willem Moreelse (Dutch, before 1630–1666)

The Netherlands became a great intellectual center in the seventeenth century, with five universities founded during the years of struggle against Spain. The most famous was at Leyden, but the present scholar may be a new doctor of the University of Utrecht, where the little-known painter Willem Moreelse worked. Crowned with laurel, the successful candidate proudly displays his thesis, on which the Latin words announce that "any plant shows the presence of God." The bringing of hitherto unknown plants from the rest of the world to Europe contributed strongly not only to science but to medicine, food supply, and the pleasures of chocolate, tea, and coffee. Courtesy of The Toledo Museum of Art, Gift of Edward Drummond Libbey, 1962.

poets; their harmony was the "music of the spheres." These spheres all revolved about the earth, each sphere containing, set in it as a jewel, a luminous heavenly body or orb which moved about the earth with the movement of its transparent sphere. Nearest to the earth was the sphere of the moon; then, in turn, the spheres of Mercury and Venus, then the sphere of the sun, then those of the outer planets. Last came the outermost sphere containing all the fixed stars studded in it, all moving majestically about the earth in daily motion, but motionless with respect to each other because held firmly in the same sphere. Beyond the sphere of the fixed stars, in general belief, lay the "empyrean," the home of angels and immortal spirits; but this was not a matter of natural science.

A person standing on the earth, and looking up into the sky, thus felt himself to be enclosed by a dome of which his own position was the center. In the blue sky of day he could literally see the crystalline spheres; in the stars at night he could behold the orbs which these spheres carried with them. All revolved about him, presumably at no very alarming distance. The celestial bodies were commonly supposed to be of different material and quality from the earth. The earth was of heavy dross; the stars and planets and the sun and moon seemed made of pure and gleaming light, or at least of a bright ethereal substance almost as tenuous as the crystal spheres in which they moved. The cosmos was a hierarchy of ascending perfection. The heavens were purer than the earth.

This system corresponded to actual appearances, and except for scientific knowledge would be highly believable today. It was formulated also in rigorous mathematical terms. Ever since the Greeks, and becoming increasingly intricate in the Middle Ages, a complex geometry had grown up to explain the observed motion of the heavenly bodies. The Ptolemaic system was a mathematical system. And it was for purely mathematical reasons that it first came to be reconsidered. There was a marked revival of mathematical interest at the close of the Middle Ages, in the fourteenth and fifteenth centuries, a renewed concentration on the philosophical traditions of Pythagoras and Plato. In these philosophies could be found the doctrine that numbers might be the final key to the mysteries of nature. With them went a metaphysical belief that simplicity was more likely to be a sign of truth than complication, and that a simpler mathematical formulation was better than a more complex one.

These ideas motivated Nicholas Copernicus, born in Poland of German and Polish background, who, after study in Italy, wrote his epochal work *On the Revolutions of the Heavenly Orbs*. In this book, published in 1543 after his death, he held the sun to be the center of the solar system and fixed stars, and the earth to be one of the planets revolving in space around it. This view had been entertained by a few isolated thinkers before. Copernicus gave a mathematical demonstration. To him it was a purely mathematical problem. With increasingly detailed knowledge of the actual movement of the heavenly bodies it had become necessary to make the Ptolemaic system more intricate by the addition of new "cycles" and "epicycles," until, as John Milton expressed it later, the cosmos was

> *With Centric and Concentric scribbled o'er,*
> *Cycle and Epicycle, Orb in Orb.*

Copernicus needed fewer such hypothetical constructions to explain the known movements of the heavenly bodies. The heliocentric or sun-centered theory was mathematically a little simpler than the geocentric or earth-centered theory hitherto held.

The Copernican doctrine long remained a hypothesis known only to experts. Most astronomers for a time hesitated to accept it, seeing no need, from the evidence yet produced, of so overwhelming a readjustment of current ideas. Tycho Brahe (1546–1601), the greatest authority on the actual positions and movements of the heavenly bodies in the generations immediately after Copernicus, never accepted the Copernican system in full. But his assistant and follower, John Kepler (1571–1630), not only accepted the Copernican theory but carried it further.

Kepler, a German, was a kind of mathematical mystic, part-time astrologer, and scientific genius. He felt ecstasy at the mysterious harmonies of mathematical forms. He built upon the exact observations of Tycho Brahe. Copernicus had believed the orbits of the planets about the sun to be perfect circles. Tycho showed that this belief did not fit the observable facts. Kepler discovered that the orbits of the planets were ellipses. The ellipse, like the circle, is an abstract mathematical figure with knowable properties. Kepler demonstrated that, as a planet moves in its elliptical path about the sun, the straight line connecting it with the sun sweeps through an area of space proportional to the time taken by the planet's motion; that is, that a planet sweeps equal areas in equal times; or, more simply, that the closer a planet is to the sun in its elliptical orbit, the faster it moves. Kepler further showed that the length of time in which the several planets revolve about the sun varies proportionately with their distance from the sun: the square of the time is proportional to the cube of the distance.

It is not possible for most people to understand the mathematics involved, but it is possible to realize the astounding implications of Kepler's laws of planetary motion. Kepler showed that the actual world of stubborn facts, as observed by Tycho, and the purely rational world of mathematical harmony, as surmised by Copernicus, were not really in any discrepancy with each other; that they really corresponded exactly. Why they should be did not know; it was the mystery of numbers. He digested an overwhelming amount of hitherto unexplained information into a few brief statements. He showed a cosmic mathematical relationship between space and time. And he described the movement of the planets in explicit formulas, which any competent person could verify at will.

The next step was taken by Galileo (1564–1642). So far the question of what the heavenly bodies were made of had hardly been affected. Indeed, they were not thought of as bodies at all, but rather as orbs. Only the sun and moon had any dimension; stars and planets were only points of light; and the theories of Copernicus and Kepler, like those of Ptolemy, might apply to insubstantial luminous objects in motion. In 1609 Galileo built a telescope. Turning it to the sky, he perceived that the moon had a rough and apparently mountainous surface, as if made of the same kind of material as the earth. Seeing clearly the dark part of the moon in its various phases, and noting that in every position it only reflected the light of the sun, he concluded that the moon was not itself a luminous object, another indication that it might be made of earth-like substance. He saw spots on the sun, as if the sun were not pure and perfect. He found that the planets had visible breadth when seen in the telescope, but that the fixed stars remained only points of light, as if incalculably further away. He discovered also that Jupiter had satellites, moons moving around it like the moon around the earth. These discoveries reassured him of the validity of the Copernican theory, which he had in any case already accepted. They suggested also that the heavenly bodies might be of the same substance as the earth, masses of matter moving in space. Contrariwise, it became easier to think of the earth as itself a kind of heavenly body revolving about the sun. The difference between the earth and the heavens was disappearing. This struck a terrifying blow at all earlier philosophy and theology. Some professors were afraid to look through the telescope, and Galileo was condemned and forced to an ostensible recantation by his church.

Moreover, where Kepler had found mathematical laws describing the movement of planets, Galileo found mathematical laws describing the movement of bodies on the earth. Formerly it had been thought that some bodies were by nature heavier than others, and that heavier bodies fell to the ground faster than light ones. Galileo in 1591, according to the story, dropped a ten-pound and a one-pound weight simultaneously from the top of the Leaning Tower of Pisa. The truth of this story has been questioned, but in any case Galileo showed that despite all previous speculation on the subject two bodies of different weights, when allowance was made for differences in air resistance due to differences of size or shape, struck the ground at the same time. His further work in dynamics, or the science of the motion of bodies, took many years to accomplish. He had to devise more refined means for measuring small intervals of time, find means of estimating the air resistance, friction, and other impediments which always occur in nature, and conceive of pure or absolute motion, and of force and velocity, in abstract mathematical terms. He made use of a new conception of inertia, in which only *change* in motion, not the origination of motion, had to be explained. This dispensed with the need of an Unmoved Mover felt in the older philosophy. Of bodies moving on the earth, Galileo discovered that when falling freely they fall with a velocity that increases according to mathematical formula.

The Achievement of Newton: The Promise of Science

It was the supreme achievement of Newton to bring Kepler and Galileo together, that is, to show that Kepler's laws of planetary motion and Galileo's laws of terrestrial motion were two aspects of the same laws. Galileo's findings, holding that moving bodies move uniformly in a straight line unless deflected by a definite force, made it necessary to explain why the planets, instead of flying off in straight lines, tend to fall toward the sun, the result being their elliptical orbits— and why the moon, similarly, tends to fall toward the earth. Newton seems early to have suspected that the answer would be related to Galileo's laws of falling bodies —that is, that gravity, or the pull of the earth upon objects on earth, might be a form of a universal gravitation, or similar pull, characterizing all bodies in the solar system. Great technical difficulties stood in the way, but finally, after inventing calculus, and using a new measurement of the size of the earth made by a Frenchman and experiments with circular motion made by the Dutch Huyghens on the pendulum, Newton was able to bring his calculations to fruition, and to publish, in 1687, his *Mathematical Principles of Natural Philosophy.*

This stupendous book showed that all motion that could then be timed and measured, whether on the earth or in the solar system, could be described by the same mathematical formulas. All matter moved as if every particle attracted every other particle with a force proportional to the product of the two masses, and inversely proportional to the square of the distance between them. This "force" was universal gravitation. What it was Newton did not pretend to explain. For two hundred years the law stood unshaken, always verified by every new relevant discovery. Only in the last century have its limitations been found; it does not hold good in the infinitesimal world of subatomic structure or in the macrocosm of the whole physical universe as now conceived.

With Newton's work (which affected other fields than are here mentioned) the promise of science seemed fulfilled. Even in purely practical affairs conveniences followed, as anticipated by the Baconians. The tides could now be understood and predicted by the gravitational interplay of earth, moon, and sun. Exact mathematical knowledge of the solar system was of great help to navigation. In the eighteenth century chronometers were developed, making possible the finding of precise longitude at sea. Merchant ships and naval squadrons could thus operate with more assurance. Better determination of longitude, at sea and on land, was of great value to cartography, the science of map making, since it is by differences of longitude that more accurate east-west distances are ascertained. Eighteenth-century Europeans were the first human beings to have a fairly accurate idea of the shapes and sizes of continents and oceans. Or again, mathematical advance, including the development of calculus, which allowed an exact treatment of curves and trajectories, reinforced by technical discoveries in the working of metals, led to an increased use of artillery. Armies in 1750 used twice as many cannon per soldier as in 1650. Naval ordnance also improved. These were items making armed forces more expensive to maintain, requiring governments to increase their taxes, and hence producing constitutional crises. Improved firearms likewise heightened the advantage of armies over insurrectionists or private fighting bands, thus strengthening the sovereignty of the state. They gave Europeans the military advantage over other peoples, in America, India, or elsewhere, on which the world ascendancy of Europe in the European age was built. This example, chosen somewhat at random, suggests the almost inconceivable ramifications of the practical consequences of science.

The instance of the steam engine may also be cited. Steam power was eventually almost literally to move the world. In 1700 it was a cloud no bigger than a man's hand. Yet it was in sight on the horizon. A Frenchman, Denis Papin, in 1681 invented a device in which steam moved a piston, but it produced so little power that it was used only in cooking. British scientists turned their minds to it. Robert Boyle, discoverer of "Boyle's law" on the pressure of gases, studied the problem; scientists, mechanics, and instrument makers collaborated. In 1702 Thomas Newcomen, a man without scientific training but associated with scientists, produced the steam engine known thereafter as Newcomen's engine, from which, as will be seen, James Watt developed the steam engine as we know it. Newcomen's engine was primitive according to later ideas. It burnt so much fuel that it could be used only in coal mines. But it was used. Not long after 1700 it was widely employed to pump water from the coal pits. It saved labor, cheapened production, and opened hitherto unusable deposits to exploitation. It was the first application of steam to an economic purpose.

The faith in natural knowledge was becoming institutionalized. Organized bodies of men, possessing equipment and funds, were engaged in scientific study. Most notable of these were the Royal Society of London, founded in 1662, and the Academy of Sciences in France, founded in 1666. Both originated when earlier and informal groups, usually gentlemen of the landed classes, received charters from their governments to pursue scientific interests. Scientific periodicals began to be published. Scientific societies provided the medium for prompt interchange of ideas indispensable to the growth of scientific knowledge. They published articles not only on the natural sciences and mathematics, but also on paleography, numismatics, chronology, legal history, and natural law. The work of the learned had not yet yielded to specialization. All felt a common interest in the advance of all fronts of knowledge. It is to be noted also how the scientific movement was an international one, shared in by all central and western Europe except Portugal and Spain. Men of many nationalities constantly made use of each other's hypotheses or discoveries. Many or even most of the books written in this age were first published in Latin, still the international language of science and learning, and many articles in the new scientific journals were written in Latin also.

The Scientific Revolution and the World of Thought

It was perhaps in the world of thought that the revolution accomplished from Copernicus to Newton was most profound. It has been called the greatest spiritual readjustment that human beings have been required to make. The old heavens were exploded. Man was no longer the center of creation. The luminaries of the sky no longer shone to light his way or to give him beauty. The sky itself was an illusion, its color a thing in the mind only, for when a man now looked upward he was really looking only into the darkness of endless space. The old cosmos, comfortably enclosed and ranked in an ascending order of purity, gave way to a new cosmos which seemed to consist in an infinite emptiness through which particles of matter were distributed. Man was the puny denizen of a material object swinging in space along with other very distant material objects of the same kind. About the physical universe there was nothing especially Christian, nothing that the God portrayed in the Bible would be likely to have made. The gap between Christianity and natural science, always present yet always bridged in the Middle Ages, now opened wider than ever. It was felt with anguish by some in the seventeenth century, notably by the Frenchman Blaise Pascal, a considerable scientist, preeminent mathematician, and deep and troubled Christian believer. He left a record of his state of mind in his *Pensées*, or *Thoughts*, jottings from which he hoped some day to write a great book on the Christian faith. "I am terrified," he said in one of these jottings, "by the eternal silence of these infinite spaces."

But on the whole the reaction was more optimistic. Man might be merely a reed, as Pascal said, but Pascal added, "a thinking reed." Man might be no longer the physical center of the world. But it was the human mind that had penetrated the world's laws. The Newtonian system, as it became popularized, a process which took about fifty years, led to a great intellectual complacency. Never had confidence in human powers been so high. As Alexander Pope put it,

> *Nature and nature's laws lay hid in night;*
> *God said, "Let Newton be," and all was light.*

Or, according to another epigram on the subject, there was only one universe to discover, and this universe had been discovered by Newton. Everything seemed possible to the human reason. The old feeling of dependency upon God lost much of its force, or became something to be discussed by clergymen in church on

Sunday. Man was not really a little creature, a wayfarer in a world that was alien to him, yearning for the reunion with God that would bring him peace. Man was a dignified creature, one of great capacity in his own right, living in a world that was understandable and manageable by him, and in which he might install himself with quite adequate comfort. These ideas contributed greatly to the secularizing of European society, pushing religion and churches to the sidelines.

The scientific discoveries also reinforced the old philosophy of natural law. This philosophy, developed by the Greeks and renewed in the Middle Ages, held that the universe is fundamentally orderly, and that there is a natural rightness or justice, universally the same for all people, and knowable by reason. It was very important in political theory, where it stood out against arbitrariness and the mere claims of power. The laws of nature as discovered by science were somewhat different, but they taught the same lesson, namely, the orderliness and minute regularity of the world. It was reassuring to feel that everywhere throughout an infinite space, whether or not yet discovered and probed by man, every particle of matter was quietly attracting every other particle by a force proportionate to the product of the masses and inversely proportional to the square of the distance. The physical universe laid bare by science—orderly, rational, balanced, smoothly running, without strife or rivalry or contention—became a model on which many thinkers, as time went on, hoped to refashion human society. They hoped to make society also fulfill the rule of law.

In some ways it would be possible to exaggerate the impact of pure science. Scientists themselves did not usually apply their scientific ideas to religion and society. Few suffered the spiritual torment of Pascal. Both Descartes and Newton wrote placid tractates arguing for the truth of certain ecclesiastical doctrines. Bacon and Harvey were conservative politically, upholders of king against Parliament. The Englishman Joseph Glanvill, in the 1660s, used the Cartesian dualism to demonstrate the probable existence of witches. Descartes, despite his systematic doubt, held that the customs of one's country were to be accepted without question. Natural science, in the pure sense, was not inherently revolutionary or even upsetting. If Europeans in the seventeenth century began to waver in many old beliefs it was not only because of the stimulus of pure science, but also because of an increasing knowledge and study of humanity itself.

34. NEW KNOWLEDGE OF MAN AND SOCIETY

Here one of the most potent forces at work was the discovery and exploration of the world overseas. Europe was already becoming part of the world as a whole, and could henceforth understand itself only by comparison with non-European regions. Great reciprocal influences were at work. The influences of European expansion on other parts of the world are easily seen: the Indian societies of America were modified or extinguished, the indigenous societies of Africa were dislocated and many of their members enslaved and transported; in the long run even the ancient societies of Asia were to be undermined. From the beginning the counterinfluence of the rest of the world upon Europe was equally great. It took the form not only of new medicines, new diseases, new foods, new and exotic manufactures brought to Europe, and the growth of material wealth in west-European countries. It affected European thinking also. It undermined the old

Europe and its ideas, just as Europe was undermining the old cultures beyond the oceans. Vast new horizons opened before Europeans in the sixteenth and seventeenth centuries. Europeans of this period were the first people to whom it was given to know the globe as a whole, or to realize the variety of the human race and its multifarious manners and customs.

The Current of Skepticism

This realization was very unsettling. The realization of human differences had the effect, in Europe, of breaking what anthropologists call the "cake of custom." A new sense of the relative nature of social institutions developed. It became harder to believe in any absolute rightness of one's own ways. Montaigne, already mentioned, expressed the relativist outlook clearly, and nowhere more clearly than in his famous essay on cannibals. The cannibals, he said humorously, did in fact eat human flesh; that was their custom, and they have their customs as we have ours; they would think some of our ways odd or inhuman; peoples differ, and who are we to judge? Travelers' books spread the same message increasingly through the seventeenth century. As one of them observed (whether or not rightly), in Turkey it was the custom to shave the hair and wear the beard, in Europe to shave the beard and wear the hair; what difference does it really make? That the ways of non-Europeans might be good ways was emphasized by Jesuit missionaries. Writing from the depths of the Mississippi Valley or from China, the Jesuit fathers often dwelt on the natural goodness and mental alertness of the native peoples they encountered, perhaps hoping in this way to gain support in Europe for their missionary labors. Sometimes strange people appeared in Europe itself. In 1684 a delegation of aristocratic Siamese arrived in Paris, followed by another in 1686. The Parisians went through a fad for Siam; they recounted how the king of Siam, when asked by a missionary to turn Christian, replied that divine Providence, had it wished a single religion to prevail in the world, could easily have so arranged it. The Siamese seemed civilized, wise, philosophic; they allowed Christians to preach in their own country, whereas it was well known what would happen to a Siamese missionary who undertook to preach in Paris. China also was seen through an ideal glow. By 1700 there were even professors of Arabic, at Paris, Oxford, and Utrecht, who said that Islam was a religion to be respected, as good for Muslims as Christianity was for Christians.

Thus was created a strong current of skepticism, holding that all beliefs are relative, varying with time and place. Its greatest spokesman at the end of the century was Pierre Bayle (1647–1706). Bayle was influenced by the scientific discoveries also; not exactly that he understood them, for he was an almost purely literary scholar, but he realized that many popular beliefs were without foundation. Between 1680 and 1682 a number of comets were seen. The one of 1682 was studied by a friend of Newton's, Edmund Halley, the first man to predict the return of a comet. He identified the one of 1682 with the one observed in 1302, 1456, 1531, and 1607, and predicted its reappearance in 1757 (it appeared in 1759); it was seen again in 1910 and the 1980s and is still called Halley's Comet. In the 1680s people were talking of comets excitedly. Some said that comets emitted poisonous exhalations, others that they were supernatural omens of future events. Bayle, in his *Thoughts on the Comet*, argued at great length that there was no basis for any such beliefs except human credulity. In 1697 he published his *Historical and Critical Dictionary*, a tremendous repository of miscellaneous lore, conveying the message that what is called truth is often mere opinion, that most people are amazingly gullible, that many things firmly believed are really ridiculous, and that it is very foolish to hold too strongly to one's own views. Bayle's *Dictionary* remained a reservoir on which skeptical writers continued to draw for generations. Bayle himself, having no firm basis in his own mind for settled judgment, mixed skepticism with an impulse to faith. Born a Protestant, he was converted to Rome, then returned to his Calvinist background. In any case his views made for toleration in religion. For Bayle, as for Montaigne, no opinion was worth burning your neighbor for.

The New Sense of Evidence

But in the study of humankind, as in the study of physical nature, Europeans of the seventeenth century were not generally content with skepticism. They were not possessed by a mere negative and doubting mood, important and salutary as such an attitude was. In the subjects collectively called the humanities, as in pure science, they were looking not for disbelief but for understanding. They wanted new means of telling the true from the false, a new method for arriving at some degree of certainty of conviction. And here, too, a kind of scientific view of the world arose, if that term be understood in a general sense. It took the form of a new sense of evidence. Evidence is that which allows one to believe a thing to be true, or at least truer than something else for which the evidence is weaker. And if to believe without evidence is the sign of primitive or irrational thinking, to require evidence before believing is in a way to be scientific, or at least to trust and use the power of human intelligence.

The new sense of evidence, and of the need of evidence, revealed itself in many ways. One of the clearest was in the law. The English law of evidence, for example, began to take on its modern form at the close of the seventeenth century. Previously the belief had been that the more atrocious the crime the less evidence should be necessary in arriving at a verdict of guilty; this was thought necessary to protect society from the more hideous offenses. From the end of the seventeenth century, in English law, the judge lost his power of discretion in deciding what should constitute evidence, and the same rules of evidence were applied in all forms of accusation, the essential question being recognized as always the same—did such-and-such a fact (however outrageous) occur or did it not? After 1650 mere hearsay evidence, long vaguely distrusted, was ruled definitely out of court. After 1696 even persons charged with felony were allowed legal counsel.

The new sense of evidence was probably the main force in putting an end to the delusions of witchcraft. What made witchcraft so credible and so fearsome was that many persons confessed themselves to be witches, admitting to supernatural powers and to evil designs upon their neighbors.[4] Many or most such confessions were extracted under torture. Reformers urged that confessions obtained under torture were not evidence, that people would say anything to escape unbearable pain, so that no quantity of such confessions offered the slightest ground for believing in witches. As for the voluntary confessions, and even the boastings of some people of their diabolical powers, it was noted that such statements often came from half-demented old women, or from persons who would today be called hysterical or psychotic. Witches came to be regarded as self-deluded. Their ideas of

[4] See pp. 51, 246.

BEHAIM 1492   SCHÖNER 1523

THE GROWTH OF GEOGRAPHICAL KNOWLEDGE

The four maps show the best scientific knowledge at their respective dates. Behaim has no inkling of the existence of America and has filled in the hemisphere opposite to Europe with a mass of islands, representing what he has heard of the East Indies and Japan. He knows pretty well the limits of Africa. Schöner in 1523 fills in America and even distinguishes two American continents. He knows of the Gulf of Mexico but fails to realize the narrowness of the Isthmus of Panama. He knows of the Straits of Magellan (but not Cape Horn) and hopefully fills in a corresponding Northwest Passage in the

themselves were no longer accepted as evidence. But it must be added that, except in England, the use of legal torture lasted on through most of the eighteenth century, in criminal cases in which the judge believed the accused to be guilty.

History and Historical Scholarship

What are called the historical sciences also developed rapidly at this time. History, like the law, depends on the finding and using of evidence. The historian and the judge must answer the same kind of question—did such-and-such a fact really occur? All knowledge of history, so far as it disengages itself from legend and wishful thinking, rests ultimately on pieces of evidence, written records, and other works of man created in the past and surviving in some form or other in the present. On this mass of material the vast picture of the past is built, and without it men would be ignorant of their own antecedents or would have only folk tales and tribal traditions.

There was much skepticism about history in the seventeenth century. Some said that history was not a form of true knowledge because it was not mathematical. Others said that it was useless because Adam, the perfect man, had neither had nor needed any history. Many felt that what passed for history was only a mass of fables. History was distrusted also because historians were often pretentious, claiming to be high-flying men of letters, writing for rhetorical or inspirational appeal or for argumentative reasons, disdaining the hard labor of actual study. History was losing the confidence of thinking people. How was it possible, they asked, to feel even a modicum of certainty about alleged events that had happened long before any living person had been born?

This doubting attitude itself arose from a stricter sense of evidence, or from a realization that there was really no proof for much of what was said about the past. But scholars set to work to assemble what evidence there was. They hoped to create a new history, one that should contain only reliable statements. Europe was littered with old papers and parchments. Abbeys, manor houses, royal archives

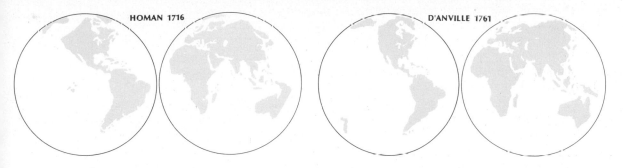

HOMAN 1716   D'ANVILLE 1761

north. His conception of the Indian Ocean is quite accurate. To Homan, two centuries later, the size and shapes of oceans and continents are well known, but he believes New Guinea joined to Australia and is frankly ignorant of the northwest coast of North America, representing it by a straight line. The Great Lakes and the interior of North America have become known to Europe. D'Anville in 1761 has no island of Tasmania, does not understand that Alaska is a peninsula, and believes the American polar regions to be impassable by sea. Otherwise his map is indistinguishable from one on the same scale today.

were full of written documents, many of them of unknown age or unknown origin, often written in a handwriting which people could no longer read. Learned and laborious enthusiasts set to work to explore this accumulation. They added so much to the efforts of their predecessors as virtually to create modern critical scholarship and erudition. The French Benedictine monk Jean Mabillon, in 1681, in his book *On Diplomatics* (referring to ancient charters and "diplomas") established the science of paleography, which deals with the deciphering, reading, dating, and authentication of manuscripts. The Frenchman DuCange in 1678 published a dictionary of medieval Latin which is still used. Others, like the Italian Muratori, spent whole lifetimes exploring archives, collecting, editing, or publishing masses of documents, comparing manuscript copies of the same text and trying to discover what the author had really said, rejecting some as fabrications or forgeries, pronouncing others to be genuine pieces of historical evidence. Others made themselves experts in ancient coins, many of which were far more ancient than the oldest manuscripts; they founded the science of numismatics. Still others, or indeed the same ones, turned to a critical examination of the inscriptions on old buildings and ruins.

Another important but little-known historical "science," namely, chronology, was greatly stimulated also. Chronology deals with the age of the world and with finding a common denominator between the dating systems of various peoples. Probably it is not natural for the human mind to think in terms of dates at all. For simple people it is enough to know that some things happened "long ago." In the seventeenth century the new interest in numbers, evident in physical science, turned also to the human past. Archbishop James Usher, an Anglican prelate of Ireland, after much study of the Bible, announced the date of 4004 B.C. as that of the creation of the world. His chronological system was later printed in the margins of the Authorized Version of the English Bible, and is still adhered to by some fundamentalists as if part of the Bible itself. But Usher's system was not accepted by scholars even in his own time. Geographical knowledge was revealing China and its dynasties to Europe; historical knowledge was beginning to discover ancient Egypt. The Chinese and Egyptian records claimed a greater antiquity for their countries than the Old Testament seemed to allow for the human race. There was much erudite conjecture; one scholar about 1700 counted seventy estimates of the age of the world, ranging as high as 170,000 years, a figure which then seemed fantastic and appalling.

The difficulty was not only in the language of the Old Testament. It was in finding the correspondence between the chronological systems of different peoples. A Chinese system of dating by dynasties might be coherent within itself, but how could it be equated with the European system of dating from the birth of Christ, a date as unknown to the Chinese as the date of Wu Wang was to Europeans? Even European records presented the same difficulty; the Romans counted by consulships, or from the supposed year of the founding of Rome; many medieval documents told only the year of some obscure ruler's reign. Only infinite patience, interminable research, and endless calculation could reduce such a jumble to the simple system of modern textbooks. This is of more importance than may be at first thought. A common system of dating is a great aid to thinking of human history as an interconnected whole. An overall conception of the human race is made easier by the dating of all events according to the Christian era. This itself, it may be pointed out, is an arbitrary and conventional scale, since Christ is now thought to have been born not in A.D. 1, but in 4 B.C.

Common dating was of importance in practical affairs as well as in historical knowledge. Europe was disunited even on the Christian calendar. Protestant and some Orthodox countries followed the old or Julian calendar, Catholic countries the corrected or Gregorian calendar, issued in the sixteenth century under authority of Pope Gregory XIII. The two calendars varied in the seventeenth century by ten days. Only gradually was the Gregorian calendar accepted, by England in 1752, by Russia in 1918. Most other peoples today, in China, India, the Arabic world, and elsewhere, use or recognize the Gregorian calendar. Without a uniform way of specifying days and years it would be less easy to transact international affairs, hold international conferences, make plans, or pay and receive money. This common dating, easily taken for granted, was a consequence of the predominance of Europe in modern times. It is a sign of growing unity in world civilization.

The Questioning of Traditional Beliefs

The historical sciences provided a foundation on which a knowledge of human activities in the past could be built, and the growing geographical knowledge spread a panorama of man's diverse activities and peculiarities in the present. This new knowledge of man shared with natural science, and probably derived from it, or from philosophers of science like Descartes and Bacon, the view that many traditional ideas were erroneous, but that much could be known by a disciplined use of the human mind. The humanities and the sciences were alike in demanding evidence for belief and in trusting to the power of reason. In their impact on the old certainties of European life, the studies of man exerted possibly a greater direct force than those of nature. Pascal, in his attempt to defend the Christian faith, feared the spirit of Montaigne, the mood of skepticism and denial, which he felt himself, more than he feared the findings of mathematical and physical science. And the movement of historical thought, with its insistence on textual criticism, threw doubt on much of the Christian religion, or at least on the sacred history related in the Bible, which was considered to be part and parcel of religion itself.

In 1678 a French priest, Richard Simon, published a pioneering work in Biblical criticism, his *Critical History of the Old Testament*. Though his book was condemned both by the church and by the government of Louis XIV, Richard Simon always felt himself to be orthodox; Catholic faith, he insisted, depended more on church tradition than on the literal statements of the Bible. He simply applied to the Old Testament the methods of textual criticism which others were applying to secular documents. He concluded that the Old Testament, as known, rested on medieval manuscripts many of which were of unknown or doubtful origin, that monkish copyists had brought in errors and corruptions, and that the books thought to have been written by Moses could not have been written by him, since they contained obvious contradictions and matter clearly inserted after his death. Others went further, questioning not merely the evidence of the Biblical text, but the very possibility of some events that it related. From the scientific idea of the absolute regularity of nature on the one hand, and from a strong sense of human credulity on the other, they denied that miracles had ever occurred and looked upon oracles and prophecies among either the Greeks or the Hebrews with a dubious eye.

The most profoundly disturbing of all thinkers of the time was Baruch Spinoza (1632–1677), the lens grinder of Amsterdam, a Jew who was excommunicated by his own synagogue and who refused a professorship at the University of Heidelberg, craving only the quiet to think in peace. Spinoza drew on both the scientific and humanistic thought of his day. He arrived at a philosophy holding that God had no existence apart from the world, that everything was itself an aspect of God, a philosophy technically called pantheism but considered by many to be really atheistic. He denied the inspiration of the Bible, disbelieved in miracles and the supernatural, rejected all revelation and revealed religion, Jewish or Christian, and held that few if any governments of the day were really just. He taught a pure, stern, and intellectual ethical code, and one which had few consolations for the average man. His name became a byword for impiety and horrendous unbelief. People were literally afraid to read his works, even when they could find them, which was not often because of the censorship. His influence spread slowly, through the mediation of other writers.

More widely read, less abstruse, more reassuring, dwelling on the merits of common sense, were the writings of the Englishman John Locke (1632–1704), who summarized many of the intellectual trends of his lifetime and exerted a strong influence for the following hundred years. He combined practical experience and theoretical interests. Educated in medicine, he kept in touch with the sciences and was acquainted with Newton. He was associated with the great Whig noblemen who were the main authors of the English revolution in 1688. For political reasons he spent several years in the 1680s in the Netherlands, where he became familiar with thought on the Continent. He wrote on many subjects—finance, economics, education, religious policy, political theory, general philosophy—always with an engaging directness and sober air of the sensible man of the world. In his *Letter on Toleration* (1689) he advocated an established church, but with toleration of all except Roman Catholics and atheists; these he held to be dangerous to society, the former because of a foreign allegiance, the latter because they lacked a basis of moral responsibility. In his *Reasonableness of Christianity* he argued that Christianity, rightly considered, is after all a reasonable form of religion; this softened the friction between religion and natural knowledge but tended to shut out the supernatural and merge religious feeling into an unruffled common sense.

Locke's deepest book was his *Essay Concerning the Human Understanding* (1690). Here he faced the great problem of the day, the problem of knowledge; he asked what it was possible for men to know with certainty, and how certain knowledge was arrived at. His answer was that true or certain knowledge is derived from experience—from perceptions of the sense organs and reflection of the mind on these perceptions. Locke at the end of the century thus echoed Bacon at the beginning; they became the two great pillars of empirical philosophy, insisting on experience and observation as the source of truth. Locke denied Descartes' doctrine of innate ideas, or inevitable disposition of the human mind to think in certain ways. He held that the mind at birth is a blank tablet or *tabula rasa*, and that what a person comes to think or believe depends on the environment in which he lives. Locke's environmentalist philosophy became fundamental to liberal and reforming thought in later years. It seemed that false ideas or superstitions were the result of bad environment and bad education. It seemed that the evil in human actions was due to bad social institutions, and that an improvement in human society would improve human behavior. This philosophy, whether or not wholly true in the final analysis, was largely true with respect to many practical conditions. It gave confidence in the possibility of social progress and turned attention to a sphere in which planned and constructive action was possible, namely, the sphere of government, public policy, and legislation. Here we touch on political theory, to which Locke contributed *Two Treatises of Government*. These are discussed below.

35. POLITICAL THEORY: THE SCHOOL OF NATURAL LAW

Political theory can never be strictly scientific. Science deals with what does exist or has existed. It does not tell what ought to exist. To tell what society and government ought to be like, in view of man's nature and his capacity to be miserable or contented, is a main purpose of political theory. Political theory is in a sense more practical than science. It is the scientists and scholars who are most content to observe facts as they are. Practical people, and scientists and scholars so far as they have practical interests, must always ask themselves what ought to be done, what policies ought to be adopted, what measures taken, what state of affairs maintained or brought about. Conservatives and radicals, traditionalists and innovators, are alike in this respect. It is impossible in human affairs to escape the word "ought."

But political theory was affected by the scientific view. The Renaissance Italian, Niccolò Machiavelli (1469–1527), had opened the way in this direction.[5] Machiavelli too had his "ought"; he preferred a republican form of government in which citizens felt a patriotic attachment to their state. But in his book, *The Prince*, he disregarded the question of the best form of government, a favorite question of Christian and scholastic philosophers of the Middle Ages. He sepa-

[5] See pp. 60–61.

rated the study of politics from theology and moral philosophy. He undertook to describe how governments and rulers actually behaved. He observed that successful rulers behaved as if holding or increasing power were their only object, that they regarded all else as means to this end. Princes, said Machiavelli, kept their promises or broke them, they told the truth or distorted or colored it, they sought popularity or ignored it, they advanced public welfare or disrupted it, they conciliated their neighbors or destroyed them, depending merely on which course of action seemed the best means of advancing their political interests. All this was bad, said Machiavelli; but that was not the question, for the question was to find out what rulers really did. Machiavelli, in *The Prince*, chose to be nonmoral in order to be scientific. To most readers he seemed to be simply immoral. Nor was it possible to draw the line between *The Prince* as a scientific description of fact and *The Prince* as a book of maxims of conduct. In telling how successful rulers obtained their successes, Machiavelli also suggested how rulers *ought* to proceed. And though governments did in fact continue to behave for the most part as Machiavelli said, most people refused to admit that they ought to.

Natural Right and Natural Law

Political theory in the seventeenth century did not embrace the cynicism attributed to Machiavelli. Nor did it fall into the skepticism of those who said that the customs of one's country should be passively accepted, or that one form of government was about as good as another. It directly faced the question, What is right? The seventeenth century was the classic age of the philosophy of natural right or of natural law.

The idea of natural law has underlain a good deal of modern democratic development, and its decline in the last century has been closely connected with many of the troubles of recent times. It is not easy to say in what the philosophy of natural law essentially consisted. It held that there is, somehow, in the structure of the world, a law that distinguishes right from wrong. It held that right is "natural," not a mere human invention. This right is not determined, for any country, by its heritage, tradition, or customs, nor yet by its actual laws (called "positive" laws) of the kind that are enforced in the law courts. All these may be unfair or unjust. We detect unfairness or injustice in them by comparing them with natural law as we understand it; thus we have a basis for saying that cannibalism is bad, or that a law requiring forced labor from orphan children is unjust. Nor is natural law, or the real rightness of a thing, determined by the authority of any person or people. No king can make right that which is wrong. No people, by its will as a people, can make just that which is unjust. Right and law, in the ultimate sense, exist outside and above all peoples. They are universal, the same for all. No one can make them up to suit himself. A good king, or a just people, is a king or people whose actions correspond to the objective standard. But how, if we cannot trust our own positive laws or customs, or our leaders, or even our collective selves, can we know what is naturally right? How do we discover natural law? The answer, in the natural law philosophy, is that we discover it by reason. Man is considered to be a rational animal. And all men are assumed to have, at least potentially and when better enlightened, the same powers of reason and understanding—Germans or English, Siamese or Europeans. This view favored a cosmopolitan outlook and made international agreement and general world progress seem realizable goals. As time went on, the premises of this philosophy came to be questioned. By the twentieth century it was widely thought that man was not an especially rational being but was motivated by drives or urges or instincts, and that human differences were so fundamental that men of different nationalities or classes could never expect to see things in the same way. When this happened the older philosophy of natural law lost its hold on many minds.

In the seventeenth and eighteenth centuries it was generally accepted. Some, carrying over the philosophy of the Middle Ages, thought of natural law as an aspect of the law of God. Others, more secular in spirit, held that the natural law stood of itself. These included even some churchmen; a group of theologians, mainly Jesuits, were condemned by the pope in 1690 for holding that universal right and wrong might exist by reason only, whether God existed or not. The idea of natural law and the faith in human reason went side by side, and both were fundamental in the thought of the time. They were to be found everywhere in Europe, in their religious or their secular form.

On the basis of natural law some thinkers tried to create an international law or "law of nations," to bring order into the maze of sovereign territorial states, great and small, that was developing in Europe. Hugo Grotius, in 1625, published the first great book devoted exclusively to this subject, his *Law of War and Peace*. Samuel Pufendorf followed with his *Law of Nature and of Nations* in 1672. Both held that sovereign states, though bound by no positive law or authority, should work together for the common good, that there was a community of nations as of individuals, and that in the absence of a higher international sovereignty they were all still subordinate to natural reason and justice. Certain concrete doctrines, such as the freedom of the seas or the immunity of ambassadors, were put forward. The principles of international law remained those of natural law. The content came to include specific agreements between governments, certain kinds of admiralty and maritime law, and the terms of treaties such as the treaties of Westphalia, Utrecht, and others. The means of enforcement, to be sure, remained weak or nonexistent in crises.

Hobbes and Locke

In domestic affairs the philosophy of natural law, though it rather favored constitutionalism, was used to justify both constitutional and absolutist governments. Right itself was held to be in the nature of things, beyond human power to change. But forms of government were held to be means to an end. No philosopher at the time thought the state to have an absolute value in itself. The state had to be "justified," made acceptable to the moral consciousness or the reason. There were, indeed, important competing philosophies. On the side of absolutism was the doctrine of the divine right of kings. On the side of constitutionalism were arguments based on heritage or custom, emphasizing the charters, bulls, or compacts of former times and the historic powers of parliaments and estates. But neither the supernatural argument of the divine right of kings, nor the historical argument pointing back to liberties of the Middle Ages, was entirely satisfactory in the scientific atmosphere of the seventeenth century. Neither carried complete conviction to the reason or moral sense of the most acute thinkers. Both were reinforced by arguments of natural law. Two Englishmen stand out above all others in this connection. Absolutism was philosophically justified by Thomas Hobbes, constitutionalism by John Locke.

Hobbes (1588–1679) followed the scientific and mathematical discoveries of his time with more than an amateur interest. In philosophy he held to a materialistic and even atheistic system. In English politics he sided with king against Parliament; he disliked the disorder and violence of the civil war of the 1640s and the unstable conditions of the English republic of the 1650s.[6] He concluded that men have no capacity for self-government. His opinion of human nature was low; he held that men in the "state of nature," or as imagined to exist without government, were quarrelsome and turbulent, forever locked in a war of all against all. In his famous phrase, life in the state of nature was "solitary, poor, nasty, brutish and short." From fear of each other, to obtain order, and enjoy the advantages of law and right, men came to a kind of agreement or "contract" by which they surrendered their freedom of action into the hands of a ruler. It was necessary for this ruler to have unrestricted or absolute power. Only thus could he maintain order. It was intolerably dangerous, according to Hobbes, for anyone to question the actions of government, for such questioning might reopen the way to chaos. Government must in fact be a kind of Leviathan (the monster mentioned in the Bible, Job 41); and it was by the word *Leviathan* that Hobbes entitled his principal book, published in 1651, two years after the execution of King Charles I.

By this book Hobbes became the leading secular exponent of absolutism and one of the principal theorists of the unlimited sovereignty of the state. His influence on later thinkers was very great. He accustomed political theorists to the use of purely natural arguments. He quoted freely from the Bible, but the Bible had no influence on his thought. After Hobbes, all advanced political theorists regarded government as a thing created by human purpose. It was no longer considered, except popularly and except by professional theologians, as part of a divine dispensation of God to man. Hobbes also affected later theorists by his arguments for a sovereign authority, and, more negatively, by obliging them to refute his idea of an unlimited personal sovereign. But he was never a popular writer. In England the cause which he favored was lost. In those Continental countries where royal absolutism prevailed his arguments were received with secret gratification, but his irreligion was too dangerous to make public, and the absolutist argument, on the popular level, remained that of the divine right of kings. In any case Hobbes's arguments were in some ways insufficient for real monarchs. Hobbes abhorred struggle and violence. His case for absolutism required absolutism to produce civil peace, individual security, and a rule of law. He also held that absolute power depended on, or had at least originated in, a free and rational agreement by which people accepted it. An absolute monarchy that flagrantly violated these conditions could with difficulty be justified even by the doctrines of Hobbes. It is in these respects that Hobbes differs from totalitarian theorists of recent times. For Hobbes, in the final analysis, absolute power was an expedient to promote individual welfare. It was a means necessary to the realization of natural law.

John Locke (1632–1704), as has been seen, also stood in the main current of scientific thought and discovery. But in his political philosophy he carried over many ideas of the Middle Ages, as formulated in the thirteenth century by St. Thomas Aquinas[7] and kept alive in England by successive thinkers of the Anglican church. Medieval philosophy had never favored an absolute power. With Hobbes, Locke shared the idea that good government is an expedient of human purpose, neither provided by divine Providence nor inherited by a national tradition. He

[6] See pp. 169–171.
[7] See pp. 41–43.

held, too, like Hobbes and the whole school of natural law, that government was based on a kind of contract, or rational and conscious agreement upon which authority was based. In contrast to Hobbes, he sided with Parliament against king in the practical struggles of politics. About 1680, in the course of these disputes, he wrote *Two Treatises of Government*, which however were not published until shortly after the parliamentary revolution of 1688–1689.[8]

Locke took a more genial view of human nature than Hobbes. As he showed in his other books, he believed that a moderate religion was a good thing, and above all that men could learn from experience and hence could be educated to an enlightened way of life. These ideas favored a belief in self-government. Locke declared (in contradiction to Hobbes) that men in the "state of nature" were reasonable and well disposed, willing to get along with one another though handicapped by the absence of public authority. Men likewise had a moral sense, quite independently of government; and they also possessed by nature certain rights, quite apart from the state. These rights were the rights to life, liberty, and property. Locke threw very heavy emphasis on the right of property, by which he usually meant the possession of land. His philosophy can in fact be regarded as an expression of the landed classes of England in their claims against the king; it should be noted that land ownership in England was more widespread in 1690 than it later became. Men, as individuals in the state of nature, are not altogether able, according to Locke, to win general respect for their individual natural rights. They cannot by their own efforts protect what is "proper" to them, i.e., their property. They agree to set up government to enforce observance of the rights of all. Government is thus created by a contract, but the contract is not unconditional, as claimed by Hobbes. It imposes mutual obligations. The people must be reasonable; only rational beings can be politically free. Liberty is not an anarchy of undisciplined will; it is the freedom to act without compulsion by another. Only rational and responsible creatures can exercise true freedom; but adult human beings, according to Locke, are or can be educated to be rational and responsible. They therefore can and should be free. On government, also, certain conditions and obligations are imposed. If a government breaks the contract, if it threatens the natural rights which it is the sole purpose of government to protect, if, for example, it takes away a man's property without his consent, then the governed have a right to reconsider what they have done in creating the government and may even in the last extremity rebel against it. The right to resist government, Locke admits, is very dangerous, but it is less dangerous than its opposite, which would lead to enslavement; and in any case we are talking about reasonable and responsible people.

If Locke's ideas seem familiar, especially to Americans, it is because of the wide popularizing of his philosophy in the century after his death. Nowhere was his influence greater than in the British colonies. The authors of the American Declaration of Independence and of the Constitution of the United States knew the writings of Locke very thoroughly. Some phrases of the Declaration of Independence echo his very language. In Great Britain also, and in France and elsewhere, in the course of time, Locke's influence was immense.

What Locke did was to convert an episode in English history into an event of universal meaning. In England, in 1688, certain great lords, winning the support

8 See pp. 173–177.

of the established church, gentry, and merchants, put out one king and brought in another. On the new king they imposed certain obligations—specified in the Bill of Rights of 1689, and all dealing with legal or technical interpretations of the English constitution. The Revolution of 1688 was a very English affair. England in 1688 was still little known to the rest of Europe. The proceedings in England, so far as known, might seem no different from a rebellion of the magnates of Hungary. Locke, in arguing that Parliament had done right to eject James II, put the whole affair on a level of reason, natural right, and human nature. It thus came to have meaning for everyone. At the same time, Locke made the English revolution a sign of progress rather than reaction. The new and modern form of government in 1690 was royal absolutism, with its professional bureaucracy and corps of paid officials. Almost everywhere there was resistance to the kings, led by landed interests and harking back to earlier freedoms. Such resistance seemed to many Europeans to be feudal and medieval. Locke made the form taken by such resistance in England, namely, the Revolution of 1688 against James II, into a modern and forward-looking move. He checked the prestige of absolutism. He gave new prestige to constitutional principles. He carried over, in modified form, many ideas from the scholastic philosophers of the Middle Ages, who had generally maintained that kings had only a relative and restricted power and were responsible to their peoples. To these ideas he added the force of the newer scientific view of the world. He did not rest his case on supernatural or providential arguments. He did not say that constitutional government was the will of God. He said that it rested on experience and observation of human nature, on recognition of certain individual rights and especially the right of property, and on the existence of a purely natural law of reason and justice. He was an almost entirely secular thinker.

One must not claim too much for Locke, or for any writer. England was in fact, in 1688, more modern in many ways than other countries in Europe. The Glorious Revolution was in fact not exactly like uprisings of the landed and propertied classes elsewhere. England in the following century did in fact create a form of parliamentary government that was unique. But facts go together with the theories that give them an understandable meaning. Events in England, as explained by Locke, and as seen in other countries and even in England and its colonies through Locke's eyes, launched into the mainstream of modern history the superb tradition of constitutional government, which has been one of the principal themes in the history of the modern world ever since.

By 1700, at the close of the "century of genius," some beliefs that were to be characteristic of modern times had clearly taken form, notably a faith in science, in human reason, in natural human rights, and in progress. The following period, generally known as the Age of Enlightenment, was to be a time of clarifying and popularizing ideas which the more creative seventeenth century had produced. These ideas were eventually to revolutionize Europe, America, and the world. They were also in subsequent years to be modified, amended, challenged, and even denied. But they are still very much alive today.

VIII.
The Age of Enlightenment

The eighteenth century, or at least the years of that century preceding the French Revolution of 1789, is commonly known as the Age of Enlightenment, and though that name raises more than the usual difficulties, still there is no other that describes so many features of the time so well. People strongly felt that theirs was an enlightened age, and it is from their own evaluation of themselves that our term Age of Enlightenment is derived. Everywhere there was a feeling that Europeans had at last emerged from a long twilight. The past was regarded as a time of barbarism and darkness. The sense of progress was all but universal among the educated classes. It was the belief both of the forward-looking thinkers and writers known as the philosophes and of the forward-looking kings and empresses, the "enlightened despots," together with their ministers and officials.

36. THE PHILOSOPHES—AND OTHERS

The Spirit of Progress and Improvement

The spirit of the eighteenth-century Enlightenment was drawn from the scientific and intellectual revolution of the seventeenth century. The Enlightenment carried over and popularized the ideas of Bacon and Descartes, of Bayle and Spinoza, and, above all, of Locke and Newton. It carried over the philosophy of natural

Chapter Emblem: A French snuffbox showing miniature portraits on tortoise shell of three famous philosophers, Voltaire, Rousseau, and Benjamin Franklin.

law and of natural right. Never was there an age so skeptical toward tradition, so confident in the powers of human reason and of science, so firmly convinced of the regularity and harmony of nature, and so deeply imbued with the sense of civilization's advance and progress.

The idea of progress is often said to have been the dominant or characteristic idea of European civilization from the seventeenth century to the twentieth. It is a belief, a kind of nonreligious faith, that the conditions of human life become better as time goes on, that in general each generation is better off than its predecessors and will contribute by its labor to an even better life for generations to come, and that in the long run all mankind will share in the same advance. All the elements of this belief had been present by 1700. It was after 1700, however, that the idea of progress became explicit. In the seventeenth century it had shown itself in a more rudimentary way, in a sporadic dispute, among men of letters in England and France, known as the quarrel of Ancients and Moderns. The Ancients held that the works of the Greeks and Romans had never been surpassed. The Moderns, pointing to science, art, literature, and invention, declared that their own time was the best, that it was natural for men of their time to do better than the ancients because they came later and built upon their predecessors' achievements. The quarrel was never exactly settled, but a great many people in 1700 were Moderns.

Far-reaching also was the faith of the age in the natural faculties of the human mind. Pure skepticism, the negation of reason, was overcome. Nor were the educated, after 1700, likely to be superstitious, terrified by the unknown, or addicted to magic. The witchcraft mania abruptly died. Indeed all sense of the supernatural became dim. "Modern" people not only ceased to fear the devil; they ceased also to fear God. They thought of God less as a Father than as a First Cause of the physical universe. There was less sense of a personal God, or of the inscrutable imminence of divine Providence, or of man's need for saving grace. God was less the God of Love; He was the inconceivably intelligent being who had made the amazing universe now discovered by human reason. The great symbol of the Christian God was the Cross, on which a divine being had suffered in human form. The symbol which occurred to people of scientific view was the Watchmaker. The intricacies of the physical universe were compared to the intricacies of a watch, and it was argued that just as a watch could not exist without a watchmaker, so the universe as discovered by Newton could not exist without a God who created it and set it moving by its mathematical law. It was almighty intelligence that was thought divine.

Of course not everyone was primarily moved by such ideas. The first half of the eighteenth century was in fact also a time of continuing religious fervor. Isaac Watts wrote many hymns that are still familiar in English-speaking churches; the great church music of J. S. Bach was composed mainly in the 1720s; Handel's oratorio, *The Messiah*, was first performed in 1741; and it was at about this time that congregations first sang the *Adeste fideles* ("O Come, All Ye Faithful"), originally Catholic in inspiration but soon adopted by Protestants also. The Lutherans of Germany were stirred by the movement known as Pietism, which stressed the inner experience of ordinary persons as distinct from the doctrines taught and debated in theological faculties. The quest for an "inner light," or illumination of the soul rather than of the reason, was somewhat contrary to the main thrust of the Age of Enlightenment, and a religious urge for improvement of the individual rather than of social institutions was hardly central to the idea of progress, but such ideas were by no means merely conservative, for they were in general highly critical of the existing order.

Within the Church of England John Wesley, while a student at Oxford, joined a group of like-minded young men for prayer and meditation. They engaged in good works to relieve the sufferings of prisoners and the poor, to whom they distributed food and clothing, while also teaching them how to read. Going outside the restrictive system of parishes, Wesley and others took to "itinerant" preaching, often to immense crowds in open fields. Wesley is said to have traveled 250,000 miles within Great Britain over a period of fifty years. He and the similarly inclined George Whitfield preached also in the English American colonies, where they helped to arouse the Great Awakening of the 1740s. Such movements had a kind of democratizing effect in stressing individual worth and spiritual consciousness independently of the established religious authorities. Indeed, the spokesmen for older churches dismissed such movements as "enthusiasm," which was then a word of reproach. By the end of his long life (he died in 1791), Wesley had about half a million followers in what were called Methodist societies. Wesley himself tried to keep them within the Church of England, but separate Methodist churches were already founded in England and the United States.

In a way these expressions of religious feeling reflected differences between the popular and elite cultures such as have already been described. While some of the elite joined in the new movements, it was on the whole those of the least comfortable classes who did so. The official churches, Anglican, Lutheran, Catholic, did not wish to be disturbed by religious revivalism. Bishops were cultivated gentlemen of the age. But the most vehement intellectual leaders pushed all churches aside.

Oddly enough, in this age of reason, there was also a taste for mystification. A Swiss pastor, J. C. Lavater, attracted attention with his supposed science of "physiognomy," by which character could be read in the play of the facial features. An Austrian physician, A. F. Mesmer, created a stir in Paris by arranging seances where people were touched by a wand, or sat in tubs, to receive "animal magnetism" in the hope of curing various ills. His "mesmerism" was an early stage in the discovery of hypnosis, but it is significant that a committee of the Royal Academy of Sciences, after investigation, concluded that Mesmer's own theories to explain these strange phenomena were without foundation. There was a somewhat gullible vogue for popular science in the 1780s, shared in by a few who soon became famous in the Revolution, such as Marat and Brissot. Popular science simply exaggerated the claims of real science for the control of nature by human manipulation.

More in the mainstream was Freemasonry, which took form in England and soon spread to the Continent. The Masons were generally men of typical Enlightenment views, well disposed toward reason, progress, toleration, and humane reforms, and respectful toward God as architect of the universe, but they met secretly in lodges, in an atmosphere of mysterious rituals and occult knowledge. Men of all walks of life, nobles, clergy, and middle classes, belonged to the lodges, which had the effect of bringing persons of different social classes together, somewhat harmlessly for self-improvement and the improvement of others. Masonry, however, aroused suspicion because of its secrecy, and a small deviant offshoot, the Illuminati of south Germany, was considered so dangerous that the Bavarian government suppressed it in 1786. There were later some who insisted that the French Revolution had been caused by a conspiracy of Illuminati, philosophes, and other clandestine plotters, but this idea was never any more than the belief of a few frightened conservatives. The word Illuminati meant "the enlightened ones," but the notion of secrecy was foreign to the Enlightenment, which relied above all else on publicity.

The Philosophes

Philosophe is simply French for philosopher, but to be "philosophical" in the eighteenth century meant to approach any subject in a critical and inquiring spirit. The French word is used in English to denote a group of writers who were not philosophers in the sense of treating ultimate questions of existence. They were men of letters, popularizers and publicists. Though often learned, they wrote to gain attention, and it was through the philosophes that the ideas of the Enlightenment spread. Formerly authors had generally been gentlemen of leisure, or talented protégés of aristocratic or royal patrons, or professors or clerics supported by the income from religious foundations. In the Age of Enlightenment a great many were free-lancers, grub-streeters, or journalists. They wrote for "the publick."

The reading public had greatly expanded. The educated middle class, commercial and professional, was much larger than ever before. Country gentlemen were putting off their rustic habits, and even noblemen wished to keep informed. Newspapers and magazines multiplied, and people who could not read them at home could read them in coffeehouses or in reading rooms organized for that purpose. There was a great demand also for dictionaries, encyclopedias, and surveys of all fields of knowledge. The new readers wanted matters made interesting and clear. They appreciated wit and lightness of touch. From such a public, literature itself greatly benefited. The style of the eighteenth century became admirably fluent, clear, and exact, neither ponderous on the one hand nor frothy on the other. And from writings of this kind the readers benefited also, from the interior of Europe to the America of Benjamin Franklin. The bourgeois middle class was becoming not only educated but thoughtful. But the movement was not a class movement only.

There was another way in which writings of the day were affected by social conditions. They were all written under censorship. The theory of censorship was to protect people from harmful ideas as they were protected from shoddy merchandise or dishonest weights and measures. In England the censorship was so mild as to have little effect. Other countries, such as Spain, had a powerful censorship but few original writers. France, the center of the Enlightenment, had both a complicated censorship and a large reading and writing public. The church, the Parlement of Paris, the royal officials, and the printers' guilds all had a hand in the censoring of books. French censorship, however, was very loosely administered, and after 1750 writers were disturbed by it very little. It cannot be compared to censorship in some countries in the twentieth century. Yet in one way it had an unfavorable effect on French thought and letters. It discouraged writers from addressing themselves, in a common-sense way, to a serious consideration of concrete public questions. Legally forbidden to criticize church or state, they threw their criticisms on an abstract level. Debarred from attacking things in particular, they tended to attack things in general. Or they talked of the customs of the Persians and the Iroquois but not the French. Their works became full of double meanings, sly digs, innuendoes, and jokes, by which an author, if questioned, could declare that he did not mean what all the world knew he did mean. As for readers, they developed a taste for forbidden books, which were always easy enough to obtain through illicit channels.

Paris was the heart of the movement. Here, in the town houses of the well-to-do, there occurred a coming together of literary and social celebrities such as had hardly ever before been seen. It might even happen, though rarely, that a notable philosophe was also wealthy; such was the case of Helvetius, who not only wrote books *On the Mind* and *On Man*, but also gave grand entertainments at which such matters were discussed. Mainly, however, this mingling of people and ideas went on in salons conducted by women who became famous as hostesses. Mme. de Geoffrin, for example, for a period of twenty-five years beginning about 1750, entertained artists and writers at dinner, sometimes helped them financially, and introduced them to persons of influence in high society or in government. She welcomed visiting foreigners also, such as Horace Walpole and David Hume from England, and young Stanislas Poniatowski before he became king of Poland. Since other women held similar salons, philosophes and other writers had frequent opportunity to meet and exchange ideas. Salons of this kind survived the Revolution. In 1795, after the Terror, the widows of two eminent philosophes, Helvetius and Condorcet, opened or reopened their salons in Paris for people of moderate republican or liberal sentiments. Sophie Condorcet became a writer herself and a translator of Adam Smith. Her salon remained a center of liberal opposition during the years of Napoleon. More short-lived was the salon of the even more famous Mme. de Staël, who also wrote widely read books and who, among her many other ideas, deplored the subordination of women to men that the Revolution had done little to change. In these post-Revolutionary salons much of the French liberalism of the nineteenth century was born.

In Paris also, in the mid–eighteenth century, was published the most serious of all philosophe enterprises, the *Encyclopédie*, edited by Denis Diderot in seventeen large volumes and completed over the years 1751 to 1772. It was a great compendium of scientific, technical, and historical knowledge, carrying a strong undertone of criticism of existing society and institutions and epitomizing the skeptical, rational, and scientific spirit of the age. It was not the first encyclopedia, but it was the first to have a distinguished list of contributors or to be conceived as a positive force for social progress. Virtually all the French philosophes contributed—Voltaire, Montesquieu, Rousseau, d'Alembert (who assisted in the editing), Buffon, Turgot, Quesnay, and many others, all sometimes collectively called the Encyclopedists. But although edited in Paris the *Encyclopédie* became very widely known and read. About 25,000 multivolumed sets were sold before the Revolution, about half of them outside of France, since French had become an international language understood by educated persons all over Europe. Within France itself the *Encyclopédie* was read in all parts of the country and in the most influential ranks of society. At Besançon, for example, a city of about 28,000 inhabitants, 137 sets were sold to local residents, of whom 15 were members of the clergy, 53 were of the nobility, and 69 were lawyers, doctors, merchants, government officials, or others of what was called the Third Estate. The privileged groups of whom the Encyclopedists were the most critical, that is, the clergy and the nobility, read it or at least purchased it far out of proportion to their numbers in the population as a whole.

Men and women who considered themselves philosophes, or close to the philosophes in spirit, were found all over Europe. Frederick the Great was an eminent philosophe; not only was he the friend of Voltaire and host to a circle of literary and scientific men at Potsdam, but he himself wrote epigrams, satires, dissertations, and histories, as well as works on military science, and he had a gift of wit, a sharp tongue, and a certain impishness toward the traditional and the pompous. Catherine the Great, empress of Russia, was also a philosophe for much the same reason. Maria Theresa, of Austria, was not a philosophe; she was too religious and too little concerned with general ideas. Her son Joseph, on the other hand, as we shall see, proved to be a philosophe enthroned. In England Bishop Warburton was considered by some of his friends as a philosophe; he held that the Church of England of his day, as a social institution, was exactly what pure reason would have invented. The Scottish skeptical philosopher David Hume counted as a philosophe, as did Edward Gibbon, who shocked the pious by his attacks on Christianity in his famous *Decline and Fall of the Roman Empire*. Dr. Samuel Johnson was not a philosophe; he worried over the supernatural, adhered to the established church, deflated pretentious authors, and even declared that Voltaire and Rousseau were bad men who should be sent "to the plantations." There were also Italian and German philosophes, like the Marquis di Beccaria who sought to humanize the criminal law, or Baron Grimm who sent a literary newsletter from Paris to his many subscribers.

Montesquieu, Voltaire, and Rousseau

Most famous of all philosophes were the French trio, Montesquieu (1689–1755), Voltaire (1694–1778), and Rousseau (1712–1778). They differed vehemently with each other. All were hailed as literary geniuses in their own day. All turned from pure literature to works of political commentary and social analysis. All thought that the existing state of society could be improved.

Montesquieu, twice a baron, was a landed aristocrat, a seigneur or manorial lord of southern France. He inherited from his uncle a seat in the Parlement of Bordeaux and sat actively in that parlement in the days of the Regency.[1] He was part of the noble resurgence which followed the death of Louis XIV and continued on through the eighteenth century. Although he shared many of the ideas in the stream of aristocratic and antiabsolutist thought, he went beyond a mere self-centered class philosophy. In his great work, *The Spirit of Laws*, published in 1748, he developed two principal ideas. One was that forms of government varied according to climate and circumstances, for example, that despotism was suited only to large empires in hot climates, and that democracy would work only in small city-states. His other great doctrine, aimed against royal absolutism in France (which he called "despotism"), was the separation and balance of powers. In France he believed that power should be divided between the king and a great many "intermediate bodies"—parlements, provincial estates, organized nobility, chartered towns, and even the church. It was natural for him, a judge in parlement, a provincial and a nobleman, to favor the first three and reasonable for

[1] See pp. 256–257.

him to recognize the position of the bourgeoisie of the towns; as for the church, he observed that, while he took no stock in its teachings, he thought it useful as an offset to undue centralization of government. He greatly admired the English constitution as he understood it, believing that England carried over, more successfully than any other country, the feudal liberties of the early Middle Ages. He thought that in England the necessary separation and balance of powers was obtained by an ingenious mixture of monarchy, aristocracy, and democracy (king, lords, and commons), and by a separation of the functions of the executive, legislature, and judiciary. This doctrine had a wide influence and was well known to the Americans who in 1787 wrote the Constitution of the United States. Montesquieu's own philosophe friends thought him too conservative and even tried to dissuade him from publishing his ideas. He was, indeed, technically a reactionary, favoring a scheme of things that antedated Louis XIV, and he was unusual among contemporaries in his admiration of the "barbarous" Middle Ages.

Voltaire was born in 1694 into a comfortable bourgeois family and christened François-Marie Arouet; "Voltaire," an invented word, is simply the most famous of all pen names. Until he was over forty he was known only as a smart writer of epigrams, tragedies in verse, and an epic. Thereafter he turned increasingly to philosophical and public questions. His strength throughout lay in the facility of his pen. He is the easiest of all great writers to read. He was always trenchant, logical, and incisive, sometimes scurrilous; mocking and sarcastic when he wished, equally a master of deft irony and of withering ridicule. However serious in his purpose, he achieved it by creating a laugh.

In his youth Voltaire spent eleven months in the Bastille for what was considered to be impertinence to the Regent, who, however, in the next year rewarded him with a pension for one of his dramas. He was again arrested after a fracas with a nobleman, the Chevalier de Rohan. He remained an incorrigible bourgeois, while never deeply objecting to the aristocracy on principle. Through his admirer Mme. de Pompadour (another bourgeois, though the king's favorite) he became a gentleman of the bedchamber and royal historian to Louis XV. These functions he fulfilled *in absentia*, when at all, for Paris and Versailles were too hot for him. He was the personal friend of Frederick the Great, with whom he lived for about two years at Potsdam. The two finally quarreled, for no stage was big enough to hold two such prima donnas for very long. Voltaire made a fortune from his writings, pensions, speculations, and practical business sense. In his later years he purchased a manor at Ferney near the Swiss frontier. Here he became, as he said, the "hotel keeper of Europe," receiving the streams of distinguished admirers, favor hunters, and distressed persons who came to seek him out. He died at Paris in 1778, at the age of eighty-four, by far the most famous man of letters in Europe. His collected writings fill over seventy volumes.

Voltaire was mainly interested in the freedom of thought. Like Montesquieu, he was an admirer of England. He spent three years in that country, where, in 1727, he witnessed the state funeral accorded to Sir Isaac Newton and his burial in Westminster Abbey. Voltaire's *Philosophical Letters on the English* (1733) and *Elements of the Philosophy of Newton* (1738) not only brought England increasingly before the consciousness of the rest of Europe, but also popularized the new scientific ideas—the inductive philosophy of Bacon, the physics of Newton, and the sensationalist psychology of Locke,[2] whose doctrine that all true ideas arose

[2] See pp. 295–296.

from sense experience undercut the authority of religious belief. What Voltaire mainly admired in England was its religious liberty, its relative freedom of the press, and the high regard paid to men of letters like himself. Political liberty concerned him much less than it did Montesquieu. Louis XIV, a villain for Montesquieu and the neoaristocratic school, was a hero for Voltaire, who wrote a laudatory *Age of Louis XIV* (1751) praising the Sun King for the splendor of art and literature in his reign. Voltaire likewise continued to esteem Frederick the Great, though he quarreled with him personally. Frederick was in fact almost his ideal of the enlightened ruler, a man who sponsored the arts and sciences, recognized no religious authority, and granted toleration to all creeds, welcoming Protestants and Catholics on equal terms if only they would be socially useful.

After about 1740 Voltaire became more definitely the crusader, preaching the cause of religious toleration. He fought to clear the memory of Jean Calas, a Protestant put to death on the charge of murdering a son to prevent his conversion to Rome. He wrote also to exonerate a youth named La Barre, who had been executed for defiling a wayside cross. *Écrasez l'infâme!* became the famous Voltairean war cry—"crush the infamous thing!" The *infâme* for him was bigotry, intolerance, and superstition, and behind these the power of an organized clergy. He assaulted not only the Catholic church but the whole traditional Christian view of the world. He argued for "natural religion" and "natural morality," holding that belief in God and the difference between good and evil arose from reason itself. This doctrine had in fact long been taught by the Catholic church. But Voltaire insisted that no supernatural revelation in addition to reason was desirable or necessary, or rather, that belief in a special supernatural revelation made men intolerant, stupid, and cruel. He was the first to present a purely secular conception of world history. In his *Essai sur les moeurs*, or "Universal History," he began with ancient China and surveyed the great civilizations in turn. Earlier writers of world history had put human events within a Christian framework. Following the Bible, they began with the Creation, proceeded to the Fall, recounted the rise of Israel, and so on. Voltaire put Judeo-Christian history within a sociological framework. He represented Christianity and all other organized religions as social phenomena or mere human opinions. Spinoza had said as much; Voltaire spread these ideas through Europe.

In matters of politics and self-government Voltaire was neither a liberal nor a democrat. His opinion of the human race was about as low as his friend Frederick's. If only a government was enlightened he did not care how powerful it was. By an enlightened government he meant one that fought against sloth and stupidity, kept the clergy in a subordinate place, allowed freedom of thought and religion, and advanced the cause of material and technical progress. He had no developed political theory, but his ideal for large civilized countries approached that of enlightened or rational despotism. Believing that only a few could be enlightened, he thought that these few, a king and his advisers, should have the power to carry their program against all opposition. To overcome ignorance, habit, credulity, and priestcraft it was necessary for the state to be strong. It may be said that what Voltaire most desired was liberty for the enlightened.

Jean-Jacques Rousseau was very different. Born in Geneva in 1712, he was a Swiss, a Protestant, and almost of lower-class origin. He never felt at ease in France or in Paris society. Neglected as a child, a runaway at sixteen, he lived for years by odd jobs, such as copying music, and not until the age of forty did he have any success as a writer. He was always the little man, the outsider. In addition, his sex life was unsatisfactory; he finally settled down with an uneducated girl named Thérèse Levasseur, and with her mother, who kept interfering with his affairs. By Thérèse he had five children, whom he deposited at an orphanage. He had no social status, no money, and no sense of money, and after he became famous he lived largely by the generosity of his friends. He was pathetically and painfully maladjusted. He came to feel that he could trust no one, that those who tried to befriend him were deriding or betraying him behind his back. He suffered from what would now be termed complexes; possibly he was paranoiac. He talked endlessly of his own virtue and innocence and complained bitterly that he was misunderstood.

But unbalanced though he was, he was possibly the most profound writer of the age and was certainly the most permanently influential. Rousseau felt, from his own experience, that in society as it existed a good person could not be happy. He therefore attacked society, declaring that it was artificial and corrupt. He even attacked reason, calling it a false guide when followed alone. He felt doubts on all the progress which gave satisfaction to his contemporaries. In two "discourses," one on the *Arts and Sciences* (1750), the other on the *Origin of Inequality Among Men* (1753), he argued that civilization was the source of much evil, and that life in a "state of nature," were it only possible, would be much better. As Voltaire said, when Rousseau sent him a copy of his second discourse (Voltaire who relished civilization in every form), it made him "feel like going on all fours." To Rousseau the best traits of human character, such as kindness, unselfishness, honesty, and true understanding, were products of nature. Deep below reason, he sensed the presence of feeling. He delighted in the warmth of sympathy, the quick flash of intuition, the clear message of conscience. He was religious by temperament, for though he believed in no church, no clergy, and no revelation he had a respect for the Bible, a reverent awe toward the cosmos, a love of solitary meditation, and a belief in a God who was not merely a "first cause" but also a God of love and beauty. Rousseau thus made it easier for serious-minded people to slip away from orthodoxy and all forms of churchly discipline. He was feared by the churches as the most dangerous of all "infidels" and was condemned both in Catholic France and at Protestant Geneva.

In general, in most of his books, Rousseau, unlike so many of his contemporaries, gave the impression that impulse is more reliable than considered judgment, spontaneous feeling more to be trusted than critical thought. Mystical insights were for him more truthful than rational or clear ideas. He became the "man of feeling," the "child of nature," the forerunner of the coming age of romanticism, and an important source of all modern emphasis on the nonrational and the subconscious.

In the *Social Contract* (1762) Rousseau seemed to contradict all this. In it he held, somewhat like Hobbes,[3] that the "state of nature" was a brutish condition without law or morality. In other works he had held that the badness of men was due to the evils of society. He now held that good men could be produced only by an improved society. Earlier thinkers, such as John Locke, for example, had thought of the "contract" as an agreement between a ruler and a people. Rousseau thought of it as an agreement among the people themselves. It was a social, not merely a political, contract. Organized civil society, i.e., the community,

[3] See p. 299.

rested upon it. It was an understanding by which all individuals surrendered their natural liberty to each other, fused their individual wills into a combined General Will, and agreed to accept the rulings of this General Will as final. This General Will was the sovereign; and true sovereign power, rightly understood, was "absolute," "sacred," and "inviolable." Government was secondary; kings, officials, or elected representatives were only delegates of a sovereign people. Rousseau devoted many difficult and abstruse pages to explaining how the *real* General Will could be known. It was not necessarily determined by vote of a majority. "What generalizes the will," he said, "is not the number of voices but the common interest that unites them." He said little of the mechanism of government and had no admiration for parliamentary institutions. He was concerned with something deeper. Maladjusted outsider that he was, he craved a commonwealth in which every person could feel that he belonged. He wished a state in which all persons had a sense of membership and participation.

By these ideas Rousseau made himself the prophet of both democracy and nationalism. Indeed, in his *Considerations on Poland*, written at the request of Poles who were fighting against the partitions, Rousseau applied the ideas of the *Social Contract* in more concrete form and became the first systematic theorist of a conscious and calculated nationalism.[4] In writing the *Social Contract* he had in mind a small city-state like his native Geneva. But what he did, in effect, was to generalize and make applicable to large territories the psychology of small city republics— the sense of membership, of community and fellowship, of responsible citizenship and intimate participation in public affairs—in short, of common will. All modern states, democratic or undemocratic, strive to impart this sense of moral solidarity to their peoples. Whereas in democratic states the General Will can in some way be identified with the sovereignty of the people, in dictatorships it becomes possible for individuals (or parties) to arrogate to themselves the right to serve as spokesmen and interpreters of the General Will. Both totalitarians and democrats have regarded Rousseau as one of their prophets.

The *Social Contract* was little read and almost unknown in its own time. Rousseau's influence on his contemporaries was spread by his other writings and especially his novels, *Émile* (1762) and the *Nouvelle Héloïse* (1760). The novels were widely read in all literate classes of society, especially by the women, who made a kind of cult of Jean-Jacques, while he was living and after his death, which occurred in 1778. He was a literary master, able to evoke shades of thought and feeling that few writers had touched before, and by his literary writings he spread in the highest circles a new respect for the common man, a love of common things, an impulse of human pity and compassion, a sense of artifice and superficiality in aristocratic life. Women took to nursing their own babies. Even men spoke of the delicacy of their sentiments. Tears became the fashion. The queen, Marie Antoinette, built herself a village in the gardens at Versailles where she pretended to be a simple milkmaid. In all this there was much that was ridiculous or shallow. Yet it was the wellspring of modern humanitarianism, the force leading to a new sense of human equality. Rousseau estranged the French upper classes from their own mode of life. He made many of them lose faith in their own superiority. That was his main direct contribution to the French Revolution.

[4] See pp. 238–240.

Political Economists

In France, somewhat apart from the philosophes, were the Physiocrats, whom their critics called "economists," a word originally thought to be mildly insulting. Many of the Physiocrats, unlike the philosophes, were close to the government as administrators or advisers. Quesnay was physician to Louis XV, Turgot was an experienced official who became minister to Louis XVI, and Dupont de Nemours, an associate of Turgot's, became the founder of the industrial family of the Du Ponts in the United States. Such men concerned themselves with fiscal and tax reform, and with measures to increase the national wealth of France. They opposed guild regulations and price controls as impediments to the production and circulation of goods, and so were the first to use the term *laissez faire* ("let them do as they see fit") as a principle of economic activity. They favored strong government, however, relying on it to overcome traditional obstructions and to provide inducements for the establishment of new industries.

Economics, or what was long called political economy, arose from these activities of the Physiocrats, from the somewhat similar work of "cameralists" in the German states, and from the collection and analysis of quantitative data, that is, the birth of statistics. A good example of the latter was Sir William Petty's *Political Arithmetic*, published in 1690. Economic thinking flourished especially in Great Britain, where Adam Smith's *Enquiry into the nature and causes of the wealth of nations* appeared in 1776. By 1800 the *Wealth of Nations* had been translated into every West European language except Portuguese.

Adam Smith's purpose, like that of the French Physiocrats, was to increase the national wealth by the reduction of barriers that hindered its growth. He undercut the premises of what we have called "the struggle for wealth and empire" in Chapter VI, since he argued that to build up a nation's wealth it was unnecessary to have an empire. He attacked most of the program of mercantilism that had obtained since the sixteenth century, and he expected that Britain's American colonies would soon become independent without loss to British trade. Where others looked to planning by an enlightened government, Adam Smith preferred to limit the functions of government to defense, internal security, and the provision of reasonable laws and fair law courts by which private differences could be adjudicated. For innovation and enterprise he counted more on private persons than on the state. He became the philosopher of the free market, the prophet of free trade. If there was a shortage of a given commodity its price would rise, and so stimulate producers to produce more, while also attracting new persons into that line of production. If there was an excess, if more was produced than purchasers would buy, both capital and labor would withdraw and gradually move into another area where demand was stronger. Demand would increase with lower prices, which depended on lower costs, which in turn depended on the specialization of labor. His most famous example was that of the pin factory of his time, where each of a dozen workers engaged in only one part of the process of manufacture, so that together they produced far more pins than if each man produced whole pins; the price of pins then fell, and more pins could be used by more people. The same principle held in international trade; some countries or climates could produce an article more cheaply than others, so that if each specialized and then exchanged with the others, all would have more. The motivation for all such production and exchange was to be the self-interest of the participants. As he said, we rely for our meat not on the good will of the butcher but on his concern for his own income. To those who might object that this was a system of selfishness Adam Smith would reply (being a professor of moral philosophy at the University of Glasgow) that it was at least realistic, describing how people really behaved, and that it was morally justified since it ultimately produced a maximum both of freedom and of abundance. The mutual interaction of the enlightened self-interest of millions of persons would in the end, as if by an "invisible hand," he said, result in the highest welfare of all. Among problems that Smith minimized, or accepted as lesser evils, were the insecurity of individuals and the dangers of excessive dependency of a whole country on imports of essentials, such as food; and if the visible hand of government continued to regulate the price of bread it was not for economic reasons, but to prevent rioting and obtain social peace.

Main Currents of Enlightenment Thought

It is clear that the currents of thought in France and Europe were divergent and inconsistent. There was a general belief in progress, reason, science, and civilization. Rousseau had his doubts and praised the beauties of character. Montesquieu thought the church useful but did not believe in religion; Rousseau believed in religion but saw no need for any church. Montesquieu was concerned over practical political liberty; Voltaire would surrender political liberty in return for guarantees of intellectual freedom; Rousseau wanted emancipation from the trivialities of society and sought the freedom that consists in merging willingly with nature and with one's fellows. Most philosophes were closest to Voltaire. They were concerned also for equality. It was not a very far-reaching equality, but it meant equality of rights for persons of different religions, a reduction of privileges enjoyed by nobles but not by commoners, more equality of status in law courts and in the payment of taxes, and more opportunity for middle-class persons to rise to positions of honor.

France was the main center of the Enlightenment. French philosophes traveled all over Europe. Frederick II and Catherine II invited French thinkers to their courts. French was the language of the academies of St. Petersburg and Berlin. Frederick wrote his own works in the French language. There was a uniform cosmopolitan culture among the upper classes of Europe, and this culture was predominantly French. But England was important also. Hitherto somewhat on the fringes of the European consciousness, England now moved closer to the center. Montesquieu and Voltaire may be said to have "discovered" England for Europe. Through them the ideas of Bacon, Newton, and Locke, and the whole theory of English liberty and parliamentary government became matters for general discussion and comment. We have seen, too, how Adam Smith's *Wealth of Nations* was soon translated into many languages.

The main agency of progress was thought to be the state. Whether in the form of limited monarchy on the English model favored by Montesquieu, or of an enlightened despotism preferred by Voltaire, or of the ideal republican commonwealth portrayed by Rousseau, the rightly ordered government was considered the best guarantee of social welfare. Even the political economists needed the state to shake people out of the habits of ages, sweep away a mass of local regulation, preserve law and order and the enforcement of contracts, and so assure the existence of a free market. But if they relied on the state, they were not nationalists in any later sense of the word. As "universalists," they believed in the unity of mankind under a natural law of right and reason. In this they carried over the classical and Christian outlook in a secular way. They supposed that all peoples would participate eventually in the same progress. No nation was thought to have a peculiar message. French ideas enjoyed a wide currency, but no one thought of them as peculiarly French, arising from a French "national character." It was simply thought that the French at the time were in the vanguard of civilization. Such was the idea of Condorcet, one of the later philosophes, a leading spokesman of the Enlightenment, who became an active figure in the French Revolution, and also one of its victims, and who in 1794, while in hiding from the guillotine, wrote the great testament to the Enlightenment, his *Sketch of the Progress of the Human Mind.*

37. ENLIGHTENED DESPOTISM: FRANCE, AUSTRIA, PRUSSIA

The Meaning of Enlightened Despotism

Enlightened despotism is hard to define, because it grew out of the earlier absolutism represented by Louis XIV or Peter the Great. Characteristically, the enlightened despots drained marshes, built roads and bridges, codified the laws, repressed provincial autonomy and localism, curtailed the independence of church and nobles, and built up a trained and salaried officialdom. All these things had been done by kings before. The typical enlightened despot differed from his "unenlightened" predecessor mainly in attitude and tempo. He said little of a divine right to his throne. He might even not emphasize his hereditary or dynastic family right. He justified his authority on grounds of usefulness to society, calling himself, as Frederick the Great did, the "first servant of the state."

Enlightened despotism was secular; it claimed no mandate from heaven and recognized no especial responsibility to God or church. The typical enlightened despot consequently favored toleration in religion, and this was an important new emphasis after about 1740; but here again there was precedent in the older absolutism, for the rulers of Prussia had been inclined toward toleration long before Frederick, and even the French Bourbons had recognized a degree of religious liberty for almost a century following the Edict of Nantes.[5] The secular outlook of the enlightened governments is again seen in the common front they adopted against the Jesuits. High papalists and ultramontanes,[6] affirming the authority of a universal church, and at the same time intellectually and in other ways the strongest religious order in the Catholic world, the Jesuits were distasteful to the enlightened monarchs and their civil officials and in the 1760s the order was banned in almost all Catholic countries. In 1773 the pope was persuaded to dissolve the Society of Jesus entirely. The various governments concerned, in France, Austria, Spain, Portugal, and Naples, confiscated the Jesuit property and took over the Jesuit schools. Not until 1814 was the order reconstituted.

Enlightened despotism was also rational and reformist. The typical despot set out to reconstruct his state by the use of reason. Sharing the current view of the past as benighted, he was impatient of custom and of all that was imbedded in custom or claimed as a heritage from the past, such as systems of customary law

[5] See pp. 135–137, 184–185.
[6] See p. 90.

and the rights and privileges of church, nobles, towns, guilds, provinces, assemblies of estates, or, in France, the judicial bodies called parlements. The complex of such institutions was disparagingly referred to as "feudalism." Monarchs had long struggled against feudalism in this sense, but in the past they had usually compromised. The enlightened despot was less willing to compromise, and herein lay the difference in tempo. The new despot acted abruptly, desiring quicker results.

Enlightened despotism, in short, was an acceleration of the old institution of monarchy, which now put aside the quasi-sacred mantle in which it had clothed itself and undertook to justify itself in the cold light of reason and secular usefulness. In theory even the dynastic claim was awkward, for it rested on inheritance from the past. Under enlightened despotism the idea of the state itself was changing, from the older notion of an estate belonging by a kind of sanctified property right to its ruler, to a newer notion of an abstract and impersonal authority exercised by public officers, of whom the king was simply the highest.

The trend to enlightened despotism after 1740 owed a great deal to writers and philosophes, but it arose also out of a very practical situation, namely, the great war of the mid-eighteenth century.[7] War, in modern history, has usually led to concentration and rationalizing of government power, and the wars of 1740–1748 and 1756–1763 were no exception. Under their impact even governments where the rulers were not considered by philosophes to be enlightened, notably those of Louis XV and Maria Theresa, and even the government of Great Britain, which was certainly not despotic, embarked on programs which all bear features in common. They attempted to augment their revenues, devise new taxes, tax persons or regions hitherto more or less tax-exempt, limit the autonomy of outlying political bodies, and centralize and renovate their respective political systems. The workings of enlightened despotism might be seen in many states, in Habsburg Tuscany under Leopold, in Bourbon Naples and Spain under Charles III, in Portugal under the minister Pombal, in Denmark under Struensee. But it seems best to consider only the more important countries at some length—France and Austria, Prussia and Russia—and then the rather different, yet not wholly different, course of events in the British empire.

The Failure of Enlightened Despotism in France

It was in France that enlightened despotism had the least success. Louis XV, who had inherited the throne in 1715 and lived until 1774, though by no means stupid, was indifferent to most serious questions, absorbed in the daily rounds at Versailles, disinclined to make trouble for people that he saw personally, and interested in government only by fits and starts. His remark, *après moi le déluge*, whether or not he really said it, sufficiently characterizes his personal attitude to conditions in France. Yet the French government was not unenlightened, and many capable officials carried on its affairs all through the century. These men generally knew what the basic trouble was. All the practical difficulties of the French monarchy could be traced to its system of taxation. The most important impost, the taille, a kind of land tax, was generally paid only by the peasants. Nobles were exempt from it on principle, and office-holders and bourgeois, for

[7] See pp. 264–275.

one reason or another, were generally exempt also. In addition, the church, which owned between 5 and 10 percent of the land of the country, insisted that its property was not taxable by the state; it granted to the king a periodic "free gift" which, though sizable, was less than the government might expect from direct taxation. The consequence of the tax exemptions was that, although France itself was wealthy and prosperous, the government was chronically poor, because the social classes which enjoyed most of the wealth and prosperity did not pay taxes corresponding to their incomes. Louis XIV, under pressure of war, had tried to tax everybody alike by creating new levies—the capitation or poll tax and the *dixième* or tenth, both of which were assessed in proportion to income; but these taxes had been widely evaded. A similar effort was made in 1726, but it too had failed. The propertied classes resisted taxation because they thought it degrading. France had succumbed to the appalling principle that to pay direct taxes was the sure mark of inferior status. Nobles, churchmen, and bourgeois also resisted taxation because they were kept out of policymaking functions of government and so had no sense of political responsibility or control. There were good historical reasons for this, but the result was financially ruinous.[8]

In 1748, under pressure of the heavy war costs, and at the prompting of Mme de Pompadour, Louis XV bestirred himself to appoint a controller general of finance who devised a tax to be paid by all persons receiving income from property—land, manorial rights, business investments, and offices such as parlementary judgeships—irrespective of class status, provincial liberties, or previous exemptions of any kind. A clamor arose from the Parlement of Paris, the eleven provincial parlements, the estates of Brittany, and the church. All these were dominated by noblemen and because of the aristocratic resurgence that had begun with the Regency, were politically stronger than in the days of Louis XIV. They could also now cite Montesquieu to justify their opposition to the crown. The Parlement of Paris ruled the new tax unconstitutional, or incompatible with the laws of France and liberties of Frenchmen. The estates of Brittany, and of other *pays d'états*, i.e., provinces having assemblies of estates, declared that their customary and historic liberties were being outraged. The church protested with vehemence. After several years of wrangling, Louis XV decided to push the matter no further; he withdrew his support from his finance minister, and the whole project collapsed.

The 1750s and 1760s saw continued friction between the ministry and the various semiautonomous bodies within the country. Meanwhile came the enormous costs and humiliating reverses of the Seven Years' War. The government renewed its determination to win effective centralized control. It was decided to eliminate

[8] See pp. 69, 182–183, 260.

EUROPE, 1740

Boundaries are as of 1740. There were now three Bourbon monarchies (France, Spain, and the Two Sicilies), while the Austrian monarchy possessed most of what is now Belgium, and in Italy the duchy of Milan and grand duchy of Tuscany, where the Medici family had recently died out. Prussia expanded by acquiring Silesia in the war of the 1740s. The first partition of Poland in 1772 enlarged Prussia, Austria, and Russia (see maps, pp. 216, 222–223, 234–235, 328). France acquired Lorraine in 1766 and Corsica in 1768. Otherwise there were no changes until the Revolutionary-Napoleonic wars of 1792–1814.

Bourbon Dominions

Habsburg Dominions

Boundary of Holy Roman Empire

SWEDEN

NORWAY

St. Petersburg

KINGDOM OF
DENMARK AND NORWAY

Stockholm

Riga

NORTH SEA

BALTIC SEA

LITHUANIA

Edinburgh

SCOTLAND

Memel

PRUSSIA

Minsk

DENMARK

Copenhagen

EAST
PRUSSIA

IRELAND   GREAT BRITAIN

SCHLESWIG

Danzig

Dublin   Liverpool
ENGLAND

Hamburg

Thorn

POLAND

Warsaw

WALES

Bremen
HANOVER
(Britain)

Elbe R.

BRANDENBURG

UNITED
PROVINCES

London

Amsterdam   Utrecht

Magdeburg   Berlin

Lublin

Vistula R.

ATLANTIC OCEAN

AUSTRIAN
NETHERLANDS

Oudenarde   Antwerp

Cologne

Leipzig   SAXONY

SILESIA

Breslau

Cracow

Lemberg

PODOLIA

CHANNEL I.
(Britain)

CAPE
DE LA HOGUE

Malplaquet

Ramillies

MINOR
GERMAN STATES

Dresden

Prague

Rhine R.

Oder R.

Rouen

Reims

Frankfurt

BOHEMIA

MORAVIA

Munkacz

Quiberon

Paris

Metz

PALATI-
NATE R.

Blenheim

AUSTRIA

Pressburg

Seine R.

Orléans

LORRAINE
(France 1766)

Strasbourg

Vienna

Budapest

Loire R.

Tours

BAVARIA

Besançon

Munich

AUSTRIAN MONARCHY

TRANSYLVANIA

Limoges

FRANCE

Geneva

SWITZERLAND

TYROL

KINGDOM
OF HUNGARY

BANAT

Bordeaux

Lyons

SAVOY

Garonne R.

Rhone R.

PO R.

MILAN

VENETIA

Croatia   Save R.

Belgrade

WALLACHIA

Santiago

León

Pamplona

Toulouse

Turin

PAR-
MA

Venice

Bologna

BOSNIA

SERBIA

Danube R.

OTTOMAN EMPIRE

Burgos

Ebro R.

Avignon

Genoa

TUSCANY

PAPAL
STATES

DALMATIA
(Venice)

PORTUGAL

SPAIN

ARAGON

Marseilles

Toulon

CORSICA
(Genoa)

MONTENEGRO

Sofia

Lisbon

Tagus R.

Madrid

CATALONIA

Rome

ALBANIA

Almanza

Barcelona

KINGDOM OF SARDINIA

Benevento

Naples

Bari

Salonica

Cadiz

Guadalquivir R.

Seville

Toledo

Granada

BALEARIC I.

MINORCA
(Britain)

NAPLES

IONIAN I.
(Venice)

Gibraltar (Britain)

MAJORCA
(Spain)

SARDINIA

ADRIATIC SEA

Tangier

MEDITERRANEAN

Cagliari

KINGDOM
OF THE TWO SICILIES

Palermo

Athens

MOREA

Algiers

Tunis

SICILY

SEA

MOROCCO
(Independent)

ALGERIA
(Turkish)

TUNISIA
(Turkish)

MALTA (Knights of St. John)

0   100   200   300   miles

the parlements as a political force, and for this purpose, in 1768, Louis XV called to the chancellorship a man named Maupeou, who simply abrogated the old parlements and set up new ones in their place. Maupeou had the sympathy of Voltaire and most of the philosophes. In the "Maupeou parlements" the judges had no property rights in their seats but became salaried officials appointed by the crown with assurances of secure tenure, and they were forbidden to reject government edicts or to pass on their constitutionality, being confined to purely judicial functions. Maupeou likewise proposed to make the laws and judicial procedure more uniform throughout the whole country. Meanwhile, with the old parlements out of the way, another attempt was made to tax the privileged and exempted groups.

But Louis XV died in 1774. His grandson and successor, Louis XVI, though far superior in personal habits to his grandfather, and possessed by a genuine desire to govern well, resembled Louis XV in that he lacked sustained will power and could not bear to offend the people who could get to see him personally. In any case he was only twenty in 1774. The kingdom resounded with outcries against Maupeou and his colleagues as minions of despotism and with demands for the immediate restoration of the old Parlement of Paris and the others. Louis XVI, fearful of beginning his reign as a "despot," therefore recalled the old parlements and abolished those of Maupeou. The abortive Maupeou parlements represented the farthest step taken by enlightened despotism in France. It was arbitrary, highhanded, and despotic for Louis XV to destroy the old parlements, but it was certainly enlightened in the sense then connoted by the word, for the old parlements were strongholds of aristocracy and privilege and had for decades blocked programs of reform.

Louis XVI, in recalling the old parlements in 1774, began his reign by pacifying the privileged classes. At the same time he appointed a reforming ministry. At its head was Turgot, a philosophe and Physiocrat and a widely experienced government administrator. Turgot undertook to suppress the guilds, which were privileged municipal monopolies in their several trades. He allowed greater freedom to the internal commerce in grain. He planned to abolish the royal corvée (a requirement that certain peasants labor on the roads a few days each year), replacing it by a money tax which would fall on all classes. He began to review the whole system of taxation and was known even to favor the legal toleration of Protestants. The Parlement of Paris, supported by the Provincial Estates and the church, vociferously opposed him, and in 1776 he resigned. Louis XVI, by recalling the parlements, had made reform impossible. In 1778 France again went to war with Britain. The same cycle was repeated: war costs, debt, deficit, new projects of taxation, resistance from the parlements and other semiautonomous bodies. In the 1780s the clash led to revolution.[9]

Austria: The Reforms of Maria Theresa (1740–1780) and of Joseph (1780–1790)

For Maria Theresa the war of the 1740s proved the extraordinary flimsiness of her empire.[10] Had the Continental allies won a more smashing victory, not only would Silesia have been lost to Prussia, but Belgium would have gone to France, Bohemia and Austria to the elector of Bavaria supported by France, and the emperorship of the Holy Roman Empire, long a source of prestige to the Habsburgs, would have passed permanently in all probability to a Bavarian or other pro-French German prince. Maria Theresa would have become queen of Hungary only. Nor did her subjects show much inclination to remain together under her rule. In Breslau, the capital of Silesia, after the Prussian attack of 1740, the citizens stood so stubbornly by their town liberties that they would not admit her army within their walls. In Bohemia almost half the nobles welcomed the invading Franco-Bavarians. In Hungary Maria Theresa won support but only by confirming the historic Hungarian liberties. The empire was only a loose bundle of territories, without common purpose or common will. The Pragmatic Sanction devised by Charles VI, it should be recalled, had been meant not only to guarantee the Habsburg inheritance against foreign attack, but also to secure the assent of the several parts of the empire to remain united under the dynasty.[11]

The war of the 1740s led to internal consolidation. The reign of Maria Theresa set the course of all later development of the Austrian empire and hence of the many peoples who lived within its borders. She was aided by a notable team of ministers, whose origin illustrated the nonnational character of the Habsburg system. Her most trusted adviser in foreign relations, the astute Kaunitz,[12] was a Moravian; her main assistants in domestic affairs were a Silesian and a Bohemian-Czech. They worked smoothly with the German archduchess-queen and with German officials in Vienna. Their aim was primarily to prevent dissolution of the monarchy by enlarging and guaranteeing the flow of taxes and soldiers. This involved breaking the local control of territorial nobles in their several diets, which corresponded somewhat to the French Provincial Estates. Hungary, profoundly separatist, was let alone. But the Bohemian and Austrian provinces were welded together. The kingdom of Bohemia, in 1749, lost the constitutional charter which it had received in 1627.[13] The several Bohemian and Austrian diets lost their right to consent to taxes. The separate offices, or "chancelleries," by which their affairs had been separately handled at Vienna, were abolished. Formerly local affairs, recruiting, and tax collecting had been dominated by committees of the diets, made up of landed noblemen of the neighborhood, gentlemen amateurs who were often negligent or indifferent, and who, since they served without pay, were impervious to official discipline, reprimand, or coordination. They were replaced by salaried administrators. Bureaucracy took the place of local self-government. Officials (following the form of mercantilist doctrine called "cameralism" in central Europe) planned to augment the economic strength of the empire by increasing production. They checked the local guild monopolies, suppressed brigandage on the roads, and in 1775 produced a tariff union of Bohemia, Moravia, and the Austrian duchies. This region became the largest area of free trade on the European continent, since even France was still divided by internal tariffs. Bohemia, industrially the most advanced part of the empire, benefited substantially; one of its cotton manufacturing plants, at the end of Maria Theresa's reign, employed 4,000 persons.

The great social fact, both in the Habsburg lands and in all eastern Europe, was the serfdom into which the rural masses had progressively fallen during the

[11] See pp. 219, 265–266.
[12] See p. 268.
[13] See pp. 139–140, 218.

past 200 years.[14] Serfdom meant that the peasant belonged more to his landlord than to the state. The serf owed labor to his lord, often unspecified in amount or kind. The tendency, so long as the landlords ruled locally through their diets, was for the serf to do six days a week of forced labor on the lord's land. Maria Theresa, from humane motives, and also from a desire to lay hands on the manpower from which her armies were recruited, launched a systematic attack on the institutions of serfdom, which meant also an attack on the landed aristocracy of the empire. With the diets reduced in power, the protests of the nobles were less effective; still, the whole agricultural labor system of her territories was involved, and Maria Theresa proceeded with caution. Laws were passed against abuse of peasants by lords or their overseers. Other laws regularized the labor obligations, requiring that they be publicly registered and usually limiting them to three days a week. The laws were often evaded. But the peasant was to some extent freed from arbitrary exactions of the lord. Maria Theresa accomplished more to alleviate serfdom than any other ruler of the eighteenth century in eastern Europe, with the single exception of her own son, Joseph II.

The great archduchess-queen died in 1780, having reigned for forty years. Her son, who had been co-regent with his mother since 1765, had little patience with her methods. Maria Theresa, though steady enough in aim, had always been content with partial measures. Instead of advertising her purposes by philosophical generalization she disguised or understated them, never carrying matters to the point of arousing an unmanageable reaction or of uniting against her the vested interests that she undermined. She backed and filled, watched and waited. Joseph II would not wait. Though he thought the French philosophes frivolous, and Frederick of Prussia a mere clever cynic, he was himself a pure representative of the Age of Enlightenment, and it is in his brief reign of ten years that the character and the limitations of enlightened despotism can best be seen. He was a solemn, earnest, good man, who sensed the misery and hopelessness of the lowest classes. He believed existing conditions to be bad, and he would not regulate or improve them; he would end them. Right and reason, in his mind, lay with the views which he himself adopted; upholders of the old order were self-seeking or mistaken and to yield to them would be to compromise with evil.

"The state," said Joseph, anticipating the Philosophical Radicals in England, meant "the greatest good for the greatest number." He acted accordingly. His ten years of rule passed in a quick succession of decrees. Maria Theresa had regulated serfdom. Joseph abolished it. His mother had collected taxes from nobles as well as peasants, though not equally. Joseph decreed absolute equality of taxation. He insisted on equal punishment for equal crimes whatever the class status of the offender; an aristocratic army officer, who had stolen 97,000 gulden, was exhibited in the pillory, and Count Podstacky, a forger, was made to sweep the streets of Vienna chained to common convicts. At the same time many legal punishments were made less physically cruel. Joseph granted complete liberty of the press. He ordered toleration of all religions, except for a few popular sects which he thought too ignorant to allow. He granted equal civil rights to the Jews, and equal duties, making Jews liable, for the first time in Europe, to service in the army. He even made Jewish nobles, an amazing phenomenon to those of aristocratic "blood." He clashed openly and rudely with the pope, supporting a movement

---

[14] See pp. 122–123, 204–205, 217–218, 226.

called Febronianism which urged more national independence from Rome for German Catholic prelates, on the model of the French Gallican liberties. He demanded increased powers in the appointment and supervision of bishops, and he suppressed a good many monasteries, using their property to finance secular hospitals in Vienna, and thus laying the foundations of Viennese excellence as a medical center. He attempted also to develop the empire economically and built up the port of Trieste, where he even established an East India Company, which soon failed for obvious reasons—neither capital nor naval support being forthcoming from central Europe. His attempts to reach the sea commercially through Belgium, like those of his grandfather at the time of the Ostend Company, were blocked by the Dutch and British interests.[15]

To force through his program Joseph had to centralize his state, like earlier rulers, except that he went farther. Regional diets and aristocratic self-government fared even worse than under his mother. Where she had always sagaciously let Hungary go its own way, he applied most of his measures to Hungary also—what was right must be right everywhere. His ideal was a perfectly uniform and rational empire, with all irregularities smoothed out as if under a steam roller. He thought it reasonable to have a single language for administration and naturally chose German; this led to a program of Germanizing the Czechs, Poles, Magyars, and others, which in turn aroused their nationalistic resistance. Using the German language, pushing the emperor's program against regional and class opposition, was a hard-pressed, constantly growing, and increasingly disciplined body of officials. Bureaucracy became recognizably modern, with training courses, promotion schedules, retirement pensions, efficiency reports, and visits by inspectors. The clergy likewise were employed as mouthpieces of the state to explain new laws to their parishioners and teach due respect for the government. To watch over the whole structure Joseph created a secret police, whose agents, soliciting the confidential aid of spies and informers, reported on the performance of government employees, or on the ideas and actions of nobles, clergy, or others from whom trouble might be expected. The police state, so infamous to the liberal world, was first systematically built up under Joseph as an instrument of enlightenment and reform.

Joseph II, the "revolutionary emperor," anticipated much that was done in France by the Revolution and under Napoleon. He could not abide "feudalism" or "medievalism"; he personally detested the nobility and the church. But few of his reforms proved lasting. He died prematurely in 1790, at the age of forty-nine, disillusioned and broken-hearted. Hungary and the Belgian provinces were in revolution against him. They held that their old constitutional liberties had been outraged—that they were being governed without their consent. In Hungary all the good will won by Maria Theresa seemed to be lost; in Belgium the provinces stood stubbornly by the same medieval privileges, the old *Joyeuse Entrée*, which they had vindicated 200 years before against the king of Spain.[16] Noble landlords throughout the Habsburg empire, having lost their control over labor by the abolition of serfdom, and their caste status by legal and fiscal reforms, naturally were indignant. The church believed itself to be prostituted and despoiled. The peasants were grateful for their new personal liberty but balked at the official attitude

[15] See p. 219.
[16] See pp. 126–128.

of condescending uplift, and often, in real life, sympathized with their priests and their gentlefolk. The officials were unequal to the task demanded of them. There were too few bourgeois in most parts of the empire to staff the civil service, so that many functionaries were members of the landowning nobility which Joseph humiliated; and in any case they frequently found the directives that flowed from Vienna impossible to enforce or even to understand. Joseph was a revolutionist without a party. He failed because he could not be everywhere and do everything himself. His reign demonstrated the limitations of a merely despotic enlightenment. It showed that a legally absolute ruler could not really do as he pleased. It suggested that drastic and abrupt reform could only come with a true revolution, on a wave of public opinion, and under the leadership of men who shared in a coherent body of ideas.

Joseph was succeeded by his brother Leopold, one of the ablest rulers of the century, who for many years as grand duke of Tuscany had given that country the best government known in Italy for generations. Now, in 1790, Leopold was plagued by outcries from his sister, Marie Antoinette, caught in the toils of a real revolution in France.[17] He refused to interfere in French affairs; in any case, he was busy dealing with the uproar left by Joseph. He abrogated most of Joseph's edicts, but he did not yield entirely. The nobles did not win back full powers in their diets. The peasants were not wholly consigned to the old serfdom; Joseph's efforts to provide them with land and to rid them of forced labor had to be given up, but they remained personally free, in law, to migrate, marry, or choose an occupation at will. Leopold died in 1792 and was followed by his son Francis II. Under Francis the aristocratic and clerical reaction gathered strength, terrified by the memory of Joseph II and by the spectacle of revolutionary France, with which Austria went to war soon after Leopold's death.

Prussia under Frederick the Great (1740–1786)

In Prussia, Frederick the Great continued to reign for twenty-three years after the close of the Seven Years' War. "Old Fritz," as he was called, spent the time peaceably, writing memoirs and histories, rehabilitating his shattered country, promoting agriculture and industry, replenishing his treasury, drilling his army, and assimilating his huge conquest of Silesia, and, after 1772, that part of Poland which fell to him in the first partition. Frederick's fame as one of the most eminent of enlightened despots rests, however, not so much on his actual innovations as on his own intellectual gifts, which were considerable, and on the admiring publicity which he received from such literary friends as Voltaire. "My chief occupation," he wrote to Voltaire, "is to fight ignorance and prejudices in this country. . . . I must enlighten my people, cultivate their manners and morals, and make them as happy as human beings can be, or as happy as the means at my disposal permit." He did not conceive that sweeping changes were necessary to happiness in Prussia. The country was docile, for its Lutheran church had long been subordinate to the state, its relatively few burghers were largely dependents of the crown, and the independence of the Junker landlords, as expressed in provincial diets, had been curtailed by Frederick's predecessors.[18] Frederick

[17] See p. 367.
[18] See pp. 225–226.

simplified and codified the many laws of the kingdom and made the law courts cheaper, more expeditious, and more honest. He kept up a wholesome and energetic tone in his civil service. He gave religious freedom, and he decreed, though he did not realize, a modicum of elementary education for all children of all classes. Prussia under Frederick was attractive enough for some 300,000 immigrants to seek it out.

But society remained stratified in a way hardly known in western Europe. Nobles, peasants, and burghers lived side by side in a kind of segregation. Each group paid different taxes and owed different duties to the state, and no person could buy property of the type pertaining to one of the other two groups. Property was legally classified, as well as persons; there was little passing from one group to another. The basic aim of these policies was military, to preserve, by keeping intact their respective forms of property, a distinct peasant class from which to draw soldiers and a distinct aristocratic class from which to draw officers. The peasants, except in the western extremities of the kingdom, were serfs holding patches of land on precarious terms in return for obligations to labor on the estates of the lords. They were likewise considered the lord's "hereditary subjects" and were not free to leave the lord's estate, to marry, or to learn a trade except with his permission. Frederick in his early years considered steps to relieve the burden of serfdom. He did relieve it on his own manors, those belonging to the Prussian crown domain, which comprised a quarter of the area of the kingdom. But he did nothing for serfs belonging to the private landlords or Junkers. No king of Prussia could fundamentally antagonize the Junker class which commanded the army. On the other hand, even in Prussia, the existence of a monarchical state was of some advantage to the common man; the serf in Prussia was not so badly off as in adjoining areas—Poland, Livonia, Mecklenburg, or Swedish Pomerania—where the will of the landlords was the law of the land, and which therefore have not inaptly been called Junker republics. In these countries cases came to light in which owners sold their serfs as movable property, or gambled or gave them away, breaking up families in the process, as Russian landlords might do with their serfs or American plantation owners with their slaves. Such abuses were unknown in Prussia.

Frederick's system was centralized not merely at Potsdam but in his own head. He himself attended to all business and made all important decisions. None of his ministers or generals ever achieved an independent reputation. As he said of his army, "no one reasons, everyone executes"—that is, no one reasoned except the king himself. Or again, as Frederick put it, if Newton had had to consult with Descartes he would never have discovered the law of universal gravitation. To have to take account of other people's ideas, or to entrust responsibilities to men less capable than himself, seemed to Frederick wasteful and anarchic. He died in 1786, after ruling forty-six years and having trained no successors. Twenty years later Prussia was all but destroyed by Napoleon.[19] It was not surprising that Napoleon should defeat Prussia, but Europe was amazed, in 1806, to see Prussia collapse totally and abruptly. It was then concluded, in Prussia and elsewhere, that government by a mastermind working in lofty and isolated superiority did not offer a viable form of state under modern conditions.

---

[19] See pp. 412–414, 417–418.

38. ENLIGHTENED DESPOTISM: RUSSIA

The Russian empire has long been out of sight in the preceding pages. There are reasons for its absence, for it played no part in the intellectual revolution of the seventeenth century, and its role in the struggle for wealth and empire, which reached a climax in the Seven Years' War, was somewhat incidental. In the Age of Enlightenment the role of Russia was passive. No Russian thinker was known to Europe. But European thinkers were well known in Russia. The French-dominated cosmopolitan culture of the European upper classes spread to the upper classes of Russia. The Russian court and aristocracy took over French as their common conversational language. With French (German was also known, and sometimes English, for the Russian aristocrats were remarkable linguists) all the ideas boiling up in western Europe streamed into Russia. The Enlightenment, if it did not affect Russia profoundly, yet affected it significantly. It continued the westernization so forcibly pushed forward by Peter and carried further the estrangement of the Russian upper classes from their own people and their own native scene.

Russia after Peter the Great

Peter the Great died in 1725.[20] To secure his revolution he had decreed that each tsar should name his successor, but he himself had named none and had put to death his own son Alexis to prevent social reaction. Peter was succeeded by his wife, a woman of peasant origin, who reigned for two years as Catherine I. Then came the boy Peter II, son of Alexis and grandson of Peter I. Peter II reigned only from 1727 to 1730. He was followed by Anna, 1730–1740; in her reign the old native Russian party tried to surround the tsardom with various constitutional checks. They failed; Anna was followed by Ivan VI, who was tsar for a few months only, during which his mother, a German woman, ran affairs according to the views of the German party in Russia, which was indispensable to the westernization program and was resented by the Russian nativists. A palace revolution in 1741 brought to the throne Peter the Great's daughter, Elizabeth, who managed to hold power until her death twenty-one years later. In her reign the military power of Russia expanded, and she entered into European diplomacy and joined in the Seven Years' War against Prussia, fearing that the continued growth of Prussia would endanger the new Russian position on the Baltic. Her nephew, Peter III, was almost immediately dethroned, and probably assassinated, by a group acting in the name of his young wife, Catherine. The victorious coterie gave it out that Peter III had been almost a half-wit, who at the age of twenty-four still played with paper soldiers. Catherine was proclaimed the Empress Catherine II and is called "the Great." She enjoyed a long reign from 1762 to 1796, during which she acquired a somewhat exaggerated reputation as an enlightened despot.

The names of the tsars and tsarinas between Peter I and Catherine II are of slight importance. But their violent and rapid sequence tells a story. With no principle of succession, dynastic or other, the empire fell into a lawless struggle of parties, in which plots against rulers while living alternated with palace

[20] See pp. 237–238.

revolutions upon their death. In all the confusion an underlying issue was always how the westernizing program of Peter would turn out. To western Europe Russia still seemed Byzantine and barbaric.

Catherine the Great (1762–1796): Domestic Program

Catherine the Great was a German woman, of a small princely house of the Holy Roman Empire. She had gone to Russia at the age of fifteen to be married. She had immediately cultivated the good will of the Russians, learned the language, and embraced the Orthodox church. Early in her married life, disgusted with her husband, she foresaw the chance of becoming empress herself. She was nothing like her feminine contemporary Maria Theresa, except possibly in having much the same practical sense. Hearty and boisterous, she wore out a long succession of many lovers, mixing them freely with politics and using them in positions of state. When she died at the age of sixty-seven, of a stroke of apoplexy, she was still living with the last of these venturesome paramours. Her intellectual powers were as remarkable as her physical vigor; even after becoming empress she often got up at five in the morning, lighted her own fire, and turned to her books, making a digest, for example, of Blackstone's *Commentaries on the Laws of England*, published in 1765. She corresponded with Voltaire and invited Diderot, editor of the *Encyclopédie*, to visit her at St. Petersburg, where, she reported, he thumped her so hard on the knee in the energy of his conversation that she had to put a table between them. She bought Diderot's library, allowing him to keep it during his lifetime, and in other ways won renown by her benefactions to the philosophes, whom she probably regarded as useful press agents for Russia. Her gifts to them were substantial, though dwarfed by the £12,000,000 she is estimated to have bestowed on her lovers.

When she first came to power she publicized an intention to make certain enlightened reforms. She summoned a great consultative assembly, called a Legislative Commission, which met in the summer of 1767. From its numerous proposals Catherine obtained a good deal of information on conditions in the country and concluded, from the profuse loyalty exhibited by the deputies, that though a usurper and a foreigner she possessed a strong hold upon Russia. The reforms which she subsequently enacted consisted in a measure of legal codification, restrictions on the use of torture, and a certain support of religious toleration, though she would not allow Old Believers to build their own chapels. Such innovations were enough to raise an admiring chorus from the philosophes, who saw in her, as they saw retrospectively in Peter the Great, the standard-bearer of civilization among a backward people. Like other enlightened despots, Catherine turned assiduously to administrative questions also. Consolidating the machinery of state, she replaced Peter's ten *gubernii* with fifty, each subdivided into districts, and all equipped with appropriate sets of governors and officials.

Whatever ideas Catherine may conceivably have had at first, as a thoughtful and progressive young woman, on the fundamental subject of reforming serfdom in Russia, did not last long after she became empress, and dissolved with the great peasant insurrection of 1773, known as Pugachev's rebellion. The condition of the Russian serfs was deteriorating. Serf owners were increasingly selling them apart from land, breaking up families, using them in mines or manufactures, disciplining and punishing them at will, or exiling them to Siberia. The serf population was restless, worked upon by Old Believers and cherishing distorted popular memories of the mighty hero, Stephen Razin, who a century before had led an uprising against the landlords.[21] Class antagonism, though latent, was profound, nor was it made less when the rough muzhik, in some places, heard the lord and his family talking French so as not to be understood by the servants or saw them wearing European clothes, reading European books, and adopting the manners of a foreign and superior way of life.

In 1773 a Don Cossack, Emelian Pugachev, a former soldier, appeared at the head of an insurrection in the Urals. Following an old Russian custom, he announced himself as the true tsar, Peter III (Catherine's deceased husband), now returned after long travels in Egypt and the Holy Land. He surrounded himself with duplicates of the imperial family, courtiers, and even a secretary of state. He issued an imperial manifesto proclaiming the end of serfdom and of taxes and military conscription. Tens and hundreds of thousands, in the Urals and Volga regions, Tartars, Kirghiz, Cossacks, agricultural serfs, servile workers in the Ural mines, fishermen in the rivers and in the Caspian Sea, flocked to Pugachev's banner. The great host surged through eastern Russia, burning and pillaging, killing priests and landlords. The upper classes in Moscow were terrified; 100,000 serfs lived in the city as domestic servants or industrial workers, and their sympathies went out to Pugachev and his horde. Armies were at first unsuccessful. But famine along the Volga in 1774 dispersed the rebels. Pugachev, betrayed by some of his own followers, was brought to Moscow in an iron cage. Catherine forbade the use of torture at his trial, but he was executed by the drawing and quartering of his body, a punishment, it should perhaps be noted, used at the time in western Europe in cases of flagrant treason.

Pugachev's rebellion was the most violent peasant uprising in the history of Russia, and the most formidable mass upheaval in Europe in the century before 1789. Catherine replied to it by repression. She conceded more powers to the landlords. The nobles shook off the last vestiges of the compulsory state service to which Peter had bound them. The peasants were henceforth the only bound or unfree class. As in Prussia, the state came more than ever to rest on an understanding between ruler and gentry, by which the gentry accepted the monarchy, with its laws, officials, army, and foreign policy, and received from it, in return, the assurance of full authority over the rural masses. Government reached down through the aristocracy and the scattered towns, but it stopped short at the manor; there the lord took over and was himself a kind of government in his own person. Under these conditions the number of serfs increased, and the load on each became more heavy. Catherine's reign saw the culmination of Russian serfdom, which now ceased to differ in any important respect from the chattel slavery to which blacks were subject in the Americas. One might read in the Moscow *Gazette* such advertisements as the following: "For sale, two plump coachmen; two girls eighteen and fifteen years, quick at manual work. Two barbers; one, twenty-one, knows how to read and write and play a musical instrument; the other can do ladies' and gentlemen's hair."

Catherine the Great: Foreign Affairs

Territorially Catherine was one of the main builders of Russia. When she became tsarina in 1762 the empire reached to the Pacific and into central Asia, and it

[21] See p. 231.

touched upon the Gulf of Riga and the Gulf of Finland on the Baltic, but westward from Moscow one could go only 200 miles before reaching Poland, and no one standing on Russian soil could see the waters of the Black Sea.[22] Russia was separated from central Europe by a wide band of loosely organized domains, extending from the Baltic to the Black Sea and the Mediterranean and nominally belonging to the Polish and Turkish states. Poland was an old enemy, which had once threatened Muscovy, and in both Poland and the Ottoman Empire there were many Greek Orthodox Christians with whom Russians felt an ideological tie. In western Europe the disposal of the whole Polish-Turkish tract, which stretched through Asia Minor, Syria, and Palestine into Egypt, came to be called the Eastern Question. Though the name went out of use after 1900, the question itself has never ceased to exist.

Catherine's supreme plan was to penetrate the entire area, Polish and Turkish alike. In a war with Turkey in 1768 she developed her "Greek project," in which "Greeks," i.e., members of the Greek Orthodox Church, would replace Muslims as the dominant element throughout the Middle East. She defeated the Turks in the war, but was herself checked by the diplomatic pressures of the European balance of power. The result, as has been explained, was the first partition of Poland.[23] The three eastern monarchs began to divide up the territory between them. Frederick took Pomerelia, which he renamed West Prussia; Catherine took parts of White Russia; Maria Theresa, Galicia. Frederick digested his portion with relish, realizing an old dream of the Brandenburg house; Catherine swallowed hers with somewhat less appetite, since she had satisfactorily controlled the whole of Poland before; to Maria Theresa the dish was distasteful, and even shocking, but she could not see her neighbors go ahead without her, and she shared in the feast by suppressing her moral scruples. "She wept," said Frederick cynically, "but she kept on taking." Catherine, in 1774, signed a peace treaty with the defeated Turks at Kuchuk Kainarji on the Danube. The sultan ceded his rights over the Tartar principalities on the north coast of the Black Sea, where the Russians soon founded the seaport of Odessa.

Catherine had only delayed, not altered, her plans with respect to Turkey. She decided to neutralize the opposition of Austria. She invited Joseph II to visit her in Russia, and the two sovereigns proceeded together on a tour of her newly won Black Sea provinces. Her favorite of the moment, Potemkin, constructed artificial one-street villages along their way and produced throngs of cheering and happy-looking villagers to greet them, all of which enriched mankind with nothing except the phrase "Potemkin villages" to mean bogus evidence of a nonexistent prosperity. At Kherson the two monarchs passed through a gate marked "The Road to Byzantium." "What I want is Silesia," said Joseph II, but the tsarina induced him to join in a war of conquest against Turkey. This war was interrupted by the French Revolution. Both governments reduced their commitments in the Balkans to await developments in western Europe. It became Catherine's policy to incite Austria and Prussia into a war with revolutionary France, in the name of monarchy and civilization, in order that she might have a free hand in the Polish-Turkish sphere.[24] Meanwhile she contributed to killing off the nationalist and reforming movement among the Poles. In 1793 she arranged with Prussia for the

[22] See map, pp. 234–235.
[23] See pp. 238–240.
[24] See pp. 367–368.

POLAND SINCE THE EIGHTEENTH CENTURY

The top right panel shows, in simplified form, the ethnic composition of the area included in the great Poland of 1772. In addition to languages shown, Yiddish was spoken by the large scattered Jewish population. Note how the line set in 1795 as the western boundary of Russia persists through later transformations. It reappears as the eastern border of Napoleon's Grand Duchy (pp. 398–401), and of Congress Poland (pp. 422–423). After the First World War the victorious Allies contemplated much this same line as Poland's eastern frontier (the dotted line in the fourth panel, known as the Curzon Line); but the Poles in 1920–1921 conquered territory farther east (p. 715). After the Second World War the Russians pushed the Poles back to the same basic line, but compensated Poland with territory taken from Germany, as far west as the river Oder and its tributary, the Neisse. If the reader will compare the position of Warsaw in each panel he will see how Poland has been shoved westward.

second partition, and in 1795, with both Prussia and Austria, for the third. She was the only ruler who lived to take part in all three partitions of Poland.

Many advanced thinkers of the day praised the partitions of Poland as a triumph of enlightened rulers, putting an end to an old nuisance. The three partitioning powers extenuated their conduct on various grounds, and even took pride in it as a diplomatic achievement by which war was prevented between them. What seemed to be robbery was justified by the argument that the gains were equal; this was the diplomatic doctrine of "compensation." It was argued also that the partitions of Poland put an end to an old cause of international rivalry and war, replacing anarchy with solid government in a large area of eastern Europe. It is a fact that Poland had been scarcely more independent before the partitions than after. It is to be noted also, though nationalist arguments were not used at the time, that on national grounds the Poles themselves had no claim to large parts of the old Poland. The regions taken by Russia, in all three partitions, were inhabited overwhelmingly by White Russians and Ukrainians, among whom the Poles were mainly a landlord class. Russia, even in the third partition, reached only to the true ethnic border of Poland. But later, after the fall of Napoleon, by general international agreement, the Russian sphere was extended deep into the territory inhabited by Poles.

The partitions of Poland, however extenuated, were nevertheless a great shock to the old system of Europe. Edmund Burke, in England, prophetically saw in the first partition the crumbling of the old international order. His diagnosis was a shrewd one. The principle of the balance of power had been historically invoked to preserve the independence of European states, to secure weak or small ones against universal monarchy. It was now used to destroy the independence of a weak but ancient kingdom. Not that Poland was the first to be "partitioned"; the Spanish and Swedish empires had been partitioned, and during the eighteenth century there were attempts to partition Prussia and the Austrian empire also. But Poland was the first to be partitioned without war and the first to disappear totally. That Poland was partitioned without war, a source of great satisfaction to the partitioning powers, was still a very unsettling fact. It was alarming for a huge state to vanish simply by cold diplomatic calculation. It seemed that no established rights were safe even in peacetime. The partitions of Poland showed that in a world where great powers had arisen, controlling modern apparatus of state, it was dangerous not to be strong. They suggested that any area failing to develop a sovereign state capable of keeping out foreign infiltration, and so situated as to be reached by the great powers of Europe, was unlikely to retain its independence. In this way they anticipated, for example, the partitions of Africa a century later, when Africa too, lacking strong governments, was almost totally divided, without war, among half a dozen states of Europe.

Moreover the partitions of Poland, while maintaining the balance in eastern Europe, profoundly changed the balance of Europe as a whole. The disappearance of Poland was a blow to France, which had long used Poland, as it had used Hungary and Turkey, as an outpost of French influence in the East. The three Eastern powers expanded their territory, while France enjoyed henceforth no permanent growth. Eastern Europe bulked larger than ever before in the affairs of Europe. Prussia, Russia, and the Austrian empire became contiguous. They had an interest in common, the repression of Polish resistance to their rule. Polish resistance, dating from before the partitions and continuing after them, was the earliest example of modern revolutionary nationalism in Europe. The independence of Poland, and of other submerged nationalities, became in time a cause much favored in western Europe, while the three great monarchies of eastern Europe were drawn together in common opposition to national liberation; and this fact, plus the fact that the eastern monarchies were primarily landlord states, accentuated the characteristic division of Europe, in the nineteenth century, between a West that inclined to be liberal and an East that inclined to be reactionary. But these ideas anticipate a later part of the story.

As for Catherine, her own protestations of enlightenment tempt one to an ironic judgment of her career. Her foreign policy was purely expansionist and unscrupulous, and the net effect of her domestic policy, aside from a few reforms of detail, was to favor the half-Europeanized aristocracy and to extend serfdom among the people. In her defense it may be observed that unscrupulous expansion was the accepted practice of the time, and that, domestically, probably no ruler could have corrected the social evils from which Russia suffered. If there was to be a Russian empire it had to be with the consent of the serf-owning gentry, which was the only politically significant class. As Catherine observed to Diderot on the subject of reforms: "You write only on paper, but I have to write on human skin, which is incomparably more irritable and ticklish." She had reason to know how easily tsars and tsarinas could be unseated and even murdered, and that the danger of overthrow came not from the peasants but from cliques of army officers and landlords.

She remained attuned to the West. She never thought that the peculiar institutions of Russia should become a model for others. She continued to recognize the standards of the Enlightenment at least as standards. In her later years she gave careful attention to her favorite grandson, Alexander, closely supervising his education, which she planned on the Western model. She gave him as a tutor the Swiss philosophe La Harpe, who filled his mind with humane and liberal sentiments on the duties of princes. Trained by Catherine as a kind of ideal ruler, Alexander I was destined to cut a wide circle in the affairs of Europe, to defeat Napoleon Bonaparte, preach peace and freedom, and suffer from the same internal divisions and frustrations by which educated Russians seemed characteristically to be afflicted.

The Limitations of Enlightened Despotism

Enlightened despotism, seen in retrospect, foreshadowed an age of revolution and even signified a preliminary effort to revolutionize society by authoritative action from above. People were told by their own governments that reforms were needed, that many privileges, special liberties, or tax exemptions were bad, that the past was a source of confusion, injustice, or inefficiency in the present. The state rose up as more completely sovereign, whether acting frankly in its own interest or claiming to act in the interest of its people. All old and established rights were brought into question—rights of kingdoms and provinces, orders and classes, legal bodies and corporate groups. Enlightened despotism overrode or exterminated the Society of Jesus, the Parlement of Paris, the autonomy of Bohemia, and the independence of Poland. Customary and common law was pushed aside by authoritative legal codes. Governments, by opposing the special powers of the church and the feudal interests, tended to make all persons into uniform and equal subjects. To this extent enlightened despotism favored equality before the law. But it could go only a certain distance in this direction. The king was after all a hereditary aristocrat himself, and no government can be revolutionary to the point of breaking up its own foundations.

Even before the French Revolution enlightened despotism had run its course. Everywhere the "despots," for reasons of politics if not of principle, had reached a point beyond which they could not go. In France Louis XVI had appeased the privileged classes, in the Austrian empire Joseph's failure to appease them threw them into open revolt, in Prussia and in Russia the brilliant reigns of Frederick and Catherine wound up in an aggravation of landlordism for the mass of the people. Almost everywhere there was an aristocratic and even feudal revival. Religion also was renewing itself in many ways. Many were again saying that kingship was in a sense divine, and a new alliance was forming between "the throne and the altar." The French Revolution, by terrifying the old vested interests, was to accelerate and embitter a reaction which had already begun. Monarchy in Europe, ever since the Middle Ages, had generally been a progressive institution, acting along the line that Europe seemed destined to take, and in any case setting itself against the feudal and ecclesiastical powers. Enlightened despotism was the culmination of the historic institution of monarchy. After the enlightened despots, and after the French Revolution, monarchy became on the whole nostalgic and backward-looking, supported most ardently by the churches and aristocracies that it had once tried to subdue and least of all by those who felt in themselves the surge of the future.

39. NEW STIRRINGS: THE BRITISH REFORM MOVEMENT

It was not only by monarchs and their ministers, however, that the older privileged, feudal, and ecclesiastical interests were threatened. Beginning about 1760 they were challenged also in more popular quarters. Growing out of the Enlightenment, and out of the failure of governments to cope with grave social and fiscal problems, a new era of revolutionary disturbance was about to open. It was marked above all by the great French Revolution of 1789, but the American Revolution of 1776 was also of international importance. In Great Britain, too, the long-drawn-out movement for parliamentary reform which began in the 1760s was in effect revolutionary in character, though nonviolent, since it questioned the foundations of traditional English government and society. In addition, in the last third of the eighteenth century, there was revolutionary agitation in Switzerland, Belgium, and Holland, in Ireland, Poland, Hungary, Italy, and in lesser degree elsewhere. After 1800 revolutionary ferment was increasingly evident in Germany, Spain, and Latin America. This general wave of revolution may be said not to have ended until after the revolutions of 1848.

Onset of an Age of "Democratic Revolution"

For the whole period the term "Atlantic Revolution" has sometimes been used, since countries on both sides of the Atlantic were affected. It has been called also an age of "Democratic Revolution," since in all the diversity of these upheavals, from the American Revolution to those of 1848, certain principles of the modern democratic society were in one way or another affirmed. In this view, the particular revolutions, attempted revolutions, or basic reform movements are seen as aspects of one great revolutionary wave by which virtually the whole area of Western civilization was transformed. The contrary is also maintained, namely, that each country presented a special case, which is misunderstood if viewed only as part of a vague general international turmoil. Thus the American Revolution, it is argued, was essentially a movement for independence, even essentially conservative in its objectives, and thus entirely different from the French Revolution, in which a thorough renovation of all society and ideas were contemplated; and both were utterly different from what happened in England, where there was no revolution at all. There is truth in both contentions, and it need only be affirmed here that the American revolutionaries, the French Jacobins, the United Irish, the Dutch Patriots, and similar groups elsewhere, though differing from each other, yet shared much in common that can only be characterized as revolutionary and as contributing to a revolutionary age.

It is important to see in what ways the movement that began about 1760 was and was not "democratic." It did not generally demand universal suffrage, though a handful of persons in England did so as early as the 1770s and some of the American states practiced an almost universal male suffrage after 1776, as did the more militant French revolutionaries in 1792. It did not aim at a welfare state, nor question the right of property, though there were signs pointing in these directions in the extreme wing of the French Revolution. It was not especially directed against monarchy as such. The quarrel of the Americans was primarily with the British Parliament, not the king; the French proclaimed a republic by default in 1792, three years after their revolution began; the revolutionary Poles after 1788 tried to strengthen their king's position, not weaken it; and revolutionary groups could come into action where no monarchy existed at all, as in the Dutch provinces before the French Revolution, and the Swiss cantons, the Venetian Republic, or again in Holland, under French influence after 1795. Indeed the first revolutionary outbreak of the period occurred in 1768 at Geneva, a very nonmonarchical small city-republic, ruled by a close-knit circle of hereditary patricians. Royal power, where it existed, became the victim of revolutionaries only where it was used to support various privileged social groups.

The revolutionary movement announced itself everywhere as a demand for "liberty and equality." It favored declarations of rights and explicit written constitutions. It proclaimed the sovereignty of the people, or "nation," and it formulated the idea of national citizenship. In this context the "people" were essentially classless; it was a legal term, the obverse of government, signifying the community over which public authority was exercised and from which government itself was in principle derived. To say that citizens were equal meant originally that there was no difference between noble and common. To say that the people were sovereign meant that neither the king, nor the British Parliament, nor any group of nobles, patricians, regents, or other elite possessed power of government in their own right; that all public officers were removable and exercised a delegated authority within limits defined by the constitution. There must be no "magistrate" above the people, no self-perpetuation or cooptation in office, no rank derived from birth and acknowledged in the law. Social distinctions, as the French said in their Declaration of Rights of 1789, were to be based only "on common utility." Elites of talent or function there might be, but none of birth, privilege, or estate. "Aristocracy" in every form must be shunned. In representative bodies, there could be no special representation for special groups; representatives should be elected by frequent elections, not indeed usually by universal suffrage, but by a body of voters, however defined, in which each voter should count for one in a system of equal representation. Representation by numbers, with majority rule, replaced the older idea of representation of social classes, privileged towns, or other corporate groups.

In short, everything associated with absolutism, feudalism, or inherited right (except the right of property) was repudiated. Likewise rejected was any connection between religion and citizenship, or civil rights. The Democratic Revolution undermined the special position of the Catholic church in France, the Anglican in England and Ireland, the Dutch Reformed in the United Provinces; this was also the great period of what has been called Jewish "emancipation." The whole idea that government, or any human authority, was somehow willed by God and protected by religion faded away. A general liberty of opinion on all subjects was countenanced, in the belief that it was necessary to progress. Here again the secularism of the Enlightenment carried on.

On the whole, the Democratic Revolution was a middle-class movement, and indeed the term "bourgeois revolution" was later invented to describe it. Many of its leaders in Europe were in fact nobles who were willing to forgo the historic privileges of nobility; and many of its supporters were of the poorer classes, especially in the great French Revolution. But the middle classes were the great beneficiaries, and it was a kind of middle-class or bourgeois society that emerged. Persons of noble ancestry continued to exist after the storm was over, but the world of noble values was gone; and they either took part in various activities on much the same terms as others or retreated into exclusive drawing rooms to enjoy their aristocratic distinctions in private. The main drive of the working classes was still to come.

The English-Speaking Countries: Parliament and Reform

If the American Revolution was the first act of a larger drama, it must be understood also in connection with the broader British world of which the American colonies formed a part. The British Empire in the middle of the century was decentralized and composite. Thirty-one governments were directly subordinate to Westminster, ranging from the separate kingdom of Ireland through all the crown and charter colonies to the various political establishments maintained in the East by the East India Company. The whole empire, with about 15,000,000 people of all colors in 1750, was less populous than France or the Austrian monarchy. The whole tract of the American mainland from Georgia to Nova Scotia compared in the number of its white population with Ireland or Scotland—or with Brittany or Bohemia—a figure of about 2,000,000 being roughly applicable in each case.

England had its own way of passing through the Age of Enlightenment. There was general contentment with the arrangements that followed the English Revolution of 1688—it has often been remarked that nothing is so conservative as a successful revolution.[25] British thought lacked the asperity of thought on the Con-

[25] See pp. 173–177.

tinent. The writers who most resembled French philosophes, such as Hume and Gibbon, were innocuously moderate in their political ideas. The prevailing mood was one of complacency, a self-satisfaction in the glories of the British constitution, by which Englishmen enjoyed liberties unknown on the Continent.

In Britain, Parliament was supreme, as in most Continental countries, the monarch. It had the power, as one facetious journalist put it, to do all things except change a man into a woman. The British Parliament was as sovereign as any European ruler, and indeed more so, since less that could be called feudalism remained in England than on the Continent. Nor was there any "despotism" in England, enlightened or otherwise. The young George III, who inherited the throne in 1760, did feel himself to be a "patriot king." He did wish to heighten the influence of the crown and to overcome the factionalism of parties.[26] But it was through Parliament that he had to work. He had to descend into the political arena himself, buy up or otherwise control votes in the Commons, grant pensions and favors, and make promises and deals with other parliamentary politicians. What he did in effect was to create a new faction, the "king's friends." This faction was in power during the ministry of Lord North from 1770 to 1782. It is worth noting that all factions were factions of Whigs, that the Tory party was practically defunct, that Britain did not yet have a two-party system, and that the word "Tory," as it came to be used by American revolutionaries, was little more than a term of abuse.

While Parliament was supreme, and constitutional questions apparently settled, there were nevertheless numerous undercurrents of discontent. These were expressed, since the press was freer in England than elsewhere, in many books and pamphlets which were read in the American colonies and helped to form the psychology of the American Revolution. There was, for example, a school of Anglo-Irish Protestant writers, who argued that since Ireland was in any case a separate kingdom, with its own parliament, it ought to be less dependent on the central government at Westminster. The possibility of a similar separate kingdom, remaining within the British Empire, was one of the alternatives considered

[26] See pp. 257–259.

THE HON. MRS. GRAHAM
by Thomas Gainsborough (English, 1727–1788)

This picture and the three following, on pp. 343, 371, and 374, suggest what is meant by the four basic classes of preindustrial society—aristocracy, middle class, urban workers, and peasantry. High social status is very evident in this portrayal of a young gentlewoman, whose title, "The Honorable," is still used in Great Britain for the daughters of viscounts and barons. Wealth is apparent in the brooch, the plumes, the silks, bows and ruffles, and in the pearls which are both worn in strings and sewn on the hat and garments. The meticulous coiffure and complexities of dress suggest the constant attention of lady's maids. The tall stature, delicate hands, refined mouth and haughty expression all reveal high breeding, and the classical colonnade on which the lady so casually rests her arm lends an air of familiarity with magnificent surroundings. Perhaps the aristocrats of the eighteenth century did not often look like this, but this is the way they liked to imagine themselves and to be portrayed for posterity. In Gainsborough, Sir Joshua Reynolds, and Sir Thomas Lawrence, England had an unparalleled group of artists who specialized in painting the upper class. Courtesy of the National Gallery of Scotland.

by Americans before they settled on independence. In England there was the considerable body of Dissenters, or Protestants not accepting the Church of England, who had enjoyed religious toleration since 1689 but continued to labor (until 1828) under various forms of political exclusion. They overlapped with two other amorphous groups, a small number of "commonwealthmen" and a larger and growing number of parliamentary reformers. The commonwealthmen, increasingly eccentric and largely ignored, looked back nostalgically to the Puritan Revolution and the republican era of Oliver Cromwell.[27] They kept alive memories of the Levellers and ideals of equality, well mixed with a pseudo-history of a simple Anglo-Saxon England that had been crushed by the despotism of the Norman Conquest. The commonwealthmen had less influence in England than in the American colonies and especially New England, which had originated in close connection with the Puritan Revolution. The parliamentary reformers were a more diverse and influential group. They were condemned in the eighteenth century to repeated frustration; not until the First Reform Bill of 1832 was anything accomplished.

The very power of Parliament meant that political leaders had to take strong measures to assure its votes. These measures were generally denounced by their critics as "corruption," on the grounds that Parliament, whether or not truly representative, should at least be free. Control of Parliament, and especially of the House of Commons, was assured by various devices, such as patronage or the giving of government jobs (called "places"), or awarding contracts, or having infrequent general elections (every seven years after 1716); or the fact that in many constituencies there were no real elections at all. The distribution of seats in the Commons bore no relation to numbers of inhabitants. A town having the right to send members to Parliament was called a "borough," but no new borough was created after 1688 (or until 1832). Thus localities that had been important in the medieval or Tudor periods were represented, but towns that had grown up recently, such as Manchester and Birmingham, were not. A few boroughs were populous and democratic, but many had few inhabitants or none, so that influential "borough mongers" decided who should represent them in Parliament.

The reform movement began in England before the American Revolution, with which it was closely associated. Since complaints were diverse, it attracted people of different kinds. The first agitation centered about John Wilkes. Having attacked the policies of George III, been vindicated when the courts pronounced the arrest of his publisher illegal, and been expelled by a House of Commons dominated by the king's supporters, Wilkes became a hero and was three times reelected to the House, which, however, refused to seat him. In a whirl of protests and public meetings, reams of petitions supported him against the House. His followers in 1769 founded the Supporters of the Bill of Rights, the first of many societies dedicated to parliamentary reform. His case raised the question of whether the House of Commons should be dependent on the electorate and the propriety of mass agitation "out of doors" on political questions. It was in this connection, also, that debates in Parliament for the first time came to be reported in the London press. Parliament stood on the eve of a long transition, by which it was to be converted from a select body meeting in private to a modern representative institution answerable to the public and its constituents. Wilkes himself, in 1776, introduced

[27] See pp. 169–171.

the first of many reform bills of which none passed for over half a century. Meanwhile Major John Cartwright, called the "father of reform," had begun a long series of pamphlets on the subject; he lived to be eighty-four but not quite long enough to see the Reform Act of 1832. Dissenting intellectuals, such as Richard Price and Joseph Priestley, joined in the movement. Price, a founder of actuarial statistics, announced in 1776 that only 5,723 persons chose half the membership of the House of Commons. Many London merchants favored reform. So did a great many landowners and country gentry, especially in the north of England, led by Christopher Wyvil. These men objected to the fact that four-fifths of the members of the House of Commons sat for the boroughs and only one-fifth for the shires or counties. They rightly thought that the boroughs were more easily manipulated by the government; they thought that county elections were more honest; and they initiated in 1780 a movement of county associations to promote change in the electoral system.

The important Whig leaders, who had previously managed Parliament by much the same methods, began to sense "corruption" after control passed to George III and his "friends." Their most eloquent spokesman was Edmund Burke. Other reformers called for more frequent elections, "annual parliaments," a wider and more equal or even universal male suffrage, with dissolution of some boroughs in which no one was really represented. Burke favored none of these things; in fact he came strenuously to oppose them. A founder of philosophical conservatism, he was yet in his way a reformer. He was more concerned that the House of Commons should be independent and responsible than that it should be mathematically representative. He thought that the landowning interest should govern. But he pleaded for a strong sense of party in opposition to royal encroachments, and he argued that members of Parliament should follow their own best judgment of the country's interests, bound neither by the king on the one hand nor by their own constituents on the other. Like other reformers, he objected to "placemen," or jobholders dependent on their ministerial patrons, and he objected to the use made, for political purposes, of a bewildering array of pensions, sinecures, honorific appointments, and ornamental offices, ranks, and titles. In his Economical Reform of 1782 he got many of these abolished.

The reform movement, though ineffectual, remained strong. Even William Pitt, as prime minister in the 1780s, gave it his sponsorship. It took on new strength at the time of the French Revolution, spreading then to more popular levels, as men of the skilled artisan class were aroused by events in France and demanded a more adequate "representation of the people" in England. They then had upper-class support from Charles James Fox and a minority of the Whigs. But conservatism, satisfaction with the British constitution, patriotism engendered by a new round of French wars, and reaction against the French Revolution all raised an impassable barrier. Reform was delayed for another generation.

After the American Revolution, which in a way was a civil struggle within the English-speaking world, the English reformers generally blamed the trouble with America on King George III. This was less than fair, since Parliament on the American question was never dragooned by the king. The most ardent reformers later argued that if Parliament had been truly representative of the British people, the Americans would not have been driven to independence. This seems unlikely. In any case, reformers of various kinds, from Wilkes to Burke, were sympathetic to the complaints of the American colonials after 1763. There was much busy correspondence across the Atlantic. Wilkes was a hero in Boston as well as London. Burke pleaded for conciliation with the colonies in a famous speech of 1775. His very insistence on the powers and dignity of Parliament, however, made it hard for him to find a workable solution; and after the colonies became independent he showed no interest in the political ideas of the new American states. It was the more radical reformers in England, as in Scotland and Ireland, who most consistently favored the Americans, both before and after independence. They of course had no power. On the American side, for a decade before independence, the increasingly discontented colonials, reading English books and pamphlets and reports of speeches, heard George III denounced for despotism and Parliament accused of incorrigible corruption. All this seemed to confirm what Americans had long been reading anyway in the works of English Dissenters or old commonwealthmen, now on the fringes of English society but sure of a receptive audience in the American colonies. The result was to make Americans suspicious of all actions by the British government, to sense tyranny everywhere, to magnify such things as the Stamp Act into a kind of plot against American liberties.

The real drift in England in the eighteenth century, however, despite the chronic criticism of Parliament, was for Parliament to extend its powers in a general centralization of the empire. The British government faced somewhat the same problems as governments on the Continent. All had to deal with the issues raised by the great war of the mid-century, in its two phases of the Austrian Succession and Seven Years' War. Everywhere the solution adopted by governments was to increase their own central power. We have seen how the French government, in attempting to tap new sources of revenue, tried to encroach on the liberties of Brittany and other provinces and to subordinate the bodies which in France were called parlements. We have likewise seen how the Habsburg government, also in an effort to raise more taxes, repressed local self-government in the empire and even abrogated the constitution of Bohemia.[28] The same tendency showed itself in the British system. The revocation of the charter of Bohemia in 1749 had its parallel in the revocation of the charter of Massachusetts in 1774. The disputes of the French king with the estates of Brittany or Languedoc had their parallel in the disputes of the British Parliament with the provincial assemblies of Virginia or New York.

Scotland, Ireland, India

There were also problems nearer home. Scotland proved a source of weakness in the War of the Austrian Succession. The Lowlanders were loyal enough, but the Highlanders revolted with French assistance in the Jacobite rising of 1745, and by invading England threatened to take the British government in the rear as it was locked in the struggle with France.[29] The Highlands had never really been under any government, even under the old Scottish monarchy before the union of 1707 with England. Social organization, in the Highland fastnesses, followed the primitive principle of physical kinship. Men looked to their chiefs, the heads of the clans, to tell them whom and when to fight. The chiefs had hereditary jurisdiction, often including powers of life and death, over their clansmen. A few leaders could throw the whole region to the Stuarts or the French. The British govern-

[28] See pp. 315–318, 318–319.
[29] See pp. 258–259.

ment, after 1745, proceeded to make its sovereignty effective in the Highlands. Troops were quartered there for years. Roads were pushed across the moors and through the glens. Law courts enforced the law of the Scottish Lowlands. Revenue officers collected funds for the treasury of Great Britain. The chiefs lost their old quasi-feudal jurisdiction. The old system of land tenure was broken up. The holding of land from clannish chiefs was ended. The clansman swayed by his chief was turned into the subject of the crown of Great Britain. He was turned also, in many cases, into an almost landless "crofter," while some of the chiefs, or their sons, emerged as landed gentlemen of the English type. Fighting Highlanders were incorporated into newly formed Highland regiments of the British army, under the usual discipline imposed by the modern state on its fighting forces. For thirty years the Scots were forbidden to wear the kilt or play the bagpipes.

In Ireland the process of centralization worked itself out more slowly. How Ireland was subjected after the battle of the Boyne has already been described.[30] It was a French army that had landed in Ireland, supported James II and been defeated in 1690. The new English constitutional arrangements, the Hanoverian succession, the Protestant ascendancy, the church and the land settlement in Ireland, together with the prosperity of British commerce, were all secured by the subordination of the smaller island. The native or Catholic Irish remained generally pro-French. The Presbyterian Irish disliked both Frenchmen and popery, but they were alienated from England also; many in fact emigrated to America in the generation before the American Revolution. The island remained quiet in the mid-century wars. When the trouble began between the British Parliament and the American colonies the Presbyterian Irish generally took the American side. They were greatly stirred by the example of American independence. Thousands formed themselves into Volunteer Companies; they wore uniforms, armed, and drilled; they demanded both internal reform of the Irish parliament (which was even less representative than the British) and greater autonomy for the Irish parliament as against the central government at Westminster. Faced with these demands, and fearing a French invasion of Ireland during the War of American Independence, the British government made concessions. It allowed an increase of power to the Irish parliament at Dublin. But from this parliament Catholics were still excluded. In the next war between France and Great Britain, which began in 1793, many Irish felt a warm sympathy for the French Revolution. Catholics and Presbyterians, at last combining, formed a network of United Irish societies throughout the whole island. They sought French aid, and the French barely failed to land a sizable army. Even without French military support, the United Irish rose in 1798 to drive out the English and establish an independent republic. The British, suppressing the rebellion, now turned to centralization. The separate kingdom of Ireland, and the Irish parliament, ceased to exist. The Irish were thereafter represented in the imperial Parliament at Westminster. These provisions were incorporated in the Act of Union of 1801, creating the United Kingdom of Great Britain and Ireland, which lasted until 1922.

British establishments in India also felt the hand of Parliament increasingly upon them. At the close of the Seven Years' War the various British posts in and around Bombay, Madras, and Calcutta were unconnected with each other and subordinate only to the board of directors of the East India Company in London.

---

[30] See pp. 175–176.

Company employees interfered at will in the wars and politics of the Indian states and enriched themselves by such means as they could, not excluding graft, trickery, intimidation, rapine, and extortion.[31] In 1773 the ministry of Lord North passed a Regulating Act, of which the main purpose was to regulate, not Indians, but the British subjects in India, whom no Indian government could control. The company was left with its trading activities, but its political activities were brought under parliamentary supervision. The act gathered all the British establishments under a single governor general, set up a new supreme court at Calcutta, and required the company to submit its correspondence on political matters for review by the ministers of His Majesty's Government. Warren Hastings became the first British governor general in India. He was so high-handed with some of the Indian princes, and made so many enemies among jealous Englishmen in Bengal, that he was denounced at home, impeached, and subjected to a trial which dragged on for seven years in the House of Lords. He was finally acquitted. After Clive, he was the main author of British supremacy in India. Meanwhile, in 1784 an India office was created in the British ministry at home. The governor general henceforth ruled the growing British sphere in India almost as an absolute monarch but only as the agent of the ministry and Parliament of Great Britain.

Thus the trend in the British world was to centralization. Despite the flutter of royalism under George III, it was to a centralization of all British territories under authority of the Parliament. What was happening in empire affairs, as in domestic politics in England, was a continuing application of the principles of 1689. The parliamentary sovereignty established in 1689 was now, after the middle of the eighteenth century, being applied to regions where it had heretofore had little effect. And it was against the British Parliament that the Americans primarily rebelled.

40. THE AMERICAN REVOLUTION

Background to the Revolution

The behavior of the Americans in the Seven Years' War left much to be desired.[32] The several colonial legislatures rejected the Albany Plan of Union drafted by Franklin and commended to them by the British officials. During the war it was the British regular army and navy, financed by taxes and loans in Great Britain, that drove the French out of America. The war effort of the Anglo-Americans was desultory at best. After the defeat of the French the colonials had still to reckon with the Indians of the interior, who preferred French rule to that of their new British and British-colonial masters. Many tribes joined in an uprising led by Pontiac, a western chief, and they ravaged as far eastward as the Pennsylvania and Virginia frontiers. Again, the colonials proved unable to deal with a problem vital to their own future, and peace was brought about by officials and army units taking their orders from Great Britain.

The British government tried to make the colonials pay a larger share toward the expenses of the empire. The colonials had hitherto paid only local taxes. They

[31] See pp. 272–273.
[32] See pp. 269–270.

were liable to customs duties, of which the proceeds went in principle to Great Britain; but these duties were levied to enforce the Acts of Trade and Navigation, to direct the flow of commerce, not to raise revenue; and they were seldom paid, because the Acts of Trade and Navigation were persistently ignored. American merchants, for example, commonly imported sugar from the French West Indies, contrary to law, and even shipped in return the iron wares which it was against the law for Americans to manufacture for export. The colonial in practice paid only such taxes as were approved by his own local legislature for local purposes. The Americans in effect enjoyed a degree of tax exemption within the empire, and it was against this form of provincial privilege that Parliament began to move.

By the Revenue Act of 1764 (the "Sugar" Act), the British ministry, while reducing and liberalizing the customs duties payable in America, entered upon a program of actual and systematic collection. In the following year the ministry attempted to extend to British subjects in America a tax peaceably accepted by those in Great Britain and commonplace in most of Europe. This imposed on all uses of paper, as in newspapers and commercial and legal documents, the payment of a fee which was certified by the affixing of a stamp. The Stamp Act aroused violent and concerted resistance in the colonies, especially among the businessmen, lawyers, and editors who were the most articulate class. It therefore was repealed in 1766. In 1767 Parliament, clumsily casting about to find a tax acceptable to the Americans, hit upon the "Townshend duties," which taxed colonial imports of paper, paint, lead, and tea. Another outcry went up, and the Townshend duties were repealed, except the one on tea, which was kept as a token of the sovereign power of Parliament to tax all persons in the empire.

The colonials had proved stubborn, the government pliable but lacking in constructive ideas. The Americans argued that Parliament had no authority to tax them because they were not represented in it. The British replied that Parliament represented America as much as it represented Great Britain. If Philadelphia sent no actually elected deputies to the Commons, so this argument ran, neither did Manchester in England, yet both places enjoyed a "virtual representation," since members of the Commons did not in any case merely speak for local constituencies but made themselves responsible for imperial interests as a whole. To this many Americans retorted that if Manchester was not "really" represented it ought to be, which was of course also the belief of the English reformers. Meanwhile the strictly Anglo-American question subsided after the repeal of the Stamp Act and the Townshend program. There had been no clarification of principle on either side. But in practice the Americans had resisted significant taxation, and Parliament had refrained from making any drastic use of its sovereign power.

The calm was shattered in 1773 by an event which proved, to the more dissatisfied Americans, the disadvantages of belonging to a global economic system in which the main policies were made on the other side of the ocean. The East India Company was in difficulties. It had a great surplus of Chinese tea,[33] and in any case it wanted new commercial privileges in return for the political privileges which it was losing by the Regulating Act of 1773. In the past the company had been required to sell its wares at public auction in London; other merchants had handled distribution from that point on. Now, in 1773, Parliament granted the company the exclusive right to sell tea through its own agents in America to

[33] See p. 251.

American local dealers. Tea was a large item of business in the commercial capitalism of the time. The colonial consumer might pay less for it, but the intermediary American merchant would be shut out. The company's tea was boycotted in all American ports. In Boston, to prevent its forcible landing, a party of disguised men invaded the tea ships and dumped the chests into the harbor. To this act of vandalism the British government replied by measures far out of proportion to the offense. It "closed" the port of Boston, thus threatening the city with economic ruin. It virtually rescinded the charter of Massachusetts, forbidding certain local elections and the holding of town meetings.

And at the same time, in 1774, apparently by coincidence, Parliament enacted the Quebec Act. The wisest piece of British legislation in these troubled years, the Quebec Act provided a government for the newly conquered Canadian French, granting them security in their French civil law and Catholic religion, and laying foundations for the British Empire that was to come. But the act defined the boundaries of Quebec somewhat as the French themselves would have defined them, including in them all territory north of the Ohio River—the present states of Wisconsin, Michigan, Illinois, Indiana, and Ohio. These boundaries were perfectly reasonable, since the few white men in the area were French, and since, in the age before canals or railways, the obvious means of reaching the whole region was by way of the St. Lawrence valley and the Lakes. But to the Americans the Quebec Act was a pro-French and pro-Catholic outrage, and at a time when the powers of juries and assemblies in the old colonies were threatened, it was disquieting that the Quebec Act made no mention of such representative institutions for the new northern province. It was lumped with the closing of an American port and the destruction of the Massachusetts government as one of the "Intolerable Acts" to be resisted.

And indeed the implications of parliamentary sovereignty were now apparent. The meaning of centralized planning and authority was now clear. It was no longer merely an affair of taxation. A government that had to take account of the East India Company, the French Canadians, and the British taxpayers, even if more prudent and enlightened than Lord North's ministry of 1774, could not possibly at the same time have satisfied the Americans of the thirteen seaboard colonies. These Americans, since 1763 no longer afraid of the French empire, were less inclined to forgo their own interests in order to remain in the British. British

MRS. ISAAC SMITH
by John Singleton Copley (American, then English, 1737–1815)

Mrs. Smith may be contrasted with the more aristocratic Mrs. Graham, shown on p. 335. The wife of a Boston merchant, she and her husband both had their portraits painted by Copley in 1769. The picture may be taken to typify, in its portrayal of a middle-aged woman, the bourgeois family background from which came much of the leadership of the American and French revolutions. In general, it was a background of substance, comfort and hard work. Mrs. Smith's costume and surroundings, though less elegant than Mrs. Graham's, suggest her high station in New England society. Her expression is between the prim and the pleasant. She clearly represents, and expects from others, a settled standard of behavior and decorum. Copley, troubled by the rising revolutionary agitation, left America in 1774 and spent the rest of his long life in England. Courtesy of the Yale University Art Gallery, Gift of Maitland Fuller Griggs.

policies had aroused antagonism in the coastal towns and in the backwoods, among wealthy land speculators and poor squatter frontiersmen, among merchants and the workingmen who depended on the business of merchants. The freedom of Americans to determine their own political life was in question. Yet there were few in 1774, or even later, prepared to face the thought of independence.

The War of American Independence

After the "Intolerable Acts" self-authorized groups met in the several colonies and sent delegates to a "continental congress" in Philadelphia. This body adopted a boycott of British goods, to be enforced on unwilling Americans by local organizers of resistance. Fighting began in the next year, 1775, when the British commander at Boston sent a detachment to seize unauthorized stores of weapons at Concord. On the way, at Lexington, in a brush between soldiers and partisans or "minutemen," someone fired the "shot heard round the world." The Second Continental Congress, meeting a few weeks later, proceeded to raise an American army, dispatched an expedition to force Quebec into the revolutionary union, and entered into overtures with Bourbon France.

The Congress was still reluctant to repudiate the tie with Britain. But passions grew fierce in consequence of the fighting. Radicals convinced moderates that the choice now lay between independence and enslavement. It appeared that the French, naturally uninterested in a reconciliation of British subjects, would give help if the avowed aim of American rebels was to dismember the British Empire. In January 1776 Thomas Paine, in his pamphlet *Common Sense*, made his debut as a kind of international revolutionary; he was to figure in the French Revolution and to work for revolution in England. He had come from England less than two years before, and he detested English society for its injustices to men like himself. Eloquent and vitriolic, *Common Sense* identified the independence of the American colonies with the cause of liberty for all mankind. It pitted freedom against tyranny in the person of "the royal brute of Great Britain." It was "repugnant to reason," said Paine, "to suppose that this Continent can long remain subject to any external power. . . . There is something absurd in supposing a Continent to be perpetually governed by an island." *Common Sense* was read everywhere in the colonies, and its slashing arguments unquestionably spread a sense of proud isolation from the Old World. On July 4, 1776, the Congress adopted the Declaration of Independence, by which the United States assumed its separate and equal station among the powers of the earth.

The War of American Independence thereupon turned into another European struggle for empire. For two more years the French government remained ostensibly noninterventionist but meanwhile poured munitions into the colonies through an especially rigged up commercial concern. Nine-tenths of the arms used by the Americans at the battle of Saratoga came from France. After the American victory in this battle the French government concluded, in 1778, that the insurgents were a good political risk, recognized them, signed an alliance with them, and declared war on Great Britain. Spain soon followed, hoping to drive the British from Gibraltar and deciding that its overseas empire was more threatened by a restoration of British supremacy in North America than by the disturbing example of an independent American republic. The Dutch were drawn into hostilities through trading with the Americans by way of the Dutch

West Indies. Other powers, Russia, Sweden, Denmark, Prussia, Portugal, and Turkey, irked at British employment of blockade and sea power in time of war, formed an "Armed Neutrality" to protect their commerce from dictation by the British fleet. The French, in a brief revival of their own sea power, landed an expeditionary force of 6,000 men in Rhode Island. Since the Americans suffered from the internal differences inseparable from all revolutions and were in any case still unable to govern themselves to any effect, meeting with the old difficulties in raising both troops and money, it was the participation of regiments of the French army, in conjunction with squadrons of the French fleet, which made possible the defeat of the armed forces of the British Empire and so persuaded the British government to recognize the independence of the United States. By the peace treaty of 1783, though the British were still in possession of New York and Savannah, and though the governments befriending the Americans would just as soon have confined them east of the mountains, the new republic obtained territory as far west as the Mississippi. Canada remained British. It received an English-speaking population by the settlement of over 60,000 refugee Americans who remained loyal to Great Britain.

Significance of the Revolution

The upheaval in America was a revolution as well as a war of independence. The cry for liberty against Great Britain raised echoes within the colonies themselves. The Declaration of Independence was more than an announcement of secession from the empire; it was a justification of rebellion against established authority. Curiously, although the American quarrel had been with the Parliament, the Declaration arraigned no one but the king. One reason was that the Congress, not recognizing the authority of Parliament, could separate from Great Britain only by a denunciation of the British crown; another reason was that the cry of "tyrant" made a more popular and flaming issue. Boldly voicing the natural right philosophy of the age, the Declaration held as "self-evident," i.e., as evident to all reasonable people—that "all men are created equal, that they are endowed by their Creator with certain unalienable rights, that among these are life, liberty, and the pursuit of happiness." These electrifying words leaped inward into America, and outward to the world.

In the new states democratic equality made many advances. It was subject, however, to a great limitation, in that it long really applied only to white males of European origin. It was more than a century before women received the vote. American Indians were few in number, but the black population at the time of the Revolution comprised about a fifth of the whole. It was much larger proportionately than it became later, after mass immigration from Europe raised the proportion of whites. Many American whites of the revolutionary generation were indeed troubled by the institution of slavery. It was abolished outright in Massachusetts, and all states north of Maryland took steps toward its gradual extinction. But to apply the principles of liberty and equality without regard to race was beyond the powers of Americans at the time. In the South, all censuses from 1790 to 1850 showed a third of the population to be slaves. In the North, free blacks found that in fact, and often in law, they were debarred from voting, from adequate schooling, and from the widening opportunities in which white Americans saw the essence of their national life and their superiority to Europe.

For the white majority the Revolution had a democratizing effect in many ways. Lawyers, landowners, and businessmen who led the movement against England needed the support of numbers and to obtain it were willing to make promises and concessions to the lower classes. Or the popular elements, workmen and mechanics, farmers and frontiersmen, often dissidents in religion, extorted concessions by force or threats. There was a good deal of violence, as in all revolutions; the new states confiscated property from the counterrevolutionaries, called Tories, some of whom were in addition tarred and feathered by infuriated mobs. The dissolution of the old colonial governments threw open all political questions. In some states more men became qualified to vote. In some, governors and senators were now popularly elected, in addition to the lower houses of the legislatures as in colonial times. The principle was adopted, still unknown to the parliamentary bodies of Europe, that each member of a legislative assembly should represent about the same number of citizens. Primogeniture and entail, which landed families aspiring to an aristocratic mode of life sometimes favored, went down before the demands of democrats and small property owners. Tithes were done away with, and the established churches, Anglican in the South, Congregationalist in New England, lost their privileged position in varying degree. But the Revolution was not socially as profound as the revolution soon to come in France, or as the revolution in Russia in 1917. Property changed hands, but the law of property was modified only in detail. There had been no such thing in British America as a native nobleman or even a bishop; clergy and aristocracy had been incomparably less ingrained in American than in European society, and the rebellion against them was less devastating in its effect.

The main import of the American Revolution remained political and even constitutional in a strict sense. The American leaders were themselves part of the Age of Enlightenment, sharing fully in its humane and secular spirit. But probably the only non-British thinker by whom they were influenced was Montesquieu, and Montesquieu owed his popularity to his philosophizing upon English institutions. The Americans drew heavily on the writings of John Locke, but their cast of mind went back before Locke to the English Puritan movement of the first half of the seventeenth century. Their thought was formed not only by Locke's ideas of human nature and government, but, as already noted, by the dissenting literature and the neo-republican writings that had never quite died out in England. The realities of life for five generations in America had sharpened the old insistence upon personal liberty and equality. When the dispute with Britain came to a head, the Americans found themselves arguing both for the historic and chartered rights of Englishmen and for the timeless and universal rights of man, both of which were held up as barriers against the inroads of parliamentary sovereignty. The Americans came to believe, more than any other people, that government should possess limited powers and operate only within the terms of a fixed and written constitutional document.

All thirteen of the new states lost no time in providing themselves with written constitutions (in Connecticut and Rhode Island merely the old charters reaffirmed), all of which enshrined virtually the same principles. All followed the thought stated in the great Declaration, that it was to protect "unalienable" rights that governments were instituted among men, and that whenever government became destructive to this end the people had a right to "institute new government" for their safety and happiness. All the constitutions undertook to limit government by a separation of governmental powers. All appended a bill of rights, stating the natural rights of the citizens and the things which no government might justly do. None of the constitutions were as yet fully democratic; even the most liberal gave some advantage in public affairs to the owners of property.

Federalism, or the allocation of power between central and outlying governments, went along with the idea of written constitutions as a principal offering of the Americans to the world. Like constitutionalism, federalism developed in the atmosphere of protest against a centralized sovereign power. It was a hard idea for Americans to work out, since the new states carried over the old separatism which had so distracted the British. Until 1789 the states remained banded together in the Articles of Confederation. The United States was a union of thirteen independent republics. Disadvantages in this scheme becoming apparent, a constitutional convention met at Philadelphia in 1787 and drew up the constitution which is today the world's oldest written instrument of government still in operation. In it the United States was conceived not merely as a league of states, but as a union in which individuals were citizens of the United States of America for some purposes and of their particular states for others. Persons, not states, composed the federal republic, and the laws of the United States fell not merely on the states but on the people.

The consequences of the American Revolution can hardly be overstated. By overburdening the French treasury the American war became a direct cause of the French Revolution. Beyond that, it ushered in the age of predominantly liberal or democratic revolution which lasted through the European revolutions of 1848. The American doctrine, like most thought in the Age of Enlightenment, was expressed in universal terms of "man" and "nature." All peoples regardless of their own history could apply it to themselves, because, as Alexander Hamilton once put it in his youth, "the sacred rights of man are not to be rummaged for among old parchments or musty records. They are written, as with a sunbeam, in the whole volume of human nature, by the hand of Divinity itself, and can never be erased or obscured by mortal power." The Americans, in freeing themselves, had done what all men ought to do.

The revolt in America offered a dramatic judgment on the old colonial system, convincing some, in England and elsewhere, that the empires for which they had long been struggling were hardly worth acquiring, since colonies in time, in the words of Turgot, fell away from the mother country "like ripe fruit." The idea spread, since trade between Britain and America continued to prosper, that one could do business with a country without exerting political influence or control, and this idea became fundamental to the coming movement of economic liberalism and free trade. By coincidence, the book that became the gospel of the free trade movement, Adam Smith's *Wealth of Nations*, was published in England in the year 1776. The American example was pointed to by other peoples wishing to throw off colonial status—first by the Latin Americans, then by the peoples of the older British dominions, and, finally, in the twentieth century, by those of Asia and Africa also. In Europe, the American example encouraged the type of nationalism in which subjugated nations aspire to be free. And at home the Revolution did much to determine the spirit and method by which the bulk of the North American continent was to be peopled and the attitudes for which the United States, when it became a leading power a century and a half later, was to stand before the world.

More immediately, the American example was not lost on the many Europeans who sojourned in the new states during and after the war. Of these the Marquis de Lafayette was the most famous, but there were many others: Thomas Paine, who returned to Europe in 1787; the future French revolutionist Brissot; the future Polish national leader Kosciusko; the future marshals of Napoleon, Jourdan and Berthier; the future reformer of the Prussian army Gneisenau. Contrariwise various Americans went to Europe, notably the aging Benjamin Franklin, who in the 1780s was incredibly lionized in the fashionable and literary world of Paris.

The establishment of the United States was taken in Europe to prove that many ideas of the Enlightenment were practicable. Rationalists declared that here was a people, free of past errors and superstitions, who showed how enlightened beings could plan their affairs. Rousseauists saw in America the very paradise of natural equality, unspoiled innocence, and patriotic virtue. But nothing so much impressed Europeans, and especially the French, as the spectacle of the Americans meeting in solemn conclave to draft their state constitutions. These, along with the Declaration of Independence, were translated and published in 1778 by a French nobleman, the Duke de la Rochefoucauld. They were endlessly and excitedly discussed. Constitutionalism, federalism, and limited government were not new ideas in Europe. They came out of the Middle Ages and were currently set forth in many quarters, for example, in Hungary, the Holy Roman Empire, and the Parlement of Paris. But in their prevailing form, and even in the philosophy of Montesquieu, they were associated with feudalism and aristocracy. The American Revolution made such ideas progressive. The American influence, added to the force of developments in Europe, made the thought of the later Enlightenment more democratic. The United States replaced England as the model country of advanced thinkers. On the Continent there was less passive trust in the enlightened despotism of the official state. Confidence in self-government was aroused.

The American constitutions seemed a demonstration of the social contract. They offered a picture of men in a "state of nature," having cast off their old government, deliberately sitting down to contrive a new one, weighing and judging each branch of government on its merits, assigning due powers to legislature, executive, and judiciary, declaring that all government was created by the people and in possession of a merely delegated authority, and listing specifically the inalienable rights of men—inalienable in that they could not conceivably be taken away, since men possessed them even if denied them by force. And these rights were the very same rights that many Europeans wanted secured for themselves—freedom of religion, freedom of press, freedom of assembly, freedom from arbitrary arrest at the discretion of officials. And they were the same for all, on the rigorous principle of equality before the law. The American example crystallized and made tangible the ideas that were strongly blowing in Europe, and the American example was one reason why the French, in 1789, began their revolution with a declaration of human rights and with the drafting of a written constitution.

And more deeply still, America became a kind of mirage or ideal vision for Europe, a land of open opportunity and of new beginnings, free from the load of history and of the past, wistfully addressed by Goethe:

America, thou hast it better
Than has our Continent, the old one.

It is evident that this was only part of the picture. The United States, as its later history was to show, bore a heavy load of inherited burdens and unsolved problems, especially racial. But in a general way, until new revolutionary movements set in a century later, America stood as a kind of utopia of the common man, not only for the millions who emigrated to it but for other millions who stayed at home, who often wished that their own countries might become more like it, and many of whom might even agree with Abraham Lincoln in calling it the last best hope of earth.

IX.
The French Revolution

I n 1789 France fell into revolution, and the world has never since been the same. The French Revolution was by far the most momentous upheaval of the whole revolutionary age. It replaced the "old regime" with "modern society," and at its extreme phase it became very radical, so much so that all later revolutionary movements have looked back to it as a predecessor to themselves. At the time, in the age of the Democratic or Atlantic Revolution from the 1760s to 1848, the role of France was decisive. Even the Americans, without French military intervention, would hardly have won such a clear settlement from England or been so free to set up the new states and new constitutions that have just been described. And while revolutionary disturbances in Ireland and Poland, or among the Dutch, Italians, and others, were by no means caused by the French example, it was the presence or absence of French aid that usually determined whatever successes they enjoyed.

The French Revolution, unlike the Russian or Chinese revolutions of the twentieth century, occurred in what was in many ways the most advanced country of the day. France was the center of the intellectual movement of the Enlightenment.

Chapter Emblem: A cockade worn during the French Revolution, with the famous motto, and the fleur-de-lis of the monarchy embellished by the cap of liberty.

French science then led the world. French books were read everywhere, and the newspapers and political journals which became very numerous after 1789 carried a message which hardly needed translation. French was a kind of international spoken language in the educated and aristocratic circles of many countries. France was also, potentially before 1789 and actually after 1793, the most powerful country in Europe. It may have been the wealthiest, though not per capita. With a population of some 24,000,000 the French were the most numerous of all European peoples under a single government. Even Russia was hardly more populous until after the partitions of Poland. The Germans were divided, the subjects of the Habsburgs were of diverse nationalities, and the English and Scots together numbered only 10,000,000. Paris, though smaller than London, was over twice as large as Vienna or Amsterdam. French exports to Europe were larger than those of Great Britain. It is said that half the goldpieces circulating in Europe were French. Europeans in the eighteenth century were in the habit of taking ideas from France; they were therefore, depending on their position, the more excited, encouraged, alarmed, or horrified when revolution broke out in that country.

41. BACKGROUNDS

The Old Regime: The Three Estates

Some remarks have already been made about the Old Regime, as the prerevolutionary society came to be called after it disappeared, and about the failure of enlightened despotism in France to make any fundamental alteration in it.[1] The essential fact about the Old Regime was that it was still legally aristocratic and in some ways feudal. Everyone belonged legally to an "estate" or "order" of society. The First Estate was the clergy, the Second Estate the nobility, and the Third Estate included everyone else—from the wealthiest business and professional classes to the poorest peasantry and city workers. These categories were important in that the individual's legal rights and personal prestige depended on the category to which he belonged. Politically, they were obsolescent; not since 1614 had the estates assembled in an Estates General of the whole kingdom, though in some provinces they had continued to meet as provincial bodies. Socially, they were obsolescent also, for the threefold division no longer corresponded to the real distribution of interest, influence, property, or productive activity among the French people.

Conditions in the church and the position of the clergy have been much exaggerated as a cause of the French Revolution. The church in France levied a tithe on all agricultural products, but so did the church in England; the French bishops often played a part in government affairs, but so did bishops in England through the House of Lords. The French bishoprics of 1789 were in reality no wealthier than those of the Church of England were found to be when investigated forty years later. In actual numbers, in the secular atmosphere of the Age of Enlightenment, the clergy, especially the monastic orders, had greatly declined, so that by 1789 there were probably not more than 100,000 Catholic clergy of all

---

[1] See pp. 315–318.

types in the entire population. But if the importance of the clergy has often been overemphasized, still it must be said that the church was deeply involved in the prevailing social system. For one thing, church bodies—bishoprics, abbeys, convents, schools, and other religious foundations—owned between 5 and 10 percent of the land of the country, which meant that collectively the church was the greatest of all landowners. Moreover, the income from church properties, like all income, was divided very unequally, and much of it found its way into the hands of the aristocratic occupants of the higher ecclesiastical offices.

The noble order, which in 1789 comprised about 400,000 persons, including women and children, had enjoyed a great resurgence since the death of Louis XIV in 1715.[2] Distinguished government service, higher church offices, army, parlements, and most other public and semipublic honors were almost monopolized by the titled aristocracy in the time of Louis XVI, who, it will be recalled, had mounted the throne in 1774. Repeatedly, through parlements, Provincial Estates, or the assembly of the clergy dominated by the noble bishops, the aristocracy had blocked royal plans for taxation and shown a desire to control the policies of state. At the same time the bourgeoisie, or upper crust of the Third Estate, had never been so influential. The fivefold increase of French foreign trade between 1713 and 1789 suggests the growth of the merchant class and of the legal and governmental classes associated with it. As members of the bourgeoisie became stronger, more widely read, and more self-confident, they resented the distinctions enjoyed by the nobles. Some of these were financial: nobles were exempt on principle from the most important direct tax, the taille, whereas bourgeois obtained exemption with more effort; but so many bourgeois enjoyed tax privileges that purely monetary self-interest was not primary in their psychology. The bourgeois resented the nobleman for his superiority and his arrogance. What had formerly been customary respect was now felt as humiliation. And they felt that they were being shut out from office and honors, and that the nobles were seeking more power in government as a class. The Revolution was the collision of two moving objects, a rising aristocracy and a rising bourgeoisie.

The common people, below the commercial and professional families in the Third Estate, were probably as well off as in most countries. But they were not well off compared with the upper classes. Wage earners had by no means shared in the wave of business prosperity. Between the 1730s and the 1780s the prices of consumers' goods rose about 65 percent, whereas wages rose only 22 percent. Persons dependent on wages were therefore badly pinched, but they were less numerous than today, for in the country there were many small farmers and in the towns many small craftsmen, both of which groups made a living not by wages but by selling the products of their own labor at market prices. Yet in both town and country there was a significant wage-earning or proletarian element, which was to play a decisive part in the Revolution.

The Agrarian System of the Old Regime

Over four-fifths of the people were rural. The agrarian system had developed so that there was no serfdom in France, to be sure, as it was known in eastern Europe.[3] The relation of lord and peasant in France was not the relation of mas-

---

[2] See pp. 256–257.
[3] See pp. 33–34, 122–123, 204–205.

ter and man. The peasant owed no labor to the lord—except a few token services in some cases. The peasant worked for himself, either on his own land or on rented land; or he worked as a sharecropper (*métayer*); or he hired himself out to the lord or to another peasant.

The manor, however, still retained certain surviving features of the feudal age. The noble owner of a manor enjoyed "hunting rights," or the privilege of keeping game preserves, and of hunting on his own and the peasants' land. He usually had a monopoly over the village mill, bakeshop, or wine press, for the use of which he collected fees, called *banalités*. He possessed certain vestigial powers of jurisdiction in the manorial court and certain local police powers, from which fees and fines were collected. These seigneurial privileges were of course the survivals of a day when the local manor had been a unit of government, and the noble had performed the functions of government, an age that had long passed with the development of the centralized modern state.

There was another special feature to the property system of the Old Regime. Every owner of a manor (there were some bourgeois and even wealthy peasants who had purchased manors) possessed what was called a right of "eminent property" with respect to all land located in the manorial village. This meant that lesser landowners within the manor "owned" their land in that they could freely buy, sell, lease, and bequeath or inherit it; but they owed to the owner of the manor, in recognition of his "eminent property" rights, certain rents, payable annually, as well as transfer fees that were payable whenever the land changed owners by sale or death. Subject to these "eminent property" rights, landownership was fairly widespread. Peasants directly owned about two-fifths of the soil of the country; bourgeois a little under a fifth. The nobility owned perhaps a little over a fifth, and the church somewhat under a tenth, the remainder being crown lands, wastelands, or commons. Finally, it must be noted that all property rights were subject also to certain "collective" rights, by which villagers might cut firewood or run their pigs in the commons, or pasture cattle on land belonging to other owners after the crops were in, there being usually no fences or enclosures.

All this may seem rather complex, but it is important to realize that property is a changing institution. Even today, in industrialized countries, a high proportion of all property is in land, including natural resources in and below the soil. In the eighteenth century property meant land even more than it does today. Even the bourgeois class, whose wealth was so largely in ships, merchandise, or commercial paper, invested heavily in land, and in France in 1789 enjoyed ownership of almost as much land as the nobility, and of more than the church. The Revolution was to revolutionize the law of property by freeing the private ownership of land from all the indirect encumbrances described—manorial fees, eminent property rights, communal village agricultural practices, and church tithes. It also was to abolish other older forms of property, such as property in public office or in masterships in the guilds, which had become useful mainly to closed and privileged groups. In final effect the Revolution established the institutions of private property in the modern sense and benefited, therefore, most especially the landowning peasants and the bourgeoisie.

The peasants not only owned two-fifths of the soil, but occupied almost all of it, working it on their own initiative and risk. That is to say, land owned by the nobility, the church, the bourgeoisie, and the crown was divided up and leased to peasants in small parcels. France was already a country of small farmers. There was no "big agriculture" as in England, eastern Europe, or the plantations of America. The manorial lord performed no economic function. He lived (there were of course exceptions) not by managing an estate and selling his own crops and cattle, but by receiving innumerable dues, quitrents, and fees. During the eighteenth century, in connection with the general aristocratic resurgence, there took place a phenomenon often called the "feudal reaction." Manorial lords, faced with rising living costs and acquiring higher living standards because of the general material progress, collected their dues more rigorously or revived old ones that had fallen into disuse. Leases and sharecropping arrangements also became less favorable to the peasants. The farmers, like the wage earners, were under a steadily increasing pressure. At the same time the peasants resented the "feudal dues" more than ever, because they regarded themselves as in many cases the real owners of the land and the lord as a gentleman of the neighborhood who for no reason enjoyed a special income and a status different from their own. The trouble was that much of the property system no longer bore any relation to real economic usefulness or activity.

The political unity of France, achieved over the centuries by the monarchy, was likewise a fundamental prerequisite, and even a cause, of the Revolution. Whatever social conditions might have existed, they could give rise to nationwide public opinion, nationwide agitation, nationwide policies, and nationwide legislation only in a country already politically unified as a nation. These conditions were lacking in central Europe. In France a French state existed. Reformers did not have to create it but only capture and remodel it. Frenchmen in the eighteenth century already had the sense of membership in a political entity called France. The Revolution saw a tremendous stirring of this sense of membership and of fraternity, turning it into a passion of citizenship, civic rights, voting powers, use and application of the state and its sovereignty for the public advantage. At the very outbreak of the Revolution people saluted each other as *citoyen* or *citoyenne* and shouted *vive la nation!*

42. THE REVOLUTION AND THE REORGANIZATION OF FRANCE

The Financial Crisis

The Revolution was precipitated by a financial collapse of the government. What overloaded the government was by no means the costly magnificence of the court of Versailles. Only 5 percent of public expenditures in 1788 was devoted to the upkeep of the entire royal establishment. What overloaded all governments was war costs, both current upkeep of armies and navies and the burden of public debt, which in all countries was due almost totally to the war costs of the past. In 1788 the French government devoted about a quarter of its annual expenditure to current maintenance of the armed forces and about a half to the payment of its debts. British expenditures showed almost the same distribution. The French debt stood at almost four billion livres. It had been greatly swollen by the War of American Independence. Yet it was only half as great as the national debt of Great Britain, and less than a fifth as heavy per capita. It was less than the debt of the Dutch Republic. It was apparently no greater than the debt left by Louis XIV three-quarters of a century before. At that time the debt had been lightened by repudiation. No responsible French official in the 1780s even considered repudiation, a sure sign of the progress in the interim of the well-to-do classes, who were the main government creditors.

Yet the debt could not be carried, for the simple reason that revenues fell short of necessary expenditures. This in turn was not due to national poverty, but to the tax exemptions and tax evasions of privileged elements, and to complications in the fiscal system, or lack of system, by which much of what taxpayers paid never came into the hands of the treasury. We have already described how the most important tax, the taille, was generally paid only by the peasants—the nobles being exempt by virtue of their class privilege, and office holders and bourgeois obtaining exemption in various ways.[4] The church too insisted that its property was not taxable by the state; and its periodic "free gift" to the king, though substantial, was less than might have been obtained from direct taxation of the church's land. Thus, although the country itself was prosperous, the government treasury was empty. The social classes which enjoyed most of the wealth of the country did not pay taxes corresponding to their income, and, even worse, they resisted taxation as a sign of inferior status.

A long series of responsible persons—Louis XIV himself, John Law, Maupeou, Turgot—had seen the need for taxing the privileged classes. Jacques Necker, a Swiss banker made director of the finances in 1777 by Louis XVI, made moves in the same direction, and, like his predecessors, was dismissed. His successor, Calonne, as the crisis mounted, came to even more revolutionary conclusions. In 1786 he produced a program in which enlightened despotism was tempered by a modest resort to representative institutions. He proposed, in place of the taille, a general tax to fall on all landowners without exemption, a lightening of indirect taxes and abolition of internal tariffs to stimulate economic production, a confiscation of some properties of the church, and the establishment, as a means of interesting the propertied elements in the government, of provincial assemblies in which all landowners, noble, clerical, bourgeois, and peasant, should be represented without regard to estate or order.

This program, if carried out, might have solved the fiscal problem and averted the Revolution. But it struck not only at privileges in taxation—noble, provincial, and others—but at the threefold hierarchic organization of society. Knowing from experience that the Parlement of Paris would never accept it, Calonne in 1787 convened an "assembly of notables," hoping to win its endorsement of his ideas. The notables insisted on concessions in return, for they wished to share in control of the government. A deadlock followed; the king dismissed Calonne and appointed as his successor Loménie de Brienne, the exceedingly worldly-wise archbishop of Toulouse. Brienne tried to push the same program through the Parlement of Paris. The Parlement rejected it, declaring that only the three estates of the realm, assembled in an Estates General, had authority to consent to new taxes. Brienne and Louis XVI at first refused, believing that the Estates General, if convened, would be dominated by the nobility. Like Maupeou and Louis XV, Brienne and Louis XVI tried to break the parlements, replacing them with a modernized judicial system in which the law courts should have no influence over policy. This led to a veritable revolt of the nobles. All the parlements and

---

[4] See pp. 182–183, 315–318.

Provincial Estates resisted, army officers refused to serve, the intendants hesitated to act, noblemen began to organize political clubs and committees of correspondence. With his government brought to a standstill, and unable to borrow money or collect taxes, Louis XVI on July 5, 1788, promised to call the Estates General for the following May. The various classes were invited to elect representatives and also to draw up lists of their grievances.

From Estates General to National Assembly

Since no Estates General had met in over a century and a half, the king asked all persons to study the subject and make proposals on how such an assembly should be organized under modern conditions. This led to an outburst of public discussion. Hundreds of political pamphlets appeared, many of them demanding that the old system by which the three estates sat in separate chambers, each chamber voting as a unit, be done away with, since under it the chamber of the Third Estate was always outnumbered. But in September 1788 the Parlement of Paris, restored to its functions, ruled that the Estates General should meet and vote as in 1614, in three separate orders.

The nobility, through the Parlement, thus revealed its aim. It had forced the summoning of the Estates General, and in this way the French nobility initiated the Revolution. The Revolution began as another victory in the aristocratic resurgence against the absolutism of the king. The nobles actually had a liberal program: they demanded constitutional government, guarantees of personal liberty for all, freedom of speech and press, freedom from arbitrary arrest and confinement. Many now were even prepared to give up special privileges in taxation; this might have worked itself out in time. But in return they hoped to become the preponderant political element in the state. It was their idea not merely to have the Estates General meet in 1789, but for France to be governed in all the future through the Estates General, a supreme body in three chambers, one for nobles, one for a clergy in which the higher officers were also nobles, and one for the Third Estate.

This was precisely what the Third Estate wished to avoid. Lawyers, bankers, businessmen, government creditors, shopkeepers, artisans, workingmen, and peasants had no desire to be governed by lords temporal and spiritual. Their hopes of a new era, formed by the philosophy of the Enlightenment, stirred by the revolution in America, rose to the utmost excitement when "good king Louis" called the Estates General. The ruling of the Parlement of Paris in September 1788 came to them as a slap in the face—an unprovoked class insult. The whole Third Estate turned on the nobility with detestation and distrust. The Abbé Sieyès in January 1789 launched his famous pamphlet, *What Is the Third Estate?*, declaring that the nobility was a useless caste which could be abolished without loss, that the Third Estate was the one necessary element of society, that it was identical with the nation, and that the nation was absolutely and unqualifiedly sovereign. Through Sieyès the ideas of Rousseau's *Social Contract* entered the thought of the Revolution. At the same time, even before the Estates General actually met, and not from the books of philosophes so much as from the actual events and conditions, nobles and commoners viewed each other with fear and suspicion. The Third Estate, which had at first supported the nobles against the "despotism" of the king's ministers, now ascribed to them the worst possible motives.

Class antagonism poisoned the Revolution at the outset, made peaceful reform impossible, and threw many bourgeois without delay into a radical and destructive mood. And the mutual suspicion between classes, produced by the Old Regime and inflamed by the Revolution, has troubled France ever since.

The Estates General met as planned in May 1789 at Versailles. The Third Estate, most of whose representatives were lawyers, boycotted the organization in three separate chambers. It insisted that deputies of all three orders should sit as a single house and vote as individuals; this procedure would be of advantage to the Third Estate, since the king had granted it as many deputies as the other two orders combined. For six weeks a deadlock was maintained. On June 13 a few priests, leaving the chamber of the First Estate, came over and sat with the Third. They were greeted with jubilation. On June 17 the Third Estate declared itself the "National Assembly." Louis XVI, under pressure from the nobles, closed the hall in which it met. The members found a neighboring indoor tennis court, and there, milling about in a babel of confusion and apprehension, swore and signed the Oath of the Tennis Court on June 20, 1789, affirming that wherever they foregathered the National Assembly was in existence, and that they would not disband until they had drafted a constitution. This was a revolutionary step, for it assumed virtually sovereign power for a body of men who had no legal authority. The king ordered members of the three estates to sit in their separate houses. He now somewhat tardily presented a reforming program of his own, too late to win the confidence of the disaffected, and in any case continuing the organization of French society in legal classes. The self-entitled National Assembly refused to back down. The king faltered, failed to enforce his commands promptly, and allowed the Assembly to remain in being. In the following days, at the end of June, he summoned about 18,000 soldiers to Versailles.

What had happened was that the king of France, in the dispute raging between nobles and commoners, chose the nobles. It was traditional in France for the king to oppose feudalism. For centuries the French monarchy had drawn strength from the bourgeoisie. All through the eighteenth century the royal ministers had carried on the struggle against the privileged interests. Only a year before, Louis XVI had been almost at war with his rebellious aristocracy. In 1789 he failed to assert himself. He lost control over the Estates General, exerted no leadership, offered no program until it was too late, and provided no symbol behind which parties could rally. He failed to make use of the profound loyalty to himself felt by the bourgeoisie and common people, who yearned for nothing so much as a king who would stand up for them, as in days of yore, against an aristocracy of birth and status. He tried instead, at first, to compromise and postpone a crisis; then he found himself in the position of having issued orders which the Third Estate boldly defied; and in this embarrassing predicament he yielded to his wife, Marie Antoinette, to his brothers, and to the court nobles with whom he lived, and who told him that his dignity and authority were outraged and undermined. At the end of June Louis XVI undoubtedly intended to dissolve the Estates General by military force. But what the Third Estate feared was not a return to the old theoretically absolute monarchy. It was a future in which the aristocracy should control the government of the country. There was now no going back; the revolt of the Third Estate had allied Louis XVI with the nobles, and the Third Estate now feared the nobles more than ever, believing with good reason that they now had the king in their hands.

The Lower Classes in Action

The country meanwhile was falling into dissolution. The lower classes, below the bourgeoisie, were out of hand. For them too the convocation of the Estates General had seemed to herald a new era. The grievances of ages, and those which existed equally in other countries than France, rose to the surface. Short-run conditions were bad. The harvest of 1788 had been poor; the price of bread, by July 1789, was higher than at any time since the death of Louis XIV. The year 1789 was also one of depression; the rapid growth of trade since the American war had suddenly halted, so that wages fell and unemployment spread while scarcity drove food prices up. The government, paralyzed at the center, could not take such measures of relief as were customary under the Old Regime. The masses were everywhere restless. Labor trouble broke out; in April a great riot of workingmen devastated a wallpaper factory in Paris. In the rural districts there was much disorder. Peasants declared that they would pay no more manorial dues and were likewise refusing taxes. In the best of times the countryside was troubled by vagrants, beggars, rough characters, and smugglers who flourished along the many tariff frontiers. Now the business depression reduced the income of honest peasants who engaged in weaving or other domestic industries in their homes; unemployment and indigence spread in the country; people were uprooted; and the result was to raise the number of vagrants to terrifying proportions. It was believed, since nothing was too bad to believe of the aristocrats (though it was not true), that they were secretly recruiting these "brigands" for their own purposes to intimidate the Third Estate. The economic and social crises thus became acutely political.

The towns were afraid of being swamped by beggars and desperadoes. This was true even of Paris, the largest city in Europe except London. The Parisians were also alarmed by the concentration of troops about Versailles. They began to arm in self-defense. All classes of the Third Estate took part. The banker Laborde, whose career was noted in an earlier chapter,[5] and whose son sat in the Assembly at Versailles, was one of many to provide funds. Crowds began to look for weapons in arsenals and public buildings. On July 14 they came to the Bastille, a stronghold built in the Middle Ages to overawe the city, like the Tower of London in England. It was used as a place of detention for persons with enough influence to escape the common jails but was otherwise in normal times considered harmless; in fact there had been talk, some years before, of tearing it down to make room for a public park. Now, in the general turbulence, the governor had placed cannon in the embrasures. The crowd requested him to remove his cannon and to furnish them with arms. He refused. Through a series of misunderstandings, reinforced by the vehemence of a few firebrands, the crowd turned into a mob, which assaulted the fortress, and which, when helped by a handful of trained soldiers and five artillery pieces, persuaded the governor to surrender. The mob, enraged by the death of ninety-eight of its members, streamed in and murdered six soldiers of the garrison in cold blood. The governor was murdered while under escort to the Town Hall. The mayor of Paris met the same fate. Their heads were cut off with knives, stuck on the ends of pikes, and paraded about the city. While all this happened the regular army units on the outskirts of Paris did not stir, their reliability being open to question, and the authorities being in any case unaccustomed to firing on the people.

[5] See pp. 254–255.

The capture of the Bastille, though not so intended, had the effect of saving the Assembly at Versailles. The king, not knowing what to do, accepted the new situation in Paris. He recognized a citizens' committee, which had formed there, as the new municipal government. He sent away the troops that he had summoned and commanded the recalcitrants among nobles and clergy to join in the National Assembly. In Paris and other cities a bourgeois or national guard was established to keep order. The Marquis de Lafayette, "the hero of two worlds," received command over the guard in Paris. For insignia he combined the colors of the city of Paris, red and blue, with the white of the house of Bourbon. The French tricolor, emblem of the Revolution, thus originated in a fusion of old and new.

In the rural districts matters went from bad to worse. Vague insecurity rose to the proportions of panic in the Great Fear of 1789, which spread over the country late in July in the wake of travelers, postal couriers, and others. The cry was relayed from point to point that "the brigands were coming," and peasants, armed to protect their homes and crops and gathered together and working upon each other's feelings, often turned their attention to the manor houses, burning them in some cases, and in others simply destroying the manorial archives in which fees and dues were recorded. The Great Fear became part of a general agrarian insurrection, in which peasants, far from being motivated by wild alarms, knew perfectly well what they were doing. They intended to destroy the manorial regime by force.

The Initial Reforms of the National Assembly

The Assembly at Versailles could restore order only by meeting the demands of the peasants. To wipe out all manorial payments would deprive the landed aristocracy of much of its income. Many bourgeois also owned manors. There was therefore much perplexity. A small group of deputies prepared a surprise move in the Assembly, choosing an evening session from which many would be absent. Hence came the "night of August 4." A few liberal noblemen, by prearrangement, arose and surrendered their hunting rights, their *banalités*, their rights in manorial courts, and feudal and seigneurial privileges generally. What was left of serfdom and all personal servitudes was declared ended. Tithes were abolished. Other deputies repudiated the special privileges of their provinces. All personal tax privileges were given up. On the main matter, the dues arising from "eminent property" in the manors, a compromise was adopted. These dues were all abolished, but compensation was to be paid by the peasants to the former owners. The compensation was in most cases never paid. Eventually, in 1793, in the radical phase of the Revolution, the provision for compensation was repealed. In the end French peasant landowners rid themselves of their manorial obligations without cost to themselves. This was in contrast to what later happened in most other countries, where the peasants, when in turn liberated from manorial obligations, either lost part of their land or were burdened with installment payments lasting many years.

In a decree summarizing the resolutions of August 4 the Assembly declared flatly that "feudalism is abolished." With legal privilege replaced by legal equality, it proceeded to map the principles of the new order. On August 26, 1789, it issued the Declaration of the Rights of Man and Citizen.

The Declaration of 1789 was meant to affirm the principles of the new state, which were essentially the rule of law, equal individual citizenship, and collective sovereignty of the people. "Men are born and remain," declared Article I, "free and equal in rights." Man's natural rights were held to be "liberty, property, security, and resistance to oppression." Freedom of thought and religion were guaranteed; no one might be arrested or punished except by process of law; all persons were declared eligible for any public office for which they met the requirements. Liberty was defined as the freedom to do anything not injurious to others, which in turn was to be determined only by law. Law must fall equally upon all persons. Law was the expression of the general will, to be made by all citizens or their representatives. The only sovereign was the nation itself, and all public officials and armed forces acted only in its name. Taxes might be raised only by common consent, all public servants were accountable for their conduct in office, and the powers of government should be separated among different branches. Finally, the state might for public purposes, and under law, confiscate the property of private persons, but only with fair compensation. The Declaration, printed in thousands of leaflets, pamphlets, and books, read aloud in public places, or framed and hung on walls, became the catechism of the Revolution in France. When translated into other languages it soon carried the same message to all of Europe. Thomas Paine's book, *The Rights of Man*, published in 1791 to defend the French Revolution, gave the phrase a powerful impact in English.

The "rights of man" had become a motto or watchword for potentially revolutionary ideas well before 1789. The thinkers of the Enlightenment had used it, and during the American Revolution even Alexander Hamilton had spoken of "the sacred rights of man" with enthusiasm.[6] "Man" in this sense was meant to apply abstractly, regardless of nationality, race, or sex. In French as in English, then as now, the word "man" was used to designate all human beings, and the Declaration of 1789 was not intended to refer to males alone. In German, for example, where a distinction is made between *Mensch* as a human being and *Mann* as an adult male, the "rights of man" was always translated as *Menschenrechte*. Similarly the word "citizen" in its general sense applied to women, as is shown by the frequency of the feminine *citoyenne* during the Revolution, in which a great many women were very active. But when it came to the exercise of particular legal rights the Revolutionaries went no farther than contemporary opinion. Thus they assigned the right to vote and hold office only to men, and in matters of property, family law, and education it was the boys and men who had the advantages. Very few at the time argued for legal equality between the sexes.

One of them, however, was Olympe de Gouges, a woman of some prominence as a writer for the theater, who in 1791 published *The Rights of Woman*. Following the official Declaration in each of its seventeen articles, she applied them to women explicitly in each case, and she asserted also, in addition, the right of women to divorce under certain conditions, to the control of property in marriage, and for equal access with men to higher education and to civilian careers and public employments. Mary Wollstonecraft in England published a similar *Vindication of the Rights of Woman* in 1792. In France some of the secondary figures in the Revolution, and some of the teachers in boys' schools, thought that women should have greater opportunities at least in education. Among the leaders, only Condorcet argued for legal equality of the sexes. Intent on political change, the Revolutionaries thought that politics, government, law, and war

[6] See p. 347.

were a masculine business, for which only boys and young men needed to be educated or prepared.

Shortly after adoption of the Declaration of the Rights of Man the Revolutionary leadership fell apart. In September 1789 the Assembly began the actual planning of the new government. Some wanted a strong veto power for the king and a legislative body in two houses, as in England. Others, the "patriots," wanted only a delaying veto for the king and a legislative body of one chamber. Here again, it was suspicion of the aristocracy that proved decisive. The "patriots" were afraid that an upper chamber would bring back the nobility as a collective force, and they were afraid to make the king constitutionally strong by giving him a full veto, because they believed him to be in sympathy with the nobles. He was, at the moment, hesitating to accept both the August 4th decrees and the Declaration of Rights. His brother, the Count of Artois, followed by many aristocrats, had already emigrated to foreign parts and, along with these other émigrés, was preparing to agitate against the Revolution with all the governments of Europe. The patriot party would concede nothing, the more conservative party could gain nothing. The debate was interrupted again, as in July, by insurrection and violence. On October 4, a crowd of market women and revolutionary militants, followed by the Paris national guard, took the road from Paris to Versailles. Besieging and invading the château, they obliged Louis XVI to take up his residence in Paris, where he could be watched. The National Assembly also shifted itself to Paris, where it too soon fell under the influence of radical elements in the city. The champions of a one-chamber legislative body and of a suspensive veto for the king won out.

The more conservative revolutionaries, if such they may be called, disillusioned in seeing constitutional questions settled by mobs, began to drop out of the Assembly. Men who on June 20 had bravely sworn the Oath of the Tennis Court now felt that the Revolution was falling into unworthy hands. Some even emigrated, forming a second wave of émigrés that would have nothing to do with the first. So the counterrevolution gathered strength.

But those who wanted still to go forward, and they were many, began to organize in clubs. Most important of all was the Society of Friends of the Constitution, called the Jacobin club for short, since it met in an old Jacobin monastery in Paris. The dues were at first so high that only substantial bourgeois belonged; they were later lowered but never enough to include persons of the poorest classes, who therefore formed lesser clubs of their own. The most advanced members of the Assembly were Jacobins and used the club as a caucus in which to discuss their policies and lay their plans. They remained a middle-class group even during the later and more radical phase of the Revolution. Mme. Rosalie Jullien, for example, who was as excited a revolutionary as her husband and son, attended a meeting of the Paris Jacobin club on August 5, 1792. Tell your friends in the provinces, she wrote to her husband, that these Jacobins are "the flower of the Paris bourgeoisie, to judge by the fancy jackets they wear. There were also two or three hundred women present, dressed as if for the theater, who made an impression by their proud attitude and forceful speech."

Constitutional Changes

In the two years from October 1789 to September 1791 the National Assembly (or the Constituent Assembly, as it had come to be called because it was preparing a constitution) continued its work of simultaneously governing the country, devising a written constitution, and destroying in detail the institutions of the Old Regime. The old ministries, the old organization of government bureaus, the old taxes, the old property in office, the old titles of nobility, the old parlements, the hundreds of regional systems of law, the old internal tariffs, the old provinces, and the old urban municipalities—all went into the discard. Contemporaries, like Edmund Burke, were appalled at the thoroughness with which Frenchmen seemed determined to eradicate their national institutions. Why, asked Burke, should the French fanatics cut to pieces the living body of Normandy or Provence? The truth is that the provinces, like everything else, were impacted in the whole system of special privilege and unequal rights. All had to disappear if the hope of equal citizenship under national sovereignty was to be attained. In place of the provinces the Constituent divided France into eighty-three equal "departments." In place of the old towns, with their quaint old magistrates, it introduced a uniform municipal organization, all towns henceforth having the same form of government, varying only according to size. All local officials, even prosecuting attorneys and tax collectors, were elected locally. Administratively the country was decentralized in reaction against the bureaucracy of the Old Regime. No one outside Paris now really acted for the central government, and local communities enforced the national legislation, or declined to enforce it, as they chose. This proved ruinous when the war came, and although the "departments" created by the Constituent Assembly still exist, it was long traditional in France after the Revolution, as it was before, to keep local officials under strong control by ministers in Paris.

Under the constitution that was prepared, sometimes called the Constitution of 1791 because it went into effect at that date, the sovereign power of the nation was to be exercised by a unicameral elected assembly, called the Legislative Assembly. The king was given only a suspensive veto power by which legislation desired by the Assembly could be postponed. In general, the executive branch, i.e., king and ministers, was kept weak, partly in reaction against "ministerial despotism," partly from a well-founded distrust of Louis XVI. In July 1791 Louis attempted, in the "flight to Varennes," to escape from the kingdom, join with émigré noblemen, and seek help from foreign powers. He left behind him a written message in which he explicitly repudiated the Revolution. Arrested at Varennes in Lorraine, he was brought back to Paris and forced to accept his status as a constitutional monarch. The attitude of Louis XVI greatly disoriented the Revolution, for it made impossible the creation of a strong executive power and left the country to be ruled by a debating society which under revolutionary conditions contained more than the usual number of hotheads.

Not all this machinery of state was democratic. In the granting of political rights the abstract principles of the great Declaration were seriously modified for practical reasons. Since most people were illiterate it was thought that they could have no reasonable political views. Since the small man was often a domestic servant or shop assistant, it was thought that in politics he would be a mere dependent of his employer. The Constituent therefore distinguished in the new constitution between "active" and "passive" citizens. Both had the same civil rights, but only active citizens had the right to vote. These active citizens chose "electors," on the basis of one elector for every hundred active citizens. The electors convened in the chief town of their new "department," and there chose deputies to the national legislature as well as certain local officials. Males over twenty-five years of age, and well enough off to pay a small direct tax, qualified as "active" citizens; well over half the adult male population could so qualify. Of these, men paying a somewhat higher tax qualified as "electors"; even so, almost half the adult males qualified for this role. In practice, what limited the number of available electors was that, to function as such, a man had to have enough education, interest, and leisure to attend an electoral assembly, at a distance from home, and remain in attendance for several days. In any case, only about 50,000 persons served as electors in 1790–1791 because a proportion of one for every hundred active citizens yielded that figure.

Economic Policies

Economic policies favored the middle rather than the lowest classes. The public debt had precipitated the Revolution, but the revolutionary leaders, even the most extreme Jacobins, never disowned the debt of the Old Regime. The reason is that the bourgeois class, on the whole, were the people to whom the money was owed. To secure the debt, and to pay current expenses of government, since tax collections had become very sporadic, the Constituent Assembly as early as November 1789 resorted to a device by no means new in Europe, though never before used on so extensive a scale. It confiscated all the property of the church. Against this property, it issued negotiable instruments called assignats, first regarded as bonds and issued only in large denominations, later regarded as currency and issued in small bills. Holders of assignats could use them, or any money, to buy parcels of the former church lands. None of the confiscated land was given away; all was in fact sold, since the interest of the government was fiscal rather than social. The peasants, even when they had the money, could not easily buy land because the lands were sold at distant auctions or in large undivided blocks. The peasants were disgruntled, though they did acquire a good deal of the former church lands through middlemen. Peasant landowners were likewise expected, until 1793, to pay compensation for their old quitrents and many other manorial fees. And the landless peasants were aroused when the government, with its modern ideas, encouraged the dividing up of the village commons and extinction of various collective village rights, in the interest of individual private property.

The revolutionary leadership favored free economic individualism. It had had enough, under the Old Regime, of government regulation over the sale or quality of goods and of privileged companies and other economic monopolies. Reforming economic thought at the time, not only in France but in England, where Adam Smith had published his epoch-making *Wealth of Nations* in 1776, held that organized special interests were bad for society, and that all prices and wages should be determined by free arrangement between the individuals concerned.[7] The more prominent leaders of the French Revolution believed firmly in this freedom from control. The Constituent Assembly abolished the guilds, which were mainly monopolistic organizations of small businessmen or master craftsmen, interested in keeping up prices and averse to new machinery or new methods. There was also, in France, a rather highly organized labor movement. Since the masterships in the guilds were practically hereditary (as a form of property and privilege), the journeymen formed their own associations, or trade unions, called

[7] See pp. 312–313.

compagnonnages, outside the guilds. Many trades were so organized—the carpenters, plasterers, paper workers, hatters, saddlers, cutlers, nail makers, carters, tanners, locksmiths, and glassworkers. Some were organized nationally, some only locally. All these journeymen's unions had been illegal under the Old Regime, but they had flourished nevertheless. They collected dues and maintained officers. They often dealt collectively with the guild masters or other employers, requiring the payment of a stipulated wage or amendment of working conditions. Sometimes they even imposed closed shops. Organized strikes were quite common. The labor troubles of 1789 continued on into the Revolution. Business fell off in the atmosphere of disorder. In 1791 there was another wave of strikes. The Assembly, in the Le Chapelier law of that year, renewed the old prohibitions of the *compagnonnages*. The same law restated the abolition of the guilds and forbade the organization of special economic interests of any kind. All trades, it declared, were free for all to enter. All men, without belonging to any organization, had the right to work at any occupation or business they might choose. All wages were to be settled privately by the workman and his employer. This was not at all what the workingman, at that time or any other, really wanted. Nevertheless the provisions of the Le Chapelier law remained a part of French law for three-quarters of a century. The embryonic trade unions continued to exist secretly, though with more difficulty than under the hit-and-miss law enforcement of the Old Regime.

The Quarrel with the Church

Most fatefully of all, the Constituent Assembly quarreled with the Catholic church. The confiscation of church properties naturally came as a shock to the clergy. The village priests, whose support had made possible the revolt of the Third Estate, now found that the very buildings in which they worshiped with their parishioners on Sunday belonged to the "nation." The loss of income-producing properties undercut the religious orders and ruined the schools, in which thousands of boys had received free education before the Revolution. Yet it was not on the question of material wealth that the church and the Revolution came to blows. Members of the Constituent Assembly took the view of the church that the great monarchies had taken before them. The idea of separation of church and state was far from their minds. They regarded the church as a form of public authority and as such subordinate to the sovereign power. They frankly argued that the poor needed religion if they were to respect the property of the more wealthy. In any case, having deprived the church of its own income, they had to provide for its maintenance. For the schools many generous and democratic projects of state-sponsored education were drawn up, though under the troubled conditions of the time little was accomplished. For the clergy the new program was mapped out in the Civil Constitution of the Clergy of 1790.

This document went far toward setting up a French national church. Under its provisions the parish priests and bishops were elected, the latter by the same 50,000 electors who chose other important officials. Protestants, Jews, and agnostics could legally take part in the elections, purely on the ground of citizenship and property qualifications. Archbishoprics were abolished, and all the borders of existing bishoprics were redrawn. The number of dioceses was reduced from over 130 to 83, so that one would be coterminous with each department. Bishops were allowed merely to notify the pope of their elevation; they were forbidden to acknowledge any papal authority on their assumption of office, and no papal letter or decree was to be published or enforced in France except with government permission. All clergy received salaries from the state, the average income of bishops being somewhat reduced, that of parish clergymen being raised. Sinecures, plural holdings, and other abuses by which noble families had been supported by the church were done away with. The Constituent Assembly (independently of the Civil Constitution) also prohibited the taking of religious vows and dissolved all monastic houses.

Some of all this was not in principle alarmingly new, since before the Revolution the civil authority of the king had designated the French bishops and passed on the admission of papal documents into France. French bishops, in the old spirit of the "Gallican liberties," were traditionally jealous of papal power in France.[8] Many were now willing to accept something like the Civil Constitution if allowed to produce it on their own authority. The Assembly refused to concede so much jurisdiction to the Gallican church and applied instead to the pope, hoping to force its plans upon the French clergy by invoking the authority of the Vatican. But the Vatican pronounced the Civil Constitution a wanton usurpation of power over the Catholic church. Unfortunately, the pope also went further, condemning the whole Revolution and all its works. The Constituent Assembly retorted by requiring all French clergy to swear an oath of loyalty to the constitution, including the Civil Constitution of the Clergy. Half took the oath and half refused it, the latter half including all but seven of the bishops. One of the seven willing to accept the new arrangements was Talleyrand, soon to be famous as foreign minister of numerous French governments.

There were now two churches in France, one clandestine, the other official, one maintained by voluntary offerings or by funds smuggled in from abroad, the other financed and sponsored by the government. The former, comprising the nonjuring, unsworn or "refractory" clergy, turned violently counterrevolutionary. To protect themselves from the Revolution they insisted, with an emphasis quite new in France, on the universal religious supremacy of the Roman pontiff. They denounced the "constitutional" clergy as schismatics who spurned the pope and as mere careerists willing to hold jobs on the government's terms. The constitutional clergy, those taking the oath and upholding the Civil Constitution, considered themselves to be patriots and defenders of the rights of man; and they insisted that the Gallican church had always enjoyed a degree of liberty from Rome. The Catholic laity were terrified and puzzled. Many were sufficiently attached to the Revolution to prefer the constitutional clergy; but to do so meant to defy the pope, and Catholics who persisted in defying the pope were on the whole those least zealous in their religion. The constitutional clergy therefore stood on shaky foundations. Many of their followers, under stress of the times, eventually turned against Christianity itself.

Good Catholics tended to favor the "refractory" clergy. The outstanding example was the king himself. He personally used the services of refractory priests, and thus gave a new reason for the revolutionaries to distrust him. Whatever chance there was that Louis XVI might go along with the Revolution was exploded, for he concluded that he could do so only by endangering his immortal soul. Former

[8] See pp. 52, 69, 86–87, 132, 184.

aristocrats also naturally preferred the refractory clergy. They now put aside the Voltairean levities of the Age of Enlightenment, and the "best people" began to exhibit a new piety in religious matters. The peasants, who found little in the Revolution to interest them after their own insurrection of 1789 and the consequent abolition of the manorial regime, also favored the old-fashioned or refractory clergy. Much the same was true of the urban working-class families, where both men and women might shout against priests and yet want to be sure that their marriages were valid and their children properly baptized. The Constituent Assembly, and its successors, were at their wits' end what to do. Sometimes they shut their eyes at the intrigues of refractory clergy; the constitutional clergy then became fearful. Sometimes they hunted out and persecuted the refractories; in that case they only stirred up religious fanaticism.

The Civil Constitution of the Clergy has been called the greatest tactical blunder of the Revolution. Certainly its consequences were unfortunate in the extreme, and they spread to much of Europe. In the nineteenth century the church was to be officially antidemocratic and antiliberal;[9] and democrats and liberals in most cases were to be violently and outspokenly anticlerical. The main beneficiary was the papacy. The French church, which had clung for ages to its Gallican liberties, was thrown by the Revolution into the arms of the pope. Even Napoleon, when he healed the schism a decade later, acknowledged powers in the papacy that had never been acknowledged by the French kings. These were steps in the process, leading through the proclamation of papal infallibility in 1870,[10] by which the affairs of the modern Catholic church became increasingly centralized at the Vatican.

With the proclamation of the constitution in September 1791, the Constituent Assembly disbanded. Before dissolving, it ruled that none of its members might sit in the forthcoming Legislative Assembly. This body was therefore made up of men who still wished to make their mark in the Revolution. The new regime went into effect in October 1791. It was a constitutional monarchy in which a unicameral Legislative Assembly confronted a king unconverted to the new order. Designed as the permanent solution to France's problems, it was to collapse in ten months, in August 1792, as a result of popular insurrection four months after France became involved in war. A group of Jacobins, known as Girondins, for a time became the left or advanced party of the Revolution and in the Legislative Assembly led France into war.

43. THE REVOLUTION AND EUROPE: THE WAR AND THE "SECOND" REVOLUTION, 1792

The International Impact of the Revolution

The European governments were long reluctant to become involved with France. They were under considerable pressure. On the one hand, pro-French and prorevolutionary groups appeared immediately in many quarters. The doctrines of the French Revolution, as of the American, were highly exportable: they took the form of a universal philosophy, proclaiming the rights of man regardless of time

---

[9] See pp. 482–483, 598–600.
[10] See p. 600.

or place, race or nation. Moreover, depending on what one was looking for, one might see in the first disturbances in France a revolt of either the nobility, the bourgeoisie, the common people, or the entire nation. In Poland those who were trying to reorganize the country against further partition hailed the French example. The Hungarian landlords pointed to it in their reaction against Joseph II. In England, for a time, those who controlled Parliament complacently believed that the French were attempting to imitate them.

But it was the excluded classes of European society who were most inspired. The hard-pressed Silesian weavers were said to hope that "the French would come." Strikes broke out at Hamburg, and peasants rebelled elsewhere. One English diplomat found that even the Prussian army had "a strong taint of democracy among officers and men." In Belgium, where the privileged elements were already in revolt against the Austrian emperor, a second revolt broke out, inspired by events in France and aimed at the privileged elements. In England the newly developing "radicals," men like Thomas Paine and Dr. Richard Price, who wished a thorough overhauling of Parliament and the established church, entered into correspondence with the Assembly in Paris. Businessmen of importance, including Watt and Boulton, the pioneers of the steam engine, were likewise pro-French since they had no representation in the House of Commons. The Irish too were excited and presently revolted. Everywhere the young were aroused, the young Hegel in Germany, or in England the young Wordsworth, who later recalled the sense of a new era that had captivated so many spirits in 1789:

> *Bliss was it in that dawn to be alive,*
> *But to be young was very heaven!*

On the other hand the anti-Revolutionary movement gathered strength. Edmund Burke, frightened by the French proclivities of English radicals, published as early as 1790 his *Reflections on the Revolution in France*. For France, he predicted anarchy and dictatorship. For England, he sternly advised the English to accept a slow adaptation of their own English liberties. For all the world, he denounced a political philosophy that rested on abstract principles of right and wrong, declaring that every people must be shaped by its own national circumstances, national history, and national character. He drew an eloquent reply and a defense of France from Thomas Paine in the *Rights of Man*. Burke soon began to preach the necessity of war, urging a kind of ideological struggle against French barbarism and violence. His *Reflections* was translated and widely read. In the long run his book proved an influential work in the history of thought. In the short run it fell on willing ears. The king of Sweden, Gustavus III, offered to lead a monarchist crusade. In Russia old Catherine was appalled; she forbade further translations of her erstwhile friend Voltaire, she called the French "vile riffraff" and "brutish cannibals," and she packed off to Siberia a Russian named Radishchev, who in his *Voyage from St. Petersburg to Moscow* pointed out the evils of serfdom. It is said that Russians were even forbidden to speak of the "revolutions of the heavenly spheres." The terrors were heightened by plaintive messages from Louis XVI and Marie Antoinette, and by the émigrés who kept bursting out of France, led as early as July 1789 by the king's own brother, the Count of Artois. The émigrés, who at first were nobles, settled in various parts of Europe and began using their international aristocratic connections. They preached a kind of holy war. They bemoaned the sad plight of the king, but what they most wanted was to get back their manorial incomes and other rights. They hinted that Louis XVI himself was a dangerous revolutionary and much preferred his brother, the unyielding Count of Artois.

In short, Europe was soon split by a division that overran all frontiers. The same was true of America also. In the United States the rising party of Jefferson was branded as Jacobin and pro-French, that of Hamilton as reactionary and pro-British; while in colonial Spanish America ideas of independence were strengthened, and the Venezuelan Miranda became a general in the French army. In all countries of the European world, though least of all in eastern and southern Europe, there were revolutionary or pro-French elements that were feared by their own governments. In all countries, including France, there were implacable enemies of the French Revolution. In all countries were people whose loyalties lay abroad. There had been no such situation since the Protestant Reformation, nor was there anything like it again until after the Russian Revolution of the twentieth century.

The Coming of the War, April 1792

Yet the European governments were slow to move. Catherine had no intention of becoming involved in western Europe. She only wished to involve her neighbors. William Pitt, the British prime minister, resisted the war cries of Burke. Son of the Earl of Chatham, prime minister since 1784, chief founder of the new Tory party, Pitt had a reforming program of his own; he had tried and failed to carry a reform of Parliament and was now concentrating on a policy of orderly finance and systematic economy. His program would be ruined by war. He insisted that the domestic affairs of France were of no concern to the British government. The key position was occupied by the Habsburg emperor, Leopold II, brother to the French queen. Leopold at first answered Marie Antoinette's pleas for help by telling her to adjust herself to conditions in France. He resisted the furious demands of the émigrés, whom he understood perfectly, having inherited from Joseph II a fractious aristocracy himself.

Still, the new French government was a disturbing phenomenon. It openly encouraged malcontents all over Europe. It showed a tendency to settle international affairs by unilateral action. For example, it annexed Avignon at the request of local revolutionaries but without the consent of its historic sovereign, the pope. Or again, in Alsace there had been much overlapping jurisdiction between France and Germany ever since the Peace of Westphalia.[11] The Constituent Assembly abolished feudalism and manorial dues in Alsace as elsewhere in France. To German princes who had feudal rights in Alsace the Assembly offered compensation, but it did not ask their consent; and the German princes concerned, deprived by a revolutionary decree of rights guaranteed them by past treaties, appealed to the Holy Roman Emperor to protest the infringement of international understandings. Moreover, after the arrest of Louis XVI at Varennes, after his attempted flight in June 1791, it became impossible to deny that the French king and queen were prisoners of the revolutionaries.

In August Leopold met with the king of Prussia at Pillnitz in Saxony. The

[11] See maps, pp. 142–143, 183, 317.

resulting Declaration of Pillnitz rested on a famous *if:* Leopold would take military steps to restore order in France if all the other powers would join him. Knowing the attitude of Pitt, he believed that the *if* could never materialize. His aim was mainly to rid himself of the French émigrés. These perversely received the Declaration with delight. They used it as an open threat to their enemies in France, announcing that they would soon return alongside the forces of civilized Europe to punish the guilty and right the wrongs that had been done to them.

In France the upholders of the Revolution were alarmed. They were ignorant of what Leopold really meant and took the dire menaces of the émigrés at their face value. The Declaration of Pillnitz, far from cowing the French, enraged them against all the crowned heads of Europe. It gave a political advantage to the then dominant faction of Jacobins, known to history as the Girondins. These included the philosophe Condorcet, the humanitarian lawyer Brissot, and the civil servant Roland and his more famous wife, Mme. Roland, whose house became a kind of headquarters of the group. They attracted many foreigners also, such as Thomas Paine and the German Anacharsis Cloots, the "representative of the human race." In December 1791 a deputation of English radicals, led by James Watt, son of the inventor of the steam engine, received a wild ovation at the Paris Jacobin club.

The Girondins became the party of international revolution. They declared that the Revolution could never be secure in France until it spread to the world. In their view, once war had come, the peoples of states at war with France would not support their own governments. There was reason for this belief, since revolutionary elements antedating the French Revolution already existed in both the Dutch and the Austrian Netherlands, and to a lesser degree in parts of Switzerland, Poland, and elsewhere. Some Girondins therefore contemplated a war in which French armies should enter neighboring countries, unite with local revolutionaries, overthrow the established governments, and set up a federation of republics. War was also favored by a very different group, led by Lafayette, which wished to curb the Revolution by holding it at the line of constitutional monarchy. This group mistakenly believed that war might restore the much damaged popularity of Louis XVI, unite the country under the new government, and make it possible to put down the continuing Jacobin agitation. As the war spirit boiled up in France, the Emperor Leopold II died. He was succeeded by Francis II, a man much more inclined than Leopold to yield to the clamors of the old aristocracy. Francis resumed negotiations with Prussia. In France all who dreaded a return of the Old Regime listened more readily to the Girondins. Among the Jacobins as a whole, only a few, generally a handful of radical democrats, opposed the war. On April 20, 1792, without serious opposition, the Assembly declared war on "the king of Hungary and Bohemia," i.e., the Austrian monarchy.

The "Second" Revolution: August 10, 1792

The war intensified the existing unrest and dissatisfaction of the unpropertied classes. Both peasants and urban workers felt that the Constituent and the Legislative Assembly had served the propertied interests and had done little for them. Peasants were dissatisfied at the inadequate measures taken to facilitate land distribution; workers felt especially the pinch of soaring prices, which by 1792 had greatly risen. Gold had been taken out of the country by the émigrés; paper money, the assignats, was almost the sole currency, and the future of the government was so uncertain that it steadily lost value. Peasants concealed their food products rather than sell them for depreciating paper. Actual scarcity combined with the falling value of money to drive up the cost of living. The lowest income groups suffered the most. But dissatisfied though they were, when the war began they were threatened with a return of the émigrés and a vindictive restoration of the Old Regime, which at least for the peasants would be the worst of all possible eventualities. The working classes—peasants, artisans, mechanics, shopkeepers, wage workers—rallied to the Revolution but not to the revolutionary government in power. The Legislative Assembly and the constitutional monarchy lacked the confidence of large elements of the population.

In addition, the war at first went very unfavorably for the French. Prussia joined immediately with Austria, and by the summer of 1792 the two powers were on the point of invading France. They issued a proclamation to the French people, the Brunswick Manifesto of July 25, declaring that if any harm befell the French king and queen the Austro-Prussian forces, upon their arrival in Paris, would exact the most severe retribution from the inhabitants of that city. Such menaces, compounding the military emergency, only played into the hands of the most violent activists. Masses of the French people, roused and guided by bourgeois Jacobin leaders, notably Robespierre, Danton, and the vitriolic journalist Marat, burst out in a passion of patriotic excitement. They turned against the king because he was identified with powers at war with France, and also because, in France itself, those who still supported him were using the monarchy as a defense against the lower classes. Republicanism in France was partly a rather sudden historical accident, in that France was at war under a king who could not be trusted, and partly a kind of lower-class or quasi-proletarian movement, in which, however, many bourgeois revolutionaries shared.

Feeling ran high during the summer of 1792. Recruits streamed into Paris from all quarters on their way to the frontiers. One detachment, from Marseilles, brought with them a new marching song, known ever since as the *Marseillaise*, a fierce call to war upon tyranny. The transient provincials stirred up the agitation in Paris. On August 10, 1792, the working-class quarters of the city rose in revolt, supported by the recruits from Marseilles and elsewhere. They stormed the Tuileries against resistance by the Swiss Guard, many of whom were massacred, and

A WOMAN OF THE REVOLUTION
by Jacques-Louis David (French, 1748–1825)

Here is something of what historians mean by the "working class," and it may be compared with the representations of aristocracy and of the middle class already shown (see pp. 335, 343). The coarse garments and untended hair, the colorless lips, the lined forehead, and the evidences of suffering in the eyes—all reveal a life of much labor and few amenities. The woman seems to be observing something with an interest mixed with suspicion, and her air of determination and even of defiance suggests the political-mindedness aroused even in the poorest classes in time of revolution. David painted this portrait in 1795, a year after the Terror in France. He was himself an active revolutionary, a member of the Convention and of the Committee of General Security. It is rare to find portraits of people of this class of society done with so much realism, sympathy, and force. Courtesy of the Musée des Beaux-Arts, Lyon (J. Camponogara).

seized and imprisoned the king and the royal family. A revolutionary municipal government, or "Commune," was set up in Paris. Usurping the powers of the Legislative Assembly, it forced the abrogation of the constitution, and the election, by universal male suffrage, of a Constitutional Convention that was to govern France and prepare a new and more democratic constitution. The very word Convention was used in recollection of the American Constitutional Convention in 1787. Meanwhile hysteria, anarchy, and terror reigned in Paris; a handful of insurrectionary volunteers, declaring that they would not fight enemies on the frontiers until they had disposed of enemies in Paris, dragged about 1,100 persons —refractory priests and other counterrevolutionaries—from the prisons of the city and killed them after drumhead trials. These are known as the "September massacres."

For over two and a half years, since October 1789, there had been an abatement of popular violence. Now the coming of the war and the dissatisfaction of the lower classes with the course of events so far had led to new explosions. The insurrection of August 10, 1792, the "second" French Revolution, initiated the most advanced phase of the Revolution.

44. THE EMERGENCY REPUBLIC, 1792–1795: THE TERROR

The National Convention

The National Convention met on September 20, 1792; it was to sit for three years. It immediately proclaimed the Year One of the French Republic. The disorganized French armies, also on September 20, won a great moral victory in the "cannonade of Valmy," a battle that was hardly more than an artillery duel, but which induced the Prussian commander to give up his march on Paris. The French soon occupied Belgium (the Austrian Netherlands), Savoy (which belonged to the king of Sardinia who had joined with the Austrians), and Mainz and other cities on the German Left Bank of the Rhine. Revolutionary sympathizers in these places appealed for French aid. The National Convention decreed assistance to "all peoples wishing to recover their liberty." It also ordered that French generals, in the occupied areas, should dissolve the old governments, confiscate government and church property, abolish tithes, hunting rights, and seigneurial dues, and set up provisional administrations. Thus revolution spread in the wake of the successful French armies.

The British and Dutch prepared to resist. Pitt, still insisting that the French might have any domestic regime that they chose, declared that Great Britain could not tolerate the French occupation of Belgium. The British and Dutch began conversations with Prussia and Austria, and the French declared war on them on February 1, 1793. Within a few weeks the Republic had annexed Savoy and Nice, as well as Belgium, and had much of the German Rhineland under its military government.[12] Meanwhile, in eastern Europe, while denouncing the rapacity of the French savages, the rulers of Russia and Prussia came to an arrangement of their own, each appropriating a portion of Poland in the second

---

[12] See map, p. 383.

partition in January 1793.[13] The Austrians, excluded from the second partition, became anxious over their interests in eastern Europe. The infant French Republic, now at war with all Europe, was saved by the weakness of the Coalition, for Britain and Holland had no land forces of consequence, and Prussia and Austria were too jealous of each other, and too preoccupied with Poland, to commit the bulk of their armies against France.

In the Convention all the leaders were Jacobins, but the Jacobins were again splitting. The Girondins were no longer the most advanced revolutionary group as they had been in the Legislative Assembly. Beside the Girondins appeared a new group, whose members preferred to sit in the highest seats in the hall, and therefore were dubbed the "Mountain" in the political parlance of the day. The leading Girondins came from the great provincial cities; the leading Montagnards, though mostly of provincial birth, were representatives of the city of Paris and owed most of their political strength to the radical and popular elements in that city.

These popular revolutionists, outside the Convention, proudly called themselves "sans-culottes," since they wore the workingman's long trousers, not the knee breeches or *culottes*, of the middle and upper classes. They were the working class of a pre-industrial age, shopkeepers and shop assistants, skilled artisans in various trades, including some who were owners of small manufacturing or handicraft enterprises. For two years their militancy and their activism pressed the Revolution forward. They demanded an equality that should be meaningful for people like themselves, they called for a mighty effort against foreign powers that presumed to intervene in the French Revolution, and they denounced the now deposed king and queen (correctly enough) for collusion with the Austrian enemy. The sans-culottes feared that the Convention might be too moderate. They favored direct democracy in their neighborhood clubs and assemblies, together with a mass rising if necessary against the Convention itself. The Girondins in the Convention began to dismiss these popular militants as anarchists. The group known as the Mountain was more willing to work with them, so long at least as the emergency lasted.

The Convention put Louis XVI on trial for treason in December 1792. On January 15 it unanimously pronounced him guilty, but on the next day, out of 721 deputies present, only 361 voted for immediate execution, a majority of one. Louis XVI died on the guillotine forthwith. The 361 deputies were henceforth branded for life as regicides; never could they allow, in safety to themselves, a restoration of the Bourbon monarchy in France. The other 360 deputies were not similarly compromised; their rivals called them Girondins, "moderatists," counterrevolutionaries. All who still wanted more from the Revolution, or who feared that the slightest wavering would bring the Allies and the émigrés into France, now looked to the Mountain wing of the Jacobins.

Background to the Terror

In April 1793 the most spectacular French general, Dumouriez, who had won the victories in Belgium five months before, defected to Austria. The Allied armies now drove the French from Belgium and again threatened to invade France.

---

[13] See pp. 327–329.

THE GLEANERS
by Jean-François Millet (French, 1814–1875)

Three women of the poorest of the French peasantry are shown here. They may be compared with the women depicted on pp. 335, 343, and 371. Bowed with labor, reaching out with strong, muscular hands, clutching their few stalks of grain, these women are exercising a legal right, "glanage," by which poor people were allowed to glean the fields after the owners had taken in the harvest. Many of the owners were more affluent peasants. Glanage was one of the collective village rights, originally common to France, England, and most of Europe, which tended to disappear with the spread of modern private-property institutions. When the painting was first exhibited in 1857, it reminded one irate critic of the French Revolution. "Behind these three gleaning-women," he said, "against the leaden horizon, we can see silhouetted the pikes, riots and scaffolds of '93." Courtesy of the Louvre (Giraudon).

Counterrevolutionaries in France exulted. From the revolutionaries went up the cry, "We are betrayed!" Prices continued to rise, the currency fell, food was harder to obtain, and the working classes were increasingly restless. The sans-culottes demanded price controls, currency controls, rationing, legislation against the hoarding of food, and requisitioning to enforce the circulation of goods. They denounced the bourgeoisie as profiteers and exploiters of the people. While the Girondins resisted, the Mountain went along with the sans-culottes, partly from sympathy with their ideas, partly to win mass support for the war, and partly as a maneuver to get rid of the Girondins. On May 31, 1793, the Commune of Paris, under sans-culotte pressure, assembled a host of demonstrators and insurrectionists who invaded the Convention and forced the arrest of the Girondin leaders. Other Girondins fled to the provinces, including Condorcet, who, while in hiding, and before his death, found occasion to write his famous book on the *Progress of the Human Mind*.[14]

The Mountain now ruled in the Convention, but the Convention itself ruled very little. Not only were the foreign armies and the émigrés at the gates bent on destroying the Convention as a band of regicides and social incendiaries, but the authority of the Convention was widely repudiated in France itself. In the west, in the Vendée, the peasants had revolted against military conscription; they were worked upon by refractory priests, British agents, and royalist emissaries of the Count of Artois. The great provincial cities, Lyons, Bordeaux, Marseilles, and others, had also rebelled, especially after the fugitive Girondins reached them. These "federalist" rebels demanded a more "federal" or decentralized republic. Like the Vendéans, with whom they had no connection, they objected to the ascendancy of Paris, having been accustomed to more regional independence under the Old Regime. These rebellions became counterrevolutionary, since all sorts of foreigners, royalists, émigrés, and clericals streamed in to assist them.

The Convention had to defend itself against extremists of the Left as well. To the genuine mass action of the sans-culottes were now added the voices of even more excited militants called *enragés*. Various organizers, enthusiasts, agitators, and neighborhood politicians declared that parliamentary methods were useless. Generally they were men outside the Convention—and also women, for women were particularly sensitive to the crisis of food shortage and soaring prices, and an organization of Revolutionary Republican Women caused a brief stir in 1793. All such activists worked through units of local government in Paris and elsewhere, and in thousands of "popular societies" and provincial clubs throughout the whole country. They also formed "revolutionary armies," semimilitary bands of men who scoured the rural areas for food, searched the barns of peasants, denounced suspects, and preached revolution.

As for the Convention, while it cannot be said ever to have had any commanding leaders, the program it followed for about a year was on the whole that of Maximilien Robespierre, himself a Jacobin but not one to go along forever with popular revolution or anarchy. Robespierre is one of the most argued about and least understood men of modern times. Persons accustomed to stable conditions dismiss him with a shudder as a bloodthirsty fanatic, dictator, and demagogue. Others have considered him an idealist, a visionary, and an ardent patriot whose goals and ideals were at least avowedly democratic. All agree on his personal

[14] See p. 314.

honesty and integrity and on his revolutionary zeal. He was by origin a lawyer of northern France, educated with the aid of scholarships in Paris. He had been elected in 1789 to sit for the Third Estate in the Estates General, and in the ensuing Constituent Assembly played a minor role, though calling attention to himself by his views against capital punishment and in favor of universal suffrage. During the time of the Legislative Assembly, in 1791–1792, he continued to agitate for democracy and vainly pleaded against the declaration of war. In the Convention, elected in September 1792, he sat for a Paris constituency. He became a prominent member of the Mountain and welcomed the purge of the Girondins. He had always kept free of the bribery and graft in which some others became involved and for this reason was known as the Incorruptible. He was a great believer in the importance of "virtue." This term had been used in a specialized way among the philosophes: both Montesquieu and Rousseau had held that republics depended upon "virtue," or unselfish public spirit and civic zeal, to which was added, under Rousseauist influence, a somewhat sentimentalized idea of personal uprightness and purity of life. Robespierre was determined, in 1793 and 1794, to bring about a democratic republic made up of good citizens and honest men.

The Program of the Convention, 1793–1794: The Terror

The program of the Convention, which Robespierre helped to form, was to repress anarchy, civil strife, and counterrevolution at home and to win the war by a great national mobilization of the country's people and resources. It would prepare a democratic constitution and initiate legislation for the lower classes, but it would not yield to the Paris Commune and other agencies of direct revolutionary action. To conduct the government, the Convention granted wide powers to a Committee of Public Safety, a group of twelve members of the Convention who were reelected every month. Robespierre was an influential member; others were the youthful St. Just, the partially paralyzed Couthon, and the army officer Carnot, "organizer of victory."

To repress the "counterrevolution," the Convention and the Committee of Public Safety set up what is popularly known as the "Reign of Terror." Revolutionary courts were instituted as an alternative to the lynch law of the September massacres. A Committee of General Security was created as a kind of supreme political police. Designed to protect the Revolutionary Republic from its internal enemies, the Terror struck at those who were in league against the Republic, and at those who were merely suspected of hostile activities. Its victims ranged from Marie Antoinette and other royalists to the former revolutionary colleagues of the Mountain, the Girondin leaders; and before the year 1793–1794 was over, some of the old Jacobins of the Mountain who had helped inaugurate the program also went to the guillotine. The number of persons who lost their lives in the Terror, from the late summer of 1793 to July 1794, has often been exaggerated. By the standards of the twentieth century, in which governments have undertaken to extirpate whole classes or races, the Terror was fairly mild. Yet about 40,000 persons died in it; and additional hundreds of thousands were at one time or another arrested and held in custody. Most executions took place in the Vendée, at Lyons, and in other places in open rebellion, and were directed against persons in insurrection in time of war. The Terror showed no respect for, or interest in, the class origins of its victims. About 8 percent were nobles, but the nobles as a class were not molested unless suspected of political agitation; 14 percent of the victims were classifiable as bourgeois, mainly of the rebellious southern cities; 6 percent were clergy, while no less than 70 percent were of the peasant and laboring classes. A democratic republic, founded on the Declaration of the Rights of Man, was in principle to follow the Terror once the war and the emergency were over, but meanwhile, the Terror was inhuman at best and in some places atrocious, as at Nantes where 2,000 persons were loaded on barges and deliberately drowned. The Terror left long memories in France of antipathy to the Revolution and to republicanism.

To conduct the government in the midst of the war emergency the Committee of Public Safety operated as a joint dictatorship or war cabinet. It prepared and guided legislation through the Convention. It gained control over the "representatives on mission," who were members of the Convention on duty with the armies and in the insurgent areas of France. It established the *Bulletin des loix*, so that all persons might know what laws they were supposed to enforce or to obey. It centralized the administration, converting the swarm of locally elected officials, left over from the Constituent Assembly, and who were royalists in some places, wild extremists in others, into centrally appointed "national agents" named by the Committee of Public Safety.

To win the war the Committee proclaimed the *levée en masse*, calling on all able-bodied men to rally to the colors. It recruited scientific men to work on armaments and munitions. The most prominent French scientists of the day, including Lagrange and Lamarck, worked for or were protected by the government of the Terror, though one, Lavoisier, "father of modern chemistry," was guillotined in 1794 because he had been involved in tax farming before 1789. For military reasons also the Committee instituted economic controls, which at the same time met the demands of the *enragés* and other working-class spokesmen. The assignats ceased to fall during the year of the Terror. Thus the government protected both its own purchasing power and that of the masses. It did so by controlling the export of gold, by confiscating specie and foreign currency from French citizens, to whom it paid assignats in return, and by legislation against hoarding or the withholding of goods from the market. Food and supplies for the armies, and for civilians in the towns, were raised and allocated by a system of requisitions, centralized in a Subsistence Commission under the Committee of Public Safety. A "general maximum" set ceilings for prices and wages. It helped to check inflation during the crisis, but it did not work very well; the Committee believed, on principle, in a free market economy and lacked the technical and administrative machinery to enforce thorough controls. By 1794 it was giving freer rein to private enterprise and to the peasants, in order to encourage production. It tried also to hold down wages and in that respect failed to win the adherence of many working-class leaders.

In June 1793 the Committee produced, and had adopted by the Convention, a republican constitution which provided for universal male suffrage. But the new constitution was suspended indefinitely, and the government was declared "revolutionary until the peace," "revolutionary" meaning extraconstitutional or of an emergency character. In other ways the Committee showed intentions of legislating on behalf of the lower economic classes. The price controls and other economic regulations answered the demands of the sans-culottes. The last of the manorial regime was done away with; the peasants were relieved of having to pay compensation for the obligations that had been abolished at the opening of the Revolution. Purchase of land by the peasants was made somewhat easier. There were even moves, in the Ventôse laws of March 1794, to confiscate the property of suspects (not merely of the church or convicted émigrés), and to give such property gratis to "indigent patriots"; but these laws were drafted in unworkable form, never received much support from the ruling Committee, and came to very little. The Committee busied itself also with social services and measures of public improvement. It issued pamphlets to teach farmers to improve their crops, selected promising youths to receive instruction in useful trades, opened a military school for boys of all classes, even the humblest, and certainly intended to introduce universal elementary education. It was at this time, also, that slavery was abolished in the French colonies, free blacks having already received civic rights.

The Committee of Public Safety wished to concentrate the Revolution in itself. It had no patience with unauthorized revolutionary violence. With a democratic program of its own, it disapproved of the turbulent democracy of popular clubs and local assemblies. In the fall of 1793 it arrested the leading *enragés* and prohibited revolutionary women's organizations at the same time. Extreme revolutionism thereafter took the name of Hébertism, after Hébert, an officer of the Paris Commune. The Hébertists were a large and indefinable group and included many members of the Convention. They indiscriminately denounced merchants and bourgeoisie. They were the party of extreme Terror; an Hébertist brought about the drownings at Nantes. Believing all religion to be counterrevolutionary, they launched the movement of Dechristianization. Even a Republican calendar was adopted by the Convention. Its main purpose was to blot out from men's minds the Christian cycle of Sundays, saints' days, and such holidays as Christmas and Easter. It counted years from the founding of the French Republic, divided each year into new months of thirty days each, and even abolished the week, which it replaced with the *décade*.[15]

Another form taken by Dechristianization was the cult of reason which sprang up all over France at the end of 1793. In Paris the bishop resigned his office, declaring that he had been deluded; and the Commune put on ceremonies in the cathedral of Notre Dame, in which Reason was impersonated by an actress who was the wife of one of the city officials. But Dechristianization was severely frowned upon by Robespierre. He believed that it would alienate the masses from the Republic and ruin such sympathy as was still felt for the Revolution abroad. The Committee of Public Safety, therefore, ordered the toleration of peaceable Catholics, and in June 1794 Robespierre introduced the "Worship of the Supreme Being," a kind of national and naturalistic cult, in which the Republic was declared to recognize the existence of God and the immortality of the soul. Robespierre hoped that both Catholics and agnostic anticlericals could become reconciled on this ground. But Catholics were now beyond reconciliation, and the freethinkers, appealing to the tradition of Voltaire, regarded Robespierre as a reactionary mystery monger and were instrumental in bringing about his fall.

Meanwhile the Committee proceeded relentlessly against the Hébertists, whose

---

[15] Though not adopted until October 1793, the revolutionary calendar dated the Year I of the French Republic from September 22, 1792. The names of the months, in order, were Vendémiaire, Brumaire, Frimaire (autumn); Nivôse, Pluviôse, Ventôse (winter); Germinal, Floréal, Prairial (spring); Messidor, Thermidor, Fructidor (summer).

main champions it sent to the guillotine in March 1794. The paramilitary "revolutionary armies" were repressed. The extreme Terrorists were recalled from the provinces. The revolutionary Paris Commune was destroyed. Robespierre filled the municipal offices of Paris with his own appointees. This Robespierrist commune disapproved of strikes and tried to hold down wages, on the plea of military necessity; it failed to win over the ex-Hébertists and working-class spokesmen, who became disillusioned with the Revolution and dismissed it as a bourgeois movement. Probably to prevent just such a conclusion, and to avoid the appearance of deviation to the right, Robespierre and the Committee, after liquidating the Hébertists, also liquidated certain right-wing members of the Mountain who were known as Dantonists. Danton and his followers were accused of financial dishonesty and of dealing with counterrevolutionaries; the charges contained some truth but were not the main reason for the executions.

By the spring of 1794 the French Republic possessed an army of 800,000 men, the largest ever raised up to that time by a European power. It was a national army, representing a people in arms, commanded by officers who had been promoted rapidly on grounds of merit, and composed of troops who felt themselves to be citizens fighting for their own cause. Its intense political mindedness made it the more formidable and contrasted strongly with the indifference of the opposing troops, some of whom were in fact serfs and none of whom had any sense of membership in their own political systems. The Allied governments, each pursuing its own ends, and still distracted by their ambitions in Poland, where the third partition was impending, could not combine their forces against France. In June 1794 the French won the battle of Fleurus in Belgium. The Republican hosts again streamed into the Low Countries; in six months their cavalry rode into Amsterdam on the ice. A revolutionary Batavian Republic soon replaced the old Dutch provinces.

Military success made the French less willing to put up with the dictatorial rule and economic regimentation of the Terror. Robespierre and the Committee of Public Safety had antagonized all significant parties. The working-class radicals of Paris would no longer support him, and after the death of Danton the National Convention was afraid of its own ruling committee. A group in the Convention obtained the "outlawing" of Robespierre on 9 Thermidor (July 27, 1794); he was guillotined with some of his associates on the following day. Many who turned against Robespierre believed they were pushing the Revolution farther forward, as in destroying the Girondins the year before. Others thought, or said, that they were stopping a dictator and a tyrant. All agreed, to absolve themselves, in heaping all blame upon Robespierre. The idea that Robespierre was an ogre originated more with his former colleagues than with conservatives of the time.

The Thermidorian Reaction

The fall of Robespierre stunned the country, but its effects manifested themselves during the following months as the "Thermidorian reaction." The Terror subsided. The Convention reduced the powers of the Committee of Public Safety, and it closed the Jacobin club. Price control and other regulations were removed. Inflation resumed its course, prices again rose, and the disoriented and leaderless working classes suffered more than ever. Sporadic risings broke out, of which the greatest was the insurrection of Prairial in the Year III (May 1795), when a mob all but dispersed the Convention by force. Troops were called to Paris for the first time since 1789. Insurrectionists in the working-class quarters threw up barricades in the streets. The army prevailed without much bloodshed, but the Convention arrested, imprisoned, or deported ten thousand of the insurgents. A few organizers were guillotined, including one militant black. The affair of Prairial gave a foretaste of modern social revolution.

The triumphant element was the bourgeois class which had guided the Revolution since the Constituent Assembly and had not been really unseated even during the Terror. It was not mainly a bourgeoisie of modern capitalists, eager to make a financial profit by developing new factories or machinery.[16] The political victors after Thermidor were "bourgeois" in an older sense, those who had not been noble or aristocratic before 1789 yet had held a secure position under the Old Regime, many of them lawyers or officeholders, and often drawing income from the ownership of land. To them were now added new elements produced by the Revolution itself, parvenus and *nouveaux riches*, who had made money by wartime government contracts, or had profited by inflation or by buying up former church lands at bargain prices. Such people, often joined by former aristocrats, and in reaction against Robespierrist virtue, set a noisy and ostentatious style of living that gave a bad name to the new order. They also unleashed a "white terror" against Jacobins, in which many were simply murdered.

But the Thermidorians, disreputable though a few of them were, had not lost faith in the Revolution. Democracy they associated with red terror and mob rule, but they still believed in individual legal rights and in a written constitution. Conditions were rather adverse, for the country was still unsettled, and although the Convention made a separate peace with Spain and Prussia, France still remained at war with Great Britain and the Habsburg empire. But the men of the Convention were determined to make another attempt at constitutional government. They set aside the democratic constitution written in 1793 (and never used) and produced the Constitution of the Year III, which went into effect at the end of 1795.

45. THE CONSTITUTIONAL REPUBLIC: THE DIRECTORY, 1795–1799

The Weakness of the Directory

The first formally constituted French Republic, known as the Directory, lasted only four years. Its weakness was that it rested on an extremely narrow social base, and that it presupposed certain military conquests. The new constitution applied not only to France but also to Belgium, which was regarded as incorporated constitutionally into France, though the Habsburgs had not yet ceded these "Austrian Netherlands," nor had the British yielded in their refusal to accept French occupation. The constitution of 1795 thus committed the republic to a program of successful expansion. At the same time it restricted the politically active class. It gave almost all adult males the vote, but voters voted only for "electors," for whom about the same qualifications were set as in the constitution of 1791. Persons chosen as electors were usually men of some means, able to give

---

[16] On the bourgeoisie and capitalism, see pp. 114–116, 119–120, 248–249, 426.

their time and willing to take part in public life; this in effect meant men of the upper middle class, since the old aristocracy was disaffected. The electors chose all important department officials and also the members of the national Legislative Assembly, which this time was divided into two chambers. The lower chamber was called the Council of Five Hundred, the upper, composed of 250 members, the Council of Ancients—"ancients" being men over forty. The chambers chose the executive, which was called the Directory (whence the whole regime got its name) and was made up of five Directors.

The government was thus constitutionally in the hands of substantial property owners, rural and urban, but its real base was narrower still. In the reaction after Thermidor many people began to consider restoring the monarchy. The Convention, to protect its own members, ruled that two-thirds of the men initially elected to the Council of Five Hundred and Council of Ancients must be ex-members of the Convention. This interference with the freedom of the elections provoked serious disturbances in Paris, instigated by persons called royalists; but the Convention, having now accustomed itself to using the army, instructed a young general who happened to be in Paris, named Bonaparte, to put down the royalist mob. He did so with a "whiff of grapeshot." The constitutional republic thus made itself dependent on military protection at the outset.

The regime had enemies to both right and left. On the right, undisguised royalists agitated in Paris and even in the two councils. Their center was the Clichy Club, and they were in continuous touch with the late king's brother, the Count of Provence, whom they regarded as Louis XVIII (Louis XVI's son, who died in prison, being counted as Louis XVII). Louis XVIII had installed himself at Verona in Italy, where he headed a propaganda agency financed largely by British money. The worst obstacle to the resurgence of royalism in France was Louis XVIII himself. In 1795, on assuming the title, he had issued a Declaration of Verona, in which he announced his intention to restore the Old Regime and punish all involved in the Revolution back to 1789. It has been said, correctly enough in this connection, that the Bourbons "learned nothing and forgot nothing." Had Louis XVIII offered in 1795 what he offered in 1814, it is quite conceivable that his partisans in France might have brought about his restoration and terminated the war. As it was, the bulk of the French adhered not exactly to the republic as set up in 1795, but more negatively to any system that would shut out the Bourbons and former nobility, prevent a reimposition of the manorial system, and secure the new landowners, peasant and bourgeois, in the possession of the church properties which they had purchased.

The Left was made up of persons from various levels of society who still favored the more democratic ideas expressed earlier in the Revolution. Some of them thought that the fall of Robespierre had been a great misfortune. A tiny group of extremists formed the Conspiracy of Equals, organized in 1796 by "Gracchus" Babeuf. His intention was to overthrow the Directory and replace it with a dictatorial government which he called "democratic," in which private property would be abolished and equality decreed. For these ideas, and for his activist program, he has been regarded as an interesting precursor to modern communism. The Directory repressed the Conspiracy of Equals without difficulty and guillotined Babeuf and one other. Meanwhile it did nothing to relieve the distress of the lower classes, who showed little inclination to follow Babeuf but did suffer from the ravages of scarcity and inflation.

The Political Crisis of 1797

In March 1797 occurred the first really free election ever held in France under republican auspices. The successful candidates were for the most part constitutional monarchists or at least vaguely royalist. A change of the balance within the Five Hundred and the Ancients, in favor of royalism, seemed to be impending. This was precisely what most of the republicans of 1793, including the regicides, could not endure, even though they had to violate the constitution to prevent it. Nor was it endurable, for other reasons, to General Napoleon Bonaparte.

Bonaparte had been born in 1769 into the minor nobility of Corsica, shortly after the annexation of Corsica to France. He had studied in French military schools and been commissioned in the Bourbon army but would never have reached high rank under the conditions of the Old Regime. In 1793 he was a fervent young Jacobin officer, who had been useful in driving the British from Toulon, and who was consequently made a brigadier general by the government of the Terror. In 1795, as noted, he rendered service to the Convention by breaking up a demonstration of royalists. In 1796 he received command of an army, with which, in two brilliant campaigns, he crossed the Alps and drove the Austrians from north Italy. Like other generals he got out of control of the government in Paris, which was financially too harassed to pay his troops or to supply him. He lived by local requisitions in Italy, became self-supporting and independent, and in fact made the civilian government in Paris dependent on him.

He developed a foreign policy of his own. Many Italians had become dissatisfied with their old governments, so that the arrival of the French republican armies threw north Italy into a turmoil, in which the Venetian cities revolted against Venice, Bologna against the pope, Milan against Austria, and the Piedmontese monarchy was threatened by uprisings of its own subjects. Combining with some of these revolutionaries, while rejecting others, Bonaparte established a "Cisalpine" Republic in the Po valley, modeled on the French system, with Milan as its capital. Where the Directory, on the whole, had originally meant to return Milan to the Austrians in compensation for Austrian recognition of the French conquest of Belgium, Bonaparte insisted that France hold its position in both Belgium and Italy. He therefore needed expansionist republicans in the government in Paris and was perturbed by the elections of 1797.

The Austrians negotiated with Bonaparte because they had been beaten by him in battle. The British also, in conferences with the French at Lille, discussed peace in 1796 and 1797. The war had gone badly for England; a party of Whigs led by Charles James Fox had always openly disapproved it, and the pro-French and republican radicals were so active that the government suspended habeas corpus in 1794, and thereafter imprisoned political agitators at its discretion. In 1795 an assassin fired on George III, breaking the glass in his carriage. Crops were bad, and bread was scarce and costly. England too suffered from inflation, for Pitt at first financed the war by extensive loans, and a good deal of gold was shipped to the Continent to finance the Allied armies. In February 1797 the Bank of England suspended gold payments to private citizens. Famine threatened, the populace was restless, and there were even mutinies in the fleet. Ireland was in rebellion; the French came close to landing a republican army in it, and it could be supposed that the next attempt might be more successful. The Austrians, Britain's only remaining ally, were routed by Bonaparte, and at the moment the British could subsidize them no further. The British had every reason to make peace.

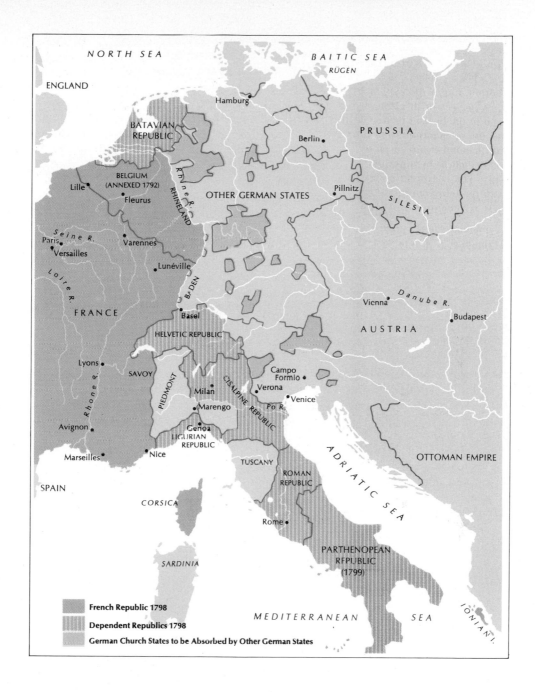

THE FRENCH REPUBLIC AND ITS SATELLITES, 1798–1799

By 1799 the French Republic had annexed Belgium (the Austrian Netherlands) and the small German bishoprics and principalities west of the Rhine, and had created, with the aid of native sympathizers, a string of lesser revolutionary republics in the Dutch Netherlands, Switzerland, and most of Italy. With the treaty of Campo Formio between France and Austria in 1797, the Holy Roman Empire began to disintegrate, for the German princes of the Left Bank of the Rhine, who were dispossessed when their territories went to France, began to be compensated with territory of the church-states of the Holy Roman Empire. These developments were carried further by Napoleon (see map, p. 401).

383

Many were inclined to settle for colonial conquests, regarding the war as a renewal of the eighteenth-century struggle for empire.

Prospects for peace seemed good in the summer of 1797, but, as always, it would be peace upon certain conditions. It was the royalists in France that were the peace party, since a restored king could easily return the conquests of the republic and would in any case abandon the new republics in Holland and the Po valley. The republicans in the French government could make peace with difficulty, if at all. They were constitutionally bound to retain Belgium. They were losing control of their own generals. Nor could the supreme question be evaded: Was peace dear enough to purchase by a return of the Old Regime, such as Louis XVIII had himself promised?

The coup d'état of Fructidor (September 4, 1797) resolved all these many issues. It was the turning point of the constitutional republic and was decisive for all Europe. The Directory asked for help from Bonaparte, who sent one of his generals, Augereau, to Paris. While Augereau stood by with a force of soldiers, the councils annulled most of the elections of the preceding spring. Two Directors were purged; one of them, Lazare Carnot, "organizer of victory" in the Committee of Public Safety, and now in 1797 a strict constitutionalist, was driven into exile. On the whole, it was the old republicans of the Convention who secured themselves in power. Their justification was that they were defending the Revolution, keeping out Louis XVIII and the Old Regime. But to do so they had violated their own constitution and quashed the first free election ever held in a constitutional French republic. And they had become more than ever dependent on the army.

After the coup d'état the "Fructidorian" government broke off negotiations with England. With Austria it signed the treaty of Campo Formio on October 17, 1797, incorporating Bonaparte's ideas. Peace now prevailed on the Continent, since only France and Great Britain remained at war, but it was a peace full of trouble for the future. By the new treaty Austria recognized the French annexation of Belgium (the former Austrian Netherlands), the French right to incorporate the Left Bank of the Rhine, and the French-dominated Cisalpine Republic in Italy. In return, Bonaparte allowed the Austrians to annex Venice and most of mainland Venetia. The Venetian possessions in the Ionian Islands, off the coast of Greece, went to France.

In the following months, under French auspices, revolutionary republicanism spread through much of Italy. The old patrician republic of Genoa turned into a Ligurian Republic on the French model. At Rome the pope was deposed from his temporal power and a Roman Republic was established. In southern Italy a Neapolitan Republic, also called Parthenopean, was set up. In Switzerland at the same time, Swiss reformers cooperated with the French to create a new Helvetic Republic.

The Left Bank of the Rhine, in the atomistic Holy Roman Empire, was occupied by a great many German princes who now had to vacate. The treaty of Campo Formio provided that they be compensated by church territories in Germany east of the Rhine, and that France have a hand in the redistribution. The German princes turned greedy eyes on the German bishops and abbots, and the almost 1,000-year-old Holy Empire, hardly more than a solemn form since the Peace of Westphalia, sank to the level of a land rush or real estate speculation, while France became involved in the territorial reconstruction of Germany.

The Coup d'État of 1799: Bonaparte

After Fructidor the idea of maintaining the republic as a free or constitutional government was given up. There were more uprisings, more quashed elections, more purgings both to Left and Right. The Directory became a kind of ineffective dictatorship. It repudiated most of the assignats and the debt but failed to restore financial confidence or stability. Guerrilla activity flared up again in the Vendée and other parts of western France. The religious schism became more acute; the Directory took severe measures toward the refractory clergy.

Meanwhile Bonaparte waited for the situation to ripen. Returning from Italy a conquering hero, he was assigned to command the army in training to invade England. He concluded that invasion was premature and decided to strike indirectly at England, by threatening India in a spectacular invasion of Egypt. In 1798, outwitting the British fleet, he landed a French army at the mouth of the Nile. Egypt was part of the Ottoman Empire, and the French occupation of it alarmed the Russians, who had their own designs on the Near East. The Austrians objected to the French rearrangement of Germany. A year and a half after the treaty of Campo Formio, Austria, Russia, and Great Britain formed an alliance known as the Second Coalition. The French Republic was again involved in a general war. And the war went unfavorably, for in August 1798 the British fleet had cut off the French army in Egypt by winning the battle of the Nile (or Aboukir), and in 1799 Russian forces, under Marshal Suvorov, were operating as far west as Switzerland and north Italy, where the Cisalpine Republic went down in ruin.

General Bonaparte's opportunity had come. He left his army in Egypt and, again slipping through the British fleet, reappeared unexpectedly in France. He found that certain civilian leaders in the Directory were planning a change. They included Sieyès, of whom little had been heard since he wrote *What Is the Third Estate?* ten years before, but who had sat in the Convention and voted for the death of Louis XVI. Sieyès' formula was now "confidence from below, authority from above"—what he now wanted of the people was acquiescence, and of the government, power to act. This group was looking about for a general, and their choice fell on the sensational young Bonaparte, who was still only thirty. Dictatorship by an army officer was repugnant to most republicans of the Five Hundred and the Ancients. Bonaparte, Sieyès, and their followers resorted to force, executing the coup d'état of Brumaire (November 9, 1799), in which armed soldiers drove the legislators from the chambers. They proclaimed a new form of the republic, which Bonaparte entitled the Consulate. It was headed by three consuls, with Bonaparte as the First Consul.

46. THE DESPOTIC REPUBLIC: THE CONSULATE, 1799–1804

The next chapter takes up the affairs of Europe as a whole in the time of Napoleon Bonaparte, the purpose at present being only to tell how he closed, in a way, the Revolution in France.

It happened that the French Republic, in falling into the hands of a general, fell also to a man of such remarkable talents as are often denominated genius. Bonaparte was a short dark man, of Mediterranean type, who would never have looked impressive in civilian clothing. His manners were rather coarse; he lost his temper, cheated at cards, and pinched people by the ear in a kind of formidable play—he was no "gentleman." A child of the Enlightenment and the Revolution, he was entirely emancipated not only from customary ideas but from moral scruples as well. He regarded the world as a flux to be formed by his own mind. He had an exalted belief in his own destinies, which became more mystical and exaggerated as the years went on. He claimed to follow his "star." His ideas of the good and the beautiful were rather blunt, but he was a man of extraordinary intellectual capacity, which impressed all with whom he came in contact. "Never speak unless you know you are the ablest man in the room," he once advised his stepson, on making him viceroy of Italy, a maxim which, if he followed it himself, still allowed him to do most of the talking. His interests ran to solid subjects, history, law, military science, public administration. His mind was tenacious and perfectly orderly; he once declared that it was like a chest of drawers, which he could open or close at will, forgetting any subject when its drawer was closed and finding it ready with all necessary detail when its drawer was opened. He had all the masterful qualities associated with leadership; he could dazzle and captivate those who had any inclination to follow him at all. Some of the most humane men of the day, including Goethe and Beethoven in Germany, and Lazare Carnot among the former revolutionary leaders, at first looked on him with high approval. He inspired confidence by his crisp speech, rapid decisions, and quick grasp of complex problems when they were newly presented to him. He was, or seemed, just what many Frenchmen were looking for after ten years of upheaval.

Under the Consulate France reverted to a form of enlightened despotism, and Bonaparte may be thought of as the last and most eminent of the enlightened despots. Despotic the new regime undoubtedly was from the start. Self-government through elected bodies was ruthlessly pushed aside. Bonaparte delighted in affirming the sovereignty of the people; but to his mind the people was a sovereign, like Voltaire's God, who somehow created the world but never thereafter interfered in it. He clearly saw that a government's authority was greater when it was held to represent the entire nation. In the weeks after Brumaire he assured himself of a popular mandate by devising a written constitution and submitting it to a general referendum or "plebiscite." The voters could take it—or nothing. They took it by a majority officially reported as 3,011,007 to 1,562.

The new constitution set up a make-believe of parliamentary institutions. It gave universal male suffrage, but the citizens merely chose "notables"; men on the lists of notables were then appointed by the government itself to public position. The notables had no powers of their own. They were merely available for appointment to office. They might sit in a Legislative Body, where they could neither initiate nor discuss legislation, but only mutely reject or enact it. There was also a Tribunate which discussed and deliberated but had no enacting powers. There was a Conservative Senate, which had rights of appointment of notables to office ("patronage" in American terms), and in which numerous storm-tossed regicides found a haven. The main agency in the new government was the Council of State, imitated from the Old Regime; it prepared the significant legislation, often under the presidency of the First Consul himself, who always gave the impression that he understood everything. The First Consul made all the decisions and ran the state. The regime did not openly represent anybody, and that was its strength, for it provoked the less opposition. In any case, the political machinery just described fell rapidly into disuse.

Bonaparte entrenched himself also by promising and obtaining peace. The military problem, at the close of 1799, was much simplified by the attitude of the Russians, who in effect withdrew from the war with France. In the Italian theater Bonaparte had to deal only with the Austrians, whom he again defeated, by again crossing the Alps, at the battle of Marengo in June 1800. In February 1801 the Austrians signed the treaty of Lunéville, in which the terms of Campo Formio were confirmed. A year later, in March 1802, peace was made even with Britain.

Peace was made also at home. Bonaparte kept internal order, partly by a secret political police, but more especially through a powerful and centralized administrative machine, in which a "prefect," under direct orders of the minister of the interior, ruled firmly over each of the departments created by the Constituent Assembly. The new government put down the guerrillas in the west. Its laws and taxes were imposed on Brittany and the Vendée. Peasants there were no longer terrorized by marauding partisans. A new peace settled down on the factions left by the Revolution. Bonaparte offered a general amnesty and invited back to France, with a few exceptions, exiles of all stripes from the first aristocratic émigrés to the refugees and deportees of the republican coups d'état. Requiring only that they work for him and stop quarreling with each other, he picked reasonable men from all camps. His Second Consul was Cambacérès, a regicide of the Terror, his Third Consul Lebrun, who had been Maupeou's colleague in the days of Louis XV.[17] Fouché emerged as minister of police; he had been an Hébertist and extreme terrorist in 1793 and had done as much as any man to bring about the fall of Robespierre. Before 1789 he had been an obscure bourgeois professor of physics. Talleyrand appeared as minister of foreign affairs; he had spent the Terror in safe seclusion in the United States, and his principles, if he had any, were those of constitutional monarchy. Before 1789 he had been a bishop and was of an aristocratic lineage almost unbearably distinguished—no one who had not known the Old Regime, he once said, could realize how pleasant it had been. Men of this sort were now willing, for a few years beginning in 1800, to forget the past and work in common toward the future.

Disturbers of the new order the First Consul ruthlessly put down. Indeed, he concocted alarms to make himself more welcome as a pillar of order. On Christmas Eve, 1800, on the way to the opera, he was nearly killed by a bomb, or "infernal machine," as people then said. It had been laid by royalists, but Bonaparte represented it as the work of a Jacobin conspiracy, being most afraid at the moment of some of the old republicans; and over a hundred former Jacobins were again deported. Contrariwise, in 1804, he greatly exaggerated certain royalist plots against him, invaded the independent state of Baden, and there arrested the Duke of Enghien, who was related to the Bourbons. Though he knew Enghien to be innocent, he had him shot. His purpose now was to please the old Jacobins by staining his own hands with Bourbon blood; Fouché and the regicides concluded that they were secure so long as Bonaparte was in power.

The Settlement with the Church; Other Reforms

For all but the most convinced royalists and republicans, reconciliation was made easier by the establishment of peace with the church. Bonaparte himself was a pure eighteenth-century rationalist. He regarded religion as a convenience. He advertised himself as a Muslim in Egypt, as a Catholic in France, and as a free-thinker among the professors at the Institute in Paris. But a Catholic revival was in full swing, and he saw its importance. The refractory clergy were the spiritual force animating all forms of counterrevolution. "Fifty émigré bishops, paid by England," he once said, "lead the French clergy today. Their influence must be destroyed. For this we need the authority of the pope." Ignoring the horrified outcries of the old Jacobins, in 1801 he signed a concordat with the Vatican.

Both parties gained from the settlement. The autonomy of the prerevolutionary Gallican church came to an end. The pope received the right to depose French bishops, since before the schism could be healed both constitutional and refractory bishops had to be obliged to resign. The constitutional or pro-revolutionary clergy came under the discipline of the Holy See. Publicity of Catholic worship, in such forms as processions in the streets, was again allowed. Church seminaries were again permitted. But Bonaparte and the heirs of the Revolution gained even more. The pope, by signing the concordat, virtually recognized the Republic. The Vatican agreed to raise no question over the former tithes and the former church lands. The new owners of former church properties thus obtained clear titles. Nor was there any further question of Avignon, an enclave within France, formerly papal, annexed to France in 1791. Nor were the papal negotiators able to undermine religious toleration; all that Bonaparte would concede was a clause that was purely factual, and hence harmless, stating that Catholicism was the religion of the majority of Frenchmen. The clergy, in compensation for loss of their tithes and property, were assured of receiving salaries from the state. But Bonaparte, to dispel the notion of an established church, put Protestant ministers of all denominations on the state payroll also. He thus checkmated the Vatican on important points. At the same time, simply by signing an agreement with Rome, he disarmed the counterrevolution. It could no longer be said that the Republic was godless. Good relations did not, indeed, last very long, for Bonaparte and the papacy were soon at odds. But the terms of the concordat proved lasting.

With peace and order established, the constructive work of the Consulate turned to the fields of law and administration. The First Consul and his advisers combined what they conceived to be the best of the Revolution and of the Old Regime. The modern state took on clearer form. It was the reverse of everything feudal. All public authority was concentrated in paid agents of government, no person was held to be under any legal authority except that of the state, and the authority of government fell on all persons alike. There were no more estates, legal classes, privileges, local liberties, hereditary offices, guilds, or manors. Judges, officials, and army officers received specified salaries. Neither military commissions nor civil offices could be bought and sold. Citizens were to rise in government service purely according to their abilities.

This was the doctrine of "careers open to talent"; it was what the bourgeoisie had wanted before the Revolution, and a few persons of quite humble birth profited also. For sons of the old aristocracy, it meant that pedigree was not enough; they must also show individual capacity to obtain employment. Qualification came to depend increasingly on education, and the secondary and higher schools were reorganized in these years, with a view to preparing young men for government service and the learned professions. Scholarships were provided, but it was mainly the upper middle class that benefited. Education, in fact, in France and in Europe generally, came to be an important determinant of social standing, with one system for those who could spend a dozen or more years at school, and another for boys who were to enter the work force at the age of twelve or fourteen.

Another deep demand of the French people, deeper than the demand for the vote, was for more reason, order, and economy in public finance and taxation. The Consulate gave these also. There were no tax exemptions because of birth, status, or special arrangement. Everyone was supposed to pay, so that no disgrace attached to payment, and there was less evasion. In principle these changes had been introduced in 1789; after 1799 they began to work. For the first time in ten years the government really collected the taxes that it levied and so could rationally plan its financial affairs. Order was introduced also into expenditure, and accounting methods were improved. There was no longer a haphazard assortment of different "funds," on which various officials drew independently and confidentially as they needed money, but a concentration of financial management in the treasury; and even in a kind of budget. The revolutionary uncertainties over the value of money were also ended. Because the Directory had shouldered the odium of repudiating the paper money and government debt, the Consulate was able to establish a sound currency and public credit. To assist in government financing, one of the banks of the Old Regime was revived and established as the Bank of France.

Like all enlightened despots, Bonaparte codified the laws, and of all law codes since the Romans the Napoleonic codes are the most famous. To the 300 legal systems of the Old Regime, and the mass of royal ordinances, were now added the thousands of laws enacted but seldom implemented by the revolutionary assemblies. Five codes emerged—the Civil Code (often called simply the Code Napoleon), the codes of civil and of criminal procedure, and the commercial and penal codes. The codes made France legally and judicially uniform. They assured legal equality; all French citizens had the same civil rights. They formulated the new law of property and set forth the law of contracts, debts, leases, stock companies, and similar matters in such a way as to create the legal framework for an economy of private enterprise. They repeated the ban of all previous regimes on organized labor unions and were severe with the individual workingman, his word not being acceptable in court against that of his employer—a significant departure from equality before the law. The criminal code was somewhat freer in giving the government the means to detect crime than in granting the individual the means of defending himself against legal charges. As for the family, the codes recognized civil marriage and divorce but left the wife with very restricted powers over property, and the father with extensive authority over minor children. The codes reflected much of French life under the Old Regime. They also set the character of France as it has been ever since, socially bourgeois, legally equalitarian, and administratively bureaucratic.

In France, with the Consulate, the Revolution was over. If its highest hopes had not been accomplished, the worst evils of the Old Regime had at least been cured. The beneficiaries of the Revolution felt secure. Even former aristocrats were rallying. The working-class movement, repeatedly frustrated under all the revolutionary regimes, now vanished from the political scene, to reappear as socialism thirty years later. What the Third Estate had most wanted in 1789 was now both codified and enforced, with the exception of parliamentary government, which after ten years of turmoil many people were temporarily willing to forgo. Moreover, in 1802, the French Republic was at peace with the papacy,

Great Britain, and all Continental powers. It reached to the Rhine and had dependent republics in Holland and Italy. So popular was the First Consul that in 1802, by another plebiscite, he had himself elected consul for life. A new constitution, in 1804, again ratified by plebiscite, declared that "the government of the republic is entrusted to an emperor." The Consulate became the Empire, and Bonaparte emerged as Napoleon I, Emperor of the French.

But France, no longer revolutionary at home, was revolutionary outside its borders. Napoleon became a terror to the patricians of Europe. They called him the "Jacobin." And the France which he ruled, and used as his arsenal, was an incomparably formidable state. Even before the Revolution it had been the most populous in Europe, perhaps the most wealthy, in the front rank of scientific enterprise and intellectual leadership. Now all the old barriers of privilege, tax exemption, localism, caste exclusiveness, and routine-mindedness had disappeared. The new France could tap the wealth of its citizens and put able men into position without inquiring into their origins. Every private, boasted Napoleon, carried a marshal's baton in his knapsack. The French looked with disdain on their caste-ridden adversaries. The principle of civic equality proved not only to have the appeal of justice, but also to be politically useful, and the resources of France were hurled against Europe with a force which for many years nothing could check.

X.
Napoleonic Europe

T he repercussions of the French Revolution had been felt throughout Europe since the fall of the Bastille, and even more definitely after the outbreak of war in 1792 and the ensuing victories of the republican armies. They became even more evident after the republican General Bonaparte turned into Napoleon I, Emperor of the French, King of Italy, and Protector of the Confederation of the Rhine. Napoleon came nearer than anyone has ever come to imposing a political unity on the European continent. Of his ascendancy of fifteen years two stories are to be told. One is a story of international relations, reflecting the diverse interests of the contending states of Europe. The other is the story of internal development of the European peoples. The French impact, though based on military success, represented more than mere forcible subjugation. Innovations of a kind made in France by revolution were brought to other countries by administrative decree. There were, for several years, Germans, Italians, Dutchmen, and Poles who worked with the French emperor to introduce the changes that he demanded, and which they themselves often desired. In Prussia it was resistance to Napoleon that gave the incentive to internal reorganization. Whether by collaboration or resistance, Europe was transformed.

It is convenient to think of the fighting from 1792 to 1814 as a "world war," as indeed it was, affecting not only all of Europe but places as remote as Spanish

Chapter Emblem: An Italian cameo of 1810, showing the idealized head of Napoleon crowned with laurels as lawgiver and culture hero.

America, where the wars of independence began, or the interior of North America, where the United States purchased Louisiana in 1803 and attempted a conquest of Canada in 1812. But it is important to realize that this world war was actually a series of wars, most of them quite short, sharp, and distinct. Only Great Britain remained continually at war with France, except for about a year of peace in 1802–1803. Never were the four great powers, Britain, Austria, Russia, and Prussia, simultaneously in the field against France until 1813.

The history of the Napoleonic period would be much simpler if the European governments had fought merely to protect themselves against the aggressive French. Each, however, in its way, was as dynamic and expansive as Napoleon himself. For some generations Great Britain had been building a commercial empire, Russia pushing upon Poland and Turkey, Prussia consolidating its territories and striving for leadership in north Germany. Austria was less aggressive, being somewhat passively preoccupied by the rise of Prussia and Russia, but the Austrians were not without dreams of ascendancy in Germany, the Balkans, and the Adriatic. None of these ambitions ceased during the Napoleonic years. Governments, in pursuit of their own aims, were quite as willing to ally with Napoleon as to fight him. Only gradually, and under repeated provocation, did they conclude that their main interest was to dispose of the French emperor entirely.

47. THE FORMATION OF THE FRENCH IMPERIAL SYSTEM

The Dissolution of the First and Second Coalitions, 1792–1802

The conflicting purposes of the powers had been apparent from the beginning. Leopold of Austria, in issuing the Declaration of Pillnitz in 1791, had believed a general European coalition against France to be impossible. When the First Coalition was formed in 1792, the Austrians and Prussians kept their main forces in eastern Europe, more afraid of each other and of Russia, in the matter of Poland, than of the French revolutionary republic. Indeed, the main accomplishment of the First Coalition was the extermination of the Polish state.[1]

In 1795 the French broke up the coalition. The British withdrew their army from the Continent. The Prussians made a separate peace; the French bought them off by recognizing them as "protectors" of Germany north of the river Main. Spain also made a separate peace in 1795. The world saw the spectacle, outrageous to all ideology or principle, of an alliance between Bourbon Spain and the republic which had guillotined Louis XVI and kept Louis XVIII from his monarchic rights. Spain simply reverted to the eighteenth-century pattern, in allying with France because of hostility to Great Britain, whose possession of Gibraltar, naval influence in the Mediterranean, and attitude toward the Spanish empire were disquieting to the Spanish government. When Austria signed the peace of Campo Formio in 1797 the First Coalition was totally dissipated, only British naval forces remaining engaged with the French.[2]

The Second Coalition of 1799 fared no better. After the British fleet defeated the French at the battle of the Nile, cutting off the French army in Egypt, the Russians saw their ambitions in the Mediterranean blocked mainly by the British,

---

[1] See pp. 239–240, 372–373.
[2] See p. 382.

and withdrew Suvorov's army from western Europe. The acceptance by Austria of the peace of Lunéville in 1801 dissolved the Second Coalition. In 1802 Great Britain signed the peace of Amiens. For the only time between 1792 and 1814 no European power was at war with another—though the British, to be sure, were at war with some Indian princes, the Russians with some Caucasian tribesmen, and the French with Toussaint l'Ouverture, the black ex-slave who was attempting to found an independent republic in Haiti.

Peace Interim, 1802–1803

Never had a peace been so advantageous to France as the peace of 1802. But Bonaparte gave it no chance. He used peace as he did war to advance his interests. He dispatched a sizable army to Haiti, ostensibly to win back a rebellious French colony, but with the further thought (since Louisiana had been ceded back by Spain to France in 1800) of reviving the French colonial empire in America. He reorganized the Cisalpine Republic into an "Italian" Republic with himself as president. He reorganized the Helvetic Republic, making himself "mediator" of the Confederation of Switzerland. He reorganized Germany; that is to say, he and his agents closely watched the rearrangement of territory which the Germans themselves had been carrying out since 1797.

By the treaty of Campo Formio,[3] it will be recalled, German princes of the Left Bank of the Rhine, expropriated by the annexation of their dominions to the French Republic, were to receive new territories on the Right Bank. The result was a scramble called by patriotic German historians the "shame of the princes." The German rulers, far from opposing Bonaparte or upholding any national interests, competed desperately for the absorption of German territory, each bribing and fawning upon the French (Talleyrand made over 10,000,000 francs in the process) to win French support against other Germans. The Holy Roman Empire was fatally mauled by the Germans themselves. Most of its ecclesiastical principalities and forty-five out of its fifty-one free cities disappeared, annexed by their larger neighbors. The number of states in the Holy Empire was greatly reduced, especially of the Catholic states, so that it could be foreseen that no Catholic Habsburg would again be elected emperor. Prussia, Bavaria, Württemberg, and Baden consolidated and enlarged themselves. These arrangements were ratified in February 1803 by the diet of the Empire. The enlarged German states now depended on Bonaparte for the maintenance of their new position.

Formation of the Third Coalition in 1805

Britain and France went to war again in 1803. Bonaparte, his communications with America menaced by the British navy, and his army in Haiti decimated by disease and by rebellious blacks, suspended his ideas for re-creating an American empire and sold Louisiana to the United States. Great Britain began to seek allies for a Third Coalition. In May 1804 Napoleon pronounced himself Emperor of the French to assure the hereditary permanency of his system, though he had no son. Francis II of Austria, seeing the ruin of the Holy Roman Empire, promulgated the Austrian Empire in August 1804. He thus advanced the long process of inte-

---

[3] See p. 384.

grating the Danubian monarchy. In 1805 Austria signed an alliance with Great Britain. The Third Coalition was completed by the accession of the Russian Tsar Alexander I, who, after Napoleon himself, was to become the most considerable figure on the European stage.

Alexander was the grandson of Catherine the Great, educated by her to be a kind of enlightened despot on the eighteenth-century model.[4] The Swiss tutor of his boyhood, La Harpe, later turned up as a pro-French revolutionary in the Helvetic Republic of 1798. Alexander became tsar in 1801, at the age of twenty-four, through a palace revolution which implicated him in the murder of his father Paul. He still corresponded with La Harpe, and he surrounded himself with a circle of liberal and zealous young men of various nationalities, of whom the most prominent was a Polish youth, Czartoryski. Alexander regarded the still recent partitions of Poland as a crime.[5] He wished to restore the unity of Poland with himself as its constitutional king. In Germany many who had first warmed to the French Revolution, but had been disillusioned, began to hail the new liberal tsar as the protector of Germany and hope of the future. Alexander conceived of himself as a rival to Napoleon in guiding the destinies of Europe in an age of change. Moralistic and self-righteous, he puzzled and disturbed the statesmen of Europe, who generally saw, behind his humane and republican utterances, either an enthroned leader of all the "Jacobins" of Europe or the familiar specter of Russian aggrandizement.

Yet Alexander, more than his contemporaries, formed a conception of international collective security and the indivisibility of peace. He was shocked when Napoleon in 1804, in order to seize the duke of Enghien, rudely violated the sovereignty of Baden.[6] He declared that the issue in Europe was clearly between law and force—between an international society in which the rights of each member were secured by international agreement and organization, and a society in which all trembled before the rule of cynicism and conquest embodied in the French usurper.

Alexander was therefore ready to enter a Third Coalition with Great Britain. Picturing himself as a future arbiter of central Europe, and with secret designs on the Ottoman Empire and the Mediterranean, he signed a treaty with England in April 1805. The British agreed to pay Russia £1,250,000 for each 100,000 soldiers that the Russians raised.

The Third Coalition, 1805–1807: The Peace of Tilsit

Napoleon meanwhile, since the resumption of hostilities in 1803, had been making preparations to invade England. He concentrated large forces on the Channel coast, together with thousands of boats and barges, in which he gave the troops amphibious training in embarkation and debarkation. He reasoned that if his own fleet could divert or cripple the British fleet for a few days he could place enough soldiers in the defenseless island to force its capitulation. The British, sensing mortal danger, lined their coasts with lookouts and signal beacons and set to drilling a home guard. Their main defense was twofold: the Austro-Russian armies and the British fleet under Lord Nelson. The Russian and Austrian armies moved westward in the summer of 1805. In August Napoleon relieved the pressure upon

[4] See p. 330.
[5] See pp. 238–240, 372–373.
[6] See p. 387.

England, shifting seven army corps from the Channel to the upper Danube. On October 15 he surrounded an Austrian force of 50,000 men at Ulm in Bavaria, forcing it to surrender without resistance. On October 21 Lord Nelson, off Cape Trafalgar on the Spanish coast, caught and annihilated the main body of the combined fleets of France and Spain.

The battle of Trafalgar established the supremacy of the British navy for over a century—but only on the proviso that Napoleon be prevented from controlling the bulk of Europe, which would furnish an ample base for eventual construction of a greater navy than the British. And to control Europe was precisely what Napoleon proceeded to do. Moving east from Ulm he came upon the Russian and Austrian armies in Moravia, where on December 2 he won the great victory of Austerlitz. The broken Russian army withdrew into Poland, and Austria made peace. By the treaty of Pressburg Napoleon took Venetia from the Austrians, to whom he had given it in 1797, and annexed it to his kingdom of Italy (the former Cisalpine and Italian Republic), which now included a good deal of Italy north of Rome. Venice and Trieste soon resounded with the hammers of shipwrights rebuilding the Napoleonic fleet. In Germany, early in 1806, the French emperor raised Bavaria and Württemberg to the stature of kingdoms and Baden to a grand duchy. The Holy Roman Empire was finally, formally, and irrevocably dissolved. In its place Napoleon began to gather his German client states into a new kind of Germanic federation, the Confederation of the Rhine, of which he made himself the "protector."

Prussia, at peace with France for ten years, had declined to join the Third Coalition. But as Napoleon's program for controlling Germany became clear after Austerlitz the war party in Prussia became irresistible, and the Prussian government, outwitted and distraught, went to war with the French unaided and alone. The French smashed the famous Prussian army at the battles of Jena and Auerstädt in October 1806. The French cavalry galloped all over north Germany unopposed. The Prussian king and his government took refuge in the east, at Königsberg, where the tsar and the re-forming Russian army might protect them. But the terrible Corsican pursued the Russians also. Marching through western Poland and into East Prussia, he met the Russian army first at the sanguinary but indecisive battle of Eylau and then defeated it on June 14, 1807, at Friedland. Alexander I was unwilling to retreat into Russia. He was unsure of his own resources; if the country were invaded there might be a revolt of the nobles or even of the serfs—for people still remembered Pugachev's rebellion.[7] He feared also merely playing the game of the British. He put aside his war aims of 1804 and signified his willingness to negotiate with Napoleon. The Third Coalition had gone the way of the two before it.

The Emperor of the French and the Autocrat of All the Russias met privately on a raft in the Niemen River, not far from the border between Prussia and Russia, the very easternmost frontier of civilized Europe, as the triumphant Napoleon gleefully imagined it. The hapless Prussian king, Frederick William III, paced nervously on the bank. Bonaparte turned all his charm upon Alexander, denouncing England as the author of all the troubles of Europe and captivating him by flights of Latin imagination, in which he set before Alexander a boundless destiny as Emperor of the East, intimating that his future lay toward Turkey, Persia, Afghanistan, and India. The result of their conversations was the treaty of Tilsit

---

[7] See pp. 325–326.

of July 1807, in many ways the high point of Napoleon's success. The French and Russian empires became allies, mainly against Great Britain. Ostensibly this alliance lasted for five years. Alexander accepted Napoleon as a kind of Emperor of the West. As for Prussia, Napoleon continued to occupy Berlin with his troops, and he took away all Prussian territories west of the Elbe, combining them with others taken from Hanover to make a new kingdom of Westphalia, which became part of his Confederation of the Rhine.

The Continental System and the War in Spain

Hardly had the "peace of the continent" been reestablished, on the foundation of a Franco-Russian alliance, when Napoleon began to have serious trouble. He was bent on subduing the British who, secure in their island, seemed beyond his reach. Since the French naval disaster at Trafalgar, there was no possibility of invading England in the foreseeable future. Napoleon therefore turned to economic warfare. He would fight sea power with land power, using his political control of the Continent to shut out British goods and shipping from all European ports. He would destroy the British trade in exports to Europe, both exports of British products and the profitable British reexport of goods from America and Asia. Thereby, he hoped, he would ruin British commercial firms and cause a violent business depression, marked by overloaded warehouses, unemployment, runs on the banks, a fall of the currency, rising prices, and revolutionary agitation. The British government, which would simultaneously be losing revenues from its customs duties, would thus find itself unable to carry the enormous national debt, or to borrow additional funds from its subjects, or to continue its financial subsidies to the military powers of Europe. At Berlin, in 1806, after the battle of Jena, Napoleon issued the Berlin Decree, forbidding the importation of British goods into any part of Europe allied with or dependent on himself. He thus formally established the Continental System.

To make the Continental System effective Napoleon believed that it must extend to all continental Europe without exception. By the treaty of Tilsit, in 1807, he required both Russia and Prussia to adhere to it. They agreed to exclude all British goods; in fact, in the following months Russia, Prussia, and Austria all declared war on Great Britain. Napoleon then ordered two neutral states, Denmark and Portugal, to adhere. Denmark was an important entrepôt for all central Europe, and the British, fearing Danish compliance, dispatched a fleet to Copenhagen, bombarded the city for four days, and took captive the Danish fleet. The outraged Danes allied with Napoleon and joined the Continental System. Portugal, long a satellite of Britain, refused compliance; Napoleon invaded it. To control the whole European coastline from St. Petersburg around to Trieste he now had only to control the ports of Spain. By a series of deceptions he got both the Bourbon Charles IV and his son Ferdinand to abdicate the Spanish throne. He made his brother Joseph king of Spain in 1808 and reinforced him with a large French army.

He thus involved himself in an entanglement from which he never escaped. The Spanish regarded the Napoleonic soldiers as godless villains who desecrated churches. Fierce guerrillas took the field. Cruelties of one side were answered by atrocities of the other. The British sent an expeditionary force of their small regular army, eventually under the Duke of Wellington, to sustain the Spanish guerrillas; the resulting Peninsular War dragged on for five years. But from the beginning the affair went badly for Napoleon. In July 1808 a French general, for the first time since the Revolution, surrendered an army corps, without fighting, by the capitulation at Baylen. In August another French force surrendered to the British army in Portugal. And these events raised hopes in the rest of Europe. An anti-French movement swept over Germany. It was felt strongly in Austria, where the Habsburg government, undaunted by three defeats, and hoping to lead a general German national resistance, prepared for a fourth time since 1792 to go to war with France.

The Austrian War of Liberation, 1809

Napoleon summoned a general congress which met at Erfurt in Saxony in September 1808. His main purpose was to talk with his ally of a year, Alexander; but he assembled numerous dependent monarchs as well, by whose presence he hoped to overawe the tsar. He even had Talma, the leading actor of the day, play in the theater of Erfurt before "a parterre of kings." Alexander was unimpressed. He was hurt in a sensitive spot because Napoleon, a few months before, had made moves to re-create a Polish state, setting up what was called the Grand Duchy of Warsaw. He had found Napoleon unwilling, despite the grandiose language of Tilsit, really to support his expansion into the Balkans. In addition, Alexander was taken aside by Talleyrand, Napoleon's foreign minister. Talleyrand had concluded that Napoleon was overreaching himself and said so confidentially to the tsar, advising him to wait. Talleyrand thus acted as a traitor, betraying the man whom he ostensibly served, and preparing a safe place for himself in the event of Napoleon's fall; but he acted also as an aristocrat of the prenationalistic Old Regime, seeing his own country as only one part of the whole of Europe, believing a balance among the several parts to be necessary, and holding that peace would be possible only when the exaggerated position of French power should be reduced. For France and Russia, the two strongest states, to combine against all other states was contrary to all principles of the older diplomacy.[8]

Austria proclaimed a war of liberation in April 1809. Napoleon advanced rapidly along the familiar route to Vienna. The German princes, indebted to the French, declined to join in a general German war against him. Alexander stood watchfully on the sidelines. Napoleon won the battle of Wagram in July. In October Austria made peace. The short war of 1809 was over. The Danubian monarchy, by no means as fragile as it seemed, survived a fourth defeat at the hands of the French without internal revolution or disloyalty to the Habsburg house. From it, in punishment, Napoleon took considerable portions of its territory. Part of Austrian Poland was used to enlarge Napoleon's Grand Duchy of Warsaw, and parts of Dalmatia, Slovenia, and Croatia, on the south, were erected into a new creation which Napoleon called the Illyrian Provinces.[9]

Napoleon at His Peak, 1809–1811

The next two years saw the Napoleonic empire at its peak. In Austria after the defeat of 1809 the conduct of foreign affairs fell to a man who was to retain it for forty years. His name was Clemens von Metternich. He was a German from west

[8] See pp. 158–159.
[9] See map, p. 401.

of the Rhine, whose ancestral territories had been annexed to the French Republic, but he had entered the Austrian service and even married the granddaughter of Kaunitz,[10] the old model of diplomatic savoir-faire, of which Metternich now became a model himself. Austria had been repeatedly humiliated and even partitioned by Napoleon, most of all in the treaty of 1809. But Metternich was not a man to conduct diplomacy by grudges. Believing that Russia was the really permanent problem for a state situated in the Danube valley, Metternich thought it wise to renew good relations with France. He was quite willing to go along with Napoleon, whom he knew personally, having been Austrian ambassador to Paris before the short war of 1809.

The French emperor, who in 1809 was exactly forty, was increasingly concerned by the fact that he was childless. He had made an empire which he pronounced hereditary. Yet he had no son. Between him and his wife Josephine whom he had married in youth, and who was six years his senior, there had long since ceased to be affection or even fidelity on either side. He divorced her in 1809, though since she had two children by a first husband she naturally protested that Napoleon's childlessness was not her fault. He intended to marry a younger woman who might bear him offspring. He intended also to make a spectacular marriage, to extort for himself, a self-made Corsican army officer, the highest and most exclusive recognition that aristocratic Europe could bestow. He debated between Habsburgs and Romanovs, between an archduchess and a grand duchess. Tactful inquiries at St. Petersburg concerning the availability of Alexander's sister were tactfully rebuffed; the tsar intimated that his mother would never allow it. The Russian alliance again showed its limitations. Napoleon was thrown into the arms of Metternich—and of Marie Louise, the eighteen-year-old daughter of the Austrian emperor and niece of another "Austrian woman," Marie Antoinette. They were married in 1810. In a year she bore him a son, whom he entitled the King of Rome.

Napoleon assumed ever more pompous airs of imperial majesty. He was now, by marriage, the nephew of Louis XVI. He showed more consideration to French noblemen of the Old Regime—only they, he said, knew really how to serve. He surrounded himself with a newly made hereditary Napoleonic nobility, hoping that the new families, as time went on, would bind their own fortunes to the house of Bonaparte. The marshals became dukes and princes, Talleyrand the Prince of Benevento, and the bourgeois Fouché, an Hébertist of '93, and more latterly a police official, was now solemnly addressed as the Duke of Otranto. In foreign affairs also the cycle had been run. With one significant exception all the powers of the successive coalitions were allied with the French, and the Son of the Revolution now gravely referred to the emperor of Austria as "my father."

48. THE GRAND EMPIRE: SPREAD OF THE REVOLUTION

The Organization of the Napoleonic Empire

Territorially Napoleon's influence enjoyed its farthest reach in 1810 and 1811, when it comprehended the entire European mainland except the Balkan peninsula. The Napoleonic domain was in two parts. Its core was the French empire;

---

[10] See pp. 268, 319.

then came thick layers of dependent states, which together with France comprised the Grand Empire. In addition, to the north and east were the "allied
states" under their traditional governments—the three great powers, Prussia, Austria, and Russia, and also Denmark and Sweden. The allied states were at war
with Great Britain, though not engaged in positive hostilities; their populations
were supposed to do without British goods under the Continental System, but
otherwise Napoleon had no direct lawful influence upon their internal affairs.

The French empire, as successor to the French Republic, included Belgium and
the Left Bank of the Rhine.[11] In addition, by 1810, it had developed two ap-
pendages which on a map looked like tentacles outstretched from it. When he
proclaimed France an empire, and turned its dependent republics into kingdoms,
Napoleon had set up his brother Louis as king of Holland; but Louis had shown
such a tendency to ingratiate himself with the Dutch, and such a willingness to let
Dutch businessmen trade secretly with the British, that Napoleon dethroned him
and incorporated Holland into the French empire. In his endless war upon British
goods he found it useful to exert more direct control over the ports of Bremen,
Hamburg, Lübeck, Genoa, and Leghorn; he therefore annexed directly to the
French empire the German coast as far as the western Baltic, and the Italian
coast far enough to include Rome. Rome he desired for its imperial rather than its
commercial value. Harking back to traditions as old as Charlemagne, he considered Rome the second city of his empire and entitled his son the "King of Rome";
and when Pope Pius VII protested, Napoleon took him prisoner and interned him
in France. The whole French empire, from Lübeck to Rome, was governed directly by departmental prefects who reported to Paris, and the eighty-three departments of France, created by the Constituent Assembly, had risen in 1810 to a
hundred and thirty.

The dependent states, forming with France the Grand Empire, were of different kinds. The Swiss federation remained republican in form. The Illyrian Provinces, which included Trieste and the Dalmatian coast, were administered in
their brief two years almost like departments of France. In Poland, since the Russians objected to a revived kingdom of Poland, Napoleon called his creation the
Grand Duchy of Warsaw. Among the most important of the dependent states in
the Grand Empire were the German states organized into the Confederation of
the Rhine. Too modestly named, the Confederation included all Germany between what the French annexed on the west and what Prussia and Austria retained on the east. It was a league of all the German princes in this region who
were regarded as sovereign, and who now numbered only about twenty, the most
important being the four newly made kings—of Saxony, Bavaria, Württemberg,
and Westphalia. Westphalia was an entirely new and synthetic state, made up of
Hanoverian and Prussian territories and of various atoms of the old Germany. Its
king was Napoleon's youngest brother Jerome.

For Napoleon used his family as a means of rule. The Corsican clan became the
Bonaparte dynasty. His brother Joseph from 1804 to 1808 functioned as king of
Naples and after 1808 as king of Spain. Louis Bonaparte was for six years king of
Holland. Jerome was king of Westphalia. Sister Caroline became queen of Naples
after brother Joseph's transfer to Spain; for Napoleon, running out of brothers
(having quarreled with his remaining brother Lucien), gave the throne of Naples

---

[11] See pp. 380–381, 383–384.

to his brother-in-law, Joachim Murat, a madcap cavalry officer who was Caroline's husband. In the "Kingdom of Italy," which in 1810 included Lombardy, Venetia, and most of the former papal states, Napoleon himself retained the title of king, but set up his stepson, Eugene Beauharnais (Josephine's son) as viceroy. "Uncle Joseph," Napoleon's mother's brother, became Cardinal Fesch. The mother of the Bonapartes, Letitia, who had brought up all these children under very different circumstances in Corsica, was suitably installed at the imperial court as Madame Mère. According to legend she kept repeating to herself, "If only it lasts!"; she outlived Napoleon by fifteen years.

Napoleon and the Spread of the Revolution

In all the states of the Grand Empire the same course of events tended to repeat itself. First came the stage of military conquest and occupation by French troops. Then came the establishment of a native satellite government with the support of local persons who were willing to collaborate with the French and who helped in the drafting of a constitution specifying the powers of the new government and regularizing its relationships with France. In some areas these two stages had been accomplished under the republican governments before Napoleon came to power. In some regions no more than these two stages really occurred, notably in Spain and the Grand Duchy of Warsaw.

The third stage was one of sweeping internal reform and reorganization, modeled on Bonaparte's program for France and hence derivatively on the French Revolution.[12] Belgium and the German territories west of the Rhine underwent this stage most thoroughly, since they were annexed directly to France for twenty years. Italy, and the main bulk of Germany west of Prussia and Austria, also experienced the third stage.

Napoleon considered himself a great reformer and man of the Enlightenment. He called his system "liberal," and though the word to him meant almost the reverse of what it meant later to liberals, he was possibly the first to use it in a political sense. He believed also in "constitutions"; not that he favored representative assemblies or limited government, but he wanted government to be rationally

---

[12] See pp. 359–364, 388–390.

NAPOLEONIC EUROPE, 1810

Napoleon extended the sphere of French power well beyond the republican expansion of 1798–1799. (See map, p. 383.) By 1810 he dominated the whole continent except Portugal and the Balkan peninsula. Russia, Prussia, and Austria had been forced into alliance with him. He made his brothers kings of Spain, Holland, and Westphalia, his brother-in-law king of Naples, and his stepson viceroy of the kingdom of Italy. He gave the title of king to the German rulers of Bavaria, Württemberg, and Saxony, each of which absorbed smaller German states, while becoming members of Napoleon's Confederation of the Rhine. The old Holy Roman Empire disappeared. In Poland Napoleon, supported by Polish nationalists, undid the partitions of the 1790s by setting up the Grand Duchy of Warsaw.

British troops were fighting in Portugal in 1810, and the British fleet controlled all the islands. To counteract British influence Napoleon extended the borders of the French empire to include the kingdom of Holland and the German cities of Bremen, Hamburg, and Lübeck, and to reach along the Italian coast to a point beyond Rome.

BALTIC SEA

0   100   200 miles

Moscow
Borodino
• Riga
COURLAND Vitebsk
Vilna   Smolensk
Tilsit Kovno • Borisov
Königsberg
RUSSIAN EMPIRE
Warsaw
Brest-Litovsk

**Napoleon's Russian Campaign
June to December, 1812**

Main map labels:

NORWAY

SWEDEN

FINLAND

St. Petersburg

ESTONIA

LIVONIA

COURLAND

KINGDOM OF DENMARK
AND NORWAY

SCOTLAND

Edinburgh

IRELAND

GREAT
BRITAIN

NORTH SEA

DENMARK • Copenhagen

BALTIC SEA

Stockholm

Memel
Tilsit Niemen R.
Königsberg • Friedland • Vilna
Danzig • Eylau

ENGLAND

ATLANTIC OCEAN

London

Plymouth

Dover

ENGLISH CHANNEL Boulogne
CHANNEL I. • Cherbourg
(Britain)

HELIGOLAND
(Britain)

Lübeck
Hamburg

Bremen

KINGDOM OF
HOLLAND

Amsterdam

Rhine R.

Antwerp
Brussels

Cologne

SWEDISH
POMERANIA

MECKLEN-
BURG

Berlin

PRUSSIA

Vistula R.

Posen • Warsaw

Oder R.

GRAND DUCHY
OF WARSAW

Brest-Litovsk

RUSSIA

Versailles Paris
Fontainebleau

Nantes Loire R. • Orleans

Amiens

Seine R.

Valmy

Metz

Mainz

K. OF
WESTPHALIA

Auerstadt
Erfurt • Jena

BERG

CONFEDERATION
OF THE
RHINE

K. OF
SAXONY
Leipzig Dresden

Breslau

Prague

BOHEMIA

Cracow GALICIA

Tarnapol

FRENCH EMPIRE

Rochefort

Strasbourg

BADEN

WÜRTTEM-
BERG
Ulm
Munich
Hohenlinden
K. OF BAVARIA

Basel

Danube R.

Austerlitz

Wagram
Vienna AUSTRIA

Budapest

HUNGARY

Bordeaux

Lyons

Garonne R.

Toulouse

Rhone R.

Avignon

SAVOY

PIEDMONT

Ebro R.

SWITZERLAND

AUSTRIA

LOMBARDY
Milan
P O.R. Genoa

VENETIA
Trieste

ILLYRIAN

SLOVENIA

Drave R.

CROATIA

Save R.

WALLACHIA

Belgrade

Danube R.

SERBIA

OTTOMAN EMPIRE

KINGDOM
OF ITALY

PROVINCES

DALMATIA

BOSNIA

CAPE
FINISTERRE

La Coruña

GALICIA

Oporto Douro R.

Burgos

Almeida • Ciudad Rodrigo

PORTUGAL

Tagus R.

• Lisbon
Elvas

Talavera Madrid

SPAIN • Ocaña

Saragossa

Marseilles

Toulon

Nice

LUCCA
Leghorn • Florence

ADRIATIC SEA

MONTENEGRO

ALBANIA

Salonica

Barcelona

CORSICA

ELBA

Rome

Bari

Taranto

Albuera Guadiana R.

• Baylen

Seville

ANDALUSIA

Cadiz

TRAFALGAR ×

• Gibraltar (Britain)

Tangier

Valencia

BALEARIC I.
(Spain)

MINORCA

IVIZA MAJORCA

KINGDOM OF
SARDINIA

Cagliari

Naples

KINGDOM
OF NAPLES

CORFU

IONIAN I.
(Britain)

MOREA

MOROCCO

Algiers

ALGERIA
(Turkish)

Tunis

Palermo

KINGDOM OF
SICILY

STRAIT OF MESSINA

TUNISIA
(Turkish)

MALTA (Britain)

MEDITERRANEAN SEA

CERIGO

Legend:

French Empire

Grand Empire

Allied with Napoleon

0   100   200   300 miles

"constituted," i.e., deliberately mapped out and planned, not merely inherited from the jumble of the past. Man on horseback though he was, he believed firmly in the rule of law. He insisted with the zeal of conviction on transplanting his Civil Code[13] to the dependent states. This code he considered to be based on the very nature of justice and human relationships and to be applicable, therefore, to all countries with no more than minor adaptation. The idea that a country's laws must mirror its peculiar national character and history was foreign to his mind, for he carried over the rationalist and universalist outlook of the Age of Enlightenment. He thought that people everywhere wanted, and deserved, much the same thing. As he wrote to his brother Jerome, on making him king of Westphalia, "the peoples of Germany, as of France, Italy and Spain, want equality and liberal ideas. For some years now I have been managing the affairs of Europe, and I am convinced that the crowing of the privileged classes was everywhere disliked. Be a constitutional king."

The same plan of reform was initiated, with some variation, in all the dependent states from Spain to Poland and from the mouth of the Elbe to the Straits of Messina. The reforms were directed, in a word, against everything feudal. They established the legal equality of individual persons, and gave governments more complete authority over their individual subjects. Legal classes were wiped out, as in France in 1789; the theory of a society made up of "estates of the realm" gave way to the theory of a society made up of legally equal individuals. The nobility lost its privileges in taxation, officeholding, and military command. Careers were "opened to talent."

The manorial system, bulwark of the old aristocracy, was virtually liquidated. Lords lost all legal jurisdiction over their peasants; peasants became subjects of the state, personally free to move, migrate, or marry, and able to bring suit in the courts of law. The manorial fees, along with tithes, were generally abolished, as in France in 1789. But whereas in France the peasants escaped from these burdens without having to pay compensation, because they had themselves risen in rebellion in 1789 and because France passed through a radical popular revolution in 1793, in other parts of the Grand Empire the peasants were committed to payment of indemnities, and the former feudal class continued to receive income from its abolished rights. Only in Belgium and the Rhineland, incorporated into France under the republic, did the manorial regime disappear without compensation as it did in France, leaving a numerous entrenched class of small landowning farmers. East of the Rhine Napoleon had to compromise with the aristocracy which he assailed. In Poland, the only country in the Grand Empire where a thoroughgoing serfdom had prevailed, the peasants received legal freedom during the French occupation; but the Polish landlords remained economically unharmed, since they owned all the land. Napoleon had to conciliate them, for there was no other effective class in Poland to which he could look for support. In general, outside of France, the assault upon feudalism was not socially as revolutionary as it had been in France. The lord was gone, but the landlord remained.

Everywhere in the Grand Empire the church lost its position as a public authority alongside the state. Church courts were abolished or restricted; the Inquisition was outlawed in Spain. Tithes were done away with, church property confiscated, monastic orders dissolved or severely regulated. Toleration became the

---

[13] See p. 389.

NAPOLEONIC GERMANY

In the panel at the left are shown, by shading, territories of the Duchy of Württemberg in 1800. Note how Württemberg had "islands" of territory unconnected with its main mass, and "holes" or enclaves formed by smaller states enclosed within the mass of Württemberg. Note, too, how Württemberg, itself only fifty miles wide, was surrounded by a mosaic of tiny jurisdictions—free cities, counties, duchies, principalities, abbacies, commanderies, bishoprics, archbishoprics, etc.—all "independent" within the Holy Roman Empire. The right-hand panel shows the Kingdom of Württemberg as consolidated and enlarged in the time of Napoleon. Similar consolidations all over Germany greatly reduced the number of states and added to the efficiency of law and government.

law; Catholics, Protestants, Jews, and unbelievers received the same civil rights. The state was to be based not on the idea of religious community but on the idea of territorial residence. With the nobility, or on economic matters, Napoleon would compromise; but he would not compromise with the Catholic clergy on the principle of a secular state. Even in Spain he insisted on these fundamentals of his system, a sure indication that he was not actuated by expediency only, since it was largely his religious program that provoked the Spanish populace to rebellion.

Guilds were generally abolished or reduced to empty forms, and the individual's right to work was generally proclaimed. Peasants, gaining legal freedom, might learn and enter any trade as they chose. The old town oligarchies and bourgeois patriciates were broken up. Towns and provinces lost their antique liberties and came under general legislation. Internal tariffs were removed, and free trade within state frontiers was encouraged. Some countries shifted to a decimal system of money; and the heterogeneous weights and measures which had originated in the Middle Ages, and of which the Anglo-American bushels, yards, ounces, and pints are living survivals, yielded to the Cartesian regularities of the metric system. Ancient and diverse legal systems gave way to the Napoleonic codes. Law courts were separated from the administration. Hereditary office and the sale of office were done away with. Officials received salaries large enough to shield them from the temptations of corruption. Kings were put on civil lists, with their personal expenses separated from those of the government. Taxes and finances were modernized. The common tax became a land tax, paid by every landowner; and governments knew how much land each owner really possessed, for they developed systematic registration of property and systematic methods of appraisal and assessment. Tax farming was replaced by direct collection. New methods of accounting and of collecting statistics were introduced.

In general, in all countries of the Grand Empire, some of the main principles of the French Revolution were introduced under Napoleon, with the notable exception that there was no self-government through elected legislative bodies. In all countries Napoleon found numerous natives willing to support him, mainly among the commercial and professional men, who were read in the writers of the Enlightenment, often anticlerical, desirous of more equality with the nobility, and eager to break down the old localisms that interfered with trade and with the exchange of ideas. He found supporters also among many progressive nobles and, in the Confederation of the Rhine, among the native rulers. His program appealed to a certain class of people everywhere, and in all parts of the Grand Empire was executed mainly by local persons. Repression went with it, though hardly on a scale to which the twentieth century has become accustomed. There were no vast internment camps, and Fouché's police were engaged more in spying and submitting reports than in the brutalizing of the disaffected. The execution of a single Bavarian bookseller, named Palm, became a famous outrage.

There was, in short, at first, a good deal of pro-Napoleonic feeling in the Grand Empire. The French influence (outside Belgium and the Rhineland) struck deepest in north Italy, where there were no native monarchist traditions, and where the old Italian city-states had produced a strong and often anticlerical burgher class. In south Germany also the French influence was profound. The French system had the least appeal in Spain, where Catholic royalist sentiment produced a kind of counterrevolutionary movement of independence. Nor did it appeal to agrarian eastern Europe, the land of lord and serf. Yet even in Prussia, as will be seen, the state was remodeled along French lines. In Russia, during the Tilsit alliance, Alexander gave his backing to a pro-French reforming minister, Speranski. The Napoleonic influence was pervasive because it carried over the older movement of enlightened despotism and seemed to confer the advantages of the French Revolution without the violence and the disorder. Napoleon, it seemed to Goethe, "was the expression of all that was reasonable, legitimate and European in the revolutionary movement."

But the Napoleonic reforms were also weapons of war. All the dependent states were required by Napoleon to supply him with money and soldiers. Germans, Dutch, Belgians, Italians, Poles, and even Spaniards fought in his armies. In addition, the dependent states defrayed much of the cost of the French army, most of which was stationed outside France. This meant that taxes in France could remain low, to the general satisfaction of the propertied interests that had issued from the Revolution.

49. THE CONTINENTAL SYSTEM: BRITAIN AND EUROPE

Beyond the tributary states of the Grand Empire lay the countries nominally independent, joined under Napoleon in the Continental System. Napoleon thought of his allies as at best subordinate partners in a common project. The great project was to crush Great Britain, and it was for this purpose that the Continental System had been established. But the crushing of Britain became in Napoleon's mind a means to a further end, the unification and mastery of all of Europe. This in turn, had he achieved it, would doubtless have merely opened the way to further conquests.

At the point where he stood in 1807 or 1810 the unification of continental Europe seemed a not impossible objective. He cast about for an ideology to inspire both his Grand Empire and his allies. He held out the cosmopolitan doctrines of the eighteenth century, spoke endlessly of the enlightenment of the age, urged all peoples to work with him against the medievalism, feudalism, ignorance, and obscurantism by which they were still surrounded. And while appealing to the sense of modernity he dwelt also on the grandeur of Roman times. The Roman inspiration reflected itself in the arts of the day. The massive "empire" furniture, the heroic canvases of David, the church of the Madeleine in Paris, resembling a classical temple and converted to a Temple of Glory, the Arch of Triumph in the same city, begun in 1806, all evoked the atmosphere of far-spreading majesty in which Napoleon would have liked the peoples of Europe to live. In addition, to arouse an all-European feeling, Napoleon worked upon the latent hostility to Great Britain. The British, in winning out in the eighteenth-century struggle for wealth and empire, had made themselves disliked in many quarters. There was the natural jealousy felt toward the successful and resentment against the high-handedness by which success had been won and was maintained. Such feelings were present among almost all Europeans. It was believed that the British were really using their sea power to win a larger permanent share of the world's sea-borne commerce for themselves. Nor, in truth, was this belief mistaken.

British Blockade and Napoleon's Continental System

The British, in the Revolutionary and Napoleonic wars, when they declared France and its allies in a state of blockade, did not expect either to starve them or to deprive them of necessary materials of war. Western Europe was still self-sufficient in food, and armaments were to a large extent produced locally, from simple materials like iron, copper, and saltpeter. Europe required almost nothing indispensable from overseas. The chief aim of the British blockade was not, therefore, to keep imports out of enemy countries; it was to keep the trade in such imports out of enemy hands. It was to kill off enemy commerce and shipping, in order, in the short run, to weaken the war-making powers of the enemy government by undermining its revenues and its navy, and in the long run to weaken the enemy's position in the markets of the world. Economic warfare was trade warfare. The British were willing enough to have British goods pass through to the enemy either by smuggling or by the mediation of neutrals.

As early as 1793 the French republicans had denounced England as the "modern Carthage," a ruthless mercantile and profit-seeking power which aspired to enslave Europe to its financial and commercial system. With the wars, the British in fact obtained a monopoly over the shipment of overseas commodities into Europe. At the same time, being relatively advanced in the Industrial Revolution, they could produce cotton cloth and certain other articles, by power machinery, more cheaply than other peoples of Europe, and so threatened to monopolize the European market for such manufactured goods. There was much feeling in Europe against the modern Carthage, especially among the bourgeois and commercial classes who were in competition with it. The upper classes were perhaps less hostile, not caring where the goods that they consumed had originated, but aristocracies and governments were susceptible to the argument that Britain was a money power, a "nation of shopkeepers" as Napoleon put it, which fought its wars with pounds sterling instead of blood and was always in search of dupes in Europe.

It was on all these feelings that Napoleon played, reiterating time and again that England was the real enemy of all Europe, and that Europe would never be prosperous or independent until relieved of the incubus of British "monopoly." To prevent the flow of goods into Britain was no more the purpose of the Continental System than to prevent the flow of goods into France was the purpose of the British blockade. The purpose of each was to destroy the enemy's commerce, credit, and public revenues by the destruction of his exports—and also to build up markets for oneself.

To destroy British exports Napoleon prohibited, by the Berlin Decree of 1806, the importation of British goods into the continent of Europe. Counted as British, if of British or British colonial origin, were goods brought to Europe in neutral ships as the property of neutrals. The British, in response, ruled by an "order in council" of November 1807 that neutrals might enter Napoleonic ports only if they first stopped in Great Britain, where the regulations were such as to encourage their loading with British goods. The British thus tried to move their exports into enemy territory through neutral channels, which was precisely what Napoleon intended to prevent. He announced, by the Milan Decree of December 1807, that any neutral vessel that had stopped at a British port, or submitted to search by a British warship at sea, would be confiscated upon its appearance in a Continental harbor.

With all Europe at war, virtually the only trading neutral was the United States, which could now trade with neither England nor Europe except by violating the regulations of one belligerent or the other. It would thus become liable to reprisals, and hence to involvement in war. President Jefferson, to avoid war, attempted a self-imposed policy of commercial isolation, which proved so ruinous to American foreign trade that the United States government took steps to renew trade relations with whichever belligerent first removed its controls over neutral commerce. Napoleon offered to do so, on condition that the United States would defend itself against the enforcement of British controls. At the same time an expansionist party among the western Americans, ambitious to annex Canada, considered that with the British army engaged in Spain the time was ripe to complete the War of Independence by driving Britain from the North American mainland. The result was the Anglo-American War of 1812, which had few results, except to demonstrate the distressing inefficiency of military institutions in the new republic.

But the Continental System was more than a device for destroying the export

trade of Great Britain. It was also a scheme—today it would be called a "plan"—
for developing the economy of continental Europe, around France as its main
center. The Continental System, if successful, would replace the national economies with an integrated economy for the Continent as a whole. It would create
the framework for a European civilization. And it would ruin the British sea
power and commercial monopoly; for a unified Europe, Napoleon thought,
would itself soon take to the sea.

The Failure of the Continental System

But the Continental System failed; it was worse than a failure, for it caused widespread antagonism to the Napoleonic regime. The dream of a united Europe,
under French rule, was not sufficiently attractive to inspire the necessary sacrifice
—even a sacrifice more of comforts than of necessities. As Napoleon impatiently
said, one would suppose that the destinies of Europe turned upon a barrel of
sugar. It was true, as he and his propagandists insisted, that Britain monopolized
the sale of sugar, tobacco, and other overseas goods, but people preferred to deal
clandestinely with the British rather than go without them. The charms of America destroyed the Continental System.

British manufactures were somewhat easier than colonial goods to replace.
Raw cotton was brought by land from the Levant through the Balkans, and the
cotton manufactures of France, Saxony, Switzerland, and north Italy were stimulated by the relief from British competition. There was a great expansion of Danish woolens and German hardware. The cultivation of sugar beets, to replace
cane sugar, spread in France, central Europe, Holland, and even Russia. Thus infant industries and investments were built up which, after Napoleon's fall, clamored for tariff protection. In general, the European industrial interests were well
disposed toward the Continental System.

Yet they could never adequately replace the British in supplying the market.
One obstacle was transportation. Much trading between parts of the Continent
had always been done by sea; this coastal traffic was now blocked by the British.
Land routes were increasingly used, even in the faraway Balkans and Illyrian
Provinces, through which raw cotton was brought; and improved roads were
built through the Simplon and Mont Cenis passes in the Alps. No less than 17,000
wheeled vehicles crossed the Mont Cenis pass in 1810. But land transport, at best,
was no substitute for the sea. Without railroads, introduced some thirty years
later, a purely Continental economy was impossible to maintain.

Another obstacle was tariffs. The idea of a Continental tariff union was put forward by some of his subordinates, but Napoleon never adopted it. The dependent
states remained insistent on their ostensible sovereignty. Each had widened its
trading area by demolishing former internal tariffs, but each kept a tariff against
the others. The kingdoms of Italy and Naples enjoyed no free trade with each
other nor did the German states of the Confederation of the Rhine. France remained protectionist; and when Napoleon annexed Holland and parts of Italy to
France, he kept them outside the French customs. At the same time Napoleon forbade the satellite states to raise high tariffs against France. France was his base,
and he meant to favor French industry, which was much crippled by its loss of its
Near Eastern and American markets.

Shippers, shipbuilders, and dealers in overseas goods, a powerful element of the older bourgeoisie, were ruined by the Continental System. The French ports were idle and their populations distressed and disgruntled. The same befell all ports of Europe where the blockade was strictly enforced; at Trieste, total annual tonnage fell from 208,000 in 1807 to 60,000 in 1812. Eastern Europe was especially hard hit. In the West there was the stimulus to new manufactures. The East, long dependent on western Europe for manufactured goods, could no longer obtain them from England legally, nor from France, Germany, or Bohemia because of the difficulties of land transport and the British control of the Baltic. Nor could the landowners of Prussia, Poland, and Russia market their produce. The aristocracy of eastern Europe, which was the principal spending and importing class, had additional reason to dislike the French and to sympathize with the British.

As a war measure against Britain the Continental System also failed. British trade with Europe was significantly reduced. But the loss was made up elsewhere because of British control of the sea. Exports to Latin America rose from £300,000 in 1805 to £6,300,000 in 1809. Here again the existence of the overseas world frustrated the Continental System. Despite the System, export of British cotton goods, rising on a continuous tide of the Industrial Revolution, more than doubled in four years from 1805 to 1809. And while part of the increase was due to mere inflation and rising prices, it is estimated that the annual income of the British people more than doubled in the Revolutionary and Napoleonic wars, leaping from £140,000,000 in 1792 to £335,000,000 in 1814.

50. THE NATIONAL MOVEMENTS: GERMANY

The Resistance to Napoleon: Nationalism

From the beginning, as far back as 1792, the French met with resistance as well as collaboration in the countries they occupied. There was resentment when the invading armies plundered and requisitioned upon the country, when the newly organized states were required to pay tribute of men and money, when their policies were dictated by French residents or ambassadors, and when the Continental System was used for the especial benefit of French manufacturers. Europeans began to feel that Napoleon was employing them merely as tools against England. And in all countries, including France itself, people grew tired of the peace that was no peace, the wars and rumors of war, the conscription and the taxes, the aloof bureaucratic government from on high, the obviously growing and insatiable appetite of Napoleon for power and self-exaltation. Movements of protest and independence showed themselves even within the Napoleonic structure. We have seen how the dependent states protected themselves by tariffs. Even the emperor's proconsuls tried to root themselves in local opinion, as when Louis Bonaparte, king of Holland, tried to defend Dutch interests against Napoleon's demands, or when Murat, king of Naples, appealed to Italian sentiment to secure his own throne.

Nationalism developed as a movement of resistance against the forcible internationalism of the Napoleonic empire. Since the international system was essentially French, the nationalistic movements were anti-French; and since Napoleon was an autocrat, they were antiautocratic. The nationalism of the period was a mixture of the conservative and the liberal. Some nationalists, predominantly conservative, insisted on the value of their own peculiar institutions, customs, folkways, and historical development, which they feared might be obliterated under the French and Napoleonic system. Others, or indeed the same ones, insisted on more self-determination, more participation in government, more representative institutions, more freedom for the individual against the bureaucratic interference of the state. Both conservatism and liberalism rose up against Napoleon, destroyed him, outlasted him, and shaped the history of the following generations.

Nationalism was thus very complex and appeared in different countries in different ways. In England the profound solidarity of the country exhibited itself; all classes rallied and stood shoulder to shoulder against "Boncy"; and ideas of reforming Parliament or tampering with historic English liberties were resolutely put aside. It is possible that the Napoleonic wars helped England through a very difficult social crisis, for the Industrial Revolution was causing dislocation, misery, unemployment, and even revolutionary agitation among a small minority, all of which were eclipsed by the patriotic need of resistance to Bonaparte. In Spain, nationalism took the form of implacable resistance to the French armies that desolated the land. Some Spanish nationalists were liberal; a bourgeois group at Cádiz, rebelling against the French regime, proclaimed the Spanish constitution of 1812, modeled on the French constitution of 1791. But Spanish nationalism drew its greatest strength from sentiments that were counterrevolutionary, aiming to restore the clergy and the Bourbons. In Italy the Napoleonic regime was better liked and national feeling was less anti-French than in Spain. Bourgeois of the Italian cities generally prized the efficiency and enlightenment of French methods, and often shared in the anticlericalism of the French Revolution. The French regime, which lasted in Italy from 1796 to 1814, broke the habit of loyalty to the various duchies, oligarchic republics, papal states, and foreign dynasties by which Italy had long been ruled. Napoleon never unified Italy, but he assembled it into only three parts, and the French influence brought the notion of a politically united Italy within the bounds of reasonable aspiration. With the Poles Napoleon positively encouraged national feeling. He repeatedly told them that they might win a restored and united Poland by faithfully fighting in his cause. A few Polish nationalists, like the aging patriot Kosciuzsko, never trusted Napoleon, and some others, like Czartoryski, looked rather to the Russian tsar for a restoration of the Polish kingdom; but in general the Poles, for their own national reasons, were exceptionally devoted to the emperor of the French and lamented his passing.

The Movement of Thought in Napoleonic Germany

By far the most momentous national movement took place in Germany. The Germans rebelled not only against the Napoleonic rule but against the century-old ascendancy of French civilization. They rebelled not only against the French armies but against the philosophy of the Age of Enlightenment. The years of the French Revolution and Napoleon were for Germany the years of its greatest cultural efflorescence, the years of Beethoven, Goethe, and Schiller, of Herder, Kant, Fichte, Hegel, Schleiermacher, and many others. German ideas fell in with all the ferment of fundamental thinking known as "romanticism," which was everywhere challenging the "dry abstractions" of the Age of Reason and about which more will be said in this and the following chapter. Germany became the most "romantic" of all countries, and German influence spread throughout Europe. In the nineteenth century the Germans came to be widely regarded as intellectual leaders, somewhat as the French had been in the century before. And most of the distinctive features of German thought were somehow connected with nationalism in a broad sense.

Formerly, especially in the century following the Peace of Westphalia, the Germans had been the least nationally minded of all the larger European peoples.[14] They prided themselves on their world citizenship or cosmopolitan outlook. Looking out from the tiny states in which they lived, they were conscious of Europe, conscious of other countries, but hardly conscious of Germany. The Holy Roman Empire was a shadow. The German world had no tangible frontiers; the area of German speech simply faded out into Alsace or the Austrian Netherlands, or into Poland, Bohemia, or the upper Balkans. That "Germany" ever did, thought, or hoped anything never crossed the German mind. The upper classes, becoming contemptuous of much that was German, took over French fashions, dress, etiquette, manners, ideas, and language, regarding them as an international norm of civilized living. Frederick the Great hired French tax collectors and wrote his own books in French.

About 1780 signs of a change set in. Even Frederick, in his later years, predicted a golden age of German literature, proudly declaring that Germans could do what other nations had done. In 1784 appeared a book by J. G. Herder, called *Ideas on the Philosophy of the History of Mankind*. Herder was an earnest soul, a Protestant pastor and theologian who thought the French somewhat frivolous. He concluded that imitation of foreign ways made people shallow and artificial. He declared that German ways were indeed different from French but not for that reason the less worthy of respect. All true culture or civilization, he held, must arise from native roots. It must arise also from the life of the common people, the *Volk*, not from the cosmopolitan and denatured life of the upper classes.[15] Each people, he thought, meaning by a people a group sharing the same language, had its own attitudes, spirit, or genius. A sound civilization must express a national character or *Volksgeist*. And the character of each people was special to itself. Herder did not believe the nations to be in conflict; quite the contrary, he simply insisted that they were different. He did not believe German culture to be the best; many other peoples, notably the Slavs, later found his ideas applicable to their own needs. His philosophy of history was very different from Voltaire's. Voltaire and the philosophes had expected all peoples to progress along the same path of reason and enlightenment toward the same civilization. Herder thought that all peoples should develop their own genius in their own way, each slowly unfolding with the inevitability of plant-like growth, avoiding sudden change or distortion by outside influence, and all ultimately reflecting, in their endless diversity, the infinite richness of humanity and of God.

The idea of the *Volksgeist* was reinforced from other and non-German sources and soon passed to other countries in the general movement of romantic thought. Like much else in romanticism, it emphasized genius or intuition rather than

---

[14] See pp. 207–211.
[15] On elite and popular cultures see pp. 242–247.

reason. It stressed the differences rather than the similarity of mankind. It broke down that sense of human similarity which had been characteristic of the Age of Enlightenment,[16] and which revealed itself in French and American doctrines of the rights of man, or again in the law codes of Napoleon. In the past it had been usually thought that what was good was good for all peoples. Good poetry was poetry written according to certain classical principles or "rules" of composition, which were the same for all writers from the Greeks on down. Now, according to Herder and to romantics in all countries, good poetry was poetry that expressed an inner genius, either an individual genius or the genius of a people—there were no more "rules." Good and just laws, according to the older philosophy of natural law, somehow corresponded to a standard of justice that was the same for all men. But now, according to Herder and the romantic school of jurisprudence, good laws were those that reflected local conditions or national idiosyncrasies. Here again there were no "rules," except possibly the rule that each nation should have its own way.

Herder's philosophy set forth a cultural nationalism, without political message. The Germans had long been a nonpolitical people. In the microscopic states of the Holy Roman Empire they had had no significant political questions to think about; in the more sizable ones they had been excluded from public affairs. The French Revolution made the Germans acutely conscious of the state. It showed what a people could do with a state, once they took it over and used it for their own purposes. For one thing, the French had raised themselves to the dignity of citizenship; they had become free men, responsible for themselves, taking part in the affairs of their country. For another, because they had a unified state which included all Frenchmen, and one in which a whole nation surged with a new sense of freedom, they were able to rise above all the other peoples of Europe. Many in Germany were beginning to feel humiliation at the paternalism of their governments. The futilities of the Holy Roman Empire, which had made Germany for centuries the battlefield of Europe, now filled them with shame and indignation. They saw with disgust how their German princes, forever squabbling with each other for control over German subjects, disgraced themselves before the French to promote their own interests. The national awakening in Germany, which set in strongly after 1800, was therefore directed not only against Napoleon and the French, but also against the German rulers and many of the half-Frenchified German upper classes. It was democratic in that it stressed the superior virtue of the common people.

Germans became fascinated by the idea of political unity and national greatness, precisely because they had neither. A great national German state, expressing the deep moral will and distinctive culture of the German people, seemed to them the solution to all their problems. It would give moral dignity to the individual German, solve the vexatious question of the selfish petty princes, protect the deep German *Volksgeist* from violation, and secure the Germans from subjection to outside powers. The nationalist philosophy remained somewhat vague, because in practice there was little that one could do. "Father" Jahn organized a kind of youth movement and became the inventor of what might be termed political gymnastics, having his young men do calisthenics for the Fatherland; he led them on open-air expeditions into the country, where they made fun of aristocrats

[16] See pp. 313–314.

in French costume; and he taught them to be suspicious of foreigners, Jews, and internationalists, and indeed of everything that might corrupt the purity of the German *Volk*. Most Germans thought him too extreme. Others collected wonderful stories of the rich medieval German past. There was an anonymous anti-French work, *Germany in Its Deep Humiliation*, for selling which the publisher Palm was put to death. Others founded the Moral and Scientific Union, generally known as the *Tugendbund* or league of virtue or manliness, whose members, by developing their own moral character, were to contribute to the future of Germany.

The career of J. G. Fichte illustrates the course of German thought in these years. Fichte was a moral and metaphysical philosopher, a professor at the University of Jena. His doctrine, that the inner spirit of the individual creates its own moral universe, was much admired in many countries. In America, for example, it entered into the transcendental philosophy of Ralph Waldo Emerson. Fichte at first was practically without national feeling. He enthusiastically approved of the French Revolution, as did Jahn and Arndt. In 1793, with the Revolution at its height and many foreign observers turning against it, Fichte published a laudatory tract on the French Republic. He saw it as an emancipation of the human spirit, a step upward in the elevation of human dignity and moral stature. He accepted the idea of the Terror, that of "forcing men to be free"; and he shared Rousseau's conception of the state as the embodiment of the sovereign will of a people. He came to see the state as the means of human salvation. In 1800, in his *Closed Commercial State*, he sketched a kind of totalitarian system in which the state planned and operated the whole economy of the country, shutting itself off from the rest of the world in order that, at home, it might freely develop the character of its own citizens. When the French conquered Germany Fichte became intensely and self-consciously German. He took over the idea of the *Volksgeist:* not only did the individual spirit create its own moral universe, but the spirit of a people created a kind of moral universe as well, manifested in its language, arts, folkways, customs, institutions, and ideas.

At Berlin, in 1808, Fichte delivered a series of *Addresses to the German Nation*, declaring that there was an ineradicable German spirit, a primordial and immutable national character, more noble than that of other peoples (thus going beyond Herder), to be kept pure at all costs from all outside influence, either international or French. The German spirit, he held, had always been profoundly different from that of France and western Europe; it had never yet really been heard from but would be some day. The French army commander then occupying the city thought the lectures too academic to be worth suppression. They had, in fact, few hearers; Fichte was considered a firebrand by most Germans; but they later regarded him as a national hero.

Reforms in Prussia

Politically, in the revolt against the French the main transformations came in Prussia. Prussia after the death of Frederick the Great had fallen into a period of satisfied inertia, such as is likely to follow upon rapid growth or spectacular success. Then in 1806, at Jena-Auerstädt, the kingdom collapsed in a single battle. Its western and most of its Polish territories were taken away. It was relegated by Napoleon to its old holdings east of the Elbe. Even here the French remained in occupation, for Napoleon stationed his Ninth Corps in Berlin. But in the eyes of German nationalists Prussia had a moral advantage. Of all the German states it was the least compromised by collaboration with the French. Toward Prussia, as toward a haven, German patriots therefore made their way. East-Elbian Prussia, formerly the least German of German lands, became the center of an all German movement for national freedom. The years after Jena contributed to the "Prussianizing" of Germany; but it is to be observed that neither Fichte nor Hegel, Gneisenau nor Scharnhorst, Stein nor Hardenberg, all rebuilders of Prussia, was a native Prussian.

The main problem for Prussia was military, since Napoleon could be overthrown only by military force. And as always in Prussia, the requirements of the army shaped the form taken by the state.[17] The problem was conceived to be one of morale and personnel. The old Prussia of Frederick, which had fallen ingloriously, had been mechanical, arbitrary, soulless. Its people had lacked the sense of membership in the state, and in the army its soldiers had held no hope of promotion and felt no patriotism or spirit. To produce this spirit was the aim of the army reformers, Scharnhorst and Gneisenau. Gneisenau, a Saxon, had served in one of the British "Hessian" regiments in the War of American Independence, during which he had observed the military value of patriotic feeling in the American soldiers. He was a close observer also of the consequences of the French Revolution, which, he said, had "set in action the national energy of the entire French people, putting the different classes on an equal social and fiscal basis." If Prussia was to strengthen itself against France, or indeed to avoid revolution in the long run in Prussia itself, it must find a means to inspire a similar feeling of equal participation in its own people, and to allow capable individuals to fill important positions in the army and government without regard to their social status.

The reconstruction of the state, prerequisite to the reconstruction of the army, was initiated by Baron Stein and continued by his successor, Hardenberg. Like Metternich, Stein came from western Germany; he had been an imperial knight of the late Holy Roman Empire, who from a bridge near his castle had beheld the domains of no less than eight German princes in one sweep of the eye. Stateless himself, he thought of Germany as a whole; he was long hostile to what he considered the barely civilized Prussia, but finally resorted to it as the hope of the future. Deeply committed to the philosophy of Kant and Fichte, he dwelt on the concepts of duty, service, moral character, and responsibility. He thought that the common people must be awakened to moral life, raised from a brutalized servility to the level of self-determination and membership in the community. This, he believed, required an equality more of duties than of rights.

Under Stein the old caste structure of Prussia became somewhat less rigid. Property became interchangeable between classes; bourgeois were allowed to buy land and serve as officers in the army. The burghers, to develop a sense of citizenship and participation in the state, were given extensive freedom of self-government in the cities; the municipal systems of Prussia, and later of Germany, became a model for much of Europe in the following century. Stein had ideas for parliamentary institutions in Prussia as a whole, thinking they would strengthen the country, but he left office before acting upon them.

His most famous work was the "abolition of serfdom." It was naturally impossible, since the whole reform program was aimed at strengthening Prussia for a war of liberation against the French, to antagonize the Junkers who commanded the army. Stein's ordinance of 1807 abolished serfdom only in that it abolished the

[17] See pp. 224–227, 322–323.

"hereditary subjection" of peasants to their manorial lords.[18] It gave peasants the right to move and migrate, marry, and take up trades without the lord's approval. If, however, the peasant remained on the land, he was still subject to all the old services of forced labor in the fields of the lord. Peasants enjoying small tenures of their own continued to be liable for the old dues and fees. By an edict of 1810, a peasant might convert his tenure into private property, getting rid of the manorial obligations, but only on condition that one-third of the land he had held should become the private property of the lord. In the following decades many such conversions took place, of which the result was that the estates of the Junkers grew considerably larger. The reforms in Prussia somewhat reduced the old patriarchal powers of the lords and gave legal status and freedom of movement to the mass of the population, thus laying the foundation for a modern state and modern economy. But the peasants tended to become mere hired agricultural laborers; and the position of the Junkers was heightened, not reduced. Prussia avoided the Revolution. Stein himself, because Napoleon feared him, was obliged to go into exile in 1808, but his reforms endured.

51. THE OVERTHROW OF NAPOLEON: THE CONGRESS OF VIENNA

The situation at the close of 1811 may be summarized as follows. Napoleon had the mainland of Europe in his grip. Russia and Turkey were at war on the Danube, but otherwise there was no war except in Spain, where four years of fighting remained inconclusive. The Continental System was working badly. Britain was hurt by it only negatively, in that, without it, British exports to Europe would have risen rapidly in these years. Well launched in the Industrial Revolution, Great Britain was amassing a vast store of national wealth, accumulating the wherewithal to assist European governments financially against Napoleon. The peoples of Europe were increasingly restless, dreaming increasingly of national freedom. In Germany, especially, many awaited the opportunity to rise in a war of independence. But Napoleon could be overthrown only by the destruction of his army, with which neither British wealth nor British sea power, nor the European patriots and nationalists, nor the Prussian nor the Austrian armed forces were able to cope. All eyes turned to Russia. Alexander I had long been dissatisfied with his French alliance. He had obtained from it nothing but the annexation of Finland in 1809. He received no assistance from France in his war with Turkey; he saw Napoleon marry into the Austrian house; he had to tolerate the existence of a French-oriented Poland at his very door. The articulate classes in Russia, namely, the landowners and serf owners, loudly denounced the French alliance and demanded a resumption of open trade relations with England. An international clientele of émigrés and anti-Bonapartists, including Baron Stein, also gradually congregated at St. Petersburg, where they poured into the tsar's ears the welcome message that Europe looked to him for its salvation.

The Russian Campaign and the War of Liberation

On December 31, 1810, Russia formally withdrew from the Continental System. Anglo-Russian commercial relations were resumed. Napoleon resolved to crush

[18] See p. 123.

the tsar. He concentrated the Grand Army in eastern Germany and Poland, a vast force of 700,000 men, the largest ever assembled up to that time for a single military operation. It was an all-European host. Hardly more than a third was French; another third was German, from German regions annexed to France, from the states of the Confederation of the Rhine, and with token forces from Prussia and Austria; and the remaining third was drawn from all other nationalities of the Grand Empire, including 90,000 Poles. Napoleon at first hoped to meet the Russians in Poland or Prussia. This time, however, they decided to fight on their own ground, and they needed in any case to delay until their forces on the lower Danube could be recalled. In June 1812 Napoleon led the Grand Army into Russia.

He intended a short, sharp war, such as most of his wars had been in the past, and carried with him only three weeks' supplies. But from the beginning everything went wrong. It was Napoleon's principle to force a decisive battle; but the Russian army simply melted away. It was his principle to live on the country, so as to reduce the need for supply trains; but the Russians destroyed as they retreated, and in any case, in Russia, even in the summer, it was hard to find sustenance for so many men and horses. Finally, not far from Moscow, Napoleon was able to join battle with the main Russian force at Borodino. Here again everything miscarried. It was his principle always to outnumber the enemy at the decisive spot; but the Grand Army had left so many detachments along its line of march that at Borodino the Russians outnumbered it. It was Napoleon's principle to concentrate his artillery, but here he scattered it instead, and to throw in his last reserves at the critical moment, but at Borodino, so far from home, he refused the risk of ordering the Old Guard into action. Napoleon won the battle, at a cost of 30,000 men, as against 50,000 lost by the Russians; but the Russian army was able to withdraw in good order.

On September 14, 1812, the French emperor entered Moscow. Almost immediately the city broke into flames. Napoleon found himself camping in a ruin, with troops strewn along a long line all the way back to Poland, and with a hostile army maneuvering near at hand. Baffled, he tried to negotiate with Alexander, who refused all overtures. After five weeks, not knowing what to do, and fearful of remaining isolated in Moscow over the winter, Napoleon ordered a retreat. Prevented by the Russians from taking a more southerly route, the Grand Army retired by the same way it had come. The cold weather set in early and was unusually severe. For a century after 1812 the retreat from Moscow remained the last word in military horror. Men froze and starved, horses slipped and died, vehicles could not be moved, and equipment was abandoned. Discipline broke down toward the end; the army dissolved into a horde of individual fugitives, speaking a babel of languages, harassed by bands of Russian irregulars, picking their way on foot over ice and snow, most of the time in the dark, for the nights are long in these latitudes in December. Of 611,000 who entered Russia 400,000 died of battle casualties, starvation, and exposure, and 100,000 were taken prisoner. The Grand Army no longer existed.

Now at last all the anti-Napoleonic forces rushed together. The Russians pushed westward into central Europe. The Prussian and Austrian governments, which in 1812 had half-heartedly supplied troops for the invasion of Russia, switched over in 1813 and joined the tsar. Throughout Germany the patriots, often half-trained boys, marched off in the War of Liberation, though it was the professional armies of the German states that made the difference. Anti-French riots broke out in Italy.

In Spain Wellington at last pushed rapidly forward; in June 1813 he crossed the Pyrenees into France. The British government, in three years from 1813 to 1815, poured £32,000,000 as subsidies into Europe, more than half of all the funds granted during the twenty-two years of the wars. An incongruous alliance of British capitalism and east-European agrarian feudalism, of the British navy and the Russian army, of Spanish clericalism and German nationalism, of divine-right monarchies and newly aroused democrats and liberals, combined at last to bring the Man of Destiny to the ground.

Napoleon, who had left his army in Russia in December 1812, and rushed across Europe to Paris, by sleigh and coach, in the remarkable time of thirteen days, raised a new army in France in the early months of 1813. But it was untrained and unsteady, and he himself had lost some of his genius for command. His new army was smashed in October at the battle of Leipzig, known to the Germans as the Battle of the Nations, the greatest battle in number of men engaged ever fought until the twentieth century. The allies drove Napoleon back upon France. But the closer they came to defeating him the more they began to fear and distrust each other.

The Restoration of the Bourbons

The coalition already showed signs of splitting. Should the allies, together or singly, negotiate with Napoleon? How strong should the France of the future be? What should be its new frontiers? What form of government should it have? There was no agreement on these questions. Alexander wanted to dethrone Napoleon and dictate peace in Paris, in dramatic retribution for the destruction of Moscow. He had a scheme for giving the French throne to Bernadotte, a former French marshal, now crown prince of Sweden, who as king of France would depend on Russian support. Metternich preferred to keep Napoleon or his son as French emperor, after clearing the French out of central Europe; for a Bonaparte dynasty in a reduced France would be dependent on Austria. The Prussian counsels were divided. The British declared that the French must get out of Belgium, and that Napoleon must go; they held that the French might then choose their own government but believed a restoration of the Bourbons to be the best solution. The three Continental monarchies had no concern for the Bourbons, and both Alexander and Metternich, if they could make France dependent respectively on themselves, were willing to see it remain strong to the extent of including Belgium. In November 1813 Metternich communicated to Napoleon a proposition known as the "Frankfurt proposals," by which Napoleon would remain French emperor, and France would retain its "natural" frontier on the Rhine. There was a chance of peace on this basis, for the allies could not shake off their old fear of Napoleon, the Prussians could be compensated elsewhere, and among the Russians many of the generals and others were impatient to go home. The British, their diplomatic influence reduced by the fact that they had few troops in Europe, faced the appalling prospect that the Continent would again make peace without them—and a peace in which France should again keep Belgium.

The British foreign minister, Viscount Castlereagh, arrived in person on the Continent in January 1814. He held a number of strong cards. For one thing, Napoleon rejected the Frankfurt proposals. He continued to fight, and the allies therefore continued to ask for British financial aid. Castlereagh skillfully used the promise of British subsidies to win acceptance of the British war aims. In addition, he found a common ground for agreement with Metternich, both Britain and Austria fearing the domination of Europe by Russia. Castlereagh's first great problem was to hold the alliance together, for without Continental allies the British could not defeat France. He succeeded, on March 9, 1814, in getting Russia, Prussia, Austria, and Great Britain to sign the treaty of Chaumont. Each power bound itself for twenty years to a Quadruple Alliance against France, and each agreed to provide 150,000 soldiers to enforce such peace terms as might be arrived at. For the first time since 1792 a solid coalition of the four great powers now existed against France. Three weeks later the allies entered Paris, and on April 4 Napoleon abdicated at Fontainebleau.

He was forced to this step by lack of support in France itself. Twenty years before, in 1793 and 1794, France had fought off the combined powers of Europe —minus Russia. It could not and would not do so in 1814. The country cried for peace. Even the imperial marshals advised the emperor's abdication. But what was to follow him? For over twenty-five years the French had had one regime after another. Now there were some who wished a republic, some who wished the empire under Napoleon's infant son, some who wished a constitutional monarchy, and some even who longed for the Old Regime. Talleyrand stepped into the breach. The "legitimate" king, he said, Louis XVIII, was after all the man who would provoke the least factionalism and opposition. The powers, likewise, had by this time concluded in favor of the Bourbons. A Bourbon king would be peaceable, under no impulse to win back the conquests of the republic and empire. He would also, as the native and rightful king of France, need no foreign support to bolster him up, so that the control of France would not arise as an issue to divide the victorious powers.

So the Bourbon dynasty was restored. Louis XVIII, ignored and disregarded for a whole generation, both by most Frenchmen and by the governments of Europe, returned to the throne of his brother and his fathers. He issued a "constitutional charter," partly at the insistence of the liberal tsar, and partly because, having actually learned from his long exile, he sought the support of influential people in France. The charter of 1814 made no concession to the principle of popular or national sovereignty. It was represented as the gracious gift of a theoretically absolute king. But in practice it granted what most Frenchmen wanted. It promised legal equality, eligibility of all to public office without regard to class, and a parliamentary government in two chambers. It recognized the Napoleonic law codes, the Napoleonic settlement with the church, and the redistribution of property effected during the Revolution. It carried over the abolition of feudalism and privilege, manorialism and tithes. It confined the vote, to be sure, to a very few large landowners; but for the time being, except for a few irreconcilables, France settled down to enjoy the blessings of a chastened revolution—and peace.

The Settlement before the Vienna Congress

It was with the government of the restored Bourbons that the powers, on May 30, 1814, signed a treaty. This document, the "first" Treaty of Paris, confined France to its boundaries of 1792, those obtaining before the wars. The allied statesmen disregarded cries for vengeance and punishment, imposed no indemnity or reparations, and even allowed the works of art gathered from Europe during the wars to remain in Paris. It was not the desire of the victors to handicap the new French government on which they placed their hopes. Napoleon meanwhile was exiled to the island of Elba on the Italian coast.

To deal with other questions, the powers had agreed, before signing the Alliance of Chaumont, to hold an international congress at Vienna after defeating Napoleon. The recession of the French flood left the future of much of Europe—Belgium, Holland, Germany, Poland, Italy, Spain—fluid and uncertain. There were many other debatable questions also, including the Russian annexation of Finland and ambitions on the Danube, the disintegration of the Spanish American empire, the British occupation of French, Dutch, and Spanish possessions, and the troublesome issue of the freedom of the seas.

Both Russia and Great Britain, before consenting to a general conference, specified certain matters that they would decide for themselves as not susceptible to international consideration. The Russians refused to discuss Turkey and the Balkans; they retained Bessarabia as the prize of their recent war with the Turks. They also kept Finland, as an autonomous constitutional grand duchy, as well as certain recent conquests in the Caucasus almost unknown to Europe. The British refused any discussion of the freedom of the seas. They also barred all colonial and overseas questions. The revolts in Spanish America were left to run their course. The British government simply announced to Europe which of its colonial and insular conquests it would keep and which it would return.

In Europe, the British remained in possession of Malta, the Ionian Islands, and Heligoland. In America, they kept St. Lucia, Trinidad, and Tobago in the West Indies and reasserted their claims to the Pacific Northwest, or Oregon country, to which claims were also made by Russia, Spain, and the United States. Of former French possessions, the British kept the island of Mauritius in the Indian Ocean. Of former Dutch territories, they kept the Cape of Good Hope and Ceylon, but returned the Netherlands Indies. During the Revolutionary and Napoleonic wars in Europe the British had also made extensive conquests in India, bringing much of the Deccan and the upper Ganges valley under their rule. The British emerged, in 1814, as the controlling power in both India and the Indian Ocean.

Indeed, of all the colonial empires founded by Europeans in the sixteenth and seventeenth centuries, and whose rivalry had been a recurring cause of war in the eighteenth, only the British now remained as a growing and dynamic system. The old French, Spanish, and Portuguese empires were reduced to mere scraps of their former selves; the Dutch still held vast establishments in the East Indies, but all the intermediate positions, the Cape, Ceylon, Mauritius, Singapore, were now British. Nor, in 1814, did any people except the British have a significant navy. With Napoleon and the Continental System defeated, with the Industrial Revolution bringing power machinery to the manufacturers of England, with no rival left in the contest for overseas dominion, and with a virtual monopoly of naval power, whose use they studiously kept free from international regulation, the British embarked on their century of world leadership, which may be said to have lasted from 1814 to 1914.

The Congress of Vienna, 1814–1815

The Congress of Vienna assembled in September 1814. Never had such a brilliant gathering been seen. All the states of Europe sent representatives; and many defunct states, such as the formerly sovereign princes and ecclesiastics of the late Holy Roman Empire, sent lobbyists to urge their restoration. But procedure was

so arranged that all important matters were decided by the four triumphant
Great Powers. Indeed it was at the Congress of Vienna that the terms great and
small powers entered clearly into the diplomatic vocabulary. Europe was at
peace, a treaty having been signed with the late enemy; France also was represented at the Congress, by none other than Talleyrand, now minister to Louis
XVIII. Castlereagh, Metternich, and Alexander spoke for their respective countries; Prussia was represented by Hardenberg. The Prussians hoped, as always,
to enlarge the kingdom of Prussia. Alexander was a question mark: he wanted
Poland, he wanted constitutional governments in Europe, he wanted some kind
of international system of collective security. Castlereagh and Metternich, with
support from Talleyrand, were most especially concerned to produce a balance of
power on the Continent. Aristocrats of the Old Regime, they applied eighteenth-
century diplomatic principles to the existing problem. They by no means desired
to restore the territorial boundaries obtaining before the wars. They did desire, as
they put it, to restore the "liberties of Europe," meaning the freedom of European
states from domination by a single power.[19] The threat of "universal monarchy," a
term which diplomats still sometimes used to signify such a system as Napoleon's,
was to be offset by an ingenious calculation of forces, a transfer of territory and
"souls" from one government to another, in such a way as to distribute and balance political power among a number of free and sovereign states. It was hoped
that a proper balance would also produce a lasting peace.

The chief menace to peace, and most likely claimant for the domination of
Europe, naturally seemed to be the late troublemaker, France. The Congress of
Vienna, without much disagreement, erected a barrier of strong states along the
French eastern frontier. The historic Dutch Republic, extinct since 1795, was revived as the kingdom of the Netherlands, with the house of Orange as a hereditary monarchy; to it was added Belgium, the old Austrian Netherlands with
which Austria had long been willing to part. It was hoped that the combined
Dutch-Belgian kingdom would be strong enough to discourage the perennial
French drive into the Low Countries. On the south, the Italian kingdom of Piedmont was restored and strengthened by the incorporation of the defunct republic
of Genoa, extinct since 1797. Behind the Netherlands and Piedmont, and further
to discourage a renewal of French pressure upon Germany and Italy, two great
powers were installed. Almost all the German Left Bank of the Rhine was ceded
to Prussia, which was to be, in Castlereagh's words, a kind of "bridge" spanning
central Europe, a bulwark against both France in the West and Russia in the
East. In Italy, again as a kind of secondary barrier against France, the Austrians
were firmly installed. They not only took back Tuscany and the Milanese, which
they had held before 1796, but also annexed the extinct republic of Venice. The
Austrian empire now included a Lombardo-Venetian kingdom in north Italy,
which lasted for almost half a century. In the rest of Italy the Congress recognized the restoration of the pope in the papal states and of former rulers in the
smaller duchies; but it did not insist on a restoration of the Bourbons in the kingdom of Naples. There Napoleon's brother-in-law Murat, with support from Metternich, managed for a time to retain his throne. The Bourbons and Braganzas restored themselves, respectively, in Spain and Portugal and were recognized by the
Congress.

As for Germany, the Congress made no attempt to put together again the

---

[19] See pp. 158–159.

Boundary of the German Confederation

0   100   200 miles

FINLAND
(Russia, 1808)

KINGDOM OF NORWAY
AND SWEDEN

St. Petersburg

Novgorod

Oslo   Stockholm

Reval

Borodino

Riga

Smolensk

SCOTLAND

Edinburgh

NORTH SEA

LITHUANIA

UNITED KINGDOM
OF GREAT BRITAIN AND IRELAND

Copenhagen
DENMARK

BALTIC SEA

Niemen R.

EAST
PRUSSIA

IRELAND   Dublin

ENGLAND

SCHLESWIG

HELIGOLAND
(Britain)

HOLSTEIN

Danzig

Vistula R.

Warsaw

Kiev

WALES

Elbe R.

Hamburg

HANOVER

KINGDOM OF THE
NETHERLANDS

Berlin

KINGDOM OF POLAND
(1815–1831)

UKRAINE

London

BELGIUM
(Ind. 1831)

Cologne

P R U S S I A

Oder R.

Breslau

Cracow

GALICIA

ENGLISH CHANNEL

LUX.

SAXON
STATES

SAXONY

Dniester R.

HESSE

Rhine R.

Prague

BESSARABIA
(Russia 1812)

Odessa

ATLANTIC OCEAN

Rouen

Seine R.

Paris

Metz

LORRAINE

Strasbourg

BADEN

ALSACE

WÜRT-
TEMBERG

BAVARIA

Munich

AUSTRIA

Vienna

Pressburg

AUSTRIAN EMPIRE

Budapest

MOLDAVIA
(Autonomous 1829)

Loire R.

Tours

F R A N C E

Berne
SWITZERLAND

TYROL

HUNGARY

TRANSYLVANIA

Lyons

Rhône R.

SAVOY

LOM-
BARDY

Milan   *Po R.*

VENETIA

CROATIA

WALLACHIA
(Autonomous 1829)

Danube R.

DOBRUJA

Bordeaux

Toulouse

PYRENEES

Marseilles

Nice

PIEDMONT

Genoa

LUCCA

PARMA

MODENA

BOSNIA

Belgrade

SERBIA
*(Autonomous
1829)*

BULGARIA

Sofia

Burgos

Ebro R.

Toulon

KINGDOM OF SARDINIA

TUSCANY

PAPAL
STATES

DALMATIA

MONTENEGRO

ADRIATIC SEA

Constantinople

PORTUGAL

Madrid

SPAIN

Tagus R.

Barcelona

ELBA

Rome

Salonica

O T T O M A N

Lisbon

Valencia

CORSICA
(France)

AEGEAN SEA

Smyrna

Seville

BALEARIC I.
(Spain)

SARDINIA

Naples

KINGDOM OF THE
TWO SICILIES

IONIAN I.
(Britain)

Athens

GREECE
(Independent 1829)

RHODES

Cadiz

Gibraltar *(Britain)*

Palermo

SICILY

MALTA
(Britain)

CRETE

Algiers

MOROCCO

ALGERIA   *(France, 1830)*

TUNIS
(Turkish)

MEDITERRANEAN SEA

TRIPOLI

TRIPOLI

EUROPE, 1815

Boundaries are those set by the Congress of Vienna in 1815. In general, a system of five "great powers" prevailed over the Napoleonic empire. France was reduced to the borders it had had before the Revolutionary-Napoleonic wars. Prussia was firmly installed on both banks of the Rhine, thus obtaining the part of Germany in which industrialization became important fifty years later. South Germany remained as reorganized under Napoleon. Poland was again partitioned. A larger share of Poland than in 1795 now went to Russia, which also acquired Finland and Bessarabia. The Austrians added Venetia to what they had held before 1796.

The union of the Dutch and Belgian Netherlands lasted only until 1831, when the kingdom of Belgium was established. Otherwise, the boundaries of 1815 lasted until the Italian war of 1859 which led to the unification of Italy.

Humpty Dumpty of the Holy Roman Empire. The pleas of the former princelings went unheeded. The French and Napoleonic reorganization of Germany was substantially confirmed. The kings of Bavaria, Württemberg, and Saxony kept the royal crowns that Napoleon had bestowed on them. The king of England, George III, was now recognized as king, not "elector," of Hanover. The German states, thirty-nine in number, including Prussia and Austria, were joined in a loose confederation in which the members remained virtually sovereign. The Congress ignored the yearnings of German nationalists for a great unified Father-land; Metternich especially feared nationalistic agitation; and in any case the nationalists themselves had no practical answer to concrete questions, such as the institutions of government and the frontiers that a united Germany should have. The Congress did declare, somewhat ineffectually, that in each of the German states there should be a representative legislative body.

The Polish-Saxon Question

The question of Poland, reopened by the fall of Napoleon's Grand Duchy of War-saw, brought the Congress almost to disaster. Alexander still insisted on undoing the crime of the partitions, which to his mind meant reconstituting the Polish kingdom with himself as constitutional king, in a merely personal union with the Russian empire. A similar arrangement was being initiated in the Grand Duchy of Finland, where Alexander reigned as a constitutional grand duke. To reunite Poland required that Austria and Prussia surrender their respective segments of the old Poland, most of which they had in any case lost to Napoleon. The Prussians were willing, with the proviso, which Alexander supported, that Prussia receive instead the whole of the kingdom of Saxony, which was considered available because the king of Saxony had been the last German ruler to abandon Napoleon. The issue presented itself as the Polish-Saxon question, with Russia and Prussia standing together to demand all Poland for Russia, and all Saxony for Prussia.

Such a prospect horrified Metternich. For Prussia to absorb Saxony would raise Prussia prodigiously in the eyes of all Germans, and it would greatly lengthen the common frontier between Prussia and the Austrian Empire. Furthermore, for Alexander to become king of all Poland, and incidentally the protector of an extended Prussia, would incalculably augment the influence of Russia in the affairs of Europe. Metternich found that Castlereagh shared these views. To Castlereagh it seemed that the main problem at Vienna was to restrain Russia. The British had not fought the French emperor only to have Europe fall to the Russian tsar. For months the Polish-Saxon question was debated, Metternich and Castlereagh exploring every device of argument to dissuade the Russo-Prussian combination from its expansionist designs. Finally they accepted the proffered assistance of Talleyrand, who shrewdly used the rift between the victors to bring France back into the diplomatic circle as a power in its own right. On January 3, 1815, Castle-reagh, Metternich, and Talleyrand signed a secret treaty, pledging themselves to go to war if necessary against Russia and Prussia. So, in the very midst of the peace conference, war again reared its head; and, in the very deliberations of the victors, one party among them allied itself with the vanquished.

No sooner had news of the secret treaty leaked out than Alexander offered to compromise. In his mixed nature he was, among other things, a man of peace, and he agreed to content himself with a reduced Polish kingdom. The Congress therefore created a new Poland (called "Congress Poland," which lasted for fifteen years); Alexander became its king, and he gave it a constitution; it comprised much the same area as Napoleon's Grand Duchy, representing in effect a transfer of this region from French to Russian control. It reached 250 miles farther west into Europe than had the Russian segment of the third partition of 1795. Some Poles still remained in Prussia and some in the Austrian Empire; Poland was not reunited. With the tsar thus content, Prussia too had to back down. It received about two-fifths of Saxony, the rest remaining to the Saxon king. The addition of both Saxon and Rhenish territories brought the Prussian monarchy into the most advanced parts of Germany. The net effect of the peace settlement, and of the Napoleonic wars, in this connection, was to shift the center of gravity of both Russia and Prussia farther west, Russia almost to the Oder, Prussia to the borders of France.[20]

With the solution of the Polish-Saxon question the main work of the Congress was completed. Other incidental matters were taken up. The Congress initiated international regulation of certain rivers. It issued a declaration against the Atlantic slave trade, which, however, remained ineffective, since the Continental powers were unwilling to grant the British navy free powers of search at sea, and the British were unwilling to put naval forces at the disposal of an international body. Committees of the Congress set to work to draft the Final Act. And at this point the whole settlement was brought into jeopardy.

The Hundred Days and Their Aftermath

Napoleon escaped from Elba, landed in France on March 1, 1815, and again proclaimed the empire. In the year since the return of the Bourbons discontent had been spreading in France. Louis XVIII proved to be a sensible man, but a swarm of unreasonable and vindictive émigrés had come back with him. Reaction and a "white terror" were raging through the country. Adherents of the Revolution rallied to the emperor on his dramatic reappearance. Napoleon reached Paris, took over the government and army, and headed for Belgium. He would, if he could, disperse the pompous assemblage at Vienna. To the victors of the year before, and to most of Europe, it seemed that the Revolution was again stirring, that the old horror of toppling thrones and recurring warfare might not after all be ended. The opposing forces met in Belgium at Waterloo, where the Duke of Wellington, commanding an allied force, won a great victory. Napoleon again abdicated, and was again exiled, this time to distant St. Helena in the south Atlantic. A new peace treaty was made with France, the "second" Treaty of Paris. It was more severe than the first, since the French seemed to have shown themselves incorrigible and unrepentant. The new treaty imposed minor changes of the frontiers, an indemnity of 700,000,000 francs, and an army of occupation.

The effect of the Hundred Days, as the episode following Napoleon's return from Elba is called, was to renew the dread of revolution, war, and aggression. Britain, Russia, Austria, and Prussia, after being almost at war with each other in January, again joined forces to get rid of the apparition from Elba, and in November 1815 they solemnly reconfirmed the Quadruple Alliance of Chaumont, adding a provision that no Bonaparte should ever govern France. They agreed

[20] See maps on pp. 222–223, 234–235, 328.

also to hold future congresses to review the political situation and enforce the peace. No change was made in the arrangements agreed to at Vienna, except that Murat, who fought for Napoleon during the Hundred Days, was captured and shot, and an extremely unenlightened Bourbon monarchy was restored in Naples. In addition to the Quadruple Alliance of the Great Powers, bound specifically to enforce or amend the terms of the peace treaty by international action, Alexander devised a vaguer scheme which he called the Holy Alliance. Long attracted to the idea of an international order, appalled by the return of Napoleon, and influenced at the moment by the pietistic Baroness von Krüdener, the tsar proposed, for all monarchs to sign, a statement by which they promised to uphold Christian principles of charity and peace. All signed except the pope, the sultan, and the prince regent of Great Britain. The Holy Alliance, probably sincerely meant by Alexander as a condemnation of violence, and at first not taken seriously by the others who signed it, and who thought it absurd to mix Christianity with politics, soon came to signify, in the minds of liberals, a kind of unholy alliance of monarchies against liberty and progress.

The Peace of Vienna, including generally the Treaty of Vienna itself, the treaties of Paris, and the British and colonial settlement, was the most far-reaching diplomatic agreement between the Peace of Westphalia of 1648 and the Peace of Paris which closed the First World War in 1919. It had its strong points and its weak ones. It produced a minimum of resentment in France; the late enemy accepted the new arrangements. It ended almost two centuries of colonial rivalry; for sixty or seventy years no colonial empire seriously challenged the British. Two other causes of friction in the eighteenth century—the control of Poland and the Austro-Prussian dualism in Germany—were smoothed over for fifty years. With past issues the peace of 1815 dealt rather effectively; with future issues, not unnaturally, it was less successful. The Vienna treaty was not illiberal in its day; it was by no means entirely reactionary, for the Congress showed little desire to restore the state of affairs in existence before the wars. The reaction that gathered strength after 1815 was not written into the treaty itself.

But the treaty gave no satisfaction to nationalists and democrats. It was a disappointment even to many liberals, especially in Germany. The transfer of peoples from government to government, without consultation of their wishes, opened the way under nineteenth-century conditions to a good deal of subsequent trouble. The peacemakers were in fact hostile both to nationalism and to democracy, the potent forces of the coming age; they regarded them, with reason, as leading to revolution and war. The problem to which they addressed themselves was to restore the balance of power, the "liberties of Europe," and to make a lasting peace. In this they were successful. They restored the European state system, or system in which a number of sovereign and independent states existed without fear of conquest or domination. And the peace which they made, though some details broke down in 1830, and others in 1848, on the whole subsisted for half a century; and not for a full century, not until 1914, was there a war in Europe that lasted longer than a few months or in which all the great powers were involved. No international disturbance comparable in magnitude to that created by the French Revolution and Napoleonic empire has yet been followed by such a protracted period of peace.

XI.
Reaction versus Progress, 1815-1848

I n the period of some thirty years preceding 1815 two "revolutions" had been taking place. One was the upheaval associated with the French Revolution and the Napoleonic empire. At bottom, it was mainly political, having to do with the organization of government, public power and authority, public finance, taxation, administration, law, individual rights, and the legal position of social classes. The other "revolution," a revolution in a more metaphorical sense, was primarily economic, having to do with the production of wealth, the techniques of manufacture, the exploitation of natural resources, the formation of capital, and the distribution of products to consumers. The political and the economic revolutions, in these years, to a surprising degree, went on independently of each other. Until 1815 the political revolution affected mainly the Continent, while the economic revolution was most active in England. The Continent, while renewing itself politically, remained economically less advanced than England. England, transformed economically, remained conservative in other respects. Hence it has been possible, in the preceding chapters, to deal with the French Revolution and its Napoleonic sequel without attending to the Industrial Revolution, as the economic changes then occurring in England are always called.

It may be (the matter is arguable) that the Industrial Revolution was more important than the French Revolution or any other. In a telescopic view of world

Chapter Emblem: A medal commemorating the Congress of Vienna, showing the victorious rulers of Austria, Russia, and Prussia.

history the two biggest changes experienced by the human race in the past ten thousand years may have been the agricultural or Neolithic revolution which ushered in the first civilizations, and the Industrial Revolution which has ushered in the civilization of the nineteenth and twentieth centuries. However that may be, it proves on closer examination that the economic and the political, the Industrial Revolution (or industrialization) and the other institutions of a society, cannot long be kept apart in an attempt at understanding. The Industrial Revolution occurred first in England, becoming evident about 1780, because of certain political characteristics of English society, because access to world markets had been gained by earlier commercial and naval successes, and because English life offered rewards to the individual for a spirit of risk taking and innovation. Nor can the effects of political and economic revolution, in England or elsewhere, be kept apart for the years after 1815.

With the defeat of Napoleon and signing of the peace treaty at Vienna in 1815, it seemed that the French Revolution was at last over. European conservatism had triumphed; since it frankly opposed the new "French ideas," it can appropriately be called "reaction." But the processes of industrialization, as they accelerated in England and spread to the Continent, worked against the politically conservative settlement. They greatly enlarged both the business and wage-earning classes, and so made it harder for monarchs and landed aristocrats to maintain their control over public power. Industrial development in the nineteenth century was often called "progress," and progress proved stronger than reaction.

Industrial society arose in England, Western Europe, and the United States, in the nineteenth century, within the system known as capitalism. In the twentieth century, since the Russian Revolution, industrial societies have been created in which capitalism is vehemently rejected. Industrialism and capitalism are therefore by no means the same. Yet all industrial societies use capital, which is defined as wealth that is not consumed but is used to produce more wealth, or future wealth. An automobile is a consumer's good; the automobile factory is the capital. What distinguishes a capitalist from a non-capitalist society is not the existence of capital, but the kinds of people who control it. The distinctions sometimes become blurred. But in one form of society the control of capital is through "private ownership" or institutions of private property, by which capital is owned by individuals or family trusts, or nowadays by foundations, pension funds, or corporations that are in turn owned by shareholders; in any case not by the state. In such societies, though ownership may be widespread, most capital is owned or at least controlled by relatively few people. In the other form of society productive capital in principle belongs to the public, and is in effect "owned" and controlled by the state or its agencies; such societies usually call themselves socialist, because the first socialists rejected the principle of private ownership of the means of production, that is, of capital. In these societies the control of capital, or decisions on saving, investment, and production, are also in the hands of relatively few.

In Europe the institutions of secure private property had been developed since the Middle Ages, and much that happened in the French Revolution was designed to protect property from the demands of the state. Possession of property was held to be the basis of personal independence and political liberty, and the expectation of keeping future profits inspired, in some, a willingness to commit their capital to new and uncertain ventures. There had been a commercial capitalism in

Europe at least since the sixteenth century.[1] Industrialization in Europe was therefore capitalistic. Countries outside the West-European orbit, and industrializing later, faced a different problem. A country in which little capital had accumulated from the trade and agriculture of previous generations, and which had few capital-owners or enterprising individuals, could hardly industrialize by European methods. If it lacked the European background, in which various political, social, legal, and intellectual features were as important as the economic, it would have to achieve industrialization by other methods. This has usually meant that innovation, planning, decision making, control, and even domination would rest with the state.

So in the short run, within a few years, the Industrial Revolution in Western Europe favored the liberal and modernizing principles proclaimed in the French Revolution. In the middle run, or in half a century, it made Europe overwhelmingly more powerful than other parts of the world, leading to a world-wide European ascendancy in the form of imperialism. In the still longer run, by the twentieth century, it provoked a retaliation, in which other countries tried hastily to industrialize in self-protection, or to improve the condition of their peoples, desperately hoping to catch up with the West while loudly denouncing it as imperialistic and capitalistic. Of these newer industrial societies the Soviet Union and the People's Republic of China would be the most prominent.

52. THE INDUSTRIAL REVOLUTION IN BRITAIN

On the whole, from the beginning of history until about 1800, the work of the world was done with hand tools. Since then it has been increasingly done by machines. Before about 1800 power was supplied by human or animal muscle, reinforced by levers or pulleys, and supplemented by the force of running water or moving air. Since then power has been supplied by the human manipulation of more recondite forms of energy found in steam, electricity, the combustion of gases, and most recently within the atom. The process of shifting from hand tools to power machinery is what is meant by the Industrial Revolution. Its beginning cannot be dated exactly. It grew gradually out of the technical practices of earlier times. It is still going on, for in some countries industrialization is barely beginning, and even in the most highly developed it is still making advances. But the first country to be profoundly affected by industrialization was Great Britain, where its effects became manifest in the half-century following 1780.

It seems likely, despite the emphasis placed on revolutionary upheavals by historians, that people are habitually quite conservative. Workingmen do not put off their old way of life, move to strange and overcrowded towns, or enter the deadly rounds of mine and factory except under strong incentive. Well-to-do people, living in comfort on assured incomes, do not risk their wealth in new and untried ventures except for good reason. The shifting to modern machine production requires in any country a certain mobility of people and of wealth. Such mobility may be produced by state planning, as in the industrialization of the Soviet Union in recent times. In England a high degree of social mobility existed in the eighteenth century in consequence of a long historical development.

[1] See pp. 112–118.

The Agricultural Revolution in Britain

The English Revolution of 1688, confirming the ascendancy of Parliament over the king, meant in economic terms the ascendancy of the more well-to-do property-owning classes.[2] Among these the landowners were by far the most important, though they counted the great London merchants among their allies. For a century and a half, from 1688 to 1832, the British government was substantially in the hands of these landowners—the "squirearchy" or "gentlemen of England." The result was a thorough transformation of farming, an Agricultural Revolution without which the Industrial Revolution could not have occurred.

Many landowners, seeking to increase their money incomes, began experimenting with improved methods of cultivation and stock raising. They made more use of fertilizers (mainly animal manure); they introduced new implements (such as the "drill seeder" and "horse-hoe"); they brought in new crops, such as turnips, and a more scientific system of crop rotation; they attempted to breed larger sheep and fatter cattle. An improving landlord, to introduce such changes successfully, needed full control over his land. He saw a mere barrier to progress in the old village system of open fields, common lands, and semicollective methods of cultivation. Improvement also required an investment of capital, which was impossible so long as the soil was tilled by numerous poor and custom-bound small farmers.

The old common rights of the villagers were part of the common law. Only an act of Parliament could modify or extinguish them. It was the great landowners who controlled Parliament, which therefore passed hundreds of "enclosure acts," authorizing the enclosure, by fences, walls, or hedges, of the old common lands and unfenced open fields. Land thus came under a strict regime of private ownership and individual management. At the same time small owners sold out or were excluded in various ways, the more easily since the larger owners had so much local authority as justices of the peace. Ownership of land in England, more than anywhere else in central or western Europe, became concentrated in the hands of a relatively small class of wealthy landlords, who let it out in large blocks to a relatively small class of substantial farmers. This development, though in progress throughout the eighteenth century, reached its height during the Napoleonic wars.

One result was greatly to raise the productivity of land and of farm labor. Fatter cattle yielded more meat, more assiduous cultivation yielded more cereals. The food supply of England was increased, while a smaller percentage of the population was needed to produce it. Labor was thus released for other pursuits. The greater number of the English country people became wage earners, working as hired men for the farmers and landlords, or spinning or weaving in their cottages for merchants in the towns. The English workingman (and woman) was dependent on daily wages long before the coming of the factory and the machine. English working people became mobile; they would go where the jobs were, or where the wages were slightly higher. They also became available, in that fewer of them were needed on the land to produce food. Such conditions hardly obtained except in Great Britain. On the Continent agricultural methods were less productive, and the rural workers were more established on the soil, whether by institutions

[2] See pp. 176–177.

of serfdom as in eastern Europe or by the possession of property or firm leaseholds as in France.[3]

Industrialism in Britain: Incentives and Inventions

Meanwhile, as the Agricultural Revolution ran its course in the eighteenth century and into the nineteenth, the British had conquered a colonial empire, staked out markets all over the Americas and Europe, built up a huge mercantile marine, and won command of the sea. The British merchant could sell more, if only more could be produced. He had the customers, he had the ships, and moreover he could obtain the capital with which to finance new ideas. The profit motive prompted the search for more rapid methods of production. The old English staple export, woolen cloth, could be marketed indefinitely if only more of it could be woven. The possibilities in cotton cloth were enormous. The taste of Europeans for cottons had been already formed by imports from Asia. By hand methods Europeans could not produce cotton in competition with the East. But the market was endless if cotton could be spun, woven, and printed with less labor, i.e., by machines. Capital was available, mobile, and fluid because of the rise of banking, credit, and stock companies. Funds could be shifted from one enterprise to another. Wealthy landowners and merchants could divert some of their profits to industry. If an invention proved a total loss, as sometimes happened, or if it required years of development before producing any income, still the investment could be afforded. Only a country already wealthy from commerce and agriculture could have been the first to initiate the machine age. England was such a country.

These conditions induced a series of successful inventions in the textile industry. In 1733 a man named John Kay invented the fly shuttle, by which only one person instead of two was needed to operate a loom. The resulting increase in the output of weaving set up a strong demand for yarn. This was met in the 1760s by the invention of the spinning jenny, a kind of mechanized spinning wheel. The new shuttles and jennies were first operated by hand and used by domestic workers in their homes. But in 1769 Richard Arkwright patented the water frame, a device for the multiple spinning of many threads. At first it was operated by water power, but in the 1780s Arkwright introduced the steam engine to drive his spinning machinery. Thus requiring a considerable installation of heavy equipment, he gathered his engines, frames, and workers into large and usually dismal buildings, called "mills" by the English, or "factories" in subsequent American usage. Mechanical spinning now for a time overwhelmed the hand weavers with yarn. This led to the development of the power loom, which became economically practicable shortly after 1800. Weaving as well as spinning was therefore done increasingly in factories. These improvements in the finishing process put a heavy strain on the production of raw cotton. An ingenious Connecticut Yankee, Eli Whitney, while acting as a tutor on a plantation in Georgia, in ten days produced a cotton gin, which by speeding up the removal of seeds greatly increased the output of cotton. The gin soon spread through the American South, where the almost decaying plantation economy was abruptly revived, becoming an adjunct to the Industrial Revolution in England. British imports of raw cotton multiplied

---

[3] See pp. 122–123.

fivefold in the thirty years following 1790. In value of manufactures, cotton rose from ninth to first place among British industries in the same years. By 1820 it made up almost half of all British exports.

The steam engine, applied to the cotton mills in the 1780s, had for a century been going through a development of its own.[4] Scientific and technical experiments with steam pressures had been fairly common in the seventeenth century, but what gave the economic impetus to invention was the gradual dwindling away of Europe's primeval stocks of timber. The wood shortage became acute in England about 1700, so that it was more difficult to obtain the charcoal needed in smelting iron, and smelters turned increasingly to coal. Deeper coal shafts could not be sunk until someone devised better methods of pumping out water. About 1702 Thomas Newcomen built the first economically significant steam engine, which was soon widely used to drive pumps in the coal mines. It consumed so much fuel in proportion to power delivered that it could generally be used only in the coal fields themselves. In 1763 James Watt, a technician at the University of Glasgow, began to make improvements on Newcomen's engine. He formed a business partnership with Matthew Boulton. Boulton, originally a manufacturer of toys, buttons, and shoe buckles, provided the funds to finance Watt's rather costly experiments, handmade equipment, and slowly germinating ideas. By the 1780s the firm of Boulton and Watt was eminently successful, manufacturing steam engines both for British use and for the export trade.

At first, until further refinements and greater precision could be obtained in the working of iron, the engines were so cumbersome that they could be used as stationary engines only, as in the new spinning mills of Arkwright and others. Soon after 1800 the steam engine was successfully used to propel river boats, notably on the Hudson in 1807, by Robert Fulton, who employed an imported Boulton and Watt engine. Experiments with steam power for land transportation began at the same time. As it was in the coal fields of England a century before that Newcomen's engine had been put to practical uses, so now it was in the coal fields that Watt's engine first became a "locomotive." Well before 1800 the mines had taken to using "rail ways," on which wagons with flanged wheels, drawn by horses, carried coal to canals or to the sea. In the 1820s steam engines were successfully placed on moving vehicles. The first fully satisfactory locomotive was George Stephenson's *Rocket*, which in 1829, on the newly built Liverpool and Manchester Railway, not only reached an impressive speed of sixteen miles per hour but met other more important tests as well. By the 1840s the era of railroad construction was under way in both Europe and the United States.

The Industrial Revolution in Great Britain in its early phase, down to 1830 or 1840, took place principally in the manufacture of textiles, with accompanying developments in the exploitation of iron and coal. The early factories were principally textile factories, and indeed mainly cotton mills; for cotton was an entirely new industry to Europe and hence easily mechanized, whereas the long established woolen trade, in which both employers and workers hesitated to abandon their customary ways, was mechanized more slowly. The suddenness of the change must not be exaggerated. It is often said that the Industrial Revolution was not a revolution at all. As late as the 1830s only a small fraction of the British working people were employed in factories. But the factory and the factory system

---

[4] See p. 287.

were even then regarded as the coming mode of production, destined to grow and expand, mighty symbols of the irresistible march of progress.

Some Social Consequences of Industrialism in Britain

The Britain that emerged fundamentally unscathed and in fact strengthened from the wars with Napoleon was no longer the "merrie England" of days of yore. The island was becoming crowded with people, as was the lesser island of Ireland. The combined population of Great Britain and Ireland tripled in the century from 1750 to 1850, rising from about 10 million in 1750 to about 30 million in 1850. The growth was distributed very unevenly. Formerly, in England, most people had lived in the south. But the coal and iron, and hence the steam power, lay in the Midlands and the north. Here whole new cities rose seemingly out of nothing. In 1785 it was estimated that in England and Scotland, outside of London, there were only three cities with more than 50,000 people. Seventy years later, the span of one lifetime, there were thirty-one British cities of this size.

Preeminent among them was Manchester in Lancashire, the first and most famous of industrial cities of modern type. Manchester, before the coming of the cotton mills, was a rather large market town. Though very ancient, it had not been significant enough to be recognized as a borough for representation in Parliament. Locally it was organized as a manor. Not until 1845 did the inhabitants extinguish the manorial rights, buying them out at that time from the last lord, Sir Oswald Mosley, for £200,000 or about 1,000,000 dollars. In population Manchester grew from 25,000 in 1772 to 455,000 in 1851. But until 1835 there was no regular procedure in England for the incorporation of cities. Urban organization was more backward than in Prussia or France. Unless inherited from the Middle Ages, a city had no legal existence. It lacked proper officials and adequate tax-raising and lawmaking powers. It was therefore difficult for Manchester, and the other new factory towns, to deal with problems of rapid urbanization, such as provision of police protection, water and sewers, or the disposal of garbage.

The new urban agglomerations were drab places, blackened with the heavy soot of the early coal age, settling alike on the mills and the workers' quarters, which were dark at best, for the climate of the Midlands is not sunny. Housing for workers was hastily built, closely packed, and always in short supply, as in all rapidly growing communities. Whole families lived in single rooms, and family life tended to disintegrate. A police officer in Glasgow observed that there were whole blocks of tenements in the city, each swarming with a thousand ragged children who had first names only, usually nicknames—like animals, as he put it.

The distressing feature of the new factories was that for the most part they required unskilled labor only. Skilled workers found themselves degraded in status. Hand weavers and spinners, thrown out of work by the new machines, either languished in a misery that was the deepest of that of any class in the Industrial Revolution or else went off to a factory to find a job. The factories paid good wages by the standards for unskilled labor at the time. But these standards were very low, too low to allow a man to support his wife and children. This had generally been true for unskilled labor, in England and elsewhere, under earlier economic systems also. In the new factories the work was so mechanical that children as young as six years old were often preferred. Women, too, worked for less and were often more adept at handling a bobbin.

BRITAIN BEFORE AND AFTER THE INDUSTRIAL REVOLUTION

In 1700 England, Scotland, and Wales had only one city with a population of more than 100,000. In 1911 they had nearly thirty. The area within the small rectangle in the right-hand panel, roughly the Midlands, is almost exactly the area of Massachusetts.

Hours in the factories were long, fourteen a day or occasionally more; and though such hours were familiar to persons who had worked on farms, or at domestic industry in rural households, they were more tedious and oppressive in the more regimented conditions that were necessary in the mills. Holidays were few, except for the unwelcome leisure of unemployment, which was a common scourge, because the short-run ups and downs of business were very erratic during this period of bewildering expansion. A day without work was a day producing nothing to live on, so that even where the daily wage was relatively attractive the worker's real income was chronically insufficient. Workers in the factories, as in the mines, were almost entirely unorganized. They were a mass of recently assembled humanity without traditions or common ties. Each bargained individually with his employer, who, usually a small businessman himself, facing a ferocious competition with others, often in debt for the equipment in his factory, or determined to save money in order to purchase more, held his "wages bill" to the lowest possible figure that he could manage.

The factory owners, the new "cotton lords," were the first industrial capitalists. They were often self-made men, who owed their position to their own intelligence, persistence, and foresight. They lived in comfort without ostentation or luxury, saving from each year's income to build up their factories and their machines. Hard-working themselves, they thought that landed gentlemen were usually idlers and that the poor tended to be lazy. They were usually honest, in a hard and exacting way; they would make money by any means the law allowed, but not beyond it. They were neither brutal nor knowingly hard-hearted. They gave to charitable and philanthropic causes. They believed that they did "the poor" a favor by furnishing them with work and by seeing to it that they worked diligently and productively. Most of them disapproved of public regulation of their business, though a few, driven by competition to expedients that they did not like, such as the employment of small children, would have accepted some regulation that fell on all competitors equally. It was a cotton magnate, the elder Robert Peel, who in 1802 pushed the first Factory Act through Parliament. This act purported to regulate the conditions in which pauper children were employed in the textile mills, but it was a dead letter from the beginning, since it provided no adequate body of factory inspectors. The English at this time, alone among the leading European peoples, had no class of trained, paid, and professional government administrators; nor did they yet want such a class, preferring self-government and local initiative. To have inspectors for one's affairs smacked of Continental bureaucracy. The fact that the older methods of economic regulation were obsolescent, actually unsuited to the new age, had the effect of discrediting the idea of regulation itself. The new industrialists wanted to be let alone. They considered it unnatural to interfere with business and believed that, if allowed to follow their own judgment, they would assure the future prosperity and progress of the country.

Classical Economics: "Laissez Faire"

The industrialists were strengthened in these beliefs by the emerging science of "political economy." In 1776 Adam Smith published his epochal *Wealth of Nations*, which criticized the older mercantilism, with its regulatory and monopolistic practices, and urged, though with moderation, that certain "natural laws" of production and exchange be allowed to work themselves out.[5] Smith was followed by Thomas R. Malthus, David Ricardo, and the so-called Manchester School. Their doctrine was dubbed (by its opponents) laissez faire and in its elaborated form is still called the classical economics. It held, basically, that there is a world of economic relationships autonomous and separable from government or politics. It is the world of the free market, and is regulated within itself by certain "natural laws," such as the law of supply and demand or the law of diminishing returns. All persons should follow their own enlightened self-interest; each knows his own interest better than anyone else; and the sum total of individual interests will add up to the general welfare and liberty of all. Government should do as little as possible; it should confine itself to preserving security of life and property, providing reasonable laws and reliable courts, and so assuring the discharge of private contracts, debts, and obligations. Not only business, but education, charity, and personal matters generally should be left to private initiative. There should be no tariffs; free trade should reign everywhere, for the economic system is world-wide, unaffected by political barriers or national differences. As for the workingman, according to classical economists before about 1850, he should not expect to make more than a bare minimum living; an "iron law of wages" brings it about that as soon as the worker receives more than a subsistence wage he breeds more children, who eat up the excess, so that he reduces himself, and the

5 See pp. 312–313.

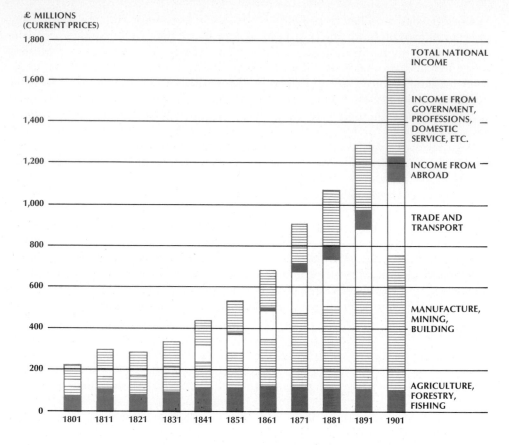

£ MILLIONS
(CURRENT PRICES)

Source: P. Deane and W. A. Cole, *British Economic Growth*
(Cambridge, Eng.: Cambridge University Press, 1962), pp. 166–167.

THE INDUSTRIAL REVOLUTION IN BRITAIN (AS SHOWN BY SOURCES OF INCOME)

Despite uncertainties in such figures several things are apparent. British national income grew about eightfold in the nineteenth century. Incomes derived from agriculture, forestry, and so forth, remained about the same, but sank from one-third to one-sixteenth of all incomes. By 1851 half the national income came from manufacturing, trade, and transportation, and by 1901 three-quarters came from these sources. The category "income from abroad" refers to interest and dividends on loans and investments outside Great Britain, that is, from the export of capital, and this source of income, insignificant in the early years of the century, grew rapidly after the 1850s.

working class generally, again to a subsistence level. The workingman, if discontented, should see the folly of changing the system, for this *is* the system, the natural system—there is no other. Political economy as taught in grim Manchester was not without reason called the "dismal science."

For working people in England the Industrial Revolution was a hard experience. It should be remembered, however, that neither low wages, nor the fourteen-hour day, nor the labor of women and children, nor the ravages of unemployment were anything new. All had existed for centuries, in England and western Europe, as agricultural and commercial capitalism replaced the more self-sufficient economies of the Middle Ages. The factory towns were in some ways better places to live than the rural slums from which many of their people came. Factory routine was psychologically deadening, but the textile mills were in some ways not worse than the domestic sweatshops in which manufacturing processes had previously been carried on. The concentration of working people in city and factory opened the way to improvement in their condition. It made their misery apparent; philanthropic sentiment was gradually aroused among the more fortunate. Gathered in cities, workers obtained more knowledge of the world. Mingling and talking together they developed a sense of solidarity, class interest, and common political aims; and in time they became organized, establishing labor unions by which to obtain a larger share of the national income.

Britain after the fall of Napoleon became the workshop of the world. Though factories using steam power sprang up in France, Belgium, New England, and elsewhere, it was really not until after 1870 that Great Britain faced any industrial competition from abroad. The British had a virtual monopoly in textiles and machine tools. The English Midlands and Scottish Lowlands shipped cotton thread and steam engines to all the world. British capital was exported to all countries, there to call new enterprises into being. London became the world's clearinghouse and financial center. Progressive people in other lands looked to Britain as their model, hoping to learn from its advanced industrial methods, and to imitate its parliamentary political system. Thus more foundations of the nineteenth century were laid.

53. THE ADVENT OF THE "ISMS"

The combined forces of industrialization and of the French Revolution led after 1815 to the proliferation of doctrines and movements of many sorts. These broke out in a general European revolution in 1848. As for the thirty-three years from 1815 to 1848, there is no better way of grasping their long-run meaning than to reflect on the number of still living "isms" that arose at that time.

So far as is known the word "liberalism" first appeared in the English language in 1819, "radicalism" in 1820, "socialism" in 1832, "conservatism" in 1835. The 1830s first saw "individualism," "constitutionalism," "humanitarianism," and "monarchism." "Nationalism" and "communism" date from the 1840s. Not until the 1850s did the English-speaking world use the word "capitalism" (French *capitalisme* is much older); and not until even later had it heard of "Marxism," though the doctrines of Marx grew out of and reflected the troubled times of the 1840s.

The rapid coinage of new "isms" does not in every case mean that the ideas they conveyed were new. Many of them had their origin in the Enlightenment, if not before. Men had loved liberty before talking of liberalism and been conservative without knowing conservatism as such. The appearance of so many "isms" shows rather that people were making their ideas more systematic. To the "philosophy" of the Enlightenment were now added an intense activism and a partisanship generated during the French Revolution. People were being obliged to reconsider and analyze society as a whole. The social sciences were taking form. An "ism" (excluding such words as "hypnotism" or "favoritism") may be defined as the conscious espousal of a doctrine in competition with other doctrines. Without the "isms" created in the thirty-odd years after the peace of Vienna it is impossible to understand or even talk about the history of the world since that event, so that a brief characterization of some of the most important is in order.[6]

Romanticism

One of the "isms" was not political. It was called "romanticism," a word first used in English in the 1840s to describe a movement then half a century old. Romanticism was primarily a theory of literature and the arts. Its great exponents included Wordsworth, Shelley, and Byron in England, Victor Hugo and Chateaubriand in France, Schiller and the Schlegels and many others in Germany. As a theory of art it raised basic questions on the nature of significant truth, on the importance of various human faculties, on the relation of thought and feeling, on the meaning of the past and of time itself. Representing a new way of sensing all human experience, it affected most thinking on social and public questions.

Possibly the most fundamental romantic attitude was a love of the unclassifiable —of moods or impressions, scenes or stories, sights or sounds or things concretely experienced, personal idiosyncrasies or peculiar customs which the intellect could never classify, box up, explain away, or reduce to an abstract generalization. The romantics, characteristically, insisted on the value of feeling as well as of reason. They were aware of the importance of the subconscious. They were likely to suspect a perfectly lucid idea as somehow superficial. They loved the mysterious, the unknown, the half-seen figures on the far horizon. Hence romanticism contributed to a new interest in strange and distant societies and in strange and distant historical epochs. Where the philosophes of the Enlightenment had deplored the Middle Ages as a time of intellectual error, the romantic generation looked back upon them with respect and even nostalgia, finding in them a fascination, a colorfulness, or a spiritual depth which they missed in their own time. The "Gothic," which rationalists thought barbarous, had a strong appeal for romantics. A Gothic Revival set in in the arts, of which one example was the British Parliament buildings, built in the 1830s.

In medieval art and institutions, as in the art and institutions of every age and people, the romantics saw the expression of an inner genius. The idea of original or creative genius was in fact another of the most fundamental romantic beliefs. A genius was a dynamic spirit that no rules could hem in, one that no analysis or classification could ever fully explain. Genius, it was thought, made its own rules and laws. The genius might be that of the individual person, such as the artist, writer, or Napoleon-like mover of the world. It might be the genius or spirit of an age. Or it might be the genius of a people or nation, the *Volksgeist* of Herder, an inherent national character making each people grow in its own distinctive way, which could be known only by a study of its history, and not by ratiocination.[7] Here again romanticism gave a new impetus to study of the past. Politically romantics could be found in all camps, conservative and radical. Let us turn to the more purely political "isms."

---

[6] For some other "isms" important after 1850, see pp. 489–495.
[7] See p. 410.

Classical Liberalism

The first Liberals, calling themselves by that name (though Napoleon used that word for his own system, as has been seen[8]), arose in Spain among certain opponents of the Napoleonic occupation. The word then passed to France, where it denoted opposition to royalism after the restoration of the Bourbons in 1814. In England many Whigs became increasingly liberal, as did even a few Tories, until the great Liberal party was founded in the 1850s. Nineteenth-century, or "classical," liberalism varied from country to country, but it showed many basic similarities.

Liberals were generally men of the business and professional classes, together with enterprising landowners wishing to improve their estates. They believed in what was modern, enlightened, efficient, reasonable, and fair. They had confidence in man's powers of self-government and self-control. They set a high value on parliamentary or representative government, working through reasonable discussion and legislation, with responsible ministries and an impartial and law-abiding administration. They demanded full publicity for all actions of government, and to assure such publicity they insisted on freedom of the press and free rights of assembly. All these political advantages they thought most likely to be realized under a good constitutional monarchy. Outside of England they favored explicit written constitutions. They were not democrats; they opposed giving every man the vote, fearing the excesses of mob rule or of irrational political action. Only as the nineteenth century progressed did liberals gradually and reluctantly come to accept the idea of universal male suffrage. They subscribed to the doctrines of the rights of man as set forth in the American and French revolutions, but with a clear emphasis on the right of property, and in their economic views they followed the British Manchester School or the French economist J. B. Say. They favored laissez faire, were suspicious of the ability of government to regulate business, wanted to get rid of the guild system where it still existed, and disapproved of attempts on the part of the new industrial laborers to organize unions.

Internationally they advocated freedom of trade, to be accomplished by the lowering or abolition of tariffs, so that all countries might exchange their products easily with each other and with industrial England. In this way, they thought, each country would produce what it was most fitted for, and so best increase its wealth and standards of living. From the growth of wealth, production, invention, and scientific progress they believed that the general progress of humanity would ensue. They generally frowned upon the established churches and landed aristocracies as obstacles to advancement. They believed in the spread of tolerance and education. They were also profoundly civilian in attitude, disliking wars, conquerors, army officers, standing armies, and military expenditures. They wanted orderly change by processes of legislation. They shrank before the idea of revolution. Liberals on the Continent were usually admirers of Great Britain.

Radicalism, Republicanism, Socialism

Radicalism, at least as a word, originated in England, where about 1820 the Philosophical Radicals proudly applied the term to themselves. These Radicals in the 1820s included not only the few working-class leaders who were beginning to emerge but also many of the new industrial capitalists, who were still unrepre-

[8] See pp. 400–402.

sented in Parliament. They took up where such English "Jacobins" as Thomas Paine had left off a generation earlier, before the long crisis of the French wars had discredited all radicalism as pro-French.[9]

The Philosophical Radicals were a good deal like the French philosophes before the Revolution. They were followers of an elderly sage, Jeremy Bentham, who in prolific writings from 1776 to 1832 undertook to reform the English criminal and civil law, church, Parliament, and constitution. The English Radicals professed to deduce the right form of institutions from the very nature and psychology of man himself. They impatiently waved aside all arguments based on history, usage, or custom. They went to the "roots" of things. ("Radical" is from the Latin word for "root.") They wanted a total reconstruction of laws, courts, prisons, poor relief, municipal organization, rotten boroughs, and fox-hunting clergy. Their demand for the reform of Parliament was vehement and insistent. They detested the Church of England, the peerage, and the squirearchy. Many radicals would just as soon abolish royalty also; not until the long reign of Queen Victoria (1837–1901) did the British monarchy become undeniably popular in all quarters. Above all, radicalism was democratic; it demanded a vote for every adult Englishman. After the Reform Bill of 1832 the industrial capitalists generally turned into liberals, but the working-class leaders remained radical democrats, as will be seen.

On the Continent radicalism was represented by militant republicanism. The years of the First French Republic, which to liberals and conservatives signified horrors associated with the Reign of Terror, were for the republicans years of hope and progress, cut short by forces of reaction. Republicans were a minority even in France; elsewhere, as in Italy and Germany, they were fewer still, though they existed. Mostly the republicans were drawn from intelligentsia such as students and writers, from working-class leaders protesting at social injustice, and from elderly veterans, or the sons and nephews of veterans, to whom the Republic of '93, with its wars and its glory, was a living thing. Because of police repression, republicans often joined together in secret societies. They looked with equanimity on the prospect of further revolutionary upheaval, by which they felt that the cause of liberty, equality, and fraternity would be advanced. Strong believers in political equality, they were democrats demanding universal suffrage. They favored parliamentary government but were much less primarily concerned with its successful operation than were the liberals. Most republicans were bitterly anticlerical. Remembering the internecine struggle between the church and the republic during the French Revolution, and still facing the political activity of the Catholic clergy (for republicanism was most common in Catholic countries), they regarded the Catholic church as the implacable enemy of reason and liberty. Opposed to monarchy of any kind, even to constitutional monarchy, intensely hostile to church and aristocracy, conscious heirs of the great French Revolution, organized in national and international secret societies, not averse to overthrowing existing regimes by force, the more militant republicans were considered by most people, including the liberals, to be little better than anarchists.

Republicanism shaded off into socialism. Socialists generally shared the political attitudes of republicanism but added other views besides. The early socialists, those before the Revolution of 1848, were of many kinds, but all had certain ideas in common. All of them regarded the existing economic system as aimless, chaotic,

[9] See pp. 367, 382.

and outrageously unjust. All thought it improper for owners of wealth to have so much economic power—to give or deny work to the worker, to set wages and hours in their own interests, to guide all the labors of society in the interests of private profit. All therefore questioned the value of private enterprise, favoring some degree of communal ownership of productive assets—banks, factories, machines, land, and transportation. All disliked competition as a governing principle and set forth principles of harmony, coordination, organization, or association instead. All flatly and absolutely rejected the laissez faire of the liberals and the political economists. Where the latter thought mainly of increasing production, without much concern over distribution, the early socialists thought mainly of a fairer or more equal distribution of income among all useful members of society. They believed that beyond the civil and legal equality brought in by the French Revolution a further step toward social and economic equality had yet to be taken.

One of the first socialists was also one of the first cotton lords, Robert Owen (1771–1858) of Manchester and the Scottish Lowlands. Appalled at the condition of the millhands, he created a kind of model community for his own employees, paying high wages, reducing hours, sternly correcting vice and drunkenness, building schools and housing and company stores for the cheap sale of workers' necessities. From such paternalistic capitalism in his early years he passed on to a long lifetime spent in crusading for social reforms, in which he was somewhat handicapped, not only by the opposition of industrialists, but by his unpopular radicalism in matters of religion.

Most of the early socialists were Frenchmen, spurred onward by the sense of an uncompleted revolution. One was a nobleman, the Count de Saint-Simon (1760–1825), who had fought in the War of American Independence, accepted the French Revolution, and in his later years wrote many books on social problems. He and his followers, who called themselves not socialists but Saint-Simonians, were among the first clear exponents of a planned society. They advocated the public ownership of industrial equipment and other capital, with control vested in the hands of great captains of industry or social engineers, who should plan vast projects like the digging of a canal at Suez, and in general coordinate the labor and resources of society to productive ends. Of a different type was Charles Fourier (1772–1837), a somewhat doctrinaire thinker who subjected all known institutions to a sweeping condemnation. His positive program took the form of proposing that society be organized in small units which he termed "phalansteries." Each of these he conceived to contain 1,620 persons, each doing the work suited to his natural inclination. Among the practical French no phalanstery was ever successfully organized. A number were established in the United States, still the land of Europe's utopian dream; the best known, since it was operated by literary people, was the Brook Farm "movement" in Massachusetts, which ran through a troubled existence of five years from 1842 to 1847. Robert Owen also, in 1825, had founded an experimental colony in America, at New Harmony, Indiana, on the then remote and unspoiled banks of the Wabash; it, too, lasted only about five years. Such schemes, presupposing the withdrawal of select spirits to live by themselves, really had little to say on the problems of society as a whole in an industrial age.

Politically the most significant form of antediluvian socialism—before the "deluge" of 1848—was the movement stirring among the working classes of France, a compound of revolutionary republicanism and socialism. The politically minded

Paris workingmen had been republican since 1792. For them the Revolution, in the 1820s, 1830s, 1840s, was not finished but only momentarily interrupted. Reduced to political impotence, discriminated against in their rights in the law courts, obliged to carry identity papers signed by their employers, goaded by the pressures of industrialization as it spread to France, they developed a deep hostility to the owning classes of the bourgeoisie. They found a spokesman in the Paris journalist Louis Blanc, editor of the *Revue de progrès* and author of the *Organization of Work* (1839), one of the most constructive of the early socialist writings. He proposed a system of "social workshops," or state-supported manufacturing centers, in which the workers should labor by and for themselves without the intervention of private capitalists. Of this kind of socialism we shall hear more as the story unfolds.

As for "communism," it was at this time an uncertain synonym for socialism. A small group of German revolutionaries, mainly exiles in France, took the name for themselves in the 1840s. They would have been historically forgotten had they not included Karl Marx and Friedrich Engels among their members. Marx and Engels consciously used the word in 1848 to differentiate their variety of socialism from that of such utopians as Saint-Simon, Fourier, and Owen. But the word "communism" went out of general use after 1848, to be revived after the Russian Revolution of 1917, at which time it received a new meaning.

Nationalism: Western Europe

Nationalism, since it arose so largely in reaction against the international Napoleonic system, has already been discussed in the preceding chapter.[10] It was the most pervasive and the least crystallized of the new "isms." In western Europe— Britain, France, or Spain—where national unity already existed, nationalism was not a doctrine so much as a latent state of mind, easily aroused when national interests were questioned, but normally taken for granted. Elsewhere—in Italy, Germany, Poland, the Austrian and Turkish empires—where peoples of the same nationality were politically divided or subject to foreign rule, nationalism was becoming a deliberate and conscious program. It was undoubtedly the example of the West, of Great Britain and France, successful and flourishing because they were unified nations, that stimulated the ambitions of other peoples to become unified nations too. The period after 1815 was in Germany a time of rising agitation over the national question, in Italy of the Risorgimento or "resurgence," in eastern Europe of the Slavic Revival.

The movement was led by intellectuals, who often found it necessary to instill in their compatriots the very idea of nationality itself. They seized upon Herder's conception of the *Volksgeist* or national spirit, each applying it to his own people. Usually they began with a cultural nationalism, holding that each people had a language, history, world view, and culture of its own, which must be preserved and perfected. They then usually passed on to a political nationalism, holding that in order to preserve this national culture, and to assure liberty and justice to its individual members, each nation should create for itself a sovereign state. Governing authorities, they held, should be of the same nationality, i.e., language, as those they governed. All persons of the same nationality, i.e., language, should be encompassed within the same state.

[10] See pp. 408–412.

Germanic
Latin (or Romance)
Slavic
Celtic

FINNISH
NORWEGIAN
SWEDISH
ESTONIAN
LETTISH
GREAT RUSSIAN
ERSE
IRISH   ENGLISH
DANISH
LITHUANIAN
WHITE RUSSIAN
WELSH
DUTCH
FLEMISH
POLISH
UKRAINIAN (LITTLE RUSSIAN, RUTHENIAN)
GERMAN
CZECH
SLOVAK
BRETON
FRENCH
MAGYAR
RUMANIAN
SLOVENE
CROATIAN
Zone of Most Extreme Local Intermixture of Languages
BASQUE
SERB
BULGARIAN
PORTUGUESE
SPANISH   CATALAN   ITALIAN   ALBANIAN
TURKISH
GREEK
GREEK

0   200   400 miles

LANGUAGES OF EUROPE

There are three main European language-families—Germanic, Latin, and Slav. It will be seen that they cover most of Europe. Language areas are shown as they were in the first part of the twentieth century, at which time they had not changed much in over five centuries. The map cannot show local complications which have been a leading source of political trouble—such as the overlapping of adjoining languages, bilingual areas, and the existence of small language "pockets," as of Turkish in the Balkans, Greek in Asia Minor, Yiddish in Poland, or German in scattered parts of eastern Europe. In the extreme northwest is the "Celtic fringe," to which the Breton, Welsh, and Gaelic languages were pushed back in the early Middle Ages. For the area within the diamond-shaped zone no map on the present scale can give a realistic idea; the reader must consult an atlas. In any case, during the Second World War and its aftermath, in Eastern Europe many language pockets were wiped out through exchange, transportation, or extermination of peoples. (See map, pp. 848–849.)

Since such ideas could not be fully realized without the overthrow of every government in Europe east of France, thoroughgoing nationalism was inherently revolutionary. Outspoken nationalists were discountenanced or persecuted by the authorities and consequently formed secret societies in large numbers. The Carbonari, organized in Italy in the time of Napoleon, was the best known. There were many others—the *Veri Italiani*, the Apophasimenes, the Sublime and Perfect Masters, etc. In some regions Masonic lodges might serve the same purpose. In many of the societies nationalism was mixed with liberalism, socialism, or revolutionary republicanism in an as yet undifferentiated way. Members were initiated by a complex ritual intended to impress upon them the dire consequences of betraying the society's secrets. They used special grips and passwords and adopted revolutionary names to conceal their identity and baffle the police. They were usually so organized that the ordinary member knew the identity of only a few others, and never of the higher-ups, so that if arrested he could reveal nothing important. The societies kept busy, circulating forbidden literature and generally maintaining a revolutionary ferment. Conservatives dreaded them, but they were not really dangerous to any government that enjoyed the support of its people.

Best known of the nationalist philosophers in western Europe was the Italian Joseph Mazzini (1805-1872), who spent most of his adult life in exile in France and England. In his youth he joined the Carbonari, but in 1831 he founded a society of his own, called Young Italy, and he edited and smuggled into Italy copies of a journal of the same name. Young Italy was soon imitated by other societies of similar aim, such as Young Germany. In 1834 Mazzini organized a filibustering expedition against the kingdom of Sardinia, hoping that all Italy would rise and join him. Undeterred by its total failure, he continued to organize, to conspire, and to write. For Mazzini nationality and revolution were a holy cause in which the most generous and humane qualities were to find expression. He was a moral philosopher, as may be judged from the title of his most widely read book, *The Duties of Man*, in which he placed a pure duty to the nation intermediate between duty to family and duty to God.

To the Germans, divided and frustrated, nationality became almost an obsession. It affected everything from folklore to metaphysics. *Grimm's Fairy Tales*, for example, was first published in 1812. It was the work of the two Grimm brothers, founders of the modern science of comparative linguistics, who traveled about Germany to study the popular dialects and in doing so collected the folk tales that for generations had been current among the common people. They hoped in this way to find the ancient, native, indigenous "spirit" of Germany, deep and unspoiled in the bosom of the *Volk*. The same preoccupation with nationhood revealed itself in the philosophy of Hegel (1770-1831), possibly the most stupendous of all nineteenth-century thinkers.

To Hegel, with the spectacle of the Napoleonic years before him, it was evident that for a people to enjoy freedom, order, or dignity it must possess a potent and independent state. The state, for him, became the institutional embodiment of reason and liberty—the "march of God through the world," as he put it, meaning not an expansion in space through vulgar conquest, but a march through time and through the processes of history. Hegel conceived of reality itself as a process, a development having an inner logic and necessary sequence of its own. He thus broke with the more static and mechanical philosophy of the eighteenth century, with its fixed categories of unchangeable right and wrong. He became a philosopher of unfolding change. The pattern of change he held to be the "dialectic," or irresistible tendency of the mind to proceed by the creation of opposites. A given state of affairs (the "thesis") would in this view inevitably produce the conception of an opposite state of affairs (the "antithesis"), which would equally inevitably be followed by a reconciliation and a fusion of the two (the "synthesis"). Thus it could be thought that the very disunity of Germany, by producing the idea of unity, would inevitably bring about the creation of a German state.

The Hegelian dialectic was soon to be appropriated by Karl Marx to new uses, but meanwhile Hegel's philosophy, with other currents in Germany, made the study of history more philosophically meaningful than it had ever been before. History, the study of time process, seemed to be the very key with which to unlock the true significance of the world. Historical studies were stimulated, and the German universities became centers of historical learning, attracting scholars from many countries. Most eminent of the German historians was Leopold von Ranke (1795–1886), founder of the "scientific" school of historical writing. Ranke, too, though intellectually scrupulous to the last degree, owed much of his incentive to his national feeling. His first youthful work was a study of the *Latin and Teutonic Peoples*; and one of his main ideas, throughout his long life, was that Europe owed its unique greatness to the coexistence and interplay of several distinct nations, which had always resisted the attempts of any one nation to control the whole. By the latter Ranke really meant France—the France of Louis XIV and Napoleon. The Germans, said Ranke in 1830, had a mission from God to develop a culture and a political system entirely different from those of the French. They were destined to "create the pure German state corresponding to the genius of the nation." Whether Western constitutional, parliamentary, and individualist principles were suited to the national character of Germany seemed to Ranke very doubtful.

In economics Friedrich List, in his *National System of Political Economy* (1841), held that political economy as taught in England was suited only to England. It was not an abstract truth but a body of ideas developed in a certain historical stage in a certain country. List thus became a founder of the historical or institutional school of economics. The doctrine of free trade, he said, was designed to make England the world's industrial center by keeping other countries in the status of suppliers of raw material and food. But any country, he held, if it was to be civilized and develop its own national culture, must have cities, factories, industries, and capital of its own. It must therefore put up high tariffs (at least temporarily, in theory) for protection. List, it should be remarked, had developed his ideas during a sojourn in the United States, where Henry Clay's "American system" was in fact a national system of political economy.

Nationalism: Eastern Europe

In eastern Europe the Poles and the Magyars had long been active political nationalists, the Poles wishing to undo the partitions and reestablish their Polish state, the Magyars insisting on autonomy of their kingdom of Hungary within the Habsburg empire.[11] But for the most part nationalism in eastern Europe long remained more cultural than political. Centuries of development had tended to submerge the Czechs, Slovaks, Ruthenians, Rumanians, Serbs, Croats, Slovenes —and even the Poles and Magyars in lesser degree. Their upper classes spoke German or French and looked to Vienna or to Paris for their ideas. The native languages had remained peasant languages, and the cultures peasant cultures, barely known to civilized Europeans. It seemed that many of these languages would disappear.[12]

But early in the nineteenth century the process began to reverse itself. Patriots began to demand the preservation of their historic cultures. They collected folk tales and ballads; they studied the languages, composing grammars and dictionaries, often for the first time; and they took to writing books in their mother tongues. They urged their own educated classes to give up "foreign" ways. They wrote histories showing the famous exploits of their several peoples in the Middle Ages. A new nationalism stirred the Magyars; in 1837 a national Hungarian

[11] On the Poles, see pp. 238–240, 327–330, 409; on the Magyars, pp. 218, 266, 321.
[12] See p. 242.

theater was established at Budapest. In what was to become Rumania a former Transylvanian peasant youth named George Lazar began as early as 1816 to teach at Bucharest. He lectured in Rumanian (to the surprise of the upper classes, who preferred Greek), telling how Rumania had a distinguished history back to the Roman emperor Trajan. As for the Greeks, they entertained visions of restoring the medieval Greek empire (known to Westerners as the Byzantine Empire) in which persons of Greek language or Greek Orthodox religion should become the predominant people of the Balkans.

The most far-reaching of the east-European movements was the Slavic Revival. The Slavs included the Russians, Poles, and Ruthenians; the Czechs and Slovaks; and the South Slavs, consisting of the Slovenes, Croats, Serbs, and Bulgars. All branches of the Slavs began to come to life. In 1814 the Serb Vuk Karajich published a grammar of his native tongue and a collection of *Popular Songs and Epics of the Serbs*; he worked out a Serbian alphabet, translated the New Testament, and declared that the dialect of Ragusa (now Dubrovnik) should become the literary language of all South Slavs. He was opposed by the Serbian clergy, who preferred to have writing confined to Slavonic, a purely learned language, like Latin; but he found much support outside Serbia, including that of the brothers Grimm. The Czechs had always been a more advanced people than the Serbs, but educated Czechs were usually half Germanized. In 1836 the historian Palacky published the first volume of his *History of Bohemia*, designed to give the Czechs a new pride in their national past. He first wrote his book in German, the common reading language of educated Czechs. But he soon recast it into Czech, significantly reentitling it a *History of the Czech People*. Among Poles the poet and revolutionary Adam Mickiewicz may be mentioned. Arrested by the Russians in 1823 for membership in a secret society, he was soon allowed by the tsarist government to pass into western Europe. From 1840 to 1844 he taught Slavic languages at the Collège de France, using his lecture platform as a rostrum to deliver eloquent pleas for the liberation of all peoples and overthrow of autocracy. He wrote epic poems on Polish historical themes and continued to be active among the revolutionary Polish exiles settled in France.

Russia itself, which Poles and Czechs regarded as very backward, was slower to develop a pronounced national sense. Under Tsar Alexander I a Western or European orientation prevailed, but in Alexander's last years and after his death the doctrines of Slavophilism began to spread. Russian Slavophilism, or the idea that Russia possessed a way of life of its own, different from and not to be corrupted by that of Europe, was simply the application to Russia of the fundamental idea of the *Volksgeist*. Such views in Russia were at least as old as the opposition to the reforms of Peter the Great.[13] In the nationalistic nineteenth century they crystallized more systematically into an "ism," and they tended to merge into Pan-Slavism, which made substantially the same assertions for the Slavic peoples as a whole. But Pan-Slavism, before 1848, was no more than embryonic.

Other "Isms"

Liberalism, radical republicanism, socialism, and nationalism were after 1815 the political forces driving Europe onward toward a future still unknown. Of

[13] See pp. 237–238, 324–325.

other "isms" less need be said. Conservatism, too, remained strong. Politically, on the Continent, conservatism upheld the institutions of absolute monarchy, aristocracy, and church and opposed the constitutional and representative government sought by liberals. As a political philosophy, conservatism built upon the ideas of Edmund Burke, who had held that every people must change its institutions by gradual adaptation, and that no people could suddenly realize in the present any freedoms not already well prepared for in the past.[14] This doctrine lacked appeal for those to whom the past had been a series of misfortunes. Conservatism sometimes passed into nationalism, since it stressed the firmness and continuity of national character. But nationalists at this time were more often liberals or republicans. "Monarchism" was conservative and even reactionary. Gone was the enlightened despotism of the last century, when kings had boldly irritated their nobles and defied their churches. After the thunders of the French Revolution aristocracy and monarchy huddled together, and their new watchword was to maintain "the throne and the altar."

Deeper than other "isms," a feeling shared in varying ways by people of all parties, was the profound current of humanitarianism. It consisted in a heightened sense of the reality of cruelty inflicted upon others. Here the thought of the Age of Enlightenment suffered no reversal. Torture was gone, and even backward governments showed no inclination to restore it. Conditions in prisons, hospitals, insane asylums, and orphanages improved. People began to be moved by the misery of pauper children, chimney sweeps, women in the mines, and black slaves. Russian serf owners and American slave owners began to show psychological signs of moral doubt. To degrade human beings, use them as work animals, torture them, confine them unjustly, hold them as hostages for others, tear apart their families, and punish their relatives were regarded by Europeans as foreign to true civilization, something distant, "Turkish" or "Asiatic," like the castration of eunuchs, the impressment of janissaries, or the burning of widows. The Christian sense of the inviolability of the human person was now again, in a mundane way, beginning to relieve the sufferings of humanity.

54. THE DIKE AND THE FLOOD: DOMESTIC

It is time now to resume the narrative of political events, broken off at the close of the last chapter with the peace settlement of 1814–1815. The governments that defeated Napoleon wanted to assure themselves above all else that the disturbances of the past twenty-five years would not be renewed. In France the restored Bourbon king, Louis XVIII, aspired to keep his throne for himself and his successors. In Great Britain the Tory governing class hoped to preserve the old England that they had so valiantly saved from the clutches of Bonaparte. In Germany, Austria, Italy, and central Europe the chief aim of Metternich, who for another thirty-three years remained the mastermind of these regions, was to maintain a system in which the prestige of the Habsburg dynasty should be supreme. The aims of the tsar, Alexander, were less clear. He was feared by representatives of the other powers as a dreamer, a self-chosen world savior, a man who said he wanted to bring Christianity into politics, a crowned Jacobin, and even a liberal. It became one of Metternich's chief hopes to convert Alexander to conservatism.

[14] See p. 367.

The arrangements made by the victorious powers were in some ways moderate, at least when the provocations they had undergone in the late wars are considered. Partly by the tsar's insistence written constitutions existed after 1814 in France and in Russian or "Congress" Poland. Some of the rulers of south German states allowed a measure of representative government. Even the king of Prussia promised a representative assembly for his kingdom, though the promise was not kept. But it was difficult to maintain any kind of stability. The forces of the political right, the privileged classes (or in France the former privileged classes) denounced all signs of liberalism as dangerous concessions to revolution. Those of the political left—liberals, nationalists, republicans—regarded the newly installed regimes as hopelessly reactionary and inadequate. Statesmen were jittery on the subject of revolution, so that they met every sign of agitation with attempts at repression, which though they might drive agitation temporarily underground really only made it worse by creating additional grievances. A vicious circle was set endlessly revolving.

Reaction after 1815: France, Poland

In France Louis XVIII in 1814 granted an amnesty to the regicides of 1793. But the regicides, like all republicans, found the France of 1814 an uncomfortable place to live in, exposed as they were to the unofficial vengeance of counterrevolutionaries, and in 1815 most of them rallied to Napoleon when he returned from Elba. This exasperated the royalist counterrevolutionaries beyond all measure. A brutal "white terror" broke out. Upper-class youths murdered Bonapartists and republicans, Catholic mobs seized and killed Protestants at Marseilles and Toulouse. The Chamber of Deputies chosen in 1815 (by the tiny electorate of 100,000 well-to-do landowners) proved to be more royalist than the king—*plus royaliste que le roi.* The king himself could not control the mounting frenzy of reaction, which he was sensible enough to realize would only infuriate the revolutionary element still further, as in fact happened. In 1820 a fanatical workingman assassinated the king's nephew, the Duke de Berry. Those who said that all partisans of the French Revolution were criminal extremists seemed to be justified. The reaction deepened, until in 1824 Louis XVIII died and was succeeded by his brother Charles X. Not only was Charles X the father of the recently murdered Duke de Berry, but for over thirty years he had been the acknowledged leader of implacable counterrevolution. As the Count of Artois, youngest brother of Louis XVI, he had been among the first to emigrate in 1789. He was the favorite Bourbon among the most obstinate ex-seigneurs, nobles, and churchmen. Regarding himself as hereditary absolute monarch by the grace of God, he had himself crowned at Reims with all the romantic pomp of ages past, and proceeded to stamp out not only revolutionary republicanism but liberalism and constitutionalism as well.

In Poland, it will be recalled, the Vienna settlement created a constitutional kingdom, with Alexander as king, joined in merely personal union with the Russian empire. The new machinery did not work very well. The Polish constitution provided for an elected diet, a very wide suffrage by the standards of the day, the Napoleonic civil code, freedom of press and religion, and exclusive use of the Polish language. But the Poles discovered that Alexander, though favoring liberty, did not like to have anyone disagree with him. They could make little use of their much touted freedom in any actual legislation. The elected diet could not get along with the viceroy, who was a Russian. In Russia the serf-owning aristocracy viewed Alexander's idea of a constitutional kingdom in Poland with a jaundiced eye. They wanted no experimentation with liberty on the very borders of Russia. The Poles themselves played into the hands of their enemies. For the Poles were nationalist at least as much as they were liberal. They were dissatisfied with the boundaries accorded to Congress Poland. They dreamed of the vast kingdom that had existed before the First Partition and so agitated the interminable question of the Eastern Border, laying claim to huge territories in the Ukraine and White Russia.[15] At the University of Vilna professors and students began to join secret societies. Some members of these societies were revolutionaries aiming at driving out Alexander, reuniting with Prussian and Austrian Poland, and reconstituting an independent Polish state. It was in the discovery and breaking up of one such society, the Philarets of Vilna, that Adam Mickiewicz was arrested in 1823. Reaction and repression now struck the University of Vilna.

Reaction after 1815: The German States, Britain

In Germany those who had felt national stirrings during the Wars of Liberation were disillusioned by the peace treaty, which maintained the several German principalities about as Napoleon had left them and purposely united them only in a loose federation, or Bund. National ideas were most common in the numerous universities, where students and professors were more susceptible than most people to the doctrines of an eternal *Volksgeist* and a far-flung *Deutschtum*. National ideas, being a glorification of the German common people, carried with them a kind of democratic opposition to aristocrats, princes, and kings. Students in many of the universities in 1815 formed college clubs, called collectively the *Burschenschaft*, which, as centers of serious political discussion, were to replace the older clubs devoted to drinking and dueling. The *Burschenschaft*, a kind of German youth movement, held a nationwide congress at Wartburg in 1817. Students listened to rousing speeches by patriotic professors, marched about in "Teutonic" costume, and burned a few reactionary books. This undergraduate performance was no immediate threat to any established state, but the nervous governments took alarm. In 1819 a theology student assassinated the German writer Kotzebue, known as an informer in the service of the tsar. The assassin received hundreds of letters of congratulation, and at Nassau the head of the local government barely escaped the same fate at the hands of a pharmacy student.

Metternich now chose to intervene. He had no authority in Germany except in that Austria was a member of the Germanic federation. He regarded all these manifestations of German national spirit, or of any demand for a more solidly unified Germany, as a threat to the favorable position of the Austrian Empire and to the whole balance of Europe. He called a conference of the principal German states at Carlsbad in Bohemia; the frightened conferees adopted certain resolutions, proposed by Metternich, which were soon enacted by the diet of the Bund. These Carlsbad Decrees (1819) dissolved the *Burschenschaft* and the equally nationalistic gymnastic clubs (some of whose members thereupon joined secret societies); and they provided for government officials to be placed in the universities to watch them and for censors to control the contents of books and of the

---

[15] See map, p. 328.

periodical and newspaper press. The Carlsbad Decrees remained in force for many years, and they imposed an effective check on the growth of liberal and nationalist ideas in Germany.

Metternich was unable to persuade the south German rulers to retract the constitutions they had granted. The rulers here, in Bavaria, Württemberg, and elsewhere, found that with representative government they could rally popular support as well as assimilate the numerous new territories that they had obtained from Napoleon. But in general, throughout Germany, after 1820, repression of new or unsettling ideas was the rule. Still more so was this true of the Austrian Empire, which Metternich could more directly control.

Nor did Great Britain escape the dreary rounds of agitation and repression. As elsewhere, radicalism produced reaction, and vice versa. Britain after Waterloo was still a country of the old regime but one afflicted by the most advanced social evils. In 1815, at the close of the wars, the landed classes feared an inrush of imported agricultural products and consequent collapse of farm prices and rentals. The gentry who controlled Parliament enacted a new Corn Law, raising the protective tariff on imports of grains to the point where importation became impossible unless prices were very high. Landlords and their farmers benefited, but wage earners found the price of breadstuffs soaring out of reach. At the same time there was a postwar depression in industry. Wages fell and many were thrown out of work. These conditions naturally contributed to the spread of political radicalism, which looked first of all to a drastic reform of the House of Commons, in order that thereafter a radical program of social and economic legislation might be enacted.

A riot broke out in London in December 1816. In the following February the Prince Regent was attacked in his carriage. The government suspended habeas corpus and employed *agents provocateurs* to obtain evidence against the agitators. Industrialists of Manchester and the new factory towns, determined to force through the reform of parliamentary representation, took the chance offered by the distress of the working classes to organize mass meetings of protest. At Birmingham a crowd elected a mock member of Parliament. At sprawling Manchester 80,000 people staged an enormous demonstration at St. Peter's Fields in 1819; they demanded universal male suffrage, annual election of the House of Commons, and the repeal of the Corn Laws. Although perfectly orderly they were fired upon by soldiers; 11 persons were killed and about 400 wounded, including 113 women. Radicals called this episode the Peterloo massacre in derisive comparison with the battle of Waterloo. The frightened government thanked the soldiers for their brave upholding of the social order. Parliament rushed through the Six Acts (1819), which outlawed "seditious and blasphemous" literature, put a heavy stamp tax on newspapers, authorized the search of private houses for arms, and rigidly restricted the right of public meeting. A group of revolutionaries thereupon plotted to assassinate the whole cabinet at a dinner; they were caught in Cato Street in London in 1820—whence the name "Cato Street Conspiracy." Five of them were hanged. Meanwhile, for publishing the writings of Thomas Paine, Richard Carlisle spent seven years in prison.

"Our example," wrote the Duke of Wellington to a Continental correspondent in 1819, "will be of value in France and Germany, and it is to be hoped that the world will escape from the general revolution with which we all seem to be threatened."

In summary, reactionary policies entrenched themselves everywhere in the years following the peace. The reaction was due only in part to memories of the French Revolution. It was due even more to the living fear of revolution in the present. This fear, though exaggerated, was no mere hallucination. Sensing the rising flood, the established interests desperately built dikes against it in every country. The same is true of international politics at the time.

55. THE DIKE AND THE FLOOD: INTERNATIONAL

At the Congress of Vienna the powers agreed to hold meetings in the future to enforce the treaty and take up new issues as they arose. A number of congresses of the Great Powers resulted, which are of significance as an experimental step toward international regulation of the affairs of Europe. The congresses resembled, in a tentative and partial way, the League of Nations that arose after the First World War of 1914–1918, or the United Nations that arose during and after the war of 1939–1945. The powers had also, in 1815, in alarm after the return of Napoleon, subscribed to Alexander I's Holy Alliance, which became the popular term for the collaboration of the European states in the congresses.[16] The Holy Alliance, on the face of it a statement of Christian purpose and international concord, gradually became an alliance for the suppression of revolutionary and even liberal activity, following in that respect the trend of the governments which made it up.

The Congress of Aix-la-Chapelle, 1818

The first general postwar assemblage of the powers took place at the Congress of Aix-la-Chapelle (or Aachen) in 1818. The principal item on the agenda was to withdraw the allied army of occupation from France. The French argued that Louis XVIII would never be popular in France so long as he was supported by a foreign army. The other powers, since they all desired the French to forget the past and accept the Bourbons, withdrew their military forces without disagreement. They arranged also to have private bankers take over the French reparations debt (the 700 million francs imposed by the second Treaty of Paris); the bankers paid the allied governments, and the French in due time paid the bankers. On a few other smaller matters international collective action proved successful.

Tsar Alexander was still the most advanced internationalist of the day. He suggested at Aix-la-Chapelle a kind of permanent European union and even proposed the maintenance of international military forces to safeguard recognized states against changes by violence. Governments if thus reassured against revolution, he argued, would more willingly grant constitutional and liberal reforms. But the others demurred, especially the British foreign minister Lord Castlereagh. The British declared themselves willing to make international commitments against specified contingencies, such as a revival of aggression on the part of France. But they would assume no obligations to act upon indefinite and unforeseeable future events. They reserved the right of independent judgment in foreign policy. Concretely, the congress addressed itself to the problems of the

<hr>

[16] See p. 424 and map, pp. 420–421.

Atlantic slave trade and of the recurring nuisance of the Barbary pirates. It was unanimously agreed that both should be suppressed. To suppress them required naval forces, which only the British possessed in adequate amount, and it meant also that naval captains must be authorized to stop and search vessels at sea. The continental states, always touchy on the subject of British sea power, refused to countenance any such uses of the British fleet. They feared for the freedom of the seas. As for the British, they would not even discuss placing British warships in an international naval pool or putting British squadrons under the authority of an international body. Nothing therefore was done; the slave trade continued, booming illicitly with the endless demand for cotton; and the Barbary pirates were not disposed of until the French occupied and annexed Algeria some years later. The growth of international institutions was blocked by the separate interests of the sovereign states.

Revolution in Southern Europe: The Congress of Troppau, 1820

Scarcely had the Congress of Aix-la-Chapelle disbanded when revolutionary agitation came to a crisis in southern Europe. It was not that revolutionary or liberal sentiment was stronger here than in the north, in the sense of having more followers, but rather that the governments in question, those of Spain, Naples, and the Ottoman Empire, were inefficient, ignorant, flimsy, and corrupt. Many of the revolutionaries were hardly more than middle-class liberals; indeed, the Spaniards at this time were the first to use the word "liberal" in this modern political sense. Many of them had at first accepted the Napoleonic occupation of Spain as a progressive development, but had then turned against it and proclaimed a new constitution in 1812, modeled on the French revolutionary constitution of 1789–1791.[17] After Napoleon's final defeat they attempted to force the restored Bourbon kings of Spain and Naples to adopt this constitution of 1812.

In 1820 the governments of both Spain and Naples collapsed with remarkable ease before the demonstrations of revolutionaries. The kings of both countries reluctantly took oaths to the Spanish constitution of 1812. But Metternich saw the insurrections as the first symptoms of a revolutionary seizure against which Europe should be quarantined. It was a fact that revolutionary agitation was international, easily leaping across frontiers, because of the operations of secret societies and of political exiles, and because in any case the same ideas had been aroused in all countries by the French Revolution. Metternich considered Italy in particular, since the ejection of Napoleon, to be within the legitimate sphere of influence of the Austrian Empire. He therefore called a meeting of the Great Powers at Troppau, hoping to use the authority of an international congress to put down the revolution in Naples. The governments of Great Britain and France, not eager to play Austria's game, sent only observers to the congress. Metternich's main problem was, as usual, Alexander. What would be the attitude of the liberal tsar, the friend and patron of constitutions, toward the idea of a constitutional monarchy in Naples? At an inn in Troppau Metternich and Alexander met alone, and there held a momentous interview over the teacups. Metternich reviewed the horrors of revolutionism, the unwisdom of granting any concessions lest revolutionaries be encouraged. Alexander was already somewhat disillusioned by the

[17] See pp. 361–363.

ungrateful feelings of the Poles. He was troubled by rumors of disaffection among officers in his own army. He had always believed that constitutions should be granted by legitimate sovereigns, not extorted from them by revolutionaries, as had happened in Naples. He allowed himself to be persuaded by Metternich. He declared that he had always been wrong, and that Metternich had always been right; and he announced himself ready to follow Metternich's political judgment. The triumph of the Austrian chancellor was complete. The radical tsar now turned reactionary.

Thus fortified, Metternich drew up a document, the protocol of Troppau, for consideration and acceptance by the five Great Powers. It held that all recognized European states should be protected by collective international action, in the interests of general peace and stability, from internal changes brought about by force. It was a statement of collective security against revolution. Neither France nor Great Britain accepted it. Castlereagh wrote to Metternich that if Austria felt its interests to be threatened in Naples it should intervene in its own name only. It was not the repression of the Neapolitan revolution that the Tories of 1820 objected to, so much as the principle of a binding international collaboration. Metternich could get only Russia and Prussia to endorse his protocol, in addition to Austria. These three, acting as the Congress of Troppau, authorized Metternich to dispatch an Austrian army into Naples. He did so; the Neapolitan revolutionaries were arrested or put to flight; the incompetent and brutal Ferdinand I was restored as "absolute" king; the demon of revolution was seemingly exorcised. Reaction won out. But the Congress of Troppau, ostensibly a Europe-wide international body, had in effect functioned as an antirevolutionary alliance of Austria, Russia, and Prussia. A gap opened between the three Eastern autocracies and the two Western powers—even when the latter consisted of Tories and Bourbons.

Spain and the Near East: The Congress of Verona, 1822

Thousands of revolutionaries and liberals fled from the terror raging in Italy. Many went to Spain, now dreaded by conservatives as the main seat of revolutionary infection. The Near East also seemed about to ignite in conflagration. Alexander Ypsilanti, a Greek who had spent his adult life in the military service of Russia, in 1821 led a band of armed followers from Russia into Rumania (still a part of Turkey), hoping that all Greeks and pro-Greeks in the Turkish empire would join him. He expected Russian support, since the penetration of Turkey by the use of Greek Christians had long been a pet project of Russian foreign policy.[18] The possibility of a Turkish empire converted into a "Greek" empire and dependent on Russia was naturally unpleasant to Metternich. To deal with all these matters an international congress met at Verona in 1822.

Alexander, in shifting from liberal to reactionary views, had not changed his belief in the need of international government. Had pure power politics determined his decisions he would doubtless have favored Ypsilanti's Grecophile revolution. But he stood by the principle of international solidarity against revolutionary violence. He refused to support Ypsilanti, who found less enthusiasm for Greek culture among the Rumanians and Balkan peoples than he had expected and was soon defeated by the Turks. As for intervention to repress the uprising in

[18] See p. 327.

Greece itself, the question did not arise, since the Turkish government proved quite able for a time to handle the matter without assistance.

The question of the revolution in Spain was settled by foreign intervention. The Bourbon regime in France had no taste for a Spain in which revolutionaries, republicans, political exiles, and members of secret societies might be harbored. The French government proposed to the Congress of Verona that it be authorized to dispatch an army across the Pyrenees. The Congress welcomed the offer, and despite many dire predictions of ruin, arising from memories of Napoleon's disaster, a French army of 200,000 men moved into Spain in 1823. The campaign proved to be a military promenade through a cheering country. Spanish liberals, constitutionalists, or revolutionaries were a helpless minority. The mass of the people saw the invasion as a deliverance from Masons, Carbonari, and heretics and shouted with satisfaction at the restoration of church and king. Ferdinand VII, unscrupulous and narrow-minded, repudiated his constitutional oath and let the vindictive ecclesiastics, grandees, and hidalgos have their way. The revolutionaries were savagely persecuted, exiled, or jailed.

Latin American Independence

The disturbances in Europe had their repercussions in all parts of America. While Great Britain was engaged against Napoleon, the United States fought its inconclusive War of 1812 against the former mother country, and a few years later, after minor military operations, obtained the cession of Florida from Spain. Latin America was affected more positively. The Portuguese royal family, to escape Napoleon, took refuge in its Brazilian empire, but when the dynasty was restored at Lisbon one of its members refused to leave Brazil, which remained as an "empire" independent of Portugal until succeeded by a republican regime in 1889.

Spanish America reached over the enormous area from San Francisco to Buenos Aires. Here, too, the thought of the Enlightenment, the news of the American and French Revolutions, the Napoleonic occupation of Spain, and the restoration in 1814 of the Bourbon Ferdinand VII to the Spanish throne all had their effects. The British had been penetrating Spanish America commercially for over a century, and during the Napoleonic wars they had increased their exports to it twentyfold.[19] There were thus business interests in Spanish America that resisted any return to the old Spanish imperial system of trade controls. More fundamental was the resentment, growing up over several generations, felt by the "creoles" for the "peninsulars," the creoles being the whites of Spanish descent born in America, and the peninsulars those born in Spain who were sent out to occupy the highest offices in the empire. In many places most of the people were native Indians or mestizos of mixed Spanish and Indian origin, often living in depressed conditions and far from the capital cities, so that the movement for independence never took on the widespread popular character that it did in the British colonies that became the United States. It was mainly led by creoles who were active in municipal governments in the towns. At times, as when the revolt was against the Napoleonic government in Spain or against the ephemeral liberal regime in Spain in 1820, the movement for independence recruited some very conservative elements among large landowners and high churchmen. But the

[19] See p. 408.

important leaders, such as Simón Bolívar and José de San Martín, were men who had spent years in Europe and preferred the new constitutional principles, but were in the end frustrated in their aspirations for their own country. The dissensions that long continued to afflict Spanish America were all present within the independence movement itself.

Because of its vast extent, over six thousand miles interrupted by mountain barriers, there could be less unity in the liberation of Spanish America than had been possible, however difficult, in the North American rebellion against England. There could be no Continental Congress such as had met in Philadelphia in 1774. Revolts took place separately within the great vice-royalties: New Spain (Mexico), New Granada (Colombia and Venezuela), Peru (including Ecuador and most of Bolivia and Chile), and La Plata (Argentina, with claims over what are now Uruguay and Paraguay).

The first revolts were against Joseph Bonaparte after Napoleon made him king of Spain in 1808. The rebels proclaimed their loyalty to the deposed Ferdinand VII, who, however, when restored in 1814, refused to make any concessions to American demands, so that revolutionary sentiment turned against him also. There followed a series of disconnected struggles between those fighting for independence (with or without much internal change) and combinations of officials, army officers, landowners, and churchmen who remained loyal to the Spanish crown. Bolívar became the liberator of Venezuela and Colombia, San Martín of Argentina and Chile, and both combined in the liberation of Peru. In Mexico, by way of exception, there was a true mass rising of Indians and mestizos, which was put down by the middle- and upper-class leaders, so that independent Mexico entered upon a long period of chronic turmoil. All Spanish America was troubled by disputes over boundaries, federations formed only to dissolve, and attempted conquests and secessions, so that it was only later in the nineteenth century that the map of South and Central America took form as we know it today.

Let us return to the congress of European powers meeting in Verona in 1822. At the very time when a French army suppressed the revolution in Spain the revolutionaries in Spanish America were declaring their independence. At Verona, the tsar Alexander urged the Congress to mediate between Spain and its colonies. This was a euphemistic way of suggesting military intervention in Spanish America, following the principle of the protocol of Troppau. The British objected. Even the Tory government favored revolutions that might break up the Spanish empire into independent states, with which free trade treaties might be negotiated. Without at least benevolent neutrality from the British fleet no armed force could sail to America. The Spanish Americans therefore maintained their independence, thanks in part to the use made by the British of their sea power on this occasion.

The new republics received strong moral support from the United States also. In December 1823 President James Monroe, in a message to Congress, announced the "Monroe Doctrine." It stated that attempts by European powers to return parts of America to colonial status would be viewed as an unfriendly act by the United States. The British foreign minister George Canning (who had just succeeded Castlereagh) had at first proposed a joint statement by Great Britain and the United States against the East European powers on the Spanish American question. President Monroe, at the advice of his secretary of state John Quincy Adams, decided instead to make a unilateral statement in the form of a message to Congress. They intended to aim their "doctrine" at Great Britain as well as the Continental states, since the British, with their command of the sea, were in fact the only power by which the independence of American states could in practice be threatened. Canning, having no such threats in mind, and concerned more with the Congress of Verona, accepted the line taken by the United States. Indeed, he declared with a flourish that he had "called the New World into existence to redress the balance of the Old." The Monroe Doctrine, at its inception, was a kind of counterblast to the Metternich doctrine of the protocol of Troppau. Where the latter announced the principle of intervention against revolution, the Monroe Doctrine announced that revolutions in America, if they resulted in regimes recognized by the United States, were outside the pale of attention of European powers. In any case the efficacy of the Monroe Doctrine long depended on the tacit cooperation of the British fleet.

Over three hundred years of European colonial empires in America now came to an end, with few exceptions, in the half-century following the United States declaration of independence. One exception was Canada, where membership in the British empire was voluntary, at least for the English-speaking inhabitants, and where both the English and French Canadians resisted threats of annexation by the United States. The other exceptions were in the West Indies, where Haiti was independent, the smaller islands remained British, French, or Dutch, and the large islands of Cuba and Puerto Rico remained Spanish until the Spanish-American War of 1898.

The End of the Congress System

After the Congress of Verona no more such meetings were held. The attempt at a formal international regulation of European affairs was given up. In the broadest retrospect, the congresses failed to make progress toward an international order because, especially after Alexander's conversion to conservatism, they came to stand for nothing except preservation of the status quo. They made no attempt at accommodation with the new forces that were shaping Europe. It was not the policy of the congresses to forestall revolution by demanding that governments institute reforms. They simply repressed or punished all revolutionary agitation. They propped up governments that could not stand on their own feet.

In any case the congresses never succeeded in subordinating the separate interests of the Great Powers. Perhaps Alexander's repudiation of Ypsilanti was a sacrifice of Russian advantage to international principle; but when the Austrian government intervened to crush the revolution in Naples, and when the French government crushed the revolution in Spain, though in both cases they acted with an international mandate, each was really promoting what it conceived to be its own interests. The interest of Great Britain was to pull away from the system entirely. As defined by Castlereagh and by Canning after him, it was to stand aloof from permanent international commitments, to preserve a free exercise of sea power and foreign policy, and to take a benevolent view toward revolution in other countries. Since France eventually pulled away also, the Holy Alliance ceased to be even ostensibly a European system and became no more than a counterrevolutionary league between the three east-European autocracies. With a majority of the five Great Powers highly illiberal, the cause of liberalism in Europe was advanced by the collapse of the international system. At the same time the collapse of the system opened the way to the uncontrolled nationalism of the sovercign states. "Things are getting back to a wholesome state again," wrote George Canning in 1822. "Every nation for itself and God for us all!"

Russia: The Decembrist Revolt, 1825

Alexander I, "the man who defeated Napoleon," the ruler who had led his armies from Moscow to Paris, who had frightened the diplomats by the Russian shadow that he threw over the Continent, and who yet in his way had been the great pillar of constitutional liberalism and international order, died at Taganrog in 1825. His death was the signal for revolution in Russia. Officers of the Russian army, during the campaigns of 1812–1815 in Europe, had become acquainted with many unsettling ideas. Secret societies were formed even in the Russian officer corps; their members held all sorts of conflicting ideas, some wanting a constitutional tsardom in Russia, some demanding a republic, some even dreaming of an emancipation of the serfs. When Alexander died it was for a time uncertain which of his two brothers, Constantine or Nicholas, should succeed him. The restless coteries in the army preferred Constantine, who was thought to be more favorable to innovations in the state. In December 1825 they proclaimed Constantine at St. Petersburg, having their soldiers shout "Constantine and Constitution!" The soldiers, it is said, thought that Constitution was Constantine's wife.

But the fact was that Constantine had already renounced his claims in favor of Nicholas, who was the rightful heir. The uprising, known as the Decembrist revolt, was soon put down. Five of the mutinous officers were hanged; many others were condemned to forced labor or interned in Siberia. The Decembrist revolt was the first manifestation of the modern revolutionary movement in Russia —of a revolutionary movement inspired by an ideological program, as distinguished from the elemental mass upheavals of Pugachev or Stephen Razin. But the immediate effect of the Decembrist revolt was to clamp repression upon Russia more firmly. Nicholas I (1825–1855) maintained an unconditional and despotic autocracy.

Ten years after the defeat of Napoleon the new forces issuing from the French Revolution seemed to be routed, and reaction, repression, and political immobility seemed everywhere to have prevailed. The dike—a massive dike—seemed to be containing the flood.

56. THE BREAKTHROUGH OF LIBERALISM IN THE WEST: REVOLUTIONS OF 1830–1832

The dike broke in 1830, nor in western Europe was the stream thereafter stopped. The seepage, indeed, had already begun. By 1825 Spanish America was independent. The British and the French had pulled away from the congress system. The Greek nationalist movement against the Turks had broken out in the early 1820s.

With the defeat of Ypsilanti in 1821 the Greek nationalists turned somewhat away from the idea of a neo-Greek empire and more toward the idea of independence for Greece proper, the islands and peninsulas where Greek was the predominant language. Tsar Nicholas was more willing than Alexander to assist this movement. The governments of Great Britain and France were not inclined to let Russia stand as the only champion of Balkan peoples. Moreover, liberals in the

West thought of the embattled Greeks as ancient Athenians fighting the modern oriental despotism of the Turkish empire.

The result was a joint Anglo-French-Russian naval intervention, which destroyed the Turkish fleet at Navarino Bay in 1827. Russia again, as often in the past, sent armies into the Balkans. A Russo-Turkish war and a great Near Eastern crisis followed, in the course of which the rival powers agreed in 1829 to recognize Greece as an independent kingdom. The Balkan states of Serbia, Wallachia, and Moldavia were also recognized as autonomous principalities within the badly shaken Ottoman Empire.[20] From the same crisis Egypt emerged as an autonomous region under Mehemet Ali. Egypt in time became a center of Arabic nationalism, which cut down Ottoman power in the south just as Balkan nationalism did in the north.

France, 1824–1830: The July Revolution, 1830

It was in 1830, and first of all in France, that the wall of reaction really collapsed. Charles X became king in 1824.[21] In the next year the legislative chambers voted an indemnity, in the form of perpetual annuities totaling 30 million francs a year, to those who as émigrés thirty-odd years before had had their property confiscated by the revolutionary state. Catholic clergy began to take over classrooms in the schools. A law pronounced the death penalty for sacrilege committed in church buildings. But the France of the restored Bourbons was still a free country, and against these apparent efforts to revive the Old Regime a strong opposition developed in the newspapers and in the chambers. In March 1830 the Chamber of Deputies, in which the bankers Laffitte and Casimir-Périer led the "leftist" opposition, passed a vote of no confidence in the government. The king, as was his legal right, dissolved the Chamber and called for new elections. The elections repudiated the king's policies. He replied on July 26, 1830, with four ordinances issued on his own authority. One dissolved the newly elected Chamber before it had ever met; another imposed censorship on the press; the third so amended the suffrage as to reduce the voting power of bankers, merchants, and industrialists and to concentrate it in the hands of the old-fashioned aristocracy; the fourth called for a new election on the new basis.

These July Ordinances produced on the very next day the July Revolution. The upper bourgeois class was of course desperate at being thus brazenly ousted from political life. But it was the republicans—the nucleus of revolutionary workingmen, students, and intelligentsia in Paris—that actually moved. For three days, from July 27 to 29, barricades were thrown up in the city, behind which a swarming populace defied the army and the police. Most of the army refused to fire. Charles X, in no mood to be made captive by a revolution like his long-dead brother Louis XVI, precipitately abdicated and headed for England.

Some of the leaders wished to proclaim a democratic republic. Working people hoped for better conditions of employment. The political liberals, supported by bankers, industrialists, various journalists, and intellectuals, had other aims. They had been satisfied in general with the constitutional charter of 1814; it was only to the policies and personnel of the government that they had objected, and they wished now to continue with constitutional monarchy, somewhat liberalized,

---

[20] See maps, pp. 420–421, 625.
[21] See p. 446.

LIBERTY LEADING THE PEOPLE
by Eugène Delacroix (French, 1798–1863)

Delacroix, a founder of the romantic school of painting, painted this picture soon after the July Revolution in Paris in 1830 (see pp. 456–458). It well illustrates the idealistic conception of revolution which prevailed among revolutionaries before 1848, in sharp contrast to the "realistic," "scientific," or "materialistic" conception of revolution that set in after 1848 and was typified by Karl Marx. (See pp. 491–495.) Revolution is shown as a noble and moral act. The figures express determination and courage, but show no sign of hatred or even anger. They are not a class (note how the costume varies from the top hat to the semi-nude); they are the People, affirming the rights of man. Liberty, holding the tricolor aloft, is a composed and even rational goddess. Romantic though the painter was, he represents the insurgents as realizing an abstract idea—Liberty, or the Republic. It is to this idea that the half-recumbent and presumably wounded figure directs his gaze. Courtesy of the Louvre (Giraudon).

457

and with a king whom they could trust. A solution to the deadlock was found by the elderly Marquis de Lafayette, the aging hero of the American and the French revolutions, who now came forward as symbol of national unity. Lafayette produced the Duke of Orleans on the balcony of the Paris Hôtel de Ville, embraced him before a great concourse of people, and offered him as the answer to France's need. The duke was a collateral relative of the Bourbons; he had also, as a young man, served in the republican army of 1792. The militant republicans accepted him, willing to see what would develop; and the Chamber of Deputies on August 7 offered him the throne, on condition that he observe faithfully the constitutional charter of 1814. He reigned, until 1848, under the title of Louis Philippe.

The regime of Louis Philippe, called the Orléanist, bourgeois, or July Monarchy, was viewed very differently by different groups in France and in Europe. To the other states of Europe and to the clergy and legitimists within France, it seemed shockingly revolutionary. The new king owed his throne to an insurrection, to a bargain made with republicans, and to promises made to a parliament. He called himself not king of France but king of the French, and he flew not the Bourbon lily but the tricolor flag of the Revolution. The latter produced an effect on the established classes not unlike that of the hammer and sickle of a later day. He cultivated a popular manner, wore sober dark clothing (the ancestor of the modern "business suit"), and carried an umbrella. Though in private he worked stubbornly to maintain his royal position, in public he adhered scrupulously to the constitution.

The constitution remained substantially what it had been in 1814. The main political change was one of tone; there would be no more absolutism, with its notion that constitutional guarantees could be abrogated by a reigning prince. Legally the main change was that the Chamber of Peers ceased to be hereditary, to the chagrin of the old nobility, and that the Chamber of Deputies was to be elected by a somewhat enlarged body of voters. Where before 1830 there had been 100,000 voters, there were now about 200,000. The right to vote was still based on the ownership of a considerable quantity of real estate. About one-thirtieth of the adult male population (the top thirtieth in the possession of real property) now elected the Chamber of Deputies. The beneficiaries of the new system were the upper bourgeoisie—the bankers, merchants, and industrialists. The big property owners constituted the *pays légal*, the "legal country," and to them the July Monarchy was the consummation and stopping place of political progress. To others, and especially to the radical democrats, it proved as the years passed to be a disillusionment and an annoyance.

Revolutions of 1830: Belgium, Poland, and Elsewhere

The immediate effect of the three-day Paris revolution of 1830 was to set off a series of similar explosions throughout Europe. These in turn, coming after the collapse of the Bourbons in France, brought the whole peace settlement of 1815 into jeopardy. It will be recalled that the Congress of Vienna had joined Belgium with the Dutch Netherlands to create a strong buffer state against a resurgent France and had also done what it could to prevent direct pressure of Russian power upon central Europe by way of Poland.[22] Both these arrangements were now undone.

[22] See pp. 418–422.

The Dutch-Belgian union proved economically beneficial, for Belgian industry complemented the commercial and shipping activity of the Dutch, but politically it worked very poorly, especially since the Dutch king had absolutist and centralizing ideas. The Belgians, though they had never been independent, had always stood stiffly for their local liberties under former Austrian rulers (and Spanish before them); now they did the same against the Dutch. The Catholic Belgians disliked Dutch Protestantism; those Belgians who spoke French (the Walloons) objected to regulations requiring the use of Dutch. About a month after the July Revolution in Paris disturbances broke out in Brussels. The leaders asked only for local Belgian self-government, but when the king took arms against them they went on to proclaim independence. A national assembly met and drafted a constitution.

Nicholas of Russia wished to send troops to stamp out the Belgian uprising. But he could not get his forces safely through Poland. In Poland, too, in 1830, a revolution broke out. The Polish nationalists saw in the fall of the French Bourbons a timely moment for them to strike. They objected also to the appearance of Russian troops bound presumably to suppress freedom in western Europe. One incident led to another, until in January 1831 the Polish diet proclaimed the dethronement of the Polish king (i.e., Nicholas), who thereupon sent in a large army. The Poles, outnumbered and divided among themselves, could put up no successful resistance. They obtained no support from the West. The British government was unsettled by agitation at home. The French government, newly installed under Louis Philippe, had no wish to appear disturbingly revolutionary, and in any case feared the Polish agents who besought its backing as international firebrands and republicans. The Polish revolution was therefore crushed. Congress Poland disappeared; its constitution was abrogated, and it was merged into the Russian empire. Thousands of Poles settled in western Europe, where they became familiar figures in republican circles. In Poland the engines of repression rolled. The tsar's government exiled some thousands to Siberia, began to Russify the Eastern Border, and closed the universities of Warsaw and Vilna. Since meanwhile it was too late for the tsar any longer to contemplate intervention in Belgium, it may be said that the sacrifice of the Poles contributed to the success of the west-European revolution of 1830, as it had done to that of the great French Revolution of 1789–1795.[23]

It was true enough, as Nicholas maintained, that an independent Belgium presented great international problems. Belgium for twenty years before 1815 had been part of France. A few Belgians now favored reunion with it, and in France the republican left, which regarded the Vienna treaty as an insult to the French nation, saw an opportunity to win back this first and dearest conquest of the First Republic. In 1831, by a small majority, the Belgian national assembly elected as their king the son of Louis Philippe, who, however, not wishing trouble with the British, forbade his son to accept it. The Belgians thereupon elected Leopold of Saxe-Coburg, a German princeling who had married into the British royal family and become a British subject. He was in fact the uncle of a twelve-year-old girl who was to be Queen Victoria. The British negotiated with Talleyrand, sent over by the French government (it was his last public service); and the result was a treaty of 1831 (confirmed in 1839) setting up Belgium as a perpetually neutral

---

[23] See pp. 372–373 and map on p. 328.

state, incapable of forming alliances and guaranteed against invasion by all five of the Great Powers. The aim intended by the Treaty of Vienna, to prevent the annexation of Belgium to France, was thus again realized in a new way. Internally Belgium presently settled down to a stable parliamentary system, somewhat more democratic than the July Monarchy in France but fundamentally offering the same type of bourgeois and liberal rule.

Revolutionary disturbances also took place in 1830 in Germany, Italy, Switzerland, Spain, and Portugal. To trace them in any detail is not necessary. In a word, a greater measure of liberalism was established in Switzerland; Spain entered a long period of tortuous parliamentary development confused by civil wars, which arose from a disputed succession to the throne; and in Italy and Germany the 1830 uprisings were quickly put down, showing only the continuance of a radical dissatisfaction still held in check by the authorities. It was in Great Britain that sweeping changes really came.

Reform in Great Britain

The three-day Paris revolution of 1830 had direct repercussions across the Channel. The quick results following on working-class insurrection gave radical leaders in England the idea that threats of violence might be useful. On the other hand, the ease and speed with which the French bourgeoisie gained the upper hand reassured the British middle classes, who concluded that they might unsparingly embarrass the government without courting a mass upheaval.

The Tory regime in England had in fact already begun to loosen up. A group of younger men came forward in the 1820s in the Tory party, notably George Canning, the foreign minister, and Robert Peel, son of one of the first cotton manufacturers.[24] This group was sensitive to the needs of British business and to the doctrines of liberalism.[25] They reduced tariff duties and liberalized the old Navigation Acts, permitting British colonies to trade with countries other than Britain. By repealing certain old statutes, they made it lawful for skilled workmen to emigrate from England, taking their skills with them to foreign parts, and for manufacturers to export machinery to foreign countries, even though English industrial secrets would thus be given away. By such measures they advanced the liberal conception of a freely exchanging international system; they moved toward freedom of trade. The Liberal Tories also undermined the legal position of the Church of England, forwarding the conception of a secular state, though such was hardly their purpose. They repealed the old laws (which dated from the seventeenth century) forbidding dissenting Protestants to hold public office except through a legal fiction by which they pretended to be Anglicans. They even allowed the Test Act of 1673 to be repealed and Catholic Emancipation to be adopted. Catholics in Great Britain and Ireland received the same rights as others.[26] Capital punishment was abolished for about a hundred offenses. A professional police force was introduced, in place of the old-fashioned and ineffectual local constables. (It is after Robert Peel that London policemen came to be called "bobbies.") The new police were expected to handle protest meetings, angry crowds, or occasional riots without having to call for military assistance.

[24] See p. 433.
[25] See p. 437.
[26] See pp. 172–173.

There were two things that the Liberal Tories could not do. They could not question the Corn Laws, and they could not reform the House of Commons. By the Corn Laws, which set the tariff on imported grain, a tariff raised to new heights in 1815, the gentlemen of England protected their rent rolls; and by the existing structure of the House of Commons they governed the country, expecting the working classes and the business interests to look to them as natural leaders.

Never in the five hundred years of its history had the Commons been so unrepresentative. No new borough had been created since the Revolution of 1688. The boroughs, or urban centers having the right to elect members of Parliament, were heavily concentrated in southern England. With the Industrial Revolution, population was shifting noticeably to the north. The new factory towns were unrepresented. Of the boroughs, many had decayed over the centuries; some were quite uninhabited, and one was under the waters of the North Sea. In a few boroughs real elections took place, but in some of them it was the town corporation, and in others the owners of certain pieces of real estate, that had the right to name members of Parliament. Each borough was different, carrying over the local liberties of the Middle Ages. Many boroughs were entirely dominated by influential persons called borough-mongers by their critics. As for the rural districts, the "forty-shilling freeholders" chose two members of Parliament for each county, in a convivial assembly much influenced by the gentlefolk. It was estimated about 1820 that less than 500 men, most of them members of the House of Lords, really selected a majority of the House of Commons.

Some two dozen bills to reform the House of Commons had been introduced in the half-century preceding 1830. They had all failed to pass. In 1830, after the Paris revolution, the issue was again raised by the minority party, the Whigs. The Tory prime minister, the Duke of Wellington, the victor of Waterloo and a most extreme conservative, so immoderately defended the existing system that he lost the confidence even of some of his own followers. The existing methods of election in England, he declared, were more perfect than any that human intelligence could contrive at a single stroke. After this outburst a Whig ministry took over the government. It introduced a reform bill. The House of Commons rejected it. The Whig ministry thereupon resigned. The Tories, fearing popular violence, refused to take the responsibility for forming a cabinet. The Whigs resumed office and again introduced their reform bill. This time it passed the Commons but failed in the House of Lords. An angry roar went up over the country. Crowds milled in the London streets, rioters for several days were in control at Bristol, the jail at Derby was sacked, and Nottingham castle burned. Only the passage of the bill, it seemed, could prevent an actual revolution. Using this argument the Whigs got the king to promise to create enough new peers to change the majority in the House of Lords.[27] The Lords yielded rather than be swamped, and in April 1832 the bill became law.

The Reform Bill of 1832 was a very English measure. It adapted the English or medieval system rather than following new ideas let loose by the French Revolution. On the Continent, where constitutions existed at all (as in France), the idea was that each representative should represent roughly the same number of voters, and that voters should qualify to vote by a flat uniform qualification, usually the

[27] See note, p. 189.

payment of a stated amount of property taxes. The British held to the idea that members of the House of Commons represented boroughs and counties, in general without regard to size of population (with exceptions); in other words, no attempt was made to create equal electoral districts. The qualification for voting was enormously simplified, but it still remained rather complex. The franchise, or right to vote, depended on whether one lived in a borough or in a county. It was defined also very largely in terms of rents, because in England, with the high concentration of landownership in the old landowning class, many important people did not own any land at all.

In a borough, under the new law, a man could vote for a member of Parliament if he occupied premises for which he paid £10 annual rental. In a county (a rural area or a small town not considered a borough), a man could vote if he paid £10 annual rental for land held on a long-term sixty-year lease; but he had to pay as high as £50 rental for land occupied on a shorter-term lease in order to be eligible to vote. If he himself owned the land, he could vote if its annual rental value was £2 a year (the old forty-shilling freehold). Thus the vote was nicely distributed according to evidences of economic substance, reliability, and permanence. The total effect on the size of the electorate was to raise the number of voters in the British Isles from about 500,000 to about 813,000. Some persons actually lost their votes, namely, the poorer elements in the handful of old boroughs which had been fairly democratic, like the borough of Westminster in greater London.

The most important thing was not the increased size of the electorate but its redistribution by region and by class. The Reform Bill reallocated the seats in the House of Commons. Fifty-six of the smallest older boroughs were abolished, their inhabitants thereafter voting as residents of their counties. Thirty other small boroughs kept the right to send only one burgess to Parliament instead of the historic two. The 143 seats thus made available were given to the new industrial towns. Here it was the £10-householders who voted, i.e., the middle classes—factory owners and businessmen and their principal employees; doctors, lawyers, brokers, merchants, and newspaper people; relatives and connections of the well-to-do.

The Reform Bill of 1832 was more sweeping than the Whigs would have favored except for their fear of revolution. It was more conservative than the democratic radicals would have accepted, except for their belief that the suffrage might be widened in the future. Great Britain in 1830 was probably nearer to real revolution than any country of Europe—for the revolutions of 1830 on the Continent were in reality only insurrections and readjustments. In Britain a distressed mass of factory workers, and of craft workers thrown out of employment by factory competition, was led by an irate manufacturing interest, grown strong by industrial changes and determined no longer to tolerate its exclusion from political life. Had these elements resorted to general violence a real revolution might have occurred. Yet there was no violent revolution in Britain. The reason probably lies first of all in the existence of the historic institution of Parliament, which, erratic though it was before the Reform Bill, provided the means by which social changes could be legally accomplished and continued, in principle, to enjoy universal respect. Conservatives, driven to the wall, would yield; they could allow a revision of the suffrage because they could expect to remain themselves in public life. Radicals, using enough violence to scare the established interest, did not thereafter face a blank wall; they could expect, once the breach was made, to carry some day a further democratization of Parliament and with it their social and economic program by orderly legislation.

Britain after 1832

But the Reform Bill of 1832 was in its way a revolution. The new business interests, created by industrialization, took their place alongside the old aristocracy in the governing elite of the country. The aristocratic Whigs who had carried the Reform Bill gradually merged with formerly radical industrialists and with a few Liberal Tories to form the Liberal party. The main body of the Tories, joined by a few old Whigs and even a few former radicals, gradually turned into the Conservative party. The two parties alternated in power at short intervals from 1832 to the First World War, this being the classic period in Great Britain of the Liberal-Conservative two-party system.

In 1833 slavery was abolished in the British Empire. In 1834 a new Poor Law was adopted. In 1835 the Municipal Corporations Act, second only to the Reform Bill in basic importance, modernized the local government of English cities; it broke up the old local oligarchies and brought in uniform electoral and administrative machinery, enabling city dwellers to grapple more effectively with the problems of urban life. In 1836 the House of Commons allowed the newspapers to report how its members voted—a long step toward publicity of government proceedings was thus taken. Meanwhile an ecclesiastical commission reviewed the affairs of the Church of England; financial and administrative irregularities were corrected, together with the grosser inequalities between the income of upper and lower clergy, all of which had made the church formerly a kind of closed preserve for the landed gentry.

The Tories, thus assaulted in their immemorial strongholds of local government and the established church, carried a counteroffensive into the strongholds of the new liberal manufacturing class, namely, the factories and the mines. Tories became champions of the industrial workers. Landed gentlemen, of whom the most famous was Lord Ashley, later seventh Earl of Shaftesbury, took the lead in publicizing the social evils of a rapid and indeed ruthless industrialization. They received some support from a few humanitarian industrialists; indeed, the early legislation tended to follow practices already established by the best or strongest business firms. A Factory Act of 1833 forbade the labor of children less than nine years old in the textile mills. It was the first effective piece of legislation on the subject, for it provided for paid inspectors and procedures for enforcement. An act of 1842 initiated significant regulation in the coal mines; the employment underground of women and girls, and of boys under ten, was forbidden.

The greatest victory of the working classes came in 1847 with the Ten Hours Act, which limited the labor of women and children in all industrial establishments to ten hours a day. Thereafter men commonly worked only ten hours also, since the work of men, women, and young people was too closely coordinated for the men to work alone. The great Liberal John Bright, Quaker and cotton magnate, called the Ten Hours Act "a delusion practiced on the working classes." To regulate the hours of labor was contrary to the accepted principles of laissez faire, economic law, the free market, freedom of trade, and individual liberty for employer and worker. Yet the Ten Hours Act stood, and British industry continued to prosper.

Gathering their strength, the Whig-liberal-radical combination established in 1838 an Anti–Corn Law League. Wage earners objected to the Corn Laws because the tariff on grain imports kept up the price of food. Industrial employers objected to them because, in keeping up food prices, they also kept up wages and cost of production in England, thus working to England's disadvantage in the export trade. Defenders of the Corn Laws argued that protection of agriculture was necessary to maintain the natural aristocracy of the country (most land being owned by peers and gentry, as has been seen), but they also sometimes used more widely framed economic arguments, affirming that Britain should preserve a balanced economy as between industry and farming, and avoid becoming too exclusively dependent on imported food. The issue became a straight contest between the industrialists, acting with working-class support, and the aristocratic and predominantly Tory landowning interest. The Anti–Corn Law League, whose headquarters were at Manchester, operated like a modern political party. It had plenty of money, supplied by large donations from manufacturers and small ones from laboring people. It sent lecturers on tour, agitated in the newspapers, and issued a stream of polemical pamphlets and educational books. It held political teas, torchlight processions, and open-air mass meetings. The pressure proved irresistible and received a final impetus from a famine in Ireland. It was a Tory government, headed by Sir Robert Peel, which in 1846 yielded before so vociferous a demand.

The repeal of the Corn Laws in 1846 stands as a symbol of the change that had come over England. It reaffirmed the revolutionary consequences of the Reform Bill of 1832. Industry was now a governing element in the country. Free trade was henceforth the rule. Great Britain, in return for the export of manufactures, became deliberately dependent on imports for its very life. It was committed henceforth to an international and even world-wide economic system. The first to undergo the Industrial Revolution, possessing mechanical power and methods of mass production, the British could produce yarn and cloth, machine tools and railroad equipment, more efficiently and more cheaply than any other people. In Britain, the workshop of the world, people would pour increasingly into mine, factory, and city, live by selling manufactures, coal, shipping, and financial services to the other peoples of the earth, and obtain raw cotton, rare ores, meat, cereals, and thousands of lesser but still vital necessities from the rest of the earth in exchange. The welfare of Britain depended on the maintenance of a freely exchanging world-wide economic system.

It depended also, more than ever, on British control of the sea, which was rarely mentioned by the civilian-minded Anti–Corn Law League, but which, firmly

BIG INVESTMENTS
by Honoré Daumier (French, 1808–1879)

The Revolution of 1830, romanticized by Delacroix, was in fact followed by a period of moneymaking and business ferment (as well as genuine economic development) made famous in the novels of Balzac and the graphic art of Daumier. This lithograph of 1837 shows a financier, with bundles of stock certificates piled beside him, offering to sell shares in factories, foundries, breweries, etc., to a skeptical client. Daumier was a satirist and caricaturist of bourgeois society. Where Rembrandt in the seventeenth century could portray businessmen with a high seriousness (as on p. 161), artists since the 1830s have been generally alienated from such subjects. Courtesy of the Bibliothèque Nationale, Paris.

Grand placement d'actions.

J'ai aujourd'hui de bien bonnes actions à placer, M. Desrognaires, en voulez vous ? — C'est selon. Qu'avez-vous en actions ?
— J'ai 3000 actions de fonderies. — Affaire fondue ! — 3000 actions des usines — Usé, usé ! — 10,000 actions des
brasseries, opérations magnifiques. — Ou faites les mousser ! — J'en ai du recueil des connaissances. — Connu
comme ! Enfin, combien cela fait il en bloc — Un milliard ou deux pas plus. — Un milliard. le papier
se mieux ... cela doit donner une livres à 4 sous ça vaut 2 francs — Deux milliards pour 2 francs !
Y pensez-vous mon cher ? Mettez au moins 25 francs ! — Pas un liard. — Allons, enlevez. Vous faites
en marche d'or ! — Parceu ! vous me dites tous les jours la même chose.

established in the long duel with Napoleon, was now an assumed postulate of economic discussion. No one understood this better than Lord Palmerston, a flamboyant Anglo-Irish Whig aristocrat, who by risky and audacious moves that alarmed his colleagues and threw Queen Victoria into consternation, came forward as the very British bulldog in defense of Britain's name. For example, in 1850 a Moroccan Jew known as Don Pacifico, who was a British subject, got into trouble in Greece because of certain debts owed to him by the Greek government. Though the claim was not above question, Palmerston unloosed the thunders of the British fleet. He sent a squadron to the Piraeus, the port of Athens, and forbade Greek vessels the use of their own harbor until the matter was settled. On another occasion, in 1856, when Chinese authorities arrested a Chinese ship called the *Arrow*, which, though without due right, was flying the British flag, Palmerston again called on the navy, which proceeded to bombard Canton and precipitated the Second Anglo-Chinese War. In other connections, as a good mid–nineteenth-century liberal, Palmerston favored movements for national independence, including that of the Confederate States of America, expecting them to result in the further extension of free trade.

57. TRIUMPH OF THE WEST-EUROPEAN BOURGEOISIE

In both Great Britain and France (as also in Belgium) the revolutionary agitation of 1830–1832 ushered in a period of ascendancy for the bourgeois or propertied classes. The reigning liberal doctrine was the "stake in society" theory: those should govern who have something to lose. In the France of the July Monarchy (1830–1848) about one adult male in thirty could vote, in the Britain of the first Reform Bill (1832–1867) about one in eight. In Britain virtually the whole middle class was now enfranchised, in France only the most well-to-do. In Britain the continuation of the Tory landed interests in politics somewhat blunted the edge of capitalist and managerial rule, resulting in the passage of significant legislation for the protection of industrial labor. In France the aristocratic landed interest, weaker and less public spirited than in England in any case, lost much of its influence by the revolution of 1830. France under Louis Philippe was a more purely bourgeois country than Great Britain, and less was done to relieve the condition of labor.

In general, the decades following 1830 may be thought of as a kind of golden age of the west-European bourgeoisie. It left its mark on Europe in many ways. For one thing, western Europe continued to accumulate capital and build up its industrial plant. National income was constantly rising, but a relatively small share went to the laboring class, and a relatively large share went to owners of capital. This meant that less was spent on consumers' goods—housing, clothing, food, recreation—and that more was saved and available for reinvestment. New stock companies were constantly formed, and the law of corporations was amended, allowing for the extension of corporate enterprise to new fields. The factory system spread from Britain to the Continent and within Britain from the textile industry to other lines of production. The output of iron, a good index to economic advancement in this phase of industrialism, rose about 300 percent in Great Britain between 1830 and 1848 and about 65 percent in France between 1830 and 1845. (All the German states combined, at the latter date, produced about a tenth as much iron as Great Britain, and less than half as much as France.) Railroad building set in in earnest after 1840. In 1840 Samuel Cunard put four steamships in regular transatlantic service. Much capital was exported, as early as 1839 an American estimated that Europeans (mainly British) owned $200,000,000 worth of stocks in American companies. Such investments financed the purchase of British and other goods and helped to rivet together a world economic system, in which western Europe and especially England took the lead, with other regions remaining in a somewhat subordinate status.

The Frustration and Challenge of Labor

The bourgeois age had the effect also of estranging the world of labor. The state in Britain and France was as near as it has ever been to what Karl Marx was soon to call it—a committee of the bourgeois class. Already in France people spoke worriedly of the *prolétaires*, those at the bottom of society, who had nothing to lose. Republicans in France, radical democrats in Britain, felt cheated and imposed upon in the 1830s and 1840s. They had in each country forced through a virtual revolution by their insurrections and demonstrations and then in each country had been left without the vote. Some lost interest in representative institutions. Excluded from government, they were tempted to seek political ends through extragovernmental, which is to say revolutionary or utopian, channels. Social and economic reforms seemed to the average worker far more important, as a final aim, than mere governmental innovations. Workers were told by respected economists that they could not hope to change the system in their own favor. They were tempted, therefore, to destroy the system, to replace it utterly with some new system conceived mainly in the minds of thinkers. They were told by the Manchester School, and by its equivalent in France, that the income of labor was set by ineluctable natural laws, that it was best and indeed necessary for wages to remain low, and that the way to rise in the world was to get out of the laboring class altogether, by becoming the owner of a profitable business and leaving working people about where they were.[28]

The reigning doctrine emphasized the conception of a labor market. The worker sold labor, the employer bought it. The price of labor, or wage, was to be agreed upon by the two individual parties. The price would naturally fluctuate according to changes in supply and demand. When a great deal of a certain kind of labor was required the wage would go up, until new persons moved into the market offering more labor of this type, with the result that something like the old wage would again be established. When no labor was needed none should be bought, and persons who could not sell labor might then subsist for a time by poor relief. The new Poor Law of 1834 was especially repugnant to the British working classes. It corrected crying evils in the old system, which had pauperized and demoralized millions of people. But the new law followed the stern precepts of the dismal science; its main principle was to safeguard the labor market by making relief more unpleasant than any job. It granted relief only to persons willing to enter a workhouse, or poorhouse; and in these establishments the sexes were segregated and life was in other ways made noticeably less attractive than in the outside world. The workers considered the new law an abomination. They

[28] See pp. 433–435, 437.

called the workhouses "bastilles." They resented the whole conception of a labor market, in which labor was to be bought and sold (or remain unsold) like any other commodity.

In the long run it would be the increase of production in Europe that was to relieve the condition of the workers. Meanwhile there were two means of escape. One was to improve the position of labor in the market. This led to the formation of labor unions for control of the labor supply and collective bargaining with employers. Such unions, illegal in France, were barely legal in Great Britain after 1825, though it was still illegal in both countries to strike. The other means of escape was to repudiate the whole idea of a market economy and of the capitalist system. It was to conceive of a system in which goods were to be produced for use, not for sale; and in which working people should be compensated according to need, not according to the requirements of an employer. This was the basis of most forms of nineteenth-century socialism.[29]

Socialism and Chartism

Socialism spread rapidly among the working classes after 1830. In France it blended with revolutionary republicanism. There was a revival of interest in the great Revolution and the democratic Republic of 1793. Cheap reprints of the writings of Robespierre began to circulate in the working-class quarters of Paris. Robespierre was now seen as a people's hero. The socialist Louis Blanc, for example, who in 1839 published his *Organization of Work*, recommending the formation of "social workshops," also wrote a long history of the French Revolution, in which he pointed out the equalitarian ideals that had inspired the National Convention in 1793. In Britain, as befitted the different background of the country, socialistic ideas blended in with the movement for further parliamentary reform. This was advanced by the working-class group known as the Chartists, from the People's Charter which they drafted in 1838. Between the British Chartists and the French socialists there was considerable coming and going. One Chartist, the Irish-born journalist Bronterre O'Brien, translated a French book on the "conspiracy of Babeuf" of 1796, which itself was a source and inspiration of the rising socialism of France.[30]

Chartism was far more of a mass movement than the French socialism of the day. Only a few Chartists were clearly socialists in their own minds. But all were anticapitalistic. All could agree that the first step must be to win working-class representation in Parliament. The Charter of 1838 consisted of six points. It demanded (1) the annual election of the House of Commons by (2) universal suffrage for all adult males, through (3) a secret ballot and (4) equal electoral districts; and it called for (5) the abolition of property qualifications for membership in the House of Commons, which perpetuated the old idea that Parliament should be composed of gentlemen of independent income, and urged instead (6) the payment of salaries to the elected members of Parliament, in order that people of small means might serve. A convention composed of delegates sent by labor unions, mass meetings, and radical societies all over the country met in London in 1839. "Convention" was an ominous word, with French revolutionary and even terrorist overtones; some members of this British convention regarded it as the

[29] See pp. 438–440.
[30] See p. 381.

body really representing the people, and favored armed violence and a general strike, while others stood only for moral pressure upon Parliament.

A petition bearing over a million signatures, urging acceptance of the Charter, was submitted to the House of Commons. The violent and revolutionary wing, or "physical force" Chartists, precipitated a wave of riots which were effectively quelled by the authorities. In 1842 the petition was again submitted. This time, according to the best estimate, it was signed by 3,317,702 persons. Since the entire population of Great Britain was about 19 million it is clear that the Charter, whatever the exact number of signatures, commanded the explicit adherence of half the adult males of the country. The House of Commons nevertheless rejected the petition by 287 votes to 49. It was feared, with reason, that political democracy would threaten property rights and the whole economic system as they then existed. The Chartist movement gradually died down in the face of firm opposition by the government and the business classes, and was weakened by mutual fears and disagreements among its own supporters. It had not been entirely fruitless; for without popular agitation and the publicizing of working-class grievances, the Mines Act of 1842 and the Ten Hours Act of 1847 might not have been enacted. These measures in turn alleviated the distress of industrial workers and kept alive a degree of confidence in the future of the economic system. Chartism revived briefly in 1848, as will be seen in the next chapter; but in general, in the 1840s, British working people turned from political agitation to the forming and strengthening of labor unions, by which they could deal directly with employers without having to appeal to the government. Not until 1867 was the suffrage extended in Great Britain, and it took about eighty years to realize the full program of the Charter of 1838, except for the annual election of Parliament, for which there soon ceased to be any demand.

It is not easy to summarize the history of Europe between 1815 and 1848. Among all the forces set free by the French and Industrial revolutions—liberalism, conservatism, nationalism, republicanism, democracy, socialism—no stabilization had been achieved. No international system had been created; Europe had rather fallen into two camps, composed of a West in which liberal conceptions moved forward, and an East in which three autocratic monarchies held sway. Western Europe favored the principles of nationality; governments in central and eastern Europe still opposed them. The West was growing collectively richer, more liberal, more bourgeois. Middle-class people in Germany, central Europe, and Italy (as well as in Spain and Portugal) did not enjoy the dignities and emoluments that they enjoyed in Great Britain or France. But the West had not solved its social problem; its whole material civilization rested upon a restless and sorely tried working class. Everywhere there was repression, in varying degree, and everywhere apprehension, more in some places than in others; but there was also hope, confidence in the progress of an industrial and scientific society, and faith in the unfinished program of the rights of man. The result was the general Revolution of 1848.

XII.
Revolution and the Reimposition of Order, 1848-1870

ears haunting the established classes of Europe for thirty years came true in 1848. Governments collapsed all over the Continent. Remembered horrors appeared again, as in a recurring dream, in much the same sequence as after 1789 only at a much faster rate of speed. Revolutionaries milled in the streets, kings fled, republics were declared, and within four years there was another Napoleon. Soon thereafter came a series of wars.

Never before or since has Europe seen so truly universal an upheaval as in 1848. While the French Revolution of 1789 and the Russian Revolution of 1917 both had immediate international repercussions, in each of these cases a single country took the lead. In 1848 the revolutionary movement broke out spontaneously from native sources from Copenhagen to Palermo and from Paris to Budapest. Contemporaries sometimes attributed the universality of the phenomenon to the machinations of secret societies, and it is true that the faint beginnings of an international revolutionary movement existed before 1848; but the fact is that revolutionary plotters had little influence upon what actually happened, and the

Chapter Emblem: A medal showing St. Paul's Church at Frankfurt, then a new building in the neoclassic style, where the German National Assembly met in 1848–1849.

nearly simultaneous fall of governments is quite understandable from other causes. Many people in Europe wanted substantially the same things—constitutional government, the independence and unification of national groups, an end to serfdom and manorial restraints where they still existed. With some variation, there was a common body of ideas among politically conscious elements of all countries. Some of the powers that the new forces had to combat were themselves international, notably the Catholic church and the far-spreading influence of the Habsburgs, so that resistance to them arose independently in many places. In any case, only the Russian empire and Great Britain escaped the revolutionary contagion of 1848, and the British received a very bad scare.

But the Revolution of 1848, though it shook the whole Continent, lacked basic driving strength. It failed almost as rapidly as it succeeded. Its main consequence, in fact, was to strengthen the more conservative forces that viewed all revolution with alarm. Revolutionary ideals succumbed to military repression. To some extent the governments of the 1850s and 1860s, while hostile to revolution, satisfied some of the aims of 1848, notably in national unification and constitutional government with limited representation, but they did so in a mood of calculated realism, and while reasserting their own authority. The repressed Revolution of 1848 also left a legacy of class fears and class conflict, in which prophets of a new society also became more realistic, as when Karl Marx, branding earlier forms of socialism as "utopian," offered his own views as hard-headed and "scientific."

58. PARIS: THE SPECTER OF SOCIAL REVOLUTION IN THE WEST

The July Monarchy in France was a platform of boards built over a volcano. Under it burned the repressed fires of the republicanism put down in 1830, which since 1830 had become steadily more socialistic.[1]

Politics in the July Monarchy became increasingly more unreal. So few interests were represented in the Chamber of Deputies that the most basic issues were seldom debated. Even most of the bourgeois class had no representation. Graft and corruption were more common than they should have been, as economic expansion favored stockjobbing and fraud by business promoters and politicians in combination. A strong movement set in to give the vote to more people instead of to only one man in thirty. Radicals wanted universal suffrage and a republic, but liberals asked only for a broadening of voting rights within the existing constitutional monarchy. The king, Louis Philippe, and his prime minister, Guizot, instead of allying with the latter against the former, resolutely and obtusely opposed any change whatsoever.

The "February" Revolution in France

Reformers, against the king's expressed wishes, planned a great banquet in Paris for February 22, 1848, to be accompanied by demonstrations in the streets. The government on February 21 forbade all such meetings. That night barricades were built in the working-class quarters. These consisted of paving blocks, build-

---

[1] See pp. 456–458, 466–468.

ing stones, or large pieces of furniture thrown together across the narrow streets and intersections of the old city, and constituting a maze within which insurgents prepared to resist the authorities. The government called out the National Guard, which refused to move. The king now promised electoral reform, but republican firebrands took charge of the semimobilized working-class elements, which held a demonstration outside the house of Guizot. Someone shot at the guards placed around the house; the guards replied, killing twenty persons. The republican organizers put some of the corpses on a torch-lit cart and paraded them through the city, which, armed and barricaded, soon began to swarm in an enormous riot. On February 24 Louis Philippe, like Charles X before him, abdicated and made for England. The February Revolution of 1848, like the July Revolution of 1830, had unseated a monarch in three days.

The constitutional reformers hoped to carry on with Louis Philippe's young grandson as king, but the republicans, now aroused and armed, poured into the Chamber of Deputies and forced the proclamation of the Republic. Republican leaders set up a provisional government of ten men, pending election by all France of a Constituent Assembly. Seven of the ten were "political" republicans, the most notable being the poet Lamartine. Three were "social" republicans, the most notable being Louis Blanc. A huge crowd of workers appeared before the Hôtel de Ville, or city hall, demanding that France adopt the new socialist emblem—the red flag. They were dissuaded by the eloquence of Lamartine, and the tricolor remained the republican standard.

Louis Blanc urged the Provisional Government to push through a bold economic and social program without delay. But since the "social" republicans were in a minority in the Provisional Government (though probably not among Paris republicans generally), Louis Blanc's ideas were very much watered down in the application. He wanted a Ministry of Progress to organize a network of "social workshops," the state-supported and collectivist manufacturing establishments that he had projected in his writings. All that was created was a Labor Commission, with limited powers, and a system of shops significantly entitled "national" rather than "social." The National Workshops, as they are always called in English (though "workshop" suggests something more insignificant than Louis Blanc had in mind), were agreed to by the Provisional Government only as a political concession, and no significant work was ever assigned them to do, for fear of competition with private enterprise and dislocation of the economic system. Indeed, the man placed in charge of them admitted that his purpose was to prove the fallacies of socialism. Meanwhile the Labor Commission was unable to win public acceptance for the ten-hour day, which the British Parliament had enacted the year before.

The National Workshops became in practice only an extensive project in unemployment relief. Men of all trades, skilled and unskilled, were set to work digging on the roads and fortifications outside of Paris. They were paid two francs a day. The number of legitimate unemployed increased rapidly, for 1847 had been a year of depression and the revolution prevented the return of business confidence. Other needy persons also presented themselves for remuneration, and soon there were too many men for the amount of "work" made available. From 25,000 enrolled in the workshops by the middle of March, the number climbed to 120,000 by mid-June, by which time there were also in Paris another 50,000 whom the bulging workshops could no longer accommodate. In June there were probably almost 200,000 essentially idle but able-bodied men in a city of about a million people.

The Constituent Assembly, elected in April by universal male suffrage throughout France, met on May 4. It immediately replaced the Provisional Government with a temporary executive board of its own. The main body of France, a land of provincial bourgeois and peasant landowners, was not socialist in the least. The new temporary executive board, chosen by the new Constituent Assembly in May, included no "social" republicans. All five of its members, of whom Lamartine was the head, were known as outspoken enemies of Louis Blanc. Blanc and the socialists could no longer expect even the grudging and insincere concessions that they had so far obtained.

The battle lines were now drawn, after only three months of revolution, somewhat as they had been drawn in 1792 after three years.[2] Paris again stood for a degree of revolutionary action in which the rest of the country was not prepared to share. Revolutionary leaders in Paris, in 1848 as in 1792, were unwilling to accept the processes of majority rule or slow parliamentary deliberation. But the crisis in 1848 was more acute than in 1792. A larger proportion of the population were wage earners. Under a system of predominantly merchant capitalism, in which machine industry and factory concentration were only beginning, the workers were tormented by the same evils as the more industrialized working classes of England. Hours were if anything longer, and pay less, in France than in Great Britain; insecurity and unemployment were at least as great; and the feeling that a capitalist economy held no future for the laboring man was the same. In addition, where the English workingman shrank from the actual violation of Parliament, the French workingman saw nothing very sacrilegious in the violation of elected assemblies. Too many regimes in France since 1789, including those preferred by the comfortable classes, had been based on insurrectionary violence for the French workingman to feel much compunction over using it for his own ends.

The "June Days" of 1848

On the one hand stood the nationally elected Constituent Assembly. On the other, the National Workshops had mobilized in Paris the most distressed elements of the working class. Tens of thousands had been brought together where they could talk, read journals, listen to speeches, and concert common action. Agitators and organizers naturally made use of the opportunity thus presented to them. Men in the workshops began to feel desperate, to sense that the social republic was slipping from them perhaps forever. On May 15 they attacked the Constituent Assembly, drove its members out of the hall, declared it dissolved, and set up a new provisional government of their own. They announced that a social revolution must follow the purely political revolution of February. But the National Guard, a kind of civilian militia, turned against the insurgents and restored the Constituent Assembly. The Assembly, to root out socialism, prepared to get rid of the National Workshops. It offered those enrolled in them the alternatives of enlistment in the army, transfer to provincial workshops, or being put out of Paris by force. The whole laboring class in the city began to resist. The government proclaimed martial law, the civilian executive board resigned, and all power was given to General Cavaignac and the regular army.

[2] See pp. 369–372.

There followed the "Bloody June Days"—June 24–26, 1848—three days during which a terrifying class war raged in Paris. Over 20,000 men from the workshops took to arms (more would doubtless have done so had not the government continued to pay wages in the workshops during the insurrection), and they were joined by other unnumbered thousands from the working-class districts of the city. Half or more of Paris became a labyrinth of barricades defended by determined men and equally resolute women. Military methods of the time made it possible for civilians to shoot it out openly with soldiers; small arms were the main weapons, and armies had no armored vehicles or even any very devastating artillery. The soldiers found it a difficult operation, even several generals being killed, but after three days the outcome was in doubt no longer. Ten thousand persons had been killed or wounded. Eleven thousand insurgents were taken prisoner. The Assembly, refusing all clemency, decreed their immediate deportation to the colonies.

The June Days sent a shudder throughout France and Europe. Whether the battle in Paris had been a true class struggle, how large a portion of the laboring class had really participated (it was large in any case), how much they had fought for permanent objectives, and how much over the temporary issue of the workshops—all these are secondary questions. It was widely understood that a class war had in fact broken out. Militant workers were confirmed in a hatred and loathing of the bourgeois class, in a belief that capitalism existed in the last analysis by the callous shooting of laboring men in the streets. People above the laboring class were thrown into a panic. They were sure that they had narrowly escaped a ghastly upheaval. The very ground of civilized living seemed to have quaked. After June 1848, wrote a Frenchwoman of the time, society was "a prey to a feeling of terror incomparable to anything since the invasion of Rome by the barbarians."

Nor were the signs in England much more reassuring. There the Chartist agitation was revived by the February Revolution in Paris.[3] "France is a Republic!" cried the Chartist Ernest Jones; the Chartist petition was again circulated and was soon said to have 6 million signatures. Another Chartist convention met, considered by its leaders to be the forerunner of a Constituent Assembly as in France. The violent minority was the most active; it began to gather arms and to drill. The old Duke of Wellington swore in 70,000 special constables to uphold the social order. Clashes occurred at Liverpool and elsewhere; in London the revolutionary committee laid plans for systematic arson and organized men with pickaxes to break up the pavements for barricades. Meanwhile the petition, weighing 584 pounds, was carried in three cabs to the House of Commons, which estimated that it contained "only" 2 million signatures and again summarily rejected it. The revolutionary menace passed. One of the secret organizers in London proved to be a government spy; he revealed the whole plan at the critical moment, and the revolutionary committee was arrested on the day set for insurrection. Most Chartists had in any case refused to support the militants, but the truculent minority of radical workers and journalists had a deeper sense of envenomed class consciousness. The word "proletarian" was imported from France. "Every proletarian," wrote the Chartist editor of *Red Revolution*, "who does not see and feel that he belongs to an enslaved and degraded class is a *fool*."

The specter of social revolution thus hung over western Europe in the summer

---

[3] See pp. 468–469.

of 1848. Doubtless it was unreal; in all probability there could have been no successful socialist revolution at the time. But the specter was there, and it spread a sinking fear among all who had something to lose. This fear shaped the whole subsequent course of the Second Republic in France and of the revolutionary movements that had by this time begun in other countries as well.

The Emergence of Louis Napoleon Bonaparte

In France, after the June Days, the Constituent Assembly (keeping General Cavaignac as a virtual dictator) set about drafting a republican constitution. It was decided, in view of the disturbances just passed, to create a strong executive power in the hands of a president to be elected by universal male suffrage. It was decided also to have this president elected immediately, even before the rest of the constitution was finished. Four candidates presented themselves: Lamartine, Cavaignac, Ledru Rollin and Louis Napoleon Bonaparte. Lamartine stood for a somewhat vaguely moral and idealistic republic, Cavaignac for a republic of disciplined order, Ledru-Rollin for somewhat chastened "social" ideas. What Bonaparte stood for was not so clear. He was, however, elected by an avalanche of votes in December 1848, receiving over 5,400,000, to only 1,500,000 for Cavaignac, 370,000 for Ledru-Rollin, and a mere 18,000 for Lamartine.

Thus entered upon the European stage the second Napoleon. Born in 1808, Louis Napoleon Bonaparte was the nephew of the great Napoleon. His father, Louis Bonaparte, was at the time of his birth the king of Holland. When Napoleon's own son died in 1832 Louis Napoleon assumed the headship of the Bonaparte family. He resolved to restore the glories of the empire. With a handful of followers he tried to seize power at Strasbourg in 1836 and at Boulogne in 1840, leading what the following century would know as *Putsches*. Both failed ridiculously. Sentenced to life imprisonment in the fortress of Ham, he had escaped from it as recently as 1846 by simply walking off the grounds dressed as a stonemason. He expressed advanced social and political ideas, had probably joined the Carbonari in his youth, and had taken part in the Italian revolutionary uprising of 1830. He wrote two books, one called *Napoleonic Ideas*, claiming that his famous uncle had been misunderstood and checkmated by reactionary forces, and one called the *Extinction of Poverty*, a somewhat anticapitalistic tract like so many others of its time. But he was no friend of "anarchists," and in the spring of 1848, while still a refugee in England, he enrolled as one of Wellington's special constables to oppose the Chartist revolution. He soon returned to France. Compromised neither by the June Days nor by their repression, he was supposed to be a friend of the common people and at the same time a believer in order; and his name was Napoleon Bonaparte.

For twenty years a groundswell had been stirring the popular mind. It is known as the Napoleonic Legend. Peasants put up pictures of the emperor in their cottages, fondly imagining that it had been Napoleon who gave them the free ownership of their land. The completion of the Arch of Triumph in 1836 drove home the memory of imperial glories, and in 1840 the remains of the emperor were brought from St. Helena and majestically interred at the Invalides on the banks of the Seine. All this happened in a country where, government being in the hands of a few, most people had no political experience or political sense except what they had gained in revolution. When millions were suddenly, for the first time in their lives, asked to vote for a president in 1848, the name of Bonaparte was the only one they had ever heard of. "How should I not vote for this gentleman," said an old peasant, "I whose nose was frozen at Moscow?"

So Prince Louis Napoleon became president of the republic, by an overwhelming and indubitable popular mandate, in which an army officer was his only even faintly successful rival. He soon saw the way the wind was blowing. The Constituent Assembly dissolved itself in May 1849 and was replaced by the Legislative Assembly provided for in the new constitution. It was a strange assembly for a republic. It may be recalled that in 1797 the first normal election in the First Republic had produced a royalist majority.[4] Now in the Second Republic, under universal male suffrage, the result was the same. Five hundred of the deputies, or two-thirds, were really monarchists, but they were divided into irreconcilable factions—the Legitimists, who favored the line of Charles X, and the Orléanists, who favored that of Louis Philippe. One-third of the deputies called themselves republicans. Of these, in turn, about 180 were socialists of one kind or another; and only about 70 were political or old-fashioned republicans to whom the main issue was the form of government rather than the form of society itself.

The president and the Assembly at first combined to conjure away the specter of socialism, with which republicanism itself was now clearly associated. An abortive insurrection of June 1849 provided the chance. The Assembly, backed by the president, ousted thirty-three socialist deputies, suppressed public meetings, and imposed controls on the press. In 1850 it went so far as to rescind universal male suffrage, taking the vote away from about a third of the electorate—naturally the poorest and hence most socialistic third. The Falloux Law of 1850 put the schools at all levels of the educational system under supervision of the Catholic clergy; for, as M. Falloux said in the Assembly, "lay teachers have made the principles of social revolution popular in the most distant villages," and it was necessary "to rally around religion to strengthen the foundations of society against those who want to divide up property." The French Republic, now actually an antirepublican government, likewise intervened against the revolutionary republic established by Mazzini in the city of Rome. French military forces were sent to Rome to protect the pope; they remained there twenty years.

To the conservatives Bonaparte knew that he was virtually indispensable. They were so sharply divided between two sets of monarchists—Legitimist and Orléanist—that each would accept any antisocialist regime rather than yield to the other. Bonaparte's problem was to win over the radicals. He did so by urging in 1851 the restoration of universal suffrage, which he had himself helped repeal in 1850. He now posed as the people's friend, the one man in public life who trusted the common man. He let it be thought that greedy plutocrats controlled the Assembly and hoodwinked France. He put his lieutenants in as ministers of war and of the interior, thus controlling the army, the bureaucracy, and the police. On December 2, 1851, the anniversary of Austerlitz, he sprang his coup d'état. Placards appeared all over Paris. They declared the Assembly dissolved and the vote for every adult Frenchman reinstated. When members of the Assembly tried to meet, they were attacked, dispersed, or arrested by the soldiers. The country did not submit without fighting. One hundred and fifty persons were killed in Paris, and throughout France probably 100,000 were put under arrest. But on December 20 the voters elected Louis Napoleon president for a term of ten years, by a vote officially stated as 7,439,216 to 646,737. A year later the new Bonaparte proclaimed the empire, with himself as emperor of the French. Remembering Napoleon's son, he called himself Napoleon III.

How the empire functioned will be seen below. Not only the republic was dead. The republic as republicans understood it, an equalitarian, anticlerical regime with socialist or at least antibourgeois tendencies, had been dead since June 1848. Feeble anyway, it was killed by its reputation for radicalism. Liberalism and constitutionalism were dead also. Bourgeois and property-owning monarchists were greater sticklers for constitutional liberalism than were the republicans or the Bonapartists or than town laborers or rural peasants. But the monarchists, hopelessly divided among themselves, were now pushed aside. For the first time since 1815 France ceased to have any parliamentary life. It was ruled by a dictatorship, more demagogic, more calculating, more hollow, and more modern than any that the first Napoleon had ever imagined.

59. VIENNA: THE NATIONALIST REVOLUTION IN CENTRAL EUROPE AND ITALY

The Austrian Empire in 1848

The Austrian Empire of the Habsburgs, with its capital at Vienna, was in 1848 the most populous European state except Russia. Its peoples, living principally in the three major geographical divisions of the empire, Austria, Bohemia, and Hungary, were of about a dozen recognizably different nationalities or language groups— Germans, Czechs, Magyars, Poles, Ruthenians, Slovaks, Serbs, Croats, Slovenes, Dalmatians, Rumanians, and Italians.[5] In some parts of the empire the nationalities lived in solid blocks, but in many regions two or more were interlaced together, the language changing from village to village, or even from house to house, in a way quite unknown in western Europe.

Germans, the leading people, occupied all of Austria proper and considerable parts of Bohemia, and were scattered also in small pockets throughout Hungary. The Czechs occupied Bohemia and the adjoining Moravia. The Magyars were the dominant group in the historic kingdom of Hungary, which contained a mixture of nationalities with a considerable number of Slavic peoples. Two of the most advanced parts of Italy also belonged to the empire—Venetia, with its capital at Venice, and Lombardy, whose chief city was Milan.

The Czechs, Poles, Ruthenians, Slovaks, Serbs, Croats, Slovenes, and Dalmatians in the empire were all Slavs; i.e., their languages were all related to one another and to the several forms of Russian. Neither the Magyars nor the Rumanians were Slavs. The Magyars, as national sentiment grew, prided themselves on the uniqueness of their language in Europe and the Rumanians on their linguistic affiliations with the Latin peoples of the West. Rumanians, Magyars, and Germans formed a thick belt separating the South Slavs (in later years called Yugoslavs) from those of the north. Germans and Italians within the empire were in continual touch with Germans and Italians outside. The peoples of the empire

[5] See maps, pp. 216, 420–421, 441; and pp. 215–219, 265–268, 318–322, 397–398, 422.

represented every cultural level known to Europe. Vienna, where the Waltz King Johann Strauss was reigning, recognized no peer except Paris itself. Milan was a great center of trade. Bohemia had long had a textile industry of importance, which was beginning to be mechanized in the 1840s; but 200 miles to the south a Croatian intellectual remarked, about the same time, that the first steam engine he ever saw was in a picture printed on a cotton handkerchief imported from Manchester. In 1848, some denied that any such people as the Ruthenians existed at all. Nor was it clear exactly what groups made up the South Slavs. No such word as Yugoslavia or Czechoslovakia had been invented, and Rumania was a term used only by professors.

Thus the empire ruled from Vienna included, according to political frontiers established seventy years later, in 1918, all of Austria, Hungary, and Czechoslovakia, with adjoining portions of Poland, Rumania, Yugoslavia, and Italy. But the political authority of Vienna reached far beyond the borders of the empire. Austria since 1815 had been the most influential member of the German confederation, for Prussia in these years was content to look with deference upon the Habsburgs. The influence of Vienna was felt throughout Germany in many ways, as in the enactment and enforcement of the Carlsbad Decrees mentioned in the last chapter.[6] It reached also through the length of Italy. Lombardy and Venetia were part of the Austrian Empire. Tuscany, ostensibly independent, was governed by a Habsburg grand duke. The kingdom of Naples or the Two Sicilies, comprising all Italy south of Rome, was virtually a protectorate of Vienna. The papal states looked politically to Vienna for leadership, at least until 1846, when the College of Cardinals elected a liberal-minded pope, Pius IX—the one contingency upon which Metternich confessed he had failed to reckon. In all Italy there was only one state ruled by a native Italian dynasty and attempting any consistent independence of policy—the kingdom of Sardinia (called also Savoy or Piedmont) tucked away in the northwest corner around Turin. Italy, said Metternich blandly, was only a "geographical expression," a mere regional name. He might have said the same of Poland, or even of Germany, though Germany was tenuously joined in the Bund, or loose confederation, of 1815.

These peoples since the turn of the century had all felt the flutters of the *Volksgeist*, persistent stirrings of a cultural nationalism, and among Germans, Italians, Poles, and Hungarians a good deal of political agitation and liberal reformism had been at work. Metternich, in Vienna, had discouraged such manifestations for over thirty years, ominously predicting that if allowed to break out they would produce the *bellum omnium contra omnes*—"the war of all against all." As a prophet he was not wholly mistaken, but if it is the business of statesmanship not merely to prophesy events but to control them it cannot be said that the regime of Metternich was very successful. The whole nationalities question was evaded. The fundamental problem of the century, the bringing of peoples into some kind of mutual and moral relationship with their governments—the problem of which nationalism, liberalism, constitutionalism, and democracy were diverse aspects—remained unconsidered by the responsible authorities of central Europe. All that Metternich offered was the idea that a reigning house, with an official bureaucracy, should rule benevolently over peoples with whom it need have no connection and who need have no connection with each other. They

[6] See pp. 447–448.

were the ideas of the eighteenth century, dating from before the French Revolution and best suited to an agricultural and localistic society.

The March Days

In March 1848, everything collapsed with incredible swiftness. At that time the diet of Hungary had been sitting for some months, considering constitutional reforms and, as usual, debating further means of keeping German influence out of Hungary. Then came news of the February Revolution in Paris. The radical party in the Hungarian diet was aroused. Its leader, Louis Kossuth, on March 3 made an impassioned speech on the virtues of liberty. This speech was immediately printed in German and read in Vienna, where restlessness was also heightened by the news from Paris. On March 13 workingmen and students rose in insurrection in Vienna, manned barricades, fought off soldiers, and invaded the imperial palace. So flabbergasted and terrified was the government that Metternich, to the amazement of Europe, resigned and fled in disguise to England.

The fall of Metternich proved that the Vienna government was entirely disoriented. Revolution swept through the empire and through all Italy and Germany. On March 15 rioting began in Berlin; the king of Prussia promised a constitution. The lesser German governments collapsed in sequence. On the last day of March a Pre-Parliament met to arrange the calling of an all-German national assembly. In Hungary, aroused by Kossuth's national party, the diet on March 15 enacted the March Laws, by which Hungary assumed a position of complete constitutional separatism within the empire, while still recognizing the Habsburg house. The harassed Emperor Ferdinand a few days later granted substantially the same status to Bohemia. At Milan between March 18 and 22 the populace drove out the Austrian garrison. Venice proclaimed itself an independent republic. Tuscany drove out its grand duke and also set up as a republic. The king of Sardinia,[7] Charles Albert (who, stimulated by the Paris revolution, had granted a constitution to his small country on March 4) declared war on Austria on March 23 and invaded Lombardy-Venetia, hoping to bring that area under the house of Savoy. Italian troops streamed up from Tuscany, from Naples (where revolution had broken out as early as January), and even from the papal states (the new pope being in some sympathy with national and liberal aims) to join in an all-Italian war against the seemingly helpless Austrian government.

Thus in the brief span of these phenomenal March Days the whole structure based on Vienna went to pieces. The Austrian Empire had fallen into its main components, Prussia had yielded to revolutionaries, all Germany was preparing to unify itself, and war raged in Italy. Everywhere constitutions had been wildly promised by stupefied governments, constitutional assemblies were meeting, and independent or autonomous nations struggled into existence. Patriots everywhere demanded liberal government and national freedom—written constitutions, representative assemblies, responsible ministries, a more or less extended suffrage, restrictions upon police action, jury trial, civil liberty, freedom of press and assembly. And where it still existed—in Prussia, Galicia, Bohemia, Hungary—serfdom

---

[7] "Sardinia" was in the northwest corner of the Italian mainland. See the note on p. 189 for an explanation of how this state, with its capital at Turin and its seaport at Genoa, came to be called after the rather desolate island of Sardinia. Of the king and kingdom we must say "Sardinia"; of the dynasty, "Savoy"; the state was often also called "Piedmont."

was declared abolished and the peasant masses became legally free from control by their local lords.

The Turning of the Tide after June

The revolution, as in France, surged forward until the month of June, and then began to ebb. For its steady reflux there are many reasons. The old governments had been only stunned in the March Days, not really broken. They merely awaited the opportunity to take back promises extorted by force. The force originally imposed by the revolutionaries could not be sustained. The revolutionary leaders were not really very strong. Middle-class, bourgeois, property-owning, and commercial interests were nowhere nearly as highly developed as in western Europe. The revolutionary leaders were to a large extent writers, editors, professors, and students, men of ideas rather than spokesmen for large positive interests. In Vienna, Milan, and a few other cities the working class was numerous and socialist ideas fairly common; but the workers were not as literate, organized, politically conscious, or irritated as in Paris or Great Britain. They were strong enough, however, to disquiet the middle classes; and especially after the specter of social revolution rose over western Europe, the middle-class and lower-class revolutionaries began to be afraid of each other. The liberated nationalities also began to disagree. The peasants, once emancipated, had no further interest in revolution. Nor were the peasants at this time conscious of nationality; nationalism was primarily a doctrine of the educated middle classes or of the landowning classes in Poland and Hungary. Since the old internationally minded aristocracy furnished the bulk of officers in the armies, and the peasants the bulk of the soldiers, the armies remained almost immune to nationalist aspirations. This attitude of the armies was decisive.

The tide first turned in Prague. The all-German national assembly met at Frankfurt-on-the-Main in May. Representatives from Bohemia had been invited to come to Frankfurt, since many Germans had always lived in Bohemia, and since Bohemia formed part of the confederation of 1815 as it had of the Holy Roman Empire before it. But the idea of belonging to a national German state, a Germany based on the principle that the inhabitants were Germans (which had not been the principle of the Holy Roman Empire or of the confederation of 1815) did not appeal to the Czechs in Bohemia. They refused to go to the all-German congress at Frankfurt. Instead, they called an all-Slav congress of their own. At Prague, in June 1848, this first Pan-Slav assembly met. Most of the delegates were from the Slav communities within the Austrian Empire, but a few came from the Balkans and non-Austrian Poland. Only one Russian was present, the anarchist revolutionary Michael Bakunin. Slavs generally did not at this time look with favor upon Russia, the oppressor of Poles; nor did the tsarist government, under Nicholas I, think well of Pan-Slavism, seeing in it a subversive popular agitation.

The spirit of the Prague congress was that of the Slavic Revival described in the last chapter;[8] the Czech historian Palacky was in fact one of its most active figures. The congress was profoundly anti-German, since the essence of the Slavic Revival was resistance to Germanization. But it was not profoundly anti-Austrian or anti-Habsburg. A few extremists, indeed, maintained that Slavdom should be

[8] See pp. 443-444.

the basis of political regeneration, and that the world therefore had no place for an Austrian empire. But the great majority at the Prague congress were Austroslavs. Austroslavism held that the many Slavic peoples, pressed on two sides by the population masses of Russians and Germans, needed the Austrian Empire as a political frame within which to develop their own national life. It demanded that the Slavic peoples be admitted as equals with the other nationalities in the Austrian Empire, enjoying local autonomy and constitutional guarantees.

The Germans of Bohemia, the Sudeten Germans, were of course attracted to the Frankfurt Assembly. They were eager to be included in the unified Germany about to be formed. As the Bohemian Czechs would be a minority in a German Germany, so the Bohemian Germans would be a minority in a Czech Bohemia. There was therefore friction among the mixed people of Bohemia and in Prague, a bilingual city.

Victories of the Counterrevolution, June–December

But the Emperor Ferdinand, and the advisers on whom he chose to rely, would have nothing to do with national movements, since they were also liberal, bristling with restrictions upon the powers of the state. All therefore were to be resisted. The first victory of the old government came at Prague. In that city a Czech insurrection broke out on June 12, at the time when the Slav congress was sitting, and was made worse by local animosities between Czechs and Germans. Windischgrätz, the local army commander, bombarded and subdued the city. The Slav congress dispersed. The Habsburg army was in control.

The next victory of the counterrevolution came in north Italy in the following month. Only Lombardy-Venetia, of all parts of the empire, had declared independence from the Habsburgs during the upheavals of March. The diminutive kingdom of Sardinia had lent support and had declared war on Austria. Italians from all over the peninsula had flocked in to fight; and until after the June Days in Paris it seemed not impossible that republican France might intervene, to befriend fellow revolutionaries, as in 1796. But in France no radical or expansionist revolution succeeded. The Italians were left to themselves. Radetsky, the Austrian commander in Italy, overwhelmingly defeated the king of Sardinia at Custozza on July 25. The Sardinian king, Charles Albert, retreated into his own country. Lombardy and Venetia were restored with savage vengeance to the Austrian Empire.

The third victory of the counterrevolution came in September and October. The Hungarian radical party of Louis Kossuth was liberal and even democratic in many of its principles, but it was a Magyar nationalist party above all else. Triumphant in the March Days, it completely shook off the German connection. It moved the capital from Pressburg near the Austrian border to Budapest in the center of Hungary. It changed the official language of Hungary from Latin to Magyar. Less than half the people of Hungary were Magyars, and Magyar is an extremely difficult language, quite alien to the Indo-European tongues of Europe. It soon became clear that one must be a Magyar to benefit from the new liberal constitution, and that the Magyars intended to denationalize and Magyarize all others with whom they shared the country. Slovaks, Rumanians, Germans, Serbs, and Croats violently resisted, each group determined to keep its own national identity unimpaired. The Croats, who had enjoyed certain Croatian liberties before the Magyar revolution, took the lead under Count Jellachich, the "ban," or provincial governor, of Croatia. In September Jellachich raised a civil war in Hungary, leading a force of Serbo-Croatians, supported by the whole non-Magyar half of the population. Half of Hungary, alarmed by Magyar nationalism, now looked to the Habsburgs and the empire to protect them. Emperor Ferdinand made Jellachich his military commander against the Magyars. Hungary dissolved into the war of all against all.

At Vienna the more clear-sighted revolutionaries, who had led the March rising, now saw that Jellachich's army, if successful against the Magyars, would soon be turned against them. They therefore rose in a second mass insurrection in October 1848. The emperor fled; never had the Viennese revolution gone so far. But it was already too late. The Austrian military leader Windischgrätz brought his intact forces down from Bohemia. He besieged Vienna for five days and forced its surrender on October 31.

With the recapture of Vienna the upholders of the old order took heart. Counterrevolutionary leaders—large estate holders, Catholic clergy, high-ranking army men—decided to clear the way by getting rid of the Emperor Ferdinand, considering that promises made in March by Ferdinand might be more easily repudiated by his successor. Ferdinand abdicated and on December 2, 1848, was succeeded by Francis Joseph, a boy of eighteen, destined to live until 1916 and to end his reign in a crisis even more shattering than that in which he began it.

Final Outburst and Repression, 1849

For a time in that first part of 1849 the revolution in many places seemed to blaze more fiercely than ever. Republican riots broke out in parts of Germany. In Rome someone assassinated the reforming minister of Pius IX. The pope fled from the city, and a radical Roman Republic was proclaimed under three Triumvirs, one of whom was Mazzini, who hastened from England to take part in the republican upheaval. In north Italy Charles Albert of Sardinia again invaded Lombardy. In Hungary, after the revived Habsburg authorities repudiated the new Magyar constitution, the Magyars, led by the flaming Kossuth, went on to declare absolute independence. But all these manifestations proved short-lived. German republicanism flickered out. Mazzini and his republicans were driven from Rome, and Pius IX was restored, by intervention of the French army.[9] The Sardinian king was again defeated by an Austrian army on March 23, 1849. In Hungary the Magyars put up a terrific resistance, which the imperial army and the anti-Magyar native irregulars could not overcome. The Habsburg authorities now renewed the procedures of the Holy Alliance. The new Emperor Francis Joseph invited the Tsar Nicholas to intervene. Over a hundred thousand Russian troops poured over the mountains into Hungary, soon defeated the Magyars, and laid the prostrate country at the feet of the court of Vienna. This was in August 1849.

The nationalist upheaval of 1848 in central Europe and Italy was now over. The Habsburg authority had been reasserted over Czech nationalists in Prague, Magyars in Hungary, Italian patriots in north Italy, and liberal revolutionists in Vienna itself. Reaction, or antirevolutionism, became the order of the day. Pius IX, the "liberal pope" of 1846, resumed the papal throne, disillusioned in his liberal ideas. The breach between liberalism and Roman Catholicism, which had

⁹ See p. 476.

opened wide in the first French Revolution, was made a yawning chasm by the revolutionary violence of Mazzini's Roman Republic and by the measures taken to repress it. Pius IX now reiterated the anathemas of his predecessors. He codified them in 1864 in the *Syllabus of Errors*, which warned all Catholics, on the authority of the Vatican, against everything that went under the names of liberalism, progress, and civilization. As for the nationalists in Italy, many were disillusioned with the firecracker methods of romantic republicans and inclined to conclude that Italy would be liberated from Austrian influence only by an old-fashioned war between established powers.

In the Austrian Empire, under Prince Schwarzenberg, the emperor's chief minister, the main policy was now to oppose all forms of popular self-expression, with a sophistication, in view of the events of 1848, that Metternich had never known, and with a candid reliance on military force. Constitutionalism was to be rooted out, as well as all forms of nationalism—Slavism, Magyarism, Italianism, and also Germanism, which would draw the sentiments of Austrian Germans from the Habsburg empire to the great kindred body of the German people. The regime came to be called the Bach system, after Alexander Bach, the minister of the interior. Under it, the government was rigidly centralized. Hungary lost the separate rights it had had before 1848. The ideal was to create a perfectly solid and unitary political system. Bach insisted on maintaining the emancipation of the peasants, which had converted the mass of the people from subjects of their landlords into subjects of the state. He drove through a reform of the legal system and law courts, created a free trading area of the whole empire with only a common external tariff, and subsidized and encouraged the building of highways and railroads. The aim, as in France at the same time under Louis Napoleon, was to make people forget liberty in an overwhelming demonstration of administrative efficiency and material progress. But some, at that time, would not forget. A liberal said of the Bach system that it consisted of "a standing army of soldiers, a sitting army of officials, a kneeling army of priests, and a creeping army of informers."

60. FRANKFURT AND BERLIN: THE QUESTION OF A LIBERAL GERMANY

The German States

Meanwhile, from May 1848 to May 1849, the Frankfurt Assembly was sitting at the historic city on the Main. It was attempting to bring a unified German state into being, one which should also be liberal and constitutional, assuring civil rights to its citizens and possessing a government responsive to popular will as manifested in free elections and open parliamentary debate. The failure to produce a democratic Germany was long one of the overshadowing facts of modern times.

The convocation of the Frankfurt Assembly was made possible by the collapse of the existing German governments in the March Days of 1848. These governments, the thirty-nine states recognized after the Congress of Vienna, were the main obstacles in the way of unification. The reigning princes and their ministers enjoyed a heightened political stature from political independence. The German states resisted the surrender of sovereignty to a united Germany just as national states in the next century were to resist the surrender of sovereignty to a United Nations. In another way Germany was a miniature of the political world. It consisted of both great and small powers. Its great powers were Prussia and Austria. Austria was the miscellaneous empire described above. Prussia after 1815 included the Rhineland; the central regions around Berlin; West Prussia and Posen (acquired in the partitions of Poland); and historic East Prussia. The former Polish areas were inhabited by a mixture of Germans and Poles.[10] Neither of these great powers could submit to the other or allow the other to dominate its lesser German neighbors. The small German powers, in turn, upheld their own independence in the balance between the two great ones.

This German "dualism," or polarity between Berlin and Vienna, had been somewhat abated under the common menace of the Napoleonic empire. The whole German question had lain dormant, so far as the governments were concerned, nor did it agitate the old aristocracies. In Prussia the Junkers, the owners of great landed estates east of the Elbe, were singularly indifferent to the all-German dream. Their political feeling was not German but Prussian. They were making a good thing of Prussia for themselves and could expect only to lose by absorption into Germany as a whole, for in Germany west of the Elbe the small peasant holding was the basis of society, and there was no landowning element corresponding to the Junkers. The rest of Germany looked upon Prussia as somewhat uncouth and Eastern; but this feeling, too, had been abated in the time of Napoleon, when patriots from all over Germany enlisted in the Prussian service.[11]

Berlin: Failure of the Revolution in Prussia

Prussia was illiberal but not backward. Frederick William III repeatedly evaded his promise to grant a modern constitution. His successor, Frederick William IV, who inherited the throne in 1840, and from whom much was at first hoped by liberals, proved to be a somewhat cloudy and neomedieval romantic, equally determined not to share his authority with his subjects. At the same time the government, administratively speaking, was efficient, progressive, and fair. The universities and elementary school system surpassed those of western Europe. Literacy was higher than in England or France. The government followed in mercantilist traditions of evoking, planning, and supporting economic life.[12] In 1818 it initiated a tariff union, at first with tiny states (or enclaves) wholly enclosed within Prussia. This tariff union, or *Zollverein*, was extended in the following decades to include almost all Germany.

On March 15, 1848, as noted above, rioting and street fighting broke out in Berlin. For a time it seemed as if the army would master the situation. But the king, Frederick William IV, a man of notions and projects, and erratically conscientious, called off the soldiers and allowed his subjects to elect the first all-Prussian legislative assembly. Thus though the army remained intact, and its Junker officers unconvinced, revolution proceeded superficially on its way. The Prussian Assembly proved surprisingly radical, since it was dominated by anti-Junker lower-class extremists from East Prussia. These men were supporting Polish revolutionaries and exiles who sought the restoration of Polish freedom.

---

[10] See maps, pp. 222–223, 420–421; and see pp. 220–227, 239, 422–423.
[11] See pp. 412–413.
[12] See pp. 116–118, 225, 322–323.

Their main belief was that the fortress of reaction was tsarist Russia—that the whole structure of Junkerdom, landlordism, serf-owning, and repression of national freedom depended ultimately on the armed might of the tsarist empire. (The subsequent intervention of Russia in Hungary indicated the truth of this diagnosis.) Prussian radicals, like many elsewhere, hoped to smash the Holy Alliance by raising an all-German or even European revolutionary war against Russia, to precipitate which they supported the claims of the Poles.

Meanwhile the radical-dominated Berlin Assembly granted local self-government to the Poles of West Prussia and Posen. But in those areas Germans and Slavs had long lived side by side. The Germans in Posen refused to respect the authority of Polish officials. Prussian army units stationed in Posen supported the German element. As early as April 1848, a month after the "revolution," the army crushed the new pro-Polish institutions set up in Posen by the Berlin Assembly. It was clear where the only real power lay. By the end of 1848, in Prussia as in Austria, the revolution was over. The king again changed his mind; and the old authorities, acting through the army, were again in control.

The Frankfurt Assembly

Meanwhile a similar story was enacted on the larger stage of Germany as a whole. The disabling of the old governments left a power vacuum. A self-appointed committee convoked a Pre-Parliament, which in turn arranged for the election of an all-German assembly. Bypassing the existing sovereignties, voters throughout Germany sent delegates to Frankfurt to create a federated superstate. The strength and weakness of the resulting Frankfurt Assembly originated in this manner of its election. The Assembly represented the moral sentiment of people at large, the liberal and national aspirations of many Germans. It stood for an idea. Politically it represented nothing. The delegates had no power to issue orders or expect compliance. Superficially resembling the National Assembly which met in France in 1789, the German National Assembly at Frankfurt was really in a very different position. There was no preexisting national structure for it to work with. There was no all-German army or civil service for the Assembly to take over. The Frankfurt Assembly, having no power of its own, became dependent on the power of the very sovereign states that it was attempting to supersede.

The Assembly met in May 1848. Its members with a handful of exceptions were not at all revolutionary. They were overwhelmingly professional people—professors, judges, lawyers, government administrators, clergy both Protestant and Catholic, and prominent businessmen. They wanted a liberal, self-governing, federally unified, and "democratic" though not equalitarian Germany. Their outlook was earnest, peaceable, and legalistic; they hoped to succeed by persuasion. Violence was abhorrent to them. They wanted no armed conflict with the existing German states. They wanted no war with Russia. They wanted no general international upheaval of the working classes. The example of the June Days in Paris, and of the Chartist agitation in Great Britain, coinciding with the early weeks of the Frankfurt Assembly, increased the dread of that body for radicalism and republicanism in Germany. The tragedy of Germany (and hence of Europe) lies in the fact that this German revolution came too late, at a time when social revolutionaries had already begun to declare war on the bourgeoisie, and the bourgeoisie was already afraid of the common man. It is the common man, not the professor or respectable merchant, who in unsettled times actually seizes firearms and rushes to shout revolutionary utterances in the streets. Without lower-class insurrection not even middle-class revolutions have been successful. The combination effected in France between 1789 and 1794, an unwilling and divergent combination of bourgeois and lower-class revolutionaries, was not and could not be effected in Germany in 1848. One form of revolutionary power—controlled popular turbulence—the Germans of the Frankfurt Assembly would not or could not use. Quite the contrary: when radical riots broke out in Frankfurt itself in September 1848 the Assembly undertook to repress them. Having no force of its own, it appealed to the Prussian army. The Prussian army put down the riots, and thereafter the Assembly met under its protection.

But the most troublesome question facing the Frankfurt Assembly was not social but national. What, after all, was this "Germany" which so far existed only in the mind? Where was the line really to be drawn in space? Did Germany include Austria and Bohemia, which belonged to the Bund of 1815 and had in former days belonged to the Holy Roman Empire?[13] Did it include all Prussia, although eastern Prussia had lain outside the Empire and did not now belong to the Bund? On the side toward Denmark, did it include the duchies of Schleswig and Holstein, which belonged to the Danish king, who was therefore himself, as ruler of Holstein, a member of the 1815 confederation? And if, as poets said, the Fatherland existed wherever the German tongue was spoken, what of the German communities in Hungary and Moravia, or along the upper Baltic and in the city of Riga, or in some of the Swiss cantons and the city of Zurich, or for that matter in Holland, which had left the Holy Roman Empire only two hundred years before —not long as time is measured in Europe.

These last and most soaring speculations, though they had already been launched by a few bold spirits, were put out of mind by the men of the Frankfurt Assembly. The other questions remained. The men at Frankfurt, eager to create a real Germany, naturally could not offer one smaller than the shadow Germany that they so much deplored. Most therefore were Great Germans; they thought that the Germany for which they were writing a constitution should include the Austrian lands, except Hungary. This would mean that the federal crown must be offered to the Habsburgs. Others, at first a minority, were Little Germans; they thought that Austria should be excluded, and that the new Germany should comprise the smaller states and the entire kingdom of Prussia. In that case the king of Prussia would become the federal emperor.

The desire of the Frankfurt Assembly to retain non-German peoples in the new Germany, at a time when these peoples also were feeling national ambitions, was another reason for its fatal dependency upon the Austrian and Prussian armies. The Frankfurt Assembly applauded when Windischgrätz broke the Czech revolution. It expressed its satisfaction when Prussian forces put down the Poles in Posen. On this matter the National Assembly at Frankfurt and the Prussian Assembly at Berlin did not agree. The men of Frankfurt, thinking the Prussian revolutionary assembly too radical and pro-Polish, and wanting no war with Russia, in effect supported the Prussian army and the Junkers against the Berlin revolution, without which the Frankfurt Assembly itself could never have existed.

[13] See maps, pp. 317, 420–421, 522.

A still clearer case arose over Schleswig-Holstein. These duchies belonged to the Danish king. Schleswig, the northern of the two, had a mixed population of Danes and Germans. The Germans in Schleswig rebelled in March 1848; and the Danes, who also had a constitutional upheaval at the time, proceeded to incorporate Schleswig integrally into their modernized Danish state. When the Frankfurt Assembly met, it found that the Pre-Parliament had already declared an all-German war upon Denmark in defense of fellow Germans in Schleswig. Having no army of its own, the Frankfurt Assembly invited Prussia to fight the war; and the revolutionary Prussian government in Berlin was at first able to persuade the Prussian generals to initiate a campaign. Great Britain and Russia prepared to intervene to keep control of the mouth of the Baltic out of German hands. The Prussian army simply withdrew from the war. Its officers had no desire to antagonize Russia or to advance the interests of nationalist revolutionaries in Germany. The Frankfurt Assembly, humiliated and helpless, was obliged to accept the armistice concluded by the Prussian generals. Radical socionationalistic riots broke out against the Junkers, the tsar, and the Frankfurt Assembly; and it was at this time that the Assembly called in Prussian forces for its own protection.

The Failure of the Frankfurt Assembly

By the end of 1848 the debacle was approaching. The nationalists had checkmated each other. Everywhere in central Europe, from Denmark to Naples and from the Rhineland to the Transylvanian forests, the awakening nationalities had failed to respect each other's aspirations, had delighted in each other's defeats, and by quarreling with each other had hastened the return of the old absolutist and nonnational order. At Berlin and at Vienna the counterrevolution, backed by the army, was in the saddle. At this very time, in December, the Frankfurt Assembly at last issued a Declaration of the Rights of the German People. It was a humane and high-minded document, announcing numerous individual rights, civil liberties, and constitutional guarantees, much along the line of the French and American declarations of the eighteenth century, but with one significant difference—the French and Americans spoke of the rights of man, the Germans of the rights of Germans. In April 1849 the Frankfurt Assembly completed its constitution. It was now clear that Austria must be excluded, for the simple reason that the restored Habsburg government refused to come in. The Danubian empire, as already seen, was as profoundly opposed to Germanism as to any other nationalistic movement. The Little Germans in the Assembly therefore had their way. The hereditary headship of a new German empire, a constitutional and federal union of German states minus Austria, was now offered to Frederick William IV, the king of Prussia.

Frederick William was tempted. The Prussian army officers and East-Elbian landlords were not. They had no wish to lose Prussia in Germany. The king himself had his scruples. If he took the proffered crown he would still have to impose himself by force on the lesser states, which the Frankfurt Assembly did not represent and could not bind, and which were in fact still the actual powers in the country. He could also expect trouble with Austria. He did not wish war. Nor was it proper for an heir to the Hohenzollerns to accept a throne circumscribed with constitutional limitations and representing the revolutionary conception of the sovereignty of the people. Declaring that he could not "pick up a crown from the gutter," he turned it down. It would have to be offered freely by his equals, the sovereign princes of Germany.

Thus all the work of the Frankfurt Assembly went for nothing. Most members of the Assembly, having never dreamed of using violence in the first place, concluded that they were beaten and went home. A handful of extremists remained at Frankfurt, promulgated the constitution on their own authority, urged revolutionary outbreaks, and called for elections. Riots broke out in various places. The Prussian army put them down—in Saxony, in Bavaria, in Baden. The same army drove the rump Assembly out of Frankfurt, and that was the end of it.

In summary, Germany in 1848 failed to solve the problem of its unification in a liberal and constitutional way. Liberal nationalism failed, and a less gentle kind of nationalism soon replaced it. The German movement of 1848, like so much else in German history, in the long run contributed to a fateful estrangement between Germany and the West. Thousands of disappointed German liberals and revolutionaries migrated to the United States, which came to know them as the "Forty-eighters." They brought to the new country, besides a ripple of revolutionary agitation, a stream of men trained in science, medicine, and music, and of highly skilled craftsmen like silversmiths and engravers.

The Prussian Constitution of 1850

In Prussia itself the ingenious monarch undertook to placate everybody by issuing a constitution of his own, one that should be peculiarly Prussian. It remained in effect from 1850 to 1918. It granted a single parliament for all the miscellaneous regions of Prussia. The parliament met in two chambers. The lower chamber was elected by universal male suffrage, not along the individualist or equalitarian principles of the West, but by a system that in effect divided the population into three estates—the wealthy, the less wealthy, and the general run of the people. Division was made according to payment of taxes. Those few big taxpayers who together contributed a third of the tax returns chose a third of the members of district electoral colleges, which in turn chose deputies to the Prussian lower house. In this way one large property owner had as much voting power as hundreds of working people. Large property in Prussia in 1850 still meant mainly the landed estates of the East-Elbian Junkers, but as time went on it came to include industrial property in the Rhineland also. The Junkers likewise were not harmed by the final liquidation of serfdom. They increased the acreage of their holdings, as after the reforms of Stein;[14] and the former servile agricultural workers turned into free wage earners economically dependent on the great landowners.

For 1850 the Prussian constitution was fairly progressive. If the mass of the people could elect very few deputies under the indirect system described, the mass of the British people, until 1867 or even 1884, could elect no deputies to Parliament at all. But the Prussian constitution remained in force until 1918. By the close of the nineteenth century, with democratic advances making their appearance elsewhere, the electoral system in Prussia, remaining unchanged, came to be reactionary and illiberal, giving the great landowners and industrialists an unusual position of special privilege within the state.

[14] See pp. 413–414.

61. THE NEW TOUGHNESS OF MIND: REALISM, POSITIVISM, MARXISM

The Revolution of 1848 failed not only in Germany but also in Hungary, in Italy, and in France. The "springtime of peoples," as it was called, was followed by chilling blasts of winter. The dreams of half a century, visions of a humane nationalism, aspirations for liberalism without violence, ideals of a peaceful and democratic republican commonwealth, were all exploded. Everywhere the cry had been for constitutional government, but only in a few small states—Denmark, Holland, Belgium, Switzerland, Piedmont—was constitutional liberty more firmly secured by the Revolution of 1848. Everywhere the cry had been for the freedom of nations, to unify national groups or rid them of foreign rule; but nowhere was national liberty more advanced in 1850 than it had been two years before. France obtained universal male suffrage in 1848, and kept it permanently thereafter; but it did not obtain democracy; it obtained a kind of popular dictatorship under Louis Napoleon Bonaparte. One accomplishment, however, was real enough. The peasantry was emancipated in the German states and the Austrian Empire. Serfdom and manorial restraints were abolished, nor were they reimposed after the failure of the revolution. This was the most fundamental accomplishment of the whole movement. The peasant masses of central Europe were thereafter free to move about, find new jobs, enter a labor market, take part in a money economy, receive and spend wages, migrate to growing cities—or even go to the United States. But the peasants, once freed, showed little concern for constitutional or bourgeois ideas. Peasant emancipation, in fact, strengthened the forces of political counterrevolution.

The most immediate and far-reaching consequence of the 1848 revolutions, or of their failure, was a new toughness of mind. Idealism was discredited. Revolutionaries became less optimistic, conservatives more willing to exercise repression. It was now a point of pride to be realistic, emancipated from illusions, willing to face facts as they were. The future, it was thought, would be determined by present realities rather than by imaginings of what ought to be. Industrialization went forward, with England still far in the lead, but spreading to the Continent and initiating the momentous transformation of Germany. The 1850s were a period of rising prices and wages, thanks in part to the gold rush in California. There was more prosperity than in the 1840s; the propertied classes felt secure, and spokesmen for labor turned from theories of society to the organizing of viable unions, especially in the skilled trades.

Materialism, Realism, Positivism

In basic philosophy the new mental toughness appeared as materialism, holding that everything mental, spiritual, or ideal was an outgrowth of physical or physiological forces. In literature and the arts it was called "realism." Writers and painters broke away from romanticism, which they said colored things out of all relation to the real facts. They attempted to describe and reproduce life as they found it, without intimation of a better or more noble world. More and more people came to trust science, not merely for an understanding of nature, but for insights into the true meaning of man and society. In religion the movement was toward skepticism, renewing the skeptical trend of the eighteenth century, which had been somewhat interrupted during the intervening period of romanticism.[15] It was variously held, not by all but by many, that religion was unscientific and hence not to be taken seriously; or that it was a mere historical growth among peoples in certain stages of development and hence irrelevant to modern civilization; or that one ought to go to church and lead a decent life, without taking the priest or clergyman too seriously, because religion was necessary to preserve the social order against radicalism and anarchy. To this idea the radical counterpart was of course that religion was a bourgeois invention to delude the people.

"Positivism" was another term used to describe the new attitude. It originated with the French philosopher Auguste Comte, who had begun to publish his numerous volumes on *Positive Philosophy* as long ago as 1830 and was still writing in the 1850s. He saw human history as a series of three stages, the theological, the metaphysical, and the scientific. The revolutions in France, he thought, both of 1789 and of 1848, suffered from an excess of metaphysical abstractions, empty words, and unverifiable high-flying principles. Those who worked for the improvement of society must adopt a strictly scientific outlook, and Comte produced an elaborate classification of the sciences, of which the highest would be the science of society, for which he coined the word "sociology." This new science would build upon observation of actual facts to develop broad scientific laws of social progress. Comte himself, and his closest disciples, envisaged a final scientific Religion of Humanity, which, stripped of archaic theological and metaphysical concerns, would serve as the basis for a better world of the future. More generally, however, "positivism" came to mean an insistence on verifiable facts, an avoidance of wishful thinking, a questioning of all assumptions, and a dislike of unprovable generalizations. Positivism in a broad sense, both in its demand for observation of facts and testing of ideas, and in its aspiration to be humanly useful, contributed to the growth of the social sciences as a branch of learning.

In politics the new toughness of mind was called by the Germans *Realpolitik*. This simply meant a "politics of reality." In domestic affairs it meant that people should give up utopian dreams, such as had caused the debacle of 1848, and content themselves with the blessings of an orderly, honest, hard-working government. For radicals it meant that people should stop imagining that the new society would result from goodness or the love of justice, and that social reformers must resort to the methods of politics—power and calculation. In international affairs *Realpolitik* meant that governments should not be guided by ideology, or by any system of "natural" enemies or "natural" allies, or by any desire to defend or promote any particular view of the world; but that they should follow their own practical interests, meet facts and situations as they arose, make any alliances that seemed useful, disregard tastes and scruples, and use any practical means to achieve their ends. The same men who, before 1848, had been not ashamed to express pacifist and cosmopolitan hopes now dismissed such ideas as a little softheaded. War, which governments since the overthrow of Napoleon had successfully tried to prevent, was accepted in the 1850s as an obvious means sometimes necessary to achieve a purpose. It was not especially glorious; it was not an end in itself; it was simply one of the tools of the statesman. *Realpolitik* was by no means confined to Germany, despite its German name and despite the fact that the famous German chancellor Bismarck became its most famous practitioner. Two

[15] See pp. 302–303, 305–311, 436.

other tough-minded thinkers, each in his own way, were Karl Marx and Louis Napoleon Bonaparte.

Early Marxism

Karl Marx and Friedrich Engels were among the disappointed revolutionaries of 1848. Marx (1818–1883), son of a lawyer in the Prussian Rhineland, was a democratic-radical newspaperman, who had studied law and philosophy. Engels (1820–1893) was the son of a well-to-do German textile manufacturer who owned a factory at Manchester, which the young Engels went to England to manage. Marx and Engels met in Paris in 1844. There they began a collaboration in thinking and writing that lasted for forty years. In 1847 they joined the Communist League, a tiny secret group of revolutionaries, mainly Germans in exile in the more liberal western Europe. The League, according to Engels, was at first "not actually much more than the German branch of the French secret societies." It aspired to become international and worked by tactics of infiltration. It agitated like other societies during the Revolution of 1848, and issued a set of "Demands of the Communist Party in Germany," which urged a unified indivisible German republic, democratic suffrage, universal free education, arming of the people, a progressive income tax, limitations upon inheritance, state ownership of banks, railroads, canals, mines, etc., and a degree of large-scale, scientific, collectivized agriculture. It was such obscurely voiced radicalism that alarmed the Frankfurt Assembly. With the triumph of counterrevolution in Germany the Communist League was crushed.

It was for this League that Marx and Engels wrote their *Communist Manifesto*, which was published in January 1848. But there was as yet no Marxism, and Marxism played no role in the Revolution of 1848. As a historical force Marxism set in during the 1870s. Meanwhile, with the failure of the revolution, Engels returned to his factory at Manchester, and Marx also settled in England, spending the rest of his life in London, where, after long labors in the British Museum, he finally produced his huge work called *Capital*, of which the first volume was published in German in 1867.

Sources and Content of Marxism

Marxism may be said to have had three sources or to have merged three national streams: French revolutionism, the British Industrial Revolution, and German philosophy. Without the massive fact of the Great French Revolution standing at the opening of the nineteenth century it is doubtful whether anyone would have developed so improbable a doctrine as the abrupt and total renovation of human affairs by the Revolution. But revolution had in fact occurred; it therefore might occur again. What the bourgeois class had done, the workers could do too. And Marxism, along with all early forms of socialism, saw an unredeemed promise in the French Revolution, believing that social and economic equality should follow the civil and legal equality already won.[16] In addition, and in keeping with the general movement of romanticism, the concept of liberty began also to mean a more personal emancipation. Marx, especially in his youthful writings, developed

---

[16] See pp. 438–440.

the idea of psychological alienation, a state of mind produced when a human being becomes divorced from the object on which he works, through the historic process of mechanization and commercialization of labor.

The revolutionary outbreaks of 1848, coming within a few weeks of the publication of the *Communist Manifesto*, naturally confirmed Marx and Engels in their beliefs, and the actual class war that shook Paris in the June Days was taken by them as a manifestation of a universal class struggle. But Marx was no mere insurrectionary schemer, like the "revolution-makers," as he contemptuously called them. His mature thought was a system for producing revolution, but it showed how the future revolution must come by the operation of vast impersonal forces.

Engels, engaged in the Manchester cotton industry, possessed a personal knowledge of the new industrial and factory system in England. He was in touch with a few of the most radical Chartists, though he had no respect for Chartism itself as a revolutionary movement. In 1844 he published a revealing book on *The Condition of the Working Classes in England.* The depressed condition of labor, to which Marxism like all forms of socialism called emphatic attention, was an actual fact.[17] It was a fact that labor received a relatively small portion of the national income, and that much of the product of society was being reinvested in capital goods, which belonged as private property to private persons. Government and parliamentary institutions, also as a matter of fact, were in the hands of the well-to-do in both Great Britain and France. Religion was commonly held to be necessary to keep the lower classes in order. The churches at the time, as a matter of fact, took next to no interest in problems of the workers. At best, evangelical sects taught the poor that they must be patient. The family, as an institution, was in fact disintegrating among laboring people in the cities, through exploitation of women and children and the overcrowding in inadequate and unsanitary living quarters. All these facts were seized upon and dramatized in the *Communist Manifesto:* The worker is deprived of the wealth he has himself created! The state is a committee of the bourgeoisie for the exploitation of the people! Religion is a drug to keep the workingman quietly dreaming upon imaginary heavenly rewards! The worker's family, his wife and children, have been prostituted and brutalized by the bourgeoisie! It seemed to Marx and Engels that the uprooted workingman should be loyal to nothing—except his own class. Even country had become meaningless. The proletarian had no country. Workers everywhere had the same problems and faced everywhere the same enemy. Therefore "let the ruling classes tremble at a communist revolution. The proletarians have nothing to lose but their chains. They have a world to win. Workingmen of all countries, unite!" So closed the *Manifesto.*

It was from English sources that Marx also took over much of his economic theory. From British political economy he adopted the subsistence theory of wages, or Iron Law, which orthodox economists presently abandoned since wages did in fact begin to rise.[18] It held that the average workingman could never obtain more than a minimum level of living—of which the corollary, for those who wished to draw it, was that the existing economic system held out no future for the laboring class as a class. Marx likewise took over from orthodox economists the labor theory of value, holding that the value of any man-made object depended ultimately on the amount of labor put into it—capital being regarded as the stored up labor

[17] See pp. 431–433, 467–468.
[18] See pp. 433–434, 589.

of former times. Orthodox economists soon discarded the labor theory of value, preferring the theory that value is determined psychologically by satisfaction of human wants or tastes. Marx, from the labor theory, developed his doctrine of surplus value. This was very intricate; but "surplus value" meant in effect that the workingman was being robbed. He received in wages only a fraction of the value of the product which his labor produced. The difference was "expropriated" by the bourgeois capitalists—the private owners of the factories and the machines. And since workers never received in wages the equivalent of what they produced, capitalism was constantly menaced by overproduction, the accumulation of goods that people could not afford to buy. Hence it ran repeatedly into crises and depressions and was obliged also to be constantly expanding in search of new markets. It was the depression of 1847, according to Marx, that had precipitated the Revolution of 1848; and with every such depression during the rest of his life-time Marx hoped that the day of the great social revolution was drawing nearer.

What brought all these observations together in a unified and compelling doctrine was the philosophy of dialectical materialism. By dialectic, Marx meant what the German philosopher Hegel had meant,[19] that all things are in movement and in evolution, and that all change comes through the clash of antagonistic elements. The word itself, coming from the Greek, meant originally a way of arriving at a higher conclusion through debate. The implications of the dialectic, for both Hegel and Marx, were that all history, and indeed all reality, is a process of development through time, a single and meaningful unfolding of events, necessary, logical, and deterministic; that every event happens in due sequence for good and sufficient reason (not by chance); and that history could not and cannot happen any differently from the way it has happened and is still happening today. This, it need hardly be said, cannot be demonstrated on any basis of knowable fact.

Marx differed from Hegel in one vital respect. Whereas Hegel emphasized the primacy of "ideas" in social change, Marx gave emphasis to the primacy of material conditions. By materialism, Marx meant that the basic element in society is economic. It is not primarily by having ideas that men create the social world in which they live. On the contrary, their form of society, especially their economic institutions, predisposes them to have certain ideas. At bottom, it is the "relations of production" (technology, invention, natural resources, property systems, etc.) that determine what kind of religions, philosophies, governments, laws, and moral values men accept. To believe that ideas precede and generate actualities was, according to Marx, the error of Hegel. Hegel had thought, for example, that the mind conceives the idea of freedom, which it then realizes in the Greek city-state, in Christianity, in the French Revolution, and in the kingdom of Prussia. Not at all, according to Marx: the idea of freedom, or any other idea, is generated by the actual economic and social conditions. Conditions are the roots, ideas the trees. Hegel had held the ideas to be the roots and the resulting actual conditions to be the trees. Or as Marx and Engels said, they found Hegel standing on his head and set him on his feet again.

The picture of historical development offered by Marx was somewhat as follows. Material conditions, or the relations of production, give rise to economic classes. Agrarian conditions produce a landholding or feudal class, but with changes

in trade routes, money, and productive techniques a new commercial or bourgeois class arises. Each class, feudal and bourgeois, develops an ideology suited to
its needs. Prevailing religions, governments, laws, and morals reflect the outlook
of these classes. The two classes inevitably clash. Bourgeois revolutions against
feudal interests break out—in England in 1642, in France in 1789, in Germany in
1848, though the bourgeois revolution in Germany proved abortive. Meanwhile,
as the bourgeois class develops, it inevitably calls another class into being, its dialectical antithesis, the proletariat. The bourgeois is defined as the private owner
of capital, the proletarian as the wage worker who possesses nothing but his own
hands. The more a country becomes bourgeois, the more it becomes proletarian.
The more production is concentrated in factories, the more the revolutionary laboring class is built up. Under competitive conditions the bourgeois tend to
devour and absorb each other; ownership of the factories, mines, machines, railroads, etc. (capital) becomes concentrated into very few hands. Others sink into
the proletariat. In the end the proletarianized mass simply takes over from the
remaining bourgeois. It "expropriates the expropriators," and abolishes the old
private property in the means of production. The social revolution is thus accomplished. It is inevitable. A classless society results, because class arises from economic differences which have been done away with. The state and religion, being
outgrowths of bourgeois interests, also disappear. For a time, until all vestiges of
bourgeois interests have been rooted out, or until the danger of counterrevolution
against socialism has been overcome, there will be a "dictatorship of the proletariat." After that the state will "wither away," since there is no longer an exploiting
class to require it.

Meanwhile the call is to war. Bourgeois and proletarian are locked in a universal struggle. It is really war, and as in all war all other considerations must be
subordinated to it. Periods of social calm are not peace; they are merely inter-
ludes between battles. The workers must not be allowed to grow soft or conciliatory, any more than an army should be allowed to forget its primary function of
fighting. Workers and labor unions must be kept in a belligerent and revolutionary mood. They must never forget that the employer is their class enemy, and
that government, law, morality, and religion are merely so much artillery directed against them. Morals are "bourgeois morals," law is "bourgeois law," government is an instrument of class power, and religion is a form of psychological
warfare, a means of providing "opium" for the masses. Workers must not let
themselves be fooled; they must learn how to detect the class interest underlying
the most exalted institutions and beliefs. In this piece of military intelligence, ferreting out the ways of the enemy, they will be helped by intellectuals especially
trained in explaining it to them. Like all fighting forces, the workers need a disciplined solidarity. Individuals must lose themselves in the whole—in their class. It
is a betrayal of their class for workers to rise above the proletariat, to "improve
themselves," as the bourgeois says. It is dangerous for labor unions merely to obtain better wages or hours by negotiation with employers, for by such little gains
the war itself may be forgotten. It is likewise dangerous, and even treasonous, for
workers to put faith in democratic machinery or "social legislation," for the state,
an engine of repression, can never be made into an instrument of welfare. Law is
the will of the stronger (i.e., the stronger class); "right" and "justice" are thin
emanations of class interest. We must hold, wrote Marx in 1875, to "the realistic
outlook which has cost so much effort to instill into the party, but which has now

taken root in it"; and we must not let this outlook be perverted "by means of ideological nonsense about 'right' and other trash common among the democrats and French Socialists."

The Appeal of Marxism: Its Strength and Weaknesses

The original Marxism was a hard doctrine, with both advantages and handicaps in the winning of adherents. One of its advantages was its claim to be scientific. Marx classified earlier and rival forms of socialism[20] as utopian: they rested on moral indignation, and their formula for reforming society was for men to become more just, or for the upper classes to be converted to sympathy for the lower. His own doctrine, Marx insisted, had nothing to do with ethical ideas; it was purely scientific, resting upon the study of actual facts and real processes, and it showed that socialism would be not a miraculous reversal but a historical continuation of what was already taking place. He also considered it utopian and unscientific to describe the future socialist society in any detail. It would be classless, with neither bourgeois nor proletarian; but to lay any specific plans would be idle dreaming. Let the revolution come, and socialism would take care of itself.

Marxism was a strong compound of the scientific, the historical, the metaphysical, and the apocalyptic. But some elements of Marxism stood in the way of its natural propagation. The working people of Europe were not really in the frame of mind of an army in battle. They hesitated to subordinate all else to the distant prospect of a class revolution. They were not exclusively class-people, nor did they behave as such. Enough of Christianity was still alive in them, and of older natural-law ideas, to inhibit the belief that morality was a class weapon, or right and justice "trash." They had national loyalties to country; they could with difficulty associate themselves emotionally with a world proletariat in an unrelenting struggle against their own neighbors.

The cure for the revolutionism of 1848 proved in time to be the admission of the laboring classes to a fuller membership in society. Wages generally rose after 1850, labor unions were organized, and by 1870 in the principal European countries the workingman very generally had a vote. Through their unions, workers were often able to get better wages and working conditions by direct pressure upon employers. Having the vote, they gradually formed working-class parties, and as they proceeded to act through the state they had less inclination to destroy it. Marx's word for such maneuvers was "opportunism." Opportunism, the tendency of working people to better themselves by dealing with employers and by obtaining legislation through existing government channels, was the most dangerous of all dangers to the Revolution. For in war people do not negotiate or pass laws; they fight. From Marxism the working classes absorbed much, including a watchful hostility to employers and a sense of working-class solidarity; but on the whole, as Marxism spread at the close of the nineteenth century it ceased to be really revolutionary.[21] Had the old Europe not gone to pieces in the twentieth-century wars, and had Marxism not been revived by Lenin and transplanted to Russia, it is probable that Marx's ideas would have been domesticated into the general body of European thought, and that much less would be said about them in this book.

[20] See pp. 438–440.
[21] See pp. 588–591.

62. BONAPARTISM: THE SECOND FRENCH EMPIRE, 1852–1870

We have seen how Louis Napoleon Bonaparte, elected president of the republic in 1848, in 1852 made himself emperor of the French with the title of Napoleon III.[22] Those willing to fight for the parliamentary and liberal institutions which he crushed in 1851 proved helpless. There is no doubt that he became "dictator" on a wave of popular acclaim.

Political Institutions of the Second Empire

Indeed the dubious title of first modern dictator fits Napoleon III far better than it fits Napoleon I. The new Napoleon was not at all like his great uncle. He was no soldier, no administrator, and though intelligent enough he had no especial distinction or force of mind. He was a politician. He had led *Putsches* against the July Monarchy, for which he had been imprisoned. The first Napoleon came to power in the course of a war that he had not started. The second Napoleon made himself dictator in time of peace, by playing on social fears in a country divided by an abortive revolution. The first Napoleon, it is hardly too much to say, never in his life condescended to make a public speech. Louis Napoleon made them all the time; the political rostrum was his natural habitat. Public opinion was more of a force in 1850 than in 1800. Louis Napoleon recognized it as an opportunity, not merely as a nuisance. He appealed to the masses by promises and by pageantry; he cultivated, solicited, directed, and manufactured popular favor. He understood perfectly that a single leader exerts more magnetism than an elected assembly. And he knew that a Europe still shuddering over the June Days was hoping desperately for order in France.

He gloried in modern progress. Toward the changes coming over Europe the monarchs of the old school usually showed an attitude of timidity and doubt if not positive opposition. Napoleon III boldly offered himself as the leader in a brave new world. Like his uncle, he announced that he embodied the sovereignty of the people. He said that he had found a solution to the problem of mass democracy. In all the other great Continental states and in Great Britain, in 1852, universal suffrage was thought to be incompatible with intelligent government and economic prosperity. Napoleon III claimed to put them together. Like Marx and other "realists" after 1848 he held that elected parliamentary bodies, far from representing an abstract "people," only accentuated class divisions within a country. He declared that the regime of the restored Bourbons and the July Monarchy had been dominated by special interests, that the Republic of 1848 had first been violent and anarchic, then fallen into the hands of a distrustful assembly that robbed the laboring man of his vote, and that France would find in the empire the permanent, popular, and modern system for which it had been vainly searching since 1789. He affirmed that he stood above classes and would govern equally in the interests of all. In any case, like many others after 1848, he held that forms of government were less important than economic and social realities.

The political institutions of the Second Empire were therefore authoritarian, modeled on those of the Consulate of the first Bonaparte. There was a Council of State, composed of experts who drafted legislation and advised on technical mat-

[22] See pp. 475–477.

ters. There was an appointive Senate with few significant functions. There was a Legislative Body elected by universal male suffrage. The elections were carefully managed. The government put up an official candidate for each seat whom all officeholders in the district were required to support. Other candidates might offer themselves for election, but there could be no political meetings of any kind, and if the independent candidate put up posters he had to use a different kind of paper from the official candidate. Few ventured in these circumstances to differ with the government.

The Legislative Body had no independent powers of its own. It could not initiate legislation but only consider what was submitted to it by the emperor. It had no control over the budget, for the emperor was legally free to borrow money as he saw fit. It had no power over the army or the foreign office or the making of war and peace. To publish speeches made in the legislative chamber was against the law. Any five members, by requesting a secret session, could exclude the public from the galleries. Parliamentary life sank toward absolute zero.

To captivate public attention and glorify the Napoleonic name the new emperor set up a sumptuous court at the Tuileries. Balked in the ambition to marry into one of the great dynasties, Napoleon III chose as his empress a young Spanish beauty, Eugénie, who was destined to outlive the empire by fifty years, dying in 1920. It was said to be a love match—a sure sign of popularized royalty. The court life of the empire was brilliant, gay, luxurious, and showy beyond anything known at the time in St. Petersburg or Vienna. The note of pageantry was further struck in the embellishment of the city of Paris. Baron Haussmann, one of the most creative of city planners, gave Paris much of the appearance that it has today. He built roomy railway stations with broad approaches, and he constructed a system of boulevards and public squares offering long vistas ending in fine buildings or monuments, as at the Place de l'Opéra. He also modernized the sewers and the water supply. The building program, like the expensive court, had the additional advantage of stimulating business and employment. And the cutting of wide avenues through the crooked streets and congested old houses would permit easier military operations against insurrectionists entrenched behind barricades, should the events of 1848 ever be repeated.

Economic Developments under the Empire

It was as a great social engineer that Napoleon III preferred to be known. In his youth he had tried to read the riddle of modern industrialism, and now, as emperor, he found some of his main backers in former Saint-Simonians, who called him their "socialist emperor." Saint-Simon, it may be recalled, had been among the first to conceive of a centrally planned industrial system.[23] But the Saint-Simonians of the 1850s shared in the new sense of being realistic, and their most signal triumph was the invention of investment banking, by which they hoped to guide economic growth through the concentration of financial resources. They founded a novel kind of banking institution, the *Crédit Mobilier*, which raised funds by selling its shares to the public, and with the funds thus obtained bought stock in such new industrial enterprises as it wished to develop. A land bank, or

[23] See p. 439.

Crédit Foncier, was likewise established to lend funds to landowners for the improvement of agriculture.

The times were exceedingly favorable for expansion, for the discovery of gold in California in 1849, and in Australia soon afterward, together with the newly organized credit facilities, brought a substantial increase in the European money supply, which had a mildly inflationary effect. The steady rise of prices and all money values encouraged company promotion and investment of capital. Railway mileage, increasing everywhere in the Western world, increased in France from 3,000 to 16,000 kilometers in the 1850s. The demand for rolling stock, iron rails, auxiliary equipment, and building materials for stations and freight houses kept the mines and factories busy. The railway network was rationalized, fifty-five small lines in France being merged into six big regional trunks. Iron steamboats replaced wooden sailing ships. Between 1859 and 1869 a French company built the Suez Canal, which it continued to own for almost a century, though the British government after 1875 was the principal stockholder.

Large corporations made their appearance, in railroads and banking first of all. In 1863 the law granted the right of "limited liability," by which a stockholder could not lose more than the par value of his stock, however insolvent or debt-burdened the corporation might become. This encouraged investment by persons of small means, and by capitalists large and small in enterprises of which they knew very little; thus the wealth and savings of the country were more effectively mobilized and put to work. Stocks and shares became more numerous and diversified. The Stock Exchange boomed. Financiers—those whose business was to handle money, credit, and securities—assumed a new eminence in the capitalistic world. A good many people became very rich, richer perhaps than anyone had ever been in France before.

The emperor aspired also to do something for the workingman, within the limits of the existing system. The land bank was of some use to the more substantial peasants. Jobs were plentiful and wages good, by the ideas of the day, at least until the temporary depression of 1857. The emperor had a plan, as did some of the Saint-Simonians, for organizing forces of workers in military fashion and setting them to clear and develop uncultivated land. Not much was done in this direction. More was accomplished in the humanitarian relief of suffering. Hospitals and asylums were established, and free medicines were distributed. The outlines of a social-service state began somewhat vaguely to appear. Meanwhile the workers were building up unions. All combinations of workingmen had been prohibited during the French Revolution, and the Le Chapelier Law of 1791 was deemed to be still in force.[24] Gradually the ambiguous legal position of labor unions was clarified. In 1864 it even became legal for organized workers to go on strike. Large labor units, or unions, and large business units, or corporations, were thus legalized at the same time. Napoleon III hardly did enough for labor to rank as a working-class hero, but he did enough to be suspected as "socialistic" by many middle-class people of the day.

Later dictatorships, bent like the Second Empire on a program of economic development, were usually highly protectionist, unwilling to face open competition with the rest of the world. Napoleon III believed in freedom of international trade. He had a project for a tariff union with Belgium, which some Belgians also

---

[24] See p. 364.

supported. Belgium was already well industrialized, and a Franco-Belgian union, especially since Belgium had the coal that France lacked, would have formed a trading area of very great strength. But the plan was blocked by private interests in both countries, and strongly opposed by both Great Britain and the German *Zollverein.* The emperor then turned to an all-around reduction of import duties. Since the repeal of the Corn Laws in 1846 the free traders were in power in England.[25] They were eager to abolish trade barriers between Britain and France. Napoleon III, overriding opposition in his Legislative Body, concluded a free trade treaty with Great Britain in 1860. He set aside 40 million francs of government funds to assist French manufacturers in making adjustments to British competition; but this sum was never spent in full, and it has hence been concluded that French industry was able to compete successfully with the more intensively mechanized industry of Britain. The Anglo French treaty was accompanied by lesser trade agreements with other countries. It looked, in the 1860s, as if Europe might actually be about to enter the promised land of freedom of trade.

Internal Difficulties and War

But by 1860 the empire was running into trouble. It took a few years to overcome the depression of 1857. By his free trade policy the emperor made enemies among industrialists in certain lines. The Catholics did not like his policy in Italy.[26] After 1860 opposition mounted. The emperor granted more leeway to the Legislative Body. The 1860s are called the decade of the Liberal Empire—all such terms being relative. How the empire would have fared had purely internal causes been left free scope we shall never know. Louis Napoleon actually ruined himself by war. His empire evaporated on the battlefield in 1870. But he was at war long before that.

"The empire means peace," he had assured his audiences in 1852: *l'empire, c'est la paix.* But war is after all the supreme pageantry (or was then); France was the strongest country of Europe, and the emperor's name was Napoleon. Less than a year and a half after the proclamation of the empire France was at war with a European state for the first time since Waterloo. The enemy was Russia, and the war was the Crimean War. Napoleon III did not alone instigate the Crimean War. Many forces in Europe after 1848 made for war; but Napoleon III was one of these forces. In 1859 the new Napoleon was fighting in Italy, from 1862 to 1867 in Mexico, and in 1870 in France itself, in a war with Prussia which he could easily have avoided. These wars form part of the story of the following chapter.[27]

It is enough to say here that in 1870 the Second Empire went the way of the First, into the limbo of governments tried and discarded by the French. It had lasted eighteen years, exactly as long as the July Monarchy, and longer than any other regime known in France, up to that time, since the fall of the Bastille. Not until the 1920s and 1930s, when dictators sprouted all over Europe, did the world begin to suspect what Louis Napoleon had really been, an omen of the future rather than a bizarre reincarnation of the past. It is only right to add that some, like Alexis de Tocqueville, suspected it even then.

[25] See p. 464.
[26] See p. 515.
[27] See pp. 515, 524–525; for Mexico, see p. 617.

Early Industrialism and Social Classes

Industrialization, as it appeared first in England in the nineteenth century, rested on a combination of coal and iron, of which the steam engine was the most portentous offspring. Steam engines provided power to the textile mills, and when put on wheels they revolutionized transportation. In the factories a new kind of wage-earning working class was assembled. The railway train, powered by steam, running on rails at first made of wood, then of iron, then of steel, carried people and goods at a speed and in a volume never known in the past. It made possible the concentration of population in cities, both gigantic cities such as London, and clusters of smaller cities in which manufacturing processes were carried on. In this urban world, while polite architecture ran through a series of classical, Gothic, Renaissance, and other revivals, more utilitarian structures of a novel kind were built of iron, and then of structural steel. The new habitat provided luxury for a few, comfort for some, and misery for all too many.

Class conflict therefore raged throughout the nineteenth century, but most acutely in the first half. One difficulty was that, though there had long been talk of the progress of science and invention, the actual difficulties of industrialization had been unforeseen. As the first people to undergo the Industrial Revolution, the English had no experience on which to draw. The English imagination dwelt by preference on rural rather than urban themes, especially in the early part of the century, and under the influence of literary romanticism. Government until 1832 was in the hands of a landed aristocracy and country gentry, made conservative in their politics by the French Revolution. Priding themselves on their English liberties, and fearing anything like Continental bureaucracy, the English only gradually endowed their government with adequate powers of regulation, inspection, enforcement, and police.

After 1850 some of the more favorable consequences of modern industry and technology became apparent. While poverty remained chronic, and the working class struggled to better itself, the middle classes grew in numbers and enjoyed new amenities and conveniences. The following pages illustrate the life of social classes in England, and also in France, in this new Age of Iron. The medium here is part of the message, since the nineteenth-century innovations of lithography, photography, and low-cost printing for a wide market are to be observed.

At the left, this piece of popular art (a song-book cover) points up the exciting contrast between new and old. An express train rushes at night, on a high bridge, with the city behind it, through an English countryside illuminated by the moon.

   Above: The newly organized London police, in the 1840s, await the arrival of a Chartist procession. Between 1832 and 1848 the Chartists organized mass demonstrations in the vain attempt to democratize the electoral laws and so obtain legislation designed to favor the working classes. The government introduced a more modern and better disciplined police force as a measure of crowd control, and to avoid the kind of chaotic confrontation shown on the following page. The men are in a kind of civilian uniform complete with stovepipe hats.

503

Upper left: The "Peterloo Massacre" of 1819, as caricatured by Cruikshank. A peaceable crowd in St. Peter's Fields, Manchester, was fired upon and dispersed by the yeomanry, a militia of nonprofessional part-time soldiers, mostly rural people out of sympathy with modern cities.

Lower left: These primitive trains, about 1840, are running on wooden rails with "guidance wheels" at an apparently crazy angle to help keep them on the track.

Above: London, or rather one of its poorer quarters, as seen by the French artist Gustave Doré about 1880. The omnipresent railroad is in the background, while in the foreground the mass housing, with the little yards, or rather pens, evokes the atmosphere of a prison.

505

Upper left: A workers' meeting in Paris, as seen by the painter Jean Béraud in 1884. The audience is probably hearing some socialist speeches.

Lower left: The future King Edward VII, then Prince of Wales, with his wife, comfortably installed in box seats, observes the new Bessemer steel-making process at Sheffield in 1875.

Above: The Bon Marché department store in Paris about 1880. The new era is evident in the vast expanse, the proliferation of merchandise, and the presence of affluent women, who have come downtown with their children to shop.

507

508

Buildings of cast iron and glass, appearing about 1850, represented the most significant technical innovation in architecture in centuries. The department store on page 507 was of this kind. At the left, above, is the famous Crystal Palace in Hyde Park, London, built to house the Great Exhibition of 1851. The world's fair, or industrial exposition, was another product of the revolution in transportation.

Lower left: The Café de la Rotonde in Paris about 1860. The new French café was designed to be large, airy, open, cosmopolitan, suitable for ladies, and not necessarily alcoholic.

Above: The Eiffel Tower, built for the Paris exposition of 1889, with elevators to carry visitors to the top 984 feet above the ground, long remained the world's highest structure, and still stands as a symbol of nineteenth-century civilization. It was at first criticized as ungainly and vulgarly colossal. A later generation, accustomed to an architecture of concrete slabs and oblong cages, sees its graceful curves and the delicate tracery of its four immense legs.

XIII.
The Consolidation of Large Nation-States, 1859-1871

nly a dozen years, from 1859 to 1871, were enough to see the formation of a new German empire, a unified kingdom of Italy, a Dual Monarchy of Austria-Hungary, drastic internal changes in tsarist Russia, the triumph of central authority in the United States, the creation of a united Dominion of Canada, and the modernizing or "Europeanization" of the empire of Japan. All these disparate events reflected profound changes brought in by the railroad, steamship, and telegraph, which made the communication of ideas, exchange of goods, and movement of people over wide areas more frequent and easier than ever before. Politically, all represented the advancing principle of the nation-state.

63. BACKGROUNDS: THE IDEA OF THE NATION-STATE

Before 1860 there were two prominent nation-states—Great Britain and France. Spain, united on the map, was internally so miscellaneous as to belong to a different category. Portugal, Switzerland, the Netherlands, and the Scandinavian

Chapter Emblem: Medallion to celebrate the Prussian defeat of Austria in 1866, and featuring the King of Prussia, William I, who later became the first German Emperor.

countries were nation states, but small and peripheral. The characteristic political organizations were small states comprising fragments of a nation, such as were strewn across the middle of Europe—Hanover, Baden, Sardinia, Tuscany, or the Two Sicilies—and large sprawling empires made up of all sorts of peoples, distantly ruled from above by dynasties and bureaucracies, such as the Romanov, Habsburg, and Ottoman domains.[1] Except for recent developments in the Americas the same mixture of small nonnational states and of large nonnational empires was to be found in most of the rest of the world.

Since 1860 or 1870 a nation-state system has prevailed. The consolidation of large nations became a model for other peoples large and small. In time, in the following century, other large peoples undertook to establish nation-states in India, Pakistan, Indonesia, and Nigeria. Small and middle-sized peoples increasingly thought of themselves as nations, entitled to their own sovereignty and independence; the result, also accomplished in the following century, was the appearance of such states as Czechoslovakia, the Turkish Republic, Israel, and the Republic of Ireland. Some of these sovereignties comprise fewer people than a large modern city. The idea of the nation-state has served both to bring people together into larger units and to break them apart into smaller ones. In the nineteenth century, outside the disintegrating Ottoman Empire, from which Greece, Serbia, Bulgaria, and Rumania became independent, and in which an Arabic national movement also began to stir, the national idea served mainly to create larger units in place of small ones. The map of Europe, from 1871 to 1918, was the simplest it has ever been before or since.[2]

About the idea of the nation-state and the movement of nationalism much has been said already in this book. Earlier chapters have described the ferment of national ideas and movements stirred up by the French Revolution and by the Napoleonic domination of Europe, the nationalist agitation and repression of the years after 1815, and the frustration and failure of patriotic aspirations in Germany, Italy, and central Europe in the Revolution of 1848.[3] For many in the nineteenth century, nationalism, the winning of national unity and independence and the creation of the nation-state, became a kind of secular faith.

A nation-state may be thought of as one in which supreme political authority somehow rests upon and represents the will and feeling of its inhabitants. There must be a people, not merely a swarm of human beings. The people must basically will and feel something in common. They must sense that they belong—that they are members of a community, participating somehow in a common life, that the government is their government, and that outsiders are "foreign." The outsiders or foreigners are usually (though not always) those who speak a different language. The nation is usually (though not always) composed of all persons sharing the same speech. A nation may also possess a belief in common descent or racial origin (however mistaken), or a sense of a common history, a common future, a common religion, a common geographical home, or a common external menace. Nations take form in many ways. But all are alike in feeling themselves to be communities, permanent communities in which individual persons, together with their children and their children's children, are committed to a collective destiny on earth.

[1] See map, pp. 420–421.
[2] See map, pp. 528–529.
[3] See pp. 354, 366–368, 408–414, 440–460, 477–488.

In the nineteenth century governments found that they could not effectively rule, or develop the full powers of state, except by enlisting this sense of membership and support among their subjects. The consolidation of large nation-states had two distinguishable phases. Territorially, it meant the union of preexisting smaller states. Morally and psychologically it meant the creation of new ties between government and governed, the admission of new segments of the population to political life, through the creation or extension of liberal and representative institutions. This happened even in Japan and in tsarist Russia. National consolidation in the nineteenth century favored constitutional progress. Although there was considerable variation in the real power of the new political institutions and in the extent of self-government actually realized, parliaments were set up for the new Italy, the new Germany, the new Japan, the new Canada; and the movement in Russia was in the same direction. In Europe, some of the aims which the revolutionists of 1848 had failed to achieve were now realized by the established authorities.

They were realized, however, only in a series of wars. To create an all-German or an all-Italian state, as the revolutions of 1848 had already shown, it was necessary to break the power of Austria, render Russia at least temporarily ineffective, and overthrow or intimidate those German and Italian governments which refused to surrender their sovereignty. In the United States, to maintain national unity as understood by President Lincoln, it was necessary to repress the movement for Southern independence by force of arms. For forty years after 1814 there had been no war between established powers of Europe. Then in 1854 came the Crimean War, in 1859, the Italian War, in 1864 the Danish War, in 1866 the Austro-Prussian War, and in 1870 the Franco-Prussian War. Concurrently the Civil War raged in the United States. After 1871, for forty-three years there was again no war between European powers.

The Crimean War, 1854–1856

Before moving on to the first of the national consolidation movements, the Italian, we must examine the Crimean War which, though seemingly remote and unconnected, helped to make possible the success of the European national movements. Its chief significance in the story of the present chapter is that it seriously weakened both Austria and Russia, the two powers most bent on preserving the peace settlement of 1815 and on preventing national changes. It was also the first war covered by newspaper correspondents, and the first in which women, led by Florence Nightingale, established their position as army nurses.

The pressure of Russia upon Turkey was an old story. Every generation saw its Russo-Turkish war.[4] In the last Russo-Turkish war, to go back no further, that of 1828–1829, the Tsar Nicholas I protected the independence newly won by Greece and annexed the left bank of the mouth of the Danube. Now, in 1853, Nicholas again made demands upon the still large but decaying Ottoman Empire, moving in on the two Danubian principalities, Wallachia and Moldavia (later to be known as Rumania), with military forces.[5] The dispute this time ostensibly in-

[4] See pp. 232–233, 326–327, 394, 414, 451–452, 455–456.
[5] See maps, pp. 420–421, 625.

volved the protection of Christians in the Ottoman Empire, including the foreign Christians at Jerusalem and in Palestine. Over these Christians the French also claimed a certain protective jurisdiction. The French had for centuries been the principal Western people in the Near East. They had often furnished money and advisers to the sultan, they carried on a huge volume of trade, they staffed and financed Christian missions, and they were continually talking of building a Suez canal. Napoleon III had especial reason to resent the Tsar Nicholas, who regarded him as a revolutionary adventurer. Napoleon III encouraged the Turkish government to resist Russian claims to protect Christians within Turkey. War between Russia and Turkey broke out late in 1853. In 1854 France joined the side of the Turks, as did Great Britain, whose settled policy was to uphold Turkey and the Near East against penetration by Russia. The two Western powers were soon joined by a small ally, Piedmont, which had no visible interest in the issues in the Near East and entered the war mainly for the purpose of advancing the Italian question.

The British fleet successfully blockaded Russia in both its Baltic and Black Sea outlets. French and British armies invaded Russia itself, landing in the Crimean peninsula, to which all the important fighting was confined. The Austrian Empire had its own reasons not to wish Russia to conquer the Balkans and Constantinople, or to see Britain and France master the situation alone; Austria therefore, though not yet recovered from the upheaval of 1848–1849, mobilized its armed forces at a great effort to itself and occupied Wallachia and Moldavia, which the Russians evacuated under this threat of attack by a new enemy. Tsar Nicholas died in 1855, and his successor Alexander II sued for peace.

A congress of all the great powers made peace at Paris in 1856. By the treaty the powers pledged themselves jointly to maintain the "integrity of the Ottoman Empire." The Russian tide ebbed a little. Russia ceded the left bank of the mouth of the Danube to Moldavia and gave up its claim to the special protection of Christians in the Turkish empire. Moldavia and Wallachia (united as "Rumania" in 1858), together with Serbia, were recognized as self-governing principalities under protection of the European powers. It was agreed that Russia should maintain no warships on the Black Sea, and that the Danube should be an international river open to commercial shipping of all nations. At the Congress of Paris all seemed harmonious. There seemed to be such a thing as Europe, undertaking collective obligations, protecting small states, rationally and peaceably conducting its affairs.

But trouble was in the making. Napoleon III needed glory. The Italians wanted some kind of unified Italy. The Prussians, who had done nothing in the Crimean War, and were only tardily invited to the Congress of Paris, feared that their status as a great power might be slipping away. Napoleon III, the Italian nationalists, the Prussians, all stood to gain by change. Change in central Europe and Italy meant a tearing up of the Treaty of Vienna of 1815, long guarded by Metternich and unsuccessfully challenged by the revolutionaries of 1848. Now, after the Crimean War, the forces opposing change were very weak. It was the Russian and Austrian empires that had stood firmly for the status quo. But these two powers, which had most seriously attempted to uphold the Vienna settlement, could do so no longer. The first proof came in Italy.

64. CAVOUR AND THE ITALIAN WAR OF 1859: THE UNIFICATION OF ITALY

Italian Nationalism: The Program of Cavour

In Italy there had long been about a dozen sizable states, together with a few very small ones. Several of them had dissolved in the Italian movements that accompanied the wars of the French Revolution. All had been reorganized, first by Napoleon and then by the Congress of Vienna. In the northwest lay the kingdom of Sardinia, more commonly known as Piedmont. Its royal house of Savoy was the only native Italian dynasty in Italy. East of it lay Lombardy, and east of that, Venetia. Since 1814 Lombardy and Venetia belonged to the Austrian Empire. South of Lombardy, in the northwest corner of the "leg" of the peninsula, was the duchy of Tuscany with its capital at Florence. The smaller duchies of Modena, Parma, and Lucca filled the interstices between Tuscany and the northern states. Across the middle of the peninsula were spread the papal states, the hereditary temporal possession of the Roman See. Further south, comprising half of all Italy, lay the large kingdom of Naples or the Two Sicilies, ruled since 1735 by a branch of the Bourbons. The governments of these states were generally content with their separate independence. But the governments were remote from their peoples.

There was a widespread disgust in Italy with the existing authorities, and a growing desire for a liberal national state in which all Italy might be embodied and which might resurrect the Italian grandeur of ancient times and of the Renaissance. This sentiment, the dream of an Italian Risorgimento, or resurgence, had become very heated at the time of the French Revolution and Napoleon, then had been transformed into a moral purpose by the writings of Mazzini.[6] Mazzini, who had invested the cause of Italian unity with almost a holy character, had seen his hopes for a unified republican Italy elevated for a brief moment and then blasted in the general debacle of 1848. In the stormy events of 1848 the papacy had been frightened off by the radical romantic republicanism of Mazzini, Garibaldi, and other firebrands and could no longer be expected to support the cause of Italian nationalism. And in the same events the kingdom of Sardinia had failed in its vow to oust Austria from the Italian peninsula without the aid of any outside great power.[7]

These lessons were not lost on the prime minister of Piedmont (or "Sardinia"), which was ruled since 1848 as a constitutional monarchy and was now under King Victor Emmanuel. This prime minister after 1852 was Camillo di Cavour, one of the shrewdest political tacticians of that or any age. Cavour was a liberal of Western type. He tried to make Piedmont a model of progress, efficiency, and fair government that other Italians would admire. He worked hard to plant constitutional and parliamentary practices in Piedmont. He favored the building of railroads and docks, the improvement of agriculture, and emancipation of trade. He followed a strongly anticlerical policy, cutting down the number of religious holidays, limiting the right of church bodies to own real estate, abolishing the church courts—all without negotiation with the Holy See. A liberal and constitutional monarchist, a wealthy landowner in his own right, he had no sympathy for the revolutionary and republican nationalism of Mazzini. To him it did not seem

---

[6] See p. 442.
[7] See pp. 479–483, and the note on p. 189.

that Italy would be united by the methods of conspiracy and secret societies, by hortatory literature smuggled in from political exiles, or by the proclamation of idealistic radical republics, as in 1848, which alarmed the most influential people in the country.[8]

Cavour shared in that new toughness of mind described in the last chapter. He embraced a "politics of reality." He did not approve of republicans but was willing to work with them surreptitiously. He did not idealize war but was willing to make war to unify Italy under the house of Savoy. With unruffled calculation he took Piedmont into the Crimean War, sending troops to Russia, in the hope of winning a place at the peace table and raising the Italian question at the Congress of Paris. It was evident to him that against one great power one must pit another, and that the only way to get Austria out of Italy was to use the French army. It became his master plan deliberately to provoke war with Austria, after having assured himself of French military support.

It was not difficult to persuade Napoleon III to collaborate. The Bonapartes looked upon Italy as their ancestral country, and Napoleon III, in his adventurous youth, had traveled in conspiratorial Italian circles and even participated in an Italian insurrection in 1831. Now, as emperor, in his role of apostle of modernity, he entertained a "doctrine of nationalities" which held the consolidation of nations to be a forward step at the existing stage of history. To fight reactionary Austria for the freedom of Italy would also mollify liberal opinion in France, which in other ways Napoleon was engaged in suppressing. The last note in persuasion was furnished by an Italian republican named Orsini, who in 1858, finding the French emperor too slow to make up his mind, attempted to assassinate him with a bomb. Napoleon III reached a secret agreement with Cavour. In April 1859, Cavour tricked Austria into a declaration of war. The French army poured over the Alps.

There were two battles, Magenta and Solferino, both won by the French and Piedmontese. But Napoleon III was now in a quandary. The Prussians began to mobilize on the Rhine, not wishing France to create an Italian sphere of influence for itself. In Italy, with the defeat of the Austrians, revolutionary agitation broke out all over the peninsula, as it had a decade before—and the French emperor was no patron of popular revolution. The revolutionaries overthrew or denounced the existing governments and clamored for annexation to Piedmont. In France, as elsewhere, the Catholics, fearful that the pope's temporal power would be lost, upbraided the emperor for his godless and unnecessary war. The French position was indeed odd, for while the bulk of the French army fought Austria in the north, a detachment of it was still stationed in Rome, sent there in 1849 to protect the pope against Italian republicanism.[9] Napoleon III, in July 1859, at the height of his victories, stupefied Cavour. He made a separate peace with the Austrians.

The Franco-Austrian agreement gave Lombardy to Piedmont but left Venetia within the Austrian Empire. It offered a compromise solution to the Italian question, in the form of a federal union of the existing Italian governments, to be presided over by the pope. This was not what Cavour, or the Piedmontese, or the more fiery Italian patriots wanted. Revolution continued to spread. Tuscany, Modena, Parma, and Romagna drove out their old rulers. They were annexed to

8 See pp. 481, 483.
9 See p. 476.

Piedmont, after plebiscites or general elections in these regions had shown an overwhelming popular favor for this step. Since Romagna belonged to the papal states the pope excommunicated the organizers of the new Italy. Undeterred, representatives of all north Italy except Venetia met at the Piedmontese capital of Turin in 1860 in the first parliament of the enlarged kingdom. The British government hailed these events with enthusiasm, and Napoleon III also recognized the expanded Piedmontese state, in return for the transfer to France of Nice and Savoy, where plebiscites disclosed enormous majorities for annexation to France.

The Completion of Italian Unity

There were now, in 1860, a north Italian kingdom, the papal states in the middle, and the kingdom of the Two Sicilies still standing in the south. The latter was being undermined by revolutionary agitation, as often in the past.[10] A Piedmontese republican, Giuseppe Garibaldi, brought matters to a head. Somewhat like Lafayette, Garibaldi was a "hero of two worlds," who had fought for the independence of Uruguay, lived in the United States, and been one of the Triumvirs in the short-lived Roman Republic of 1849. He now organized a group of about 1,150 personal followers—"Garibaldi's Thousand," or the Red Shirts—for an armed expedition to the south. Cavour, unable openly to favor such filibustering against a neighboring state, connived at Garibaldi's preparations and departure. Garibaldi landed in Sicily and soon crossed to the mainland. Revolutionists hastened to join him, and the government of the Two Sicilies, backward and corrupt, commanding little loyalty from its population, collapsed before this picturesque intrusion.

Garibaldi now prepared to push from Naples up to Rome. Here, of course, he would meet not only the pope but the French army, and the international scandal would reverberate throughout the globe. Cavour decided that so extreme a step must be averted, but that Garibaldi's successes must at the same time be used. Anticipating Garibaldi, a Piedmontese army entered the papal states, carefully avoiding Rome, and proceeded onward into Naples. Garibaldi, though not all his followers, was now ready to accept a monarchy as the best solution to the problem of Italian unification. The chief of the Red Shirts, the one-time foe of kings, consented to ride in an open carriage with Victor Emmanuel through the streets of Naples amid cheering thousands. Plebiscites held in the Two Sicilies showed an almost unanimous willingness to join with Piedmont. In the remainder of the papal states, except for Rome and its environs, plebiscites were held also, with the same result. A parliament representing all Italy except Rome and Venetia met in 1861, and the Kingdom of Italy was formally proclaimed, with Victor Emmanuel II as king "by grace of God and the will of the nation." Venetia was added in

[10] See pp. 450–451, 479.

NATION BUILDING, 1859–1867

In eight years from 1859 to 1867 Italy was unified (except for the city of Rome, annexed in 1870), the Habsburg government tried to solve its nationalities problem by creating a Dual Monarchy of Austria-Hungary, the United States affirmed its unity by defeating the Southern secessionist movement, and the Dominion of Canada was formed to include all British North America (with dates shown for accession of provinces) except Newfoundland and Labrador, which were added in 1949. For Germany see the map on p. 522.

UNIFICATION OF ITALY, 1859-1870

PIEDMONT
LOMBARDY
Turin
Milan
VENETIA
Venice
PARMA
MODENA
Florence
TUSCANY
PAPAL STATES
KINGDOM OF SARDINIA
ROME
SARDINIA
NAPLES
SICILY

FORMATION OF DUAL MONARCHY OF AUSTRIA-HUNGARY, 1867

AUSTRIA
Vienna
Budapest
HUNGARY

FORMATION OF DOMINION OF CANADA, 1867

NORTHWEST TERRITORIES

LABRADOR
1949

NEWFOUND-LAND
1949

BRITISH COLUMBIA
1871

ALBERTA
1905

SASKATCHEWAN
1905

MANITOBA
1870

QUEBEC
1867

MARITIME PROVINCES
1867

ONTARIO
1867

Ottawa

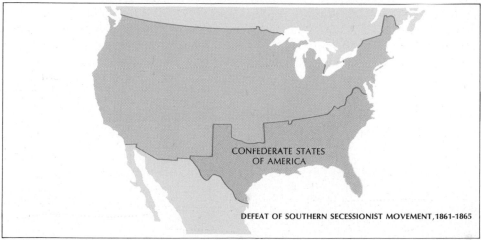

CONFEDERATE STATES OF AMERICA

DEFEAT OF SOUTHERN SECESSIONIST MOVEMENT, 1861-1865

1866, as a prize for Italian aid to Prussia in a war against Austria, and Rome was annexed in 1870 after the withdrawal of French troops in the Franco-Prussian War of 1870.[11]

So Italy was "made," as the phrase of the time expressed it. It had been made by the long high-minded apostolate of Mazzini, the audacity of Garibaldi, the cold policy of Cavour, by war and insurrection, by armed violence endorsed by popular vote.

Persistent Problems after Unification

Very little was settled or ended by unification. Even territorially, the more pronounced nationalists refused to believe that Italian unity was completed. They looked beyond, to regions of mixed population where Italians were numerous or preponderant—to the Trentino, to Trieste, to certain Dalmatian islands, or to Nice and Savoy. They saw in these regions an *Italia irredenta*, "an unredeemed Italy," awaiting in its turn the day of incorporation. "Irredentism" even passed into the English language as a word signifying a vociferous demand, on nationalist grounds, for annexation of regions beyond one's own frontiers.

The occupation of Rome in 1870 by the Italian government opened the rift between church and state still wider. The pope, deprived of territories he had held for a thousand years, renewed his condemnations and chose to remain in lifelong seclusion in the Vatican. His successors followed the same policy until 1929. Hence good Italian patriots were bound to be anticlerical, and good Catholics were bound to look upon the Italian state with unfriendly eyes. The regional differences between northern and southern Italy did not disappear with unification. The north looked upon the agrarian south, the land of priest, landlord, and impoverished peasant, as disgracefully backward. Lawlessness in Sicily and Naples did not disappear with the overthrow of the Bourbons.

The new Italy was parliamentary but not democratic. At first the vote was only given to some 600,000 persons out of more than 20 million. Not until 1913 was the suffrage significantly broadened. Meanwhile parliamentary life, confined to a few, was somewhat unrealistic and frequently corrupt. With the mass of the population excluded from the vote, the revolutionary agitation continued unabated after the unification. Garibaldi himself, in the 1860s, made two more attempts to seize Rome by violence. In general, the revolutionary movement shifted from the older republican nationalism to the newer forms of Marxian socialism, anarchism, or syndicalism.

But the dream of ages was realized. Italy was one. The period that seemed so shameful to patriots, the long centuries that had elapsed since the Renaissance, were now terminated in the glories of a successful Risorgimento.

65. BISMARCK: THE FOUNDING OF A GERMAN EMPIRE

To play upon the divisions among the Germans, keeping them in rivalry with each other and dependent upon outside powers, had been the policy of France ever since the Reformation and of Russia since it began to take part in the affairs of Europe. The pulverization of the Germanic world was in fact a kind of negative prerequisite to the development of modern history as we know it, for without

[11] See pp. 523–524, 600–602.

it the economic and cultural leadership of Europe would hardly have become concentrated along the Atlantic seaboard, or a great military empire have arisen in Russia and spread along the Baltic and into Poland.

Gradually, as we have seen, the Germans became dissatisfied with their position. They became nationalistic.[12] Many German thinkers held that Germany was different from the West, destined some day to work out a peculiarly German way of life and political system of its own. To the Slavs the Germans felt immeasurably superior. German philosophy, as shown most clearly in Hegel, took on a certain characteristic tone. It pronounced individualism to be Western; it skipped lightly over individual liberty; it tended to glorify group loyalties, collectivist principles, and the state. It made a great to-do about History, which in the thought of Hegel, and after him Marx, became a vast force almost independent of human beings. History was said to ordain, require, necessitate, condemn, justify, or excuse. What one did not like could be dismissed as a mere historical phase, opening into a quite different and more attractive future. What one wanted, in the present or future, could be described as historically necessary and bound to come.

The German States after 1848

In 1848 a series of revolutions unseated the several governments of Germany. At the Frankfurt Assembly a group composed essentially of private citizens undertook to organize a united Germany by constitutional methods. They failed because they had no power. Hence after 1848 the Germans began to think in terms of power, developing a somewhat extreme admiration for *die Macht*. The men of Frankfurt failed also, perhaps, because they were insufficiently revolutionary. The Germans were a sober, orderly, and respectful people. They were still attached emotionally to their several states. What happened in Italy, a revolutionary extermination of all the old governments except that of Piedmont, could not happen in Germany.[13]

After the failure of the 1848 revolution German nationalists and liberals were confused. By 1850 the old states were restored—Austria and Prussia, the kingdoms of Hanover, Saxony, Bavaria, and Württemberg, together with about thirty other states ranging in size down to the free cities of Hamburg and Frankfurt. The loose confederation of 1815, linking all these states together, was restored also.[14] But within this framework great economic and social changes were occurring. Between 1850 and 1870 the output of both coal and iron in Germany multiplied sixfold. In 1850 Germany produced less iron than France, in 1870 more. Germany was overcoming the economic and social lag which had characterized it for 300 years. A *Zollverein*, formed by Prussia in 1834, included almost all Germany outside of Austria and Bohemia and provided a large measure of economic unity. The German cities were growing, bound together by railroad and telegraph, requiring larger supporting areas on which to live. Industrial capitalists and industrial workingmen were becoming more numerous. With the advantages of unity more obvious than ever, with the ideals of 1848 badly compromised, with an exaggerated respect for the state and for power, and with a habit of accepting the

[12] See pp. 408–414, 442–443.
[13] See pp. 442–443.
[14] See pp. 419–422, 487–488 and map, p. 522.

successful event as the "judgment of history," the Germans were ripe for what happened. They did not unify themselves by their own exertions. They fell into the arms of Prussia.

Prussia in the 1860s: Bismarck

Prussia had always been the smallest and most precarious of the great powers. Ruined by Napoleon, it had risen again. It owed its international influence and internal character to its army. Actually it had fought rather fewer wars than other great powers, but, with its army in being, it had followed a program of expansion by conquest or diplomacy. The taking of Silesia in 1740, of parts of Poland in the 1770s and 1790s, of the Rhineland in 1815 by an international bargain were the highlights of Prussian growth.[15] After 1850 those who controlled the destinies of Prussia were apprehensive. Their state had been shaken by revolution. In the Crimean War and at the Congress of Paris they were hardly more than spectators. Italy was unified without any Prussian saying yes or no. It seemed as if the hard-won and still relatively recent position of Prussia might be waning.

Since 1815 the population of Prussia had grown from 11 to 18 million, but the size of the army had not changed. Merely to enforce existing principles of conscription would therefore almost double the army. But this would require increased financial appropriations. After 1850 Prussia had a parliament.[16] It was a parliament, to be sure, dominated by men of wealth; but some of the wealthy Prussians, notably the capital owners of the Rhineland, were liberals who wished the parliament to have control over government policies. These men did not like professional armies and considered the Prussian Junkers, from whom the officer corps was recruited, as their main rivals in the state. The parliament refused the necessary appropriations. The king at this juncture, in 1862, appointed a new chief minister, Otto von Bismarck.

Bismarck was a Junker from old Brandenburg east of the Elbe. He cultivated the gruff manner of an honest country squire, though he was in fact an accomplished man of the world. Intellectually he was far superior to the rather slow-witted landlord class from which he sprang, and for which he often felt an impatient contempt. He shared in many Junker ideas. He advocated, and even felt, a kind of stout Protestant piety. Although he cared for the world's opinion, it never deterred him in his actions; criticism and denunciation left him untouched. He was in fact obstinate. He was not a nationalist. He did not look upon all Germany as his Fatherland. He was a Prussian. His social affinities, as with the Junkers generally, lay to the East with corresponding landowning elements of the Baltic provinces and Russia.[17] The West, including the bulk of Germany, he neither understood nor trusted; it seemed to him revolutionary, turbulent, free-thinking, materialistic. Parliamentary bodies he considered ignorant and irresponsible as organs of government. Individual liberty seemed to him disorderly selfishness. Liberalism, democracy, socialism were repugnant to him. He preferred to stress duty, service, order, and the fear of God. The idea of forming a new German union developed only gradually in his mind and then as an adjunct to the strengthening of Prussia.

[15] See maps, pp. 222–223.
[16] See p. 488.
[17] See map, p. 206.

Bismarck thus had his predilections, and even his principles. But no principle bound him, no ideology seemed to him an end in itself. He became the classic practitioner of *Realpolitik.* The time came when the Junkers thought him a traitor to his class, when even the king was afraid of him, when he outraged and then mollified the august house of Habsburg, when he made friends with liberals, democrats, and even socialists, and in turn made enemies of them. First he made wars, then he insisted upon peace. Enmities and alliances were to him only matters of passing convenience. The enemy of today might be the friend of tomorrow. Far from planning out a long train of events, then following it step by step to a grand consummation, he seems to have been practical and opportunistic, taking advantage of situations as they emerged and prepared to act in any one of several directions as events might suggest.

In 1862, as minister president, it was his job, or duty, to outface the liberals in the Prussian parliament. For four years, from 1862 to 1866, Bismarck waged this "constitutional struggle." The parliament refused to vote the proposed taxes. The government collected them anyway. The taxpayers paid them without protest—it was the orderly thing to do, and the collectors represented public authority. The limitations of Prussian liberalism, the docility of the population, the respect for officialdom, the belief that the king and his ministers were wiser than the elected deputies, all clearly revealed themselves in this triumph of military policy over the theory of government by consent. The army was enlarged, reorganized, retrained, and reequipped. Bismarck fended off the showers of abuse from the liberal majority in the chamber. The liberals declared that the government's policy was flagrantly unconstitutional. The constitution, said Bismarck, could not have been meant to undermine the state. The government, said the liberals, was itself undermining Prussia, for the rest of Germany hoped to find in Prussia, as Italy had found in Piedmont, a model of political freedom. What the Germans admired in Prussia, replied Bismarck coldly, was not its liberalism but its power. He declared that the Prussian boundaries as set in 1815 were unsound, that Prussia must be prepared to seize favorable opportunities for further growth.[18] And he added one of his most memorable utterances: "Not by speeches and majority votes are the great questions of the day decided—that was the great error of 1848 and 1849—but by blood and iron."

Bismarck's Wars: The North German Confederation, 1867

A favorable opportunity was not long in presenting itself. The Schleswig-Holstein question arose again. We have seen how it had arisen in 1848, and how even the mild men of Frankfurt had insisted, to the point of war, upon the incorporation of the two duchies into their German union.[19] Now in 1863 the story was repeated. The Danes, engaged in a process of national consolidation of their own, wished to make Schleswig an integral part of Denmark. The population of Schleswig was part Dane and part German. The diet of the German confederation, unwilling to see Germans thus annexed outright to Denmark, called for an all-German war upon the Danes, just as the revolutionary Frankfurt Assembly had done. Bismarck had no desire to support or strengthen the existing German confederation. He wanted not an all-German war but a Prussian war. To disguise

---

[18] See maps, pp. 223, 522.
[19] See p. 487.

THE GERMAN QUESTION, 1815–1871

From 1815 to 1866 there were thirty-nine states in Germany (of which only the largest are shown) joined in the Confederation of 1815. At the Frankfurt Assembly in 1848 (see pp. 485–486) two groups developed: the Great Germans who adhered to the idea of an all-German union, to include the Austrian lands except Hungary; and the Little Germans who were willing to exclude Austria and its empire. Bismarck was a Little German but a Great Prussian. He (1) enlarged Prussia by conquest in 1866, (2) joined Mecklenburg, Saxony, etc., with his enlarged Prussia in a North German Confederation of 1867, (3) combined this in turn with Bavaria, Württemberg, etc., to form the German empire of 1871, (4) conquered Alsace-Lorraine from France, and (5) ejected Austria. The boundaries of Bismarck-ian Germany remained unchanged until 1918. (See also maps, pp. 222–223, 420–421, 528–529, 692–693.)

his aims he acted jointly with Austria. In 1864 Prussia and Austria together went to war with Denmark, which they soon defeated. It was Bismarck's intention to annex both Schleswig and Holstein to Prussia, gaining whatever other advantages might present themselves from future trouble with Austria. He arranged a provisional occupation of Schleswig by Prussia, and of Holstein by Austria. Disputes soon arose over rights of passage, the keeping of internal order, and other problems with which occupying forces are commonly afflicted. While pretending to try to regulate these disputes he allowed them to ripen.

He now proceeded to discredit and isolate Austria. The British government was at the time following a policy of nonintervention in the affairs of the Continent. The Russian empire was in no position for action; it was divided internally by a reform program then at its height; it was in a mood of hostility to Austria, because of events of the Crimean War, and well disposed toward Prussia and Bismarck, because Bismarck in 1863 took care to support it against an uprising of the Poles. To win over the new kingdom of Italy Bismarck held out the lure of Venetia. As for France, Napoleon III was embarrassed by domestic discontents and had his army committed to adventures in Mexico. In addition, Bismarck charmed him at a confidential interview at Biarritz, where vague oral intimations of French expansion were exchanged, and the two men seemed to agree to a needed modernization of the map of Europe. To weaken Austria within Germany, Bismarck presented himself as a democrat. He proposed a reform of the German confederation, recommending that it have a popular chamber elected by universal male suffrage. He calculated that the mass of the German people were wedded neither to the well-to-do capitalistic liberals, nor to the existing government structures of the German states, nor to the house of Habsburg. He would use "democracy" to undermine all established interests that stood in his way.

Meanwhile the occupying powers continued to quarrel over Schleswig-Holstein. Austria finally raised the matter formally in the German federal diet, one of whose functions was to prevent war between its members. Bismarck declared that the diet had no authority, accused the Austrians of aggression, and ordered the Prussian army to enter Holstein. The Austrians called for federal sanctions in the form of an all-German force to be sent against Prussia. The result was that Prussia, in 1866, was at war not only with Austria but with most of the other German states. The Prussian army soon proved its superiority. Trained to an unprecedented precision, equipped wth the new needle-gun, by which the infantryman could deliver five rounds a minute, brought into the zone of combat by an imaginative strategy that made use of the new railroads, commanded by the skill of von Moltke, the Prussian army overthrew the Austrians at the battle of Sadowa (or Königgrätz) and defeated the other German states soon thereafter. The Austro-Prussian, or Seven Weeks' War, was amazing in its brevity. Bismarck hastened to make peace before the other European powers could realize what had happened.

Prussia annexed outright, together with Schleswig-Holstein, the whole kingdom of Hanover, the duchies of Nassau and Hesse-Cassel, and the free city of Frankfurt. Here the old governments simply disappeared before the axe of the "red reactionary." The German federal union disappeared likewise. In its place, in 1867, Bismarck organized a North German Confederation, in which the newly enlarged Prussia joined with twenty-one other states, all of which combined it greatly outweighed. The German states south of the river Main—Austria, Bavaria, Baden, Württemberg, and Hesse-Darmstadt—remained outside the new organization, with no kind of union among themselves. Meanwhile the kingdom of Italy annexed Venetia.

For the North German Confederation Bismarck produced a constitution. The new structure, though a federal one, was much stronger than the now defunct Confederation of 1815. The king of Prussia became its hereditary head. Ministers were responsible to him. There was a parliament with two chambers. The upper chamber, as in the United States, represented the states as such, though not equally. The lower chamber, or Reichstag, was deemed to represent the people and was elected by universal male suffrage. Such flirting with democracy seemed madness to both conservative Junker and liberal bourgeois. It was indeed a bold step, for only France at the time illustrated universal suffrage in Europe on a large scale, and in the France of Napoleon III neither old-fashioned conservatives nor genuine liberals could take much satisfaction. As for Great Britain, where voting rights were extended in this same year, 1867, they were still given to less than half the adult male population. Bismarck sensed in the "masses" an ally of strong government against private interests. He negotiated even with the socialists, who had arisen with the industrialization of the past decade, and who, in Germany at this time, were mainly followers of Ferdinand Lassalle. The Lassallean socialists, unlike the Marxian, believed it theoretically possible to improve working-class conditions through the action of existing governments. To the great annoyance of Marx, then in England (his *Capital* first appeared in 1867), the bulk of the German socialists reached an understanding with Bismarck. In return for a democratic suffrage they agreed to accept the North German Confederation. Bismarck, for his part, by making use of democratic and socialist sentiment, won popular approval for his emerging empire.

The Franco-Prussian War

It was clear that the situation was not yet stable. The small south German states were left floating in empty space; they would sooner or later have to gravitate into some orbit or other, whether Austrian, Prussian, or French. In France there were angry criticisms of Napoleon III's foreign policy. French intervention in Mexico had proved a fiasco.[20] A united Italy had been allowed to rise on France's borders. And now, contrary to all principles of French national interest observed by French governments for hundreds of years, a strong and independent power was being allowed to spread over virtually the whole of Germany. Everywhere people began to feel that war was coming between France and Prussia. Bismarck played on the fears of France felt in the south German states. South Germany, though in former times often a willing satellite to France, was now sufficiently nationalistic to consider such subservience to a foreign people disgraceful. To Bismarck it seemed that a war between Prussia and France would frighten the small south German states into a union with Prussia, leaving only Austria outside— which was what he wanted. To Napoleon III, or at least to some of his advisers, it seemed that such a war, if successful, would restore public approval of the Bonapartist empire. In this inflammable situation the responsible persons of neither country worked for peace.

Meanwhile a revolution in Spain had driven the reigning queen into exile, and a Spanish provisional government invited Prince Leopold of Hohenzollern, the

[20] See p. 617.

king of Prussia's cousin, to be constitutional king of Spain. To entrench the Prussian royal house in Spain would naturally be distasteful to France. Three times the Hohenzollern family refused the Spanish offer. Bismarck, who could not control such family decisions, but who foresaw the possibility of a usable incident, deviously persuaded the Spanish to issue the invitation still a fourth time. On July 2, 1870, Paris heard that Prince Leopold had accepted. The French ambassador to Prussia, Benedetti, at the direction of his government, met the king of Prussia at the bathing resort of Ems, where he formally demanded that Prince Leopold's acceptance be withdrawn. It was withdrawn on July 12. The French seemed to have their way. Bismarck was disappointed.

The French government went still further. It instructed Benedetti to approach the king again at Ems and demand that at no time in the future would any Hohenzollern ever become a candidate for the Spanish throne. The king politely declined any such commitment and telegraphed a full report of the conversation to Bismarck at Berlin. Bismarck, receiving the telegram, which became famous as the "Ems dispatch," saw a new opportunity, as he put it, to wave a red flag before the Gallic bull. He condensed the Ems telegram for publication, so reducing and abridging it that it seemed to newspaper readers as if a curt exchange had occurred at Ems, in which the Prussians believed that their king had been insulted, and the French that their ambassador had been snubbed. In both countries the war party demanded satisfaction. On July 19, 1870, on these trivial grounds, and with the ostensible issue of the Spanish throne already settled, the irresponsible and decaying government of Napoleon III declared war on Prussia.

Again the war was short. Again Bismarck had taken care to isolate his enemy in advance. The British generally felt France to be in the wrong. They had been alarmed by French operations in Mexico, which suggested an ambition to recreate a French American empire. The Italians had long been awaiting the chance to seize Rome; they did so in 1870, when the French withdrew their troops from Rome for use against Prussia. The Russians had been awaiting the chance to upset the clause of the Peace of 1856 which forbade them to keep naval vessels in the Black Sea. They did so in 1870.

The War of 1870, like the others of the time, failed to become a general European struggle. Prussia was supported by the south German states. France had no allies. The French army proved to be technically backward compared with the Prussian. War began on July 19; on September 2, after the battle of Sedan, the principal French army surrendered to the Germans. Napoleon III was himself taken prisoner. On September 4 an insurrection in Paris proclaimed the Third Republic. The Prussian and German forces moved into France and laid siege to the capital. Though the French armies dissolved, Paris refused to capitulate. For four months it was surrounded and besieged.

The German Empire, 1871

With their guns encircling Paris, the German rulers or their representatives assembled at Versailles. The château and gardens of Versailles, since Louis XVI's unceremonious departure in October 1789, had been little more than a vacant monument to a society long since dead. Here, in the most sumptuous room of the palace, the resplendent Hall of Mirrors, where the Sun King had once received the deferential approaches of German princes, Bismarck on January 18, 1871, caused the German Empire to be proclaimed. The king of Prussia received the hereditary title of German emperor. The other German rulers (excepting, to be sure, the ruler of Austria, and those whom Bismarck had himself dethroned) accepted his imperial authority. Ten days later the people of Paris, shivering, hungry, and helpless, opened their gates to the enemy. France had no government with which Bismarck could make peace. It was not at all clear what kind of government the country wanted. Bismarck insisted on the election of a Constituent Assembly by universal suffrage. He demanded that France pay the German Empire a war indemnity of five billion gold francs (then an enormous and unprecedented sum) and cede to it the border region of Alsace and most of Lorraine. Though the Alsatians spoke German, most of them felt themselves to be French, having shared in the general history of France since the seventeenth century. There was strong local protest at the transfer to Germany, and the French never reconciled themselves to this cold-blooded amputation of their frontier. The peace dictated by Bismarck was embodied in the treaty of Frankfurt of May 10, 1871. Thereafter, as will be seen, the French Constituent Assembly gradually proceeded to construct the Third Republic.[21]

The consolidation of Germany transformed the face of Europe. It reversed the dictum not only of the Peace of Vienna but even of the Peace of Westphalia.[22] The German Empire, no sooner born, was the strongest state on the continent of Europe. Rapidly industrialized after 1870, it became more potent still. Bismarck, by consummate astuteness, by exploiting the opportunities offered by a Europe in flux, and with no more fighting than that involved in a few weeks in three short wars, had brought about what European statesmen of many nationalities had long said should at all costs be prevented. He outwitted everybody in turn, including the Germans. The united all-German state that issued from the nationalist movement was a Germany conquered by Prussia. Prussia, with its annexations of 1866, embraced almost all Germany north of the Main. Within the empire it had about two-thirds of the area. Before such unanswerable success the Prussian liberals capitulated, and the Prussian parliament passed an "indemnity act"; the gist of it was that Bismarck admitted to a certain high-handedness during the constitutional struggle but that the parliament legalized the disputed tax collections *ex post facto*, agreeing to forgive and forget, in view of the victory over Austria and its consequences. Thus liberalism withered away before nationalism.

The German Empire received substantially the constitution of the North German Confederation. It was a federation of monarchies, each based in theory on divine or hereditary right. At the same time, in the Reichstag elected by universal male suffrage, it rested on a kind of mass appeal and was in a sense democratic. Yet the country's ministers were responsible to the emperor and not to the elected chamber. Moreover, it was the rulers who joined the empire, not the peoples. There were no popular plebiscites as in Italy. Each state kept its own laws, government, and constitution. The people of Prussia, for example, remained for Prussian affairs under the rather illiberal constitution of 1850,[23] while in affairs of the Reich, or empire, they enjoyed an equal vote by universal suffrage. The emperor, who was also the king of Prussia, had legal control over the foreign and military policy of the empire. The German Empire in effect served as a mechan-

[21] See pp. 572–574.
[22] See pp. 141–145, and map, pp. 142–143.
[23] See p. 488.

ism to magnify the role of Prussia, the Prussian army, and the East-Elbian Prussian aristocracy in world affairs.

66. THE DUAL MONARCHY OF AUSTRIA-HUNGARY

The Habsburg Empire after 1848

Bismarck united Germany, but he also divided it, for he left about a sixth of the Germans outside his German Empire. These Germans of Austria and Bohemia had now to work out a common future with the dozen other nationalities in the Danubian domain.

The clumsiness of the old Habsburg multinational empire is clear enough, but more impressive is its astonishing capacity to live and to survive. Prussia and France, in the 1740s, had tried unsuccessfully to dismember it. Smashed four different times by the French between 1796 and 1809, it outlived this crisis, and after 1815, under Metternich, it guided the counsels of Europe.[24] Broken up in 1848, restored by the intervention of Russia in 1849, dislocated by its effort at mobilization in 1855, attacked by Napoleon III in 1859 and by Bismarck in 1866, it still continued to hold together and disappeared finally only in 1918 in the cataclysm of the First World War.[25] But the events of the 1850s and 1860s greatly altered its character.

The essential question, in a nationalist age, was how the Habsburg government would react to the problems raised by national self-expression. The nationalities did not wish to destroy the empire. Among the Hungarians after 1848–1849, only a handful of extreme radicals dreamed of a Hungary entirely independent. Most of them desired constitutional autonomy for Hungary but were not prepared to sever the link with Vienna. Slav opinion, at the Slav Congress of Prague in 1848, went basically no further than Austroslavism.[26] The peoples of the empire, while increasingly insistent on certain national rights—such as a degree of local self-government, and schools, law courts, and administration in their own language—felt an underlying need for the large political structure which the empire gave.

By Habsburg, in this period, one means primarily Francis Joseph, who as emperor from 1848 to 1916 reigned even longer than his famous contemporary,

---

[24] See pp. 265–268, 382–384, 392–395, 397–398, 445–455.
[25] See pp. 477–483, 513, 515–516, 521–523, 681–682.
[26] See pp. 480–481.

EUROPE, 1871

The new features on this map, as compared to the Europe of 1815 (see pp. 420–421), are the existence of a unified German Empire and a unified Kingdom of Italy. The German domain was enlarged by the incorporation of Schleswig (in the neck of the Danish peninsula) and the annexation from France of Alsace and parts of Lorraine, the regions respectively around Strassburg (French Strasbourg) and Metz on the map. From 1871 to 1914 Europe had fewer separate states, fewer land frontiers, and a simpler political geography than at any other time in its history. Except for the voluntary separation of Norway and Sweden in 1905 there were no changes in this period outside the Balkans. (See map, p. 667.)

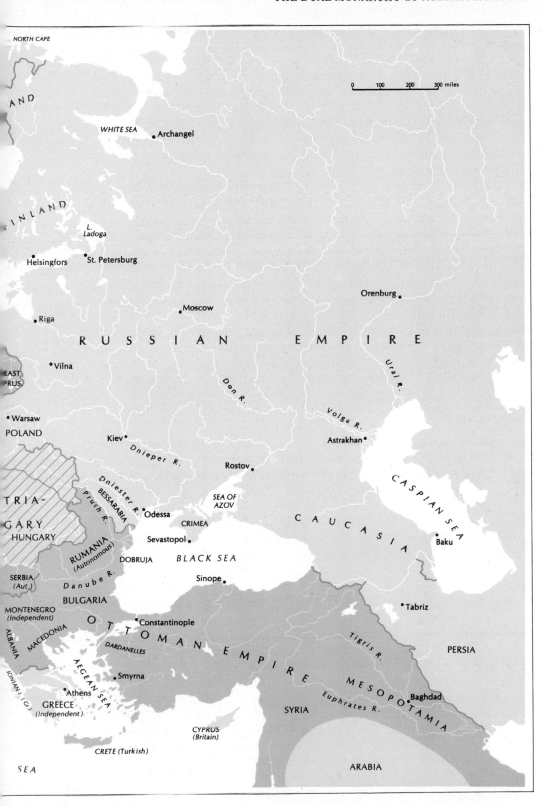

NORTH CAPE

WHITE SEA • Archangel

0   100   200   300 miles

...AND

...INLAND

L.
Ladoga

• Helsingfors   • St. Petersburg

Orenburg •

• Riga   • Moscow

R U S S I A N   E M P I R E

• Vilna

Ural R.

EAST
PRUS.

• Warsaw   Don R.
POLAND   Volga R.

Kiev •   Astrakhan •

Dnieper R.   Rostov •

Dniester R.   SEA OF
BESSARABIA   AZOV
TRIA-   Pruth R.   CAUCASIA
GARY   • Odessa
HUNGARY   CRIMEA   CASPIAN SEA
    Sevastopol •
SERBIA   BLACK SEA   • Baku
(Aut.)   Danube R.   • Sinope
RUMANIA   DOBRUJA
(Autonomous)
MONTENEGRO   BULGARIA   • Tabriz
(Independent)   O T T O M A N   E M P I R E
ALBANIA   • Constantinople   Tigris R.   PERSIA
MACEDONIA   DARDANELLES
IONIAN I. (Gr.)   AEGEAN   • Smyrna   M E S O P O T A M I A
    SEA
    • Athens   Euphrates R.   • Baghdad
GREECE   SYRIA
(Independent)   CYPRUS
    (Britain)
SEA   CRETE (Turkish)   ARABIA

Queen Victoria. Francis Joseph, like many others, could never shake off his own tradition. His thoughts turned on his house and on its rights. Buffeted unmercifully by the waves of change, he cordially disliked everything liberal, progressive, or modern. He allied himself with the Catholic hierarchy and the Vatican, which also, for decades after 1848, and for understandable reason, set itself bluntly against compromise with the new age. Personally, Francis Joseph was incapable of enlarged views, ambitious projects, bold decisions, or persevering action. And he lived in a pompous dream world, surrounded in the imperial court by great noblemen, high churchmen, and bespangled personages of the army.

Yet the government was not idle; it was, if anything, too fertile in devising new deals and new dispensations. Various expedients were tried after 1849, but none was tried long enough to see if it would work. For several years the ruling idea was centralization—to govern the empire through the German language and with German efficiency, maintaining the abolition of serfdom as accomplished in 1848 (and which required a strong official control over the landlords if it was to work in practice) and favoring the building of railroads and other apparatus of material progress.[27] This Germanic and bureaucratic centralization was distasteful to the non-German nationalities, and especially to the Magyars. It is important to say Magyars, not Hungarians, because the Magyars composed less than half the very mixed population of Hungary within its then existing borders. Nevertheless the Magyars, as the strongest of the non-German groups, and hence the most able to maintain a political system of their own, felt the Germanic influence as most oppressive. In the war of 1859 the Magyars sympathized with the Italians.

The Compromise of 1867

In 1867 a compromise was made, known as the *Ausgleich*. It was essentially a bargain between the Germans of Austria-Bohemia and the Magyars of Hungary. It worked to the common disadvantage of the Slavs. Both Germans and Magyars looked upon the Slavs somewhat as many whites in the United States then looked upon blacks, seeing in them a people who had shown no aptitude for civilization except under tutelage. In fact the word "slave" in many languages (German *Sklave*) had originated from the word "Slav." As Count Beust, the Austrian negotiator, put it in 1867, the idea of the Compromise was that each people, Germans and Magyars, should thereafter govern its own barbarians in its own way.

The Compromise created a Dual Monarchy, of a kind unparalleled in Europe. West of the river Leith was the Empire of Austria, east of it the Kingdom of Hungary. The two were now judged exactly equal. Each had its own constitution and its own parliament, to which in each country the governing ministry was henceforth to be responsible. The administrative language of Austria would be German, of Hungary, Magyar. Neither state might intervene in the other's affairs. The two were joined by the fact that the same Habsburg ruler should always be emperor in Austria and king in Hungary. Yet the union was not personal only; for, though there was no common parliament, delegates of the two parliaments were to meet together alternately in Vienna and Budapest, and there was to be a common ministry for finance, foreign affairs, and war. To this common ministry of Austria-Hungary both Austrians and Hungarians were to be appointed.

[27] See p. 483.

In effect, the Compromise treated Austria as a kind of German nation-state and Hungary as a Magyar nation-state. It furnished each with parliamentary and constitutional organs, by which the leading nationality was made to feel a sense of participation in government. But the Germans formed less than half the people of Austria, as did the Magyars of Hungary. Austria included the Slovenes, Czechs, Poles, and Ruthenians (and a few Italians); Hungary the Slovaks, the Croats and Serbs, and the Transylvanians, who were essentially Rumanians.[28] All these people felt aggrieved.

Both Austria and Hungary, under the Dual Monarchy, were in form constitutional parliamentary states, although the principle of ministerial responsibility was not consistently honored. Neither was democratic. In Austria, after much juggling with voting systems, a true universal male suffrage was instituted in 1907. In Hungary, when the First World War came in 1914, still only a quarter of the adult male population had the vote. Socially, the great reform of 1848, the abolition of serfdom, was not allowed to lead on to upsetting conclusions. The owners of great landed estates, especially in Hungary (but also in parts of the Austrian Empire) remained the unquestionably dominant class. They were surrounded by landless peasants, an agrarian proletariat, composed partly of lower classes of their own nationality, and partly of entire peasant peoples, like the Slovaks and Serbs, who had no educated or wealthy class of their own. National and social questions therefore came together. For some nationalities, and for none more than the Magyars, not only a national but a social and economic ascendancy was at stake. Landlordism became the basic social issue. A landowning class, educated and civilized, faced a peasant mass that was generally ignorant, rude, and left out of the advancing civilization of the day.

67. LIBERALIZATION IN TSARIST RUSSIA: ALEXANDER II

Tsarist Russia after 1856

For Russia also the Crimean War set off a series of changes. The ungainly empire, an "enormous village" as it has been called, stretching from Poland to the Pacific, had proved unable to repel a localized attack by France and Great Britain, into which neither of the Western powers had put anything like its full resources. Alexander II (1855–1881), who became tsar during the war, was no liberal by nature or conviction. But he saw that something drastic must be done. The prestige of western Europe was at its height. There the most successful and even enviable nations were to be found. The reforms in Russia therefore followed, at some distance, the European model.

Imperial Russia was a political organization very difficult to describe. Its own subjects did not know what to make of it. Some, called Westernizers in the mid-nineteenth century, believed Russia destined to become more like Europe. Others, the Slavophiles, believed Russia to be entrusted with a special destiny of its own, which imitation of Europe would only weaken or pervert.

That Russia differed from Europe at least in degree was doubted by nobody. The leading institution was the autocracy of the tsar. This was not exactly the absolutism known in the West. In Russia certain very old European conceptions

---

[28] See maps, pp. 441, 528–529.

were missing, such as the idea that spiritual authority is independent of even the mightiest prince or the old feudal idea of reciprocal duties between king and subject.[29] The notion that men have rights, claims for justice at the hands of power, which no one in Europe had ever expressly repudiated, was in Russia a somewhat doctrinaire importation from the West. The tsardom did not rule by law; it ran the country by ukase, police action, and the army. The tsars, since Peter and before, had built up their state very largely by importing European technical methods and technical experts, often against strong objection by native Russians of all classes, upon whom the new methods were, when necessary, simply forced. More than any state in Europe, the Russian empire was a machine superimposed upon its people without organic connection—bureaucracy pure and simple. But as the contacts with Europe were joined, many Russians acquired European ideas of a kind in which the autocracy was not interested—ideas of liberty and fraternity, of a just and classless society, of individual personality enriched by humane culture and moral freedom. Many people, with such sentiments, found themselves chronically critical of the government and of Russia itself. The government, massive though it seemed, was afraid of such people. Any idea arising outside of official circles seemed pernicious, and the press and the universities were as a rule severely censored.

A second fundamental institution, which had grown up with the tsardom, was legalized bondage or serfdom. The bulk of the population were serfs dependent upon masters. Russian serfdom was more onerous than that found in east-central Europe until 1848.[30] It resembled the slavery of the Americas in that serfs were "owned"; they could be bought and sold and used in other occupations than agriculture. Some serfs worked the soil, rendering unpaid labor service to the gentry. Others could be used by their owners in factories or mines or rented out for such purposes. Others were more independent, working as artisans or mechanics, and even traveling about or residing in the cities, but from their earnings they had to remit certain fees to the lord, or return home when he called them. The owners had a certain paternalistic responsibility for their serfs, and in the villages the gentry constituted a kind of personal local government. The law, as in the American South, did little or nothing to interfere between gentry and servile mass, so that the serf's day-to-day fortunes depended on the personality or economic circumstances of his owner.

By the mid-nineteenth century both conservative and liberal Russians were agreeing that serfdom must some day end. Serfdom was in any case ceasing to be profitable; some two-thirds of all the privately owned serfs (i.e., those not belonging to the tsar or state) were mortgaged as security for loans at the time of Alexander II's accession. Increasingly serfdom was recognized as a bad system of labor relations, making the muzhiks into illiterate and stolid drudges, without incentive, initiative, self-respect, or pride of workmanship, and also very poor soldiers for the army.

Educated Russians, full of Western ideas, were estranged from the government, from the Orthodox church, which was an arm of the tsar, and from the common people of their own country. They felt ill at ease in a mass of ignorance and obscurantism and a pang of guilt at the virtual slavery on which their own

[29] See pp. 18–19, 30. On Russia in the sixteenth and seventeenth centuries, see pp. 227–228.
[30] See pp. 230–231, 325–326.

position rested. Hence arose, at about the time under discussion, another distinctive feature of Russian life, the "intelligentsia." In Russia it was thought so exciting to be educated, to have ideas, to subscribe to magazines, or engage in critical conversation that the intelligentsia sensed themselves as a class apart. They were made up of students, university graduates, and persons who had a good deal of leisure to read. Such people, while not very free to think, were more free to think than to do almost anything else. The Russian intelligentsia tended to sweeping and all-embracing philosophies. They believed that intellectuals should play a large role in society. They formed an exaggerated idea of the direct influence of thinkers upon the course of historical change. Their characteristic attitude was one of opposition. Some, overwhelmed by the mammoth immobility of the tsardom and of serfdom, turned to revolutionary and even terroristic philosophies. This only made the bureaucrats more anxious and fearful, and the government more fitfully repressive.

The Emancipation Act of 1861 and Other Reforms

Alexander II, on becoming tsar, attempted to enlist the support of the liberals among the intelligentsia. He gave permission to travel outside of Russia, eased the controls on the universities, and allowed the censorship to go relatively unenforced. Newspapers and journals were founded, and those written by Russian revolutionaries abroad, like the *Polar Star* of Alexander Herzen in London, penetrated more freely into the country. The result was a great outburst of public opinion, which was agreed at least on one point, the necessity of emancipating the peasants. This was in principle hardly a party question. Alexander's father, Nicholas I, had been a noted reactionary, who abhorred Western liberalism and is memorable for having organized, as the "Third Section" of his chancellory, a system of secret political police until then unparalleled in Europe for its arbitrary and inquisitorial methods. Yet Nicholas I had taken serious measures to alleviate serfdom. Alexander II, basically conservative on Russian affairs, proceeded to set up a special branch of the government to study the question. The government did not wish to throw the whole labor system and economy of the country into chaos, nor to ruin the gentry class without which it could not govern at all. After many discussions, proposals, and memoranda, an imperial ukase of 1861 declared serfdom abolished and the peasants free.

By this great decree the peasants became legally free in the Western sense. They were henceforth subjects of the government, not subjects of their owners. It was hoped that they would be stirred by a new sense of human dignity. As one enthusiastic official put it shortly after emancipation: "The people are erect and transformed; the look, the walk, the speech, everything is changed." The gentry lost their old quasi-manorial jurisdiction over the villages. They could no longer exact forced and unpaid labor or receive fees arising from servitude.

It is important to realize what the Act of Emancipation did and did not do. Roughly (with great differences from region to region) it allocated about half the cultivated land to the gentry and half to the former serfs. The latter had to pay redemption money for the land they received and for the fees which the gentry lost. The Russian aristocracy was far from weakened; in place of a kind of human property largely mortgaged anyway, they now had clear possession of some half the land, they received the redemption money, and were rid of obligations to the peasants.

The peasants, on the other hand, now owned some half the arable land in their own right—a considerable amount by the standards of almost any European country. They did not, however, possess it according to the principles of private property or independent farming that had become prevalent in Europe. The peasant land, when redeemed, became the collective property of the ancient peasant village assembly, or *mir*. The village, as a unit, was responsible to the government for payment of the redemption and for collection of the necessary sums from its individual members. The village assembly, in default of collection, might require forced labor from the defaulter or a member of his family; and it could prevent peasants from moving away from the village, lest those remaining bear the whole burden of payment. It could (as in the past) assign and reassign certain lands to its members for tillage and otherwise supervise cultivation as a joint concern. To keep the village community intact, the government presently forbade the selling or mortgaging of land to persons outside the village. This tended to preserve the peasant society but also to discourage the investment of outside capital, with which equipment might be purchased, and so to retard agricultural improvement and the growth of wealth. Not all peasants within the village unit were equal. As in France before the Revolution, some had the right to work more land than others. Some were only day laborers. Others had rights of inheritance in the soil (for not all land was subject to reassignment by the commune) or rented additional parcels of land belonging to the gentry. These lands they worked by hiring other peasants for wages. These more substantial peasants, as agricultural entrepreneurs, resembled farmers of the type found in France or the United States. None of the Russian peasants, however, after the emancipation, possessed full individual freedom of action. In their movements and obligations, as in their thoughts, they were restricted by their villages as they had once been restricted by their lords.

Alexander II proceeded to overhaul and westernize the legal system of the country. With the disappearance of the lord's jurisdiction over his peasants a new system of local courts was needed in any case, but the opportunity was taken to reform the courts from bottom to top. The arbitrariness of authority and defenselessness of the subject were the inveterate evils. They were greatly mitigated by the edict of 1864. Trials were made public, and private persons received the right to be represented in court by lawyers of their own choosing. All class distinctions in judicial matters were abolished, although in practice peasants continued to be subject to harsh disadvantages. A clear sequence of lower and higher courts was established. Requirements were laid down for the professional training of judges, who henceforth received stated salaries and were protected from administrative pressure. A system of juries on the English model was introduced.

While thus attempting to establish a rule of law, the tsar also moved in the direction of allowing self-government. He hoped to win over the liberals and to shoulder the upper and middle classes with some degree of public responsibility. He created, again by an edict of 1864, a system of provincial and district councils called zemstvos. Elected by various elements, including the peasants, the zemstvos gradually went into operation and took up matters of education, medical relief, public welfare, food supply, and road maintenance in their localities. Their great value was in developing civic sentiment among those who took part in them. Many liberals urged a representative body for all Russia, a Zemsky Sobor or Duma, which, however, Alexander II refused to concede. After 1864 his policy became more cautious. A rebellion in Poland in 1863 inclined him to take advice from those who favored repression. He began to mollify the vested interests that had been disgruntled by the reforms and to whittle down some of the concessions already granted. But the essence of the reforms remained unaffected.

Revolutionism in Russia

The autocrat who thus undertook to liberalize Russia barely escaped assassination in 1866, had five shots fired at him in 1873, missed death by half an hour in 1880 when his imperial dining room was dynamited, and in 1881 was to be killed by a bomb. The revolutionaries were not pleased with the reforms, which if successful would merely strengthen the existing order. Dissatisfied intelligentsia in the 1860s began to call themselves "nihilists": they believed in "nothing"—except science—and took a cynical view of the reforming tsar and his zemstvos. The peasants, saddled with heavy redemption payments, remained basically unsatisfied, and intellectuals toured the villages fanning this discontent. Revolutionaries developed a mystic conception of the revolutionary role of the Russian masses. They reminded the peasants of the vast rebellions of Stephen Razin and Pugachev, in which they saw a native Russian revolutionary tradition.[31] Socialists, after the failure of socialism in Europe in the Revolution of 1848, came in many cases to believe, as Alexander Herzen wrote, that the true and natural future of socialism lay in Russia, because of the very weakness of capitalism in Russia and the existence of a kind of collectivism already established in the village assemblies or communes.

More radical than Herzen were the anarchist Bakunin and his disciple Nechaiev. In their *People's Justice* these two called for terrorism not only against tsarist officials but against liberals also. As they wrote in the *Catechism of a Revolutionist*, the true revolutionary "is devoured by one purpose, one thought, one passion—the revolution. . . . He has severed every link with the social order and with the entire civilized world. . . . Everything which promotes the success of the revolution is moral, everything which hinders it is immoral." Terrorism (which is really to say assassination) was rejected by many of the revolutionaries, especially by those who in the 1870s took up the scientific socialism of Karl Marx. To Marx it did not seem that frantic violence would advance an inevitable social process. But other groups, recognizing the inspiration of men like Bakunin and Nechaiev, organized secret terroristic societies. One of these, the People's Will, determined to assassinate the tsar. In an autocratic state, they held, there was no other road to justice and freedom.

Alexander II, alarmed by this underground menace, which of course did not escape the attention of the police, again turned for support to the liberals. The liberals, who were themselves threatened by the revolutionaries, had become estranged from the government by its failure to follow through with the reforms of the early 1860s. Now, in 1880, to rally support, the tsar again relaxed the autocratic system. He abolished the dreaded Third Section or secret police set up by his father, allowed the press to discuss most political subjects freely, and encour-

[31] See pp. 231, 325–326.

aged the zemstvos to do the same. Further to associate representatives of the public with the government, he proposed, not exactly a parliament, but two nationally elected commissions to sit with the council of state. He signed the edict to this effect on March 13, 1881, and on the same day was assassinated, not by a demented individual acting wildly and alone, but by the joint efforts of the highly trained members of the People's Will.

Alexander III, upon his father's death, abandoned the project for elected commissions and during his whole reign, from 1881 to 1894, reverted to a program of brutal resistance to liberals and revolutionaries alike. The new regime established by peasant emancipation, judicial reform, and the zemstvos was nevertheless allowed to continue. How Russia finally received a parliament in 1905 is explained below in the chapter on the Russian Revolution. At present it is enough to have seen how even tsarist Russia, under Alexander II, shared in a liberal movement that was then at its height. The abolition of serfdom, putting both aristocrat and peasant more fully on a money economy, opened the way for capitalistic development within the empire. And between the two confining walls of autocracy and revolutionism—equally hard and unyielding—European ideas of law, liberty, and humanity inserted themselves in a tentative way.

68. THE UNITED STATES: THE AMERICAN CIVIL WAR

The history of Europe, long interconnected with that of the rest of the world, by the early twentieth century became merged with it entirely. Similarly the development of non-European regions, long a collection of separate stories, was to fuse into a single world-wide theme, to which later chapters of this book are largely devoted. It is no great leap at this point to pass to a treatment of areas overseas (as seen from Europe), some of which underwent in the 1860s the same process of national consolidation, or attempted consolidation, already traced in Italy and Germany, Austria, Hungary, and the Russian empire. In particular, foundations were laid for two new "powers" like those of Europe—the United States of America and the Empire of Japan. The huge Dominion of Canada was also established.

Growth of the United States

As in the time of the American Revolution and Napoleon, the history of the United States in the nineteenth century reflected that of the European world of which it formed a part. The most basic fact, besides territorial expansion, was rapid growth. This was so obvious as to lead a French observer in the 1830s, Alexis de Tocqueville, to make a famous prediction: that within a century the United States would have 100 million people and would, along with Russia, be one of the two leading powers of the world. By 1860, with 31 million, the United States was almost as populous as France and more so than Great Britain.

The growth in numbers was due to a prolific birth rate, but also to the arrival of immigrants, who became prolific in their turn. The immigrants—except for an uncounted, because illegal, importation of slaves—came almost entirely from Europe, and before 1860 almost entirely from Great Britain, Ireland, and Germany. The immigrants did not desire to surrender their native ways. Some brought skills that the new country greatly needed, but immigration also presented a true social problem, obliging peoples to live together without common tradition. On the whole, it appears that the older Americans accepted the reshaping of their country rather calmly, with anti-foreign movements occasionally surfacing but then quickly subsiding. Few concessions were made. English was the language of the public schools, the police, law courts, local government, and public notices and announcements. Usually the immigrant had to know some English to hold a job. On the other hand no one was exactly forced to become "Americanized"—the new arrivals were free to maintain churches, newspapers, and social gatherings in their own tongues. The fact that the English, Scots, and Irish already spoke English, and that the Germans readily learned it, alleviated the language issue. The immigrants did not constitute minorities in the European sense. They were more than willing to embrace American national attitudes as formed in the eighteenth century—the national traditions of republicanism and self government, of individual liberty, free enterprise, and unbounded opportunity for self-improvement. The old America impressed itself on the new, being somewhat impressed itself in the process. In this sense a new nationality was being consolidated.

The Estrangement of North and South

But at the same time the nation was falling to pieces. North and South became completely estranged. The Industrial Revolution had contrary effects on the two regions. It turned the South into an economic associate of Great Britain. The South became the world's chief producer of raw cotton for the Lancashire mills. The Southerners, living by the export of a cash crop, and producing virtually no manufactures, wished to purchase manufactured goods as cheaply as possible. Hence they favored free trade, especially with Great Britain. In the North, the Industrial Revolution led to the building of factories. Northern factory owners, usually backed by their workers, demanded protection from the inflow of British goods, with which no other country at the time could easily compete. The North therefore favored a high tariff, which the South declared to be ruinous.

More fundamental was the difference in the status of labor. As the demand for raw cotton reached astronomical magnitudes the South fell more deeply under the hereditary curse of the Americas—the slave and plantation system.[32] In the nineteenth century slavery increasingly revolted the moral conscience of the white man's world. It was abolished in the British colonies in 1833, in the French colonies in 1848, and in the Latin American republics at different dates in the first half of the century. Similarly, serfdom was abolished in the Habsburg possessions in 1848 and in Russia in 1861. The American South could not, and after about 1830 no longer even wished to shake the system off. The South was the Cotton Kingdom whose "peculiar institution" was unfree labor of blacks. Whites were hurt by the system as well as blacks. Few free men could prosper alongside a mass of subservient and virtually uncompensated labor. The incoming Europeans settled overwhelmingly in the North, the South remaining more purely "Anglo-Saxon"—except that in its most densely peopled areas some half of the people were of African descent.

[32] See pp. 251–252.

In the movement westward, common in North and South, the pressure in the South came mainly from planters wishing to establish new plantations, in the North from persons hoping to set up small farms and from businessmen bent on founding new towns, building railroads, and creating markets. As once France and Great Britain had fought for control beyond the Alleghenies, so now North and South fought for control beyond the Mississippi. In 1846 the United States made war upon Mexico by methods at which Bismarck would not have blushed. The North widely denounced the war as an act of Southern aggression, but was willing enough to take the ensuing conquests, which comprised the region from Texas to the Pacific. The first new state created in this region, California, prohibited slavery. Since 1820 the United States had held together precariously by the "Missouri Compromise," under which new states, as set up in the West, were admitted to the Union in pairs, one "slave" and one "free," so that a rough equality was maintained in the Senate and in the presidential electoral vote. With the creation of California this balance of power was upset in favor of the North, so that in return, by the "compromise of 1850," the North agreed to enforce the laws on runaway slaves to the satisfaction of the South. But the new strictness toward fugitive slaves ran against mounting sentiment in the North. Attempts to arrest blacks in free states and return them to slavery aroused abolitionist sentiment to a higher pitch. The abolitionists, a branch of the humanitarian movement then sweeping the European world, and somewhat resembling the radical democrats who came forward in Europe in 1848, demanded the immediate and total elimination of slavery, without concession, compromise, or compensation for the property interests of the slave owners. Abolitionists denounced the Union itself as the unholy accomplice in a social abomination.

By 1860 a sense of "sectionalism" had developed in the South not different in principle from the nationalism felt by many peoples in Europe. In their proud insistence on states' rights and constitutional liberties, their aristocratic and warlike codes of ethics, their demand for independence from outside influence and for freedom in ruling their own subject people, the Southern whites suggested nothing in Europe so much as the Magyars of the Austrian Empire. They now wondered whether their way of life could be safely maintained within the Union which they had helped to create. They sensed Northerners as outsiders, unsympathetic, foreign, hostile, and the South as potentially an independent and distinct nation. They were aware that within the Union they were increasingly a minority; for where in 1790 North and South had been approximately equal, by 1860 the North had outrun the South in population, mainly because of the stream of migration from Europe. The incipient nationalism of the South was of the type of the small nation struggling against the great empire. In the North, nationalism was a sentiment in favor of maintaining the whole existing territory of the United States. Northerners by 1860, with a few exceptions, refused to admit that any state of the Union could withdraw, or secede, for any reason.

In 1860 the new Republican party elected Abraham Lincoln president. It advanced a program of free Western lands for small farmers, a higher tariff, transcontinental railroad building, and economic and capitalistic development on a national scale. The new party's radical wing, to which Lincoln himself did not belong, was vehemently abolitionist and anti-Southern in sentiment. Southern leaders, after the election of Lincoln, brought about the formal withdrawal of their states from the United States of America and the creation of the Confederate States of America reaching from Virginia to Texas. Lincoln ordered the armed forces to defend the territory of the United States, and the resulting Civil War, or war of Southern independence, lasting for four years and involving battles as great as those of Napoleon, was the most harrowing struggle of the nineteenth century with the exception of the Taiping rebellion in China.[33]

European governments, while never recognizing the Confederacy, were partial to the South. The United States stood for principles still considered revolutionary in Europe, so that, while the European working classes generally favored the North, the upper classes were willing enough to see the North American republic end in collapse and failure. In addition, Great Britain and France saw in the breakup of the United States the same advantages that they had formerly seen in the breakup of the Spanish empire.[34] In the Confederate States the British, and the French to a lesser degree, expected to find another free trade country, supplying western Europe with raw materials and buying its manufactures; in short, they saw not a competitor like the North, but a complementary partner to the industry of the Old World. It was likewise during the American Civil War that a French army sent by Napoleon III invaded Mexico to create a puppet empire under an Austrian archduke.[35] Thus the only serious attempt to ignore the Monroe Doctrine, violate the independence of Latin America, and revive European colonialism in the Americas occurred at the time when the United States was in dissolution.

But the North won the war and the Union was upheld. The Mexicans rid themselves of their unwanted emperor. Tsar Alexander II sold Alaska to the United States. The war ended the idea of the Union as a confederation of member states from which members might withdraw at will. In its place triumphed the idea that the United States was a national state, composed not of member states but of a unitary people irrevocably bound together. This doctrine was written explicitly into the Fourteenth Amendment to the Constitution, which pronounced all Americans to be citizens not only of their several states but of the United States and forbade any state to "deprive any person of life, liberty or property without due process of law"—"due process" to be determined by authority of the national government. The new force of central authority was felt first of all in the South. President Lincoln, using his war powers, issued the Emancipation Proclamation in 1863, abolishing slavery in areas engaged in hostilities against the United States. The Thirteenth Amendment in 1865 abolished slavery everywhere in the country. No compensation was paid to the slave owners, who were therefore ruined. The legal authority of the United States was thus used for an annihilation of individual property rights without parallel (outside of modern communism) in the history of the Western world; for neither the nobility in the French Revolution, nor the Russian serf owners in 1861, nor the slave owners of the West Indies in the nineteenth century, nor the owners of businesses nationalized by twentieth-

[33] See p. 639.
[34] See pp. 191, 452–454.
[35] See p. 617.

century socialists in western Europe had to face such a total and overwhelming loss of property values as the slave owners of the American South.

After the Civil War: Reconstruction; Industrial Growth

The assassination of Lincoln in 1865 by a fanatical Southern patriot strengthened those radical Republicans who said that the South must be drastically reformed. With the old Southern upper class completely ruined, Northerners of many types poured into the defeated country. Some came to represent the federal government, some to dabble in local politics, some to make money, and a great many out of democratic and humanitarian impulses, to teach the distressed ex-slaves the elements of reading and writing or of useful trades. Blacks in the South voted, sat in legislatures, occupied public office. This period, called Reconstruction, may be compared to the most advanced phase of the French Revolution, in that "radical republicans" undertook to press liberty and equality upon a recalcitrant country, under conditions of emergency rule and under the auspices of a highly centralized national government with a mobilized army. The Southern whites strenuously objected, and the Northern radicals discredited themselves and gradually lost their zeal. Reconstruction was abandoned in the 1870s, and, by what Europeans would call a counterrevolution, the Southern whites gradually regained control.

The Northern business interests—financiers, bankers, company promoters, railway builders, manufacturers—expanded greatly with the wartime demand for munitions and military provisioning. They received protection by the Morrill tariff of 1861. In the next year, partly as a war measure, the Union Pacific Railroad was incorporated, and in 1869, at a remote spot in Utah, the last spike was driven in the first railroad to span the American continent. The Homestead Act, providing farms to settlers on easy conditions, and the granting of public lands to certain colleges (ever since called "land-grant colleges"), largely for the promotion of agricultural sciences, encouraged the push of population and civilization into the West. Vast tracts of land were given by the government to subsidize railway building. With the destruction of the Southern slaveholders, who before the war had counterbalanced the rising industrialists, it was now industry and finance that dominated national politics in the increasingly centralized United States. The Fourteenth Amendment, for many years, was mainly interpreted not to protect the civil rights of individual persons, but the property rights of business corporations against restrictive legislation by the states. The shift of political power from the states to the federal government accompanied and protected the shift of economic enterprise from local businesses to far-flung and continent-embracing corporations. As in France under Napoleon III, there was a good deal of corruption, fraud, speculation, and dishonestly or rapaciously acquired wealth; but industry boomed, the cities grew, and the American mass market was created. On Fifth Avenue in New York, and in other Northern cities, rose the pretentious and gaudy mansions of the excessively rich.

In short, the American Civil War, which might have reduced English-speaking America to a scramble of jealously competing minor republics, resulted instead in the economic and political consolidation of a large nation-state, liberal and democratic in its political principles, and committed enthusiastically to private enterprise in its economic system.

69. THE DOMINION OF CANADA, 1867

North of the United States, at the time of the Civil War, lay a number of British provinces unconnected with one another, and each in varying degree dependent on Great Britain. The population had originated in three great streams. One part was French, settled in the St. Lawrence valley since the seventeenth century. A second part was made up of descendants of United Empire Loyalists, old seaboard colonists who, remaining faithful to Britain, had fled from the United States during the American Revolution.[36] They were numerous in the Maritime Provinces and in Upper Canada, as Ontario was then called.[37] A third part consisted of recent immigrants from Great Britain, men and women of the working classes who had left the home country to improve themselves in America.

The French firmly resisted assimilation to the English-speaking world around them. Their statute of freedom was the Quebec Act of 1774, which had been denounced as "intolerable" by the aroused inhabitants of the Thirteen Colonies, but which put the French civil law, French language, and French Catholic church under the protection of the British Crown.[38] The French looked with apprehension upon the stream of immigrants, English-speaking and Protestant, which began to flow into Canada about 1780 and thereafter never stopped. There was constant irritation between the two nationalities.

The British government tried various expedients. In 1791 it created two provinces in the St. Lawrence and Great Lakes region—a Lower Canada to remain French, and an Upper Canada to be English. They received the same form of government as that enjoyed by the Thirteen Colonies before their break from the empire. Each colony, that is, had a locally elected assembly with certain powers of taxation and lawmaking, subject to veto by the British authorities, as represented either by the governor or by the London government itself. For many years there was no objection to these arrangements. The War of 1812, in which the United States embarked on the conquest of Canada, aroused a national sentiment among both French and English in that country, together with a willingness to depend politically upon Great Britain for military security. But the internal political differences continued. In Lower Canada the French feared the English-speaking minority. In Upper Canada the old aristocracy of United Empire Loyalists, who had carved the province from the wilderness, hesitated to share control with the new immigrants from Great Britain. Between the provinces there were grievances also, since Lower Canada stood in the way of Upper Canada's outlet to the sea. In 1837 a superficial rebellion broke out in both provinces. It was put down virtually without bloodshed.

Lord Durham's Report

In Great Britain at this time the reforming Whigs were busily renovating many ancient English institutions.[39] Some of them had definite views on the administra-

---

[36] See p. 345.
[37] See map, p. 517.
[38] See p. 342.
[39] See pp. 460–466.

tion of colonies. In general, they held that it was not necessary to control a region politically in order to trade with it. This was an aspect of the free trade doctrine, separating economics from politics, business from power. The Whig reformers were rather indifferent to empire, unconcerned with military, naval, or strategic considerations. A few even thought it natural for colonies, when mature, to drop away entirely from the mother country. Whigs, liberals, and radicals all wished to economize on military expenditure, to relieve British taxpayers by cutting down British garrisons overseas.

After the Canadian insurrection of 1837 the Whig government sent out the Earl of Durham as governor. Durham, one of the framers of the parliamentary Reform Bill of 1832, published his views on Canadian affairs in 1839. Durham's Report has ever since been regarded as one of the classic documents in the rise of the British Commonwealth of Nations. He held that in the long run French separatist feeling in Canada should be extinguished and all Canadians brought to feel a common citizenship and national character. He therefore called for the reuniting of the two Canadas into one province. To consolidate this province he proposed an intensive development of railways and canals. In political matters he urged the granting of virtual self-government for Canada and the introduction of the British system of "responsible government," in which the elected assembly should control the executive ministers in the province, the governor becoming a kind of legal and ceremonial figure like the sovereign in Great Britain.

Most of Durham's Report was accepted immediately, and a united Canada was given the machinery of self-government in 1840. The British army was withdrawn. The Canadians undertook to maintain their own military establishment, still regarded as necessary, since the era of the famous undefended frontier between Canada and the United States had not yet dawned. The Webster-Ashburton treaty of 1842 put an end to the long dispute over the Maine border. But as late as 1866 the Canadians had to repel armed invaders from the United States, when several hundred Irish Americans, members of the Fenians, an Irish republican secret society, staged a Garibaldi-like attempt to detach Canada from the British Empire. Local Canadian forces proved sufficient to this threat.

The principle of responsible government was established in the late 1840s, the governors of Canada allowing the elected assembly to adopt policies and appoint or remove ministers as it chose. Responsible government, still confined to internal matters, worked satisfactorily from the beginning. But one feature of the new plan, the union of the two Canadas, began to produce friction as the English-speaking immigration continued. The French were afraid of being outnumbered in their own country. Many Canadians therefore turned to the idea of a federation, in which the French and English areas might each conduct its own local affairs, while remaining joined for larger purposes in a superior government.

Founding of the Dominion of Canada

Federalism in Canada was thus partly a decentralizing idea, aimed at satisfying the French element by a redivision into two provinces, and in part a plan for a new centralization or unification, because it contemplated bringing all the provinces of British North America into union with the St. Lawrence and Great Lakes region, to which alone the term Canada was then applied. While British North

Americans discussed federation the Civil War was disrupting the United States. In the face of this unpleasant example, the British North Americans formed a strong union in which all powers were to rest in the central government except those specifically assigned to the provinces. The federal constitution, drafted in Canada by Canadians, was passed through the British Parliament in 1867 as the British North America Act, which constitutionally established the Dominion of Canada. In 1982 the British North America Act was replaced by new arrangements, which explicitly recognized the sovereign independence of Canada and its power to frame a constitution for itself.

The new dominion received a common parliament, in which the majority party controlled a responsible ministry according to British principles of cabinet government. The original provinces were Quebec and Ontario, formed from the old Canada, and Nova Scotia and New Brunswick, which joined on the understanding that a railroad be built to connect them with Quebec. The old Hudson's Bay Company, founded in 1670, transferred its rights of government over the vast Northwest to the dominion in 1869. From these territories the province of Manitoba was created in 1870 and British Columbia in 1871. To link them solidly with the rest of the dominion the Canadian Pacific Railway was completed in 1885. It made possible the development of the prairies, where the provinces of Saskatchewan and Alberta were added in 1905.

The Dominion of Canada, though not large in population, possessed from the beginning a significance beyond the mere number of its people. It was the first example of successful devolution, or granting of political liberty, within one of the European colonial empires. It embodied principles which Edmund Burke and Benjamin Franklin had vainly recommended a century before to keep the Thirteen Colonies loyal to Great Britain. The dominion after 1867 moved forward from independence in internal matters to independence in such external affairs as tariffs, diplomacy, and the decisions of war and peace. It thus pioneered in the development of "dominion status," working out precedents later applied in Australia (1901), New Zealand (1907), the Union of South Africa (1910), and in the 1920s, temporarily, in Ireland. By the middle of the twentieth century the same idea, or what may be called the Canadian idea, was even applied to the worldwide problem of colonialism as it affected non-European peoples, notably in India, Pakistan, Ceylon, and the former British colonies in Africa, until all these peoples chose to become republics, though still loosely and voluntarily joined together and to Great Britain in a Commonwealth of Nations.

More immediately, in America, the founding of the dominion, a solid band of self-governing territory stretching from ocean to ocean, stabilized the relations between British North America and the United States. The United States regarded its northern borders as final. The withdrawal of British control from Canadian affairs furthered the United States conception of an American continent entirely free from European political influence.

70. JAPAN AND THE WEST

The Japanese, when they allowed the Westerners to discover them, were a highly civilized people living in a complex society. They had many large cities, they enjoyed the contemplation of natural scenery, they went to the theater, and they read novels. With their stylized manners, their fans and their wooden temples, their lacquer work and their painting on screens, their tiny rice fields and their curious and ineffectual firearms, they seemed to Europeans to be the very acme of everything quaint. This feeling is immortalized in *The Mikado* of Gilbert and Sullivan, first performed in 1885. Not long thereafter the idea of Japanese quaintness, like the idea of the Germans as an impractical people given mainly to music and metaphysics, had to be revised. The Europeans, in "opening" Japan, opened up more than they knew.

In 1853, the American Commodore Perry forced his way with a fleet of naval vessels into Yedo Bay, insisted upon landing, and demanded of the Japanese government, somewhat peremptorily, that it engage in commercial relations with the United States and other Western powers. In the next year the Japanese began to comply, and in 1867 an internal revolution took place, of which the most conspicuous consequence was a rapid westernizing of Japanese life and institutions. But if it looked as if the country had been "opened" by Westerners, actually Japan had exploded from within.

Background: Two Centuries of Isolation, 1640–1854

For over two centuries Japan had followed a program of self-imposed isolation. No Japanese was allowed to leave the islands or even to build a ship large enough to navigate the high seas. No foreigner, except for handfuls of Dutch and Chinese, was allowed to enter. Japan remained a sealed book to the West. The contrary is not quite so true, for the Japanese knew rather more about Europe than Europeans did about Japan. The Japanese policy of seclusion was not merely based upon ignorance. Initially, at least, it was based on experience.

The first Europeans—three Portuguese in a Chinese junk—are thought to have arrived in Japan in 1542. For about a century thereafter there was considerable coming and going. The Japanese showed a strong desire to trade with the foreigners, from whom they obtained clocks and maps, learned about printing and shipbuilding, and took over the use of tobacco and potatoes. Thousands also adopted the Christian religion as preached to them by Spanish and Portuguese Jesuits. Japanese traveled to the Dutch Indies and even to Europe. The Japanese in fact proved more receptive to European ideas than other Asian peoples. But shortly after 1600 the government began to drive Christianity underground; in 1624 it expelled the Spaniards, in 1639 the Portuguese, and in 1640 all Europeans except for a few Dutch merchants who were allowed to remain at Nagasaki under strict control. From 1640 to 1854 these few Dutch at Nagasaki were the only channel of communication with the West.[40]

The reasons for self-seclusion, as for its abandonment later, arose from the course of political events in Japan. The history of Japan showed an odd parallel to that of Europe. In Japan, as in Europe, a period of feudal warfare was followed by a period of government absolutism, during which civil peace was kept by a bureaucracy, an obsolescent warrior class was maintained as a privileged element in

[40] See p. 162.

society, and a commercial class of native merchants grew wealthier, stronger, and more insistent upon its position.

When the first Europeans arrived, the islands were still torn by the wars and rivalries of the numerous clans into which the Japanese were organized. Gradually one clan, the Tokugawa, gained control, taking over the office of "shogun." The shogun was a kind of military head who governed in the name of the emperor, and the hereditary Tokugawa shogunate, founded in 1603, lasted until 1867. The early Tokugawa shoguns concluded from a good deal of evidence that the Europeans in Japan, both merchants and missionaries, were engaging in feudal or interclan politics and even aspiring to dominate Japan by helping Christian or pro-European Japanese to get into power. The first three Tokugawa shoguns, to establish their own dynasty, to pacify and stabilize the country, and to keep Japan free from European penetration, undertook to exterminate Christianity and adopted the rigid policy of nonintercourse with the rest of the world.

Under the Tokugawa Japan enjoyed peace, a long peace, for the first time in centuries. The Tokugawa shoguns completed the detachment of the emperor from politics, building him up as a divine and legendary being, too august and too remote for the hurly-burly of the world. The emperor remained shut in at Kyoto on a modest allowance furnished by the shoguns. The shoguns established their own court and government at Yedo (later called Tokyo); and as Louis XIV brought nobles to Versailles, or Peter the Great forced his uncouth lords to build town houses in St. Petersburg, so the shoguns required the great feudal chieftains and their men-at-arms to reside at least part of the year in Yedo.

The shoguns administered the country through a kind of military bureaucracy or dictatorship. This formidable instrument of state watched over the great lords (called daimyo), who, however, retained a good deal of feudal authority over their subjects in the regions most distant from Yedo. The great lords and their armed retainers (the samurai), having no further fighting to occupy them, turned into a landed aristocracy which spent a good deal of its time in Yedo and other cities. As a leisure class, they developed new tastes and standards of living and hence needed more income, which they obtained by squeezing the peasants, and which they spent by buying from the merchants.

The merchant class greatly expanded by catering to the government and the gentry. Japan in the seventeenth century passed on to a money economy. Many lords fell seriously into debt to the merchants. Many samurai, like lesser nobles in France or Poland at the time, were almost ridiculously impoverished, hard-pressed to keep up appearances, with nothing except social status to distinguish them from commoners. The law, as in Europe under the Old Regime, drew a sharp line between classes. Nobles, merchants, and peasants were subject to different taxes and were differently punished for different offenses. What was a crime for a commoner would be excusable for a samurai; or what in a samurai would be a punishable breach of honor would be accepted in a common person. The samurai had the right to carry two swords as a mark of class and could in theory cut down an impudent commoner without arousing further inquiry. In practice the shoguns repressed violence of this kind, but there was much less development of law and justice than in the European monarchies of the Old Regime. Economically the merchants and artisans prospered. By 1723 Yedo was a city with 500,000 people; by 1800 with over 1,000,000, it was larger than London or Paris, and twenty times as large as the largest city in the United States. After 1800 some merchants were able to purchase the rank of samurai for money. The old class lines were beginning to blur.

Though deliberately secluded, the economic and social life of Japan was thus by no means static. The same is true of its intellectual life. Buddhism, the historic religion, lost its hold on many people during the Tokugawa period, so that Japan in its way underwent, like the West, a "secularization" of ideas. As a code of personal conduct there was a new emphasis on Bushido, the "way of the warrior," a kind of nonreligious moral teaching which exalted the samurai virtues of honor and loyalty. With the decline of Buddhism went also a revival of the cult of Shinto, the "way of the gods," the ancient indigenous religion of Japan, which held, among much else, that the emperor was veritably the Son of Heaven. There was much activity in the study and writing of history, arousing, as in Europe, an acute interest in the national past. History, like Shinto, led to a feeling that shoguns were usurpers and that the emperor, obscurely relegated to Kyoto, was the true representative of everything highest and most lasting in the life of Japan.

Meanwhile, through the crack left open at Nagasaki, Western ideas trickled in. The shogun Yoshimune in the mid-eighteenth century permitted the importation of Occidental books, except those relating to Christianity. A few Japanese learned Dutch and began to decipher Dutch books on anatomy, surgery, astronomy, and other subjects. In 1745 a Dutch-Japanese dictionary was completed. For European manufactures also—watches, glassware, velvets, woolens, telescopes, barometers—there came to be an eager demand, satisfied as much as possible by the methodical Dutch. Nor were the Japanese wholly uninformed about politics in the West. While the most assiduous Westerner could learn nothing of the internal affairs of Japan, an educated Japanese could, if he wished, arrive at some idea of the French Revolution, or know who was president of the United States.

The Opening of Japan

When Perry in 1853 made his unwanted visit he therefore had many potential allies within Japan. There were nobles, heavily in debt, unable to draw more income from agriculture, willing to embark upon foreign trade and to exploit their property by introducing new enterprises. There were penurious samurai, with no future in the old system, ready and willing to enter upon new careers as army officers or civil officials. There were merchants hoping to add to their business by dealing in Western goods. There were scholars eager to learn more of Western science and medicine. There were patriots fearful that Japan was becoming defenseless against Western guns. Spiritually the country was already adrift from its moorings, already set toward a course of national self-assertion, restlessly susceptible to hazily understood new ideas. Under such pressures, and from downright fear of a bombardment of Yedo by the Americans, which if it would not subdue Japan would at least ruin the declining prestige of the shogunate, the shogun Iesada in 1854 signed a commercial treaty with the United States. Similar treaties were soon signed with the Europeans.

In the following years were sown the seeds of much later misunderstanding between Japan and the West. The whites in those days—European and American—

were somewhat trigger-happy in the discharge of naval ordnance against backward peoples. The Japanese, a proud and elaborately civilized nation, soon found that the whites considered them backward. They found, for example, as soon as they learned more of the West by reading and travel, that the treaties they signed in the 1850s were not treaties between equals as understood in the West. These first treaties provided that Japan should maintain a low tariff on imports and not change it except with the consent of the foreign powers. To give outsiders a voice in determining tariff policy was not the custom among sovereign states of the West. The early treaties also provided for extraterritoriality. This meant that Europeans and Americans residing in Japan were not subject to Japanese law but remained under the jurisdiction of their respective homelands as represented by consular officials. Such extraterritorial provisions had long been established in Turkey and were currently taking in root in China.[41] Europeans insisted upon them in countries where European principles of property, debt, or security of life and person did not prevail. At the same time, of course, no civilized state ever permitted a foreign power to exercise jurisdiction within its borders. Extraterritoriality was a mark of inferiority, as the Japanese soon discovered.

A strong antiforeign reaction developed after 1854. It was at first led by certain nobles of the western islands, the lords of Choshu and Satsuma, who had never been fully subordinated to the shogun at Yedo, and who now dreamed of overturning the Tokugawa shogunate and leading a national revival with the emperor as its rallying point. Their first idea was to check Western penetration (as two and a half centuries before) by driving the Westerners out. But in 1862 some Englishmen unintentionally violated a small point of Japanese etiquette. One of them was killed. The British government demanded punishment for the offending Japanese, who were followers of the lord of Satsuma. The shogun proved unable to arrange this, and the British navy thereupon itself sailed up and bombarded the capital of Satsuma. In the same year the lord of Choshu, who commanded the straits of Shimonoseki with some ancient artillery, ordered it to fire on passing vessels. The British, French, Dutch, and United States governments immediately protested, and, when the embarrassed shogun proved unable to discipline Choshu, they dispatched an allied naval force to Shimonoseki. The forts and shipping of Choshu were destroyed, and an indemnity of $3,000,000 was imposed. These incidents were remembered in Japan long after they were forgotten in Europe and the United States. It was likewise remembered that the Western powers, discovering that the shogun was not the supreme ruler of the country, sent a naval expedition to Kyoto itself and required the emperor to confirm the treaties signed by the shogun and to reduce import duties, under threat of naval bombardment.

The Meiji Era (1868–1912): The Westernization of Japan

The lords of Choshu and Satsuma now concluded that the only way to deal with the West was to adopt the military and technical equipment of the West itself. They would save Japan for the Japanese by learning the secrets of the Western power. First they forced the resignation of the shogun, whose prestige had long been undermined anyway, and who had now discredited himself first by signing undesirable treaties with the West and then failing to protect the country from

---

[41] See pp. 214, 642.

outrage. The last shogun abdicated in 1867. The reformers declared the emperor restored to his full authority. It was their intention to use the plenitude of imperial power to consolidate and fortify Japan for its new position in the world. In 1868 a new emperor inherited the throne; his name was Mutsuhito, but according to Japanese custom a name was given to his reign also, which was called Meiji. The Meiji era (1868–1912) was the great era of the westernization of Japan.

Japan turned into a modern national state. Feudalism was abolished, most of the great lords voluntarily surrendering into the emperor's hands their control over samurai and common people. "We abolish the clans and convert them into prefectures," declared one imperial decree. The legal system was reorganized and equality before the law introduced, in the sense that all persons became subject to the same rules regardless of class. In part with the hope of getting rid of extraterritoriality, the reformers recast the criminal law along Western lines, deleting the bizarre and cruel punishments which Europeans considered barbaric. A new army was established, modeled mainly on the Prussian. The samurai in 1871 lost his historic right to carry two swords; he now served as an army officer, not as the retainer of a clannish chief. A navy, modeled on the British, followed somewhat later. Control of money and currency passed to the central government, and a national currency, with decimal units, was adopted. A national postal service began to function and above all a national school system, which soon brought a high rate of literacy to Japan. Buddhism was discouraged, and the property of Buddhist monasteries was confiscated. Shinto was the cult favored by the government. Shinto gave a religious tincture to national sentiment and led to a renewed veneration of the imperial family. In 1889 a constitution was promulgated. It confirmed the civil liberties then common in the West and provided for a parliament in two chambers, but it stressed also the supreme and "eternal" authority of the emperor, to whom the ministers were legally responsible. In practice, in the new Japan, the emperor never actively governed. He remained aloof, as in the past; and political leaders, never fully responsible to the parliament, tended to govern freely in what they conceived to be the interests of the state.

Industrial and financial modernization went along with and even preceded the political revolution. In 1858 the first steamship was purchased from the Dutch. In 1859 Japan placed its first foreign loan, borrowing 5 million yen by a bond issue floated in England. In 1869 the first telegraph connected Yokohama and Tokyo. The first railroad, between the same two cities, was completed in 1872. In 1870 appeared the first spinning machinery. Foreign trade, almost literally zero in 1854, was valued at $200 million a year by the end of the century. The population rose from 33 million in 1872 to 46 million in 1902. The island empire, like Great Britain, became dependent on exports and imports to sustain its dense population at the level of living to which it aspired.

The westernization of Japan still stands as the most remarkable transformation ever undergone by any people in so short a time. It recalls the westernizing of Russia under Peter over a century before, though conducted somewhat less brutally, more rapidly, and with a wider consent among the population. For Japan, as formerly for Russia, the motive was in large measure defense against Western penetration, together with an admiration for Western statecraft and an ambition to become a "power."[42] What the Japanese wanted from the West was primarily

⁴² See pp. 227–238.

science, technology, and organization. They were content enough with the innermost substance of their culture, their moral ideas, their family life, their arts and amusements, their religious conceptions, though even in these they showed an uncommon adaptability. Essentially it was to protect their internal substance, their Japanese culture, that they took over the external apparatus of Western civilization. This apparatus—science, technology, machinery, arms, political and legal organization—was the part of Western civilization for which other peoples generally felt a need, which they hoped to adopt without losing their own spiritual independence, and which therefore, though sometimes rather scornfully dismissed as materialistic, became the common ground for the interdependent world-wide civilization that emerged at the close of the nineteenth century.

In brief, to conclude a long chapter, the world between 1850 and 1870, revolutionized economically by the railroad and steamship, was revolutionized politically by the formation of large and consolidated nation-states. These states at the time all embodied certain liberal and constitutional principles, or at least the machinery of parliamentary and representative government. But the whole earth had also become an arena in which certain mighty beings, called nations or powers, were to act. The Great Powers in 1871 were Great Britain, Germany, France, Austria-Hungary, and Russia. Britain had produced a daughter nation in Canada. Whether Italy was to be called a Great Power was not yet clear. No one knew what Japan would do. All agreed that the United States would one day play a large role in international politics, but the time was not yet.

XIV.
European
Civilization,
1871-1914

alf a century elapsed between the period of national consolidation described in the last chapter and the outbreak of the First World War in 1914. In this half-century Europe in many ways reached the climax of the modern phase of its civilization, and also exerted its maximum influence upon peoples outside Europe. The present chapter will attempt a description of European civilization in these years, the next chapter an account of the world-wide ascendancy which Europe enjoyed at this time.

For Europe and the European world the years 1871 to 1914 were marked by hitherto unparalleled material and industrial growth, international peace, domestic stability, the advance of constitutional, representative, and democratic government, and continued faith in science, reason, and progress. But in these very years, in politics, economics, and basic thinking there were forces operating to undermine the liberal premises and tenets of this European civilization. Most of the present chapter will be devoted to the continuing triumphs of liberalism, but the signs of its transformation and wane will be pointed out too.

Chapter Emblem: A painting called "The Last of England," dated 1852, by Ford Madox Brown, showing two emigrants looking back from their departing ship.

71. THE "CIVILIZED WORLD"

Materialistic and Nonmaterialistic Ideals

With the extension of the nation-state system Europe was politically more divided than ever. Its unity lay in the sharing by all Europeans of a similar way of life and outlook, which existed also in such "European" countries as the United States, Australia, and New Zealand. Europe and its offshoots constituted the "civilized world." Other regions—Africa, China, India, the up-country of Peru—were said to be "backward." (They are today referred to as "less developed.") Europeans were extremely conscious and inordinately proud of their civilization in the half-century before 1914. They believed it to be the well-deserved outcome of centuries of progress. Feeling themselves to be the most advanced branch of mankind in the important areas of human endeavor, they assumed that all peoples should respect the same social ideals—that so far as they were unwilling or unable to adopt them they were backward, and that so far as they did adopt them they became civilized in their turn.

These ideals of civilization were in part materialistic. If Europeans considered their civilization to be better in 1900 than in 1800, or better in 1900 than the ways of non-Europeans at the same time, it was because they had a higher standard of living, ate and dressed more adequately, slept in softer beds, and had more satisfactory sanitary facilities. It was because they possessed ocean liners, railroads, and streetcars, and after about 1880 telephones and electric lights. But the ideal of civilization was by no means exclusively materialistic. Knowledge as such, correct or truthful knowledge, was held to be a civilized attainment—scientific knowledge of nature, in place of superstition or demonology; geographical knowledge, by which civilized people were aware of the earth as a whole with its general contours and diverse inhabitants. The ideal was also profoundly moral, derived from Christianity, but now secularized and detached from religion. An Englishman, Isaac Taylor, in his *Ultimate Civilization* published in 1860, defined this moral ideal by listing the contrasting "relics of barbarism" which he thought were due to disappear—"Polygamy, Infanticide, Legalized Prostitution, Capricious Divorce, Sanguinary and Immoral Games, Infliction of Torture, Caste and Slavery." The first four of these had been unknown to the approved customs of Europe at least since the coming of Christianity. Torture went out of use about 1800, even in the illiberal European states, and legalized caste and slavery in the course of the nineteenth century. But there were few non-European peoples, in 1860, among whom two or three of Taylor's "relics" could not be found.

There are certain other indices, more purely quantitative, worked out by sociologists to show the level of advancement of a given society. One of these is the death rate, or number of persons per thousand of population who die each year. In England, France, and Sweden the "true" death rate (or death rate regardless of the proportion of infants and old people, who are most susceptible to death) is known to have fallen from about 25 (per 1,000 per year) before 1850, to 19 in 1914 and 18 in the 1930s. Indeed, before the Second World War, it stood seemingly stabilized at about 18 in all countries of northwestern Europe, the United States, and the British dominions. Death rates in countries not "modern" run over 40 even in favorable times. A closely related index is infant mortality, which fell rapidly after 1870 in all countries affected by medical science. Thus a woman under civilized conditions had to go through pregnancy and childbirth less often to produce the same number of surviving children. Another index is life expectancy, or the number of years of age which a person has an even chance of attaining. In England the expectation of life at birth rose from 40 years in the 1840s to 59 in 1933 and 73 in 1980. In India in 1931 it was less than 27 years. It had risen to about 50 in 1980. Still another index is the literacy rate, or proportion of persons above a certain age (such as ten) able to read and write. In northwestern Europe by 1900 the literacy rate approached 100. In some countries it still does not rise very far above zero. A further basic index is the productivity of labor, or amount produced by one worker in a given expenditure of time. This is difficult to compute, especially for earlier periods for which statistical data are lacking. In the 1930s, however, the productivity of a farmer in Denmark was over ten times that of a farmer in Albania. All northwestern Europe was above the European average in this respect with the exception of Ireland, whereas Ireland, Spain, Portugal, Italy, and all eastern Europe were below it.

The essence of civilized living doubtless is in the intangibles, in the way in which people use their minds, and in the attitudes they form toward others or toward the conduct and planning of their own lives. The intangibles, however, are not always agreed upon by persons of different culture or ideology. On the quantitative criteria there is less disagreement; all, with few exceptions, wish to lower the death rate, raise the literacy rate, and increase the productivity of human exertion. Even if we apply quantitative or sociological indices alone, we can say that after 1870 there was in fact, and not merely in the opinion of Europeans, a civilized world of which Europe was the center.

The "Zones" of Civilization

Or rather, a certain region of Europe was the center. For there were really two Europes, an inner zone and an outer. A Frenchman writing in the 1920s, describing the two Europes that had risen since 1870, called the inner zone the "Europe of steam," and bounded it by an imaginary line joining Glasgow, Stockholm, Danzig, Trieste, Florence, and Barcelona. It included not only Great Britain but Belgium, Germany, France, northern Italy, and the western portions of the Austrian Empire. Virtually all heavy European industry was located in this zone.

TRAIN IN THE SNOW
by Claude Monet (French, 1840–1926)

With the Impressionists, and notably with Claude Monet, some of the conventions of Western painting since the Renaissance began to fade. Emphasis shifted from the representation of objects to the perception of them as experienced through the eye. Solid masses melted into the play of light under a variety of atmospheric conditions. The railway age, which developed rapidly in Monet's youth, furnished many subjects to excite his imagination. In this picture the solid iron of the locomotive merges into the indeterminate grays of a dull day in winter. The chill and the low visibility are conveyed as much as the visual images themselves. Courtesy of the Musée Marmottan, Paris (Giraudon). Permission S.P.A.D.E.M. 1970 by French Reproduction Rights, Inc.

Here the railway network was thickest. Here was concentrated the wealth of Europe, in the form both of a high living standard and of accumulations of capital. Here likewise were almost all the laboratories and all the scientific activity of Europe. Here, in the same zone, lay the strength of constitutional and parliamentary government and of liberal, humanitarian, socialist, and reformist movements of many kinds. In this zone the death rate was low, life expectancy high, conditions of health and sanitation at their best, literacy almost universal, productivity of labor very great. To the same zone, for practical purposes, belonged certain regions of European settlement overseas, especially the northeastern part of the United States.

The "outer zone" included most of Ireland, most of the Iberian and Italian peninsulas, and all Europe east of what was then Germany, Bohemia, and Austria proper. The outer zone was agricultural, though the productivity of agriculture, per farm worker or per acre, was far less than in the inner zone. The people were poorer, more illiterate, and more likely to die young. The wealthy were landlords, often absentees. The zone lived increasingly after 1870 by selling grain, livestock, wool, or lumber to the more industrialized inner zone but was too poor to purchase many manufactured products in return. To obtain capital it borrowed in London or Paris. Its social and political philosophies were characteristically imported from Germany and the West. It borrowed engineers and technicians from the first zone to build its bridges and install its telegraph systems and sent its youth to universities in the first zone to study medicine or other professions. Many areas of European settlement overseas, for example in Latin America and the southern part of the United States, may also be thought of as belonging to this outer zone.

Beyond the European world lay a third zone, the immense reaches of Asia and Africa, all "backward" by the standards of Europe, with the exception of the recently Europeanized Japan, and all destined, with the exception of Japan, to become heavily dependent upon Europe in the half-century after 1870. Much of the world's history since 1870 could be written as the story of relations among these three zones; but it is necessary in all human things to guard against formulas that are too simple.

72. BASIC DEMOGRAPHY: THE INCREASE OF THE EUROPEANS

European and World Population Growth, 1650–1980

All continents except Africa grew enormously in population in the three centuries following 1650, but it was Europe that grew the most. There is little doubt that the proportion of Europeans in the world's total reached its maximum for all time between 1850 and the Second World War. Estimates are given in the following table, beginning with 1650.

The causes of sudden rise in world population after 1650 are not known. Some of them must obviously have operated in Asia as well as Europe. All students agree in attributing the increase to falling death rates rather than to increasing birth rates. Populations grew because more people lived longer, not because more were born. It is probable that a better preservation of civil order reduced death

ESTIMATED POPULATION OF THE WORLD BY CONTINENTAL AREAS

	1650	1750	1850	1900	1950	1980
	MILLIONS					
Europe	100	140	266	401	532	684
United States and Canada	1	1	26	81	166	251
Australasia-Oceania	2	2	2	6	13	23
Predominantly "European"	103	143	294	488	711	958
Latin America	12	11	33	63	162	364
Africa	100	95	95	120	217	469
Asia	330	479	749	937	1,396	2,624
Predominantly "Non-European"	442	585	877	1,120	1,775	3,457
World Total	515	728	1,171	1,608	2,486	4,415
	PERCENTAGES					
Europe	18.3	19.2	22.7	24.9	21.5	15.5
United States and Canada	.2	.1	2.3	5.1	6.7	5.7
Australasia-Oceania	.4	.3	.2	.4	.5	.5
Predominantly "European"	18.9	19.6	25.2	30.4	28.7	21.7
Latin America	2.2	1.5	2.8	3.9	6.5	8.3
Africa	18.3	13.1	8.1	7.4	8.7	10.6
Asia	60.6	65.8	63.9	58.3	56.1	59.4
Predominantly "Non-European"	81.1	80.4	74.8	69.6	71.3	78.3
World Total	100.0	100.0	100.0	100.0	100.0	100.0

SOURCE: Figures for 1650–1900 are from A. N. Carr-Saunders, *World Population* (Oxford: Oxford University Press, 1936), p. 42. Those for 1950 and 1980 are from the *United Nations Demographic Yearbook*. Neither source attempts a breakdown between "Europeans" and "non-Europeans," which as presented here is significant only in very rough outline for comparative purposes. Figures for the U.S.S.R. are divided in the table between Europe and Asia. Population of the United States and Canada before the eighteenth century, and of Australasia before the nineteenth, was of course almost entirely non-European. Distinctions are further blurred when it is remembered that millions of Europeans (i.e., Russians) have long lived in the Asian parts of the U.S.S.R., that there are more than 4 million whites in South Africa, that the population of the United States has always been of both European and African descent, and that Latin America is so mixed that it could as accurately be placed, especially on cultural grounds, in the European category. For world population in the twentieth century, see also pp. 931–932. For population changes in particular countries, see Appendix III below.

rates in both Asia and Europe. In Europe the organized sovereign states, as established in the seventeenth century, put an end to a long period of civil wars, stopping the chronic violence and marauding, with the accompanying insecurity of agriculture and of family life, which were more deadly than wars fought by armies between governments. Similarly, the Tokugawa kept peace in Japan, and the Manchu dynasty brought a long period of order to China. The British rule in India, and that of the Dutch in Java, by curbing famine and violence, allowed the populations to mount very rapidly. Only in Africa, where the slave trade removed over 10 million persons of the childbearing ages in three or four centuries, and where slave raiding led to intertribal warfare and the disruption of African cultures, did the growth of population fail to keep pace with the world's average. The fate of the American aborigines was somewhat the same.

In Europe, sooner than in Asia, other causes of growth were at work beyond the maintenance of civil peace. They included the liberation from certain endemic diseases, beginning with the subsiding of bubonic plague in the seventeenth century and the retreat of smallpox in the eighteenth; the improvement of agricultural output, beginning notably in England about 1750; the improvement of transportation, which, by road, canal, and railroad, made localized famine a thing of the past since food could be moved into areas of temporary shortage; and, last, the development of machine industry, which allowed large populations to subsist in Europe by trading with peoples overseas.

Consequently, while it seems that the death rate fell in Asia as well as in Europe after 1650, it fell much more substantially in Europe, and since the European birth rate long remained at a high level, the result was a tremendous swelling of population. Approximate figures are given in the preceding table. Asia, by these estimates, increased less than threefold in population between 1650 and 1900, but Europe increased fourfold, and the total number of Europeans, including the descendants of Europeans who migrated to other continents, increased almost fivefold. In 1650 the Europeans comprised only about a fifth of the world's population. In 1900 the proportion of "Europeans" on all continents was approaching a third of the human race. Since 1900 this proportion has been falling. But the ascendancy of European civilization, or roughly of the white races, in the two or three centuries after about 1650, was due in some measure to merely quantitative growth.

Stabilization of European Population

This advantage of a higher growth rate began to disappear in the middle of the twentieth century. As early as 1910 it was possible to anticipate that the population of Europe, or, more accurately, of the most advanced "inner zone," would soon grow less rapidly, because the children being born about 1910, who would become the parents of 1940, were not sufficiently numerous to maintain growth at the birth rates which then existed. At the same time death rates began to fall dramatically in Asia. With a large population base to begin with, non-Europeans by the mid-twentieth century were multiplying faster than Europeans.

Stabilization and relative decline of European population followed from a fall in the birth rate. We have seen how the persistence of high birth rates, while death rates fell, accounted for a long period of rapid expansion. But European birth rates began to fall about 1880. As early as 1830 they began noticeably to drop in France, with the result that France, long the most populous European state, was surpassed in population by Russia in the eighteenth century, by Germany about 1870, by the British Isles about 1895, and by Italy about 1930. France, once thought to be decadent for this reason, was in fact only the leading country in a population cycle through which the European countries seemed to pass. The birth rate, which had fallen below 30 per 1,000 in France in the 1830s, fell to that level in Sweden in the 1880s, in England in the 1890s, and in Germany, Bohemia, and the Netherlands between 1900 and 1910. After the Second World War there was a temporary rise, but in 1980 the birth rate was only 15 per 1,000 or less in European countries.

The reduced birth rate is not a mere dry statistical item, nor does it affect populations merely in the mass. It is one of the indices of modern civilization, first appearing in that inner European zone in which the other indices were also highest, and thence spreading outward in a kind of wave. Concretely, a low birth rate means that families average from two to four children, where in former times, or today under conditions not "modern," families are commonly found to consist of ten children or even more. The low birth rate means the small family system, than which few things are more fundamental to modern life. The principal means used to hold down the birth rate, or to limit the family, is the practice of contraception. But the true causes, or reasons why parents wish to limit their families, are deeply embedded in the codes of modern society.

Historical demographers have detected a "European family pattern" as far back as the seventeenth century. It was a pattern in which, in comparison to other societies, Europeans married later, and a larger number never married at all. Late marriage shortened the number of years during which a woman bore children, and enabled young people to acquire skills or accumulate savings (as in tools and household goods) before setting up new families. The effect was a less explosive population growth, and less extreme poverty, than occurred in some other parts of the world. Evidence indicating the practice of contraception can be found in the eighteenth century among the upper classes, by study of the number and spacing of their children. The practice seems to have spread to other social classes during the French Revolution. The Code Napoleon then required that inheritances be divided among all sons and daughters. The French peasants, many of them owners of land, began to limit themselves to two or three children, in order that all children (by inheritance, marriage, and dowries) might remain in as high an economic and social position as their parents. It was thus economic security and the possession of a social standard that led to the reduced birth rate in France.

In the great cities of the nineteenth century, in which standards of life for the working classes often collapsed, the effect might at first be a proliferation of offspring. But life in the city, under crowded conditions of housing, also set a premium on the small family. There were many activities in the city that people with many children could only with difficulty enjoy. After about 1880 child labor became much less frequent among the working classes. When children ceased to earn part of the family income parents tended to have fewer of them. About the same time governments in the advanced countries began to require universal compulsory schooling. The number of years spent in education, and hence in economic dependency upon parents, grew longer and longer, until it became common even for young adults to be still engaged in study. Each child represented many years of expense for its parents. The ever rising idea of what it was necessary to do for one's children, and the desire of parents to give them every possible advantage in a competitive world, were probably the most basic causes of voluntary limitation of the family. Hardly less basic was the desire to lighten the burdens upon mothers. The small family system, together with the decline of infant mortality, since they combined to free women from the interminable bearing and tending of infants, probably did more than anything else to improve the position of civilized women.

But the effects of the small family system upon total population became manifest only slowly. More people lived on into the middle and older age groups, and the fall of the birth rate was gradual, so that in all the leading countries total numbers continued to rise, except in France, which hardly grew between 1900 and 1945. The persistent note was one of superabundant increase. In five generations, between 1800 and 1950, some 200 million "Europeans" grew into 700 million. Since productivity increased even more rapidly, the standard of living for most of these "Europeans" rose in spite of the increase of numbers, and there was no general problem of overpopulation.

Growth of Cities and Urban Life

Where did so many people go? Some stayed in the rural areas where most people had always lived. Rural populations in the "inner zone" became more dense, turning to the more intensive agriculture of truck gardening or dairy farming, leaving products like wool and cereal grains to be raised elsewhere and then imported. But it is estimated that of every seven persons added to the western European population only one stayed on the land. Of the other six, one left Europe altogether and five went to the growing cities.[1]

The modern city is mostly the child of the railroad, for with the railroads it became possible for the first time to concentrate manufacturing in large towns, to which bulky goods such as foods and fuel could now be moved in great volume. The growth of cities between 1850 and 1914 was phenomenal. In England two-thirds of the people lived in places of 20,000 or less in 1830; in 1914 two-thirds lived in places of 20,000 or more. Germany, the historic land of archaic towns carried over from the Middle Ages, rivaled England after 1870 in modern industrial urbanization. Whereas in 1840 only London and Paris had a million people, the same could be said by 1914 of Berlin, Vienna, St. Petersburg, and Moscow.[2] Some places, like the English Midlands and the Ruhr valley in Germany, became a mass of contiguous smaller cities, vast urban agglomerations divided only by municipal lines.

The great city set the tone of modern society. City life was impersonal and anonymous; people were uprooted, less tied to home or church than in the country. They lacked the country person's feeling of deference for aristocratic families. They lacked the sense of self-help characteristic of older rural communities. The hungry, the jobless, the miserable could expect little comfort from neighbors. It was in the city that the daily newspaper press, which spread rapidly in the wake of the telegraph after 1850, found its most habitual readers. The so-called yellow or sensational press appeared about 1900. Articulate public opinion was formed in the cities, and city people were on the whole disrespectful of tradition, receptive to new ideas, having in many cases deliberately altered their own lives by moving from the country or from smaller towns. That socialism spread among the industrial masses of European cities is hardly surprising. It is less often realized that some of the more blatant nationalism that arose after 1870 was stimulated by city life, for people felt increasingly detached from all institutions except the

---

[1] See Appendix III for the growth of cities and the map on p. 432 for England.

[2] And, outside Europe, of New York, Chicago, Philadelphia, Rio de Janeiro, Buenos Aires, Calcutta, Tokyo, and Osaka.

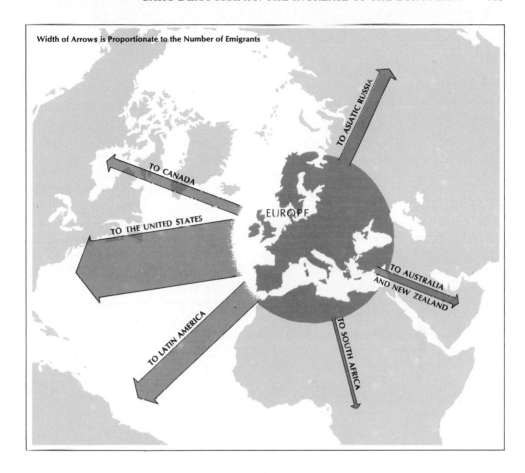

Width of Arrows is Proportionate to the Number of Emigrants

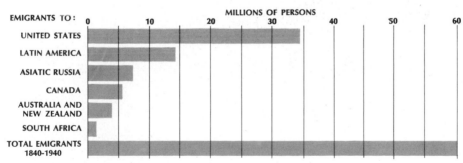

EMIGRANTS TO:	MILLIONS OF PERSONS
UNITED STATES	
LATIN AMERICA	
ASIATIC RUSSIA	
CANADA	
AUSTRALIA AND NEW ZEALAND	
SOUTH AFRICA	
TOTAL EMIGRANTS 1840-1940	

MIGRATION FROM EUROPE, 1840–1940

Over 60 million people left Europe in the century preceding the Second World War, distributing themselves as shown in the diagram above. (See figures on p. 560.) About half went to the United States. This huge wave of settlement built up, outside of Europe, populous "European" countries which produced foods and raw materials for Europe and borrowed capital and bought manufactures from Europe, thus helping to support the increasingly dense European population and to build up a world-wide economic system.

state. At the same time city life, by its greater facilities for schooling, reading, and discussion, made for a more alert and informed public opinion of an enlightened kind.

Migration from Europe, 1840–1940

During the same period in which the cities were rising, approximately 60 million people left Europe altogether, of whom possibly a fifth sooner or later returned. This Atlantic Migration—aptly so called, because all crossed the ocean except those who moved from European to Asiatic Russia—towers above all other historical migrations in magnitude, and possibly also in significance, for it was the means by which earlier colonial offshoots of Europeans were transformed into new Europes alongside the old. All parts of Europe contributed, as is shown in the table below, which comprises the years from 1846 to 1932. Before 1846 the movement had scarcely begun, though over a million immigrants had entered the United States at that time since the close of the Napoleonic wars. After 1932 it was greatly reduced until after the Second World War.

The British and Irish (inseparable in the statistical records) went to the British dominions and to the United States. The Italians divided between the United States and Latin America. Spaniards settled overwhelmingly in the Spanish Amer-

MIGRATION FROM EUROPE,* 1846–1932

FROM:	Great Britain and Ireland	18,000,000
	Italy	10,100,000
	Russia†	9,200,000
	Austria-Hungary	5,200,000
	Germany	4,900,000
	Spain	4,700,000
	Portugal	1,800,000
	Sweden	1,200,000
	Norway	850,000
	Poland‡	640,000
	France	520,000
	Denmark	390,000
	Finland	370,000
	Switzerland	330,000
	Holland	220,000
	Belgium	190,000
	Total	58,610,000

* Carr-Saunders, *World Population*, pp. 49 and 56.
† Including 7 million from European to Asiatic Russia up to 1914 only. It is thought that 3 million went from European to Asiatic parts of the U.S.S.R. between 1926 and 1939.
‡ 1920–1932 only. The figures above for Russia, Austria-Hungary, and Germany include the emigration to all countries of ethnic Poles and East European Jews, of whom about 3 million Poles and 2 million Jews came to the United States in the forty years before 1914. Were it possible to allocate these emigrants among the three segments of partitioned Poland, the figures for Russia especially, but also for Austria-Hungary and Germany, would be correspondingly reduced.

ican republics, and Portuguese in Brazil. The Germans moved overwhelmingly to the United States, though some went to Argentina and Brazil. The new countries received the following influxes of people:

IMMIGRATION INTO OTHER COUNTRIES
FROM EUROPE*

TO:		
	United States	34,000,000
	Asiatic Russia (to 1914 only)	7,000,000
	Argentina	6,400,000
	Canada	5,200,000
	Brazil	4,400,000
	Australia	2,900,000
	Cuba	860,000
	South Africa	852,000
	Uruguay	713,000
	New Zealand	594,000

* Carr-Saunders, *World Population*, p. 49.

The extraordinary preponderance of the United States is apparent. At the same time, it is well to rectify the impressions of most Americans on the subject. Almost half the European migration was directed elsewhere than to the United States. Asiatic Russia was second only to the United States in the receipt of new settlers. Germany was by no means a chief source of emigration, especially in proportion to total national population from which emigrants came. Canada received fewer immigrants than Argentina, Australia fewer than Brazil, New Zealand fewer than Uruguay. The new worlds were not peculiarly Anglo-Saxon.

The exodus from Europe was due to a remarkable and temporary juxtaposition of causes. One fundamental cause, or precondition, was that before 1914 the new countries welcomed immigration. Hands were wanted to farm the land, build houses, dig in the mines. This was least true of Australia and New Zealand, which preferred to limit themselves to English-speaking settlers, and which also pioneered as social democracies, becoming models, even before 1900, of legislation to protect the working classes. One result was that no inrush of outsiders to compete for jobs at low wages was desired. A similar combination of national preferences and labor protectionism led to laws restricting immigration in the United States in 1921 and 1924. Thereafter immigrants could enter only under quotas, and the quotas were lowest for eastern and southern Europe from which most emigration was then forthcoming.

In Europe there were many conditions propelling emigrants outward. Physically, the steamship made it easier and cheaper to cross the sea, and the railroad helped people to get to the ports as well as to distribute themselves after landing in the new countries. Economically, people in the mass could for the first time afford a long journey. People migrated to improve their material circumstances; but the great crests in the wave of emigration coincided with crests in the business cycle in Europe, when jobs in Europe were plentiful and wages at their highest. Of the opposite case, of actual flight from economic ruin or starvation, the emigration from Ireland after 1846 is the best example. After the revolutions of 1848 a certain number left Europe for political reasons, and, later on, to avoid compulsory military service. The best example of flight from actual persecution is that of the Jews of Russia and Russian Poland, of whom a million and a half moved to the United States in the fifteen years preceding the First World War.

But perhaps most basic in the whole European exodus was the underlying liberalism of the age. Never before (nor since) had people been legally so free to move. Old laws requiring skilled workmen to stay in their own countries were repealed, as in England in 1824.[3] The old semicommunal agricultural villages, with collective rights and obligations, holding the individual to his native group, fell into disuse except in Russia. The disappearance of serfdom allowed the peasant of eastern Europe to change his residence without obtaining a lord's permission.[4] Governments permitted their subjects to emigrate, to take with them their savings of shillings, marks, kronen, or lire, and to change nationality by becoming naturalized in their new homes. The rise of individual liberty in Europe, as well as the hope of enjoying it in America, made possible the great emigration. For so huge a mass movement the most remarkable fact is that it took place by individual initiative and at individual expense. Individuals and family groups (to borrow the metaphor of one authority) detached themselves atom by atom from the mass of Europe, crossed the seas on their own, and reattached themselves atom by atom to the accumulating mass of the New World.

73. THE WORLD ECONOMY OF THE NINETEENTH CENTURY

How did the swelling population of Europeans manage to feed itself? How, in fact, did it not merely feed itself but enjoy an incomparably higher standard of living in 1900 than in 1800? By science, industry, transportation, and communications. And by organization—in business, finance, and labor.

The "New Industrial Revolution"

The Industrial Revolution entered upon a new phase. The use of steam power, the growth of the textile and metallurgical industries, and the advent of the railroad had characterized the early part of the century. Now, after 1870, new sources of power were tapped, the already mechanized industries expanded, new industries appeared, and industry spread geographically.

The steam engine itself was refined and improved. By 1914 it still predominated over other power machinery, but electricity with its incomparable advantages came into use. The invention of the internal combustion (or gasoline) engine and the diesel engine gave the world automobiles, airplanes, and submarines in the two decades before 1914; the advent of the automotive and aviation industries made oil one of the most coveted of natural resources. In the new chemical industries industrial research laboratories were replacing the individual inventor. Chemists discovered new fertilizers, and from coal tar alone produced a bewildering array of new products ranging from artificial food flavors to high explosives. With the latter the first great tunnels were built, the Mount Cenis in 1873, the Simplon in 1906—both in the Alps; and great new canals, the Suez in 1869,

---

[3] See p. 460.
[4] See pp. 479–480, 489.

CLASSIC LANDSCAPE
by Charles Sheeler (American, 1883–1965)

This landscape depicts the River Rouge plant of the Ford Motor Company in 1931, but it also symbolizes what has been called the Second Industrial Revolution, in which electricity, the internal combustion engine, and the automobile were important, and industry spread beyond its original centers in Britain and Western Europe. The picture is "classic" in its clear delineation, its array of familiar mathematical forms, and the universality of its message. The plant seems rational and precise, but the absence of human beings is to be noted; it is as if the machine had a life of its own and could do without human hands. The sharp shadows suggest bright sunshine, despite the smoke pouring from the tall chimney. When the picture was painted no one was alarmed about atmospheric pollution. Courtesy of Mrs. Edsel B. Ford.

the Kiel in 1895, the Panama in 1914. Chemistry made possible the production of synthetic fabrics like rayon which revolutionized the textile industry. Electricity transformed all indoor and outdoor lighting. There was a communications revolution too. The telephone appeared in the 1870s. Marconi brought the continents closer together, successfully transmitting wireless signals across the Atlantic in 1901. The moving picture and the radio modestly presented themselves before 1914. Medicine ran a tongue-twisting alphabetical gamut from anesthetics to x-rays; yellow fever was overcome. Vastly improved processes for refining iron ore made possible a great expansion in the production of steel, the key product of the new industrial age; aluminum and other metal alloys were also being produced. Railroad mileage multiplied; the European network, including the Russian, increased from 140,000 miles in 1890 to 213,000 in 1914.

In the new phase of the Industrial Revolution machine industry spread geographically from Britain and Belgium, the only truly industrial countries in 1870, to France, Italy, Russia, Japan, and, most markedly, to Germany and the United States. In Europe industrial production was concentrated in the "inner zone." Three powers alone—Britain, Germany, and France—accounted in 1914 for more than seven-tenths of all European manufactures and produced over four-fifths of all European coal, steel, and machinery. Of the major European powers Germany was now forging ahead. To use steel alone as a criterion, in 1871 Germany was producing annually three-fifths as much steel as Britain; by 1900 it was producing more, and by 1914 it was producing twice as much as Britain—but only half as much as the new industrial giant, the United States. By 1914 American steel output was greater than that of Germany, Britain, and France combined. Britain, the pioneer in mechanization, was being outstripped in both the old world and the new. The three European powers increased their industrial production by about 50 percent in the two decades before 1914, but the United States had a far higher annual growth rate from 1870 to 1913, 4.3 percent as compared to the next leading powers, Germany with 2.9 percent, Britain with 2.2 percent, and France with 1.6 percent.[5] By 1914 the United States had moved ahead of Europe in the mechanization of agriculture, in manufactures, and in coal and steel production, in which it was producing over two-fifths of the world's output. The Americans were pioneering also in assembly-line, conveyor-belt techniques for the mass production of automobiles and all kinds of consumer goods.

Free Trade and the European "Balance of Payments"

It was Britain in the mid-nineteenth century, then the workshop of the world, that had inaugurated the movement toward free trade. It will be recalled that in 1846, by the repeal of the Corn Laws, the British embarked upon a systematic free trade policy, deliberately choosing to become dependent upon overseas imports for their food.[6] France adopted free trade in 1860.[7] Other countries soon followed. It is true that by 1880 there was a movement back to protective tariffs, except in Britain, Holland, and Belgium. But the tariffs were impediments rather than barriers, and until 1914 the characteristic of the economic system was the

---

[5] *The New Cambridge Modern History*, Volume XII, rev. ed. (Cambridge: Cambridge University Press, 1968), p. 40.
[6] See p. 464.
[7] See pp. 498–499.

extreme mobility of goods across political frontiers. Politically, Europe was more than ever nationalistic; but economic activity, under generally liberal conditions in which business was supposed to be free from the political state, remained predominantly international and globe-encircling.

Broadly speaking, the great economic accomplishment of Europe before 1914 was to create a system by which the huge imports used by industrial Europe could be acquired and paid for. All European countries except Russia, Austria-Hungary, and the Balkan states imported more than they exported. It was the British again that had led in this direction. Britain had been a predominantly importing country since the close of the eighteenth century. That is to say, despite the expanding export of cotton manufactures and other products of the Industrial Revolution, Britain consumed more goods from abroad than it sent out. Industrialization and urbanization in the nineteenth century confirmed the same situation. Between 1800 and 1900 the value of British exports multiplied eightfold, but the value of imports into Great Britain multiplied tenfold, and in the decade before 1914 the British had an import surplus of about three-quarters of a billion dollars a year. Great Britain and the industrial countries of Europe together (roughly Europe's "inner zone"), at the beginning of the twentieth century, were drawing in an import surplus, measured in dollars, of almost $2 billion every year (the dollar then representing far more goods than it came to represent later). The imports into Europe's inner zone consisted of raw materials for its industries and of food and amenities for its people.

How were the imports paid for? How did Europe enjoy a favorable "balance of payments" despite an unfavorable balance of trade in commodities? Export of European manufactures paid for some imports, and even most, but not all. It was the so-called invisible exports that made up the difference, that is, shipping and insurance services rendered to foreigners, and interest on money lent out or invested, all bringing in foreign exchange. Shipping and insurance were important. An Argentine merchant in Buenos Aires, to ship hides to Germany, might employ a British vessel; he would pay the freight charges in Argentine pesos, which might be credited to the account of the British shipowner in an Argentine bank; the British shipowner would sell the pesos to someone, in England or elsewhere in Europe, who needed them to buy Argentine meat. The far-flung British merchant marine thus earned a considerable amount of the food and raw materials needed by Britain. To insure themselves against risks of every conceivable kind people all over the world turned to Lloyds of London. With the profits drawn from selling insurance the British could buy what they wished. Governments or business enterprises borrowed money in Europe, mainly in England; the interest payments, putting foreign currencies into European and British hands, constituted another invisible export by which an excess of imports could be financed. But the lending of money to foreigners is only part of a larger phenomenon, the export of capital.

The Export of European Capital

The migration of millions of Europeans had the effect of creating new societies, basically European in character, which both purchased manufactures from Europe and produced the food, wool, cotton, and minerals that Europe needed. It could not have had this effect if Europe had exported people only, especially people of such small means as most emigrants were. Europe also exported the capital necessary to get the new settlers and the new worlds into production.

The export of capital meant that an older and wealthier country, instead of using its whole annual income to raise its own standard of living, or to add to its own capital by expanding or improving its houses, factories, machinery, mines, transportation, etc., diverted some of its income to expanding or improving the houses, factories, machinery, mines, and transportation of foreign countries. It meant that British, French, Dutch, Belgian, Swiss, and eventually German investors in the desire to increase their income bought the stocks of foreign business enterprises and the bonds of foreign businesses and governments; or they organized companies of their own to operate in foreign climes; or their banks granted loans to banks in New York or Tokyo, which then lent the funds to local users. Capital arose in Europe to some extent from the savings of quite small people, especially in France, where peasants and modest bourgeois families were notably thrifty. But most capital accumulated from savings by the well-to-do. The owners of a business concern, for example, instead of spending the concern's income by paying higher wages, took a portion of it in profits or dividends, and instead of spending all this on their own living, reinvested part of it in domestic or foreign enterprises. The gap between rich and poor was thus one cause of the rapid accumulation of capital, though the accumulation of capital, in the nineteenth century, produced in turn a steady rise of living standards for the working classes. In a sense, however, the common people of western Europe, by forgoing the better housing, diet, education, or pleasures that a more democratic or consumer-oriented society might have planned for them, made possible the export of capital and hence the financing and building up of other regions of the world.

The British were the chief exporters of capital, followed at some distance by the French, and at the close of the century by the Germans. As early as the 1840s half the annual increase of wealth in Great Britain was going into foreign investments. By 1914 the British had $20 billion in foreign investments, the French about $8.7 billion, the Germans about $6 billion. A quarter of all the wealth owned by the inhabitants of Great Britain consisted in 1914 of holdings outside the country. Almost a sixth of the French national wealth lay in investments outside of France. All three countries had given hostages to fortune, and fortune proved unkind, for in the First World War the British lost about a quarter of their foreign investments, the French about a third, the Germans all.

These huge sums, pouring out from Europe's inner zone for a century before 1914, at first went mainly to finance the Americas and the less affluent regions of Europe.[8] No country except Great Britain completely built its railways with its own resources. In the United States the railway system was built very largely with capital obtained from England. In central and eastern Europe British companies often constructed the first railways, then sold out to native operating companies or to governments which subsequently ran them. In the Argentine Republic the British not merely financed and built the railways, but long continued to operate and own them. In addition, up to 1914 the British sold about 75 million tons of coal a year to South America to keep the railways going, not to mention items for replacement and upkeep of equipment. Docks, warehouses, mines, plantations,

---

[8] The penetration of European capital into Asia and Africa, after about 1890, is considered in the following chapter.

Width of Arrow Segments is Proportionate to the Amount of Capital Export

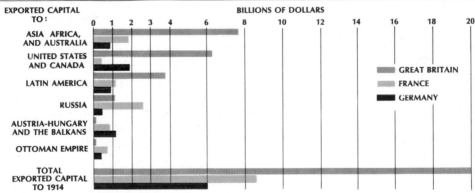

EXPORT OF EUROPEAN CAPITAL TO 1914

In 1914 the British, French, and Germans held upwards of $30 billion in foreign and colonial loans and investments, distributed as shown on the map. Dutch investments, especially in the Netherlands Indies, together with Swiss, Belgian, and Scandinavian holdings, would add several billion dollars more. Proceeds from such investments helped Europeans to pay for the excess of their imports over exports. New and undeveloped countries were built up by capital borrowed from Europe. British capital predominated in the overseas world, while the less advanced regions of eastern Europe and the Near East were financed mainly from Germany and France. Much of the investment shown on this map was lost or expended in the First World War. See pp. 684–685, 690.

processing and manufacturing establishments all over the world were similarly built up with capital drawn from Europe. European capital also helped emigrants in the new countries to live in a civilized fashion. In the United States, for example, state and local governments very commonly sold their bonds in Europe, to build roads, pave streets, or construct school systems for the westward-moving population. A few of these American bonds proved a partial or total loss to European investors. On the whole, by 1914, the United States had paid back a good deal of its indebtedness. Even so, in 1914, Americans still owed about $4 billion to Europeans—a sum three times as large as the national debt of the United States at the time.

An International Money System: The Gold Standard

The international economy rested upon an international money system, based in turn upon the almost universal acceptance of the gold standard. England had adopted the gold standard in 1816, when the pound sterling was legally defined as the equivalent of 113 grains of fine gold. Western Europe and the United States adopted an exclusively gold standard in the 1870s. A person holding any "civilized" money—pounds, francs, dollars, marks, etc.—could turn it into gold at will, and a person holding gold could turn it into any money. The currencies were like so many different languages all expressing the same thing. All had substantially the same value, and until 1914 the exchange rates between currencies remained highly stable. It was assumed that no civilized country's currency ever "fell"; such things might happen in Turkey or China, or in the French Revolution, but not in the world of practical men, modern progress, and civilized affairs.

The important currencies were all freely exchangeable. A Frenchman, selling silks to a German, and hence receiving German marks, could turn the marks into francs, pounds sterling, or dollars. That is, he was not obliged to buy from Germany or spend his money in Germany but could use the proceeds of his German sale to buy French, British, or American goods or services as he chose. Trade was multilateral. A country needing imports from another country, such as American cotton, did not have to sell to that country to obtain them; it could sell its own goods anywhere and then import according to its needs.

It was the acceptance of the gold standard, and the fact that all important countries possessed a sufficient share of gold to support their currencies, that made possible so fluid an interchange. At the same time the gold standard had less wholesome effects. It was hard on countries that lacked gold. And it produced a gradual fall of prices, especially between 1870 and 1900, because (until the gold discoveries in South Africa, Australia, and Alaska in the 1890s) the world's production of gold lagged behind the expanding production of industrial and agricultural goods. Persistently declining prices were a hardship to those who habitually worked with borrowed money—many farmers, many businessmen, and debtor nations as a whole. A famous speech of William Jennings Bryan in the United States in 1896, declaring that mankind should not be crucified "upon this cross of gold," expressed a restlessness that was world-wide. But falling prices were an advantage to the wage-earning class, which generally improved its position in these years, and also to the wealthy, the owners and lenders of capital, the bankers and financiers, who so long as prices were falling were repaid in money of more value than that which they had lent.

The center of the global economic and financial system was London. The London banks came forward in consequence of the defeat of Napoleon, the older financial centers in Amsterdam having been ruined in the Revolutionary and Napoleonic wars. It may be recalled also that the victors in 1815 imposed upon France an indemnity of 700 million francs, which in 1818 was taken over by a syndicate of private bankers; the London banks played a leading part in this affair and so developed their connections with many government treasuries.[9] In the Crimean War of 1854–1856, with England at war with Russia, the London banks floated loans for the Russian government—so independent were business and politics at the time. The early adoption of the gold standard in England meant that many people, British and foreign, kept their funds in the form of sterling on deposit in London, where quantities of available capital therefore accumulated.

The banks, too, grew up in the financing of the British export trade, itself borne on the tide of the Industrial Revolution. A small Lancashire manufacturer, for example, might receive an order for a gross of scissors from an unknown merchant in Trieste. He would draw a bill or "sight draft" against the Trieste merchant, and take this bill to a financial institution known as an acceptance house. The acceptance house, which in the course of its business had acquired a microscopic knowledge of the credit of thousands of individuals and firms in all parts of the world, would then "discount" the bill, giving cash to the Lancashire manufacturer and collecting from the Trieste merchant through international banking channels. In this way the bank took a burden off the British manufacturer, and extended short-term credit to foreigners for the purchase of British goods. Many acceptance houses gradually went into the business of long-term foreign lending also. London became the apex of a pyramid which had the world for its base. It was the main center of exchange of currencies, the clearinghouse of the world's debts, the depository from which all the world borrowed, the banker's bank, the insurance man's resort for reinsurance, as well as the world's shipping center and the headquarters of many international corporations.

A World Market: Unity, Competition—and Insecurity

Never had the earth been so unified economically, with each region playing its due role in a global specialization. Western Europe, and in 1870 mainly Great Britain, was the world's industrial workshop. Other parts of the earth supplied its many needs. An English economist marveled in 1866 that Britain now had its granaries in Chicago and Odessa, its forests in Canada and the Baltic, its sheep farms in Australia, and its gold and silver mines in California and Peru, while drinking tea brought from China and coffee from East Indian plantations. The same could have been said of most of Europe's "inner zone" by the time of the First World War.

A true world market had been created. Goods, services, money, capital, people moved back and forth almost without regard to national boundaries. Articles were bought and sold at uniform world prices. Dealers in wheat, for example, followed prices in Minneapolis, Liverpool, Buenos Aires, and Danzig as reported by telegraph and cable from day to day. They bought where it was cheapest, and sold where it was dearest. In this way the world's wheat supply was distributed roughly according to need or ability to pay. The worker of Milan, if the Italian

[9] See pp. 423, 449.

crop was poor and prices high, was fed from another source. On the other hand, the Italian wheat grower would in this case feel the pinch of world competition. The world market, while it organized the world into a unified economic system, at the same time brought distant regions into competition for the first time. The producer—whether businessman, factory employee, farmer, or coffee planter— had no secure outlet for his product, as had generally been true in the past. He was in competition not only with the man across the street or down the road, but with the world.

The creation of an integrated world market, the financing and building up of countries outside of Europe, and the consequent feeding and support of Europe's increasing population were the great triumphs of the nineteenth-century system of unregulated capitalism. The system was intricate, with thousands and even millions of individuals and business firms supplying each other's wants without central planning. But it was extremely precarious, and the position of most people in it was exceedingly vulnerable. Region competed against region, and person against person. A fall of grain prices in the American Middle West, besides ruin- ing a few speculators, might oblige the Prussian or Argentine wheat grower to sell at a price at which he could not live. A factory owner might be driven out of busi- ness if his competitor successfully undersold him or if a new commodity made his own product obsolete. The workingman, hired only when needed by an em- ployer, faced unemployment when business slackened, or the permanent dis- appearance of his job by the next labor-saving invention. The system went through cycles of boom and depression, the most notable example of the latter be- ing the long depression that set in about 1873 and lasted to about 1893. It rested on expansion and on credit; but sometimes people could not pay their debts, so that credit collapsed, and sometimes expansion failed to keep pace with expecta- tions, and anticipated profits proved to be losses. To combat the essential in- security of private capitalism, all manner of devices were resorted to. Govern- ments adopted protective tariffs on the one hand and social insurance and welfare legislation on the other; trade unionism and socialist movements grew; business mergers took place. These and other measures, to which we shall return, signal- ized the gradual decline in the years after 1880 of nineteenth-century unregu- lated, laissez-faire capitalism.

Changes in Organization: Big Business

A great change came over capitalism itself about 1880 or 1890. Formerly charac- terized by a very large number of very small units, small businesses run by indi- viduals, partnerships, or small companies, it was increasingly characterized by large and impersonal corporations. The attractions of the "limited liability" cor- poration as a form of business organization and as a means of encouraging invest- ment arose from laws, enacted by most countries in the nineteenth century, which limited the individual investor's personal loss in the event of a bankruptcy to the amount of his shares of stock in the enterprise. The corporation, in its mod- ern form appearing first with the railroads, became the usual form of organiza- tion for industry and commerce. As machinery grew more complicated only a large pool of capital could finance it. And as corporations grew in size and num- ber, relying on the sale of stock and the issue of bonds, the influence of banking and financial circles was enhanced. Financiers, using not so much their own money as the savings of others, had a new power to create or to extinguish, to stimulate, discourage, or combine corporate enterprises in various industries. Industrial capitalism brought finance capitalism with it.[10]

Corporate organization made it possible to concentrate economic processes under unified management. In retail commerce, large department stores appeared about 1890 in the United States and France. In industry, steel offers a good example. Steel became in any case a big business when heavy blast furnaces were introduced. It was not safe for the steel business, or for the blast furnaces, to rely for iron and coal on independent producers who might sell to whomsoever they pleased. The steel works therefore began to operate mines of their own or to buy out or otherwise reduce coal and iron mines to subsidiary status. Some, to assure their markets, began to produce not merely steel but steel manufactures as well—steel ships, railway equipment, naval and military ordnance. Thus entire processes from mining to finished product became concentrated in a "vertical" integration. By "horizontal" integration concerns at the same level combined with each other to reduce competition and to protect themselves against fluctuations in prices and in markets. Some fixed prices, some agreed to restrict production, some divided up markets among themselves. They were called trusts in the United States, cartels in Europe. They were common in many of the new industries at the close of the century, such as chemicals, aluminum, and oil. In steel such combinations produced the great interests of Krupp in Germany, Schneider-Creusot in France, Vickers-Armstrong in Great Britain. It was in the United States that such big business developed furthest, headed by "captains" of industry and "titans" of finance. Andrew Carnegie, by origin a poor Scottish immigrant boy, produced more steel than all England; in 1901 he sold out to an even more colossal organization, the United States Steel Corporation, formed by the financier J. P. Morgan. It was in the United States, too, that concern over monopoly and the power of big business in general was felt most strongly; antitrust legislation, beginning with the Sherman Act of 1890, was enacted but never with any substantial effect.

Many of the new combinations were beneficial in making the ups and downs of business less erratic, and so providing more stable prices and more continuous and secure employment. Generally they reduced the costs of production; but whether the savings went into higher profits, higher wages, or lower prices depended on numerous factors. Some trusts were more greedy than others or confronted with only weakly organized or unorganized labor. In any case, for good or ill, decisions rested with management and finance. A new kind of private power had arisen, which its critics liked to call "feudal." Since no economic system had ever been so centralized up to that time, never in fact had so few people exercised so much economic power over so many. The middle class, with the rise of great corporations, came typically to consist of salaried employees; the salaried man might spend a lifetime with the same company, and feel toward it, in its disputes with labor or government, a loyalty not unlike that of a lord's retainer in feudal times. The laboring class was less amenable; labor attempted to organize unions capable of dealing with increasingly gigantic employers. It also after about 1880 played an increasingly decisive role in the politics of all advanced nations.

---

[10] See pp. 497–498, 540.

74. THE ADVANCE OF DEMOCRACY: THIRD FRENCH REPUBLIC, UNITED KINGDOM, GERMAN EMPIRE

In the years from 1815 to 1870 European political life had been marked by liberal agitation for constitutional government, representative assemblies, responsible ministries, and guarantees of individual liberties. In the years from 1871 to 1914, even where these liberal objectives were not fully achieved but remained as goals, the most notable political development was the democratic extension of the vote to the working class—the adoption of universal male suffrage, which in turn meant for the first time the creation of mass political parties and the need for political leaders to appeal to a wide electorate. The extension of the suffrage in these years did not take place because of popular agitation as in the days of the Chartists or of the radical reformers in France. Governments for a variety of reasons extended the suffrage on their own. Often democratization took place in a continuing monarchical and aristocratic framework, but almost everywhere by 1914 the machinery at least of democratic self-government was being established. In addition, to counter the growing strength of socialism after 1871, and for humanitarian reasons, governments were also assuming responsibility for the social and economic problems arising from industrialism. The welfare state in its modern form was taking shape.

France: The Establishment of the Third Republic

In France the democratic republic was not easily established, and its troubled early years left deep cleavages within the country. It will be recalled that in September 1870, when the empire of Napoleon III revealed its helplessness in the Franco-Prussian War, insurrectionaries in Paris, as in 1792 and 1848, again proclaimed the Republic.[11] A provisional government of national defense sought desperately to continue the war, but the cause was hopeless. By January 1871, a bitter siege of Paris came to an end and an armistice was signed. Bismarck, insisting that only a properly constituted government could make peace, permitted the election, by universal male suffrage, of a National Assembly which was to consider his peace terms and draft a constitution for the new French state. When the elections were held in February, it was found, as in 1848 (and, indeed, 1797), that republicanism was so distrusted by the French people as a whole, and most especially in the provinces and rural areas, that a free election brought monarchist elements into power.[12] Republicanism was still thought to be violent—bellicose in its foreign policy, turbulent in its political workings, unfriendly to the church, and socialistic or at least equalitarian in its views of property and private wealth. The new Assembly contained only about 200 republicans out of more than 600 deputies.

But the Paris republicans, who had defended France when Napoleon III failed to do so, who for four months had been besieged, starved, and frozen by the Germans, and who still refused to make peace on the harsh terms imposed by Bismarck and about to be accepted by the Assembly, refused to recognize the latter's authority. A civil war broke out between the National Assembly, now sitting at

---

[11] See p. 525.
[12] See pp. 382, 473, 475.

THE ADVANCE OF DEMOCRACY 573

Versailles, and the city of Paris, where a revolutionary municipal council or "Commune" was set up. Paris, so lately attacked by German soldiers, was now attacked by French.

The Paris Commune, which lasted from March to May 1871, seemed to be another explosion of social revolution. Actually, it was in essence a revival of the Jacobinism of 1793. It was fiercely patriotic and republican, anti-German, opposed to wealthy bourgeois, aristocrats, and clergy, in favor of government controls upon prices, wages, and working conditions, but still not socialist in any sweeping or systematic way. Among its leaders, however, there were a few of the new international revolutionary socialists, who saw in a Jacobin or democratic republic a step toward their new order. Marx in England, and others elsewhere, hopefully read into the Commune the impending doom of the bourgeoisie. This was precisely what more conservative elements feared. To many of the French middle and peasant class, and to people like them all over Europe, it seemed that the "Communards" were wild and savage destroyers of nineteenth-century civilization. The fighting in Paris was atrocious beyond anything known in any preceding French revolution. The Communards, in final desperation, burned a number of public buildings and put to death the archbishop of Paris, whom they held as a hostage. The forces of the National Assembly, when finally triumphant, were determined to root out the inveterate revolutionism of Paris. Some 330,000 persons were denounced, 38,000 arrested, 20,000 put to death, and 7,500 deported to New Caledonia. The Third Republic was born in an atmosphere of class hate and social terror.

The form of government for the new regime still had to be established. The monarchist majority in the Assembly was itself evenly divided between those who favored a restoration of the Bourbon family and those who favored the Orléanist. In the end, even after they were reconciled, the Bourbon candidate alienated everyone by his stiff insistence on a return to the white flag of the Bourbons. The monarchists checkmated each other. Meanwhile, after extended discussion of various constitutional projects, the Assembly adopted in 1875 not a constitution, but certain constitutive laws. By a margin of one vote, a resolution indirectly amounting to the establishment of a republic was passed. The new laws provided for a president, a parliament in two chambers, and a council of ministers, or cabinet, headed by a premier. The Senate was to be elected by a complicated and indirect system of election, the Chamber of Deputies by universal, direct, male suffrage.

Within two years, in 1877, the role of the president, the ministers, and the parliament was further clarified as a result of an unsuccessful attempt by an early president, Marshal MacMahon, to dismiss a premier of whom he did not approve but who had the backing of the Chamber. MacMahon proceeded to dissolve the Chamber and to hold new elections, but the example of Napoleon III's transformation of the Second Republic into a personal dictatorship was still fresh. The elections vindicated the principle of parliamentary primacy and of the responsibility of the premier and his cabinet to the legislature, a responsibility which in France meant generally but not exclusively to the lower house. The true executive in republican France was to be the premier and his cabinet, themselves held strictly to account by a majority of the legislature. Unfortunately, that majority, in a parliament where a dozen or so parties were represented, was always difficult to form and could be created only by unstable, temporary, shifting party alliances, coalitions, or blocs. No president, and indeed no premier, could henceforth dissolve the Chamber in order to hold new elections and consult the country as could be done in Britain. Actually, under the Third Republic the substantial machinery of state—ministries, prefectures, law courts, police, army, all under highly centralized control—was carried over virtually untouched as in all upheavals since the time of Napoleon I. France in the nineteenth century, so volatile in appearance, in effect underwent less extensive reorganization than any other leading country in Europe.

Troubles of the Third French Republic

Yet the Third Republic was precarious. The government had changed so often since 1789 that all forms of government seemed to be transitory. Questions which in other countries were party questions became in France questions of "regime"—monarchy versus republic. Many people, especially those influenced by the upper classes, the Catholic clergy, and the professional army officers, continued to feel a positive aversion to the republic. On the other hand, the unmerciful and vindictive repression of the Commune made many middle-class people sympathetic to the republicans. Many turned republican simply because no other form of government established itself, or because it was the form of government that divided the country the least. As republicanism took in wider elements of society, it became less revolutionary and less fearsome. In 1879, for the first time, republicans won control of both houses of the government. In the 1880s their radicalism hardly went further than the founding of a democratic and compulsory school system at government expense and the passage of anticlerical legislation intended to curb church influence in education.

For over a quarter of a century, however, republican energies had to be expended in defense of republican institutions in order to ensure the survival of the regime. An initial crisis arose in 1886–1889, when General Boulanger gathered around him an incongruous following that included not only Bonapartists, monarchists, and aristocrats but also extreme radical republicans, who wished a war of revenge against Germany, and workers disgruntled over their general lot. Boulanger became a popular figure and seemed for a moment about to seize power as a dictator. But the menace collapsed in a comical failure as the general lost heart at the crucial hour and fled into exile. Meanwhile, in the 1880s and 1890s scandals and revelations of corruption in high republican circles provided ammunition for the antirepublicans. Moreover, the hope that unsympathetic French Catholics would rally to the republic, as urged by French prelates and by Pope Leo XIII in 1892, was shattered by the Dreyfus Affair, which in the late 1890s rocked the country and indeed the world.

In 1894 Captain Dreyfus, a Jewish army officer, was found guilty of treason by a military court and deported to Devil's Island. Evidence accumulated showing his innocence and pointing to the guilt of another officer, a Major Esterhazy, an adventurer known to be riddled with gambling debts. But the army refused to reopen the case, unwilling to admit it had erred; a staff officer, Major Henry, even forged documents to confirm Dreyfus' guilt. Meanwhile anti-Semites, royalists, traditionalists, militarists, and most of the "best" people fought the reopening of the case, deeming it unpatriotic to shake the nation's confidence in the army and wishing also to disgrace the republican regime. The partisans of Dreyfus stubbornly upheld him, both because they believed in justice and because they wished to discredit their adversaries. The country was deeply split. Finally, in 1899, Dreyfus was pardoned, and in 1906, fully exonerated. In the aftermath of the affair the left republicans and socialists revenged themselves by blocking the promotions of antirepublican officers and by anticlerical legislation. In 1905, in a series of laic laws, they "separated" church and state, ending the close relationship established under Napoleon's concordat a century earlier.

The Strength and Weakness of the Republic

The Third Republic, when the First World War came in 1914, a test which it was successfully to meet, had lasted over twice as long as any French regime since 1789. Born unwanted and accidentally, though it still had its opponents, it now commanded the loyalty of the overwhelming mass of the French people. What it had done, since 1871, was to domesticate democratic republicanism in Europe. Republicanism, one of the most militant of revolutionary movements down to 1870, had been shown in France to be compatible with order, law, parliamentary government, economic prosperity, and a mutual tolerance between classes, to the extent at least that they no longer butchered each other in the streets. Industrial workers were in many ways less well off than in England or Germany, but there were fewer of them; and for most people France in these years was a pleasant country, full of painters, writers, scholars, and scientists, full of bankers, bourgeois and well-established farmers, a country living comfortably and unhurriedly on the savings of generations, and one in which, in a close-knit family group, the average man could plan securely for his own and his children's future.

But the very comforts and values of bourgeois France were not those that would equip it for leadership in the modern age of technology and industrial power. Though substantial economic progress was made, the country lagged behind Germany in industrial development; the French entrepreneur showed little inclination to take the business risks needed for industrial growth. Politically, the fragmentation of political parties, itself a democratic reflection of a divided public opinion, and the distrust for historic reasons of a strong executive power led to the rise and fall of numerous short-lived ministries—no fewer than fifty in the years between 1871 and 1914. Ministerial instability was to be a chronic symptom of the Third Republic both before and after 1914; continuity of government policy was, however, generally maintained because of stability in certain key ministries and because of the permanent civil service.

French labor remained a steady source of discontent. Although French workers benefited from some labor legislation in the two decades after 1890, they continued to feel frustrated at the failure to establish a "social republic." Socialist representation in the Chamber grew. However, the most important single party of the republic, the Radicals, or Radical Socialists, were in actuality radical republicans —patriotic, anticlerical, spokesmen for the small shopkeepers and the lesser propertied interests; they drew the line at the advanced social legislation that labor expected from them, and on occasion their leaders even took positive steps to prevent unionization and to suppress strikes. Since some of these Radicals had started out as socialists, the distrust of French workers for all politicians and even for political processes was intensified. But the difficulties of the republic went deeper. The political energies of the republican statesmen had gone into liquidating the past, into curbing the political strength of the monarchists, the church, and the army; by the turn of the century, even before these older issues were fully resolved, the republic was compelled to meet the challenge of labor and to face other domestic and international pressures that were to try it sorely. The Third Republic was to weather the crisis of the First World War but not that of the Second.

The British Constitutional Monarchy

The British constitutional monarchy in the half-century before 1914 was the great exemplar of reasonable, orderly, and peaceable self-government through parliamentary methods. For over sixty years, spanning two-thirds of the nineteenth century, Victoria reigned (1837–1901) and gave her name to a distinguished era of material progress, literary accomplishment, and political stability. The two great parties, Liberal and Conservative, the heirs roughly of the Whigs and Tories, took form in the 1850s, the former producing its great leader in William E. Gladstone, the latter, a series of leaders of whom the most colorful was Benjamin Disraeli.

The advance toward an equalitarian political democracy in Britain was more cautious and slower than in France. The Reform Bill of 1832 had granted the vote to about an eighth of the adult male population. The democratic Chartist agitation of the 1830s and 1840s came to nothing.[13] In 1867, in response to continued demand for a wider suffrage, the Second Reform Bill was passed, Conservatives as well as Liberals outdoing one another in an effort to satisfy the country and to win new political strength for their own party. The bill, adopted under Disraeli's Conservative ministry, extended the suffrage from about 1 million eligible voters to about 2 million, or over a third of the adult males in the United Kingdom, reaching down far enough to include most workingmen in the cities. Disraeli's colleague Lord Derby called it a "leap in the dark." In 1884, under Liberal auspices,

---

[13] See pp. 468–469, 474.

SUNDAY AFTERNOON ON THE ISLAND OF LA GRANDE JATTE
by Georges Seurat (French, 1859–1891)

This picture of sunny calm, painted in 1886, suggests something of the well-being brought to a great many people by the European civilization of the late nineteenth century. Whether boating, or idly fishing, or quietly sitting and watching, or strolling alone or in pairs or in families with their children, the figures seem to live in a peaceable world which a later age of war, speed, and mechanical amusements has made to seem far away. Technically this is one of the most remarkable pictures ever painted. The artist, an impressionist, created it without the use of lines by filling the canvas with thousands of minute dots of the primary colors, which so blur and mix in the eye as to produce the forms and hues of nature. As a result it seems to be a picture of light itself, with an actual shimmer on the water, an astonishing "grassiness" in the grass, with shadows that seem to be real shadows, and distant figures looking really distant as if seen through the intervening air. Courtesy of The Art Institute of Chicago.

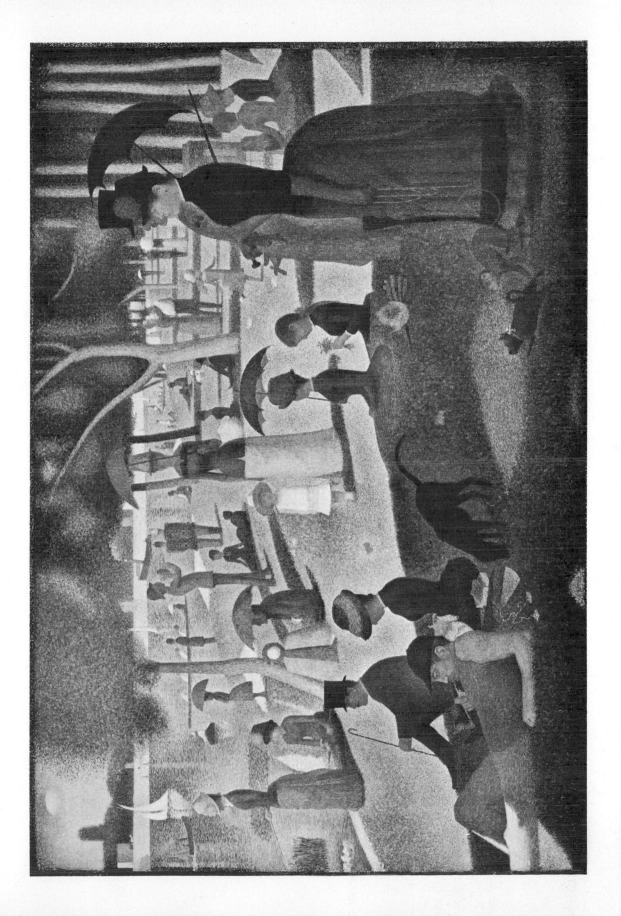

the suffrage was again broadened, this time in the rural areas, adding some 2 million additional voters and enfranchising over three-fourths of all adult males in the country. The suffrage still excluded agricultural workers who did not have a fixed residence, servants living with employers, and such people as unmarried grown sons who lived in the homes of their parents. Not until 1918 did Great Britain adopt universal male suffrage, as generally understood; and at that time women over thirty were given the vote too.

Despite the extension of the suffrage, the leadership of the country at the turn of the century was still in the hands of the upper and wealthier classes. Until 1911 the government paid no salaries to members of the House of Commons, who therefore, in both great parties, were usually gentlemen with private incomes, possessing the same family background and education. An attitude of sportsmanship and good feeling was characteristic of British politics. The two parties alternated in power at regular intervals, each indulgent toward the other, carrying over and developing rather than reversing the policies of its predecessor in office. Both parties sought support where they could find it, the Liberals leaning somewhat more on the industrial and commercial interests, the Conservatives on the landed aristocracy; both sought and succeeded in winning their share of the new working-class vote. It was in these years that both parties, when parliamentary reversals occurred, increasingly appealed to the country in general elections; the traditional crown and cabinet basis of British parliamentary government was being transformed into crown, cabinet, and country.

The Liberals were usually the more willing to pioneer, the first of the four ministries of Gladstone being especially notable in this respect. Gladstone in this first ministry (1868-1874) developed the principle of state-supported public education under the Forster Education Act of 1870, introduced the secret ballot, formally legalized labor unions, promoted competitive examinations for civil service posts, reorganized the upper judiciary, eliminated the purchase and sale of commissions in the army (a form of property in office), and by abolishing religious tests enabled persons not members of the Church of England to graduate from Oxford and Cambridge. The Conservative party, less sensitive to pressure from business interests for a laissez-faire policy in economic matters, and continuing the tradition of early Tory reformers, took the initiative in further labor legislation. Under Disraeli's second ministry (1874-1880), the existing acts regulating public sanitation and conditions in mines and factories were extended and codified, safety measures were enacted to protect sailors, and the first attempt to regulate housing conditions for the poorer classes was initiated. But the Liberals, it must be added, protected the workers' interests too. In Gladstone's second ministry (1880-1885) workingmen were assured of compensation for injuries not of their own responsibility, and in 1892, before the formation of his fourth ministry (1892-1894), Gladstone campaigned to shorten labor hours and to extend employers' liability in accidents.

British Political Changes after 1900

At the turn of the century important changes were discernible on the British political scene. Labor emerged as an independent political force, the Labour party itself being organized shortly after 1900.[14] The rise of labor had a deep impact

[14] See pp. 586-587.

upon the Liberal party, and indeed upon liberalism itself. With many persons insisting that protective measures be taken to counteract the poor health, low income, and economic insecurity of the British working people, the Liberals abandoned their traditional position of laissez faire and sponsored a policy of government intervention and social legislation in behalf of the workingman. The Liberals, though they acted in part for humanitarian reasons, were aware that with the emergence of the Labour party workingmen who customarily had voted for them might readily transfer their allegiance.

In control of the government from 1906 to 1916, with Herbert Asquith as prime minister and David Lloyd George as chancellor of the exchequer during most of this time, the Liberals put through a spectacular program of social welfare. Sickness, accident, old-age, and a degree of unemployment insurance were adopted, and a moderate minimum wage law was enacted. Labor exchanges, or employment bureaus, were set up over the country. Restrictions on strikes and other trade union activities were removed. To meet the costs of the new program as well as of other government expenditures, Lloyd George's budget of 1909 called for progressive income and inheritance taxes: the wealthier the taxpayer, the higher the rate at which he was taxed. He was in effect advancing the then novel idea of using taxation to modify the extremes of wealth and poverty. It was a "war budget," he said, intended "to wage war against poverty." Its fiscal measures were directed primarily at the landed aristocracy, and it aroused great opposition, especially in the House of Lords, where the contest over the budget led to a further constitutional curtailment of the power of the upper house. The Parliament Act of 1911 deprived the Lords of all veto power in money matters and of all but a two-year delaying veto on action of the Commons in other legislation. At this time, too, the government voted to pay salaries to members of the House of Commons, making it possible for workers and others without independent incomes to take seats in Parliament. This last measure was enacted because of a court ruling, the Osborne Judgment of 1909, that trade unions could not pay the salaries of workingmen elected to Parliament.

The Liberal party was embracing a program of positive state intervention in social and economic matters that the older liberalism, nurtured on the doctrines of laissez faire and the Manchester School, would not have accepted. With the Liberals actively seeking the support of labor and altering much in their traditional program, the Conservatives in the twentieth century tended to become the party of industry as well as of landed wealth and to replace the Liberals as the champions of economic liberalism and laissez faire. In the next generation, after the First World War, the Conservatives were to remain one of the two major parties of the country; the Liberals were to be far outstripped by the Labour party.

Meanwhile, despite its gains, labor was not pacified. Real wages showed a tendency to fall after 1900, and great coal and railway strikes broke out in 1911 and 1912. The British capacity to survive crises without violence, while still conspicuous, was being strained. An even more serious threat came from Ireland.

The Irish Question

Britain suffered from one of the worst minorities questions in Europe—the Irish question. After 1801 Britain was known as the United Kingdom of Great Britain and Ireland, Ireland having been incorporated into the United Kingdom as a defensive measure against pro-French sympathies in Ireland during the wars of the French Revolution.[15] The Irish representatives who sat in Parliament were generally obstructionist in their tactics. The Irish had many substantial grievances, among which two were conspicuous. The Irish peasant was defenseless against his landlord, far more so, for example, than the French peasant before 1789; and the Irish people, though predominantly Catholic, were obliged to pay tithes to the established Church of Ireland (an Anglican sister church to the Church of England), which also owned a good deal of the land.

Gladstone, in his first ministry, disestablished the Church of Ireland. He also initiated measures to protect the Irish farm tenant. By 1900, under Conservative auspices, Irish tenants were being assisted by the British government to buy out their landlords—often Englishmen or Anglicized and absentee Irishmen. The Irish also wanted home rule, or a parliament of their own. Gladstone, in trying to give it to them in 1886, split his Liberal party, part of which went along with the Conservatives, not wishing political division of the British Isles. Home rule was finally granted to Ireland in 1914. But the Ulstermen, Presbyterians of north Ireland, objected vehemently to inclusion in an autonomous Ireland, in which they would be outnumbered by the Catholics of the south. The latter, however, insisted with equal vehemence on the inclusion of Ulster, not wishing a political division of Ireland.

The Ulstermen, backed by British Conservatives, started arming and drilling to resist the act of Parliament that authorized home rule. Great Britain, in 1914, was about to see a civil war on its own doorstep. It suffered from something of the insoluble nationalistic disputes that afflicted Austria-Hungary. During the First World War home rule was suspended, and after considerable violence on both sides Catholic Ireland (Eire) received dominion status in 1922, but eventually dissolved all ties with Britain. Ulster remained in the United Kingdom and was dominated by Protestants, so that its Catholic minority remained discontented. No satisfactory solution has yet been found to the "Irish question."

Bismarck and the German Empire, 1871–1890

The German Empire, as put together by Bismarck in 1871 with William I, king of Prussia, as Kaiser, was a federation of monarchies, a union of twenty-five German states, in which the weight of monarchical Prussia, the Prussian army, and the Prussian landed aristocracy was preponderant. It developed neither the strong constitutionalism of England nor the democratic equality that was characteristic of France. To win popular support for his projects, Bismarck exploited existing democratic and socialist sentiment and provided that members of the Reichstag, the lower chamber, be elected by universal male suffrage.[16] Remaining chancellor of the united empire for some twenty years, from 1871 to 1890, he usually tried to have a majority in the Reichstag on his side, but he recognized no dependence on a majority in principle, holding to the doctrine that it was the emperor and his chancellor who were to govern the country. Moreover, in practice, the legislative powers of the lower house were severely restricted, and the upper chamber, representing the princes and not the people, and favored by the govern-

---

[15] See pp. 339, 382.
[16] See pp. 524, 526.

ment, tended to be more important. Despite the nature of the empire, the Prussian conservatives, the East-Elbian Junker landlords, were at first by no means enthusiastic over Bismarck's unified Germany.[17] They opposed his democratic concessions and were left horrified when in 1872 he undertook to extinguish what was left of their manorial jurisdiction over their peasants.

Bismarck in the 1870s therefore leaned not on the Conservatives but on the National Liberals. With their aid he put through a number of economic and legal measures designed to consolidate the unity of the new empire. Bismarck's first serious conflict developed with the Catholic church. At the very time that he was bent on subordinating all groups within the state to the sovereign power of the new empire, the church had spoken out. In 1864 in the *Syllabus of Errors*, it denounced the encroachment of all governments on educational and church affairs; in 1870 the new dogma of papal infallibility made it incumbent on Catholics to accept unreservedly the pope's pronouncements in matters of faith and morals.[18] To many, the implication was that the new empire could not count on the undivided loyalty of its Catholic citizens. To defend Catholic interests and those of the south German states where Catholicism predominated, Catholic elements had organized the strong Center party, which now upheld the church pronouncements. In 1871 Bismarck launched the so-called *Kulturkampf*, or "battle for modern civilization." The Liberals joined in eagerly. Like nineteenth-century liberals elsewhere (Gladstone's campaign against Anglican privilege and the French laic laws have just been mentioned), they were strongly anticlerical and disapproved of the influence of organized churches in public and private life. Laws were put through imposing restrictions upon Catholic worship and education, the Jesuits were expelled, and many Catholic bishops throughout Germany were arrested or went into exile. But Bismarck gradually concluded that the anti-Catholic legislation was fruitless, that he had overestimated the danger to the state of organized Catholicism, and that he needed the support of the Center party for other parts of his program.

In 1879, with the support of the Center and Conservative parties but to the dismay of many of his erstwhile Liberal allies, Bismarck abandoned free trade and adopted a protective tariff that provided needed revenues for the government and gave satisfaction both to agricultural and industrial interests. Meanwhile, the country's rapid and spectacular industrial expansion had stimulated the growth of the German working class, and to Bismarck's alarm, socialism was spreading.

The German Social Democratic party had been founded in 1875 by a fusion of Marxian socialists and the reformist followers of Ferdinand Lassalle on an essentially moderate program which Marx had denounced. But even a moderate socialism was mistrusted by Bismarck. He shared in the European horror at the recent Paris Commune, he feared socialism as anarchy, and he knew that socialism was in any case republican, and in that alone a potentially revolutionary movement in an empire of monarchies. Two radical attempts on the emperor's life (in neither case by Social Democrats) provided him with all the excuse he needed. In 1878, having already made peace with the Catholics, he set out to eradicate socialism. Antisocialist laws from 1878 to 1890 prohibited socialist meetings and socialist newspapers. For twelve years socialism was driven underground. But

---

[17] See pp. 484, 520–521.
[18] See p. 600.

repression was not his only weapon; he turned also to another tactic. Bismarck sought to persuade the workers to place their faith in him and the German Empire rather than in Marx and the prophets of socialism. To that end, in the 1880s, he initiated an extensive program of social legislation. Workingmen were insured by the state against sickness, accident, and incapacity in old age. "Our democratic friends," said Bismarck, "will pipe in vain when the people see princes concerned with their well-being." In social insurance imperial Germany was, from whatever motives, years ahead of more democratic England, France, and the United States.

Bismarck failed to kill socialism. The number of socialists elected to the Reichstag was greater in 1890 than in 1878—for Bismarck's antisocialist campaign, in deference to the then current standards of civilized government, never suppressed the voter's freedom to vote as he chose. It seems, however, that Bismarck by the later 1880s was more apprehensive than ever of social revolution that would destroy his empire and contemplated some kind of coup d'état in which the Reichstag would be throttled. He never reached this point because in 1890, at the age of seventy-five, he was obliged by the new emperor, William II, to retire.

The German Empire after 1890: William II

William I died in 1888 and was succeeded by his son Frederick III who, incurably ill of cancer, died some three months after his accession. Frederick's son, William II, the last king of Prussia and the last German Kaiser, began his reign (1888–1918) as a young man of twenty-nine, full of startling ideas about his personal power and privileges. He was uncomfortable in the presence of an elder statesman who had made the German Empire, who had been his grandfather's aide and adviser, and whom he regarded partly with veneration and partly as an old fogy. William soon quarreled with Bismarck over continuation of the antisocialist laws and over matters of foreign affairs. When Bismarck forbade his ministers to meet with the emperor on policy matters unless he was present, William resolved that he, and not Bismarck, would rule the empire, and in 1890 he ordered Bismarck to resign, "dropping the pilot," in the celebrated phrase. Under the four chancellors who succeeded Bismarck, it was William who dominated policy.

After 1890 Germany embarked upon what was termed a "new course." In foreign affairs this meant a more aggressive and ambitious colonial, naval, and diplomatic policy, as will appear in the next two chapters. In domestic affairs it meant a more conciliatory attitude toward the masses. The antisocialist laws were dropped, and the system of social security legislation was enlarged and codified. But no democratic adjustment seemed possible. William II believed in the divinely ordained prerogatives of the house of Hohenzollern, and the empire still rested on the power of the federated princes, on the Junkers, the army, and the new industrial magnates. But the Social Democrats, the Progressive party, and other democratic forces were growing in strength. They demanded, for Prussia, a reform of the illiberal constitution of 1850,[19] and for the Reich, real control over the federal chancellor by the majority party in the Reichstag. In the election of 1912 the Social Democrats reached a new high by polling four and a quarter million votes, about one-third of the total, and by electing 110 members to the

[19] See p. 488.

Reichstag, in which they now formed the largest single party; yet they were excluded from the highest posts of government. Even had war not come in 1914, it is clear that the imperial Germany created by Bismarck was moving toward a constitutional crisis in which political democracy would be the issue.

Developments Elsewhere; General Observations

Of political developments in other European states before 1914, something has already been said in the preceding chapter. Italy had become a constitutional monarchy in the 1860s and completed its unification by the forceful seizure of Rome in 1870.[20] Despite parliamentary forms, Italian political life in substance was characterized by unstable majorities and by opportunistic maneuvering and manipulation by moderate liberal political leaders, who maintained themselves in office for long periods of time by shuffling and reshuffling political coalitions. Deputies, in a form of parliamentary politics that was baptized *trasformismo* (or a kind of "crossing over") moved readily from one party group to another—for favors granted. Giovanni Giolitti, a shrewd tactician who headed several cabinets, governed in this way with only a few interruptions from 1903 to 1914. The liberal leaders were anticlerical, and the quarrel with the papacy over the seizure of the papal territories remained unsettled. The popes refused to recognize the Italian kingdom and forbade Catholics to participate in its affairs or even to vote in elections. Catholics voted nonetheless and in 1907 bishops in each diocese were permitted to relax the ban, as they increasingly did.

Industry had begun to make an appearance in the northern cities like Milan. More as a matter of expediency than out of any democratic impulse, the government moved to extend the franchise to the working classes. The narrow suffrage of 1861 was broadened, first in 1882, and then in 1912, when the new reform increased the number of eligible voters from three to eight million, or virtually universal male suffrage. Because of illiteracy and political inertia not all of the newly enfranchised hastened to exercise their voting privilege. The social problem remained serious, too, despite some modest labor legislation. Poverty and illiteracy, especially in the agrarian south, were grievous problems and radical unrest appeared in the industrial cities. In 1900 Victor Emmanuel's son and successor Humbert was assassinated. The first manifestations of an antiparliamentary ideology, chauvinistic nationalism, and explosive irrationalism appeared in the writings and political activism of literary men like Gabriele d'Annunzio and Filippo Marinetti, the latter publishing in 1909 the manifesto of a violently nihilistic movement he called "futurism." The machinery of political democracy was established in Italy but there could be no assurance about the direction Italian parliamentary democracy was taking.

In the Dual Monarchy of Austria-Hungary, created by the Compromise of 1867, Austria and Hungary were each in form constitutional parliamentary states.[21] In theory, the Emperor-King Francis Joseph ruled through ministries responsible to the legislature in each state. However, in the important sphere of matters affecting the empire as a whole, such as foreign affairs and military questions, there was little parliamentary restraint on the emperor. Here he had vir-

---

[20] See pp. 516–518, 525, 600–602.
[21] See pp. 530–531.

tually final authority; moreover, in all matters he still had broad powers to govern by decree, which he exercised. As in Germany, the tide of socialism was held back both by repressive laws and by social insurance and benevolent legislation. The most serious problem in the empire remained not socialism but agitation by the various subject nationalities, the Czechs and other Slavic peoples. Political democracy took a different course in Austria than in Hungary. In the former, partly as an effort to placate nationalist sentiment, universal male suffrage was introduced in 1907. In the latter it was bitterly and successfully resisted by the Magyars, who saw in it a weapon that could be employed by the Slavs to contest and destroy their preponderance. Austria itself, despite the democratic suffrage, was ruled very much like the German Empire, with the legislature able to debate and criticize but not control policy.

Of other countries it can be said that the political forms of democracy showed signs of advancing everywhere. Universal male suffrage was adopted in Switzerland in 1874, in Belgium in 1893 (though plural voting was still permitted), in the Netherlands in 1896; and in the next few years in Norway and Sweden (Norway was peacefully separated in 1905 from Sweden). In southern Europe, besides Italy, universal manhood suffrage was introduced in Spain, Greece, Bulgaria, Serbia, and after the revolt of 1908, in Turkey. Although both Spain and Portugal were beset by civil wars, constitutional forms were eventually adopted in both countries, universal male suffrage being introduced in Spain in 1890 and a liberal suffrage in Portugal under a republic in 1911. Even tsarist Russia, after the Revolution of 1905, received a Duma, or national parliament, elected on a wide franchise but on an indirect and undemocratic class basis, and with narrow powers.[22] Among states west of the Russian empire, only Hungary and Rumania had a highly restricted suffrage on the eve of the First World War. The vote for women progressed more slowly. Women voted before 1914 only in certain western states of the United States, in Australia, New Zealand, Finland, and Norway. Not until after the First World War did female suffrage begin to make significant advances.

The progress of representative and democratic institutions did not mean an end to the rule of monarchs, landed aristocrats, and other minority interests. For one thing, with the exception of France and Switzerland, Europe remained monarchical. Second, despite the growing importance of parliaments, parliamentary control over political life was far from guaranteed; emperors and kings still ruled through their chancellors and prime ministers. Of the major world powers it was mainly in the United States (at least for whites), Britain, and France that democratic and popular control was something of a reality. But the extension of the suffrage, by the relaxation of property qualifications, had a dynamic of its own and was altering the framework of politics everywhere; mass political parties, including socialist parties and confessional, or religious-oriented parties, were replacing the older, narrowly oligarchic political organizations, and support now had to be sought on a wider electoral basis. In almost all Europe, and in many of the outlying areas peopled by European descendants, democracy was advancing, even within the older framework. By 1871, most European nations, with the notable exception of Russia, had already won written constitutions, guarantees of

[22] See pp. 707–708.

personal freedom, parliamentary and representative institutions, and limitations on absolutism; in the years between 1871 and 1914 the most significant new political factor was the advance of male suffrage.

75. THE ~~ADVANCE OF DEMOCRACY~~ SOCIALISM AND LABOR UNIONS

The artisan and laboring classes had never viewed with much pleasure the rise of capitalism or of "bourgeois" liberalism. They had always been doubtful of free competition, unrestrained private enterprise, the Manchester School, laissez faire, the laws of supply and demand, the free market for goods and labor, the idea of an economy independent of states and governments. These were the ideas of middle-class liberals, not of radical democrats. Popular leaders had opposed them in the French Revolution in 1793. The English Chartists had been outspokenly anticapitalistic, and on the Continent the ideas of socialism had been spreading. In 1848 there was a strong movement among the working classes for a "social" republic, and, though the social revolution failed in 1848, the force of it was enough to terrify the possessing classes and shape the philosophy of Karl Marx.[23] With the advent of the ballot, workers pressed for social legislation and used their political power to gain a greater measure of social democracy.

But in addition, before and after obtaining the ballot, working people resorted to other devices for the improvement of their position. Against the owners of capital, who controlled the giving of jobs, there were two principal lines of action. One was to abolish the capitalists, the other to bargain with them. The former led to socialism, the latter to the formation of labor unions. Socialism, in logic, meant the extinction of the private employer as such.[24] Trade unionism, in logic, meant that the workingman had every reason to keep his employer prosperously in business in order that bargaining with him might produce more results. The working-class movement thus contained an internal contradiction which was never completely resolved.

Middle-class and educated people who took up the workers' cause, the "intellectuals" of the movement—Karl Marx, Friedrich Engels, Louis Blanc, Ferdinand Lassalle, and thousands of less famous names—tended more to socialism than to unionism. They thought of society as a whole, they saw the economic system as a system, they thought of the future in long-run terms, and their time scale allowed generously for whole historical epochs to come and go. The actual workingman, put to work at an early age, barely educated if at all, with the waking hours of his adult life spent on a manual job, was inclined to keep his attention more on unionism than on socialism. To earn a shilling more every week beginning next week, to be spared the nervous strain and physical danger of constant exposure to unprotected machinery, to have fifteen minutes more every day for lunch, were likely to seem more tangible and important than far-reaching but distant plans for a reconstructed society. The worker looked on the intellectual as an outsider, however welcome; the intellectual looked on the worker as shortsighted and timid, however much in need of help.

---

[23] See pp. 466–469, 472–475, 491–495.
[24] See pp. 438–440, 468.

After the failures of 1848 the socialist and trade union movements diverged for a generation. The 1850s, compared with the hungry '40s, were a time of full employment, rising wages, and increasing prosperity for all classes. Workers set to organizing unions, socialist thinkers to perfecting their doctrines.

The Trade Union Movement and Rise of British Labor

Organizations of wage workers, or labor unions in the modern sense (as distinguished from medieval craft guilds), had long maintained a shadowy and sporadic existence, as in the old French journeymen's associations.[25] But they had always been extralegal, frowned upon or actually prohibited by governments. French revolutionaries in the Le Chapelier Act of 1791, British Tories in the Combination Act of 1799, had been as one in forbidding workers to unite. It was the rise of "bourgeois" liberalism, so insensitive to the worker in most ways, that first gave legal freedom to labor unions. The British unions received a tacit recognition from the Liberal Tories in 1825 and explicit recognition from Gladstone's Liberal ministry in 1871. French unions were recognized by Napoleon III in 1864, then restrained in the reaction caused by the Commune, then fully legalized in 1884. In Germany Bismarck negotiated with labor leaders to find support against the vested interests that stood in his way.

The prosperity of the 1850s favored the formation of unions, for workers can always organize most easily when employers are most in need of their services. The craft union—or union of skilled workers in the same trade, such as carpenters—was at first the typical organization. It was most fully developed in England, where a "new model" unionism was introduced by the Amalgamated Society of Engineers (i.e., machinists) in 1851. It was the policy of the "new model" union officials to take the unions out of politics, to forget the semisocialism of the Chartists, to abandon Robert Owen's grandiose idea of "one big union" for all workers, and to concentrate on advancing the interests of each separate trade. The new leaders proposed to be reasonable with employers, avoid strikes, accumulate union funds, and build up their membership. In this they were very successful; the unions took root; and the two governing parties in England, reassured by the unexpected moderation of working-class spokesmen, combined to give the town workman the vote in 1867.

In the 1880s, and especially with the great London dock strike of 1889, which closed the port of London for the first time since the French Revolution, unions of unskilled workers began to form. Industrial unionism, or the joining in one union of all workers in one industry, such as coal or transportation, regardless of the skill or job of the individual worker, began to take shape at the same time. In some cases the older skilled unionists joined with unskilled laborers who worked beside them. Thus gradually arose, for example, the Transport Workers Union, which half a century later was to give a foreign secretary to the government in the person of Ernest Bevin. By 1900 there were about 2,000,000 union members in Great Britain, compared with only 850,000 in Germany and 250,000 in France.

It was largely because British workers were so far advanced in trade unionism, and so successful in forcing collective bargaining upon their employers, that they were much slower than their Continental counterparts in forming a workers'

---

[25] See pp. 363–364, 498.

political party. By the 1880s, when avowed socialists were already sitting in French, Belgian, and German parliaments, the only corresponding persons in Britain were a half-dozen "Lib-Labs," as they were called, laboring men elected on the Liberal ticket. The British Labour party was formed at the turn of the century by the joint efforts of trade union officials and middle-class intellectuals.[26] Where on the Continent the labor unions were often led, and even brought into being, by the socialist political parties, in Britain it was the labor unions that brought into being, and subsequently led, the Labour party. Hence for a long time the Labour party was less socialistic than working-class parties on the Continent. Its origin and rapid growth were due in large measure to a desire to defend the unions as established and respectable institutions. The unions were threatened in their very existence by a ruling of the British courts in 1901, the Taff Vale decision, which held a union financially responsible for business losses incurred by an employer during a strike. The shortest and most orderly strike, by exhausting a union's funds, might ruin the union. The year before, steps had been taken to bring together the unions and all other existing labor and socialist organizations into a labor representation committee, in preparation for the elections of 1900; the effort was not very successful and only two of the fifteen labor candidates were returned. But the Taff Vale decision unified all ranks and precipitated the formation of the modern Labour party. In the election of 1906 the new Labour party sent twenty-nine members to Parliament, which thereupon overruled the Taff Vale decision by new legislation. The social legislation put through Parliament by the Liberal party government in the next few years, in good part under pressure from labor, has already been described.[27]

European Socialism after 1850

As for socialism, which had so frightened the middle and upper classes in 1848, it seemed in the 1850s to go into abeyance. Karl Marx, after issuing the *Communist Manifesto* with Engels in 1848, and agitating as a journalist in the German revolution of that year, withdrew to the secure haven offered by England, where, after years of painstaking research, he published the first volume of his *Capital* in 1867. This work, of which the succeeding volumes were published after his death, gave body, substance, and argument to the principles announced in the *Manifesto*.[28] Marx, during more than thirty years in London, scarcely mixed with the labor leaders then building up the English unions. Hardly known to the English, he associated mainly with political exiles and temporary visitors of numerous nationalities.

In 1864 there took place in London the first meeting of the International Working Men's Association, commonly known as the First International. It was sponsored by a heterogeneous group, including the secretary of the British carpenters' union, Robert Applegarth; the aging Italian revolutionary, Mazzini; and Karl Marx. With the union officials absorbed in union business, leadership in the Association gradually passed to Marx, who used it as a means of publicizing the ideas about to appear in his *Capital*. At subsequent annual congresses, at Geneva, Lau-

[26] See p. 589.
[27] See pp. 578–579.
[28] See p. 492.

sanne, Brussels, and Basel, Marx built up his position. He made the Mazzinians unwelcome, and he denounced the German Lassalleans for their willingness to co-operate with Bismarck, arguing that it was not the business of socialists to cooperate with the state but to seize it. His sharpest struggle was with the Russian Bakunin. With his background in tsarist Russia, Bakunin believed the state to be the cause of the common man's afflictions; he was hence an "anarchist," holding that the state should be attacked and abolished. To Marx anarchism was abhorrent; the correct doctrine was that the state—tsarist or bourgeois—was only a product of economic conditions, a tool in the class struggle, a weapon of the propertied interests, so that the true target for revolutionary action must be not the state but the capitalist economic system. Marx drove Bakunin from the International in 1872.

Meanwhile members of the First International watched with great excitement the Paris Commune of 1871, which they hoped might be the opening act of a European working-class upheaval. Members of the International infiltrated the Commune, and the connection between the two, though rather incidental, was one reason why the French provisional government repressed the Commune with such terrified ferocity. But the Commune actually killed the First International. The Commune had been bloody and violent, an armed rebellion against the democratically elected National Assembly of France. Marx praised it as a stage in the international class war. He even saw in it a foretaste of what he was coming to call the "dictatorship of the proletariat." He thus frightened many possible followers away. Certainly British trade unionists, sober and steady men, could have nothing to do with such doings or such doctrines. The First International faded out of existence after 1872.

But in 1875, at the Gotha conference, Marxian and Lassallean socialists effected enough of a union to found the German Social Democratic party, whose growth thereafter, against Bismarck's attempts to stop it, has already been noted. About 1880 socialist parties sprouted up in many countries. In Belgium, highly industrialized, a Belgian Socialist party appeared in 1879. In the industrial regions of France some workingmen were attracted to Jules Guesde, a self-taught worker, former Communard, and now a rigid Marxist, who held it impossible to emancipate the working class by compromise of any sort; others followed the "possibilist" Dr. Brousse, who thought it possible for workers to arrive at socialism through parliamentary methods; still others supported Jean Jaurès, who eloquently linked social reform to the French revolutionary tradition and the defense of republican institutions. Not until 1905 did the socialist groups in France form a unified Socialist party. In England, in 1881, H. M. Hyndman founded a Social Democratic Federation on the German model and with a Marxist program; it never had more than a handful of members. In 1883 two Russian exiles in Switzerland, Plekhanov and Axelrod, recent converts to Marxism, founded the Russian Social Democratic party, from which the communism of the following century was eventually to be derived. The socialist parties all came together to establish an international league in 1889, known as the Second International, which thereafter met every three years and lasted until 1914.

Revisionist and Revolutionary Socialism, 1880–1914

The new socialist parties of the 1880s were all Marxist in inspiration. Marx died in 1883. Marxism or "scientific socialism," by the force of its social analysis, the mass of Marx's writings over forty years, and an attitude of unyielding hostility to competing socialist doctrines, had become the only widely current form of systematic socialism. Strongest in Germany and France, Marxism was relatively unsuccessful in Italy and Spain, where the working class, less industrialized anyway, more illiterate, unable to place its hopes in the ballot, and habituated to an excitable insurrectionism in the manner of Garibaldi, turned more frequently to the anarchism preached by Bakunin.

Nor was Marxism at all successful in England; workers stood by their trade unions, and middle-class critics of capitalism followed the Fabian Society, established in 1883. The Fabians (so called from the ancient Roman general Fabius Cunctator, the "delayer," or strategist of gradual methods) were very English and very un-Marxist. George Bernard Shaw, H. G. Wells, and Sidney and Beatrice Webb were among early members of the Society. For them socialism was the social and economic counterpart to political democracy, as well as its inevitable outcome. They held that no class conflict was necessary or even existed, that gradual and reasonable and conciliatory measures would in due time bring about a socialist state, and that improvement of local government, or municipal ownership of such things as waterworks and electric lighting, were steps toward this consummation. The Fabians, like the trade union officials, were content with small and immediate satisfactions. They joined with the unions to form the Labour party. At the same time, by patient and detailed researches into economic realities, they provided a mass of practical information on which a legislative program could be based.

The Marxist or Social Democratic parties on the Continent grew very rapidly. Marxism turned into a less revolutionary "parliamentary socialism"—except indeed for the Russian Social Democratic party, since Russia had no parliamentary government. For the growth of socialist parties meant that true workingmen, and not merely intellectuals, were voting for socialist candidates for the Reichstag, Chamber of Deputies, or whatever the lower house of parliament might be called; and this in turn meant that the psychology and influence of labor unions within the parties were increased. The workers, and their union officials, might in theory consider themselves locked in an enormous struggle with capital; but in practice their aim was to get more for themselves out of their employers' business. They might believe in the internationalism of the workers' interests; but in practice, acting through the parliaments of national states, they would work for orderly legislation benefiting the workers of their own country only—social insurance, factory regulation, minimum wages, or maximum hours. Nor was it possible to deny, by the close of the century, that Marx's anticipations (based initially on conditions of the 1840s) had not come true, at least not yet; the bourgeois was getting richer, but the proletarian was not getting poorer. Real wages—or what the wage earner's income would actually buy, even allowing for the losses due to unemployment—are estimated to have risen about 50 percent in the industrialized countries between 1870 and 1900. The increase was due to the greater productivity of labor through mechanization, the growth of the world economy, the accumulation of capital wealth, and the gradual fall in prices of food and other items that the workers had to buy.

Repeatedly, but in vain, the Second International had to warn its component socialist parties against collaboration with the bourgeoisie. Marxism began in the 1890s to undergo a movement of revisionism, led in France by Jean Jaurès,

socialist leader in the Chamber of Deputies, and in Germany by Eduard Bernstein, Social Democratic member of the Reichstag and author in 1898 of *Evolutionary Socialism*, an important tract setting forth the new views. The revisionists
held that the class conflict might not be absolutely inevitable, that capitalism
might be gradually transformed in the workers' interest, and that now that the
workers had not only the vote but a political party of their own, they could obtain their ends through democratic channels, without revolution and without any
dictatorship of the proletariat. Most socialists or social democrats followed the
revisionists.

This tendency to "opportunism"[29] among Marxists drove the really revolutionary spirits into new directions. Thus there arose revolutionary syndicalism, of
which the main intellectual exponent was a Frenchman, Georges Sorel. "Syndicalism" is simply the French word for trade unionism (*syndicat*, a union), and the
idea was that the workers' unions might themselves become the supreme authoritative institutions in society, replacing not only property and the market economy, but government itself. The means to this end was to be a stupendous general
strike, in which all workers in all industries should simultaneously stop work,
thus paralyzing society and forcing acceptance of their will. Syndicalism made
most headway where the unions were weakest, as in Italy, Spain, and France,
since here the unions had the least to lose and were most in need of sensational
doctrines to attract members. Its strongest base was in the French General Confederation of Labor, founded in 1895.

Among orthodox Marxists there was also a revival of Marxist fundamentals in
protest against revisionism. In Germany Karl Kautsky arraigned the revisionists
as compromisers who betrayed Marxism for petty-bourgeois ends. In 1904 he and
other rigorists prevailed upon the Second International to condemn the political
behavior of the French socialist Alexandre Millerand who in 1899 had accepted a
ministerial post in a French cabinet. Socialists might use parliaments as a forum,
the International ruled, but socialists who entered the government itself were un-
pardonably identifying themselves with the enemy bourgeois state. Not until the
First World War did socialists henceforth join the cabinet of any European country. In the Russian Social Democratic party the issue of revisionism came to a
head in 1903, at a party congress held in London—for the most prominent Russian Marxists were mainly exiles. Here a group led by Lenin demanded that revisionism be stamped out. Lenin won a majority, at the moment at least, and hence
the uncompromising Marxists were called Bolsheviks (from the Russian word for
majority), while the revisionist or conciliatory Russian Marxists, those willing to
work with bourgeois liberals and democrats, were subsequently known as Mensheviks or the "minority" group.[30] But in 1903 the Russian Marxists were considered very unimportant.

In general, in Europe's "inner zone," by the turn of the century, most people
who called themselves Marxists were no longer actively revolutionary. As revolutionary republicanism had quieted down in the Third French Republic, so revolutionary Marxism seemed to have quieted down into the milder doctrines of
social democracy. What would have happened except for the coming of war in
1914 cannot be known; possibly social revolutionism would have revived, since

[29] See p. 495.
[30] See p. 703.

real wages no longer generally rose between 1900 and 1914, and considerable restlessness developed in labor circles, punctuated by great strikes. But in 1914 the working class as a whole was in no revolutionary mood. Workers still sought a greater measure of social justice, but the social agitation so feared or hoped for in 1848 had subsided. There seem to have been three principal reasons. Capitalism had worked well enough to raise the workers' living standard above what they could remember of their fathers' or grandfathers'; workers had the vote and so felt that they participated in the state, could expect to benefit from the government, and had little to gain by its overthrow; and third, they had their interests watched over by organized and increasingly powerful unions, by which a larger share in the national income could be demanded and passed on to them.

76. SCIENCE, PHILOSOPHY, THE ARTS, AND RELIGION

Faith in the powers of natural science has been characteristic of modern society for over three centuries, but never was there a time when this faith spread to so many people, or was held so firmly, so optimistically, and with so few qualms or mental reservations as in the half-century preceding the First World War. Science lay at the bottom of the whole movement of industrialization; and if science became positively popular after about 1870, in that persons ignorant of science came to look upon it as an oracle, it was because it manifested itself to everybody in the new wonders of daily life. Hardly had the world's more civilized regions digested the railroad, the steamship, and the telegraph when a whole series of new inventions already described[31] had begun to unfold itself. In thirty years following 1875 the number of patents tripled in the United States, quadrupled in Germany, and multiplied in all the civilized countries. The scientific and technical advance was as completely international (though confined mainly to the "inner zone") as any movement the world has ever seen. Never had the rush of scientific invention been so fundamentally useful, so helpful to the constructive labors and serious problems of mankind, and in that sense human.

In more basic scientific thinking important changes set in about 1860 or 1870. Up to that time, generally speaking, the underlying ideas had been those set forth by Isaac Newton almost two centuries before.[32] The law of universal gravitation reigned unquestioned, and with it, hardly less so, the geometry of Euclid and a physics that was basically mechanics. The ultimate nature of the universe was thought to be regular, orderly, predictable, and harmonious; it was also timeless, in that the passage of ages brought no change or development. By the end of the epoch considered here, that is, by 1914, the old conceptions had begun to yield on every side.

The Impact of Evolution

In impact upon general thinking the greatest change came in the new emphasis upon biology and the life sciences. Here the great symbolic date is the publication by Charles Darwin of the *Origin of Species* in 1859. Evolution, after Darwin,

---

[31] See pp. 562–564.
[32] See pp. 286–289.

became the order of the day. Evolutionary philosophies, holding that the way to understand anything was to understand its development, were not new in 1859. Hegel had introduced the evolutionary conception into metaphysics; and he and Marx, into theories of human society.[33] The idea of progress, taken over from the Age of Enlightenment, was a kind of evolutionary philosophy; and the great activity in historical studies, under romantic and nationalistic auspices, had made people think of human affairs in terms of a time process.[34] In the world of nature, the rise of geology after 1800 had opened the way to evolutionary ideas, and venturesome biologists had allowed themselves to speculate on an evolutionary development of living forms. What Darwin did was to stamp evolution with the seal of science, marshaling the evidence for it and offering an explanation of how it worked. In 1871, in his *Descent of Man*, he applied the same hypotheses to human beings.

By evolution, Darwin meant that species are mutable; that no species is created to remain unchanged once and for all; and that all species of living organisms, plant and animal, microscopic or elephantine in dimensions, living or extinct, have developed by successive small changes from other species that went before them. An important corollary was that all life was interrelated and subject to the same laws. Another corollary was that the whole history of living things on earth, generally held by scientists in Darwin's time to be many millions of years, was a unified history unfolding continuously in a single meaningful process of evolution.

Darwin thought that species changed, not by any intelligent or purposeful activity in the organism, but essentially by a kind of chance. Individual organisms, through the play of heredity, inherited slightly different characteristics, some more useful than others in food getting, fighting, or mating; and the organisms that had the most useful characteristics tended to survive, so that their characteristics were passed on to offspring, until the whole species gradually changed. Certain phrases, not all of them invented by Darwin, summed up the theory. There was a "struggle for existence" resulting in the "survival of the fittest" through "natural selection" of the "most favored races"—races meaning not human races but the strains within a species. The struggle for existence referred to the fact that, in nature, more individuals were born in each species than could live out a normal life span; the "fittest" were those individual specimens of a species having the most useful characteristics, such as fleetness in deer or ferocity in tigers; "natural" selection meant that the fittest survived without purpose in themselves or in a Creator; the "favored races" were the strains within a species having good survival powers.

Darwin's ideas precipitated a great outcry. Scientists rushed to defend and churchmen to attack him. The biologist T. H. Huxley became the chief spokesman for Darwin—"Darwin's bulldog." He debated with, among others, the bishop of Oxford. Darwin was denounced, with less than fairness, for saying that men came from monkeys. It was feared that all grounds of human dignity, morality, and religion would collapse. Darwin himself remained complacent on this score. Under civilized conditions, he said, the social and cooperative virtues were useful characteristics assisting in survival, so that "we may expect that virtuous habits will grow stronger, becoming perhaps fixed by inheritance." Much of the

[33] See pp. 442–443, 493–494.
[34] See pp. 303, 314, 410, 442–443.

outburst against Darwin was somewhat trivial, nor were those who attacked him generally noted for spiritual insight; yet they were not mistaken in sensing a profound danger.

That Darwinism said nothing of God, Providence, or salvation was not surprising; no science ever did. That evolution did not exactly square with the first chapter of Genesis was disturbing but not fatal; much of the Old Testament was already regarded as symbolic, at least outside certain fundamentalist circles. Even the idea that man and the animals were of one piece was not ruinous; the animal side of human nature had not escaped the notice of theologians. The novel and upsetting effect of evolutionary biology was to change the conception of nature. Nature was no longer a harmony, it was a scene of struggle, "nature red in tooth and claw." Struggle and elimination of the weak were natural, and as means toward evolutionary development they might even be considered good. There were no fixed species or perfected forms, but only an unending flux. Change was everlasting; and everything seemed merely relative to time, place, and environment. There were no norms of good and bad; a good organism was one that survived where others perished; adaptation replaced virtue; outside of it there was nothing "right." The test was, in short, success; the "fit" were the successful; and here Darwinism merged with that toughness of mind, or *Realpolitik*, which came over Europe at the same time from other causes.[35]

Such at least were the implications if one generalized from science, carrying over scientific findings into human affairs, and the prestige of science was so great that this is precisely what many people wished to do. With the popularization of biological evolution, a school known as Social Darwinists actively applied the ideas of the struggle for existence and survival of the fittest to human society. Social Darwinists were found all over Europe and the United States. Their doctrines were put to various uses, to show that some peoples were naturally superior to others, such as whites to blacks, or Nordics to Latins, or Germans to Slavs (or vice versa), or non-Jews to Jews; or that the upper and middle classes, comfortable and contented, deserved these blessings because they had proved themselves "fitter" than the shiftless poor; or that big business in the nature of things had to take over smaller concerns; or that some states, such as the British or German Empire, were bound to rise; or that war was morally a fine thing, proving the virility and survival value of those who fought.

Anthropology and Psychology

The newer life sciences, such as anthropology and psychology, developed very rapidly in the latter part of the nineteenth century. Their effect upon the civilization of the day was not unlike that of Darwinism. Both accepted biological evolution. Both, as the price of being truly scientific, eschewed standards of right and wrong and set themselves to finding out and explaining the mere facts of human behavior.

Anthropology set itself the task of studying the physical and cultural characteristics of all branches of mankind. Physical anthropologists became interested in the several human "races," some of which they considered might be "favored" in the Darwinian sense, that is, superior in inheritance and survival value. It was

[35] See pp. 489–490.

often concluded, even by scientists at the time, that the whites were the most competent race, and among the whites the Nordics, Teutons, or Germans and Anglo-Saxons. The public, more or less exaggerating such ideas, became more race conscious than Europeans had ever been before. On the other hand the cultural anthropologists, surveying all manner of primitive or complex societies with scientific disinterest, seemed sometimes to teach a more deflating doctrine. Scientifically, it seemed, no culture or society was "better" than any other, all being adaptations to an environment, or merely a matter of custom—of the *mores*, as people said in careful distinction from "morals." The effect was again a kind of relativism or skepticism—a negation of values, a belief that right and wrong were matters of social convention, psychological conditioning, mere opinion, or point of view. We are describing, let it be repeated, not the history of science itself but the effects of science upon European civilization at the time.

The impact of anthropology was felt keenly in religion too. Sir James Frazer (1854–1941) in his multivolumed *The Golden Bough* could demonstrate that some of the most sacred practices, rites, and ideas of Christianity were not unique but could be found among primitive societies, and that, moreover, only the thinnest of lines divided magic from religion. Anthropology, like Darwinian evolution, undermined traditional religious beliefs.

Psychology, as a science of human behavior, led to thoroughly upsetting implications about the very nature of man. It was launched in the 1870s as a natural science by the German physiologist Wilhelm Wundt (1832–1920), who developed various new experimental techniques. The Russian Ivan Pavlov (1849–1936) conducted a famous series of experiments in which he "conditioned" dogs to salivate automatically at the ringing of a bell once they had become accustomed over a period of time to associate the sound with the serving of their food. Pavlov's observations were important. They implied that a great part of animal behavior, and presumably human behavior, could be explained on the basis of conditioned responses. In the case of human beings these are responses which humans make automatically by virtue of their earlier environment and training and not through choice or conscious reasoning.

Most significant of all the developments in the study of human behavior was the work of Sigmund Freud (1856–1939) and those influenced by him. Freud, a Viennese physician, founded psychoanalysis at the turn of the century. He came to believe that certain forms of emotional disturbance like hysteria were traceable to earlier forgotten episodes of patients' lives. After first trying various techniques such as hypnosis, which he soon abandoned, he employed free association, or free recall. If patients could be helped to bring these suppressed experiences into conscious recall, the symptoms of illness would often disappear. From these beginnings Freud and his followers explored the role that the unconscious played in all human behavior, he himself stressing the sexual drive. In one of his most famous books, *The Interpretation of Dreams* (1900), he stressed dreams as a key to understanding the unconscious; elsewhere he related his findings to religion, education, art, and literature. Freud and Freudian ideas had great influence on the social and behavioral sciences, and a good deal of the Freudian vocabulary later entered into everyday language and popular culture. In its deepest significance psychoanalysis, by revealing the wide areas of human behavior outside conscious control, suggested that human beings were not essentially rational creatures at all.

The New Physics

The revolution in biology of the nineteenth century, together with the developments in psychology and anthropology, were soon to be matched and surpassed by the revolution in physics. In the late 1890s physics was on the threshold of a revolutionary transformation. Like Newtonian mechanics in the seventeenth century and Darwinian evolution in the nineteenth, the new physics represented one of the great scientific revolutions of all time. There was no single work comparable to Newton's *Principia* or Darwin's *Origin of Species* unless Albert Einstein's theory of relativity, propounded in a series of scientific papers in 1905 and 1916, might be considered as such. Instead there were a series of discoveries and findings, partly mathematical and then increasingly empirical, that threw new light on the nature of matter and energy. In Newtonian physics the atom, the basic unit of all matter, which the Greeks had hypothesized in ancient times, was like a hard, solid, unstructured billiard ball, permanent and unchanging; and matter and energy were separate and distinct. But a series of discoveries from 1896 on profoundly altered this view. In 1896 the French scientist Antoine Henri Becquerel discovered radioactivity, observing that uranium emitted particles or rays of energy. In the years immediately following, from the observations and discoveries of the French scientists Pierre and Marie Curie and the Englishmen J. J. Thomson and Lord Rutherford, there emerged the notion that atoms were not simple but complex, and, moreover, that various radioactive atoms were by nature unstable, releasing energy as they disintegrated. The German physicist Max Planck demonstrated in 1900 that energy was emitted or absorbed in specific and discrete units or bundles, each called a quantum; moreover, energy was not emitted smoothly and continuously as previously thought, nor was it as distinguishable from matter as once supposed. In 1913, the Danish physicist Niels Bohr postulated an atom consisting of a nucleus of protons surrounded by electrically charged units, called electrons, rotating around the nucleus, each in its orbit, like a minuscule solar system.

With radioactivity scientists were being brought back to the idea long rejected, the favored view of the alchemists, that matter was transmutable; in a way undreamed of even by the alchemists, it was convertible into energy. This the German-born Jewish scientific genius Albert Einstein (1879–1955) expressed in a famous formula $e = mc^2$. From his theory of relativity emerged also the profoundly revolutionary notion that time, space, and motion were not absolute in character but were all relative to the observer and the observer's own movement in space. In later years, in 1929 and in 1954, Einstein brought together into one common set of laws, as Newton formerly had done, a unified field theory, an explanation of gravitation, electromagnetism, and subatomic behavior. Difficult as it was to grasp, and a great deal was still the subject of scientific controversy, it modified much that had been taken for granted since Newton. The Newtonian world was being replaced by a four-dimensional world, a kind of space-time continuum; and in mathematics, non-Euclidean geometries were being developed. It turned out, too, that neither cause and effect nor time and space nor Newton's law of universal gravitation meant very much in the subatomic world nor indeed in the cosmos when objects moved with the speed of light. It was impossible, as the German scientist Werner Heisenberg demonstrated a little later, in 1927, by his principle of uncertainty, or indeterminacy, to ascertain simultaneously both the position and the velocity of the individual electron. On these foundations established before the First World War there developed the new science of nuclear physics and the tapping of the atom's energy. The atom was soon discovered to be even more complex than conceived of before 1914, and its potentialities even greater.

Trends in Philosophy and the Arts

The step from pure science to philosophy is a long one, but one that many were prepared to take. Not only was the faith in science widespread but it was widely held that science was the only means of certain knowledge, and that anything unknowable to science must remain unknowable forever—a doctrine called agnosticism, or the acknowledgment of ignorance. Herbert Spencer (1820–1903) in England and Ernst Haeckel (1834–1919) in Germany were widely read popularizers of agnosticism; both also pictured a universe governed by Darwinian evolution. For Spencer especially, all philosophy could be unified, organized, and coordinated through the doctrine of evolution; this doctrine he applied not only to all living things but to sociology, government, and economics as well. The evolution of society, he felt, was toward the increasing freedom of the individual, the role of governments being merely to maintain freedom and justice; they were not to interfere with natural social and economic processes, nor to coddle the weak and unfit. Yet, like Darwin himself, Spencer believed that altruism, charity, and good will as individual ethical virtues were themselves useful and laudable products of evolutionary development.

These latter views were not shared by another of the serious writers of the age, also much influenced by evolutionary ideas, the German philosopher Friedrich Nietzsche (1844–1900). More a philosopher of art than of science, and drawing from many intellectual currents of the century, Nietzsche was an unsystematic and unclear thinker to whom it is easy to do less than justice. It is evident, however, that his opinion of mankind was a low one, and that from a background of evolutionary thinking he developed some kind of doctrine of a Superman, a noble being who, in a final triumph of world history, should issue from, lead, dominate, and dazzle the multitude. Qualities of humility, patience, brotherly helpfulness, hope, and love, in short the specifically Christian virtues, Nietzsche described as a slave morality concocted by the weak to disarm the strong. Qualities of courage, love of danger, intellectual excellence, and beauty of character he considered much better. Such views, for better or worse, were actually a new form of classical paganism. Nietzsche was neither much read nor much respected by his contemporaries, who considered him unbalanced or even insane; but he nevertheless expressed with unshrinking frankness many ideas implied in the outlook of his day.

As in the sciences, so in works of creative imagination—pure literature and the fine arts—the changes at the dawn of the twentieth century ushered in the contemporary age. Some writers, like Zola in France or Ibsen in Scandinavia, turned to the portrayal of social problems, producing a realistic literature dealing with industrial strife, strikes, prostitution, divorce, or insanity. Freudian and other views of psychology slowly made themselves felt in works of fiction; the new novels were often more lifelike than the old even though they added little to one's faith in human nature. The arts followed the intellectual developments of the age, reflecting, as they do today, attitudes of relativism, irrationalism, social determinism, and interest in the subconscious. On the other hand, never had artist and society been so far apart. The painter Gauguin, an extreme case, fled to the South Seas, went primitive, and reveled in the stark violence of tropical colors. Others became absorbed in technicalities or mere capricious self-expression. Art at its extreme fringe became incomprehensible and the average person was deprived of a means (as old as the cave paintings of the Stone Age) of perceiving, seizing, and enjoying the world about him. After the First World War, and on into the present, the same trends of subjectivism in the arts attracted a wider, if still skeptical, audience. People read books without punctuation (or with peculiar punctuation), listened to music called atonal and deliberately composed for effects of discord and dissonance, and studied intently abstract or "nonobjective" paintings and sculpture to which the artists themselves often refused to give titles.

The problem of communication remained serious. The arts suffered from the specialization of the modern world. The artist was not thought of as a collective spokesman or creator of something for common use but as a specialist plying his own trade and pursuing his own concerns. Society itself was divided into busy, self-centered groups, unable to communicate except on superficial matters, and hence in the long run less able to work in common.

The Churches and the Modern Age

Religion, too, was displaced. It was now a long time since almost everyone had looked to religion for guidance. But religion was more threatened after 1860 or 1870 than ever in the past, because never before had science, or philosophies drawing upon science, addressed themselves so directly to the existence of life and of man. Never before had so many of the fundamental premises of traditional religion been questioned or denied. Darwinian evolution had challenged the traditional picture of Creation, and anthropologists had questioned the uniqueness of the most sacred Christian tenets. There developed also the "higher" criticism of the Bible, an effort to apply to the Scriptures the techniques of scholarship long applied to secular documents, to incorporate archeological discoveries, and to reconstruct a naturalistic, historical account of ancient religious times. The movement, going back at least to the seventeenth century,[36] now took on significant proportions and was applied both to the Old Testament and the New. In the case of the Old Testament the patient scrutiny of style and language cast doubt on the validity of certain prophecies; and in the New the inconsistencies of the several Gospel sources were made patent. The German theologian David Friedrich Strauss (1808–1874), one such critical scholar, was the author of a widely discussed *Life of Jesus*, in which many miraculous and supernatural episodes were reverently but firmly explained away as "myth." The sensitive French historian and man of letters Ernest Renan (1823–1892) in a somewhat similar vein wrote on the origins of Christianity and on the life of ancient Israel. The ordinary person's long-established articles of faith were being further undermined. Moreover, the whole tenor of the time, its absorption in material progress, likewise kept people away from church; and the wholesale uprooting, the movement from country to city, often broke religious ties.

[36] See pp. 294–295.

The Protestant churches were less successful than the Catholic in protecting their membership from the disintegrating effects of the age. Church attendance among Protestants became increasingly casual, and the doctrines set forth in sermons seemed increasingly remote. Protestant laymen traditionally trusted their own private judgment and regarded their clergy as their own agents, not as authoritative teachers placed above them. Protestants also had always set special emphasis on the Bible as the source of religious belief; and as doubts accumulated on the literal truth of Biblical narratives there seemed no other source on which to rely.

Protestants tended to divide between modernists and fundamentalists. The fundamentalists, as they were called in the United States, in an effort to defend the literal word of Scripture, were often obliged to deny the most indubitable findings of science. The modernists were willing enough to be scientific and to interpret much of the Bible as allegory, but only with difficulty could they recapture any spirituality or urgent feeling of Christian truth. Most Protestant churches were slow to face the social problems and wholesale injustices produced by the economic system, though a group of "Christian socialists" developed, notably within the Church of England. And as education and the care of orphans, aged, sick, and insane persons passed to the state, Protestant groups had less to do in the relief of suffering and upbringing of the young. Protestantism, to the regret of many Protestants, became increasingly a customary observance by people whose minds were elsewhere. Not until after the First World War could a strong Protestant revival be discerned, with a reaffirmation of basic doctrines by thinkers like Karl Barth, and a movement on the part of divergent Protestant churches to combine.

The Roman Catholic church proved more resistant to the trends of the age. We have seen how Pope Pius IX (1846–1878), after being driven from Rome by republicans in 1848, gave up his inclinations to liberalism.[37] In 1864, in the *Syllabus of Errors*, he denounced as erroneous a long list of widely current ideas, including the faith in rationalism and science, and he vigorously denied that the head of the church "should reconcile and align himself with progress, liberalism,

[37] See pp. 482–483.

PAINTING #198 (AUTUMN)
by Vasily Kandinsky (Russian, then in Germany and France, 1866–1944)

What is loosely called modern art dates from the early twentieth century. Where the Impressionists continued to represent objects while losing interest in objective representation, in the next generation many painters gave up the objects themselves, thus launching various nonobjective or "abstract" styles. This "Painting #198" was done in 1914 by Kandinsky, one of the first practitioners of purely abstract painting. Since it is meant to convey color, without reference to physical objects, it does not lend itself to the kind of reproduction here used. Color at this time had a deep and vital meaning for Kandinsky though he later turned to the invention of geometric or linear images as well. For the commonly perceived world of external objects he substituted a universe of his own. "To create a body of artistic work," he said, "is to create a world." Or again, speaking of nature, "it is not enough to see it; we must live it." With such sentiments Kandinsky shared in the antirationalist or vitalistic philosophies of the period. Courtesy of the The Solomon R. Guggenheim Museum. Permission A.D.A.G.P. 1970 by French Reproduction Rights, Inc.

599

and modern civilization." The *Syllabus* was in form a warning to Catholics, not a matter of dogma incumbent upon them to believe. In dogma, the Immaculate Conception of the Virgin Mary was announced as dogmatic truth in 1854; a century later, in 1950, the bodily assumption of Mary into heaven was proclaimed. Thus the Catholic church reaffirmed in a skeptical age, and against Christian modernists, its faith in the supernatural and miraculous.

Pius IX also convened an ecumenical church council which met at the Vatican in 1870. It was the first such council since the Council of Trent some 300 years before.[38] The Vatican Council proclaimed the dogma of papal infallibility, which holds that the pope, when speaking *ex cathedra* on matters of faith and morals, speaks with a final and supernatural authority that no Catholic may question or reject. The Vatican Council, and the acceptance of papal infallibility by Catholics, was only the climax of centuries of development within the church. In brief, as the world grew more national, Catholicism became more international. As state sovereignty and secularism grew, Catholic clergy looked increasingly to the spiritual powers of Rome for protection against alien forces. Much in the past 300 years had made Catholics distrustful of their own governments or of non-Catholics in their midst—the Protestantism and the state churches of the sixteenth century, the Jansenist movement of the seventeenth, the anticlericalism of enlightened despotism in the eighteenth, the hostility to the church shown by the French Revolution, and by liberalism, republicanism, and socialism in the nineteenth century. By 1870 the net effect was to throw Catholics into the arms of the Holy See. Ultramontanism, the unconditional acceptance of papal jurisdiction, prevailed over the old Gallican and other national tendencies within the church.

In 1870, while the 600 prelates of the Vatican Council were sitting, the new Italian state unceremoniously entered and annexed the city of Rome.[39] The pope's temporal power thus disappeared. It is now widely agreed that with the loss of local temporal interests the spiritual hold of the papacy on Catholics throughout the world has been enhanced. The popes long refused, however, to recognize the

[38] See pp. 87–88.
[39] See p. 525.

COMPOSITION WITH THE ACE OF CLUBS
by Georges Braque (French, 1882–1963)

This painting, of about the same date as the preceding one by Kandinsky, represents a quite different direction in modern art. It is one of the great works of the Cubist movement. Where the Kandinsky painting presents color without line and seeks to express life and feeling, Braque and the Cubists break up the visual world into lines and planes, in a more analytic and intellectual fashion. Objects recede or disappear, not into an impressionist blur nor a burst of color, but into a carefully contrived and almost mathematical pattern. In the new movement, it made sense to "see" things from more than one direction at a time, as the mind conceives them. Perception is not enough; as Braque once wrote, "the senses deform, but the mind forms." In any case, innovative artists after 1900 turned away from the main concerns of Western painting since the Renaissance: realistic representation of persons, places, or objects; natural color; illusionistic three-dimensional volume; a humanly occupied space with perspectives, horizons, location, and distance as seen by the eye from a single fixed viewpoint. Courtesy of the Musée d'Art Moderne, Paris (Service Photographique). Permission A.D.A.G.P. 1970 by French Reproduction Rights, Inc.

loss of Rome; and each pope in turn, from 1870 to 1929, adopted a policy of self-imprisonment in the Vatican grounds. By the Lateran treaty of 1929 the papacy finally recognized the Italian state, and Italy conceded, along with much else, the existence of a Vatican City about a square mile in area, as an independent state not legally within Italy at all. The papacy thus gained that independence from national or secular authority deemed necessary by Catholics to the performance of its role.

Pius IX's successor, Leo XIII (1878–1903), carried on the counteroffensive against irreligion, and instituted a revival of medieval philosophy as represented by Thomas Aquinas.[40] But Leo XIII is chiefly remembered for formulating Catholic social doctrine, especially in the encyclical *Rerum Novarum* ("of modern things") of 1891, to which subsequent pontiffs have adhered, and from which various movements of Catholic socialism are derived. *Rerum Novarum* upheld private property as a natural right, within the limits of justice; but it found fault with capitalism for the poverty, insecurity, and even degradation in which many of the laboring classes were left. It declared that much in socialism was Christian in principle; but it criticized socialism insofar as (like Marxism) it was materialistic and antireligious. The pope therefore recommended that Catholics, if they wished, form socialist parties of their own, and that Catholic workingmen form labor unions under Catholic auspices. Since the 1830s there had been individual Catholics and Catholic clergy who were socialists, or at least severe critics of the then emerging social order; these were encouraged by the encyclical of 1891, and Catholic (or Christian, as they were often called) socialist parties and labor unions began to appear at the turn of the century. The Roman church thus undertook to free itself from dependency upon capitalism. At the same time it took steps to insure that a future society, if socialist, might be Catholic also.

As for Judaism, the Jews were a small minority, but their condition had always been a kind of barometer reflecting changes in the atmosphere of Europe as a whole. In the nineteenth century the basic trend was toward "emancipation" and "assimilation." Science and secularism had the same dissolving effect upon Orthodox Judaism as upon traditional Christianity. Reform Judaism grew up as the Jewish counterpart to "modernism" in other faiths. Individual Jews increasingly gave up their old distinctive Jewish way of life. In society at large, the prevalence of liberalism allowed them to act as citizens and to enter business or the professions like everybody else. Jews were thus freed from old legal discriminations that had been imposed on them for centuries.

Toward the end of the century two tendencies, counter to assimilation, became evident. One, a cultural and political nationalism, originated with Jews themselves, some of whom feared an assimilation that would lead to a loss of Jewish identity and perhaps even the disappearance of Judaism itself. The other countertendency, or barrier to assimilation, was the rise of anti-Semitism, noticeable in many quarters by 1900. Racist theories, dislike for Jewish competitors in business and the professions, socialist scorn for Jewish capitalists like the Rothschilds, upper-class fears of Jewish revolutionaries and Marxists, together with a growth of ethnic nationalism, which held that France should be purely French and Latin, Germany purely German and Nordic, or Russia purely Russian and Slav, all combined to raise an anti-Semitic hue and cry. In Russia there were actual

[40] See pp. 41–42.

pogroms, or massacres of Jews. In France the Dreyfus case, dragged out from 1894 to 1906, revealed unsuspected depths of anti-Semitic fury. Many Jews were forced by such hostility into a new sense of Jewish identity. The Hungarian-born Jewish journalist Theodor Herzl was one. Appalled by the turbulence of the Dreyfus affair in civilized France, which he observed firsthand as a reporter for a Vienna newspaper, he founded modern, or political, Zionism when he organized the first international Zionist congress at Basel in 1897. Zionists hoped to establish a Jewish state in Palestine, in which Jews from all the world might find refuge, although there had been no independent Jewish state there since ancient times.

Many Jews, wishing civic assimilation yet despairing of obtaining it, began to sympathize with the Jewish nationalist movement, looking to Zionism and a Jewish renascence as a way to maintain their own dignity. Others insisted that Judaism was a religious faith, not a nationality by itself; that Jews and non-Jews within the same country shared in exactly the same nationality, citizenship, and political and social outlook. Liberals and democrats were of the same opinion. On the integration of Jews into the larger community the traditions of the Enlightenment, the American and French revolutions, the empire of Napoleon I, and the liberalism of the nineteenth century all agreed.

77. THE WANING OF CLASSICAL LIBERALISM

The net effect of the political, economic, and intellectual trends described above was twofold. There was a continued advance of much that was basic to liberalism and at the same time a weakening of the grounds on which liberalism had firmly rested ever since the seventeenth and eighteenth centuries. A third effect might be noted too. Even where the essentials of liberalism persisted, in program and doctrine it underwent important changes; liberalism persisted but the classical type of liberalism was in eclipse.

Classical liberalism, the liberalism in its heyday in the nineteenth century, went back at least as far as John Locke in the seventeenth century and the philosophes of the eighteenth, and found its highest nineteenth-century expression in the writings of men like John Stuart Mill and in the political outlook of men like William Gladstone. Classical liberalism had as its deepest principle the liberty of the individual person.[41] Man, or each specimen of mankind, according to liberals, was or could become a freestanding human being. "Man" meant for them any member of the human race, *homo sapiens*, though in practice, except for a few like Mill, they were thinking of adult males. The very principle of liberalism, however, with its stress on the autonomy of the individual, contributed to the still small but growing movement of women's rights.

The individual, in this view, was not simply formed by race, class, church, nation, or state but was ultimately independent of all such things. Individuals did not have such and such ideas because they belonged to such and such a group, but were capable of the free use of reason or of thinking things out independently, apart from their own interests, prejudices, or subconscious drives. And, since this was so, people of different interests could reasonably and profitably discuss their

---

[41] See pp. 360, 437.

differences, make compromises, and reach solutions by peaceable agreement. It was because they thought all persons potentially reasonable that liberals favored education. They opposed all imposition of force upon the individual, from physical torture to mental indoctrination.

In religion, liberals thought each individual should adopt any faith or no faith as he or she chose, and that churches and clergy should play little or no part in public affairs. In politics, they thought that governments should be constitutional and limited in power, with individuals governing themselves through their chosen representatives, with issues presented, discussed, and decided by the use of intelligence, both by the voters in election campaigns and by elected deputies in parliamentary debate. The will of a majority, or larger number of individuals, was taken as decisive, with the understanding that the minority might become a majority in its turn through individual changes of opinion. At first distrustful of democracy, fearing the excesses of popular rule, and eager to limit political power and the suffrage to the propertied classes, in the course of the nineteenth century liberals had accepted the democratic principle of universal male suffrage. In economics, liberals thought of the whole world as peopled by individuals doing business with one another—buying and selling, borrowing and lending, hiring and firing—without interference from governments and without regard to religion or politics, both of which were thought to impose superficial differences upon the underlying uniformity of mankind. The practical consequences of liberalism were toleration, constitutionalism, laissez faire, free trade, and an international or non-national economic system. It was thought that all peoples would progress to these same ends.

There never was a time, even in one country, when all liberal ideas were simultaneously triumphant. Pure liberalism has never existed except as a doctrine. Advancing in one way, liberalism would be blocked or reversed in another. One the whole, Europe before 1914 was predominantly liberal. But signs of the wane of liberalism set in clearly about 1880; some, like the changing conceptions of human behavior, have already been mentioned.

The Decline of Nineteenth-Century Liberalism: Economic Trends

The free economy produced many hardships. The workingman tossed by the ups and downs of a labor market, the producer tossed by those of a world commodity market, alike clamored for protection against exposure. A severe depression in 1873 sent prices and wages into collapse, and the economy did not fully recover until 1893. European farmers, both small French farm owners and big Junker landlords of East Germany, demanded tariff protection: they could not compete with the American Middle West or the steppes of South Russia, both opened up by rail and steamship, and both of which after 1870 poured their cereals at low prices into Europe. The revival of tariffs and decline of free trade, very marked in Europe about 1880, thus began with the protection of agricultural interests. Industry soon demanded the same favors. In Germany the Junkers and the rising Rhineland industrialists joined forces in 1879 to extort a tariff from Bismarck. The French in 1892 adopted a high tariff to shelter both manufacturing and agricultural interests. The United States, rapidly industrializing, also put up protective tariffs beginning in the 1860s, the earliest of all.

The Industrial Revolution was now definitely at work in other countries than Great Britain. There was an increasing resistance to buying manufactures from England, selling only raw materials and foodstuffs in return. Everywhere there was a revival of the arguments of the German economist Friedrich List, who a half-century before, in his *National System of Political Economy* (1840), had branded free trade as a system mainly advantageous to the British and declared that no country could become strong, independent, or even fully civilized if it remained a semi-rustic supplier of unfinished goods.[42] With Germany, the United States, and Japan manufacturing for export, a nationalist competition for world markets set in, contributing also to the drive for colonies and the phenomena of imperialism described in the next chapter. The new imperialism was another sign of the waning of liberalism, which had been largely indifferent to colonies.

In all these respects the division between politics and economics, postulated by liberals, began to fade. A kind of neomercantilism arose, recalling the attempts of governments in the seventeenth and eighteenth centuries to subordinate economic activity to political ends. A better term is economic nationalism, which became noticeable by 1900. Nations struggled to better themselves by tariffs, by trade rivalries, and by internal regulation, without regard to the effect upon other nations. And for the individual worker or businessman also, in purely economic matters, it now made a great difference to what nation he belonged, by what government he was backed, and under what laws he lived.

It was of course to protect themselves against insecurity and abuse as individuals that workers formed labor unions. It was likewise to protect themselves against the uncertainties of uncontrolled markets that business interests began to merge, to concentrate in large corporations, or to form monopolies, trusts, or cartels. The rise of big business and organized labor undermined the theory and practice of individual competition to which classical liberalism had been attached. Organized labor, socialist parties, universal male suffrage, and a sensitivity to social distress all obliged political leaders to intervene increasingly in economic matters. Factory codes became more detailed and better enforced. Social insurance, initiated by Bismarck, spread to other countries. Governments regulated the purity of food and drugs. The social service state developed, a state assuming responsibility for the social and economic welfare of the mass of its own subjects. The "new" liberalism, that of the Liberals in England of the David Lloyd George era, of the Republican President Theodore Roosevelt and the Democratic President Woodrow Wilson in the United States, accepted the enlarged role of the government in social and economic matters. Both Theodore Roosevelt and Wilson, and others, sought also to reestablish economic competition by government action against monopolies and trusts. The new liberals were generally less well disposed toward business than toward workers and the depressed classes; the improvement of the workers' lot would vindicate the old humanitarian concern of liberalism with the dignity and worth of the individual person. The welfare state, remote as it was from the older liberalism, was the direction taken by the new liberals. Others, liberal and otherwise, viewed with concern the growing power of governments and centralized authority and were apprehensive for individual liberties.

[42] See p. 443.

Intellectual and Other Currents

Liberalism, both old and new, was undermined also by many developments in the field of thought described earlier in this chapter—Darwinian evolution, the new psychology, trends in philosophy and the arts. Paradoxically, this great age of science found that man was not a rational animal. Darwinian theory implied that man was merely a highly evolved organism whose faculties were merely adaptations to an environment. Psychology seemed to teach that what was called reason was often only rationalization, or a finding of alleged "reasons" to justify material wants or emotional and unconscious needs, and that conscious reflection dominated only a narrow part of human behavior. Ideas themselves were said to be the products of conditioning. There were English ideas or Anglo-Saxon ideas, or bourgeois or progressive or reactionary ideas. In politics, some believed that parties or nations with conflicting interests could never reasonably agree on a program common to both, since neither could ever get beyond the limitations of its own outlook. It became common to dismiss the arguments of an adversary without further thought and without any expectation that thought could overcome difficulties. This insidious "anti-intellectualism" was destructive to liberal principles. If, because of prior conditioning, it was impossible for anyone to change his mind, then there was no hope of settling matters by persuasion.

From the view that man was not essentially a rational being, which in itself was only a scientific attempt at a better understanding of human behavior, it was but a short step deliberately to reject reason and to emphasize and cultivate the irrational, to stress the will, intuition, impulse, and emotion, and to place a new value on violence and conflict. A philosophy of "realism," a kind of unrealistic faith in the constructive value of struggle and a tough-minded rejection of ideas and ideals, spread. It was not new. Marxism, since the 1840s, had taught that class war, latent or open, was the motivating power of history. Now Nietzsche rejected the ordinary virtues in favor of courage and daring; and the Social Darwinists glorified the successful and the dominant in all phases of human activity as the "fit" in the perpetual struggle for existence. Other thinkers embraced a frank irrationalism. Georges Sorel, the philosopher of syndicalism, in his *Reflections on Violence* in 1908, declared that violence was good irrespective of the end accomplished (so much did he hate existing society), and that workers should be kept alert in the class war through believing in the "myth" of a future general strike. They should believe in such a strike, with its attendant debacle of bourgeois civilization, even though it was known to be only a "myth." The function of thought, in this philosophy of the social myth, was to keep people agitated and excited and ready for action, not to achieve any correspondence with rational or objective truth. Such ideas passed into the fascism and other activist movements of the twentieth century.

Thus the end of the nineteenth century, the greatest age of peace in Europe's history, abounded in philosophies glorifying struggle. Men who had never heard a shot fired in anger solemnly announced that world history moved forward by violence and antagonism. They said not merely that struggle existed (which would have been a purely factual statement) but that struggle was a positive good through which progress was to be accomplished. The popularity of struggle was due not only to the intellectuals but in part to actual historical events. People remembered that before 1871 certain weighty questions had been settled by force, that the movements of social revolution in 1848 and in the Paris Commune of 1871 had been put down by the military, and that the unity of Italy and Germany, as well as of the United States, had been confirmed by war. In addition, after 1871, all continental European states maintained large standing armies, the largest ever maintained until then in time of peace.

In economic and political matters, even in England, the homeland of liberalism, there were numerous signs between 1900 and 1914 that the older liberalism was on the wane. Joseph Chamberlain led a movement to return to tariff protection (to repeal, so to speak, the repeal of the Corn Laws); it failed at the time, but was strong enough to disorient the Conservative party in 1906. The Liberal party abandoned its traditional laissez-faire policy in sponsoring the labor legislation of the years following 1906. The new Labour party required its members in Parliament to vote as directed by the party, thus initiating a system of party solidarity, eventually copied by others, that hardened the lines of opposition, denied that individuals should freely change sides, and hence reduced the practical significance of parliamentary discussion. The Irish nationalists had long used unparliamentary methods; in 1914, when Parliament at last enacted Irish home rule, the anti-Irish and Conservative interests prepared to resist parliamentary action by force. The suffragettes, as women pioneering for female suffrage were called, despairing of ever getting the men to listen to reason, resorted to amazingly "un-English" and unreasonable arguments. They chained themselves to public buildings, smashed the store fronts in Bond Street, threw acid into mailboxes, and broke porcelains in the British Museum. When arrested they went on hunger strikes, threatening self-starvation, to which the police replied by "forcible feeding" through tubes lowered into their stomachs. And in 1911 and 1912 great railway and coal strikes disclosed the sheer power of organized labor.

Still, it is the persistence of liberalism rather than its wane that should be emphasized at the close of a chapter on European civilization in the half-century before 1914. Tariffs existed, but goods still circulated freely in world trade. Nationalism was heightened, but there was nothing like totalitarianism. Racist ideas were in the air, but they had little political importance. Anti-Semitism was sometimes vocal; but all governments except the Russian protected the rights of Jews, and the years from 1848 to 1914 were in fact the great period of Jewish integration into general society. The laissez-faire state was disappearing, but social legislation continued the humanitarian strain that had always been the essence of liberalism. A few advanced revolutionaries preached social catastrophism, but social democrats and laboring men were overwhelmingly revisionist, loyal to parliamentary procedures and to their existing states. Doctrinaires exalted the grim beauty of war, but all governments down to 1914 tried to prevent war among the great powers. And there was still a supreme faith in progress.

XV.
Europe's
World
Supremacy

uropean civilization, as described in the last chapter, spread to the whole earth after about 1870. The large nation-states whose consolidation was described in the chapter before last, and now equipped with the overwhelming new powers of science and industry, gained empires for themselves throughout the globe. The history of Europe—as of Asia, Africa, and America—became more involved in the history of the world.

For a while the most active of the imperial nation-states were located in Europe, and the forty years preceding the First World War were the years of Europe's world supremacy. With the rise of the United States the term "Western" came into use, signifying European in an expanded sense. The arrival of Japan made the term "Western" inappropriate for some purposes, and later the industrialization of the Soviet Union created similar verbal embarrassments, so that by the mid–twentieth century it was customary to speak of "developed" parts of the earth, alongside which others were seen as "developing" or "less developed." There even came to be a "Third World," which had no geographic identity of its

Chapter Emblem: A medal commemorating the opening of the Suez Canal in 1869.

own, but which did not wish to be identified with either the Western or the Soviet form of modern society. All these terms represented efforts to deal with the same basic reality, namely, a bifurcation between modern and traditional societies, rich countries and poor ones, or between the powerful and the weak.

For the first time in human history, by 1900, it was possible to speak of a world civilization. All countries were drawn into a world economy and a world market. The attributes of modernity, where they existed at all, were much the same everywhere—modern science, modern weapons of warfare, machine industry, fast communications, industrial organization, efficient forms of taxation and law enforcement, and of public hygiene, sanitation, and medicine.

But not all peoples participated in this global evolution on equal terms. It was the Europeans (or "Westerners") who reaped the greatest rewards. Under the impact of modernity both tribal societies and massive old civilizations began to come apart. Scientific ideas changed ways of thinking everywhere, as they had done in Europe. In India, China, or Africa the native industries often suffered, and many people found it harder than ever to subsist even at a low level. The building of railways in China, for example, threw boatmen, carters, and innkeepers out of work. In India, the hand spinners and weavers of cotton could not compete in their own villages with the machine-made products of Lancashire. In parts of Africa, native tribes that had lived by owning herds of cattle, moving from place to place to obtain grazing lands, found white farmers or plantation or mine owners occupying their country and were often forced by the white man's law to give up their migratory habits. Peoples of all races began to produce for export—rubber, raw cotton, jute, petroleum, tin, gold—and hence were exposed to the rise and fall of world prices. A depression tended to become a world depression, dragging all down alike.

Imperialism, or the colonialism of the late nineteenth century, may be briefly defined as the government of one people by another. European imperialism proved to be transitory. It was a phase in the world-wide spread of the industrial and scientific civilization which had originated in Europe's "inner zone."[1] That it was not the last phase became clear as the twentieth century unfolded. The subordinated peoples, forcibly introduced to the West by imperialism, came to feel a need for modernizing and industrializing their own countries and for the aid of Western science, skill and capital; but they wished to get rid of imperialists, govern themselves, and control the conditions under which modernization and borrowing should take place. In opposition to European empires, subject peoples began to assert ideas learned from Europe—ideas of liberty and democracy, and of an anticapitalism that passed easily into socialism. Many such ideas were derived from the French and American revolutions, or from Marxism, or the whole record of Europe itself.

The present chapter deals only with the imperialist phase of the global transformation. By one of the ironies of history, the imperialist rivalries of the European powers, while representing Europe's world supremacy, also contributed to the disaster of the First World War, and so to the collapse of such supremacy as Europe had enjoyed.

[1] See pp. 156, 552.

78. IMPERIALISM: ITS NATURE AND CAUSES

European civilization had always shown a tendency to expand. In the Middle Ages Latin Christendom spread by conquest and conversion to include the whole area from Spain to Finland. Then came the age of overseas discoveries and the founding of colonial empires, whose struggles filled the seventeenth and eighteenth centuries, and of which the Europeanization of the Americas was the most far-reaching consequence. At the same time European culture spread among the upper classes of Russia. The defeat of Napoleon left only one of the old colonial empires standing in any strength, namely, the British. For sixty years after 1815 there were no significant colonial rivalries. In many circles there was an indifference to overseas empire. Under principles of free trade, it was thought unnecessary to exercise political influence in areas in which one did business. Actually, in these years, the French moved into Algeria, the British strengthened their Indian empire, the Dutch developed Java and the neighboring islands more intensively, and the Western powers "opened" Japan and began to penetrate China. But there was no overt conflict among Europeans, and no systematic program, doctrine, or "ism."

Rather suddenly, about 1870 or 1880, colonial questions came again to the fore. In the short space of two decades, by 1900, the advanced countries partitioned most of the earth among themselves. A world map by 1900 showed their possessions in some nine or ten colors.

The New Imperialism

The new imperialism differed both economically and politically from the colonialism of earlier times. The older empires had been maritime and mercantile. European traders, in India, Java, or Canton, had simply purchased the wares brought to them by native merchants as produced by native methods. They operated on a kind of cash-and-carry basis. European governments had had no territorial ambitions beyond the protection of way stations and trading centers. To these generalizations America had been an exception. It had neither native states which Europeans respected, nor native industries in which Europeans were interested. Europeans therefore developed territorial claims, and invested capital and brought in their own methods of production and management, especially in the then booming sugar islands of the West Indies.[2]

Under the new imperialism Europeans were by no means content simply to purchase what native merchants provided. They wanted goods of a kind or in a quantity that preindustrial handicraft methods could not supply. They moved into the "backward" countries more thoroughly. They invested capital in them, setting up mines, plantations, docks, warehouses, factories, refineries, railroads, river steamships, and banks. They built offices, homes, hotels, clubs, and cool mountain resorts suitable for white men in the tropics. Taking over the productive life of the country, they transformed large elements of the local population into the wage employees of foreign owners and so introduced the class problems of industrial Europe in a form accentuated by racial difference. Or they lent money to native rulers—the khedive of Egypt, the shah of Persia, the emperor of

[2] See pp. 250–252.

China—to enable them to hold up their tottering thrones or simply to live with more pleasure and magnificence than they could pay for from their usual revenues. Europeans thus developed a huge financial stake in governments and economic enterprises outside the pale of Western civilization.

To secure these investments, and for other reasons, in contrast to what had happened under the older colonialism, the Europeans now aspired to political and territorial domination. Some areas became outright "colonies," directly governed by white men. Others became "protectorates": here the native chief, sultan, bey, rajah, or prince was maintained and guaranteed against internal upheaval or external conquest. A European "resident" or "commissioner" usually told him what to do. In other regions, as in China or Persia, where no single European state could make good its claims against the others, they arranged to divide the country into "spheres of influence," each European power having advisory privileges and investment and trade opportunities within its own sphere. The sphere of influence was the vaguest of all forms of imperial control; supposedly, it left the country independent.

An enormous differential opened up, about 1875, between the power of European and non-European states. Queen Elizabeth had dealt with the Great Mogul with genuine respect. Even Napoleon had pretended to regard the shah of Persia as an equal. Then came the Industrial Revolution in Europe, iron and steel ships, heavier naval guns, more accurate rifles. Democratic and nationalistic movements produced large and solid European peoples, united in the service of their governments as no "backward" people ever was. Seemingly endless wealth, with modern administration, allowed governments to tax, borrow, and spend almost without limit. The civilized states loomed as enormous power complexes without precedent in the world's history. At the same time it so happened that all the principal non-European empires were in decay. They were receiving a minimum of support from their own subjects. As in the eighteenth century the disintegration of the Mogul empire had enabled the British to take over India,[3] so in the nineteenth century the decrepitude of the sultan of Turkey, the sultan of Zanzibar, the shah of Persia, the emperor of China, and the shogun of Japan made European intervention easy. Only the Japanese were able to revolutionize their government in time to ward off imperialist penetration. Even the Japanese, thanks to early treaties, remained unfree to determine their own tariff policy until after 1900.[4]

So great was the difference in the sheer mechanics of power that usually a mere show of force allowed the whites to impose their will. A garrison of only 75,000 white troops long held India for the British. Numerous sporadic little wars were constantly fought—Afghan wars, Burmese wars, Zulu wars—which passed unnoticed by Europeans in the home country and were no more like true war than the operations of the United States army against the Indians of the western plains. The Spanish-American War of 1898 and the Boer War of 1899 were also wars of colonial type, fought between entirely unequal parties. Often a show of naval strength was enough. It was the classic age of the punitive or minatory bombardment. We have seen how the American Commodore Perry threatened to bombard Tokyo in 1854.[5] In 1856 the British consul at Canton, to punish acts of violence

[3] See pp. 271–273, 339–340.
[4] See pp. 546–547.
[5] See pp. 544, 546–547.

against Europeans, called upon the local British admiral to bombard that Chinese city. In 1863 the British bombarded Satsuma, and in 1864 an allied force including Americans bombarded Choshu—precipitating revolution in Japan. Similarly, Alexandria was bombarded in 1882 and Zanzibar in 1896. The usual consequence was that the local ruler signed a treaty, reorganized his government, or accepted a European (usually British) adviser.

Incentives and Motives

Behind the aggressiveness lay many pressures. Europeans could not maintain, for themselves in Europe, the style of life to which they had become accustomed, except by bringing the rest of the world within their orbit. But many other needs felt in Europe drove men into distant and savage places. Catholic and Protestant groups sent growing numbers of missionaries to regions increasingly remote and wild. The missionaries sometimes got into trouble with the natives, and some were even killed. Public opinion in the home countries, soon learning of such events by ocean cable, might clamor for political action to suppress such vestiges of barbarism. Similarly, science required scientific expeditions for geographical exploration, or for botanical, zoological, or mineral discoveries, or for astronomical or meteorological observations. Wealthy persons traveled more, now that travel was so easy; they hunted tigers or elephants, or simply went to see the sights. It seemed only reasonable, at the close of the nineteenth century, that all civilized persons wherever they might choose to go should enjoy the security of life and limb and the orderly procedures that only European supervision could provide.

Economically, European life required material goods, many of which only tropical regions could supply. Even the working classes now drank tea or coffee every day. After the American Civil War Europe relied for its cotton increasingly on Africa and the East. Rubber and petroleum became staple needs. The lowly jute, which grew only in India, was used to make burlap, twine, carpets, and the millions of jute bags employed in commerce. The lordly coconut tree had innumerable common uses, which led to its intensive cultivation in the Dutch Indies. Various parts of it could be eaten, or manufactured into bags, brushes, cables, ropes, sails, or doormats or converted into copra and coconut oil, which in turn went into the making of candles, soap, margarine, and many other products.

Industrial countries also attempted to sell their own products, and one of the reasons given by imperialists, in support of imperialism, was the urgent necessity of finding new markets. The industrialization of Germany, the United States, Japan, and other countries, after about 1870, meant that they competed with each other and with Great Britain for foreign trade.[6] The slowly declining price level after 1873 meant that a business firm had to sell more goods to turn over the same amount of money. Competition was more intense. The advanced countries raised tariffs to keep out each other's products. It was therefore argued that each industrial country must develop a colonial empire dependent on itself, an area of "sheltered markets," as the phrase went in England, in which the home country would supply manufactured goods in return for raw materials. The idea was to create a large self-sufficient trading unit, embracing various climates and types of resources, protected if necessary from outside competition by tariffs, guaranteeing a market for all its members and wealth and prosperity for the home country.

[6] See p. 605.

This phase of imperialism is often called neomercantilism, since it revived in substance the mercantilism of the eighteenth and earlier centuries.[7]

Purely financial considerations also characterized the new imperialism. Money invested in "backward" countries, by the close of the nineteenth century, brought a higher rate of return than if invested in the more civilized ones. For this there were many reasons, including the cheap labor of non-European regions, the heavy and unsatisfied demand for non-European products, and the greater risk of losses in half-unknown areas where European ideas of law and order did not prevail. By 1900 western Europe and the northeastern United States were equipped with their basic industrial apparatus. Their railway networks and first factories were built. Opportunities for investment in these countries became stabilized. At the same time, these countries themselves accumulated capital seeking an outlet. In the mid century most exported capital was British-owned. By the close of the century more French, German, American, Dutch, Belgian, and Swiss investors were investing or lending outside their own borders. In 1850, most exported capital went to build up Europe, the United States, Canada, Australia, or the Argentine—the white man's world. By 1900 more of it was going to the undeveloped regions. This capital was the property of small private savers or of large banking combinations. Investors preferred "civilized" political control over the parts of Asia, Africa, or Latin America in which their railroads, mines, plantations, government loans, or other investments were situated. Hence the profit motive, or desire to invest "surplus" capital, promoted imperialism.

This analysis was put forward by critics like the English socialist J. A. Hobson, who wrote an influential book on imperialism in 1903, and later by Lenin, in his *Imperialism, the Highest Stage of World Capitalism*, written in 1916. They ascribed imperialism primarily to the accumulation of surplus capital and condemned it on socialist grounds. Argued Hobson especially, if more of the national income went to workers as wages, and less of it to capitalists as interest and dividends, or if wealthy people were more heavily taxed and the money used for social welfare, there would be no surplus of capital and no real imperialism. Since the working class, if this were done, would also have more purchasing power, it would be less necessary to look endlessly for new markets outside the country. But the "surplus capital" explanation of imperialism was not entirely convincing. That investors and exporters were instrumental in the rise of imperialism was of course very true. That imperialism arose essentially from the capitalists' pressure to invest abroad was more doubtful. Perhaps even more basic was Europe's need for imports—only by enormous imports could Europe sustain its dense population, complex industry, and high standard of living. It was the demand for such imports—cotton, cocoa, coffee, copper, or copra drawn from the "colonies"—that made investment in the colonies financially profitable. Moreover, non-Europeans themselves often asked for the capital, glad though the European lenders were to lend it at high rates. In 1890 this might mean merely that a shah or sultan wanted to build himself a new palace, but the need of non-Europeans for Western capital was basic, nor was it to decline as the world became more democratic. Lastly, the imperialism of some countries, notably Russia and Italy, which had little capital and few modern-type capitalists of their own, could not reasonably be attributed to pressure for lucrative foreign investments.

For the British, however, the capitalistic incentive was of great importance.

[7] See pp. 116–118, 248–252.

We have seen how the British, in 1914, had $20 billion invested outside of Great Britain, a quarter of all their wealth.[8] About half, or $10 billion, was invested in the British Empire. Only a tenth of French foreign investments was in French colonies. French investment in the colonial world in general, however, including Egypt, Suez, South Africa, and Asia in addition to the French colonies, amounted to about a fifth of all French foreign investments. Only an infinitesimal fraction of German foreign investment in 1914 was in German colonies, which were of slight value. A fifth of German foreign investments, however, was placed in Africa, Asia, and the Ottoman Empire. These sums are enough to suggest the pressures upon the European governments to assert political influence in Africa, Turkey, or China.

In addition, French investors (including small bourgeois and even affluent peasants) had in 1914 a huge stake in the Russian empire. Russia, an imperial power with respect to adjoining countries in the Balkans and Asia, occupied an almost semicolonial status with respect to western Europe. The tsardom in its last twenty years, not unlike the Ottoman sultanate or the Manchu dynasty, was kept going by foreign loans, predominantly French. The French in 1914 had lent over $2 billion to Russia, more than to all colonial regions combined. For these huge outlays the motivation was at least as much political as economic. The French government often urged French banks to buy Russian bonds. The aim was not merely to make a profit for bankers and savers, but to build up and hold together a military ally against Germany.

Politics went along with economics in the whole process of imperialist expansion. National security, both political and economic, was as important an aim as the accumulation of private wealth. So, too, was the growing concern in many quarters over the economic security and welfare of the working classes. The ideas of the British statesman Joseph Chamberlain (1836–1914) illustrated how these motives entered into imperialist thinking.

Chamberlain, father of Neville Chamberlain who was to be prime minister of Britain in the years just prior to the Second World War, began as a Birmingham manufacturer, the type of man who a generation before would have been a staunch free trader and upholder of laissez faire. Discarding the old individualism, he came to believe that the community should and could take better care of its members, and, in particular, that the British community (or empire) could advance the welfare of Britons. As mayor of Birmingham he introduced a kind of municipal socialism, including public ownership of utilities. As colonial secretary from 1895 to 1903, he preached Britain's need for "a great self-sustaining and self-protecting empire" in an age of rising international competition—a world-wide British trading area, developed by British capital, which would give a secure source of raw materials and food, markets for exports, and a steady level of profits, wages, and employment.

Chamberlain saw with misgivings the tendencies toward independence in Canada, New Zealand, and the Australian Commonwealth. For these dominions he favored complete self-government, but he hoped that, once assured of virtual independence, they would reknit their ties with each other and with Great Britain. Such a reintegration of the empire he called "imperial federation." Britain and its dominions, in Chamberlain's view, should pool their resources not only for mili-

[8] See p. 566.

tary defense but also for economic well-being. The dominions had already levied tariffs against British manufactures in order to build up their own. Chamberlain, to favor British exports, urged the dominions to charge a lower duty on British wares than on the same wares coming from foreign countries. In return, he even proposed that Great Britain adopt a protective tariff, so that it might then favor Canadian or Australian goods by imposing on them a lower rate. His plan was to bind the empire together by economic bonds, making it a kind of tariff union, or system of "imperial preference." Since Britain imported mainly meat and cereals from the dominions, Chamberlain was obliged to recommend a tariff even upon these—to "tax the people's food," repudiating the very ark of the covenant of Free Trade upon which the British economy had rested for half a century.[9] The proposal was rejected. Chamberlain died in 1914, his goal unaccomplished. But after the First World War the British Empire, or Commonwealth of Nations, followed closely along the lines he had mapped out.[10]

Whether the economic welfare and security of the European working classes was advanced by imperialism is still debated. It is probable that the workingman in western Europe did benefit from imperialism. Socially conservative imperialists were joined in this belief by thinkers of the extreme Left. Marx himself, followed by Lenin, thought that the European worker obtained higher real wages through the inflow of low-priced colonial goods. To Marxists this was unfortunate, for it gave European workers a vested interest in imperialism, made the European proletariat "opportunistic" (i.e., unrevolutionary), and blocked the formation of a true international world proletariat of all races.

Another imperialist argument much heard at the time held that European countries must acquire colonies to which surplus population could migrate without altogether abandoning the native land. It seemed unfortunate, for example, that so many Germans or Italians emigrating to the United States should be lost to the fatherland. This argument was purely specious. No European country after 1870 acquired any colony to which European families in any numbers wished to move. The millions who still left Europe, up to 1914, persisted in heading for the Americas, where in the circumstances no European colony could be founded.[11]

The competitive nature of the European state system introduced other almost exclusively political elements. The European states had to guard their security against each other. They had to keep some kind of balance among themselves, in the overseas world as in Europe. Hence, as in the scramble for Africa, one government often hurriedly annexed territory simply for fear that another might do so first. Or again, colonies came to have an intangible but momentous value in symbolism and prestige. To have colonies was a normal criterion of greatness. It was the sign of having arrived as a Great Power. Britain and France had had colonies for centuries. Therefore the new powers formed in the 1860s—Germany, Italy, Japan, and in a sense the United States—had to have colonies also.

Imperialism as Crusade

Imperialism arose from the commercial, industrial, financial, scientific, political, journalistic, intellectual, religious, and humanitarian impulses of Europe com-

[9] See pp. 464, 564–565.
[10] See p. 765.
[11] See map, p. 559.

pounded together. It was an outthrust of the whole white man's civilization. It would bring civilization and enlightened living to those who still sat in darkness. Faith in "modern civilization" had become a kind of substitute religion. Imperialism was its crusade.

So the British spoke of the White Man's Burden, the French of their *mission civilisatrice*, the Germans of diffusing *Kultur*, the Americans of the "blessings of Anglo-Saxon protection." Social Darwinism and popular anthropology taught that white races were "fitter" or more gifted than colored.[12] Others argued, more reasonably, that the backwardness of non-Europeans was due to historical and hence temporary causes, but that for a long period in the future the civilized whites must keep a guardianship over their darker protégés. In the psychology of imperialism there was much that was not unworthy. Young men of good family left the pleasant lands of Devonshire or Poitou to spend long and lonely years in hot and savage places, sustained by the thought that they were advancing the work of humanity. It was a good thing to bring clearer ideas of justice to barbaric peoples, to put down slave raiding, torture, and famine, to combat degrading superstitions or fight the diseases of neglect and filth. But these accomplishments, however real, went along all too obviously with self-interest and were expressed with unbearable complacency and gross condescension to the larger part of the human race. As Rudyard Kipling wrote in 1899:

> *Take up the White Man's burden—*
> *Send out the best ye breed—*
> *Go bind your sons to exile,*
> *To serve your captives' need;*
> *To wait in heavy harness,*
> *On fluttered folk and wild—*
> *Your new-caught sullen peoples,*
> *Half devil and half child.*

79. THE AMERICAS

After the general considerations above, let us examine each of the earth's great regions in turn, and first the Americas, where we must begin our discussion earlier in the century, before the age of the "new imperialism."

In America the breakup of the Spanish and Portuguese empires in the first quarter of the nineteenth century, during and after the Napoleonic wars, left the vast tract from Colorado to Cape Horn very unsettled. Most of the people were Indian or a mixture of Indian and white (*mestizo*), with clusters here and there of pure European stock, which the nineteenth-century immigration was greatly to increase.[13] Except in inaccessible spots, the Spanish culture and language predominated. In Brazil the culture was Portuguese, and the country, though independent after 1822, remained a monarchy or "empire" until 1889, when it became a republic. In the former Spanish domains the disappearance of royal control left a large number of flaccid and shifting republics, chronically engaged

---

[12] See pp. 592, 594.
[13] See pp. 108–112, 452–454.

in border disputes with one another. Fortunately for these republics, at the time of independence in the 1820s, European imperialism was at a low ebb. We have seen how the Congress of Verona considered ways of returning them to Spain but was opposed by Great Britain; and how the United States, in 1823, supplemented the British action by announcing the Monroe Doctrine. But it was by the United States that one of the new republics was first threatened from the outside.

The United States and Mexico

Mexico, on becoming independent of Spain, reached almost to the Mississippi and the Rocky Mountains. Hardly was it independent when land seekers from the United States swarmed over its northeastern borders. They brought with them their slaves, to grow the cotton so voraciously demanded in industrial England. The Mexican Republic did not allow slavery. The newcomers proclaimed their own republic, which they called Texas. Agitation developed for annexation to the United States. Mexico objected, but in 1845 the United States annexed Texas. A war followed, in which Mexico lost to the United States not only Texas but the whole region from Texas to the California coast. As is usual in such affairs, the loser preserved a longer memory than the winner. It soon seemed only natural in the United States to possess these regions; in Mexico many decades had to pass before the wound was healed. Mexico had lost half its territory within the first generation of its independence. It was argued at the time that the United States had far better facilities than Mexico for civilizing the region.

The next threat to Mexico came from Europe. Political leaders in Mexico, at a time of internal disorders, contracted large loans in Europe on exorbitant terms, the European leaders rightly estimating Mexican credit to be highly unsound. When the liberal leader Juárez (a pure-blooded Indian, at least racially "non-European") repudiated the loans, the European bondholders demanded satisfaction from their governments. The United States was paralyzed by the Civil War. Great Britain, France, and Spain, which had never recognized the Monroe Doctrine, in 1861 sent combined military forces to Veracruz. The British proposed seizure of the customs houses in Mexican ports, and appropriation of the customs revenues to pay off the debt (an expedient introduced in China three years before); but the French had more ambitious designs. Unknown both to the British, who wanted only to collect debts, and to the Spanish, who dreamed of setting up a new Bourbon monarchy in Mexico, the Emperor Napoleon III had a secret project for establishing a French satellite state in Mexico, which French capital and exports might subsequently develop.[14] He planned to create a Mexican empire with the Austrian archduke Maximilian as its figurehead emperor. The British and Spanish disapprovingly withdrew their forces. The French army proceeded into the interior. Maximilian reigned for some years, but Napoleon III gradually concluded that conquest of Mexico was impossible, or too expensive. It further appeared, by 1865, that the United States was not going to collapse after all, as expected and even hoped for by the European governing classes. The United States protested strongly to the French government. The French withdrew, Maximilian was captured and shot, and Juárez and the Mexican liberals came back to power.

[14] See pp. 498–499.

United States pressure, before 1870, had thus in turn both despoiled and protected the adjoining part of Latin America. This ambivalent situation became characteristic of the New World. As the United States became a great power the Monroe Doctrine became an effective barrier to European territorial ambitions. Latin America never became subject to imperialism as completely as did Asia and Africa. On the other hand, the United States became the imperialist power feared above all others south of the border. It was the *Yanqui* menace, the Colossus of the North.

In the 1870s in the course of its turbulent politics, both natives of Mexico and foreign residents were obliged to pay forced loans to rival leaders. The State Department at Washington demanded that American citizens be reimbursed by the Mexican government. The double standard characteristic of imperialism—one standard for civilized and one for uncivilized states—became clear in the exchange of notes. The Mexican government, now under Porfirio Díaz, attempted to lay down the principle that "foreigners locating in a country accepted the mode of life of the people . . . and participated not only in the benefits of such residence but also in the adversities. Foreigners should enjoy the same guarantees and the same legal protection as natives, but no more." The Mexicans observed that the United States had never recognized the claims of foreigners for losses sustained in its Civil War. The United States, under President Hayes, held on the other hand that citizens of advanced states, operating in more primitive regions, should continue to enjoy the security of property characteristic of their home countries. When on another occasion the United States sent troops to the border, and the Mexicans objected, the secretary of state remarked on "the volatile and childish character of these people and their incapacity to treat a general question with calmness and without prejudice." Mexico retorted that the United States had "disregarded all the rules of international law and practice of civilized nations and treated the Mexicans as savages, as Kaffirs of Africa."

It was, in fact, a principle of international law in the nineteenth century that civilized states might not intervene in each other's affairs but had the right of intervention in "backward" countries. In the dispute of 1877 the United States classified Mexico as backward, "volatile and childish." What the Mexicans objected to was being treated like "savages and Kaffirs," and not like a civilized nation. They differed on which of the two standards should apply.

United States Imperialism in the 1890s

The 1890s saw a crescendo of imperialism both in Europe and in the United States. In 1895, in a resounding restatement of the Monroe Doctrine, President Cleveland forbade the British to deal directly with Venezuela in a boundary dispute affecting British Guiana. The British were obliged to accept international arbitration. When, however, the adjacent Colombia faced a revolution in the Isthmus of Panama the United States supported the revolutionaries and, consulting nobody, recognized Panama as an independent republic. Here the United States leased and fortified a Canal Zone, and proceeded to build the Panama Canal. Panama became in effect what Europeans would call a protectorate of the United States.

Meanwhile what was left of the old Spanish American empire, confined to Cuba and Puerto Rico, was agitated by revolutionary disturbances looking to independence. Sympathies in the United States lay with the revolutionaries. Every sign of the new imperialism showed itself unmistakably. Americans had $50 million invested in Cuba. They bought the bonds issued by Cuban revolutionaries in New York. Cuban sugar, whose production was interfered with by political troubles, was necessary to the famed American standard of living. An orderly and amenable Cuba was vital to American strategic interests in the Caribbean, in the soon to be built canal, and in the Pacific. The barbarity of the Spanish authorities was deplored as an outrage to modern civilization. The newspapers, especially the new "yellow" press, roused the American public to a fury of moral indignation and imperial self-assertion. The climax came when an American warship, the *Maine*, sank under mysterious circumstances in Havana harbor.

The United States easily won the ensuing war with Spain in 1898. Puerto Rico was annexed outright, as were the Philippine Islands on the other side of the world. Cuba was set up as an independent republic, subject to the Platt Amendment, a series of provisions by which the United States obtained the right to oversee Cuba's relations with foreign powers, and to intervene in Cuba in matters of "life, property, individual liberty" and "Cuban independence." Thus the United States obtained another protectorate in the Caribbean. The right of intervention in Cuba was exercised several times in the following two decades, until the growth of Cuban nationalism and subsiding of American imperialism led to abrogation of the Platt Amendment in 1934. Later, after the Second World War, the Philippines formally received independence in 1946 and Puerto Rico became a self-governing commonwealth in 1952.

It was under President Theodore Roosevelt, the peppery "hero of San Juan hill," that the imperial greatness of the United States was most emphatically trumpeted. He announced in 1904 that weakness or misbehavior "which results in a general loosening of the ties of civilized society may . . . require intervention by some civilized nation," and that the Monroe Doctrine might force the United States "to the exercise of an international police power." In the following year Santo Domingo fell into such financial disorder that European creditors were alarmed. To forestall any pretext for European intervention, the United States sent a financial administrator to Santo Domingo, reformed the economy of the country, and impounded half the customs receipts to pay its debts. Roosevelt declared—in what came to be known as the "Roosevelt Corollary" to the Monroe Doctrine—that, since the United States would not permit European states to intervene in America to collect debts, it must itself assume the duty of intervention to safeguard the investments of the civilized world. The Monroe Doctrine, initially a negative warning to Europe, now stood with the new corollary as a positive notice of supervision of all America by the United States. A quarter of a century of "dollar diplomacy" followed, in which the United States repeatedly intervened, by military or other means, in the Caribbean and Mexico. But the Roosevelt Corollary, like the Platt Amendment, created so much bad feeling in Latin America that the Washington government finally repudiated it.

The story of the Hawaiian Islands was as typical of the new imperialism as any episode in the history of any of the European empires. Known originally to outsiders as the Sandwich Islands, these spots of land long enjoyed isolation in the vastnesses of the mid-Pacific. The growth of navigation in the nineteenth century introduced them to the world. Sailors, whalers, missionaries, and vendors of rum and cloth filled Honolulu by 1840. The native ruler, confused and helpless in the new situation, almost accepted a British protectorate in 1843 and in 1875 did accept a virtual protectorate by the United States, which guaranteed Hawaiian independence against any third party, obtained trading privileges, and acquired Pearl Harbor as a naval base. American capital and management entered the island. They created huge sugar and pineapple industries, entirely dependent on export to, and investment by, the United States. In 1891, when Queen Liliuokalani came to the throne, she tried to check westernization and Americanization. The American interests, endangered by her nativist policies, overthrew the queen and set up an independent republic, which soon sought annexation to the United States. It was the story of Texas reenacted. For several years the issue hung in the balance because of lingering disapproval in the United States for such strong-arm methods. But with Japan revealing imperial designs in 1895, the rush of the other powers into China, the Spanish-American War, acquisition of the Philippines, and plans for the Panama Canal, the United States "accepted its destiny" in the Pacific, and annexed the Hawaiian Republic by joint resolution of Congress in 1898. Hawaii became a state in the American union in 1959.

80. THE DISSOLUTION OF THE OTTOMAN EMPIRE

The Ottman Empire in the 1850s

Of all parts of the non-European world, the Ottoman, or Turkish, Empire was the nearest to Europe, and with it Europeans had for centuries had close relations. It had for long extended from Hungary and the Balkan peninsula to the south Russian steppes and from Algeria to the Persian Gulf. The empire was not at all like a European state. Immense in extent, it was a congeries of religious communities. Most of its people were Muslim, including both orthodox Muslims and such reform sects as Druses and Wahabis; some were Jews who had always lived in the Near East; many were Christian, principally Greek Orthodox and Armenian. The Turks were the ruling class and Islam the dominant religion. Only Muslims, for example, could serve in the army; non-Muslims were known as *raya*, the "flock" or "herd"—they paid the taxes. Persons of different religion lived side by side, each under the laws, courts, and customs of his own religious group. Religious officials—patriarchs, bishops, rabbis, imams, ulemas—were responsible to the Turkish government for their own people, over whom therefore they had a great deal of authority.[15]

Western Europeans had their own special rights. Roman Catholic clergy, living mainly in Palestine, looked to the pope in religion and to France for a mundane protector. Western merchants enjoyed the regime of the "capitulations," or special rights granted by the Ottoman government in numerous treaties going back to the sixteenth century. By the capitulations Turkey could not levy a tariff of more than 8 percent on imported goods. Europeans were exempt from most taxes. Cases involving two Europeans, civil or criminal, could be settled only in a court held by a European consul under European law. Disputes between a European and an Ottoman subject were settled in Turkish courts, but in the presence of a European observer.

---

[15] See pp. 213–214.

The Ottoman Empire, in short, completely lacked the European idea of nationalism or national unity. The European idea of sovereignty and a uniform law for all its peoples were also absent, as was the idea of the secular state, or of law and citizenship separated from religion. The empire had fallen behind Europe in scientific, mechanical, material, humanitarian, and administrative achievements.

Turkey was the "sick man of Europe," and its long decline constituted the Eastern Question. Since the loss of Hungary in 1699 the Ottoman Empire had entered on a long process of territorial disintegration. That the empire lasted another two centuries was due to the European balance of power.[16] But by the 1850s the empire was falling away at the edges. Russia had advanced in the Crimea and the Caucasus. Serbia was autonomous, Greece independent, and Rumania recognized as a self-governing principality. The French occupied Algeria. A native Arab dynasty, the Sauds, of the Wahabi reform sect, ruled over much of Arabia. A former Turkish governor of Egypt, Mehemet Ali, had established his family as hereditary khedives in the Nile valley.[17] Notwithstanding these changes, the Ottoman Empire in the 1850s was still huge. It encompassed not only the Turkish or Anatolian peninsula (including Armenia and territory south of the Caucasus) but also the central portion of the Balkan peninsula from Constantinople to the Adriatic where many Christians of Slavic nationality lived, Tripoli (Libya) in North Africa, and the islands of Crete and Cyprus. Egypt and Arabia, though autonomous, were still under the nominal suzerainty of the sultan.

The Crimean War of 1854–1856 opened a new phase in Ottoman history as in that of Europe.[18] We have seen how this war was followed by the consolidation of great nation-states in Europe, and how even the United States, Canada, and Japan consolidated or modernized themselves at the same time. The Turks tried to do the same between 1856 and 1876.

In the Crimean War the Turks were on the winning side, but the war affected them as it affected Russia, the loser. Exposing their military and political weakness, it pointed up the need of organization. The outcome of the war was taken to prove the superiority of the political system of England and France. It was therefore on Western lines that Turkish reformers wished to remodel. It was not merely that they wished to defend themselves against another of the periodic wars with Russia. They wished also to avoid being periodically saved from Russia by the West, a process which if continued could lead only to French or British control of Turkey.

Attempts at Reform and Revival, 1856–1876

In 1856 the Ottoman government issued the Hatt-i Humayun, the most far-reaching Turkish reform edict of the century. Its purpose was to create an Ottoman national citizenship for all persons in the empire. It abolished the civil authority of religious hierarchs. Equality before the law was guaranteed as was eligibility

---

[16] See pp. 215–217, 327, 455–456, and map, p. 625.

[17] See p. 456. The Egyptian ruler, as viceroy under the Ottoman Empire, did not adopt the title of "khedive" until 1867; he was called "sultan" from 1914 to 1922; and thereafter "king" until the overthrow of the monarchy in 1952.

[18] See pp. 512–513.

to public office without regard to religion. The army was opened to Christians and Muslims alike and steps were even taken to include both in nonsegregated military units. The edict announced a reform of taxes, security of property for all, abolition of torture, and reform of prisons. It promised to combat the chronic evils of graft, bribery, and extortion by public officials.

For twenty years there were serious efforts to make the reform decree of 1856 a reality. Western and liberal ideas circulated freely. Newspapers were founded. Writers called for a national Turkish revival, threw off the old Persian style in literature, composed histories of the Ottomans, translated Montesquieu and Rousseau. Foreign loans entered the country. Railroads joined the Black Sea and the Danube. Abdul Aziz (1861–1876), the first sultan to travel to Europe, visited Vienna, London, and the great Paris world's fair of 1867. But powerful resistance developed against such radical changes. Also, the best efforts of the Turkish reformers miscarried. There were too few Turks with skill or experience in the work required. Abdul Aziz took to spending his borrowed money somewhat too freely for purposes of the harem. In 1874 the Ottoman government, having recklessly overborrowed, repudiated half its debt.

A new and more determined reforming minister, Midhat Pasha, goaded by opposition and desperate at the weight of inertia, deposed Abdul Aziz in 1876, deposed the latter's nephew three months later, and set up Abdul Hamid II as sultan. The new sultan at first briskly went along with the reform movement, proclaiming a new constitution in 1876. It declared the Ottoman Empire to be indivisible, and promised personal liberty, freedom of conscience, freedom of education and the press, and parliamentary government. The first Turkish parliament met in 1877. Its members earnestly addressed themselves to reform. But they reckoned without Abdul Hamid, who in 1877 revealed his true intentions. He got rid of Midhat, packed off the parliament, and threw away the constitution.

Repression after 1876

Abdul Hamid reigned for thirty-three years, from 1876 to 1909. For all this time he lived as a terrified animal, fighting back blindly and ferociously against forces that he could not understand. Once when a consignment of dynamos reached the Turkish customs it was held up by fearful officials, because the contents were declared to make several hundred revolutions per minute. Again, chemistry books for use in the new American college were pronounced seditious, because their chemical symbols might be a secret cipher. The sultan sensed that tampering with the old Ottoman way would lead to ruin. He dreaded any moves to check his own whim or power. He was thrown into a panic by Turkish reformers and westernizers, who became increasingly terroristic in the face of his opposition. Driven away by Abdul Hamid, some tens of thousands of Young Turks, the activists of the reform era before 1876, or their children and successors, lived in exile in Paris, London, or Geneva, plotting their return to Turkey and vengeance upon Abdul the Damned. The sultan was frightened also by agitation among his non-Turkish subjects. Nationalist Armenians, Bulgars, Macedonians, and Cretans defied and taunted the Ottoman authorities, which responded with the Bulgarian massacres of 1876 and the Armenian massacres of 1894. These horrible butcheries of thousands of peasants by Ottoman troops came as a shock to a Europe unused to such violence. Lastly, and with good reason, Abdul Hamid lived in a creeping fear of the designs of the imperialist European powers upon his dissolving empire.

A thoroughly reformed, consolidated, and modernized Ottoman Empire was the last thing that European governments desired. They might wish for humanitarian reforms in Turkey, for more efficiency and honesty in Turkish government and finance, and even for a Turkish parliamentary system. Such demands were eloquently expressed by liberals like Gladstone in England. But no one wanted what Turkish reformers wanted, a reinvigorated Ottoman Empire that could deal with Europe politically as an equal.

The Russo-Turkish War of 1877–1878: The Congress of Berlin

In Russia, since the time of Catherine II, many had dreamed of installing Russia on the shores of the Bosporus.[19] Constantinople they called Tsarigrad, the Imperial City, which Orthodoxy was to liberate from the infidel. Crusading motives, in a nationalist and imperialist age, reappeared anew in the form of Pan-Slavism.[20] This was now a doctrine preached by leading Russians, including the novelist Dostoevski, the poet Tyutchev, and the publicist Danilevsky. Danilevsky's *Russia and Europe*, published in 1871, predicted a long war between Europe and Russia, to be followed by a grand federation of the East, in which not only Slavs, but Greeks, Hungarians, and parts of Asiatic Turkey would be included under Russian control. This type of Pan-Slavism was favored and patronized by the Russian government, because it diverted attention from internal and revolutionary troubles. As for the Slav peoples of the Ottoman Empire, they were willing to use Russian Pan-Slavism as a means of combating their Turkish rulers. Insurrection against the Turks broke out in Bosnia in 1875, in Bulgaria in 1876. In 1877 Russia declared war on Turkey. Russia was again on the move against the Ottoman Empire for the sixth time in a hundred years.

The British, who had fought Russia over Turkey in 1854, were prepared to do so again. A number of recent developments added to their apprehension. The Suez Canal was completed in 1869. It was within the territory of the Ottoman Empire. It restored the Near East to its ancient position as a crossroads of world trade. The British also took alarm when Russia, in 1870, in the confusion of the Franco-Prussian War, repudiated a clause in the treaty of 1856 and began to build a fleet on the Black Sea. In 1874 Benjamin Disraeli, a Conservative and an imperialist, became prime minister of Great Britain. By a sudden coup in the following year he was able to buy up, from the almost bankrupt khedive of Egypt, 44 percent of the shares of the Suez Canal Company. In 1876, in a dramatic affirmation of imperial splendor, he had Queen Victoria take the title of empress of India. British commercial and financial interests in India and the Far East were growing, and the Suez Canal, of which the British government was now the principal stockholder, was becoming the "lifeline" of empire. But the Ottoman state, and hence the whole Near East, was now collapsing before the Russians, whose armies advanced rapidly through the Balkans in 1877, reached Constantinople, and forced the Turks to sign a treaty, the treaty of San Stefano. By this treaty Turkey ceded to Russia Batum and Kars on the south side of the Caucasus Mountains, gave full independence to Serbia and Rumania, promised reforms in

---

[19] See pp. 327, 512–513.
[20] On earlier Pan-Slavism, see p. 480.

Bosnia, and granted autonomy to a new Bulgarian state, whose boundaries were to be very generously drawn, and which everyone expected to be dominated by Russia. England seethed with a popular clamor for war against Russia. The outcry gave the word "jingoism" to the language:

> *We don't want to fight, but by jingo, if we do,*
> *We've got the men, we've got the ships, we've*
>   *got the money too.*

It now appeared that the weakness of Turkey, its inability to fend off foreigners from its borders, would precipitate at least an Anglo-Russian and possibly a general European war. But war was averted by diplomacy. Bismarck assembled a congress of all the European great powers at Berlin. Once again Europe attempted to assert itself as a unity, to restore life to the much-battered Concert of Europe by dealing collectively with the common problem presented by the Eastern Question. The immediate need was to mediate between the Russians and Turks and to placate the British. To prevent any single power from gaining unequal advantage, and to win the acceptance of all powers for the arrangements agreed to, it was deemed necessary to give something to all, or almost all. The congress in effect initiated a partition of the Ottoman domain. It kept peace in Europe at the expense of Turkey. The European balance now both protected and dismembered Turkey at the same time.

The Russians were persuaded at Berlin to give up the treaty of San Stefano that they had imposed on the Turks, but they still obtained Batum and Kars and won independence for the Serbs and Rumanians. Montenegro, too, was recognized as an independent state. They compromised on Bulgaria, which was divided into three zones with varying degrees of autonomy, all still nominally within the Ottoman Empire. Austria-Hungary was authorized by the congress to "occupy and administer" Bosnia (but not annex it) in the interests of civilization and in compensation for the spread of Russian influence in the Balkans. To the British (Disraeli boasted he brought home "peace with honor") the Turks ceded Cyprus, a large island not far from the Suez Canal. The French were told that they might expand from Algeria into Tunisia. To the Italians (who counted least) it was more vaguely hinted that some day, somehow, they might expand across the Adriatic into Albania. As Bismarck put it, "the Italians have such a large appetite and such poor teeth." Germany took nothing. Bismarck said he was the "honest broker," with no interest except in European peace.

The treaty of Berlin in 1878 dispelled the immediate threat of war. But it left many continuing problems for later statesmanship to deal with, problems which, because they were not dealt with successfully, became a principal cause of the First World War thirty-six years later. Neither the Balkan nationalists nor the Russian Pan-Slavs were satisfied. The Turks, both reactionaries like Abdul Hamid and the revolutionary Young Turks in exile, were indignant that peace had been made by further dismemberment of their territory. The demonstrated weakness of Turkey was a constant temptation to all concerned. In the years before 1914 German influence grew. Germans and German capital entered Turkey, projecting, and partially completing, a great Berlin to Bagdad railway to be accompanied by the exploitation of Near Eastern natural resources. The railroad was all

THE DISSOLUTION OF THE OTTOMAN EMPIRE, 1699–1914

Beginning in 1699, with the loss of Hungary to the House of Austria, the Ottoman Empire entered upon a long process of territorial disintegration which lasted for over 200 years. Dates shown are those at which territories dropped away. In general, regions lost from 1699 to the fall of Napoleon, 1812–1815, were annexed directly by Austria and Russia. European territories lost in the nineteenth century emerged as independent states, owing to the rise of nationalism and the balance among the great European powers. (See maps, p. 667.) In the Arabic world, reaching from Algeria to the Persian Gulf, regions lost before the First World War were absorbed into European colonial empires; those lost in the First World War (1918) were at first mostly assigned to France and Britain as mandates, but after the Second World War emerged as independent Arabic states, as did the Republic of Israel (see pp. 872–873). During the First World War Britain, France, Italy, Russia, and Greece took steps to partition Turkey proper, but a Turkish nationalist movement blocked these designs and established a Turkish republic (see pp. 627, 667, 753–754).

but completed before 1914 despite the protests and representations of the Russians, the French, and particularly the British, who saw in it a direct threat to their empire in India.

Egypt and North Africa

For Egypt, technically autonomous within the Ottoman Empire, the 1850s and 1860s were a time of progress in the Western sense as they had been for the empire as a whole. The Egyptian government modernized its administration, court system, and property law, cooperated with the French in building the Suez Canal, encouraged shipping on the Red Sea, and let British and French interests construct railroads. Between 1861 and 1865, while the American South was unable to export raw cotton, the annual export of Egyptian cotton rose from 60 million to 250 million pounds. Egypt more than Turkey was drawn into the world market, and the khedive more than the sultan became a Western type of man. The khedive Ismail built himself a fine new opera house in Cairo, where, in 1871, two years after the opening of the Suez Canal, Verdi's *Aïda*, written at the khedive's request, was resoundingly performed for the first time.

Such improvements cost a good deal of money, borrowed in England and France. The Egyptian government was soon in financial straits, only temporarily relieved by the sale of Canal shares to Disraeli. By 1879 matters reached the point where Western banking interests forced the abdication of Ismail and his replacement by Tewfik, who, with a childlike fascination for the new Western marvels, soon let himself become thoroughly enmeshed by his creditors. This led to nationalistic protests within Egypt, headed by Colonel Arabi. In a pattern repeated in many parts of the colonial world, especially in Manchu China, the nationalists opposed both the foreigners and their own government, charging it with being a mere front for foreign interests. Arabi's movement, an early expression of Arab nationalism, led to riots in Alexandria, where Europeans had to flee aboard British and French shipping in the harbor. A British squadron then unceremoniously bombarded Alexandria. British troops (the French, though invited to take part, refused) disembarked in 1882 at Suez and Alexandria, defeated Arabi, and took Tewfik under their protection. The military intervention of 1882 was said by the British to be temporary, but British troops remained there for a long time, through two world wars and well into the twentieth century, not leaving until 1956.

Egypt became a British protectorate. The British protected the khedive from discontent within his own country, from the claims of the Ottoman Porte, and from the rival attentions of other European powers. The British resident from 1883 to 1907, an exceptionally capable administrator named Evelyn Baring, the first Earl of Cromer, did much to reconstruct the economy of the country, reform its taxation, ease the burdens on the peasants and raise their productivity, while encouraging the growth of raw materials wanted by England and assuring regular payment of interest to British, French, and other holders of Egyptian bonds.

The French strenuously objected when the British stayed on so long in Egypt. It had long been the French who had the greatest investments in the Near East, and Near Easterners who were at all westernized—Egyptian, Syrian, Turkish—overwhelmingly preferred the French language and culture to the English. The French, harboring deep suspicion of British designs in Egypt, compensated themselves by building a North African empire farther west. They developed Algeria, assumed a protectorate over Tunisia, and began to penetrate Morocco. Upon these French advances the British, and soon the Germans, looked with unmitigated disfavor. Rivalry for the spoils of the Ottoman Empire thus created enmity among the Great Powers and constituted a fertile source of the war scares, fears, and diplomatic maneuvers that preceded the First World War. These are related in the following chapter.

The dissolution of the Ottoman Empire became indistinguishable from the whole chronic international crisis before 1914. It is enough to say here, to keep the fate of the Ottoman Empire in focus, that Abdul Hamid's frantic policies came to nothing and that the Young Turks won control of the Ottoman government in 1908. They forced the restoration of the constitution of 1876 and introduced many reforms. In the midst of the revolutionary disturbances of 1908 Bulgaria proclaimed its full independence and Austria annexed Bosnia. In the Turco-Italian War of 1911–1912 Italy took Libya and the Dodecanese Islands from the Turks. In two successive Balkan Wars (1912–1913) Turkey lost nearly all its territory in Europe to Bulgaria, Serbia, Greece, and Albania, the latter becoming an independent state in 1912.[21] Finally, when all Europe became involved in war in 1914, Russia again declared war on Turkey, and the Turks came into the war on the side of Germany, whose political and economic influence in the empire had been steadily growing. During the war, with British aid, the Arabs detached themselves from the empire, becoming eventually independent Arab states. Egypt, too, ended all connections with the empire. In 1923 a Turkish republic was proclaimed. It was confined to Constantinople and the Anatolian peninsula, where the bulk of the true Turkish people lived. The new republic proceeded to undergo a thorough nationalist and secular revolution.[22]

81. THE PARTITION OF AFRICA

South of Mediterranean Africa lay the Sahara, and south of that lay Black Africa, the Dark Continent for Europeans. For centuries Europeans knew only its coasts —the Gold Coast, Ivory Coast, Slave Coast—to which from an inexhaustible interior had come shackled processions of captive slaves, as well as the swelling waters of enormous rivers, like the Nile and the Congo, whose sources in the dim hinterland were a subject of romantic speculation. The population was black, except that Arabic-speaking whites were found on the east coast; and in the southern part of the continent (at the time of the founding of the Union of South Africa in 1910) about 1.1 million Europeans lived along with about 5 million blacks. The native peoples were agricultural or pastoral, without written language or enduring political states but with bold and remarkable art forms and a memory of great kingdoms in earlier times.

The Opening of Africa

Missionaries, explorers, and individual adventurers first opened this world to Europe. The historic pair, Livingstone and Stanley, well illustrate the drift of events. Long before the imperialist age, in 1841, the Scot David Livingstone arrived in southeast Africa as a medical missionary. He gave himself to humanitarian and religious work, with a little occasional trading and much travel and discovery, but without political or true economic aims. Exploring the Zambesi River, he was the first white man to look upon the Victoria Falls. Fully at home in inner Africa, safe and on friendly terms with its native people, he was quite content to be let alone. But the hectic forces of modern civilization sought him out. Word spread in Europe and America that Dr. Livingstone was lost. The New York *Herald*, to manufacture news, sent the roving journalist H. M. Stanley to

[21] See p. 666.
[22] See pp. 753–755.

find him, which he did in 1871. Livingstone soon died, deeply honored by the natives. Stanley was a man of the new era. Seeing vast possibilities in Africa, he went to Europe to solicit backers. In 1878 he found a man with the same ideas, who happened to be a king, Leopold II, king of the Belgians.

Leopold, for all his royalty, was at heart a promoter. China, Formosa, the Philippines, and Morocco had in turn attracted his fancy, but it was the central African basin of the Congo that he decided to develop. Stanley was exactly the man he was looking for, and the two founded at Brussels, with a few financiers, an International Congo Association in 1878. It was a purely private enterprise; the Belgian government and people had nothing to do with it. All Africa inland from the coasts was considered to be, like America in the time of Columbus, a *terra nullius*, without government and claimed by nobody, wide open to the first civilized persons who might arrive. Stanley, returning to the Congo in 1882, in a year or two concluded treaties with over 500 chiefs, who in return for a few trinkets or a few yards of cloth put their crude marks on the mysterious papers and accepted the blue-and-gold flag of the Association.

Since the Dark Continent was still innocent of internal frontiers, no one could tell how much ground the Association might soon cover by these methods. The German explorer Karl Peters, working inland from Zanzibar, was signing treaties with the chiefs of East Africa. The Frenchman Brazza, departing from the west coast and distributing the tricolor in every village, was claiming on the Congo River itself a territory larger than France. The Portuguese aspired to join their ancient colonies of Angola and Mozambique into a trans-African empire, for which they required a generous portion of the interior. Britain supported Portugal. In every case the home governments in Europe were still hesitant over involvement in the African wilds, but they were pushed on by small organized minorities of colonizing enthusiasts, and they faced the probability that if they missed the moment it would be too late.

Bismarck, who personally thought African colonies an absurdity, but was sensitive to the new pressures, called another conference at Berlin in 1885, this time to submit the African question to international regulation. Most European states, as well as the United States, attended. The Berlin conference attempted to do two things: to set up the territories of the Congo Association as an international state, under international auspices and restrictions; and to draft an international code governing the way in which European powers wishing to acquire African territory should proceed.

The Congo Free State, which in 1885 took the place of the International Congo Association, was not only an international creation but embodied, in principle, what were to be known after the First World War as international mandates or international trusteeships for "backward" peoples. The Berlin conference specified that the new state should have no connection with any power, including Belgium. It delegated the government to Leopold. It drew the boundaries, making the Congo Free State almost as large as the United States east of the Mississippi, and it added certain specific provisions: the Congo River was internationalized, persons of all nationalities should be free to do business in the Congo state, there should be no tariff levied on imports, and the slave trade should be suppressed. Leopold in 1889 reassembled the signatory powers in a second conference, held at Brussels. The Brussels conference took further steps to root out the slave trade, which remained a stubborn though declining evil, because the Muslim world was

PRE-COLONIAL AFRICA: SITES AND PEOPLES

This map is meant to show Africa before penetration by the Europeans in the nineteenth century. It does not refer to any particular date. Names in brown designate ancient or medieval centers, like the Ghana and Mali empires, which no longer existed in modern times. Even the most extensive African kingdoms had indefinite and shifting boundaries which are hard to indicate on a map. Bantu peoples were moving toward the southern tip of the continent in the nineteenth century, at the time when Europeans began to move northeastward into the interior from the Cape.

several generations behind the Christian in abolishing slavery. The Brussels conference also undertook to protect native rights, correct certain glaring abuses, and reduce the traffic in liquor and firearms.

This attempt at internationalism failed, because Europe had no international machinery by which the hard daily work of executing general agreements could be carried out. Leopold went his own way in the Congo. His determination to make it commercially profitable led him to unconscionable extremes. Europe and America demanded rubber, and the Congo was at the time one of the world's few sources of supply. The Congo people, among the least advanced in Africa, and afflicted by the disease and enervation of a lowland equatorial climate, could be made to tap enough rubber trees only by inhuman severity and compulsion. The trees themselves were destroyed without thought of replacement. Leopold, by ravaging its resources and virtually enslaving its people, was able to draw from the Congo a princely income to be spent in Brussels, but he could never make the enterprise self-supporting. Consumed with debt, he borrowed another 25 million francs from the kingdom of Belgium, agreeing that Belgium should inherit the Congo on his death if the debt was unpaid. In 1908, the reluctant Belgians thus found themselves heirs to some "tropical gardens" to which they had been consistently indifferent. The Free State became the Belgian Congo, and under Belgian administration the worst excesses of Leopold's regime were removed.

The Berlin conference of 1885 had also laid down, for expansion in Africa, certain rules of the game—a European power with holdings on the coast had prior rights in the back country; occupation must not be on paper only, through drawing lines on a map, but must consist in real occupation by administrators or troops; and each power must give proper notice to the others as to what territories it considered its own. A wild scramble for "real occupation" quickly followed. In fifteen years the entire continent was parceled out. The sole exceptions were Ethiopia and, technically, Liberia, founded in 1822 as a colony for emancipated American slaves and virtually a protectorate of the United States.

Everywhere a variant of the same process was repeated. First, somewhere in the wilderness, would appear a handful of white men, bringing their inevitable treaties—sometimes printed forms. To get what they wanted, the Europeans commonly had to ascribe powers to the chief which by the customs of the tribe he did not possess—powers to convey sovereignty, sell land, or grant mining concessions. Thus the Africans were baffled at the outset by foreign legal conceptions. Then the Europeans would build up the position of the chief, since they themselves had no influence over the people. This led to the widespread system of "indirect rule," by which colonial authorities acted through the existing chiefs and tribal forms. There were many things that only the chief could arrange, such as security for isolated Europeans, porter services, or gangs of workmen to build roads or railroads.

Labor was the overwhelming problem. For pure slavery Europeans now had an abhorrence, and they abolished it wherever they could. But the African, so long as he lived in his traditional way, did not react like the free wage earner postulated in civilized business and economics. He had little sense of individual gain and almost no use for money. He worked rather sporadically according to European ideas; work, continuous and laborious work, was in many African societies left to the women. The result was that Europeans all over Africa resorted to forced labor. For road building, systems like the French *corvée* before the Revolution reappeared. Or the chief would be required to supply a quota of able-bodied men for a certain length of time, and frequently he did so gladly to raise his own importance in the eyes of the whites. More indirect methods were also used. The colonial government might levy a hut tax or a poll tax, payable only in money, to obtain which the native would have to seek a job. Or the new government, once installed, might allocate so much land to Europeans as private property (another foreign conception) that the local tribe could no longer subsist on the lands that remained to it. Or the whole tribe might be moved to a reservation, like Indians in the United States. In any case, while the women tilled the fields or tended the stock at home, the men would move off to take jobs under the whites for infinitesimal pay. The men then lived in "compounds," away from family and tribal kindred; they became demoralized; and the labor they gave, unintelligent and unwilling, would scarcely have been tolerated in any more civilized community. In these circumstances everything was done to uproot the Africans, and little was done to benefit them. The old tribal or village society collapsed, and nothing replaced it.

Conditions improved with the twentieth century, as traditions of enlightened colonial administration were built up. Colonial officials even came to serve as buffers or protectors of the natives against the white man's interest. Throughout, it was part of the ethos of imperialism to put down slavery, tribal warfare, superstition, disease, and illiteracy. Slowly a westernized class of Africans grew—chiefs and the sons of chiefs, Catholic priests and Protestant ministers, warehouse clerks and government employees. Young men from Nigeria or Uganda appeared as students at Oxford, the University of Paris, or universities in the United States. Westernized Africans usually resented both exploitation and paternalism. They showed signs of turning nationalistic, like their counterparts in the Ottoman Empire and Asia. If they wanted westernization, it was at a pace and for a purpose of their own. As the twentieth century progressed, nationalism in Africa grew more vocal and more intense.

Friction and Rivalry between the Powers

Meanwhile, in the fifteen years from 1885 to 1900, the Europeans in Africa came dangerously near to open blows. The Portuguese annexed huge domains in Angola and Mozambique. The Italians took over two barren tracts, Italian Somaliland and Eritrea on the Red Sea. They then moved inland, in quest of more imposing possessions, to conquer Ethiopia and the headwaters of the Nile. Some 80,000 Ethiopians, however, slaughtered and routed 20,000 Italians in pitched battle at Adowa in 1896. It was the first time that native Africans successfully defended themselves against the whites, and it discouraged invasion of Ethiopia by the Italians (or other Europeans) for forty years. Italy and Portugal, like the Congo Free State and Spain (which retained a few vestiges of former days), were able to enjoy sizable holdings in Africa because of mutual fears among the principal contenders. The principal contenders were Great Britain, France, and Germany. Each preferred to have territory held by a minor power rather than by one of its significant rivals.

The Germans were latecomers in the colonial race, which Bismarck entered with reluctance. By the 1880s all the usual imperialist arguments were heard in Germany, though most of them, such as the need of new markets, of outlets for emigration, or for the investment of capital, had little or no application in tropical Africa. The Germans established colonies in German East Africa, and in the Cameroons and Togo on the west coast, along with a desert area that came to be called German Southwest Africa. It did not escape the notice of German imperial planners that some day the Congo and the Portuguese colonies might be joined with German East Africa and the Cameroons in a solid German belt across the African heartland. The French controlled most of West Africa, from Algeria across the Sahara and the Sudan to various points on the Guinea coast. They also occupied Obok on the Red Sea, and after the Italian defeat in 1896 their influence in Ethiopia grew. French planners therefore dreamed of a solid French belt across Africa from Dakar to the Gulf of Aden. The French government in 1898 dispatched Captain J. B. Marchand with a small party eastward from Lake Chad, to hoist the tricolor far away on the upper Nile, in the southern part of the Sudan, which no European power as yet "effectively" occupied.

The two presumptive east-and-west belts, German and French, were cut (presumptively) by a north-and-south belt, projected in the British imperial imagination as an "Africa British from the Cape to Cairo." From the Cape of Good Hope Cecil Rhodes pushed northward into Rhodesia. Kenya and Uganda in the mid-continent were already British. In Egypt, a British protectorate since 1882, the British began to support old Egyptian claims to the upper Nile. The first venture proved a disaster, when in 1885 a British officer, "Chinese Gordon," leading an Egyptian force, was killed by aroused Muslims at Khartoum. In the following decade British opinion turned imperialist in earnest. Another British officer, General Kitchener (with a young man named Winston Churchill under his command), again started southward up the Nile and defeated the local Muslims in 1898 at Omdurman. He then pushed on further upstream. At a place called Fashoda he met Marchand.

The ensuing Fashoda crisis brought Britain and France to the verge of war. Already at odds over Egypt and Morocco,[23] the two governments used the encounter at Fashoda to force a showdown. It was a test of strength, not only for their respective plans for all Africa, but for their relative position in all imperialist and international issues. Both at first refused to yield. The British virtually threatened to fight. The French, fearful of their insecurity against Germany in Europe, at last decided not to take the risk. They backed down and recalled Marchand from Fashoda. A wave of hatred for the British swept over France.

The British no sooner won this Pyrrhic victory than they became involved in more unpleasantness at the other end of the African continent. In 1890 Cecil Rhodes had become prime minister of the Cape Colony. He was a principal sponsor of the Cape-to-Cairo dream. Two small independent neighboring republics, the Transvaal and the Orange Free State, stood in his way. Their people were Afrikaners—Dutch who had originally settled the Cape in the seventeenth century, then after 1815, when England annexed the Cape of Good Hope, had made the "great trek" to escape from British rule. The Boers, as the English called them, from the Dutch word for "farmer," were simple, obstinate, and old-fashioned. They thought slavery not ungodly and disliked promoters, fortune hunters, foot-loose adventurers, mining-camp people, and other Uitlanders.

The discovery of diamonds and gold in the Transvaal brought the issue to a head. British capital and British people poured in. The Transvaal refused to pass legislation needed by the mining corporations and their employees. In 1895 Rhodes, attempting to precipitate revolution in the Transvaal, sent a party of armed irregulars, under Dr. Jameson, over its borders. This Jameson Raid was a

[23] See p. 626.

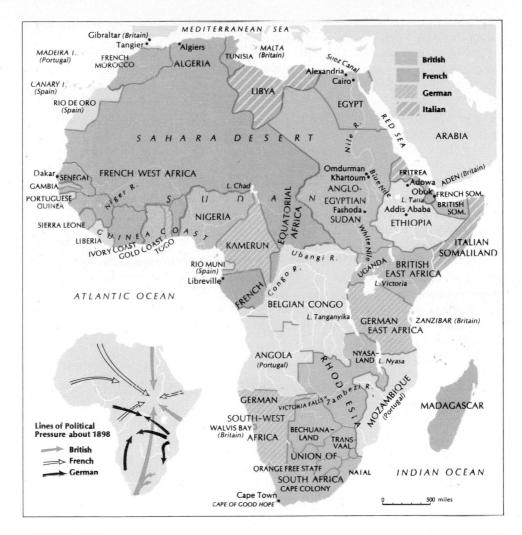

AFRICA, 1914

The map shows the recognized holdings of the Powers in 1914. The inset suggests the directions of political pressure about 1898. These pressures led to the Fashoda crisis in 1898 and the Boer War in 1899. In 1898 the British and German governments held secret discussions on the possible partitioning of the Portuguese colonies, which, however, never came to pass since the British greatly preferred to have the Portuguese colonies remain in the hands of Portugal.

failure, but in Europe a great cry went up against British bullying of a small inoffensive republic. The German emperor, William II, dispatched a famous telegram to Paul Kruger, president of the Transvaal, congratulating him on his driving off the invaders "without having to call for the support of friendly powers" —i.e., Germany. Three years later the British Empire went to war with the two Boer republics. It took another three years to subdue them. Once conquered and brought within the British Empire they were left with their self-governing institutions, and in 1910 they were joined with the Cape Colony and the predominantly

English Natal into the Union of South Africa, which received a semi-independence along the lines of the Dominion of Canada.

The Fashoda crisis and the Boer War, coming in rapid succession, revealed to the British the bottomless depths of their unpopularity in Europe. All European governments and peoples were pro-Boer; only the United States, involved at the time in a similar conquest of the Philippines, showed any sympathy for the British. The British, after the Boer War, began to rethink their international position, as will soon be seen.

As in the case of the Ottoman Empire, rivalry between the Great Powers over the spoils of Africa embittered international relations and helped prepare the way for the First World War. The rivalry over Morocco involving France and Germany entered into the general prewar crisis and will be related in the following chapter. As for Africa as a whole, there was little territorial change after the Boer War, although in 1911 Italy took Libya from the Turks. In 1914 the Germans were excluded from their short-lived empire. Had the Germans won the First World War, the map of Africa would probably have been greatly revised, but since they lost it the only change was to assign the German colonies, under international mandate, to the French and British. With this change, and except for Italy's ephemeral conquest of Ethiopia in 1935, the map of Africa remained what the brief years of partition had made it until the spectacular end of the European empires after the Second World War.[24]

82. IMPERIALISM IN ASIA: THE DUTCH, THE BRITISH, AND THE RUSSIANS

The Dutch East Indies and British India

British India and the Dutch East Indies, in the half-century before the First World War, were the world's ideal colonies. They illustrated the kind of empire that all imperialists would have wished to have, and a glance at them suggests the goal toward which imperialism was logically moving.

Whereas all countries of western Europe showed a surplus of imports, receiving more goods from the rest of the world than they sent out, India and Indonesia invariably, year after year and decade after decade, showed a surplus of exports, sending out far more goods than they took in. This export surplus was the hallmark of the developed colonial area, geared closely into the world market, with low purchasing power for the natives and kept going by foreign investment and management. Both regions, in addition, were so large as to have a good deal of internal business—commerce, insurance, banking, transportation—which never appeared in the statistics for world trade, but which, being dominated by Europeans, added immeasurably to their profits. Both had rich and varied natural resources, tropical in character, so that they never competed with the products of Europe—though India even before 1914 showed tendencies to industrialization. In both regions the people were adept and quick to learn. But they were divided by religion and language, so that, once conquered, they were relatively easy for Europeans to govern. Neither region before the First World War had any self-

---

[24] See pp. 876–882, and map, p. 879.

government at the highest levels. Both were ruled by a civil service, honest and high-minded by its own lights, in which the most illustrious, most influential, and best paying positions were reserved for Europeans. Hence upper-class families in England and the Netherlands valued their empires as fields of opportunity for their sons—somewhat as they had formerly valued an established church. In both India and Indonesia the governments were more or less benevolent despotisms, which, by curbing warfare, plague, and famine, at least allowed the population to grow in numbers. Java, with 5 million people in 1815, had 48 million in 1942. India's population in the same years probably grew from less than 200 million to almost 400 million. Finally, as the last virtue of a perfect colony, no foreign power directly challenged the British in India or the Dutch in their islands.

The Dutch in 1815 occupied little more than the island of Java itself.[25] In the following decades the British moved into Singapore, the Malay peninsula, and north Borneo, and made claims to Sumatra. The French in the 1860s appeared in Indochina. The Germans in the 1880s annexed eastern New Guinea and the Marshall and Solomon islands. Ultimately it was the mutual jealousy of these three that preserved the Dutch position. The Dutch, however, took the initiative themselves. To forestall occupation by other Europeans, and to put down native pirates and find raw materials that the world demanded, the Dutch spread their rule over the whole 3,000-mile extent of the archipelago. They created an empire, in place of the old chain of trading posts concerned only with buying and selling. Revolts were suppressed in 1830, 1849, and 1888; not till the twentieth century was northern Sumatra or the interior of Celebes brought under control. For some decades the Dutch exploited their huge empire by a kind of forced labor, the "culture system," in which the authorities required farmers to deliver, as a kind of tax, stated amounts of stated crops, such as sugar or coffee. After 1870 a freer system was introduced. The Dutch also, as an important matter of policy, favored instruction in the Malay and Javanese languages, not in Dutch. This preserved the native cultures from westernizing disintegration but at the same time meant that Western ideas of nationalism and democracy entered more slowly.

In India, in 1857, the British faced a dangerous rebellion, commonly called the Indian Mutiny, as if it had been a revolt of undisciplined soldiers only. The Indian army, with its sepoys, was the only organization through which Indians could exert any collective pressure.[26] The proportion of sepoys in the army was high in 1857 (about five-sixths) because British units had been withdrawn for the Crimean War and for action in China. Many Indians, outside the army, had been restless for decades. Rulers had been conquered and dethroned. Landowners had lost their property and been replaced by new ones more friendly to the British. Religious sentiments were inflamed. The British too obviously regarded Indian beliefs as repulsive; they had outlawed suttee, or widow burning, suppressed the Thugs, a small sect of holy assassins, and one British officer even declared that in ten years the government would abolish caste. The Muslims were agitated by Wahabi fundamentalism. Mysterious propaganda circulated over India. It infiltrated the sepoys, announcing to Muslim soldiers that certain newly issued cartridges were greased with the fat of a pig and to Hindus that the same cartridges were greased with the fat of a cow. Since for Hindus the cow was sacred, and for

25 See p. 162.
26 On the sepoys see p. 272.

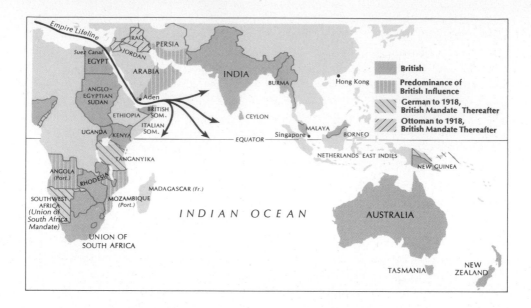

"THE BRITISH LAKE," 1918

This small map shows almost half the surface of the earth. All the most important parts of the British Empire are visible except Canada and the United Kingdom itself. All shores of the Indian Ocean are shown to be British, except for French Madagascar, the politically weak Portuguese, Italian, and Dutch colonies, and the Arabian and Persian coasts, in which British influence was strong. It is easy to see why the Mediterranean and the Suez Canal, leading from Europe into this half-world, were called the lifeline of the British Empire.

Muslims to touch pork was profane, much agitation was produced. The sepoys mutinied in the Ganges valley; and with them the other injured interests, including the far-faded Great Mogul and his court, rose against the British.

The British put down the rebellion, aided by the fact that western and southern India took no part in it. But the uprising persuaded the British to a radically new course of policy, pursued basically until the end of the Indian empire almost a century later. The British East India Company and the Mogul empire were both finally and forever done away with. British authorities ruled directly. But the British concluded that they must rule India with and through the Indians themselves, not against them. This in practice meant a collaboration between the imperial power and the Indian upper classes. The British began to shelter Indian vested interests. They supported the Indian landlords and became more indulgent toward Indian "superstition." Where before 1857, when they conquered an Indian state, they had simply abolished it and incorporated its territories, after the Mutiny they kept the remaining Indian states as protectorates. States existing in 1857, such as Hyderabad and Kashmir and over 200 others, with their galaxy of rajahs and maharajahs, carried on to the end of British rule in 1947. It was largely to provide a fitting summit for this mountain of Indian royalty that Queen Victoria was proclaimed empress of India in 1877.

India had been a considerable manufacturing country by preindustrial standards. Indian merchants had once been important throughout the Indian Ocean, and before 1800 Indian exports to Europe had included many textiles and other finished goods.[27] The native crafts collapsed before modern industrialism reinforced by political power. "India," observed a British expert in 1837, "can never again be a great manufacturing country, but by cultivating her connection with England she may be one of the greatest agricultural countries in the world." Free trade (made possible by military superiority, usually overlooked by the economists) turned Britain into the world's workshop and India into a supplier of raw materials. Indian exports, in the latter part of the nineteenth century, consisted increasingly of raw cotton, tea, jute, oilseeds, indigo, and wheat. The British shipped their manufactures in return. Business in India boomed; India came to have the densest railway network outside of Europe and North America. It is important to note, however, as a commentary on dealing with poor countries, that Britain in 1914 did far more trading with the 6 million people of Australia and New Zealand than with the 315 million impoverished people of India.

The British, in contrast to the Dutch, decided in 1835 to favor instruction in English, not in the native languages. The historian Macaulay, one of the commission to make this recommendation, branded the Indian languages as vehicles of barbarous and unenlightened ideas—a bar to progress. The British also, after the Mutiny, admitted Indians to the civil service and to governors' councils—sparingly indeed, but more than the Dutch in Indonesia. There were also many Indian businessmen. A class of westernized Indians grew up, speaking perfect English, and often educated in England. They demanded more of a role in the affairs of their country. In 1885 the predominantly Hindu Indian National Congress was organized; in 1906, the All-India Muslim League. Muslim separatism, while favored by the British and sometimes even blamed upon them, was natural to India and exploited by some Indian leaders. Nationalism spread. It became increasingly anti-British, and radical nationalism turned also against the Indian princes, capitalists, and businessmen, as accomplices in imperialism, and so took on the color of socialism. In the period of the First World War, under nationalist pressure, the British granted more representation to Indians, especially in provincial affairs, but the movement toward self-rule was never fast enough to overcome the basic anti-British feeling of the Indian peoples.

Conflict of Russian and British Interests

While no outsider yet threatened the British in India, British statecraft discerned in the northern sky a large cloud which was clearly approaching. The Russian empire had occupied northern Asia since the seventeenth century.[28] About 1850 Russian pressure on inner Asia was resumed. It was a type of imperialism in which neither the demand for markets nor for raw materials, nor for the investment of capital, counted for much. In these matters Russia was itself semicolonial with respect to the West. The Russians had, like the Westerners, a sense of spreading their type of civilization; but Russian expansion was distinctively political in that most of the initiative came from the government. Russia was an icebound

[27] See pp. 250–251.
[28] See pp. 228–229.

empire, craving "warm-water ports." It was a landlocked empire, so that which-ever way it turned it moved toward one ocean or another. The ocean was the do-main of the Westerners, and in particular the British. In the large picture, Russia pushed by land against the Ottoman Empire, Persia, India, and China, all of which the British (and others) reached by sea. In 1860, on the shores of the Sea of Japan, the Russians founded Vladivostok, the farthest-flung of all Slavic cities, whose name meant Lord of the East. But their advance in the mid-century was mainly in the arid and thinly settled regions of western Asia. The British had al-ready fought two Afghan wars to keep Afghanistan as a no man's land between Russia and India. In 1864 the Russians took Tashkent, in Turkestan. A decade later they touched India itself but were kept away by an Anglo-Russian agreement, which allotted a long tongue of land to Afghanistan and so separated the Indian and Russian empires by twenty miles—the new frontier, in the high Pamirs, on the Roof of the World, was to be sure, scarcely adapted to military operations.

Russian advances in Turkestan, east of the Caspian, increased the pressure on Persia, which had long felt the same pressure west of the Caspian, where cities like Tiflis and Baku, now Russian, had once been Persian. If Tiflis and Turkestan could fall to the Russian empire, there was no reason why Persia should not do so next—except that Persia had a seacoast and so might also be available for occu-pancy by the British. In 1864 a British company completed the first Persian tele-graph as part of the line from Europe to India. Other British investments and interests followed. Oil became important about 1900. In 1890, to bolster the Per-sian government against Russia, the British granted it a loan—taking the customs in Persian Gulf ports as collateral. In 1900 the Russian government granted the same favor, making its own loan to Persia, and appropriating as security all Per-sian customs except those of the Gulf. Russian ships appeared in the Persian Gulf in 1900, a demonstration soon countered by a state visit to Persia of the Viceroy of India, Lord Curzon. Clearly Persia was losing control of its own affairs, falling into zones, turning ripe for partition. A Persian nationalist revolution, directed against all foreigners and against the subservient government of the shah, broke out in 1905 and led to the assembly of the first parliament but hardly settled the question of Persian independence. In 1907 the British recognized a Russian "sphere of influence" in northern Persia, the Russians a British sphere in the south.[29]

Imperial ambitions had deepened the hostility between Great Britain and Rus-sia, with disputes over Persia and the Indian borderlands adding fuel to the quar-rel they had long waged over the Ottoman Empire. We have seen how the strug-gle for Africa had at the same time estranged Britain from France and indeed from all Europe.

83. IMPERIALISM IN ASIA: CHINA AND THE WEST

China before Western Penetration

But the biggest bone of imperialist contention was offered by China. On this bone every Great Power without exception tried to bite. The Manchu dynasty held a suzerainty over the whole area affected by Chinese civilization, from the mouth

---

[29] See p. 664, and map, 640.

of the Amur River (as far north as Labrador) to Burma and Indochina (as far south as Panama), and from the ocean westward into Mongolia and Tibet. In the old Chinese view China was the world itself, the Middle Kingdom between the upper and nether regions. The Europeans were outlandish barbarians. A few had trickled through to China since the European Middle Ages. But the Chinese people persistently wanted nothing to do with them.

China was moving into an upheaval of its own even before Western influence became of any importance. For 2,000 years the country had seen dynasties come and go in a kind of cycle. The Manchu dynasty in the nineteenth century was clearly nearing its end. It was failing to preserve order or to curb extortion. About 1800 a White Lotus Society revolted and was suppressed. In 1813 a Heavenly Reason Society attempted to seize Peking. In the 1850s a Muslim rebellion set up a temporary independent state in the southwest. Greatest of all the upheavals was the Taiping Rebellion of 1850, in which as many as 20 million people, approximately the population of Great Britain at the time, are thought to have perished. Except that some fragmentary Christian ideas, obtained from missionaries, were expressed by some of the Taipings, the rebellion was due entirely to Chinese causes. The rebels attacked the Manchus, who had come from Manchuria two centuries before, as corrupt foreigners ruling over China. Their grievances were poverty, extortion, rack-renting, and absentee landlords. The Taipings at first set up a state in south China, and their armies were at first disciplined, but the fighting lasted so long that both the Taiping leaders and the Manchu commanders sent against them got out of control, and much of the country sank into chronic banditry and disorder. It was in this period that China's war lords, men controlling armed forces but obeying no government, appeared. The Manchus managed to put down organized Taiping resistance after fourteen years, with some European assistance, led by the British General Gordon, the "Chinese Gordon" who later died at Khartoum. But it is clear that Chinese social confusion, agrarianism, and nationalism (the latter at first only anti-Manchu) antedated the impact of European imperialism.

Into this distracted China the Europeans began to penetrate about 1840. It became their policy to extort concessions from the Manchu empire but at the same time to defend the Manchu empire against internal opposition, as was shown by the exploits of Gordon. This was because they needed some kind of government in China with which they could make treaties, legalizing their claims and binding upon the whole country.

IMPERIALISM IN ASIA, 1840–1914

Boundaries and possessions are as of 1914. During these years the British and Dutch filled out their holdings in India and the East Indies, in each case moving outward from establishments founded long before. The Russians, who had long occupied Siberia, pressed southward in Central Asia, founded Vladivostok in 1860, and penetrated Manchuria at the close of the century. The French built an empire in Indochina, while the United States acquired the Philippines, and the Germans, as latecomers, were confined to miscellaneous parts of the western Pacific. The Japanese won control of Korea and replaced the Russians as the chief outside influence in Manchuria. Meanwhile all obtained special rights and concessions in China. A bid for such concessions by Italy was refused.

0 100 200 300 400 500 miles

ARCTIC

Archangel

St. Petersburg

Moscow

S I B

Yenisei R.

Ob R.

• Tobolsk

R   U   S   S   I   A   N   E   M   P

Samara

EUROPE

ASIA

Omsk

• Tomsk

TRANS-SIBERIAN RAILROAD

MEDITERRANEAN SEA

BLACK SEA

Constantinople

• Astrakhan

CASPIAN SEA   1846

ARAL SEA   1873

L. Balkhash

1854

OTTOMAN

Mosul

Baku   1873

1881   1864   Tashkent   1860-65

SINKIANG

EMPIRE

1884

1876

Cairo

Suez Canal

Jerusalem

Baghdad

Teheran

RUSSIAN SPHERE, 1907

Merv

BOKHARA

1885   1868

1895

Kashgar

Basra

PERSIA

BRITISH SPHERE, 1907

Kabul

AFGHAN-

ISTAN

Indus R.

KASHMIR

1846

T I

HIMALAYAS

HEJAZ

RED SEA

ARABIA

PERSIAN GULF

BALUCHISTAN

1883

PUNJAB

Delhi

NEPAL

Ganges R.

Mecca

OMAN

Karachi

INDIA

Calcut

A   F   R   I   C   A

YEMEN

Diu

(Portugal)

Bombay •

Hyderabad •

B   R   I   T   I   S   H

Yanaon

(France)

BAY OF

Aden *(Britain, 1839)*

Goa

(Portugal)

Madras

Pondicherry

(France)

Karikal *(France)*

CEYLON

JEHOL

MANCHURIA

Mukden

GREAT WALL

Kinchow

Peking

Tientsin   Taku

GULF OF CHILI

Dairen

Port Arthur

(Lease to Russia, 1898; Japan, 1905)

KOREA

Grand Canal

Tsinan

Chifu

• Wei-hai-wei

(Britain, 1898)

Kiao-chow

(Germany, 1898)   Tsingtao

YELLOW SEA

SHANTUNG

CRITICAL AREA, 1895-1905

0   100   200 miles

INDIAN OCEAN

OCEAN

ALASKA
(Purchased by U.S.A.
from Russia, 1867)

BERING SEA

ALEUTIAN I. (U.S.A., 1867)

KAMCHATKA

SEA OF
OKHOTSK

SAKHALIN

KURILE I.
(Japan, 1875)

KARAFUTO
(Japan, 1905)

Lena R.

Yakutsk

E R I A

I R E

L. Baikal
Irkutsk   Chita

AMUR PROVINCE
1858

Amur R.
MANCHURIA

Khabarovsk

MARITIME
PROVINCE
(Russia, 1868)

Vladivostok
1860

SEA OF
JAPAN

JAPANESE EMPIRE

Harbin

Urga

OUTER MONGOLIA
(Autonomous, 1912 Russian Sphere)

INNER MONGOLIA

Mukden

JEHOL

KOREA
(Japan, 1905, 1910)

Tokyo

Peking
Tientsin

Port Arthur
(Japan, 1905)

Kiao-chow
(Germany, 1898)

PACIFIC OCEAN

C H I N A

Hankow

Huang Ho

Nanking

Shanghai
(Britain, 1842)

Ningpo
1842

EAST
CHINA
SEA

RYUKYU I.

Chungking

Yangtse R.

Foochow

Lhasa

T

Amoy

FORMOSA (Japan, 1895)

PESCADORES (Japan, 1895)

MARIANA I.
(Germany, 1899)

Canton
(Britain, 1842)

YÜNNAN   KWANGSI
(French Sphere)

Hong Kong (Britain, 1842)

Maçao (Portugal, 1557)

GUAM
(U.S.A., 1898)

BHUTAN

Brahmaputra R.

Kwang-chow
(Lease to France, 1898)

HAINAN

BURMA
(Britain, 1852, 1885)

Hanoi

ANNAM

Mekong R.

FRENCH
INDOCHINA
1884, 1907

Manila

PHILIPPINE I.
(U.S.A., 1898, 1899)

CAROLINE I.
(Germany, 1899)

INDIA
1852

Rangoon

SIAM

1826
Bangkok

SOUTH
CHINA SEA

Saigon

YAP

PALAU I.

BENGAL

ANDAMAN I.
(Britain)

BRITISH
NORTH BORNEO
1888

NEW GUINEA

KAISER WILHEMSLAND
(Germany, 1884)

SARAWAK
1888

MALAY STATES
(Britain, 1800, 1824)

BORNEO

CELEBES

Singapore
(Britain, 1819)

SUMATRA

D U T C H   E A S T   I N D I E S

(Portugal, 1859)

TIMOR   Darwin

AUSTRALIA

Batavia

JAVA

The Opening of China to the West

The modern phase of Chinese relations with the West was inauspiciously opened by the Opium War of 1839–1841. We have already observed how, though Europeans wanted Chinese products, the Chinese had no interest in buying European products in return. Trade therefore was difficult, and the British East India Company had for decades solved the problem of getting Chinese tea for Europe by shipping Indian-grown opium in return, since opium was one available commodity for which a Chinese demand existed.[30] When the Chinese government attempted to control the inflow of opium the British government went to war. Fifteen years later, in 1857, Britain and France combined in a second war upon China to force the Chinese to receive their diplomats and deal with their traders. The Chinese proving contumacious, 17,000 French and British soldiers entered Peking and deliberately burned the emperor's very extensive Summer Palace, an appalling act of vandalism from which soldiers brought back so much loot—vases, tapestries, porcelain, enamels, jades, wood carvings—as to set a fashion in Europe and America for Chinese art.

From the first of these wars arose the treaty of Nanking (1842), from the second the treaties of Tientsin (1857), whose terms were soon duplicated in still other treaties signed by China with other European powers and with the United States. The resulting complex of interlocking agreements imposed certain restrictions on China, or conferred certain rights upon foreigners, which came to be known as the "treaty system." To the British in 1842 the Chinese ceded the island of Hong Kong outright, and somewhat later granted adjoining territories on a long lease. They opened over a dozen cities, including Shanghai and Canton, to Europeans as "treaty ports." In these cities Europeans were allowed to make settlements of their own, immune to all Chinese law. Europeans traveling in the Chinese empire remained subject only to their own governments, and European and American gunboats began to police the Yangtse River. The Chinese likewise paid large war indemnities, though it was they themselves who suffered most of the damages. They agreed to levy no import duty over 5 percent and so became a free trade market for European products. To administer and collect the customs a staff of European experts was introduced. Money from the customs, collected with a new efficiency, on a swelling volume of imports, went in part to the British and French in payment of the indemnities, but part remained with the Manchu government, which, as noted, the Europeans had no desire to overthrow.

Annexations and Concessions

While China was thus permeated at the center like an aging cheese, by extraterritorial and other insidious privileges for Europeans, whole slabs of it were cut away at the outer rim. The Russians moved down the Amur River, established their Maritime Province, and founded Vladivostok in 1860. The Japanese, now sufficiently westernized to behave like Europeans in such matters, in 1876 recognized the independence of Korea. The British annexed Burma in 1886. The French in 1883 assumed a protectorate over Annam despite Chinese protests; they soon combined five areas—Annam, Cochin China, Tonkin, Laos, and Cambodia

---

[30] See pp. 251, 341.

—into French Indochina. (The first three were known also as Vietnam, a word not familiar in the West until after the Second World War.) These outlying territories had never, it is true, been integral parts of China proper; but it was with China that they had had their most important political and cultural relations and to the Chinese emperor that they had paid tribute.

Japan, whose modernization has been described already, lost little time in developing an imperialistic urge.[31] An expansionist party already looked to the Chinese mainland and to the south. Japanese imperialism first revealed itself to the rest of the world in 1894, when Japan went to war with China over disputes in Korea. The Japanese soon won, equipped as they were with modern weapons, training, and organization. They obliged the Chinese to sign the treaty of Shimonoseki in 1895, by which China ceded Formosa and the Liaotung peninsula to Japan and recognized Korea as an independent state. The Liaotung was a tongue of land reaching down from Manchuria to the sea; at its tip was Port Arthur. Manchuria was the northeastern part of China itself.

This sudden Japanese triumph precipitated a crisis in the Far East. No one had realized how strong Japan had become. All were astounded that a people who were not "European," i.e., white, should show such aptitude for modern war and diplomacy. It was to be supposed that Japan had designs on Manchuria.

Now it so happened that Russia, not long before, in 1891, had begun to build the Trans-Siberian Railway, whose eastern terminus was to be Vladivostok, the "Lord of the East." Manchuria extended northward in a great hump between central Siberia and Vladivostok. The Russians, whether or not they ever dominated Manchuria themselves, could not allow its domination by another Great Power. It happened also that Germany was at this time looking for a chance to enter the Far Eastern arena, and that France had formed an alliance with Russia, whose good will it was eager to retain.[32]

Russia, Germany, and France therefore registered an immediate joint demurrer with the Tokyo Foreign Office. They demanded that Japan give up the Liaotung peninsula. The Japanese hesitated; they were indignant, but they yielded. The Liaotung went back to China.

In China many alert people were humiliated at the defeat by the Japanese whom they had despised. The Chinese government, at last facing the inevitable, began madly to plan westernization. Huge loans were obtained from Europe—the customs being pawned as security, following the pattern well established in Turkey, Persia, and Santo Domingo. But the European powers did not wish China to become consolidated too soon. Nor had they forgotten the sudden apparition of Japan. The result was a frantic scramble for further concessions in 1898.

It seemed in 1898 as if the Chinese empire in its turn would be partitioned. The Germans extorted a ninety-nine-year lease on Kiaochow Bay, plus exclusive rights in the Shantung peninsula. The Russians took a lease on the Liaotung peninsula from which they had just excluded Japan; they thus obtained Port Arthur and rights to build railroads in Manchuria to interlock with their Trans-Siberian system. The French took Kwangchow and the British Wei-hai-wei, in addition to confirming their sphere of influence in the Yangtse valley. The Italians demanded a share but were refused. The United States, fearing that all China

---

[31] See pp. 548–549.
[32] See pp. 661–662.

NORTHEAST CHINA AND ADJOINING REGIONS, 1895–1914

This area has long been one of the world's trouble zones. Note how Vladivostok is shut off from the ocean by the Japanese islands and Korea, and almost shut off from the mass of Russia by the intervening bulk of Manchuria. Manchuria, which began to be industrialized about 1900, became an object of dispute between China, to which it belonged historically, the Russian empire, to which it had strategic value and offered an access to the open ocean, and the Japanese empire, which found in it an outlet for commercial and military expansion and a buffer against Russia. Manchuria was dominated by the Russians from 1898 to 1905, by the Japanese from 1905 to 1945, and again by the Russians from 1945 to 1950, when they handed over their concessions and privileges to the Chinese Communist government. Korea was dominated by Japan after its victories over China in 1895 and over Russia in 1905. After World War II, Korea was promised independence but was divided at the 38th parallel into a Russian occupation zone and an American zone. After the Korean War (1950–1953, see pp. 915–917) the country remained divided at roughly the same parallel with a Communist regime in the north and a Western-sponsored regime in the south.

might soon be parceled out into exclusive spheres, announced its policy of the Open Door. The idea of the Open Door was that China should remain territorially intact and independent, and that powers having special concessions or spheres of influence should maintain the 5 percent Chinese tariff and allow businessmen of all nations to trade without discrimination. The British supported the Open Door, as a means of discouraging actual annexations by Japan or Russia, which, as the only Great Powers adjacent to China, were the only ones that could dispatch real armies into its territory. The Open Door was a program not so much of leaving China to the Chinese, as of assuring that all outsiders should find it literally "open."

If the reader will imagine what the United States would be like if foreign warships patrolled the Mississippi as far as St. Louis, if foreigners came and went throughout the country without being under its laws, if New York, New Orleans, and other cities contained foreign settlements outside its jurisdiction, but in which all banking and management were concentrated, if foreigners determined the tariff policy, collected the proceeds, and remitted much of the money to their own governments, if the western part of the city of Washington had been burned (the Summer Palace), Long Island and California annexed to distant empires (Hong Kong and Indochina), and all New England were coveted by two immediate neighbors (Manchuria), if the national authorities were half in collusion with these foreigners and half victimized by them, and if large areas of the country were the prey to bandits, guerrillas, and revolutionary secret societies conspiring against the helpless government and occasionally murdering some of the foreigners—then he can understand how observant Chinese felt at the end of the last century, and why the term "imperialism" came to be held by so many of the world's peoples in abomination.

One Chinese secret society, its name somewhat literally translated as the Order of Literary Patriotic Harmonious Fists, and so dubbed the Boxers by the amused Westerners, broke out in insurrection in 1899. The Boxers pulled up railway tracks, fell upon Chinese Christians, besieged the foreign legations, and killed about 300 foreigners. The European powers, joined by Japan and the United States, sent a combined international force against the insurgents, who were put down. The victors imposed still more severe controls on the Chinese government

Spheres of Influence About 1900

	Russian
	British
	German

and inflicted an indemnity of $330 million. Of this the United States received $24 million, of which, in 1924, it canceled the balance that was still due. On the other hand, as a consequence of the Boxer Rebellion, the Manchu officials strove desperately to strengthen themselves by westernization, while at the same time the revolutionary movement in China, aiming at expulsion of Manchus and foreigners alike, spread rapidly throughout the country, especially in the south, under the leadership of Sun Yat-sen.

84. THE RUSSO-JAPANESE WAR AND ITS CONSEQUENCES

Meanwhile Russia and Japan opposed each other's intrigues in Manchuria and Korea. The Japanese felt a need for supplying their new factories with raw materials and markets on the Asian mainland, for employment for their newly westernized army and navy, and for recognized status as a Great Power in the Western sense. The Russian government needed an atmosphere of crisis and expansion to stifle criticism of tsarism at home; it could not abide the presence of a strong power directly on its East Asian frontier; it could use Manchuria and Korea to strengthen the exposed outpost of Vladivostok, which was somewhat squeezed against the sea and landlocked by Japanese waters. The Russians had obtained a concession from China to build the Chinese Eastern Railway to Vladivostok across the heart of Manchuria. A railway, in Manchuria, implied special zones, railway guards, mining and timber rights, and other auxiliary activities. The Japanese saw the fruits of their successful war of 1895 against China greedily enjoyed by their rival. In 1902 Japan signed a military alliance with Great Britain. We have seen how the British were alarmed by their diplomatic isolation after Fashoda and the Boer War, and how for many years, in the Far East, the Middle East, and the Near East, they had been expecting to have trouble with Russia. The Anglo-Japanese military alliance lasted twenty years.

War broke out in 1904, undeclared, by Japanese naval attack on Russian installations at Port Arthur. Both sides sent large armies into Manchuria. The battle of Mukden, in the number of men engaged, which was 624,000, was the largest battle that human experience had thus far witnessed. Military observers were present from all countries, anxiously trying to learn what the next war in Europe would be like. The Russians sent their Baltic fleet around three continents to the Far East, but to the world's amazement the Russian fleet was met and destroyed at Tsushima Strait by the new and untested navy of Japan. Russian communications by sea were thereby broken, and since the Trans-Siberian Railway was unfinished, and since the Japanese also won the battle of Mukden, Russia was beaten.

At this point the president of the United States, Theodore Roosevelt, stepped upon the scene. With an outpost in the Philippines and growing interests in China, it was to the American advantage to have neither side win too overwhelming a victory in the Far East. The most imperially minded of all American presidents offered his mediation, and plenipotentiaries of the two powers met at Portsmouth, New Hampshire. By the treaty of Portsmouth, in 1905, Japan recovered from Russia what it had won and lost in 1895, namely, Port Arthur and the Liaotung peninsula, a preferred position in Manchuria, which remained nominally Chinese, and a protectorate in Korea, which remained nominally independent, although a few years later in 1910, it was annexed by Japan. Japan also received from Russia the southern half of the island of Sakhalin. Much of what Russia lost to Japan in 1905 was regained forty years later at the end of the Second World War.

The Russo-Japanese War was the first war between Great Powers since 1870. It was the first war fought under conditions of developed industrialism. It was the first actual war between westernized powers to be caused by competition in the exploitation of undeveloped countries. Most significant of all (except for the Ethiopian rout of the Italians), it was the first time that a nonwhite people had defeated a white people in modern times. Asians had shown that they could learn and play, in less than half a century, the game of the Europeans.

The Japanese victory set off long chains of repercussions in at least three different directions. For one thing, the Russian government, frustrated in its foreign policy in East Asia, shifted its attention back to Europe, where it resumed an active role in the affairs of the Balkans. This contributed to a series of international crises in Europe, of which the result was the First World War. Second, the tsarist government was so weakened by the war, both in prestige and in actual military strength, and opinion in Russia was so disgusted at the clumsiness and incompetency with which the war had been handled, that the various underground movements were able to come to the surface, producing the Revolution of 1905. This in turn was a prelude to the great Russian Revolution twelve years later, of which Soviet communism was the outcome. Third, news of Japan's victory over Russia electrified those who heard of it throughout the non-European world. The fact that Japan was itself an imperialist power was overlooked in the excited realization that the Japanese were not white. Only half a century ago the Japanese, too, had been "backward"—defenseless, bombarded, and bulldozed by the Europeans. The moral was clear. Everywhere leaders of subjugated peoples concluded, from the Japanese precedent, that they must bring Western science and industry to their own countries, but that they must do it, as the Japanese had done, by getting rid of control by the Europeans, supervising the process of modernization themselves, and preserving their own native national character. Nationalist revolutions began in Persia in 1905, in Turkey in 1908, in China in 1911. In India and Indonesia many were stirred by the Japanese achievement. In the face of rising agitation, the British admitted an Indian to the Viceroy's executive Council in 1909, and in 1916 the Dutch created a People's Council, to include Indonesian members, in the Indies. The self-assertion of Asians was to grow in intensity after the First World War.

The Japanese victory and Russian defeat can therefore be seen as steps in three mighty developments, the First World War, the Russian Revolution, and the Revolt of Asia. These three together put an end to Europe's world supremacy and almost to European civilization; or at least they so transmuted them as to make the world of the twentieth century far different from that of the nineteenth.

The British in India

The British presence in India, reaching over three centuries, spanned the whole period from the early trading empires to the latest phases of European imperialism. In the seventeenth century the Indian subcontinent was held together by a Muslim empire whose ruler was known in Europe as the Great Mogul. His revenues, in 1605, were some twenty times greater than those of the King of England. The Europeans were for a long time only handfuls of foreigners operating out of small coastal stations. After 1700 the Mogul authority fell to pieces, leaving a disorganized situation in which the British emerged as the supreme power throughout the country.

India in the nineteenth century represented, in its full form, the European imperialism that by 1900 reached throughout Asia and Africa. Parts of it were ruled by the British directly, parts through the rajahs and maharajahs of Indian states. British power prevented internal warfare and subordinated the conflicts between Hindus and Muslims. Peace generally prevailed except for the great Mutiny, or rebellion, of 1857, which was quickly suppressed. The British introduced their own ideas of law, government, civil service, and education. With food production increased by irrigation and famine relieved by transport of provisions by railroad, population grew very rapidly.

The British invested a great deal of capital in India, in railroads, coal mines, and tea plantations. There was also much development of Indian capital, especially in the new jute, cotton, and steel industries. As the railroad opened the interior to the cheaper products of Lancashire, the old handicraft and village industries were destroyed, to be symbolically revived by Gandhi and his spinning wheel in the 1920s, and in fact replaced by an extensive development of modern manufactures. India moved into the twentieth century as a land of violent contrasts, of endless villages interrupted by teeming cities, with staggering problems of poverty and overpopulation, yet also as an important industrial country with a heavy involvement in world trade.

The British, throughout their rule in India, lived very much to themselves, occasionally mixing with the Indian upper classes but avoiding intimate or even equal relationships. For many Indians, nevertheless, English became a second language, used both for contacts with the Western world and as a common medium among themselves. A modern Indian upper class, largely English-speaking, grew up with the development of business, government, and the professions. It ultimately took the lead in the national movement against foreign rule. But historic divisions within the country, between Hindu and Muslim, dating back to the Mogul empire and before, brought it about that upon the British withdrawal, in 1947, what had formerly been known as India became the separate states of India and Pakistan. Later Bangladesh was formed by secession from Pakistan.

The gorgeous East, as Milton called it, had been fabled in Europe for its riches since ancient times. Above, right, we see the weighing of the Great Mogul on his birthday, upon which he was to receive an equal weight in gold and jewels. The picture is from an English geography of 1782. As the French "Encyclopédie" put it at about this time: "The most solemn day of the year was when the emperor was weighed in golden balances in the presence of the people; on that day he received over 50 millions in presents."

At the left is the English factory at Surat, near Bombay, in the early seventeenth century. A "factory" was only a trading center where the agents, or factors, of the East India Company stored their goods.

Calcutta, now the largest city in India, is far from being one of the oldest. It was founded by the English East India Company in 1690, and acquired many Western-style buildings in the two following centuries. At the left above is the Old Court House; at the right the early nineteenth-century Government House, with a large British lion astride the neo-classic gate. At the left an English lady is carried in a palanquin, and in both pictures important persons ride by in carriages, surveyed at a distance by some of the plain people of India, one of them with a bullock cart. The two cultures never really merged.

Darjeeling, in the mountains 300 miles north of Calcutta, grew up after 1840 as a cool retreat for Britons in refuge from the Indian heat. At the left is the "big loop" of the Darjeeling Railway, a substantial feat of engineering, by which the imperial rulers were able to make the journey more comfortably. The clouds probably obscure a view of the Himalayas for which Darjeeling is famous.

653

The railroad also had a transforming impact on India as a whole. By carrying goods it brought the interior into the world market, breaking up old native industries while creating new ones, and by transporting persons it drew together the members of diverse religions, castes, and linguistic groups. A passenger train of 1863 appears above. In its crowded coaches Indians who in former times would have kept scrupulously apart, for fear of pollution, had to rub elbows together, and on long journeys even eat together and breathe the same tainted air. Such proximity, together with the increasing adoption of English, produced a new basis for Indian unity which in the end was to make the British position untenable.

At the right, before the track is laid, a team of elephants hauls the first locomotive into Indore in Central India.

Above left: Queen Victoria is proclaimed Empress of India at Bombay in 1877. The neo-Gothic canopy, built for the occasion, under which an effigy of the queen is enthroned, seems incongruous in the circumstances. It reminds us, together with the more permanent church in the background, that the British maintained their own ways with supreme confidence, making few concessions to the alien culture over which they presided.

In the nineteenth century the traveling Englishwoman became legendary for her indomitability. At the right, two of them go on a jungle picnic. The pith helmets of their escorts, and the bearer carrying the refreshments on his head, may be taken as symbols of the heyday of empire.

656

The two scenes depicted in the drawings above represent the administration of justice, with a British magistrate at the left, a native magistrate at the right. They seem much alike, and their purpose may be to show how under British rule the Indian judicial system was brought up to British standards of legal procedure.

Many Indians received a thoroughly English education. At the far right is Jawaharlal Nehru at Harrow about 1905. Nehru, born in 1889 of Brahmin parents, his father a wealthy lawyer, was educated at home by English tutors, then sent to Harrow and Cambridge. He joined Gandhi in the independence movement in the 1920s, and served as first prime minister of independent India from 1947 until his death in 1964. British India dug its own grave, or prepared its own successors.

658

XVI.
The First
World War

S omewhere before 1914 Europe went off its course. Europeans believed themselves to be heading for a kind of high plateau, full of a benign progress and more abundant civilization, in which the benefits of modern science and invention would be more widely diffused, and even competitive struggle worked out somehow for the best. Instead, Europe stumbled in 1914 into disaster. It is not easy to see exactly where Europe went astray, at what point, that is, the First World War became inevitable, or (since the human mind does not know what is truly inevitable) so overwhelmingly probable that only the most Olympian statesmanship could have avoided it.

85. THE INTERNATIONAL ANARCHY

After 1870 Europe lived in a repressed fear of itself. The great questions of the mid-century had been settled by force. The German Empire was only the strongest and most obvious of the new structures which armed power had reared. Never had the European states maintained such huge armies in peacetime as at the beginning of the twentieth century. One, two, or even three years of compulsory

Chapter Emblem: A German medal to celebrate the sinking of the Lusitania in 1915, showing the Cunard Line as a skeleton selling tickets, under an inscription, "Business First."

military service for all young men became the rule. In 1914 each of the Continental Great Powers had not only a huge standing army but millions of trained reserves among the civilian population. Few people wanted war; all but a few sensational writers preferred peace in Europe, but many took it for granted that war would come some day. In the last years before 1914 the idea that war was bound to break out sooner or later probably made some statesmen, in some countries, more willing to unleash it.

Rival Alliances: Triple Alliance versus Triple Entente

Political diagnosticians, from Richelieu to Metternich, had long thought that an effective union of Germany would revolutionize the relationships of Europe's peoples. After 1870 their anticipations were more than confirmed. Once united (or almost united), the Germans entered upon their industrial revolution. Manufacturing, finance, shipping, population grew phenomenally. In steel, for example, of which Germany in 1865 produced less than France, by 1900 Germany produced more than France and Great Britain combined. Germans felt that they needed and deserved a "place in the sun," by which they vaguely meant some kind of acknowledged supremacy like that of the British. Neither the British nor the French, the leaders of modern Europe since the seventeenth century, could share wholeheartedly in such German aspirations. The French had the chronic grievance of Alsace and Lorraine, annexed to Germany in 1871. The British as the years passed saw German salesmen appear in their foreign markets, selling goods often at lower prices and by what seemed ungentlemanly methods; they saw Germans turn up as colonial rivals in Africa, the Near East, and the Far East; and they watched other European states gravitate into the Berlin orbit, looking to the mighty German Empire as a friend and protector to secure or advance their interests.

Bismarck after 1871 feared that in another European war his new German Empire might be torn to pieces. He therefore followed, until his retirement in 1890, a policy of peace. We have seen him as the "honest broker" at the Berlin Congress of 1878, helping to adjudicate the Eastern Question, and again offering the facilities of Berlin in 1885 to regulate African affairs.[1] To isolate France, divert it from Europe, and keep it embroiled with Britain, he looked with satisfaction on French colonial expansion. He took no chances, however; in 1879 he formed a military alliance with Austria-Hungary, to which Italy was added in 1882. Thus was formed the Triple Alliance, which lasted until the First World War. Its terms were, briefly, that if any member became involved in war with two or more powers its allies should come to its aid by force of arms. To be on the safe side, Bismarck signed a "reinsurance" treaty with Russia also; since Russia and Austria were enemies (because of the Balkans), to be allied to both at the same time took considerable diplomatic finesse. After Bismarck's retirement his system proved too intricate, or too lacking in candor, for his successors to manage. The Russo-German agreement lapsed. The French, faced by the Triple Alliance, soon seized the opportunity to form their own alliance with Russia, the Franco-Russian Alliance signed in 1894. In its time this was regarded as politically almost impossible. The French Republic stood for everything radical, the Russian empire for every-

---

[1] See pp. 624, 628–630.

thing reactionary and autocratic. But ideology was thrown to the winds, French capital poured into Russia, and the tsar bared his head to the *Marseillaise.*

The Continent was thus divided by 1894 into two opposed camps, the German-Austrian-Italian against the Franco-Russian. For a time it seemed that this rigid division might soften. Germany, France, and Russia cooperated in the Far Eastern crisis of 1895.[2] All were anti-British at the time of Fashoda and the Boer War. The Kaiser, William II, outlined tempting pictures of a Continental league against the global hegemony of England and her empire.

Much depended on what the British would do. They had long prided themselves on a "splendid isolation," going their own way, disdaining the kind of dependency that alliance with others always brings. Fashoda and the Boer War came as a shock. British relations with France and Russia were very bad. Some in England, including Joseph Chamberlain, therefore thought that a better understanding with Germany was to be sought. Arguments of race, in this race-conscious age, made Englishmen and Germans feel akin.[3] But politically it was hard to cooperate. The Kaiser's Kruger Telegram of 1896 was a studied insult.[4] Then in 1898 the Germans decided to build a navy.

A new kind of "race" now entered the picture, the naval competition between Germany and Great Britain. British sea power for two centuries had been all too successful. The American Admiral Mahan, teaching at the Naval War College, and taking his examples largely from British history, argued that sea power had been the foundation of Britain's greatness, and that in the long run sea power must always choke off and ruin a power operating on the land. Nowhere were Mahan's books read with more interest than in Germany. The German naval program, mounting rapidly after 1898, in a few years became a source of concern to the British, and by 1912 was felt as a positive menace. The Germans insisted that they must have a navy to protect their colonies, secure their foreign trade, and "for the general purposes of their greatness." The British held with equal

---

[2] See pp. 643–644.

[3] The will of Cecil Rhodes, who died in 1902, illustrates this point. Rhodes left most of his fortune (£6 million) to establish scholarships at Oxford to be awarded to students in the United States, as an Anglo-Saxon country, the British dominions and colonies, and Germany. The German Rhodes Scholarships were suspended from 1914 to 1930 and again after 1938. The same feeling that Germans were racially akin was common in the United States also; a prominent example of this viewpoint was President Theodore Roosevelt.

[4] See p. 633.

ANGLO-GERMAN INDUSTRIAL COMPETITION, 1898 AND 1913

This diagram really shows two things: first, the huge increase in world trade in the last fifteen years before the First World War, shared in by all countries; and second, the fact that German exports grew more rapidly than British. The exports of both countries together, as shown on the diagram, multiplied no less than threefold in these fifteen years. The increase, while due in small part to a slight rise of prices, was mainly due to a real increase in volume of business. If the reader will compare the shaded bands within the large arrows he will see that, for the countries shown, British exports about doubled, but those of Germany multiplied many times. In 1913 total German exports about equaled the British, but German exports to the United States and Russia greatly exceeded the British. Note how the Germans even gained in exports to British India, where the liberalism of British policy freely admitted competitive goods. In merchant marine, though the Germans doubled their tonnage, the British continued to enjoy an overwhelming lead.

EXPORTS TO:

HUNDRED MILLIONS OF DOLLARS

0 1 2 3 4 5 10 15 20 25

UNITED STATES
1898
1913
1898
1913

BRITISH INDIA
1898
1913
1898
1913

RUSSIA
1898
1913
1898
1913

ARGENTINE
1898
1913
1898
1913

CHINA
1898
1913
1898
1913

TOTAL EXPORTS
TO ALL COUNTRIES,
FOREIGN AND
COLONIAL,
1898 AND 1913
1898
1913
1898
1913

GREAT BRITAIN
GERMANY

MILLIONS OF TONS

MERCHANT MARINE

0 1 2 3 4 5 6 7 8 9 10 15

GREAT BRITAIN
1898
1913

GERMANY
1898
1913

resolution that England, as a densely populated industrial island, dependent even for food upon imports, must at all costs control the sea in both peace and war. They adhered stubbornly to their traditional policy of maintaining a navy as large as the next two combined. The naval race led both sides to enormous and increasing expenditures. In the British it produced a sense of profound insecurity, driving them as the years passed ever more inescapably into the arms of Russia and France.

Slowly and cautiously the British emerged from their diplomatic isolation. In 1902 they formed a military alliance with Japan against their common enemy, Russia.[5] The decisive break came in 1904, from which may be dated the immediate series of crises issuing in the World War ten years later.

In 1904 the British and French governments agreed to forget Fashoda and the accumulated bad feeling of the preceding twenty-five years. The French recognized the British occupation of Egypt, and the British recognized the French penetration of Morocco. They also cleared up a few lesser colonial differences and agreed to support each other against protests by third parties. There was no specific alliance; neither side said what it would do in the event of war; it was only a close understanding, an *entente cordiale*. The French immediately tried to reconcile their new friend to their ally, Russia. After defeat by Japan the Russians proved amenable. The British, increasingly uncertain of German aims, proved likewise willing. In 1907 Britain and Russia, the inveterate adversaries, settled their differences in an Anglo-Russian Convention. In Persia, the British recognized a Russian sphere of influence in the north, the Russians a British sphere in the south and east. By 1907 England, France, and Russian were acting together. The older Triple Alliance faced a newer Triple Entente, the latter somewhat the looser, since the British refused to make any formal military commitments.

The Crises in Morocco and the Balkans

The Germans, who already felt encircled by the alliance of France and Russia, naturally watched with concern the drift of England into the Franco-Russian camp. The Entente Cordiale was barely concluded when the German government decided to test it, to find out how strong it really was, or how far the British would really go in support of France. The French, now enjoying British backing, were taking over more police powers, concessions, and loans in Morocco. In March 1905 William II disembarked from a German warship at Tangier, where he made a startling speech in favor of Moroccan independence. To diplomats everywhere this carefully staged performance was a signal: Germany was attempting not primarily to keep France out of Morocco, nor even to reserve Morocco for itself, but to break up the new understanding between France and England. The Germans demanded and obtained an international conference at Algeciras (at which the United States was represented), but the conference, which met in 1906, supported the French claims in Morocco, only Austria voting with Germany. The German government had thus created an incident and been rebuffed. The British, disturbed by German diplomatic tactics, stood by the French all the more firmly. French and British army and naval officers now began to discuss common plans. Distrust of Germany also inclined the British to bury

[5] See p. 646.

the hatchet with Russia in the next year. The German attempt to break the Entente simply made it more solid.

In 1911 came a second Morocco crisis. A German gunboat, the *Panther*, arrived at Agadir "to protect German interests." It soon developed that the move was a holdup; the Germans offered to make no further trouble in Morocco if they could have the French Congo. The crisis passed, the Germans obtaining some trifling accessions in Africa. But a member of the British cabinet, David Lloyd George, made a rather inflammatory speech on the German menace.

Meanwhile a series of crises rocked the Balkans. Here at the opening of the twentieth century the situation was very confused. The Ottoman Empire, in an advanced state of dissolution, still held a band of territory from Constantinople westward to the Adriatic.[6] South of this band lay an independent Greece. North of it, on the Black Sea side, lay an autonomous Bulgaria and an independent Rumania. In the center and west of the peninsula, north of the Turkish belt, was the small, landlocked independent kingdom of Serbia, adjoined by Bosnia-Herzegovina, which belonged legally to Turkey but had been "occupied and administered" by Austria since 1878. Within the Austro-Hungarian Empire, adjoining Bosnia on the north, lay Croatia and Slovenia.

Serbs, Bosnians, Croats, and Slovenes all spoke basically the same language, the main difference being that Serbs and Bosnians wrote with the eastern or Cyrillic alphabet, the Croats and Slovenes with the western or Roman. With the Slavic Revival and general growth of nationalism these peoples came to feel that they were really one people, for which they took the term South Slavs or Yugoslavs. We have seen how when the Dual Monarchy was formed in 1867, the Slavs of the Habsburg empire were kept subordinate to the German Austrians and to the Magyars.[7] By 1900 the most radical Slav nationalists within the empire had concluded that the Dual Monarchy would never grant them equal status, that it must be broken up, and that all South Slavs should form an independent state of their own. Concretely, this meant that an element of the Austro-Hungarian population, namely, the Croatian and Slovenian nationalists, wished to get out of the empire and join with Serbia across the border. Serbia became the center of South Slav agitation. The Serbs conceived of their small kingdom as the Piedmont of a South Slav Risorgimento, the nucleus around which a new national state could be formed, at the expense of Austria-Hungary, which, to repeat, contained Croatia-Slovenia within its own frontiers and "occupied" Bosnia.

This brew was brought to a boil in 1908 by two events. First, the Young Turks, whose long agitation against Abdul Hamid has been noted, managed in that year to carry through a revolution.[8] They obliged the sultan to restore the liberal-parliamentary constitution of 1876. They showed, too, that they meant to stop the dissolution of the Ottoman Empire, by taking steps to have delegates from Bulgaria and Bosnia sit in the new Ottoman parliament. Second, Russia, its foreign policy in the Far East ruined by the Japanese war, turned actively to the Balkan and Turkish scene. Russia, as always, wanted control at Constantinople. Austria wanted full annexation of Bosnia, the better to discourage Pan-Yugoslav ideas. But if the Young Turks really modernized and strengthened the Ottoman Empire, Austria would never get Bosnia nor the Russians Constantinople.

[6] See maps, pp. 441, 625, and 667.
[7] See p. 530.
[8] See pp. 622–623.

The Russian and Austrian foreign ministers, Isvolsky and Aehrenthal, at a conference at Buchlau in 1908 came to a secret agreement. They would call an international conference, at which Russia would favor Austrian annexation of Bosnia, and Austria would support the opening of the Straits to Russian warships. Austria, without waiting for a conference, proclaimed the annexation of Bosnia without more ado. This infuriated the Serbs, who had marked Bosnia for their own. Meanwhile, that same year, the Bulgarians and the Cretans broke finally with the Ottoman Empire, Bulgaria becoming fully independent, Crete uniting with Greece. Isvolsky was never able to realize his plans for Constantinople. His partners in the Triple Entente, Britain and France, refused to back him; the British in particular were evasive on plans for opening the Straits to the Russian fleet. The projected international conference was never called. In Russia itself public opinion knew nothing of Isvolsky's secret deal. The known fact in Russia was that the Serbs, the little Slav brothers of Russia, had their toes rudely stepped on by the Austrians by the annexation of Bosnia.

This "first Balkan crisis" presently passed. The Russians, weakened by the Japanese war and by recent revolution,[9] accepted the Austrian *fait accompli*. Russia protested but backed down. Austrian influence in the Balkans seemed to be growing. And South Slav nationalism was frustrated and inflamed.

In 1911 Italy declared war on Turkey, from which it soon conquered Tripoli and the Dodecanese Islands. With the Ottomans thus embarrassed, Bulgaria, Serbia, and Greece joined forces in their own war against Turkey, hoping to annex certain Balkan territories to which they believed they had a right. Turkey was soon defeated, but the Bulgarians claimed more of Macedonia than the Serbs would yield, so that the first Balkan war of 1912 was followed in 1913 by a second, in which Serbia, Greece, Rumania, and Turkey turned upon and defeated Bulgaria. Albania also, a mountainous region on the Adriatic, mainly Muslim, and known as the wildest place in all Europe, was the subject of angry discord. The Serbs occupied part of it in the two Balkan wars, but the Greeks also claimed a part, and it had also on several occasions been vaguely promised to Italy.[10] Russia supported the Serbian claim. Austria was determined to shut off the Serbs from access to the sea, which they would obtain by annexation of Albanian territory. An agreement of the great powers, to keep the peace, conjured up an independent kingdom of Albania. This confirmed the Austrian policy, kept Serbia from the sea, and aroused vehement outcries in both Serbia and Russia. But Russia again backed down. Serbian expansionism was again frustrated and inflamed.

The third Balkan crisis proved to be the fatal one. It was fatal because two others had gone before it, leaving feelings of exasperation in Austria, desperation in Serbia, and humiliation in Russia.

The Sarajevo Crisis and the Outbreak of War

On June 28, 1914, a young Bosnian revolutionary, a member of the Serbian secret society called "Union or Death," and commonly known as the Black Hand, acting with the knowledge of certain Serbian officials, assassinated the heir to the Habsburg empire, the Archduke Francis Ferdinand, in the streets of Sarajevo, the Bos-

[9] See pp. 646–647, 705–707.
[10] See p. 624.

THE BALKANS, 1878 AND 1914

The Ottoman Empire, under the blows of Austria and Russia, had been receding from Europe since 1699 (see map, p. 625). The Congress of Berlin of 1878 undertook to stabilize the situation by recognizing Rumania, Serbia, and Montenegro as independent monarchies, and northern Bulgaria as an autonomous principality within the Ottoman Empire. The ambitions of these new states (and of Greece, independent since 1829), together with the discontents of all non-Turkish peoples remaining under Ottoman rule, led to successive altercations culminating in the Balkan wars of 1912–1913. Albania then became independent, and Serbia, Bulgaria, and Greece contiguous. Austrian and Russian pressures meanwhile continued; in 1908 Austria annexed Bosnia, where the South Slav population was related to the Serbs. In Bosnia, at Sarajevo, six years later, the assassination of an Austrian archduke by a South Slav patriot precipitated the First World War.

nian capital, in the Austrian Empire. The world was shocked at this terrorist outrage and at first sympathized with the protests of the Austrian government. Francis Ferdinand, who would soon have become emperor, was known to favor some kind of transformation of Austria-Hungary, in which a more equal place might be given to the Slavs; but the reformer who makes a system work is the most dangerous of all enemies to the implacable revolutionary, and it is perhaps for this reason that the archduke was killed by the Black Hand.

The Austrian government was determined to make an end to the South Slav separatism that was gnawing its empire to pieces. It decided to crush the independence of Serbia, the nucleus of South Slav agitation, though not to annex it, since there were now thought to be too many Slavs within the empire already. The Austrian government consulted the German to see how far it might go with the support of its ally. The Germans, issuing their famous "blank check," encouraged the Austrians to be firm. The Austrians, thus reassured, dispatched a drastic ultimatum to Serbia, demanding among other things that Austrian officials be permitted to collaborate in investigating and punishing the perpetrators of the assassination. The Serbs counted on Russian support, even to the point of war, judging that Russia could not again yield in a Balkan crisis, for the third time in six years, without losing its influence in the Balkans altogether. The Russians in turn counted on France; and France, terrified at the possibility of being some day caught alone in a war with Germany, and determined to keep Russia as an ally at any cost, in effect gave a blank check to Russia. The Serbs rejected the critical item in the Austrian ultimatum as an infringement on Serbian sovereignty, and Austria thereupon declared war upon Serbia. Russia prepared to defend Serbia and hence to fight Austria. Expecting that Austria would be joined by Germany, Russia rashly mobilized its army on the German as well as the Austrian frontier. Since the power which first mobilized had all the advantages of a rapid offensive, the German government demanded an end to the Russian mobilization on its border and, receiving no answer, declared war on Russia on August 1, 1914. Convinced that France would in any case enter the war on the side of Russia, Germany also declared war on France on August 3.

The German decisions were posited on a reckless hope that Great Britain might not enter the war at all. England was bound by no formal military alliance. Even the French did not know for certain, as late as August 3, whether the British would join them in war. The British clung to scraps of their old proud isolation; they hesitated to make a final choice of sides; and as the foreign secretary, Sir Edward Grey, repeatedly explained, in England only Parliament could declare war, so that the foreign office could make no binding promise of war in advance. It has often been said that, had the German government known as a positive fact that England would fight, the war might not have come. Hence the evasiveness of British policy is made a contributing cause of the war. In reality, the probability that England would fight was so great that to underestimate it, as the Germans did, was an act of supreme folly. The British were deeply committed to France, especially through naval agreements. As the German High Seas Fleet grew, the British had been obliged to concentrate naval forces in the North Sea. They had therefore had to withdraw forces from the Mediterranean. In 1914, by agreement with France, the French fleet was concentrated in the Mediterranean, watching over British interests, while the British fleet attended to French interests in the north. The French Channel coast was therefore open to German naval attack, unless the British defended it. Sir Edward Grey accepted this moral obligation, but what swept the British public was the invasion of Belgium. The German plan to crush France quickly was such that it could succeed only by crossing Belgium. When the Belgians protested, the Germans invaded anyway, violating the treaty of 1839 which had guaranteed Belgian neutrality.[11] England declared war on Germany on August 4.

The mere narration of successive crises does not explain why the chief nations of Europe became locked in combat over the murder of an imperial personage within a few days. Among more obvious general causes, the alliance system may be singled out. Europe was divided into two camps. Every incident tended to become a test of strength between the two. A given incident, such as German intervention in Morocco, or the assassination of Francis Ferdinand, could not be

[11] See pp. 459–460.

settled on its own merits, merely by the parties concerned; however it was dealt with, one of the two camps was deemed to have lost or gained and hence to have lost or gained in influence in other incidents, of perhaps greater purport, that would arise in the future. Each power felt that it must stand by its allies whatever the specific issue. This was because all lived in the fear of war, of some nameless future war in which allies would be necessary. The Germans complained of being "encircled" by France and Russia. They dreaded the day when they might have to face a war on two fronts. Willing to accept even a European-wide war to break their threatened "encirclement" by the Entente powers, they were obliged to hold to their one ally, Austria-Hungary, which was in turn able to sell its support at its own price. The French dreaded a coming conflict with Germany, which in forty years had far surpassed France in population and industrial strength; they were obliged to cling to their ally Russia, which therefore could oblige the French to yield to Russian wishes. As for Russia and Austria, they were both tottering empires. Especially after 1900, the tsarist regime suffered from endemic revolutionism, and the Habsburg empire from chronic nationalistic agitation. Authorities in both empires became desperate. Like the Serbs, they had little to lose and were therefore reckless. It was Russia that drew France and hence England into war in 1914, and Austria that drew in Germany. Seen in this light, the tragedy of 1914 is that the most backward or politically bankrupt parts of Europe, through the alliance system, dragged the more advanced parts automatically into ruin.

The German Empire, too, faced an internal crisis. The Social Democrats became the largest party in the Reichstag in 1912.[12] Their sentiments for the most part were antimilitarist and antiwar. But the German imperial government recognized no responsibility to a majority in the chamber. Policy was determined by men of the old unreconstructed upper class, in which army and navy interests, now reinforced by the new business interests, were very strong; and even moderates and liberals shared in the ambition to make Germany a world power, the equal of any. The perplexities the ruling groups faced at home, the feeling that their position was being undermined by the Social Democrats, may have made them less unwilling to view war as a way out. And while it is not true that Germany started the war, as its enemies in 1914 popularly believed, it must be granted that its policies had for some years been rather peremptory, arrogant, devious, and obstinate. In a broad sense, the emergence of a consolidated industrial Germany after 1870, making its bid for world-power status relatively late, was a distant and basic cause of the war.

The alliance system was only a symptom of deeper trouble. In a word, the world had an international economy but a national polity. Economically, each European people now required habitual contact with the world as a whole. Each people was to that extent dependent, and insecure. Industrial countries were especially vulnerable, relying as they did on import of raw materials and food, and on export of goods, services, or capital in return. There was, however, no world state to police the world-wide system, assuring participation in the world economy to all nations under all conditions. Each nation had to take care of itself. Hence came much of the drive for imperialism, in which each Great Power tried to stake out part of the world system for itself. And hence also came the quest for allies and for binding alliances. The alliances, in a world that was in the strict

---

[12] See pp. 582–583.

WORLD WAR I

Land fighting in the First World War was mainly confined to the areas shown by the darker horizontal shading. The huge battles on the Western Front, which in expenditure of manpower exceeded those of the Second World War in the West, for four years swayed back and forth over the small area indicated, less than a hundred miles wide.

sense anarchic (and seemed likely to remain so), were a means by which each nation attempted to bolster up its security; to assure that it would not be cut off, conquered, or subjected to another's will; to obtain some hope of success in the competitive struggle for use of the world's goods.

86. THE ARMED STALEMATE

The First World War lasted over four years, from 1914 to the end of 1918, the United States entering with effective result in the last year. Germany and its allies were called the Central Powers, while the Entente governments were termed the Allies. The war was appalling in its human costs; on the Western Front, more men were used and killed in the First World War than in the Second.

At first a short war, as in 1870, was universally expected. The German General Staff had its plans ready for a two-front struggle against France and Russia. The disadvantage of fighting on two fronts was offset by the possession of good rail lines, which allowed the rapid shuttling of troops from one front to the other. The German war plan, known as the Schlieffen Plan, rested upon this fact. The idea was first to defeat France by the rapid wheeling motion of a tremendous army through Belgium and then to turn at more leisure against Russia, whose great size and less developed railways would make its deployment much slower.

The War on Land, 1914–1916

On August 3, 1914, the Germans launched 78 infantry divisions in the West. They were opposed by 72 French divisions, 5 British, and 6 Belgian. The Germans swept irresistibly forward. The Schlieffen Plan seemed to be moving like clockwork. The civilian authorities made plans for the conquest and annexation of large parts of Europe. Then a hitch occurred: the Russians were fulfilling the terms of their alliance; the 10 billion francs invested by Frenchmen in Russia now paid their most significant dividend. The Russians pushed two armies into Germany, penetrating into East Prussia. Moltke withdrew forces from the German right wing in France, on August 26, for service in the east. The Germans moved on, but their striking arm was weakened, and their lines of communication were already overextended. Joffre, the French commander, regrouping his forces, with strong support from the relatively small British contingent, and at exactly the right moment, ordered a counterattack. The ensuing battle of the Marne, fought from September 5 to 12, changed the whole character of the war. The Germans were obliged to retreat. The hope of felling France at a single blow was ended. Each side now tried to outflank and destroy the other until the battle lines extended to the sea. The Germans failed to win control of the Channel ports; French and British communications remained uninterrupted. For these reverses the great victories meanwhile won by the Germans in the east, though of gigantic proportions (the battles of Tannenberg and the Masurian Lakes, at which 225,000 Russians were captured), were in the long run small consolation.

In the West the war of movement now settled into a war of position. The armies on the Western Front became almost immobile. The units of horse cavalry—the uhlans, hussars, and lancers that had pranced off to war in high spirits—disappeared from the field. Since aviation was barely beginning, and motor transport was still new (the armies had trucks, but no self-propelled guns, and no tanks until very late in the war), the basic soldier more than ever was the man on foot. The most deadly new weapon was the machine gun, which made it impossible for foot soldiers to advance across open fields without overwhelming artillery preparation. The result was a long stalemate of war in the trenches in which the indispensable infantry sought protection.

In 1915 the Germans and Austro-Hungarians put their main effort into an attempt to knock out Russia. They pressed far into the tsarist empire. The Russian losses were enormous—2 million killed, wounded, or captured in 1915 alone. But at the end of the year the Russian army was still fighting. Meanwhile the British and French, hoping to open up communications with Russia, launched a naval attack on Turkey, aiming at Constantinople by way of the Dardanelles. They poured 450,000 men into the narrow peninsula of Gallipoli, of whom 145,000 were killed or wounded. After almost a year the enterprise was given up as a failure.

In 1916 both sides turned again to northern France in an attempt to break the deadlock. The Allies planned a great offensive along the river Somme, while the Germans prepared one in the neighborhood of Verdun. The Germans attacked Verdun in February. The French commander, Joffre, put in General Pétain to defend it but resisted committing his main reserves, holding them for the coming offensive on the Somme. Pétain and his troops, held to minimum numbers, thus had to take the full weight of the German army. The battle of Verdun lasted six months, it drew the horrified admiration of the world, and it became a legend of determined resistance ("they shall not pass"), until the Germans finally abandoned the attack because they sustained almost as many casualties as the French —330,000 to 350,000—so that their purpose was baffled. While the inferno still raged at Verdun the Allies opened their offensive on the Somme in July. They brought up unheard of amounts of artillery, and the newly raised British army was present in force. The idea was to break through the German line simply by stupendous pressure; on both sides, Allied and German, the art of generalship had sunk to an all-time low. Despite a weeklong artillery bombardment the British lost 60,000 men on the first day of the attack. In a week they had advanced only a mile along a six-mile front. In a month they had advanced only two miles and a half. The battle of the Somme, lasting from July to October, cost the Germans about 500,000 men, the British 400,000, and the French 200,000. Nothing of any value had been gained. It was, indeed, at the Somme that the British first used the tank, an armored vehicle with caterpillar tracks that could crash through barbed wire, lunge over trenches, and smash into machine gun nests; but the tanks were introduced in such small numbers, and with such skepticism on the part of many commanders, that they had no effect on the battle.

The War at Sea

With land armies thus helpless, both sides looked to the sea. The long preponderance of British sea power, and the more recent Anglo-German naval race, would now be tested. The British, with French aid, imposed a strict naval blockade. International law at the time placed goods headed for a country at war into two classes. One class was called "contraband"; it included munitions and certain specified raw materials which might be used in the manufacture of military equipment. The other class, including foodstuffs and raw cotton, was defined as "noncontraband." A country was supposed, by international law, to be able to import noncontraband goods even in wartime. These terms of wartime law had been set forth as recently as 1909 at an international conference held in London. The purpose was to make it impossible for a sea power (that is, the British) to starve out an enemy in wartime, or even to interfere with normal civilian production. The jealousy of Continental Europe for British sea power was an old story.

Such law, if observed, would make the blockade of Germany entirely ineffective, and the Allies did not observe it. To starve out the enemy and ruin his economy was precisely their purpose. Economic warfare took its place alongside armed attack as a military weapon, as in the days of Napoleon.[13] The Allies announced a new international law. The distinction between contraband and noncontraband was gradually abolished. The British navy (aided by the French) proceeded to stop all goods of whatever character destined for Germany or its allies. Neutrals, among whom the Americans, Dutch, and Scandinavians were the ones mainly affected, were not allowed to make for German ports at all.

The United States protested vehemently against these regulations. It defended the rights of neutrals. It reasserted the distinction between contraband and noncontraband, claimed the right to trade with other neutrals, and upheld the "freedom of the seas." Much mutual bad feeling resulted between the American and British governments in 1915 and 1916. But when the United States entered the war it adopted the Allied position, and its navy joined in enforcing exactly the same regulations. International law was in fact changed. In the Second World War the very words "contraband" and "freedom of the seas" were never heard.

The Germans countered with an attempt to blockade England. A few isolated German cruisers were able for some time to destroy British shipping in the several oceans of the world. But the Germans relied mainly on the submarine, against which the British naval power at first seemed helpless. The submarine was an unrefined weapon; a submarine commander could not always tell what kind of ship he was attacking, nor could he remove passengers, confiscate cargo, escort the vessel, or indeed do much except sink it. Citing British abuses of international law in justification, the German government in February 1915 declared the waters surrounding the British Isles to be a war zone, in which Allied vessels would be torpedoed and neutral vessels would be in grave danger. Three months later the liner *Lusitania* was torpedoed off the Irish coast. About 1,200 persons were drowned, of whom 118 were American citizens. The *Lusitania* was a British ship; it carried munitions of war manufactured in the United States for Allied use; and the Germans had published ominous warnings in the New York papers that Americans should not take passage upon it. Americans then believed that they should be able to sail safely, on peaceable errands, on the ship of a belligerent power in wartime. The loss of life shocked the country. President Wilson informed the Germans that another such act would be considered "deliberately unfriendly." The Germans, to avoid trouble, refrained for two years from making full use of their submarines. For two years the Allied use of the sea was only partly impeded.

Allied access to the sea was confirmed by the one great naval engagement of the war, the battle of Jutland. The German admirals became restless at seeing their newly built navy skulking behind minefields on the German shores, yet they could not presume to challenge the superior British Grand Fleet, posted watchfully at Scapa Flow. They hoped, however, to decoy smaller formations of British ships, destroy them one by one, and perhaps eventually obtain enough of a naval

---

[13] See pp. 405–408.

balance in the North Sea to loosen the British blockade, by which Germany was slowly being strangled. They were themselves, however, trapped into a major engagement in which the British Grand Fleet of 151 ships took them by surprise. After a few hours of furious combat the Germans were able to withdraw into mined waters. They had lost less tonnage and fewer men than the British. They had proved themselves to be dangerously proficient in naval combat. But they had failed to undermine the British preponderance at sea.

Diplomatic Maneuvers and Secret Agreements

With no military solution in sight, both sides looked about for new allies. The Ottoman Empire, fearing Russia, had joined Germany and Austria-Hungary as early as October 1914. Bulgaria, being anti-Serb, had done the same in 1915.

The leading new prospect was Italy, which, though formally a member of the Triple Alliance, had long ago drifted away from it. Both sides solicited the Italian government, which bargained imperturbably with both. The Italian public was divided. Both Catholic and socialist leaders recommended staying at peace, but extreme nationalists saw a chance to obtain their *irredenta*, the border regions in which Italians lived, but which had not been incorporated in the time of Cavour.[14] The Italian government cast its lot with the Allies in the secret treaty of London of 1915. It was agreed that if the Allies won the war Italy would receive (from Austria) the Trentino, the south Tyrol, Istria and the city of Trieste, and some of the Dalmatian Islands. If Britain and France took over Germany's African colonies, Italy should receive territorial increases in Libya and Somaliland. The treaty of London, in short, carried on the most brazen prewar practices of territorial expansionism. It must be remembered that the Allies were desperate. Italy, thus bought, and probably against the will of most Italians, opened up a front against Austria-Hungary in May 1915.

The Allies likewise made plans for a final partition of the Ottoman Empire, which still reached from Constantinople through the Middle East into Arabia and modern Iraq. Britain and France were so dependent on Russia that they gave up their age-old opposition to Russian domination of the Straits. By a secret treaty of 1915 they agreed that, upon an Allied victory, Russia might proceed to the annexation of Constantinople, along with the whole Bosporus, the Sea of Marmara, and the Dardanelles. By another agreement Mesopotamia was to go to Britain, Syria and southeastern Asia Minor to France, small portions to Italy, and Kurdistan and Armenia to Russia.[15]

Each side tampered with minorities and discontented groups living within the domains of the other. The Germans promised an independent Poland, to embarrass Russia. They stirred up local nationalism in the Ukraine. They raised up a pro-German Flemish movement in Belgium. They persuaded the Ottoman sultan, as caliph, to proclaim a holy war in North Africa, hoping that irate Muslims would drive the British from Egypt and the French from Algeria. This had no success. German agents worked in Ireland, and one Irish nationalist, Sir Roger Casement, landed in Ireland from a German submarine, precipitating the Easter Rebellion of 1916, which was suppressed by the British.

[14] See p. 518.
[15] See map on p. 625.

To Americans the most amazing of similar activities was the famous Zimmermann telegram. In 1916 an American military force had crossed the Mexican border in pursuit of bandits, against protests by the Mexican government. Relations between the United States and Germany were also deteriorating. In January 1917 the German state secretary for foreign affairs, Arthur Zimmermann, dispatched a telegram to the German minister at Mexico City, telling him what to say to the Mexican president. He was to say that if the United States went to war with Germany, Germany would form an alliance with Mexico and if possible Japan, enabling Mexico to get back its "lost territories." These latter referred to the region conquered by the United States from Mexico in 1848—Texas, New Mexico, and Arizona (California was not mentioned by Zimmermann, who was no doubt somewhat vague on the exact history and location of these Alsace-Lorraines of America). Zimmermann's telegram was intercepted and decoded by the British, and passed on by them to Washington. Printed in the newspapers, it shocked public opinion in the United States.

The Allies were more successful in appealing to nationalist discontent, for the obvious reason that the most active national minorities were within the lands of their enemies. They were able to promise restoration of Alsace-Lorraine to France without difficulty. They promised independence to the Poles, though with some difficulty as long as the Russian monarchy stood. It was easier for them to favor national independence for Czechs, Slovaks, and Yugoslavs, since an Allied victory would dissolve the Austro-Hungarian empire.

Within the Ottoman Empire the British aroused Arab hopes for independence. The British Colonel T. E. Lawrence led an insurrection in the Hejaz against the Turks; and the emir Hussein of Hejaz, with British support, in 1916 took the title of king of the Arabs, with a kingdom reaching from the Red Sea to the Persian Gulf. Zionists saw in the impending Ottoman collapse the opportunity to realize their dream for Palestine.[16] Since Palestine was peopled by Arabs (and had been for over 1,000 years) the Zionist program conflicted with British plans to sponsor Arab nationalism. Nevertheless, in the Balfour note of 1917, the British government promised support for the idea of a "Jewish homeland" in Palestine. For the Armenians these years were especially disastrous. They were a Christian people living in the eastern part of the Anatolian peninsula where it abuts on Russia, and like other peoples in the Ottoman Empire, including the Turks themselves, they had developed aspirations for a national state of their own, which conflicted with the plans of Turkish reformers to Turkify the empire. It was only twenty years since such clashes had produced the Armenian massacres of 1894 which had horrified Europe. Now in 1915 the Turkish government, as the Russian army threatened its eastern frontier, ordered the deportation of Armenians from the war zone as potential sympathizers with Russia and the Western Allies. Supposedly they were to be resettled in Syria and Palestine. In fact, in the atmosphere of military crisis, political hatred, bureaucratic contempt, and wartime scarcities hundreds of thousands of Armenians perished. It is a fact also that virtually no Armenians remained within what became the Turkish republic a few years later. The surviv-

---

[16] See p. 603, and for Israel pp. 869–874 below.

ing Armenians became another of the world's scattered peoples, with no state of their own, except for the small Armenian republic within the Soviet Union, with which few other Armenians could feel any sympathy or connections.

Meanwhile during the war the British and French easily moved into the German colonies in Africa. The British foreign secretary, Sir Edward Grey, revealed to Colonel House, President Wilson's personal emissary, that the Allies did not intend that Germany should ever get its colonies back.

In China, too, the third important area of imperialist competition, the war accelerated the tendencies of preceding years. The Japanese saw their own opportunity in the self-slaughter of the Europeans. Japan had also been allied to Britain since 1902. In August 1914 Japan declared war on Germany. It soon overran the German concessions in China and the German islands in the Pacific, the Marshalls and Carolines. In January 1915 Japan presented its Twenty-One Demands on China, a secret ultimatum most of which the Chinese were obliged to accept. Japan thereby proceeded to turn Manchuria and north China into an exclusive protectorate.

As for the Germans, their war aims were even more expansionist, and more menacing to existing boundaries in Europe itself. Early in September 1914, when a quick victory seemed within their grasp, Bethmann-Hollweg, who remained chancellor until the summer of 1917, drew up a list of German war aims which stayed unaltered until the end of hostilities. The plans called for an enlarged German Empire dominating all central Europe, and annexations or satellites in both western and eastern Europe. In the east, Lithuania and other parts of the Baltic coast were to become German dependencies, large sections of Poland were to be directly annexed, and the remainder joined with Austrian Galicia to form a German-dominated Polish state. In the west, Belgium was to become a German dependency to provide more direct access to the Atlantic, and French Lorraine with its rich iron ore was to be added to the already German parts of Alsace-Lorraine. Colonial adjustments, including the acquisition of most of central Africa from coast to coast, were also projected. The political map of Europe and of colonial Africa would thus be transformed.

All these developments, especially the Allied negotiations, whether accomplished facts or secret agreements, affecting Europe, Asia, or Africa, became very troublesome later at the peace conference. They continued some of the most unsettling tendencies of European politics before the war. It does not appear that the Allies, until driven by Woodrow Wilson, gave any thought to means of controlling anarchic nationalism or of preventing war in the future. As president of the United States, Wilson for a long time could see little to choose between the warring alliances, though his personal sympathies were with England and France. In 1916 he attempted to mediate, entering into confidential discussions with both sides; but both still hoped to win on their own terms, so that negotiation was fruitless. Wilson judged that most Americans wished to remain uninvolved, and in November 1916 he was reelected to a second term, on the popular cry, "he kept us out of war." Wilson urged a true neutrality of thought and feeling, or a settlement, as he said, that should be a "peace without victory."

As of the end of 1916, it is hard to see how the First World War would have turned out, had not two new sets of forces been brought in.

87. THE COLLAPSE OF RUSSIA AND THE INTERVENTION OF THE UNITED STATES

The Withdrawal of Russia: Revolution and the Treaty of Brest-Litovsk

The first victim of the First World War, among governments, was the Russian empire. As the Russo-Japanese War had led to the Revolution of 1905 in Russia, so the more ruinous conflict in Europe led to the far greater Revolution of 1917. The story of the Russian Revolution is told in the following chapter. It is enough to say here that war offered a test that the tsarist government could not meet. Bungling, dishonest, and secretive, incapable of supplying the materiel required for modern fighting, driving hordes of peasants into battle in some cases even without rifles, losing men by the millions yet offering no goal to inspire sacrifice, the tsarist regime lost the loyalty of all elements of its people. In March 1917 the troops in St. Petersburg mutinied, while strikes and riots desolated the city. The Duma, or Russian parliament, used the occasion to press its demands for reform. On March 15 Nicholas II abdicated. A Provisional Government took over, made up of liberal noblemen and middle-class leaders, generally democrats and constitutionalists, with at first only one socialist. The Provisional Government remained in office from March to November 1917. Its members, who shared in the liberalism of western Europe, believed that a liberal and parliamentary regime could not succeed in Russia unless the German Empire were defeated. They took steps, therefore, to prosecute the war with a new vigor. In July 1917 an offensive was opened in Galicia, but the demoralized Russian armies again collapsed.

The mass of the Russian people were wearied of a war in which they were asked to suffer so much for so little. Nor did the Russian peasant or workingman feel any enthusiasm for the westernized intellectuals and professional men who manned the Provisional Government. The ordinary Russian, so far as he had any politics, was drawn to one or another of numerous forms of socialism, Marxist and non-Marxist. The Russian Marxist party, the Social Democrats, was divided between Menshevik and Bolshevik factions, the latter being the more extreme. The Bolshevik leaders had for some time lived as exiles in western Europe. Their principal spokesman, V. I. Lenin, with a few others, had spent the war years in Switzerland. In April 1917 the German government offered safe passage to Lenin through Germany to Russia. A railway car full of Bolsheviks, carefully "sealed" to prevent infection of Germany, was thus hauled by a German train to the frontier, whence it passed on to St. Petersburg, or Petrograd, as the city was renamed during the war. The aim of the Germans in this affair, as in the sending of Roger Casement to Ireland in a submarine, was of course to use a kind of psychological warfare against the enemy's home front. It was to promote rebellion against the Provisional Government and thus at last to eliminate Russia.

The position of the Provisional Government became rapidly more untenable, from many causes, until by November 1917 the situation was so confused that Lenin and the Bolsheviks were able to seize power. The Bolsheviks stood for peace with Germany, partly to win popular favor in Russia, and partly because they regarded the war impartially, as a struggle between capitalist and imperialist powers which should be left to exhaust and destroy each other for the benefit of socialism. On December 3, 1917, a peace conference opened between the Bolsheviks and the Germans at Brest-Litovsk. Meanwhile the peoples within the western border of the old Russia—Poles, Ukrainians, Bessarabians, Estonians, Latvians, Finns—with German backing, proclaimed their national independence. The Bolsheviks, since they would not or could not fight, were obliged to sign with Germany a treaty to which they vehemently objected, the treaty of Brest-Litovsk of March 3, 1918. By this treaty they acknowledged the "independence," or at least the loss to Russia, of Poland, the Ukraine, Finland, and the Baltic provinces.

For the Germans the treaty of Brest-Litovsk represented their maximum success during the First World War; it accomplished some of the war aims formulated at the beginning of hostilities. Not only had they neutralized Russia; they also now dominated eastern Europe through puppets placed at the head of the new independent states. They relieved the effects of the naval blockade by drawing considerable quantities of foodstuffs from the Ukraine, though less than they expected. A certain number of German troops remained in the East to preserve the new arrangements. But it was no longer a two-front war. Masses of the German army were shifted from east to west. The High Command, under Hindenburg and Ludendorff since August 1916, prepared to concentrate for a last blow in France to end the war in 1918.

The year 1918 was essentially a race to see whether American aid could reach Europe soon enough, in sufficient amount, to offset the added strength which Germany drew from the collapse of Russia. In March of that year the Germans, beginning with gas attacks and a bombardment by 6,000 artillery pieces, opened a formidable offensive before which the French and British both recoiled. On May 30, 1918, the Germans again stood at the Marne, thirty-seven miles from Paris. At this time there were only two American divisions in action, though the United States had been at war over a year. At this point in the story there are therefore two open questions: how the United States entered the war, and the length of time required for the build-up of its forces overseas.

The United States and the War

We have seen how President Wilson clung persistently to neutrality. The American people were divided. Many had been born in Europe or were the children of immigrants. Those of Irish origin were anti-British; those of German origin were often sympathetic to Germany. On the other hand, since the time of the Spanish-American and Boer Wars, a noticeable current of friendliness to the English had been running, more than ever before in American history. The sale of war materials to the Allies, and the purchase of the bonds of Allied governments, had given certain limited though influential circles a material interest in an Allied victory. The idealism of the country was on the side of England and France, so far as it was not isolationist. An Allied victory would clearly advance the cause of democracy, freedom, and progress far more than a victory of the German Empire. On the other hand, England and France were suspected of somewhat impure motives, and they were allied with the Russian autocracy, the reactionary and brutal tsardom.

The fall of tsarism made a great impression. Democratic and progressive men now came forward even in Russia. No one had ever heard of Lenin or foresaw the

Bolshevik Revolution. It seemed in the spring of 1917 that Russia was struggling along the path that England, France, and America had already taken. An ideological barrier had dropped away, and the demand for American intervention to safeguard democracy became more insistent.

The Germans gave up the attempt to keep the United States out. Constricted ever more tightly by the blockade, and failing to get a decision on land, the German government and High Command listened more readily to the submarine experts, who declared that if given a free hand they could force British surrender in six months. It was the chief example in the First World War of the claim that one branch of the service could win the war alone. Civilian and diplomatic members of the government objected, fearing the consequences of war with the United States. They were overruled; it was a good example of the way in which, in Germany, the army and navy had taken the highest policy into their hands. Unrestricted submarine warfare was to be resumed on February 1, 1917. It was foreseen that the United States would declare war, but the German High Command believed that this would make no immediate difference. They estimated in 1917 (correctly) that between the time when the United States entered a European war and the time when it could take part with its own army about a year must intervene. Meanwhile, the planners said, in six months they could force Britain to accept defeat.

On January 31, 1917, the Germans notified Wilson of the resumption of unrestricted submarine attacks. They announced that they would sink on sight all merchant vessels found in a zone around the British Isles or in the Mediterranean. Wilson broke off diplomatic relations and ordered the arming of American freighters. Meanwhile, the publication of the Zimmermann telegram convinced many Americans of German aggressiveness. German secret agents also had been at work in America, fomenting strikes and causing explosions in factories engaged in the manufacture of munitions for the Allies. In February and March several American ships were sunk. Americans regarded all these activities as an interference with their rights as neutrals. Wilson at last concluded that Germany was a menace. Having made his decision, Wilson saw a clear-cut issue between right and wrong, and he obtained a rousing declaration of war from Congress, on April 6, 1917. The United States went to war "to make the world safe for democracy."

At first the German campaign realized and even exceeded the predictions of its sponsors. In February 1917 the Germans sank 540,000 tons of shipping, in March 578,000 tons, in April, as the days grew longer, 874,000 tons. Something akin to terror, with difficulty concealed from the public, seized on the government in London. Britain was reduced to a mere six-weeks' reserve of food. Gradually countermeasures were developed—mine barrages, hydrophones, depth charges, airplane reconnaissance, and most of all the convoy. It was found that a hundred or more freighters together, though all had to steam at the pace of the slowest, could be protected by a sufficient concentration of warships to keep submarines away. The United States navy, which, unlike the army, was of considerable size and ready for combat, supplied enough additional force to the Allies to make convoying and other antisubmarine measures highly effective. By the end of 1917 the submarine was no more than a nuisance. For the Germans the great plan produced the anticipated penalty without the reward—its net result was only to add America to their enemies.

On the Western Front in 1917, while the Americans desperately got themselves ready for the war they had entered, the French and British continued to hold the line. The French, finding in General Nivelle a commander who still believed in the breakthrough, launched an offensive so unsuccessful and so bloody that mutiny spread through the French army. Pétain then replaced Nivelle and restored discipline to the exhausted and disillusioned soldiers, but he had no thought of further attack. "I am waiting for the Americans and the tanks," he said. The British then assumed the main burden. For three months late in 1917 they fought the dismal battle of Passchendaele. They advanced five miles, near Ypres, at a cost of 400,000 men. At the very end of 1917 the British surprised the Germans with a raid by 380 tanks, which penetrated deep into the German lines, but were obliged to withdraw, since no reserve of fresh infantry was at hand to exploit their success. Meanwhile the Austro-Hungarians, strongly reinforced by German troops, overwhelmed the Italians at the disastrous battle of Caporetto. The Central Powers streamed into northern Italy, but the Italians, with British and French reinforcements, were able to hold the line. The net effect of the campaigns of 1917, and of the repulse of the submarine at the same time, was to reemphasize the stalemate in Europe, incline the weary Allies to await the Americans, and give the Americans what they most needed—time.

The Americans made good use of the time given them. Conscription, democratically entitled selective service, was adopted immediately after the declaration of war. The United States army, whose professionals in 1916 numbered only 130,000, performed the mammoth feat of turning over 3.5 million civilians into soldiers. With the navy, the United States came to have over 4 million in its armed services (which may be compared with over 12 million in the Second World War). Aid flowed to the Allies. To the loans already made through private bankers were added some $10 billion lent by the American government itself. The Allies used the money mainly to buy food and munitions in the United States. American farms and factories, which had already prospered by selling to the Allies during the period of neutrality, now broke all records for production. Civilian industry was converted to war uses; radiator factories turned out guns, and piano factories airplane wings. Every possible means was employed to build up ocean shipping, without which neither American supplies nor American armies could reach the theater of war. Available shipping was increased from 1 million to 10 million tons. Civilian consumption was drastically cut. Eight thousand tons of steel were saved in the manufacture of women's corsets, and 75,000 tons of tin in the making of children's toy wagons. Every week people observed meatless Tuesday, and sugar was rationed. Daylight-saving time, invented in Europe during the war, was introduced to save coal. By such means the United States made enormous stocks available for its Allies as well as itself, though for some items, notably airplanes and artillery ammunition, the American armies, when they reached France, drew heavily on British and French manufactures.

The Final Phase of the War

The Germans, as we have seen, victorious in the East, opened a great final offensive in the West in the spring of 1918, hoping to force a decision before American participation turned the balance forever. To oppose it, a unity of command was at last achieved, for the first time, when a French general, Ferdinand Foch, was made commander in chief of all Allied forces in France, with the national commanders subordinate to him, including Pershing for the Americans. In June the Germans first made contact with American troops in significant force, meeting the Second Division at Château-Thierry. The German position was so favorable that civilians in the German government thought it opportune to make a last effort at a compromise peace. The military, headed by Hindenburg and Ludendorff, successfully blocked any such attempts; they preferred to gamble on one final throw. The German armies reached their farthest advance on July 15 along the Marne. There were now nine American divisions in the Allied line. Foch used them to spearhead his counterattack on July 18. The badly overstrained Germans began to falter. Over 250,000 American troops were now landing in France every month. The final Allied offensive which opened in September, with American troops in the Argonne occupying an eastern sector, proved more than the Germans could withstand. The German High Command notified its government that it could not win the war. The German foreign office made peace overtures to President Wilson. An armistice was arranged, and on November 11, 1918, firing ceased on the Western Front.

Since Germany's allies had surrendered during the preceding weeks, the war, or at least the shooting war in western Europe, was now over. The horror it brought to individual lives cannot be told by statistics, which drily report that almost 10 million men had been killed, and 20 million wounded. Each of the European Great Powers (except Italy) lost from 1 million to 2 million in killed alone. The United States, with some 330,000 casualties of all types (of whom 115,000 died) lost in the entire war fewer men than the main combatants had lost in such a single battle as Verdun or Passchendaele.[17] American assistance was decisive in the defeat of Germany. But it came so late, when the others had been struggling for so long, that the mere beginnings of it were enough to turn the scale. On the date of the armistice there were 2 million American soldiers in France, and another 1 million were on the way. But the American army had really been in combat only four months. During the whole year 1918, out of every hundred artillery shells that were fired by the three armies, the French fired 51, the British 43, and the Americans only 6.

88. THE COLLAPSE OF THE AUSTRIAN AND GERMAN EMPIRES

The war proved fatal to the German and Austro-Hungarian empires, as to the Russian. The subject Habsburg nationalities, or the "national councils" representing them in the Western capitals, obtained increasing recognition from the Allies, and in October 1918 declared their independence. The last Austrian emperor, Charles I, abdicated on November 12, and on the next day Austria was proclaimed a republic, as was Hungary in the following week. Before any peace conference could convene, the new states of Czechoslovakia, Yugoslavia, an enlarged

---

[17] Of the 115,000 American deaths only 50,000 represented men killed in battle, the remainder representing mainly deaths by disease. The great influenza epidemic of 1918, which brought death to over 20 million people, civilians and military alike, in all parts of the world, probably accounted for 25,000 deaths in the American army.

Rumania, a republican Hungary, and a miniature republican Austria were in existence by their own action.

The German Empire stood solid until the closing weeks. Liberals, democrats, and socialists had lately begun to press for peace and democratization. Yet it was the High Command itself that precipitated the debacle. In the last years of the war dictatorial powers had become concentrated in the hands of General Ludendorff, and in September 1918 only he and his closest military associates realized that the German cause was hopeless. On September 29, at supreme headquarters at Spa in Belgium, Ludendorff informed the Kaiser that Germany must ask for peace. He urged that a new government be formed at Berlin, reflecting the majority in the Reichstag, on democratic parliamentary principles.

In calling for immediate peace negotiations, he seems to have had two ideas in mind. First, he might win time to regroup his armies and prepare a new offensive. Or if collapse became unavoidable, then the civilian or democratic elements in Germany would be the ones to sue for peace.

The liberal Prince Max of Baden was found to head a cabinet in which even socialists were included. In October various reforms were enacted, the Bismarckian system was ended, and Germany became a liberal constitutional monarchy. For Ludendorff the changes were not fast enough. What was happening was essentially simple. The German military caste, at the moment of Germany's crisis, was more eager to save the army than to save the empire. The army must never admit surrender; that was an affair for small men in business suits. Emperor, High Command, officers, and aristocrats were unloading frantically upon civilians.

President Wilson unwittingly played into their hands. Speaking now as the chief of the Allied coalition, the one to whom peace overtures were first made, he insisted that the German government must become more democratic. It may be recalled how Bismarck, after defeating France in 1871, demanded a general election in France before making peace.[18] Wilson, unlike Bismarck, really believed in democracy; but in a practical way his position was the same. He wanted to be sure that he was dealing with the German people itself, not with a discredited elite. He wanted it to be the real Germany that applied for and accepted the Allied terms. In Germany, as realization of the military disaster spread, many people began to regard the Kaiser as an obstacle to peace. Or they felt that Germany would obtain better terms if it appeared before the Allies as a republic. Even the officer corps, to halt the fighting before the army disintegrated, began to talk of abdication. Sailors mutinied at Kiel on November 3, and councils of workers and soldiers were formed in various cities. The socialists threatened to withdraw from the newly formed cabinet (i.e., go into opposition and end the representative nature of the new government) unless William II abdicated. A general strike, led by minority socialists and syndicalists, began on November 9. "Abdication," Prince Max told the emperor, "is a dreadful thing, but a government without the socialists would be a worse danger for the country." William II abdicated on November 9, and slipped across the frontier into Holland, where despite cries to try him as a "war criminal" he lived quietly until his death in 1941. Germany was proclaimed a republic on the same day. Two days later the war stopped.

[18] See pp. 526, 572.

The fall of the empire in Germany, with the consequent adoption of the republic, did not arise from any basic discontent, deep revolutionary action, or change of sentiment in the German people. It was an episode of the war. The republic (soon called the Weimar Republic) arose because the victorious enemy demanded it, because the German people craved peace, because they wished to avoid forcible revolution, and because the old German military class, to save its face and its future strength, wished at least temporarily to be excused. When the war ended, the German army was still in France, its discipline and organization still apparently unimpaired. No hostile shot had been fired on German soil. It was said later, by some, that the army had not been defeated, that it had been "stabbed in the back" by a dissolving civilian home front. This was untrue; it was the panic-stricken Ludendorff who first cried for "democracy." But the circumstances in which the German republic originated made its later history, and hence all later history, very troubled.

89. THE ECONOMIC AND SOCIAL IMPACT OF THE WAR

Effects on Capitalism: Government-Regulated Economies

European society was forced by the First World War into many basic changes that were to prove more lasting than the war itself. First of all, the war profoundly affected capitalism as previously known. Essential to the older capitalism (or economic liberalism, or free private enterprise) had been the idea that government should leave business alone, or at the most regulate certain general conditions under which businessmen went about their affairs. Before 1914 governments had increasingly come into the economic field. They had put up tariffs, protected national industries, sought for markets or raw materials by imperialist expansion, or passed protective social legislation to benefit the wage-earning classes. During the war all belligerent governments controlled the economic system far more minutely. Indeed, the idea of the "planned economy" was first applied in the First World War. For the first time (with such rare and archaic precedents as the French dictatorship of 1793)[19] the state attempted to direct all the wealth, resources, and moral purpose of society to a single end.

Since no one had expected a long war, no one had made any plans for industrial mobilization. Everything had to be improvised. By 1916 each government had set up a system of boards, bureaus, councils, and commissions to coordinate its war effort. The aim was to see that all manpower was effectively utilized, and that all natural resources within the country, and all that could possibly be imported, were employed where they would do the most good. In the stress of war free competition was found to be wasteful and undirected private enterprise too uncertain and too slow. The profit motive came into disrepute. Those who exploited shortages to make big profits were stigmatized as "profiteers." Production for civilian use, or for mere luxury purposes, was cut to a minimum. Businessmen were not allowed to set up or close down factories as they chose. It was impossible to start a new business without government approval, because the flotation of stocks and

[19] See pp. 376–378.

bonds was controlled, and raw materials were made available only as the government wished. It was equally impossible to shut down a business engaged in war production; if a factory was inefficient or unprofitable the government kept it going anyway, making up the losses, so that in some cases management came to expect government support. Here too the tests of competition and profitableness were abandoned. The new goal was coordination or "rationalization" of production in the interests of the country as a whole. Labor was discouraged from protesting against hours or wage rates, and the big unions generally agreed to refrain from strikes. For the upper and middle classes it became embarrasssing to show their comforts too openly. It was patriotic to eat meagerly and to wear old clothes. War gave a new impetus even to the idea of economic equality, if only to enlist rich and poor alike in a common cause.

Military conscription was the first step in the allocation of manpower. Draft boards told some men to report to the army, granting exemptions to others to work safely in war industries. Given the casualty rates at the front, state determination over individual life could hardly go farther. With the insatiable need for troops, drawing in men originally exempted or at first rejected as physically inadequate, great numbers of women poured into factories and offices, and in Britain even into newly organized women's branches of the armed forces. Women took over many jobs which it had been thought only men could do. Women did not remain in the labor force after the war in such large numbers, most making way for the returning veterans but the wartime experience in this and the Second World War was part of the process by which the labor force in all countries was enlarged, women's place in society revolutionized, and the lives and outlook of millions of individual women turned outward from the home. It was a process that would be intensified during the Second World War and in the years that followed. During the war governments did not directly force men or women to drop one job and take another. There was no systematic labor conscription except in Germany. But by influencing wage scales, granting draft exemptions, forcing some industries to expand and others to contract or stand still, and propagandizing the idea that work in an arms factory was patriotic, the state shifted vast numbers of workers to war production. Impressed or "slave" labor was not used in the First World War nor were prisoners of war obliged to give labor service, though there were some abuses of these rules of international law by the Germans, who were possibly the least scrupulous and certainly the most hard pressed.

Governments controlled all foreign trade. It was intolerable to let private citizens ship off the country's resources at their own whim. It was equally intolerable to let them use up foreign exchange by importing unneeded goods, or to drive up prices of necessities by competing with one another. Foreign trade became a state monopoly, in which private firms operated under strict licenses and quotas. The greatest of the exporting countries was the United States, whose annual exports rose from $2 billion to $6 billion between 1914 and 1918. The endless demand for American farm and factory products naturally drove up prices, which, however, were fixed by law in 1917, for the most important items.

As for the European Allies, which even before the war had exported less than they imported, and were now exporting as little as possible, they could make purchases in the United States only by enormous loans from the American government. British and French citizens, under pressure from their own governments, sold off their American stocks and bonds, which were bought up by Americans.[20] The former owners received pounds sterling or francs from their own governments, which in return took and spent the dollars paid by the new American owners. In this way the United States ceased to be a debtor country (owing some $4 billion to Europeans in 1914), and became the world's leading creditor country, to which by 1919 Europeans owed about $10 billion.

The Allies controlled the sea, but they never had enough shipping to meet rising demands, especially with German submarines taking a steady though fluctuating toll. Each government set up a shipping board, to expand shipbuilding at any cost and to assign available shipping space to whatever purposes—troop movements, rubber imports, foodstuffs—the government considered most urgent in view of overall plans. Control and allocation eventually became international under the Interallied Shipping Council, of which the United States was a member after entering the war. In England and France, where all manufactures depended on imports, government control of shipping and hence of imports was itself enough to give control over the whole economy.

Germany, denied access to the sea and also to Russia and western Europe, was obliged to adopt unprecedented measures of self-sufficiency. The oil of Rumania and grain of the Ukraine, which became available late in the war, were poor substitutes for the world trade on which Germany had formerly depended. The Germans went with less food than other belligerents. Their government controls became more thorough and more efficient, producing what they called "war socialism." In Walter Rathenau they found a man with the necessary ideas. He was a Jewish industrialist, son of the head of the German electrical trust. One of the first to foresee a long war, he launched a program for the mobilization of raw materials. Early in the war it seemed that Germany might be soon defeated by lack of nitrogen, necessary to make explosives. Rathenau sweepingly requisitioned every conceivable natural source, including the very manure from the farmers' barnyards, until German chemists succeeded in extracting nitrogen from the air. The German chemical industry developed many other substitute products, such as synthetic rubber. German production was organized into War Companies, one for each line of industry, with private business firms working under close government supervision.

The other belligerent governments also replaced competition between individual firms and factories with coordination. "Consortiums" of industrialists in France allocated raw materials and government orders within each industry. The War Industries Board did the same in the United States. In Britain, similar methods became so efficient that by 1918, for example, the country produced every two weeks as many shells as in the whole first year of the war and turned out seventy times as much heavy artillery.

Inflation, Industrial Changes, Control of Ideas

No government, even by heavy taxes, could raise all the funds it needed except by printing paper money, selling huge bond issues, or obliging banks to grant it credit. The result, given heavy demand and acute shortages, was rapid inflation of prices. Prices and wages were regulated but were never again so low as before

---

[20] See pp. 566–568.

1914. The hardest hit by this development were those whose money income could not easily be raised—people living on "safe" investments, those drawing annual salaries, professional people, government employees. These classes had been one of the most stabilizing influences in Europe before the war. Everywhere the war threatened their status, prestige, and standard of living. The huge national debts meant higher taxes for years to come. The debt was most serious when it was owed to a foreign country. During the war the Continental Allies borrowed from Britain, and they and the British both borrowed from the United States. They thereby mortgaged their future. To pay the debt, they were bound for years to export more than they imported—or, roughly, to produce more than they consumed. It may be recalled that in 1914 every advanced European country habitually imported more than it exported.[21] That fact, basic to the European standard of life, was now threatened with reversal.

Moreover, with Europe torn by war for four years, the rest of the world speeded up its own industrialization. The productive capacity of the United States increased immensely. The Japanese began to sell in China, in India, in South America the cotton textiles and other civilian goods which these countries for the time being could not obtain from Europe. Argentina and Brazil, unable to get locomotive parts or mining machinery from England, began to manufacture them themselves. In India the Tata family, a group of wealthy Parsees controlling $250 million of native Indian capital, developed numerous manufacturing enterprises, one of which became the largest iron and steel works in the British Empire. With Germany entirely out of the world market, with Britain and France producing desperately for themselves, and with the world's shipping commandeered for war uses, the position of western Europe as the world's workshop was undermined. After the war Europe had new competitors. The economic foundations of the nineteenth century had slipped away. The age of European supremacy was in its twilight.

All the belligerent governments during the war attempted to control ideas as they did economic production. Freedom of thought, respected everywhere in Europe for half a century, was discarded. Propaganda and censorship became more effective than any government, however despotic, had ever been able to devise. No one was allowed to sow doubt by raising any basic questions.

It must be remembered that the facts of the prewar crises, as related above, were then largely unknown. People were trapped in a nightmare whose causes they could not comprehend. Each side wildly charged the other with having started the war from pure malevolence. The long attrition, the fruitless fighting, the unchanging battle lines, the appalling casualties were a severe ordeal to morale. Civilians, deprived of their usual liberties, working harder, eating dull food, seeing no victory, had to be kept emotionally at a high pitch. Placards, posters, diplomatic white papers, schoolbooks, public lectures, solemn editorials, and slanted news reports conveyed the message. The new universal literacy, the mass press, the new moving pictures, proved to be ideal media for the direction of popular thinking. Intellectuals and professors advanced complicated reasons, usually historical, for loathing and crushing the enemy. In Allied countries the Kaiser was portrayed as a demon, with glaring eyes and abnormally bristling mustaches, bent on the mad project of conquest of the world. In Germany people

[21] See p. 565.

were taught to dread the day when Cossacks and Senegalese should rape German women and to hate England as the inveterate enemy which inhumanly starved little children with its blockade. Each side convinced itself that all right was on its side and all wrong, wickedness, and barbarity on the other. An inflamed opinion helped to sustain men and women in such a fearsome struggle. But when it came time to make peace the rooted convictions, fixed ideas, profound aversions, hates, and fears became an obstacle to political judgment.

90. THE PEACE OF PARIS, 1919

The late ally, Russia, was in the hands of the Bolsheviks, ostracized like a leper colony, and taking no part in international relations. The late German and Austro-Hungarian empires were already defunct, and more or less revolutionary regimes struggled to establish themselves in their places. New republics already existed along the Baltic coast, in Poland, and in the Danube basin but without effective governments or acknowledged frontiers. Europe east of France and Italy was in a state approaching chaos, with revolution on the Russian style threatening. Western Europe was wrenched out of all resemblance to its former self. The Allied blockade of Germany continued. In these circumstances the victors assembled in Paris, in the bleak winter of 1919, to reconstruct the world. During 1919 they signed five treaties, all named after Paris suburbs—St.-Germain with Austria, Trianon with Hungary, Neuilly with Bulgaria, Sèvres with Turkey (1920), and most especially, with Germany, the Treaty of Versailles.

The world looked with awe and expectation to one man—the president of the United States. Wilson occupied a lone eminence, enjoyed a universal prestige. Victors, vanquished, and neutrals admitted that American intervention had decided the conflict. Everywhere people who had been long tried, confused, bereaved, were stirred by Wilson's thrilling language in favor of a higher cause, of a great concert of right in which peace would be forever secure and the world itself at last free. Wilson reached Europe in January 1919, visiting several Allied capitals. He was wildly acclaimed, and almost mobbed, greeted as the man who would lead civilization out of its wasteland.

The Fourteen Points and the Treaty of Versailles

Wilson's views were well known. He had stated them in January 1918 in his Fourteen Points—principles upon which, after victory, peace was to be established. The Fourteen Points demanded an end to secret treaties and secret diplomacy (or in Wilsonian language, "open covenants openly arrived at"); freedom of the seas "alike in peace and in war"; removal of barriers and inequalities in international trade; reduction of armaments by all powers; colonial readjustments; evacuation of occupied territory; self-determination of nationalities and a redrawing of European boundaries along national lines; and, last but not least, an international political organization to prevent war. On the whole, Wilson stood for the fruition of the democratic, liberal, progressive, and nationalistic movements of the century past, for the ideals of the Enlightenment, the French Revolution, and of 1848. As Wilson saw it, and as many believed, the World War should end in a new type of treaty. There was thought to be something sinister about peace conferences of the past, for example, the Congress of Vienna of 1815.[22] The old diplomacy was blamed for leading to war. Lenin in his own way and for his own purposes was saying this in Russia too. It was felt that treaties had too long been wrongly based on a politics of power, or on unprincipled deals and bargains made without regard to the people concerned. Democracy having defeated the Central Powers, people hoped that a new settlement, made in a democratic age, might be reached by general agreement in an atmosphere of mutual confidence. There was a real sense of a new era.

Wilson had had some difficulty, however, in persuading the Allied governments to accept his Fourteen Points. The French demanded a guarantee of German payment for war damages. The British vetoed the freedom of the seas "in peace and war"; it was naval rivalry that had estranged them from Germany, and they had fought the war to preserve British command of the sea. But with these two reservations the Allies expressed their willingness to follow Wilson's lead. The Germans who asked for the armistice believed that peace would be made along the lines of the Fourteen Points with only the two modifications described. The socialists and democrats now trying to rule Germany thought also that, having overthrown the Kaiser and the war lords, they would be treated by the victors with some moderation, and that a new democratic Germany would reemerge into the place in the world which they considered to be due it.

Twenty-seven nations assembled at Paris in January 1919, but the full or plenary sessions were unimportant. Matters were decided by conferences among the Big Four—Wilson himself, Lloyd George for England, Clemenceau for France, Orlando for Italy. The conjunction of personalities was not a happy one. Wilson was sternly and stubbornly righteous; Lloyd George, a fiery and changeable Welshman; Clemenceau, an aged patriot, the "tiger of France," who had been not exactly young in the War of 1870 (he was born in 1841); Orlando, a passing phenomenon of Italian politics. None of them was especially equipped for the task in hand. Clemenceau was a pronounced nationalist, Lloyd George had always been concerned with domestic reforms, Orlando was by training a professor like Wilson, and Wilson, a former college president, lacked concrete knowledge or intimate feeling for peoples other than his own. However, they democratically represented the governments and peoples of their respective countries, and thus spoke with an authority denied to professional diplomats of the old school.

Wilson first fought a hard battle for a League of Nations, a permanent international body in which all nations, without sacrificing their sovereignty, should meet together to discuss and settle disputes, each promising not to resort to war. Few European statesmen had any confidence in such a League. But they yielded to Wilson, and the covenant of the League of Nations was written into the treaty with Germany. In return, Wilson had to make concessions to Lloyd George, Clemenceau, Orlando, and the Japanese. He was thus obliged to compromise the idealism of the Fourteen Points. Probably compromise and bargaining would have been necessary anyway, for such general principles as national self-determination and colonial readjustment invariably led to differences of opinion in concrete cases. Wilson allowed himself to believe that, if a League of Nations

[22] See pp. 417–423.

were established and operating, faults in the treaty could later be corrected at leisure by international discussion.

The great demand of the French at the peace conference was for security against Germany. On this subject the French were almost rabid. The war in the West had been fought almost entirely on their soil. To trim Germany down more nearly to French size, they proposed that the part of Germany west of the Rhine be set up as an independent state under Allied auspices. Wilson and Lloyd George objected, sagely observing that the resulting German resentment would only lead to another war. The French yielded, but only on condition that they obtain their security in another way, namely, by a promise from both Britain and the United States to join them immediately if they were again attacked by the Germans. An Anglo-French-American guarantee treaty, with these provisions, was in fact signed at Paris. France obtained control over the Saar coal mines for fifteen years; during that time, a League commission would administer the Saar territory and in 1935 a plebiscite would be held. Lorraine and Alsace were returned to France. German fortifications and troops were banned from a wide belt in the Rhineland. Allied troops would occupy the Rhineland for fifteen years to assure German compliance with the treaty.

In the east the Allies wished to set up strong buffer states against Bolshevism in Russia. Sympathies with Poland ran very high. Those parts of the former German Empire that were inhabited by Poles, or by mixed populations of Poles and Germans—Posen and West Prussia—were assigned to the new Polish state. This gave Poland a corridor to the sea, but at the same time cut off the bulk of Germany from East Prussia.[23] Danzig, an old German town, became a free city, belonging to no country. Memel also was internationalized; it was soon seized by Lithuania. Upper Silesia, a rich mining country, went to Poland after a disputed plebiscite. In Austria and among the Sudeten Germans of Bohemia, now that there was no longer a Habsburg empire (whose existence had blocked an all-German union in 1848 and in the time of Bismarck),[24] a feeling developed for annexation to the new German republic. But the feeling was unorganized, and in any case the Allies naturally refused to make Germany bigger than it had been in 1914. Austria remained a dwarf republic, and Vienna a former imperial capital cut off from its empire—a head severed from its body, and scarcely more capable of sustaining life. The Bohemian Germans became disgruntled citizens of Czechoslovakia.

Germany lost all its colonies. Wilson and the South African General Smuts, to preserve the principle of internationalism against any imputation of raw conquest, saw to it that the colonies were actually awarded to the League of Nations. The League, in turn, under "mandates," assigned them to various powers for administration. In this way France and Great Britain divided the best of the African colonies; the Belgian Congo received a slight enlargement; and the Union of South Africa took over German Southwest Africa. In the colonial world, Italy got nothing. Japan received the mandate for the German Pacific islands north of the equator, Australia for German New Guinea and the Solomon Islands, New Zealand for German Samoa. The Japanese claimed rights over the German concessions in China. The Chinese at the Paris conference tried to get all special con-

---

[23] See maps, pp. 328, panel 4, and 692–693.
[24] See pp. 483–487, 519–524.

cessions and extraterritorial rights in China abolished.[25] No one listened to such proposals. By a compromise, Japan received about half the former German rights. The Japanese were dissatisfied. The Chinese walked out of the conference.

The Allies took over the German fleet, but the German crews, rather than surrender it, solemnly scuttled it at Scapa Flow. The German army was limited to 100,000. Since the Allies forbade conscription, or the annual training of successive groups of young civilians, the army became exclusively professional, the officer class retained political influence in it, and the means used by the Allies to demilitarize Germany served if anything the contrary purpose. The treaty forbade Germany to have any heavy artillery, aviation, or submarines. Wilson saw his plan for universal disarmament applied to Germany alone.

The French, even before the armistice, had stipulated that Germany must pay for war damages. The other Allies made the same demand. Wilson, at the conference, was stupefied at the size of the bills presented. The Belgians suggested, for their own share, a sum larger than the entire wealth of all Belgium according to officially published Belgian statistics. The French and British proposed to charge Germany with the entire expenses, including war pensions, incurred by them during the war. Wilson observed that "total" reparation, while not strictly unjust, was absolutely impossible, and even Clemenceau noted that "to ask for over a trillion francs would lead to nothing practical." The insistence on enormous reparations was in fact largely emotional. No one knew or considered how Germany would pay, though all dimly realized that such sums could only be made up by German exports, which would then compete with the Allies' own economic interests. The Germans, to avoid worse, even offered to repair physical damages in Belgium and France, but were brusquely refused on the ground that the Belgians and French would thereby lose jobs and business. No total at all was set for reparations in the treaty; it was made clear that the sum would be very large, but it was left for a future commission to determine. The Allies, maddened by the war, and themselves loaded with fantastic debts to the United States, had no desire in the matter of reparations to listen to economic reason and regarded the reparations as simply another means of righting a wrong and of putting off the dangers of a German revival. As a first payment on the reparations account the treaty required Germany to surrender most of its merchant marine, make coal deliveries, and give up all property owned by German private citizens abroad. This last proviso ended Germany's prewar career as an exporter of capital.

It was with the specific purpose of justifying the reparations that the famous "war guilt" clause was written into the treaty. By this clause Germany explicitly "accepted the responsibility" for all loss and damage resulting from the war "imposed upon them (the Allies) by the aggression of Germany and her allies." The Germans themselves felt no such responsibility as they were now obliged formally to accept. They considered their honor as a people to be impugned. The "war guilt" clause gave a ready opening to agitators in Germany and made even moderate Germans regard the treaty as something to be escaped from as a matter of self-respect.

The Treaty of Versailles was completed in three months. The absence of the Russians, the decision not to give the Germans a hearing, and the willingness of Wilson to make concessions in return for obtaining the League of Nations, made

[25] See pp. 642–644.

it possible to dispose of intricate matters with considerable facility. The Germans, when presented with the completed document in May 1919, refused to sign. The Allies threatened a renewal of hostilities. A government crisis ensued in Berlin. No German wished to damn himself, his party, or his principles, in German eyes, by putting his name to a document which all Germans regarded as outrageous. A combination drawn from the Social Democratic and Catholic parties finally consented to shoulder the hateful burden. Two abashed and virtually unknown representatives appeared at the Hall of Mirrors at Versailles, and signed the treaty for Germany in the presence of a large concourse of Allied dignitaries.

The other treaties drafted by the Paris conference, in conjunction with the Versailles treaty, laid out a new map for eastern Europe and registered the recession of the Russian, Austrian, and Turkish empires. Seven new independent states now existed: Finland, Estonia, Latvia, Lithuania, Poland, Czechoslovakia, and Yugoslavia. Rumania was enlarged by adding areas formerly Hungarian and Russian; Greece was enlarged at the expense of Turkey. Austria and Hungary were now small states, and there was no connection between them. The Ottoman Empire presently disappeared: Turkey emerged as a republic confined to Constantinople and Asia Minor, Syria and Lebanon went to France as mandates of the League of Nations, Palestine and Iraq to Great Britain on the same basis.[26] The belt of states from Finland to Rumania was regarded as a *cordon sanitaire* (sanitary zone) to prevent the infection of Europe by communism. The creation of Yugoslavia realized the aims of the South Slav or Pan-Serb movement which had set off the fatal crisis of 1914. The fact, however, that Italy received Trieste and some of the Dalmatian Islands (in keeping with the secret treaty of 1915) left the more ambitious Yugoslavs discontented.

Significance of the Paris Peace Settlement

The most general principle of the Paris settlement was to recognize the right of national self-determination, at least in Europe. Each people or nation, as defined

[26] The secret treaty of 1916 (p. 674) promising the Straits to Russia lapsed with the Revolution, neither the Bolsheviks nor the Allies recognizing an agreement made with the tsarist government.

EUROPE, 1923

The map shows European boundaries between the two World Wars, after the Peace of Versailles and certain other agreements. Comparison with the language map (p. 441) will suggest how the principle of nationality was recognized. Germany returned Alsace-Lorraine to France and lost the region around Danzig (the "Polish corridor") to Poland—essentially the area taken by Prussia in the First Partition of 1772 (see map, p. 222.) In place of the Austro-Hungarian empire we find the "succession states," Austria, Hungary, Czechoslovakia, Yugoslavia, and Rumania. Austria-Hungary also lost Trieste and some of the Dalmatian Islands to Italy. Poland regained its independence, and Finland and the three Baltic states, Estonia, Latvia, and Lithuania, emerged from the tsarist empire. Most of Ireland became a "free state" in the British Commonwealth of Nations, only Ulster remaining in the United Kingdom.

These boundaries lasted until 1938, when, as the Second World War approached, the Germans annexed Austria and the Sudeten part of Czechoslovakia.

ARCTIC OCEAN

0   100   200   300 miles

Narvik

Reykjavik   ICELAND
             (Denmark)

NORWAY

SWEDEN

FAEROE I.
(Denmark)

BALTIC SEA

ORKNEY I.
SCAPA FLOW

Oslo

Stockholm

Edinburgh   NORTH SEA

ULSTER   GREAT BRITAIN   DENMARK   Copenhagen

IRISH
FREE STATE

ATLANTIC OCEAN   Dublin   Liverpool   Danzig
                                          POLISH
                                          CORRIDOR

                             Hamburg
                             Bremen

                   NETHERLANDS   GERMANY   Berlin
           London   Amsterdam Rhine
                                 WEIMAR REPUBLIC
                     Brussels   RUHR   Weimar   Dresden
                     BELGIUM   Cologne
                             LUX.   Frankfurt
                   Paris Metz SAAR   Prague
         Versailles   Stuttgart   CZECHOSLO
                              Strasbourg
                              Munich

                   F R A N C E   Vienna
                                            AUSTRIA   Budapest
                         Geneva SWITZERLAND
                                Locarno   HUN
           Bordeaux   Trent
                                            Trieste
                                            Fiume
                                                      YUGOS
           Bilbao
                                            Zara
                        Marseilles   Florence (Italy)   ADRIATIC SEA

PORTUGAL   CORSICA
        Madrid   (France)   Rome   ITALY
   Lisbon   S P A I N   Barcelona
                                                   Naples

        Seville   BALEARIC I.   SARDINIA
Cadiz   (Spain)
Tangier   Gibraltar (Britain)

SPANISH
MOROCCO   Algiers   SICILY

                                                   MALTA (Britain)

MOROCCO   ALGERIA   TUNISIA   MEDITERRANEAN
(France)   (France)   (France)

NORTH CAPE

• Murmansk

• Archangel

FINLAND

Areas Lost by Germany
Areas Lost by Russia
Areas Lost by Ottoman Empire
Austria and Hungary plus areas lost by
Austro-Hungarian Empire

Sverdlovsk •

L. Onega

L. Ladoga

• Volgoda

• Helsinki
• Reval
ESTONIA

• Leningrad

S O V I E T   U N I O N

Orenburg •

• Moscow

• Samara

Volga R.

Riga •
LATVIA

• Saratov

Memel
LITHUANIA
• Kaunas
E.
RUS.   • Vilna

WHITE
RUSSIAN
S.S.R.

KAZAK S.S.R.

POLAND
• Warsaw   • Brest-
          Litovsk

• Kiev

UKRAINIAN S.S.R.

• Tsaritsyn

• Astrakhan

GALICIA

Dniester R.

C A S P I A N   S E A

AKIA

BUKO
VINA

BESSARABIA

CRIMEA

CAUCASIA

ARY

TRANSYLVANIA

• Sevastopol

GEORGIAN S.S.R.
    Tiflis •

• Baku

RUMANIA

DOBRUJA

BLACK SEA

Batum •

AZERBAIJAN
S.S.R.

• Belgrade   • Bucharest

Danube R.

ARMENIAN S.S.R.

AVIA
SERBIA   • Sofia
         BULGARIA

• Tabriz

(Turkey) • Istanbul

• Ankara

ALBANIA

T U R K E Y

IRAN

• Mosul

GREECE   • Smyrna

AEGEAN SEA

• Athens

SYRIA AND
LEBANON

Baghdad •

Tigris R.

Euphrates R.

DODECANESE I
    (Italy)

CYPRUS
(Britain)

IRAQ

CRETE (Greece)

LEBANON

SEA

PALESTINE

TRANS-
JORDAN

SAUDI ARABIA

by language, was in principle set up with its own sovereign and independent national state. Nationalism triumphed in the belief that it went along naturally with liberalism and democracy. It must be added that the peacemakers at Paris had little choice in this matter, for the new states had already declared their independence. Since in eastern Europe the nationalities were in many places intermixed, and since the peacemakers did not contemplate the actual movement and exchange of populations to sort them out, each new state found alien minorities living within its borders or could claim that people of its own kind still lived in neighboring states under foreign rule. There were Hungarians in Czechoslovakia, Ruthenians in Poland, Poles in Lithuania, Bulgars in Rumania—to cite only a few examples. Hence minority problems and irredentism troubled eastern Europe, as they had before 1914. Eventually it was the complaint of Germans in Czechoslovakia that they were an oppressed minority, together with the irredentist demand of Germany to join these outlying brothers to the Fatherland, that produced the Munich crisis preceding the Second World War.[27]

The Treaty of Versailles was designed to put an end to the German menace. It was not a successful treaty. The wisdom of it has been discussed without end, but a few comments can safely be made. For practical purposes, with respect to Germany, the treaty was either too severe or too lenient. It was too severe to conciliate and not severe enough to destroy. Possibly the victors should have dealt more moderately with the new German republic, which professed their own ideals, as the monarchical victors over Napoleon, in 1814, had dealt moderately with the France of the restored Bourbons, regarding it as a regime akin to their own. As it was, the Allies imposed upon the German republic about the same terms that they might have imposed upon the German Empire. They innocently played the game of Ludendorff and the German reactionaries; it was the Social Democrats and liberals who bore the "shame" of Versailles. The Germans from the beginning showed no real intention to live up to the treaty. On the other hand, the treaty was not sufficiently disabling to Germany to destroy its economic and political strength. Even the degree of severity that it incorporated soon proved to be more than the Allies were willing to enforce. The treaty makers at Paris in 1919, working hastily and still in the heat of war, under pressure from press and propaganda in their own countries, drafted a set of terms which the test of time showed that they themselves did not in the long run wish to impose. As the years passed, many people in Allied countries declared various provisions of the Versailles treaty to be unfair or unworkable. The loss of faith by the Allies in their own treaty only made easier the task of those German agitators who demanded its repudiation. The door was opened for Adolf Hitler.

Even at the beginning the Allies showed doubts. Lloyd George, in the last weeks before the signing, tardily called for certain amendments, though in vain; for in 1919 British opinion shifted somewhat from fear of Germany to the fear of Bolshevism, and already the idea of using Germany as a bulwark against communism was expressed. The Italians disliked the whole settlement from the beginning; they observed that the spoils of Africa and the Near East went only to France and Great Britain. The Chinese were also dissatisfied. The Russians, when they reentered the international arena some years later, found a situation that they did not like and had had no part in making. They objected to being faced

[27] See pp. 801–803.

with a *cordon sanitaire* from Finland to Rumania and soon remembered that most of this territory had once belonged to the Russian empire.

The United States never ratified the Treaty of Versailles at all. A wave of isolationism and disgust with Europe spread over the country; and this feeling, together with some rational criticism of the terms, and a good deal of party politics, caused the Senate to repudiate Wilson's work. The Senate likewise refused to make any advance promises of military intervention in a future war between Germany and France, and hence also declined to ratify the Anglo-French-American guarantee treaty on which Wilson had persuaded Clemenceau to rely. The French considered themselves duped, deprived both of the Rhineland and of the Anglo-American guarantee. They raised more anguished cries over their insecurity. This led them to try to hold Germany down while it was still weak, in turn raising many further complications.

The League of Nations was established at Geneva. Its mere existence marked a great step beyond the international anarchy before 1914. Wilson's vision did not die. But the United States never joined; Germany was not admitted until 1926, or Russia until 1934. The League could handle and dispatch only such business as the Great Powers were willing to allow. It was associated with a west-European ascendancy that no longer corresponded to the facts of the world situation. Its covenant was part of the Versailles treaty, and many people in many countries, on both sides in the late war, saw in it, not so much a system for international adjudication, as a means for maintaining a new status quo in favor of Britain and France.

The First World War dealt a last blow to the ancient institutions of monarchy and aristocratic feudalism. Thrones toppled in Turkey, in Russia, in Austria-Hungary, in the German Empire and the individual German states; and with the kings went the courtly retainers and all the social preeminence and special advantage of the old landed aristocracies. The war was indeed a victory for democracy, though a bitter one. It carried further a process as old as the French and American revolutions. But for the basic problems of modern civilization, industrialism and nationalism, economic security and international stability, it gave no answer.

XVII.
The Russian
Revolution
and the
Soviet Union

o less powerful than the First World War as a force shaping
the twentieth century has been the revolution in Russia, of
which the decisive step was the seizure of power by the Bolshevik party in November 1917. The Russian Revolution of
1917 can be compared in its magnitude only with the French
Revolution of 1789. Both originated in deep-lying and distant
causes, and both made their repercussions felt in many countries for many years.
The present chapter will set forth the revolutionary process in Russia over half a
century. We shall begin with the old regime before 1900, pass through the two
revolutions of 1905 and 1917, and survey the Union of Soviet Socialist Republics
down to 1939, at which time a new order had been consolidated under Joseph
Stalin, a form of "planned economy" successfully realized, and the last of the
original revolutionaries, or Old Bolsheviks, either silenced or put to death.

The comparison of the Russian Revolution to the French is enlightening in
many ways. Both were movements of liberation, the one against "feudalism" and
"despotism," the other against "capitalism" and "imperialism." Neither was a
strictly national movement dealing with merely domestic troubles; both addressed
their message to all the world. Both attracted followers in all countries. Both
aroused a strong reaction on the part of those whose view of life was endangered.
And both showed the same pattern of revolutionary politics: a relative unity of

*Chapter Emblem: One of a series of bronze medals issued by the Leningrad mint in honor of Lenin
and the Russian Revolution of 1917.*

opinion so long as the problem was to overthrow the old regime, followed by disunity and conflict over the founding of the new, so that one set of revolutionaries
eliminated others, until a small, organized, and determined minority (Jacobin
democrats in 1793, Bolshevik communists in 1918) suppressed all opposition in
order to defend or advance the revolutionary cause; and in short order (within a
matter of months in France, years in Russia), many of the most intensely revolutionary leaders were themselves suppressed or liquidated.

The differences are equally deserving of notice. Relatively speaking, or compared in general civilization with other European countries, Russia in 1900 was
in the rear, and France in 1780 in many ways in the lead. The main strength of
the French Revolution lay in the middle classes, who soon managed to prevail
over more extreme pressures. In the Russian Revolution middle-class people were
also active, especially at first, but they proved unable to cope with mass discontents, and succumbed to a more radical party which appealed to workers and
peasants. In France, so to speak, the revolution just "happened," in that ordinary
people from many walks of life unexpectedly found themselves in a revolutionary
situation, and even the Jacobin dictatorship was improvised by men who had
spent their lives thinking of other things. In Russia professional revolutionaries
worked for the revolution long in advance, and the dictatorship of the Bolsheviks
realized the plans and preparations of twenty years. In France the revolution was
followed by a reaction in which émigrés returned, dispossessed classes reappeared
in politics, and even the Bourbons were restored. The French Revolution was followed by a century of uneasy compromise. The Russian Revolution effectively
wiped out its opposition; no once discredited class ever came back, few émigrés
returned, no Romanovs regained their throne. The Russian Revolution was in this
sense more immediately successful.

The repercussions of the Russian Revolution were the more far-reaching because of the very ambivalence of Russia itself. Since the days of Peter the Great
and before, it had always faced toward both Europe and Asia. It was European,
yet it was also outside Europe, and even opposed to it. If about 1900 it was the
least developed of the major European countries, it was at the same time the most
developed, industrialized, or modernized part of the non-European world. Its
revolution could win sympathy on the Left in Europe because it reinforced the
old European socialist objections to capitalism. It aroused the interests of submerged peoples in other continents because it also denounced imperialism (i.e.,
the possession of colonies by Europeans), affirming that imperialism was merely
the "highest stage" of capitalism, and that both must be overthrown together.
The Soviet Union, once established, came to occupy an intermediate position between the West and the Third World. In the West it could long be feared or admired as the last word in social revolution. In the Third World it suggested new
beginnings, a new way to become modern without being capitalistic or European, a step in a world-wide rebellion against European supremacy. The Russian
Revolution thus not only produced communism and hence fascism in Europe, but
added strength to the revolt of Asia, as explained in the following chapters.

Although professional revolutionaries worked for revolution in Russia, they did
not "cause" it. Lenin and the Bolsheviks did not bring about the Russian Revolution. They captured it after it had begun. They boarded the ship in midstream.
The Russian Revolution, like all great revolutions, originated in a totality of previous history and in the prolonged dissatisfaction of many kinds of people.

91. BACKGROUNDS

Russia after 1881: Reaction and Progress

We have seen in earlier chapters how the tsarist autocracy arose, how it ruled as a machine superimposed upon its subjects, how the upper class became westernized while the masses sank further into serfdom, and how an intelligentsia developed, divorced both from the work of government and the activities of the people.[1] It has been explained in Chapter XIII how Alexander II freed the serfs in 1861 and created provincial and district councils or zemstvos, elected mainly by landowners, which attended to such matters as roads, schools, and hospitals.[2]

In 1881 Alexander II was assassinated by members of the People's Will. His son, Alexander III (1881–1894), tried to stamp out revolutionism and to silence even peaceable criticism of the government. Revolutionaries and terrorists were driven into exile. The People's Will as an organized group became extinct. Jews were subjected to pogroms, by far the worst of any (until then) in modern times. For the first time the empire adopted a program of systematic Russification. Poles, Ukrainians, Lithuanians, Caucasians, the scattered German communities, the various Muslim groups, all faced the prospect of forcible assimilation to the Great Russian culture. The philosopher and chief official of this movement was Pobiedonostsev, procurator of the Holy Synod, or layman head, under the tsar, of the Russian Orthodox Church. Pobiedonostsev saw in the West something alien and doomed. Drawing on such old enemies of the French Revolution as Edmund Burke, he attacked Western rationalism and liberalism in his writings, declared that Slavs had a peculiar national character of their own, and dreamed of turning Holy Russia into a kind of churchly community, in which a disciplined clergy should protect the faithful from the insidious influences of the West.

This is not, however, what happened. In the closing decades of the nineteenth century Russia became more than ever before a part of European civilization. Almost overnight it presented Europe with great works of literature and music that Europeans could understand. The Russian novel became known throughout the Western world. All could read the novels of Tolstoy (1828–1910) without a feeling of strangeness; and if the characters of Turgenev (1818–1883) and of Dostoevski (1821–1881) behaved more queerly, the authors themselves were obviously within the great European cultural family. The melodies of Tchaikovsky (1840–1893) and of Rimsky-Korsakov (1844–1908) became very familiar throughout Europe and America; if they sometimes seemed hauntingly wild, distant, or sad, they still betrayed no more than the usual amount of national idiosyncrasy. Russians also contributed to the sciences, notably chemistry. They were considered to be especially talented in the more abstruse intellectual exercises, such as higher mathematics, physics, or chess.

Russia also, from the 1880s, began to pass through the Industrial Revolution and take its place as an integral part of the world economic system. European capital entered the country, financing railways, mines, and factories (as well as government and the army) until by 1914 Europeans had about the same amount invested in Russia as in the United States, some four billion dollars in each case.[3]

---

[1] See pp. 227–238, 324–331, 531–536.
[2] See pp. 534–535.
[3] See pp. 565–568, 614.

In 1897, under the reforming ministry of Count Witte, Russia adopted the gold standard, making its currency readily convertible with all others. In the quarter-century between 1888 and 1913 the Russian railway mileage more than doubled, the miles of telegraph wires multiplied fivefold, the number of post offices trebled, and the number of letters carried by the mails multiplied seven times. Although still industrially undeveloped by Western standards, without, for example, any machine tool industry or chemical plants, Russia was industrializing rapidly. Exports rose in value from 400 million rubles in 1880 to 1.6 billion in 1913. Imports, though smaller, grew more rapidly, quintupling in the same period. They consisted of such items as tea and coffee and of the machines and industrial goods made in western Europe. For a long time after the Revolution, the Soviet Union conducted less foreign trade than did the Russian empire on the eve of the First World War. The Soviet regime, to keep control over its own economic system, tried to depend as little as possible on outside markets and sources of supply.

Industrialization, in Russia as in all countries, brought an increase both of the business and of the wage-earning classes, or, in socialist terminology, of the bourgeoisie and of the proletariat. Though growing, they were still not numerous by standards of the West. Factory workers, laboring for eleven or more hours a day, for low wages under hard conditions, were in somewhat the same position as in England or France before 1850.[4] Unions were illegal, and strikes prohibited. Nevertheless, great strikes in the 1890s called attention to the misery of the new industrial workers. There was one distinctive feature to the Russian proletariat. Russian industry was heavily concentrated; half of Russia's industrial workers were employed in factories employing over 500 persons. It was easier for workers under such circumstances to be organized economically and at the proper time to be mobilized politically. As for the Russian business and capitalist class, it was relatively the weaker because of several features in the situation. Ownership of much of Russia's new industrial plant was in foreign hands. Much was owned by the tsarist government itself; Russia already had the largest state-operated economic system in the world. Moreover, in Russia (unlike the United States at the time) the government itself was a heavy borrower from Europe; hence it was less dependent financially on its own people and more able to maintain an absolutist regime.

Nevertheless, the rising business and professional classes, reinforced by enterprising landowners, were strong enough to form a liberal segment of public opinion, which emerged in 1905 as the Constitutional Democratic party (the K.D.'s or "Cadets"). Many of those who were active in the provincial zemstvos also became Constitutional Democrats. They were liberals, progressives, or constitutionalists in the Western sense, thinking less about the troubles of factory workers and peasants than about the need of a nationally elected parliament to control the policies of state.

Russia remained predominantly agricultural. Its huge exports were mainly farm and forest products. The peasants formed four-fifths of the population. Free from their former lords since 1861, they lived in their village communes or *mirs*.[5] In most communes the land was divided and redivided among peasant households by agreement of the village community, nor could anyone leave without communal permission. The peasants still carried a considerable burden. Until 1906

[4] See pp. 431–432, 463–469, 471–475.
[5] See pp. 533–534.

they paid redemption money arising from the Emancipation of 1861, and even after that other forms of onerous payments. They also paid high taxes, for the government defrayed the interest on its foreign loans from taxes raised at home. The constantly rising export of cereals (also used to pay off debts contracted by Russia in the West) tended to keep food from the farmer's table; many a peasant raised the best wheat for sale and ate black bread himself. The farm population, in short (as in other countries in similar stages of their development), bore a considerable share of the costs of industrialization.

Under such pressures, and because of their crude methods of cultivation, the peasants were forever demanding more land. "Land hunger" was felt both by individual families and by the *mirs*. The Emancipation had turned over roughly half the land to peasant ownership, individual and collective; and in the following half-century the peasants added to their share by buying from nonpeasant owners. The *mirs* were by no means obsolescent. They were in fact flourishing; they acquired far more land by purchase than did individual buyers, and perhaps half or more of the peasants valued communal security above the uncertain pleasures of private property. The exceptions were the minority of more enterprising and wealthier peasants, later called the kulaks. Such a one was Leon Trotsky's father, who, a hard-working, plain, and illiterate man, owned or leased the equivalent of a square mile of land, employed scores of field hands at harvest time, and permanently maintained a large domestic staff. That such a "big farmer" could afford so many employees suggests the poverty in which the bulk of the peasants lived. Not all of the well-to-do peasants were as affluent as Trotsky's father, but the big farmers stood out conspicuously from the mass, by whom they were not liked.

The Emergence of Revolutionary Parties

The peasants were the ancient source of revolutionary disturbance in Russia. Fables about Pugachev and Stephen Razin circulated in peasant legend.[6] After the Emancipation the peasants continued to believe that they had some kind of rights in *all* the land of former estates on which they had formerly been serfs — not merely in the portion that had been allotted to peasant possession. They demanded (and obtained) credit from the government to buy from the big landowners or former masters. Their land hunger could not be appeased. They remained jealous of the landed aristocrat's very existence. In Russia, as elsewhere in Europe, and unlike the United States, the rural population was divided into two sharply distinct classes, on the one hand the peasants of all types, who worked the soil, and on the other the gentry who resided upon it. The two never intermarried. They differed not merely economically but in speech, dress, and manners, and even in the looks of their faces and hands. But in the last three decades of the nineteenth century the Russian peasants were notably quiet, insurrectionism seemingly having subsided.

The other traditional source of revolutionary disturbance lay among the intelligentsia.[7] In the conditions in which the Russian empire had grown up, many of the best and purest spirits were attracted to violence. Revolutionary intelligentsia (as distinguished from those who were simply liberal or progressive) yearned for a

[6] See pp. 231, 325–326.
[7] See pp. 532–533.

catastrophic overthrow of the tsardom. Since the days of the Decembrists[8] they had formed secret organizations, comprising a few hundreds or thousands of members, engaged in outwitting the tsarist police, by whom they were bafflingly interpenetrated. For example, at a Bolshevik party congress held in 1913, out of twenty-two delegates present, no less than five, unknown to the others, were government spies.

The revolutionary intelligentsia, since there was normally little that they could do, spent their time in vehement discussion and interminable refinement of doctrine. By 1890 the terrorism and nihilism of the 1870s were somewhat passé. The great question was where these willing officers of a revolutionary movement could find an army. Disputation turned upon such topics as whether the peasants or the new factory workers were the true revolutionary class, whether the peasants were potentially proletarian or incurably petty bourgeois, whether Russia was bound to experience the same historical process as the West, or whether it was different; and, specifically, whether Russia had to go through capitalism or might simply skip the capitalist stage in reaching the socialist society.

Most of the revolutionary intelligentsia were "populists." Some had once belonged to the now broken People's Will. Some continued to approve of terrorism and assassination as morally necessary in an autocratic country. They generally had a mystical faith in the vast inchoate might of the Russian people, and since most Russians were peasants, the populists were interested in peasant problems and peasant welfare. They believed that a great native revolutionary tradition existed in Russia, of which the peasant rebellion of Pugachev, in 1773, was the chief example.[9] The populists admired the Russian communal village or *mir*, in which they saw the European socialist idea of a "commune" represented. They read and respected Marx and Engels (indeed, a populist first translated the *Communist Manifesto* into Russian); but they did not believe that an urban proletariat was the only true revolutionary class. They did not believe that capitalism, by creating such a proletariat, had inevitably and logically to precede socialism. They said that, in Russia, the horrors of capitalism could be skipped. They addressed themselves to the plight of the farmer and the evils of landlordism, favored strengthening the *mir* and equalizing the shares of all peasants in it, and, since they did not have to wait for the prior triumph of capitalism in Russia, they thought that revolution might come quite soon. This populist sentiment crystallized in the founding in 1901 of the Social Revolutionary party.

Two populists, Plekhanov and Axelrod, fleeing to Switzerland in the 1870s, there became converted to Marxism. In 1883 they founded in exile the organization from which the Russian Social Democratic or Marxist party was to grow. A few Marxists began to declare themselves (though not publicly) in Russia itself. When the youthful Lenin met his future wife Krupskaya in 1894, she already belonged to a circle of argumentative Marxists. The fact that the peasants in the 1890s were disappointingly quiescent, while machine industry, factory labor, and strikes were developing rapidly, turned many of the revolutionary intelligentsia, though only a minority, from populism to Marxism. To Plekhanov and Axelrod were added, as young leaders, Lenin (1870–1924), Trotsky (1879–1940), Stalin (1879–1953), and others.

Of these it was Lenin who, after Marx, was to be claimed by communism as a

[8] See p. 455.
[9] See pp. 325–326.

father. Lenin was a short almost rotund man, with a small man's bounding quickness and intense, penetrating gaze. High cheekbones and somewhat slanting eyes showed an Asiatic strain on the paternal side; Russian friends at first said that he looked "like a Kalmuck." His hair receded in early youth, leaving a massive forehead, behind which a restless mind was inexhaustibly at work. Even in his twenties he was called the Old One. He was of upper-middle-class origin, son of an inspector of schools who rose in the civilian bureaucracy to a rank equivalent to major general. His boyhood was comfortable and even happy, until the age of seventeen, when his elder brother, a student at St. Petersburg, became somewhat incidentally involved in a plot to assassinate Alexander III, for which he was put to death by order of the tsar himself. Because of the blot on the family record it became impossible for Lenin to continue with his law studies. He soon joined the ranks of professional revolutionaries, having no other occupation and living precariously from the party funds, which came mainly from the donations of well-to-do sympathizers.

Arrested as a revolutionary, he spent three years of exile in Siberia. Here the tsarist government treated educated political prisoners with an indulgence not later shown by the Soviet regime. Lenin and most of the others lived in cottages of their own or boarded with local residents. No labor was required of them. They borrowed books from Europe; met and visited with one another; debated, played chess, went hunting, meditated, and wrote. They chafed, however, at being cut off from the mainstream of Russian political life back home. Lenin, his term over, proceeded in 1900 to western Europe, where except for short secret trips to Russia he remained until 1917. His intellectual vigor, irresistible drive, and shrewdness as a tactician soon made him a force in the party. Genius has been called the faculty for everlasting concentration upon one thing. Lenin, said his one-time close associate Axelrod, "for twenty-four hours of the day is taken up with the revolution, has no thoughts but thoughts of revolution, and even in his sleep dreams of nothing but revolution."

In 1898 the Marxists in Russia, spurred on by émigrés, founded the Social Democratic Labor party. They were not more revolutionary than the larger group of Social Revolutionaries. They simply had a different conception of the revolution. First of all, as good Marxists, they were more inclined to see the revolution as an international movement, part of the dialectical process of world history in which all countries were involved. Russia for them was no different from other countries except that it was less advanced. They expected the world revolution to break out first in western Europe. They particularly admired the German Social Democratic party, the largest and most flourishing of all the parties that acknowledged the fatherhood of Marx.[10]

If the Social Democrats were more oriented to Europe than the Social Revolutionaries, it was because so many of their spokesmen lived there in exile. They tended to think that Russia must develop capitalism, an industrialist proletariat, and the modern form of class struggle before there could be any revolution. Seeing in the urban proletariat the true revolutionary class, they looked upon all peasantry with suspicion, ridiculed the mir, and abhorred the Social Revolutionaries. "Marxism," said Lenin, "has forever shaken itself loose from the nonsensical patter of the populists and anarchists to the effect that Russia can escape a capi-

---

[10] See pp. 581–583, 588–591.

talist development." (Russian Marxists were on this point more Marxist than Marx and Engels, both of whom, when urged, refused to pronounce on the merits of the *mir* or on the need of capitalism as a precondition to socialism in Russia.) Like Marx himself, the Russian Marxists disapproved of sporadic terrorism and assassination. For this reason, and because their doctrine seemed somewhat academic and their revolution rather conditional and far in the future, the Marxists were for a time actually favored by the tsarist police, who regarded them as less dangerous than the Social Revolutionaries.

Split in the Social Democrats: Bolsheviks and Mensheviks

The Russian Marxists held a second party congress in Brussels and London in 1903, attended by émigrés like Lenin and delegates from the underground in Russia, and by Social Democrats and members of lesser organizations. The purpose of the congress was to unify all Russian Marxism, but in fact it split it forever. The two resulting factions called themselves Bolsheviks, or majority men, and Mensheviks, or minority men. Lenin was the main author of the split and hence the founder of Bolshevism. Although he obtained his majority after one participating organization, the Jewish Bund, had seceded in indignation, and by calling for surprise votes on tactical issues, and although after 1903 it was usually the Mensheviks who had the majority, Lenin clung proudly and stubbornly to the term Bolshevism, with its favorable connotations of a majority in his support. For a number of years after 1903 the Social Democrats remained at least formally a single Marxist party, but they were irreconcilably divided into two wings. In 1912 the Bolshevik wing organized itself as a separate party.

Bolshevism, or Leninism, originally differed from Menshevism mainly on matters of organization and tactics. Russian Marxists referred to each other as "hards" and "softs." The "hards" were attracted to Lenin, the "softs" repelled by him. Lenin believed that the party should be a small revolutionary elite, a hard core of reliable and zealous workers. Those who wished a larger and more open party, with membership for mere sympathizers, became Mensheviks. Lenin insisted upon a strongly centralized party, without autonomy for national or other component groups. He demanded strong authority at the top, by which the central committee would determine the doctrine (or "party line") and control personnel at all levels of the organization. The Mensheviks favored a greater degree of influence by the membership as a whole. Lenin thought that the party would strengthen itself by purges, expelling all who developed deviations of opinion. The Mensheviks favored covering up or bridging over all but the most fundamental disagreements. The Mensheviks came to recommend cooperation with liberals, progressives, and bourgeois democrats. Lenin regarded such cooperation as purely tactical and temporary, never concealing that in the end the Bolsheviks must impose their views through a dictatorship of the proletariat. The Mensheviks, in short, came to resemble the Marxists of western Europe, so far as that was possible under Russian conditions.[11] Lenin stood for the rigid reaffirmation of Marxian fundamentals—dialectical materialism and irreconcilable class struggle.

If we ask what Leninism added to the original Marxism,[12] the answer is not easy to find. Lenin accepted Marx's governing ideas: that capitalism exploited the

[11] See pp. 588–591.
[12] See pp. 491–495.

workers, that it necessarily produced and preceded socialism, that history was logically predetermined, that class struggle was the law of society, that existing forms of religion, government, philosophy, and morals were weapons of the ruling class. He did, however, develop and transform into a first-rank element of Marxism certain theories of "imperialism" and of the "uneven development of capitalism" that had been propounded in only general terms by Marx and Engels. In the Marxist-Leninist view, "imperialism" was exclusively a product of monopoly capitalism, that is, capitalism in its big business, "highest," and "final" stage, which develops differently and at different times in each country. Monopoly capitalism is bent on exporting surplus capital and investing it in underdeveloped areas for greater profits.[13] The unceasing drive for colonies and markets in a world already almost completely partitioned leads inevitably to international "imperialist" wars for the "redistribution" of colonies, as well as to intensified national colonial struggles for independence; both provide new revolutionary opportunities for the proletariat.

In other respects, Lenin roundly denounced all who attempted to "add" anything to the fundamental principles of Marx. Nothing infuriated him so much as revisionist efforts to tone down the class struggle, or hints that Marxism might in the last analysis perhaps find room for some kind of religion. As he wrote in 1908: "From the philosophy of Marxism, cast of one piece of steel, it is impossible to expunge a single basic premise, a single essential part, without deviating from objective truth, without falling into the arms of bourgeois-reactionary falsehood." Lenin was a convert. He discovered Marxism; he did not invent it. He found in it a theory of revolution which he accepted without reservation as scientific and on which he was more outspokenly dogmatic even than Marx himself. His powers of mind, which were very great, were spent in demonstrating how the unfolding events of the twentieth century confirmed the analysis of the master.

But it was by his powers of will that Lenin was most distinguished, and if Leninism contributed little to Marxism as a theory it contributed a great deal to it as a movement. Lenin was an activist. He was the supreme agitator, a field commander in the class war, who could dash off a polemical pamphlet, dominate a party congress, or address throngs of workingmen with equal ease. Beside him, Marx and Engels seem almost to be mere recluses or sociologists. Marx and Engels had preferred to believe that the dictatorship of the proletariat, when it came, would represent the wishes of the great majority in a society in which most people had become proletarians. Lenin more frankly foresaw the possibility that the proletarian dictatorship might represent the conscious wishes of a small vanguard and might have to impose itself on great masses by an unshrinking use of force.

Above all, Lenin developed Marx's idea of the role of the party. He drew on the rich experience of pre-Marxist revolutionaries in Russia—the mysterious use of false names, invisible ink, secret ciphers, forged passports, and hidden rendezvous —the whole conspiratorial wonderland which, when it existed to a lesser degree in the West before 1848, drew Marx's scorn and laughter. Lenin's conception of the party was basically Marx's, reinforced by his own experience as a Russian. The party was an organization in which intellectuals provided leadership and understanding for workers, who could not see for themselves. For trade unionism, concerned only with the day-to-day demands of workingmen, Lenin had

---

[13] See pp. 613–614.

even less patience than Marx. "The unconscious growth of the labor movement," he wrote, "takes the form of trade unionism, and trade unionism signifies the mental enslavement of the workers to the bourgeoisie." The task of intellectuals in the party, the elite, or experts, was to make the trade unions and the working class "conscious" and hence revolutionary. Armed with "objective" knowledge, known to be correct, the party leadership naturally could not listen to the subjective opinions of others—the passing ideas of laborers, of peasants, of mistaken party subordinates, or of other parties pretending to know more than Marx himself. The idea that intellectuals supply the brains and workers the brawn, that an elite leads while the toilers meekly follow, is understandable enough in view of the Russian background, which had created on the one hand a painfully self-conscious intelligentsia, and on the other a repressed working class and peasantry deprived of all opportunity for political experience of their own. It was one of the most distinctive traits of Leninism and one of the most foreign to the democratic movement of the West.

Leninism accomplished the marriage of Russian revolutionary traditions with the Western doctrine of Marxism. It was an improbable marriage, whose momentous offspring was to be communism. But at the time, when Bolshevism first appeared in 1903, it had little or no effect. A real revolution broke out in Russia in 1905. It took the revolutionary émigrés almost entirely by surprise.

92. THE REVOLUTION OF 1905

Background and Revolutionary Events

The almost simultaneous founding at the turn of the century of the Constitutional Democratic, Social Revolutionary, and Social Democratic parties was clearly a sign of mounting discontent. None of these was as yet a party in the Western sense, organized to get men elected to office, for there were no elections in Russia above the provincial zemstvo level. All three parties were propaganda agencies, made up of leaders without followers, intellectuals who followed various lines of thought. All, even those who became Constitutional Democrats, were watched by the police and obliged to do most of their work underground. At the same time, after 1900, there were signs of growing popular unrest. Peasants were trespassing on lands of the gentry and even rising in local insurrections against landlords and tax collectors. Factory workers sporadically refused to work. But with these popular movements none of the new parties had formed any solid links.

The government refused to make concessions of any kind. The tsar, Nicholas II, who had mounted the throne in 1894, was a man of narrow outlook. To the Little Father all criticism seemed merely childish. Tutored in his youth by Pobiedonostsev,[14] he regarded all ideas questioning autocracy, Orthodoxy, and Great Russian nationalism as un-Russian. That persons in the government should be controlled by interests outside the government—the mildest liberalism or most orderly democracy—seemed to the tsar, the tsarina, and the leading officials to be a monstrous aberration. Autocracy, for them, was the best and only, as it was the God-given, form of government for Russia.

[14] See p. 698.

The chief minister, Plehve, and the circles at court, hoped that a short success-ful war with Japan would create more attachment to the government. The war went so badly that its effect was the reverse.[15] Critics of the regime (except for the handful of the most internationalist Marxists) were sufficiently patriotic to be ashamed at the ease with which Russia was defeated by an upstart and Asian power. As after the Crimean War, there was a general feeling that the govern-ment had exposed its incompetence to all the world. Liberals believed that its secret methods, its immunity to criticism or control, had made it sluggish, torpid, obstinate, and inefficient, unable either to win a war or to lead the economic modernization that was taking place in Russia. But there was little that the lib-erals could do.

The police had recently allowed a priest, Father Gapon, to go among the St. Petersburg factory workers and organize them, hoping thus to counter the propa-ganda of revolutionaries. Father Gapon took up their grievances in all serious-ness. They believed, as simple peasants only recently transplanted to the city, that if only they could reach the ear of the Little Father, the august being high above all hard capitalists and stony officials, he would hear their complaints with shocked surprise and rectify the evils that afflicted Russia. They drew up a petition, asking for an eight-hour day, a minimum daily wage of one ruble (fifty cents), a repudi-ation of bungling bureaucrats, and a democratically elected Constituent Assem-bly to introduce representative government into the empire. Unarmed, peace-able, respectful, singing "God save the Tsar," a crowd of 200,000—men, women, and children—gathered before the tsar's Winter Palace one Sunday in January 1905. But the tsar was not in the city, and his officials were afraid. Troops marched up and shot down the demonstrators in cold blood, killing several hundred.

"Bloody Sunday" in St. Petersburg snapped the moral bond upon which all sta-ble government rests. The horrified workers saw that the tsar was not their friend. The autocracy stood revealed as the force behind the hated officials, the tax collectors, the landlords, and the owners of the industrial plants. A wave of political strikes broke out. Social Democrats (more Mensheviks than Bolsheviks) appeared from the underground or from exile to give revolutionary direction to these movements. Councils or "soviets" of workers were formed in Moscow and St. Petersburg. The peasants, too, in many parts of the country spontaneously be-gan to erupt, overrunning the lands of the gentry, burning manor houses and do-ing violence to their owners. Social revolutionaries naturally tried to take this movement in charge. The liberal Constitutional Democrats, professors, engi-neers, businesspeople, lawyers, leaders in the provincial zemstvos founded forty years before, tried also to seize leadership or at least use the crisis to force the gov-ernment's hand. All agreed on one demand—that there should be more demo-cratic representation in the government.

The tsar yielded grudgingly and as little as possible. In March 1905 he prom-ised to call to office men "enjoying the confidence of the nation." In August (after the ruinous battle of Tsushima) he agreed to call a kind of Estates General, for which peasants, landowners, and city people should vote as separate classes. Still the revolution raged unchecked. The St. Petersburg Soviet, or workers' council, led mainly by Mensheviks (Lenin had not yet reached Russia), declared a great general strike in October. Railroads stopped, banks closed, newspapers ceased to

[15] See pp. 646–647.

appear, and even lawyers refused to go to their offices. The strike spread to other cities and to the peasants. With the government paralyzed, the tsar issued his October Manifesto. It promised a constitution, civil liberties, and a Duma to be elected by all classes alike, with powers to enact laws and control the administration.

The tsar and his advisers intended to divide the opposition by releasing the October Manifesto, and in this they succeeded. The Constitutional Democrats, with a Duma promised, allowed themselves to hope that social problems could henceforth be dealt with by parliamentary methods. Liberals were now afraid of revolutionaries; industrialists feared the strength shown by labor in the general strike, and landowners demanded a restoration of order among the peasants. Aroused peasants and workers were not yet satisfied; the former still wanted more land and less taxation, the latter a shorter working day and a living wage. The several branches of revolutionary intellectuals worked upon the continuing popular agitation, hoping to carry matters forward until the tsarist monarchy was abolished and a socialist republic established with themselves at its head. They believed also (and correctly) that the October Manifesto was in any case a deception, which the tsar would refuse to adhere to as soon as revolutionary pressure was removed. The soviets continued to seethe, local strikes went on, and there were mutinies among soldiers at Kronstadt and sailors in the Black Sea fleet.

But the government was able to maintain itself. With the middle-class liberals now inactive or demanding order, the authorities arrested the members of the St. Petersburg Soviet. Peace was hastily made with Japan, and reliable troop units were recalled from the Far East. The revolutionary leaders fled back to Europe, or again went underground, or were caught and sent to prison or to Siberia; executions were carried out in the countryside.

The Results of 1905: The Duma

The chief apparent result of the Revolution of 1905 was to make Russia, at least ostensibly, into a parliamentary type of state, like the rest of Europe. The promised Duma was convoked. For ten years, from 1906 to 1916, Russia had at least the superficial attributes of a semiconstitutional monarchy.

But Nicholas II soon showed that he did not intend to yield much. He drew the teeth of the new Duma before the creature could even be born, by announcing in advance, in 1906, that it would have no power over foreign policy, the budget, or government personnel. His attitude toward constitutional monarchy continued until 1917 to be entirely negative; the one thing that tsarism would not allow was any real participation in government by the public. Within this "public" the two extreme fringes were equally impervious to liberal constitutionalism. On the right, stubborn upholders of pure autocracy and the Orthodox church organized the Black Hundreds, terrorizing the peasantry and urging them to boycott the Duma. On the left, in 1906, the Social Revolutionaries and both the Bolshevik and Menshevik wings of the Social Democrats likewise refused to recognize the Duma, urged workers to boycott it, and refused to put up any candidates for election.

The short-lived first Duma was elected in 1906 by a system of indirect and unequal voting, in which peasants and workers voted as separate classes, and with proportionately far less representation than was granted to the landlords. In the absence of socialist candidates, workers and peasants voted for all sorts of people, including the liberal Constitutional Democrats (the "Cadets"), who obtained a sweeping majority. The Cadets, when the Duma met, found themselves still fighting for the bare principle of constitutional government. They demanded true universal male suffrage and the responsibility of ministers to a parliamentary majority. The tsar's response was to dismiss the Duma after two months. The Cadets fled to Viborg in autonomous Finland, which the tsarist police generally let alone. It is significant that these constitutional liberals and democrats, in council at Viborg, again appealed for a general strike and nonpayment of taxes—that is, for mass revolution. But real revolutions are not easy to start, and nothing happened.

A second Duma was elected in 1907, with the government trying to control the elections through suppression of party meetings and newspapers, but since Social Revolutionaries and Mensheviks now consented to take part, some eighty-three socialists were elected. The Cadets, becoming fearful of the revolutionary left, concluded that constitutional progress must be gradual and showed a willingness to cooperate with the government. But the Duma came to an abrupt end when the government denounced and arrested some fifty socialists as revolutionaries bent only on destruction. A third Duma, elected after an electoral change that gave increased representation to the landed propertied class and guaranteed a conservative majority, managed to hold several sessions between 1907 and 1912, as did a fourth Duma from 1912 to 1916. The deputies, by following the lead of the government, by addressing themselves only to concrete issues, by losing themselves in committee work, and by avoiding the basic question of where supreme power lay, kept precariously alive a modicum of parliamentary institutions in the tsarist empire.

The Stolypin Reforms

Some officials believed that the way to checkmate the revolutionaries, and strengthen the hold of the monarchy, was for the government, while keeping all controls in its own hands, to attract the support of reasonable and moderate people by a program of reforms. One of these was Peter Stolypin, whom the tsar retained as his principal minister from 1906 to 1911. It was Stolypin who dissolved the first two Dumas. But it was not his policy merely to stand still. His aim was to build up the propertied classes as friends of the state. He believed, perhaps rightly, that a state actively supported by widespread private property had little to fear from doctrinaire intellectuals, conspirators, and émigrés. As he said in a speech to the Third Duma in 1908: "The government has placed its wager, not on the needy and the drunken, but on the sturdy and the strong—on the sturdy individual proprietor who is called upon to play a part in the reconstruction of our Tsardom."

Stolypin therefore favored and broadened the powers of the provincial zemstvos, in which the larger landowners took part in administering local affairs. For the peasantry he put through legislation more sweeping than any since the Emancipation.

Seeing in the *mir* the source of communal agrarian restlessness, Stolypin hoped to replace this ancient institution with a regime of private individual property. He abolished what was left of the redemption payments for which the *mirs* had been collectively responsible.[16] He allowed each peasant to sell his share of the

[16] See pp. 533–534.

communal rights and to leave the commune at will. He authorized peasants to buy land freely from the communes, from each other, or from the gentry. He thus favored the rise of the class of "big farmers," the later kulaks, men who obtained control of large tracts, worked them with hired help, and produced cash crops for the market. These were "the sturdy and the strong" upon whom Stolypin pinned his hopes. At the same time, by allowing peasants to sell out and leave the *mir* (it would generally be the worst farmers or most improvident persons who did so), he hastened the formation of a migratory wage-earning class, which would either seek work from the big farmers or go off to take jobs in the city. The creation of a mobile labor force, and of a food supply raised by big farmers for the market, would thus advance the industrialization of Russia.

The Stolypin policy was successful. Between 1907 and 1916, 6.2 million families out of 16 million who were eligible applied for legal separation from the *mir*. There was no mistaking the trend toward individual property and independent farming. But the results of the Stolypin program must not be exaggerated. The *mir* was far from broken. A vast majority of peasants were still involved in the old system of common rights and communal restrictions. The land shortage was still acute in the agricultural areas where yields were highest. Land hunger and poverty continued in the countryside. There were kulaks, to be sure, to be resented and envied, but the largest landed proprietors were still the gentry. About 30,000 landlords owned nearly 200 million acres of land, and another 200 million acres made up other large landed estates.

Stolypin was not left long to carry on his program. The tsar gave him only an unwilling support. Reactionary circles disliked his tampering ways and his Western orientation. Social Revolutionaries naturally cried out against dissolution of the communes. Even Marxists, who should in theory have applauded the advance of capitalism in Russia, feared that Stolypin's reforms might do away with agrarian discontent. "I do not expect to live to see the revolution," said Lenin in these years. Stolypin was shot dead while attending the theater in Kiev, in the presence of the tsar and tsarina, in 1911. The assassin, a member of the terrorist wing of the Social Revolutionaries, is thought also to have been a secret agent of the reactionary tsarist police. It may be added that Stolypin's predecessor, Plehve, and about a dozen other high officials within the past few years had similarly died at the hands of assassins.

But all in all, violent and half barbaric though it still was, the Russian empire on the eve of the First World War was moving in a Western direction. Its industries were growing, its railways expanding, its exports almost half as great in value as those of the United States. It had a parliament, if not a parliamentary government. Private property and individualist capitalism were spreading to new layers of the people. There was a guarded freedom of the press, illustrated, for example, by the legal and open establishment of the Bolshevik party paper, *Pravda*, in St. Petersburg in 1912. It is not possible to say how far this development might have gone, for it was menaced on both the right and the left by obstinate and obscurantist reactionaries upholding the absolute tsardom and by revolutionaries whom nothing but the end of tsardom and wholesale transformation of society could appease. But both extremes were discouraged. The desperation of extreme reactionaries in the government, the feeling that they might in any case soon lose their position, perhaps made them the more willing to precipitate a European war by armed support of Serbian nationalists. As for the revolutionary parties, and especially the Bolsheviks, they were losing in membership on the eve of the war, their leaders lived year after year in exile, dreaming of the great days of 1905 which stubbornly failed to repeat themselves and sometimes pessimistically admitting, as Lenin did, that there might be no revolution in their time.

93. THE REVOLUTION OF 1917

End of the Tsardom: The Revolution of March 1917

War again put the tsarist regime to a test that it could not meet. In this war, more "total" than any had ever been, willing cooperation between government and people was indispensable to success. This essential prerequisite the tsarist empire did not have. National minorities, Poles, Jews, Ukrainians, Caucasians, and others, were disaffected. As for the socialists, who in every other European parliament voted for funds to finance the war, the dozen otherwise disunited socialists in the Duma refused to do so and were promptly jailed.[17] The ordinary workingman and peasant marched off with the army, but without the sense of personal conviction felt by common people in Germany and the West. More decisive was the attitude of the middle class. Because they patriotically wished Russia to win, the glaring mismanagement of the government was the more intolerable to them. The disasters with which the war opened in 1914, at Tannenberg and the Masurian Lakes, were followed by the advance of the Central Powers into Russia in 1915, at the cost of 2 million Russian soldiers killed, wounded, or captured.[18]

At the war's outbreak middle-class people, as in all countries, offered their assistance to the government.[19] The provincial zemstvos formed a union of all zemstvos in the empire to facilitate the mobilization of agriculture and industry. Business groups at Petrograd (St. Petersburg lost its Germanic name at this time) formed a Commercial and Industrial Committee to get the factories into maximum production. The government distrusted these signs of public activity arising outside official circles. On the other hand, organized in this way, middle-class people became conscious of their own strength and more critical of the bureaucracy. Rumors spread that some officials in the war ministry itself were pro-German, reactionaries who feared the liberalism of England and France, with which Russia was allied.

Life at court was bizarre even for Russia. The tsarina Alexandra, German by origin, looked upon all Russians outside her own circle with contempt, incited her husband to play the proud and pitiless autocrat, and took advice from a self-appointed holy man, the mysterious Rasputin. She was convinced that Rasputin possessed supernatural and prophetic powers, because he had apparently cured her young son, the tsarevitch, of hemophilia. Rasputin, by his influence over her, had a voice in appointments to high office. All who wished an audience with the imperial pair had to go through him. Patriotic and enlightened persons of all classes vainly protested. In these circumstances, and given the military defeats, the union of zemstvos and other such war-born bodies complained not merely of faults of administration but of fundamental conditions in the state. The govern-

---

[17] See pp. 708, 735.
[18] See p. 672.
[19] See pp. 681–685.

ment responded by holding them at arm's length. The tsarist regime, caught in a total war, was afraid of the help offered by its own people.

During the war, in September 1915, the Duma was suspended. It was known that reactionaries—inspired by the tsarina, Rasputin, and other sinister forces—expected that a victory in the war would make it possible to kill liberalism and constitutionalism in Russia. The war thus revived all the basic political issues that had been latent since the Revolution of 1905. The union of zemstvos demanded the assembly of the Duma. The Duma reassembled in November 1916 and, conservative though it had always been, expressed loud indignation at the way affairs were conducted. Among all elements of the population, dissatisfaction with the course of the war and with the government's ineptitude mounted. In December Rasputin was assassinated by nobles at the court. The tsar began to consider repression and again adjourned the Duma. Machine guns were issued to the police. Members of the Duma, and of the new extragovernmental bodies, concluded that the situation could be saved only by force. It is when moderate persons, normally concerned with their own business, come to such conclusions that revolution becomes a political possibility. The shift of moderates and liberals, their need of a coup d'état to save themselves from reactionaries, likewise raised the long failing prospects of the minority of professional revolutionaries.

Again it was the workers of Petrograd who precipitated the crisis. Food had become scarce, as in all the belligerent countries. But the tsarist administration was too clumsy and too demoralized by graft to institute the controls that had become usual elsewhere, such as maximum prices and ration cards. It was the poorest who felt the food shortage most keenly. On March 8, 1917, food riots broke out, which soon developed, doubtless with the help of revolutionary intellectuals, into political insurrections. Crowds shouted, "Down with the tsar!" Troops within the city refused to fire on the insurgents; mutiny and insubordination spread from unit to unit. Within a few days a Soviet of Workers' and Soldiers' Deputies, on the model of 1905, had been organized in Petrograd.

Middle-class leaders, with the government now helpless, demanded dismissal of the ministry and formation of a new one commanding the confidence of a majority of the Duma. The tsar retaliated by disbanding the Duma. The Duma set up an executive committee to take charge until the situation clarified. There were now two new authorities in the city: one, the Duma committee, essentially moderate, constitutionalist, and relatively legal; the other, the Petrograd Soviet, representing revolutionary forces arising by spontaneous upsurge from below. The Petrograd Soviet (or workers' "council") was to play in 1917 a role like that of the Paris Commune of 1792, constantly pushing the supposedly higher and more nationwide authority to the left. The Soviet became the public auditorium and administrative center of the working-class upheaval. Since it was generally socialist in its outlook, all the factions of doctrinaire socialists—Social Revolutionaries, Mensheviks, Bolsheviks—tried to win it over and utilize it for their own ends.

The Duma committee, under pressure from the Petrograd Soviet, on March 14 set up a Provisional Government under Prince Lvov. The Duma liberals, as a concession to the Soviet, admitted one socialist to the new government, Alexander Kerensky, a moderate, legal-minded Social Revolutionary, and they furthermore consented to demand the abdication of Nicholas II. The tsar was then at the front. He tried to return to his palace near Petrograd, but the imperial train was stopped and turned back by troops. The army, fatefully, was taking the side of the Revolution. The very generals in the field, unable to vouch for the loyalty of their men, advised abdication. Nicholas yielded; his brother the grand duke declined to succeed him; and on March 17, 1917, Russia became a republic.

The Bolshevik Revolution: November 1917

The Provisional Government, following the best precedents of European revolutions, called for elections by universal male suffrage to a Constituent Assembly, which was to meet late in the year and prepare a constitution for the new regime. It tried also to continue the war against Germany. In July an offensive was mounted but the demoralized armies were quickly routed. Pending final decision by the Constituent Assembly, the Provisional Government promised wholesale redistribution of land to the peasants but took no action. Meanwhile, the peasants, driven by the old land hunger, were already overrunning the rural districts, burning and looting. At the front the armies melted away; many high officers refused to serve the republic, and masses of peasant soldiers simply turned their backs and went home, unwilling to be absent while farmlands were being handed out. The Petrograd Soviet, opposing the Provisional Government, called for speedy termination of the war. Fearing reactionary officers, it issued on March 14 its Order No. 1, entrusting command within the army to committees elected by both officers and men. Discipline collapsed.

The Revolution was thus already well advanced when Lenin and the other Bolsheviks arrived in Petrograd in the middle of April.[20] They immediately took sides with the Petrograd Soviet against the Provisional Government, and with similar soviets that had sprung up in other parts of the country. In July an armed uprising of soldiers and sailors, which the Bolshevik central committee disapproved of as premature, was put down. The Bolsheviks were blamed, and Lenin had to flee to Finland. But as a bid for popular support the Provisional Government named the socialist Kerensky as its head in place of Prince Lvov in an uneasy coalition of moderate socialists and liberals. Kerensky's middle position was next threatened from the right. The newly appointed military commander, General Kornilov, dispatched a force of cavalry to restore order. Not only conservatives but liberals wished him success in the hope that he would suppress the soviets. Kornilov's movement was defeated, but with the aid of the Bolsheviks, who rallied with other socialists, and of revolutionary-minded soldiers in the city who offered armed resistance. Radicals denounced liberals as accomplices in Kornilov's attempt at counterrevolution, and both camps blamed Kerensky for having allowed the plot to be hatched under his government. Both liberals and moderate socialists abandoned Kerensky, and he had to form a government of uncertain political support. Meanwhile the food shortage worsened, with transport disarranged and the farm population in turmoil, so that workers in the city listened more willingly to the most extreme speakers.

The Bolsheviks adapted their program to what the most aroused elements in a revolutionary people seemed to want. Lenin concentrated on four points: first, immediate peace with the Central Powers; second, redistribution of land to the peasants; third, transfer of factories, mines, and other industrial plants from the capitalists to committees of workers in each plant; and, fourth, recognition of the

[20] See pp. 677, 701–705.

soviets as the supreme power instead of the Provisional Government. Lenin, though a rigid dogmatist on abstract questions, was a flexible and bold tactician; and his program in 1917 was dictated more by the immediate situation in Russia than by considerations of theoretical Marxism. What was needed was to win over soldiers, peasants, and workers by promising them "peace, land, and bread." With this program, and by infiltration and parliamentary stratagems, as well as by their accuracy as political prophets—predicting the Kornilov counterrevolution and "unmasking" the trend of middle-way liberals to support it—the Bolsheviks won a majority in the Petrograd Soviet and in soviets all over the country.

Lenin thereupon raised the cry, "All power to the Soviets!" to crush Kerensky and forestall the coming Constituent Assembly. Kerensky, to broaden the base on which he stood, and unable to wait for the Constituent Assembly, convoked a kind of preparliament representing all parties, labor unions, and zemstvos. Lenin and the Bolsheviks boycotted his preparliament. Instead they called an all-Russian Congress of Soviets.

Lenin now judged that the hour had come for the seizure of power. The Bolsheviks themselves were divided, many like Zinoviev and Kamenev opposing the move, but Lenin was backed by Trotsky, Stalin, and a majority of the party Central Committee. Troops garrisoned in Petrograd voted to support the soviets, which the Bolsheviks now controlled. On the night of November 6–7, 1917, the Bolsheviks took over telephone exchanges, railway stations, and electric lighting plants in the city. A warship turned its guns on the Winter Palace, where Kerensky's government sat. The latter could find almost no one to defend it. The hastily assembled Congress of Soviets pronounced the Provisional Government defunct and named in its place a Council of People's Commissars, of which Lenin became the head. Trotsky was named commissar for foreign affairs, Stalin commissar for nationalities. Kerensky fled, eventually arriving in the United States, where he lived until 1970.

At the Congress of Soviets Lenin introduced two resolutions. One called upon the belligerent governments to negotiate a "just democratic peace," without annexations and without indemnities; the second "abolished all landlord property" immediately and without compensation. Although determined to establish a proletarian dictatorship, the Bolsheviks knew the importance of the Russian peasants. The millions of acres belonging to the large estates that were now expropriated provided a base of support for the new regime without which it could hardly have survived.

Thus was accomplished the Bolshevik or November Revolution.[21] But the long awaited Constituent Assembly remained to be dealt with. It met in January 1918. Thirty-six million persons had voted for it. Of these, 9 million had voted for Bolshevik deputies, showing that the Bolshevik program, launched less than a year before by a small band of émigrés, had a widespread mass appeal. But almost 21 million had voted for Kerensky's party, the agrarian-populist, native Russian, peasant-oriented Social Revolutionaries. However, said Lenin, "to hand over power to the Constituent Assembly would again be compromising with the malignant bourgeoisie." The Assembly was broken up on the second day of its sessions; armed sailors dispatched by the people's commissars simply surrounded it. The

---

[21] Also known as the October Revolution, since according to the Julian calendar, used in Russia until 1918, the events described took place in October.

dissolution of the Constituent Assembly was a frank repudiation of majority rule in favor of "class rule"—to be exercised for the proletariat by the Bolsheviks. The dictatorship of the proletariat was now established. Two months later, in March 1918, the Bolsheviks renamed themselves the Communist party.

The New Regime: The Civil War, 1918–1922

In these same months, the Communists, or Bolsheviks, made the peace of Brest-Litovsk with Germany, surrendering to Germany control over the Baltic provinces, Poland, and the Ukraine.[22] The conquests of two centuries were thus abandoned; not since the days of Peter the Great had the Russian frontier been so far from central Europe. To Lenin it made no difference. He was convinced that the events that he had just mastered in Russia were the prelude to a general upheaval; that the war, still raging in the west, would bring all Europe to the inevitable proletarian or Marxist revolution; that Imperial Germany was therefore doomed; and that Poles, Ukrainians, and others would soon emerge, like the Germans themselves, as free socialist peoples. In any case, it was largely by promising peace that Lenin had won enough backing to overthrow Kerensky, who on this deep popular demand had delayed too long, waiting for England and France to release Russia from its treaty obligations as an ally. But real peace did not come, for the country sank immediately into civil war.

Not only old tsarist reactionaries, and not only liberals, bourgeois, zemstvo men, and Constitutional Democrats, but all types of anti-Leninist socialists as well, Mensheviks and Social Revolutionaries, scattered in all directions to organize resistance against the regime of soviets and people's commissars, and they obtained aid from the Western Allies. Both sides competed for the support of the peasants.

As for the new regime, the oldest of its institutions was the party, founded as a wing of the Social Democrats in 1903; the next oldest were the soviets, dating from 1905 and 1917; and then came the Council of People's Commissars set up on the day of the coup d'état. The first institution founded under the new order was a political police, an Extraordinary All-Russian Commission of Struggle Against Counterrevolution, Speculation, and Sabotage, commonly known from its Russian initials as the Cheka and in later years, without basic change of methods or purpose, under such successive names as the OGPU, the NKVD, the MVD, and the KGB. It was established on December 7, 1917. In January 1918 the Red Army was founded, with Leon Trotsky as war commissar and virtually its creator. In July a constitution was promulgated.

In social policy the Bolsheviks at first adopted no long-range plans, contenting themselves with a mixture of principle and expediency known as "war communism." They nationalized some of the largest industrial enterprises but left the bulk under the control of workers' committees. The pressing problem was to find food, which had ceased to move through any normal channels. The peasants, very much as in the French Revolution under similar conditions—worthless money, insecure property titles, unruly hired men, armed marauding, and a doubtful future —were producing less food than usual, consuming it themselves, or hoarding it on their own farms. The response of the government and city workers was also much

[22] See p. 678.

as in 1793. The new government levied requisitions, required the peasants to make stated "deliveries," and invited labor unions to send armed detachments into the country to procure food by force. Since it was naturally the big farmers who had the surplus, they came into disrepute as starvers of the people. Class war broke out, rabid, ferocious, and elemental, between farmers who feared that their very subsistence as well as their property would be taken away, and city people, often supported by hungry agricultural laborers, who were driven to desperation by famine. Many peasants, especially the larger farmers, therefore rallied to anti-Bolshevik political leaders.

Centers of resistance developed on every side. In the Don valley a small force assembled under Kornilov and Denikin, with many army officers, gentry landowners, and expropriated business people taking part in it. The Social Revolutionaries gathered followers on the middle Volga. At Omsk a disaffected group proclaimed the independence of Siberia. As a military organization the most significant was a force of some 45,000 Czechs, who had deserted or been captured from the Austro-Hungarian armies and had then been organized as a Czech Legion to fight on the side of Russia and the Allies. After the November Revolution and the peace of Brest-Litovsk, these Czechs decided to leave Russia by way of the Trans-Siberian Railroad, return to Europe by sea, and resume fighting on the Western Front. When Bolshevik officials undertook to disarm them they allied with the Social Revolutionaries on the Volga.

The Allied governments believed that Bolshevism was a temporary madness that with a little effort could be stopped. They wished above all to bring Russia back into the war against Germany. So long as the war in Europe lasted, they could not reach Russia by the Black or Baltic Sea. A small Allied force took Murmansk and Archangel in the north. But for Allied military intervention the best opening was in the Far East, through Vladivostok. The Japanese, who had declined military aid to their Allies in any other theater, received this proposal with enthusiasm, seeing in the ruin of the Russian empire a rare opportunity to develop their sphere of influence in East Asia. It was agreed that an interallied military force should land at Vladivostok, cross Siberia, join with the Czechs, break up Bolshevism, and fall upon the Germans in eastern Europe. For this ambitious scheme Britain and France could supply no soldiers, engaged as they were on the Western Front; the force turned out to be American and Japanese, or rather almost purely Japanese, since Japan contributed 72,000 men and the United States only 8,000. They landed at Vladivostok in August 1918.

The civil war lasted until 1920, or even later in some places. It became a confused melee in which the Bolsheviks struggled against dissident Russians and against foreign intervention. They fought in the Ukraine first against the Germans, and then against the French, who occupied Odessa as soon as the war ended in Europe. They reconquered the Ukraine, Armenia, Georgia, and Azerbaidzhan, which had declared their independence; put to flight a hundred thousand "Whites" under Wrangel in the south; and fought off Admiral Kolchak, who, with a White army in Siberia, proclaimed himself ruler of all Russia. In 1920, the Bolsheviks carried on a war with the new republic of Poland, which was scarcely organized when it set out to recover the huge Ukrainian and White Russian territories that had been Polish before 1772.[23] British, French, and American troops

[23] See map, p. 328.

remained at Archangel until the end of 1919, the Japanese at Vladivostok until the end of 1922.

But the anti-Bolshevik forces could never unite. The anti-Communist Russians represented every hue of the political spectrum from unregenerate tsarists to left-wing Social Revolutionaries. Many of the rightist anti-Bolsheviks openly antagonized the peasants by proceeding to restore expropriated landed estates in areas they occupied; many engaged in vindictive reprisals in a kind of "white terror." The Allies themselves could not agree; the French sent troops to the Ukraine and gave aid to the Poles, but the British and Americans wanted to be rid of all military entanglements as soon as the armistice with Germany was signed. Leon Trotsky, on the other hand, forged in the crucible of the civil wars the hard and solid metal of the Red Army, recruiting it, organizing it, restoring its discipline, equipping it as best he could, assigning political commissars to watch it, and assuring that trustworthy officers occupied its high command. The Bolsheviks could denounce the foreign intervention and appeal to national patriotism; and they could win peasant support by the distribution of land. By 1922 the Bolsheviks, or Communists, had established themselves up to the frontiers of the former tsarist empire in every direction except on the European side. There the band of Baltic states in the *cordon sanitaire* remained independent; Rumania had acquired Bessarabia, the new Rumanian frontier reaching now almost to Odessa; and Poland, as a result of the war of 1920, retained a frontier farther east than the Allies themselves had intended. Russia had lost thousands of square miles of territory and buffer areas acquired over the centuries by the tsars.[24] They were to remain lost until the Second World War. But peace was won and the regime stood.

It was during these civil wars that the Red Terror broke out in Russia. Like the famous Terror in France in 1793, it was in part a response to civil and foreign war. Before the Bolshevik Terror, the old Jacobin Terror paled. They differed as the cruelty and violence endemic in the old Russia differed from the more humane or law-abiding habits of western Europe. Thousands were shot merely as hostages (a practice unknown to Europe for some centuries); and other thousands without even the summary formalities of revolutionary tribunals. The Cheka was the most formidable political police that had yet appeared. The Bolshevik Terror was aimed at the physical extermination of all who opposed the new regime. A bourgeois class background would go far to confirm the guilt of the person charged with conspiring against the Soviet state. As a chief of the Cheka said: "The first questions you should put to the accused person are, To what class does he belong, what is his origin, what was his education, and what is his profession? These should determine the fate of the accused. This is the essence of the Red Terror." But a working-class background made little difference. In 1918 a young woman named Fanny Kaplan shot at Lenin and wounded him. She deposed that she had favored the Constituent Assembly, that her parents had emigrated to America in 1911, that she had six working-class brothers and sisters; and she admitted that she had intended to kill Lenin. She was of course executed, as were others in Petrograd. When the sailors at Kronstadt, who were among the first adherents won by the Bolsheviks, rose in 1921, objecting to domination of the soviets by the party (threatening a kind of leftist renewal of the revolution, like the Hébertists

[24] See p. 691 and map on pp. 692–693.

who had opposed Robespierre), they were branded as petty-bourgeois and shot down by the thousands. The Terror struck at the revolutionists themselves quite as much as it did the bourgeoisie; it was to continue to do so long after the Revolution was secured.

The Terror succeeded in its purpose. Together with the victories of the Red Army, it established the new regime. Those "bourgeois" who survived took on the protective coloration of "toilers." No bourgeois as such ever again presumed to take part in the politics of Russia. Mensheviks and other socialists fleeing to Europe told appalling stories of the human toll taken by Lenin. Horrified European socialists repudiated communism as an atrocious, Byzantine, Asiatic perversion of Marxism. But, at whatever cost, Lenin and his followers were now able to start building the socialist society as they understood it.

94. THE UNION OF SOVIET SOCIALIST REPUBLICS

Government: The Nationalities and Federalism

With the end of the civil wars and foreign intervention, and with the termination of the war with Poland, it became possible in 1922 to establish the Union of Soviet Socialist Republics. Its first members were four in number: the Russian Soviet Federated Socialist Republic, the Ukrainian Soviet Socialist Republic, the White Russian Soviet Socialist Republic, and the Transcaucasian Soviet Socialist Republic.[25] In the new Union, which geographically replaced the old Russian empire, the name Russia was not officially used. The guiding conception was a blend of the national and the international: to recognize nationality by granting autonomy to national groups, while holding these groups together in a higher union and allowing new groups to enter regardless of historic frontiers. In 1922 the expectation of world revolution was still alive. The constitution, formally adopted

[25] The original Russian and Transcaucasian federal republics were subsequently reorganized to create additional soviet republics, so that by the constitution of 1936 the S.S.R.'s were eleven in number, to which five more were added in 1940; the Karelo-Finnish S.S.R. lost this status, however, in 1956. There have come to be fifteen soviet republics in the U.S.S.R., with population figures in 1940 and 1980, as follows:

	1940	1980
Russian S.F.S.R.	109,000,000	139,100,000
Ukrainian S.S.R.	40,000,000	50,100,000
White Russian (Byelorussian) S.S.R.	10,000,000	9,700,000
Armenian S.S.R.	1,250,000	3,100,000
Georgian S.S.R.	3,500,000	5,100,000
Azerbaidzhan S.S.R.	3,200,000	6,200,000
Uzbek S.S.R.	6,300,000	16,200,000
Turkmen S.S.R.	1,200,000	2,900,000
Tadzhik S.S.R.	1,500,000	4,000,000
Kazakh S.S.R.	6,100,000	15,000,000
Kirghiz S.S.R.	1,500,000	3,700,000
ADDED IN 1940:		
Karelo-Finnish S.S.R.	500,000	——
Moldavian S.S.R.	2,500,000	4,000,000
Lithuanian S.S.R.	2,900,000	3,400,000
Latvian S.S.R.	2,000,000	2,500,000
Estonian S.S.R.	1,100,000	1,500,000
TOTAL U.S.S.R.	192,550,000	266,500,000

in 1924, pronounced the founding of the U.S.S.R. to be "a decisive step by way of uniting the workers of all countries into one World Soviet Socialist Republic." It made the Union, in principle, fluid and expansible, declared that any member republic might secede (none ever has) and that newly formed soviet socialist republics might join. When, in connection with the Second World War, the U.S.S.R. took back territories detached from tsarist Russia after the First World War—Bessarabia from Rumania, Karelia from Finland, parts of White Russia and the Ukraine from Poland, and Estonia, Latvia, and Lithuania after two decades of independence—these territories were sovietized and added to the Union as republics on a footing of legal equality with the old ones.

The federal principle in the U.S.S.R. was designed to answer the problem of nationalism. The tsardom, in its last decades, had tried to deal with this problem by systematic Russification. The nationalities had resisted, and nationalist discontent had been one of the forces fatally weakening the empire. Nationalism, or the demand that national groups should have their own political sovereignty, had not only broken up the Austro-Hungarian empire but "Balkanized" central and eastern Europe. In 1922 the U.S.S.R., occupying a sixth of the world's land area, was adjoined on the west by a Europe which in one twenty-seventh of the world's land surface contained twenty-seven independent states.

A hundred languages were spoken in the Soviet Union, and fifty distinct nationalities were recognized within its borders. Many of these were extremely small, splinter groups or isolated communities left by the ebb and flow of mankind in inner Asia over thousands of years. Many were very primitive, without political consciousness. All recognized nationalities received a cultural autonomy, or the right to use their own language, have their own schools, wear their own dress, and follow their own folkways without interference. Indeed, the Soviet authorities favored the growth of cultural nationalism. Some fifty languages were reduced to writing for the first time, and the new regime encouraged the singing of national songs, performance of dances, and collection of folklore. Administratively the nationalities were put on various levels, with varying degrees of separate identity according to their size, degree of civilization, or importance. Some constituted only "national districts," others "autonomous regions," still others "autonomous republics" within a federated soviet republic. The most important were the federated soviet republics themselves. The second constitution, adopted in 1936, created an upper legislative house, the Soviet (or Council) of Nationalities, to which each Union republic sent twenty-five delegates, each "autonomous republic" eleven, each "autonomous region" five, and each "national district" one. In practice, the Russian S.F.S.R., with over half the population and three-quarters of the territory of the Union, predominated over the others. When to the Russian were added the Ukrainian (or Little Russian) and White Russian republics, whose people were not very different from the Great Russians, the overwhelmingly Russian and Slavic character of the Union became marked.

The federal structure undoubtedly gave some dignity, self-respect, and sense of equal cooperation to many of the numerous minorities. Yet political rights were severely limited by the centralization of authority in the hands of the federal government and the Communist party, as well as by the overwhelming Slavic preponderance. There was no substance to the formal claim that each constituent republic was sovereign, had the right to secede, and had the right to conduct its own foreign affairs, on the basis of which the Soviets demanded sixteen (and received three) votes in the United Nations when it was formed in 1945. Moreover, there was evidence in the Second World War that separatism had not wholly died down, remaining especially alive in the Ukraine. Four autonomous republics and one autonomous region were officially dissolved for separatist as well as collaborationist activities. Grievances persisted on the part of many minorities on political and even on cultural grounds; the Soviet Jews in later years had many complaints. Yet, on balance, the Soviets accomplished much to prevent the disintegration of their multinational state by granting the nationalities a measure of political and cultural self-expression while on fundamental matters consolidating central authority and control within the communist framework as a whole.

Government: Parallelism of State and Party

Government in the Union, and in each component republic, followed a pattern worked out during the Revolution and written into the constitution of 1924 and the later constitution promulgated in 1936. Its chief feature was a system of parallelism. On the one hand was the state; on the other, paralleling the state but technically not part of it, was the party. There was a close interlocking relationship between the two.

On the side of the state, the distinctive institution was the council or soviet. Here elections took place, and authority proceeded from the bottom upward to the top. Under the constitution of 1924 only "toilers" had the right to vote. Surviving bourgeois, private traders, "persons using the labor of others to make a profit," as well as priests, were excluded from the suffrage. An indirect system of elections prevailed. In each village and town the voters chose a local soviet; the local soviet elected delegates to a provincial soviet, which in turn sent delegates to a soviet of the republic (Russian or other); the soviets of these republics sent delegates to a Union-wide Congress of Soviets, the supreme law-enacting body of the country. Soviets at all levels chose executive officials; the Congress of Soviets chose the Council of People's Commissars, or ministry.

In the constitution of 1936 a more direct democratic procedure was introduced —for the state side of the parallelism. Voters henceforth directly elected members of the higher soviets, a secret ballot was adopted, and no class was any longer denied the vote. A bicameral parliament was created, with an upper chamber, the Soviet of Nationalities, and a lower chamber, a Soviet of the Union, in which there was one representative for every 300,000 persons in the whole country. The Supreme Soviet, with its two chambers, chose a smaller body, the Presidium, to function while the chambers were not in session. The chairman of the Presidium served as "president," or nominal head, of the U.S.S.R. The Presidium supervised the Council of People's Commissars or Council of Ministers, as it came to be called after 1946, which the Supreme Soviet continued to elect. The chairman of the Council of Ministers was in Western terms the premier or prime minister. On the state side, as set forth in the constitution, especially the constitution of 1936, the government embodied many seemingly democratic features.

Yet alongside the state, at all levels and in all localities, was the party. Only one party was allowed, the Communist, though nonparty members might be elected to the soviets or to other official positions. In the party, authority began at the top and proceeded downward. At its apex stood the Central Committee, whose membership varied from about seventy in the 1930s to more than double that in later

THE UNION OF SOVIET SOCIALIST REPUBLICS

The U.S.S.R. is over 5,000 miles long and covers one-sixth of the land area of the globe, including 42 percent of Europe and 43 percent of Asia, though the conventional distinction between Europe and Asia is not officially recognized in the Soviet Union. It is the only state that immediately adjoins so many important political regions—Europe in the west, the Near and Middle East in the south, China along a long frontier, Japan across a narrow sea, and the United States on the side toward Alaska and the Aleutian Islands. The Union has fifteen member republics, of which the Russian is by far the largest, embracing more than three-fourths of the territory and over half the population. Most of it lies farther north than Lake Superior, but around Tashkent, in the latitude of New York and Chicago, cotton and citrus fruits are grown.

years. The Central Committee worked through an executive secretariat headed by a general secretary and through an Orgburo and a Politburo, subcommittees handling, respectively, matters of party organization and party policy. The Central Committee itself, or an inside group within it, and especially the general secretary, determined the membership of the Committee and of its subcommittees. It likewise assigned, transferred, and gave orders to party members through the successive lower levels of its organization. Although party congresses were held every few years before the Second World War, they generally simply registered decisions already made by the Central Committee. Actually it was the Politburo[26] of about a dozen men that dominated the Central Committee. Power and authority flowed downward and outward, as in an army, or as in a highly centralized government agency or large private corporation in the West, except that the party was not subject to any outside control. Discipline was likewise enforced in ways not used in liberal countries, the fearsome machinery of the secret police being available for use in extreme cases against party members as well as those outside.

The number of party members, men and women, which could not have been more than 70,000 at the time of the Revolution, rose to about 2 million by 1930, 3 million by 1940, 8 million by 1960, and 18 million by the early 1980s. The Leninist ideal of a small, compact, and manageable party, made up of faithful and zealous workers who willingly carried out orders, the ideal on which the Bolsheviks had separated from the Mensheviks in 1903, continued to characterize the Communist party in the Soviet Union. Old Bolsheviks, those who had been members in the lean years before 1917, long continued to occupy the seats in the Politburo and other important party positions. The problem, once it was clear that the Revolution had come to stay, was to prevent an inrush of careerists, persons who simply wished to belong to the new governing elite, old Mensheviks, Social Revolutionaries, or even former bourgeois now flying Communist colors. A party of 2 million members, though small in contrast to the population of the U.S.S.R., still represented an enormous growth for the party itself, in which for each old member (who had joined before 1917) there were thousands of new ones. To preserve party unity under the new conditions strict uniformity was enforced. Members made an intensive study of the principles of Marxism-Leninism, embraced dialectical materialism as a philosophy and even a kind of religion, learned how to take orders without question or compunction, and to give authoritative leadership, assistance, or explanations of policy to the mass of nonparty members among whom they worked. The bottom of the party structure consisted of small nuclei or cells. In each factory, in each mine, in each office, in each class at the universities and technical schools, in each labor union, in each at least of the larger villages, one, two, or a dozen of the local people (factory workers, miners, office workers, students, etc., as the case might be) belonged to the party and imparted party views and party momentum to the whole.

The function of the party, in Marxist terms, was to carry out the dictatorship of the proletariat. It was to lead the people as a whole to the realization of socialism and, in day-to-day affairs, to coordinate the ponderous mechanism of government and make it work. Party members were present at all levels. The same men sat, in the party, in the Politburo of the Central Committee, and, in the state, in the Council of People's Commissars. At the next lower level, in the soviets of the

---

[26] For a time, during the years from 1952 to 1966, it was called the Presidium.

Union and of the component republics, party members were numerous. Lower down, party members became more rare. In a small rural soviet there might be no one belonging to the party at all; the village councilmen would receive instructions, exhortations, or "pep talks" from itinerant party members. In any event, throughout the whole structure, the party decided what the state should do.

The role of the party in the U.S.S.R. has been called, at its best, a "vocation of leadership." Those joined it who were willing to work hard, to devote themselves to party matters day and night, to absorb and communicate the party policy (or "line"), to go where they were sent, to attend meetings, speak up, and remain until all others had left for home, to perceive and explain the significance of small passing events for the future of Russia or the world revolution, to master intricate technical details of farming, manufacturing, or the care of machinery, so that others would look to them willingly for advice. The party was a specially trained elite whose members were in constant touch with each other. It was the thin stream of lifeblood which, circulating through all the diverse tissues of the U.S.S.R.—the multitudinous republics, soviets, bureaus, army, industrial and other enterprises owned under socialism by the state—kept the whole complex body unified, organic, functioning, and alive.

To the country as a whole the party undoubtedly represented the vocation of leadership. The corollary was that more than ninety-five out of a hundred persons were condemned to be followers, and while it is perhaps true (as apologists for the system have said) that under any system true leadership is exercised by a tiny fraction of people, the difference between Communist and non-Communist in the U.S.S.R. became a clear matter of social status. As the years passed, by the 1930s, many Communists in the U.S.S.R. were less of the type of revolutionary firebrand than of the successful and the efficient man or woman in any social system. They represented the satisfied, not the dissatisfied. Frequently they enjoyed material privileges, such as access to the best jobs, better housing, special food coupons, or priorities on trains. They worked faithfully for recognition and promotion in the party. They developed a bourgeois concern for the advantages of their own children. They became a new vested interest. Within the party, members had to be not so much leaders as followers. A homogeneous and monolithic organization was desired, presenting a solid front to the far more numerous but unorganized outsiders. Within the party, from time to time, a great deal of difference of opinion and open discussion was tolerated (indeed, since there was only one party all political questions were intraparty disputes), but in the end the entire membership had to conform. The party favored a certain initiative of action, and a certain fertility of mind in inventing ways to get things done, but it did not favor, and in fact repressed, originality, boldness, or freedom of thought or action.

The New Economic Policy, 1921–1927

By 1920 "war communism," as we have seen, had hopelessly antagonized the peasants, who, it was estimated, were cultivating only 62 percent as much land as in 1914.[27] This fact, together with a severe drought and the breakdown of transportation, produced a great famine. Four or five million people died. The ravages of eight years, of the World War, the Revolution, the civil wars, the Terror, had

---

[27] See pp. 714–715.

left the country in ruins, its productive facilities thrown back by decades as compared with the point reached in 1914. The rising of the Kronstadt sailors in 1921 revealed profound disillusionment in the revolutionary ranks themselves. Lenin concluded that socialization had advanced too fast. He openly advocated a compromise with capitalism, a strategic retreat. The New Economic Policy, or Nep, adopted in 1921, lasted until 1927. Most of the decade of the 1920s saw a relaxation of tempo for most people in the U.S.S.R.

Under the Nep, while the state controlled the "commanding heights" of the economy, maintaining state ownership of the basic productive industries, it allowed a great deal of private trading for private profit. The basic problem was to restore trade between town and country. The peasant would produce nothing beyond the needs of his own subsistence unless he could exchange his surplus for city-made wares such as clothing or tools. The city people had to be fed from the country if they were to turn out factory products or even continue to live in the city. Under the Nep, peasants were allowed to sell their farm products freely. Middlemen were allowed to buy and sell farm products and manufactured articles at will, to whom they pleased, at market prices, and at a profit to themselves. The Nep therefore favored the big individualist farmer or kulak. Indeed, rural changes initiated before 1914 were still at work;[28] peasant families consolidated millions of acres as private property in 1922, 1923, and 1924. Correspondingly, other peasants became "proletarians," wage-earning hired hands. The Nep also favored the sprouting of a new-rich commercial class, neobourgeois who ate expensive dinners in the restaurants of Moscow, and whose very existence seemed to explode the dream of a classless society. Under the Nep the worst damages of war and revolution were repaired. But there was no real progress, for in 1928 Russia was producing only about as much grain, raw cotton, cattle, coal, and oil as in 1913, and far less than it presumably would have produced (given the rate of growth before 1913) had there been no revolution.

Stalin and Trotsky

Lenin died in 1924 prematurely at the age of fifty-four after a series of paralyzing strokes that left him incapacitated in the last two years of his life. His embalmed remains were put permanently on view in the Kremlin; Petrograd was renamed Leningrad; a leader cult was built up around his name and image; the party presented him as a deified equal of Marx himself; and it became necessary for all schools of communist thought to claim unflinching fidelity to the Leninist tradition. Actually, in his own lifetime, the Old Bolsheviks had never regarded Lenin as infallible. They had often differed with him and with each other. As he lay dying, and after his death, his old companions and contemporaries, men in their prime, carrying on the feuding habits of the émigré days, fought with each other for control of the party in Lenin's name. They disputed over Lenin's intentions. Had he secretly thought of the Nep as a permanent policy? If not, how would he have modified it, and, most especially, how soon? Quietly, behind the scenes, as secretary of the party, without much attention to broader problems, a hitherto relatively modest member named Joseph Stalin, of whom Lenin had never had an enthusiastic opinion, was drawing all the strings of party control into his own

[28] See pp. 708–709.

hands. More openly and vociferously Leon Trotsky, who as war commissar in the critical years had been only less conspicuous than Lenin himself, raised the basic issues of the whole nature and future of the movement.

Trotsky, in 1925 and 1926, inveighed against the lassitude that had descended upon socialism.[29] The Nep with its tolerance of bourgeois and kulaks excited his contempt. He developed his doctrine of "permanent revolution," an incessant drive for proletarian objectives on all fronts in all parts of the world. He stood forth as the exponent of world revolution, which many in the party were beginning to discard in favor of first building socialism in one country. He denounced the tendency to bureaucratic ossification in the party and urged a new movement of the masses to give it life. He called for more forceful development of industry and for the collectivization of agriculture, which had figured in Communist manifestos ever since 1848.[30] Above all, he demanded immediate adoption of an overall plan, a central control and operation of the whole economic life of the country.

Trotsky failed to carry the party with him. He was charged with leftist deviationism, machinations against the Central Committee, and inciting to public discussion of issues outside the party. Stalin wove his web. At a party congress in 1927, 854,000 members dutifully voted for Stalin and the Central Committee and only 4,000 for Trotsky. Trotsky was first exiled to Siberia, then banished from the U.S.S.R.; he lived first in Turkey, then France, then Mexico, writing and propagandizing for the "permanent revolution," stigmatizing developments in the U.S.S.R. as "Stalinism," a monstrous betrayal of Marxism-Leninism, organizing an underground against Stalin as he had done in former days against the tsar. He was murdered in Mexico in 1940 under mysterious circumstances, presumably by a Soviet agent or sympathizer.

95. STALIN: THE FIVE-YEAR PLANS AND THE PURGES

Economic Planning

Hardly had the party expelled Trotsky when it appropriated certain fragments of his program. In 1928 it launched the First Five-Year Plan, aimed at rapid industrialization and the collectivization of agriculture. "Planning," or the central planning of a country's whole economic life by government officials, was to become the distinctive feature of Soviet economics and the one that was to have the greatest influence in the rest of the world.

In retrospect, it seems strange that the Communists waited ten years before adopting a plan. The truth seems to be that the Bolsheviks had only confused ideas of what to do after their seizure of power. Marxism for the most part gave only general hints. Marxism was primarily an analysis of existing or bourgeois society. It was also a theory of class war. But to portray any details of a future society, or specify what should be done after the class war had been won by the proletariat, was according to Marx and Engels sheer utopian fantasy. The bour-

---

[29] For communists, though not for socialists, the terms "communism" and "socialism" are almost interchangeable, since Russian Communists regard their own system as true socialism and all other socialism as opportunistic, reactionary, or false. Communism is also defined, in the U.S.S.R., as a future state of society toward which socialism, i.e., Soviet socialism, is the intermediate stage.

[30] See pp. 491–492.

geoisie, to be sure, would be destroyed; there would be "social ownership of the means of production," and no "exploitation of man by man"; everyone would work, and there would be neither leisure class nor unemployment. This was not much to go on in the operation of a modern industrial system.

One great constructive idea had been mapped out, most clearly by Engels. *Within* each private enterprise, Engels had observed, harmony and order reigned; it was only *between* private enterprises that capitalism was chaotic. In the individual factory, he noted, the various departments did not compete with each other; the shipping department did not purchase from the production department at prices fluctuating according to daily changes in supply and demand; the output of all departments was planned and coordinated by management. In a larger way, the great capitalist mergers and trusts, controlling many factories, prevented blind competition between them, assigned specific quotas to each, anticipated, coordinated, and stabilized the work of each plant and each person by an overall policy. With the growth of large corporate enterprise, observed Engels, the area of economic life under free competition was constantly reduced, and the area brought under rational planning was constantly enlarged. The obvious next step, according to Engels and other socialists, was to treat *all* the economic life of a country as a single factory with many departments, or a single enormous monopoly with many members, under one unified, vigorous, and far-seeing management.

During the First World War the governments of belligerent countries had in fact adopted such centralized controls.[31] They had done so not because they were socialistic, but because in time of war people were willing to subordinate their usual liberties to a single overwhelming and undisputed social purpose—victory. The "planned society" therefore made its first actual (though incomplete) appearance in the First World War. It was partly from socialist doctrine as exemplified by Engels, partly from experience of the war, and in even larger measure from the irresistible pressure to meet the continuing chronic problems of the country by raising its productive level that Stalin and the party in Russia gradually developed the idea of a plan. The war experience was especially valuable for the lessons it gave on technical questions of economic planning, such as what kind of bureaus to set up, what kind of forecasts to make, and what kind of statistics to collect.

In the U.S.S.R. it was decided to plan for five years into the future, beginning with 1928. The aim of the plan was to strengthen and enrich the country, make it militarily and industrially self-sufficient, lay the groundwork for a true workers' society, and overcome the Russian reputation for backwardness. As Stalin said in a speech in 1929: "We are becoming a country of metal, a country of automobiles, a country of tractors. And when we have put the U.S.S.R. in a motor car and the *muzhik* in a tractor . . . we shall see which countries may then be 'classified' as backward and which as advanced."

The First Five-Year Plan was declared fulfilled in 1932, and a Second Five-Year Plan was launched, lasting until 1937. The Third, inaugurated in 1938, was interrupted by the war with Germany in 1941. New plans were introduced after 1945.[32]

The First Five-Year Plan (like its successors) listed the economic goals to be

---

[31] See pp. 683–685.
[32] See pp. 856–857.

achieved. It was administered by an agency called the Gosplan. Within the frame of general policy set by the party, the Gosplan determined how much of every article the country should produce, how much of the national effort should go into the formation of capital, and how much into producing articles for daily consumption, what wages all classes of workers should receive, and at what prices all goods should be exchanged. At the bottom level, in the individual factory, the local management drew up its "requirements," or estimates of what it would need, in raw material, machinery, trained workers, plant facilities, and fuel, if it was to deliver the planned quantity of its product at a stated date. These estimates were passed up the planning ladder (or, thousands of such estimates up thousands of ladders) until they reached the Gosplan, which, balancing them against each other and against other needs as seen at the top, determined how much steel, coal, etc., should be produced, and in what qualities and grades; how many workers should be trained in technical schools and in what particular skills; how many machines should be manufactured and how many spare parts; how many new freight cars should be constructed and which lines of railway track needed repair; and how, where, when, and to whom the steel, coal, technicians, machines, and rolling stock should be made available. The plan, in short, undertook to control, by conscious management, the flow of resources and manpower which under free capitalism was regulated by shifts in demand and supply, through changes in prices, wage levels, profits, interest rates, or rent.

The system was exceedingly intricate. It was not easy to have the right number of ball bearings, for example, arrive at the right place at the right time, in exact correspondence to the amounts of other materials or to the number of workers waiting to use them. Sometimes there was overproduction, sometimes underproduction. The plan was often amended as it was applied in action. Countless reports, checkups, and exchanges of information were necessary. A huge class of white-collar office workers came into existence to handle the paperwork. The plan achieved some of its goals, exceeded a few, and failed in some.

The primary objective of the First Five-Year Plan was to build up the heavy industry, or capital wealth, of the U.S.S.R. The aim was to industrialize without the use of foreign loans.[33] Russia in 1928 was still chiefly an agricultural country. The world offered hardly any case of a country shifting from agriculture to industry without borrowing capital from abroad. Great Britain, the original home of the Industrial Revolution, was the best example, although even there, in the eighteenth century, a great deal of capital invested in England was owned by the Dutch. An agricultural country could industrialize from its own resources only by drawing upon agriculture itself. An agricultural revolution had been prerequisite to an industrial revolution in England.[34] By enclosure of land, the squeezing out of small independent farmers, and the introduction of scientific cultivation, under the auspices of a growing class of wealthy landowners, England had both increased its production of food and released many of the rural population to find employment in industry. The First Five-Year Plan called for a similar agricultural revolution in Russia, without benefit to landlords and under the auspices of the state.

---

[33] The Bolsheviks had repudiated the entire debt of the tsarist empire. Their credit in capitalist countries was therefore not good, so that, in addition to fearing dependence upon foreign lenders, they were in any case for a long time unable to borrow large sums.

[34] See pp. 428–429.

The Collectivization of Agriculture

The plan, as originally conceived, called for the collectivization of only one-fifth of the farm population, but it was suddenly revised in the winter of 1929 to include the immediate collectivization of the greater part of the peasantry. The plan set up collective farms, averaging a few thousand acres apiece, which were considered to be the property not of the state but of the peasants collectively who resided on them. Individual peasants were to pool their privately owned fields and livestock in these collectives. Those peasants who possessed fields or stock in considerable amount, the prosperous peasants or kulaks, resisted surrendering them to the new collectives. The kulaks were therefore liquidated as a class. Zealous detachments of Communists from the cities often used more violence than the plan envisaged; poor peasants turned upon rich ones; hundreds of thousands of kulaks and their families were killed and many more transported to labor camps in remote parts of the Soviet Union. The trend that had gone on since Stolypin and indeed since the Emancipation, building up a class of property-owning, labor-hiring, and "bourgeois" peasants, was now abruptly reversed. Politically, the obstinate obstruction of individualistic farmers was removed, and the peasantry was converted into a class more nearly resembling the proletariat of Marxian doctrine, a class of people who as individuals owned no capital and employed no labor, and so were better able to feel the advantages of a proletarian state. The year 1929, not 1917, was the great revolutionary year for most people in Russia.

Collectivization was accomplished at the cost of village class war in which the most capable farmers perished, and at the cost also of a wholesale destruction of livestock. The big farmers slaughtered their horses, cattle, pigs, and poultry rather than give them up. Even middling and small farmers did the same, caring nothing about animals that were no longer their own, or naïvely expecting that under collectivism the state would soon furnish a new supply. The ruinous loss of animals was the worst unforeseen calamity of the First Five-Year Plan. Agricultural disorder, together with two summers of bad weather, was followed in 1932 by temporary but deadly famine in southeast Russia that took the lives of an estimated 2 million to 3 million persons; the government meanwhile refused to cut back on export quotas because they were needed to pay for industrial imports under the Five-Year Plan. Agriculture long remained the weakest sector of the Soviet economy.

By introducing thousand-acre units in place of very small ones, collectivization made it possible to apply capital to the soil. Formerly the average peasant had been far too poor to buy a tractor and his fields too tiny and dispersed for him to use one, so that only a few rare kulaks had employed any machinery. In the course of the First Five-Year Plan hundreds of Machine Tractor Stations were organized throughout the country. Each, in its region, maintained a force of tractors, harvesting combines, expert agronomists, etc., which were dispatched from one collective farm to another by local arrangement. The application of capital increased the output per peasant. It was also much easier administratively for higher authorities to get control over the agricultural surplus (products not consumed by the village itself) from a single collective farm than from numerous small and unorganized peasants. Each collective was assigned a quota on which it contracted in advance to make delivery. Members of the collective could sell in a free market any products they raised beyond this quota; but meanwhile the government knew the quantity of agricultural produce it could count on, either to feed the cities and other regions that did not produce their own food, or for export in the world market to pay for imports of machinery from the West. By 1939 all but a negligible fraction of the peasantry were collectivized. Although collectivization failed to increase agricultural output, it accomplished the goal of insuring state control over agricultural production. Simultaneously, it made possible the success of industrialization by augmenting the supply of industrial workers. Since the villages needed less labor, 20 million people moved from country to city between the years 1926 and 1939 and were available for jobs in the new industries.

It was the peasants who bore the burden of collectivization. Not only had they been subjected to violence and expropriation, but the new collectives threw the peasant back into something like the *mir*, condemning him to the rounds of communal living, robbing him of the chance to make any decisions of his own. By obliging peasants to make "deliveries" below market prices, it even revived some features of the type of serfdom and forced labor that had prevailed a century before over most of eastern Europe.[35] On the other hand, although the collectives varied widely in their degree of prosperity, it is probable that by 1939 a great many of the rural people were better housed and better fed than they had been before the Revolution. Kulaks who might have remembered better conditions had not survived.

The Growth of Industry

While the agricultural base was being revolutionized, industrialization went rapidly forward. At first there was considerable dependence on the capitalist countries. Engineers and other technicians from western Europe and the United States took service in the Soviet Union. Much machinery was at first imported. But the world-wide depression that set in about 1931, bringing a catastrophic fall of agricultural prices, meant that foreign-made machines became more costly in terms of the cereals that were the chief Soviet export. The international situation also deteriorated. Both Japan and Germany in the 1930s showed an increasing hostility to the U.S.S.R. From the beginning the Five-Year plans had as one of their objectives the industrial and military self-sufficiency of the country. The Second Five-Year Plan, launched in 1933, though in some ways less ambitious than the first, showed an even greater determination to cut down imports and achieve national self-sufficiency, especially in the heavy industry that was basic to war production.

No ten years in the history of any Western country ever showed such a rate of industrial growth as the decade of the first two plans in the Soviet Union. In Great Britain industrialization had been gradual; in Germany and the United States it had been more rapid, and in each country there had been decades in which output of coal or iron doubled; but in the U.S.S.R., from 1928 to 1938, production of iron and steel expanded four times and that of coal three and a half times. In 1938 the U.S.S.R. was the world's largest producer of farm tractors and railway locomotives. Four-fifths of all its industrial output came from plants built in the preceding ten years. Two plants alone, at the new cities of Magnitogorsk in the Urals and Stalinsk 1,000 miles farther east, produced as much iron and steel as the whole Russian empire in 1914. In 1939 the U.S.S.R. was surpassed in gross industrial output only by the United States and Germany.

---

[35] See pp. 479–480, 533–534.

The plans called for a marked development of industry east of the Urals, and so brought a modernization of life for the first time to inner Asia, in a way comparable only to the movement of machine industry into the once primitive Great Lakes region of the American Middle West. Pittsburghs, Clevelands, and Detroits rose in the old Turkestan and Siberia. Copper mines were opened in the Urals and around Lake Balkhash, lead mines in the Far East and in the Altai Mountains. New grain-producing regions were developed in Siberia and in the Kazakh S.S.R., whence grain was shipped westward to Russia proper, or southward to the Uzbek S.S.R., which was devoted mainly to cotton. Tashkent, the Uzbek capital, formerly a remote town of bazaars and caravans, grew to be a city of over half a million, a center of cotton culture, copper mining, and electrical industries, connected with the north by the newly built Turksib Railway. The Kuznetsk basin, 2,000 miles inland from every ocean, was found to possess coal deposits of high grade. Kuznetsk coal and the iron ores of the Urals became complementary, though separated by a thousand miles, somewhat like Pennsylvania coal and Minnesota iron in the United States. The opening of all these new areas, requiring the movement of food to Uzbekistan in exchange for cotton, or of Ural iron to the new Kuznetsk cities, demanded a revolution in transportation. The railroads in 1938 carried five times as much freight as in 1913.

These astounding developments were enough to change the relative economic strength of the world's peoples with respect to one another. It was significant that inner Asia was for the first time turning industrial. It was significant, too, that although the U.S.S.R. had less foreign trade than had the Russian empire, it had more trade than the old Russia with its Asian neighbors, with which it formed new and close connections. The Russia that went to war with Germany in 1941 proved to be a different antagonist from the Russia of 1914. Industrialization in the Urals and in Asia enabled the U.S.S.R. (with a good deal of Allied assistance) to survive the German occupation and destruction of the older industrial areas in the Don valley. The new "socialist fatherland" proved able to absorb the shock and strike back. A great deal of the increased industrial output had gone to equip and modernize the Red Army.

At the same time, the degree of industrialization of the U.S.S.R. can easily be exaggerated. It was phenomenal because it started from so little. Qualitatively, by Western criteria, standards of production were low. Many of the hastily constructed, new plants were shoddy and suffered from rapid depreciation. In efficiency, as shown by output per worker employed, the U.S.S.R. continued to lag behind the West. In intensity of modernization, as shown by output of certain items in proportion to the whole population, it also lagged. Per capita of its huge population, in 1937, the U.S.S.R. produced less coal, electricity, cottons, woolens, leather shoes, or soap than did the United States, Britain, Germany, France, or even Japan, and less iron and steel than any of them except Japan. Production of paper is revealing because paper is used in so many "civilized" activities—in books, newspapers, magazines, schools, correspondence, placards, maps, pictures, charts, business and government records, and household articles and amenities. Where the United States about 1937 produced 103 pounds of paper per person, Germany and Great Britain each 92, France 51, and Japan 17, the U.S.S.R. produced only 11.

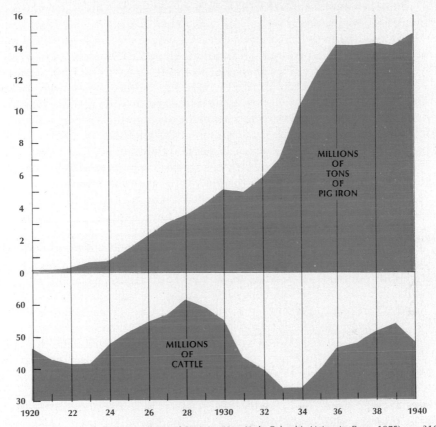

Source: B. R. Mitchell, *European Historical Statistics* (New York: Columbia University Press, 1975), pp. 316, 396.

PIG IRON AND CATTLE IN THE SOVIET UNION, 1920–1940

If pig iron is taken as a measure of industrial activity and number of cattle as a similar indication for agriculture, the chart reveals clearly what happened in the twenty years after the Revolution—an enormous build-up of heavy industry at the expense of food supplies. Iron mines and forges, in the disorganization of the Revolution and civil war, were producing almost nothing in 1920. By the late 1920s, output of pig iron regained the pre-Revolutionary level, but the great upsurge came with the Second Five-Year Plan. By 1940 Russia produced more pig iron than Germany, and far more than Britain or France. Numbers of cattle grew in the 1920s, but fell catastrophically during the collectivization of agriculture after 1929, and by 1940 hardly exceeded the figure for 1920. Since 1940 the industrial development of the Soviet Union has been impressive, but agricultural production has continued to be a problem.

Social Costs and Social Effects of the Plans

Industrialization in Russia demanded a huge and continuing sacrifice on the part of the people. It was not merely that kulaks lost their lives, or that others, whose numbers have never been known, were found to be enemies of the system and sent off to correctional labor camps. All were required to accept a program of austerity and self-denial, going without the better food, housing, and other consumers' goods that might have been produced, in order that the capital wealth and heavy industry of the country might be built up. As much as a third of the national income was reinvested in industry every year—twice as much as in the England of 1914, though probably not more than in the England of 1840. The plan required hard work and low wages. People looked to the future, to the time when, the basic industries having been built, better housing, better food, better clothing, and more leisure would follow. Morale was sustained by propaganda. One of the chief functions of party members was to explain why sacrifices were necessary. In the late 1930s life began to ease; food rationing was abolished in 1935, and a few more products of light industry, such as dishes and fountain pens, began to appear in Soviet retail stores. Living standards were at least up to those of 1927 with prospects brighter for raising them. But the need for war preparations, as the world again approached chaos, again drove back the vision of the Promised Land.

Socialism, as realized in the plans, did away with some of the evils of unrestrained free enterprise. There was no unemployment. There was no cycle of boom and depression. There was less misuse of women and children than in the early days of industrialism in the West. There was no absolute want or pauperization, except for political undesirables and except for temporary conditions of famine. There was a minimum below which no one was supposed to fall. On the other hand, there was no economic equality. Marxism, indeed, had never seen complete equality of income as a principal objective. While there was no handful of very rich people, as in the West (where the income of the rich came from property), the differences in income were nevertheless very great. High government officials, managers, engineers, and favored intellectuals received the highest rewards. People with large incomes, by buying government bonds or accumulating personal possessions, could build up precarious little fortunes for themselves and their children. They could not, however, under socialism, own any industrial capital.

Competition persisted. In 1935 a miner named Stakhanov greatly increased his daily output of coal by devising improvements in his methods of work. He also greatly increased his wages, since Soviet workers were paid at piece rates. His example proved contagious; workers all over the country began to break records of all kinds. The government publicized their achievements, called them Stakhanovites and "labor heroes," and pronounced the movement to be "a new and higher stage of socialist competition." In labor circles in the United States such straining to increase output would be called a speed-up, and piecework wages had long been anathema to the organized labor of all countries. Nor was management free from competitive pressure. A factory manager who failed to show the net income (or "profit") upon which the plan counted, or who failed to meet his quota of output, might lose not only his job but his social status or even his life. Poor management was often construed as sabotage. Insufficient use of the men and resources allocated to a factory was considered a betrayal of Soviet workers and a waste of the property of the nation. The press, not otherwise free, freely denounced whole industries or individual executives for failures to meet the plan.

Foreign observers often found the distinctive feature of the new system to lie in this kind of competition or emulation, or in a feeling that everybody was busily toiling and struggling to create a socialist fatherland. Workers in the 1930s, it seemed, had a real belief that the new industrial wonders were their own. People rejoiced at every new advance as a personal triumph. It became a national pastime to watch the mounting statistics, the fulfilling of quotas or hitting of "targets." Newspaper readers read no comic strips; they read eagerly about the latest doings (or misdoings) on the economic front. Never had there been such unalloyed delight in material and mechanical progress, not even in America in the Gilded Age.

How real the feeling of solidarity was, how much of it was spontaneous, and how much was inculcated by a watchful and dictatorial government, are questions on which there has been much difference of opinion. There is no doubt that unity was purchased at the price of totalitarianism.[36] The government supervised everything. There was no room for skepticism, eccentricity of thought, or any basic criticism that weakened the will to achieve. As in tsarist times, no one could leave the country without special permission, which was given far more rarely than before 1914. There was only one party. There were no free labor unions, no free press, no freedom of association, and at best only an irritable tolerance for religion. Art, literature, and even science became vehicles of political propaganda. Dialectical materialism was the official philosophy. Conformity was the ideal, and the very passion for solidarity made for fear and suspicion of all who might go astray. As for the number of people sacrificed to the Juggernaut—liquidated bourgeois, liquidated kulaks, purged party members, disaffected persons sentenced to long terms in labor camps—a precise figure is difficult to arrive at, but it certainly reached many millions over the years.

The Purge Trials of the 1930s

In 1936 socialism was judged to have proved so successful that a new constitution for the U.S.S.R. was proclaimed. It enumerated, as rights of Soviet citizens, not merely the usual civil liberties of Western democracy but the rights to steady employment, rest, leisure, economic security, and a comfortable old age. All forms of racism were condemned. It reorganized the soviet republics and granted equal and direct universal suffrage, as explained above.[37] The new constitution of 1936 was favorably commented upon in the West, where it was hoped that the Russian Revolution, like former revolutions, had at last turned into more peaceable and quiet channels. It was nonetheless apparent that the Communist party remained the sole governing group in the country, that Stalin was tightening his dictatorship, and that the party was racked by internal troubles.

It was natural that the complex and multifarious operations of the Five-Year plans should produce divergences of opinion among the men who carried them out. The party elders, however, were engaged not merely in discussions of policy but in the older game of the seizure of power. On the right, led by Bukharin, was a group that believed in more gradual methods of collectivizing the peasants. More important was the element described as leftist. Its mastermind and rallying point was the exiled Trotsky. Probably there was some kind of secret Trotskyist machine within the U.S.S.R. and within the party, even if there is no evidence for the charge that some Trotskyists had intrigued with Germans and other foreigners to overthrow and replace Stalin. As early as 1933 the party underwent a drastic purge, in which a third of its members were expelled. Even faithful associates

---

[36] On totalitarianism, see pp. 790–793.
[37] See p. 719.

of Stalin were appalled at his growing ruthlessness. Serge Kirov, an old friend and revolutionary companion of Stalin since 1909, recently elected a key member of the party secretariat, showed signs of leading the disaffected; in 1934 he was assassinated in his office, very probably by a police agent of Stalin's. Stalin used the assassination to strike out at his opponents, imagined or real, by a revival of terror, immediately executing over a hundred persons and launching the extraordinary "purges" of the 1930s.

A series of sensational trials took place. In 1936 sixteen Old Bolsheviks were brought to trial. Some, like Zinoviev and Kamenev, had been expelled from the party in 1927 for supporting Trotsky and subsequently, after the proper recantations, had been readmitted. Now they were charged with the murder of Kirov, with plotting the murder of Stalin, and with having organized, in 1932, under Trotsky's inspiration, a secret group to disorganize and terrorize the Central Committee. To the amazement of the world, all the accused made full confession to the charges in open court. All blamed themselves as unworthy and erring reprobates. All were put to death. In 1937, after similar trials, seventeen other Old Bolsheviks met the same fate or received long prison sentences; and in 1938 Bukharin and the rightists, charged with wanting to restore bourgeois capitalism and conspiring with Trotsky to revolutionize the U.S.S.R., were executed. The same confessions and self-accusations followed in almost every case, with no other verifiable evidence adduced. How these confessions were obtained in open court, from men apparently in full possession of their faculties and bearing no sign of physical harm, long remained one of the great mysteries of modern statecraft. Later revelations of psychological torture and physical mistreatment that broke their will and destroyed their reasoning powers gave some insight into the techniques used. In addition to these public trials there were thousands of arrests, private inquisitions, and executions. In 1937, in a secret court-martial, Marshal Tukhachevski and seven other ranking generals were accused of Trotskyism and of conspiring with the Germans and Japanese and were shot. The purges not only included men who had held the highest rank in party, government, and military circles but reached down into the lesser echelons of all these groups as well. Before the purges were over late in 1938, an unknown number of persons, but probably in the millions, were either executed or sent off into prison labor camps. Years later the innocence was established of many of the victims of Stalin's almost paranoid suspicion, and their reputations were posthumously restored.

By these famous "purge trials" Stalin's dictatorship and party discipline were reinforced. It may be that a real danger of renewed revolution was averted. Had the tsarist government dealt as summarily with Bolsheviks as Bolsheviks dealt with one another there could have been no November Revolution. Above all, Stalin rid himself by the trials of all possible rivals for his own position. He disposed of the embarrassment of having men about him who could remember the old days, who could quote Lenin as a former friend, or belittle the reality of 1937 by recalling the dreams of 1917. After 1938 there were virtually no Old Bolsheviks left. The aging but still explosive professional revolutionaries were now dead. A younger group, products of the new order, successful men of affairs, practical, constructive, impatient of "agitators," and acquiescing in Stalin's dictatorship, were operating what was now an established system.

96. THE INTERNATIONAL IMPACT OF COMMUNISM, 1919–1939

Socialism and the First World War

Marxism had always been international in its outlook. To Marx, and the early Marxists, existing states (like other institutions) owed their character to the class struggle. They were committees of the bourgeoisie to govern the proletariat. National states were regarded as frameworks, destined to be dismantled and pass away in the course of inevitable historic processes. After Marx's death, as Marxist parties grew in numbers, and as states of western Europe became more democratic, most people who called themselves Marxists actually accepted the national state, seeing in it a means by which the workers' lot could be gradually improved. This view was part of the movement of "revisionism," or what more rigorous Marxists called "opportunism."[38] In the First World War national loyalty proved its strength. The socialist parties in the Reichstag, the French Chamber, and other parliamentary bodies voted for war credits without hesitation. Socialist workers reported for mobilization like everyone else. In Germany socialists said that the reactionary Russian tsardom must be resisted; in France, that the Germans menaced all Frenchmen alike. In general, all political parties, including the socialists, declared a moratorium on party politics during the war.

Small minorities of socialists in every country, however, refused to accept the war. Marxian socialism had long taught that workingmen of all nations were bound by the supreme loyalty of class, that their real enemies were the capitalists of their own countries, that international wars were capitalist and "imperialist" quarrels, and that class struggle was the only kind of warfare that the proletarian should accept. These socialists denounced the action of the socialist majorities as a sellout to capitalism and imperialism. They met in international conferences with each other and with socialists from the neutral countries. Active among them were Lenin and other Russian Social Democrats then in Switzerland. "The only task for socialists," wrote Lenin in 1914, "is to convert the war of peoples into a civil war." The minority or antiwar socialists met at the small Swiss town of Zimmerwald in 1915, where they drew up a "Zimmerwald program," calling for immediate peace without annexations or indemnities. This had no effect on most socialists in the belligerent countries. The Zimmerwald group itself soon began to split. Most Zimmerwalders regarded peace, or the repudiation of the war, as their aim. But a "Zimmerwald Left" began to develop, inspired mainly by Lenin and the Russian émigrés. This faction made its aim not peace but revolution. It hoped that the war would go on until it caused social revolution in the belligerent countries.

Then in April 1917, with the German imperial government wishing them *bon voyage*, Lenin and the other Bolsheviks went back to Russia and accomplished the November Revolution. Lenin, until his death in 1924, believed that the Russian Revolution was only a local phase of a world revolution—of *the* revolution of strict Marxian doctrine. Russia, for him, was the theater of currently most active operations in the international class war. Because he expected proletarian upheaval in Germany, Poland, the Danube valley, and the Baltic regions, he accepted without compunction the treaty of Brest-Litovsk. He took no pride in

---

[38] See pp. 495, 588–591.

Russia; he was no patriot or "social-chauvinist," to use his own term. In the founding of the U.S.S.R. in 1922 he saw a nucleus around which other and greater soviet republics of any nationality might coalesce. "Soviet republics in countries with a higher degree of civilization," he wrote, "whose proletariat has greater social weight and influence, have every prospect of outstripping Russia as soon as they start upon the road of proletarian dictatorship."

The First World War was in fact followed by attempted revolutions in Germany and eastern Europe. With the German and Austro-Hungarian empires wrecked, socialists and liberals of all descriptions strove to establish new regimes. Among socialists the old differences persisted, between Social Democrats favoring gradual, nonviolent, and parliamentary methods, and a more extreme (and smaller) group which saw in postwar disintegration a chance to realize the international proletarian revolution. The first group looked upon the Bolshevik Revolution with horror. The second looked upon it with admiration. The first group included not only trade union officials and practical socialist politicians, but such prewar giants of Marxian exegesis as Karl Kautsky and Eduard Bernstein. Even Kautsky, who had upheld pure Marxism against the revisionism of Bernstein, could not stomach the methods of Lenin. The mass of European socialists, with their fiercest leaders removed, were to remain characterized by relative moderation. Marxist in principle, they were in fact more than ever wedded to gradual, peaceable, and parliamentary methods.

In the second group, the sifted residue of uncompromising Leninist neo-Marxists, who accepted the Bolshevik Revolution, were Karl Liebknecht and Rosa Luxemburg. Organizing the Spartacist movement[39] in Germany, they attempted, in January 1919, to overthrow the majority socialist government in Germany, as Lenin had overthrown the Provisional Government in Russia in November 1917. In the second group also was Béla Kun, who had turned Bolshevik during a sojourn in Russia, and who set up and maintained a soviet regime in Hungary for several months in 1919.

Lenin and the Bolsheviks, though absorbed in their own revolution, gave all possible aid to the fringe of left socialists of Europe. They sent large sums of money to Germany, to Sweden, to Italy. When the Bolshevik Radek was arrested in Berlin he was said to have a plan for proletarian revolution in all central Europe in his possession. The party considered sending Russian troops to Hungary to support Béla Kun. But the chief instrument of world revolution, created in March 1919, was the Third or Communist International.

The Founding of the Third International

The Second International, which since its foundation in 1889 had met every two or three years until 1914, held its first postwar meeting at Berne in 1919.[40] It represented socialist parties and labor organizations of all countries. The Berne meeting was stormy, for a small minority vehemently demanded "revolution as in Russia, socialization of property as in Russia, application of Marxism as in Russia." Overruled at Berne, they repaired to Moscow and there founded a new International in conjunction with the Russian Communist party, and with Lenin and the Russians dominating it completely. It was Lenin's hope, by founding a

[39] See p. 746 and note.
[40] See pp. 588–590.

new International of his own, to discredit moderate socialism and to claim for the Communists the true line of succession from the First International of Karl Marx. The First International, he declared, had laid the foundations for proletarian struggle, the Second had broadened it, the Third "took over the work of the Second International, cut off its opportunistic, social-chauvinist, bourgeois and petty-bourgeois rubbish, and began to carry into effect the dictatorship of the proletariat."

The first congress of the Third International in 1919 was somewhat haphazard, but at the second, in 1920, the extreme left parties of thirty-seven countries were represented. The Russian party was supposedly only one component. Actually, it supplied most of the personnel and most of the funds; the Bolshevik Zinoviev was its first president, remaining in this office until his disgrace as a Trotskyist in 1927. The Third or Communist International—the Comintern—was in part a spontaneous rallying of Marxists from all countries who accepted the Bolshevik Revolution as the true fruition of Marxism and so were willing to follow the Russian lead; but, even more, it was the creation and weapon of the Bolsheviks themselves, by which to discredit and isolate the moderate socialists and bring about world revolution. Of all enemies the Communists hated the socialists most, reserving for them even choicer epithets than they bestowed upon capitalists and imperialists, because Communists and socialists were competing for the same thing, the leadership of the world's working class.

Parties adhering to the Comintern were obliged to drop the old name "socialist" and call themselves Communist. They were obliged to accept strong international centralization. Where the Second International had been a loose federation, and its congresses hardly more than forums, the Third International put strong powers in the hands of its Executive Committee, whose orders the Communist parties of all countries had to obey. Since there was a kind of interlocking directorate by which members of the Central Committee of the party in Russia sat also as members of the Executive Committee of the Third International, the top Communists in Russia had, in the Comintern, an "apparatus" by which they could produce desired effects in many countries—the use of party members to penetrate labor unions, foment strikes, propagandize ideas, or interfere in elections.

The second congress of the International, in 1920, endorsed a program of Twenty-One Points, written by Lenin. These included the requirements that each national party must call itself Communist, repudiate "reformist" socialism, propagandize labor unions and get Communists into the important union offices, infiltrate the army, impose an iron discipline upon members, require submission of each party worker to his national committee and to the orders of the international Executive, use both legal channels and secret underground methods, and expel promptly any member not hewing to the party line. Making no pretense of respect for parliamentary democracy, the second congress ruled that "the only question can be that of utilizing bourgeois state institutions for their own destruction." As for the labor movement, Lenin wrote that "the struggle against the Gomperses, the Jouhaux, the Hendersons[41] . . . who represent an *absolutely*

---

[41] Samuel Gompers (1850–1924), began as a cigar maker, president of the American Federation of Labor, 1886–1924; Léon Jouhaux (1879–1954), began as a factory worker, secretary general of the French General Confederation of Labor, 1909–1947, resigned in 1947 to found a new labor organization in opposition to communism; Arthur Henderson (1863–1935), began as an iron-molder's apprentice, chairman of the Parliamentary Labour Party, 1908–1910, 1914–1917, Member of Parliament, 1903–1931, Secretary of State for Foreign Affairs, 1929–1931.

similar social and political type as our Mensheviks . . . must be waged without mercy to the end." The Comintern was not an assemblage of humanitarians engaged in welfare work; it was a weapon for revolution, organized by revolutionaries who knew what revolution was.

For several years the U.S.S.R., using the Comintern or more conventional diplomatic channels, promoted world revolution as best it could. Communists from many countries went to Russia for indoctrination. Native-born or Russian agents proceeded to the Dutch Indies, to China, to Europe, to America. Until 1927 the Chinese revolutionists welcomed assistance from Moscow; the Russian Borodin became an adviser in their affairs. In 1924, in England, publication of the "Zinoviev letter," in which, at least allegedly, the Comintern urged British workers to provoke revolution, led to a great electoral victory for the Conservative party. The Bolshevik menace, real and imagined, produced everywhere a strong reaction. It was basic to the rise of fascism described in the following chapters.

In 1927, with the suppression of Trotskyism and world revolutionism in Russia, and with the concentration under Stalin on a program of building socialism in one country, the Comintern entered upon a period of inaction. About 1935, as fascist dictators became more noisily bellicose, the U.S.S.R. turned to a policy of international collective security, and the Comintern instructed all Communist parties, each in its own country, to enter into coalitions with socialists and advanced liberals, in what were called "popular fronts," to combat fascism and reaction. During the Second World War (in 1943), as a gesture of good will to Great Britain and the United States, the U.S.S.R. abolished the Comintern entirely, but it reappeared for a few years from 1947 to 1956 under a new name, the Communist Information Bureau or Cominform.[42]

It was not through the Comintern that the U.S.S.R. exerted its greatest influence on the world. It exerted its influence by the massive fact of its very existence. By 1939 it was clear that a new type of economic system had appeared. Before 1917 no one in Europe or Asia had thought that anything was to be learned from Russia. Twenty years later even critics of the U.S.S.R. feared that it might represent the wave of the future. Its sheer power was soon demonstrated in the Second World War. However one judged the U.S.S.R., no one could dismiss its socialism as visionary or impracticable. An alternative to free enterprise and capitalism had been brought into being. Marxism was not merely a theory; there was an actual society, embracing a sixth of the globe, which called itself Marxist.

In every country those who were most critical of capitalist institutions compared them unfavorably to those of the Soviet Union. Most of those who in the 1930s hoped to profit from the Soviet experience were not actually communist. Some believed that something like Soviet results might be obtained without the use of Soviet methods, which were dismissed as typically Russian, a deplorable heritage from the Byzantine Empire and the tsars. With the appearance of Communism and Communist parties, socialism and socialist ideas seemed in contrast to be middling and respectable. Everywhere in the 1930s the idea of "planning" began to find favor. Workers obtained more security against the fluctuations of capitalism. The so-called backward peoples, especially in Asia, were particularly impressed by the achievement of the U.S.S.R., which had shown how a tradi-

---

[42] For the U.S.S.R. and for international communism after 1945, see pp. 852–866.

tional society could modernize without falling under the influence of foreign capital or foreign guidance.

For a long time, and long after the abolition of the Comintern, the Communist party in Russia tried to present itself as the leader of world revolution and to exert control over Communist parties in other countries. After the Second World War this became increasingly difficult. Over half a century after the November Revolution the U.S.S.R. no longer seemed very innovative, and in some ways not even efficient; and the later revelations from within the Soviet system itself of the persecution and deaths of millions of innocent victims cast doubt upon its self-assumed leadership of oppressed peoples. European Communist parties sought to establish their independence from Moscow, a Communist revolution triumphed in China, and new movements of the Left emerged by which even the Soviets were called bourgeois and Soviet society was denounced as state capitalism. But all Communist parties derived from the establishment of the Third International in 1919; they all professed adherence to Marxism; and for all of them the Russian Revolution stood as the first great victory over capitalism and imperialism.

XVIII.
The
Apparent
Victory of
Democracy

We have followed events in the Soviet Union to about the year 1939 but have left the story of Europe and the rest of the world at the signing of the peace treaties of 1919. We must deal now with the period of just twenty years that elapsed between the formal close of the First World War in 1919 and the outbreak of the Second World War in 1939. In these twenty years the world made a dizzy passage from confidence to disillusionment and from hope to fear. It went through a few years of superficial prosperity, abruptly followed by unparalleled economic disaster. For a time, in the 1920s, democracy seemed to be advancing almost everywhere; then, in the 1930s, the new phenomenon of totalitarianism began to spread. Let us first examine the apparent triumphs of democracy in the 1920s, turn next to the devastating world-wide effects of the great depression that began in 1929, and then, in the following chapter, trace the painful decade of the 1930s.

97. THE ADVANCE OF DEMOCRACY AFTER 1919

Gains of Democracy and Social Democracy

The first years following the war were troubled. Even the victors faced serious difficulties in reconversion from war to peace. Men demobilized from the huge armies found themselves unemployed and psychologically restless. Farms and

Chapter Emblem: A medal struck in honor of the Peace of Versailles, 1919.

factories geared to maximum production during the war faced a sudden disappearance of markets. They produced more than could now be sold, so that the war was followed by a sharp postwar depression, which, however, had run its course by 1922. Basically, the economic position even of the victors was seriously damaged, for the war had disjointed the world of 1914, in which industrial western Europe had lived by exchange with eastern Europe and with overseas countries.

The war, President Wilson had said, had been fought to make the world safe for democracy. Political democracy now made advances everywhere. The new states that emerged from the war all adopted written constitutions and universal suffrage. Democracy made advances even in countries that had long been in large measure democratic. The last significant steps toward universal male suffrage were taken in Great Britain in 1918. The most conspicuous innovation was the growing enfranchisement of women. In 1918 female suffrage with certain restrictions was adopted in Great Britain; in 1928 the restrictions were dropped and the vote was granted on an equal basis with men. In 1920, through an amendment to the constitution, female suffrage became general in the United States. Women voted also in Germany and in most of the new states of Europe. In the Soviet Union women received the vote on an equal basis with men after the Revolution in 1917.

In most European countries the successors of the old prewar socialists gained in strength. With the left of the old socialists generally seceding, calling themselves communists, and affiliated with each other and with Moscow in the Communist International, the European socialists or social democrats were preponderantly a party of peaceable or revisionist Marxism, entirely willing to carry on the class conflict by parliamentary and legislative methods. Labor unions, with new self-confidence gained from the role they had played in the war, grew in membership, prestige, and importance.

Social legislation which before the war would have seemed radical was now enacted in many places. An eight-hour legal working day became common, and government-sponsored insurance programs against sickness, accident, and old age were either adopted or extended; an act of 1930, in France, insured almost 10 million workers. An air of progressive democracy pervaded Europe and the European world. The social service, or welfare, state, already under way in the late nineteenth century, was becoming more firmly established.

Only in Italy in the early postwar years, of the states that might have been expected to continue their prewar democratic gains, did democracy receive a sharp setback. Italy had been a parliamentary state since 1861 and had introduced a democratic suffrage in the elections of 1913. In 1919 the Italians held their second elections under universal male suffrage. But Italian democracy was abruptly ended. In 1922 an agitator named Benito Mussolini, leading a movement which he called Fascism, killed off the Italian parliament.[1] Lenin had already founded the first single-party state; Mussolini became the first of the personal dictators of postwar Europe outside Russia. Fascist Italy, in the 1920s, was the chief exception in what seemed to be a rising tide of democracy.

The New States of Central and East-Central Europe

In central and east-central Europe—in Germany, in the territory of the former Austro-Hungarian empire, and in the western fringe of former tsarist Russia—

[1] See pp. 518, 780–784.

entirely new states and new governments struggled to establish themselves. The new states included, besides republican Germany, the four successor states to the Habsburg empire—Austria, Hungary, Czechoslovakia, and Yugoslavia; and the five states that had broken away from the Russian empire Poland, Finland, Estonia, Latvia, and Lithuania.[2] The other small states in eastern Europe, Rumania, Bulgaria, Greece, and Albania, had already been independent before 1914; their boundaries underwent some modification and their governments considerable reorganization after the war. The Turkish Republic is considered elsewhere.[3]

The new states were to a large extent accidents of the war. Nowhere, except possibly in Poland, did they represent a deeply felt, long-maturing, or widespread revolutionary sentiment. Only an infinitesimal number of Germans in 1914 would have voted for a republic. Even among the nationalities of Austria-Hungary in 1914 few persons would have chosen the complete breakup of the Habsburg empire. The republicans, moderate socialists, agrarians, or nationalists who now found themselves in power had to improvise governments for which there had been little preparation. They had to contend with reactionaries, monarchists, and members of the old aristocracy. They had also to deal with the real revolutionaries, who, inspired by Lenin's success, hoped to bring about the dictatorship of the proletariat. A communist revolt broke out in Germany in 1919 but was quickly suppressed; soviet regimes were actually set up but soon crushed in Hungary and in the German state of Bavaria; and as late as 1923 there was a communist uprising in the German state of Saxony.

The new states all embodied the principle of national self-determination, which held that each nationality should enjoy political sovereignty—one nation, one government. But people in this region were and always had been locally intermixed.[4] Each of the new states therefore included minority nationalities; for, with the exception of an exchange of populations between Greece and Turkey, arranged in 1923, there was no thought of the actual physical removal of "alien" groups. Poland and Czechoslovakia were the most composite of the new states. Each of these two possessed, in particular, among its several minorities, a considerable population of disaffected Germans.

[2] See map, pp. 692–693.
[3] See pp. 753–755.
[4] See map, p. 441.

AUTOUR d'ELLE
by Marc Chagall (Russian, then French, 1887–   )

Where some painters departed from the Western tradition by cultivating pure abstraction or geometrized patterns (see pp. 596 601, 906 909), others did so by evoking unconscious or dreamlike mental phenomena. This picture was painted by Chagall in France in 1945 in memory of his wife. The houses in the center represent the Russian city of Smolensk, where they had been married thirty years before. The surrounding faces and figures are individually quite distinct, but they float disconnectedly like the vivid images in a dream, without location in space or time, or any rational relationship to each other. Past and present, memory and perception, fantastic and real objects flow together in a kind of free play of the unconscious mind. These qualities characterized surrealism, of which Chagall in his younger days had been a forerunner. Courtesy of the Musée d'Art Moderne, Paris (Service Photographique). Permission A.D.A.G.P. 1970 by French Reproduction Rights, Inc.

Nevertheless, despite economic and nationalist troubles, the new states and governments attempted at the outset to make themselves democratic. Except for the German republic they were all relatively small. All the newly created states were republics except Yugoslavia, which was under the older Serbian dynasty. Hungary started out in 1918 as a republic, but the attempt of Béla Kun to found a Hungarian Soviet Republic in 1919 brought back the counterrevolutionaries who restored the Habsburg monarchy in principle, though they were prevented by foreign pressure from restoring the king in person. Hungary emerged in 1920 as a monarchy with a perennially vacant throne, under a kind of dictatorship exercised by Admiral Horthy. All smaller states of Europe, including Hungary, possessed at least the external apparatus of democracy until the 1930s; that is, they had constitutions, parliaments, elections, and a diversity of political parties. If civil liberty was sometimes violated, the right to civil liberty was not denied; and if the elections were sometimes rigged, they were at least in principle supposed to be free.

Economic Problems of Eastern Europe: Land Reform

Eastern Europe for centuries had been an agrarian region of large landed estates, which supported on the one hand a wealthy landowning aristocracy of almost feudal outlook, and on the other an impoverished mass of agricultural workers with little or no property of their own. The landed aristocracy had been the chief support of the Austro-Hungarian empire and an important pillar of the old order in the tsarist empire and in eastern Prussia. The mass of the rural population, through all this region, had been free from serfdom, or released from subjection to manorial landlords, only since the middle of the preceding century.[5] The middle class of business and professional men was small except in Austria and Bohemia, the western portion of Czechoslovakia. In general, the whole region was conscious of lagging behind western Europe, not only in industry, factories, railroads, and great cities, but also in literacy, schooling, reading habits, health, death rates, length of life, and material standard of living.[6]

The new states set out to modernize themselves, generally on the model of the West. They introduced democratic and constitutional ideas. They put up protective tariffs, behind which they tried to develop factories and industries of their own. But the new national boundaries created difficulties. Where Europe in 1913 had had 6,000 miles of frontiers, after the war it had almost 10,000, and all the increase was in eastern Europe. Goods circulated much less easily. Protected industries in the old agricultural regions produced inefficiently and at high cost. Old and established industries, in Austria, Czechoslovakia, and western Poland, cut off by the new frontiers and new tariffs from their former markets, fell upon hard times. The working class of Vienna lived in misery, because Vienna, a city of 2 million persons, formerly the capital of an empire of 50 million, was now the capital of a republic of 6 million. In Czechoslovakia the German minority, the Sudetens, complained that in hard times the German businessmen and workers, because of government policies, always suffered more than their Czech counterparts. Economically, the carving up of eastern Europe into a dozen independent states was self-defeating.

The greatest of reforms undertaken by the new east-European states was the reform of landownership. Although it far from solved basic economic problems in

[5] See pp. 483, 489, and map, p. 206.
[6] See pp. 552–554.

the area, it did have substantial effect on the pattern of land distribution. The whole traditional agrarian base of society was overturned. The work of the revolutions of 1848, which, in the Habsburg lands, had liberated the peasants but left them landless, was now carried a step further. The example of the Russian Revolution gave a powerful stimulus, for in Russia in 1917 peasants had driven off landlords, and communists and communist sympathizers won a hearing among discontented and propertyless peasants from Finland to the Balkans. Not until 1929, it should be recalled, did the Soviet Union embark on the collectivization of agriculture; until then, communism appeared to favor the small individual farmer. But it may be said with equal truth that the model for agrarian reform lay in the West, especially in France, the historic land of the small peasant proprietor.

Land reform worked out differently in different countries. In the Baltic states the big properties belonged almost entirely to German families, the "Baltic barons," descendants or at least successors to the medieval Teutonic Knights.[7] In Estonia, Latvia, and Lithuania the nationalist dislike for Germans thus made it easier to liquidate landlords. Small farms here became the rule. In Czechoslovakia over half the arable land was transferred from large to small owners; here again, the fact that many great landowners had been German, in some cases since the days of the Thirty Years' War,[8] made the operation in a sense more palatable, though it inflamed the German minority in Bohemia. In Rumania and Yugoslavia the breakup of large estates, though considerable, was less thorough. In Finland, Bulgaria, and Greece the issue hardly arose, since small landownership was already common. Land reform had least success in Poland and Hungary, where the landed magnates were exceptionally strong and well rooted.

After the land reforms, political parties of peasants or small landholders became the chief democratic force within the various states on the western border of Russia. Often they inclined to socialism, especially since capitalism was associated in their minds with foreign investors and outsiders. On the other hand, the great landowners, the former aristocrats of the prewar empires, whether already expropriated or merely threatened with expropriation, were confirmed in a reactionary outlook. The land reforms did not solve basic economic problems. The new small farms were very small, frequently no more than ten acres. The peasant owners lacked capital, agricultural skill, and knowledge of the market. Farm productivity did not rise. In place of old differences between landlord and tenant there developed new differences between the more comfortable peasant and the proletarian hired man—between the kulak and the toiler, in communist parlance. The continuance of relative poverty, the obstinacy of reactionary upper classes, the new stresses and strains among the peasants themselves, the economic distortions produced by numerous tariff walls, and the lack of any sustained tradition of self-government all helped to frustrate the democratic experiments launched in the 1920s.

98. THE GERMAN REPUBLIC AND THE SPIRIT OF LOCARNO

The keystone of Europe was Germany. Germany, too, had its revolution in 1918. But it was a revolution without revolutionaries, a negative revolution caused more by the disappearance of the old than by any vehement arrival of the new.

[7] See p. 78 and map, p. 44.
[8] See pp. 139–140, 218.

The emperor and the High Command of the army, in the last weeks of the war, had bowed out of the picture, leaving it to others to face defeat and humiliation.[9] For a time, after November 1918, the men in charge of affairs were mainly Social Democrats. The Social Democrats were Marxists, but their Marxism was the tamed, toned down, and revisionist Marxism that had prevailed for twenty years before the advent of Lenin. They were trade union officials and party managers. They could look back, in 1918, on decades spent in developing labor organizations and building up the Social Democratic party, which in 1912 had become the largest single party in the Reichstag.[10] Now, in 1918, they were a cautious and prudent group, essentially conservative, more anxious to preserve what they had already achieved than to launch audacious new social experiments. Before 1917 the Social Democrats considered themselves well to the left. But the Bolshevik Revolution in Russia, and the emergence of a pro-Bolshevik or communist element in Germany, put the Social Democrats in the middle. The middle is an awkward spot, especially in disturbed times; the Communists regarded the Social Democrats as reactionaries, despicable traitors to the working-class movement; whereas the true reactionaries, recruited from old monarchists, army officers, Junker landowners, and big business groups, saw in social democracy, or professed to see in it, a dangerous flirtation with Bolshevism.

The middle group in Germany, the Social Democrats reinforced by the Catholic Center party and others, was more afraid of the left than of the right. They were appalled, in 1918 and 1919, by the stories brought out of Russia, not merely by fugitive bourgeois or tsarist aristocrats, but by refugee Social Democrats, Mensheviks, and anti-Leninist Bolsheviks, men whom all socialists had long known and trusted in the Second International. In January 1919 the Spartacists,[11] led by Karl Liebknecht and Rosa Luxemburg, attempted to bring about a proletarian revolution in Germany, like that in Russia. Lenin and the Russian Bolsheviks lent their aid. For a time, there seemed to be a possibility that Germany might go communist, that the Spartacists might succeed in imposing a dictatorship of the proletariat. But the Social Democratic Provisional Government crushed the Spartacist uprising, turning for that purpose to demobilized army officers and volunteer vigilantes recruited from the disbanding army. The Spartacist leaders Liebknecht and Luxemburg were arrested and shot while in police custody. The events of "Spartacus Week" widened a chasm between Social Democrats and Communists which was not to be bridged even in Hitler's concentration camps.

Shortly after, elections were held for a National Constituent Assembly. No single party received a majority, but the Social Democrats were the leading party. A coalition of Social Democrats, Center party, and liberal democrats dominated the Assembly. After several months of deliberations at the city of Weimar, in July 1919, a constitution was adopted establishing a democratic republic. The Weimar Republic (as the regime in Germany from 1919 to the advent of Hitler in 1933 is called) was soon threatened ominously from the right. In 1920 a group of disaffected army officers staged a *Putsch*, or armed revolt, put the republican government to flight, and attempted to place a puppet of their own, one Dr. Kapp, at the head of the state. The Berlin workers, by turning off public utilities, stopped the Kapp *Putsch* and saved the republic. But the Weimar government

[9] See pp. 682–683.
[10] See pp. 581–583, 588–591.
[11] So named from Spartacus, a Roman slave who led a slave revolt in south Italy in 72 B.C.

never took sufficiently firm measures to put down private armed bands led by reactionary or outspokenly antidemocratic agitators. One of these was soon to be Adolf Hitler, who as early as 1923 staged an abortive revolt in Munich.[12] Nor, being democratic and liberal, did it ever deny the rights of election to the Reichstag, and of free speech in the Reichstag and in public, either to communists or to antidemocratic reactionaries.

The Weimar Republic was in principle highly democratic. The constitution embodied all the devices then favored by the most advanced democrats, not only universal suffrage, including the vote for women, but proportional representation and the initiative, referendum, and recall. But except for the legal eight-hour day and a few other such safeguards to the workers' welfare (and traditional demands of organized labor) the republic of which the Social Democrats were the main architects in its formative years was remote from anything socialistic. No industries were nationalized. No property changed hands. No land laws or agrarian reforms were undertaken, as in the new states of eastern Europe; the East-Elbian Junkers remained untouched in their landed estates. There was almost no confiscation even of the property of the former kaiser and other ruling dynasties of Bismarck's federal empire. The very statues of emperors, kings, princes, and grand dukes were left standing in the streets and squares. Officials, civil servants, police agents, professors, schoolteachers of old imperial Germany remained at their respective duties. The army, though limited by the Versailles treaty to 100,000 men, remained the old army in miniature, with all its essential organs intact, and lacking only in mass. The soldiers were peasant youths enlisted for long terms and soon formed to German and Prussian military traditions. In the officer corps the old professional and aristocratic influences remained strong.

Never had there been a revolution so mild, so reasonable, so tolerant. There was no terror, no fanaticism, no stirring faith, no expropriation, no émigrés. There had in truth been no revolution at all, in the sense in which France, England, the United States, Russia, and other countries, either recently or in the more distant past, had experienced revolutions.

The German Democracy and Versailles

The supreme question, for Europe and the world, was how Germany would adjust itself to the postwar conditions. How would the Germans accept the new internal regime of democracy? How would they accept the new German frontiers and other provisions of the Treaty of Versailles? These two questions were unfortunately interconnected. The Weimar Republic and the Treaty of Versailles were both products of the defeat of Germany in the war. There were many in Germany who favored democracy, notably the numerous Social Democrats, and many more possibly could have been won over to it, given time and favorable conditions. But no one, not even the Social Democrats, accepted the Treaty of Versailles or the new German frontiers as either just or final. If "democracy" in Germany meant the perpetual acceptance of the treaty without amendment, or if it meant economic distress or hardship which could either reasonably or unreasonably be explained as consequences of the treaty, then "democracy" would lose such appeal as it had for the Germans.

[12] See p. 786.

The German republicans, we have seen, protested against the Versailles treaty before signing, and signed only under pressure.[13] The Allies continued the wartime naval blockade after the armistice; this confirmed, in German eyes, the argument that the Treaty of Versailles was a *Diktat*, a dictated peace, Carthaginian, ruthless, and vengeful. The "war guilt" clause, while it perhaps on the one hand satisfied a peculiar Anglo-American sense of morality, on the other hand offended a peculiar German sense of honor. Neither the reparations demanded of them, nor the new frontiers, were accepted by the Germans as settled. Reparations they regarded as a perpetual mortgage on their future. They generally expected, some day, to revise their eastern frontier, get back at least the Polish corridor, and incorporate Austria.

The French lived in terror of the day when Germany would recover. Their plans for their own security, and for the collective security of Europe against a German revival, had been disappointed. They had been unable to detach the Rhineland from Germany. The United States Senate had refused to ratify the treaty, signed at Paris by Wilson, by which the United States was to guarantee France against German invasion in the future.[14] Both Britain and the United States showed a tendency to isolation, to pull away from the Continent, to get back to "normalcy," to work mainly for a restored trade in which a strong Germany would be a large customer. The League of Nations, of which the United States was not a member, and in which every member nation had a veto, offered little assurance of safety to a people so placed as the French. The French began to form alliances, against a potentially resurgent Germany, with Poland, Czechoslovakia, and other east-European states. They insisted also on German payment of reparations. The amount of reparations, left unstated in the treaty, was fixed by a Reparations Commission in 1921 at 132 billion gold marks. This sum, the equivalent of $35 billion, was soon pronounced by various Western economists to be more than Germany could possibly contrive to pay.

The Weimar government in these circumstances looked to Russia, which had been no party to the Versailles treaty and claimed no reparations. The Soviet government meanwhile, concluding from the failure of proletarian revolution in Germany and Hungary that the time was not ripe for the sovietizing of Europe, prepared to enter into normal diplomatic relations with established governments. Germany and Russia, despite ideological repugnance, thus signed the treaty of Rapallo in 1922. In the following years the Soviet Union obtained needed manufactures from Germany, and German factories and workers were kept busy by orders from Russia. The German army dispatched officers and technicians to give instruction to the Red Army. Obliged by the Treaty of Versailles to restrict its activities, the German army was in fact able, through its work in Russia, and through a number of subterfuges at home, to maintain a high standard of training, planning, technical knowledge, and familiarity with new weapons and equipment. The good understanding between Germany and Russia naturally caused apprehension in the West.

Reparations, the Great Inflation of 1923, Recovery

The French, blocked in the attempt to collect reparations, and assisted by the Belgians, in 1923 sent units of the French army to occupy the industrial sites of

[13] See p. 691.
[14] See pp. 687–689, 695.

the Ruhr valley. The Germans responded by general strikes and passive resistance. To sustain the workers in this patriotic idleness the Weimar government paid them benefits, grinding paper money off the printing presses for this purpose. Germany, like other belligerent countries, had suffered from inflation, i.e., rising prices, during and after the war; neither the imperial government nor the Weimar statesmen had been willing to impose heavier taxes to offset inflation. But what now swept Germany was different from ordinary inflation. It was of catastrophic and utterly ruinous proportions. Paper money became literally worthless. By the end of 1923 it took over 4 trillion paper marks to equal a dollar.

This inflation brought far more of a social revolution than the fall of the Hohenzollern empire had ever done. Debtors paid off debts in worthless money. Creditors received baskets full of meaningless paper. Salaries even when raised lagged behind the soaring cost of living. Annuities, pensions, proceeds of insurance policies, savings accounts in the banks, income from bonds and mortgages—every form of revenue which had been arranged for at some time in the past, and which often represented the economy, foresight, and personal planning of many years—now turned to nothing. The middle class was pauperized and demoralized. Middle-class people were now materially in much the position of day workers and proletarians. Their whole view of life, however, made it impossible for them to identify themselves with the laboring class or to accept its Marxist or socialist ideologies. They had lost faith in society itself, in the future, in the old burgher codes of self-reliance and rational planning of their own lives in an understandable world. A kind of moral void was created, with nothing for them to believe in, hope for, or respect.

The inflation, however, by wiping out all outstanding indebtedness within the country, made it possible, once the losses were written off and accepted, to start up economic production afresh. The United States was persuaded to play a reluctant role. The United States, in these years, demanded payment of the huge war debts owed to it by the Allies.[15] The Allies—Britain, France, Belgium—insisted that they could not pay debts to the United States unless they collected reparations from Germany. In 1924 the Dawes Plan, named for the American Charles G. Dawes, was instituted in Germany to assure the flow of reparations. By the Dawes Plan the French evacuated the Ruhr, the reparations payments were cut down, and arrangements made for the German republic to borrow abroad. A good deal of American private capital was invested in Germany in the following years, both in German government bonds and in German industrial enterprises. Gradually, so at least it seemed, Germany was put on its feet. For four or five years the Weimar Republic even enjoyed a bustling prosperity, and there was a good deal of new construction in roads, housing, factories, and ocean liners. But the prosperity rested in good measure on foreign loans, and the great depression that began in 1929 reopened all the old questions.

The Spirit of Locarno

These years of economic prosperity were years also of relative international calm. No issue, in truth, was dealt with fundamentally. The universal German hatred for the Treaty of Versailles elicited no concessions from the Allies. Conceivably, had the Allies been willing at this time to amend the treaty by international

[15] See pp. 685–686, 690.

agreement, they might have taken wind from the sails of nationalistic rabble-rousers in Germany and so spared themselves much later grief. It may be, however, that no possible concession would have sufficed. The great problem was to prevent a German overthrow of the treaty structure by violence, especially in eastern Europe where the Germans regarded the new frontiers as basically subject to reconsideration. After the Ruhr incident, and adoption of the Dawes Plan, a group of moderate and peace-loving men shaped the foreign policy of the principal countries—Gustav Stresemann in Germany, Édouard Herriot and Aristide Briand in France, Ramsay MacDonald in England.

The charter of the League of Nations provided for international sanctions against potential aggressors. Like the system of congresses after the Peace of Vienna, the League was supposed to assure peaceable compliance with the peace treaties, or their modification without resort to force.[16] No one expected the League, by any authority of its own, to prevent war between Great Powers, but the League achieved various minor pacifications in the 1920s, and in any case its headquarters at Geneva offered a convenient meeting place in which statesmen could talk.

As a further assurance against war, in 1925 at Locarno, the European powers signed a number of treaties. These marked the highest point in international good will reached between the two World Wars. Germany signed a treaty with France and Belgium guaranteeing their respective frontiers unconditionally. It signed arbitration treaties with Poland and Czechoslovakia—not guaranteeing these frontiers as they stood, but undertaking to attempt changes in them only by international discussion, agreement, or arbitration. France signed treaties with Poland and Czechoslovakia promising military aid if they were attacked by Germany. France thus fortified its policy of balancing German power in the East by its own diplomatic alliances and by supporting the Little Entente, as the postwar alliance of Czechoslovakia, Yugoslavia, and Rumania was called. Great Britain "guaranteed"—i.e., promised military aid in the event of violation—the frontiers of Belgium and France against Germany. It did not give an equivalent guarantee with respect to Czechoslovakia or Poland. The British took the view that their own basic security would be threatened by German expansion westward, but not by German expansion to the east. It was on the borders of Czechoslovakia and Poland, fourteen years later, that the Second World War began. Had Britain gone along with France in 1925 in guaranteeing these two countries, then stuck to the guarantee, the Second World War might possibly have been prevented. On the other hand, no war ever depends on any single decision; it is the accumulation of many decisions that matters.

In 1925 people talked with relief of the "spirit of Locarno." In 1928 international harmony was again strengthened when the French foreign minister Briand and the United States Secretary of State Frank B. Kellogg arranged for the Pact of Paris. Ultimately signed by sixty-five nations, it condemned recourse to war for the solution of international controversies. Although no measures of enforcement were provided and a number of reservations were added before certain countries signed, the Pact solemnly affirmed the will of the nations to renounce war as an instrument of national policy.

In the mid-1920s the outlook was indeed full of hope. At Locarno, Germany

---

[16] See pp. 449–452, 454.

had of its own volition (and not by the *Diktat* of Versailles) accepted its borders both east and west, to the extent of abjuring violence and unilateral action even in the east. In 1926 Germany joined the League of Nations. Germany was a going concern as a democratic republic. Democracy seemed to work, as well as could be expected, in most of the new states of eastern Europe—the *cordon sanitaire* against Communist Russia, which itself had halted its postwar revolutionary offensive. The world was again prosperous, or seemed to be so. World production was at or above the prewar level. In 1925 the world's production of raw materials, it was estimated, was 17 percent greater than in 1913. World trade, by 1929, measured in hard money—gold—had almost doubled since 1913. The war and the postwar troubles were remembered as a nightmare escaped from. It seemed that, after all, the world had been made safe for democracy.

But complacency was shattered by the great world depression, by the growth of a malignant nationalism in Germany, due in some part to the depression, and by the assertion of a new militancy in Japan, which also was not unrelated to the depression. But let us turn first to the postwar years in Asia.

99. THE REVOLT OF ASIA

Resentments in Asia

The peoples of Asia had never been satisfied with the position in which the great European expansion of the nineteenth century had placed them.[17] Increasingly they condemned everything associated with "imperialism." In this respect there was little difference between countries actually governed by Europeans as parts of European empires, such as British India, the Netherlands Indies, French Indochina (or the American Philippines), and countries that remained nominally independent under their own government, such as China, Persia, and the Ottoman Empire. In the former, as political consciousness awakened, there was objection to the monopoly of Europeans in the important offices of government. In the latter, there was objection to the special rights and privileges enjoyed by Europeans, the widespread impounding of customs revenues to pay foreign debts, the capitulations in Turkey, the extraterritorial rights in China, the spheres of influence in Persia which divided the country between British and Russians.

By imperialism, in either case, aroused Asians meant a system whereby the affairs of their own country were conducted, its resources exploited, its people employed, for the benefit of foreigners, Europeans, or white men. They meant the system of absentee capitalism, by which the plantations, docks, or factories before their eyes, and on which they themselves labored, were the property of owners thousands of miles away whose main interest in them was a regular flow of profits. They meant the constant threat that an alien civilization would disintegrate and eat away their own ancient cultures. They meant the nuisance of having to speak a European language, or the calamity of having to fight in wars originated by Europeans. And they meant the airs of superiority assumed by white men, the race consciousness exhibited by all whites, though perhaps most of all the British and Americans, the color line that was everywhere drawn, the

---

[17] See pp. 608–616, 634–645.

attitudes varying between contempt and condescension, the relation of native "boy" and European "sahib." Imperialism to them signified the gentlemen's clubs in Calcutta to which no Indian was ever admitted, the hotels in Shanghai from which Chinese were carefully kept out, the park benches in various cities on which no "native" could ever sit. In deeper psychology, as well as in economics and in politics, the revolt of self-conscious Asians was a rebellion against social inferiority and humiliation.

The revolt against the West was generally ambivalent or two-sided. It was a revolt against Western supremacy, but at the same time, in most cases, those who revolted meant to learn from and imitate the West, in order that, by taking over Western science, industry, organization, and other sources of Western power, they might preserve their own identity and emerge as the West's equals.

The crisis in Asia had broken out with the Russo-Japanese War, when an Asian people, in 1905, defeated a great European power for the first time.[18] In 1906 revolution began in Persia, leading to the assembly of the first majlis, or parliament. In 1908 the Young Turks staged a successful revolution in Constantinople and summoned a parliamentary assembly to represent all regions then in the Ottoman Empire. In 1911 the revolutionists in China, led by Sun Yat-sen, overthrew the Manchu dynasty and proclaimed the Chinese Republic. In each case the rebels charged their old monarchs—shah, sultan, emperor—with subservience to Western imperialists. In each case they summoned national assemblies on the prevailing democratic model of Europe, and they proposed to revive, modernize, and westernize their countries to the degree necessary to avoid domination by the West.

First World War and Russian Revolution

In the First World War almost all the Asian peoples were somehow involved. The Ottoman Empire, allied with Germany, immediately repudiated all the capitulations, or special legal rights of Europeans. Persia attempted to remain neutral and to get rid of the partition made in 1907 between British and Russian spheres, but it became a battleground of British, Russian, and Turkish forces. China, which joined the Allies, attempted at the peace conference to have the extraterritorial rights in China abolished. We have seen how this request of the Chinese Republic was refused, and how the Allies, instead, transferred many of the prewar German concessions to the Japanese.[19] The dependent regions of Asia, the Dutch, French, and British possessions, were stimulated economically by the war.[20] The Netherlands Indies, though remaining neutral, increased its output of foodstuffs, oil, and raw materials. India developed its steel industry and textile manufactures and contributed over a million soldiers, combat and service troops, to the British cause. All the dependent regions were stirred by Woodrow Wilson's call to make the world safe for democracy.

The home governments made concessions. They were naturally afraid to go too far; they insisted that their subject peoples were not yet capable of self-government. They had huge investments at stake, and the whole world economy depended on the continuing production of tropical and subtropical countries. But

[18] See pp. 646–647.
[19] See pp. 689–690.
[20] See p. 686.

they did compromise. In 1916 the Dutch created a legislative assembly to advise the governor general of the Indies; half its members were elected from native races. In 1917 the British agreed to a measure of self-government in India; an Indian legislative assembly was set up with 140 members, of whom 100 were elected, and in the provinces of British India the number of elected representatives and of native Indian officials was increased. The French in 1922 provided for a somewhat similar assembly in Indochina. Thus all three imperial powers, at about the same time, began to experiment with consultative bodies whose membership was partly elective, partly appointive, and partly native, partly European. The United States introduced an elected assembly in the Philippine Islands in 1916.

The Russian Revolution added a new stimulus to unrest in Asia. The Bolsheviks denounced not only capitalism but also imperialism. In Marxist-Leninist ideology imperialism was an aspect of capitalism.[21] Colonial peoples also tended to identify the two, not so much for Marxist reasons as because modern capitalism was a foreign or "imperialist" phenomenon in colonial countries, where the ownership and the management of large enterprises were both foreign. Nationalism in Asia, the movement for independence or for more equality with the West, thus easily shaded off into socialism and the denunciation of capitalistic exploitation. The Bolsheviks were quick to see the advantages for themselves in this situation. As it became clear that the world revolution, as expected by Lenin, would not soon come to pass in Europe, the Russian communists turned to Asia as the theater in which world capitalism might be attacked by a great flanking movement. In September 1920 a "congress of oppressed Eastern peoples" assembled at Baku, on the coast of the Caspian Sea. Zinoviev, head of the Communist International, called for war upon "the wild beasts of British capitalism." Not much was accomplished at the conference. But a few extremists from Asian countries in the following years sojourned in Moscow, and a few communists dispatched from Moscow stirred up the discontents which existed, quite without Russian instigation, all over Asia.

The postwar situation in Asia was thus extremely fluid. Men who were not communists hailed communism as a liberating force. Anti-westerners declared that their countries must westernize. Nationalism overshadowed all other isms. In the Indian National Congress rich Indian capitalists consorted with socialist leaders, with whom they were held together in relative harmony so long as the common enemy was the British.

The Turkish Revolution: Kemal Atatürk

The most immediately successful of the revolutionary movements was the one in Turkey. The Young Turks at first, in 1908, had meant to prevent the further dissolution of the Ottoman Empire.[22] This proved to be impossible. In the Balkan wars of 1912–1913 the Ottoman power was almost totally excluded from the Balkan peninsula. In the World War, in which the Turks were on the losing side, the Arabs with a great deal of British assistance broke away. After the war the Greeks invaded the Anatolian peninsula. They dreamed of a Great Greece embracing both sides of the Aegean. Europeans still regarded Turkey as the sick man of Europe, the Ottoman state as doomed to extinction, and the Turkish people as

---

[21] See p. 704.
[22] See pp. 622–623, 665, and maps, pp. 625, 667.

barbarous and incompetent. The Allies had agreed in 1915 to partition Turkey; and after the war the Western powers favored the Greek invasion. Italian and French forces occupied parts of Anatolia, and Italians, French, and British undertook to take Constantinople from Turkish rule, though its disposition remained uncertain. (It had been promised to Russia in 1915, before the Bolshevik Revolution.[23]) In these circumstances a powerful army officer named Mustapha Kemal rallied Turkish national resistance. Gradually, and with aid from Soviet Russia, the Turks drove the Greeks and the Western Allies away. They affirmed their hold on the Anatolian peninsula, and on both shores of the Straits, including Constantinople, which was renamed Istanbul.[24]

The Nationalists, under the energetic drive of Mustapha Kemal, now put through a sweeping revolution. They abolished the sultanate and the caliphate, since the sultan had somewhat compromised himself with foreigners, and was also, as caliph or commander of the faithful, a religious functionary for all Islam and hence a conservative influence. The Turkish Republic was promulgated in 1923.

Where the Ottoman Empire had been a composite organization made up of diverse religious communities, among which the Muslims were the ruling group, the Turkish Republic was conceived as a national state in which the "people," i.e., the Turkish people, were sovereign. Universal suffrage was introduced, along with a parliament, a ministry, and a president with strong powers. Non-Turks in Asia Minor now became "foreign" in a way they had not been before. We have seen the fate of the Armenians during the First World War.[25] The other large non-Turkish and Christian people were the Greeks. After the war about 1.4 million Greeks either fled or were officially transported from Asia Minor to Greece, and, in exchange, some 400,000 Turks residing in northern Greece were transported to Turkey. The exchange of populations caused great hardship, it uprooted most of the Greek element that had lived in Asia Minor since 1000 B.C., and it overwhelmed the impoverished Greek kingdom by obliging it suddenly to absorb a mass of destitute refugees, who were a quarter as numerous as the population of Greece itself. But it enabled the Turkish Republic to acquire a relatively homogeneous population, ending minority disputes between Greece and Turkey until Cyprus posed new problems after the Second World War.

For the first time in any Muslim country the spheres of government and religion were sharply distinguished. The Turkish Republic affirmed the total separation of church and state. It declared religion to be a private belief, and it tolerated all religions. Government was reorganized on secular and nonreligious principles stemming from the French Revolution. The law of the Koran was thrust aside. The new law was modeled on the Swiss Code, the most recently codified European legislation, itself derived from the Code Napoleon.

Mustapha Kemal urged women to put aside the veil, to come out of the harem, to vote, and to occupy public office. He made polygamy a crime. Men he required by law to discard the fez. He fought against the fez as Peter the Great had fought against the beard, and for the same reason, seeing in it the symbol of conservative and backward habits. The hat, "headgear of civilization," correspondingly became the symbol of progress. The people shifted to Western dress. The Western

[23] See p. 674.
[24] See map, p. 625.
[25] See pp. 675–676. On the multinational character of the Ottoman Empire see pp. 213–214 and 620–621.

alphabet became mandatory; literate Turks had to learn to read again, and illiteracy was reduced. The Western calendar and the metric system were adopted. Turks were required to assume hereditary family surnames, like Westerners; Kemal himself took the name Atatürk, or Great Turk. The capital was moved from Istanbul to Ankara. The republic put up a high tariff. In 1933 it adopted a five-year plan for economic development. The Turks, having shaken off foreign influence, were determined not to become again dependent on Western capital or capitalism. The five-year plan provided for mines, railroads, and factories, mainly under government ownership. At the same time, while willing to accept Russian aid against the Western powers, the republic had no patience with communism, which it suppressed. The Turks wanted a modern Turkey—by and for the Turks.

Persia experienced a similar revolution, somewhat less drastic. The old concessions, capitulations, and spheres were done away with, and the Persian government renegotiated its oil contracts, asserting more control over foreign corporations and receiving a larger return from them in taxes and royalties. In 1935, to emphasize its break with the past, Persia took the name of Iran.

The National Movement in India: Gandhi and Nehru

India at the close of the World War was on the verge of revolution against British rule.[26] Discontented Indians looked for leadership to Mohandas K. Gandhi, the Mahatma, or Holy One, who in the following decades, though hardly typical of modern Asia, attained a world-wide eminence as the spokesman of subjected peoples. Gandhi had been educated in England in the 1890s and had practiced law in South Africa, where he became aware of racial discrimination as a world-wide problem. In India, after 1919, he led a movement for self-government, for economic and spiritual independence from Great Britain, and for greater tolerance within India itself both between Hindus and Muslims and between upper-caste Hindus and the depressed outcastes and untouchables. The weapons he favored were those of the spirit only; he preached nonviolence, passive resistance, civil disobedience, and the boycott. He took to self-imposed fasts and hunger strikes to break the firmness of British jailers, and later of Indians themselves. He and his most loyal followers, as the troubles mounted, refused to be elected or take part in the partially representative institutions that the British cautiously introduced and also boycotted the British economic position in India, by refusing to buy or use goods imported from England. The latter touched the British in a sensitive spot. Before the World War half of all exports of British cotton cloth had gone to India. By 1932 this proportion fell to a quarter. Gandhi turned against all industrialism, even the mechanized industry that was growing up in India itself. He put aside Western costume, took to using a spinning wheel and living on goat's milk, urged Indian peasants to revive their old handicrafts, and appeared on solemn occasions clad in no more than a homespun loincloth. By the high level of his principles Gandhi made himself an inspiration to many groups that differed on more mundane matters. Even in the West he was regarded as one of the great religious teachers of all time.

India was very much divided within, and the British maintained that because of these divisions the ending of British rule would precipitate anarchy. There

[26] See pp. 634–637, 647.

were Hindus and Muslims, between whom clashes and terrorist outrages were chronic. (Gandhi was himself murdered in 1948 by an anti-Muslim Hindu fanatic.) There were the hundreds of oriental potentates of the native states. There were Indian capitalists, like the Tata family, and growing masses of proletarians produced by Indian industrialization.[27] There were the higher castes and the outcastes, and there were hundreds of millions of peasants living in a poverty unimaginable in the West. In politics, there were those who demanded full independence, boycotted the British, and spent years in jail, as did Gandhi and his more practical-minded but devoted follower, Jawaharlal Nehru; and there were the moderates who believed that they might best advance the welfare of India by accepting government office, cooperating with the British, and working for dominion status within the British Empire. Marxism exerted a strong appeal, not indeed on the spiritual and pacific Gandhi, but on Nehru and even many of the less radical leaders. In the 1920s the Soviet Union stood in their eyes for the overthrow of imperialism; in the 1930s it pointed the way by its adoption of five-year plans. For a people wishing to raise itself by its own bootstraps, to move from poverty to industrial strength and higher living standards without loss of time, and without dependence on foreign capital and capitalism, the Soviet Union with its economic planning seemed to offer a more appropriate model and more practical lessons than the rich democracies of the West, with their centuries of gradual progress behind them.

The twenty years between world wars were years of repeated disturbance, of rioting and repression, of sporadic violence despite the exhortations of Gandhi, of conferences and round tables, reforms and promises of reform, with a drift in the 1930s toward more participation of Indians in the affairs of the Indian empire. Independence was not won until after the Second World War; with it took place a partition of the Indian subcontinent into two new nations, a predominantly Hindu India and a predominantly Muslim Pakistan.[28]

In the Netherlands Indies, where the nationalist movement was less developed than in India,[29] the interwar years were more quiet. A serious rebellion, in which communists took part, broke out in 1922 but was suppressed by the Dutch. The peoples of the archipelago were almost as diverse as those of India. Only the Dutch empire had brought them politically together. Opposition to the Dutch gave them a common program. In 1937 the legislative council petitioned for the grant of dominion status. But not until after the Second World War and the failure of a military effort to repress the nationalists did the Dutch concede independence.[30]

The Chinese Revolution: The Three People's Principles

The Chinese Revolution had opened in 1911 with the overthrow of the Manchu dynasty, which itself had belatedly begun to introduce westernizing reforms. The Chinese Republic was proclaimed, but the first immediate result was the establishment in Peking of a military dictatorship exercised by General Yüan Shih-kai, who had been a close adviser to the Manchus and who, until his death in 1916,

[27] See p. 686.
[28] See pp. 866–867.
[29] See pp. 634–635.
[30] See p. 868.

never ceased to cast covetous eyes on the now empty imperial throne itself. In the south the veteran revolutionary Dr. Sun Yat-sen reorganized the Kuomintang (National People's, or Nationalist party), successor to the prerevolutionary network of underground societies of which he had been the chief architect. Sun, elected the first president of the republic by a revolutionary provisional assembly, resigned within a few months in favor of General Yüan, who he mistakenly believed would unite the country under a parliamentary regime. Subsequently, in the confusion that followed the struggle for power in Peking after Yüan's death in 1916, Sun was proclaimed president of a rival government in the south at Canton, which exercised a nominal power over the southern provinces. Not until 1928 could any government have any basis for claiming actual rule over China—and even then, there were important exceptions. For most of these years the country was virtually in the hands of contending war lords, each of whom pocketed the customary taxes in his own locality, maintained his own army, and recognized no superior authority.

It was Sun Yat-sen who best expressed the ideas of the Chinese Revolution. Born in 1867 and educated under American influence in the Hawaiian Islands, he had received a medical degree at Hong Kong, had traveled extensively about the world, studied Western ideas, lectured to Chinese audiences in America, collected money for his conspiracies against the Manchus, and had returned from Europe to take part in the revolution. Shortly before his death in 1925 Sun gathered the lectures which he had been expounding for years into a book, *The Three People's Principles.* The book sheds much light on the revolt of China, and of all Asia, against the supremacy of the West.

The three people's principles, according to Sun Yat-sen, were democracy, nationalism, and livelihood. Livelihood meant social welfare and economic reform—a more equitable distribution of wealth and land, a gradual end to poverty and unjust economic exploitation. By nationalism Dr. Sun meant that the Chinese who had always lived mainly in the clan and family had now to learn the importance of the nation and the state. They were in fact a great nation, he thought, the world's most cultured, and had once prevailed from the mouth of the Amur to the East Indies. But they had never been cohesive. The Chinese had been "a sheet of loose sand"; they must now "break down individual liberty and become pressed together into an unyielding body like the firm rock which is formed by the addition of cement to sand."

By democracy Sun Yat-sen meant the sovereignty of the people. Like Rousseau, he gave little attention to voting, elections, or parliamentary processes. He believed that while the people were sovereign, the able should govern. Government should be conducted by experts, a principle he criticized the West for neglecting. Dr. Sun felt a warm sympathy for Lenin. Yet he was by no means a doctrinaire Marxist. Marxism he thought inapplicable to China, arguing that the Chinese must take Marxism as they took all other Western ideas, avoiding slavish imitation, using, adapting, amending, rejecting as they saw fit. China had no native capitalism in any Marxist or Western sense. The "capitalists" in China, he said, were owners of land, especially in the cities, such as Shanghai, where the coming of Westerners had raised land values to dizzy heights. Hence if China could get rid of imperialism it would take a long step toward getting rid of capitalism also; it could begin to equalize landowning and confiscate unearned rents. Since China, he observed, had no true capitalists the state itself must undertake capitalist and industrial development. This would require loans of foreign capital and the services of foreign managers and technicians, adding another reason why the Chinese state, to maintain control, must be strong.

With Sun Yat-sen, in short, democracy easily shaded off into a theory of benevolent and constructive dictatorship. Marxism, communism, socialism, "livelihood," the planned society, welfare economics, and antiforeign and anti-imperialist sentiment were all mixed together—in some ways as the ideas of the Chinese Communists would later be.

The first aim of Sun Yat-sen and of the revolutionists in China was to shake off the "treaty system" that had bound China to outside interests since 1842.[31] In this respect the Paris peace conference had been disappointing; the Chinese not only failed to obtain the abolition of Western privileges and extraterritorial rights but could not block the retention by Japan of many of the former German concessions that the Japanese had taken over during the war.[32] Widespread student and worker demonstrations directed against the Western powers took place on May 4, 1919. The May Fourth movement heightened the antiforeign consciousness.

As the Western powers proved obdurate, Sun and the Kuomintang turned to Russia. They declared the Russian and Chinese revolutions to be two aspects of the same world-wide movement of liberation. The Chinese Communist party, organized in 1921, became allied with the Kuomintang in 1923. The latter accepted Russian communist advisers, notably the veteran revolutionist Borodin, whom Sun Yat-sen had known years before in the United States.[33] The Soviet Union, following its strategy of outflanking world capitalism by penetrating Asia, sent military equipment, army instructors, and party organizers into China. It also surrendered the Russian concessions and extraterritorial rights acquired in China by the tsars. The Chinese policy of friendliness to Russia began to produce the hoped for effects; the British, to draw China from Russia, gave up a few of their lesser concessions at Hankow and other cities.

China: Nationalists and Communists

The Kuomintang, its armies reorganized and strengthened, now displayed a fresh vitality and after 1924 launched a military and political offensive, planned by the ever active Russian advisers, supported by the Chinese Communists, and headed by Chiang Kai-shek, who succeeded to the leadership of the Kuomintang upon Sun's death in 1925. Chiang's main objectives were to compel the independent war lords and the regime still holding office in Peking to accept the authority of a single Nationalist government. By the end of 1928 Chiang's armies had swept northward, occupied Peking, and transferred the seat of government to Nanking. Chiang now exercised at least nominal control over most of China, although effective control was still limited by the recalcitrance of many provincial war lords. The outside powers, acknowledging the accomplishments of the Kuomintang, extended diplomatic recognition to the Nanking government and conceded its right to organize and run the country's tariff and customs affairs. They also partially surrendered their extraterritorial privileges and pledged to abolish them completely in the near future.

[31] See pp. 642–645.
[32] See pp. 689–690.
[33] See p. 738.

In 1927, while a measure of national unity was being forged in the country, an open break occurred between the Kuomintang and its left wing. In the course of the northern military campaign, and particularly in the seizure of Nanking, popular disturbance and excesses, including the killing of a number of foreigners, had taken place, allegedly fomented by the Communists. These radical disturbances frightened and alienated the wealthier and more conservative element in the Kuomintang and so jeopardized Chiang's chief source of financial assistance for his government and army. Chiang himself, also, had never apparently considered the alliance with either the Communists or the Russians as anything more than one of convenience. Now Chiang took decisive action. Communists, and Russian advisers, were forthwith purged from the Kuomintang; many were executed; Borodin and others fled to Moscow; and a Communist-led uprising in Canton was forcefully suppressed. A number of armed Communist groups fled to the safety of the mountain regions in the south and joined other guerrilla contingents. In that way the Chinese Red Army was formed; among its leaders were Mao Tse-tung, a former librarian, teacher, newspaper editor, and union organizer, who had been one of the founding members of the party, and Chu Teh, who had held high rank in the Kuomintang armies and who had traveled and studied in Germany and elsewhere in Europe.

Chiang, with the renewed financial and moral support of the Kuomintang bankers, resumed the northern offensive whose success by 1928 has been described. But the original revolutionary impulse of the Kuomintang was now very much dissipated. Made up of men who feared social upheaval and who often regarded their own maintenance in power as their chief problem, it exercised a kind of one-party dictatorship over most of China under Chiang's leadership. Chiang himself recognized mounting popular dissatisfaction with the reluctance or inability of the Kuomintang to initiate reforms, but he was still busy consolidating the regime and after 1931 he had to contend with Japanese aggression. During these years he conceived a deadly hatred for Communists and those who actively agitated for revolutionary reform.

The Communists, operating now in southeast China, fed on popular discontent and drew support from the poor peasantry by a systematic policy of expropriation and distribution of large landed estates as well as by intensive propaganda. They succeeded in fighting off Chiang's armies and even in winning over part of his troops. Organizing a network of local soviets, in 1931 they proclaimed a Chinese Soviet Republic in the southeast. When after many years the Nationalist armies succeeded in dislodging them, the Communists, under Mao's leadership, undertook in 1934–1935 an amazing 6,000-mile march over near-insuperable terrain in north-central Yenan, closer, it was said, to Soviet supply lines. About 90,000 began the Long March, of which only half survived. They entrenched themselves again, fought off the Nationalist armies, and built up a strong popular following among the rural masses. With the Japanese invasion of north China well under way they abandoned their revolutionary offensive and pressed Chiang to end the civil war and to create a united front against the Japanese aggressor. Chiang reluctantly consented, so that by 1937 an alliance was formed between the Kuomintang and the Communists; the Chinese Red Army was placed under Nationalist control and disposition; a united China would face the Japanese. But the uneasy alliance between Kuomintang and Communists was not to last even until the defeat of the common Japanese foe in the Second World War, and the

Chinese Revolution was about to enter a new, dynamic, and vastly different phase.[34]

Japan: Militarism and Aggression

The Nationalist movement in China caused apprehension in Japan, whose rise as a modern power has already been traced.[35] The Japanese, at least since the Sino-Japanese War of 1895, had looked upon the huge disintegrating area of China as a field for expansion of their own interests, in this scarcely differing from Europeans, except that they were closer to the scene. During the World War they had presented their Twenty-One Demands on China, taken over the German concessions in Shantung, and sent troops into eastern Siberia.[36] During the war the industrialization of Japan proceeded apace; Japan captured many markets while the Europeans were locked in the struggle; and after the war the Japanese remained one of the chief suppliers of textiles for the rest of Asia. The Japanese could produce at lower prices than the Europeans, prices at which the penniless masses of Asia were more able to buy. Densely packed in their mountainous islands, they sustained their standard of living by importing raw materials and selling manufactures. But the Chinese Nationalists hoped to erect a protective tariff; it was for this reason, among others, that they denounced the treaty system, which for almost a century had bound China to international free trade. The Chinese, like the Turks, hoped to industrialize and westernize their own country behind a high tariff wall, which would shut out Japanese manufactures as well as others.

During the 1920s the civilian, liberal, Western-oriented element in Japan remained in control of the government. In 1925 universal male suffrage was adopted. It was still the fashion in Europe and America to view the Japanese with sympathetic approval, as the most progressive of all non-Europeans, the one Asian people who had ably learned to play its part in the advancing world-wide civilization. But there was another facet to Japan. The constitution of 1889 and parliamentary operations were but a façade that concealed political realities. Only in Japan of all modern countries did a constitutional law prescribe that the war and navy ministers must be active generals or admirals. The diet itself had sharply restricted powers. Ministers governed in the name of the supreme and sacred authority of the emperor, to whom they were alone responsible. Economically, the government's sponsorship of industrial growth had resulted in a tremendous concentration of economic power in the hands of four family trusts known collectively as the Zaibatsu. The business interests and the civilian political leaders all looked to an expanding empire and growing markets, but the most restless group in Japan drew its strength from the nationalist revival which, even before the "opening" of Japan in 1854, had cultivated Shinto, emperor worship, and the way of the warrior as a new and modern way of life.[37] This element was recruited in large part from the old clansmen and samurai, whom the "abolition of feudalism" had uprooted from their accustomed ways, and who in many cases found no satisfying field of effort in the new regime. Many of these men now served as officers in the army. Often they regarded the West as decadent. They dreamed of the day when Japan would dominate all East Asia.

---

[34] See pp. 860–866.
[35] See pp. 543–549.
[36] See pp. 676, 689–690, 715–716.
[37] See pp. 546, 548.

About 1927 this group began to hold ministries in the Japanese government and to turn Japanese policy into increasingly aggressive and militaristic attitudes toward China. In 1931 Japanese army units stationed in southern Manchuria (where the Japanese had been since defeat of the Russians in 1905), alleging the mysterious murder of a Japanese officer at Mukden, began to seize Chinese arsenals and spread northward over all Manchuria. In 1932, charging the Chinese with economic warfare against Japan (Chinese boycotts were in fact damaging the Japanese export trade materially), the Japanese landed 70,000 troops at Shanghai. They soon withdrew, preferring to concentrate at this stage on the occupation of the northern part of China. They declared Manchuria to be an independent state under an emperor picked by themselves, renaming it Manchukuo.

After the Manchurian invasion the Chinese appealed to the League of Nations. The League sent a commission of inquiry, which, under Lord Lytton, found Japan at fault for disturbing the peace. Japan defiantly withdrew from the League. The small powers in the League generally cried for military sanctions, but the Great Powers, knowing that they would be the ones to bear the burden of military intervention against Japan, and in any case inclined to see no threat to their own immediate security, refused to take any stronger measures, so that, in effect, the Japanese remained in occupation of Manchuria and northeast China. With the Japanese conquest of Manchuria one tributary of the coming torrent had begun to flow. But the world at this time was also stunned by economic depression. Each government was preoccupied with its own internal social problems.

100. THE GREAT DEPRESSION: COLLAPSE OF THE WORLD ECONOMY

The capitalist economic system was a delicate and interlocking mechanism, in which any disturbance was rapidly transmitted with accelerating impact through all the parts.[38] For many basic commodities prices were determined by the free play of supply and demand in a world-wide market. There was much regional division of labor; large areas lived by producing a few specialized articles for sale to the world as a whole. A great deal of production, both local and international, especially in the 1920s, was financed by credit, which is to say by promises of repayment in the future. The system rested upon mutual confidence and mutual exchange—on the belief of the lender, creditor, or investor that he would get his money back, on the belief of the borrower that he could pay his debts, on the ability of farms and factories to market their products at prices high enough to bring a net return, so that farmers and factory people might purchase the output of other factories and farms, and so on round and round in countless circles of mutual interdependence, and throughout the world as a whole.

The Prosperity of the 1920s and Its Weaknesses

The five years after 1924 were a period of prosperity, in that there was a good deal of international trade, building, and development of new industries. The automobile, for example, still an oddity in 1914, became an article of mass production after the war; and its widespread use increased the demand for oil, steel,

[38] See pp. 562–570, 683–687.

rubber, and electrical equipment, caused the building or rebuilding of tens of thousands of miles of roads, and created whole new secondary occupations for thousands of men as truckdrivers, garage mechanics, or filling-station attendants. Similarly the mass popularity of radios and moving pictures had repercussions in all directions. The ensuing expansion was most phenomenal in the United States, but almost all countries enjoyed it in greater or lesser degree. "Prosperity" became a mystic term, and some thought that it would last indefinitely, that the secret of human plenty and of progress had been found, and that science and invention were at last realizing the hopes of ages.

But there were weaknesses in this prosperity, various imperfections in this or that gear or valve of the mechanism, flaws which, under stress, were to bring the whole intricate structure to a halt. The expansion was largely financed by credit, or borrowing. Laboring people received less than a balanced share; wages lagged behind profits and dividends, so that mass purchasing power, even when inflated by installment buying (another form of credit), could not absorb the vast output that it was technically possible to produce. And throughout the world the whole decade of the 1920s was a time of chronic agricultural depression, so that farmers could neither pay their debts nor purchase manufactures to the degree required for the smooth functioning of the system.

Military operations in the First World War had reduced wheat fields under cultivation in Europe by a fifth. The world price of wheat went up, and farmers in the United States, Canada, and elsewhere increased their acreage. Often, to acquire land at high prices, they gave mortgages which in later years they were unable to repay. After the war Europe restored its own wheat production, and eastern Europe reentered the world market. Agriculture was increasingly mechanized. Where, in the nineteenth century, one man could cut ten times as much grain with a single horse-drawn reaper as with a scythe, and where, before 1914, he could cut fifty times as much with a combined reaper and binder, he could again increase his output fivefold after the war, by using a tractor-drawn harvester-thresher combine. At the same time dry farming opened up new land, and agronomic science increased the yield per acre. The result of all these numerous developments was a superabundant output of wheat. But the demand for wheat was what economists call "inelastic." By and large, within the area of the Western world, people already ate as much bread as they wanted and would buy no more; and the undernourished masses of Asia, who in pure theory could have consumed the excess, could not pay even low costs of production or transportation. The world price of wheat fell incredibly. In 1930 a bushel of wheat, in terms of gold, sold for the lowest price in four hundred years.

Wheat growers in all continents were faced with ruin. Growers of many other crops faced the same dismal prospect. Cotton and corn, coffee and cocoa all collapsed. Brazilian and African planters were caught by overproduction and falling prices. In Java, where not only had the acreage in sugar been extended, but the unit yield of sugar from the cane had multiplied ten times under scientific cultivation over the past century, the bottom dropped out of prices in the world market. There were indeed other and more profitable forms of agricultural production— for example, in oranges and eggs, of which world consumption was steadily growing. But the coffee planter could not shift to eggs, nor the Iowa farmer to oranges. Not to mention the requirements of climate, the ordinary farmer or peasant lacked the capital, the special knowledge, or the access to refrigerated transportation that these newer branches of agriculture demanded. For the one thing that the average farmer or peasant knew how to do—grow wheat and other cereals—the new wonderful world of science and machinery had too little place.

The acute phase of the great depression, which began in 1929, was made worse by this chronic background of agricultural distress, since there was no reserve of purchasing power on the farms. The farmer's plight became even worse when the city people, struck by depression in industry, cut down their expenditures for food. Agricultural depression, rather than industrial depression, was at the bottom of widespread troubles in the interwar years throughout eastern Europe and the colonial world.

The Crash of 1929 and the Spread of Economic Crisis

The depression, in the strict sense, began as a stock market and financial crisis. Prices of stocks had been pushed upward by years of continuing expansion and high dividends. At the beginning of 1929 prices on the European stock exchanges began to weaken. But the real crisis, or turning point, came with the crash on the New York Stock Exchange in October 1929. Here values had been driven to fantastic heights by excessive speculation. Not only professional speculators, but quite ordinary people, in the United States, as an easy way to make a good deal of money, bought stock with borrowed funds. Sometimes, trading on "margin," they "owned" five or ten times as much stock as the amount of their own money put into it; the rest they borrowed from brokers, and the brokers borrowed from banks, the purchased stock in each case serving as collateral. With money so easy to obtain, people pushed up stock prices by bidding against each other and enjoyed huge fortunes on paper; but if prices fell, even a little, the hapless owners would be obliged to sell their stock to pay off the money they had borrowed. Hence the weakening of values on the New York Stock Exchange set off uncontrollable tidal waves of selling, which drove stock prices down irresistibly and disastrously. In a month stock values dropped by 40 percent, and in three years, from 1929 to 1932, the average value of fifty industrial stocks traded on the New York Stock Exchange dropped from 252 to 61. In these same three years 5,000 American banks closed their doors.

The crisis passed from finance to industry, and from the United States to the rest of the world. The export of American capital came to an end. Americans not only ceased to invest in Europe but sold the foreign securities that they had. This pulled the foundations from under the postwar revival of Germany and hence indirectly of much of Europe. Americans, their incomes falling, ceased to buy foreign goods; from Belgium to Borneo people saw their American markets slip away, and prices tumbled. In 1931 the failure of a leading Vienna bank, the *Creditanstalt*, sent a wave of shivers, bankruptcies, and business calamities over Europe. Everywhere business firms and private people could not collect what was owed them, or even draw on money that they thought they had in the bank. They could not buy, and so the factories could not sell. Factories slowed down or closed entirely. Between 1929 and 1932, the latter year representing the depth of the depression, world production is estimated to have declined by 38 percent, and the world's international trade fell by two-thirds. In the United States the national income fell from $85 billion to $37 billion.

Unemployment, a chronic disease ever since the war, now assumed the proportion of pestilence. In 1932 there were 30 million unemployed persons statistically reported in the world; and this figure did not include the further millions who could find work only for a few hours in the week, or the masses in Asia or Africa for whom no statistics were to be had. The worker's wages were gone, the farmer's income now touched bottom; and the decline of mass purchasing power forced more idleness of machinery and more unemployment. Men in the prime of life spent years out of work. Young people could not find jobs or establish themselves in an occupation. Skills and talents of older people grew rusty, young people found no opportunity to learn. Millions were reduced to living, and supporting their families, on the pittances of charity, doles, or relief. Great modern cities saw an outburst of sidewalk art, in which, at busy street corners, jobless able-bodied men drew pictures on the pavement with colored chalk, in the hope of attracting a few sixpence or dimes. People were crushed in spirit by a feeling of uselessness; months and years of fruitless job hunting left them demoralized, bored, discouraged, embittered, frustrated, and resentful. Never had there been such waste, not merely of machinery which now stood still, but of the trained and disciplined labor force on which all modern societies were built. And people chronically out of work naturally turned to new and disturbing political ideas.

Reactions to the Crisis

Optimists at the time, of whom President Herbert Hoover in the United States was one, declared that this depression, though a severe one, was basically only another periodic low point in the business cycle, or alternation of expansion and contraction, which had ebbed and flowed in the Western world for over a century. Prosperity, they plaintively said, was "just around the corner." Others felt that the crisis represented the breakdown of the whole system of capitalism and free private enterprise. These people, in many cases, looked for signs of the future in the planned economy then being introduced in the U.S.S.R. There was something in both views. After 1932, in part for purely cyclical reasons—because the depression cut down indebtedness and reduced the costs of doing business—it again became possible to produce and sell. World steel production, for example, which had stood at 121 million tons in 1929, and then collapsed to 50 million in 1932, by 1936 again reached 122 million. (To what degree revival was due to armament building is debated.) On the other hand, the Great Depression did put an end to the old economic system in the old sense. Even if such a stricken economy had internal powers of full recuperation after a few years, people would not stand for such terrifying insecurity in their personal lives. The horrors of mass unemployment were long remembered.

All governments took steps to provide work and incomes for their people. All, in one way or another, strove to free themselves from dependency on the uncertainties of the world market. The interlocking world economy collapsed both from the depression itself and from the measures adopted to cure it. The most marked economic consequence of the depression was a strong movement toward economic nationalism—toward greater self-sufficiency within the sphere which each government could hope to control.

The internationalism of money, the gold standard, and the free convertibility of currencies one into the other were gradually abandoned. Countries specializing in agricultural exports were among the first to be pinched. Agricultural prices were so low that even a large quantity of exports failed to produce enough foreign currency to pay for needed imports; hence the exporting country's currency fell in value. The currencies of Argentina, Uruguay, Chile, Australia, and New Zealand all depreciated in 1929 and 1930. Then came the turn of the industrial countries. England, as the depression went on, could not sell enough exports to pay for imports. It had to pay for imports in part by sending gold out of the country; thus the gold reserve supporting the pound sterling declined, and people who had pounds sterling began to convert their pounds into dollars or other currencies for which they thought the gold basis was more secure. This was known, in the poetic language of economics, as the "flight from the pound." In 1931 Great Britain went off the gold standard, which is to say that it devaluated the pound. But after Britain devaluated, some twenty-odd other countries, to protect their own exports and their own industries, did the same. Hence somewhat the same relative position reappeared. Even the United States, which possessed most of the world's gold supply, abjured the gold standard and devalued the dollar in 1934. The purpose was mainly to help American farmers, for with dollars cheaper in terms of foreign currencies, foreigners could afford to buy more American agricultural products. But it became harder for foreigners to sell to the United States.

Hence the depression, adding its effects to those of the World War and postwar inflation, led to chaos in the international monetary exchanges. Governments manipulated their currencies to uphold their sagging exports. Or they imposed definite exchange controls: they required that foreigners from whom their own people purchased, and to whom they thus gave their own currency, should use this currency to buy from them in return. Trade, which had been multilateral, became increasingly "bilateral." That is, where a Brazilian importer of steel, for example, had formerly bought steel wherever he wished, at such price or of such quality as he preferred, he now had to obtain steel, often regardless of price or precise quality, from a country to which Brazil had sold enough of its own products to make payment possible. Sometimes, notably in the relations between Germany and east-European countries in the 1930s, bilateralism degenerated into actual barter. The Germans would exchange a certain number of cameras with Yugoslavia in return for a certain number of pigs. In such cases the very conception of a market disappeared.

Currency control was one means of keeping one's own factories from idleness, by holding or capturing export markets in time of depression. Another way of keeping one's own factories going (or farms, or mines, or quarries) was to shut out competitive imports by the old device of protective tariffs. The United States, hit by depression in 1929, enacted the unprecedentedly high Hawley-Smoot tariff in 1930. Other countries, equally or more distressed, now could sell less to America and hence buy less American goods. Other countries likewise raised their own tariffs, in the desperate hope of reserving national markets for their own people. Even Great Britain, citadel of free trade in the nineteenth century, turned to protectionism. It also revived and adopted Joseph Chamberlain's old idea of an imperial tariff union, when in 1932, by the Ottawa agreements, Britain and the British dominions adopted a policy of having lower tariffs against one another than against the world outside.[39]

Even tariffs were not always enough. Quotas or quantitative restrictions were

---

[39] See pp. 614–615.

adopted in many states. By this system a government said in effect not merely that goods brought into the country must pay a high tariff duty, but that above a certain amount no goods could be brought in at all. Increasingly both importers and exporters worked under government licenses, in order that a country's entire foreign trade could be centrally planned and managed. Such methods approached those of the Soviet Union, which asserted a government monopoly of all foreign trade, exported only in order to finance imports, and determined, without the bother of tariffs, the exact quantity of imported commodities that it would take.

Thus the world economy disintegrated into fiercely competing national economic systems. In the oceanic wreckage of the great depression, each state tried to create an island of economic security for its own people. Some efforts were made to break down the rising barriers. An International Monetary and Economic Conference, meeting in London in 1933, attempted to open the clogged channels of world trade; it ended in failure, as did attempts to stabilize the exchange rates of various currencies. Soon thereafter, the wartime Allies defaulted on their debt payments to the United States.[40] Legislation in Congress then denied them the right to float bonds, or obtain new loans, in the American securities market. American actions thus reinforced economic nationalism. The era that had opened with Woodrow Wilson's dream of international economic cooperation was ending with an unprecedented intensification of economic rivalry and national self-centeredness; it was only one of the promises of the twentieth century to be blasted by the Great Depression.

[40] See pp. 684–685, 690, 745.

XIX.
Democracy and Dictatorship

I n the 1920s, people in a general way believed that the twentieth century was realizing all those goals summed up in the idea of progress; in the 1930s, they began to fear that "progress" was a phantom, to speak the word self-consciously with mental quotation marks, and to be content if only they could prevent a relapse into positive barbarization and a new world war.

The Great Depression ushered in the nightmare of the 1930s. Everywhere the demand was for security. Each nation tried to live economically, so far as possible, within itself. Each regulated, controlled, guided, planned, and tried to rescue its own economic system, attempting to be as little influenced as possible by the unpredictable behavior of other countries, or by the free rise and fall of prices in an uncontrolled world market. Within each country the same search for security encouraged the advancement of the welfare state and social democracy. Where democratic institutions were strong and resilient, governments took steps to protect individuals against the ravages of unemployment and destitution, and to help guard against future catastrophes. These governments remained democratically controlled but they assumed heavy new social responsibilities. On the other hand, where democratic governments were not well established or taken for granted, which was the case in many countries after the First World War, dictatorship spread alarmingly in the 1930s with the coming of the depression. Democracy was said to be suited only to wealthy or prosperous countries. Unemployed people generally cared far more for economic help, or for promises of economic help, than for any theory of how persons wielding public power should be selected. The cry was for a leader, someone who would act, make decisions, assume responsibilities,

Chapter Emblem: A postage stamp featuring Hitler and Mussolini, and reading "Two Peoples, One War," for use in Italian East Africa about 1940.

get results, inspire confidence, and restore national pride. The Great Depression opened the way for unscrupulous and ambitious political adventurers, for dictators like Adolf Hitler in Germany, whose solution to all problems, economic, political, and international, it turned out, was war.

101. THE UNITED STATES: DEPRESSION AND NEW DEAL

Profound changes took place in the United States, where the stock market crash of 1929 had precipitated the great economic collapse. In 1932 national income had dropped to less than half of what it had been in 1929; 12 million to 14 million were unemployed. The Republican President Herbert Hoover, elected in 1928 at the floodtide of prosperity, was identified in the public mind with the hard times. Hoover viewed with disfavor any large-scale government intervention, convinced that the business cycle that had brought the depression would in turn bring prosperity, and that once business confidence was restored recovery would begin. Eventually his administration did act, proposing for the world economy a one-year suspension of payments on all intergovernmental debts and at home giving financial assistance to banks and railroads, expanding credit facilities, and helping to save the mortgages of some farmers and small home owners. But Hoover would not go further; he opposed immediate direct federal relief to the jobless; veterans seeking payment of their wartime bonuses to tide them over the bad times were ejected from Washington; unemployment, business failures, and farm foreclosures continued. In the election of 1932 the millions of unemployed workers, disheartened urban lower middle classes, and distressed farmers swept the Republican administration from office and elected the first Democratic president since Woodrow Wilson. The new president was Franklin Delano Roosevelt. The combination of recovery, relief, and reform legislation that he inaugurated is known as the New Deal.

The new president embarked on a program of improvisation and experimentation, but with such dispatch and vigor as to generate at once an electric enthusiasm. Within a short time an impressive array of legislation was put through Congress. The program of assistance to farmers, small home owners, and

THE ASSEMBLY LINE
by Diego Rivera (Mexican, 1886–1957)

Not all twentieth-century artists have been attracted to pure abstraction or exploration of the unconscious. Among others, social activists and revolutionaries have continued to engage in narrative painting and realistic representation. Diego Rivera was one of the great painters of the Mexican Revolution. Regarded as the greatest living muralist and known also for his Marxist opinions, he was commissioned in 1931 by The Detroit Institute of Arts to decorate the walls of a large new hall. The fragment reproduced here shows part of the assembly line in an automobile plant, with workers of various races working speedily and as a team, while "bourgeois" visitors in the background somewhat stupidly watch and marvel. It was the machine age that Rivera meant to portray, rendering it with a mixture of realism and artistic heightening, and a sense of automatism, movement, and power. Courtesy of The Detroit Institute of Arts.

industry initiated under the Hoover administration was expanded so that it was no longer recognizable.

The government provided financial assistance for the relief of the unemployed and sponsored a broad public works program to absorb the jobless, first by loans to the states for the construction of housing, roads, bridges, and schools, later by a direct federal works program. To meet the financial crisis, the banks were temporarily closed and then reopened under stricter supervision. The dollar was taken off the gold standard and devalued, principally to help the farmers compete in foreign markets. In agriculture the government gave subsidies to farmers who agreed to curtail farm production, even subsidizing the destruction of crops and livestock, so that ruinous surpluses which had been one cause of the agricultural distress might be eliminated. It was a paradox, to be sure, for the government to reduce acreage and destroy agricultural products while city populations were in want. But the administration was endeavoring not only to cope with the immediate situation but also to meet the deep-seated agricultural crisis that antedated the depression. Subsequently, farmers received subsidies for devoting part of their land to soil-conserving crops. A Civilian Conservation Corps also promoted conservation and reforestation, and relieved unemployment by giving jobs to almost 3 million young people. For industry a National Recovery Administration (the NRA) for a time encouraged business firms to set up voluntary "codes of fair competition," which helped to regulate prices and production.

All these measures were designed to set the ailing capitalist system on its feet again by creating purchasing power and stimulating industrial activity. The major innovation was government spending, or "deficit financing." Although never following any consistent economic philosophy, the New Deal policies indirectly reflected the theories of the British economist John Maynard Keynes. In his earlier writings and in his most famous book, *The General Theory of Employment, Interest, and Money,* published in 1936, he argued that if private investment funds were idle, government funds must be employed to encourage economic activity and to increase purchasing power until such time as private funds flowed again. In order to get money into circulation and to "prime the pump" of industrial production, the government undertook a huge borrowing and spending program. Unorthodox as "deficit financing" was, it seemed to many at the time the only direct and rapid method of preventing economic collapse in a capitalist system. In all these recovery and reform activities the federal government assumed a role that it had hitherto played only in wartime. Alphabetical agencies proliferated; the federal payroll grew; the government debt mounted—between 1932 and 1940 it more than doubled.

From the beginning, some longer-range reform measures were adopted in addition to the recovery measures. To prevent overspeculation and the recurrence of a crash such as that of 1929, a Securities and Exchange Commission was created to regulate the issuance of stock and to supervise the operations of the stock exchange. Bank deposits were guaranteed by federal insurance so that depositors would never again lose their lifetime savings. A Tennessee Valley Authority served as a pilot program in flood control, regional economic development, and cheap public power production—a yardstick, it was said, for the private utility companies.

After 1935 the focus shifted to regulation and reform. Sound economic recovery had not been achieved; there were still at least 5 million persons who could not find jobs in private industry. Businessmen who at first had been responsive to the government's leadership were now resisting the government's regulation of finance and industry. The Supreme Court declared the NRA and other New Deal measures unconstitutional.

Some of the major New Deal reforms after 1935 were laws to improve the condition of labor and to moderate the insecurity of the ordinary citizen. A broad national Social Security Act in 1935 provided for unemployment, old-age, and disability insurance. Here the United States was a latecomer. Germany, Britain, and other European countries had had such legislation since before the First World War. A Fair Labor Standards Act established forty hours as a maximum normal workweek and set a minimum hourly wage; child labor was abolished. With the passage of a third measure, the National Labor Relations (or Wagner) Act, the American industrial scene was virtually transformed. For the first time the unions found the federal government and the law solidly aligned on their side in the campaign to organize labor. Under the new act, which guaranteed the right of workers to set up and bargain through unions of their own choice, company unions were outlawed and employers were forbidden to interfere with union organization or discriminate against union members. Under its aegis the older American Federation of Labor (AFL) was revitalized and a new vigorous organization came into being, the Congress of Industrial Organizations (CIO), organizing workers on an industry-wide basis and reaching down to unskilled workers in such industries as automobile, steel, textile, maritime, and rubber. Millions never before organized, including women and black workers, became part of powerful labor unions with expanding treasuries. Total union membership rose from about 4 million in 1929 to 9 million by 1940; in 1980 it was about 22 million. Militant and conscious of its new strength but hardly touched by revolutionary ideology, American labor chose not to create a third party but to operate within the traditional two-party system.

Other reforms included a tax revision bill, which arranged for steeply graduated income taxes, levies on corporate profits, and the plugging of various corporate tax-evasion loopholes. The New Deal later tried also to reverse the trend toward the concentration of economic power, which it had itself stimulated under the NRA, by an investigation into monopoly and monopoly practices, and a trust-busting campaign. A program of slum clearance and low-cost housing made a start toward providing adequate housing. Aid was given to the tenant farmer and the sharecropper. All this was undertaken to help those whom the president described in 1937 as "one-third of a nation ill-nourished, ill-clad, ill-housed." If the New Deal did not feed, clothe, and house them, or strike at the deeper roots of American poverty, urban decay, and racial discrimination, as many later argued, it at least demonstrated that the national community cared, and it showed the enormous potential for government action along all those fronts.

Government spending and renewed confidence in the soundness of the country's institutions created a slow, gradual, and partial recovery. In mid-1937, however, a recession occurred, i.e., business activity slid backward, when government spending slowed down; the recession did not end until 1938 when government spending was resumed. National income reached $71 billion by 1939, double what it had been at the depth of the depression but still short of 1929. Despite substantial progress, business activity did not regain the high-water mark of June 1929. Resistance from the business community itself may have played a part. The rising public debt, antibusiness pronouncements by the government, heavier cor-

porate and income taxes, and the many concessions to labor undoubtedly frightened off business investments and led to what was called a "sit-down strike" of
capital. Some claimed that wage rates had risen too sharply, adding to production costs and therefore discouraging business expansion. The New Deal did much
to help economic recovery, but it did not end the depression. Complete recovery,
the elimination of unemployment, the full use (and expansion) of the nation's
productive capacity had to wait upon the huge war expenditures, by which depression spending was to be dwarfed. By 1938 or so the New Deal was over; the
administration turned its attention from domestic reform to the gathering storm
in Europe and the Far East.

The changes were substantial under what some called the "Roosevelt Revolution." Carrying forward a process that went back at least to the era of Theodore
Roosevelt, but enlarging the role of the federal government as no previous administration had done, the New Deal transformed the noninterventionist state into a
social service or welfare state. The government imposed controls on business, entered business itself (as in the TVA), used its powers to redistribute wealth, and
introduce a broad social security system. Labor's power and political influence
grew. The responsibility of public authority for the social and economic welfare
of the people was clearly established. Here perhaps was the essence of the New
Deal. When the Republican party later returned to power, it opposed in principle
the further growth of the welfare state and the expanding role of the federal government, but it retained the New Deal reforms, a tacit admission that the New
Deal had not intended to destroy capitalism but to revive it.

The New Deal, however, engendered violent feelings, which lingered on.
Roosevelt, himself of patrician and well-to-do background, denounced the "economic royalists"; in turn he was called a "traitor to his class." When the Supreme
Court declared New Deal measures unconstitutional, he made plans to reorganize
and enlarge the court, which aroused more political hostility. Despite vociferous
opposition, in the election of 1936 Roosevelt won all but two states, and he was
subsequently reelected in 1940 and 1944 (during the wartime emergency, to be
sure, and with increasingly smaller majorities) for an unprecedented four terms.
Such an occurrence was later barred for the future by a constitutional amendment of 1951.

Roosevelt's opponents, at the time and later, argued that the New Deal had
created an enormous regulatory bureaucracy, expensive and cumbersome, a
threat to the freedom and self-reliance of the citizenry. But, others contended, despite its waste and inconsistencies, costliness and unorthodox financial policies,
enlargement of the executive power and expansion of the bureaucracy, it represented a bold and humanitarian way of meeting the greatest crisis the American
republic had ever faced short of the challenge of arms; it preserved and reaffirmed American faith in its democratic system—and that at a time when
democracy was succumbing elsewhere.

102. TRIALS AND ADJUSTMENTS OF DEMOCRACY IN BRITAIN AND FRANCE

British Politics: The 1920s and the Depression

Britain, like the United States, even in the troubles of the depression, remained
firmly attached to representative institutions and democratic principles. The

Great Depression aggravated and intensified Britain's older economic difficulties. More dependent on overseas markets than any other people, the British until 1914 had managed to hold their lead, exporting industrial products and capital, selling insurance and other services, and importing foodstuffs. But in the years before 1914 the British were increasingly losing their markets because of many circumstances: the emergence of other economically aggressive industrial nations, the growth of tariff barriers, the development of indigenous textile and other industries in India and elsewhere in the East, the competition of new textile products with British cottons and woolens, and the substitution of new sources of fuel for British coal. The losses were accelerated by the economic disruption of the First World War, the disappearance of many investments, and the postwar disorganization and impoverishment of markets, though British trade for about a year enjoyed a short lived boom caused by pent-up demands that could not be satisfied during the war. The general rise in tariffs after the war and the customs barriers raised in the new small states of Europe also hurt British exports. After 1918 Britain lived in a world no longer dependent on, or eager for, its manufactures. Britain's very historical primacy as the pioneer industrial country was also a handicap. Both labor and management had become adjusted to older conditions, and the more recently industrialized countries had less antiquated techniques and machinery.

The net result of all this was that in the interwar years, even in times of relative prosperity for the rest of the world, Britain was in depression and suffered severely from unemployment. The unemployment insurance adopted in 1911 was called heavily into play. By 1921 over 2 million unemployed were receiving benefit payments, contemptuously called the "dole" by those who disliked it. Unemployment insurance, an expanded old-age pension system, medical aid, government-subsidized housing, and other social welfare measures helped to relieve economic distress and to prevent any drastic decline in the living standards of British workers. The welfare state was well under way in Britain before the Labour party took office after the Second World War.

The labor unions made a strenuous effort to retain wage gains and other concessions won in wartime. Industry, hard-pressed itself, resisted. This situation reached a climax in 1926 in the coal-mining industry, which was in a particularly bad plight; government subsidies had not helped and even conservative investigators had recommended some form of amalgamation and public management. A strike by the coal miners led to a "general strike" supported by the other British unions; about half of the 6 million organized workers in Britain left their jobs as a token of their sympathy and solidarity. But the government declared a state of emergency and made use of army and navy personnel and middle-class volunteers to take over essential services. The strike ended in failure, and even in a setback for the trade unions, which were put under stricter control by the Trades Disputes Act of 1927, a measure that declared all general or sympathy strikes illegal and even forbade the unions from raising money for political purposes. The act remained in effect until repealed after the Second World War.

After the election of 1922, the Labour party displaced the Liberal party as the second of the two great parties of the country and faced the Conservatives as the official opposition.[1] The Labour party could more consistently and more actively champion both labor legislation and bolder measures to deal with Britain's troubled economic state. The Labour party, moreover, which had been no more than

[1] See pp. 578–579, 586–587, 606–607.

a loose federation of trade union and socialist organizations before the war, tightened its organizational structure and, bridging the gap between the trade unionists and the socialists, committed itself in 1918 to a program of socialism. But it was a program of gradualist, democratic socialism operating through customary British parliamentary procedures and hence able to gain the good will of large sections of the middle classes.

Twice, in 1924 and in 1929, Labour governed the country with Ramsay MacDonald as prime minister, in each case as a coalition government, with Labour dependent on the support of the Liberals for its majority. In 1924 the Labourites proved their moderation. Their administration went no further than an extension of unemployment relief and the inauguration of housing and public works projects; indeed the Labour government acted firmly in the face of a series of strikes that broke out. Its overthrow was precipitated by its diplomatic recognition of the Soviet Union and the pledge of a loan to the Soviets for the purchase of British goods. Defeat was ensured by the preelection publication of the so-called Red (or Zinoviev) letter purporting to be secret instructions to British labor groups from the head of the Communist International urging preparations for a Communist uprising in Britain.[2] The document's authenticity has never been established, but the Conservatives successfully exploited it and won the election of 1924.

In the election of May 1929, however, Labour's representation almost doubled, and the Conservative representation dropped proportionately. MacDonald again became prime minister of a Labour-dominated coalition government. Thus the Wall Street crash and the world-wide depression came while the Labour party government was in office. The effects of the depression were quickly felt. Unemployment, which had hovered about the 1 million mark in 1929, soon approached the 3 million figure. The government expended large sums to supplement the unemployment insurance payments. Gold flowed out of the country, tax receipts declined, the public debt grew. Alarmed at the mounting deficit, MacDonald took the advice of a committee of financial experts and made plans to introduce a severe retrenchment policy, even to the extent of reducing the "dole" payments. The Labour party was outraged; some of the Labour ministers in his cabinet refused to support him. He was read out of the party, along with those ministers who had gone along with him. MacDonald thereupon formed an all-party coalition cabinet known as the National government, which in an election of 1931 won an overwhelming victory, the Conservative members of the coalition alone winning a majority of the seats in Parliament.

The new government, though Conservative in essence, represented an effort to maintain national unity in the face of economic emergency, within the framework of the British parliamentary democracy. Not a single seat in Parliament in the depression election of 1931 went to either the Communists or to a British Fascist party organized by Sir Oswald Mosley; in 1935 the Communists won one seat.

The National government coped with the depression chiefly along retrenchment lines, under Ramsay MacDonald from 1931 to 1935, Stanley Baldwin to 1937, and Neville Chamberlain after 1937. In addition to retrenchment and budget balancing, the government encouraged industry to reorganize and rationalize production by providing low-interest loans. Mainly, the government concentrated on the kind of economic nationalist measures that have already been

[2] See p. 738.

described.[3] As in the United States, despite some recovery from the depths of the depression, none of the steps taken brought full recovery or full employment. Unemployment persisted until military conscription and an expanded armament program absorbed the jobless. The Labour party, partially recovering its strength in the election of 1935, denounced the timid expedients of the Conservatives, whom it held responsible for the apathy and gloom gripping the country.

Britain and the Commonwealth: Imperial Relations

To the older British Empire—India, the crown colonies, protectorates, and spheres of influence—the postwar settlement added a number of League of Nations mandates. British rule in its various forms extended to almost 500 million people, a fourth of the earth's population and land surface. It was principally in Ireland, Egypt, India, and Palestine that the British faced complex imperial problems after the First World War. In Palestine, where the British exercised a League of Nations mandate, Arabs and Jews fought with each other and with Britain. In Egypt, in 1922, Britain, although retaining the right to station some troops there, formally ended the protectorate it had established forty years earlier; but many questions, especially the status of the Sudan, remained unresolved. In India the agitation for national independence, as we have seen, grew more intense. In these areas nothing resembling a solution was arrived at until after the Second World War. In Ireland the independence movement managed to establish a separate republic.

The Irish question had disoriented English politics for forty years.[4] Irish home rule, authorized by Parliament in 1914, had been deferred for the duration of the war. Irish nationalists, during the war, had accepted German support and had risen in rebellion in 1916. After the war, in 1919 and 1920, the Irish Nationalist or Sinn Fein party fought a small but savage war of independence against the British forces known as "Black and Tans." The British blocked independence, but in 1922 recognized the Irish Free State, granting it dominion status. The Protestant majority in Ulster, the northern counties where Presbyterians of Scottish origin had lived for three centuries, preferred to remain outside the Free State and continued to be joined in the United Kingdom of Great Britain and Northern Ireland, to the vehement dissatisfaction of the Irish republicans. In 1937 a new constitution for the Irish Free State affirmed the full sovereignty of Ireland (or Eire, as it was for a time called), the country remaining, however, in the British Commonwealth of Nations. Politics remained unsettled, for the Irish agitated for the annexation of Ulster, conducted tariff wars with a Britain from which they were now cut off, strove to revive Celtic in place of the English language, and fell into disputes in which Irish moderates were pitted against Irish extremists, the latter perpetrating an occasional assassination, or other outrage, to further their cause. The last formal ties with the British Commonwealth were severed in 1949, when the Republic of Ireland was proclaimed. The Irish continued to claim jurisdiction over Ulster and to support the cause of the Irish Catholic minority there.

As for the dominions, the political status of these areas of white settlement overseas was now more clearly defined than ever before. The dominions—Canada, Australia, New Zealand, and the Union of South Africa—had long pursued

[3] See pp. 764–766.
[4] See pp. 579–580, 607, 674; for developments after 1945, see p. 889.

their own policies, even levying tariffs against British goods. They had all joined loyally with Great Britain in the First World War, but all were stirred by a nationalism of their own and desired their virtual independence to be regularized and promulgated to the world. An imperial conference of 1926 defined "dominion status," which was corroborated by the Statute of Westminster of 1931. The dominions became legally equal with each other and with Great Britain. No act passed by the British Parliament could apply to a dominion save by the dominion's own consent. Despite independent policies in economic matters and even in foreign affairs, the bonds between the dominions and Britain were firm; the support of the dominions in the Second World War was to be vital in Britain's survival. After the war the Commonwealth was to become a larger and even more flexible institution.

France: The 1920s and the Coming of the Depression

When the depression came to France, agitation of fascist type made more headway there than in Britain or the United States. Earlier, in the 1920s, France was preoccupied with recovery from the physical destruction of the war, the instability of public finances, and the fear of a resurgent Germany. Immediately after 1919, and for most of the 1920s, the government was run by coalitions of parties of the conservative right, i.e., parties supported by business and financial interests, well disposed toward the army and church, and interested in economy and stability in domestic affairs. For about two years, from 1924 to 1926, the Radical Socialists were in control; this party of the moderate left, whose leader was Edouard Herriot, served as spokesman for the lower middle classes, the small businessmen and farmers; it advocated progressive social legislation so long as increased taxes were not necessary. Despite its name, a carryover from an earlier era, it was firmly committed to private enterprise and private property; it was staunch in its defense of individual liberties and was fervently anticlerical; sometimes, it seemed, its anticlericalism was a substitute for any more positive program. Although the Radical Socialists could cooperate in elections with the Socialists, the other major party of the left, the two parties differed too profoundly on economic policies to preserve stable coalitions. In the 1920s the Socialists, led by Léon Blum, were still recovering from the secession of the more orthodox Marxists who had formed a French Communist party. Both left and right in France shaded off into antidemocratic groups that were hostile to the parliamentary republic as such. These included the Communists on the left, who sat in parliament and took part in elections; and on the extreme right, royalists of the Action Française and other antirepublican organizations, which operated principally outside the Chamber as militant and noisy pressure groups.

The outstanding figure of the moderate conservative right was Raymond Poincaré; it was he who sent troops into the Ruhr in 1923, when the Germans failed to pay reparations; and it was he who now "saved" the franc. The reparations question was extremely important for French finances. The country had undertaken a large-scale reconstruction program to repair the wartime devastation of northern and eastern France, and had counted upon the defeated enemy to pay. When German reparations were not paid as anticipated, the public debt mounted, a balanced budget became impossible, and the franc declined precipitously. The huge war expenditures, heavy wartime investment losses, notably in Russia, and an outmoded taxation program which invited widespread evasion added to French difficulties. After 1926, when the financial crisis reached a climax, a "national union" ministry under Poincaré inaugurated new taxes, tightened tax collection somewhat, cut down drastically on government expenditures in order to balance the budget, and eventually stabilized the franc—at about one-fifth of its prewar value. The internal debt was thus in effect largely repudiated, to the despair of many bondholders, but the threat of a runaway inflation, like that of the Weimar Republic, and of national bankruptcy was avoided. From 1926 to 1929 the country prospered. New factories, replacing those destroyed in the war, were modern and up to date. The index of industrial production rose; tourists flocked in. As in many other countries, workers did not share proportionately in the prosperity of the 1920s. The unions received a sharp setback when, immediately following the war, a series of strikes of major proportions ended in failure; the unions were also divided between a Communist and non-Communist national confederation; collective bargaining in the country was virtually unknown. The workers were not mollified by a social insurance program adopted by a reluctant parliament, which went into effect in 1930.

The Great Depression came later to France and was less severe than in the United States or Germany. Trade declined. Unemployment and part-time employment increased; at the worst period, in 1935, close to 1 million workers were unemployed; perhaps half of those employed worked part-time. Industrial production, which in 1930 was 40 percent above the prewar level, sank by 1932 back to the 1913 figure. The government displayed the usual pattern of unstable, shifting, short-lived ministries; in 1933 five ministries rapidly succeeded one another (there were some forty all told in the twenty interwar years). The cabinets formed after 1932 followed a policy of retrenchment and economy, and clung to the gold standard. Meanwhile, in Germany Adolf Hitler had become chancellor in 1933; France's domestic difficulties were intensified by mounting international tension.

Depression Ferment and the Popular Front

In the uneasy years of the depression, the latent hostility to the republic came to the surface. Fascist-type "leagues" appeared in open imitation of Italian and German fascist organizations, many obtaining funds from wealthy industrialists; the older *Action Française* and right-wing veterans' associations like Colonel de la Rocque's *Croix de Feu* were also active. The same elements that had been antirepublican, antidemocratic, or monarchist since the French Revolution and which had rallied behind Boulanger and denounced Dreyfus[5] now grew more strident in their attacks on the parliamentary republic.

In 1934 it seemed for a moment that the opportunity awaited by the antirepublican elements had come. A political and financial scandal of the kind familiar in prewar French public life broke over the country. A financial manipulator and adventurer with excellent political connections, Stavisky by name, induced the municipal authorities at Bayonne to launch a flotation of worthless bonds. Faced with exposure, he fled and apparently committed suicide; the sensationalist press encouraged the rumor that he had been shot by the police to prevent the implication of high-ranking politicians. A clamor went up accusing the government of

[5] See pp. 574–575.

involvement in the financial scandal. Where elsewhere such an affair would have called only for turning the incumbents out of office, in France it supplied ammunition for those who demanded the end of the republic itself, which was equated with corruption and venality.

The agitation reached a climax in the riots of February 1934. A mob of fascist tendency assembled in the Place de la Concorde, threatened the Chamber, and battled with the police; several were killed and hundreds injured. French liberals and democrats, organized labor, and the Socialist party were outraged by the threat to the republic. The Communists, hostile to the fascist groups, were unfriendly to the government too, but soon, along with the Comintern, they sensed the danger to themselves and to the Soviet Union in the event of a French fascist triumph and joined with the antifascists. As elsewhere, in the 1930s the Communists emerged from their sectarian revolutionary isolation, became intensely patriotic, and widened their prestige, influence, and appeal. An impressive labor-sponsored general strike was held a week after the riots. Shortly thereafter, the Radical Socialists, Socialists, and Communists drew together in a political coalition that came to be known as the Popular Front, of the kind that was being organized, or advocated, in many countries in the 1930s. It campaigned on a pledge to defend the republic against fascism, to take measures against the depression, and to introduce labor reforms. In the spring of 1936 it won a decisive victory at the polls. The French Socialists for the first time in their history became the leading party in the Chamber; their chief, Léon Blum, long a spokesman for democratic and reformist socialism, became premier of a coalition cabinet of Socialists and Radical Socialists; the Communists, who had increased their representation in the Chamber from 10 to 72 seats, did not join the cabinet but pledged their support.

The Popular Front and After

Blum's Popular Front ministry, although it lasted little more than a year, put through a program of far-reaching legislation. In part, this was due to the Popular Front election program, in part to unforeseen events, for the tremendous enthusiasm generated by the victory led to a spontaneous nationwide wave of "sit-down strikes," which did not subside until Blum pledged a number of immediate reforms.

Through Blum's mediation, industry at once awarded a blanket wage increase to all workers and promised to cooperate with social legislation passed by parliament. Parliament in short order passed laws providing for a forty-hour week, vacations with pay, and a collective bargaining law. As in the case of the Wagner Act in the United States, the encouragement given to collective bargaining led to the nationwide signing of collective contracts for the first time in the country's history and to an enormous growth in trade union membership, from about 1 million to 5 million in a year's time. Labor's strength was increased also by a re-unification of the Communist and non-Communist labor confederations. Other legislation was important too. Steps were taken to nationalize the armaments and aviation industry; the fascist armed leagues were, at least in theory, dissolved; the Bank of France was reorganized and placed under government control to break the power of the "two hundred families." Machinery was established for the arbitration of labor disputes. Aid was given to farmers through price fixing and government purchases of wheat. As in the United States all these measures aimed at both recovery and reform; Blum spoke openly of his program as a "French New Deal." But French conservatives, and the quasi fascists to their right, cried revolution; they uttered dark predictions that a French Lenin would follow Blum. They did not conceal their sullen resentment at what had come to pass: the fate of Catholic France was in the hands of a leftist, a Socialist, and a Jew. Even salvation by a warrior from outside the country, one who had demonstrated his anti-Bolshevism, would be preferable. They envied the protection given to established interests by Mussolini, and there were those who even muttered "better Hitler than Léon Blum."

In all truth the Popular Front reforms, long overdue though they were, came to France at a time when the sands were rapidly running out. While France had a forty-hour week, German arms plants were operating at full capacity. In the shadow of Nazi remilitarization a rearmament program had to be undertaken at the very same time as reform; even moderates argued that the country could not afford both. Opposition from many quarters hindered success. French employers balked at cooperating in the new reforms and tried to pass on rising production costs to the consumer. Labor was disgruntled at the rise in prices that canceled out their wage gains. Both employers and labor applied the forty-hour week in such a manner that plants were shut down for two days a week instead of operating in shifts, as the law had intended. Nothing could check the flight of gold from the country. Industrial production hardly rose; even in 1938, when it had shown substantial recovery in other countries, it was only 5 percent higher in France than at the depth of the depression. The Communists attacked the Blum government for refusing aid to the hard-pressed Spanish Popular Front government across the Pyrenees; Blum, following the lead of Britain and fearing involvement, resisted. In 1937, after a year in office, the Blum government was overthrown by the Senate, which refused to grant it emergency financial powers. The Popular Front coalition rapidly disintegrated. By mid-1938 the Radical Socialists had abandoned their allies on the left, and under Édouard Daladier formed a conservative ministry, whose attention was increasingly occupied by the international crisis. Little remained of the Popular Front, or indeed of the strength of labor, which declined rapidly and exhausted itself further by an unsuccessful general strike in 1938 in protest against nullification of the forty-hour week. For the French worker, 1936 had gone the way of other "great years"; the comfortable classes had been thrown into panic by the social turmoil; internal division and class hatreds had grown sharper. Yet the French democracy, the Third Republic itself, had been successfully preserved and its domestic enemies repulsed, at least for a time.

Western Europe and the Depression

Britain and France, and indeed all western Europe, Europe's "inner zone," never fully recovered from the Great Depression before the Second World War came. When economic expansion later resumed after the war, the interwar years seemed like a deep trough in Europe's economic history. Western Europe barely maintained its old inherited equipment in the depression and was unable to utilize even its existing machinery to capacity. Moreover, as the events of 1929 had clearly shown, Europe's economic dependence on the United States was pronounced, and the U.S.S.R. was becoming an industrial giant. The economic destiny of Europeans in the 1930s was very much in doubt.

There were other signs of decline. The birth rate in western Europe in the 1930s declined to its lowest recorded levels as young people postponed marriage and married people limited the size of their families because of economic and psychological stresses. Birth rates did not run significantly higher than death rates, the population stagnating and growing older. There was a scarcity of men of vigorous middle age because of the casualties of the First World War. Politically neither British nor French democratic political leaders were able to cope successfully with the economic dilemmas of the depression era. Nor could the Socialists, who found neither Marxian economics nor class struggle ideas helpful but who failed to renew or reinvigorate their doctrines in any significant way.

103. ITALIAN FASCISM

Though they shade into each other imperceptibly, it is well to distinguish dictatorship from totalitarianism. Dictatorship, an old phenomenon in history, has commonly been regarded as a mere expedient, designed for emergencies and believed to be temporary; at most, it is a theory of government. Totalitarianism, as it arose after the First World War, was not merely a theory of government but a theory of life and of human nature. It claimed to be no expedient but a permanent form of society and civilization, and so far as it appealed to emergency for justification, it regarded life itself as an everlasting emergency. Let us first review the pertinent events in Italy and Germany, return next to the general ideas of totalitarianism, and then, in the following chapter, trace the crises that in 1939 again led to a world war.

The belief widely held in the 1920s that democracy was generally advancing was not deeply disturbed by the failure of Russia or Turkey or China to develop effective parliaments or liberal institutions. These were backward countries, in the throes of revolution; some day, when conditions quieted down, it could be supposed, they would move forward to democracy as known in the West. The first jarring exception to the apparent victory of democracy was furnished by Italy, a country that was an integral part of civilized Europe, one that since 1861 had accepted parliamentary liberalism, but where, as early as 1922, Benito Mussolini seized control of the government and proclaimed *Fascismo*.

Mussolini, born in 1883, the son of a blacksmith, was a fiery and pugnacious character, who before the war had followed the career of professional revolutionary, left-wing socialist, and radical journalist. He had read and digested such works as Sorel's *Reflections on Violence* and Nietzsche's writings.[6] During the war he turned intensely nationalist, clamored for intervention on the side of the Allies, and demanded the conquest from Austria of *Italia irredenta*, the "unredeemed" Italian lands to the north and across the Adriatic. In the war he rose to the rank of corporal. In March 1919 he organized, mainly from demobilized and restless ex-soldiers, his first fighting band, or *fascio di combattimento*. *Fascio* meant a bunch or bundle, as of sticks; it called to mind the Latin *fasces*, or bundle of rods, carried by the lictors in ancient Rome as a symbol of state power—for Mussolini loved to conjure up ancient glories.

[6] See pp. 596, 606.

In 1919 Italian glories were dim. Italy had entered the war on the side of the Allies quite frankly for territorial and colonial spoils; the secret treaty of London in 1915 promised the Italians certain Austrian lands and a share in German and Turkish possessions. During the war Italian arms did not especially shine; Italian troops were routed at Caporetto in 1917. Yet Italy lost over 600,000 lives in the war, and the Italian delegates came to the peace conference confident that their sacrifices would be recognized and their territorial aspirations satisfied. They were rapidly disappointed. Wilson refused to honor the provisions of the London secret treaty and other demands of the Italians. Britain and France displayed no eagerness to side with Italy. The Italians received some of the Austrian territories promised to them, but they were given no part of the former German or Turkish possessions as mandates.

After the war Italy, like other countries, suffered from the burden of wartime debt and from acute postwar depression and unemployment. Social unrest spread. In the countryside land seizures took place, not in any significant proportions but enough to spread concern among landowners; tenant farmers refused to pay rents; peasants burned crops and destroyed livestock. In the cities great strikes broke out in heavy industry and in transportation. Some of the strikes turned into sit-down strikes, the workers refusing to leave the plants; demands were raised even for worker control of the factories. Moderate socialist and labor leaders disavowed all such extremism, but left-wing socialists who, as elsewhere, had turned communist and joined the Third International, fanned the existing discontents. Meanwhile, armed bands of young men, most prominent of whom were the Blackshirts or Fascists, brawled with Communists and ordinary workers in the streets. By the late summer of 1920 the strikes and the agrarian unrest had subsided, although violence in the streets persisted.

During the months of turmoil the government refrained from any bold action. The Italian parliamentary system in the prewar years had never functioned impressively nor commanded widespread esteem; now respect for parliament and the weak, shifting, coalition ministries sank even lower. In 1919 the first postwar election had been held, under a law that added proportional representation to the universal male suffrage introduced in 1913. The Socialists and a new Catholic Popular, or Christian Socialist, party made an impressive showing. In 1921, in the wake of the postwar disturbances, new elections were held. Liberals and democrats, moderate socialists, and the Catholic Popular party were all returned in large numbers. Mussolini's Fascist movement won 35 of the 500-odd seats. Despite this less than impressive showing (the best ever made by the Fascists in a totally free election), the Fascist ranks had been swelling, in the backwash, as it were, of the postwar unrest. Although the social agitation died down, burning itself out on its own, and there had never been any real threat of a Soviet-style revolution, the propertied classes went through a great fright; they found comfort in the Fascist movement and were willing to lend it financial support.

Mussolini and the Fascists had at first gone along with the radical tide; they had not disapproved the factory seizures; they had inveighed against plutocracy and war profiteers and called for a high levy on capital and profits. But Mussolini, never one to sacrifice opportunity for principles or doctrine, soon came forward with his Fascists as the upholders of national law and order, and hence property; he pledged battle "against the forces dissolving victory and nation." The propertied interests gave financial aid to the self-styled bulwark against Bolshevism;

patriots and nationalists of all classes rallied to it; and the lower middle class, pinched by economic inflation and, as elsewhere, unable to find protection or solace in labor unions or socialist movements, joined too. The black-shirted upholders of national order meanwhile proceeded methodically to administer beatings (and doses of castor oil) to Communists and alleged Communists, to Socialists and Christian Socialists, and to ordinary persons who did not support them; nor did they refrain from arson and murder. Vigilante squadrons, the *squadristi*, broke up strikes, demolished labor union headquarters, and drove from office duly elected Socialist and Communist mayors and town officials. Mussolini reinforced his claim as paladin of law, authority, and order by declaring his loyalty to king and church; a few years earlier he had been a rabid republican and anticlerical.

In October 1922 the "March on Rome" took place. The Blackshirts mobilized for a threatened coup and began to converge from various directions on the capital; Mussolini remained at a safe distance in Milan. The liberal-democratic coalition cabinet had viewed the events of the past two years with disapproval but at the same time with the undeniable satisfaction that the Blackshirts were serving something of a useful national purpose by suppressing trouble-makers on the left. Now they made belated but ineffectual gestures to save the situation by an effort to have martial law declared; the king refused to approve. The cabinet resigned and Mussolini was named premier. It was all quite legal, or almost so. Indeed Italy was still in form a constitutional and parliamentary government. Mussolini headed only a coalition ministry and received from parliament no more than a year's grant of full emergency powers to restore order and introduce reforms.

But soon it was clear in whose hands power rested. Before the expiration of his emergency powers Mussolini forced through parliament a law providing that any party securing the largest number of votes in an election should automatically receive two-thirds of the seats in the legislature. This was Mussolini's solution to the instability of coalitions and blocs in parliamentary governments like those of Italy and France (and indeed of most other Continental democracies), where a single party hardly ever enjoyed a majority. The two-thirds law was not even necessary. In the 1924 elections, although seven opposition slates appeared, the Fascists received well over three-fifths of the total vote, aided by government control of the electoral machinery and the use of *squadristi*.

After the elections of 1924 the highly respected Socialist deputy Matteotti publicly exposed hundreds of cases of armed Fascist violence, and of fraud and chicanery at the polls. He was murdered by Fascists. There was widespread indignation in the country, and the press clamored for Mussolini's resignation. The opposition parties even seceded from the Chamber, wanting to have nothing to do with such a government. Mussolini, not directly involved in the assassination, was at first dismayed by the event and was even willing to punish the perpetrators, but he eventually took full responsibility and moved to consolidate his dictatorship. Within a few years he reduced the Italian parliament to a nonentity, put the press under censorship, destroyed the labor unions, deprived labor of the right to strike, and abolished all political parties except the Fascist party.

Fascism in the 1920s was an innovation which the rest of the world was slow to understand. In his more flamboyant moments Mussolini strutted, stuck out his jaw, and glared ferociously; he jumped through flaming hoops to show his virility and had his chief subordinates do likewise; to the outside world this seemed an odd way of demonstrating fitness for public office. He denounced democracy as historically outmoded and declared that it accentuated class struggle, split people into countless minority parties, and led to selfishness, futility, evasion, and empty talk. In place of democracy he preached the need of vigorous action, under a strong leader; he himself took the title of Leader, or *Duce*. He denounced liberalism, free trade, laissez faire, and capitalism, along with Marxism, materialism, socialism, and class consciousness, which he said were the evil offspring of liberal and capitalistic society. In their place he preached national solidarity and state management of economic affairs, under the same Leader's farseeing and audacious vision. And in fact Mussolini seemed to bring a kind of efficiency to easygoing Italy; as the saying went, at least he made the trains run on time.

Mussolini introduced, at least in theory, the syndical, or corporative state. This had been discussed in both left- and right-wing circles for many years. Left-wing syndicalism, especially before the First World War, looked to revolutionary labor unions to expropriate the owners of industry and then to assume the direction of political and economic life. A more conservative syndicalism was endorsed and encouraged by the Catholic church, with which, as has been noted in a previous chapter, Mussolini made his peace with the signing of the Lateran accord in 1929.[7] The conservative type looked nostalgically toward a revival of the medieval guilds, or "corporations," in which master and journeymen, employer and employees, had labored side by side in a supposedly golden age of social peace. The Fascist corporative system really resembled neither, because in it the hand of the state was writ large, something that none of the older corporative doctrines had anticipated. It went through a number of complicated stages, but as it finally emerged in the 1930s, it provided for the division of all economic life into twenty-two major areas, for each of which a "corporation" was established. In each corporation representatives of the Fascist-organized labor groups, the employers, and the government determined working conditions, wages, prices, and industrial policies; and in a national council these representatives were supposed jointly to devise plans for Italy's economic self-sufficiency. In each case the role of government was decisive and the whole structure was under the jurisdiction of the minister of corporations. As a final step, these corporative economic chambers were integrated into the government proper so that in 1938 the old Chamber of Deputies was superseded by a Chamber of Fasces and Corporations representing the corporations and the Fascist party, its members selected by the government and not subject to popular ratification.

None of this was democratic, but this was an improvement over democracy, the Fascists asserted. A legislature in an advanced economic society, they said, should be an economic parliament; it should represent not political parties and geographical constituencies but economic occupations. Organization along such lines would do away with the anarchy and class conflict engendered by free capitalism, which only sap the strength of the national state. Real authority in any event rested with the government—the Head of the Government, who settled most matters by decree. In point of fact, social unrest and class conflict were "ended," not by the corporative system as such, but by the prohibition of strikes and lockouts and the abolition of independent labor unions. The corporative system represented the most extreme form of state control over economic life within a framework of private enterprise and a relatively capitalistic economy, that is, one

[7] See pp. 600–602.

in which ownership continued to rest in private hands. It was the Fascist answer to Western-style democracy and to Soviet proletarian dictatorship. Fascism, said Mussolini, is the "dictatorship of the state over many classes cooperating."

When the depression struck, none of Italy's economic controls availed very much. Mussolini was eager to lay upon the world depression the blame for Italy's continuing economic ills. He turned to a vigorous program of public works and to increasing economic self-sufficiency. A "battle of wheat" was launched as a campaign to increase food production; progress was made in reclaiming swamp areas in central Italy and in developing hydroelectric power as a substitute for the coal that Italy lacked. Throughout the Fascist era no fundamental reform took place in the position of the peasants. The existing structure of society, which in Italy meant social extremes of wealth and poverty, remained unaltered. Fascism failed to provide either the economic security or the material well-being for which it had demanded the sacrifice of individual freedom. But it undeniably substituted a widespread psychological exhilaration, a feeling that Italy was undergoing a heroic national revival; and after 1935 to support that feeling Mussolini turned increasingly to military and imperialist adventures.

Fascism came to be regarded in other countries as a possible alternative to democratic or parliamentary government, as an actual corrective to troubles whose reality no one could deny. All communists hated it, and so did all socialists, labor leaders, moderate leftists, and idealistic liberals; wealthier or established people, because of fear of Bolshevism, made more allowances in its favor. In east-European countries, often highly nationalistic, or influenced by disgruntled land-owners, or simply unused to settling questions by majority vote, Fascism made a considerable appeal. In the Latin countries, in Spain, Portugal, and France, Mussolini's corporative state found champions and admirers. Sometimes, in Europe and elsewhere, intellectuals spun refined, respectable theories about the new order of discipline and authority, forgetting how Mussolini himself with unusual candor had written, "Fascism was not the nursling of a doctrine worked out beforehand with detailed elaboration; it was born of the need for action."

104. TOTALITARIANISM: GERMANY'S THIRD REICH

The Rise of Adolf Hitler

It was in Germany that Mussolini found his aptest pupil. Born in Austria in 1889, Adolf Hitler did little before the war. He was not an intellectual, like the prewar journalist Mussolini. He was never a socialist, but he fell into a restless and somewhat ignorant type of radicalism. Son of an Austrian customs official, he lost his father at fourteen and his mother a few years later. He dropped out of high school at sixteen and at nineteen came to the great metropolis of Vienna as an art student but was never accepted into the academy to which he sought admission. When the small inheritance left by his parents ran out and a government grant for orphan students ended, he drifted into various menial jobs, occasionally selling a few of his postcard and poster paintings but mainly eking out a marginal existence with hardly any friends, money, or livelihood. The young Hitler did not like what he saw in Vienna: neither the trappings of the Habsburg court, nor the noblemen of eastern Europe who rode by in their carriages, nor the mixed nationalities of the

Danubian empire, nor the Vienna workingman's attachment to international Marxism, nor above all the Jews, who thanks to a century of liberal influences had become assimilated to the German culture and now occupied many distinguished positions in business, law, medicine, and journalism in the city. He became exceedingly race conscious, like many others in many countries at the time;[8] the youthful Hitler took a special satisfaction in thinking of himself as a pure German of the good old German stock. He became violently anti-Semitic, and he also disliked aristocracy, capitalism, socialism, cosmopolitanism, internationalism, and "hybridization."

His aversion for Austria led him in 1913 to move to Munich, capital of the South German state of Bavaria. Once again he drifted without livelihood except by occasionally selling a few of his watercolors. When the war broke out, he volunteered for the Germany army. He was a good soldier, serving as a dispatch runner to the front line, and at one point was the victim of a gas attack that temporarily blinded him and injured his vocal cords. Although he did not rise higher in rank than to what is roughly equivalent to corporal (the rank was actually closer to private first class), he received important military decorations for his services. For Hitler, as for Mussolini and others, the war was a thrilling, noble, and liberating experience. The average man, in modern society, led a pretty dull existence. Peace, for many, was a drab routine from which war was an exciting emancipation. Human atoms, floating in an impersonal and unfriendly world, they were stirred by the nationalism which the war aroused into a sense of belonging to, believing in, fighting for something greater than themselves, but which was yet their own. When peace returned, they felt a moral letdown.

When the war ended, Hitler remained for a time on active duty and was transferred to Munich. Bavaria in 1919 was a principal focus of the Communist offensive in central Europe; a Bavarian Soviet Republic even existed for about three weeks until crushed by the federal government in Berlin. The Communist threat made Bavaria a busy center for anticommunist, antisocialist, antirepublican, and antidemocratic agitation of all kinds, and the seat of a disgruntled illiberalism. It swarmed with secret societies and paramilitary organizations led by discontented army officers or others who fitted with difficulty into the new Weimar democracy. Hitler, working with the army's political instruction program which had been created to combat socialist and democratic propaganda among the demobilized veterans and workers and to keep alive a patriotic and military spirit, joined at the army's behest a tiny party called the German Workers' party and soon became its leader. Early in 1920 he proclaimed its 25-point program, the party now calling itself the National Socialist German Workers' party. Thus were born the Nazis, so called from the German way of pronouncing the first two syllables of *National*. Now demobilized, Hitler was fully launched on a career of radical politics.

In earlier pages we have noted the beginnings of the Weimar Republic and the burdens it was compelled to bear from the start—the Versailles peace, reparations, the catastrophic inflation of 1923.[9] Something has been said also of the failure of the republicans to inaugurate the kind of deep social changes that might have democratized the political and social structure of German society and thereby strengthened republican forces. For five years after the war, violence remained sporadic in Germany. Communist agitation continued; but more danger-

---

[8] See pp. 593–594, 602–603, 616, 662, 751–752.
[9] See pp. 748–749.

ous, because they attracted more sympathy among the Germans, were the maneuvers of monarchist and antirepublican organizations, which maintained armed bands and threatened uprisings like the Kapp *Putsch* of 1920.[10] (One such private "army" was the Brownshirts or Storm Troopers maintained by the Nazis.) Such bands even resorted to assassination. Thus Walter Rathenau was murdered in 1922; he had organized German production during the war, and in 1922 he was foreign minister, but he had democratic and internationalist inclinations—and was a Jew. Another victim was Matthias Erzberger, a leading moderate politician of the Catholic Center party—he had helped "betray" the army by signing the armistice.

In 1923, when reparations payments were not forthcoming, the French army occupied the Ruhr. A clamor of national indignation swept over Germany. Hitler and the National Socialists, who since 1919 had obtained a considerable following, denounced the Weimar government for shameful submission to the French. They judged the moment opportune for seizing power, and at the end of 1923, in imitation of Mussolini's march on Rome the year before, the Brownshirts staged the "beer hall *Putsch*" in Munich. Hitler jumped on the platform, fired a revolver at the ceiling, and shouted that the "national revolution has broken out." But the police suppressed the disturbance, and Hitler was sentenced to five years in prison. He was released in less than a year; the Weimar democracy dealt mildly with its enemies. In prison he wrote his book, *Mein Kampf (My Struggle)*, a turbid stream of personal recollection, racism, nationalism, collectivism, theories of history, Jew baiting, and political comment. *Mein Kampf* sold widely. The book and the publicity that had accompanied the five-week trial converted Hitler into a political figure of national prominence. The former soldier was not alone in his ideas; no less a person than General Ludendorff, who had distinguished himself in the war,[11] and after the war became one of the most grotesquely unbalanced of the old officer class, gave his warm support to Hitler and even took part in the beer hall *Putsch*.

Beginning in 1924, with the French out of the Ruhr, reparations adjusted, a new and stable currency adopted, and loans from foreign countries, mainly America, Germany began to enjoy an amazing economic revival. National Socialism lost its appeal, the party lost members, Hitler was regarded as a charlatan and his followers as a lunatic fringe. All seemed quiet. Then came the Great Depression in 1929. Adolf Hitler, who might have faded out of history, was made by the circumstances attending the depression in Germany into a figure of Napoleonic proportions.

No country suffered more than Germany from the world-wide economic collapse. Foreign loans abruptly ceased or were recalled. Factories ground to a halt. There were 6 million unemployed. The middle class had not really recovered from the great inflation of 1923;[12] when struck again, after so brief a respite, they lost all faith in the economic system and in its future. The Communist vote steadily mounted; the great middling masses, who saw in communism their own death warrant, and who are extremely numerous in any highly developed society, looked about desperately for someone to save them from Bolshevism. The depression also stirred up the universal German loathing for the Treaty of Versailles. Many

[10] See pp. 746–747.
[11] See pp. 681–682.
[12] See pp. 748–749.

Germans explained the ruin of Germany by the postwar treatment it had received from the Allies—the constriction of its frontiers, the loss of its colonies, markets, shipping, and foreign investments, the colossal demand for reparations, the occupation of the Ruhr, the inflation, and much else.

Any people in such a trap would have been bewildered and resentful. But the way out chosen by the Germans was perhaps a product of deeper attitudes formed by German experience in the past centuries. Democracy—the agreement to obtain and accept majority verdicts, to discuss and compromise, to adjust conflicting interests without wholly satisfying or wholly crushing either side—was hard enough to maintain in any country in a true crisis. In Germany democracy was itself an innovation, which had yet to prove its value, which could easily be called un-German, an artificial and imported doctrine, or even a foreign system foisted upon Germany by the victors in the late war.

Hitler inflamed all such feelings by his propaganda. He denounced the Treaty of Versailles as a national humiliation. He denounced the Weimar democracy for producing class struggle, division, weakness, and wordy futility. He called for "true" democracy in a vast and vital stirring of the people, or *Volk*, behind a Leader who was a man of action. He declared that Germans, pure Germans, must rely only on themselves. He inveighed against Marxists, Bolsheviks, communists, and socialists, throwing them all together in a deliberate beclouding of the issues; but he claimed to favor the right kind of socialism for the little man, i.e., the doctrine of the National Socialist German Workers' party. He ranted against unearned incomes, war profits, the power of the great trusts and chain stores, land speculators, interest slavery, and unfair taxes. Above all, he denounced the Jews. Jews, like others, were found in all political camps. To the left, Jewish capitalists were anathema. To the right, Jewish revolutionaries were a horror. In anti-Semitism Hitler found a lowest common denominator upon which to appeal to all parties and classes. At the same time the Jews were a small minority (only 600,000 in all Germany), so that in an age of mass politics it was safe enough to attack them.

In the election of 1930 the Nazis won 107 seats in the Reichstag; in 1928 they had won only 12; their popular vote went up from 800,000 to 6.5 million. The Communist representation rose from 54 to 77. By July 1932 the Nazis more than doubled their popular vote, won 230 seats, and were now by far the largest single party though because of the multiplicity of parties they fell well short of a majority. In another election, in November 1932, the Nazis, though still well out in front, showed some loss of strength, losing 2 million votes, and dropping to 196 seats. The Communist vote had risen progressively to a peak of 100 in November 1932.

After the relative setback of November 1932 Hitler feared that his moment was passing. But certain conservative, nationalist, and antirepublican elements—old aristocrats, Junker landowners, army officers, Rhineland steel magnates, and other industrialists—had conceived the idea that Hitler could be useful to them. From such sources came a portion of Nazi funds. This group of big men, mainly of the small Nationalist party, imagined that they would be able to control Hitler and hence control the wave of mass discontent of which in such large measure he had made himself the leader; they were little disturbed by his anticapitalist program.

After Bruening's resignation in June 1932, Franz von Papen headed a Nationalist cabinet with the backing of the influential army leader General Kurt von Schleicher. In December 1932 Schleicher forced Papen's downfall and succeeded him. When he, too, was compelled to resign a month later, both men, intriguing separately, prevailed upon President Hindenburg to name Hitler chancellor of a coalition cabinet. On January 30, 1933, by entirely legal means, Adolf Hitler became chancellor of the German Republic; other positions in the new cabinet were occupied by the Nationalists, with whom the Nazis were to share power. But to share power was not their aim. Hitler called for another election. A week before election day the Reichstag building caught fire. The Nazis, without any real evidence, blamed it on the Communists. They raised up a terrific Red scare, suspended freedom of speech and press, and set loose the Brownshirts to bully the voters. Even so, in the election, the Nazis won only 44 percent of the vote; with their Nationalist allies, they had 52 percent. Hitler, trumpeting a national emergency, was voted dictatorial powers by a pliant Reichstag from which the Communist deputies had been excluded. The Nazi revolution now began.

The Nazi State

Hitler called his new order the Third Reich. He declared that, following on the First Reich, or Holy Roman Empire, and the Second Reich, or empire founded by Bismarck, the Third Reich carried on the process of true German history, of which, he said, it was the organic outgrowth and natural culmination. The Third Reich, he prophesied, would last a thousand years.

Like Mussolini, Hitler took the title of Leader, or, in German, the *Führer*. He claimed to represent the absolute sovereignty of the German people. Jews were considered un-German. Democracy, parliamentarianism, and liberalism were stigmatized as "Western" and together with communism labeled as "Jewish." The new "racial science," whose high priest was Alfred Rosenberg, classified Jews as non-Aryan[13] and included as Jewish anyone who had one Jewish grandparent. The Nuremberg laws of 1935 deprived Jews of all citizenship rights and forbade intermarriage between Jews and non-Jews. Jews were beaten up, hounded, driven from public office, ruined in private business, fined as a community, put to death, or allowed to flee the country after being stripped of all their possessions. The anti-Semitism of some fanatics descended to positive bestiality; it foreshadowed the wartime physical extermination of millions of German and east-European Jewry.

The new order was thought of as absolutely solid, or monolithic, like one huge single slab of rock in which no particle had any separate structure. Germany ceased to be federal; all the old states such as Prussia and Bavaria were abolished, so that the historic process of German unification was carried forward. All political parties except the National Socialists were destroyed. The Nazi party was itself violently purged on the night of June 30, 1934, when many of the old Brownshirt leaders, those who represented the more social revolutionary wing of the movement, were accused of plotting against Hitler and were summarily shot. A secret political police, the Gestapo *(Geheime Staatspolizei)*, together with People's Courts, and a system of permanent concentration camps in which thousands were

[13] See note p. 13.

detained without trial or sentence, suppressed all ideas at variance with the Leader's. Law itself was defined as the will of the German people operating in the interests of the Nazi state. Churches, both Protestant and Catholic, were "coordinated" with the new regime; their clergy were forbidden to criticize its activities, international religious ties were discouraged, and efforts were made to keep children out of religious schools. The government encouraged anti-Christian pagan movements, in worship of the old Teutonic gods, but nothing was sponsored so much as worship of Nazism and its *Führer*. A Nazi Youth Movement, and schools and universities, indoctrinated the rising generation in the new concepts. The total, all-encompassing repression thwarted the efforts of a few dedicated men to develop a broad resistance movement.

Labor unions also were "coordinated"; they were replaced by a National Labor Front. Strikes were forbidden. Under the "leadership principle" employers were set up as small-scale *Führers* in their factories and industries and given extensive control, subject to close government supervision. An extensive public works program was launched, reforestation and swamp drainage projects were organized, housing and superhighways were built. A vast rearmament program absorbed the unemployed and within a short time unemployment had significantly declined. Even under Nazi statistics labor's share in the national income was reduced, but workers had jobs; and an organization called Strength Through Joy attended to the needs of people with small incomes, providing entertainment, vacations, and travel for many who could never otherwise afford them.

The government assumed increasing controls over industry, while leaving ownership in private hands. In 1936 it adopted a Four-Year Plan of economic development. All countries after the Great Depression tended to economic nationalism, but Nazi Germany set up the goal of autarchy and self-sufficiency—absolute independence from foreign trade. German chemists developed artificial rubber, plastics, synthetic textiles, and many other substitute products to enable the country to do without raw materials imported from overseas. Germany took advantage of its position as the chief market on which east Europeans were dependent. Mixing political threats with ordinary business, the Nazis bartered for Polish wheat, Hungarian lumber, or Rumanian oil, often giving in return such articles as it was convenient for Germany to dispose of, rather than those that the east Europeans wanted. For Europe as a whole one of the basic economic problems, especially after the World War, was that while the Continent was economically a unit dependent on exchange between diverse regions, politically it was cut to pieces by tariff restrictions, currency differences, and hothouse industries artificially nurtured by nationalist ambition. The Nazis claimed to have a solution for this problem in a network of bilateral trade agreements assuring all neighboring peoples an outlet for their products. But it was a solution in which Germans were to be the most industrial, most advanced, most powerful, and most wealthy, and other Europeans relegated to permanently inferior status. And what could not be accomplished under trade agreements and economic penetration could be accomplished by conquest and war. Within a few years after 1933, although the regime had its share of confusion and personal rivalries, the Nazi revolution had turned Germany into a huge disciplined war machine, its internal foes liquidated or silenced, its mesmerized masses roaring their approval in giant demonstrations, ready to follow the Führer in storming new Valkyrian heights. "Today Germany," went an ominous Nazi phrase, "tomorrow the whole world."

Totalitarianism: Some Origins and Consequences

Totalitarianism was a many-sided thing. It had appeared first with the Bolshevik Revolution, for in the denial of individual liberty the Soviet regime did not differ from the most extreme anti-Soviet or fascist totalitarianism as manifested in Germany. There were at first important differences in principle. Theoretically, the proletarian dictatorship was temporary; it did not glorify the individual Leader-Hero; and it was not nationalistic, for it rested on a principle of world-wide class struggle in all nations alike. It adopted a democratic-sounding constitution and paid at least lip service to the idea of a bill of rights. Its constitution officially condemned racism, and it did not deliberately and consciously cultivate an ethics of war and violence. But as time passed, Soviet totalitarianism became harder to distinguish from others. The Soviet dictatorship and one-party state seemed as permanent as any political system; the hollowness of the constitution and bill of rights became more apparent; a cult developed around the person of Stalin; and the emphasis became more nationalistic, falling less on the workers of the world and more on the glories of the Soviet Fatherland.

Totalitarianism, as distinct from mere dictatorship, though it appeared rather suddenly after the First World War, was no historic freak. It was an outgrowth of a good deal of development in the past. The state was an institution that had continuously acquired new powers ever since the Middle Ages; step by step, since feudal times, it had assumed jurisdiction over law courts and men at arms, imposed taxes, regulated churches, guided economic policy, operated school systems, and devised schemes of public welfare. The First World War had continued and advanced the process.[14] The twentieth-century totalitarian state, mammoth and monolithic, claiming an absolute domination over every department of life, now carried this old development of state sovereignty to a new extreme. For centuries, for example, the state had clashed with the church; from Philip the Fair of France in 1303, down through Henry VIII, the enlightened despots, the French Revolutionaries, Napoleon, Mazzini, Bismarck—the list was a long one of those who had come into conflict with the Christian churches. The twentieth-century dictators did the same. In addition, however, they were in most cases not merely anticlerical but explicitly anti-Christian, offering, or rather imposing, a "total" philosophy of life.

This new philosophy drew heavily upon a historic nationalism which it greatly exaggerated. It derived in part from the organic theory of society, which held that society (or the nation or state) was a kind of living organism within which the individual person was but a single cell. The individual, in this theory, had no independent existence; he received life itself, and all his ideas, from the society, people, nation, or culture into which he was born and by which he was nurtured. In Marxism, the absolute subordination of the individual to his class came to much the same thing. The individual was a microscopic cell, meaningless outside the social body. He was but clay to be molded by the imprint of his group. It made little sense, given such theories, to speak of the individual's "reason" or "freedom," or to allow individuals to have their own opinions (which were formed for them by environment), or to count up individual opinions to obtain a merely numerical majority. Valid ideas were those of the group as a whole, of the people or nation (or, in Marxism, the class) as a solid block. Even science was a product

---

14 See pp. 683–687.

of specific societies; there was a "Nazi science" which was bound to differ in its conclusions from democratic, bourgeois, Western, or "Jewish" science; and for the Soviets there was a Soviet science, consistent with dialectical materialism, and better equipped to see the truth than the decadent bourgeois, capitalistic, or "fascist" science of the non-Soviet world. All art, too—music, painting, poetry, fiction, architecture, sculpture—was good art insofar as it expressed the society or nationality in which it grew.

The avowed philosophy of totalitarian regimes (like much modern thought) was basically subjective. Whether an idea was held to be true depended on whose idea it was. Ideas of truth, or beauty, or right were not supposed to correspond to any outer or objective reality; they had only to correspond to the inner nature, interests, or point of view of the people, nation, society, or class that entertained such ideas. The older concepts of reason, natural law, natural right, and the ultimate alikeness of all mankind, or of a common path of all mankind in one course of progress, disappeared.[15]

The totalitarian regimes did not simply declare, as a dry finding of social science, that peoples' ideas were shaped by environment. They set about shaping them actively. Propaganda became a principal branch of government. Propaganda was hardly new, but in the past, and still in the democratic countries, it had been a piecemeal affair, urging the public to accept this or that political party, or to buy this or that brand of coffee. Now, like all else, it became "total." Propaganda was monopolized by the state, and it demanded faith in a whole view of life and in every detail of this coordinated whole. Formerly the control of books and newspapers had been mainly negative; under Napoleon or Metternich, for example, censors had forbidden statements on particular subjects, events, or persons. Now, in totalitarian countries, control of the press became frighteningly positive. The government manufactured thought. It manipulated opinion. It rewrote history. Writers were required to present whole ideologies, and books, newspapers, magazines, and the radio diffused an endless and overwhelming cloud of words. Loudspeakers blared in the streets, gigantic blown-up photographs of the Leader looked down in public places. The propaganda experts were sometimes fanatics, but often they were cynics like Dr. Goebbels in Germany, too intelligent to be duped by the rubbish with which they duped their country.

The very idea of truth evaporated. No norm of human utterance remained except political expediency—the wishes and self-interest of the men in power. No one could learn anything except what the government wanted him to know. No one could escape the omnipresent official doctrine, the insidious penetration of the very recesses of the mind by ideas planted by outsiders for their own purposes. People came to accept, and even to believe, the most extravagant statements when they were endlessly repeated, year after year. Barred from all independent sources of information, having no means by which any official allegation could be tested, the peoples of totalitarian countries became increasingly in fact, and not merely in sociological theory, incapable of the use of reason.

Racism, more characteristic of Nazi Germany than of totalitarianism in general, was a further exaggeration, or degradation, of older ideas of nationalism and national solidarity. It defined the nation in a tribal sense, as a biological entity, a group of persons possessing the same physical ancestry and the same or similar

[15] See pp. 297–298, 301, 303, 313–315, 360, 445, 551, 603.

physical characteristics. Anti-Semitism was the most venomous form of racism in Europe. While a latent hostility to Jews had always been present in the Christian world, modern anti-Semitism had little to do with Christianity. It arose in part from the fact that, in the nineteenth century, with the general removal of religious disabilities, the Jews entered into general society and many of them achieved positions of prominence, and nowhere more so than in Germany, so that from the point of view of any individual non-Jew they could be represented as dangerous competitors in business or the professions. But most of all, anti-Semitism was inflamed by propagandists who wished people to feel their supposed racial purity more keenly or to forget the deeper problems of society, including poverty, unemployment, and economic inequities.

For totalitarianism was an escape from the realities of class conflict. It was a way of pretending that differences between rich and poor were of minor importance. Typically, a totalitarian regime came into power by stirring up class fears, then remained in power, and represented itself as indispensable, by declaring that it had settled the class problem. Thus Mussolini, Hitler, and certain lesser dictators, before seizing office, pointed alarmingly to the dark menace of Bolshevism; and, once in power, declared that all classes stood shoulder to shoulder in slablike solidarity behind the Leader. Nor were events in Russia altogether different. The Bolsheviks in 1917, armed with the ideas of Karl Marx, aroused the workers against capitalists, landlords, middle-class people, and rich peasants; then, once in power, and after extensive liquidations, they declared that the classless society had arrived, that no true social classes any longer existed, and that all Soviet citizens stood solidly behind a regime from which, they said, all good citizens benefited equally. Only the democracies admitted that they suffered from internal class problems, from maladjustments between rich and poor or between favored and unfavored groups in society.

The dictatorships blamed their troubles on forces outside the country. They accused dissatisfied persons of conspiring with foreigners or refugees—with being the tools of Trotskyism, imperialism, or international Jewry. Or they talked of the struggle between rich nations and poor nations, the "have" and the "have not" countries, and thus transformed the problem of poverty into an international struggle. In the distinction between "have" and "have-not" countries there was, of course, more than a grain of truth; in more old-fashioned language some countries (in fact the European democracies, as well as the United States and the British dominions of the 1930s) had "progressed" farther than others. It is probable that any propaganda is more effective if partly true. But when the totalitarians blamed their troubles on other countries and transformed the conflict between "have" and "have not" into a struggle between nations, they gave the impression that war might be a solution for social ills.

Violence, the acceptance and even glorification of violence, was indeed the characteristic most clearly distinguishing the totalitarian from the democratic systems. We have seen how a cult of violence, or belief that struggle was beneficial, had arisen before the First World War.[16] The war itself habituated people to violence and direct action. Lenin and his followers showed how a small group could seize the helm of state under revolutionary or chaotic conditions. Mussolini in 1922 taught the same lesson, with further refinements; for the Italy in which he

[16] See pp. 606–607.

seized power was not at war, and it was merely the threat or possibility of revolution, not revolution itself, that provided him with his opportunity. In the 1920s, for the first time since the seventeenth century, some of the most civilized parts of Europe, in time of peace, saw private armies marching about the country, bands of uniformed and organized ruffians, Blackshirts or Brownshirts, who manhandled, abused, and even killed law-abiding citizens with impunity. Nor would anyone in the 1920s have believed that, by the 1930s, Europe would see the reintroduction of torture.

The very ethics of totalitarianism was violent and neopagan. It borrowed from Nietzsche and other prewar theoreticians, who, safe and civilized, had declared that men should live dangerously, avoid the flabby weakness of too much thought, throw themselves with red-blooded vigor into a life of action. The new regimes all instituted youth movements. They appealed to a kind of juvenile idealism, in which young people believed that by joining some kind of squad, donning some kind of uniform, and getting into the fresh air they contributed to a great moral resurgence of their country. Young men were taught to value their bodies but not their minds, to be tough and hard, and to regard mass gymnastics as patriotic demonstrations. Young women were taught to breed large families without complaint, to be content in the kitchen, and to look with awe upon their virile mates. The body cult flourished while the mind decayed. Especially in National Socialism the ideal was to turn the German people into a race of splendid animals, pink-cheeked, Nordic, and upstanding. Contrariwise, euthanasia was adopted for the insane and was proposed for the aged. Later, in the Second World War, when the Nazis overran eastern Europe, they committed Jews to the gas chambers, destroying some 6 million human beings by the most scientific methods. Animals were animals; one bred the kind one wanted and killed the kind one did not.

The Spread of Dictatorship

The trend of dictatorship spread over Europe in the 1930s. By 1938 only ten out of twenty-seven European countries remained democratic, in the sense that different political parties honestly competed for office and that citizens within generous limits thought and acted as they pleased. They were Great Britain and France; Holland, Belgium, and Switzerland; Czechoslovakia and Finland; and the three Scandinavian countries. The Soviet Union still exemplified the dictatorship of the proletariat, and all other European countries possessed more or less dictatorial regimes somewhat vaguely called, with more or less accuracy, "fascist."

The promise of the early 1920s that constitutional and democratic government would flourish was thwarted. The weakness or absence of a parliamentary or democratic tradition, low education and literacy standards, the hostility of reactionary elements, the fear of Bolshevism, and the dissatisfaction of existing national minorities, all coupled with economic strains, many resulting from the Great Depression, contributed to the collapse of the new representative institutions. Apart from the avowedly totalitarian or fascist regimes of Germany and Italy, the new dictatorships and authoritarian systems generally rested on a combination of personal and military power. To name but a few, this was true of Poland under Marshal Pilsudski and his successor, General Smigly-Rydz; Hungary under General Julius Gömbös, successor to Count Bethlen; Greece under General Metaxas; Spain (after a bloody civil war to be described), under General Franco; and Yugoslavia, Bulgaria, and Rumania under their respective kings. In Portugal, Salazar began a clerical-corporative dictatorship in 1932 that lasted for over four decades. In Austria, Dollfuss fused various right-wing political and military elements into a clerical-fascist "Christian" dictatorship which violently suppressed the Socialists and sought in vain with this dictatorship to counter the German threat; assassinated in July 1934, he was succeeded by Kurt von Schuschnigg, who headed a similar regime until the German annexation of Austria in 1938. In many respects the dictatorships of Latin America under a diversity of caudillos and military juntas, in both origin and character, resembled the European dictatorships.

The authoritarian regimes were alike in repressing individual liberties, banning opposition parties, and abolishing or nullifying parliamentary institutions. Many borrowed features of the corporative state, outlawing independent labor organizations and forbidding strikes; many, like Hungary, Rumania, and Poland, instituted anti-Semitic legislation. None went so far in the total coordination of all political, economic, intellectual, and biological activities in a revolutionary mass-based dictatorship as did Hitler's Third Reich.

The acceptance and glorification of violence, it has been noted, was the feature most clearly distinguishing the totalitarian from the democratic systems. War in the Nazi and Fascist ethics was a noble thing, and the love of peace a sign of decadence. (The Soviet regime, while by its own theory it regarded war with non-Soviet powers as inevitable some day, did not preach it as a positive moral good.) The exaltation of war and struggle, the need for maintaining national solidarity, the habit of blaming foreign countries for social troubles, together with the considerable armaments program in which the dictatorships engaged, plus the personal ambition and egotistical mania of individual dictators, made the decade of the 1930s a time not only of domestic reaction but of recurrent international crises, of which the last one led to war.

XX.
The
Second
World War

Peace in the abstract, the peace that is the mere absence of war, does not exist in international relations. Peace is never found apart from certain conditions; it means peaceable acceptance of given conditions, or peaceable and orderly transformation of conditions by negotiation and agreement. The conditions, in the 1930s, were basically those laid down by the Paris peace conference of 1919—the states recognized, the frontiers drawn, the terms agreed to, at the close of the First World War. In the 1930s neither Germany, Italy, Japan, nor the U.S.S.R. was content with these conditions; they were "revisionist" or dissatisfied powers; and the first three were willing to undertake war itself to make a change. Great Britain, France, and the United States were satisfied powers, expecting no benefit from change in the conditions; but on the other hand they had lost faith in the conditions and were unwilling to risk war for the sake of upholding them. They had made a treaty in 1919 which a dozen years later they were unwilling to enforce. They stood idly by, as long as they could, while the dissatisfied powers tore to pieces the states recognized, the frontiers drawn, and the terms agreed to at the Peace of Paris. From the Japanese invasion of Manchuria in 1931 to the outbreak of European war in 1939, force was used by those who wished to upset international order, but never by those who wished to maintain it.

Chapter Emblem: A clock stopped when the atomic bomb was dropped on Hiroshima, Japan, in 1945.

105. THE WEAKNESS OF THE DEMOCRACIES: AGAIN TO WAR

The Pacifism and Disunity of the West

While dictators stormed, the Western democracies were swayed by a profound pacifism, which may be defined as a somewhat doctrinaire insistence on peace regardless of consequences. Many people now believed, especially in England and the United States, that the First World War had been a mistake, that little or nothing had been gained by it, that they had been deluded by wartime propaganda, that wars were really started by armaments manufacturers, that Germany had not really caused the war of 1914, that the Treaty of Versailles was too hard on the Germans, that vigorous peoples like the Germans or Italians needed room for expansion, that democracy was after all not suited to all nations, that it took two to make a quarrel, and that there need be no war if one side resolutely refused to be provoked—a whole system of pacific and tolerant ideas in which there was perhaps the usual mixture of truth and misunderstanding.

The pacifism of the West had other roots, most evident in France. About 1.4 million Frenchmen had died in World War I; half of all French males between the ages of 20 and 32 in 1914 had been killed. To the French it was inconceivable that such a holocaust should be repeated. French strategy was therefore defensive and sparing of manpower. If war came, the French expected to fight it mainly in the elaborate fortifications, called the Maginot Line, which they built on their eastern frontier facing Germany, from the Swiss to the Belgian border; to its north the Ardennes forest was to be a barrier to any invader. Moreover, as we have seen, during the depression France was torn by internal class conflict and by fascist and quasi-fascist agitation.[1] Many Frenchmen of the right, historically unsympathetic to the republic and seeing, or claiming to see, in such movements as the Popular Front the threat of social revolution, did not conceal their admiration for Mussolini or even for Hitler. Abandoning their traditional role as ardent nationalists, they would do nothing to oppose the dictators. On the other hand, many on the left looked with sympathy upon the Soviet Union. France was ideologically too divided in the 1930s to possess any firm foreign policy, and all elements took false comfort from the supposed impregnability of the French Chinese Wall.

A similar situation, in lesser degree, prevailed in Great Britain and the United States. The loss and bloodshed of the First World War were remembered. It was well known that another world war would be even more horrible; there was an unspeakable dread of the bombing of cities. Typical of the time was a resolution adopted by students at Oxford in 1933 that they would never take up arms for their country under any conditions; peace movements appeared among American college students too. The pull between left and right was felt in England and America. In the 1930s, when any international action seemed to favor either the U.S.S.R. on the one hand, or Hitler and Mussolini on the other, it was hard to establish any foreign policy on a firm basis of national unity. In Britain some members of the upper classes were overtly sympathetic to the fascist dictators, or at least saw in them a bulwark against communism. The government itself tried to be noncommittal; it believed that some means of satisfying or appeasing the

---

[1] See pp. 777–779.

more "legitimate" demands of the dictators might be found. Neville Chamberlain, prime minister after 1937, became the principal architect of the appeasement policy.

The United States government, despite President Roosevelt's repeated denunciation of the aggressors, followed in practice a policy of rigid isolation. Neutrality legislation, enacted by a strong isolationist bloc in Congress in the years 1935 to 1937, forbade loans, export of munitions, and use of American shipping facilities to any belligerent once the president had recognized a state of war in a given area. It was then believed, by many, that the United States had been drawn into the First World War by such economic involvement. From this American neutrality legislation the aggressors of the 1930s were to derive great benefit, but not the victims of aggression.

As for the men who ruled the U.S.S.R., they were revisionist and dissatisfied in that they did not accept the new frontiers of eastern Europe nor the territorial losses incurred by Russia in the First World War. They resented the *cordon sanitaire* created in 1919 against the spread of Bolshevism, the ring of small states on their borders from Finland to Rumania, which were almost without exception vehemently anti-Soviet. They had no fondness for the international status quo nor had they abandoned their long-range revolutionary objectives. But, as Communists and as Russians, they were obsessed by fear of attack and invasion. Their Marxist doctrine taught the inherent hostility of the entire capitalist world; the intervention of the Western Allies in the Revolution and civil wars confirmed their Marxist theory. And long before the Bolshevik Revolution, in the days of Napoleon and earlier, the fertile Russian plains had tempted ambitious conquerors. Resentful and suspicious of the outside world, in the 1930s the men in the Kremlin were alarmed primarily by the signs of aggressive intentions in Germany. Hitler, in *Mein Kampf* and elsewhere, had declared that he meant to obliterate Bolshevism and subordinate large stretches of eastern Europe to Germany.

The Soviets became interested in collective security, in international action against aggression. In 1934 they joined the League of Nations. They instructed Communist parties to work with socialists and liberals in popular fronts.[2] They offered assistance in checking fascist aggressors, signing mutual assistance pacts with France and Czechoslovakia in 1935. But many people fled from the Soviet embrace with a shudder. They distrusted Soviet motives, or they were convinced that the purges and trials of the 1930s had left the Soviets weak and undependable as allies, or they felt that the fascist dictators might be diverted eastward against the Soviets and so spare the Western democracies. Here again, though the Russians were ostensibly willing, no effective coalition against aggression could be formed.

The March of Nazi and Fascist Aggression

Adolf Hitler perceived these weaknesses with uncanny genius. Determined to wreck the whole treaty system, he employed tactics of gradual encroachment that played on the hopes and fears of the democratic peoples. He inspired in them alternating tremors of apprehension and sighs of relief. He would rage and rant, arouse the fear of war, take just a little, declare that it was all he wanted, let the

[2] See p. 738.

former Allies naïvely hope that he was now satisfied and that peace was secure; then rage again, take a little more, and proceed through the same cycle.

Each year he precipitated some kind of emergency, and each time the French and British saw no alternative except to let him have his way. In 1933, soon after seizing power, he took Germany out of the League and out of the Disarmament Conference then taking place. He successfully wooed Poland, long France's ally, and in 1934 the two countries signed a nonaggression treaty. That same year the Nazis of Austria attempted a *Putsch*, assassinated the Austrian chancellor, Dollfuss, and demanded the union of Austria with Germany. The Western powers did nothing. It was Mussolini who acted. Not desiring to see Germany installed at the Brenner Pass, he mobilized large Italian forces on the frontier; he thus discouraged Hitler from intervening openly in Austria and so preserved the independence of Austria for four more years. In January 1935 a plebiscite was conducted in the Saar by the League of Nations as stipulated under the Versailles treaty. Amidst intense Nazi agitation, the Saar voted for reunion with the Reich. Two months later, in March 1935, Hitler dramatically repudiated those clauses in the Versailles treaty intended to keep Germany disarmed; he now openly built up the German armed forces. France, England, and Italy protested at such arbitrary and one-sided denunciation of an international treaty but did nothing specifically about it. Indeed, Great Britain entered into a naval agreement with Germany, to the consternation of the French.

On March 7, 1936, using as his justification the new Franco-Soviet pact, Hitler repudiated the Locarno agreements[3] and reoccupied the Rhineland; i.e., he sent German troops into the German territory west of the Rhine, which by the Treaty of Versailles was supposed to be a demilitarized zone. There was talk in the French government of action, and at this time Hitler might have been checked, for German military strength was still weak and the German army was prepared to withdraw, or at least consult, at signs of resistance. But the French government was divided and unwilling to act without Britain; and the British would not risk war to keep German troops from occupying German soil. The next year, 1937, was a quiet one, but Nazi agitation flared up in Danzig, which the Treaty of Versailles had set up as a free city. In March 1938 German forces moved into Austria, and the union of Austria and Germany, the *Anschluss*, was at last consummated. In September 1938 came the turn of Czechoslovakia and the Munich crisis. To understand it we must first pick up other threads in the story.

Mussolini, too, had his ambitions and required sensational foreign triumphs to magnetize the Italian people. Since 1919 the Italians had been dissatisfied with the peace arrangements. They had received nothing of the former Turkish territories and former German colonies that had been liberally parceled out, as mandates, to Great Britain, France, Belgium, and Japan, and even to South Africa, Australia, and New Zealand.[4] They had never forgotten the humiliating defeat of Italian forces by Abyssinia at Adowa in 1896.[5] Ethiopia, as Abyssinia was now called, remained the only part of black Africa (with the exception of Liberia) that was still independent.

In 1935 Italy went to war with Ethiopia. The League of Nations, of which Ethiopia was a member, pronounced the Italian action an unwarranted aggression

[3] See pp. 750–751.
[4] See pp. 689–690, 781
[5] See p. 631.

and imposed sanctions on Italy, by which members of the League were to refrain from selling Italy either arms or raw materials—oil was excepted. The British even gathered large naval forces in the Mediterranean in a show of strength. In France, however, there was considerable sympathy for Mussolini in important quarters, and in England there was the fear that if sanctions became too effective, by refusal of oil or by closure of the Suez Canal, Italy might be irritated into a general war. Mussolini was thus able to defeat Ethiopia in 1936 and to combine it with Italian Somaliland and Eritrea in an Italian East African empire. The Ethiopian Emperor Haile Selassie made futile pleas for further action at Geneva. The League of Nations again failed, as in the case of the occupation of Manchuria by Japan, to provide machinery for disciplinary action against a wayward Great Power.[6]

The Spanish Civil War, 1936–1939

Hardly had the Ethiopian crisis been disposed of, to the entire satisfaction of the aggressor, when an even more serious crisis broke out in Spain. In 1931, after a decade of political disturbance, a rather mild revolution had driven out Alfonso XIII, of the Bourbon family, and brought about the establishment of a democratic Spanish Republic. Old hostilities within the country came to a head. The new republican government undertook a program of social and economic reform. To combat the ancient entrenched power of the church, anticlerical legislation was enacted; church and state were separated, the Jesuit order was dissolved and its property confiscated, and the schools were removed from clerical control. The old movement for Catalan independence was somewhat mollified by the grant of considerable local autonomy. To placate the peasantry the government began to break up some of the larger landed estates and to redistribute the land. The government's program was never pushed vigorously enough to satisfy extremist elements, who manifested their dissatisfaction in strikes and uprisings, particularly in industrial Barcelona, the Catalan capital, and the mining areas of the Asturias, but it was radical enough to antagonize the great property owners and the churchmen. After 1933 the government fell into the hands of rightist and conservative parties, who ruled through ineffective and unpopular ministries. An insurrection of the miners in the Asturias was put down with much brutality. Agitation for complete Catalan independence was repressed.

In February 1936 new general elections were held. All elements of the left—republicans, socialists, syndicalists, anarchists, communists—joined in a Popular Front against monarchists, clericals, army officers, other adherents of the old regime, and Falangists, or Spanish fascists. The left won a victory at the polls. Thereupon, in July 1936, a group of military men led an insurrection against the republican government; General Francisco Franco emerged as leader. The parties of the left united in resistance and the whole country fell into civil war. It was the most devastating war in all Spanish history; over 600,000 human beings lost their lives, and it was accompanied by extreme cruelties on both sides. For nearly three years the republican or loyalist forces held their own before finally succumbing to the insurgents led by Franco, who in March 1939 established an authoritarian, fascist-type rule over the exhausted country.

---

[6] See p. 761.

Spain provided a rehearsal for the greater struggle soon to come. The republican government could legitimately have looked forward to the purchase of arms abroad to suppress the rebellion, but Britain and France were resolved not to let the war expand into a general conflict. They forbade the shipment of war materials to the republican government; even the French Popular Front government put obstacles in the way of aid to the hard-pressed Spanish Popular Front. The United States extended its neutrality legislation to cover civil wars and placed an embargo on the export of arms to Spain despite much pressure in the country for support to the loyalists. At British and French instigation twenty-seven nations, including all the major European powers, agreed not to intervene or take sides. But the nonintervention policy proved a fiasco. Germany, Italy, and the Soviet Union intervened anyway. The former two supported Franco and denounced the republicans as the tools of Bolshevism, while the U.S.S.R. supported the republic and stigmatized the rebels under Franco as the agents of international fascism. Germans, Italians, and Russians sent military equipment to Spain, testing their tanks and planes in actual battle. The fascist bombings of Guernica, Madrid, and Barcelona horrified the democratic world. The Germans and Italians sent troops (the Italians over 50,000); the Soviets if only for geographical reasons could not do likewise but sent technicians and political advisers. Thousands of volunteers of leftist or liberal sympathy, from the United States and Europe, went to Spain as individuals to serve with the loyalist republican forces. Spain became the battlefield of contending ideologies. The Spanish Civil War split the world into fascist and antifascist camps.

Like Ethiopia, the war in Spain helped bring Germany and Italy together. Mussolini had at first, like others, feared the revival of a militant Germany. He had been the one who outfaced Hitler when the latter threatened to absorb Austria in 1934. The Ethiopian war, Italian ambitions in Africa, and a clamorous Italian demand for ascendancy in the Mediterranean, the *mare nostrum* of the ancient Romans, estranged Italy from France and Britain. In 1936, soon after the outbreak of the Spanish Civil War, Mussolini and Hitler came to an understanding, which they called the Rome-Berlin Axis—the diplomatic axis around which they hoped the world might turn. That year Japan signed with Germany an Anti-Comintern Pact, soon ratified by Italy too; ostensibly an agreement to oppose communism, it was actually the foundation for a diplomatic alliance. Each, thus furnished with allies, was able to push its demands with more success. In 1938 Mussolini accepted the German absorption of the very Austria which in 1934 he had denied to Hitler.

And in 1937 Japan, using as a pretext the firing upon Japanese troops at the Marco Polo Bridge near Peking, launched a new full-scale invasion of China. Within a short time, despite resistance from the Chinese forces, both Kuomintang and Communist, the invader controlled most of China. The Chinese fought on from the hinterland, obtaining equipment and supplies by difficult and devious routes. The League again ineffectually condemned the Japanese action. The United States refrained from applying its neutrality legislation, since no war was officially declared. This made possible the extension of loans to the Chinese government, but it also made possible the purchase by the Japanese of vitally needed scrap iron, steel, oil, and machinery from American industrial firms. The Japanesc profited from the tension in the Western world; and in 1938 the tension in Europe was rapidly mounting.

The Munich Crisis: The Climax of Appeasement

By annexing Austria in March 1938 Hitler added about 6 million Germans to the Reich. Another 3 million Germans lived in Czechoslovakia.[7] All those who were adults in 1938 had been born under the Habsburg empire. They had never, since 1918, been contented with their new position as a minority in a Slavic state, and they had long complained against various forms of subtle discrimination. There were Polish, Ruthenian, and Hungarian minorities also, and since even the Slovaks felt a basic separation from the Czechs, there was in truth no preponderant national majority of any kind. The fact that Czechoslovakia had one of the most enlightened minorities policies in Europe, enjoyed the highest living standard east of Germany, and was the only country in central Europe in 1938 that was still democratic only demonstrated the difficulty of maintaining a multinational state under the most favorable of conditions.

Czechoslovakia was strategically the keystone of Europe. It had a firm alliance with France, which had repeatedly guaranteed to defend it against German attack, and an alliance with the Soviet Union; Soviet aid was made dependent on the functioning of the French alliance. With Rumania and Yugoslavia it formed the Little Entente, upon which France relied to maintain the existing boundaries in that part of Europe. It had a well-trained army, important munitions industries, and strong fortifications against Germany, which, however, were located in precisely the Sudeten border area where the population was almost all German. When Hitler annexed Austria—since Vienna is further east than Prague—he enclosed Czechoslovakia in a vise. From the German point of view it could now be said that Bohemia-Moravia, which was almost a third German anyway, formed a bulge protruding into the German Reich.

The Sudeten Germans of Czechoslovakia, whether Nazis or not, fell under the influence of agitators whose aim was less to relieve their grievances than to promote National Socialism. Hitler fomented their demands for union with Germany. In May 1938 rumors of an imminent German invasion caused the Czechs to mobilize; Russia, France, and England issued warnings. Hitler, not actually intending to invade at that time, was forced to issue assurances but was nevertheless determined to smash the Czechs in the autumn. France and England, instead of rejoicing in having prevented aggression, were appalled by their narrow escape from war. The French were nervous and acquiesced in the leadership of Britain, which in the following months strove to avoid any firm stand that might precipitate war. The Czechs, under pressure from Britain and France, accepted British mediation on the Sudeten issue and in the summer of 1938 offered wide concessions to the Sudeten Germans amounting to regional autonomy; but these were never enough to satisfy Hitler, who loudly proclaimed that the plight of the Germans in Czechoslovakia was intolerable and must be corrected. The Soviets urged a firm stand, but the Western powers had little confidence in Soviet military strength and, given the Soviet geographical situation, their ability to render

[7] See pp. 689, 691–694, 743–745, and maps, pp. 441 and 692–693.

assistance to Czechoslovakia; moreover, they feared a firmness that might mean war. They could not be sure whether Hitler was bluffing. He might, if opposed, back down; but it seemed equally likely, or indeed more so, that he was entirely willing to fight. The Western powers discounted intelligence reports, which happened to be true, of a military-civilian plot to unseat Hitler if, in the event of Western firmness, a war broke out over Czechoslovakia.

As the tension mounted in September 1938, the British prime minister, Neville Chamberlain, who had never flown in his life before, flew to Germany twice to sound out Hitler on his terms; the second time Hitler raised his demands so that even the British and French could not accept them. Mobilization began; war seemed imminent. Suddenly, in the midst of the unbearable tension, Hitler invited Chamberlain and Édouard Daladier, the French premier, to a four-power conference at Munich, to be attended by his ally, Mussolini. The Soviet Union, and Czechoslovakia itself, were excluded. At Munich Chamberlain and Daladier accepted Hitler's terms and then put enormous pressure on the Czech government to yield, to sign its own death warrant in cold blood. France, urged on by England in a pacific course that it was only too willing to follow, repudiated its treaty obligation to protect Czechoslovakia, ignored the Russians who had reaffirmed their willingness to aid the Czechs if the French acted, and abandoned its whole system of a Little Entente in the East. It was agreed at Munich that Germany should annex the adjoining fringe of Bohemia in which the majority of the people were Germans. This fringe contained the mountainous approaches and the fortifications, so that its loss left Czechoslovakia militarily defenseless. After promises to guarantee the integrity of what remained of Czechoslovakia, the conference disbanded. Chamberlain and Daladier were received with cheers at home. Chamberlain happily reported that he had brought "peace in our time." Again the democracies sighed with relief, hoped that Hitler had made his last demand, and told themselves that, with wise concessions, there need be no war.

The Munich crisis, with its death sentence to Czechoslovakia, revealed the helpless weakness into which the Western democracies had fallen by 1938. There was, in fact, little that the French and British could do, at Munich, to save Czechoslovakia. Their countries lagged behind Germany in military preparedness. They were impressed by the might of the German army and air force. Bolder men than Daladier and Chamberlain, knowing the state of their own armed forces, would have declined to risk a quarrel. They loved peace and would buy it at a high price, not daring to believe that they were dealing with a blackmailer whose price would always be raised. They suffered, too, from another moral uncertainty; by the very principle of national self-determination, accepted by the victors after the First World War, Germany had a right to all that it had hitherto demanded. Hitler, in sending German troops into the German Rhineland, in annexing Austria, stirring up Danzig, incorporating the Bohemian Germans, had only asserted the right of the German people to have a sovereign German state. Moreover, if Hitler could be diverted eastward, enmeshed in a war with Russia, then communism and fascism might destroy each other—so one might hope. Possibly it was one of Hitler's motives, in the Munich crisis, to isolate Russia from the West and the West from Russia. If so, he succeeded well enough.

In the weeks following Munich the international commission set up to arrange the new boundaries worked further injustices on Czechoslovakia, dispensing even with the plebiscites which had been agreed to for disputed areas. Meanwhile the

Poles and Hungarians brought forth their demands on the hapless Czechs. The Poles seized the Teschen district; and Hungary, under a German and Italian award, took 7,500 square miles of Slovakia. France and Britain were not consulted and did not seriously protest.

The End of Appeasement

The final disillusionment came in March 1939. Hitler marched into Bohemia-Moravia, the really Czech part of Czechoslovakia, which he transformed into a German protectorate. Exploiting Slovak nationalism, he declared Slovakia "independent." Czechoslovakia, merely trimmed down at Munich, now disappeared from the map. Having promised to take only a bite, Hitler swallowed the whole. He then seized Memel from Lithuania and raised demands for Danzig and the Polish Corridor. A horrible realization now spread in France and Britain. It was clear that Hitler's most solemn guarantees were worthless, that his designs were not limited to Germans, but reached out to all eastern Europe and beyond, that he was essentially insatiable, that he could never be appeased. In April 1939 his partner in aggression, Mussolini, took over Albania.

The Western powers now began to make military preparations. Britain, changing its East European policy at the eleventh hour, now gave a guarantee to Poland, and followed that with guarantees to Rumania and Greece. That spring and summer the British tried to form an anti-German alliance with the U.S.S.R. But Poland and the Baltic states were unwilling to allow Soviet armies within their borders, even for the purpose of defending them against the Germans. The Anglo-French negotiators refused to put pressure on them. Since the Poles, in 1920, had conquered more territory than the Allies had meant them to have,[8] pushing their eastern border well into White Russia, almost to Minsk, the Anglo-French scruples seemed to the Soviets unnecessarily delicate. The Russians did not wish the Germans to launch an attack on them from a point as far east as Minsk. They thought, too, with good reason, that what the French and British really wanted was for the Soviet Union to take the brunt of the Nazi attack. They considered it an affront that the British sent lesser officials as negotiators to Moscow when the prime minister himself had three times flown personally to deal with Hitler. Having quietly undertaken negotiations earlier that spring, the Soviets, on August 23, 1939, openly signed a treaty of nonaggression and friendship with Hitlerite Germany. In a protocol kept secret at the time, it was agreed that in any future territorial rearrangement the Soviet Union and Germany would divide Poland between them, that the Soviet Union would enjoy a preponderant influence in the Baltic states and have its claim to Bessarabia, lost to Rumania in 1918, recognized. In return the Soviets pledged to stay out of any war between Germany and Poland, or between Germany and the Western democracies.

The Nazi-Soviet Pact stupefied the world. Communism and Nazism, supposed to be ideological opposites, had come together. A generation more versed in ideology than in power politics was dumbfounded. The pact was recognized as the signal for war; all last minute negotiations failed. The Germans invaded Poland on September 1. On September 3 Great Britain and France declared war on Germany. The second European war in a generation, soon to be a world war, had begun.

[8] See p. 715, and map, p. 328.

106. THE YEARS OF AXIS TRIUMPH

Nazi Europe, 1939–1940: Poland and the Fall of France

The Second World War opened with the assault on Poland. German forces totaling over 1 million men, spearheaded by armored divisions and supported by the massed air power of the *Luftwaffe,* rapidly overran western Poland and subdued the ill-equipped Polish armies. The outcome of the campaign, a spectacular, perfectly executed example of *Blitzkrieg,* or lightning warfare, was clear within the first few days; organized resistance ended within a month. The Germans undertook to integrate their Polish conquest into the Reich.

Simultaneously, the Soviet Union, acting under the secret clauses of the Nazi-Soviet Pact, moved into the eastern half of Poland two weeks after the German invasion; the territory occupied was roughly equivalent to that lost to Poland in 1920. The Soviets proceeded also to establish fortified bases in the Baltic states—Estonia, Latvia, and Lithuania. Finland alone resisted Soviet demands. The Finns refused to cede border territories sought by the Russians or to yield military rights within their country. The Soviets insisted; Leningrad, the second major city of the U.S.S.R., lay only twenty miles from the Finnish frontier. When negotiations foundered, the Soviets attacked in November 1939. Finnish resistance was valiant and at first effective, but the small country was no match for the U.S.S.R., even though the latter used only limited forces in the war. Western democratic sympathies were with the Finns; the British and French sent equipment and supplies and even planned an expeditionary force. The Soviet Union was expelled from the League of Nations for the act of aggression—the only power ever to be expelled. By March 1940 the fighting was over. The Finns had to yield somewhat more territory to the U.S.S.R. than originally demanded but retained their independence.

Meanwhile all was deceptively quiet in the West. The pattern of 1914, when the Germans reached the Marne in the first month of hostilities, failed to repeat itself. The French sat behind their Maginot Line; the British had few troops; the Germans did not stir from behind their Siegfried Line, or West Wall, in the Rhineland. Hardly any air action took place. It was called the "phony war." The two great Western democracies rejected Hitler's peace overtures after the conquest of Poland but still clung to their peacetime outlook. The mad hope still lingered that somehow a real clash might even yet be averted. During this same strange winter, a cold and bitter one, the Germans put their forces through special training, whose purpose became apparent in the spring.

On April 9, 1940, the Germans suddenly attacked and overran Norway, ostensibly because the British were laying mines in Norwegian waters in an endeavor to cut off German sources of Swedish iron ore. Denmark, too, was overrun, and an Allied expeditionary force with inadequate air strength had to withdraw. Then on May 10, the Germans delivered their main blow, striking at the Netherlands, Belgium, Luxembourg, and France itself. Nothing could stand against the German armored divisions and dive bombers. The Nazi use of massed tanks, though already demonstrated in Poland, took the French and British by surprise. Strategically, the Allies expected the main advance to be in central Belgium, as in 1914, and indeed as in the original German plan, which had been altered only a few months earlier. Hence the French and British sent into Belgium the best-equipped troops they had. But the Germans delivered their main armored thrust, seven divisions, through Luxembourg and the Ardennes forest, long considered by the French General Staff impassable to tanks. In France, skirting the north-western end of the Maginot Line, which had never been extended to the sea, the German armored divisions crossed the Meuse, drove deep into northern France against confused and ineffective resistance and, racing westward toward the Channel ports, cut off the Allied armies in Belgium. The Dutch, fearful of further air attack on their crowded cities, capitulated. The Belgian king sued for an armistice, and a large part of the French armies surrendered. The British fell back upon Dunkirk and could hope only to salvage their broken forces before the trap closed completely. They were able to accomplish their rescue operation only because Hitler had some days earlier halted the advance of his armored divisions. In the week ending June 4 an epic evacuation of over 330,000 British and French troops was successfully executed from the beaches of Dunkirk, under air cover, with the help of all kinds of British vessels, manned in part by civilian volunteers, but the precious equipment of the shattered army was all but totally abandoned.

In June the German forces drove relentlessly southward. Paris itself was occupied on June 13, Verdun two days later; by June 22 France had sued for peace and an armistice had been signed. Hitler danced with glee.

France, obsessed by a defensive military psychology at the outset of the war, its armies unprepared for mechanized warfare, lacking armored divisions and an adequate air force, its government divided, its people split into hostile and suspicious factions, had fallen into the hands of a group of men who were openly defeatist. The fall of France left the world aghast. Everyone knew that France was no longer its former self, but it had still been considered a great power, and its collapse in one month seemed inconceivable. Some Frenchmen, fleeing to England, established a Free French movement under General Charles de Gaulle; others formed a Resistance movement in France. The British made the bitter decision to destroy a part of the French fleet anchored in the Algerian harbor of Oran to prevent its falling into enemy hands.

France itself under the terms of the armistice was occupied in its northern two-thirds by the Germans. The Third Republic, its capital now at Vichy in the unoccupied southern third, was transformed by vote of a confused and stunned parliament into an authoritarian regime headed by the eighty-four-year-old Marshal Pétain and the cynical and unscrupulous Pierre Laval. The republic was dead; the very slogan *Liberty, Equality, Fraternity* was banned from official use. Pétain, Laval, and others proceeded to collaborate with the Nazis and to integrate Vichy France into the Nazi "new order" in Europe.[9]

Mussolini attacked France in June 1940, as soon as it was clear that Hitler had defeated it. Shortly thereafter, he invaded Greece and moved against the British in Africa. The *Duce* tied his own destinies, for good or ill, to those of the *Führer*. Since the Germans were emphatically the senior partner in this combination, since they were on good terms with Franco in Spain, and since the U.S.S.R. was benevolently neutral, they now dominated the European continent. History seemed to repeat itself, in the distant and unreal way in which it ever repeats. The Germans controlled almost exactly the same geographical area as Napoleon. Organizing a new "continental system," which they called the "new order," they made plans to govern, exploit, and coordinate the resources, industry, and labor

[9] See maps, pp. 810–811 and 894–895.

of Europe. Not having made plans for a long war, and only belatedly mobilizing their resources for a sustained military effort, they had to intensify the exploitation of their conquered subjects. They garrisoned Europe with their soldiers, creating what they called *Festung Europa*, the Fortress of Europe. In every country they had their sympathizers, collaborators, or "quislings"—the prototype was Vidkun Quisling, who had organized a Norwegian Fascist party in 1933, and was premier of Norway from 1942 to 1945. But Hitler never commanded the following of Napoleon. He never remotely approached Napoleon in raising an international army to fight his battles. Instead, by what the West called slave labor, he impressed millions of French, Russians, Poles, Czechs, and others, prisoners of war or civilians, to work under close control in his war industries, in one of the largest forcible displacements of population in all history.

The Battle of Britain and American Aid

In 1940, as in 1807, only Great Britain remained at war with the conqueror of Europe. After Dunkirk the British awaited the worst, momentarily expecting invasion. Winston Churchill, who had replaced Chamberlain as prime minister in May 1940 during the military debacle, rose to the summit of leadership in adversity. To Parliament and the British people he promised nothing but "blood, toil, tears, and sweat." He pledged implacable war against "a monstrous tyranny, never surpassed in the dark, lamentable catalogue of human crime." To the American democracy across the Atlantic he appealed "Give us the tools, and we will finish the job." The United States began to respond.

Since 1939, and even before, the American government had been anything but neutral. Opinion was excitedly divided. One group, called isolationist, opposed any involvement in the European war, believing that Europe was hopeless, or that the United States could not save it, or that the Germans would win anyway before America could act, or that Hitler, even if victorious in Europe, constituted no danger to the United States. Another group, the interventionists, urged immediate aid to the Allies, believing that Hitler was an actual menace, that fascism must be destroyed, or that the Nazis, if they subjected all Europe, would soon begin to tamper with the American republics. President Roosevelt was an interventionist, convinced that American security was endangered; he tried to rally national opinion by declaring that the United States might openly assist the Allies without itself fighting, by using "measures short of war."

The neutrality legislation of the mid-1930s was amended in November 1939, when the ban on the sale of arms was repealed. Britain and the British Empire the President described as "the spearhead of resistance to world conquest"; the United States was to be "the great arsenal of democracy." Both were fighting for a world, he said, in which the Four Freedoms were to be secure—freedom of speech, freedom of worship, freedom from want, and freedom from fear. In June 1940, immediately after Dunkirk, the United States sent a small initial shipment of arms to Britain. A few months later the United States gave the British fifty overage destroyers in return for the right to maintain American bases in Newfoundland, the Bermudas, and the British Caribbean islands. In 1941 it adopted Lend-Lease, a policy of providing arms, raw materials, and food to powers at war with the Axis. At the same time, in 1940 and 1941, the United States introduced conscription, built up its army and air force, and projected a two-ocean navy. Plans for joint hemisphere defense were developed with the Latin American republics. To protect its shipping it secured bases in Greenland and Iceland and convoyed Allied shipping as far as Iceland. In October 1941 German submarines sank an American destroyer. It is likely that the Germans, as in 1917, would have eventually provoked war with the United States to stop the flow of aid to their enemies even had war not come from another quarter.

Meanwhile, after the fall of France, the Germans stood poised for the invasion of Britain. But they had not calculated on such rapid and easy successes in Europe, they had no immediately practical plan for an invasion, and they needed to win control of the air before a sea invasion could take place. Moreover, there was always the hope that the British might sue for peace, or even become an ally of Germany—so Hitler's mind ran. The assault on Britain, which began that summer and reached its climax in the autumn of 1940, took the form of an air offensive. Never until then had any bombing been so severe. But the Germans were unable to win control over the air in the battle of Britain. Gradually the British Royal Air Force fought off the bombers with more success; new radar devices helped detect the approach of enemy planes, as did a remarkable British intelligence operation called Ultra, by which the British early in the war broke the code of an important German communications device used for military conversations at the highest level. Although Coventry was wiped out, the life and industry of other cities badly disrupted, and thousands of people killed (20,000 in London alone), still the productive activity of the country carried on. Nor, contrary to the predictions of theorists of air power, did the bombings break the morale of the civilian population.

In the winter of 1940–1941 the Germans began to shift their weight to the east. Hitler postponed indefinitely the planned invasion of Britain for which he seems never to have had much enthusiasm anyway. He had already decided, like Napoleon before him, that before committing his resources to an invasion of England he must dispose of Russia, a project much closer to his heart.

The Nazi Invasion of Russia: The Russian Front, 1941–1942

The Nazi-Soviet Pact of 1939 which had precipitated the war, like the alliance between Napoleon and Alexander I, was never a warm or harmonious understanding. Both parties probably entered it mainly to gain time. The Soviets gained space as well, pushing their borders westward. Stalin seems to have convinced himself that he could remain uninvolved in the war going on. But he and the Nazis soon began to dispute over eastern Europe. The Soviets, with the Nazis preoccupied by the war, hoped to win more influence in the Baltic, as promised them, and in the Balkans. They had already occupied eastern Poland and the three Baltic states and won territory from Finland. In June 1940, to the chagrin of the Germans, they had quietly sovietized and converted the three Baltic states into member republics of the U.S.S.R. The old German landowning class, the famous "Baltic barons," who had lived there for centuries, were uprooted and were returned to German soil. At the same time the Soviets seized from Rumania the Bessarabian province that they had lost in the First World War and incorporated it as a Soviet republic. The Russians were expanding toward the Balkans, another area of historic Russian interest, and seemed bent on winning control over eastern Europe.

This the Germans viewed with dismay. They wished to reserve eastern Europe for themselves as a counterpart to industrial Germany. Hitler moved to bring the Balkans under German control. By early 1941 he had blackmailed or, by territorial concessions, cajoled Rumania, Bulgaria, and Hungary into joining the Axis; they became Axis lesser partners and were occupied by German troops; Yugoslavia also was occupied despite resistance by the army and population. Greece too was subjugated, the Germans coming to the rescue of Mussolini's hard-pressed troops. Hitler thus barred Russian expansion in the Balkans and made them part of the Nazi new order. The Balkan campaigns delayed his plans, but now, to end the threat from the East, and to gain the wheat harvests of the Ukraine and the oil wells of the Caucasus, the core of the Eurasian "heartland," Hitler struck, and on June 22, 1941, invaded Russia. Stalin, ignoring warnings he had received, was caught completely by surprise and momentarily seemed incapable of mounting any kind of defense.

The German army threw 3 million men into Russia along a vast 2,000-mile front. The Russians gave way. One swift moving battle melted into another. By the autumn of 1941 the Germans had overrun White Russia and most of the Ukraine. In the north, Leningrad was in a state of siege; in the south, the Germans had entered the Crimean peninsula and were besieging Sebastopol. And toward the center of the vast front, the Germans stood, exhausted, but apparently victorious, within twenty-five miles of Moscow. But the overconfident German forces had not calculated on the stubbornness of Russian resistance once Stalin rallied the country and replaced some of his ineffective military commanders, nor were they prepared to fight in an early and extraordinarily bitter Russian winter, which suddenly came upon them. A counteroffensive, launched by the Russians in the winter of 1941, saved Moscow. Hitler, disgusted and impatient with his subordinates, took over direct command of military operations; he shifted the main attack to the south and began a great offensive in the summer of 1942 directed toward the oil fields of the Caucasus. Sebastopol soon fell; the siege of Stalingrad began. After the failure to take Moscow, Hitler, aware now that the war would not be brief, also took steps to mobilize the German economy on a full wartime basis. Germany had been ready for war in 1939 as no other major power had been, but without preparations in depth for a protracted conflict. In the early months of 1942 Hitler found in Albert Speer an organizing genius who, despite all kinds of obstacles from party leaders and government functionaries, coordinated manpower and resources in the next two years and tripled armaments production.

1942, The Year of Dismay: Russia, North Africa, the Pacific

A year after the invasion, in the fateful summer of 1942, the German line reached from beleaguered Leningrad in the north, past the western outskirts of Moscow, past Stalingrad on the Volga southward to the Caucasus Mountains; the Germans were within a hundred miles of the Caspian Sea. But the Russians had traded space for time. Though the industrial Don basin and the food-producing Ukraine were overrun, the deliveries of Caucasus oil rendered hazardous and uncertain, still the Russians continued to fight; industries were shifted to the new Ural and Siberian cities; and neither the Soviet economy nor the Soviet government was yet struck in a vital spot. A "scorched earth" policy, in which the retreating Russians destroyed crops and livestock and guerrilla units wrecked industrial and transportation facilities, guaranteed that Russian resources would not fall into the hands of the advancing conqueror.

Simultaneously, late in 1942 the Axis also was moving forward in North Africa. Here the desert campaigns had started in September 1940 with an Italian eastward offensive mounted from Libya, which succeeded in crossing over into Egypt. The stakes here too were high—control over Suez and the Mediterranean. At the height of the battle of Britain, Churchill had made the decision to send vitally needed supplies and men to North Africa. To the satisfaction of the British, a counteroffensive against vastly superior numbers swept the Italians out of Egypt and by early 1941 the British moved deep into Libya. Shortly thereafter the British overran Ethiopia and ended entirely Mussolini's short-lived East African empire; the Italian navy suffered reverses as well. But in North Africa fortunes were fickle. A German elite force, the Afrika Korps under General Rommel, reorganized the Axis armies and in the spring of 1941 attacked in Libya. The British, their forces depleted by transfers that had been made to the Greek front, were driven back to the Egyptian frontier. Then, a few months later, in a second successful offensive, the British once more advanced into Libya. Again fortunes shifted. By mid-1942 Rommel had repulsed the British and penetrated Egypt. The British took up a stand at El Alamein, seventy miles from Alexandria, their backs to the Suez Canal. Here they held the Germans.

But it seemed in 1942 that the Axis armies, breaking through the Soviet Caucasus and across the isthmus of Suez in North Africa, might enclose the whole Mediterranean and Middle East in a gigantic vise, and even, moving farther east, somehow make contact with their allies the Japanese, who were at this time penetrating into the Indian Ocean. For the Pacific situation in the latter half of 1941 had also exploded. It was Japan that finally drew the United States into war.

The Japanese, in 1941, had conducted a war against China for ten years. In the second war in Europe, as in the first, Japanese expansionists saw a propitious moment to assert themselves throughout the Far East. In 1940 they had cemented their alliance with Germany and Italy in a new three-power pact; the following year they had concluded a neutrality treaty with Russia. From the Vichy French government the Japanese obtained a number of military bases and other concessions in Indochina and began the occupation of that area. The United States belatedly placed an embargo on the export of such materials as scrap iron and steel to Japan. Hesitating to precipitate any all-out drive of the Japanese toward the Dutch East Indies and elsewhere, the United States government still sought some definition of Japanese ambitions in southeast Asia. The new Japanese prime minister, General Hideki Tojo, a staunch champion of the Axis, publicly proclaimed that the influence of Britain and the United States was to be totally eliminated from the Orient, but he agreed to send representatives to Washington for negotiations.

EUROPE, 1942

The map shows Europe at the height of Axis military successes during World War II, just before the Soviet victory at Stalingrad and the Western invasion of North Africa. Austria, the Sudetenland, Bohemia-Moravia, Poland, and Alsace-Lorraine were all joined to Hitler's Reich. The Atlantic Coast from southern France to northern Norway was under German military occupation, as was much of Russia almost to the Caspian Sea. Southern Europe from Vichy France to Rumania was also occupied or allied.

ARCTIC OCEAN

ICELAND
Reykjavik

Hitler's "Empire"
Allied With Germany
Occupied by the Axis
At War Against the Axis

Relations between the Axis and Vichy France
were governed by the Armistice of June 1940,
but Germany occupied the whole of France
in November 1942.

0   100   200   300 miles

Narvik

NORWAY

SWEDEN

FAEROE I.
(Denmark)

SHETLAND I.
(Britain)

Bergen

Oslo

Stockholm

ORKNEY I.

NORTH
SEA

DENMARK
Copenhagen

BALTIC SE

Danzig

ATLANTIC OCEAN

NORTHERN
IRELAND

EIRE

UNITED
KINGDOM

Coventry

London

ENGLISH CHANNEL   Dunkirk

Brest

Paris

Hamburg

Elbe R.

Berlin

NETHERLANDS
Rotterdam

Essen   GERMANY   Breslau
Cologne
BELGIUM
LUX. Nuremburg   BOHEMIA
Sedan   SUDETEN-
LAND
MORAVIA
SLO

FRANCE

Munich   Vienna

Vichy   AUSTRIA   Budape

Rhine R.

SWITZERLAND

H

Bordeaux

Bilbao

CROATIA

Toulon

ADRIATIC SEA

PORTUGAL

Lisbon

Madrid

SPAIN

Barcelona

CORSICA
(Vichy France)

ITALY

Rome
Anzio
Salerno

Cassino
Taranto

SARDINIA
(Italy)

BALEARIC I.
(Spain)

Cadiz

Tangier

Gibraltar (Britain)

SPANISH
MOROCCO

Oran

Algiers

Palermo

Bizerte   SICILY

Casablanca

MOROCCO
(Vichy France)

ALGERIA
(Vichy France)

TUNISIA
(Vichy France)

MALTA (Britain)

MEDITERRANEAN

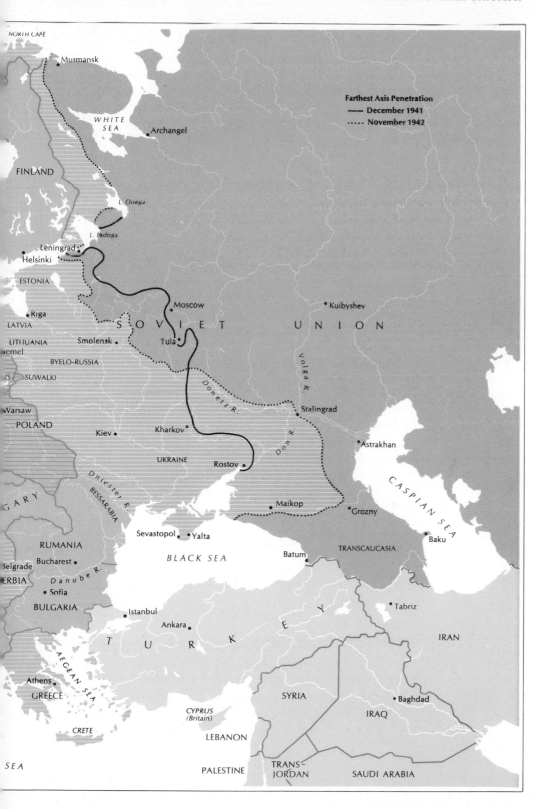

Farthest Axis Penetration

——— December 1941

.... November 1942

At the very time that the Japanese representatives in Washington were carrying on conversations with the American Secretary of State Cordell Hull, on December 7, 1941, without warning, the Japanese launched a heavy air raid on the American naval base at Pearl Harbor in Hawaii and began to invade the Philippines. Simultaneously, they launched attacks on Guam, Midway, Hong Kong, and Malaya. The Americans were caught off guard at Pearl Harbor; close to 2,500 were killed; the fleet was crippled; and the temporary disablement of the American naval forces allowed the Japanese to roam at will in the western Pacific. The United States and Great Britain declared war on Japan on December 8. Three days later Germany and Italy declared war on the United States, as did the Axis puppet states.

The Japanese, working overland through Malaya, two months later captured Singapore, a British naval base long fabulous for its supposed impregnability, the veritable Gibraltar of the East. The sinking by air of the mighty British battleship *Prince of Wales*, a feat often pronounced by naval experts to be impossible, added to the general consternation. In 1942 the Japanese conquered the Philippines, Malaya, and the Netherlands Indies. They invaded New Guinea and threatened Australia; they moved into the Aleutians. They streamed into the Indian Ocean, occupied Burma, and seemed about to invade India. Everywhere they found ready collaborators among enemies of European imperialism. They held up the idea of a Greater East Asia Co-Prosperity Sphere under Japanese leadership, in which the one clear element was that the European whites should be ejected. Meanwhile, as noted, the Germans stood at the Caucasus and almost at the Nile. And in the Atlantic, even to the shores of the United States and the American republics, German submarines were sinking Allied ships at an unprecedented and disastrous rate. The Mediterranean was unusable. For the Soviet-Western alliance, 1942 was the year of dismay. Despite Allied naval and air victories in the Pacific, the late summer and autumn of 1942 was the worst period of the war. Few realized, wrote the United States Chief of Staff General George C. Marshall some years later, how "close to complete domination of the world" were Germany and Japan and "how thin the thread of Allied survival had been stretched." That Germany and Japan had no plans to concert their strategy and operations was no small factor in the eventual Allied victory.

107. THE WESTERN-SOVIET VICTORY

Plans and Preparations, 1942–1943

But by January 1942 twenty-six nations, including the three Great Powers—Britain, the United States, and the U.S.S.R.—and representing Europe, Asia, and both Americas, were aligned against the Axis, a combination to which President Roosevelt gave the name the United Nations. Each pledged to use all its resources to defeat the Axis and never to make a separate peace. The Grand Alliance against the Axis aggressors, which could not be created in the 1930s, had at last been consummated.

The two Atlantic democracies, the United States and Great Britain, pooled their resources under an organization called the Combined Chiefs of Staff. Never had any two sovereign states formed so intimate a coalition. In contrast with the

First World War an overall strategy was in effect from an early date. It was decided that Germany was the main enemy, against which it was necessary to concentrate first. For the time being the Pacific war was relegated to the background. Australia became the chief base for operations against the Japanese. The American General Douglas MacArthur, who had been ordered to abandon the doomed American garrison in the Philippines, assumed command in the southwest Pacific; Admiral Chester Nimitz was in command of the Pacific naval forces. A separate organization was established for the China-Burma-India theater. The American navy and air force soon brought Japanese southward expansion to a halt and frustrated Japanese efforts to cut off supply lines to Australia; impressive naval and air victories were won in the spring of 1942 in the battle of the Coral Sea and at Midway, the only relief to the overall gloom of that period. In the summer American forces landed at Guadalcanal in the Solomon Islands. A long ordeal of "island hopping" with inadequate forces began.

In Europe the first point of concentration was an air bombardment of Germany. The Russians, dissatisfied, called for a true "second front," an immediate invasion by ground forces that would relieve the pressure of the many German divisions that were devastating their country. Suspicious of the West as ever, doubly suspicious since the Munich conference of 1938, in which they saw a Western attempt to deflect the Germans into an attack on Russia, they regarded the failure to establish a second front as new evidence of anti-Soviet feeling.

But neither the United States nor Britain, in 1942, was ready to undertake land action by a direct assault on *Festung Europa*. Although in the Second World War, as in the First, more than two years elapsed between the outbreak of war in Europe and the intervention of the United States, and although in the second war American military preparations began much sooner, the United States in 1942 was still involved in the cumbersome processes of mobilization, converting industry to the production of war materials for itself and its Allies, imposing controls on its economy to prevent a runaway inflation, and giving military training to its profoundly civilian-minded people, of whom over 12 million eventually served in the armed forces—over three times as many as in the First World War. Large numbers of women, as in Britain, and more so than in the First World War, took wartime jobs in defense and other industries. (To the end, Nazi ideology placed obstacles in the way of utilizing women in German factories.) In any case, for a year after the United States entered the war, German submarines enjoyed enough control of the Atlantic to make large shipments of troops too risky. In effect, they blockaded the American army in the United States. The American and British navies gradually won the battle of the Atlantic; the submarine menace was reduced to tolerable proportions by the first part of 1943. The Americans and British decided to begin the assault upon Germany, from Great Britain as a base, with a massive and prolonged air bombardment of its factories and cities. Because precision bombardment of factories and other military targets proved difficult either by day or by night, the air assaults became area bombings; German cities were bombed mercilessly and civilians were the largest casualties. In Hamburg in 1943 fires raged on and destroyed most of the city after several days of incessant bombing. Since not everything could be shipped across the Atlantic at the same time, and since the United States and Britain were engaged in war with Japan as well, land invasion had to be deferred until 1944. The embattled Russians questioned whether the Western Allies ever really meant to face the German army at all.

The Turning of the Tide, 1942–1943: Stalingrad, North Africa, Sicily

Meanwhile, at the end of 1942 the tide began to turn. In November an Anglo-American force effected a surprise invasion of Algeria and Morocco in an amphibious operation of hitherto unparalleled proportions. The Allies, failing to win the cooperation of the French in North Africa as they had hoped to do, turned to the Vichy French political leader Admiral Darlan in a calculated act of expediency that brought a loud outcry of protest in many quarters. Darlan assisted the Allies in assuming control but was assassinated in late December. In the competition that developed in the succeeding months for leadership of the French liberation committee, newly established in Algiers, General de Gaulle, though mistrusted and virtually ignored by President Roosevelt, easily pushed aside all rivals.

On the Continent, after the North African landings, the Germans took over control of unoccupied France as well; they were frustrated, however, in the effort to obtain possession of the remainder of the French fleet by the action of French crews who scuttled their ships at Toulon. In North Africa the invading forces under the command of General Dwight D. Eisenhower fought their way eastward into Tunisia. Meanwhile the British forces under General Montgomery, having held the Germans at El Alamein in June 1942, had already launched their third (and final) counteroffensive in October, even before the invasion; they now pushed the Germans westward from Egypt until a large German force was crushed between the two Allied armies and destroyed in Tunisia. By May 1943 Africa was cleared of Axis forces. Mussolini's dream of an African empire had been thwarted; the Mediterranean was open; the threat to Egypt and the Suez Canal was ended.

At the same time it became clear, in the winter of 1942–1943, that the Germans had suffered a catastrophic reversal in the Soviet Union in the titanic battle of Stalingrad. In August 1942 massive German forces, an army of over a quarter million, began an all-out assault on Stalingrad, the vital key to all transport on the lower Volga; by September they had penetrated the city itself. Stalin, who from the start of the war personally commanded military operations in Russia, ordered his namesake city held at all costs; Russian soldiery and the civilian population took a desperate stand. Hitler, still gambling on one big victory, was as obstinate in ordering the city taken. After weeks of fighting the Germans had occupied most of the city when suddenly a great Russian counterattack, led by General Zhukov, trapped the German army, and took a terrible toll; fewer than 100,000 were left to surrender in February 1943. The Russians followed up their victory with a new counteroffensive, a great westward drive that netted them wholesale advances and regained for them what they had initially lost in the first year of the war. After Stalingrad, despite some setbacks, the Russians were on the offensive for the remainder of the war. Stalingrad (or Volgograd as it was later renamed) was a turning point not only in the history of the war but in the history of central and eastern Europe as well.

American equipment meanwhile all through 1943 was arriving in Russia in prodigious quantities. The terms of Lend-Lease were liberally extended to the Soviets; a stream of American vehicles, clothing, food, and supplies of all kinds made its way laboriously to Russia through the Arctic Ocean and through the Persian Gulf. Machinery and equipment were sent for the Soviet arms plants, which were themselves tremendously increasing their output. Anglo-American bombing was crippling the German aviation industry at home. The Allied contribution to the Soviet war effort was indispensable, but Russian human losses were tremendous. The Russians lost more men in the battle of Stalingrad than the United States lost in combat during the entire war, in all theaters combined.

With contemporary American successes in the Solomon Islands at the end of 1942 and the slow throttling of German submarines in the Atlantic, the beginning of the year 1943 brought new hope for the Allies in all quarters. In a spectacular campaign of July–August 1943, the British, Canadians, and Americans conquered the island of Sicily. Mussolini immediately fell; the twenty-one-year-old Fascist regime came to an end. Mussolini set up an "Italian Social Republic" in the north, but it was no more than a German puppet government. (Some months later, in April 1945, the Duce, as he attempted to flee the country, was seized, shot, and strung up like a slaughtered pig by anti-Fascist Italians.) The new Italian government under Marshal Badoglio, in August 1943, tried to make peace. The German army then occupied Italy. The Allies, having crossed to the Italian mainland, attacked from the south. In October the Badoglio government declared war on Germany, and Italy was recognized by the Allies as a "cobelligerent." But the Germans stubbornly blocked the advance of the Allies to Rome despite new Allied landings and beachheads. The Italian campaign turned into a long and disheartening stalemate because the Western Allies, concentrating troops in Great Britain for the approaching cross-Channel invasion, could never spare enough for the Italian front.

The Allied Offensive, 1944–1945: Europe and the Pacific

Festung Europa, especially along its western approaches, the coasts of Holland, Belgium, and France, bristled with every kind of fortification that German scientific and military ingenuity could devise. A seaborne attack upon Europe was an operation of wholly unprecedented kind. It differed from the earlier amphibious attacks on Algeria, Sicily, or the Pacific islands in that the defender in Europe, in the very part of Europe where the road and railway network was thickest, could immediately rush overwhelming reserves to the spot attacked—except insofar as feinting tactics kept him uncertain, air power destroyed his transport, or the Russians held the bulk of his forces in the East. Precise and elaborate plans had been worked out. Ten thousand aircraft were to provide aerial protection, scores of warships were to bombard the coast, 4,000 ships were to carry the invading troops and their supplies across the Channel, artificial harbors were to be created where none existed.

The invasion of Europe began before dawn on June 6, 1944. The spot selected was the coast of Normandy directly across the Channel from England; false intelligence reports, planted by the Allies, led the Germans to expect the main thrust at Calais. An unparalleled combination of forces, British, Canadian, and American, land, sea, and air, backed up by huge accumulations of supplies and reserves of men assembled in Great Britain, and the whole under the unified command of the American General Eisenhower, assaulted the French coast, established a beachhead, and maintained a front. The Allies poured in their strength, over 130,000 men the first day, 1 million within a month. The Germans were at first thrown back more easily than had been expected. By August Paris was liberated, by September the Allies crossed the frontier of Germany itself. In France, Italy, and Belgium the Resistance movements, which had grown up in secret during the

Map labels:

NORTH POLE

SOVIET UNION

CANADA

GREENLAND
(Denmark)

• Murmansk

4. Greatest Axis Expansion,
December 1941–November 1942

NORWAY

FIN-
LAND

• Kuibyshev

• Moscow

SWEDEN

• Stalingrad

ICELAND

1. Hitler Invades Poland
September 1, 1939

UNITED KINGDOM

DEN.

GERMANY

6. Germany Surrenders,
May 8, 1945

IRAN

UNITED
STATES

2. France Surrenders
June 22, 1940

FRANCE

TURKEY

5. Allies Invade:
North Africa, November 8, 1942
Normandy Coast, June 6, 1944

ITALY

SPAIN

El Alamein

Suez Canal

PORTUGAL

TUNISIA

3. United States:
Bases-Destroyer Deal, September 2, 1940
Enacts Lend Lease March 11, 1941
Enters the War December 8, 1941

AZORES
(Portugal)

Casablanca •

Oran

EGYPT

FRENCH
MOROCCO

ALGERIA
(France)

LIBYA

CUBA

CANARY I.
(Spain)

ATLANTIC OCEAN

Panama Canal

VENEZUELA

FRENCH WEST AFRICA

ITALIAN
SOM.

CAPE VERDE I.
(Portugal)

Dakar

FRENCH
EQUATORIAL
AFRICA

← Allied Thrusts

← Lend Lease Supply Lines

Hitler's "Empire"

Allied with Germany

Occupied by the Axis

At War Against the Axis

BRAZIL

WORLD WAR II

These two maps show the global character of the war and the central position of the United States with respect to the European and Pacific theaters. The numbered legends summarize the successive stages of the war in both the Eastern and Western hemispheres. In 1942, with the Germans reaching as far east as Egypt and Stalingrad, and the Japanese as far west as Burma, the great danger to the Soviet-Western alliance was that these two might join forces, dominate southern Asia, control the oil resources of the Persian Gulf, and stop the flow of Western supplies to the Soviet Union from this direction. The almost simultaneous Soviet-Western successes, late in 1942, at Stalingrad and El Alamein, and in the invasion of Morocco-Algeria and of Guadalcanal, proved to be the turning point of the war. In 1943 the German submarine campaign in the Atlantic was defeated, so that American troops and supplies could move more freely to Europe. The invasion of Normandy in June 1944, with continuing Soviet pressure from the east, brought about German surrender in May 1945. Meanwhile, in the Pacific, American occupation of the islands and reoccupation of the Philippines prepared the way for the surrender of Japan, consummated by two atomic bombs in August 1945.

later years of German occupation, now came into the open and drove out Germans and pro-German collaborators. In Germany itself no widespread or deeply rooted Resistance movement ever developed, but a small group of men, military and civilian, formed an underground group. On July 20, 1944, after the failure of several earlier efforts, it attempted to assassinate Hitler by exploding a bomb at his military headquarters in East Prussia; Hitler was only injured and took a fearsome revenge on the conspirators.

In August, in another amphibious operation, the Allies landed on the French Mediterranean coast and swept up from southern France to join the Allied forces advancing against stiffening resistance. At one point, momentarily, the Allied offensive even suffered a serious reversal. A sudden German drive under Hitler's direct personal orders in December 1944, unleashed under radio silence to thwart Allied intelligence, was launched against thinly held American lines on the Belgian sector in the Ardennes, created a "bulge" in the advancing armies, and caused heavy losses and confusion. But the Allies rallied, and Hitler used up his armored reserves in the effort. Neither the Ardennes counteroffensive nor the use of new destructive weapons rained on Britain, jet-propelled flying bombs and rockets, availed the Germans. All this time the American and British kept up their massive air bombardments, killing over 50,000 civilians in the fire-bombing of Dresden in February 1945. On the ground they pushed on and smashed through the heavily fortified Siegfried Line. The last natural obstacle, the Rhine, was crossed when in March 1945 American forces by a stroke of luck discovered an undestroyed bridge at Remagen; they poured troops over it and established a bridgehead—the first troops to cross the Rhine in combat since the armies of Napoleon. The main crossing, under the British, subsequently took place farther to the north. Soon the Allies were accepting wholesale surrenders in the Ruhr valley.

Meanwhile in 1944 the Russian armies swept the Germans from the Ukraine, White Russia, the Baltic states, and eastern Poland. By August they reached the suburbs of Warsaw. The Polish underground rose against the Germans but the Russians, determined that Poland must not be liberated by noncommunist Polish leadership, refused to permit aid to the rising, and it was crushed, with a heavy loss of Polish lives. The Polish martyrdom was severe; earlier the mass graves of 12,000 Polish army officers were found in the Katyn Forest, the evidence indicating, despite Soviet denials, that they were the victims of the retreating Russian armies after the German invasion began. The Russians, their lines overextended, and checked for several months by German strength in Poland, pushed southward into Rumania and Bulgaria; both countries changed sides and declared war against Germany. Early in 1945 the Russians, reopening their offensive, forced their way into East Prussia and Silesia and by February they reached the Oder, forty miles from Berlin, where Zhukov paused to regroup his forces. In March and April Russian forces occupied Budapest and Vienna.

The final drive on Germany began. Hitler moved troops from the collapsing western front to reinforce the stand on the Oder and to protect his capital. The German population did little to impede Western advances, hopeful that the Western allies might reach Berlin and indeed occupy as much of their country as possible before the Russians. In April the Americans drew up on the Elbe, about sixty miles from Berlin, with hardly any obstacles before them; but here they halted, by decision of General Eisenhower, who was without any firm political guidance from home. The Americans, whose supply lines were already overextended,

NORWAY
9

BALTIC
STATES
228

RUSSIAN S.S.R.
107

WHITE
RUSSIAN
S.S.R.
245

NETHERLANDS
105

GERMANY AND
AUSTRIA
210

BELGIUM
40

POLAND
3,000

UKRAINIAN S.S.R.
900

CZECHOSLOVAKIA
155

FRANCE
90

HUNGARY
450

RUMANIA
300

YUGOSLAVIA
26

BULGARIA
14

ITALY
8

GREECE
54

Percentage of Jewish Population
Annihilated

83-90

65-77

50-60

11-26   Figures Indicate Number of Jews Killed
under Nazi Racial Policies (In Thousands)

THE HOLOCAUST

The map shows what the Nazis called their Final Solution, that is, their program of exterminating the Jews and Judaism. Before the Second World War most European Jews lived in Poland and the adjoining parts of the Soviet Union which the Germans occupied during the war, so that most of the deaths occurred in these areas. The map shows both the number killed in each country and the percentage of its Jewish population that were victims of this deliberate genocide. The numbers add up to 5,933,900 men, women, and children, or an estimated two-thirds of the Jewish population of Europe as a whole. Although word of this extermination policy reached the outside world through the Vatican and other sources, the Allied leaders at first disbelieved the reports, and then, giving priority to their military objectives, did nothing to stop the systematic slaughter.

wanted a clear line of demarcation from the Russians; they also believed it necessary to divert some forces southward against a possible German last stand in the Alps. But mainly the decision was a gesture of good will toward the Russians, who were to be permitted to take Berlin as compensation for the heavy sacrifice in the common cause. Similarly, the American troops that moved southward were held back from taking Prague and the Russians were permitted to take the Czech capital too. By some it was later said that the fate of central Europe was determined by the war in the Far East; the Americans sought Russian aid against Japan, which it turned out, could readily have been dispensed with. In any event, the Russians were in control of all the major capitals of central and eastern Europe; in the case of Berlin and Prague it need not have been that way.

The Western Allies and the Soviets offered no terms to Hitler, nor to any Germans. They demanded unconditional surrender, and the Germans fought on in the very streets of Berlin. On the last day of April Hitler perished by his own hand in the ruins of his capital after denouncing some of his closest party subordinates as traitors. Admiral Doenitz, designated by Hitler as his successor, went through the formalities of surrender on May 8, 1945. Since fighting had already ceased on the Italian front a few days earlier, the war in Europe was now over.

Meanwhile a generation reared to mistrust the fabricated atrocity tales of the First World War painfully became aware of the real German horrors of the Second—hostages rounded up and shot in reprisal for resistance; whole villages like Lidice in Czechoslovakia or Oradour-sur-Glane in France razed to the ground and their inhabitants killed or deported; concentration camps constructed as or converted into mass extermination centers, with gas chambers and crematory ovens, at Auschwitz (where at its peak 12,000 victims a day were put to death), Maidanek, Treblinka, Belzec, Dachau, Buchenwald, and elsewhere, where "inferior" peoples could be systematically liquidated. Before the war was over in the areas of Nazi domination millions of human beings, men, women, and children, were transported to these centers of destruction in cattle cars where some were worked to death and others destroyed immediately; by far the largest proportion killed were almost 6 million Jews, but Poles, Russians, Gypsies, and others were destroyed as well. All this was done in the effort to "Germanize" Europe, to make it work and sacrifice for the greater glory of the *Herrenvolk*, the master race. For the Jews, the annihilation policy, decided upon at a high-level Nazi meeting in January 1942, was to be the "Final Solution" to the Jewish problem over which Hitler had agitated for so many years. Genocide, the effort to destroy a whole people, was the greatest of the Nazi sins against mankind.

In the Pacific, against Japan, operations had dragged on for three years, hampered by the strategic decision to concentrate against Germany first. Slowly, from points in the Solomon Islands, the easternmost fringe of the Indonesian archipelago, American forces, at first very small, worked their way in a northwesterly direction toward faraway Japan. They had to fight in turn for Guadalcanal, for New Guinea, for the reconquest of the Philippines. They had to fight for the Japanese islands and atolls in the mid-Pacific (taken by Japan from the Germans after the First World War and converted into powerful naval bases), the Gilbert Islands, the Marshalls, the Carolines, the Marianas. In October 1944 they won a great naval victory at the battle of Leyte Gulf. Finally, in one of the war's greatest and final battles, they won the island of Okinawa, only 300 miles from Japan itself. Okinawa was captured just as the Germans collapsed in Europe. From the new Allied bases that had been won, from Saipan, from Iwo Jima, and from Okinawa, and from aircraft carriers a heavy bomber offensive was launched against Japan, such as had devastated Germany in the preceding two years, shattering Japanese industry, destroying the remnants of the Japanese navy, and compelling the Japanese government to give serious thought to suing for peace. The Allied leaders refused to believe that Japanese defenses were ready to crumble or that the Japanese were ready to negotiate. The American army prepared to shift combat troops from the European theater to the Far East. The stage was being set for a full-scale invasion of Japan itself.

THE SURVIVOR

by George Grosz (German, then American, 1893–1959)

George Grosz, born in Germany, came to the United States in 1932 to avoid the Nazis. He painted this powerful picture in 1945 at the close of the Second World War. It suggests what is meant by the collapse of civilization. The hideous figure crawling out of the wreckage, according to the artist's own explanation, is insane with fear. He is starving, filthy, abandoned, and alone. In his teeth he desperately clasps a knife, which he will use to fight another terrified survivor, should he meet one, or to hunt for and cut up food. Note the symbolism of a broken swastika in the arrangement of the man's body and the debris. The picture is of course meant to be repulsive, to show the depths to which humanity can be degraded, and so shock people into constructive action. Courtesy of Mrs. Marc J. Sandler.

Then, on August 6, 1945, an atomic bomb, prepared in utmost secrecy by American and European refugee scientists, hit the city of Hiroshima, with a population of 200,000 people. The city was destroyed in this single explosion, and 78,000 lives were lost. Two days later, the Soviet Union, which had pledged itself to enter the conflict in the East within three months after the surrender of Germany, declared war on Japan and invaded Manchuria. On August 9 an even more powerful atomic bomb struck Nagasaki and killed many more thousands. The Japanese made peace at once. On September 2, 1945, the formal surrender was signed. The emperor was permitted to remain as head of the state, but the Japanese islands were placed under the rule of a United States army of occupation.

The Second World War of the twentieth century was over, the greatest conflict in human history. The same cold impersonal statistics that had recorded 10 million killed in the First World War now reported 15 million military deaths and (unlike the First World War) at least that many civilian fatalities. Russian military deaths were estimated at over 7 million (and total deaths at 20 million), German at 3.5 million, Chinese at 2.2 million, Japanese at 1.3 million; British and Commonwealth losses were about 350,000, American about 300,000, French about 200,000. The military death figures would have been greater except that one of every two soldiers seriously wounded was saved by new sulfa and penicillin drugs and by blood plasma transfusions. None of these statistics could be more than approximate and no one could begin to estimate the complete toll of human lives lost in the war, directly or indirectly, from the Allied and Axis bombings, the Nazi mass exterminations, the Nazi and Soviet deportation policies, and the postwar famines and epidemics. Some estimates place the total at 45 million men, women, and children, but at such figures the human mind retreats and human sensitivities are dulled. It is enough to say that peace had come.

108. THE FOUNDATIONS OF THE PEACE

Whereas the First World War had been concluded by a peace conference a few months after the close of hostilities, the Second World War ended in no such clear-cut settlement. Nothing like the Treaty of Versailles of 1919 followed the defeat of Germany in 1945. The terms of peace, as they gradually developed, left no such single symbol of humiliation as the Versailles treaty had represented. The peace terms emerged episodically, at first during a series of conferences among the victors during the war, and then in a series of de facto arrangements in the years after 1945.

The foundations of a peaceable postwar world had been laid, it was then thought, at a number of meetings where the war itself was being planned. In August 1941 Roosevelt and Churchill had met at sea off the coast of Newfoundland and had drawn up the Atlantic Charter. There were meetings in 1943 at Casablanca, at Cairo, and at Teheran (in the latter Stalin participated for the first time); and in the final phase of the war, in February 1945, at Yalta, and in July 1945, at Potsdam, in the environs of shattered Berlin.

The Atlantic Charter, issued jointly by Roosevelt and Churchill at their first meeting, resembled in spirit the Fourteen Points of Woodrow Wilson. It pledged that sovereign rights and self-government would be restored to all who had been forcibly deprived of them, that all nations would have equal access to world trade and world resources, that all peoples would work together to achieve improved living standards and economic security. The postwar peace, it promised, would assure for men in all lands freedom from fear and want and would end force and aggression in international affairs. Here, and in the Four Freedoms enunciated earlier by President Roosevelt, the ideological basis of the peace was proclaimed. At the 1943 conferences, and through other consultations, the Allies endeavored to concert their military plans. At Casablanca, in January 1943, they resolved to accept nothing less than the "unconditional surrender" of the Axis powers. This vague formula, adopted somewhat cavalierly at American initiative, and without much thought to possible political implications, was intended mainly to prevent a recurrence of anything like the ambiguity surrounding the armistice of 1918.[10] Though much criticized in later years (and not fully applied in the case of Japan), it is doubtful whether the decision had any true bearing on the outcome of events. German resistance was stubbornly prolonged because of Hitler's fierce obstinacy and his support by the military, not because responsible leaders would have been willing or able to sue for peace if the Allies had offered them appropriate terms.

At Teheran, in December 1943, Roosevelt and Churchill met with Stalin for the first of two wartime meetings. They discussed the postwar occupation and de-militarization of Germany, laid plans for a postwar international organization, and debated strategy for winning the war. Throughout the war Roosevelt, un-willing to disturb the unity of the Western-Soviet coalition in the global struggle America was engaged in, followed a policy of postponing controversial territorial and political decisions until victory was assured. Churchill was more apprehen-sive. Steeped in traditional balance-of-power politics, he sensed that without prior diplomatic bargaining and political arrangements, the victory over the Nazis would leave Russia dominant over all eastern Europe. At Teheran he pro-posed operations in the Mediterranean and an invasion through the Balkans, for political reasons but also out of concern for the casualties that a cross-Channel in-vasion would involve. But Roosevelt overcame his objections. It was agreed that a landing in France would take place in the spring of 1944; thus the major second front that Stalin had been promised would be opened. Stalin, gratified, pledged that he would launch a simultaneous offensive on the eastern front at that time.

The strategy that would win the war in the next eighteen months was decided upon at Teheran, but that strategy, without political agreements, all but guaran-teed the Russian domination of eastern Europe. Later, in October 1944, as the Russian armies advanced westward, Churchill, acting on his own, visited Stalin and sketched out a demarcation of spheres of influence for the Western powers and the Soviets in the Balkan states (a Russian preponderance in Rumania and Bulgaria, a Western preponderance in Greece, and an even division of influence in Hungary and Yugoslavia). Russian control over the Baltic states had virtually been conceded by the British earlier. But Roosevelt and the State Department would not ratify any such agreement; it was considered old-fashioned and a dan-gerous revival of the worst features of pre-1914 diplomacy. Soon, however, politi-cal decisions had to be made. The two conferences that arrived at the most im-portant political decisions were the meetings at Yalta and at Potsdam in 1945.

The Yalta meeting in February 1945 took place when the Allies were close to final victory—closer, events disclosed, than anyone at the time realized. The three

[10] See p. 688.

Allied statesmen met at an old tsarist Crimean summer resort on the Black Sea, toasted their common triumphs, and took the measure of each other. Roosevelt thought of himself in the role of a mediator between Churchill and Stalin where European issues were involved. He took pains to avoid giving Stalin the impression that he and Churchill were in any sense united against him; in point of fact, Roosevelt was suspicious of Churchill's devotion to empire and colonial ties, which he considered anachronistic for the postwar world. Despite differences, the Big Three reached agreements, at least formally, on Poland and eastern Europe, the future of Germany, the war in the Far East, and the projected postwar international organization, the United Nations.

The discussion of Poland and eastern Europe raised the most serious difficulties. Stalin's armies, having driven the Nazi forces to within forty miles of Berlin, were in control of Poland and almost all eastern and central Europe. The Russians remembered these areas as anti-Soviet, and Poland particularly as the perpetrator of aggression against Soviet territory in 1920, and as the ancient corridor of attack upon Russia. Stalin had already taken steps to establish a "friendly" government in Poland, i.e., a government subservient to the Soviets. Neither Roosevelt nor Churchill had fought the war against the Nazis to leave the Soviet Union the undisputed master of all eastern Europe and in a position to impose a totalitarian political system on all this vast area. At Yalta, Roosevelt and Churchill extracted from Stalin a number of promises for the areas he controlled. In accordance with the Atlantic Charter, the liberated states were to be permitted provisional governments "broadly representative of all democratic elements in the population," i.e., not consisting merely, as in the case of the provisional government of Poland already established, of authorities subservient to the Soviets. They pressed Stalin to pledge also the "earliest possible establishment through free elections of governments responsive to the will of the people." The pledge was a verbal concession that cost the Russian leader little; he rejected the suggestion of international supervision over the elections. The Declaration on Liberated Europe, promising sovereign rights of self-determination, provided a false sense of agreement.

A number of territorial changes were also accepted, pending final settlement at a postwar peace conference. It was agreed that the Russian-Polish, or eastern, boundary of Poland should be set roughly at the so-called Curzon line, the frontier contemplated by the Allies in 1919 before the Poles conquered territory to their east. The Poles were to be compensated, in the north and west, at the expense of Germany.[11] On this and on other matters relating to Germany there was a large area of accord; the three were united in their hatred of German Nazism and militarism. Germany was to be disarmed and divided into four occupation zones under the administration of the Big Three powers and France—the latter at the insistence of Churchill. There was vague talk, at Yalta and earlier, of dismembering Germany, of undoing the work of Bismarck, but the difficulties of such an undertaking were understood and the proposal was postponed, later to be discarded completely. Also discarded, as impracticable, was the Morgenthau plan, seriously considered as late as 1944, which was designed to transform industrial Germany back into an eighteenth-century pastoral and agricultural economy. The Americans and British rejected as excessive the demands for reparations raised by the Soviets, a sum of $20 billion to be paid in kind, half to the Soviets. It

[11] See maps, pp. 328 and 895.

was agreed, however, that reparations would go to those countries that had borne the main burdens of the war and suffered the heaviest losses. The Soviet Union was to receive half of whatever total sum was set.

To the satisfaction of everyone, the participants agreed on plans for a postwar international organization, to be called the United Nations. Roosevelt believed it essential to win the Soviets over to the idea of an international organization. He was convinced that the great powers, cooperating within the framework of the United Nations, and acting as international policemen, could alone preserve the future peace and security of the world. No less than Stalin or Churchill, he emphasized the importance of the great powers in the new organization, although he accepted a dignified role for the smaller nations as well. All agreed that each of the great powers, the permanent members of the new organization's Security Council, would have a veto power on important decisions. The Soviets pressed for sixteen votes in the General Assembly of the new organization, arguing that their constitution gave sovereign rights to each of their constituent republics and that the British dominions would each have a seat. In the interests of harmony they were given three seats.

Critical agreements were reached on the Far East. Here political and military decisions were inextricably linked. In April 1941 the Soviets had concluded a non-aggression treaty with Japan and had remained neutral in the Pacific war despite their historic interests in the Far East. Given the magnitude of the war effort on the European front, no one pressed the Soviets to enter the Pacific war. It was agreed to wait at least until the Germans were on the verge of defeat. At Yalta, Stalin agreed to enter the war against Japan, but Soviet "public opinion," he averred, would demand compensation. It was stipulated that the U.S.S.R. would enter the war against Japan "two to three months" after Germany had surrendered. In return, the Soviets were to have restored to them territories and rights that tsarist Russia had lost to Japan forty years before in the Russo-Japanese war of 1904–1905—the southern half of Sakhalin Island, and in Manchuria special concessions at the warm-water port of Dairen and at the naval base of Port Arthur, as well as joint control with China over the Manchurian railroads leading to these ports; in addition, the Soviets were to receive the Kurile Islands, which had not been Russian before.[12] The Russian position in Outer Mongolia was also to remain unaltered. Meanwhile Stalin confirmed Chinese political sovereignty over Manchuria, despite the privileges granted to the Soviets, and pledged Soviet support for the Nationalist government of China, then on uneasy terms with the Chinese Communists.[13]

But China was not a party to any of these concessions, which for a time were kept secret. Roosevelt took it upon himself to secure the consent of Chiang Kai-shek, which he subsequently did. By the territorial concessions to the Soviets in the Far East, the Western powers seemed to be sanctioning the replacement of Japanese imperialism by Russian imperialism in the long contested area of northeast China, and without China having any voice in the matter at all. The concessions were the price to be paid for Soviet assistance against the Japanese, assistance then considered indispensable for the final defeat of Japan. What really exasperated so many in later years was that Russia's entry into the war, as pledged, was not of any military consequence; it came two days after the atomic bomb

[12] See pp. 646–647 and map, p. 645.
[13] See pp. 758–759, 860–861.

had been dropped and at a time when the Japanese were in a desperate state, near collapse and surrender, even without the dropping of the atomic bomb. The concessions in the Far East need not have been made. Even without the Yalta agreement, nothing perhaps except outright force could have deterred Stalin from moving into Manchuria after the Japanese collapse, or indeed from controlling eastern Europe as he wished. The Yalta agreement, however, lent an aura of respectability to Soviet expansion.

Roosevelt made concessions at Yalta not only because he appreciated the Soviet war effort against the Germans but because he believed that he needed their support in the last phase of the war against the Japanese; he wished to preserve the Western-Soviet coalition until final victory was guaranteed. Above all else, he believed that wartime harmony would produce postwar cordiality, especially if all the participating personalities remained alive to assure it. Churchill, less certain of the future and of "diplomacy by friendship," would have preferred a franker recognition and definition of spheres of influence. Such ideas were ruled out as the thinking of a bygone era. Yet the spirit of the Atlantic Charter, so closely identified with the American president, the pledge of sovereign self-determination for all peoples, was contravened at Yalta in many ways. Like the Versailles treaty of 1919, the decisions at Yalta would not have been so disappointing had the ideals not been set so high.

At Potsdam, in July 1945, after the German collapse, the Big Three met again. A new American president, Harry S. Truman, represented the United States; President Roosevelt had died in April, on the eve of final victory. Churchill, in the midst of the conference, was replaced by a new British prime minister, Clement Attlee, after the Labour party's victory at the polls. Stalin still represented Russia. By now, disagreements between the Western Allies and the Soviets had deepened, not only over Soviet control in Poland, eastern Europe, and the Balkans, but over German reparations and other matters. Yet the Western leaders were still prepared to make concessions in the hope of establishing harmonious relations. Agreements were announced on the postwar treatment of Germany, on German disarmament, demilitarization, "denazification," and the punishment of war criminals. It was agreed that each power might take reparations in kind from its occupation zone and that the Russians would get substantial additional deliveries from the Western zones so that the original $10 million Soviet demand was virtually met. Pending the final peace treaty, German territory east of the Oder-Neisse rivers was committed to Polish administration. The details of this decision had earlier been postponed; now the Polish-German boundary was set at the western Neisse, even further west than originally envisaged. Poland thus extended its territorial boundaries about a hundred miles westward as compensation for Russian westward expansion at Polish expense. German East Prussia was similarly divided between Russia in the north and Poland in the south. Königsberg, founded by the Teutonic Knights, for centuries the ducal seat of Prussian dukes and the coronation city of Prussian kings, became the Russian city of Kaliningrad. The ancient German cities of Stettin and Breslau became the Polish cities of Szczecin and Wroclaw. The de facto administration of these areas hardened into permanent rule. The transfer of the German population in these eastern areas was supposed to be effected in an orderly and humane fashion; but millions of Germans were driven from their homes or fled within a few months. For them (and for the Germans who were expelled from the Sudetenland) it was the final consummation of the war that Hitler had unleashed.

It was agreed at Potsdam that peace treaties would be signed as soon as possible with the former German satellite states; the task of preparing them was entrusted to a Council of Foreign Ministers representing the United States, Britain, France, the Soviet Union, and China. In the months that followed, the widening chasm between the Soviets and the West manifested itself in stormy meetings of the Foreign Ministers' Council in London, Paris, and New York, as well as in a peace conference held in Paris in 1946, at which were represented the twenty-one states that had contributed substantial military forces to the defeat of the Axis powers. Eighteen months after Potsdam, in February 1947, treaties were signed with Italy, Rumania, Hungary, Bulgaria, and Finland. All these states paid reparations and agreed to certain territorial adjustments. In 1951 a peace treaty was signed with Japan, but not by the Soviets, who made their own peace in 1956. The years went by but no final peace treaty was signed with Germany, a Germany divided into two. For the wartime Western-Soviet coalition had fallen apart, shattering the dreams and aspirations of those who had fought the Second World War to a resounding triumph over one kind of aggression and totalitarianism, and then found themselves confronted with a new age of crisis.

The Modern World in Varied Settings

Evidences of modernity have spread by the late twentieth century to all parts of the world. Among them are airplanes and oil derricks, computer technology and carbonated soft drinks, such as may be seen in different continents in the following pages.

There is a new global uniformity in certain aspects of civilization. It is no longer a matter of Westernization, as used to be said of what happened in Japan and Russia, nor of the Americanization of the world that has sometimes been pointed to with alarm. It is a process in which Europeans and Americans have been instrumental, but which arises from the effects of modern science, engineering, medicine, transportation, television, and almost instantaneous communications. It seems that human beings of all cultures and races may develop an aptitude to pursue these activities, and that they have wants that such activities can supply.

But as modern civilization becomes more widespread it must adapt to a variety of traditional cultural settings, which must in turn adapt to it. Cultures interpenetrate each other. Older ones are eroded not only in Asia and Africa but in the West itself, where practices that have characterized Europe at least since the Renaissance—in painting, sculpture, architecture, literature, religion, personal values, child rearing, and family life—have increasingly been called into question. Some may resist modernization by reaffirming their own identity, and so may feel a new attachment to their own background, especially in religion. Accepting the interdependence of a world civilization, they strive not only for political but for cultural and spiritual independence.

To operate an airline, or any other appurtenance of modern civilization, requires a high degree of accuracy, division of labor, and the synchronization of the efforts of many persons who must perform certain actions at a given time. These in turn presuppose the objectivity of knowledge and rationality of behavior, and an acceptance of discipline, foresight, organization, and management. But these very qualities generate their opposite. It is a paradox that new philosophies of subjectivity and irrationalism, revolts against form, and demands for free self-expression have also been thought of as signs of modernity in the twentieth century. Organization restricts liberty, yet is necessary to modern life. It is not easy to adapt to the social environment created to improve the human condition. The paradox is as old as Rousseau, yet is felt increasingly every day.

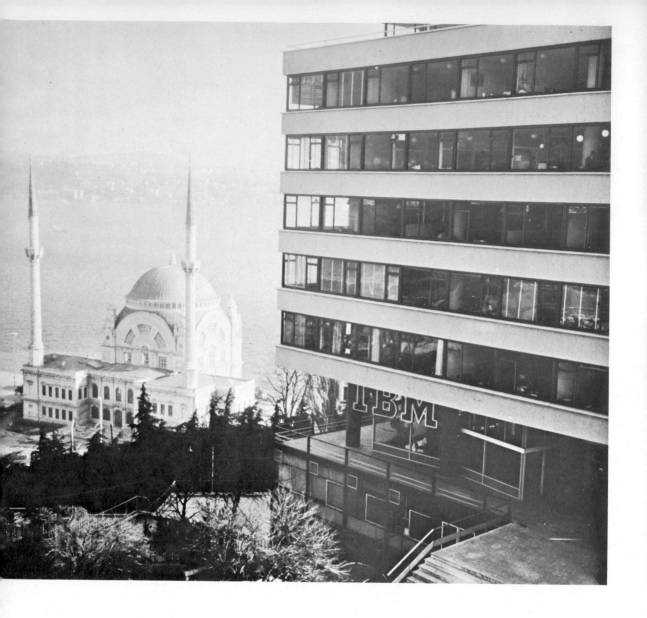

The office of International Business Machines seems in strange company alongside the mosque in Istanbul, Turkey, but it would seem no more so alongside a Gothic church in Europe. Here there is the additional juxtaposition of East and West.

Nigeria, the most populous state in Black Africa, has become one of the most important producers and exporters of crude oil. Here is an oil derrick in the swampy area of the delta of the Niger river. As other countries become dependent on Nigeria for energy, so Nigeria becomes vulnerable to fluctuations in the demand for oil.

The older centers of industrial production in Europe, North America, and Japan all feel the pressure from newer competitors. Here Brazilian workers assemble a Volkswagen in São Paulo.

Right: Pope John Paul II upholds the traditional values of Roman Catholic Christianity by using the most advanced technology in his frequent travels. He is shown here arriving in Warsaw.

Below: At Jiddah on the Red Sea, now a city with high rise apartments, automobiles, and parking problems, a group of Muslims engage in one of the daily prayers prescribed by Islam. They may be on their way to Mecca, only a few miles away.

The assumptions underlying Western art since the Renaissance have perhaps been abandoned most fully in sculpture. The statue which celebrated a great man or an allegorical figure from the fifteenth century through the nineteenth has become even more rare than the realistic portrait painting; it might even be thought ludicrous today.

Henry Moore, at the left, born in England in 1898, is one of the leading sculptors of the twentieth century. He is shown in a room where he keeps his collection of plaster maquettes, the working models for the finished products over his long career. As early as 1920, breaking with European traditions of sculpture, he became interested in the art of pre-Columbian America, Black Africa, and archaic or preclassical Greece. The models on these shelves reveal influences of this kind. In the quest for a new accent, for boldness of line or emphatic abstraction, the modern and the primitive come together.

Above: Ayatollah Khomeini's revolution in Iran brought out violent anti-Western demonstrations. Depicted here is a group of Iranian women, wearing the chador to assert their traditional Islamic values, which they mean to enforce with these modern and imported weapons.

Left: One effect of modern medicine and public hygiene has been a huge growth of population. At New Delhi in India a large sign, promoting a government campaign for family planning, poses a question: Do you want joy and comfort with two children, or destitution with four?

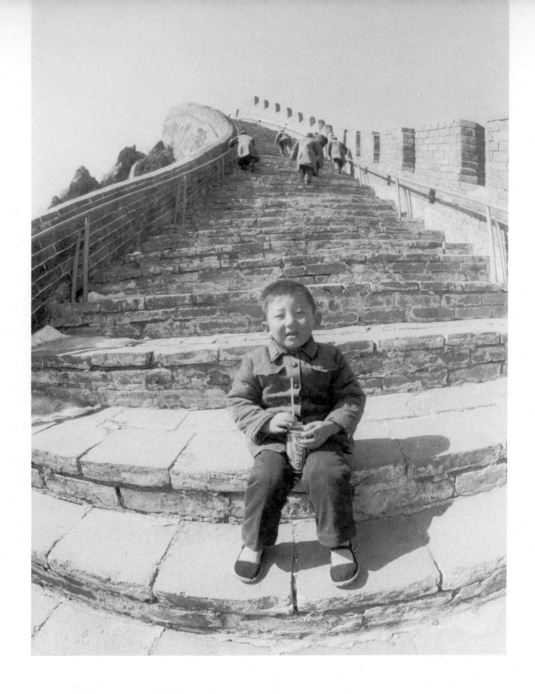

Above: Life goes on as this Chinese boy enjoys a Western beverage while sitting on the Great Wall of China, built two thousand years ago to protect Chinese culture from the barbarians of that day.

Right: Two youths work on a computer problem at Ibadan University in Nigeria. Their costumes reflect their own time and place, but the young man at the right shows a concentration and perplexity that are universal. Ibadan University is relatively new, dating from 1962, but the multiplication of universities, with their attendant problems, is a sign of modernization in all countries.

A Japanese super-express passes Mt. Fuji between Tokyo and Osaka. Some forms of modernization have been introduced sooner in Japan than in Europe or North America.

Right: These apartments in the South Bronx in New York City, built at the beginning of the present century, have proved less durable than most human constructions. The decay is not in the masonry of the buildings but in economic and social conditions.

Below: This pyramid at Giza, near Cairo, was built about 2500 B.C., some two thousand years before the introduction of the camel into Egypt and more than four thousand before the motor car. It will outlast "modern times."

XXI.
The
Contemporary
Age: Cold War,
Communism,
and Colonial
Revolution

A cataclysm, according to Webster's dictionary, is "any violent change involving sudden and extensive alterations of the earth's surface; hence, any upheaval, especially a social or political one." A cataclysm in nature, as we may imagine it, is a time when volcanoes erupt, earthquakes rumble, old mountain systems are broken down, new peaks and ranges thrust themselves upward, the very coastlines assume new shapes, living creatures flee from destruction, old forms of life become extinct, and new forms of life, at first unnoticed, enter upon careers in which they are later to flourish. The human world has been in the grip of such a cataclysm since 1914. The two World Wars, the Russian and Chinese Revolutions, the Great Depression, the Nazi and Fascist dictatorships, the Hiroshima bomb, the end of the European colonial empires in Asia and Africa, and the emergence of dozens of new nations—all are part of the changes that have altered the coastlines of modern human society beyond recognition, and for which "cataclysm" is not too strong a word.

Many of the changes have taken place since 1945. It is difficult to do justice to the complexities of recent history and to keep current with the onrushing events of our own times. The following two chapters attempt to sketch the most memorable developments of what we have called the contemporary age.

Chapter Emblem: The earth as seen from a satellite 22,300 miles away, transmitting a photograph to a station in North Carolina.

109. THE COLD WAR AND THE RECOVERY OF WESTERN EUROPE

Peoples and Nations

Broadly speaking, the world in the second half of the twentieth century faced no wholly new problems, yet certain problems that had troubled mankind for over a century became even more complex and more urgent. Three can be singled out— science, the organization of industrial society, and national sovereignty.

The problem of science was dramatized by the atomic bomb. The world shuddered at the instantaneous destruction of Hiroshima. The postwar contest to produce even more sophisticated atomic and hydrogen bombs spurred the realization that a third world war would be unimaginably more awful. The use of intercontinental guided missiles, electronic controls, proximity fuses, and probably biological warfare could be foreseen. Human beings now possessed the means to annihilate not only their civilizations but even human existence on the planet. This thought was especially shocking to a world that had set its highest values on scientific progress.

The problem of science was not new. Science, and its partner, invention, had for a long time transformed both industry and war. It had conquered many of the dreaded plagues and diseases of the world. Observant people had long known that science could be applied either constructively or destructively. It was the magnitude of destructive possibilities that made formerly indifferent persons now worry over the problem. The accumulation of scientific knowledge, instead of heightening the quality of human life, had taken on the ghastly distortions of a nightmare. Scientists themselves, after the first atomic explosion, affirmed the need for a moral regeneration. They insisted that science was neutral, free from blame for the horror of Hiroshima, that the trouble lay not with science but the uses to which scientific knowledge was put.

The problem of organizing industrial society was also unresolved. There were in theory two opposite social poles. At one, best represented by the U.S.S.R., all capital was owned by the state and supplied to workers as needed, and all interchange was carefully planned by public authorities in advance. At the other pole, best demonstrated by the United States, capital was owned by private persons who chose the channels of investment and hence determined the availability of jobs, and interchange took place through the mechanism of the market. Neither system was pure in practice, and mixed economics became the rule in many countries, but the differences remained pronounced. The chief drawback in the Soviet system was its lack of freedom, in the American its lack of stability and economic security. Americans spent a good deal more time trying to correct the lack of security than the Soviets did in trying to correct the lack of freedom.

Another question hinged on the unity and diversity of the modern world. Was the modern world really "one world," or was it not? It was one world in the sense that it required a good deal of economic exchange, political events affected the whole globe, and world cultures interacted as never before. But it was far from homogeneous; all admired the steam turbine, and stood in awe of nuclear fission, but beyond the material level schemes of values diverged. No people wished to be subordinated to another or to lose its way of life in a uniform world civilization. Here lay the root of the problem of national independence and of its corollary, world organization.

After the Second World War, as after the First, an international organization was set up to prevent war in the future.[1] A conference of all anti-Axis powers, held at San Francisco in 1945, established the United Nations and drew up its Charter. The new organization was designed to maintain international peace and security, encourage cooperation in solving international social, economic, and cultural problems, and work for equality and the expansion of human freedom. Of its numerous agencies, two were central. The General Assembly was a deliberative body in which all member states, however small, were considered equal. The Security Council, whose primary responsibility was to preserve peace, consisted of fifteen members, the five Great Powers who were permanent members, and ten rotating members chosen by the Assembly for two-year terms. Apart from the United States and the U.S.S.R., it was not easy to define the Great Powers in 1945, but the permanent seats were assigned to the United States, the Soviet Union, Great Britain, France, and Nationalist China.

Each permanent member had a veto power. Thus the Security Council could act on important matters only if the Great Powers were unanimous. Although widely criticized, the veto was considered necessary. In major crises the agreement of the Great Powers would be needed to maintain world peace. The U.S.S.R. demanded the veto most frankly (and used it most freely), but the United States, too, would not have joined without this safeguard. Many remembered that the old League was weak because the United States had never joined, and the Soviet Union had been admitted only belatedly. In the following years even small countries refused to abide by judgments of the United Nations. The fact was that no nation, large or small, was willing to forgo its independence or submerge itself in a world state with authority to put down violence anywhere— as the national state could do within its own borders.

The United Nations had fifty-one original members—the countries involved in some way in the war against the Axis. Its headquarters was located in New York. The Charter provided for the admission of new members, including the former Axis countries and their satellites, and also wartime neutrals, so that it could be truly international. From 1947 to 1955 a few additional states were admitted, in 1955 sixteen additional nations, and then in the following decades, with decolonization, the organization expanded to over three times its original number. Not only in membership but in other ways the United Nations, and especially the General Assembly, evolved along lines unanticipated in 1945. But for the most part, in the postwar period, it was the rivalry between the two superpowers, the United States and the Soviet Union, that frustrated efforts to bring about disarmament and peace.

The Struggle for Europe

The Second World War, in effect, left only two Great Powers still standing in any strength, the United States and the Soviet Union. Since the seventeenth century the world has normally had about a half-dozen Great Powers. That there were only two in the years after 1945 made a great difference. Moreover, the two were superpowers, continental land giants, possessing enormous resources and military strength, overshadowing all other states, including the powers of Europe that had

---

[1] See pp. 688, 695, 825.

long been dominant in the modern centuries. The characteristic of a two-state system, not found in a multiple-state system, is that each superpower knows in advance who its only dangerous enemy can be. In such a situation diplomatic delicacy breaks down. Measures taken by either power for its security seem to be provocations to the other. After the war the United States and the U.S.S.R. fell into this unhappy dualistic relationship; a diplomatic and ideological clash of interests and ideas set in that came to be known as the Cold War.

At the close of hostilities Russian armies occupied eastern Europe as far west as the river Elbe; American, British, and French armies held the remainder of Germany, most of Austria, and all of Italy.[2] The movement of ground armies during the fighting generally determined the spheres of influence after the peace, except that the four Allied powers shifted troops in order to occupy the zones of Germany agreed upon at Potsdam. The Soviets in August 1945, as agreed to at Yalta, declared war on Japan; they then moved into Manchuria and Korea. In the two years following the war, from 1945 to 1947, they pressed the Turks for joint control of the Turkish straits; supported the Communists in a civil war in Greece; forced Communist governments upon the countries of eastern Europe; refused to cooperate in economic policies for occupied Germany; installed a Communist regime in East Germany; and rejected atomic disarmament proposals. In Asia they lent aid to separatists in northern Iran, supported Communist-led independence movements in French Indochina and elsewhere, and helped to establish a Communist regime in North Korea.

It was not possible for anyone (even in the U.S.S.R.) to know what Stalin and his associates in the Kremlin really believed or intended. Probably, as confirmed Marxist-Leninists, they considered a clash between the U.S.S.R. and the Western powers to be inevitable at some indefinite future date. Probably they were disturbed by the American monopoly of the atomic bomb, and possibly by the economic strength of American capitalism, which might seek to recapture markets in eastern Europe and elsewhere. Probably they felt that the fluid postwar situation gave them a chance to establish an outer buffer zone favorable to the U.S.S.R., a program on which they had already embarked in their alliance with Germany in 1939, which had allowed them to absorb eastern Poland and the Baltic states (or to reabsorb them, since these regions had been Russian for over a century before 1918). Probably they saw in the aftermath of the Second World War, as in the First, an opportunity to advance the international Marxist revolution in Europe and Asia. Whether the Russians were acting defensively to protect their own national security or aggressively to promote communism on a world scale, President Truman and his advisers became convinced that the Soviets were embarked on a universal Communist offensive which it was their responsibility to halt.

One of the early casualties of the rift was a plan for international supervision over atomic weapons. To prevent the manufacture of atomic bombs the United States proposed an international control body with the right to send inspectors at will into all countries and to enforce sanctions, regardless of the veto, against any country found guilty of unauthorized uses of atomic power. To the Soviets the idea of having foreigners freely examine their society had always been repugnant. They declared that inspection would violate national sovereignty, and they questioned the good faith of the American proposal, especially since the Americans

[2] See pp. 818–820.

alone possessed the atomic bomb. Rejecting the proposal, they proceeded with their own atomic research, and by 1949 they were equipped to conduct atomic warfare. The atomic armaments race, universally dreaded, began.

The Soviet Union, to protect its interests in the United Nations, where the over-whelming majority at the time was consistently against it, made frequent use of its veto. From 1945 to 1955 the Soviets used the veto seventy-five times, the United States three. The United States nonetheless found the United Nations in-adequate as an instrument to check Communist expansion. With Britain unable to help in any meaningful way because of economic weakness, the United States formulated a positive national policy of its own to "contain" communism, com-mitting itself to new global responsibilities. In 1947, under the "Truman Doc-trine," it supplied military equipment and professional military advisers to Greece and Turkey, and announced a policy of assisting all peoples to prevent forcible capture of their governments by minority parties. That same year an American program of broad economic aid to all European countries—including the Soviet satellites if they would accept it—was announced; it was called the Marshall Plan, after the American Secretary of State George Marshall. The hope was that the economic reconstruction of Europe would prevent Communist gains from hunger and distress.

The Soviets for their part denounced the American capitalist and imperialist "warmongers." With the United States arming Greece and Turkey, with Ameri-can carriers able to sail the length of the Mediterranean or lie off the coast of Murmansk, with American air bases established or easy to establish in the Middle East, with the Americans in occupation of southern Korea and Japan and virtu-ally annexing Okinawa, and with the bulk of the United States lying across the North Pole from the vital centers of the Soviet Union, and the American capacity for long-range bombardment already sufficiently demonstrated, the Soviets felt encircled. Soviet suspicions—dating from Western intervention in the Russian civil wars of 1918–1920, the Munich Pact of 1938, the second-front controversy in the Second World War, the abrupt cessation of Lend-Lease at the end of the war, and other sources of friction—became inflamed.[3]

The great object of rivalry in the early postwar years was Europe. Europe, the main protagonist of this long history, was in ruins in 1945. The Second World War left it in a worse state of disorder than the First. Physical destruction was in-comparably greater. In the First World War trench warfare had thoroughly de-stroyed limited regions. In the Second the ground fighting devastated large areas and made a ruin of western Russia, and the air bombing reduced whole cities, especially in Germany, to piles of debris. The strategic bombing of the Allies had blighted the productive industry and transport facilities of the Continent. Goods, even if produced, could not be moved; millions of refugees sought desperately for an asylum. The war had ruined one of the world's chief industrial areas and brought its economic system to collapse.

In a year or two the worst local devastation was repaired, but the problems of transportation and exchange remained. Industrial Europe was unable to trade with agricultural eastern Europe or with the world. The Continent was in the position in which the First World War had left Vienna. Europe was a world metropolis, a kind of huge continental city, cut off from the areas with which it

---

[3] See pp. 715–716, 801–803, 812–813.

had carried on its trade. It had long lived by imports for which it could no longer afford to pay. Even more than in the First World War, Europeans lost their overseas investments, and overseas countries built up their own industries and needed those of Europe less.

At the same time, Europe was not to be written off; its combined population exceeded that of either of the superpowers, and even in ruins it possessed one of the world's leading industrial plants. One of the chief postwar questions was therefore the rescue of Europe, or, in practical politics, who Europe's "rescuer" would be. Europeans did not relish the prospect of being rescued by either the U.S.S.R. or the United States. Most Europeans regarded communism as slavery. In France and Italy, to be sure, almost a quarter of the people voted Communist in the early postwar years, and Communists held important positions in labor unions; but the number of those actually desirous of a Communist society was not large, and much of the Communist vote was a protest against traditional ways of handling social and economic problems. Social cleavages existed between the classes, but short of catastrophe, Europe would not go Communist. Nor was the number large of those who wished to be remodeled according to the economy or culture of the United States. Dependency even on the benefactions of the United States they feared as a gamble; remembering the depression of 1929, and how all Europe had gone down after the cessation of American loans, they had no desire to be dependent upon American capitalism. Europe wished to preserve its identity and its spiritual independence. But between the programs of the two superpowers there was the difference that the Soviets had more to gain by chaos in Europe, and the United States more to gain by its rebuilding. Immediately after the war the United States sent billions of dollars' worth of goods to relieve the distress of Europe and then embarked on the Marshall Plan. Its motives were much discussed and even impugned. In effect, the Americans satisfied their humanitarian impulse, found markets for their own industries, and reduced the drift of working-class Europeans into the Communist camp. The Marshall Plan made possible an amazing and rapid revival of industrial Europe.

The key to the rebuilding of Europe was Germany. The Ruhr was still Europe's industrial heartland. The former Allies had agreed to have common policies and joint control for Germany even though each occupied a separate zone. They agreed that Germany should pay reparations, especially to the Soviet Union, which had suffered most from German military power. The Americans, to make Europe self-supporting and less dependent on American aid, and overcoming French objections, came to favor the economic reconstruction of Germany. The Russians wished to use Germany to rebuild the Soviet Union. The Americans did not wish to pour aid into Germany to have it drained off as reparations to the U.S.S.R. By 1946 joint administration of Germany broke down. The Russians reaffirmed their hold on eastern Germany; the Americans, British, and French went their own way in the western zones. Each side competed for the good will of the late enemy. Each accused the other of partitioning the country in violation of their agreements.

In 1947 relations between the two superpowers deteriorated further. In France and Italy the Communists, who had earlier cooperated in postwar reconstruction, now encouraged quasi-insurrectionary strikes, and Communist ministers were dropped from the cabinet. Early in 1948 the Czech Communist party seized power in Prague, ending a democratic coalition experiment and turning Czecho-

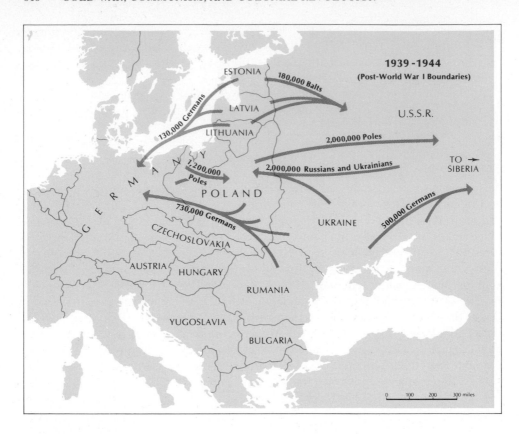

1939-1944
(Post-World War I Boundaries)

ESTONIA
180,000 Balts
130,000 Germans
LATVIA
LITHUANIA
U.S.S.R.
2,000,000 Poles
G E R M A N Y
1,200,000 Poles
2,000,000 Russians and Ukrainians
TO →
SIBERIA
POLAND
730,000 Germans
UKRAINE
500,000 Germans
CZECHOSLOVAKIA
AUSTRIA HUNGARY
RUMANIA
YUGOSLAVIA
BULGARIA

0   100   200   300 miles

DEPORTATION AND RESETTLEMENT, 1939–1950

The age-old distribution of nationalities in Central and Eastern Europe was radically transformed between 1939 and 1950. Not only were about 6,000,000 Jews put to death, with over 300,000 of the survivors emigrating to Israel by 1950, but millions of Germans, Poles, and others were forcibly uprooted.

The first stage, shown in the left-hand panel, began with the Nazi-Soviet Pact of 1939, after which the Germans occupied western Poland, while the Russians annexed eastern Poland and the three Baltic republics. Western Poland received Poles expelled from Germany, while in eastern Poland about 2,000,000 Poles were deported to Siberia, being replaced by about the same number of Russians and Ukrainians. Many Estonians, Latvians, and Lithuanians were moved to other parts of the Soviet Union. Germans who had lived in Eastern Europe for centuries were displaced. Thousands "returned" to Germany from the Baltic republics and from places in Rumania and elsewhere where they had long formed German enclaves. The "Volga Germans" and others in south Russia were sent to Siberia.

slovakia into a Communist-dominated regime. The Soviets forbade their satellites to participate in the Marshall Plan. In the summer of 1948, retaliating for the American, British, and French unification of western Germany and the introduction of currency reform there, the Soviets blockaded Berlin and cut off all rail and

A second stage (right-hand panel) came with the Soviet victory and the collapse of Hitler's Reich. The German-Polish frontier was now moved westward to the Oder River. Millions of Germans from east of the Oder, along with more millions from the Sudeten regions of Czechoslovakia and a continuing stream from Hungary and Rumania, were thrown back into what remained of Germany, most of them fleeing to the Western zone, but some to what was the Soviet zone in 1945. Poles streamed into what had been Germany east of the Oder; others came into Poland from the Ukraine. Russians moved into what had been eastern Poland and the Baltic states. Ukrainians and various non-Russian minorities were sent to Siberia. Some Balts escaped to the West (including the United States); others were redistributed to various places in the Soviet Union.

There was a considerable resettlement also of Hungarians, Slovaks, and Finns. The most conspicuous changes, however, in addition to the virtual disappearance of East European Jewry, were the expulsion of the Germans from Eastern Europe and a westward movement of Poles and Russians. (Source: *Westermanns Atlas zur Weltgeschichte.*)

road routes through East Germany to the western sectors of the city. The Western powers, notably the United States, responded with a massive "air lift," daily flying in thousands of tons of supplies. After almost a year, the blockade was lifted; but it was only the first of several crises over Berlin. Meanwhile, the

United States and the Western European powers proceeded with plans for the economic reconstruction and defense of Europe, and the U.S.S.R. drew its satellites closer together.

The Recovery of Western Europe

Under the Marshall Plan, which went into effect in 1948, American loans to Europe no longer were regarded as stopgap relief. American aid was coordinated with each country's policies and with joint European policies in order to enable Europe to stand on its own feet and play its own part in international trade. The United States also encouraged the Europeans to reduce tariff barriers against each other. Only by creating a free internal market could Europeans obtain the advantages of mass production and lower costs such as prevailed in the United States.

The results exceeded the boldest anticipations of its sponsors. The trend after the First World War toward high tariffs and economic rigidity, the United States taking the lead, had culminated in the Great Depression and with it had come an intensification of economic nationalism. Under the Marshall Plan the trend was reversed. Freer trade conditions prevailed among the participating Western European countries, and freer international trade as well. In Western Europe industrial production rose dramatically. By 1950, industrial production in West Germany reached and exceeded prewar levels; by the early 1950s the boom spread to France and Italy and, although to a lesser degree, to Britain. Western Europeans began to enjoy a remarkable prosperity; their economies grew at unprecedented rates, and living standards and consumption levels rose strikingly, even if not rapidly enough to satisfy all the expectations aroused. For over twenty years this economic growth and prosperity continued without serious interruption. The Marshall Plan was in a sense revolutionary; the United States used its economic resources to revive its competitors, but it served American interests also by restoring a world market, of which the United States was one of the chief beneficiaries.

Having received their initial impulse from the Marshall Plan, the countries of Western Europe took additional steps on their own toward economic integration. In 1952, under a French plan developed by Robert Schuman and Jean Monnet, the six Continental industrial countries—France, Italy, West Germany, Belgium, the Netherlands, and Luxembourg—set up a European Coal and Steel Community to control and allocate their coal and steel resources. Not only were the production results significant, but the supranational agencies established in Luxembourg became the groundwork for increased economic and political cooperation. In 1957, under treaties signed at Rome, an even more ambitious step by the same six countries created the European Economic Community, or Common Market, which aimed at the elimination of all internal tariff barriers, the development of a common tariff system with respect to the outside world, and the free movement of labor and capital within the Common Market itself. Moreover, the six signatories pronounced economic union the avenue to political unity. Under the same treaties, they agreed also to coordinate their atomic research and technology.

The Common Market, in operation by 1958, became one of the thriving economic aggregates of the world. By 1968 the last internal tariff was dropped; over 175 million people were joined in a large free-trade area. Britain, undecided whether its Commonwealth ties and dependence on low-priced agricultural imports made it feasible to link up with Continental Europe, at first refrained from joining. Subsequently, in the 1960s, its bid for membership was twice blocked by France, then under the leadership of General de Gaulle, who regarded Britain as a bridgehead for excessive American influence on the Continent and believed that Continental unity would be weakened by British affiliation; not until 1973 did Britain become a member.

Many were confident that Western Europe might move from customs union to political unity, as individual nations once had. The supranational economic and political machinery of the European Economic Community, the day-to-day cooperation of a European bureaucracy in Luxembourg, Brussels, and Strasbourg, and the close consultation on common interests, were favorable signs of European unification. The likelihood of any real European unity, however, was still remote. The European governments showed no haste to surrender their national sovereignty and independence. Moreover, in later years emergent sources of friction clouded the prospects even for continued economic cooperation.

The nations of Western Europe also made military arrangements with each other and with the United States, at first as insurance against any military revival of Germany, but soon directed against Soviet expansion. Under the Brussels treaty of 1948, Britain, France, Belgium, the Netherlands, and Luxembourg agreed to consult on mutual defense matters. In 1949 the United States took the lead in creating the North Atlantic Treaty Organization (NATO). The military alliance, of which the United States, Canada, and ten European nations were the original members, was soon joined by West Germany (after 1949, the Federal Republic of Germany), Greece, and Turkey. The United States agreed to supply equipment for European rearmament and to guarantee Western Europe against invasion. In 1950 the United States pressed to rearm West Germany. When a French plan for a European Defense Community (with a common "European" army, in which the German military would serve as "European" soldiers) failed to pass the French legislature, the Federal Republic of Germany was authorized to create a national army under the overall command of NATO. With American and British commitments to the defense of the Continent, and with European anxiety directed at Soviet expansion, concern over a resurgent German militarism was laid to rest; there remained, however, an agreement prohibiting Germany from manufacturing atomic weapons.

In less than a decade after the most devastating war in its history, Western Europe had recovered economically, regained its identity, and was advancing toward economic and political unity. The U.S.S.R. could not be expected to view with equanimity the reinvigoration of Western Europe. American encouragement to the unification of Europe seemed to the U.S.S.R. another hostile act. The Soviets drew their own satellites closer together. They formalized economic ties by creating a Council for Mutual Economic Aid in 1949, and consummated a network of military alliances in the Warsaw Pact of 1955. But these were only a part of the vast changes taking place in the Communist worlds that had come into being after 1945.

110. THE COMMUNIST WORLDS: EASTERN EUROPE AND THE SOVIET UNION

Eastern Europe, 1945–1953

If after the Second World War there was nothing so epochal as the Russian Revolution of 1917, the triumph of communism in Eastern Europe in the years after 1945 and in China by 1949 was equally momentous. Whereas communism in 1918 had been chaos, in 1945 it was the way of life of an organized Great Power. The Communist flare-ups after the First World War had flickered out,[4] but in 1945 communism materialized in Eastern and Central Europe, not through spontaneous popular revolution but through Soviet military strength and the backing the Soviets gave to local Communist leaders.

The Soviets came to control Eastern Europe in the sweep of military operations against the Germans in the last months of the war. The states that fell into the orbit of Soviet influence included Poland, Hungary, Rumania, Bulgaria, and Czechoslovakia; East Germany (after 1949, the German Democratic Republic) was also shaped into a Soviet satellite. In all these states Communist-dominated coalition governments were established, closely bound to the Soviet Union. Yugoslavia and Albania, liberated by their own partisan leaders and not by the Red Army, were governed by single-party Communist regimes but were not tied to the Soviet Union. Since the three Baltic states had been incorporated into the Soviet Union in 1940, an additional 100 million Europeans and eleven European states were under Communist-style governments after the Second World War. The areas considered in 1919 a protective buffer against Bolshevism were now under Russian domination. An "iron curtain" was said to have descended, roughly along the old Elbe-Trieste line, sharpening and deepening the centuries-old divergencies in the development of Western and Eastern Europe.[5] Finland, Austria, and Greece escaped Communist domination, Greece only after a fierce civil war that dragged on to 1949, in which anti-Communist forces, aided by a British army, defeated the Communists. Finland acquiesced in its wartime territorial losses to Russia, maintaining a discreetly correct relationship with the Soviets. Austria was at first occupied by the four wartime allies but regained full independence in 1955.

The consolidation of Communist control in Eastern Europe took place in stages. During the war it was understood that the power or powers liberating an area would temporarily exercise political control until the peace treaties were signed. In that way the Western powers controlled political events in Italy without consultation with the Soviets. In Poland, Bulgaria, Rumania, and Hungary, Soviet military occupation made it possible for local Communist leaders, many trained in Moscow and returning from exile, to dominate united-front coalition governments. In a state like Bulgaria, Communist domination was complete from the beginning. In the case of Poland, pressure at Yalta and Potsdam forced the Soviets to give some representation to the Western-sponsored government-in-exile then in London; the leader of the agrarian party returned to Poland as deputy premier. In the postwar coalition governments, the Communists shared power but held the key ministries of interior, propaganda, and justice, and controlled the police, the army, and the courts. Elements alleged to have been "fascist" or to

---

[4] See pp. 743–744.
[5] See pp. 204–240, 552–553, and map, p. 206.

have collaborated with the Nazis were barred from public life and even from voting. Although many of the nationalist and rightist political elements so excluded were undoubtedly guilty, the loose definition of "fascist" and "reactionary" made it possible to bar many who were only anti-Communist. In the first elections, in Poland and elsewhere, purges and disfranchisement of political "undesirables" made a mockery of Stalin's pledge at Yalta to hold free and unfettered elections in Eastern Europe. This the United States and Great Britain pointed out in strong but ineffectual protests.

The new regimes introduced important reforms. Continuing the land distribution programs begun after the First World War under non-Communist regimes,[6] they confiscated and redistributed numerous large estates and put uncultivated land to use so that 3 million peasant families acquired about 6 million acres of land; the agrarian reforms were the final blow to the landed aristocracy that had once ruled in the east. Relatively inefficient small farms probably would not raise productivity, but the reforms, pressed by the agrarian and small landowners' parties, were popular. The new regimes, taking advantage of the fact that industry had been in foreign hands or run by collaborators, also nationalized much of the economy. Struggling with the burden of postwar reconstruction, they even lent a sympathetic ear to the American invitation in the summer of 1947 to accept Marshall Plan aid. But Stalin was not disposed to permit these countries to drift into the Western economic orbit, nor did he view favorably the growing strength of the small landowners, or the movement toward free elections in which the Communists could lose their hold. After the summer of 1947, wherever non-Communist elements were still strong, the Communists ousted their political rivals, banned or reduced to impotence all other political parties, and set up single-party Communist regimes, which were styled "people's democracies." In Czechoslovakia, where liberal leaders like Eduard Beneš and Jan Masaryk (the son of the country's prewar president) hoped for a time that their country would serve as a bridge between the Soviets and the West, the coalition government lasted longer than elsewhere but ended with a Communist coup in February 1948 and the death of the young Masaryk.

With the Communists in control, the leaders of the opposition political parties, especially the agrarian leaders, were forced into flight, imprisoned, or in other ways silenced. The people's democracies clashed also with the Catholic church; high-ranking prelates were denounced, brought to public trial and imprisoned, and church property confiscated. As in the Russian Revolution, the Communist leaders themselves soon became victims. From 1949 to 1953, reflecting the tightening repression in the Soviet Union itself in Stalin's last years, there occurred in the highest ranks of each party the familiar pattern of purges, arrests, trials, confessions, and executions. Party leaders were accused of nationalist deviations and of conspiring with Tito, the independent-minded Communist leader of Yugoslavia. Later, after Stalin's death, many received the somewhat dubious consolation of posthumous rehabilitation.

The tempo of change quickened under the new regimes. As in the Soviet Union collectivization of land was a prelude to industrialization; collectivization and mechanization would enable fewer farms to produce more crops, release surplus workers for industrial production, and provide capital from agricultural

[6] See pp. 744–745.

surpluses for industrial investment. Though never applied as brutally as in the Soviet Union in 1929, collectivization was accompanied by pressure and coercion. The results varied. In Bulgaria, the most docile of the satellites, over half the arable land was collectivized by the end of 1952, but in Hungary by 1953 only about a third. In Poland, where resistance was strongest, collectivization was halted, and 85 percent of the land remained in private possession. Collectivization delayed the postwar recovery of Eastern Europe, and agriculture in that region, no less than in the Soviet Union, remained the weakest part of the socialist economies. Peasants diligently cultivated the land permitted them on an individual basis and worked reluctantly on the large collectives. On the other hand, industry made striking gains. The Eastern European countries all launched Soviet-type five-year plans. But because of the emphasis on heavy industry and pressures to contribute to the economy of the Soviet Union, industrialization for a number of years brought little improvement in living standards; in the last years of Stalin's life, economic and national discontent mounted in the Soviet Union's Eastern European satellites.

For a time the policies of the new regimes were coordinated through a new international organization created in 1947 and given the innocuous name of the Cominform, or Communist Information Bureau. Although more loosely organized than the Comintern,[7] which had been dissolved by Stalin in 1943 as a gesture of wartime harmony, it became the chief center of the propaganda war against the West until its dissolution in 1956. The relationship of the people's democracies to the Soviets was formalized also by military alliances under the Warsaw Pact and by trade agreements and economic projects under the Council for Mutual Economic Aid, which, to the chagrin of the satellite states, principally benefited the Soviet Union.

In the early postwar years, Yugoslavia, freed from the Nazis largely by its own partisan armies, made a remarkable and successful show of resistance to the Soviets. The Yugoslav Communist leader, Marshal Tito, built a more flexible and less centralized Communist society in his own country. Demonstrating the centrifugal power of nationalism even in the Communist international order, he openly defied Moscow. The Soviet leadership excommunicated and anathematized the heretic in 1948, and then after Stalin's death sought to woo him back to the fold. The first major Communist figure to declare his independence of Moscow, Tito established a model that other Communist leaders and parties would later follow.

The Soviet Union: The Post-Stalin Era

In March 1953 Russia's twentieth-century Peter the Great died. Stalin's accomplishments during his close to thirty years in power had been massive—the industrialization of Russia, the rallying of the country in the Great Patriotic War, postwar reconstruction, and the expansion of communism.[8] At the same time it was Stalin's mistrust of the West and his rigidity that aggravated the tensions of the postwar international atmosphere and the Cold War. Inside his own country his dictatorial ruthlessness and paranoid suspicions, growing sharper with the passage of years, filled even his closest associates with dismay. Economic reconstruction

[7] See pp. 736–738.
[8] See pp. 725–733, 808, 814–827, 843–846.

after the war was accompanied by tightened ideological restrictions. Controls over all phases of intellectual life multiplied and grew more repressive. The emphasis was vehemently nationalistic and xenophobic; deviations in economics, music, genetics, linguistics were condemned on grounds of "cosmopolitanism." An officially inspired anti-Semitism made an appearance, thinly disguised as anti-Zionism, and became a continuing feature of Soviet life. Plots were fabricated to create an atmosphere of terror, as in the revelation of an alleged "doctors' plot" in 1952, most of the doctors being Jewish, to poison Stalin and other Kremlin leaders. Forced labor camps were again filled with suspected dissidents. The Soviets claimed a leadership in technological inventiveness, denying even that the Russia of Peter the Great had ever been "Europeanized" by borrowings from the West.[9]

Three years after Stalin's death, Nikita S. Khrushchev, his successor as party secretary, in a speech to the party on the "crimes of the Stalin era," made partial but nonetheless startling disclosures of Stalin's dictatorial rule that confirmed the worst speculations of Western critics over the years. Stalin had been personally responsible for the purges and executions of the 1930s, the victims of which had all been innocent of the charges against them. He had built up a cult of personality around himself and created an atmosphere of terror so that his most intimate colleagues lived in fear for their own lives. His initial loss of nerve and ineptitude at the time of the German invasion in 1941 were also revealed for the first time.

After Stalin's death in 1953 a struggle for power ensued. At first Georgi Malenkov served as premier but the party leaders exercised collective control behind the scenes; all agreed that no one should dominate the regime as Stalin had. To prevent a seizure of power by Lavrenti Beria, head of the secret police and one of Stalin's principal lieutenants, the new leaders arrested and executed him. Malenkov, who tried to ease the austerity of postwar reconstruction by providing greater quantities of consumer goods at the expense of heavy industry and military needs, was ousted after two years. Marshal Nikolai Bulganin, who succeeded him for the next three years, was only a figurehead. Gradually, authority had shifted to Khrushchev, secretary of the party in 1954 and after 1958 head of the government as well. Rotund, jovial, and ebullient, he was in actuality a shrewd, tough, pragmatic realist who had governed the Ukraine for Stalin in the years from 1939 to 1950. His ascent was as much a personal victory as a triumph of the party over other competing institutions in Soviet society—the army, the bureaucracy, and the secret police.

In 1964 Khrushchev too fell from command, the victim of rebellion in the party at his accumulation of power, his economic failures, especially in agriculture, and his foreign policy miscalculations; ousted, he lived quietly in Moscow until his death in 1971. In replacing him, the party apparatus separated the top governmental and party posts, and again stressed collective leadership. Leonid I. Brezhnev became party secretary and Aleksei N. Kosygin premier. Brezhnev soon eclipsed all others, heading the party and for many years the government until his death in 1982. A tough-minded, unassuming, somewhat colorless political personality, he provided close to eighteen years of stability, quietly building the military strength of the country during a period of comparatively relaxed tensions with the West, overseeing a troubled but growing economy, and keeping a firm hand on dissent at home and in the satellites. A new constitution,[10] adopted in 1977,

[9] See pp. 227–238, 531–533.
[10] See pp. 717–718, 719.

made explicit the dominance of the Communist party and subordinated individual freedoms to duties and responsibilities to the Soviet state. After Brezhnev's death the party leadership, confident in its collective control, and with most other candidates no longer surviving Brezhnev's long tenure, chose as party secretary Yuri V. Andropov, head of the state security police but with experience in diplomatic affairs as well.

In the years after 1953 Stalin's successors softened many aspects of the older tyrant's reign and even rehabilitated the reputations of many of his victims. For a time the Soviet leaders permitted something of a "thaw," a greater literary and intellectual freedom, but nonetheless continued to maintain vigilant supervision. Controls were alternately relaxed and tightened. In 1958 Boris Pasternak was forbidden to accept the Nobel Prize in literature because his writings, notably *Dr. Zhivago*, which had been published abroad, implicitly condemned Soviet society by stressing individual freedom. Other intellectuals were similarly repressed and some imprisoned. The writer Alexander Solzhenitsyn, who himself spent years as a prisoner in forced labor camps after the war, devoted his prodigious literary talents to describing the human suffering in the world of the Soviet concentration camps—the Gulag Archipelago, as he called it. Forbidden to go to Stockholm to accept a Nobel Prize, in 1974 he was arrested, accused of treason, and forcibly deported. The physicist Andrei Sakharov, another outspoken critic of the regime, was also refused permission to leave the country to accept a Nobel Prize, and was the victim of continued harassment.

The finest minds and talents in the Soviet Union found the atmosphere oppressive. Although the arbitrary, capricious, and unbridled repression of the Stalin era diminished, the essential features of totalitarianism persisted. The control of the party pervaded all aspects of Soviet life, and many ugly features of repression, including the psychiatric confinement of dissident intellectuals and anti-Semitic persecution, were common. Soviet Jews, seeking permission to leave for Israel, were subjected to many restrictions.

The system of centralized economic planning inaugurated under the five-year plans of the 1930s[11] was resumed after the war. The Soviet economy continued to expand. Between the Fourth Five-Year Plan (1946–1950) and the Eleventh (1981–1985), once wartime devastation was repaired, economic growth, especially in heavy industry, was impressive, the gross national product growing at an annual rate of close to 5 percent over three decades, slowed down somewhat in later years by agricultural weaknesses. By the 1970s the Soviet Union was the world's leading producer of steel, pig iron, coal, cotton, and oil. Whereas in 1950 the Soviet gross national product was only 30 percent of the American, in 1975 it was close to 60 percent. The attempt to strike a better balance between heavy industry and consumer goods, however, was less successful; consumer goods amounted to little more than a fourth of the total economic output. The Tenth Five-Year Plan (1976–1980) stressed quality in industrial production more explicitly than ever before, a tacit admission of the previous emphasis on quantity alone and the inferiority of much that had been produced. The Eleventh Plan, anticipating a slower rate of growth, focused on labor productivity even though capital investment remained high. Under the later postwar plans, the government permitted a greater degree of decentralization in economic decisions and delegated authority to regional and

[11] See pp. 725–733.

local planning agencies, and even to management at the factory level, an admission that excessive centralization had hampered production.

Agriculture persisted as the weakest part of the economy. Despite massive investments in collectivized mechanized farms, agricultural production did not keep pace with industrial and urban growth. The system of collective farms failed to provide adequate incentives for increased production, and there was some evidence of the poor use, or even abuse, of farm machinery. Inadequate roads made it difficult to transport farm products to markets and processing plants. Production on the small, privately owned, half-acre plots, which the collectivized peasants were permitted to cultivate, often showed larger yields in proportion to the size of the holdings—as in the case of the farms in Eastern Europe. Harvest failures not only slowed overall economic growth but necessitated grain purchases from the United States and elsewhere. The difference in productivity as compared to American agriculture remained striking. Whereas one Soviet agricultural worker fed seven persons in the U.S.S.R., one agricultural worker fed forty-six in the United States; one-fourth of the labor force in the Soviet Union was employed in agriculture as against a comparable one twenty-fifth in the United States.

Expenditures on heavy industry and on armaments, as well as agricultural weakness—all features of the Soviet economy since the 1930s—made it difficult for living standards to rise in ways that might have been expected in an industrialized society. Yet living conditions improved in the three decades after 1950, consumption per capita tripling. People were better clothed and had a more varied diet. Some problems remained urgent, especially urban housing. Inadequate distribution systems and intense demand for consumer goods encouraged a black market and an underground economy. When harvests were poor, rationing was at times reintroduced. After more than sixty-five years of the Communist regime, despite industrialization and military strength that made the country one of the world's two superpowers, the Soviet citizen could still purchase only half the consumer goods and services that the average American could, and living standards remained well below those of the United States, Japan, and most of the European countries, including several of the East European satellites.

The U.S.S.R. also found itself lagging in newer industrial technology and in the late 1960s, in a significant economic shift, it welcomed capital investment and advanced technology from the Western countries. The future of the Soviet economy also continued to depend heavily on resources in its eastern regions. For cities like Kazakhstan, Samarkand, and Tashkent, the pace of modernization proceeded rapidly. The Asian parts of the U.S.S.R. furnished over half the country's iron and steel, cement, and hydroelectric power, and almost all of its magnesium and aluminum; rich new mineral resources were constantly being discovered, like copper, found in eastern Siberia in 1975. The population here was also growing rapidly, posing future challenges to the Soviet multinational state.

Soviet industrial advances were crowned by remarkable achievements in nuclear power and space technology. In 1949 the Soviets successfully tested their first atomic bomb, in 1953 their first hydrogen bomb, and they proceeded to build a formidable nuclear arsenal. In 1957 the U.S.S.R. successfully launched *Sputnik*, the world's first artificial earth satellite, alerting even the most skeptical to the advanced state of Soviet science and technology. In 1961 they orbited the first man around the earth and in the 1960s launched manned space flights of an extent and duration that for a time overshadowed American accomplishments.

Less efficient than the capitalist West in some ways, the Soviets could effectively marshal the country's resources for military and scientific objectives.

The People's Democracies after 1953

The changes in the Soviet Union after Stalin's death in 1953 directly affected the Soviet satellites. Riots in East Berlin that year served notice that the brutal exploitation of Eastern Europe for the benefit of the U.S.S.R. could not continue without protest. Discontent mounted over forced industrialization and land collectivization, and over repression by Stalinist-type leaders who continued to rule even after Stalin's death. The Eastern Europeans sought a relaxation of controls, economic concessions, and relief from their austere living standards. The ferment rose to the surface after Khrushchev himself denounced the brutal character of the Stalin dictatorship and, in an attempt to win back Yugoslavia, made the official concession that "different roads to socialism" were possible. The "de-Stalinization" program opened a Pandora's box; destroying Stalin's infallibility destroyed Soviet infallibility as well. In October 1956 open revolt broke out in Poland and Hungary.

In Poland the demand for greater independence emerged within the Polish party itself. The Polish Communist leader Wladyslaw Gomulka, once discredited and imprisoned for his nationalist deviationism, pressed for greater Polish independence. Khrushchev blustered and threatened military action, but backed down. Gomulka received wide backing in Poland, even from the church, most of the population viewing him as a desirable alternative to the return of Moscow control. He halted collectivization of the farms, curbed police terror, and for a time created a freer political and intellectual atmosphere; but this was only the prelude to continuing political ferment.

In Hungary events in 1956 took a different course. Only a few days after the news of the Polish success, rioting broke out in the streets of Budapest and other cities. The moderate-minded Communist leader Imre Nagy, whose earlier efforts to liberalize the Hungarian regime had failed, returned to power. He undertook a policy of liberal concessions, even freeing political prisoners, but the concessions only increased revolutionary pressures. When new riots erupted, threatening to end the Communist regime, establish parliamentary government, and cut ties with Moscow, Khrushchev dispatched an army of tanks and artillery, suppressed the revolt, and forcefully reestablished Communist rule. The tougher János Kadár, subservient to Moscow, replaced Nagy, who later was executed. The open show of force by Moscow in Budapest destroyed illusions about the benevolence and liberalism of Stalin's successors and shook the Communist faithful in Western Europe and elsewhere.

Despite the Hungarian episode and the limits placed by the Soviets on the independence of the satellites, many liberalizing changes were introduced after 1956. The Soviets allowed more flexible economic policies adapted to the needs of each country; the pace of collectivization slowed down. A freer atmosphere, most remarkably in Hungary, came to prevail. The government in Rumania, repressive at home, showed independence in foreign affairs and resisted Soviet pressures for closer economic integration. Of all the regimes, Czechoslovakia democratized its government more than any other in the late 1960s, permitting freedom of the press and allowing non-Communist political organizations to flourish.

Here liberalization went too far for the Soviets, who saw their grip on Eastern Europe threatened. They viewed the liberalization of the Czech regime both as a threat to socialism and as a subversion of the Warsaw Pact. In August 1968 they ended the "Prague spring." It was Brezhnev now who dispatched 250,000 troops, including token Polish, Hungarian, Bulgarian, and East German contingents, to crush the incipient revolution. The Czechs, stunned and infuriated, were forced to accept Soviet demands for a restoration of censorship and an end to democratization. The "Brezhnev doctrine" served notice that the Soviets reserved the right to intervene in the affairs of any of the East European satellites if communism seemed threatened, and that the satellites were to enjoy only a qualified sovereignty. It served notice also of the limits within which freedom and independence would be tolerated in Eastern Europe.

By the mid-1960s, the years of forced industrialization yielded important social and economic results. Eastern Europe was being transformed from a rural agrarian society into an urban industrial one. Consumer goods were in greater supply, often, as in the case of Hungary or East Germany, more abundantly available than in the Soviet Union itself. The German Democratic Republic emerged as one of the world's leading industrial powers; Poland's economy grew. Like the U.S.S.R. itself, the other East European countries sought capital and advanced technology from the West. All traded with countries outside the Soviet sphere and encouraged foreign tourists. The value of trade between the Soviet bloc and the outside world increased fourfold in the 1970s, and the East European countries borrowed heavily from the West. When in the general world economic decline in the mid-1970s, they could no longer export, they found it difficult to pay back these loans. In the mid-1970s the East European countries, like the Western industrial countries, entered a period of retrenchment and slower economic growth.

Meanwhile the countries of Eastern Europe were further loosening their bonds to the Soviet Union, but Poland once more learned the limits to independence and liberalization tolerable to the Soviets. Gomulka, who governed Poland for fourteen years after 1956, met continuing economic scarcities by reintroducing repression, persecuting the church, and even embarking on an anti-Semitic campaign against the small number of Jews still remaining in Poland after the Nazi wartime extermination. In 1970 Edmund Gierek for a time created a freer atmosphere which made it possible for an aggressive trade union federation, independent of party control, to flourish and win legal recognition, the only one of its kind in Eastern Europe. Called Solidarity, it had church and popular backing and counted 9.5 million members. When at a national congress in December 1981 it called boldly for free elections and for a nationwide referendum on the establishment of a non-Communist parliamentary government, the Soviets furiously denounced it and brought pressure upon the Polish government and party to curb it. A new Polish government imposed martial law, banned the widespread public demonstrations that had become common, and dissolved the trade union federation. The threat of Soviet invasion hung over the country if the Polish government did not itself end the agitation for freedom.

The successive acts of intervention in Eastern Europe shattered Soviet leadership of the world Communist movement. Tito had earlier rejected Soviet leadership, as had the Chinese Communists, and there had been protests by the Western Communist parties over the intervention in Hungary in 1956. In 1968 only seven of the world's Communist parties, in addition to those of the five participating countries, supported the intervention in Czechoslovakia. The large Communist parties of France and Italy openly protested. In the 1970s many Communist parties made explicit their determination to pursue an independent role in advancing communism. No longer was the U.S.S.R. an unquestioned political, social, and economic model. Loyal Communists questioned the bureaucratic inertia, cultural repression, and social inequities in the U.S.S.R. The once monolithic Communist world of the 1930s was becoming increasingly fragmented. A Reformation had taken place in Marxism, the authority of Moscow to speak for world communism succumbing to national and doctrinal challenges. Many of the West European Communist parties even repudiated the concept of the dictatorship of the proletariat as a universally valid goal, or necessary revolutionary stage, for all national parties. The Soviet Union, accepting the changed situation, nominally acquiesced in the theory that each party was free to find its own path to socialism, and that Moscow was not the sole interpreter of Marxist ideology. It was clear, however, that in Eastern Europe, where Soviet troops had already intervened, or threatened intervention, and where ideology and Soviet state power were blurred, Soviet authority could not be undermined with impunity.

When in 1979 the Soviet Union, alleging a threat to its security, suddenly invaded Afghanistan, its Muslim neighbor to the south, and a link to the Persian Gulf, it gave added evidence of its capacity for aggression and reinforced Communist skepticism about its claim to world revolutionary leadership. Although there remained sentimental attachments to the Soviet Union, it became commonplace for Western Communist leaders to criticize and even denounce Moscow.

111. THE RISE OF COMMUNIST CHINA

The Civil War

The proclamation of the People's Republic of China in October 1949 was among the most momentous of postwar events. The Communist triumph was the final episode in the long civil war between the Kuomintang, or Nationalists, and the Communists that began in 1927.[12] An uneasy alliance, formed between the two groups in 1937 to fight the Japanese, barely held together through the war years. The Communists had placed their armies under the nominal command of the Kuomintang. But retaining actual control and waging successful guerrilla warfare against the Japanese, they moved deep into the Japanese zones, organized villages and local governments along Communist lines, and mobilized support among the peasants through popular land reforms. The Nationalists deteriorated in morale and efficiency and lost popular support. Expelled by the Japanese from their industrial and financial bases in eastern China, they suffered from chaotic economic conditions, inflation, and outright corruption. To the growing strength of the Communists, the Nationalist government responded with repression that transformed it into an increasingly authoritarian regime.

The victory over Japan set the stage for renewed civil war. Nationalist troops, with United States aid, took over the big cities in eastern and northern China, but

[12] See pp. 758–759.

the Communist forces, moving out from their guerrilla bases, poured into the hinterland of the northern Chinese provinces and also moved into Manchuria, where they made contact with the Russians. The Soviets at this juncture, however, were maintaining correct relations with the Kuomintang and refused direct encouragement to the Communists. Mao Tse-tung, the indomitable Communist leader, declined to surrender the northern provinces, disband his army, or accept Kuomintang political control over the country; in the autumn of 1945 fighting broke out. An American-sponsored truce temporarily halted hostilities, but with the withdrawal of the U.S.S.R. from Manchuria in the spring of 1946, many months after it had pledged to do so and after it had removed Manchurian industrial assets as reparations, Nationalists and Communists again clashed over control of that important border province. The Communists were quite willing to plunge the country into civil war to achieve their ends, but it was also true that political power in the Kuomintang remained concentrated in the hands of an inner group bent on repressing all opposition, even non-Communist. One of the tragedies of the postwar era was that the anti-Communist forces in China, and in other parts of Asia, were themselves undemocratic.

In the fighting, which lasted for more than three years from 1946 to 1949, the Nationalists lost ground steadily. The United States gave large sums of money to bolster the Kuomintang but to no avail; the Nationalists seemed to lack the ability or will to resist. On the other hand, the Red Army, equipped with American supplies obtained through mass surrenders and sales by corrupt Kuomintang functionaries, moderated their propaganda to attract wide sections of the population and pressed forward. They routed the Kuomintang armies in the north and, moving south, occupied the Nationalist capital at Nanking. By the autumn of 1949 Nationalist resistance ended on the Chinese mainland and Chiang withdrew his shattered forces to the island of Taiwan, where with American help he established a small but soon prospering Republic of China, which for the next twenty-two years held the permanent seat in the UN assigned to China.

The New Regime

The Chinese Communist leader, Mao Tse-tung, and his lieutenants proceeded to shape the People's Republic of China. For twenty-seven years Mao guided the destinies of the new state, its national capital reestablished in the ancient northern city of Peking.

For the first time since the Revolution of 1911, and indeed for generations, a unified central government controlled China, able to direct and mobilize the most populous nation in the world. The Chinese Communists might be a small hardened group of successful Marxist-Leninist revolutionaries exercising supreme power over the submissive Chinese masses, but they were not as alien to the Chinese cultural tradition as many Westerners believed. They continued a long pattern of bureaucratic government that stretched back for centuries, articulated a universal hostility to Western imperialism that had all but carved their country to pieces in the nineteenth century,[13] and were the legatees of an ancient tradition of Chinese political and cultural preeminence in the east Asian world. With traditional ways of life already disrupted by revolution, civil struggle, and the war

[13] See pp. 638–645, 751–752, and maps, pp. 640–641, and 645.

against Japan, the Communists accelerated the disintegration of older Confucian values but provided a stability unknown to the country for years and launched one of the most extraordinary political experiments of the twentieth century.

The Chinese Communists leaned on Russian experience but added innovations of their own. They promulgated a Soviet-type constitution, providing a parallel structure of party and government, with party officials controlling each level of governmental organization. The apparatus of totalitarianism appeared. The party manipulated all organs of information for indoctrination purposes. Political education was accompanied by mass arrests and executions, forced labor, the liquidation of anti-Communist opponents, and internal party purges, styled "rectification" drives. In 1957 Mao conceded that in the first five years of the Revolution excesses had been committed and that hundreds of thousands of opponents had been purged. As the years passed, repression continued, but coercion was often less important in China than the mobilization of social pressures for conformity. Political opponents were rehabilitated rather than liquidated, and often permitted to return to positions of responsibility.

As the Soviet Union had earlier, the leaders of the new Communist regime mobilized the nation in a vast program of economic development designed to transform China from an agricultural country into an industrial power. As a first step, from 1949 to 1952, the regime restored and rehabilitated the war-devastated economy that it had inherited. At the same time it inaugurated a vast land redistribution program, establishing cooperatives as a preliminary to collectivization and eliminating the old landlord class. The country's initial Five-Year Plan was launched in 1953. Concentrating on heavy industry, the plan, with Soviet economic and technical assistance, had considerable success; substantial advances were recorded in the output of coal, electric power, iron ore, and steel. Not all targets were reached, especially not in agriculture, where the same floods and droughts that had troubled China for centuries refused to obey government decrees.

In 1958 a second, more radical plan, heralded as the "great leap forward," was launched. Faced with a serious lack of balance between the growth of industry and the lag in agriculture, the planners determined to continue industrial expansion and simultaneously to revolutionize agricultural production by mass mobilization of the countryside. Mao, the champion of the peasantry, was resolved to avoid the Soviet experience of industrialization at the expense of the peasants and small farmers. The government began to amalgamate the existing cooperatives into far larger and more comprehensive units, "people's communes," which would be responsible not only for agricultural mechanization and improvement but for local industrialization and many other social and economic functions. Intended to be a self-sufficient rural city, tightly organized in military fashion with a hierarchy of production brigades and battalions, the commune was to use the reservoir of local labor and resources to raise agricultural and industrial production. Communal kitchens, nurseries, and boarding schools were established to free women from household chores and child care so that they too could work on an equal basis in the fields and factories.

All kinds of obstacles thwarted the communal experiment. In 1960 the government, acknowledging the stubborn resistance it was encountering from a recalcitrant peasantry that had learned over the centuries to reject external compulsion, backed down. By 1961 the "great leap forward" was in retreat. With successive years of crop failures and deficiencies, some of which were caused by natural disasters, the government abandoned the communal program. Agriculture continued to be organized along collective lines, but peasants were permitted to sell or barter surplus products as an added incentive to production. Handicrafts and manufactures were still encouraged. In that way the regime industrialized the countryside itself, utilizing the labor power always available in rural areas. The government stressed the fundamental importance of agriculture as the necessary prerequisite for future economic development, but it did not abandon its ambitious plans for industrial growth. By the 1960s the Chinese economy had made significant progress toward industrialization. In the years before the Communist regime, annual steel production had never reached 1 million tons; by 1960 the official figures set it at over 18 million tons. Although per capita output was understandably low, given its huge population, China by 1960 already ranked among the top ten powers in the world in total industrial output. An industrial base for further expansion had been built even if only modest annual growth rates were achieved under successive five-year plans. Nor was the country's scientific prowess to be minimized; it successfully tested an atomic bomb in 1964 and a hydrogen bomb in 1967, and orbited unmanned satellites in the 1970s.

The most serious problem, as in other developing countries, was the pressure of the expanding population on the economy. Of all the larger developing countries, China was the most successful in coping with population growth. Through a unique system involving central directives and local controls, economic incentives and penalties, massive education programs, social pressures, and the ready availability of a wide variety of contraceptive devices, a slowdown in the birth rate was achieved, which in China's case significantly affected global statistics as well. Nonetheless it remained a serious problem. The Chinese population, one-fourth the world's total, was estimated to have passed the 1 billion mark in 1982, and was growing at a rate of 1.5 percent per year. The regime had to feed its enormous population. Through irrigation schemes, fertilizers, and the harnessing of the vast peasant labor power, the land was more efficiently cultivated than before. Nor were the cities permitted to swell with urban consumers; 80 percent of the population remained rural and worked the land.

The regime transformed life in many ways. Road, rail, and air transport physically unified the country. Impressive strides were made in public sanitation and in public health, which was highly organized and given a top national priority. Labor gangs systematically drained and filled infested canals. The government made progress in overcoming illiteracy, reforming and simplifying the written Chinese language, and moving toward a single spoken tongue. It also adopted a new transliteration system for Chinese names spelled in the Roman alphabet.[14] Women received legal equality with men and played a large role in political and economic life, sharing in the sacrifices imposed and the progress achieved in the new regime. Old abuses like child marriage and concubinage were outlawed. More profoundly than the Russian, the Chinese Revolution was refashioning the habits and ethos of a gigantic population, reaching remote villages and hamlets untouched for centuries. Within a generation an agrarian, semifeudal country

---

[14] The Pinyin ("transliteration") system, which more closely approximates Mandarin Chinese pronunciation, replaced the older Wades-Giles spelling in 1978. It is increasingly common now to see Mao Tse-tung rendered as Mao Zedong, the city of Peking as Beijing, Liu Shao-ch'i as Liu Shaoqi, Chou En-lai as Zhou Enlai, Chiang Ch'ing as Jiang Qing, Teng Hsiao-p'ing as Deng Xiaoping, etc.

was becoming a modern industrial society; the full transformation was promised before the end of the century.

For a decade beginning in 1966, in a period of great turmoil known as the Cultural Revolution, progress was seriously set back. The turbulence was unleashed by Mao himself. The aging leader, fearful that he would lose his grip after the failure of the country's more extreme economic experiments, or that the social revolution would not survive him, or that the purity of the Revolution would be tarnished by material success and a new elitism, called for a purge of the highest ranks of government and party, directed against all who lacked the zeal to push on with the Revolution, or who had succumbed to bureaucratic routine. A principal target of abuse was Liu Shao-ch'i, president of the republic since 1959, a leading party theoretician, and once Mao's heir apparent. In 1966 Mao and his closest followers, and most notably his wife, Chiang Ch'ing, mobilized hundreds of thousands of young people and galvanized them into action as Red Guards or shock troops to take up the Maoist revolutionary cause. Converging on Peking and other cities, they denounced the old ways, attacked the vestiges of Western imperialist culture, and harassed and humiliated their opponents. When the uncontrolled mobs threatened to tear the country apart, committees of party functionaries, army leaders, and government officials gradually restored order in the capital and in the provinces. But the Cultural Revolution continued. Because Mao proclaimed the virtues of the land, white-collar workers, students, and party officials were sent off to the countryside to till the soil and labor in the fields. The economy and the entire educational system broke down in the chaos. By the time the worst of the disturbances were over in 1969, thousands of lives had been lost, close to three million persons had been arrested and sent to labor camps, and more than two-thirds of the party's central committee had been replaced. Mao believed that his control was assured and his revolutionary legacy reinforced, but the country suffered serious reversals for almost a decade.

When Mao died in 1976, long ailing and in his eighties, he was widely mourned as the towering father of the Revolution and as one of the great figures in the centuries-old history of China. In dedicated service of over half a century he had forged a revolutionary party and a revolutionary army, led the Long March, defeated the Nationalists, and presided over a revolution that unified, transformed, and strengthened the country. His theoretical teachings on the struggle against imperialism and his practical successes in guerrilla warfare influenced revolutionaries all over the world. His homilies, published in a little red book called *The Living Thoughts of Chairman Mao*, were widely quoted and assiduously studied. Mao's revolution had brought equality for the peasants, emancipation for women, a sense of dignity for labor, technological progress, unity, and pride. But the uncontrolled violence he had unleashed was costly. As the years went by, his successors tempered their praise for Mao, lauding his monumental achievements but criticizing him for his errors—the radical utopianism of the "great leap forward," the excesses of the Cultural Revolution, the accumulation of personal power, and even some of his theoretical teachings on the need to continue the class struggle after the Revolution. They also imprisoned and put on trial his closest associates, whom they called the "gang of four," and rehabilitated many of those earlier condemned.

Of all the party leaders, Chou En-lai had complemented Mao most closely in the councils of government and party; for many years he was premier and foreign minister. Chou helped balance the moral and the practical aspects of the Revolution. He died a few months before Mao. Other once-designated successors to Mao had earlier fallen out of favor or had not survived. After Mao's death those close to him were pushed aside and a group of pragmatic leaders came forward, led by Teng Hsiao-p'ing, who sought to curb the more radical and utopian phases of the Revolution and who viewed modernization and economic progress as the country's necessary goals. Economic realities forced a slowdown in agricultural and industrial growth, but modernization and economic development, and not ideology, were the highest priorities for Mao's successors. They pledged to quadruple the output of the nation's farms and factories by the end of the century, and to stabilize population growth as well.

The existence of a second major Communist power, with the world's largest population and the world's largest Communist party (40 million members in the early 1980s), and championing the emergent nations of the former colonial world, further undermined the ideological leadership of the Soviet Union. The Soviets had not wholeheartedly supported the Chinese Communists in their civil war with the Kuomintang at the end of the Second World War, but once the Communist regime was established, the U.S.S.R. in 1950 surrendered the rights and concessions in Manchuria it had acquired by the Yalta agreement in 1945.[15] Relations between the two countries remained cool but correct. In the 1950s the Chinese were dependent on the Soviets for military aid, capital loans, and technical assistance. Hostility to the United States also caused the Chinese Communists for a time to draw closer to the Soviet Union. The Chinese Communists resented the United States' efforts to block them from representation in the United Nations and its continued support for the Nationalist regime in Taiwan; in 1950, as we shall see, they openly entered the Korean War.

Mao never considered himself subordinate to the Soviet leaders. He projected himself as a new prophet of Marxism-Leninism, adapting the "revolution" to Asian conditions, where the peasant masses and not the proletariat represented the engine for social change. After Stalin's death the Chinese Communists openly asserted their independence of Soviet control. Mao echoed Khrushchev's pronouncement in 1956 that there were "different roads to socialism" with: "Let a hundred flowers bloom, let a hundred schools of thought contend." Neither, of course, believed in toleration of differences or in mere ideological debate.

In the 1960s relations between the two Communist countries became strained. The Soviets, who were viewed as "half-Asian" by many in the West, were repudiated as Westerners by the Chinese Communists and denounced as "social imperialists." The two major Communist states were not only ideological rivals but disputed the lands of inner Asia into which Russia had expanded in the age of the tsars. In 1960 the Chinese Communists and the Soviets were hurling polemics at each other; in 1968 they clashed in armed conflict over border territory that divided Manchuria and Russia's maritime provinces, and continued to confront each other with large armies in these border areas. Not until the early 1980s were there even tentative signs of reconciliation. With the United States, diplomatic channels of communication were opened in 1972, following a visit to China by

[15] See p. 825.

President Nixon. In 1971 the People's Republic of China replaced Nationalist China in the United Nations and took a permanent seat as one of the Great Powers on the Security Council.

China was a vast new center of Communist power, with one-fourth the world's people. With the satellite states of Eastern Europe reasserting their national identities, and with the Communist parties of Western Europe pronouncing their freedom to criticize the Soviet Union and make their own decisions, a "polycentrism," unheard of in Stalin's day, had emerged.

112. EMPIRES INTO NATIONS: ASIA AND AFRICA

The colonial revolt in Asia and Africa, having built up pressure in the years after the First World War, reached a flood tide in the years after the Second.[16] The British, French, Dutch, and Belgian empires in Asia and Africa all but disappeared in the amazingly short span of fifteen years, from 1947 to 1962, and the Portuguese left Africa in 1975. In some instances the liquidation of these empires occurred peacefully, the imperial power resigned to the end of colonial rule, as in the British withdrawal from the Indian subcontinent. In other instances the Western powers withdrew only after long and protracted bloody wars, as in the case of the Dutch in Indonesia, the French in Indochina and Algeria, and the Portuguese in Angola and Mozambique. Everywhere the end of empire came as a result of rising nationalist agitation reinforced by the wartime Atlantic Charter. Western political ideas of sovereignty, independence, and freedom were blended with antagonism toward European whites and denunciation of imperialism. After the war Europeans could rule in their empires only at prohibitive military cost, if at all, and in blatant contradiction to their own professed ideas of self-government.

Asia: End of the British and Dutch Empires

The peaceful end in 1947 of British rule in India, the largest and most populous of all colonial areas directly ruled by Europeans, was epoch-making. The drive for self-government and independence gathered momentum in the 1930s and resulted in the grant of a constitution, a legislature, and other concessions to self-government. The British had also trained an Indian civil service to carry on the functions of a modern state. In the Second World War India rendered substantial aid to the British. To rally Indian support and to counter Japanese propaganda demanding the expulsion of Europeans from Asia, the British promised dominion status to take effect at the war's end, a pledge that did not satisfy the Indian Congress party leaders agitating for immediate independence. Meanwhile the Muslim League, which claimed to speak for 100 million Muslims unwilling to live in an India dominated by the Hindus and the Congress party, insisted on a state of their own. After the war the British decided on partition.

In 1947 the Indian empire was dissolved and the subcontinent was divided into two dominions, both of which shortly thereafter became republics—India, predominantly Hindu, with 350 million people at the time of independence, and

[16] See pp. 751–759.

Pakistan, mainly Muslim, with a population of 75 million. Because of the Muslim distribution in the old Indian empire, Pakistan (the made-up name means "land of the pure" in Urdu) had to be established in two disconnected parts separated by 1,000 miles of Indian territory; even so, almost 40 million Muslims were left in India, which helped keep India a multireligious and secular state. As the British had warned, independence resulted in bloody riots between the religious communities, forcible mass expulsions and migrations involving millions, and the deaths of hundreds of thousands. The uglier features of the communal rivalry subsided, although religious tension remained high and later flared up on several occasions. Relations between the two nations were also strained because of a quarrel that dragged on for years over the status of the disputed border state of Kashmir, a dispute settled by a partition agreed upon in 1972.

Politically, the Republic of India under Jawaharlal Nehru and the Congress party offered an example of parliamentary democracy, humanitarian leadership, and slow evolutionary progress in meeting enormous problems of poverty, overpopulation, and linguistic and cultural diversity. After Nehru's death in 1964 his successors continued his policies, but restlessness mounted. By 1966 Nehru's daughter, Indira Gandhi (her married patronym only coincidentally the same as that of the founder of Indian nationalism[17]), came forward as prime minister and as leader of the Congress party. Economic progress remained uneven despite significant growth in areas of industry such as steel production and in agriculture, where the country became close to self-sufficient in food crops. The huge increase in population, which nearly doubled in the first thirty-five years after independence, threatened always to outstrip economic advances. A compulsory birth control program aroused resentment. In 1975, when the courts found Indira Gandhi guilty of electoral improprieties, she peremptorily set aside constitutional government, proclaimed emergency rule, and silenced opponents by arrest and imprisonment. When she relented and permitted parliamentary elections in 1977, the opposition parties united to win control of the legislature and drove her from office. Returned three years later by the voters, she governed constitutionally. The courage of the opposition in combatting authoritarianism preserved parliamentary democracy in India.

Pakistan, after a decade of turmoil, came to be governed under a paternalistic military dictatorship. Despite a written constitution and parliamentary forms, there were few illusions about parliamentary democracy. The most critical problem, not unexpectedly, was the division between West Pakistan, where the federal government was located, and East Pakistan, the eastern part of the old Indian state of Bengal, 1,000 miles away. Friction between the two states exploded into secession and civil war. The eastern rice-producing state, with more than half the nation's population, was crowded into an area one-sixth that of the western. The Bengali political leaders of East Pakistan pressed for autonomy. When their demand was rejected, they proclaimed independence in 1971 as the new state of Bangladesh (or "Bengali nation"). The government in Karachi dispatched an army to suppress the rebellion; hundreds of thousands were killed in the unequal civil war and over 10 million refugees, mostly Hindu, crossed the border to West Bengal in India. But India intervened, quickly defeated the Pakistani army, and forced the recognition of the new state. Bangladesh remained impoverished,

[17] See pp. 755–756.

crowded into a small area with a rapidly growing population, and subject to political violence, assassinations, and military rule.

The other major parts of the British empire in Asia, Malaya, Ceylon (later renamed Sri Lanka), and Burma, also became independent in 1948, or shortly thereafter. Malaya (now Malaysia) suffered from a decade of internal strife that delayed independence until 1957; it joined in 1963 with Singapore and other former British dependencies to form a federation, but Singapore soon withdrew to become a small but thriving independent nation on its own.

Most of the new states in Asia (and in Africa), even after their progression from self-governing dominions to independent republics, retained a voluntary association with the Commonwealth of Nations, as the British Commonwealth was now called. The adherence of the newly independent states made the Commonwealth an even more flexible institution than it had been.[18] In the decades after 1947 it grew into an association of over forty independent communities, most of them republics, which accepted the British sovereign as symbolic head of the Commonwealth and agreed to consult, though not necessarily to act in concert, on matters of common concern. Although the new members of the Commonwealth lacked the tie of sentiment that bound Australians, New Zealanders, and Canadians of European descent to Great Britain, the Commonwealth remained one of the world's significant political groupings, helping to transmit Western technology, political institutions, and economic aid, and furthering the interaction of Western and non-Western ideas in parts of the world as far flung as the British empire had once been. Not all the former members of the British empire joined or stayed in the Commonwealth. Burma from the beginning chose to remain outside, and as the years went by, the Commonwealth lost Ireland in 1949, South Africa in 1961, and Pakistan in 1975.

Another great empire in the East, the Netherlands Indies, which the Dutch had been consolidating since the early modern centuries, also came to an end.[19] In 1942 the Dutch abandoned the Indonesian archipelago to the Japanese under humiliating circumstances. At the war's end the Japanese proclaimed Indonesian independence, and the Indonesian nationalist leader, Sukarno, who had been agitating for independence since the 1920s, took control. The Dutch tried to return and reconquer the country, and for four years there was open warfare. In 1949 the Dutch recognized Indonesia as an independent republic joined in a tenuous union with the Dutch crown; in 1954 even these ties were dissolved. In Indonesia, as elsewhere in the former colonial world, independence was won but constitutional democracy and economic welfare were not assured. Sukarno, elected president in 1949, governed dictatorially under a policy variously called "guided democracy" and "Indonesian socialism," setting aside the constitution, suspending the elected parliament, and exercising unrestricted powers as "president for life." Here and elsewhere, the leadership upon which the former colonial countries relied in the struggle for national independence turned into personal dictatorship once independence was won. After much bloodshed, including the slaughter by extremist Muslim groups of suspected leftist sympathizers, Sukarno was overthrown in 1966. His successors restored political stability, permitted national elections, and resumed some of the country's unfulfilled social and economic programs. Here, too, the population doubled in size in the three and a half decades after independence.

[18] See pp. 543, 775–776.
[19] See pp. 162, 635, 756.

End of the French Empire in Indochina

French domination of the colonial union of French Indochina ended in 1954, but not until after seven and a half years of fighting between French armies and Communist-led nationalist forces. The leader of the nationalist forces in Vietnam was the Paris-educated, Moscow-trained Communist, Ho Chi Minh, who, after waging guerrilla warfare against the Japanese during the war, proclaimed an independent republic at the war's end. The French in Paris were willing to concede a large measure of self-rule to the peoples of Indochina, but not independence. Negotiations broke down and fighting began at the end of 1946. Because the leadership of the independence movement fell into the hands of Ho Chi Minh and the Communists, the French could claim that they were not fighting to preserve nineteenth-century colonial privileges but to stem the tide of world communism. Yet the advance of communism in Asia, as distinct from its advance in Eastern Europe, was closely linked to nationalism, anticolonialism, and genuine popular discontent.

The United States, anticolonialist but ready to champion anti-Communist movements, gave considerable financial aid to the French but refrained from open intervention. The war severely drained French morale and resources. After a disastrous French defeat at the battle of Dien Bien Phu in 1954, a truce was negotiated, and at an international conference in Geneva the independence of Vietnam, Laos, and Cambodia was recognized. Vietnam, the state most seriously contested, was partitioned at the seventeenth parallel into a Communist-governed North Vietnam and a non-Communist South Vietnam. The partition was to be temporary, to last only until elections could be held. The armistice of 1954 proved to be an uneasy one. Vietnam remained in turmoil and an even bloodier war soon broke out, as we shall see in the chapter that follows.

The Arab States, Pan-Arabism, Israel

In the Muslim states nationalism also grew in intensity, as did the self-consciousness of the Islamic world as a political entity. The Muslim world included Arabs and non-Arabs and stretched from Morocco on the Atlantic Ocean to Indonesia in Asia; it embraced the Arab states of the Middle East and stretched north to include the non-Arab states of Iran and Afghanistan on the borders of the Soviet Union. Within the Muslim world the Arab states made efforts to create a united bloc. Syria, Jordan, and Lebanon (which had a large Christian population as well) emerged from the old Turkish empire in 1919 as European mandates and became independent countries after the Second World War. Iraq had been independent since 1937. Egypt, where the British for a time retained treaty rights, was in other respects independent.[20] In 1945 the seven principal Arab states, Egypt, Iraq, Syria, Jordan, Lebanon, Saudi Arabia, and Yemen formed an Arab League to act jointly in international affairs and to advance Arab interests. In the following three decades other Arab states joined so that by the 1980s the League had twenty-two members. Within this Middle Eastern area, Arab and non-Arab, lay two-thirds of the world's petroleum reserves, on which much of the economic activity of the industrial West and of Japan depended.

The Arab countries were aroused most by the emergence of a Jewish state in

[20] See pp. 625–626, 691, 775.

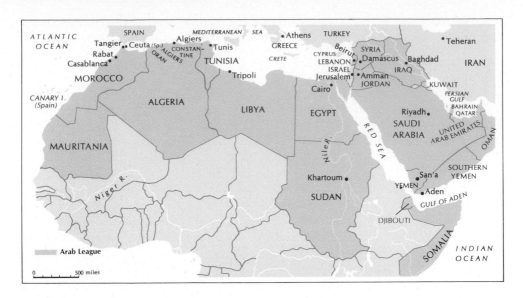

THE ARAB WORLD

The Arabic language zone is one of the most extensive in the world, reaching from the Atlantic Ocean to the Persian Gulf. In 1945 the Arab states formed a League, whose members are shown on the map. In 1983 there were twenty-two members, including the Palestinian Liberation Organization. The League has proved to be rather loose, with much disagreement among its members, but it has been opposed to the establishment of an Israeli state in the midst of an otherwise predominantly Arab world.

Israel. After the war the homeless survivors of the Nazi Holocaust sought out Palestine as a place of refuge that they considered pledged to them as a Jewish homeland in the First World War.[21] The Arabs objected to making territorial sacrifices because of Europe's persecution of the Jews. Britain, which held a mandate over Palestine, sought to placate the Arabs by limiting Jewish immigration. After unsuccessful negotiations, the British turned the problem over to the United Nations, which in 1947 voted for partition. When the British ended their mandate and withdrew a few months later, the Zionist leaders on May 14, 1948, proclaimed the republic of Israel but had to defend themselves against sizable invading Arab armies. At the cease-fire Israel increased its original territory by about half, taking over western Galilee in the north, a corridor of land in central Palestine to the city of Jerusalem, and the western part of the city, where they established their capital. Jordan meanwhile annexed land in eastern and central Palestine, including the west bank of the Jordan River, which had been designated under the partition for a Palestinian Arab state, and took over the eastern part of Jerusalem. In the founding of the Israeli state, over half a million Arabs were dispossessed and remained disgruntled; Israeli offers to relocate the refugees were spurned. To the Arabs, the state of Israel seemed like a new form of Western invasion of the Middle East. The Israelis saw themselves not only as creating a Jewish homeland to guarantee against another Holocaust but as building a bridgehead

[21] See pp. 602–603, 675, 820, and map, p. 872.

for Western scientific, technological, and democratic advances in an economically underdeveloped, semifeudal area. They succeeded in developing modern industry and in reclaiming vast stretches of the Negev desert, where they grew citrus fruits and other crops. They made progress also in creating a democratic society out of widely disparate elements and they developed powerful modern military forces. The Arab countries refused even to recognize the state and worked for its destruction. Four more Arab-Israeli wars were fought after 1948—in 1956, 1967, 1973, and 1982. All had international ramifications because the United States supported Israel and the U.S.S.R. gave aid to the Arab states.

Egypt at first took the lead in the holy war against Israel. When in 1956 the British evacuated the Suez Canal zone, the Egyptian leader Colonel Nasser announced that the canal would be nationalized and placed under Egyptian control. The British prime minister, Anthony Eden, haunted by the appeasement of the European dictators in the 1930s, retaliated with military intervention. Joining with him were the French, who were irritated at the flow of Egyptian aid to Algerian nationalists, then fighting against France, and the Israelis, who saw their security imperiled by permanent Egyptian control over the canal. The Soviet Union backed Nasser, as did many of the states of Asia and Africa who looked upon the Egyptian leader as resisting an old-fashioned imperialist invasion. When the United States refused to support the intervention, Britain, France, and Israel were compelled to withdraw. Although the Egyptians agreed to operate the canal on an impartial basis, they continued to bar Israeli shipping.

In 1967 the Egyptians moved to close the Gulf of Aqaba. This action, combined with the continued barring of the Suez Canal to Israeli shipping, threatened to strangle the Israeli economy, and Israel retaliated. In a quick six-day war the Israelis shattered the Egyptian, Syrian, and Jordanian armies, captured vast amounts of equipment, mostly of Soviet origin, and occupied extensive territories belonging to the three Arab states, taking over the west bank of the Jordan River and the eastern part of Jerusalem from Jordan, the Golan Heights from Syria, and the Sinai Peninsula and the Gaza Strip from Egypt. Over 1 million additional Arabs came under Israeli rule. The Arab states, smarting under the humiliating defeat, refused to sign a peace treaty or recognize Israel.

The Palestinian refugees added a highly volatile element to the situation. Concentrated in camps in neighboring Arab states, their leadership became increasingly militant, conducting guerrilla warfare, making armed incursions into Israel, and carrying on terrorist activities in many parts of the world. In 1964 they organized themselves as a government-in-exile, the Palestinian Liberation Organization (PLO), which became a member of the Arab League and received official recognition from many quarters, including eventually the United Nations. Refusing to recognize the existence of Israel, they professed to speak for 2.5 million Palestinians and demanded the establishment of a Palestinian state on the west bank of the Jordan River.

After the 1967 war Egypt received massive military and economic aid from the Soviet Union. When Nasser died in 1970 his successor, Anwar-al-Sadat, for a few years continued the tough line against Israel, but concerned over the Soviet penetration of Egypt, terminated almost two decades of close ties to the U.S.S.R. Though less flamboyant than Nasser, Sadat also tried to project himself as leader of the Arab crusade against Israel. In 1973 Egyptian forces surprised the Israelis by attacking on the Jewish holy day Yom Kippur, moved eastward across the Suez

Canal and established a bridgehead on the Sinai peninsula; Syria simultaneously attacked in the north on the Golan Heights. Israel, after recovering from the surprise attack, stabilized the Syrian front, and reoccupied the Golan Heights, crossed the Suez Canal, and trapped the Egyptian forces that had invaded the east bank.

With the Israelis near victory and in control of still more Arab territory, the oil-producing Arab countries supporting Egypt and Syria dramatically resorted to a new strategic weapon, an embargo on oil shipments. They hoped to pressure the United States and Western Europe into demanding Israeli withdrawal from all Arab territories occupied since 1967, including the newly conquered ones: Although the embargo was lifted a few months later in the winter of 1974, the oil-producing nations had meanwhile quadrupled the price of oil. The embargo and the rise in world oil prices opened a new era in international economic and political relations and had implications far beyond the conflict in the Middle East.

The United States and the Soviet Union both supported a United Nations resolution calling for a cease-fire. The war ended with an American-mediated settlement, the United States persuading Israel to withdraw from the occupied west bank of the Suez Canal to the east bank, behind an Egyptian zone and a UN-patrolled buffer area; negotiations continued on further withdrawals.

The united Arab front against Israel was broken when Sadat encouraged friendly relations with Israel. The other Arab states, rejecting any settlement with Israel, lobbied for Israeli withdrawal from all occupied Arab territories and even persuaded the General Assembly of the United Nations to adopt a resolution in 1975 condemning Zionism as a form of racism and racial discrimination—even though Zionism had come into being as a defense against anti-Semitism, and Israel as a result of the Nazi persecution of the Jews.

The conviction grew that unless a comprehensive settlement was negotiated in the Middle East, new and even more deadly conflicts would explode. To be settled was the demand of the Palestinian refugees for an independent national state, the recognition and guarantee of Israel's legitimacy and security, and the disposition of the territories occupied by Israel since 1967. Neither Sadat nor the conservative Zionist militant, Menachem Begin, whose party in 1977 displaced the Labor party in Israel for the first time since independence, seemed a likely spokesman for peace or reconciliation. Begin, more intransigent than many of his countrymen, encouraged the Israelis to make permanent settlements on the west bank of the Jordan. Yet he persuaded Sadat to visit Jerusalem, to the outrage of other Arab leaders, and he himself visited Egypt. With the encouragement of the United States, the two leaders signed the Camp David accords in Washington in 1979, closing thirty years of hostile relations. Israel agreed to withdraw from the Sinai Peninsula completely, which it did in 1982, and was guaranteed the free use of the Suez Canal. Many differences persisted, however, and Egypt also pressed for recognition of the PLO. Begin continued to encourage settlements on the west

ISRAEL AND ADJOINING REGIONS

"Palestine" is the term by which Europeans long designated a small region of mixed population, but predominantly Arab, which belonged to the Ottoman Empire until the First World War. European Jews, with the Zionist movement, began to migrate to it in the nineteenth century. In 1922 the League of Nations "mandated" it to the British, who tried to restrict Jewish immigration in an attempt to satisfy the Arabs. After the death of millions of Jews during the Second World War the Zionist idea of an independent Jewish state won increasing numbers of adherents. In 1947 the United Nations proposed a partition between Jewish and Arab states, with Jerusalem as a separate zone. The Arabs rejected the plan, and in the Arab-Israeli war of 1948 the Israelis won recognition of wider boundaries than those first proposed. The Arab states still refused recognition of Israel. In the Six-Day War of 1967 the Israelis occupied additional territory as shown in the lower lefthand panel. In 1973, in the "Yom Kippur" war, Egypt and Syria attacked Israel, but Israel defeated them and continued to occupy the Sinai except that in the peace negotiations that followed Egypt was allowed to regain the east bank of the Suez Canal, and a United Nations demilitarized zone was set up between the two adversaries. In 1982 Israel returned the Sinai to Egypt, but retained the small area known as the Gaza Strip.

bank, unified the Israeli capital by formally annexing East Jerusalem, and moved aggressively in other ways, alienating even the United States, his principal ally. When Sadat was assassinated in 1981 by fundamentalist Egyptian army officers, his successor was less friendly to Israel. But Israel now had to turn its attention to Lebanon, its northern neighbor, with which for many years it had enjoyed its only peaceful border.

Lebanon was in turmoil after two years of civil war, which began in 1975 as a rebellion of leftist Muslims against the moderate Arab Christians who, although a minority, controlled the Lebanese government. The war was rapidly transformed and enlarged. The Palestinian Liberation Organization, which had settled in large numbers in Lebanon after its expulsion from Syria for stirring up Arab extremists, entered the fighting. In the near anarchy, the authority of the Lebanese government disappeared. Syrian troops eventually intervened and ended the fighting, but the Syrians and the PLO now controlled separate areas of the troubled country. The Israelis felt menaced. When PLO guerrillas, based in Lebanon, made terrorist sorties, Israel retaliated, invading southern Lebanon twice and then withdrawing, and later bombing PLO strongholds. In 1982 Israel launched a full-scale land, sea, and air invasion designed to strike at the heart of the PLO. The Israeli army quickly moved north and closed in on the capital city of Beirut. The trapped PLO forces, after surrendering, were permitted to embark for various Arab states under the supervision of a multinational peacekeeping force. But the war was not over. When the newly elected president of the Lebanese government was assassinated, the Israelis, fearing new chaos, pushed further into the capital; in one tragic episode Lebanese Christian militia entered Palestinian refugee camps to root out remaining PLO guerrillas and vindictively massacred over three hundred Palestinian civilians. The Israelis, themselves divided over the aggressiveness of their own government, demonstrated against the war and forced a full inquiry into the civilian massacre. Although Israel had once again won a striking military victory, it was far from certain that its security had been strengthened, or that Syria and the returning PLO would not maintain their presence in Lebanon. The Soviet Union, which had not intervened directly in the fighting, continued to provide arms to Syria and the PLO. The United States, although impatient with many of Israel's unilateral actions, continued to support Israel but intensified efforts to mediate a settlement, difficult and elusive though that might be, that would satisfy Arab demands as well.

The Islamic Revival: Iran

In all parts of the Muslim world, Arab and non-Arab in Asia and in Africa, the older age of imperialism had ended. A powerful new sense of identity swept Islam. Pride in its great cultural heritage was reinforced by the huge wealth pouring in from its oil resources. It moved to redress its industrial backwardness by rapid modernization, but it was determined to share in Western material advances on its own terms. Arab states such as Kuwait, Saudi Arabia, and Libya were so rich in oil resources that they were pressed to help less favored Islamic nations. Within these countries, however, still elitist in social organization, wealth remained in the hands of the privileged classes and only slowly trickled down to alleviate the lot of the impoverished, often illiterate, lower classes. In many of the Muslim countries numerous obstacles to modernization remained, including traditional religious and cultural barriers to the full absorption of women into society. The pace of change in the Muslim world was uneven, and the Islamic countries differed very much from each other, but older life styles were visibly undermined everywhere by the new wealth, industry, urbanization, and the spread of education.

In some Islamic countries, where change occurred rapidly, resentments ran deep over modernization, the intrusion of the West, with which it was equated, and the destruction of older religious and cultural values. No one, however, could have predicted the deep fury of the fundamentalist Islamic and anti-Western revolution that shook Iran in the late 1970s when the Shah and the Pahlavi dynasty were overthrown by the followers of the Islamic religious leader, the Ayatollah Ruhollah Khomeini. Iran (or Persia) had had a long history of foreign domination and of movements to shake off foreign control.[22] The Shah had succeeded his father, an army officer who seized power and became hereditary ruler in 1925 but was ousted in 1941 for pro-Axis activities by the British and Russians. The Shah identified himself with the West. When the Iranian parliament and a reform prime minister sought to nationalize the oil industry after the end of the war, the Shah, with American and British encouragement, blocked them and assumed full control. Embarking on an extensive modernization program, he introduced Western-style industry and education and, with American aid, revamped the armed forces. Using the oil wealth of the country for his economic and military plans, he also received loans and technical assistance from the United States. At the same time he solidified authoritarian rule, crushing opposition from traditionalist clerical leaders (the *mullahs*) and from leftists. A ruthless secret police tracked down opponents, thousands were arrested and tortured, and hundreds were executed. The United States, pleased with the economic and military progress of its ally in a crucial area of the world, ignored the swelling tides of resentment. In 1978 the opposition forces coalesced and riots and strikes broke out. The Shah invoked martial law, but was soon forced to flee the country. The aged Ayatollah Khomeini returned from his exile in Paris and quickly assumed full authority. Revolutionary guards defeated troops loyal to the Shah. Although a constitution was written for a new Islamic republic, the Ayatollah and a clerical-dominated revolutionary council remained supreme. The revolutionary authorities revitalized Islamic ways of life: women were directed to cover their heads with the veil (or *chador*); alcoholic beverages, mixed bathing, and Western music were banned. Revolutionary justice took a terrible toll, with drumhead trials and immediate execution for religious or other offenses. For a time the schools and universities were closed and, when reopened, concentrated on indoctrination in Islamic fundamentalism.

Much of the fury was antiforeign and turned against the United States ("the Great Satan," it was called). When despite warnings the United States admitted the ailing exiled Shah, armed revolutionary guards and militants seized the American embassy in Teheran and detained fifty-two Americans as hostages for 444 days, insisting upon the return of the Shah and his wealth to Iran. The hostages were released only after the United States agreed to return several billions of dollars of frozen Iranian assets; the Shah meanwhile had died. Before long many of the highest civilian officials of the new regime, including the president and the foreign affairs minister, fled the country or were executed; some of the clergy themselves fell victim; bombings and other acts of terrorism were commonplace.

[22] See pp. 611, 638, 647, 751–752, 755.

In 1980 the country became involved in a war with Iraq. Whether the revolution would settle down or enter a military expansionist phase, whether the death of the Ayatollah would bring renewed chaos, or whether traditional Islamic values could be brought into balance with modern ways of life—all remained unanswered questions. The events in Iran, which threatened to unloose Islamic revivalism elsewhere, were unsettling to the entire Islamic world as well as to the West.

The French in North Africa: The Algerian War

The postwar history of Morocco, Tunisia, and Algeria (the Maghreb, as these Arab states of North Africa along with Libya are called) belongs at once to the history of the Muslim world, emergent Africa, and France. Morocco and Tunisia, never outright colonies, were French protectorates under their traditional rulers, the Moroccan sultan and the Tunisian bey. North African nationalists, who had been educated in France and had discussed freedom and independence in Paris cafés after the First World War, were bent on achieving these goals after the Second.[23] The decision by the wartime Allies to grant independence to the former Italian colony of Libya in 1951, and agitation for the British to end the vestiges of their control in Egypt, galvanized North Africa in the 1950s. To mollify the rising nationalist agitation, the French offered various political concessions and in 1956 granted complete independence to Morocco and Tunisia.

Algeria, however, the French considered an integral part of France; it was represented in the French assembly like any constituency of metropolitan France (except that the vote for representatives was heavily weighted in favor of the European settlers and to the disadvantage of the Arab majority). Of the 9 million inhabitants, at least 1 million were European settlers, or *colons*, mostly French who, like the family of the French writer Albert Camus, had lived there for generations. Since the European settlers controlled the economy and owned most of the land and industry, they feared for their political and economic privileges if Algeria were cut loose from France and governed by an Arab majority smarting from years of unequal treatment. At a moment when France and the French army had barely recovered from the disastrous rout in Indochina, large-scale revolt broke out in Algeria in the autumn of 1954.

The French-Algerian War lasted seven and a half years, involving 500,000 French troops at its peak, and costing the lives of at least 100,000 Arab and 10,000 French soldiers, and of additional thousands of civilians. The Algerian Liberation Front received aid and support from Egypt and other sympathetic Arab states. Torture and cruelty were common on both sides; the violence spread to Paris as extremist Algerians attacked moderates. The French were confronted with a choice of losing Algeria or of continuing to bear the military, financial, and moral strain of a divisive colonial war. In the midst of a prolonged cabinet crisis in Paris, an insurrection on May 13, 1958, led by die-hard settlers and army leaders in Algiers, brought General Charles de Gaulle to power.

At first pressing on with the war, de Gaulle spoke of autonomy for the Algerians once the rebellion had ended, then spoke of self-determination and a referendum when a truce had been arranged. In 1961 he won the backing of the French electorate for independence. Army leaders rebelled, and some of his closest former

---

[23] See pp. 621, 625–627.

associates helped form a secret army of terrorists that bombed and killed, and even attempted his assassination, but in 1962 French rule dating back to the 1830s ended.[24] After independence there was a mass exodus of Europeans from Algeria, but most of the French and Algerians were grateful that de Gaulle had ended the ordeal. The new regime in Algeria narrowly escaped civil war; for the first three years the country was under the authoritarian rule of an army-backed leftist regime, which nationalized much of the economy. After 1965 it was governed by a military dictatorship that emphasized rapid industrial development, in part based on the country's oil resources. The French accepted the loss of Algeria and, with a prospering economy, turned their attention to other matters.

Sub-Saharan Africa: End of British, French, Belgian, and Portuguese Rule

In Asia and in North Africa nationalist agitation for independence and the end of colonial empires might have been expected, but in black Africa south of the Sahara the movement for liberation was nothing short of breath-taking. In 1945, and even in 1950, Africa, politically, was scarcely different from what it had been in 1914: with the exception of Ethiopia, Liberia, and Egypt, it was all European governed or controlled.[25] By the early 1960s the opposite was true; most of Africa was independent or close to achieving independence. In the 1980s there were over fifty independent sovereign states in Africa, a third of the membership of the United Nations. In many ways the new states differed from the older European states. Almost without exception they united diverse tribal, ethnic, and linguistic groups, some antagonistic to each other. Because African geographical boundaries had been drawn by the European colonial powers, peoples and tribes were often distributed over several countries. The new states enjoyed less of a unified national heritage than older nations in Europe and elsewhere. But once the African states obtained independence from Western rule, they rapidly assumed the complete panoply of national sovereignty and moved to weld their disparate peoples into nationhood.

The winning of independence in Arab North Africa in the 1950s spurred nationalist movements in sub-Saharan Africa, where black populations lived in colonial empires carved out by the British, French, Belgians, and Portuguese either in the early modern centuries or in the decade and a half of imperialist scramble after 1885.[26] The British led the way in granting independence. After dissolving their Indian empire and cutting their other imperial commitments for economic reasons, they yielded to mounting pressures and prepared for African self-rule through a gradual transfer of authority to local officials and through economic development programs.

In 1957 the Gold Coast became the first British African colony to achieve dominion status. It immediately shed a name identified with imperialist exploitation and took for itself the name of Ghana, recalling an African kingdom that had flourished on the Niger River from the fourth to the eleventh century A.D. In 1960 Ghana became a republic, retaining its voluntary association with the Commonwealth, the first of the new Commonwealth's African members. After independ-

---

[24] See pp. 621, 625–627.
[25] See map, p. 633, and pp. 631–634.
[26] See pp. 627–634; for earlier years, see pp. 105–107, 162, 251–252, 423.

ence, the American-educated Kwame Nkrumah, who had led the nationalist movement, gathered extensive powers into his own hands. He became president for life, banned opposition parties, and governed as a dictator. After a decade, his arbitrary government, unbridled extravagances, and cult of personality led to his overthrow in 1966; a military dictatorship, despite sporadic efforts at resuming constitutional government, persisted for years.

In 1960 Nigeria moved from colonial status to independence, first as a dominion and, three years later, as a republic. Nigeria, with by far the largest population of any country in Africa, had numerous ethnic groups. In the mid-1960s ethnic antagonisms flared into open violence. The Ibos, the most advanced people economically, made a bid for independence in 1967, proclaiming the secession of their eastern region as the state of Biafra. A civil war lasted two and a half years, resulting in as many as one million casualties, before the federal troops crushed the outnumbered rebels. In the age of African independence Africans, tragically, destroyed Africans. After the war the government embarked on a policy of reconstruction and reconciliation, reintegrating the Ibos into national life, but not until 1979 did the country return to civilian rule and constitutional government.

In East Africa the independence movements of the 1950s encountered obstacles. In Kenya (as in South Africa and Rhodesia), a minority of white settlers set themselves against a government of black Africans. The nationalist movement responded with violence. The British imprisoned Jomo Kenyatta and other nationalist leaders for a time and forcibly suppressed the extremists, but after a decade of unrest, they granted independence in 1963. For the next fifteen years, until his death, Kenyatta headed the government, ruling firmly and paternalistically but within a parliamentary framework.

Of the other important colonial areas of East Africa, Uganda became independent in 1962. A struggle ensued between the central government and the centuries-old kingdom of Buganda, which had been promised autonomy in the new state. The central government triumphed, but itself fell under dictatorship. In 1971 a relatively obscure army sergeant, Idi Amin, seized power and for eight years tyrannized the country as a capricious and brutal dictator, destroying what had been a prosperous agricultural economy. He was overthrown in 1979 only when Tanzanian forces, with the tacit support of other African states, invaded the country. Continuing instability and economic chaos made difficult the restoration of constitutional rule, and even the activities of everyday life.

Tanzania had come into existence when Tanganyika (once German East Africa) and Zanzibar, a former British protectorate, merged in 1964 shortly after independence. For a time Tanzania served as a bridgehead for Chinese Communist influence on the continent. In 1975 an important rail link from the port capital of Dar-es-Salaam to Zambia was completed with the help of the Chinese. Zambia, another new nation, once known as Northern Rhodesia, became independent in 1964; Kenneth Kaunda, a former schoolteacher and independence leader, was its first president. Unlike Nkrumah and the leaders in so many of the new nations who established open dictatorships, Kaunda in Zambia, Kenyatta in Kenya, and Nyerere in Tanzania all emerged from their role as independence leaders to govern their respective countries for many years with a general respect for parliamentary and constitutional forms, although not encouraging genuine political ferment, an active opposition, or meaningful social change.

During all these years the white colonial settlers in southern Africa—in Rhodesia

CONTEMPORARY AFRICA

This map should be compared with those for Pre-Colonial Africa (p. 629) and for Africa in 1914 at the height of European colonialism (p. 633). The first of the new states was Ghana, the former British Gold Coast, which became independent in 1957 and took its name from a medieval African kingdom that had been located further north. The following decades saw the independence of Algeria and of numerous republics in black Africa in place of the French, British, Belgian, and Portuguese colonial empires.

and South Africa, and in the South African trusteeship over Southwest Africa (once German Southwest Africa)—held out longest against granting majority rule to the black population. In South Africa the dominant political leaders, the Afrikaner descendants of the Boer settlers, upheld a policy of apartheid, or racial segregation, under which 5 million whites ruled 21 million blacks and an additional 3 million mixed peoples treated as nonwhites. They conceded, at best, autonomous homelands for the black peoples, who remained excluded from participation in political life and suffered blatant forms of discrimination; opponents of the policy, black and white, were silenced by imprisonment and even torture. The regime, increasingly isolated, withdrew in 1961 from the Commonwealth, whose members were critical of its racial policies, and proclaimed itself a republic. Over two decades later, despite some progress in the opening up of economic opportunities, the tensions remained unresolved.

South Africa also refused to give up the trusteeship it held since 1919 over what had formerly been German Southwest Africa. In 1974 the United Nations declared South African rule at an end and took steps to create an independent Namibia. The South African government, however, refused to negotiate with the black independence organizations, fought the nationalist guerrilla forces, and raided their military bases in bordering countries like Angola, where Soviet-backed Cuban troops were a presence.

In Southern Rhodesia, unlike Northern Rhodesia and Nyasaland, where the independent states of Zambia and Malawi with black majority governments emerged in 1964, a small white minority also refused to surrender its rule over 6 million blacks. The British sought to negotiate political rights for the black majority before independence but were unsuccessful. In 1965 the white political leaders unilaterally proclaimed independence from Britain. Continuing guerrilla warfare, supported at times by the People's Republic of China, and international pressures finally forced the recalcitrant white leaders to yield, and the independent state of Zimbabwe, with a black majority government, was formed in 1980.

Meanwhile the French dissolved their colonial empire in West and Equatorial Africa, reacting very differently here than in other parts of their empire. For years the French hoped that a French-educated African elite would maintain strong ties to France. After the war they gave the overseas territories representation in the French assemblies and promises of self-governing institutions. But effective control remained centralized in Paris and by the mid-1950s the sub-Saharan African colonies, inspired by the example of events elsewhere in Africa, sought full independence.

In 1958 de Gaulle offered the African colonies the right of self-determination and voluntary association with France, which they accepted. Guinea alone insisted on secession. The French African states moved quickly from autonomy to complete independence and sovereignty, some choosing to remain associated with France and with each other in a loosely organized association known as the French Community; even those who withdrew retained economic and cultural ties with France. In the decades that followed France remained an economic and military presence in eighteen francophone nations, retaining military bases, lending economic aid, and profiting from extensive economic privileges. On occasion the French even intervened with military force; in 1979, they helped overthrow the dictator Bokassa, who in 1965 had seized power in the Central African Republic.

Belgium's withdrawal from the Congo, and the emergence of the new state of Zaire, was accompanied by tragedy and bloodshed. The Belgian Congo had once been a byword for imperialist exploitation.[27] The most abusive features had been remedied, but political control remained concentrated in Brussels and few steps were taken to assist the colony in self-administration. When nationalist agitation for independence erupted in 1959, the Belgian government in panic decided

[27] See pp. 628–630.

against gradualism and precipitously announced withdrawal in six months' time. The nationalist leadership was itself divided, there were ethnic and regional antagonisms, and no one was prepared to take over the function of governing. The Belgian withdrawal in 1960 led to anarchy, riots, looting, and atrocities. The wealthy mining province of Katanga (now Shaba) seceded; Belgian troops flew back in American planes to restore order; and the Soviet Union threatened to intervene to defend the new state against Western imperialism. A United Nations international police force, composed chiefly of Africans, averted what might have been a civil war, especially dangerous because of the Soviet-Western confrontation. After two and a half years order returned to Zaire, but in 1965 an army leader, Colonel Mobutu, established a strong personal dictatorship and nationalized much of the economy. He also Africanized all geographical names: the country was renamed Zaire, as was the famous river; Leopoldville, the capital, and Stanleyville, with names reminiscent of European imperialism, became Kinshasa and Kisangani. Zaire, the second largest country in Africa, its cities widely separated and without adequate transportation facilities, had vast copper, cobalt, and other mineral resources, but its great potential riches, like those in other parts of Africa, were still underdeveloped.

Of all the older colonial powers, Portugal, itself under an authoritarian dictatorship until the 1970s, clung longest to its colonies, symbols of Portuguese grandeur in the early age of European expansion. To retain Angola and Mozambique, two large colonies on the southwestern and southeastern coasts of Africa respectively which had once flourished on the slave trade, the Portuguese dictatorship fought a war which lasted over ten years. In the course of the struggle revolutionary elements in the army, disaffected by the prolonged colonial war, turned against the regime and in 1974 overthrew it. In 1975 the new revolutionary regime granted independence to Angola, Mozambique, and its other African colonies.

During its war for independence Angola became a battleground for competing nationalist groups, each backed by outside powers, one of them supported by the Soviet Union and Cuba. The Soviets sent weapons and advisers, and the Cuban leader Fidel Castro, who advanced himself as a spokesman for the colonial peoples, dispatched 15,000 troops. In the end the Soviet- and Cuban-backed group won and consolidated control over the country; the Cuban troops were not withdrawn. It was from guerrilla bases in Angola that raids were launched to end South African control over Namibia, the South Africans retaliating with attacks on Angola. Angola and Mozambique were under leftist governments, strongly susceptible to Communist influence, but both countries traded with and accepted economic aid from the West.

Africa remained an arena of rivalry for the superpowers. The Soviets maintained a military and economic presence not only in Angola and Mozambique but in Ethiopia and Libya as well. Although many of the African governments were professedly Marxist-oriented or vaguely socialist, few wished to be client states of the Soviet Union; they had not ousted their earlier European rulers to replace them with new ones. But many African leaders were resentful of the United States for its wealth and power. Alarmed by the continuing cultural and economic dependence on the West, and by the continuing economic privileges still enjoyed by former colonial rulers, some Africans believed themselves threatened by a revived imperialism, or neocolonialism.

But the European political empires were gone. Only the new map of contemporary Africa could communicate the transformation that had occurred. The unfinished agenda for the African revolution included the extension of political rights to the black majority in South Africa, South Africa's withdrawal from Namibia, and above all, the struggle everywhere to make independence a prelude to the improvement of human lives.

For independence was not enough. To be sure it provided a source of great pride. The poet-president of Senegal, Léopold Senghor, spoke of *négritude*, a powerful, far-reaching black self-consciousness, a pride in ancient cultural roots and modern achievements, which struck responsive chords in Americans of African descent whose ancestors had been brought in chains from some of the very lands that had now become modern nations. But in the years that followed independence, frustrations mounted. The end of colonialism did not bring individual freedoms or democratic government. Although most of the new nations began with constitutions, elected parliaments, independent judiciaries, and guarantees of civil liberties, much of the machinery of constitutional government was quickly submerged under one-party rule and often under military regimes. In some, civil wars erupted; ethnic loyalties frequently transcended national loyalties in states whose boundaries had been artificially drawn in the nineteenth century. Some argued that strong centralized governments were needed rather than multiparty democratic systems to counter tribalism and regionalism and to cope with severe economic problems. The decades of independence did not bring economic well-being; poverty and hunger were present in many parts of Africa and elsewhere in the colonial world. Young people with secondary school or university education found few job opportunities. The cities were overcrowded and sprawling slums multiplied because large numbers fled the bushland for the presumed attractions of urban life; twenty years after independence twice as many people lived in cities in Africa as before. Agriculture was neglected in the race to industrialize; and production of food and other crops declined when they were most needed to feed the needs of growing populations. The African economies remained dependent on exports in the world market, as in colonial times, and when economic reverses occurred, as they did in the mid-1970s, the new countries suffered further setbacks and miseries.

The End of Empire

Of all the great political changes in the history of the modern world, affecting hundreds of millions of people, nothing was more revolutionary, more dramatic, or more sudden than the end of the European overseas colonial empires. The German and Turkish empires had disappeared with military defeat in the First World War, the Italian and the Japanese in the Second. But in 1945 the British, the French, the Dutch, the Belgians, and the Portuguese still governed more than a quarter of the world's population. Within three decades after 1945, however, the European empires had disappeared. The United States in the postwar years also played a part in the transformation; it withdrew from the Philippines, granted Puerto Rico commonwealth status, took in Alaska and Hawaii as equal members of the federal union, and surrendered special privileges in the Panama Canal Zone.

At the beginning of the twentieth century, or even in 1945, few would have predicted the nature or extent of the colonial revolution. The colonial empires seemed at best susceptible only to slow evolution toward independence. To be sure, the Marxists stressed the relationship of imperialism to capitalism and predicted the decline of both, but they, too, failed to foresee the rapidity or completeness with which the end of the colonial empires took place. The two World Wars, by weakening the European powers and by encouraging nationalism, played a vital part; it was difficult to wage war in the name of self-determination and democracy, often with the colonial countries as allies, without reinforcing such ideas among subject peoples. The end of the colonial empires and the emergence of the new nations have to be counted among the most far-reaching consequences of the two wars, and especially of the Second.

The age of imperialism dated to the fifteenth century when the Europeans first set sail on their voyages of discovery; it reached a climax from 1885 to 1900 when Europeans penetrated the interior of Africa and expanded their influence in Asia, and Americans took the Philippines and asserted their power in the Caribbean and Latin America.[28] It had its share of exploitation, brutality, and degradation that left a permanent scar, yet it was also the instrument whereby many of the scientific, material, intellectual, and humanitarian advances of Western Europe spread to the rest of the world. The West no longer dominated these areas politically, but Western civilization, technology, and institutions were still important everywhere. Industry, science, secularization, social mobility, individual freedoms, long accepted as accomplishments, or as goals, of the West, now reached remote parts of the world. The impact of the new values and institutions brought dislocations and tensions, and transformed the landscape of the non-Western world. In some places, as in the Islamic reaction in Iran, there was deep resentment at the intrusion of the West, but mostly there was the expectation that some amalgam could be found of modernization and traditional values.

---

[28] See pp. 105–112, 264–275, 608–647.

XXII.
The Contemporary Age:
Crises and Coexistence

For over twenty years, from the postwar recovery in the early 1950s to the mid-1970s, the West (and Japan) experienced a period of remarkable prosperity, economic growth, and rising living standards and were able to enjoy democratic government without the strain of economic tensions. The nations of Western Europe absorbed the momentous loss of their colonial empires with a minimum of shock, and the emergent nations embarked on their independent paths, facing new challenges and problems. But in the mid-1970s a world-wide recession sharply slowed economic growth everywhere and in some cases undermined political stability. After close to four decades the Cold War continued, and the two heavily armed superpowers confronted each other in many parts of the globe, but avoided direct conflict.

113. THE DEMOCRACIES SINCE 1945

In the domestic affairs of the Western countries there were again, as after the First World War, decisive democratic advances in the early postwar years. To have rid the world of the aggressive dictatorships and military regimes in Germany, Italy, and Japan and to have restored constitutional government where it had been crushed for many years was a triumph for democracy. Another advance was the widening of the suffrage. Women received the vote in France, Italy, and Japan immediately after the war, and in Switzerland in 1971, and the franchise broadened even further in the early 1970s when the legal voting age for men and women was reduced to eighteen in many countries. The postwar democracies concerned themselves also with the welfare of their citizens. The memories of the

Chapter Emblem: The official symbol for the World Population Year, 1974.

Great Depression, the sacrifices demanded in the war, and the desire for protection against economic insecurity imposed new responsibilities on democratic governments everywhere.

The United States

For the United States, and indeed for much of the world, the most important single fact in the early postwar years was the productivity of the American economic system. The American economy, after recovering partially from the Great Depression during the New Deal years and expanding enormously to meet military needs during the Second World War, continued to grow rapidly after 1945. War damage in such industrial countries as the U.S.S.R., Germany, Britain, and Japan made United States economic superiority for a time greater than ever. Income per capita in the United States in 1938 had been only a little higher than in Great Britain, Sweden, or Switzerland, the next wealthiest countries. In 1948 it was about twice as high. Even after Western Europe and Japan embarked on a period of rapid industrial expansion, the United States retained a substantial lead in per capita output, wealth, and consumption levels. Per capita output in the 1970s was still twice as high as that of Western Europe, its closest competitor, but the gap was narrowing.

The great wealth and vast resources of the United States provoked in other countries a suspicious and hostile view of American policies, but it was American financial assistance that made possible the recovery, modernization, and expansion of the Western European economies. In the early postwar years the economic ascendancy of the United States produced problems. Exporting far more than it imported, it tended to unbalance world exchanges by its very productivity. Until 1957 there was a chronic "dollar shortage," in that other countries could not earn dollars with which to buy American goods. By the early 1960s, because of the economic recovery of Western Europe and American military expenditures abroad, the American balance of payments shifted unfavorably and the dollar weakened. The Europeans meanwhile accumulated large dollar reserves, for which they had the right to demand gold—as France did in 1965. American gold and foreign currency reserves declined dramatically. In 1971 the United States unilaterally suspended gold convertibility and devalued the dollar. Later, in the mid-1970s, because of expensive oil imports the balance of payments weakened further. The image of the American dollar as an unassailable citadel of strength no longer held, and the international monetary system set up at Bretton Woods in 1945, when the dollar was accepted as the equivalent of gold itself, broke down. As the world-wide recession spread, however, and other currencies weakened, it once again regained its strength. The American economy, despite the recession, was still strong, but it was vulnerable to international financial and energy crises, and it faced new technological challenges at home and mounting competition from abroad.

President Truman, taking office at Roosevelt's death in 1945, and then elected in 1948, attempted in his Fair Deal to continue the New Deal of his predecessor.[1] After the presidency of the wartime hero Dwight D. Eisenhower (1952–1960), no other president in the next two decades served two full terms. John F. Kennedy was assassinated in 1963 in his first term; Lyndon B. Johnson, beset by the unpopular Vietnam War, chose not to run for reelection in 1968; Richard M. Nixon re-

---

[1] See pp. 768–772.

signed his presidency in 1974 to avoid impeachment after the Watergate scandal; Gerald Ford was defeated for reelection in 1976 by his Democratic opponent, Jimmy Carter, who in turn was defeated by Ronald Reagan four years later. In these presidencies, despite variations in their pro-business or pro-labor orientation, the welfare state continued to grow, although military expenditures in these decades diverted funds from domestic needs. In 1980 a Republican administration committed itself to check the growth of big government and the welfare state. Despite its generally high standard of living, the United States was troubled by poverty, decaying cities, and economically depressed regions, and for a time was shaken by the long, divisive war in Vietnam, discussed later in the chapter.

It also continued to grapple with the challenge of fully integrating its minorities, black and Hispanic, into the American mainstream. In May 1954 a Supreme Court decision prescribed equal access to the nation's public schools, and Presidents Eisenhower and Kennedy both used federal troops to enforce the ruling. Under President Johnson, beginning in 1964, Congress adopted legislation to halt discrimination in employment, housing, and public accommodations. But there were many setbacks. In 1968 the assassination of the American black leader Martin Luther King shocked the country. In the 1970s and on into the 1980s, while more blacks and Hispanics moved into middle-class positions, the situation for most members of these minority groups hardly improved. The industrial slowdown, unemployment, and inflation that afflicted the world economy worked especially to their disadvantage. In 1982 the unemployment rate in the United States stood at its highest in fifty years, and most alarmingly so for black youth. The high interest rates and restrictive monetary policies that helped reduce inflation at home aggravated unemployment and also made world recovery more difficult.

Great Britain

In Great Britain, even before the Second World War ended, an election in July 1945, the first in ten years, unseated Winston Churchill and voted in a Labour government under Clement Attlee. Once the center of high capitalism, Britain for a time became the world's chief exemplar of parliamentary socialism. The Labour party, governing from 1945 to 1951 for the first time in history with a majority of its own,[2] enacted a broad social program that left permanent changes in British society. Insisting that in an ailing economy the country's basic industries could not be left to the unplanned anarchy of capitalism and free competition, the Labour government brought under public ownership an important segment of the economy, including the Bank of England, the coal mines, such public utilities as electricity and gas, communications and transportation, and iron and steel production. Since four-fifths of the economy remained in private hands, what emerged was not socialism but a mixed economy. Even in the private branches of the economy, however, steps were taken to influence the direction and amount of private investment on the theory that it was in the national interest to supplement the self-interest of private enterprise and the profit motive. At the same time the Labour government greatly expanded and revamped the program of social insurance inherited from the Liberal reforms of 1906–1914.[3] All parties had committed themselves during the war to an extension of these welfare services. The Beveridge Report in 1942 had sketched a program to guarantee "full employment in a

[2] See pp. 586–587, 773–775.
[3] See pp. 576–579.

free society" and social security for all from cradle to grave. The Labour government now extended insurance coverage for unemployment, old age, and other contingencies, and inaugurated a comprehensive free medical and health service for the entire population. Income and inheritance taxes were also sharply increased. The only constitutional change under the Labour government was an act of 1949 to reduce the power of the House of Lords to delay legislation from three years to one; it was not invoked until a quarter of a century later. Restrictions on labor activities dating from the general strike of 1926 were repealed.[4] The Labour program—the public ownership of an important sector of the economy, governmental controls over the economy as a whole, the extensive social security system, and the use of taxation to redistribute wealth—furthered the idea of the welfare state, described by some as a demonstration that political democracies could protect the social and economic welfare of their citizens and thereby ensure an even greater devotion to democratic processes, and by others as an oppressive, regimented, bureaucratic apparatus, the road to a "new serfdom."

After six years, the electorate returned the Conservatives to office in 1951, and they governed uninterruptedly to 1964, with Churchill, Eden, Harold Macmillan, and Alec Douglas-Home serving as successive prime ministers. After 1964 the two parties alternated. Labour, under Harold Wilson, held office from 1964 to 1970 and the Conservatives with Edward Heath from 1970 to 1974. When Labour regained power in 1974, its margin was so narrow that Wilson and his successor James Callaghan could govern only with the support of the small Liberal party. The shifting electoral fortunes of the two parties stemmed partly from division over the welfare state set up by Labour but even more fundamentally from concern over the economy.

During their years in office, the Conservatives halted the nationalization program, restored iron and steel production and the trucking industry to private control, introduced fees into the national health insurance program, and encouraged private construction over public housing. Although critical in principle of the welfare state, they did no more than modify it. Labour, in office, encouraged public housing and slum clearance, renationalized steel, restored free medical services, and reorganized the educational system along more democratic lines. A Labour reform dropped the voting age to eighteen in 1970; the first election under the reform was won by the Conservatives.

Both parties recognized that social reforms were possible only if the economy prospered, but both faced nagging economic problems, which grew even more acute in the mid-1970s. The country was in a much worse state after the Second World War than after the First because most of its foreign holdings had been liquidated, and a large part of its merchant marine lost. Britain remained dependent on imports for its food and raw materials; the loss of interest on its investments and the reduced income from its shipping adversely affected its balance of payments.[5] However, with American financial aid, postwar European economic cooperation, an intensified export drive, and a curtailment of military and imperial commitments, the British economy and trade position improved. The country experienced a modest prosperity which, despite some weaknesses, exceeded anything it had known since before the First World War.

Despite the economic improvement, the country could not pay for its imports, sustain prosperity, and support the heavy burden of public services except with a

[4] See p. 574.
[5] See pp. 564–570, 764–766, 772–775.

modern, expanding economy. But British industry was outstripped in the contest for export markets by other Western Europeans and the Japanese, and was unable to compete even in its home market. The economy grew more slowly than that of the rest of Western Europe and Japan, and was less productive and efficient. When out of power, the Labour party argued that the Conservatives lacked economic dynamism and were responsible for the lagging economy. But when Labour returned to office in 1964, it, too, faced economic troubles and in 1967 was forced to devalue the pound and extend austerity measures. Inflation set in and the militant trade unions demanded wage increases to match rising prices. In 1972, when the Conservatives tried to keep wages in line, the coal miners called a nationwide strike, and a prolonged work stoppage followed. The Arab oil embargo and the dramatic rise in oil prices in the winter of 1973–1974 aggravated the inflationary spiral.

Britain was hard hit by the combination of industrial stagnation and inflation in the mid-1970s. Of all the industrial nations, it suffered the highest rate of inflation—a staggering 27 percent in 1975. Unemployment that year passed the 1 million mark, and the pound dropped to the lowest point in its history. To avert collapse the country depended upon foreign loans and an austerity program for which it desperately needed trade union support.

No one proposed to discard entirely the national health insurance system, low income housing, or other benefits of the welfare state. Yet even Labour and the trade unions were reexamining priorities. Labour after 1974 sought to curb public expenditures, make funds available for private investment, and limit wage increases. It assigned the highest priority to industrial expansion and to support for key industries that gave promise of economic growth. Yet the trade unions were reluctant to accept the necessary sacrifices. The discovery and exploitation of oil fields in the North Sea in 1975 was one of very few cheering developments.

In 1979 the Conservatives won a substantial majority and Margaret Thatcher became the first woman prime minister in the history of any major Western country. The Conservative government followed a policy of harsh deflation, cutting government expenditures, resisting trade union demands, curbing imports, encouraging productivity, and protecting the currency. The inflation rate declined dramatically but at the expense of a large increase in unemployment, which exceeded 3 million in 1983, the highest since 1931, and contributed to riots in London and other cities. In the Labour party disaffection grew. Moderate elements, rebelling against trade union domination of the party and its growing neutralism in foreign affairs, formed a Social Democratic party in 1981 in the hope of creating an important fourth party and, with the Liberals, a centrist alliance that could challenge Conservatives and Labour alike.

Although Britain had relinquished most of its imperial commitments, the Conservative government reacted vigorously when Argentina in 1982, contesting British sovereignty, invaded the Falkland (or Malvina) Islands, 250 miles east of the southernmost part of South America. The Thatcher government dispatched a small armada the 8,000 mile distance, drove out the Argentine forces, and recaptured the islands. The victory stirred old memories and bolstered the political fortunes of the Conservatives, who won a sweeping victory at the polls in 1983.

Troubles in Northern Ireland persisted. The settlement of 1922 had left a large number of Catholics in Northern Ireland, which after the partition of Ireland became part of the United Kingdom, but with provision for self-government.[6] Of the 1.5 million inhabitants, two-thirds were Protestant and one-third Catholic. The Catholic minority militantly protested that they were victims of political and economic discrimination, and pressed for annexation to the Republic of Ireland. The Irish Republican Army, although disavowed by the Dublin government, inflamed matters, and Protestant extremists responded in kind. Open violence broke out in 1969. In the years that followed, over 2,000 persons lost their lives and no compromise was in sight.

On a less violent scale, other separatist pressures were at work. The Scots and the Welsh pressed for economic, cultural, and political autonomy, and the Scottish nationalist party, which sought independence, grew in strength. Scottish and Welsh separatism resembled political and cultural movements in France, Belgium, Spain, Canada, and other countries with long national histories, where Bretons, Corsicans, Flemish, Catalans, Basques, Québecois, and other minorities in a modern search for ethnic identity now sought autonomy or independence.

The French Republic: Fourth and Fifth

France's Fourth Republic, which lasted from 1946 to 1958, inherited most of the weaknesses of the Third.[7] Whereas the Third Republic lasted seventy years, the Fourth survived barely twelve. For two and a half years after liberation, from 1944 to 1946, a provisional government held office while a constitution was formulated. The constitution, adopted by a narrow margin, differed in only a few details from that of the Third. Once again the president of the republic was a ceremonial figure, and the premier and his cabinet responsible to the whims of the legislature. The Fourth Republic came to be dominated, as the Third had been, by an all-powerful National Assembly, as the Chamber of Deputies was now called.

As head of the provisional government, de Gaulle had governed in cooperation with three major parties of the left—the Communist party, the Socialist party, and the Popular Republican Movement (or MRP), the latter a new phenomenon in republican history, a Catholic progressive party devoted to the republic. All three had emerged from the Resistance movement enhanced in strength and prestige, but the Communists emerged as the leading party, largely on their record in the wartime Resistance movement after the German invasion of the Soviet Union in 1941. Almost a fourth of the electorate voted for the Communist party in France, as in Italy—the maximum that communism in Western Europe was able to attain in the early postwar years. De Gaulle and his successors refused the Communists key ministries in the cabinet but gave them several posts important for the rehabilitation of the national economy. After de Gaulle resigned, the three parties cooperated in governing; but in May 1947 the Communists, reflecting the heightening tension between the Soviet and Western camps, fomented a series of strikes directed against the government and were expelled from the cabinet.

Parliamentary and ministerial instability grew worse after 1947; the Socialists and MRP formed unstable coalitions with the once moribund but now reviving Radicals, and with other center parties. Periodically de Gaulle returned to the political scene, heading a movement called the "Rally of the French People,"

---

[6] See p. 775.
[7] See pp. 572–576, 776–779, 805.

which he described as "above parties." Inveighing with good cause against the instability of the regime, he nonetheless alarmed the democratic parties who saw the republic threatened by communism on the left and dictatorship on the right. By 1953 the Rally of the French People faded, and de Gaulle withdrew from the political scene. In the next few years parliamentary instability and ineffectiveness filled the public with cynicism, hostility, and indifference; the spirit of enthusiasm and regeneration carried forward from the Resistance movement flagged, except for a brief revival under the eight-month ministry of the reforming Radical Pierre Mendès-France in 1954–1955.

Yet despite its uninspiring political record, the economic and social accomplishments of the Fourth Republic were substantial. The provisional government under de Gaulle and the tripartite combination of left parties laid the foundation for a modern industrial democracy. The government nationalized a number of key industries, including the coal mines, gas and electricity, and the major banking, credit, and insurance facilities. As in Britain, a mixed economy emerged. The existing body of social security legislation was expanded, including the addition of family allowances as a supplement to the wages of heads of family. In 1946 a farsighted economic plan, drawn up by Jean Monnet, channeled investments into six key sectors of the economy, enlarging and modernizing the economic base and creating the potential for industrial expansion. The Monnet plan, along with American financial aid under the Marshall Plan, helped to modernize the French economy and to make possible a spectacular economic growth. By 1952 production levels were one and a half times those of 1938, and industrial output was growing at an annual rate of at least 5 percent. Frenchmen like Monnet and Robert Schuman took the lead in many of the proposals for European economic integration launched in the 1950s.[8] The country also showed a demographic vitality that confounded earlier pessimists.[9] The population decline in the years before the war gave way to regular annual increases so that the prewar French nation of less than 40 million counted over 54 million in the 1980s; even so, there was concern in the 1970s over slower growth rates. There were many weak spots in the economy; public finances and tax evasion remained serious problems; and labor unrest persisted, in part provoked by the Communists, in part motivated by genuine grievances, including inflation.

What rendered the Fourth Republic's political problems insoluble was the strain of trying to preserve the old French empire. The regime was unable to cope with the exhausting colonial wars that it waged in Indochina from 1946 to 1954 and in Algeria from 1954 to 1962.[10] France alone, of all the major powers, was almost continuously at war for almost fifteen years in the postwar era. It could envy the lot of the losers in the Second World War, Germany, Italy, and Japan, with no restless colonies to subdue.

The constitution of 1946 democratized the government of the French Union, but the limited reforms did not satisfy national revolutionaries pressing for independence. As we have seen, from 1946 to 1954, the French army fought the nationalists in Indochina until it finally had to withdraw. Only a few months later, the Algerian war broke out. As the fighting dragged on, savagery and brutality mounted on both sides, and the war drained the financial resources, morale, and self-esteem of the French. To check the flow of aid from Egypt to the Algerian na-

---

tionalists the French also participated in the ill-fated Suez expedition in 1956. The settlers in Algeria and the army leaders, smarting under their earlier defeat in Indochina, adamantly opposed French withdrawal, and in May 1958 they staged an insurrectionary coup in Algiers. A new cabinet, hastily formed in Paris, proved impotent against the junta in Algeria, feared a paratroop invasion of the capital, and welcomed the one man they believed could save the situation, de Gaulle. The vast majority of the French people hailed his return. The army leaders, the settlers in Algeria, and the parties of the right were convinced that with his solicitude for the army and for French national greatness he would keep Algeria French. He also mollified the left, except for the Communists and a tiny group of stubborn inflexible republicans, by recalling the democratic way in which he had governed after liberation and by insisting that he would return to power only in a legal way. In June 1958 the National Assembly invested de Gaulle as premier with emergency powers for six months and with the authority to prepare a new constitution.

In that way the Fifth Republic was born. In quick succession in the autumn of 1958 a constitution was written and accepted overwhelmingly by a popular referendum, and elections were held; a new Gaullist party (the Union for the New Republic) emerged, and de Gaulle was elected president. The presidency was the key office and focus of power in the Fifth Republic. The president, elected for a seven-year term, was empowered to dissolve the Assembly and call for new elections, submit important questions to popular referendums, and assume emergency powers, all of which de Gaulle did in his eleven years in office. Political instability disappeared; in the first ten years of the Fifth Republic there were only three premiers; in the fourteen years from 1944 to 1958 under the Fourth Republic there had been twenty-five.

In his own way, de Gaulle settled the Algerian crisis, and an independent Algeria came into existence in July 1962; even earlier, he granted independence to the former French colonies in sub-Saharan Africa. With French self-confidence restored because of the stability of the new regime, with economic prosperity continuing, and with France playing an active and independent role in world affairs, the French reconciled themselves to the loss of empire and took pride in their heightened importance on the world scene. In 1960 France became the fourth nation to develop a nuclear capacity and began to develop an independent nuclear strike force. De Gaulle, rejecting the rigid patterns of the Cold War and viewing postwar international affairs as a struggle between Great Powers rather than a clash of ideologies, declined to follow the American or British lead in Europe or Asia and aspired to a large diplomatic role for France.

After the settlement of the Algerian crisis de Gaulle made himself an even stronger master of the French domestic scene. He continued to build a kind of plebiscitary democracy by frequent direct appeals to the people and by ignoring parliament. In one major instance, bypassing parliament, he secured a constitutional amendment providing for the direct popular election of future presidents. In the elections of 1962 his party won an absolute majority in the Assembly, the first time any party had done so in republican history. Although civil liberties were for the most part preserved, and free speech and free elections maintained, the old democratic ferment was lacking; the political parties, including the Communist, seemed paralyzed or impotent. Despite sporadic street demonstrations, sterility and torpor for a time settled over French political life. Skilled technicians ran the affairs of state, and de Gaulle, an uncrowned republican monarch, presided as arbiter over the nation's destinies.

But the nation grew restless. In 1965 de Gaulle at seventy-five was reelected president, but with a runoff necessary because he failed to secure a majority on the first ballot. The labor unions chafed at inflation and inadequate attention to housing; students objected to government expenditures on nuclear arms instead of on educational facilities; opposition political leaders criticized the government's control over the mass information media. The parties of the left grew closer together. The country as a whole became impatient with de Gaulle's extravagant posturing in world affairs, as when he called for Quebec to free itself from Canada, or lectured Israel and sided with the Arab cause, or clung to doctrinaire anti-British and anti-American attitudes. Suddenly, in May 1968, grievances in the overcrowded universities sparked a revolt that led to demonstrations by hundreds of thousands of students and then brought 10 million workers out on strike, paralyzing the economy and threatening the regime itself. De Gaulle survived the revolt but only after assuring himself of army support and promising wage increases and educational and labor reforms.

Elections the next month, in which de Gaulle held out the threat of communism and chaos, resulted in an overwhelming majority for his party. The country seemed to forget the outburst. Educational changes were inaugurated, but the economic disruption of the spring hurt the economy. In 1969 de Gaulle chose to make a referendum on a complicated series of constitutional and regional reforms a vote of confidence in himself. When it was defeated by a small margin, he resigned and retired to his country estate, where he died a year later, an august, heroic, and austere figure whose exploits in war and peace assured him a lasting place in France's history.

The Gaullist Republic continued without de Gaulle. His two immediate successors as president, Georges Pompidou from 1969 to 1974, who died in office, and Valéry Giscard d'Estaing, a conservative but not a Gaullist who governed until his defeat in 1981, gave firm presidential leadership and followed de Gaulle's independent foreign policy but avoided his more extreme positions in international affairs. Like other industrial countries, France struggled from 1974 on with inflation, industrial slowdown, and unemployment. Although the Fifth Republic afforded stability under de Gaulle and his conservative successors, it permitted little latitude for constructive political opposition. The president and the technocratic regime appeared aloof from the people, concerned with technological progress but not with the quality of life, and the country appeared to be at a standstill in the 1970s. The austerity program adopted to combat inflation was unpopular, and the opposition on the left grew in strength. In 1981 François Mitterrand, a flexible, moderate Socialist who had revitalized the Socialist party and won over many independent voters, was elected president, and his party won an absolute majority in the National Assembly, ending the quarter-century supremacy of the Gaullist-conservative coalition. Not dependent on the Communists, whose representation declined to a low point, Mitterrand allowed them a few posts in the new cabinet.

Mitterrand interpreted the election results as a mandate for sweeping reform, if not for a socialist society; the government would manage the overall direction of the economy but leave ownership mostly in private hands. In office the Socialists nationalized the remaining privately owned larger commercial banks and some sectors of manufacturing, but five-sixths of the economy remained privately owned. The government funded scientific and technological research generously on the theory that the country could absorb a broad program of reforms only if it made itself the master of modern technology. Labor reforms reduced the work week from 40 to 39 hours (eventually to drop to 35), added a fifth week of paid vacations, increased social security benefits, and provided for greater labor participation in management. To meet unemployment the government established a jobs program, the Socialists adopting a course opposite to the deflationary program followed elsewhere. The government moved also to transform the centuries-old centralized administration of the country, encouraging autonomy for locally elected regional and local councils. In the meantime, Mitterrand had to cope with a steadily weakening franc, a mounting trade deficit, rising inflation, and continuing unemployment, and was forced to impose unpopular austerity measures. As in the Popular Front experience of 1936,[11] harsh economic realities checked the ardor of social reform. In foreign affairs Mitterrand made clear that, like his predecessors, he would exercise an independent role and not defer to American leadership.

The Two Germanies: Divided but Restored

In 1945 Germany was in ruins, its cities gutted, three-fourths of the homes in its great cities destroyed, its industrial plants burned and bombed, its land divided into four zones and occupied by United States, British, French, and Soviet troops. Economic chaos, a worthless currency, food and housing scarcities, an active black market, and shattered morale combined to create a grim picture. Moreover, under the arrangements at Potsdam, Germany surrendered control to Poland and the U.S.S.R. of an area along its eastern borders roughly equivalent to a fourth of the German territory as defined at Versailles. Some 12 million refugees, expelled or in flight from these eastern areas, as well as from former German population centers such as the Sudetenland, had to find homes in the bombed-out German cities.[12]

The four powers cooperated in 1946 in holding an international trial at Nuremberg of twenty-two major Nazi leaders charged with crimes against humanity and world peace, condemning twelve to execution by hanging. The evidence of evil deeds, massive and incontrovertible, was set down for posterity in many volumes of testimony, but some critics at that time and later questioned the precedent of punishing the leaders of a defeated enemy, and even the propriety of one totalitarian power, the Soviet Union, sitting in judgment over another. A "denazification" program, carried out by the occupation authorities, each in its own way, and by German courts under Allied supervision, had mixed results; sometimes lesser offenders were punished, whereas more serious offenders benefited from postponements and delays. Since so many technically trained and professional Germans had been identified with Nazi organizations, it became impossible to exclude all of them from public life. In general, the Allied countries rejected the notion of collective or mass German guilt for Nazi misdeeds. Individuals guilty of the more heinous crimes associated with the Third Reich were still being apprehended and tried three decades after the war's end—in German courts and, in the spectacular case of Adolf Eichmann, who played a leading role in the Jewish liquidation program, in Israel. In 1947 the Allied authorities formally dissolved the historic state of Prussia. The spirit of Prussian militarism and authoritarianism was thus to be exorcised from the German body politic; on this, Western and Soviet authorities were in agreement.[13]

[11] See pp. 777–779.
[12] See pp. 824, 826, maps, pp. 848–849, 895.
[13] See pp. 224–227, 412–414, 520–527.

Late in 1946 the Americans and British fused their occupation zones; the French followed in 1948. The Soviets went their separate way in their zone in East Germany. They encouraged the East German Communists to swallow up the Social Democrats and in 1949 oversaw the establishment of a German Democratic Republic. Under the stern rule of Walter Ulbricht, who dominated East German political affairs for over twenty-five years, East Germany followed the pattern of the Soviet satellites, building a disciplined one-party state and industrializing the economy. There was less liberalization here than in any of the other satellites; riots in East Berlin in 1953 and continued mass flight to West Germany were symptoms of unrest and dissatisfaction with the regime.

In West Germany, after the establishment of state governments, a constitutional convention representing the state diets met in 1948–1949, with the encouragement of the Western occupying powers, and established the Federal Republic of Germany, its capital in the Rhineland city of Bonn. The political leaders in Bonn were resolved to create an enduring German democracy, which their predecessors at Weimar in 1919 had failed to do.[14] The political fortunes of the new republic from the beginning rested largely in the hands of the Christian Democrats, heir to the old Catholic Center party. The dominating figure in postwar Germany was Konrad Adenauer, a patriarchal, strong-willed, powerful personality recalling Bismarck. Adenauer took office as chancellor at the age of seventy-three and governed with skill and shrewdness for fourteen years from 1949 to 1963, resigning reluctantly at the age of eighty-seven. For twenty years from 1949 to 1969, the elections held every four years confirmed the Christian Democrats in office, although a reinvigorated Social Democratic party supported by one-third of the voters, broadening its appeal, and growing in strength, provided a strong and energetic opposition. A small liberal party, the Free Democrats, for many years could be counted on to support the Christian Democrats. Adenauer, relegating to an indefinite future the question of German unification and the lost eastern territories, strengthened ties of friendship with France, cooperated in the movement of European political and economic integration, won the support and confidence of the Western powers, and provided the domestic stability and continuity that made possible a phenomenal German economic recovery.

[14] See pp. 745–749, 784–787.

GERMANY SINCE 1919

The upper panel shows the boundaries established after the Treaty of Versailles. Note the free city of Danzig and the Polish Corridor; for these and other areas lost in the First World War see also the map on pp. 692–693. In the middle panel we see the borders at the height of the Second World War in 1942. The Reich proper had then annexed (1) Luxembourg, (2) Alsace and Lorraine from France, (3) Carniola from Yugoslavia, (4) Austria, (5) the Sudeten regions and a Bohemian-Moravian protectorate from Czechoslovakia, (6) the free city of Danzig, and (7) Poland, which was renamed the "General Government." Beyond the borders of the Reich, the Germans occupied France, Belgium, the Netherlands, Denmark, and Norway, and in Eastern Europe had set up controls over the former Baltic states, White Russia, and the Ukraine. The lower panel shows Germany after Hitler's defeat. All conquests have been lost, and Poland now reaches westward almost to Berlin. A communist East Germany (the German Democratic Republic) and a democratic West Germany (the Federal Republic of Germany) have grown out of the zones occupied respectively by the Soviets and the West.

West Germany's industrial recovery and expansion was justifiably styled the "German miracle." In the first two postwar years, from 1945 to 1947, conditions were chaotic, but the damage to German industry, whose capacity had been greatly expanded during the war, proved less extensive than appeared on the surface; many of the German plants were usable after repairs, to which the population set itself with diligence and ingenuity. The influx of deportees and refugees from Eastern Europe turned into an asset, adding to the labor force. Reparations, over which the Western powers and the Soviets wrangled, were soon halted in the Western zone. In 1948 the Western powers effected a much needed currency reform in their zone. Then, with large sums of money provided by the United States under the Marshall Plan, West Germany embarked on an unprecedented industrial expansion, cooperating closely with other European countries in lowering trade barriers. The economic system remained capitalist, although the government shaped economic policies, channeled investments into the vital sectors of the economy, and conscientiously attended to social needs. Ludwig Erhard served as Adenauer's economics minister and from 1963 to 1968 as his successor, restoring the sense of partnership with cabinet and legislature that Adenauer had ignored. In 1968 Kurt Georg Kiesinger became chancellor, continuing the Christian Democratic ascendancy.

With the population accepting a relatively modest scale of living and thereby making imports less necessary, the industrial scene undisturbed by labor strife, the country free from the burden of military expenditures and profiting from the increased world demand for its exports, a substantial proportion of the national product was reinvested year after year and made possible continuous industrial growth and full employment. By 1950 industrial production surpassed prewar German levels; by 1958 Germany had almost doubled its output of 1938 and was the leading industrial country of Western Europe. By the 1960s it was producing more than twice as much as before the war, even though its industrial rate of growth showed signs of slowing down, largely because of a labor shortage. At the same time the West German population grew in the three decades after 1945 from 48 million to 62 million, whereas the population of East Germany, despite important economic progress, declined from 19 million to 17 million. By the 1950s, only a few years after the disastrous military defeat, the German Federal Republic had become an impressive industrial and political power, a coveted ally of the West, an equal member of Western military structures, including the North Atlantic Treaty Organization. With the passage of time a new generation appeared that felt little responsibility for the crimes of the Nazis; Chancellor Kiesinger had even once been a member of the party. Political issues of an inflammatory nature faded; material progress seemed triumphant over ideology, at least as far as older and middle-aged people were concerned. Efforts to agitate the burned-out ashes of Nazism had limited success. The real sources of discontent appeared among students and young people, who rebelled against West German society for its materialism and embraced a vaguely defined anarchism; some tiny groups of left-wing terrorists sought by violence to undermine the prospering institutions of the German republic.

In 1969 the twenty-year tenure of the Christian Democrats ended. Since 1961 the Christian Democrats were able to govern only with the support of the Free Democrats. When in 1965 the Social Democrats, for many years in the opposition, also joined the coalition, Willy Brandt, long the popular Social Democratic mayor of West Berlin, became foreign minister and launched his *Ostpolitik*, a policy of flexibility toward Eastern Europe. In 1969 with the support of the Free Democrats, he became Chancellor. To improve relations with Eastern Europe, he negotiated agreements with the Soviet Union and Poland, formally agreeing to the frontiers established at the end of the war. In Warsaw and in Israel he paid homage to the Jewish victims of the Nazis. Despite restlessness at his personal style and complaints that he was neglecting domestic affairs, his party won additional seats in 1972, but the discovery that a member of his staff was spying for East Germany cut short his chancellorship. In 1974 the less sentimental but astute Social Democratic leader, Helmut Schmidt, succeeded him and governed for the next eight years.

The German Federal Republic in 1975 was the strongest economic power in Western Europe, producing more goods and services than any other nation except the two superpowers and Japan. Its industrial output was a third that of all the members of the Common Market combined. With a population less than one-quarter the American, West Germany's gross national product was one-third that of the United States, and its volume of foreign trade nearly equal. In industrial relations it pioneered in bringing labor and capital together; a "co-determination" law gave workers an equal number of seats with management on the board of directors of firms with more than 2,000 workers. For a time West Germany coped more successfully than any other industrial power with inflation, industrial slowdown, and unemployment, and the mark remained strong. Because the self-disciplined labor movement accepted minimal wage increases, the government succeeded in controlling the rate of inflation. The political parties, and labor and industry, were all haunted by the memory of what the inflation of the 1920s, and the swollen unemployment ranks of the 1930s, had once done to their country.

But the recession strained the West German political consensus too. The labor unions were less willing to accept restraints. Unemployment rose; over 2 million West Germans were out of work in the early 1980s, more than at any time since the postwar recovery. Some feared what this might mean for political stability. Opposition also grew to Schmidt's support for American defense policy and his willingness to base nuclear missiles in West Germany. When in 1982 the Free Democrats, alarmed by the growing radicalism and neutralism of the left wing of the Social Democrats and other activist groups, shifted their support to the Christian Democrats, that party returned to office with Helmut Kohl as chancellor.

Just as Germany remained divided, so did Berlin, which lay 100 miles deep within East Germany, partitioned into a Western and a Soviet sector. In 1961 the Soviet and East German authorities erected the Berlin Wall and checked an exodus of East Germans that already amounted to 3 million people fleeing in pursuit of the more democratic atmosphere and material plenty of the West. The German Democratic Republic until the recession of the mid-1970s made remarkable economic progress under its Soviet-type centralized economic planning. By the late 1960s, despite its relatively small population, it was one of the world's ten leading industrial powers, the wealthiest country in all Eastern Europe, its standards of living higher than those in the U.S.S.R. Although Ulbricht's successors were more flexible, they firmly backed Soviet repressive policies toward the other East European satellites.

In the early postwar years Christian Democrats and Social Democrats in West Germany, and Communists in East Germany, had been at one in their determination some day to reunite their divided nation. Under Brandt's conciliatory foreign policy, communications were improved and family visits across the border of

East Germany permitted, but reunification remained remote. In 1973 the two German states recognized each other diplomatically, and were each admitted to the United Nations. The two social systems were evolving along very different lines, and each in its way, by material and other standards, was successful. If the leading industrial power of Western Europe and the leading industrial power of Eastern Europe outside the U.S.S.R. were one day to unite, the implications for European and world affairs would be far-reaching. But reunification was less in German hands than in the larger framework of international relationships. As the years passed, the two Germanies were fast developing a separate sense of national destiny and identity; they spoke of two nations and coexistence. Many remembered that Germany in modern times had been united only for the seventy-five years from 1871 to 1945, and that in the early modern centuries it had long been common to speak of the Germanies.

The Japanese Revival

In Japan, as in Germany, the Americans used military occupation in 1945 to foster democratic institutions. A new constitution promulgated in 1946 ended the divine right rule of the emperor[15] and transformed him into a constitutional sovereign. The political machinery of democratic government was established; women voted; local self-government was encouraged. Labor unions grew in size and militancy. The large industrial and banking combinations were ordered dissolved, although new forms of economic concentration took their place. A sweeping program of land redistribution was inaugurated. Unfortunately, many peasants lacked the means to purchase the holdings offered them, and larger landowners resisted the reforms. Although the moderate socialists emerged as an important party, political control remained largely in the hands of conservative groups drawn from the upper social classes who had long ruled Japan; the conservative Liberal Democratic party monopolized power in the postwar decades.

Japan, like Germany, profited from the tension between the Soviets and the Western world. In the peace treaty signed in 1951, to which the Soviets were not a party, no reparations were exacted. Japanese sovereignty was reestablished, although the United States, by treaty, retained some military rights in Japan and occupied the Ryukyu Islands, including Okinawa, until 1972. The Soviets made no move to return the Kurile Islands, which they had occupied at the end of the Second World War. Japan early recognized, and had close relations with, the People's Republic of China. A militant peace movement, stirring up memories of Hiroshima, tried to steer Japan on a neutralist course and opposed mutual defense arrangements with the United States; anti-American demonstrations and riots, led by dissatisfied university students, recurred. A sizable Communist party encouraged neutralism and anti-Americanism but maintained its independence of Moscow too.

In 1968 Japan celebrated the centennial of the Meiji Restoration,[16] which had launched the country into the mainstream of world history; in 1975 Hirohito became the first Japanese emperor to visit the United States. Despite its disastrous defeat in the Second World War, with a population close to 120 million but having successfully stabilized its population growth, Japan was the third leading industrial power of the world, surpassed only by the United States and the U.S.S.R.

---

[15] See pp. 548, 760–761.
[16] See pp. 548–549.

As in other industrial countries, the process of continuing economic expansion was interrupted in the mid-1970s, and Japan suffered from industrial slowdown and inflation. To the resentment of other industrial countries, it restricted imports and continued to enjoy a large export market for its products. Intent upon making its democratic machinery work, Japan remained, despite social ferment, a bastion of conservative stability in the troubled Asia of the postwar years.

The Italian Republic

In Italy, after more than two decades of fascism, democratic processes were resumed after the war.[17] The country adopted a new constitution, voted the Savoy monarchy out of existence in favor of an Italian Republic, and extended the suffrage to women. In the first postwar elections, held in June 1945, three parties, the Christian Democratic, the Communist, and the Socialist, came forward in that order, along with a few smaller parties. Communism would remain a powerful force in Italian political life, emerging, as in France, with great prestige from the partisan movement of the Resistance and successfully exploiting existing economic and social grievances, of which there were many in Italy; until 1947 the Communists held seats in the cabinet. In the divided Socialist party a Left majority insisted on close ties with the Communists, while a minority insisted on an independent democratic socialism. The Christian Democrats, sparked initially by a high sense of Christian idealism and social justice yet moderate enough in social and economic outlook to attract conservatives, dominated the political scene over the next four decades.

The leading figure in postfascist Italy was the Christian Democratic leader, Alcide de Gasperi, who survived the Mussolini years as a librarian in the Vatican. He provided strength and stability in the first chaotic period after the war, and for seven formative years in the life of the republic, from 1946 to 1953, presided over a strong government that advanced political freedom and introduced moderate reforms. In 1947, in the context of the Cold War, de Gasperi dismissed the Communists from his cabinet. In the 1948 elections de Gasperi, backed by the conservative parties, the Vatican, and the United States, which for the first time in its history openly intervened to influence the outcome of a European election, thwarted the Communist bid for power.

The Christian Democrats continued to govern the country, but without the majority they had won in 1948. They governed in coalition with the smaller parties of the left and left center, and by the late 1960s, often with the support of the right. Moving cautiously, they took care not to alienate propertied interests. The tempo of change in the more backward south was slow. After de Gasperi's departure in 1953, a succession of prime ministers followed one another with scarcely a year in office for each. The party was divided by factionalism and dominated by conservative interests, in which the church hierarchy played a significant role. Even when joined briefly by the Socialists in the early 1960s, in "an opening to the left," the Christian Democrats showed little enthusiasm for reform; the Socialists, meanwhile, lost working-class support and soon withdrew. The Communists, manifesting increasing independence from Moscow, gained substantial strength in each election after 1958. Supported by about a third of the electorate, they profited from restlessness with the perennial Christian Democratic coali-

[17] See pp. 780–784, 815.

tions. In the meantime the economic boom that reached a peak in Italy about 1963 began to show signs of trouble.

For almost two decades after the war, Italy enjoyed an unprecedented economic expansion. By 1949, with Marshall Plan aid, industrial production reached prewar levels. From 1953 on, Italian industrial growth rivaled that of West Germany and France. Benefiting from the Common Market, and with foreign capital streaming in, the economy flourished; by the 1960s economic output was more than double the level of the prewar years, and Italy was a leading industrial power. The south, however, remained an economic problem. Although the region made more progress in the decade from 1955 to 1965 than ever before, the gap with the industrial north widened rather than narrowed. There was a steady migration of southern workers, so that a city like Milan had to absorb a stream of untrained, often illiterate immigrants who seemed to be coming from a foreign country; others from the south, close to 3 million, found jobs as "guest workers" in the booming economies of France, Germany, and Switzerland.

In the 1960s Italy, despite many unresolved problems, was a constitutional democracy with a thriving capitalist economy, a quiet revolution elevating living standards for all classes. Most Italians hoped that continuing prosperity and close political and economic ties with the other countries of democratic Western Europe would allay social and labor unrest and frustrate the advance of a powerful and growing Communist party. But the economic boom affected Italian society unevenly, and the margin between the highest and lowest incomes remained wide. Nor did the Christian Democratic governments adequately direct public and private investment into such neglected areas as education and housing, troubled urban areas, and the agricultural south. After 1963 the economy began to weaken. Prosperity itself was partly responsible. As consumer demand rose, increased imports encouraged inflation; wages were increased to keep up with rising prices, and the inflationary spiral mounted. Italian products became less competitive, profits declined as costs rose, and investment shrank. Austerity measures undertaken in 1964 helped to curb inflation and the trade deficit, but they also postponed government spending on social needs.

Worsening economic conditions accentuated political problems. The conservatism of the Christian Democrats increased. The Socialists, who lost heavily in the 1968 elections, were no longer a major political force, while the Communists advanced in strength. In the autumn of 1969 labor discontent burst out in a great wave of strikes that subsided only after substantial wage increases, which accelerated inflation and further undermined the country's ability to compete in world markets. More dependent on oil imports than any other industrial country, Italy suffered from the oil embargo and the sudden steep oil price increases in 1973–1974. By mid-1974 it faced an economic crisis unlike anything it had known in the twenty years since postwar recovery. The inflation rate, which reached 25 percent in 1975, was still 16 percent in the early 1980s, over 1 million were unemployed, and the lira had dropped sharply in value.

Only a few years earlier Italy had looked forward to rising living standards and a resolution of its social and economic difficulties. Now the very existence of parliamentary and constitutional democracy was at stake. The Christian Democrats had previously muddled through because of widespread political apathy and a relatively quiescent labor movement, but the labor unions and the Communist party now actively mobilized mass support. The Communists, long the second largest party, had been increasing their share of the popular vote over the years.

In 1974 they proposed a reconciliation between themselves and other parties in the interests of the troubled nation. The strongest Communist party in the Western world and one of those most independent of the Soviet Union, it had condemned Soviet intervention in the East European satellites, renounced such tenets of Marxist orthodoxy as the dictatorship of the proletariat, and insisted that each country, in keeping with its political traditions, should be free to follow its own road to socialism. Communist mayors and municipal councils governed a number of major cities. Many Italians turned to the Communists to break the thirty-year tenure of the Christian Democrats, whose hold seemed to be weakening. In the elections of 1976, although the Communists did not surpass the Christian Democrats in popular vote, the margin narrowed, and the Communists sought accommodation with the Christian Democrats in an experiment in parliamentary cooperation. The short-lived experiment ended after the 1979 elections when the party suffered its first decline at the polls. It became difficult for any political leader to form a cabinet. In 1981, for the first time since 1945, a non-Christian Democrat, the leader of a small conservative party, formed one, but it too did not last. After the 1983 elections the Christian Democrats, despite a setback, helped form the country's forty-fourth cabinet. The nation was divided not only over political matters but also over laws permitting divorce and abortion. Political instability was aggravated by an atmosphere of violence, kidnappings, and terrorism, which included the seizure and slaying in 1978 of the Christian Democratic leader and former premier Aldo Moro. Terrorism, natural disasters like an earthquake in the south in 1980, and political scandals plagued the country, undermined confidence, and threatened constitutional government.

The Iberian Peninsula

Nowhere in Europe in the 1970s did political change take place so dramatically as in the Iberian peninsula. In Spain the thirty-six-year-old authoritarian rule of General Franco ended with the death of the dictator in 1975. In his last two decades Franco held power with a minimum of overt force, grudgingly accepted because the Spanish wished to wipe out memories of the bloody civil war that had torn the country apart in the previous generation.[18] Despite the political backwardness of the regime, remarkable economic progress was made. Within a decade, in the 1960s, a predominantly agricultural country became industrialized, and millions moved from the countryside to the cities. Even before Franco died, a program of political reform was put into effect, too limited, however, to satisfy democratic-minded Spaniards, working-class groups, and the unexpectedly robust political parties that emerged from their clandestine existence. After Franco's death, in accordance with the dictator's wishes, Juan Carlos I, grandson of the last Bourbon monarch, assumed the throne. The young king presided over the restoration of a constitutional monarchy. Two years later, in the first free elections in over forty years, a moderate liberal party and the Socialists emerged as the two strongest parties. When a small military group attempted a coup in 1981, the king rallied the army and the country to the defense of the constitution.

In 1982 the Socialists emerged as the leading party and formed a government, the country quietly accepting the victory of the left. The new government was faced with lagging economic growth, unemployment, inflation, and other effects of the general recession. Old separatist pressures continued; Catalans and Basques

[18] See pp. 799–801.

received home rule after 1977, but extremist Basque nationalists pressed for independence and resorted to bombings and terrorism.

In Portugal, as in Spain, an authoritarian regime survived the Second World War,[19] but, unlike Spain, Portugal remained in a state of economic backwardness. In 1961, Portugal was forced to surrender the remnants of its Indian empire to India; that year revolt broke out in the Portuguese colonies in Africa. The regime diverted its attention to subduing the African colonial rebellions, and a long, dreary, and unsuccessful military effort began. In the midst of the struggle, António Salazar, who had ruled Portugal for forty years, became incapacitated and died in 1970. His successor loosened the dictatorial controls slightly but continued the costly effort to subdue the colonies.

The colonial struggle in the next four years precipitated revolution. The army, frustrated and radicalized by the war, recognized as hopeless the thirteen-year effort to crush the independence movement. In April 1974 a group of majors and captains led a bloodless seizure of power in the capital; the following year the colonies received their independence. The officers established themselves as a Council of the Revolution but pledged democratic civilian rule in the near future. The next two years brought a succession of provisional governments, the leftist army officers and the newly emergent Communists often cooperating. In 1976 General Antonio Eanes was elected president, sympathetic to the left but not to the Communists. The economy, in difficulties even before the revolution, was in chaos. The provisional governments had introduced sweeping changes, nationalizing much of the economy, expropriating large landholdings, and awarding substantial wage increases, but they had neglected immediate problems. The country suffered from high unemployment and severe inflation. Socialists, moderates, and the more conservative governments that followed had to adopt austerity programs. In 1982 a new constitution reinforced the powers of parliament and restored civilian authority. The economic problems seemed insuperable, but Portugal was launched on a democratic political course. The advance of parliamentary democracy in Spain and Portugal in the 1970s and in Greece, where in 1974 a military junta was overthrown along with the Greek monarchy, were exceptions to the eclipse of democracy in many other parts of the world.

114. INTELLECTUAL AND SOCIAL CURRENTS

Along with sweeping political and economic changes, new cultural and intellectual currents also could be discerned. Much of contemporary twentieth-century culture had its origins in the years from 1871 to 1914,[20] but since that time science, philosophy, the arts, and religion crossed new frontiers or took new directions.

The Advance of Science: Nuclear Physics

Although science and technology expanded rapidly in the half-century before the First World War, the pace quickened in the following years and scientific discovery advanced more rapidly in the years after 1919 than in all previous human history. For one thing, more scientists were at work in the contemporary era than ever before. At the opening of the twentieth century, about 15,000 trained scien-

[19] See p. 794.
[20] See pp. 591–607.

tists were exploring scientific problems; in the latter half of the century, over a half-million scientists were engaged in research, more than in all previous centuries combined.

The average person experienced the triumphs of science most dramatically in medicine and public health. Nothing in previous medical discovery could equal the positive contributions of sulfa drugs, penicillin, cortisone, and antibiotics, used to combat formerly crippling or deadly infections and ailments; vitamins, hormones, adrenalin, and insulin were also available to promote health or relieve suffering. Vaccines combated a number of dread diseases, including, after 1955, poliomyelitis; by 1975 smallpox had been eradicated world-wide. The advances in medicine were accompanied by remarkable accomplishments in surgery, including the transplantation of vital organs. Apart from the advances in medical science, citizens in an industrial society benefited from modern technology in ways too familiar to need recounting. For entertainment radio and the motion picture were available and, after the Second World War, television. After 1947 airplanes could fly faster than the speed of sound; giant airships could traverse huge distances in a few hours; tourist travel to distant parts of the earth became commonplace. A new world of computers, rocketry, and space technology also opened, and the world seemed on the threshold of a new industrial age based on nuclear power.

The transformation of physics in the opening years of the twentieth century could be compared only to the scientific revolution of the sixteenth and seventeenth centuries and to the impact of Darwinian evolution in the nineteenth.[21] After 1919 a series of discoveries led to a deeper understanding of the structure of the atom and its nucleus. The cyclotron, developed in 1932, made it possible to penetrate or "bombard" the nucleus of the atom with high-speed particles and explore it further. The atom, it appeared, was not simply a nucleus of protons surrounded by electrons. In 1932 the British physicist Sir James Chadwick discovered that the atomic nucleus, or nucleon, consisted not only of protons but of neutrons as well. Earlier, at the turn of the century, scientists had discovered the natural radioactivity of certain elements, and Einstein had propounded his formula for the equivalence of energy and mass.

Now it was discovered that the atomic nucleus of elements like uranium, when bombarded by neutrons, could release unprecedented energy. Scientists explained that when a certain form, or isotope, of the uranium atom absorbs a neutron it becomes violently unstable and splits into two parts, releasing not only energy but neutrons of its own that then trigger the splitting of other atoms in a chain reaction, resulting in the emission of energy in prodigious amounts. In 1938 German scientists for the first time succeeded in accomplishing the fission, or splitting, of the uranium atom in the laboratory. By then the advance of atomic science, though the achievement of scientists of many different nationalities, was geared to war. Learning of the German developments, some scientists, including Albert Einstein who had fled the Nazis in 1934, prevailed upon the United States government to explore the use of atomic energy for military purposes before the Germans succeeded in doing so. In 1942 American and British scientists, together with European refugee scientists like the Italian Enrico Fermi, brought about the first sustained nuclear chain reaction; this, in turn, led to the secret preparation of the atomic bomb and, as has been related, its use in August 1945.[22]

The destructive power of the bomb dropped at Hiroshima heralded the atomic

[21] See pp. 276–289, 591–594.
[22] See p. 822.

age. The first use of atomic energy was for military purposes, but it could be used for constructive peacetime purposes as well; a tiny gram of uranium could produce power equal to almost three tons of coal. Even more staggering technical developments followed, involving nuclear fusion or the joining together of lighter atoms to form heavier ones, at great heat, with accompanying thermonuclear chain reactions. This was the basis of the hydrogen bomb developed in the 1950s in which atomic fission bombs were used as detonators. Such thermonuclear fusion was believed to be responsible for the energy of the sun itself. Twentieth-century nuclear physics had discovered the cosmic secret that the production of all energy in the universe depended on nuclear transformation. At the same time the awesome explosive powers discovered by science threatened the very survival of the human species and of the earth itself. Accidents in nuclear power plants, as had already occurred, threatened the surrounding population and environs with the release of radioactive gases; accidental bomb explosions, as reported to have occurred, were even more serious; but a true nuclear clash of arms could mean apocalypse. By the 1980s the nuclear powers possessed missiles in the thousands, each of which represented power equal to all of the explosive force used in all previous warfare since the invention of gunpowder.

Other Advances and Implications of Science

As in the case of nuclear physics, science in general in the contemporary age was closely allied with technology. There was a conscious organized effort to exploit new scientific findings. Government and industry subsidized most scientific research. Laboratory equipment was expensive, and complex investigation required large-scale collaborative efforts; the solitary scientific investigator or even inventor was disappearing. As scientific research came to be subsidized for national purposes, there was concern that scientific discoveries would serve political and not human goals.

Science had always affected the way people thought about themselves and their universe. The Copernican revolution had removed the earth from its central position in the scheme of things; Darwinian evolution had demonstrated that *Homo sapiens* was biologically a species that had survived. The philosophical implications of twentieth-century physics were only vaguely understood, yet they reinforced theories of relativism in all spheres. Ironically, at the very time that the average person was awed by the capabilities of science, scientists themselves recognized that they had no magic key to the nature of things. Generally they claimed no more than the ability to determine, or guess at, relationships which in the world of the atom were mysterious and uncertain.

In some quarters there was a tendency to question scientific and technological advance, and to ask whether modern technology had not grown beyond human control. Ecologists pointed to the wastage and spoliation of natural resources, the pollution of the atmosphere by smoke, soot, and smog, and the threat to the human environment. In another way the life-preserving features of medicine and public health threatened to result in overpopulation and in perhaps unmanageable pressure upon the limited resources of the globe. The techniques developed to save or prolong human life also raised ethical and legal questions including definitions of life and death, and the rights in such matters of patients, families, and physicians. Some, who condemned modern technology, extolled the virtues of a prescientific and preindustrial age; others called for sharper awareness of present and future dangers, and for increased controls by society. No longer was the idea of progress equated with the advance of science and technology.

Meanwhile, in the quest to understand nature the old divisions between the sciences broke down and new sciences appeared. Biochemistry, biophysics, astrophysics, geophysics, and other subdisciplines arose, and all made intensive use of mathematics. The study of genetics made great advances. While physicists discovered new atomic particles, biochemists isolated the organic substance found in the genes and chromosomes of all living cells, the chemical carriers of all hereditary characteristics. When they discovered the genetic "code," and when they synthesized the basic substance of heredity, the implications of genetic engineering for the future evolution of the race were staggering. Here, too, the destiny of all life was more than ever linked to science.

The other life sciences and social sciences also grew in importance. Psychological exploration of human behavior, as well as the applied medical sciences of psychiatry and psychoanalysis, expanded rapidly. Freud, who had first developed his theories of psychoanalysis before 1914, became widely known in the 1920s.[23] His emphasis on the human sex drive and sexual repression was much modified by disciples like Alfred Adler, Carl Jung, and many others, but the original creative concepts persisted. On the other hand, many students of human behavior rejected Freud and argued that his contributions were not universally or scientifically valid but reflected the values of pre-1914, middle-class, male-dominated Viennese society. New schools emerged with different interpretations and techniques, but the search was not abandoned for the unconscious sources of individual and collective human conduct.

As in the late nineteenth century, sociology and anthropology increasingly stressed the relativism of all culture. They denied notions of cultural superiority or hierarchies of cultural values, or even that there were objective criteria of historical progress. If Western society, they argued, made notable progress in science and technology, other cultures accomplished more in self-discipline, individual integrity, and human happiness. The very adjective "primitive," as opposed to "civilized," tended to disappear, and a new cultural humanism emerged that recognized and emphasized values distinct from the Western tradition.

Space Exploration

Among the most dramatic developments in science and technology in the second half of the twentieth century were advances in space exploration. Here competition developed between the Soviets and the Americans, who each orbited spaceships and for the first time in history crossed lunar and planetary frontiers. The Soviets pioneered with the orbiting of the first unmanned satellite in 1957 and the first manned spaceship in 1961. The Americans soon did the same.[24] Although the Soviets successfully launched rocket probes of the moon, it was American astronauts who in 1969 made the quarter-million mile journey and, while millions over the globe watched on television, walked on the lunar surface. Both countries proceeded with the deployment of space stations and with unmanned probes of the planets of the solar system as distant as Jupiter and Saturn, even making plans for spacecraft to "escape" the solar system and travel beyond. Other countries joined in the operation of artificial satellites for information-gathering and com-

[23] See p. 594.
[24] See p. 857.

munications. In 1975 Soviet and American astronauts orbited the earth simultaneously and linked their spaceships in a spectacular rendezvous before proceeding their separate ways. In 1981 the Americans began using a space shuttle capable of repeated flights to and from outer space. In 1982 Soviet cosmonauts spent a record seven months in a space station and flew home safely.

Meanwhile the information fed back to complex computer systems provided more knowledge than ever before about the planets, the structure and nature of matter, and even about the age and origins of the universe. Because space exploration could be undertaken only at enormous cost, some complained when acute social needs remained unfulfilled, but others saw it as part of the continuing human effort to cross new frontiers, expand horizons, and explore the unknown.

The Creative Arts

The revolution against older traditions in the creative arts continued. Ever since the Renaissance, artists had followed certain norms of representation and space perspective. But much of modern, or contemporary, art prided itself on being nonobjective; it rejected the idea of imitating or reconstructing nature, or mirroring it with realism or photographic fidelity. The fundamental innovations of the artistic revolution began in the decade before 1914,[25] but after 1919 the revolution in painting picked up in intensity; it seemed to mirror the political turbulence of the times and the disillusionment with rationalism and optimism. It reflected the influence of depth psychology and the emphasis on the unconscious and irrational, as well as the relativity of the new physics and the uncertainties raised about the nature of matter, space, and time. Surrealists openly derided rationality and reality, focusing on the artist's subconscious in an orgy of uncontrolled subjectivism.

Matisse, Braque, Picasso, and others continued the pre-1914 experimentation in color and form. Picasso systematically distorted and deformed his objects, as in the famous painting memorializing the German bombing of Guernica in 1937 during the Spanish Civil War, in which he strove for effects of anguish and intensity by his distortions. Chagall deliberately painted the exaggerations of a dream world. At the same time the possibilities inspired by the cubists led to a stricter sense of geometry and a focus on form alone. The results were sometimes pleasing, but often strange; but here, too, science taught that solid everyday objects have a different kind of reality in space and in movement. After the Second World War, especially in the United States, Jackson Pollock and other artists developed a new school of abstract art; it included techniques of improvisation and automation in which the unconscious was said to dictate the artist's work. Other, even broader, experimentation followed.

Beginning in the 1950s, the United States took the leadership from France in the new artistic developments. Contemporary art resulted in bold and original expressions of form and color, but the conscious subjectivism widened still further the gap between artist and public. The artist, painter, and sculptor (and the poet, musician, and novelist who were also rejecting the older conventions) were conveying their own vision of the world, not an objective reality shared by others. Perhaps the greatest innovation was that the public, baffled as it was by much of contemporary art, came to accept the avant-garde as normal. Or at least this was

---

[25] See pp. 596–597.

so in freer societies; in totalitarian societies—Nazi Germany in the 1930s or the Soviet Union—such experimentation or innovation was frowned upon and banned as degenerate or socially dangerous. Representational art, of course, never completely disappeared anywhere, and became common once again as a new pluralism emerged in contemporary artistic style.

The focus on subjectivism and the unconscious were reflected in literature too. The artistic reconstruction of lost time and the unfolding of the individual's innermost experience through a stream of consciousness and a flood of memories appeared first in the work of Marcel Proust and James Joyce. Perhaps T. S. Eliot reflected best the spiritual malaise of the contemporary age in the tone of his long poem, *The Waste Land*, written in 1922 but just as relevant sixty years later. After the Second World War advanced writers, particularly in France, experimented with novels and plays without heroes or plots in a conventional sense, often reconstructing little closed worlds shut off from reality. Film makers and directors experimented with the cinema along similar lines. All of this was in sharp contrast to the literature and entertainment provided through the mass communications media, especially popular movies and television, and hardly touched the average citizen.

Philosophy: Science, Logic, and Language

Philosophy in the mid-twentieth century seemed to contribute less to an understanding of contemporary problems than in the past. Whereas it had formerly focused on metaphysics and ethics, and shared common concerns with theology, it now sought, at least for a time, to adopt the precision of mathematics and the methodology of science. The effort to approach philosophy through empirical science, mathematics, and symbolic logic was known as logical positivism (or logical empiricism). It was developed in England by Bertrand Russell and Alfred North Whitehead, who published their *Principia Mathematica* on the eve of the First World War, and simultaneously by the Viennese philosopher Ludwig Wittgenstein, who later moved to Cambridge. Opposed to all that was metaphysical, it rejected the traditional questions of philosophy, and insisted that philosophers could not speak, in Wittgenstein's phrase, of "God, death, what is higher."

Another major development favored linguistic analysis. Rejecting the mathematical formulations of logical positivism, some philosophers, including Wittgenstein himself in his later work, argued that philosophical questions and statements could not be similar to those of science; philosophers had to explore language and the ambiguities of language. Philosophy, especially in Great Britain and the United States, for a time devoted itself almost exclusively to language, semantics, and linguistic analysis. All this was somewhat remote for the average person, and offered little enlightenment for the perplexities of the modern age. But many philosophers were becoming responsive to contemporary concerns and were grappling with unresolved human and social dilemmas.

Religion: Protestantism, Catholicism, Judaism

Christianity was in flux. With the continuing inroads of secularism and the triumph of communism in Eastern Europe and other parts of the world, Christianity suffered a number of setbacks. At the same time the Christian churches contin-

ued their older efforts to reconcile religious insights and traditional teaching with science, biblical scholarship, and comparative religion.[26]

In Protestantism in the early part of the twentieth century liberal, or modernist, thought tended to dominate. The churches absorbed the new scientific findings, minimized the supernatural and dogmatic aspects of their faith, and tried to adapt the religious teachings of the gospel to the social needs of the contemporary world. But the First World War and the disillusionment that followed dealt a blow to the social gospel and its inherent optimism. Sometime in the 1920s, as a reaction, a revived emphasis on revealed religion and the supernatural set in. The Swiss theologian Karl Barth, whose writings from 1919 to the 1960s exerted great influence, sought to lead Protestantism back to the root principles of the Reformation. After the Second World War, as a result of the work of Barth, Paul Tillich, and others, a powerful movement in Protestantism reasserted its dependence on revealed truth and denied that human reason with its fallibility and corruption could ever properly judge divine revelation. Some theologians turned also to Søren Kierkegaard, a nineteenth-century Danish theologian, who, like Luther, had resolved his own deep anguish by a commitment to religious experience. Despite these developments the liberal, or modernist, trend remained strong; the German theologian Rudolph Bultmann, who wanted readers to view the gospels as human experience, was one of its leading exemplars. The ecumenical movement, an effort to unite all branches of Protestantism and at the same time work out a rapprochement with the Roman Catholic and Eastern Orthodox churches, made slow progress. Disagreements over doctrine and over such social political issues as the ordination of women persisted.

The Roman Catholic church in the middle part of the twentieth century seemed to be in one of its great historic phases. Like Protestantism, it suffered from the secularism of the twentieth century. It lost followers, and church attendance and recruitment for the clergy declined, yet it showed much vigor. To cope with the advance of communism in the postwar years the church prohibited Catholics in 1949 from reading the Communist press, and in the 1950s suppressed the "worker-priest" movement in which a number of priests, especially in France, lived and worked among ordinary workers. Although the church no longer sought to stamp out modernism, it continued to emphasize dogmatic training in the seminaries. In 1950 the newly pronounced dogma of the Assumption (i.e., the bodily assumption of Mary to heaven) was a blow to liberal Catholics and to ecumenical-minded Protestants. But both Catholics and Protestants absorbed without great

[26] See pp. 597–602.

TWINNED COLUMN
by Antoine Pevsner (Russian, then French, 1886–1962)

Antoine Pevsner, like Kandinsky and Chagall (see pp. 599 and 742), left his native Russia after the Soviet regime began to disapprove of "modern" art. The picture here shows one of his sculptures, a bronze piece about forty inches high, constructed in 1947. The symmetry and the column recall the classical tradition, but the work also conveys the scientific and technological interests of the twentieth century. Pevsner's sculptural space is not the familiar medium in which human beings live and move, but a more abstract space, known to mathematics, quite apart from man's peculiarities of size and physical senses. Courtesy of the Solomon R. Guggenheim Museum.

shock the Dead Sea Scrolls, the first manuscripts of which were discovered in 1947, and which cast new light on the origins of Christianity.

When Pius XII (1939–1958) died, he was succeeded by John XXIII (1958–1963). Although elected at the age of seventy-seven, and reigning for only four and a half years, John was one of the most remarkable popes of modern times. To bring the church into harmony with the political and social changes of modern times, and to renew its organization and doctrine, he not only enlarged the College of Cardinals, increasing its non-Italian majority, but convened a Second Vatican Council. The Council, after careful preparation, met from 1962 to 1965, the first assembled since 1870 and the most important since the sixteenth-century Council of Trent.[27] John also issued powerful encyclicals; one, *Mater et Magistra* (1961), updating the older social teachings of the church, called upon the wealthier nations to share their resources with the world; another, *Pacem in Terris* (1963), addressed Catholics and non-Catholics alike, the first encyclical to do so, in an appeal for peace and the protection of human rights.

John, who did not live to see the Council's labors completed, was succeeded by Paul VI (1963–1978). Paul shared John's concern for reform and social progressivism and encouraged ecumenicism by visiting the centers of orthodox Christianity in the Middle East. In the Council, which completed its work under his papacy, he considered himself a mediator between conservative and liberal elements. The Council proclaimed the right to religious liberty for all religions and explicitly absolved the Jews from the charges of deicide that had inflamed anti-Semitism over the ages. It revised a number of church practices. The Mass, for example, could henceforth be said in the vernacular. It sought to affirm the principle of collegiality, that is, that the pope must share authority with the prelates of the church. Paul was unhappy about some innovations, opposing the attempt to repudiate certain tenets of orthodoxy or papal supremacy. Later, on the question of birth control, especially critical to the Catholic countries of Latin America with their expanding populations, Paul rejected the recommendations of his own commission and condemned modern birth control methods. Many Catholics remained restless and impatient with the failure to modernize the church more thoroughly. Many advocated abandoning the injunction of celibacy for the clergy; some monks, nuns, and priests set aside their vows and married. Theologians continued to reaffirm the principle of shared authority. Paul's insistence on papal obedience went unheeded, and his strictures against birth control were openly criticized and often ignored. But the Second Vatican Council opened the door to change; Catholics everywhere felt freer to question old tenets and practices.

The church in the years after 1945 suffered a special kind of martyrdom in Eastern Europe, and especially in Poland. Appropriately, after Paul's death in 1978, and after his successor, John Paul I, died after only thirty-four days in office, the new pope elected was the former archbishop of Cracow, the first Polish head of the church, and the first non-Italian pope in over four and a half centuries. In office John Paul II (1978–   ) returned to his native Poland to demonstrate his concern for his countrymen in their struggle against repression. Robust, earthy, and energetic, he traveled widely; in 1981 he narrowly escaped assassination in Rome itself. As head of the church he favored orthodoxy in doctrine and a disciplined and celibate clergy, and reaffirmed the church's opposition to birth

[27] See pp. 87–88.

control, but he gave warm and eloquent expression to the need to protect human dignity all over the globe.

Judaism, the third important faith of the Western world, was haunted in the years after 1945 by the great traumatic experience of the Nazi persecution and the wartime attempt at genocide, the Holocaust.[28] Although the older trend of assimilation to a secular society persisted, there was a revived adherence to religion, both orthodox and reform. There was also support by Jews everywhere, and especially in the United States, for the state of Israel, and not only among Zionists, although many later became increasingly troubled by Israeli militancy. Support for Israel was reinforced by the harassment and persecution of Jews in the Soviet Union and Eastern Europe, and in the Arab countries; in turn these countries used Jewish allegiance to Israel as justification for their attacks.

Like the Western religions, Islam, Hinduism, Buddhism, and the other great non-Western faiths, of which little can be said in these pages, all faced serious challenges, and were making efforts to adjust millennial old doctrines to the secularism of the contemporary age—or to resist them. Iran, where a fundamentalist Islamic reaction to modernization burst forth into revolution in the late 1970s, was one example where resistance was stronger than accommodation. Some of the Eastern religions attracted adherents in the West, Islam among American blacks, Buddhist teachings and practices among intellectuals and others. There was also a revived interest in the West in the transcendental and even the occult.

Existentialism

Outside organized religion, and generally outside professional philosophy too, a loosely organized body of ideas called "existentialism" grappled in the early postwar years with the human predicament. The existentialists formed no one school of thought and held no coherent body of principles; there were Christian, agnostic, and atheist existentialists. Yet all held some beliefs and attitudes in common. All reflected a troubled civilization, a world disturbed by war, totalitarianism, and oppression, a world of material progress and moral uncertainty in which the individual could be crushed by the triumphs of science and technology. The existentialists questioned the idea of progress or dismissed it as an illusion. Emphasizing the fact of "existence" in the present, they sometimes doubted whether a living generation could learn from the past or contribute to the future. Accepting what they liked to call the "absurdity" of the human situation, they sought to reconcile the discrepancy between human ideals and a universe they considered devoid of purpose.

Existentialist thought owed a debt to Pascal, Nietzsche,[29] and others who had underscored the tragic element in human existence and limitations on the power of human reason. More directly it owed a debt to Kierkegaard, the Danish religious philosopher, whose writings became better known when translated into German in 1909. But it was French writers like Albert Camus and Jean-Paul Sartre who, after the emergence of their country from defeat, occupation, and resistance in the Second World War, developed it in literature and philosophy in a form that gave it a wide intellectual following. In a hostile world, they contended, human beings had to reassert their freedom. They were "condemned to be free," said Sartre,

[28] See p. 820 and map, p. 819.
[29] See pp. 288–289, 596.

totally free and entirely responsible for the choices they made. The authentic existentialist, moreover, was not merely contemplative but *engagé*, committed to action, even though aware that such action could not change the world. Camus drew upon the myth of Sisyphus to communicate his message. Sisyphus was condemned to roll his stone uphill even though it rolled back down again, his very humanity growing out of courage and perseverance at a hopeless and absurd task.

Some of these beliefs were shared by Christian existentialists who adopted Nietzsche's nineteenth-century assertion that "God is dead." The universe, they asserted, was no longer ruled by a deity who decreed and revealed the rules individuals must live by; human beings had to make their own choices and commitments. They spoke even of a post-Christian era. But mainly existential ideas were part of an atheistic humanism, like that of Sartre, emphasizing the anguish of human existence, the frailty of human reason, the fragility of human institutions, and the need to reassert and redefine human freedom.

Activism: The Youth Rebellion

In the 1960s a new activism made a startling appearance, sparked by a widespread student rebellion. A generation came to college age during a period of comparative political stability and prosperity, knowing little firsthand of the Great Depression, the political turbulence of the 1930s, or the Second World War, and growing up in an era of rapid global change and scientific breakthroughs. They took for granted the scientific, technological, and other accomplishments of their world and concentrated on its deficiencies—the flagrant contradictions of wealth and poverty within nations and among nations, racial injustices, colonialism, the impersonal quality of mechanized society and bureaucratized institutions (including colleges and universities), the violence that destroyed human beings in continuing wars, and always the threat of nuclear destruction. The rebelliousness extended beyond the traditional generation gap; it was directed at all established society.

The revolt burst forth in the late 1960s in widely separate parts of the world. The Cultural Revolution in China,[30] although in an entirely different context, was not unrelated and indirectly inspired it. At the peak of the movement in 1967–1968 students demonstrated and rioted on campuses and battled the police in streets all over the world; American, West German, Italian, and French universities were most involved. Only in France in the spring of 1968 did the demonstrations reach near-revolutionary dimensions and threaten to overthrow the regime when ten million workers also went out on strike, partly in sympathy and partly for their own grievances. The ultra-militancy of the students alienated many, and the government overcame the threat and restored order.[31] Such initial grievances as inadequate facilities in the overcrowded universities and impersonal and remote instruction were almost forgotten in the upheavals in Paris and elsewhere. Some of the earliest demonstrations took place in the United States, antedating the peak of the fighting in Vietnam, and continued longer, heightened by resistance to American involvement in the war.

The rebelling students made heroes of the sworn foes of the established order: Fidel Castro and his martyred lieutenant Che Guevara, Ho Chi Minh, Mao Tsetung, revolutionary American black leaders such as the assassinated Malcolm X,

[30] See p. 864.
[31] See p. 892.

the heralds of the colonial revolution such as Frantz Fanon and others. They read the neo-Marxist philosopher Herbert Marcuse, who warned that the very tolerance of bourgeois society was a trap to prevent true protest against injustice; they learned that the industrial proletariat, embedded in the existing system, was no longer a revolutionary force. Adherents of a New Left, they dismissed older revolutionaries in the Soviet Union as timid bureaucrats who were unaware that the revolution had entered a post-Marxist phase and that leadership was to be sought in the underdeveloped Third World. They attacked modern materialism, comfort, affluence and conformity, and the power structure of contemporary society. Some turned to violence; others sang its praise; there was confrontation and action for the sake of action, recalling, if it resembled anything at all, an older anarchism and nihilism.[32] They called on each other to destroy in order to purify and to restore creative freedom by obliterating the past. The rebellion in its dramatic phase of the late 1960s subsided after a short interval, some elements of it lingering on and passing into a less activist counterculture which favored drugs, sexual permissiveness, communal living, and other forms of rejecting conventional society. A small number affiliated themselves with underground terrorist organizations and continued their assault on society. While older people shuddered at the attacks on established institutions and orderly processes, many were shaken out of their complacency about social inequities. Efforts were made subsequently in France, West Germany, and elsewhere to reform university administration and to provide more adequate teaching facilities. The youth movement, even after it subsided, had a continuing effect on all age groups in loosening older standards of language, dress, and relationships between the sexes.

The Woman's Liberation Movement

The feminist, or woman's liberation, movement was another manifestation of contemporary social ferment. From the time of the French Revolution a few thinkers in France and England had raised the question of equal rights for women.[33] The modern movement had its origin in the United States in the mid-nineteenth century, and also began its contemporary phase there. In 1848 Elizabeth Cady Stanton and a small group of associates proclaimed a declaration of independence for women, demanding the right to vote, equal compensation for work, legal equality, and expanded educational opportunities. The movement spread abroad and was taken up in Britain by the suffragettes. The right to vote was won in a few American states and smaller countries before the First World War; in Britain and the United States, among others, after the First World War; and in almost all other countries after the Second[34]; but other objectives remained unrealized. The militant contemporary phase began in the United States in the mid-1960s, sparked in part by the civil rights movement in behalf of the American black population, and took form as the woman's liberation movement. Its leaders stressed the fact that women, who comprised half or more of the human race, did not enjoy positions of authority, leadership, and power proportionate to their numbers. Although some of the more blatant forms of legal discrimination were being removed, feminists demanded an end to all barriers to equality. Discrimination in contemporary society, they also noted, was often subtle and indi-

[32] See pp. 535, 588, 606, 700–702.
[33] See pp. 360, 584, 607.
[34] See pp. 584, 884–885.

rect. Sometimes it involved acculturation patterns by which children at an early age absorbed stereotyped notions of their future lives and possible careers. The process was self-perpetuating because with few women in visible positions of leadership there were few models to emulate.

The arguments for equal rights were most meaningful in the advanced industrial countries. Elsewhere, in the poorer, less developed nations women had to overcome centuries-old neglect, oppression, abuse, and disregard of the most elementary personal rights. The United Nations, from the time of its founding in 1945, committed itself to equal political, economic, and educational rights for women. But in Africa, Asia, and Latin America adult illiteracy rates a generation later were still significantly higher for women than for men and were declining more slowly. Opportunities for higher education were also more circumscribed. In the developing areas, where a majority of the world's women lived, equal rights for women also hinged upon economic development and upon social advances for the entire population.

Discrimination was not confined to capitalist societies. In a Communist country like the Soviet Union women, at least constitutionally, were guaranteed equal rights with men. They made up over 30 percent of the elected representatives to the Supreme Soviet, whereas in the United States the corresponding figure for the American Congress was less than 3 percent. Yet there were few if any women represented in the organs of the Communist party with real power, such as the Politburo. In professional opportunities, the Soviet Union had many more women than men in medicine and dentistry, but these professions did not enjoy the high standing that they did in the United States and Western Europe, nor did women occupy many important research or administrative positions in Soviet hospitals or universities. Women were encouraged to work, and in fact had to work out of economic necessity and social pressure, but not necessarily to develop their potential or to achieve positions of responsibility. Not much more attention was paid in the Soviet Union than elsewhere to overcoming the patterns of a male-dominated society. In the People's Republic of China, women were afforded wide opportunities within the limits of a controlled society, and equality between the sexes was proclaimed as a social goal. At the same time women in China, as in the Soviet Union, worked along with men at heavier and more arduous work than in Western industrial countries. Everywhere there was much to be done, and weakened economies after the mid-1970s curtailed opportunities still further. In the United States an equal rights amendment to the Constitution, although adopted by Congress, failed of ratification by the required number of states before its deadline in 1982. Some women, more so than in the past when authority resided only with reigning women sovereigns, held positions of the highest authority in their countries in the years after 1945, among them Indira Gandhi in India, Golda Meir in Israel, Margaret Thatcher in Britain, and several less prominent women presidents or prime ministers in such widely differing countries as Sri Lanka, Malta, Yugoslavia, Portugal, and Norway. In 1981 the first woman was appointed to the Supreme Court in the United States.

The development of contraceptive devices, including the birth control pill in the early 1960s, provided a new biological freedom for women. Changing social patterns tolerating sexual freedom and new forms of marital relationships also contributed to social liberation. There remained a contradiction between the demand for equal rights and the special protection in the form of labor legislation that democratic societies had long adopted for women. Although disagreement persisted on the methods and tempo of change, wide agreement existed on the need to utilize all of society's human resources, male and female, in every part of the globe to confront the challenges of the contemporary world. If that could be accomplished, it would count among the most memorable of the revolutionary changes of the contemporary era.

115. CRISES, CLASHES, AND COEXISTENCE

The War in Korea

We have already noted the origins and course of the Cold War to about 1950.[35] In June 1950 the Korean War broke out. The Soviet-sponsored regime of North Korea crossed the border along the thirty-eighth parallel and launched an invasion of the Western-supported republic in the south. During the Second World War the Western powers and the Soviets had agreed that Korea, once a source of imperialist contention between Japan and Russia, and after 1910 under Japanese rule, would again become free and independent. At the war's end Soviet troops by arrangement occupied the northern part of the country to the thirty-eighth parallel, and United States troops the southern part. The U.S.S.R. established a satellite government under a Moscow-trained Communist leader, supported a large North Korean army, and rejected an American proposal to hold elections in a unified Korea under international supervision.

Elections in South Korea in 1948 resulted in the presidency of Syngman Rhee, who despite democratic forms governed the republic dictatorially for the next twelve years. After the election the United States withdrew its occupation forces but continued military and economic support to South Korea. The Soviet Union similarly withdrew from North Korea and continued to provide arms and economic aid to its client state. Although the American government had not explicitly included Korea, as it had Japan and the Philippines, in the perimeter defined as vital to the defense of American interests in Asia, President Truman was resolved to check the invasion when it occurred. He was convinced that it was incited by the Soviet Union as part of the Soviet world-wide offensive, a further stage in the Cold War in which communism had passed from subversion to armed aggression.

The North Korean attackers expected a quick victory because of the boldness of their initiative and their superior forces. They gambled that the United States would not intervene and that the outside world would lodge no more than a moral protest. The precise inspiration for the invasion cannot be known for certain. The U.S.S.R., concerned over American entrenchment in occupied Japan, may have encouraged it, or the North Koreans may have decided on their own to unify the country, confident that they would win Stalin's approval. In any event the Russians seemed to be caught by surprise too; boycotting the United Nations for its refusal to recognize the People's Republic of China, they were unable to exercise their veto when the American government brought the matter before the Security Council. That the North Koreans were capable of independent action was difficult for Americans to believe. The attack challenged the entire collective security system built since 1945 to stem the tide of Soviet communism. Truman, recalling the weakness and appeasement of the 1930s, prevailed on the Security

[35] See pp. 844–850.

Council to condemn North Korea as an aggressor and to take military action, simultaneously committing American troops.

In the fighting that summer the American-led United Nations forces commanded by General Douglas MacArthur were driven back at first but later pushed the North Korean armies northward, and then, in a crucial decision, crossed the thirty-eighth parallel, moving rapidly toward the Yalu River, the boundary between Korea and the Manchurian province of Communist China. In November 1950 the People's Republic of China entered the war; hundreds of thousands of Chinese Communist troops supported by Russian-made jet planes drove the American-led forces southward in what looked like a repetition of the early phase of the conflict.

Although Truman was determined to check the North Koreans, he also feared another world war, which was a possibility if Manchuria or other parts of China were bombed. When MacArthur insisted on drastic action against China, President Truman relieved him of his command. In the following months the United Nations forces fought their way back to the thirty-eighth parallel, and even slightly to its north. In July 1951 a cease-fire agreement ended large-scale fighting, but not until 1953 was an armistice signed, negotiations being snarled for two full years over the exchange and repatriation of prisoners of war. Fifteen nations participated in the Korean War, with token contingents fighting alongside the United States. The Americans suffered over 54,000 battle and battle-related deaths in this undeclared war, almost half as many as in the First World War; the American wounded were estimated at 100,000. As for the Koreans, losses were roughly equal for North and South; over 2 million Koreans were dead, wounded, or missing.

Politically, conditions reverted to what they had been before 1950. Korea was again divided roughly at the thirty-eighth parallel. The North Korean government, the People's Republic of China, and the U.S.S.R. continued to reject elections for the entire country under international supervision. It was an uneasy armistice, punctuated by numerous border and other incidents. In Western eyes a flagrant act of aggression had been checked; to the Communist world, and to many non-Communists in Asia, the great capitalist power, the United States, had been prevented from reasserting Western imperialist supremacy in the East. In practical terms the United States, both in the Korean War and in its efforts to create regional security pacts in the East, found little enthusiasm for its policies among the larger non-Communist Asian powers such as India or Indonesia. Most of them disliked communism but also distrusted the West. Although the United States had been the least involved of all the Great Powers in nineteenth-century Asian colonialism, its new leadership in the Western world, and the suspicion that it was seeking world markets for American capitalism, made it the symbol of Western oppression and exploitation, a picture assiduously cultivated by the Soviets and even more belligerently, for a time, by the Chinese Communists. On the other hand, success in deterring the North Koreans reinforced the American belief that military strength and decisiveness could check Communist expansion everywhere. The Korean War inaugurated an era of deep American entanglement in Asia; it was a prelude to a larger and more serious conflict, the war in Vietnam in the following decade.

Soviet-American Relations after Stalin

In the early 1950s Soviet-American relations and the Cold War entered a new phase. The political leaders of the U.S.S.R. who succeeded Stalin in 1953 seemed more conciliatory or at least were willing to pursue their ends in less ruthless ways.[36] Although they kept the Western powers and the world oscillating between tension, relaxation, and renewed tension, the alternative of a peaceful coexistence of competing world systems seemed possible. There were signs, too, that in the United States not all compromise was to be shunned as appeasement. At Geneva in 1955 President Eisenhower, along with British and French leaders, met face to face with the heads of the Soviet state in a friendlier atmosphere than any since the Second World War.

But the Geneva spirit did not last. Crises reopened over Western access to Berlin. In 1960 a summit conference at Paris broke up when Khrushchev produced evidence of American reconnaissance flights over Russian territory, which the Americans did not deny. The tension shifted to the Western hemisphere. In Cuba Fidel Castro had ousted a rightist dictatorship in 1959 and established a Communist regime, with an independent character of its own, supported by both the Soviet Union and the People's Republic of China. In 1961 Cuban anti-Communist exiles, encouraged by the United States, invaded the island but met with disaster. The following year President Kennedy, charging that Soviet missile bases installed in Cuba represented a direct threat to American security, placed a naval quarantine on the further shipment of military equipment to Cuba and issued stern warnings to the Soviets. Khrushchev backed down and agreed to dismantle the bases (for which he was berated as a capitulationist by the then more belligerent Chinese Communists).

The Berlin Wall, a huge concrete and barbed wire barricade, built in 1961 to prevent East Germans from traveling to West Berlin, remained a source of friction. In Korea border incidents and the seizure in 1968 of an American ship, avowedly on an intelligence-gathering mission, disturbed the armistice. The Middle East, as we have seen, broke out in recurrent open warfare, the Soviets wooing and arming the Arab states. Most of all, Southeast Asia, after the withdrawal of the French in 1954, remained a troubled area.

The Vietnam War

In Vietnam war broke out in the early 1960s. In the course of the fighting against the French, the former French colony had been divided into a Communist-dominated regime in the north and a non-Communist regime in the south, much as in the case of Korea. After the French defeat and withdrawal,[37] an international conference at Geneva in 1954 partitioned the country at the seventeenth parallel until elections could be held and the country unified. North Vietnam, or the Democratic Republic of Vietnam, with its capital at Hanoi, was presided over by Ho Chi Minh, the Communist leader who had successfully led the independence movement against the French. Below the seventeenth parallel an anti-Communist, Western-backed South Vietnam was established, with Saigon as its capital. The partition left the population divided into roughly equal halves of 20 million people each, but with little relationship to historic or ethnic differences. South Vietnam, concerned that the Communists had acquired a large popular following in the struggle against the French, and even earlier against the Japanese, refused to participate in elections for the country scheduled for 1956 on the ground that it had not been a signatory to the Geneva agreement. When the elections were not held, events took a different turn. Communist guerrilla soldiers left behind in the south when the northern armies withdrew under the Geneva agree-

[36] See pp. 854–855.
[37] See p. 869.

ment, harassed the authorities in South Vietnam. Skilled in insurgent warfare, the Viet Cong terrorized and coerced the peasantry, but they also won support by redistributing land and by denouncing the Western-backed government of South Vietnam. They were reinforced by North Vietnam regular troops, who infiltrated the south and received economic and military aid from the People's Republic of China. In 1960 a National Liberation Front projected itself as a revolutionary government for the south. South Vietnam, despite technical advice and assistance from the United States, found itself hard pressed and appealed for additional American aid.

The United States took the position that it was necessary to fill the vacuum created by the French withdrawal and to check Communist expansion in South Vietnam in order to prevent the other states in Asia from toppling one by one—like a set of dominoes, the theory went. The United States bolstered the Saigon regime with military advisers, financial backing, and arms. At the same time it sought to democratize the regime, whose authoritarian practices and widespread corruption became increasingly embarrassing.

American involvement deepened and spanned the administration of five presidents, from Eisenhower to Ford. Under Eisenhower a few hundred military advisers were present, and military and economic aid began; as early as 1959 two military advisers were killed in an attack north of Saigon. In 1961 under Kennedy the first American support troops arrived, and a year later 4,000 troops were on hand and the first battle deaths reported. The United States also involved itself actively in South Vietnam politics, first propping up and then in 1963 actively helping to overthrow the repressive government of President Ngo Dinh Diem.

Under Johnson American intervention reached a climax. In 1964, on the alleged ground that North Vietnamese torpedo boats in the Gulf of Tonkin had attacked United States destroyers, Johnson ordered immediate air strikes against North Vietnam and the next day secured support for a joint congressional resolution empowering him to take "all necessary measures" to defend the United States and its ally. The Gulf of Tonkin resolution was the only explicit congressional sanction for American involvement in the years that followed, and it was later revoked in 1970 by a disenchanted Congress. After 1965 heavy air raids on supply bases in the north and on Communist-controlled areas in the south became an almost daily occurrence. American bombers attacked as far north as Hanoi. In searching out the elusive Viet Cong in the south, incendiary materials were dropped from the air, burning and destroying entire villages, defoliating hundreds of thousands of acres of land, and turning the survivors into homeless refugees. The bombing raids, the commitment of American ground troops, and the casualties mounted. In 1966 there were close to 200,000 American troops in South Vietnam. By 1969 at the maximum there were 543,400 troops. (About 50,000 South Korean and Thai troops also participated.) In the massive bombings from 1965 to 1968 more tons of explosives were dropped than against all the Axis powers in the Second World War.

Despite United States military aid, the South Vietnamese were unable to cope with the strength and resourcefulness of North Vietnam. With aid from the Soviet Union and from the People's Republic of China the northerners rebuilt their destroyed factories and kept the supplies flowing south. Optimistic reports to Washington on the pacification of the countryside and on the number of enemy casualties were confounded by a successful Communist offensive at the opening of 1968. It became clear that a negotiated settlement had to be sought.

From the beginning America's allies in Western Europe showed a lack of enthusiasm and offered little support. In the United States the war became a root cause of riots and disorders on campuses and in the cities. Many questioned whether the United States, despite its enormous strength, should assume the responsibility, or even had the capability, to police the world against Communist aggression; whether the American presence in Vietnam was an unwanted foreign presence reminiscent of Western intrusion in the age of imperialism; whether bombing raids that reached to within ten miles of the Chinese border might provoke direct Chinese intervention and a third world war; whether the South Vietnamese regime could be stabilized and democratized to make the sacrifices worthwhile; and whether the air raids and continued hostilities might end in the utter destruction of the entire hapless country. Critics with a knowledge of Asian history argued that the Vietnamese had a long record of protecting themselves from their Chinese neighbors and that even a Vietnam united under the Communists would not mean subjugation by the Chinese, or by the Soviets.

The need to win the war became an obsession with President Johnson. But with victory remote, and with popular and congressional resentment against the war rising, he decided not to seek reelection in 1968 and announced a halt to the bombing in the north so that negotiations for peace could go forward. By November 1968 all bombing ceased—for a time. The Hanoi government and the National Liberation Front in the south opened preliminary peace talks in Paris with the United States and the Saigon government, but the fighting went on.

In 1969 President Nixon pledged an early end to the war and promised to shift to the South Vietnamese the major responsibility for their own defense, and began to withdraw troops. Yet involvement in the next three years in some ways became even more intense. In response to stalemated peace talks in Paris and continuing Communist advances Nixon ordered the resumption of heavy air attacks and widened the war by an "incursion" into Cambodia to cut off Communist supply lines. At the end of 1972 North Vietnam was subjected to the heaviest bombing of the entire war. Meanwhile Nixon's energetic and versatile secretary of state Henry Kissinger made intermittent progress in secret talks with the North Vietnamese representatives and finally reached a cease-fire agreement in January 1973, ending direct involvement for the United States and concluding the longest war— like the Korean, an undeclared one—the country had ever fought. Over eight years had elapsed from the arrival of the first Marine contingent in 1965 to the withdrawal of the last troops at the end of March 1973, or twelve, if the involvement is dated from 1961.

Even though American troops were withdrawn, hostilities between North Vietnam and South Vietnam continued as each sought additional territory before a final settlement was reached. Both sides violated the cease-fire, and fighting resumed on a major scale in 1973. Although the United States remained committed to the defense of South Vietnam, Congress refused additional expenditures for military aid. North Vietnam continued to receive support from the Communist powers, the Soviet Union and the People's Republic of China, and dominated the fighting. Corruption and demoralization in South Vietnam grew worse; army desertions mounted. Nevertheless, the end came as a surprise. At the close of 1974, the North Vietnamese captured key cities in the southern provinces. Even before their main attack, the government of South Vietnam lost heart and ordered withdrawal to the coast; a planned retreat degenerated into rout. The North Vietnamese, deciding that complete victory was in their grasp, poured thousands of troops south across the demilitarized zone. Swarms of refugees fleeing south added to the confusion. By April North Vietnam's armies controlled three-fourths of South Vietnam, and Saigon fell.

When on April 30, 1975, North Vietnamese troops entered Saigon, they renamed the capital Ho Chi Minh City in honor of the Communist leader who died in 1969 and who in 1946 had first proclaimed Vietnamese independence from the French. After thirty years of almost uninterrupted fighting, first between the French and the Vietnamese, and then in the civil war between North and South in which the United States had massively intervened, peace had finally come, and with it total Communist victory. Reunification and reorganization of the country

VIETNAM AND ITS NEIGHBORS

French Indochina, for about sixty years before World War II, comprised the old Asian territories of Cambodia, Laos, and Vietnam, though the French called northern Vietnam Tonkin and southern Vietnam Annam. Shaken by Japanese invasion in World War II, the French proved unable after a long struggle to resist the Vietnamese movement for independence that drew strength also from Communist affiliations. When the French withdrew in 1954, an international agreement (the Geneva Accords) provided for partition of Vietnam until unity could be restored. Since the north was now Communist, the United States undertook to strengthen South Vietnam by favoring reforms and by measures of economic and military assistance. This involvement grew in the 1960s into a large-scale though undeclared war, in which the United States intervened with over half a million troops. Hostilities ended in 1975 with Communist regimes established in Vietnam, Laos, and Cambodia.

along Communist lines proceeded quickly; a "political reeducation" campaign was launched and property was nationalized. Cities, crowded with refugees, were emptied by a forced resettlement campaign that moved large numbers into the countryside.

In the wake of North Vietnam's victory Cambodia and Laos also fell under Communist control. Thirty years after the end of the Second World War, all that had once been French Indochina was in Communist hands, and a reunified Vietnam emerged as an important military power in Southeast Asia.

The Vietnam War was costly; about one and a quarter million Vietnamese were estimated to have died in the fighting. For the United States the war was a searing experience. Battle and battle-related deaths were estimated at 57,000, with 900 missing and over 155,000 wounded. The number of battle deaths exceeded those of the Korean War and approached the number of Americans killed in the First World War.[38] From 1960 to 1975 the hostilities cost the United States over $140 billion. The impact of these expenditures on the American economy was heightened by the failure to place taxes on a wartime basis, contributing to the inflation that set in during the late 1960s. The political and moral costs were enormous. The war alienated young people more than any previous American war. It created also a mistrust of presidential power and of the military. The deadly bombings, the reports of enemy casualties, the gruesome war scenes visible in homes in the first war reported in detail by television, the revelation of atrocities and war crimes committed by American troops, as at My Lai in 1968, first covered up and then made the subject of a public inquiry and trial, were all deeply disturbing. America's giant industrial and military power had failed to bring victory. Unlike the war in Korea, where regular troops fought each other along recognized frontiers, in Vietnam, quite apart from the political and moral issues involved, technological superiority in armaments and air power was inadequate against an enemy skilled in insurgent warfare and imbued with a revolutionary zeal.

The travail of southeast Asia was not yet ended. During the Vietnam War the North Vietnamese infiltrated border areas of Cambodia and helped arm

[38] Department of Defense figures showed:

	Battle Deaths	Other Deaths	Wounded	Total Deaths
World War I (1917–1918)	53,402	63,114	204,002	116,516
World War II (1941–1945)	291,557	113,842	670,846	405,399
Korean War (1950–1953)	33,629	20,617	103,284	54,246
Vietnam War (1965?–1973)	47,253	10,449	155,419	57,702

Communist insurgents who, after five years of civil war, overthrew the government in 1975. The leaders of the Khmer Rouge subjected Cambodia (or Kampuchea, as they renamed it) to brutal dictatorship and terror; perhaps 2 million died in the small country from 1975 to 1978. In foreign affairs the Khmer Rouge turned out to be more pro-Chinese than suited the Vietnamese, who were expelling large numbers of Vietnamese of Chinese extraction (many fled to China and elsewhere as the "boat people"). In 1979 Vietnam, backing a dissident group of Communist rebels, and invading with large numbers of troops, helped overthrow the regime; in retaliation China attacked the border provinces of Vietnam and fighting continued sporadically for some time. The Soviet Union supported Vietnam in the United Nations, and international pressure for the withdrawal of the Vietnamese from Cambodia was without effect. Ancient rivalries between China and Vietnam, and between Vietnam and Cambodia, and contemporary tensions between the Soviet Union and the People's Republic of China prolonged the agonies of Southeast Asia.

The Superpowers: After 1962

No nuclear weapons were used in Vietnam, nor indeed in any conflict in the close to four decades after 1945, but over every crisis, large or small, hung the threat that armed conflict might escalate into nuclear catastrophe. The early atomic disarmament negotiations had been broken off in 1948.[39] The following year the Soviets exploded their first atomic bomb, and in 1952 the British. Despite the opposition of some scientists, the United States developed and in 1952 successfully tested the hydrogen bomb, which through a chain reaction and thermonuclear effect had vastly more destructive capacity than the atomic bomb. A year later the Soviets exploded a hydrogen bomb. In 1961 the Soviets tested a 50-megaton bomb, that is, one with the explosive power of 50 million tons of TNT, the largest nuclear device ever exploded before or since, dwarfing the mere 20,000 tons of the Hiroshima bomb. No one doubted that the United States, as it proceeded with its testing, could do the same.

Because continued nuclear testing of this kind threatened to poison the earth's environment and damage the genetic endowment of present and future generations, the United States, the U.S.S.R., and Britain in 1963 drew up a partial test ban treaty to permit underground testing only; the ban was later extended to outer space as well. Over 100 nations eventually subscribed but not France, which in 1960 had become a fourth atomic power, or the People's Republic of China, which in 1964 became a fifth and in 1967 successfully exploded a hydrogen bomb.

The nuclear capacity of the superpowers and the threatened spread of nuclear arms loomed menacingly over a world split by deep rivalries. On this the United States and the Soviet Union could agree, and negotiations led to an international agreement in 1977 to try to curb the proliferation of nuclear weapons; 90 states subscribed to it, but not a score or so with near-nuclear capacities. To check such proliferation was difficult so long as the peaceful use of atomic energy was encouraged. Nations purchasing nuclear power plants from any of the industrial powers, ostensibly for peaceful purposes, could reprocess the plutonium from the spent fuel and build atomic bombs. India did precisely that, and in 1974 tested an atomic bomb underground; it became the sixth atomic power. The search for alternative energy sources in the 1970s stimulated many nations to build nuclear

[39] See pp. 845–846.

power plants that could easily be diverted to non-peaceful purposes. By the end of the 1980s, it was estimated, seventeen additional countries would cross the nuclear threshold and have a nuclear military capacity of some kind. The danger also existed that terrorist and guerrilla organizations might divert explosive atomic materials for their purposes.

The United States and the Soviet Union had continued to build not only the destructive weapons but also the delivery systems that could make possible mutual annihilation and the destruction of much of the earth. In the 1960s both had learned to build and launch nuclear-tipped ballistic missiles that could with accuracy reach targets thousands of miles away. Thermonuclear strategists calculated the potential of a nuclear exchange between the superpowers in millions of deaths, or "megadeaths," and evaluated the effect of deterrents and counter-deterrents, and of "first strikes" and "second strikes," on each nation's ability to survive nuclear war. The balance of power was spoken of as a "balance of terror"; experts referred to doctrines of "mutual vulnerability" and of "mutually assured destruction." The possession by each superpower of a vast nuclear arsenal, it was argued, would deter the other from using nuclear arms for fear of instant retaliation. So delicately suspended over the human race was the nuclear sword of Damocles that a direct communication link, or "hot line," between the Kremlin and the White House was installed in 1963, and in the following decade modernized and improved, to prevent the accidental outbreak of a nuclear war because of some human error or mechanical failure, instances of which were already on record; direct communication between the tribal chieftains was necessary once mutual destruction, and the safety of the planet, was at stake. The debate over security in the nuclear age grew in intensity in the 1980s.

Expenditures on conventional arms, and international trade in all kinds of advanced weapons, with the United States and the Soviet Union the chief merchants and suppliers, also expanded rapidly. From 1960 to 1980 the world's annual military expenditures doubled; in the early 1980s the world spent $600 billion a year on armaments. The United States and the Soviet Union together accounted for 60 percent of the total, but expenditures were also substantial in the developing countries, which could afford them least because of their urgent nonmilitary needs. American financial aid, which in the earlier postwar decades went to the poorer countries for development assistance, now increasingly made its way to a selected number of nations for military aid.

After the Cuban missile confrontation of 1962, relations for a time eased again between the two superpowers. Preliminary negotiations to limit strategic nuclear arms, that is, weapon systems that could launch intercontinental nuclear warheads, were initiated. Despite the ongoing war in Vietnam, a general relaxation of tensions or détente took shape as an informal policy after 1969 under President Nixon and his chief foreign policy adviser, Henry Kissinger. Strategic arms limitation talks (SALT was the acronym) culminated after three years of negotiations in an agreement in 1972 which placed numerical limits on each nation's intercontinental ballistic missiles; it also reduced defense systems, that is, antiballistic missiles, and specified further limitations. By that time, with space satellites and monitoring stations, on-site verification was less important as an issue. In 1975 an agreement was reached limiting nuclear tests to 150 kilotons. Relations improved in other ways too. In 1972 the Soviet Union, faced with a harvest failure, negotiated a large grain purchase from the United States, and continued to rely on such purchases in subsequent years. In 1975 thirty-five nations, including the Soviet

Union and the United States, met in a cordial atmosphere at Helsinki and pledged themselves to work for permanent peace in Europe and to promote cultural cooperation and human rights. The Helsinki agreements ratified the European territorial boundaries set up after the Second World War, including the Oder-Neisse boundary between West Germany and Poland.[40] Further meetings were planned to review progress.

The years of détente, although reducing friction between the two superpowers, did not end the Cold War. The Soviet Union and the United States supported opposing sides in the Arab-Israeli conflicts. The United States made efforts to check the strength of Communist parties in Western Europe and in Central and South America, intervening in 1973 to help overthrow a liberal-left government in Chile, and attempting in various ways to counter the expanding influence of Castro's Cuba. The Soviet Union pressed for advantages in Africa and Asia. But the period was one of minimal direct confrontation.

Sometime in the late 1970s relations between the two superpowers deteriorated once again. In December 1979 the Soviet Union, alleging a threat to the security of its borders, invaded Afghanistan and fought a long and continuing war there to impose a pro-Soviet regime; it was the first direct Soviet military intervention outside Eastern Europe. Soviet efforts to thwart democratization in Poland created new tensions. In retaliation for Soviet aggression and coercion, the United States imposed an embargo on grain sales, which it dropped after pressure from American farm interests, and an embargo on the sale of high technology equipment, which it abandoned after the Western Europeans refused to cooperate. Meetings to review the Helsinki agreements foundered in the midst of Soviet-Western mutual recriminations, especially about human rights. Seven years of renewed strategic arms limitations talks led to a new agreement in 1979, but the United States Senate by then refused to ratify it. In Central America the United States actively supported governments facing what it considered to be Communist threats.

In military matters, President Reagan and his advisors grew increasingly apprehensive. During détente the Soviet Union had quietly built up its military strength so that it now clearly had nuclear parity with the United States. It had modernized its conventional fighting forces as well and had a powerful modern navy. The Americans, although able to launch thousands of missiles from submarines and long-range bombers, feared that their land-based intercontinental missiles in the United States were inferior to their Soviet counterparts, were vulnerable to destruction from a Soviet attack, and were therefore inadequate to deter a first strike. They made plans to build larger missiles, each with more nuclear warheads, and debated how best to protect them. Some observers noted that with their existing arsenals each side had the power to annihilate the other many times over, and much of the earth as well. Each superpower had about nine thousand nuclear bombs; if only a small number of these reached their targets they could destroy each other's major cities (and kill millions in the attack and the radioactive effects). Together, the two arsenals equaled 500,000 megatons (or millions of tons) of explosive power, 100,000 times the total explosive power used in all of the Second World War.

Because the Soviets in the late 1970s also deployed newly modernized intermediate-range nuclear missiles targeted on Western Europe, the United States arranged to reinforce NATO with American missiles. This too became a

[40] See pp. 826, 893, and map, p. 895.

source of contention. Discussions were resumed on strategic arms limitations and arms limitations of other kinds in the 1980s, but in an atmosphere of suspicion and strain. A comprehensive test ban treaty, the prevention of proliferation, a multilateral halt to the design, production, and deployment of all nuclear weapons were on the complete agenda if civilization were to survive. Meanwhile the fears of ordinary people about a nuclear catastrophe, dormant for many years, reawakened, and large protest demonstrations were held. Many pointed to the danger, the paradox, and even the immorality of building vast nuclear armaments to prevent nuclear war; others argued that without such armaments a nation could be subject to nuclear blackmail.

Western Europe watched the nuclear arms race with growing concern. After the 1950s it began to insist on an equal partnership in the Atlantic alliance. De Gaulle, while president of France from 1958 to 1969, had made himself a spokesman for European self-assertiveness and had called upon Europe to act as a counterpoise to the hegemony of the two superpowers. Opposed to American leadership, he ended French participation in the NATO military command and arranged for the removal of its headquarters from Paris to Brussels. Seeking to bridge the gap between Western and Eastern Europe, he called for a reuniting of Europe "from the Atlantic to the Urals." Because he was scornful of the ideological crusade of the United States in the Cold War, he sought to restore an older balance-of-power politics to international affairs.

Although de Gaulle's extremist anti-American views failed to persuade France's Continental partners, and even alarmed them by what at times seemed a bid for French hegemony, his assertion of independence from the United States struck a sympathetic chord. The French and the British had developed nuclear deterrents of their own but also wanted a share in American strategies and policies. In the 1980s these attitudes won additional support. It had long been understood that in the event of a massive Soviet invasion of Western Europe, the United States would rally to the support of NATO—with long-range nuclear arms, if necessary, in which at the time it held superiority. Many Europeans had even then been skeptical that the United States would resort to nuclear arms, inviting Soviet retaliation and the incineration of American cities and populations. With Soviet nuclear parity in the 1980s, it seemed even more implausible that the Americans would defend Western Europe by long-range nuclear arms. Some Europeans were also disturbed by American military planning for limited nuclear war and the use of tactical nuclear weapons. They came to fear nuclear exchange restricted to their own continent—the "Europeanization" of a nuclear conflict. Many objected to the deployment of American missiles in their countries, even against the Soviet threat. Antinuclear demonstrations became anti-American as well. Never sanguine about American leadership, the Western Europeans became more apprehensive. The United States had acted unilaterally in the Cuban missile crisis and had fought in Korea and Vietnam with what many considered a reckless disregard for the risks involved. The Europeans remained concerned about excessive American anti-Communist zeal and also considered it a misguided notion that economic sanctions could alter Soviet policy, or even unsettle the Soviet regime. Yet almost four decades after the end of the Second World War, they knew that they remained dependent on the United States for defense against Soviet aggression.

The U.S.S.R. itself faced disaffection in the Soviet bloc, where events had shown that it could repress liberalization only by force or the threat of force. Meanwhile the nonaligned nations, a group that had grown from a handful in

1955 to over ninety, sought to play an independent role as a power bloc too. Although many condemned the Soviet invasion of Afghanistan, they were mainly vehemently anti-American. The People's Republic of China, with which the United States established full diplomatic relations after 1972, constituted another independent element. In a military sense the bipolarity of the post–1945 world grew even sharper in the early 1980s, the two armed superpowers confronting each other in an uneasy coexistence, but the assertiveness of Western Europe and the restiveness in the Soviet empire, the existence of the People's Republic of China and of the nonaligned nations, all intent on an independent role in the world's affairs, made it difficult to speak only of bipolarity.

116. CHALLENGES AND DILEMMAS

Economic Problems

Not only was the world troubled by continuing international tension, but the global economy took a downward turn after the mid-1970s affecting all countries. Western Europe, which for over two decades had experienced unprecedented prosperity, economic advances, and a growing sense of unity, suffered sharp setbacks. In the early 1970s, before the recession hit, the European Economic Community, or Common Market,[41] was prospering, providing a mobility of labor and capital that made possible trade over one of the world's largest internal markets. Western Europe again played a central role in the world's economy, accounting for one-fourth of all imports and one-fifth of all exports, its exports equaling those of the United States and Japan combined. Its steel production surpassed that of the United States. Self-sufficient in food, it became the world's largest exporter of dairy products, even though ten million people left the farms for the cities in the two previous decades. West Germany alone was exceeded only by the United States, the U.S.S.R., and Japan in gross national product. Although the United States still led Western Europe in per capita income, the gap was narrowing.

The European economy, to be sure, did not maintain its pace in all areas. The world itself had entered a new phase of the Industrial Revolution. Progress was no longer measured in coal and steel or in ships and textiles but in nuclear energy, microelectronics, and computer and space technology. Here the Europeans found themselves outdistanced by the United States. They observed with anxiety the economic penetration of Europe by giant American industrial firms, which controlled many of the new industries.

When Britain, Denmark, and Ireland joined in 1973, and Greece in 1979, the Community grew from its original six members to ten, and counted 270 million citizens and consumers; Spain and Portugal were also expected to join. With growth and diversity, older tensions came to the fore. The food-exporting countries received large subsidies for their products and highly industrial countries like West Germany and Britain, who were food importers, paid for a disproportionate share of these subsidies in the Common Market budget. Politically, the initial enthusiasm for European unification, although not forgotten, dimmed. The citizens of the member states traveled across each other's borders without passports but were still far from enjoying common citizenship. A European Monetary System in 1979 replaced a looser arrangement to maintain exchange rates, but a common

---

[41] See pp. 850–851.

currency remained a remote goal. More symbolic than substantial, a direct European-wide election was held in 1979 for the European Parliament which helped to supervise the Common Market. Even if the more ambitious dreams were not realized, for over two decades Western Europe seemed to have submerged the fierce national antagonisms and economic rivalries that had brought two great World Wars in the twentieth century, almost destroyed Europe itself, and led to the ascendancy of the two superpowers. If in the late 1960s individual nations like Britain and Italy were suffering from economic problems and signs of an economic slowdown were on the horizon, the general picture remained one of economic prosperity and broad cooperation.

In the mid-1970s this optimistic outlook received its first rude shock. In the course of the Arab-Israeli War in the autumn of 1973,[42] the Arab oil-producing nations proclaimed an oil embargo against states accused of supporting Israel, notably the United States, and in Western Europe, the Netherlands. In addition, oil supplies were further reduced because of a cutback in production. That winter the oil-exporting countries quadrupled the price of oil. The embargo, the decline in oil supplies, and the price increases threw Western Europe into panic. With 70 percent of its oil imports dependent on Middle Eastern sources, the price rises jolted the European economy, as they did the world economy as well. Never had an essential industrial commodity risen in price so rapidly; never was the vulnerability of the whole Western industrial complex so clearly revealed. The price escalation had a devastating effect on the world's monetary markets, sharply increasing balance of payments deficits, and accelerating an inflationary spiral already under way.

The spectacular growth of the Western European economies was abruptly interrupted. The oil crisis also revealed the precarious political foundation on which European unity, and even the Atlantic alliance, was built. The Europeans resented the fact that the United States, which stood by Israel, did not consult them in the crisis. Many, apprehensive over Arab oil supplies, negotiated their own arrangements. European solidarity, tested for the first time since the 1950s, broke down.

The economic recession which almost immediately struck the Western industrial countries and Japan was the severest in over forty years. In Western Europe the recession set in and intensified from 1974 on. The American economy went through ups and downs in the 1970s suffering the severest decline from 1979 to 1982. By the late 1970s the recession was world-wide. Not since the Great Depression of the 1930s[43] had the Western industrial countries experienced such economic difficulties. Bankruptcies and threatened bankruptcies shook several countries; production declined; in the twenty-four non-Communist industrial countries the number of jobless totaled 15 million in 1975 and over 32 million in 1983. By that time close to 10 percent of the American and of the Western European labor force were without jobs, and American factories were working at only two-thirds of their capacity. The recession partly reflected the long-trend business cycle, which seemed to have reached the end of a boom period in the early 1970s. The boom itself had engendered inflationary pressures; the sharp increase in oil prices made it impossible to control a price rise already under way, and a runaway inflation raced on in many countries at double-digit annual figures, at times well over 20 percent.

Industrial stagnation and inflation ("stagflation," the journalists called it) made it difficult to cope with the recession. Government efforts to restrict borrowing in

[42] See pp. 871–872.
[43] See pp. 761–766.

order to curb inflation aggravated the business slowdown and swelled the ranks of the unemployed. On the other hand, efforts to facilitate borrowing in order to encourage investment fed inflation. When, as in the case of the United States, high interest rates and "tight money" helped bring down the inflation rate at home, and strengthened the dollar abroad, the stringent measures hurt European ability to recover. By the early 1980s the United States, Britain, and West Germany seemed able to bring inflation under control, but at the expense of rising unemployment.

The developing countries were also deeply hurt by reduced demand for their exports, the higher cost of oil and industrial imports, and cutbacks in development assistance. Even some of the oil-producing countries suffered when oil prices later declined, particularly those countries that had gone heavily into debt to finance ambitious technological expansion. The Communist nations, despite their controlled economies and access to Soviet oil resources, were also affected because of their increased links to world trade in the 1970s and heavy indebtedness to the West, especially Western Europe. Their inability to pay even the interest on these debts, as in the case of Poland and Rumania, and the insolvency of many of the developing nations further threatened the world's financial stability.

In the Western countries opinion was divided about the most effective way to revive the economy. The precepts of Keynes,[44] encouraging government spending and deficit financing in slow times, which had gained a wide following after 1945, had to be revised; they were not as readily applicable in inflationary times. Governments faced the dilemma of deciding whether to give a higher priority to the threat of inflation or unemployment.

The economic troubles were cushioned for the unemployed in almost all industrial countries. Labor unions were strong and welfare benefits more advanced than they had been in the 1930s. Unemployed automobile workers in Essen, Turin, or Detroit could count on severance pay, trade union benefits, and government unemployment compensation far beyond the welfare payments and dole of earlier generations; this not only reduced human suffering but prevented an even greater decline in consumer purchasing power. Yet these benefits were limited and unemployment remained a baneful experience. In some countries there was apprehension that inflation and unemployment could undermine social stability and threaten democratic government. There was also a growing anxiety about "structural unemployment"—that because of automation and new technology many workers would never return to their old jobs or ever again use their skills.

The electorate grew restive in the recession; but no clear trend was discernible. Socialists won office in France, Greece, Spain, and Sweden, but more conserva-

[44] See p. 770.

WHEEL MAN
by Ernest Trova (American, 1927–   )

Shown here is a somewhat dehumanized, life-size bronze figure of a human being of no particular sex, age, race, culture, or environment. Compressed between the two wheels, it seems to present humanity as the victim of its own complicated inventions. The wheels also symbolize the blind ups and downs of fortune. The date 1965 is inscribed on the base, and the whole sad assemblage seems to say that human history and civilization have not exactly turned out as was once more hopefully expected. Ernest Trova, though widely exhibited internationally, is an American sculptor living in St. Louis. Courtesy of the Solomon R. Guggenheim Museum, John V. Powers Fund.

tive governments took over in the United States, Britain, and West Germany. The economic troubles severely strained the unity of the European Economic Community and also caused friction with the United States. The Americans objected to the large Common Market agricultural subsidies which hurt American farmers in world trade. The Western Europeans objected when American economic sanctions against the Soviet Union interfered with their efforts to increase trade with the Soviets and the East European bloc; ignoring the sanctions, they continued to sell the materials needed for the construction of a Siberian natural gas pipeline to Europe until the American government backed down. Friction over trade policies developed between Japan, which had large export surpluses, and other countries, including the United States. Everywhere the old specter of economic nationalism, trade barriers, and protectionism reappeared. In the early 1980s the recession continued; when and how it would end was not known.

The Population Explosion

The less developed countries of the world were also struggling with other social and economic problems to which solutions seemed distant. The most acute was the vast growth of population. With improved health and sanitation measures and with more efficient food production and distribution, death rates declined but without a counterbalancing reduction in births. The population of the world grew so rapidly during the second half of the twentieth century that demographers spoke of a population explosion. In 1975 the world's population passed 4 billion; in the 1980s it approached 5 billion. From the first century A.D. to the sixteenth century the number of human beings increased from about a quarter billion to a half billion; by the mid-nineteenth century the half billion grew to 1 billion. Put another way, it required almost 2 million years, from the beginnings of human life on the planet (or 300,000 years from the emergence of *Homo sapiens*) to about 1850, for the world's population to reach its first billion. Only seventy-five years later, about 1925, it reached 2 billion; thirty-five years after that, in 1960, it reached 3 billion, and fifteen years later, 4 billion. If the annual global growth rate of 1.7 percent were sustained, the population would easily surpass 6 billion by the end of the century and then double again by the end of another century. If the annual growth rate were to decline to 1.5 percent by the beginning of the twenty-first century, and then continue to decline, as demographers thought it would, population estimates would be considerably lower and might then stabilize at the end of that century.

There were many examples of the utterly unprecedented fall in death rates and its impact on population growth all over the globe. In India the death rate in 1982 was half what it had been in 1950. With a population of 700 million and a growth rate of 2.1 percent, India was adding 15 million people annually, and could reach 1 billion by the end of the century. In sub-Saharan Africa, where the growth rate was 2.7 percent, the population was expected to double by the end of the century. In the industrial countries, however, population was growing only slowly because birth rates had stabilized. Industrialization, urban life, social pressures for smaller families, and easier access to contraception had slowed the birth rate since the late nineteenth century in much of Europe and North America.[45] In Asia (with some notable exceptions), Africa, and Latin America such a decline had not yet occurred.

[45] See pp. 556–557.

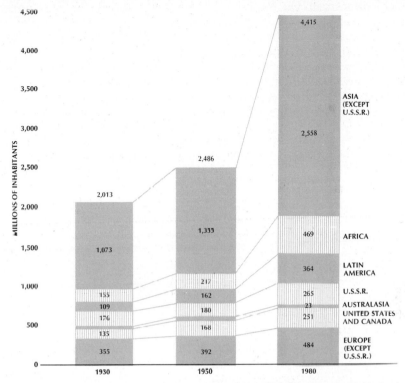

Source: *United Nations Demographic Yearbook.*

THE POPULATION EXPLOSION

As the twentieth century entered its fourth quarter the world's population passed the 4 billion mark. It had doubled in less than half a century, and more than doubled in Asia, Africa, and Latin America. Growth was most rapid in the poorer countries, where it contributed to chronic social unrest and political instability. The wealthier or "developed" part of the world, including Japan, parts of Latin America, and South Africa, had a slower growth rate, but in the 1970s they comprised only about a quarter of the world's population.

Comparison may be made with the table on page 555, where the categories are somewhat different, being designed to show the rise and decline in the proportion of "Europeans" in the global total. But the table shows no doubling of world population in any half-century from 1650 to 1950, so that the recent increase is truly an "explosion." Such a rate of increase cannot continue indefinitely; the question is whether it can be slowed down before the earth's resources are overstrained.

From the 1960s the birth control movement grew in scope. More than two-thirds of the world's population now lived in countries with some form of government-sponsored population program, which held the promise of leveling off population growth. The carefully concerted government program in the People's Republic of China reduced growth rates in the 1970s to below the world growth rate. But for population programs to be effective in most other countries it was necessary to change deeply rooted attitudes, many of them based on cultural or religious outlook, or deriving from economic dependence on grown children for support in hard times, old age, or infirmity. The assertion of women's voices in such matters was proving important. On the other hand, some political leaders, opposed to population control, argued that pressure to reduce growth rates in the less developed parts of the world represented a deliberate effort by the West to check the growth of the emergent nations.

Although experts were modifying their most extreme projections for the doubling rate of the world's population, the problem remained acute. One day, with growing standards of comfort and security, the size of families might be self-limiting everywhere, but that day was distant because such standards were nowhere in sight for the hundreds of millions who still lived on inadequate and unrelieved rations of grain or rice. While industrial and agricultural development programs were widespread, economic advances in many countries could not keep pace with population growth. The gloomy prognostications of Malthus at the end of the eighteenth century that population growth, if unchecked, would outstrip food supply,[46] a proposition that most other social thinkers had once rejected, were again much discussed. Since his day, however, technical improvements in agriculture had made possible enormous increases in food production. More food was available in the early 1980s than twenty years earlier, but distribution remained a problem, and there were striking differences in national and regional productivity. Overall productivity could be raised if everyone were to benefit from modern technology, but that was part of a larger issue—the sharing of knowledge and resources among the wealthier and poorer nations.

The Third World

The term "Third World" came to be used in the postwar years to describe the less economically advanced nations of Asia, Africa, and Latin America. The Third World countries were distinguished from the "Western," or non-Communist, bloc of industrial nations, in which the United States predominated, and the Communist bloc of industrial or industrializing nations, dominated by the Soviet Union. In the tensions of the Cold War between the Western and Soviet camps, the Third World nations drew together in the United Nations and elsewhere for mutual reinforcement. By the 1980s the Third World included over 100 independent sovereign states, almost all formerly part of the old Western colonial empires and comprising a total of over 2 billion persons, or half the world's population. They lived in the southern continents or parts of continents—in South Asia, Africa, and Latin America. The confrontation with the industrial nations, Western, Japanese, and Soviet, therefore became also a form of North-South contest.

Dependent on agriculture, the Third World countries had the lowest per capita income, the highest illiteracy rates, and the highest rates of population growth. Within the Third World itself there were divisions. Some countries, like India, Nigeria, and the oil-rich nations of the Middle East, had important natural resources; these nations, with time, capital, and technological assistance, could expect to build modern economies and had already made significant progress. A second group, a kind of "Fourth World," including such states as Pakistan, Egypt, and Peru, were without adequate resources or were so beset with growing populations that they could not feed their people or expect much economic improvement in the near future. Within this group of about forty countries, two-thirds of them in Africa, states such as Mali, Chad, Niger, Ethiopia, Somalia, Burundi, and Bangladesh formed a kind of "Fifth World"—an impoverished group of about 200 million people at the very bottom of the economic scale.

[46] See pp. 433–434.

Despite economic development programs, the gap between the Third World countries and the wealthier industrial nations, non-Communist and Communist, grew so wide that there were really only two worlds, one relatively rich and one poor. The poorer countries, with over half the world's population, had access to only a small share of the world's income. The poverty of the Third World countries had profound social and human implications. In parts of West Africa, of every 1,000 children born, over 170 died before they were one year old; in Sweden, the figure was 10. Life expectancy for a child born in Nigeria in the 1980s was about forty-six, in India about fifty-three—a higher life expectancy, to be sure, than for the European or American upper classes only a century ago, but no match for the comparable life expectancy figure of close to eighty in most modern European countries. In the twenty-four wealthiest industrial nations the gross national product on a per capita basis was $4,550 in the mid-1970s; for the twenty-five poorest countries it was $116. The distribution of wealth within all countries remained an unresolved problem, but it was particularly acute in the poorer countries where there were fewer goods and services to distribute, and where they were often distributed with gross inequity between an elite cultivating Western standards of luxury and the impoverished masses.

The Third World states pressed for a reshaping of the international economy to give them a more equitable share in the world's resources and wealth. They noted that they had shared only minimally in the postwar economic advances; even when their economies were growing in the three decades after 1945, they did not advance as rapidly as the highly productive countries. When the world recession deepened in the mid-1970s, the poorer countries suffered from the decline in international trade and received less development assistance; their economic growth rates halved; and they staggered under heavy debts. The industrial nations in the postwar years had committed a share of their gross national product to economic and technological aid, but after the mid-1970s such aid dropped to its lowest point since 1955. The United States, once the leading source of development assistance, ranked fifteenth in the 1980s. The Soviets gave far less than did the West, but not as much was expected of them.

The Third World states not only resented the decline in development assistance but even more so the notion that the resumption of their economic growth depended on the return of prosperity to the West. In calling for a new international economic order they raised demands for freer access to the investment funds, capital goods, and technology of the West and called for a shift of international financing away from agencies that they considered Western-dominated. Western governments, in the midst of their own economic troubles, were reluctant to make concessions, nor would they agree to any major economic restructuring. But without economic assistance the rising expectations and vision of hope of the post-1945 years would turn into even deeper frustrations for the poorer nations. The recession not only interrupted social and economic advances for much of the globe but dramatically demonstrated the world's interdependence.

One World: The Fate of Humanity

All the problems of the contemporary age—the awesome implications of science, the challenge of technology, the population explosion, the dangerous rivalry between nations, the quest within nations for freedom and security—were really aspects of one overriding problem, the fate of humanity. How could human beings, men and women, regardless of color, creed, or nationality—beings said by some to be made in the image of God, by others to have a natural right to liberty and

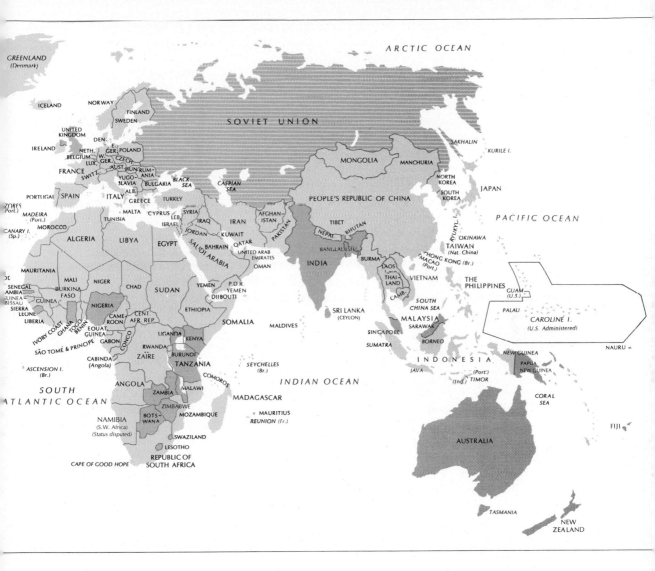

THE CONTEMPORARY WORLD

On a small political map of the contemporary world the most readily visible changes, as compared to a map of the world before the Second World War, are the breakup of the European colonial empires in Asia and Africa, the emergence of several new states in Asia, and of some fifty independent republics in Africa, the enlargement of the Commonwealth of Nations to include such new Asian and African members as India, Bangladesh, Nigeria, the peripheral expansion of the Soviet Union to include the Baltic states, and the rise of a Communist China.

happiness; by still others to have the freedom to create meaning in a meaningless universe—live out their lives and fulfill their humanity in the contemporary world, and pass on their heritage to future generations?

The worst of all eventualities would be another world war involving the super-powers and their allies. Some argued that such a war was unthinkable because of the total destruction each side could inflict on the other with modern nuclear armaments, but the danger persisted of escalation from conventional warfare. In 1945 the victors in the Second World War founded the United Nations as an instrument for preserving peace. The UN managed to play a peacekeeping role, as in the Middle East on several occasions, but only when the vital interests of the Great Powers were not directly involved; in disputes involving the major powers it proved helpless. In the 1980s even its peacekeeping mission seemed superseded when it became necessary to employ non-United Nations multinational forces in the Middle East.

The United Nations itself changed significantly from the time of its inception. The postwar colonial revolution led to a proliferation of new nations. The 51 original members tripled and grew to 157 in the early 1980s, with even a few more to be added. Most of the new members had little experience as independent states, and many fell quickly under various degrees of dictatorial government. When even very small former colonies achieved independence, as in the case of the Caribbean or Pacific island dependencies, many of these new nations had populations no larger than a small city. The eighty smallest members of the United Nations, in Africa, Asia, and Latin America and various oceanic islands, when added together represented less than 10 percent of the earth's population. Yet each member had a vote in the UN General Assembly and in that body was equal in every respect to the larger nations. An organization with such a disparity between political reality and voting strength could hardly play an effective role in international affairs. The General Assembly became a forum for the discussion of grievances against the wealthier nations, especially the United States, and even exacerbated political issues when they were brought before it. The Security Council, on the other hand, remained ineffective because of the Great Power veto, and the United States and the Soviet Union tended to negotiate with each other outside it. Few wished to see the United Nations disappear, but its impotence as an organization for world order was clear; other channels and mechanisms, not yet on the horizon, were needed to nurture international confidence, cooperation, and world organization.

These two concluding chapters began with the image of a cataclysm. The analogy is still pertinent. But even a cataclysm, as already made clear, is not a time of downfall only. Mountains crumble, but others are thrust up. Lands vanish, but others rise from the sea. So it is with the political and social cataclysm of our times. Old landmarks are worn down. The colonial empires and the gold standard pass away. The ascendancy of Europe, the West, and the white races closes; all these have learned to negotiate with others, not to rule them. Everywhere there is a fluidity in social relations: some people question older life styles and values; others wish to preserve them. Never has war been so potentially destructive, and a nuclear war would blight much of civilization, perhaps destroy it all, and even most of life on the planet; but the human species is tough, and there are billions of human beings on earth. To close this book on a note of placidity would indeed be inappropriate, but so too would it be to close it on a note of doom.

APPENDIXES, BIBLIOGRAPHY, and INDEX

Appendix I:
Chronological Tables

TABLE ONE: TO 1517

EUROPE AS A WHOLE: POLITICAL AND SOCIAL	EUROPE AS A WHOLE: THOUGHT AND LETTERS	BRITISH ISLES
	500–300 B.C. Classical Greek civilization	
146 B.C. Greeks conquered by Rome	427–347 B.C. Plato	
31 B.C. Roman Empire	384–322 B.C. Aristotle	
306–337 Emperor Constantine	106–43 B.C. Cicero	43–410 Roman Empire in Britain
	2nd century: Ptolemy and Galen	
5th century: Germanic migrations	354–430 Saint Augustine	
476 Roman Empire in West ends		
7th century: spread of Islam		596 Conversion of Anglo-Saxons
800 Coronation of Charlemagne		
9th century: Norse and Magyar invasions		871–899 Alfred the Great
1054 Schism of West and East		
	1033–1109 Anselm	
1073–1085 Pope Gregory VII (Hildebrand)		1066 Norman conquest
1095 First Crusade	1079–1142 Abelard	12th century: development of the monarchy in England
12th century: rise of towns	12th century: coming of Arabic and Greek science	
1189 Third Crusade		
1198–1216 Pope Innocent III	12th–13th century: universities, scholasticism	
13th century: rise of parliaments	1215 Fourth Lateran Council	1215 Magna Carta
1294–1303 Pope Boniface VIII	1225–1274 Thomas Aquinas	
		1295 Model Parliament
1348–1349 Black Death		1337–1453 Hundred Years' War
1378–1417 Schism of the West		
	1328–1384 John Wycliffe	
1414–1415 Council of Constance	1415 Death of John Huss	1381 Wat Tyler's rebellion
1453 Roman Empire in East ends	15th century: the Renaissance at its height	1455–1485 Wars of the Roses
	1452–1519 Leonardo da Vinci	
	1454–1455 Printing; Gutenberg Bible	
1492 Discovery of America	1466–1536 Erasmus	*1485–1603 The Tudors*
1498 Portuguese reach India	1469–1527 Machiavelli	1485–1509 Henry VII
1517 Beginnings of Reformation	1517 Luther's 95 Theses	1509–1547 Henry VIII

WESTERN EUROPE	CENTRAL EUROPE	EASTERN EUROPE
		6th–4th century B.C. Greek city-states
		4th–1st century B.C. Hellenistic Age
31 B.C.–476 Roman Empire	31 B.C.–476 Roman Empire in western and southern Germany	31 B.C.–1453 Roman Empire in East
		330 Constantinople founded
496 Conversion of Franks		
	568 Founding of Venice	
711 Muslims in Spain		
732 Muslim defeat at Tours		
768–814 Charlemagne	768–814 Charlemagne	10th century: conversion of Swedes, Poles, Hungarians to Rome; Russians to Constantinople
987–1792 Capetian monarchy in France	*962–1806 Holy Roman Empire*	
	1056–1106 Emperor Henry IV	*1001–1918 Kingdom of Hungary*
		1054 Schism of East and West
	1075–1122 Investiture struggle	
12th century: development of the monarchy in France		12th century: Teutonic Knights in Prussia
1208 Albigensian Crusade	13th century: failure of the Empire to organize Germany and Italy	13th century: conversion of East Baltic peoples to Rome
1303–1417 Papacy at Avignon		1236 Tartars in Russia
	1356 Golden Bull	1389 Turks in Balkan Peninsula
1337–1453 Hundred Years' War		
	1420–1431 Hussite Wars	
1412–1431 Joan of Arc		
	1438–1918 Habsburg Emperors	
		1453 Turks take Constantinople; end of Byzantine Empire
1461–1489 Louis XI of France		
1479–1516 Ferdinand and Isabella of Spain		
1494 French invasion of Italy		1480 Ivan the Great ends Tartar control over Russia
1515–1547 Francis I of France	1519–1556 Charles V	

TABLE TWO: 1517–1618

EUROPE AS A WHOLE: POLITICAL AND SOCIAL	EUROPE AS A WHOLE: THOUGHT AND LETTERS	BRITISH ISLES
1517 Beginnings of Reformation	1517 Luther's 95 Theses	1509–1547 Henry VIII
1519–1556 Charles V 1519–1648 Habsburg supremacy 1519–1522 Magellan circumnavigates globe		1521 Henry VIII's *Defense of Seven Sacraments*
1529 Turks besiege Vienna	1530 Loyola's *Spiritual Exercises*	
1531 First stock exchange at Antwerp	1534 Luther's German Bible 1536 Calvin's *Institutes of the Christian Religion*	1534 Act of Supremacy 1536–1539 Dissolution of monasteries 1539 Six Articles
1540 Founding of Jesuits 1541–1564 Calvin at Geneva	1543 Copernicus' *Revolutions of Heavenly Orbs* and Vesalius' *Structure of the Human Body*	1547–1553 Edward VI
1545–1563 Council of Trent	1550–1650 Golden age of Spanish literature	1553–1558 Mary I
1555 Peace of Augsburg 1556–1598 Philip II of Spain		1558–1603 Elizabeth I 1559 Knox and the Reformation in Scotland
	1561–1626 Francis Bacon	1563 The 39 Articles
	1564–1642 Galileo 1564–1616 Shakespeare	1569 Norfolk's rebellion
1571 Defeat of Turks at Lepanto	1576 Bodin's *Republic*	1577 Alliance with Netherlands
	1580 Montaigne's *Essays* 1582 Gregorian Calendar	1588 Spanish Armada
1588 Spanish Armada	1596–1650 Descartes	1603–1714 *The Stuarts* 1603–1625 James I
1607 English found Virginia 1608 French found Quebec 1609 Spanish found Santa Fé 1612 Dutch found New York	1611 King James' Bible	

WESTERN EUROPE	CENTRAL EUROPE	EASTERN EUROPE
1515–1547 Francis I of France	1519–1556 Charles V Emperor	
1516 Concordat of Bologna		1520–1566 Suleiman the Magnificent
	1521 Luther banned	
	1526 Charles V at war with Turks	1526 Turks occupy Hungary
	1529 Turks besiege Vienna	
		1533–1584 Ivan the Terrible, first Tsar of Russia
1536 Franco-Turkish alliance against Charles V		1535 First French capitulations in Turkey
1547–1559 Henry II of France	1546–1547 Schmalkaldic War	
		1553 English in White Sea
1556–1598 Philip II of Spain	1555 Peace of Augsburg	
	1556–1564 Ferdinand I	
1559–1589 Weakness of monarchy in France		
1562–1598 Wars of Religion in France		
	1564–1576 Maximilian II	
1566 Netherlands revolt begins		
1572 Massacre of St. Bartholomew		1571 Defeat of Turks at Lepanto
1574–1589 Henry III	1576–1612 Rudolf II	1574 Turks take Tunis
1589–1792 Bourbons in France		
1589–1610 Henry IV		
1598 Edict of Nantes		1604–1613 Time of troubles in Russia
1610–1643 Louis XIII		
	1608 Protestant Union	
	1609 Catholic League	
	1612–1619 Matthias	
	1618 Thirty Years' War	1613–1645 Michael Romanov, Tsar

TABLE THREE: 1618–1714

EUROPE AS A WHOLE: POLITICAL AND SOCIAL	EUROPE AS A WHOLE: THOUGHT AND LETTERS	BRITISH ISLES
	1561–1626 Francis Bacon	*1603–1714 The Stuarts*
	1564–1642 Galileo	1603–1625 James I
	1596–1650 Descartes	
1618–1648 Thirty Years' War		
17th century: English, French, Dutch in America; Dutch in South Africa and Indonesia	1623–1662 Pascal	1625–1649 Charles I
	17th century: flowering of English, French, and Dutch literature	
1619 First African slaves in Virginia	1625 Grotius' *Law of War and Peace*	1637 Ship money case
		1640–1660 Long Parliament
	1642–1727 Isaac Newton	1642–1648 Puritan rebellion and Civil War
1648 Peace of Westphalia		1649 Execution of Charles I
		1649–1658 Rule of Cromwell
1650 World population estimate: 500 million		1649–1653 Commonwealth
		1653–1660 Protectorate
	1660s Beginnings of scientific societies	1660 Restoration
1661–1715 Age of Louis XIV		1660–1685 Charles II
		1670s Rise of Whigs and Tories
		1673 Test Act
1683 Turks threaten Vienna		1685–1688 James II
	1687 Newton's *Principia*	
1689–1697 War of League of Augsburg		1688 "Glorious Revolution"
		1688–1702 William and Mary
	1690 Locke's *Treatises on Government; Human Understanding*	
	1697 Bayle's *Dictionary*	
1701–1714 War of Spanish Succession		1702–1714 Anne
		1707 Union of England and Scotland
1713–1714 Treaties of Utrecht and Rastadt		

WESTERN EUROPE	CENTRAL EUROPE	EASTERN EUROPE
1610–1643 Louis XIII of France	1618–1648 Thirty Years' War 1619 Emperor Ferdinand II 1620 Battle of White Mountain	*1613–1917 Romanovs in Russia* 1613–1645 Tsar Michael Romanov
1624–1642 Richelieu 1629 Peace of Alais 1635 France in Thirty Years' War	1629 Edict of Restitution 1640–1688 Frederick William, Great Elector of Brandenburg	17th century: spread of serfdom in Russia and Eastern Europe
1642–1661 Mazarin 1643–1715 Louis XIV of France 1648 Peace of Westphalia	1648 Peace of Westphalia 17th and 18th centuries: decline in Central Europe	
1652–1674 Three Anglo-Dutch Wars 1659 Peace of Pyrenees		
1665–1700 Charles II of Spain 1667–1668 Louis XIV's War of Devolution 1672–1678 Louis XIV's Dutch war		1667 Russian church reforms: Old Believers 1670 Revolt of Stephen Razin in Russia
1685 Revocation of Edict of Nantes	1683 Turks threaten Vienna	1682–1725 Peter the Great 1683 Turks threaten Vienna 1683–1718 Habsburg victories over Turks
1689–1714 Later wars of Louis XIV		
	1697–1733 Augustus of Saxony King of Poland	1697–1718 Charles XII of Sweden
		1699 Austro-Turkish Peace of Karlowitz
1700–1931 Bourbons in Spain 1700–1746 Philip V of Spain		
	1701–1918 Hohenzollern kings in Prussia 1701–1713 Frederick I of Prussia	

TABLE FOUR: 1714–1815

EUROPE AS A WHOLE: POLITICAL AND SOCIAL	EUROPE AS A WHOLE: THOUGHT AND LETTERS	BRITISH ISLES
1713–1714 Treaties of Utrecht and Rastadt	18th century: Age of Enlightenment	*1714–1837 Hanoverians* 1714–1727 George I 1720 South Sea Bubble 1721 Walpole's ministry
1740–1763 British-French colonial wars	1740–1789 Enlightenment at its peak	1727–1760 George II 1730 War of Jenkins' Ear
1740–1748 War of Austrian Succession	1740–1760 Voltaire at his height	
1740–1789 Enlightened despotism in Europe	1748 Montesquieu's *Spirit of Laws*	
		1745 Jacobite Rebellion
1750 World population estimate: 700 million	1751–1768 French *Encyclopedia*	
1754–1763 French and Indian War in America		
1756 Diplomatic Revolution		
		1760–1820 George III
1756–1763 Seven Years' War	1761 Rousseau's *Social Contract*	
1763 Treaties of Paris and Hubertusburg: British supremacy in Canada and India		1769 Watt's steam engine 1769 Arkwright's waterframe
1776 American Declaration of Independence	1776 Adam Smith's *Wealth of Nations*	1776 American Revolution
1776–1783 War of American Independence		
		1782–1806 Ministries of William Pitt the Younger
1789 French Revolution begins	1784 Herder's *Philosophy of History of Mankind* 1790 Burke's *Reflections on the French Revolution* 1790s Spread of French revolutionary ideas Beginnings of romanticism	
1792–1815 Revolutionary and Napoleonic wars		1793–1814 War with France
1792–1797 War of First Coalition		
1798–1801 War of Second Coalition		1798 Rebellion of Ireland 1801 Union of Great Britain and Ireland 1802–1803 Peace of Amiens
1803–1805 War of Third Coalition		
1804–1814 "Grand Empire"	1804–1811 Napoleonic codes	
1806–1812 Continental System		
		1808–1813 Peninsular War in Spain

WESTERN EUROPE	CENTRAL EUROPE	EASTERN EUROPE
	1711–1740 Charles VI of Austria	1682–1725 Peter the Great
1715–1774 Louis XV of France	1713–1740 Frederick William I	1709 Battle of Poltava
1715–1723 Regency in France	of Prussia	
1720 Mississippi Bubble	1713–1740 Pragmatic Sanction	
		1721 Russo-Swedish Treaty of
		Nystadt
18th century: culmination of	1740–1786 Frederick II of	1733–1738 War of Polish
"Old Regime" in France	Prussia	Succession
	1740–1780 Maria Theresa of	1739 Austro-Turkish Peace of
	Austria	Belgrade
	1740–1745 Silesian Wars	
	1756 Habsburg-Bourbon	
	Alliance	
	1756–1763 Seven Years' War	
		1762–1796 Catherine II of
		Russia
		1768–1774 Russo-Turkish War
		1772 First Partition of Poland
1774–1793 Louis XVI of France		1773–1774 Pugachev Rebellion
		1774 Russo-Turkish Treaty of
		Kuchuk Kainarji
1778 French-American Alliance	1780–1790 Joseph II of Austria	
	1780s Cultural revival of	1787–1792 Russo-Turkish War
1789 French Revolution begins	Germany	
1792 First French Republic		1793 Second Partition of Poland
established		1795 Third Partition of Poland
1793–1794 The Terror	1797 Treaty of Campo Formio	
1795–1799 Directory		1796–1801 Paul I of Russia
1799 Bonaparte's coup	1798–1814 French	
	predominance	
1799–1804 Consulate		
		1801–1825 Alexander I of Russia
1804–1814 Napoleon I: The		
Empire		
1807 Peace of Tilsit	1806 End of Holy Roman	1806–1812 Russo-Turkish War
	Empire	

EUROPE AS A WHOLE: POLITICAL AND SOCIAL	EUROPE AS A WHOLE: THOUGHT AND LETTERS	BRITISH ISLES
1809–1811 Napoleon at height 1812 Invasion of Russia, and retreat 1812 U.S.-British War 1813 Battle of Leipzig 1814–1815 Congress of Vienna 1815 Waterloo		1814 Alliance of Chaumont

TABLE FIVE: 1815–1871

WORLD AS A WHOLE	EUROPE AS A WHOLE	BRITISH ISLES
		1760–1820 George III 1760–1830 Beginnings of modern industry

1806–1825 Latin American
  countries win independence
	1814–1815 Congress of Vienna	1807 British slave trade ended
		1815 Corn Laws: higher taxes
		  on grain imports

	1818 Congress of Aix-la- Chapelle	
		1819 Peterloo
	1820 Congress of Troppau 1822 Congress of Verona	
1823 Monroe Doctrine		
	1830 Revolutions	
	1833 Lyell's *Principles of Geology*	1832 First Reform Bill

1839–1842 First Anglo-Chinese
  (Opium) War
		1833 Abolition Act: abolished
		  slavery
		1837–1901 Victoria
		1838–1848 Chartism
		1842 Mines Act

1842–1858 "Treaty System" established in China		1846 Repeal of Corn Laws 1847 Ten Hours Act
	1848 Revolutions; Marx and Engels' *Communist Manifesto*	

1850 World population estimate:
  1.2 billion
1850–1864 Taiping Rebellion in
  China
1854–1868 Japan opened to
  West
1857 Indian Rebellion
	1854–1856 Crimean War	1850–1873 Golden age of British
		  capitalism: free trade

1860 Russians found Vladivostok 1861–1865 American Civil War	1859 Austro-Italian War 1859 Darwin's *Origin of Species*	

WESTERN EUROPE	CENTRAL EUROPE	EASTERN EUROPE
	1806 Confederation of the Rhine	1807 Franco Russian Alliance
		1812 Napoleon's invasion of Russia
1814 Restoration of Bourbons 1815 Hundred Days; Waterloo	1813–1814 German War of Liberation: Leipzig	

WESTERN EUROPE	CENTRAL EUROPE	EASTERN EUROPE
		1801–1825 Alexander I of Russia
1814–1830 Restoration: Bourbons in France 1814–1824 Louis XVIII of France	1814–1848 Influence of Metternich	
	1819 Carlsbad Decrees	
1824–1830 Charles X of France		1825 Decembrists in Russia
1830 Revolution in France and Belgium 1830–1848 July Monarchy in France: Louis Philippe	1830 Revolutionary flurries	1825–1855 Nicholas I of Russia 1828–1829 Russo-Turkish War 1829 Independence of Greece 1830 Revolution in Poland
1848 Revolution: Second French Republic	1848 Revolution: Frankfurt Assembly 1848–1916 Francis Joseph of Austria	
1852 Napoleon III: Second French Empire	1852–1890 Bismarck active	1853 Russo-Turkish War 1854–1856 Crimean War
	1859–1870 Unification of Italy	1855–1881 Alexander II of Russia 1858 Formation of Rumania
1860 Free trade with England 1860–1870 Liberal empire		1861 Emancipation of Russian serfs

WORLD AS A WHOLE	EUROPE AS A WHOLE	BRITISH ISLES
1863–1867 French in Mexico		
	1864–1876 First International	
	1866 Austro-Prussian War	
1867 Dominion of Canada	1867 Marx's *Capital*	1867 Extension of suffrage
1870 Vatican Council I	1870 Franco-Prussian War	1870–1874 Gladstone's first
	1871–1918 German Empire	ministry

TABLE SIX: 1871–1919

WORLD AS A WHOLE	EUROPE AS A WHOLE	BRITISH ISLES
	1871 Darwin's *Descent of Man*	
	1878 Congress of Berlin, Austro-German Alliance	1874–1880 Disraeli's ministry
1880–1914 Height of imperialism	1880s Socialist parties founded: revisionism	
1883–1893 French in Indochina	1882 Triple Alliance	
		1884 Extension of suffrage
1885 Berlin Conference on Africa		
1885–1898 Partition of Africa		
	1889 Second International	
1893 New Zealand: vote to women	1894 Franco-Russian Alliance	
1895–1898 Far Eastern crisis		
1898 Fashoda crisis; Spanish-American War		
1899–1902 Boer War		1899–1902 Boer War
1900 World population estimate: 1.6 billion	1900 Freud's *Interpretation of Dreams*	
1902 Anglo-Japanese Alliance		
1902 Australia: vote to women	1904 Anglo-French Entente	
1904 Russo-Japanese War	1905 Einstein's relativity theory	
	1905 Morocco crisis	
		1906–1911 Social insurance and parliamentary reform
1907 Anglo-Russian division of Persia	1907 Triple Entente	
	1908 Bosnian crisis	
1911 Chinese Revolution	1911 Agadir crisis	
	1912–1913 Balkan crisis	
1914–1918 First World War	1914–1918 First World War	1914 Ulster crisis
		1916 Battle of Jutland
		1916–1922 Irish troubles
1917 United States enters War		
1917 Russian Revolution		
1919 Peace of Paris	1919 Peace of Paris	

WESTERN EUROPE	CENTRAL EUROPE	EASTERN EUROPE
	1866–1871 Unification of Germany	
	1867 Dual Monarchy in Austria-Hungary	
1870–1940 Third Republic in France		1870s Populism and Nihilism in Russia

WESTERN EUROPE	CENTRAL EUROPE	EASTERN EUROPE
1870–1940 Third Republic in France	1871–1918 German Empire	
1871 Paris Commune		
	1871–1883 *Kulturkampf*	1877 Russo-Turkish War
	1878–1890 Bismarck's Anti-Socialist laws	1878 Autonomy of Bulgaria; independence of Serbia
		1881 Assassination of Alexander II
	1883–1889 Bismarck's social insurance laws	
	1888–1918 William II of Germany	
1889 Boulanger in France		
1894–1906 Dreyfus affair in France		
	1898–1914 German naval race with England	
1901–1905 Laic laws separate church and state in France	1900ff. Growth of democracy: male suffrage in Austria 1907, etc.	
1900ff. Growth of democracy: male suffrage in Netherlands 1896, etc.		1903 Bolshevik-Menshevik split
		1904 Russo-Japanese War
		1905 Revolution in Russia
		1906 Finland: vote to women
		1908 Bosnian crisis
		1908 Young Turk Revolution
		1912–1913 Balkan Wars
		1913 Norway: vote to women
1914 Battle of Marne	1914 Assassination of Francis Ferdinand	1914 Battle of Tannenberg
1916 Verdun and the Somme		
		1917 Fall of Tsardom; Bolshevik Revolution
1918 Armistice	1918 Fall of German and Austro-Hungarian empires	

TABLE SEVEN: 1919–1945

WORLD AS A WHOLE	EUROPE AS A WHOLE	BRITISH ISLES
		1918 Limited suffrage for women
1919 Peace of Paris	1919 Peace of Paris 1919 Spread of democracy	
1920 U.S.: vote to women		
1922–1929 "Prosperity Decade" 1923 Turkish Republic	1922–1943 Fascism in Italy 1923 Ruhr crisis	1922 Irish Free State
1925 World population estimate: 2 billion	1925 Locarno Pacts	1924 First Labour coalition government 1926 General Strike 1926 Definition of Dominion status
		1928 Full suffrage for women
1929 Great Depression begins		1929–1931 Second Labour Government
	1930s Depression 1930s Decline of democracy: rise of dictators	1931–1940 National Government 1931 Britain leaves gold standard 1932 Britain adopts Empire tariff protection
1931–1932 Manchurian crisis 1931–1945 Japanese in China		
1933–1945 F. D. Roosevelt's presidency 1933 Failure of World Economic Conference	1933–1945 Hitler in Germany 1933 Germany leaves League of Nations and rearms	
1935–1936 Ethiopian crisis 1936–1939 Spanish Civil War	1936–1939 Popular fronts 1937 Rome-Berlin-Tokyo Axis	1936 Edward VIII abdicates; George VI
1938 Munich crisis 1939–1945 Second World War	1939 Nazi-Soviet Pact	1939–1945 Britain at war
1940–1945 Japan aims at "Greater East Asia" 1941 U.S.S.R., U.S. enter war	1940–1945 German domination of Europe: racist policies, extermination of Jews, etc.	1940 Churchill replaces Chamberlain 1940 Battle of Britain
1944 Allies invade Europe 1945 Yalta and Potsdam conferences 1945 First atomic bomb 1945 United Nations established	1945 Death of Hitler and Mussolini	1945 Labour election victory

WESTERN EUROPE	CENTRAL EUROPE	EASTERN EUROPE
1919 Paris Peace Conference	1919 Treaty of Versailles, etc.	1918–1920 Russian Civil War
		1919–1923 Greek-Turkish War
	1919–1933 Weimar Republic	
		1920–1943 Third International
		1920–1921 Russo-Polish War
		1921–1928 NEP in Russia
	1922–1943 Mussolini in power in Italy	1922 Founding of U.S.S.R.
	1923 French occupy Ruhr	1922 Russo-German treaty of Rapallo
	1923 Inflation in Germany	
	1924 Dawes Plan	1924 Death of Lenin; emergence of Stalin
1928–1974 Dictatorship in Portugal: Salazar		1927 Expulsion of Trotsky
		1928–1933 First Five-Year Plan
1930s Depression	1930s Depression	
1931 Spanish revolution		
1934 Stavisky riots in Paris	1933–1945 Third Reich: Hitler in power	
1936–1939 Spanish Civil War	1934 First Austrian crisis	1934 U.S.S.R. joins League of Nations
1936–1937 Popular Front in France	1936 Germany remilitarizes Rhineland	1936–1937 New Soviet constitution; purge trials
	1938 Germany annexes Austria	
	1938–1939 Germany annexes Czechoslovakia	
1939–1975 Spain: Franco dictatorship		1939 Nazi-Soviet Pact
		1939 Germany invades Poland
1940 Fall of France		1939–1940 Russo-Finnish War; Soviets absorb Baltic states
1940–1944 German occupation of Western Europe	1941–1944 Allies bomb Germany	1941 Germany invades Russia
		1942–1943 Battle of Stalingrad
	1943 Allies invade Italy; fall of Mussolini	1943–1945 Russian offensives
1944–1945 Allies liberate Western Europe	1944–1945 Allied and Russian offensives	

TABLE EIGHT: 1945–1959

WORLD AS A WHOLE	ASIA	AFRICA
1945 United Nations established: 51 members	1945 Arab League formed: 7 states	1945 Colonial empires continue; only four independent African states
1945–1947 Peacemaking breaks down: Cold War begins	1945–1946 Occupation of Japan; new constitution	
1945–1953 U.S.: Truman presidency; Marshall Plan, Truman Doctrine		
	1946–1954 French war in Indochina	
1947 British leave India	1947 India and Pakistan independent	
1947–1949 End of British and Dutch empires in Asia	1948 Assassination of Gandhi	
1948 UN: Declaration of Human Rights	1948 Burma an independent republic	
	1948 Israel established	
	1948 First Arab-Israeli war	
1949 Communist triumph in China: People's Republic of China	1949 People's Republic of China established	
1949 North Atlantic Treaty Organization	1949 Dutch leave Indonesia	
1950 World population estimate: 2.5 billion; beginning of population explosion	1950 India a republic	
1950–1953 Korean War	1950–1953 Korean War	
	1950s Japan: regains sovereignty; economic expansion	
1951 Japanese peace treaty	1951 China occupies Tibet	1951 Libya independent
		1952 Egypt a republic; monarchy ousted
1953 Genetics: DNA double-helix structure discovered		
1953–1961 U.S.: Eisenhower presidency		
1954 U.S. hydrogen bomb tested	1954 French leave Indochina; Vietnam partitioned: North and South Vietnam	1954–1962 French-Algerian War
		1954 British surrender Suez Canal treaty rights
	1955 Bandung Afro-Asian conference	
1956 Suez Canal crisis	1956 Suez crisis: second Arab-Israeli war	1956 Suez crisis: Britain, France, Israel vs. Egypt
	1956 Islamic Republic of Pakistan	1956 Morocco, Tunisia, Sudan independent
1957 U.S.S.R. launches space satellites		1957 Gold Coast (Ghana): first British African colony to gain independence

WESTERN EUROPE	CENTRAL EUROPE	EASTERN EUROPE
1945–1946 De facto split of Europe: east and west	1945 Allied occupation of Germany	1945–1948 Communist satellites established
1945–1946 Woman suffrage in France, Italy, Belgium, etc.	1945 Italian elections: Christian Democratic coalitions begin	1946–1950 Soviet Fourth Five-Year Plan
1945–1951 Britain: Labour Government		
1945–1958 Fourth French Republic	1946 Italian Republic	
1046 France. Monnet Plan	1946 Nuremberg trials	
	1946–1953 Italy: De Gasperi premier	
1947 Marshall Plan	1947 Peace treaties with Italy, Hungary, etc.	1947–1956 Cominform
	1948–1949 Berlin blockade and airlift	1948 Communist takeover in Czechoslovakia
	1948 Italian elections: Communist setback	1948–1955 Yugoslavia splits with U.S.S.R.
1949 Council of Europe	1949 German Federal Republic (West Germany); German Democratic Republic (East Germany)	1949 Council of Mutual Economic Assistance
1949 North Atlantic Treaty Organization		
	1949–1963 West Germany: Adenauer chancellor; economic expansion	1949 U.S.S.R. tests atomic bomb
1951 European Coal and Steel Community		1951–1955 Soviet Fifth Five-Year Plan
1951–1964 British Conservatives in office		
1952 Britain: Elizabeth II succeeds George VI	1952 Allied occupation of West Germany ends	
1953 West European economic recovery	1953 East Berlin uprising	1953 Death of Stalin
		1953 Russian hydrogen bomb
1954 Western European Union; West German rearmament		1953–1955 Malenkov premier; emergence of Khrushchev
1954 French defeat in Indochina; war in Algeria begins	1955 Austrian peace treaty	1955 Warsaw Pact
		1956 20th party congress: Khrushchev denounces Stalin regime
		1956 Polish, Hungarian risings crushed
		1956 U.S.S.R.–Japan peace treaty
1957 Rome treaties: European Economic Community (Common Market): 6 members	1957 Rome treaties: Common Market	1957 U.S.S.R. launches Sputnik I and II

WORLD AS A WHOLE	ASIA	AFRICA
1957–1962 End of British, French, Belgian colonial empires in Africa		1957–1962 African states gain independence: Ghana, Nigeria, Kenya, Uganda, etc.
1958–1963 Pope John XXIII: reforms in Catholic Church	1958–1961 Syria part of United Arab Republic	1958 French colonies vote independence; French Community formed
1959 Cuban revolution: Castro in power		1958–1961 Egypt and Syria form short-lived United Arab Republic

TABLE NINE: 1960–

WORLD AS A WHOLE	ASIA	AFRICA
1960 World population estimate: 3 billion		
1960–1962 Congo civil war		1960–1962 Republic of Congo established: civil war
1960s U.S.: Civil rights movements, feminism	1960s North-South Vietnam War	
1961–1973 U.S. involvement in Vietnam War		
1961 U.S.S.R. and U.S. space flights; Soviets launch first man in space	1961 Portuguese leave Goa	1961 South Africa a republic; white minority government
1962 U.S.-Russian crisis over Cuba		1961–1975 Portuguese colonies: struggle for independence
1962 Chinese-Soviet rift	1962 Chinese-Soviet rift	1962 Algeria independent
1962–1965 Vatican Council II: reforms in Catholic church	1962 Chinese-Indian border war	
1963–1978 Pope Paul VI		1963 Organization of African Unity formed: 32 states
1963 Partial nuclear test ban agreement		
1963 U.S.: President Kennedy assassinated		
1963–1969 U.S.: Johnson presidency		
1964 Cyprus crisis	1964 Death of Nehru	
1964–1965 Vietnam War: U.S. involvement deepens	1964 Vietnam War: U.S. commits air and ground forces	
	1964 China tests atomic bomb	
1965 United Nations: 110 members	1964 Palestinian Liberation Organization formed	1965 Rhodesia: white minority government proclaims independence
	1966 Indonesia: Sukarno ousted	1966 UN recognizes Namibia (formerly South African trust territory)
	1966–1969 Chinese Cultural Revolution at its peak	
	1966–1977 Indira Gandhi in power	1966 Nkrumah overthrown in Ghana

WESTERN EUROPE	CENTRAL EUROPE	EASTERN EUROPE
1957 Britain tests hydrogen bomb		
1958 Fifth French Republic established 1958–1969 De Gaulle president 1959 British back European Free Trade Association		1958–1964 Khrushchev in power

WESTERN EUROPE	CENTRAL EUROPE	EASTERN EUROPE
1960 Belgium withdraws from Congo 1960 France a nuclear power		
1960s Spain: industrialization		1960s Liberalization in Soviet satellites 1960s Industrialization in German Democratic Republic, Poland, Hungary, etc. 1961 U.S.S.R. launches first man in space 1961 Soviets test 50-megaton nuclear bomb 1962–1963 Chinese Communists split with U.S.S.R.
	1961– Berlin Wall	
1962 French leave Algeria		
1963 Common Market: French veto British entry	1963–1968 West Germany: Erhard succeeds Adenauer; Christian Democratic coalition continues	
1964–1970 Britain: Labour in office		1964 Khrushchev ousted 1964–1982 Brezhnev in power
1965 France: De Gaulle reelected president		

WORLD AS A WHOLE	ASIA	AFRICA
1967–1968 China and France join U.S., U.S.S.R., and Britain as thermonuclear powers	1967 Third Arab-Israeli war (Six-Day War)	1967–1970 Nigeria suppresses Biafra secession
1968 Student riots: U.S., France, Japan, etc.	1967 China tests hydrogen bomb	
1968 Vietnam peace talks in Paris; war continues	1968 Chinese-Soviet border clashes in Manchuria	
1969–1974 U.S.: Nixon presidency	1969 Death of Ho Chi Minh	
1969 Americans in successful lunar flight		
1970s Voting age lowered to 18: U.S., Britain, France, Germany, etc.		1970s Agitation for black majority rule in Rhodesia and South Africa
1971 People's Republic of China admitted to UN		1971 Republic of Congo renamed Zaïre
		1971–1979 Uganda: repressive rule of Idi Amin
1972 U.S.-U.S.S.R. Strategic Arms Limitation Treaty		
1973 U.S. troops leave Vietnam	1973 Fourth Arab-Israeli war (Yom Kippur War)	
1973 Chile: military coup overthrows leftist government		
1973–1974 Arab oil embargo		
1974– World economic recession		
1974 India becomes sixth atomic power	1974 Turkey invades Cyprus	
1974 U.S.: Resignation of President Nixon; successor: Ford		
1975 End of last European (Portuguese) empire in Africa	1975 Bangladesh established	1975 End of Portuguese rule in Angola, Mozambique, etc.
1975 Helsinki agreements	1975 End of Vietnam War: Communist victories in Vietnam, Laos, Cambodia	1975–1976 Civil war in Angola; presence of Cuban troops
	1975–1976 Civil war in Lebanon	
1975 World population approaches 5 billion	1975–1979 Cambodia: Khmer Rouge dictatorship	
	1976 Death of Mao Tse-tung	
1977 Nuclear non-proliferation treaty	1978 Revolution in Iran: overthrow of Shah; Islamic republic	
1977–1981 U.S.: Carter presidency		
1978– Pope John Paul II	1979 Camp David accords: Israel-Egypt peace treaty	
1979 U.S.-U.S.S.R. Strategic Arms Limitation Treaty (not ratified by U.S. Senate)	1979– Vietnam invades Cambodia	
1980s Continuing space explorations	1980– Indira Gandhi returns to power	1980 Zimbabwe (Rhodesia) independent under black majority government
1980s Continuing advances in molecular genetics	1980– Iran-Iraq War	1982 Organization of African Unity: 51 states
1980–1981 U.S. hostage crisis in Iran	1982 Israel returns Sinai to Egypt	
1981– U.S.: Reagan presidency	1982 Fifth Arab-Israeli War (Lebanon)	
1982 United Nations: 157 members	1982 Arab League: 22 members	
1983 World population estimate: 5 billion		

WESTERN EUROPE	CENTRAL EUROPE	EASTERN EUROPE
		1967–1974 Military dictatorship in Greece
1968 France: student and labor demonstrations 1968 France tests hydrogen bomb		1968 Soviets invade Czechoslovakia; end liberal Czech regime
1969–1981 De Gaulle resigns; successors: Pompidou, Giscard d'Estaing 1969– Northern Ireland: Catholic-Protestant clashes 1970s Voting age lowered to 18: Britain, France, West Germany, Italy 1970–1974 Britain: Conservatives in office	1969–1974 Germany: Brandt ends Christian Democratic tenure; heads Social Democratic coalition government 1970s Italy: economic difficulties, political instability	
1973 Britain, Denmark, Ireland join Common Market: 9 members 1974– Economic recession 1974 Portugal: revolution and end of dictatorship 1974–1979 Britain: Labour in office 1975 Spain: death of Franco; constitutional monarchy	1973 German Federal Republic admitted to UN 1974 Economic recession 1974–1982 Schmidt heads Social Democratic coalition government	1973 German Democratic Republic admitted to UN 1974 Greece: dictatorship ends; republic established 1975 Helsinki agreements
		1976–1980 Soviet Tenth Five-Year Plan 1977 U.S.S.R.: new constitution adopted
1979 European Economic Community: Greece 10th member; Europe-wide elections for European Parliament 1979– Britain: Conservatives in office; Margaret Thatcher prime minister 1981– France: Socialist president, Mitterrand; Socialist legislative majority 1982 Spain joins NATO: 16 members	1982– Germany: Kohl heads Christian Democratic coalition government 1982 Italy: 43rd postwar cabinet formed	1979– Soviets invade Afghanistan 1980 Yugoslavia: death of Tito 1981–1985 Soviet Eleventh Five-Year Plan 1981– Poland: Soviet pressures curb liberalization; martial law 1982 Death of Brezhnev; successor: Andropov

Appendix II:
Rulers and Regimes
In Principal European Countries since 1500

HOLY ROMAN EMPIRE

Habsburg Line

MAXIMILIAN I	1493–1519
CHARLES V	1519–1556
FERDINAND I	1556–1564
MAXIMILIAN II	1564–1576
RUDOLPH II	1576–1612
MATTHIAS	1612–1619
FERDINAND II	1619–1637
FERDINAND III	1637–1657
LEOPOLD I	1658–1705
JOSEPH I	1705–1711
CHARLES VI	1711–1740

Charles VI was succeeded by a daughter, Maria Theresa, who as a woman could not be elected Holy Roman Emperor. French influence in 1742 secured the election of

Bavarian Line

CHARLES VII	1742–1745

On Charles VII's death the Habsburg control of the Emperorship was resumed.

Lorraine Line

FRANCIS I	1745–1765

(husband of Maria Theresa)

Habsburg-Lorraine Line

JOSEPH II	1765–1790

(son of Francis I and Maria Theresa)

LEOPOLD II	1790–1792
FRANCIS II	1792–1806

The Holy Roman Empire became extinct in 1806.

AUSTRIAN DOMINIONS

The rulers of Austria from 1438 to 1740, and at least titular kings of Hungary from 1526 to 1740, were the same as the Holy Roman Emperors. After 1740:

Habsburg Line (through female heir)

MARIA THERESA	1740–1780
JOSEPH II	1780–1790
LEOPOLD II	1790–1792
FRANCIS II	1792–1835

In 1804 Francis II took the title of Emperor, as Francis I of the Austrian Empire. Austria was declared an "empire" because Napoleon proclaimed France an empire in that year, and because the demise of the Holy Roman Empire could be foreseen.

FERDINAND I	1835–1848
FRANCIS JOSEPH	1848–1916
CHARLES I	1916–1918

The Austrian Empire became extinct in 1918.

BRITISH ISLES

Tudor Line

Kings of England and Ireland

HENRY VII	1485–1509
HENRY VIII	1509–1547
EDWARD VI	1547–1553
MARY I	1553–1558
ELIZABETH I	1558–1603

In 1603 James VI of Scotland, a great-great-grandson of Henry VII, succeeded to the English throne.

Stuart Line

Kings of England and Ireland, and of Scotland
JAMES I   1603–1625
CHARLES I   1625–1649

Republican Interregnum

The Commonwealth   1649–1653
The Protectorate
OLIVER CROMWELL   1653–1658
Lord Protector
RICHARD CROMWELL   1658–1660

Restored Stuart Line

CHARLES II   1660–1685
JAMES II   1685–1688

In 1688 James II was forced out of the country, but Parliament kept the crown in a female branch of the Stuart family, calling in Mary, the daughter of James II, and her husband William III of the Netherlands.

WILLIAM III   1689–1702,
AND MARY II   1689–1694
ANNE   1702–1714

In 1707, through the Union of England and Scotland, the royal title became King (or Queen) of Great Britain and Ireland. The Stuart family having no direct Protestant heirs, the throne passed in 1714 to the German George I, Elector of Hanover, a great-grandson of James I.

Hanoverian Line

Kings of Great Britain and Ireland
GEORGE I   1714–1727
GEORGE II   1727–1760
GEORGE III   1760–1820
GEORGE IV   1820–1830
WILLIAM IV   1830–1837

William IV having no heirs, the British throne passed in 1837 to Victoria, a granddaughter of George III. Though the British family has continued in direct descent from George I, it has dropped the Hanoverian designation and is

now known as the House of Windsor. From 1877 to 1947 the British rulers bore the additional title of Emperor (or Empress) of India.

VICTORIA   1837–1901
EDWARD VII   1901–1910
GEORGE V   1910–1936
EDWARD VIII   1936
GEORGE VI   1936–1952
ELIZABETH II   1952–

FRANCE

Valois Line

LOUIS XI   1461–1483
CHARLES VIII   1483–1498
LOUIS XII   1498–1515
FRANCIS I   1515–1547
HENRY II   1547–1559
FRANCIS II   1559–1560
CHARLES IX   1560–1574
HENRY III   1574–1589

In 1589 the Valois line became extinct, and the throne passed to Henry of Bourbon, a remote descendant of French kings of the fourteenth century.

Bourbon Line

HENRY IV   1589–1610
LOUIS XIII   1610–1643
LOUIS XIV   1643–1715
LOUIS XV   1715–1774
LOUIS XVI   1774–1792

The Republic

Convention   1792–1795
Directory   1795–1799
Consulate   1799–1804

The Empire

NAPOLEON I   1804–1814
Emperor of the French
and King of Italy

Restored Bourbon Line

LOUIS XVIII   1814–1824

(Royalists count a Louis XVII, 1793–1795, and date the reign of Louis XVIII from 1795.)

CHARLES X   1824–1830

The Revolution of 1830 gave the throne to the Duke of Orleans, descendant of Louis XIII.

Orleans Line

LOUIS-PHILIPPE   1830–1848

The Second Republic

1848–1852

The Second Empire

NAPOLEON III   1852–1870
Emperor of the French

The Third Republic

1870–1940

Vichy Regime

1940–1944

Provisional Government

1944–1946

The Fourth Republic

1946–1958

The Fifth Republic

1958–

PRUSSIA (AND GERMANY)

A continuous Hohenzollern line ruled until 1918.

Electors of Brandenburg and Dukes of Prussia

GEORGE WILLIAM   1619–1640
FREDERICK WILLIAM   1640–1688
the "Great Elector"
FREDERICK III   1688–1713

In 1701 Frederick III was permitted by the Holy Roman Emperor to entitle himself King in Prussia, as Frederick I.

Kings of Prussia

FREDERICK I   1701–1713
FREDERICK WILLIAM I   1713–1740
FREDERICK II, the "Great"   1740–1786
FREDERICK WILLIAM II   1786–1797
FREDERICK WILLIAM III   1797–1840
FREDERICK WILLIAM IV   1840–1861
WILLIAM I   1861–1888

In 1871 William I took the title of German Emperor.

German Emperors

WILLIAM I   1871–1888
FREDERICK III   1888
WILLIAM II   1888–1918

The German Empire became extinct in 1918. It was succeeded by the

Weimar Republic

1919–1933

(an unofficial title for what was still called the Deutsches Reich, a phrase not easy to translate accurately)

The Third Reich

1933–1945

(an unofficial title for the Deutsches Reich under Adolf Hitler)
Allied Military Government in 1945 was followed by

German Federal Republic (West Germany)

1949–

German Democratic Republic (East Germany)

1949–

SARDINIA (AND ITALY)

In 1720 Victor Amadeus II, Duke of Savoy, took the title of King of Sardinia, having acquired the island of that name.

Kings of Sardinia

Victor Amadeus II	1720–1730
Charles Emmanuel III	1730–1773
Victor Amadeus III	1773–1796
Charles Emmanuel IV	1796–1802
Victor Emmanuel I	1802–1821
Charles Felix	1821–1831
Charles Albert	1831–1849
Victor Emmanuel II	1849–1878

In 1861 Victor Emmanuel II took the title of King of Italy.

Kings of Italy

Victor Emmanuel II	1861–1878
Humbert I	1878–1900
Victor Emmanuel III	1900–1946
Humbert II	1946

In 1936 Victor Emmanuel III took the title of Emperor of Ethiopia, which became meaningless with British occupation of Ethiopia in 1941. In 1946 the Kingdom of Italy became extinct and was succeeded by the

Italian Republic

1946–

SPAIN

Ferdinand and Isabella   1479–1504/1516

Isabella died in 1504, but Ferdinand lived until 1516, whereupon the Spanish thrones were inherited by their grandson Charles, who became Charles V of the Holy Roman Empire, but was known in Spain as Charles I.

Habsburg Line

Charles I	1516–1556
Philip II	1556–1598
Philip III	1598–1621
Philip IV	1621–1665
Charles II	1665–1700

With Charles II the Spanish Habsburg line became extinct, and the throne passed to the French Bourbon grandson of Louis XIV of France and great-grandson of Philip IV of Spain.

Bourbon Line

Philip V	1700–1746
Ferdinand VI	1746–1759
Charles III	1759–1788
Charles IV	1788–1808

Bonaparte Line

Joseph	1808–1813

(brother of Napoleon)

Restored Bourbon Line

Ferdinand VII	1813–1833
Isabella II	1833–1868

In 1868 Isabella abdicated; after a regency, and a brief reign by Amadeus I (Savoy), 1871–1873, there was a short-lived First Republic, 1873–1874, succeeded by

Alfonso XII	1874–1885
Alfonso XIII	1885–1931

In 1931 a republican revolution unseated Alfonso XIII.

Second Spanish Republic

1931–1936

Spanish Civil War

1936–1939

Regime of General Francisco Franco

1939–1975

Upon the death of Franco the Bourbon family was restored.

Juan Carlos I   1975–

RUSSIA (AND U.S.S.R.)

Grand Dukes of Moscow

Ivan III, the "Great"	1462–1505
Basil III	1505–1533
Ivan IV, the "Terrible"	1533–1584

In 1547 Ivan IV took the title of Tsar of Russia.

Tsars of Russia

Ivan IV, the "Terrible"	1547–1584
Theodore I	1584–1598
Boris Godunov	1598–1605

Time of Troubles

1604–1613

Romanov Line

MICHAEL	1613–1645
ALEXIS	1645–1676
THEODORE II	1676–1682
IVAN V AND PETER I	1682–1689
PETER I, the "Great"	1689–1725
CATHERINE I	1725–1727
PETER II	1727–1730
ANNA	1730–1740
IVAN VI	1740–1741
ELIZABETH	1741–1762
PETER III	1762
CATHERINE II, the "Great"	1762–1796
PAUL	1796–1801
ALEXANDER I	1801–1825

NICHOLAS I	1825–1855
ALEXANDER II	1855–1881
ALEXANDER III	1881–1894
NICHOLAS II	1894–1917

In 1917 the tsardom became extinct.

Provisional Government

1917

Communist Revolution

1917

Union of Soviet Socialist Republics

1922–

Appendix III:
Historical Populations of Various Countries and Cities

Figures for dates before the nineteenth century arise from estimates, in some cases subject to a wide margin of error. Those for the nineteenth and twentieth centuries generally reflect census returns, at dates within two or three years before or after the round date indicated. For cities, the figures for 1950 and 1980 refer to "urban agglomerations" as defined in the *United Nations Demographic Yearbook*. Estimates for cities for earlier dates are conveniently assembled in Tertius Chandler and Gerald Fox, *3000 Years of Urban Growth* (New York, 1974).

For countries, the use of the table is mainly for rough comparisons. It shows, for example, that France was about five times as populous as England in the Middle Ages, and was still more populous than all the German states at the time of the French Revolution, or that Spain declined under the Habsburgs in the seventeenth century, and that Ireland lost population after the famine and ensuing emigration. All countries except Ireland grew rapidly in population in the nineteenth century. For Russia, the figures from 1750 to 1950 reflect territorial expansion as well as internal growth. All figures for China are very uncertain, though unquestionably very large.

For 1950 and 1980 the figures for Ireland include both the Republic of Ireland and Northern Ireland, and "Germany" includes both East and West Germany. In 1980 the Irish Republic was about twice as populous as its northern neighbor, and West Germany was over three times as populous as East Germany.

CITIES in thousands

	LONDON	MANCHESTER	PARIS	MARSEILLES
14th Century	50	3–	200	
15th Century				
16th Century	100			
17th Century	500	15–	450	50 +
18th Century	750		500	90
1800	959	77	600	111
1850	2681	303	1422	195
1900	6581	544	3670	491
1950	8346	2421	4823	655
1980	6970	2675	8612	1077

	FLORENCE	BERLIN	VIENNA	PRAGUE
14th Century	50 +			
15th Century	60	10–	20	25 +
16th Century	65	12	40 +	40 +
17th Century	75	20	100	40 +
18th Century	75	100	220	75
1800	84	172	247	75
1850	114	500	444	206
1900	206	2712	1675	382
1950	374	3337	1766	922
1980	464	3044	1590	1191

AMSTERDAM	ANTWERP	LISBON	MADRID	ROME
	5	20 +	5–	30–
20–	35			50
35	100	100	60	100
100 +	50	73	80	130
150	50	120	120	150
201	62	180	160	153
224	88	240	281	175
511	277	356	540	463
838	584	790	1618	1652
961	1569	1612	3200	2898

WARSAW	BUDAPEST	STOCKHOLM	ST. PETERSBURG LENINGRAD	MOSCOW
70		60	100	
100	54 +	76	220	250
150	178	93	485	365
700	732	301	1150	1000
804	1571	928	3182	4847
1542	2091	1380	4588	8011

COUNTRIES in millions

	ENGLAND AND WALES	SCOTLAND	IRELAND	FRANCE
1300	3.5			15.0
1500	2.8			16.0
1700	5.5	1.2		19.0
1800	8.9	1.6	5.2	27.0
1850	17.9	2.9	6.5	34.2
1900	32.5	4.5	4.5	38.5
1950	43.0	5.0	4.3	41.8
1980	49.2	5.2	4.9	53.7

	SWEDEN	POLAND	RUSSIA U.S.S.R.	CHINA
1300		1.3		
1500		2.0		
1700	1.6		12	200
1800	2.3		30	
1850	3.5		62	400
1900	5.1	28.3	104	
1950	7.0	24.8	180	547
1980	8.3	35.6	265	995

BELGIUM	NETHERLANDS	GERMANY	SPAIN	ITALY
.7	.4	7.0		8.0
		7.0	8.3	6.0
1.6	1.8	15.0	6.0	11.0
3.0	2.0	25.0	10.5	17.2
4.3	3.1	33.8		24.3
6.7	5.1	56.3	19.1	33.6
8.6	10.1	68.3	27.9	46.8
9.9	14.1	78.3	37.4	57.1

JAPAN	EGYPT	MEXICO	BRAZIL	U.S.A.
				.3
	2.5	6.0		5.3
30.0	5.0			23.2
45.0	10.0	13.6	20.0	76.0
83.2	20.0	25.7	52.6	152.0
116.8	42.3	69.3	118.6	228.0

Bibliography

The following reading lists are intended for the convenience of students, teachers, and general readers. Although professional students of history also may find them useful, no attempt has been made to provide comprehensive coverage of any areas or topics. The aim throughout has been to call attention to the most reliable and most recent works, to which the reader may turn for more specialized bibliographies. Classification follows the plan of chapters in the present book. Few titles are intentionally repeated; to find books on some topics, it will sometimes be necessary to look in several places. For reasons of space, works in foreign languages are excluded, as are (with few exceptions) general text-books, articles in periodicals, and primary source materials.

Many of the titles listed below are now or will be available in paperback; up-to-date lists of such paperbacks may be found in the *Paperback book guide for colleges*, published and distributed by R. R. Bowker Company. An asterisk in the reading lists below indicates availability in a paperback edition.

WORKS OF GENERAL COVERAGE

Bibliographical Guides

There are literally hundreds of thousands of books on historical subjects, and it is difficult to find titles and authors on any particular topic. One useful but now outdated bibliographical tool is the American Historical Association's *Guide to historical literature* (1961). To keep up with the outpouring of historical books in recent years, one must read the book reviews and listings of new books in the *American historical review*, the *Journal of modern history*, and other periodicals; the American Historical Association (AHA) Pamphlets series is often helpful. Some of the most discerning appraisals of new history books are to be found in the (London) *Times literary supplement*.

Brief Reference Works and Atlases

W. L. Langer, *An encyclopedia of world history: ancient, medieval, and modern, chronologically arranged* (rev., 1972), is a vast table of dates and important events. A similar service is performed by S. H. Steinberg, *Historical tables, 58 B.C.-A.D. 1978* (1979), and G. S. P. Freeman-Grenville, *Chronology of world history* (1978). Convenient one-volume reference tools are the *New Columbia encyclopedia* (4th ed., 1975), and the *Random House encyclopedia* (1977).

An excellent atlas that places European history in its world setting is G. Barraclough (ed.), the (London) *Times atlas of world history* (1978). Among many other historical atlases are R. R. Palmer and others, *Atlas of world history* (1957), available also as *Abridged historical atlas** (1958); W. R. Shepherd, *Historical atlas* (rev., 1964); *Muir's Historical atlas—medieval and modern* (rev., 1964); *Chambers historical atlas of the world** (1971); and the *New Oxford atlas* (1975). H. C. Darby and H. Fullard, *Atlas** (1975), is the final volume (vol. 14) of the *New Cambridge modern history*. Geographical information can be readily located through *Webster's geographical dictionary* (rev., 1972), and current developments may be followed in J. P. Cole, *Geography of world affairs* (1979), and M. Kidron and

R. Segal, *The state of the world atlas* (1981).
An interesting introduction to cartography is
J. N. Wilford, *The mapmakers* (1981).

Geographical influences on history are
discussed in D. S. Whittlesey, *Environmental foundations of European history* (1949);
C. T. Smith, *An historical geography of
Western Europe before 1800* (1967); and
E. A. Freeman and J. B. Bury, *The historical geography of Europe* (1974). N. J. G.
Pounds, *An historical geography of Europe*
(2 vols., 1973–1979), examines economic
changes in their geographic setting from
450 B.C. to the mid-nineteenth century. An
interesting book stressing unique factors in
European development is E. L. Jones, *The
European miracle: environments, economies, and geopolitics in the history of
Europe and Asia* * (1981), while one national setting is examined in E. W. Fox, *History in geographic perspective: the other
France* (1971).

Multivolumed Encyclopedias

Among the most useful are the *Encyclopaedia Britannica* [now in its controversial
fifteenth edition (1975), of which the nineteen volumes of the *Macropaedia* provide the
longer scholarly articles]; the *Encyclopedia
Americana, Collier's encyclopedia*, and the
New international encyclopedia. Each annually publishes a yearbook that covers developments of the previous year. The *Academic American encyclopedia* (1981) is the
newest of these multivolumed works of reference. The *International encyclopedia of the
social sciences* (17 vols., 1968) may be consulted for many topics. The *Dictionary of the
history of ideas* (4 vols., 1973) has substantial
articles on important concepts, while the
Encyclopedia of philosophy (8 vols., 1967) is
valuable for philosophical thought. The
Dictionary of scientific biography (8 vols.,
1970–1980) includes scientists from antiquity to the present. The *Dictionary of national biography* (1885–1949) is informative
for British figures; a shorter version is the
Concise dictionary of national biography
(2 vols., 1961, 1982).

Multivolumed Collaborative Works and Series on Modern European History

The *Cambridge modern history* (14 vols.,
1902–1912) has been superseded by the *New
Cambridge modern history* * (14 vols., 1957–
1979). The volumes, which are described in
the appropriate sections below, contain
valuable chapters by specialists from all over
the world but often fail to provide a synthesis
for the period covered; volume 13, a companion volume [Peter Burke (ed.), 1979], is a
welcome collection of thematic essays. An
Oxford history of modern Europe, focusing
on individual nations, will also be available
soon; seven volumes have been published to
date. An important series by American scholars on Europe from 1250 to 1945 is the *Rise
of modern Europe* (20 vols. projected, 1936
ff., now all but complete), also known as the
"Langer series" for its editor, W. L. Langer;
the volumes, each with an extensive bibliography, are discussed in the chapters below.
B. C. Shafer is editing *Europe and the world
in the age of expansion* (10 vols. projected,
1975 ff.), to cover the thirteenth to twentieth
centuries. The multivolumed collaborative
UNESCO history of mankind (1963 ff.) has
suffered from the need to arrive at political
consensus on subjects covered. There are a
variety of other series.

Interpretive and Large-Scale Histories

Histories recounting and analyzing the
human story in order to show that it follows
a certain pattern or system, or that it obeys
certain laws, are generally regarded with
distrust by historians, who are not convinced
by the evidence offered. In recent years, the
most important grand-scale interpretive account has been A. J. Toynbee's monumental
A study of history * (12 vols., 1934–1961, of
which vol. 12 consists of *Reconsiderations*)
[abridgment edited by D. C. Somervell, 2
vols., 1947–1957]; Toynbee's *Mankind and
mother earth* (1976) was published posthumously. Some objections to Toynbee are discussed in M. F. Ashley-Montagu (ed.),
Toynbee and history: critical essays and reviews (1956); E. T. Gargan and others, *The
intent of Toynbee's history* (1961); and P.
Geyl, *Debates with historians* (1956) and
Encounters in history (1961). The attempt
to find patterns or laws in historical evolution is to be distinguished from large-scale
efforts to recount the scope of human history. Here two works stand out: H. A. L.
Fisher, *A history of Europe* (3 vols.,
1935–1936; 2 vols., 1949), an older, notable
effort by a single author to tell the whole
Western story from the Greeks to the twentieth century, and W. H. McNeill, *The rise of
the West: a history of the human community*
(1963), a presentation of Western history in
its world setting that stresses the interrelationships of human civilization at all stages.

McNeill has also written *The shape of European history** (1974), a briefer study of Europe from antiquity to the present stressing cultural and technological changes. Ambitious and informative but overly Eurocentric is H. Thomas, *A history of the world* (1979).

General Histories in Special Areas

[Books listed here relate to many or all of the chapters of the present work and provide additional specialized bibliographies as well.] For European economic history, a valuable collaborative work is C. M. Cipolla (ed.), *The Fontana economic history of Europe** (6 vols., 1972–1976), with chapters contributed by an international roster of experts. A useful, one-volume synthesis is S. B. Clough and R. T. Rapp, *European economic history* (rev., 1975). On economic thought, one may read: E. Roll, *A history of economic thought* (rev., 1946); C. Gide and C. Rist, *A history of economic doctrines* (2nd ed., 1948); R. L. Heilbroner, *The worldly philosophers** (1953); E. Whittaker, *Schools and streams of economic thought* (1960); E. Heimann, *History of economic doctrines* (1964); H. T. Overton, *Social ideals and economic theories from Quesnay to Keynes* (1962); D. Winch, *Economics and policy: a historical survey* (1972); and H. W. Spiegel, *The growth of economic thought* (rev., 1983).

On rural and agrarian history, the best introduction is D. B. Grigg, *The agricultural systems of the world: an evolutionary approach** (1974), which may be supplemented by B. H. S. van Bath, *The agrarian history of western Europe, 500–1850* (trans. from Dutch, 1963).

For intellectual and cultural history and the history of ideas one still reads with profit B. Russell, *A history of philosophy* (1945); J. H. Randall, Jr., *Making of the modern mind* (1926, reissued 1976); and the same author's later work, *The career of philosophy* (2 vols., 1962–1965). An impressive comprehensive survey of formal philosophy is F. C. Copleston, *A history of philosophy* (9 vols., 1946–1975). An admirable synthesis for the history of ideas in the modern period is F. L. Baumer, *Modern European thought: continuity and change in ideas, 1600–1950* (1977). C. Brinton's books, *Ideas and men: the story of Western thought* (1950, 1963), published for the modern period as *The shaping of the modern mind** (1953), and *A history of Western morals* (1959), remain

excellent introductions, as does R. N. Stromberg, *An intellectual history of modern Europe* (rev., 1975). W. W. Wagar, *World views: a study in comparative history* (1977), examines such ideas as rationalism and romanticism in four different cultural settings, while R. Nisbet, *History of the idea of progress* (1980), traces a specific idea from antiquity to the present. Recommended also: J. Bronowski and B. Mazlish, *The Western intellectual tradition: from Leonardo to Hegel* (1960); W. H. Coates, H. V. White, and J. S. Schapiro, *The emergence of liberal humanism* (1966); and the sequel volume by Coates and White, *The ordeal of liberal humanism* (1969).

On political thought, R. Berki, *The history of political thought** (1977), is an admirable brief introduction, while Q. Skinner, *The foundations of modern political thought* (2 vols., 1978), is a masterful account for the early modern centuries. One still reads with interest G. H. Sabine, *A history of political theory* (1937, reissued 1973). On the need to examine political ideas and political vocabulary in the context of their times, one should read J. G. A. Pocock, *Politics, language, and time: essays on political thought and history* (1971).

Of the many books on the arts, one may turn for syntheses to H. W. and D. J. Janson, *History of art: a survey of the major visual arts from the dawn of history to the present day* (rev., 1977); A. Hauser, *Social history of art* (4 vols., 1963); D. J. Groat, *A history of Western music* (rev., 1973); K. H. Worner, *A history of music* (1973); N. Pevsner, *An outline of European architecture* (rev., 1963); and Pevsner and others, *A dictionary of architecture* (1976).

Books on military history treating war as a social and human phenomenon include the older J. U. Nef, *War and human progress: an essay on the rise of industrial civilization* (1950, 1965); A. Vagts, *A history of militarism: romance and realities of a profession** (1937); and Q. Wright, *A study of war* (2 vols., 1942; 1 vol. abr., 1965). To these one must add J. Keegan, *The face of battle* (1977); M. Howard, *War in European history* (1976); T. Ropp, *War in the modern world** (1959, 1962); and R. A. Preston and S. Wise, *Men in arms** (4th ed., 1979). Other informative books include: A. Corvisier, *Armies and societies in Europe, 1494–1789* (trans. 1979); G. Best, *Humanity in warfare* (1980); B. and F. M. Brodie, *From crossbow to H-bomb* (rev., 1973); W. H. McNeill, *The pursuit of power: technology,* armed force, and society since A.D. 1000 (1982); and S. Mansfield, *The gestalts of war: an inquiry into its origins and meanings as a social institution* (1982).

For strategy and battle history, one may turn to B. H. Liddell Hart, *Strategy: the indirect approach* (1957); J. F. C. Fuller, *A military history of the Western world* (3 vols., 1954–1956); and R. E. and T. N. Dupuy, *Encyclopedia of military history: from 3500 B.C. to the present* (rev., 1977). F. L. Israel has edited *Major peace treaties of modern history, 1648–1967* (4 vols., 1967).

The New Social History

In recent years, stimulated by the *Annales* school of historical writing in France (the name derived from the French periodical *Annales: sociétés, economies, civilisations*) and by newer kinds of working-class history in England, historians have concerned themselves increasingly with aspects of social history distinct from older interests in the history of social classes and of labor and laboring conditions. They have been examining such subjects as the history of the family and of women; the daily lives, diet, and outlook of the urban and rural poor; sexuality and marriage; and popular culture —all viewed as history "from the bottom up." Many of these works are listed below in the appropriate chapters. Three pioneer studies have been P. Ariès, *Centuries of childhood: a social history of family life** (trans. 1962); P. Laslett, *The world we have lost: England before the industrial age* (1965); and E. P. Thompson, *The making of the English working class** (1963).

The family is studied in such recent works as L. Stone, *The family, sex, and marriage in England, 1500–1800** (1977; abr. 1979); R. Trumbach, *The rise of the egalitarian family* (1978); M. Mitterauer and R. Sieder, *The European family: patriarchy to partnership, 1400 to the present* (1982); and E. Shorter, *The making of the modern family* (1975); there are also many collections of essays on the subject, of which a recent one with a useful overview is V. C. Fox and M. H. Quitt (eds.), *Loving, parenting, and dying: the family cycle in England and America, past and present** (1981). A massive bibliographical aid is G. L. Soliday (ed.), *History of family and kinship: a select international bibliography* (1980). Related studies include J. R. Gillis, *Youth and history: tradition and change in European age relations, 1770 to the present* (rev., 1981); D. Hunt, *Parents and children in history** (1972); and I. Pinchbeck and M. Hewitt, *Children in English society* (2 vols., 1969–1973). A. Esler (ed.), *The youth revolution: the conflict of generations in modern history** (1974), is an interesting anthology.

The best introduction to the history of popular culture is P. Burke, *Popular culture in early modern Europe* (1978), which may be supplemented by J. Beauroy, M. Bertrand, and E. T. Gargan, *The wolf and the lamb: popular culture in France from the Old Regime to the twentieth century* (1977).

General introductions providing samples of the new social history include A. Mitchell and I. Deak (eds.), *Everyman in Europe: essays in social history** (2 vols.; rev., 1981); V. J. Knapp, *Europe in the era of social transformation, 1700 to the present* (1976); R. Z. Bezucha (ed.), *Modern European social history** (1972); and P. Stearns, *European society in upheaval: social history since 1800* (1967).

There has also been a considerable interest, especially by American historians in recent decades, in the history of women. A useful brief introduction to the literature is B. Sicherman, E. W. Monter, J. W. Scott, and K. K. Sklar (eds.), *Recent United States scholarship in the history of women** (1980). Mary Ritter Beard was one of the first to examine the impact of women on history and many of her insights in *Women as a force in history: a study in traditions and realities* (1946) are still provocative. Newer emphases may be sampled in three collaborative collections of essays: R. Bridenthal and C. Koonz (eds.), *Becoming visible: women in European history** (1977), with essays running from ancient times to the twentieth century; M. Hartman and L. W. Banner (eds.), *Clio's consciousness raised: new perspectives on the history of women** (1974); and B. A. Carroll (ed.), *Liberating women's history** (1976), the latter especially valuable. An important monograph is J. W. Scott and L. A. Tilly, *Women, work, and family* (1978), focusing on French and English women in the modern centuries. Two informative collections of essays are P. H. Labalme (ed.), *Beyond their sex: learned women of the European past* (1980), mainly on early modern Europe; and C. R. Berkin and C. M. Lovett (eds.), *Women, war, and revolution* (1980). Two full-length studies are S. G. Bell, *Women: from the Greeks to the French Revolution** (1980), and

P. Stock, *Better than rubies: a history of women's education* (1978), from the Renaissance to the present, incorporating revisions of traditional views of the "progress" made by women in various epochs; recommended also is M. Kinnear, *Daughters of time** (1982). S. Rowbotham, *Women, resistance, and revolution* (1974), is a stimulating series of essays ranging from the English civil wars of the seventeenth century to the twentieth; and J. B. Elstain, *Public man, private woman: women in social and political thought* (1981), is an illuminating survey of political thinkers and their treatment of the subject of women from Aristotle on. Two documentary histories available are E. S. Reimers and J. C. Fout (eds.), *European women: a documentary history, 1789–1945* (1980), and E. O. Hillerstein, L. P. Hume, and K. M. Offen (eds.), *Victorian women: a documentary account of women's lives in England, France, and the United States** (1981), both with interesting selections and extensive bibliographies. An anthology conveying the flavor of an emergent feminism is A. S. Rossi (ed.), *The feminist papers: from [Abigail] Adams to [Simone] de Beauvoir** (1974). Two useful bibliographical studies are J. Kelly, B. A. Engel, and K. Casey, *Bibliography on the history of European women** (1976), and B. Kanner (ed.), *The women of England from Anglo-Saxon times to the present: interpretive bibliographical essays* (1979). [Many other titles are included in the appropriate sections below.]

Other subjects difficult to classify but related to the newer social history are covered in P. Ariès, *Western attitudes toward death: from the Middle Ages to the present* (trans. 1976), a synopsis of his larger work in French completed in 1979 and now being translated; and in three books by M. Foucault: *Madness and civilization* (trans. 1965); *Discipline and punish: the birth of the prison* (trans. 1979); and *A history of sexuality* (trans. 1978), the first volume of a projected larger study. On the latter subject, one may also turn to V. L. Bullough, *Sexual variance in society and history* (1976), and the briefer V. L. and B. Bullough, *Sin, sickness, and sanity: a history of sexual attitudes* (1977).

The Annales School

Although the *Annales* historians have inspired much of the newer social history, they have also been important for their emphasis on long-term factors that slowly and imperceptibly influence the course of historical change, such as geography, environment, resources, climate, population, diet, and disease, which in their view often merit closer attention than "events." Moreover, they have made notable efforts, through the intensive study of limited but valuable sources, to reconstruct the lives and outlook of ordinary men and women. Two outstanding exemplars of the *Annales* school, whose writings are available in English translation, are Fernand Braudel and Emmanuel Le Roy Ladurie.

Braudel's best-known work is *The Mediterranean and the Mediterranean world in the age of Philip II** (2 vols., 1949; rev., 1966; trans. 1972–1974). He has also written *Civilization and capitalism, 15th–18th century* (3 vols., 1977–1979), a revision of an earlier study; the first two volumes are available in English as *The structures of everyday life: the limits of the possible* (trans. 1981), and *The Wheels of Commerce* (trans. 1983). The broad theme of the study as a whole appears in *Afterthoughts on material civilization and capitalism* (trans. 1977).

Two successful books in early modern history by Ladurie skillfully reconstructing ordinary lives are *Montaillou: the promised land of error** (1975, trans. 1978) and *The carnival of Romans, 1579–80** (1979, trans. 1979). He has also written *Times of feast, times of famine: a history of climate since the year 1000* (trans. 1971), and a detailed study, *The peasants of Languedoc** (1974, trans. 1977). His reflections on historical method may be read in *The territory of the historian* (trans. 1979) and *The mind and method of the historian* (trans. 1980). The contributions of the *Annales* historians may be sampled in M. Ferro (ed.), *Social historians in contemporary France: essays from* Annales (1972); P. Burke (ed.), *Economy and society in early modern Europe: essays from* Annales (1972); and in several volumes of selections from *Annales* edited by R. Forster and O. Ranum, among them *Biology of man in history** (1975), *Family and society** (1976), and *Food and drink in history** (1979). An older work in social history that deserves incidental mention is N. Elias, *The civilizing process: the history of manners* (1939; reissued, 2 vols., 1968).

Demography and Related Topics

For demography one may turn to D. V. Glass and D. E. C. Eversley, *Population in history: essays in historical demography* (1965); E. A. Wrigley, *Population and his-*

tory * (1969); C. M. Cipolla, *Economic history of world population* * (1974); and T. McKeown, *The modern rise of population* (1977). A pioneering study, A. M. Carr-Saunders, *World population: past growth and future trends* (1936), is still valuable. To keep up with current trends, one should consult the *United Nations demographic yearbook* and other periodical literature. For the impact of famines, disease, and the movements of peoples, one may read W. H. McNeill, *Plagues and peoples* (1976), the same author's *The human condition: an ecological and historical view* (1981), and the collection of essays, McNeill and R. S. Adams (eds.), *Human migration: patterns and politics* (1978). On famine and food, one may also read E. P. Prentice, *Hunger and history: the influence of hunger on human history* (1939); R. N. Salaman, *The history and social influence of the potato* (1949); E. Forster and R. Forster (eds.), *European diet from preindustrial to modern times* (1975); and R. P. Multhauf, *Neptune's gift: a history of common salt* (1978). T. Chandler and G. Fox provide statistical data and other information on the historical growth of the world's cities in *3000 years of urban growth* (1974), and B. R. Mitchell, *European historical statistics, 1750–1970* * (rev. and abr., 1978), is a valuable compendium of figures on population, trade, and other social and economic topics.

On the subject of literacy, one may read C. M. Cipolla, *Literacy and development in the West* * (1969); and on the origins of higher education from the fourteenth to the twentieth centuries, L. Stone (ed.), *The university in society* (2 vols., 1974).

Historical Manuals and Historiography

Among manuals on methods of research and on the writing of history, a spirited introduction is J. Barzun and H. F. Graff, *The modern researcher* * (rev., 1977); Barzun and G. Dunbar, *Simple and direct: a rhetoric for writers* * (1976), is an excellent guide for all writers. Other introductions include A. Nevins, *The gateway to history* * (rev., 1962); S. Kent, *Writing history* (rev., 1967); and L. Gottschalk, *Understanding history* * (rev., 1969). There is practical information in K. L. Turabian, *A manual for writers of term papers, theses, and dissertations* * (many eds.), an adaptation of a standard guide, the University of Chicago, *A manual of style* (13th ed., 1982); in M. E. Skillin and

others, *Words into type* (3rd ed., 1974); and in M-C. van Leunen, *A handbook for scholars* * (1978).

Examples of books affording insight into the study and writing of history are C. Gustavson, *A preface to history* * (1955), and *The mansion of history* * (1975), the latter on modes of historical thinking; M. Bloch, *The historian's craft* * (1953); A. L. Rowse, *The use of history* * (1946); E. H. Carr, *What is history?* * (1962); G. L. Elton, *The practice of history* (1967); H. S. Hughes, *History as art and science: twin vistas on the past* * (1967); J. H. Hexter, *The history primer* (1971); and A. J. Gilbert (ed.), *In search of a meaningful past* * (1972). For examples of historians confronting evidence, see R. W. Winks (ed.), *The historian as detective: essays on evidence* (1970); L. P. Curtis, Jr. (ed.), *The historian's workshop* * (1971); P. Gay and V. G. Wexler (eds.), *Historians at work* (4 vols., 1972–1975); D.H. Fischer, *Historians' fallacies: toward a logic of historical thought* * (1970); and J.W. Davidson and M.H. Lytle, *After the fact: the art of historical detection* (1982).

Two informative introductions to the emergence of modern historical writing are H. Butterfield, *The origins of history* (rev., 1981), and D. Hay, *Annalists and historians: Western historiography from the eighth to the eighteenth centuries* (1977). The great historians of the past and the evolution of history are discussed in detail in the encyclopedic M. A. Fitzsimons, A. G. Pundt, and C. E. Nowell (eds.), *The development of historiography* (1954), and in the older J. W. Thompson and B. H. Holm, *A history of historical writing* (2 vols., 1942). A good introductory anthology is F. Stern (ed.), *The varieties of history: from Voltaire to the present* * (1956). Special studies of the historical craft and its practitioners include E. Cochran, *Historians and historiography in the Italian Renaissance* (1981); Donald R. Kelley, *Foundations of modern historical scholarship: language, law, and history in the French Renaissance* (1969); G. P. Gooch, *History and historians in the nineteenth century* (1913); E. E. Neff, *The poetry of history* (1947); B. E. Schmitt (ed.), *Some historians of modern Europe* (1942); and S. W. Halperin (ed.), *Some twentieth-century historians* (1961). For British historians, one may read J. R. Hale (ed.), *The evolution of British historiography: from Bacon to Namier* (1967); and V. Mehta, *The fly and the fly bottle* (1962), an intriguing journalistic account. P. Gay, *Style in history* (1974) and the same author's *Art and act: on causes in history* (1976), are also informative.

The *Annales* writers and others may be examined in T. Stoianovich, *French historical method: the Annales paradigm* (1976); W. R. Keylor, *Academy and community: the foundation of the French historical profession* (1975); and in G. G. Iggers, *New directions in European historiography* (1975). J. H. Hexter, *On historians: reappraisals of some of the makers of modern history* (1979), includes a critical appraisal of many writers, including Braudel.

Among other thoughtful reflections by contemporary historians, the following sampling of titles may be suggested: H. S. Commager, *The search for a usable past and other essays in historiography* (1967); P. Smith, *The historian and history* * (1964); G. Kitson Clark, *The critical historian* (1967); C. V. Wedgwood, *The sense of the past: thirteen studies in the theory and practice of history* (1960); J. Lukacs, *Historical consciousness: or the remembered past* (1968); J. T. Marcus, *Heaven, hell, and history: a survey of man's faith in history from antiquity to the present* (1967); G. Jackson, *Historian's quest* (1969); M. Duberman, *The uncompleted past* (1970); H. Zinn, *The politics of history* * (1970); J. H. Plumb, *The death of the past* (1970); F. E. Manuel, *Freedom from history* * (1971); B. Lewis, *History remembered, recovered, invented* (1975); F. Gilbert, *History: choice and commitment* (1977); and L. Stone, *The past and the present* (1981).

Biography may be examined in C. D. Bowen, *Biography: the craft and the calling* (1968), M. Pachter, *Telling lives* (1979), and D. Beales, *History and biography* * (1981).

A number of collections of essays provide valuable insights into contemporary trends in historical writing, among them: M. Kammen (ed.), *The past before us: contemporary historical writing in the United States* * (1980); C. F. Delzell (ed.), *The future of history* (1977); G. G. Iggers and H. T. Parker (eds.), *International handbook of historical studies: contemporary research and theory* (1979); and T. K. Rabb and R. I. Rotberg (eds.), *The new history: the 1980s and beyond* * (1982). Also useful are J. Higham (ed.), *History* (1965); B. C. Shafer (ed.), *Historical study in the West: France, Western Germany, Great Britain, and the United States* (1968); W. Laqueur and G. L. Mosse (eds.), *The new history: trends in historical research and writing since*

World War II * (1968); and F. Gilbert and S. R. Graubard (eds.), *Historical studies today* * (1972).

For relationships to the social sciences, see S. R. Lipset and R. Hofstadter (eds.), *Sociology and history* (1968); D. Landes and C. Tilly (eds.), *History as a social science* (1971); and N. J. Smelser, *Comparative methods in the social sciences* (1976). Contemporary social history owes a good deal to anthropology, where a seminal book with influence on historians has been C. Geertz, *The interpretations of cultures* (1973). One will also read with profit M. Harris, *The rise of anthropological theory* (1968); and two books by R. A. Nisbet, *The sociological tradition* (1967) and *Social change and history: aspects of the Western theory of development* (1969). Examples of quantitative, psychological, and behavioral approaches are to be found in W. O. Aydelotte and others, *The dimensions of quantitative research in history* (1972); V. Lorwin and J. Price (eds.), *Dimensions of the past* (1972); R. Floud, *An introduction to quantitative methods for historians* * (rev., 1979); and R. G. Hawks, *Economics for historians* * (1980). Psychological dimensions are examined in R. J. Lifton (ed.), *Explorations in psychohistory* * (1974); B. Mazlish (ed.), *Psychoanalysis and history* (1963); S. Friedländer, *History and psychoanalysis* (1978); and R. F. Berkhofer, Jr., *A behavioral approach to historical analysis* (1969). A provocative book criticizing the impact of the newer history is J. Barzun, *Clio and the doctors: psycho-history, quanto-history, and history* (1974).

Two books on modern research tools are P. Thompson, *The voice of the past: oral history* (1978), on new ways of tapping neglected sources; and P. Sorlin, *The film in history: restaging the past* (1980).

Philosophy of History

The historical manuals listed above all provide some introduction to the philosophy and theory of history. Two convenient introductions are the anthologies edited by H. Meyerhoff, *The philosophy of history in our time* * (1959), and P. Gardiner (ed.), *Theories of history* (1959).

There are many volumes on the philosophy of history written by professional students of philosophy sometimes not directly attuned to the needs and interests of practicing historians. The best scholarly introduction is R. E. Atkinson, *Knowledge and explanation in history: an introduction to the philosophy of history** (1978), which may be compared with two other useful treatments: W. H. Dray, *Philosophy of history** (1964), and W. H. Walsh, *An introduction to the philosophy of history** (1976). Other recommended books are R. Aron, *Introduction to the philosophy of history* (1948, trans. 1961); R. G. Collingwood, *The idea of history** (1946); M. Mandelbaum, *The anatomy of historical knowledge* (1977); A. C. Danto, *Analytical philosophy of history* (1965); R. Martin, *Historical explanation: reenactment and practical inference* (1977); and P. Munz, *The shapes of time: a new look at the philosophy of history* (1977). Two intriguing studies are B. Mazlish, *The riddle of history: the great speculators from Vico to Freud* (1966), and N. O. Brown, *Life against death: the psychoanalytical meaning of history** (1959).

Readings, Source Materials, and Historical Problems

The following titles are intended to give only a sampling of anthologies available for classroom use: Columbia University, *Introduction to contemporary civilization in the West* (2 vols., many revisions), a collection of longer source selections; J. H. Hexter and others, *The traditions of the Western world** (1967); R. P. Stearns, *Pageant of Europe: sources and selections from the Renaissance to the present day** (rev., 1961); F. L. Baumer, *Main currents of Western thought: readings in Western European intellectual history from the Middle Ages to the present** (rev., 1978); E. Weber, *The Western tradition from the ancient world to the atomic age** (1959); L. S. Stavrianos, *The epic of modern man: a collection of readings** (1966), globally oriented; J. K. Sowards, *Makers of the Western tradition: portraits from history* (rev., 1983), focusing on biographical studies; and D. Sherman, *Western civilization: images and interpretations* (2 vols., 1983), with interesting visual sources.

Among the many anthologies that focus on source problems or on conflicting interpretations of historical issues, there are S. B. Clough, P. Gay, C. K. Warner, and J. M. Cammett, *The European past: reappraisals in history** (2 vols.; rev., 1970); B. D. Gooch (ed.), *Interpreting European history** (2 vols., 1967); O. Ranum, *Searching for modern times** (2 vols., 1969); L. W. Spitz and R. W. Lyman (gen. eds.), *Major crises in Western civilization** (2 vols., 1965); and B. Tierney, D. Kagan, and L. P.

Williams (eds.), *Great issues in Western civilization** (2 vols., 1976), available also in separate pamphlets. The Great Lives Observed series* (1968 ff.) consists of sources, contemporary judgments, and latter-day interpretations relating to leading historical personalities.

Two pamphlet series offering divergent interpretations of historical events are the Heath Problems in European Civilization* (1958 ff.) and European Problem Studies* (Holt, Rinehart and Winston, 1963 ff., reprinted by Krieger). By reprinting longer excerpts, the Modern Scholarship on European History series* (New Viewpoints: Franklin Watts, 1971–1978) samples recent scholarship on selected topics.

Anthologies of more specialized coverage include S. Chodorow and P. N. Stearns, *The other side of Western civilization: readings in European civilization* (2 vols., 1979), on social history and popular culture; N. F. Cantor and M. S. Werthman (eds.), *The history of popular culture* (2 vols., 1968); by the same editors, *The English tradition: modern studies in English history* (2 vols., 1967); J. Friguglietti and E. Kennedy, *The shaping of modern France: writings on French history since 1715* (1969); and M. Kranzberg and C. W. Pursell, Jr. (eds.), *Technology in Western civilization* (2 vols., 1967).

There are several series offering brief volumes on selected topics especially suitable for undergraduate reading, among which the Berkshire series has been especially useful; many titles are listed below. Two British series deserve mention: Teach Yourself History, edited by A. L. Rowse, successfully using a biographical approach to lure the reader to historical topics; and the Men in Office series, edited by R. N. Hatton, focusing on key political leaders.

I: THE RISE OF EUROPE

Prehistoric and Ancient Times

[No attempt is made here to suggest more than a few titles.] The reader may wish to consult as useful general introductions: P. Phillips, *The prehistory of Europe* (1980); C. Renfrew, *Before civilization: the radiocarbon revolution and prehistoric Europe* (rev., 1979); J. Hawkes and L. Wooley, *Prehistory and the beginnings of civilization** (rev., 1967), the first volume in the UNESCO History of Mankind series;

J. Hawkes, *The first great civilizations**
(1973), on Egypt and the Tigris-Euphrates
valley; T. B. Jones, *From the Tigris to the
Tiber: an introduction to ancient history**
(rev., 1978); and C. G. Starr, *A history of
the ancient world* (rev., 1974).

In addition to surveys of classical Greece,
such as J. B. Bury and R. Meiggs, *A history
of Greece* (rev., 1976), and N. G. Hammond, *A history of Greece to 322 B.C.** (rev.,
1967), one may profit from H. D. F. Kitto,
*The Greeks** (1951); A. Andrewes, *The
Greeks* (1967); and M. I. Finley's books: *The
world of Odysseus** (1954), *The ancient
Greeks: their life and thought** (1963), *The
ancient economy** (1973), and *Ancient slavery and modern ideology* (1980). For Alexander, as an introduction to Hellenistic
times, the older standard biography, W. W.
Tarn, *Alexander the Great* (1948), may be
compared with P. Green, *Alexander of
Macedon, 356–323 B.C.** (1973), and with
R. L. Fox's admirable account, *Alexander
the Great* (1974).

Among many surveys of Rome and Roman civilization, M. Cary and H. H. Scul-
lard, *A history of Rome* (rev., 1976), may be
mentioned. A superb volume on the end of
the Roman republic is R. Syme, *Roman
revolution** (1939), which may be supplemented by A. H. MacDonald, *Republican
Rome* (1966), and C. Nicolet, *The world of
the citizen in republican Rome* (1976, trans.
1980). Highly recommended are M. Grant's
volumes: *The Etruscans* (1981), *History of
Rome** (1978), and *The Jews in the Roman
world* (1973). Books on later Roman history
include M. P. Charlesworth, *The Roman
Empire** (1951), and A. H. M. Jones, *The
decline of the ancient world** (1966), a condensation of his larger work (3 vols., 1964).
On a special subject, one may read S. B.
Pomeroy, *Goddesses, whores, wives, and
slaves: women in classical antiquity* (1975),
a successful effort to reconstruct the lives of
women in classical antiquity. For all subjects, the *Oxford classical dictionary* (rev.,
1970) is a valuable one-volume collaborative
encyclopedia.

On the coming of Christianity, N. H.
Baynes, *Constantine the Great and the
Christian church* (1931), remains of fundamental importance, but a good, brief
account is A. H. M. Jones, *Constantine and
the conversion of Europe** (1948), in the
Teach Yourself History series. R. A. Markus,
Christianity in the Roman world (1978),
ably traces the growth of Christian self-
awareness, while M. Grant reconstructs the
historical Jesus in *Jesus: An historian's review of the gospels* (1977). On St. Augustine
and his times, there is a sensitive account by
P. R. L. Brown, *St. Augustine of Hippo**
(1967), and another illuminating study, F.
Van der Meer, *Augustine the bishop: church
and society at the dawn of the Middle Ages*
(1961).

The Middle Ages: The Formation of Europe

Considerable attention has been paid to the
emergence of Europe in the early Middle
Ages, and a number of illuminating volumes
are available. Invaluable as a guide to books
written in the last half-century on the Middle Ages is G. C. Boyce (ed.), *Literature of
medieval history, 1930–1975* (5 vols., 1981),
revising and superseding the older bibliographical guide, long standard, of L. J.
Paetow. The first volume of a multivolume
Dictionary of the Middle Ages has appeared
(1982). R. W. Southern, *The making of the
Middle Ages** (1953), is fundamental to a
reexamination of these years. Among many
surveys of the medieval era as a whole, B.
Tierney and S. Painter, *Western Europe in
the Middle Ages, 300–1475* (rev., 1983), is
outstanding; a successful effort emphasizing
social history is E. Peters, *Europe: the world
of the Middle Ages* (1977), available also in
abridged form as *Europe and the Middle
Ages** (1983). D. Gerhard, *Old Europe: a
study in continuity, 1000–1800* (1981), examines the continuity of medieval institutions in the modern centuries. Illustrative of
recent scholarship on the early medieval period are: P. R. L. Brown, *The end of antiquity** (1971); H. R. Trevor-Roper, *The rise
of Christian Europe** (1965); D. Hay, *Europe: the emergence of an idea** (rev.,
1968); G. Barraclough, *The crucible of Europe: the ninth and tenth centuries in European history** (1976); C. Brooke, *Europe in
the Central Middle Ages, 962–1154** (1968);
J. M. Wallace-Hadrill, *The barbarian West,
400–1000** (1952); A. R. Lewis, *Emerging
medieval Europe, A.D. 400–1000** (1967);
G. Duby, *The making of the Christian West,
980–1140* (trans. 1968); and S. R. Packard,
12th century Europe: an interpretive essay
(1973). [Economic histories for the period
are listed below.]

C. W. Previté-Orton in the *Shorter Cambridge medieval history* (2 vols., 1952) has
condensed for the general reader the eight
volumes of the *Cambridge medieval history*
(1911–1936). Colorful portraits of medieval

life are found in G. G. Coulton's *Medieval panorama* (1938) and his other writings, and in two books by E. E. Power, *Medieval people** (1924, 1935) and *Medieval women** [published posthumously, M. M. Postan (ed.), 1976]; on women in the Middle Ages, one may also read J. Morris, *The lady was a bishop* (1973); S. Wemple, *Women in Frankish society* (1981); and the essays in S. M. Stuard (ed.), *Women in medieval society** (1976).

Intellectual developments are discussed in the volume by R. W. Southern and in many of the books already cited, but are also examined with insight in: D. Knowles, *The evolution of medieval thought** (1962); G. Duby, *The age of the cathedrals: art and society, 980–1420* (trans. 1981); J. LeGoff, *Time, work, and culture in the Middle Ages* (trans. 1981); F. B. Artz, *The mind of the Middle Ages, 200–1500** (3rd ed., 1980); and P. Wolff, *The awakening of Europe** (1968). Other valuable studies include G. Leff, *Medieval thought* (1958), and two works by M. L. Laistner, *Thought and letters in Western Europe, A.D. 500 to 900* (rev., 1957), and *The intellectual heritage of the Early Middle Ages* (1957). On theology, J. Pelikan, *The growth of medieval theology (600–1300)* (1978), volume 2 of his projected five-volume study, *The development of Christian doctrine*, is available. For medieval political philosophy, one still reads with profit C. H. McIlwain, *The growth of political thought in the West: from the Greeks to the end of the Middle Ages* (1932), but also available are J. B. Morrall, *Political thought in medieval times* (1958), a good brief introduction; F. C. Copleston, *Medieval philosophy* (1952); the same author's *Aquinas* (1955); R. S. Hoyt (ed.), *Life and thought in the Early Middle Ages* (1967); and W. Ullmann, *A history of political thought in the Middle Ages** (1965). Useful as a guide to intellectual developments is *The history of ideas: a bibliographical introduction*, vol. 2: *Medieval and early modern Europe* (1977), published under the auspices of the American Bibliographical Center (ABC-Clio).

There are innumerable books dealing with various regions and institutions during the Middle Ages, or covering specific centuries, of which the titles given here are only a sampling. G. Barraclough, *Origins of modern Germany** (1947), is the most valuable introduction to medieval Germany, but F. Heer, *The Holy Roman Empire* (trans. 1968), also merits reading. For the Italian city-states, one may read J. K. Hyde, *Society and politics in medieval Italy . . . 1000–1350** (1973). C. Petit Dutaillis, *The feudal monarchy in France and England, from the tenth to the thirteenth century* (1933, trans. 1936), is a comparative study of the two monarchies, and S. Painter, *Rise of the feudal monarchies** (1951), is an excellent brief introduction.

For English developments, two good introductions are B. Lyon, *A constitutional and legal history of medieval England* (1960), and H. Cam, *England before Elizabeth** (1950). A valuable bibliographical tool is E. B. Graves (ed.), *A bibliography of English history to 1485* (1975). For social developments, one may consult E. Duckett, *Life and death in the tenth century* (1968); D. W. Robertson, Jr., *Chaucer's London** (1968); J. T. Rosenthal, *Angles, angels, and conquerors* (1973), covering the years 400–1154; J. Barnie, *War in medieval English society: social values in the Hundred Years' War, 1337–99* (1974); and M. M. McLaughlin, *Survivors and surrogates: children and parents from the ninth to the thirteenth centuries* (1975). S. L. Thrupp examines the guilds and other subjects in *The merchant class of medieval London, 1300–1500* (1958), and T. H. Lloyd an important economic activity in *The English wool trade in the Middle Ages* (1977). On the Carolingian era and France, see H. Fichtenau, *The Carolingian empire: the age of Charlemagne** (1949, trans. 1957); A. D. Bullough, *The age of Charlemagne* (1965); R. Fawtier, *The Capetian kings of France* (1960); R. Folz, *The coronation of Charlemagne, 25 December 800* (1964, trans. 1975), covering more than the title implies; and P. Riché, *Daily life in the world of Charlemagne** (trans. 1978).

For economic developments, the pioneering books by H. Pirenne on the origins of the cities, revival of trade, and other social and economic developments still merit reading, but they have been superseded by more recent research. Among the most useful of the newer treatments are: R. S. Lopez, *The commercial revolution of the Middle Ages, 950–1350** (rev., 1976); R. Latouche, *The birth of the Western economy** (rev., 1967); and G. Duby, *The growth of the European economy* (1974), all covering social and economic developments. Also useful are N. J. G. Pounds, *An economic history of medieval Europe* (1974), a well-balanced survey; C. M. Cipolla (ed.), *The Middle Ages** (1972, 1977), vol. I of the Fontana Economic History of Europe; the same author's *Before the Industrial Revolution: European society and economy, 1000–1700** (rev., 1980); and M. M. Postan, *Medieval trade and finance* (1973). J. Gimpel, *The medieval machine: the industrial revolution of the Middle Ages* (trans. 1976), is informative but strains to compare the age to contemporary times; it may be compared with L. White, Jr., *Medieval technology and social change** (1962). Important too are the appropriate sections of D. C. North and R. P. Thomas, *Rise of the Western world: a new economic history* (1973), which examines economic growth and other developments from 900 to 1700. The volumes in the collaborative Cambridge Economic History of Europe (1941 ff.) provide authoritative but highly specialized accounts.

The best introduction to the growth of towns is E. Ennen, *The medieval town* (trans. 1979), which incorporates the considerable research completed since Pirenne and is a more complete synthesis than F. Rörig, *The medieval town** (1967). On the complex subjects of feudalism and manorialism, the most informative introduction is F. L. Ganshof, *Feudalism** (rev., 1961). A remarkable effort at comparing ideal models and material realities is G. Duby, *The three orders: feudal society imagined* (trans. 1980); his two other books are also important: *Rural economy and country life in the medieval West* (trans. 1968), and *The early growth of the European economy: warriors and peasants from the seventh to the twelfth century* (trans. 1974). One should also read M. Bloch's important contributions: *Feudal society** (1939–1940, trans. 1961), *French rural history** (trans. 1966), *Land and work in medieval Europe* (trans. 1967), and *Slavery and serfdom in the Middle Ages* (trans. 1975); M. M. Postan, *Essays on medieval agriculture and general problems of the medieval economy* (1973); and J. L. Bolton, *The medieval economy, 1150–1500** (1980). For comparative studies emphasizing the diversity of feudalism in various ages and places, R. Coulborn (ed.), *Feudalism in history* (1956), may be supplemented by J. Critchley, *Feudalism* (1978).

For the Byzantine world, a fundamental work is G. Ostrogorsky, *History of the Byzantine state* (1950), translated in 1956 by J. M. Hussey, who herself has written a good introduction in briefer compass, *The Byzantine world** (1957), and has edited *The Byzantine empire*, vol. IV (rev., 1966–1967), in the Cambridge Medieval History. Among other narrative and topical accounts

are C. Diehl, *Byzantium: greatness and decline** (1919, trans. 1957), an older account; D. Oblensky, *The Byzantine commonwealth: eastern Europe, 500–1453* (1971); P. Lemerle, *A history of Byzantium* (1964); S. Vryonis, Jr., *Byzantium and Europe** (1967); R. Jenkins, *Byzantium: the imperial centuries, A.D. 619–1071* (1966); and D. M. Nicol, *The last centuries of Byzantium, 1261–1453* (1972). An important episode is graphically described in S. Runciman, *The fall of Constantinople, 1453* (1965). A survey stressing socioeconomic trends in the Byzantine and Islamic worlds is E. Ashtor, *A social and economic history of the Near East in the Middle Ages* (1976). Emphasizing cultural interaction is D. J. Geanokoplos, *Medieval Western civilization and the Byzantine and Islamic worlds: interaction of three cultures* (1979). On the theology of eastern Christendom, one may read J. Pelikan, *The spirit of eastern Christendom, 600–1700* (1974), the second volume of his longer study.

Good starting points for the study of Islam include H. A. R. Gibb's succinct *Mohammedanism: an historical survey* (1949); W. M. Watt, *The majesty that was Islam: the Islamic world, 661–1100* (1974); M. G. S. Hodgson, *The venture of Islam: conscience and history in a world civilization** (3 vols., 1974), comprehensive and insightful, from the beginnings to the mid-twentieth century, and free from Eurocentric bias; and B. Lewis, *Islam in history* (1973). Among many accounts of the founder of Islam, three outstanding ones are T. Andrae, *Mohammed: the man and his faith* (trans. 1936, reprinted 1957); W. M. Watt, *Muhammed: prophet and statesman** (1961), a condensation of his detailed two-volume study (1953–1956); and M. Rodenson, *Muhammad** (rev., 1980). Excellent brief surveys of Arab history are B. Lewis, *The Arabs in history** (3rd ed., 1964); B. Lewis (ed.), *Islam and the Arab world* (1978); P. K. Hitti, *The Arabs: a short history* (rev., 1968), the latter a compression of his larger work (rev., 1970); and P. Mansfield, *The Arabs** (1976). S. N. Fisher, *The Middle East: a history* (rev., 1968), covers the region from pre-Islamic times to the twentieth century. G. E. von Grunebaum in his masterful *Medieval Islam: a study in cultural orientation* (1946) compares Islamic with Byzantine and Christian civilizations, while W. C. Smith, *Islam in modern history* (1957), provides indispensable insights on religious themes. N. Daniel, *The Arabs and* medieval Europe (rev., 1979), emphasizes the unwillingness and inability of the medieval Latin West to come to terms with Islam. For Islamic philosophy and science and their impact on Europe, there are W. M. Watt's important volumes: *The formative period of Islamic thought* (1973) and *The influence of Islam on medieval Europe* (1972), as well as S. H. Nasr, *Islamic science* (1976). Books focusing on social, economic, and cultural developments include S. D. Gotein, *A Mediterranean society* (3 vols. to date, 1967–), informative on the Jewish community in Cairo and the Muslim society surrounding it; I. M. Lapidus, *Muslim cities in the later Middle Ages* (1967); and R. Bulliet, *The camel and the wheel* (1975).

Some biographical accounts for the early Middle Ages are R. Winston, *Charlemagne: from the hammer to the cross** (1954); E. S. Duckett, *Alcuin, friend of Charlemagne* (1951); F. Barlow, *William I and the Norman Conquest* (Teach Yourself History series, 1965); A. R. Kelly, *Eleanor of Aquitaine and the four kings** (1950); E. F. Jacob, *Henry V and the invasion of France** (Teach Yourself History series, 1950); A. S. Ehrenkrentz, *Saladdin* (1978); and J. H. Smith, *Joan of Arc* (1973).

The High Middle Ages

The classic expression of the spiritual unity and harmony of medieval Europe is Henry Adams, *Mont-Saint-Michel and Chartres** (1912, many reprintings). C. Dawson, in *The making of Europe* (1937), *Medieval religion* (1934), and *Medieval essays* (1954), also examines the close communion between medieval European culture and Christianity, as does P. Hughes in the relevant chapters of *A history of the church* (3 vols., 1935–1949). Two recommended books for the advanced reader are D. Matthew, *The medieval European community* (1977), successful in exploring the mentality of the medieval world; and A. Murray, *Reason and society in the Middle Ages* (1978). A valuable introduction to the church as an institution is C. Barraclough, *The medieval papacy** (1968). The appropriate volumes of R. H. Bainton, *The Penguin history of Christianity** (1960 ff.), and H. Chadwick, *The Pelican history of the church** (1967 ff.), both multivolumed works, are recommended. The most comprehensive study of the development of the papacy from the fourth to the twelfth centuries is W. Ullmann, *The growth of papal government in the Middle Ages* (1955,

1962); the same author has also written *A short history of the papacy in the Middle Ages** (1974). An attractive illustrated volume is C. Brooke, *The monastic world, 1000–1300* (1974).

A special subject is treated in A. S. Turberville, *Medieval heresy and the Inquisition* (1920, 1932), and in S. Runciman, *The medieval Manichee* (1961). Both books are more balanced treatments of the Inquisition than H. C. Lea's pioneer work, *History of the Inquisition of the Middle Ages* (3 vols., 1888; abr. ed., 1969*).

Three notable contributions to the study of medieval secular culture are by C. H. Haskins: *Normans in European civilization** (1915), *The Renaissance of the twelfth century* (1927), and *The rise of universities** (1923). The last may be supplemented by H. Rashdall, *Universities of Europe in the Middle Ages* (1895; rev., 1936); and G. Leff, *Paris and Oxford universities in the thirteenth and fourteenth centuries* (1968). Medieval science is examined in A. C. Crombie, *Medieval and early modern science** (2 vols., 1959); D. C. Lindberg (ed.), *Science in the Middle Ages* (1978); and in R. C. Dales, *The scientific achievement of the Middle Ages* (1973). A successful attempt to link medieval society, economic development, and morality is L. K. Little, *Religious poverty and the profit economy in medieval Europe* (1978); and a scholarly exploration of sexual attitudes in the medieval world is J. Boswell, *Christianity, sexual tolerance, and homosexuality: gay people in Western Europe from the beginning of the Christian era to the fourteenth century* (1980).

The Crusades may be approached through the brief Berkshire study, R. A. Newhall, *The Crusades** (1927; rev., 1963), and the detailed, colorful S. Runciman, *A history of the Crusades** (3 vols., 1951–1954). Three volumes of a collaborative, multivolumed *History of the Crusades* (K. M. Setton, gen. ed.) have appeared (1955, 1962, 1975). K. M. Setton's *The papacy and the Levant, 1204–1571* (2 of 3 vols. projected, 1976, 1978) is a monumental account, now complete through the fifteenth century. For all aspects of the expansion of Christianity, the works of K. S. Latourette are indispensable, especially his *History of Christianity* (1953) and his longer *History of the expansion of Christianity* (7 vols., 1937–1945), of which vol. II, *The thousand years of uncertainty, A.D. 500–A.D. 1500*, covers the Middle Ages. S. W. Baron's monumental history, *A social and religious history of the Jews*, covers the years 1200 to 1650 in vols. IX–XVII (rev., 1967–1980); on the same general subject, see also L. Finkelstein (ed.), *The Jews* (2 vols., 1960), and H. H. Ben Sasson (ed.), *A history of the Jewish people* (1976).

Problems and Readings*

Several pamphlets in the various problems series are relevant to this chapter: D. Kagan (ed.), *Decline and fall of the Roman Empire* (1962); A. F. Havighurst (ed.), *The Pirenne thesis* (rev., 1976); J. F. Benton (ed.), *Town origins: the evidence from medieval England* (1968); R. E. Sullivan (ed.), *The coronation of Charlemagne* (1959); R. S. Lopez (ed.), *The tenth century: how dark the Dark Ages?* (1959); C. W. Hollister (ed.), *The twelfth-century Renaissance* (1969); C. R. Young (ed.), *The Renaissance of the twelfth century* (1970); S. Williams (ed.), *The Gregorian epoch* (1966); J. A. Brundage (ed.), *The Crusades* (1964); J. M. Powell (ed.), *Innocent III* (1963); R. E. Herzstein (ed.), *The Holy Roman Empire in the Middle Ages* (1965); and G. P. Bodet (ed.), *Early English parliaments: high courts, royal councils, or representative assemblies?* (1968). M. Chambers, *Ancient Greece* (1973), and E. S. Gruen, *The Roman Republic* (1972), are contributions to the American Historical Association Pamphlets series.

II: THE UPHEAVAL IN CHRISTENDOM, 1300–1560

Important syntheses on the early modern period include M. P. Gilmore, *The world of humanism, 1453–1517* * (1952), in the Langer series; W. K. Ferguson, *Europe in transition, 1300–1520* * (1963); A. G. Dickens, *The age of humanism and reformation: Europe in the fourteenth to sixteenth centuries* * (1972); and S. E. Ozment, *The age of reform, 1250–1550: an intellectual and religious history of late medieval and Reformation Europe* (1980). Other recommended general treatments are D. Hay, *Europe in the fourteenth and fifteenth centuries* * (1966); M. Aston, *The fifteenth century: the prospect of Europe* * (1968); H. G. Koenigsberger and G. L. Mosse, *Europe in the sixteenth century* * (1968); J. R. Hale, *Renaissance Europe: the individual and society, 1480–1520* * (1971); M. L. Bush, *Renaissance, Reformation, and the outer world, 1450–1600* * (1967); E. P. Rice, Jr., *The foundations of early modern Europe,*

1460–1559 * (1970); L. W. Spitz, *The Renaissance and Reformation movements* (1971); and D. L. Jensen, *Renaissance Europe: age of recovery and reconciliation* (1981). There are informative chapters in G. R. Potter (ed.), *The Renaissance, 1493–1520* (1957), and G. R. Elton (ed.), *The Reformation, 1520–1559* (1958), vols. I and II respectively of the New Cambridge Modern History. The economic basis of the age is examined in H. Miskimin, *The economy of early Renaissance Europe, 1300–1460* * (1975), and *The economy of later Renaissance Europe, 1460–1600* * (1977), as well as in many of the economic histories listed for the previous chapter. On political thought, there is available a masterful account by Q. Skinner, *The foundations of modern political thought* (2 vols., 1978), the first volume on the Renaissance, the second on the Age of Reformation. C. M. Cipolla explores an interesting subject in *Public health and the medical profession in the Renaissance* (1976), as does G. Mattingly in *Renaissance diplomacy* * (1955). E. L. Eisenstein, *The printing press as an agent of change: communications and cultural transformations in early modern Europe* (2 vols., 1979), elaborates the thesis that the truly revolutionary event for the modernization of European culture was the invention of the printing press.

Much of the newer social history has been centered on the early modern centuries. Here P. Burke, *Popular culture in early modern Europe* (1978), cited in the introductory chapter, is fundamental. C. Ginzburg, *The cheese and the worms: the cosmos of a sixteenth-century miller* * (trans. from Italian, 1980), is a fascinating effort to reconstruct the mentality and outlook of an obscure Italian miller of the age. Other examples of topics that have been explored include: J. H. Langbein, *Prosecuting crime in the Renaissance: England, Germany, France* (1974); M. Weisser, *Crime and criminality in early modern Europe* (1978); and H. Soly and R. Lis, *Poverty and capitalism in early modern Europe* (1978). R. Kelso, *Doctrine for the lady of the Renaissance* (1956), is an older but still valuable study.

Disasters of the Fourteenth Century

A good brief introduction to the era is R. E. Lerner, *The age of adversity: the fourteenth century* * (1968), while a vivid account written for a broad audience and signaling twentieth-century parallels is B. W. Tuchman, *A distant mirror: the calamitous 14th century** (1978). G. Leff, *The dissolution of the medieval outlook: an essay on intellectual change in the fourteenth century* (1976), despite the title, stresses the continuity of medieval thought. The growing restlessness within the church is ably described in P. Hughes, *The revolt against the church: Aquinas to Luther* (1947), an outstanding Catholic account; E. F. Jacob, *Essays on the conciliar epoch* (1943, 1953); and F. Oakley, *The Western church in the later Middle Ages* (1979). National heresies of the fourteenth century may be studied in H. Kaminsky, *A history of the Hussite revolution* (1967); B. Workman, *John Wyclif: a study of the English medieval church* (2 vols., 1926); and the lively K. B. McFarlane, *John Wycliffe and the beginnings of English nonconformity** (Teach Yourself History series, 1952). The fourteenth-century plague that swept Europe and other parts of the globe is examined in W. H. McNeill, *Plagues and peoples* (1976), cited earlier; P. Ziegler, *The black death* (1969); J. Hatcher, *Plague, population, and the English economy, 1348–1530* (1979); and M. W. Dols, *The black death in the Middle East* (1977), where in contrast to Western Europe recovery was considerably slower.

The phenomenon of witchcraft in the early modern centuries has attracted a good deal of scholarly attention. Here K. Thomas, *Religion and the decline of magic** (1971) is of fundamental importance. Other important studies include R. Kieckhefer, *European witch trials: their foundation in popular and learned culture, 1300–1500* (1976); E. W. Monter, *Witchcraft in France and Switzerland: the borderlands during the Reformation* (1976); and J. B. Russell, *A history of witchcraft: sorcerers, heretics, and pagans** (1980). Kieckhefer has also written *Repression of heresy in medieval Germany* (1979), which focuses on the fourteenth century. For the later period one may read H. R. Trevor-Roper, *The European witch craze of the sixteenth and seventeenth centuries** (1969); H. C. E. Midelfort, *Witch hunting in southwestern Germany, 1562–1684* (1972); D. P. Walker, *Unclean spirits: possession and exorcism in France and England in the late sixteenth and early seventeenth centuries* (1981); and C. Larner, *Enemies of God: the witch hunt in Scotland* (1981). Two books that examine the *jacqueries* and other popular revolts are M. Mollat and P. Wolff, *The popular revolutions of the late Middle Ages* (trans. 1972), and G. Fourquin, *The anatomy of popular rebellion in the Middle Ages* (trans. 1978).

The Renaissance in Italy

In addition to the accounts cited at the beginning of this chapter, one may turn to D. Hay, *The Italian Renaissance in its historical background** (rev., 1977); R. S. Lopez, *The three ages of the Italian Renaissance* (1970); J. A. Mazzeo, *Renaissance and revolution: the remaking of European thought* (1969); and B. Pullan, *A history of early Renaissance Italy* (1973). The concept of the "Renaissance" is explored in W. K. Ferguson, *The Renaissance in historical thought: five centuries of interpretation* (1948), in which he examines, among other things, the classical accounts of the Italian Renaissance by J. A. Symonds (7 vols., 1875–1886) and J. Burckhardt (1860; new ed., 1944). An important study stressing continuity rather than rupture with the Middle Ages, and stressing lay culture rather than secularism, is M. Becker, *Medieval Italy: constraints and creativity* (1981).

The fusion of politics and humanism in Renaissance Italy is brilliantly traced in H. Baron, *The crisis of the early Italian Renaissance: civic humanism and republican liberty in an age of classicism and tyranny** (2 vols., 1955; rev. 1 vol. ed., 1966); on this subject, one also may read E. Garin, *Italian humanism: philosophy and civic life in the Renaissance* (1941, trans. 1965). Another successful synthesis stressing the relationships of politics and culture in the age is L. Martines, *Power and imagination: city-states in Renaissance Italy** (1979); here one may also turn to P. Burke, *Culture and society in Renaissance Italy, 1420–1540* (1972). The specialist cannot neglect P. O. Kristeller, *Renaissance thought: the classic, scholastic, and humanist strains* (1961) and *Eight philosophers of the Italian Renaissance* (1964), nor C. Trinkaus, *In our image and likeness: humanity and divinity in Italian humanist thought* (2 vols., 1970). On Machiavelli, there are studies by F. Chabod, *Machiavelli and the Renaissance* (trans. 1958); J. R. Hale, *Machiavelli and Renaissance Italy** (Teach Yourself History series, 1960); and F. Gilbert, *Machiavelli and Guicciardini: politics and history in sixteenth-century Florence* (1965). A profound and provocative study of political thought as it was influenced by the Renaissance from the fifteenth to the eighteenth centuries is J. G. A. Pocock, *The Machiavellian* moment: Florentine political thought and the Atlantic republican tradition* (1975). J. R. Hale (ed.), A concise encyclopedia of the Italian Renaissance (1981), is a convenient reference tool.

Numerous studies focusing on each of the Italian city-states have helped illuminate the "world of humanism," of which only a few titles can be cited here. Much of the focus has been on Florence, for which three general accounts are available: G. Holmes, The Florentine enlightenment, 1400–1450 (1969); V. Cronin, The Florentine Renaissance (1967); and G. Brucker, Renaissance Florence (1969). Among outstanding special studies are G. Brucker, Florentine politics and society, 1343–1378 (1962), and The civic world of early Renaissance Florence (1977), which carries the story to 1430; J. R. Hale, Florence and the Medici: the pattern of control (1978), a masterful account; M. Becker, Florence in transition (2 vols., 1967–1969); D. Weinstein, Savanorola and Florence (1970); C. Fusero, The Borgias (trans. 1973); and two books that focus in new ways on relationships between culture and social change: R. C. Trexler, Public life in Renaissance Florence (1980), and S. K. Cohen, Jr., The laboring classes in Renaissance Florence (1980). R. G. Witt, Hercules at the crossroads: the life, works, and thought of Coluccio Salutati (1983), studies an important Florentine humanist. R. A. Goldthwaite, The building of Renaissance Florence: an economic and social history (1981), is a thorough account of all aspects of the physical construction of the city, while R. DeRoover explores another specialized subject in The rise and decline of the Medici bank, 1307–1494* (1963). E. Cochrane examines the post-Renaissance city in Florence in the forgotten centuries, 1527–1800 (1973).

Outstanding studies of Venice with varying perspectives include: F. C. Lane, Venice: a maritime republic* (1973); W. H. McNeill, Venice: the hinge of Europe, 1081–1797 (1974); W. Bouwsma, Venice and the defense of republican liberty: Renaissance values in the age of the Counter Reformation (1968); B. Pullan, Rich and poor in Renaissance Venice (1971); R. Finlay, Politics in Renaissance Venice (1980); and J. J. Norwich, A history of Venice (1982). On Rome, one may read P. Partner, The lands of St. Peter: the papal state in the Middle Ages and the early Renaissance (1972), and Renaissance Rome, 1500–1559: a portrait of a society* (1977).

The Renaissance Outside Italy and the New Monarchies

J. Huizinga, The waning of the Middle Ages . . . life, thought, and art in France and the Netherlands in the fourteenth and fifteenth centuries* (1924, reissued 1976), and P. S. Allen, The age of Erasmus (1914), remain excellent introductions to the northern Renaissance. On Erasmus, there are available the sympathetic P. Smith, Erasmus* (1923); J. Huizinga, Erasmus* (1924); the brief, spirited M. M. Phillips, Erasmus and the northern Renaissance* (Teach Yourself History series, 1950); and R. M. Bainton, Erasmus of Christendom (1969). J. D. Tracy, The politics of Erasmus: a peaceful intellectual and his political milieu (1978), focuses on his idea of the state. On Christian humanism, one turns to E. H. Harbison, The Christian scholar in the age of the Reformation* (1956), and L. Spitz, The religious renaissance of the German humanists (1963).

The relations between banking and culture in Germany and elsewhere are examined in R. Ehrenberg, Capital and finance in the age of the Renaissance: a study of the Fuggers and their connections (1928), and in J. Strieder, Jacob Fugger the Rich (1931). G. M. Trevelyan's Illustrated English social history (4 vols., 1949 ff.) and English social history: a survey of six centuries* (rev., 1946) discuss the influence of the Continental Renaissance. Two studies by A. B. Ferguson illuminate aspects of the Renaissance in England: The articulate citizen and the English Renaissance (1965) and Clio unbound: perception of the social and cultural past in Renaissance England (1979). For France, L. Batiffol, The century of the Renaissance (trans. 1961), remains useful but see N. Z. Davis, Society and culture in early modern France: eight essays (1975), in which the lives and values of ordinary men and women are examined.

Two scholarly biographies of French monarchies are highly recommended: J. M. Tyrrell, Louis XI (1980), and R. J. Knecht, Francis I (1982), the latter a major work of scholarship. A special subject is explored in M. Wolfe, The fiscal system of Renaissance France (1972). The first Tudor monarch is examined in S. B. Chrimes, Henry VII (1972), and in M. V. C. Alexander, The first of the Tudors: a study of Henry VII and his reign (1980), a lively account. Other books on England, France, and Spain in this period are listed below and in the next chapter.

General Works on the Reformation

Besides the general accounts already listed, syntheses focusing on the Reformation proper include G. R. Elton, *Reformation Europe, 1517–1559** (1963); A. G. Dickens, *Reformation and society in sixteenth century Europe** (1960); O. Chadwick, *The Reformation** (1963); K. Holl, *The cultural significance of the Reformation* (1959); H. J. Grimm, *The Reformation era* (rev., 1965); and H. J. Hillerbrand, *The world of the Reformation* (1973). P. Hughes, *A popular history of the Reformation** (1957), and J. Lortz, *How the Reformation came* (1964), are accounts by eminent Catholic scholars. For the political background, there are H. Holborn, *A history of modern Germany: the Reformation* (1959), the first volume of a three-volume history of Germany; and F. L. Carsten, *Princes and parliaments in Germany* (1959). Two outstanding accounts of the leading ruler of the age are K. Brandi, *The Emperor Charles V** (1939), an older masterly study, and M. Fernandez Alvarez, *Charles V: elected emperor and hereditary ruler* (trans. 1975, in the Men in Office series).

An outstanding biographical account of Luther is E. G. Schwiebert, *Luther and his times* (1950). E. H. Erikson, *Young man Luther: a study in psychoanalysis and history** (1958, 1962), is a pioneering psychoanalytical study. Other lively, scholarly accounts are R. H. Bainton, *Here I stand: a life of Martin Luther* (1950); A. G. Dickens, *Martin Luther and the Reformation** (Teach Yourself History series, 1967); E. G. Rupp, *The progress of Luther to the Diet of Worms, 1521* (1951); R. H. Fife, *The revolt of Martin Luther* (1957); J. Atkinson, *Martin Luther and the birth of Protestantism** (1968); R. Marius, *Luther* (1974); M. U. Edwards, *Luther and the false brethren* (1975); and H. G. Haile, *Luther: an experiment in biography* (1980), which focuses on the reformer in his later years.

P. Blickle, *The revolution of 1525: the German peasants' war from a new perspective* (1977, trans. 1981), studies that event comprehensively but may be supplemented by the essays in B. Scribner and G. Benecke (eds.), *The German peasant war, 1525— new viewpoints* (1979). The appeal of Lutheran ideas to the uneducated classes is skillfully analyzed in R. W. Scribner, *For the sake of simple folk: popular propaganda for the German Reformation* (1981).

Among the best accounts of Calvin and his influence are J. T. McNeill, *The history and character of Calvinism* (1954); F. Wendel, *Calvin: the origins and development of his religious thought* (trans. 1963); and Q. Breen, *John Calvin: a study in French humanism* (1931). There are biographical studies by G. Harkness (1931), R. N. Carew Hunt (1933), and J. MacKinnon (1936). G. R. Potter, *Zwingli* (1977), is an outstanding biography, and W. S. Reid has written *Trumpeter of God: a biography of John Knox* (1974). R. H. Bainton, *Hunted heretic: the life and death of Michael Servetus** (1960), may be compared with J. Friedman, *Michael Servetus: a case study in total heresy* (1978).

The cities in which the major events of the Reformation occurred are examined in G. Strauss, *Nuremberg in the sixteenth century** (1966), and W. Monter, *Calvin's Geneva** (1967); and the urban element in general is analyzed in S. E. Ozment, *The Reformation in the cities: the appeal of Protestantism to sixteenth century Germany and Switzerland** (1975). R. H. Bainton studies the contributions of women to the religious changes of the era in a three-volume study, each covering different parts of Europe, in *Women of the Reformation* (1971–1977), and I. Maclean reviews the images of women in a broad range of early modern thought and writing, including theology, law, and medicine, in *The Renaissance notion of women* (1980).

The Reformation in England and Other Reformation Themes

The course of the Reformation in England may be approached through two outstanding syntheses: A. G. Dickens, *The English Reformation** (1964), and D. H. Pill, *The English Reformation, 1529–58** (1973). Other able accounts are A. G. Dickens, *Thomas Cromwell and the English Reformation* (1959); R. W. Beckingsale, *Thomas Cromwell* (1978); and F. E. Hutchinson, *Cranmer and the English Reformation** (Teach Yourself History series, 1951). Good introductions to England in this age are J. R. Lander, *Government and community: England, 1450–1509* (1980), and G. R. Elton, *Reform and reformation: England, 1509–1558* (1977); both are volumes in the New History of England series. Surveys covering all phases of English religious history are N. Sykes, *The English religious tradition*

(1953), and E. O. James, *A history of Christianity in England* (1949). R. W. Chambers, *Thomas More* (1948), is a sympathetic, moving biography; on More's contribution to his age, one also may read M. Fleisher, *Radical reform and political persuasion in the life and writings of Thomas More* (1973); J. H. Hexter, *The vision of politics on the eve of the Reformation: More, Machiavelli, and Seyssel* (1973); and J. A. Guy, *The public career of Sir Thomas More* (1980). D. Knowles, *Bare ruined choirs: the dissolution of the English monasteries* (1976), a revised version of his earlier work (1959), is informative on an important subject, as are G. W. O. Woodward, *The dissolution of the monasteries* (1967), and J. Youings, *The dissolution of the monasteries* (1971), in which some representative documents are reprinted. A distinguished biography focusing on the king as well as on the events of his reign is J. J. Scarisbrick, *Henry VIII* (1968); one also may read L. B. Smith, *Henry VIII: the mask of royalty* (1971). A detailed account of the famous divorce is provided in G. deC. Parmiter, *The king's great matter: a study of Anglo-papal relations, 1527–1534* (1967), and in H. A. Kelly, *The matrimonial trials of Henry VIII* (1975). On Henry VIII's two immediate successors, one may read W. K. Jordan, *Edward VI* (2 vols., 1968–1970), and D. M. Loades, *The reign of Mary Tudor: politics, government, and religion in England, 1553–1558* (1979). Among books focusing on religion under Elizabeth are P. Collinson, *The Elizabethan Puritan movement* (1967); P. McGrath, *Papists and Puritans under Elizabeth I* (1968); and A. Morey, *The Catholic subjects of Elizabeth I* (1978). The restlessness of the age and of the years that followed is depicted in A. Fletcher, *Tudor rebellions* (1973).

The various forms of Protestantism are placed in historical perspective in E. Troeltsch's masterpiece, *The social teachings of the Christian churches* (2 vols., reissued 1949); J. S. Whale, *The Protestant tradition* (1959); and E. G. Leonard, *A history of Protestantism* (1965). The radical movements of the era may be studied in G. H. Williams, *The radical Reformation* (1962); N. Cohn, *The pursuit of the millennium* (1957; rev., 1964); and M. A. Mulett, *Radical religious movements in early modern Europe* (1980). Another important subject is explored in H. Kamen, *The rise of toleration* (1967).

On the much-debated question concerning the relation between economic change and religious doctrine, see M. Weber, *The Protestant ethic and the spirit of capitalism** (1904, reissued 1948), which opened the controversy; R. H. Tawney, *Religion and the rise of capitalism** (1926, 1947), a brilliant work, although somewhat superseded by more recent research; and G. Marshall, *In search of the spirit of capitalism: an essay on Max Weber's Protestant ethic thesis* (1982), a balanced review of the thesis and the debate.

Two provocative books dealing with the social implications of the Reformation for England, among many other subjects, are H. R. Trevor-Roper, *Religion, the Reformation and social change* (1967), and C. Hill, *Reformation to industrial revolution: the making of modern English society* (1967).

Catholicism Reformed and Reorganized

On the Counter Reformation, one may turn to M. R. O'Connell, *The Counter Reformation, 1559–1610** (1974), in the Langer series; A. G. Dickens, *The Counter Reformation* (1969); H. O. Evennett, *The spirit of the Counter Reformation* (1968); L. Cristiani, *The revolt against the church* (trans. 1962); G. W. Searle, *The Counter Reformation* (1974); P. F. Grendler, *The Roman Inquisition and the Venetian press, 1540–1605* (1977); and P. Hughes, *Rome and the Counter Reformation in England* (1942). H. Jedin, *The Council of Trent* (2 vols., 1957–1961), is an objective treatment, narrating much more than the council itself. An introduction to the large literature on the Society of Jesus is provided in C. Hollis, *The Jesuits* (1968), and one may also read M. Foss, *The founding of the Jesuits, 1540* (1969), and W. V. Bangert, *A history of the Society of Jesus* (1972). There are biographies of Loyola by C. Hollis (1931), P. Dudon (1933), and J. Brodrick (1956).

Problems and Readings*

Among pamphlets in various problems series for subjects covered in this chapter are K. H. Dannenfeldt (ed.), *The Renaissance* (rev., 1975); D. Hay (ed.), *The Renaissance debate* (1963); D. L. Jensen (ed.), *Machiavelli: cynic, patriot, or political scientist?* (1960); L. W. Spitz (ed.), *The Reformation* (rev., 1972); K. C. Sessions (ed.), *Reformation and authority: the meaning of the Peas-*

ants' Revolt (1968); A. J. Slavin (ed.), *The new monarchies* (1964) and *Henry VIII and the English Reformation* (1968); R. W. Green, *Protestantism, capitalism, and social science: the Weber thesis controversy* (rev., 1973); and R. Kingdon, *Calvin and Calvinism: sources of democracy?* (1970). In the Anvil series, there are R. H. Bainton, *The age of the Reformation* (1956), and E. M. Burns, *The Counter Reformation* (1964). Source material and commentary are provided in H. J. Hillerbrand (ed.), *The Protestant Reformation: a narrative history related by contemporary observers and participants* (1964); L. W. Spitz (ed.), *The Protestant Reformation* (1966); and G. R. Elton (ed.), *Renaissance and Reformation, 1300–1648* (1963). S. E. Ozment (ed.), *The Reformation in medieval perspective* (1971), provides examples of recent scholarly writings on the subject. W. J. Bouwsma, *The culture of Renaissance humanism* (1973), and H. J. Grimm, *The Reformation* (1972), are two useful contributions in the American Historical Association Pamphlets series.

III: ECONOMIC RENEWAL AND WARS OF RELIGION, 1560–1648

Of general treatments for these years, covering institutional and international developments, the best guides are J. H. Elliott, *Europe divided, 1559–1598** (1969; rev., 1982); C. Wilson, *The transformation of Europe, 1558–1648* (1976); H. Kamen, *The iron century: social change in Europe, 1550–1660* (1971); R. S. Dunn, *The age of religious wars, 1559–1715** (rev., 1979); and two volumes in the Langer series: M. R. O'Connell, *The Counter Reformation, 1559–1610** (1974), already cited, and C. J. Friedrich, *The age of the baroque, 1610–1660** (1952), which is less useful for political subjects. A richly illustrated collaborative volume with chapters on the non-Western world is H. R. Trevor-Roper (ed.), *The age of expansion: Europe and the world, 1559–1660* (1968). A magisterial work stressing broad geographic, demographic, and economic developments is the study by F. Braudel, *The Mediterranean and the Mediterranean world in the age of Philip II** (2 vols., trans. 1972–1974), cited in the introductory section.

Four analytical treatments focusing on the concept of crisis in the seventeenth century (and useful for this and the following chapter) deserve mention: T. K. Rabb, *The struggle for stability in early modern Europe* (1975); G. Parker and L. M. Smith, *The general crisis of the seventeenth century* (1978); T. Aston (ed.), *Crisis in Europe, 1560–1660** (1966); and R. Forster and J. P. Greene (eds.), *Preconditions of revolution in early modern Europe* (1970). There are informative chapters by specialists in R. B. Wernham (ed.), *The Counter Reformation and price revolution, 1559–1610** (1968), and in J. P. Cooper (ed.), *The decline of Spain and the Thirty Years' War, 1609–1648/59** (1970), vols. III and IV of the New Cambridge Modern History respectively.

The Opening of the Atlantic

The best introductory account is by J. H. Parry, *The age of reconnaissance** (rev., 1981), who also has written *Europe and a wider world, 1415–1715** (1949), and *The discovery of the sea* (1974). Also useful are C. E. Nowell's brief *The great discoveries and the first colonial empires** (1954); G. J. Marcus, *The conquest of the North Atlantic from early times to the late 15th century* (1980); and G. V. Scammell, *The world encompassed: the first European maritime empire, c. 800–1650* (1982). S. E. Morison, *The European discovery of America* (2 vols., 1971, 1974), is indispensable, the first volume on the northern voyages, the second on the southern. Morison also masterfully reconstructed the life and voyages of Columbus in *Admiral of the ocean sea* (1942). C. M. Cipolla stresses the importance of technology for the explorations in *Guns, sails, and empires: 1400–1700** (1965). D. Lach, *Asia in the making of Europe* (2 vols., the second volume in three parts, 1965–1978), is an important work tracing the Asian cultural and intellectual impact on Europe through the sixteenth century.

Portuguese maritime and colonial enterprises are recounted in C. R. Boxer, *Four centuries of Portuguese expansion, 1415–1825** (1961), and *The Portuguese seaborne empire* (1969), on which one may also read B. W. Diffie and G. D. Winius, *Foundations of the Portuguese empire, 1415–1580* (1977), in the series on European expansion edited by B. W. Shafer. On Portugal itself, there are sound histories by H. V. Livermore, *A new history of Portugal** (1977); A. H. De Oliveira Marques, *History of Portugal** (rev., 1976); and on the entire Iberian peninsula, S. G. Payne, *A history of Spain and Portugal* (2 vols., 1973).

Spain in Europe and Overseas

Three books reflecting modern scholarship on Spain for the early modern centuries and superseding older works of which R. B. Merriman's were the best known are J. H. Elliott, *Imperial Spain, 1469–1716** (1964); J. Lynch, *Spain under the Habsburgs 1516–1700* (2 vols., rev., 1981); and I. A. A. Thompson, *War and government in Habsburg Spain, 1560–1620* (1976). Elliott also has written *The revolt of the Catalans: a study in the decline of Spain, 1598–1640* (1963). Recommended also are two books by J. Vicens Vives, *An economic history of Spain from earliest times to the end of the nineteenth century* (1955, trans. 1969), and *Approaches to the history of Spain** (1962, trans. 1967); and a good brief introduction to Spanish economic history is J. Harrison, *An economic history of modern Spain* (1978). R. Herr, *Spain** (1971), thoughtfully views twentieth-century Spain in historical perspective. C. Petrie's *Philip II of Spain* (1963) is an account of Spanish affairs rather than a biography; an impressive scholarly portrait of the king and his times is P. Pierson, *Philip II of Spain* (Men in Office series, 1976). G. Mattingly, *The Armada** (1959), masterfully places the dramatic episode in its European setting.

For the Spanish empire in the new world, excellent accounts are C. Gibson, *Spain in America** (1966); J. H. Parry, *The Spanish seaborne empire* (1966); and J. H. Elliott, *The old world and the new, 1492–1716* (1970). Two vivid accounts are F. A. Kirkpatrick, *The Spanish conquistadores* (1934, 1949), and J. Hemmings, *The conquest of the Incas** (1970).

L. Hanke, *The Spanish struggle for justice in the conquest of America** (1949), questions older views on the Inquisition. Spanish treatment of subject peoples in Latin America also is discussed in L. B. Simpson, *The encomienda in New Spain: forced native labor in the Spanish colonies, 1492–1550* (1929), while a comprehensive study of blacks in Spanish America from 1502 to the present is provided in L. B. Rout, Jr., *The African experience in Spanish America* (1976). F. Tannenbaum, *Slave and citizen: the Negro in the Americas** (1947), argued that in Latin America (unlike North America) there was recognition of the "moral personality" of the slave; see also, on North American attitudes, W. D. Jordan, *White over black: American attitudes toward the Negro, 1550–1812** (1968). Other key studies are D. B. Davis, *The problem of slavery in Western culture* (1966), and its sequel, *The problem of slavery in the age of revolution, 1770–1823* (1975); and E. Williams, *Capitalism and slavery** (1944). The grim story of the slave trade is told in J. Pope-Hennessy, *Sins of the fathers: a study of the Atlantic slave traders, 1441–1807** (1968); D. P. Mannix and M. Cowley, *Black cargoes* (1962); P. D. Curtin, *The Atlantic slave trade** (1969); H. S. Klein, *The middle passage: comparative studies in the Atlantic slave trade** (1978); J. A. Rawley, *The transatlantic slave trade: a history* (1981); H. Gemery and J. Hogendorn (eds.), *The uncommon market: essays in the economic history of the Atlantic slave trade* (1979); and C. A. Palmer, *Human cargoes: the British slave trade to Spanish America, 1700–1739* (1981). A thoughtful analysis is C. D. Rice, *The rise and fall of black slavery* (1975). A pioneer inquiry into the impact of the discovery of silver upon economic changes in Europe is E. J. Hamilton, *American treasure and the price revolution in Spain, 1501–1650* (1934), although some of its conclusions have been modified. The subject also is examined in P. Vilar, *A history of gold and money, 1450–1920* (trans. 1976), and in J. N. Ball, *Merchants and merchandise: the expansion of trade in Europe, 1500–1630* (1977), which explores the upswing in population, trade, and prices in the sixteenth century.

Changing Social Structures, Early Capitalism, Mercantilism

[The general economic histories cited in the introductory section and the general works cited for Chapter II and in the present chapter also should be consulted.] Among the best surveys of preindustrial economic history are R. Davis, *The rise of the Atlantic economies** (1973), covering developments from the mid-fifteenth to the eighteenth centuries; C. M. Cipolla, *Before the industrial revolution: European society and economy, 1000–1700* (1976); and J. DeVries, *The economy of Europe in an age of crisis, 1600–1750** (1976). An important work, influenced by the *Annales* school and especially by F. Braudel, whose works on the emergence of capitalism have been cited in the introductory section, is I. Wallerstein, *The modern world-system:* vol. I, *Capitalist agriculture and the origins of the European world economy in the sixteenth century** (1974), and vol. II, *Mercantilism and the consolidation of the European world econ-*

*omy, 1600–1750** (1980); additional volumes are projected. On mercantilism, E. Hecksher, *Mercantilism* (2 vols., 1935), may be supplemented by P. Buck, *The politics of mercantilism* (1942), and C. Wilson, *Profit and power* (1957). Indispensable on social structures is B. Moore, *Origins of democracy and dictatorship: lord and peasant in the making of the modern world** (1966). There are valuable chapters in C. M. Cipolla (ed.), *The Fontana economic history of Europe: the sixteenth and seventeenth centuries** (1974), and in two volumes edited by E. E. Rich and C. H. Wilson: *The economy of expanding Europe in the sixteenth and seventeenth centuries* (1967), and *The economic organization of early modern Europe* (1977), vols. IV and V respectively of the Cambridge Economic History of Europe. For early demography, one may turn to M. W. Flynn, *The European demographic system, 1500–1820* (1981).

J. U. Nef, *Industry and government in France and England, 1540–1640** (1957), argues the case for an early "industrial revolution"; for the English model, it may be compared with L. A. Clarkson, *The pre-industrial economy of England, 1500–1750* (1972); B. A. Holderness, *Pre-industrial England: economy and society, 1500–1750* (1976); and D. C. Coleman, *The economy of England, 1450–1750* (1977). A. O. Hirschman, *The passions and the interests: political arguments for capitalism before its triumph* (1977), explores the changes in intellectual climate that lent respectability to the pursuit of material gain.

Revolt of the Netherlands

G. Parker, *The Dutch revolt* (1977), is an admirable comprehensive study, which may be compared with P. Geyl's masterful longer account: *The revolt of the Netherlands, 1555–1609* (1932, trans. 1958), and *The Netherlands in the seventeenth century, 1609–1715* (2 vols., trans. 1961–1964). C. V. Wedgwood, *William the Silent** (1944), is an excellent, laudatory biography. Other books on the Netherlands appear in the following chapter.

Tudor England

Among many good books, the best recent accounts are G. R. Elton, *Reform and Reformation: England 1509–1558** (1977) cited for Chapter II, sympathetic to the Tudors; J. Hurstfield, *Elizabeth I and the unity of England** (1966), more critical; and P. Williams, *The Tudor regime** (1979), a provocative reassessment. Highly recommended also are two books by W. T. MacCaffrey, *The shaping of the Elizabethan regime** (1968), and *Queen Elizabeth and the making of policy, 1572–1588** (1981); and by J. E. Neale, *The Elizabethan House of Commons* (1949), and *Elizabeth I and her parliaments* (2 vols., 1953–1957). R. B. Wernham, *Before the armada: the emergence of the English nation, 1485–1588** (1972), is important for foreign affairs, as is P. S. Crowson, *Tudor foreign policy* (1973). L. B. Smith, *The Elizabethan world* (1967), is a colorful account. The outstanding biography of Elizabeth remains J. E. Neale's distinguished *Queen Elizabeth I** (1934, 1966), but three other scholarly and readable books deserve mention: E. Jenkins, *Elizabeth the Great** (1959), N. Williams, *Elizabeth the first, queen of England* (1968), and L. B. Smith, *Elizabeth Tudor* (1975). C. Wilson, *Queen Elizabeth and the revolt of the Netherlands* (1970), examines an important episode in her career. A. L. Rowse crowds many subjects into *The Elizabethan age* (2 vols., 1950–1955), and has also written *The Elizabethan Renaissance: the cultural achievement* (1972), as well as a highly controversial *William Shakespeare: a biography** (1963). There is a vivid biography of Mary Tudor by H. F. M. Prescott (rev., 1953) and of Mary Stuart by A. Fraser, *Mary Queen of Scots* (1969).

On the naval and imperial side, one may read J. A. Williamson, *The age of Drake* (1938, 1946), and two books by D. B. Quinn, *Raleigh and the British empire** (Teach Yourself History series, 1947) and *England and the discovery of America, 1481–1620* (1974). The religious connections of English expansionism are pointed out in L. B. Wright, *Religion and empire: the alliance between piety and commerce in English expansion, 1558–1625* (1943). T. K. Rabb, *Enterprise and empire: merchant and gentry investment in the expansion of England, 1575–1630* (1967), is a pioneering effort to apply computer techniques in the study of early modern history. A monograph illuminating more than its topic is C. E. Challis, *The Tudor Coinage* (1978).

Social and economic features of the age are treated in L. Stone, *The crisis of the aristocracy, 1558–1641* (1965; abr. ed., 1967), stressing the decline of the nobility, and a sequel volume, *Family and fortune: studies in aristocratic finance in the sixteenth and* seventeenth centuries (1973). H. R. Trevor-Roper, *The gentry, 1540–1640* (1953), should be read along with J. H. Hexter, *Reappraisals in history: new views on history and society in early modern Europe** (1961), cited in the introductory section. A provocative essay is A. Macfarlane, *The origins of English individualism: the family, property, and social transition** (1978). W. K. Jordan, *Philanthropy in England, 1480–1660* (1959), throws light on the founding of schools and on some of the Oxford and Cambridge colleges; and D. Cressy, *Literacy and the social order: reading and writing in Tudor and Stuart England* (1980), answers other questions about early English education.

New historical research based on the examination of parish records in order to reconstruct the history of the family is brilliantly exemplified in L. Stone, *The family, sex, and marriage in England, 1500–1800** (1977, abr. 1979), cited in the introductory section. Other works focusing on such subjects as trends in illegitimate births since the sixteenth century are P. Laslett, *Family life and illicit love in earlier generations: essays in historical sociology* (1977); and G. R. Quaife, *Wanton wenches and wayward wives: peasants and illicit sex in early seventeenth-century England* (1979). An important demographic study is E. A. Wrigley and R. S. Schofield, *The population history of England, 1541–1871: a reconstruction* (1981).

Disintegration and Reconstruction of France

An informative volume on the religious and dynastic turmoil in sixteenth-century France is J. H. M. Salmon, *Society in crisis: France in the sixteenth century* (rev., 1979); another recommended synthesis is R. Briggs, *Early modern France, 1560–1715** (1977). Two major French works available in abridged translations are R. Mandrou, *Introduction to modern France, 1500–1640: an essay in historical psychology* (trans. 1976), and E. Le Roy Ladurie, *The peasants of Languedoc** (trans. 1974), cited earlier. A survey of French history is provided in G. de Bertier de Sauvigny and D. H. Pinkney, *History of France* (rev., 1983). Other useful books on events, issues, and personalities of the age are: J. E. Neale, *The age of Catherine de Medici and the lost revolution** (1937); N. M. Sutherland, *The massacre of St. Bartholomew and the European conflict,* *1559–1572* (1973); the same author's *The Huguenot struggle for recognition* (1980); R. M. Kingdon, *Geneva and the consolidation of the French Protestant movement, 1564–1572* (1967); D. R. Kelley, *The beginning of ideology: consciousness and society in the French reformation* (1981); and A. N. Galpern, *The religions of the people in sixteenth-century Champagne* (1976), a successful effort to use anthropological techniques. Social history is explored in S. L. Flandrin, *Families in former times: kinship, household, and sexuality in early modern France* (trans. 1979). There are biographies of Henry of Navarre by Q. Hurst (1938) and H. Pearson (1964), and of Henry's mother by N. L. Roelker, *Queen of Navarre: Jeanne d'Albret, 1528–1572* (1968); also available is R. Mousnier, *The assassination of Henry IV* (trans. 1973).

Governmental and constitutional developments are explored in J. R. Major, *Representative government in early modern France* (1980), which stresses the vitality of the early representative bodies; P. Anderson, *Lineages of the absolutist state* (1974); J. M. Haydon, *France and the Estates General of 1614* (1974); and H. H. Rowen, *The king's state: proprietary dynasticism in early modern France* (1980), which argues that the French kings viewed the state as royal property. D. Bitton, *The French nobility in crisis, 1560–1640* (1969), describes arguments for and against nobility two centuries before the French Revolution.

The growth of centralized government is described in D. Buisseret, *Sully and the growth of centralized government in France, 1598–1610* (1968). For Richelieu, one may turn to C. V. Wedgwood's brief and balanced *Richelieu and the French monarchy** (Teach Yourself History series, 1949); G. R. R. Treasure, *Cardinal Richelieu and the development of absolutism* (1972); and W. F. Church, *Richelieu and reason of state* (1972). Other studies include D. Parker, *La Rochelle and the French monarchy: conflict and order in seventeenth-century France* (1980); R. Bonney, *Political change in France under Richelieu and Mazarin, 1624–1661* (1978), especially useful on the role of the *intendants*; and G. Dethan, *The young Mazarin* (1977). Two important specialized studies are O. Ranum, *Richelieu and the councillors of Louis XIII* (1963), and by a Russian scholar, A. D. Lublinskaya, *French absolutism: the crucial phase, 1620–1629* (trans. 1968).

The Thirty Years' War

Vivid and authoritative accounts are C. V. Wedgwood, *The Thirty Years' War** (1938); S. H. Steinberg, *The Thirty Years' War** (1966); and J. V. Polisensky, *The Thirty Years' War* (1971), by a Czech historian, which may be supplemented by his *War and society in Europe, 1618–1648* (1978). Biographical accounts include F. Watson, *Wallenstein: soldier under Saturn* (1938); G. Mann, *Wallenstein: his life narrated* (trans. 1976), a major biographical study; and N. Ahnlund, *Gustav Adolf the Great* (1932, 1940). A detailed treatment of all aspects of Swedish history is to be found in the many books of M. Roberts: *The early Vasas* (1968); *Gustavus Adolphus* (2 vols., 1953–1958); *Essays in Swedish history* (1967); and *The Swedish imperial experience, 1560–1718* (1979). Roberts also has edited *Sweden as a great power: government, society, and foreign policy, 1611–1697* (1968) and *Sweden's age of greatness, 1632–1718* (1973). The story of the conversion to Catholicism of Gustavus Adolphus's daughter and her abdication is told in G. Masson, *Queen Christina* (1968), and in S. Svolpe, *Christina of Sweden*, edited by A. Randall (1966), a condensation of the untranslated larger work by a Swedish historian. A recommended general history of Sweden is F. D. Scott, *Sweden: the nation's history* (1977).

Problems and Readings*

The following will be found useful: D. L. Jensen (ed.), *The expansion of Europe: motives, methods, and meaning* (1967); J. H. Parry (ed.), *The European reconnaissance: selections and documents* (1968); W. E. Minchitan (ed.), *Mercantilism: system or expediency?* (1969); J. M. Levine (ed.), *Elizabeth I* (Great Lives Observed, 1969); R. L. Greaves, *Elizabeth I, Queen of England* (1974); J. C. Rule and J. J. TePaske (eds.), *The character of Philip II: the problem of moral judgments in history* (1963); TePaske (ed.), *Three American empires* (1967); J. F. Bannon (ed.), *Indian labor in the Spanish Indies* (1966); J. H. M. Salmon (ed.), *The French wars of religion* (1967); and T. K. Rabb (ed.), *The Thirty Years' War* (2nd ed., 1981). The Folger Booklets on Tudor and Stuart Civilization, published by the Folger Shakespeare Library, Washington, D.C., treat many historical and literary subjects.

IV: THE ESTABLISHMENT OF WEST-EUROPEAN LEADERSHIP

[Syntheses for these years will often overlap with titles listed at the beginning of Chapter III, which should be consulted.] Informative general works for the seventeenth century include D. Ogg, *Europe in the seventeenth century** (1925, 1961); G. N. Clark, *The seventeenth century** (1929, 1961); M. Beloff, *The age of absolutism, 1660–1815** (1954); R. N. Hatton, *Louis XIV and Europe* (1976); M. Ashley, *The golden century: Europe, 1598–1715* (1969); the same author's *A history of Europe, 1648–1815* (rev., 1973); and W. Doyle, *The old European order, 1660–1800** (1978). Other useful introductions are J. Stoye, *Europe unfolding, 1648–1689** (1969); C. J. Friedrich and C. Blitzer, *The age of power, 1610–1713** (1957); and J. B. Wolf, *Toward a European balance of power, 1620–1715** (1970). Three volumes in the Langer series provide coverage for the seventeenth century: C. J. Friedrich, *The age of the baroque, 1610–1660,** already cited; F. L. Nussbaum, *The triumph of science and reason, 1660–1685** (1953); and J. B. Wolf, *The emergence of the great powers, 1685–1715** (1951).

F. L. Carsten (ed.), *The ascendancy of France, 1648–1688** (1961), and J. S. Bromley (ed.), *The rise of Great Britain and Russia, 1688–1715/25** (1970), vols. V and VI of the New Cambridge Modern History, provide authoritative chapters on many topics. For Europe overseas, one may turn to W. G. Davies, *The North Atlantic world in the seventeenth century* (1974), and for diplomatic practices and institutions of the age, W. J. Roosen, *The age of Louis XIV: the rise of modern diplomacy** (1976).

The Dutch Republic and the Empire

The second part of P. Geyl, *The Netherlands in the seventeenth century, 1609–1715*, already cited, covers the years 1648 to 1715; for seventeenth-century Netherlands' history, there also are available C. Wilson, *The Dutch Republic and the civilization of the seventeenth century** (1968), an attractive, brief introduction; K. H. D. Haley, *The Dutch Republic in the seventeenth century* (1972); and J. L. Price, *Culture and society in the Dutch Republic during the seventeenth century* (1974). Dutch economic influence is explored in the relevant chapters of J. A. van Houtte, *An economic history of* the Low Countries, 800–1800 (1977), and the agrarian economy in J. De Vries, *The Dutch rural economy in the golden age, 1500–1700* (1974). The economic and cultural life of the leading Dutch city is explored in V. Barbour, *Capitalism in Amsterdam in the seventeenth century** (1950); D. Regin, *Traders, artists, burghers: a cultural history of Amsterdam in the 17th century* (1977); and P. Burke, *Venice and Amsterdam* (1974), a comparative study. On William of Orange, the best study is S. B. Baxter, *William III and the defense of European liberty, 1650–1702* (1966). N. A. Robb, *William of Orange: a personal portrait* (2 vols., 1963–1966), is stronger on biographical than on political details, and D. Ogg, *William III** (1956), is a brief sketch. A masterful detailed biography of a leading Dutch statesman is H. H. Rowen, *John de Witt, grand pensionary of Holland, 1625–1672* (1978). On overseas exploration and colonization, an outstanding introduction is C. R. Boxer, *The Dutch seaborne empire, 1600–1800* (1965).

Seventeenth-Century England

[See also the books on England cited in Chapter III.] The best introduction is J. P. Kenyon, *Stuart England* (1978). Other recent histories of high quality are C. Hill, *The century of revolution, 1603–1714** (1962); J. R. Jones, *Country and court: England, 1658–1714** (New History of England series, 1978); B. Coward, *The Stuart age, 1603–1714* (1980); and two books by M. Ashley: *England in the seventeenth century** (rev., 1980), and *The house of Stuart: its rise and fall* (1980). Ashley also has prepared a survey of seventeenth-century social history with many contemporary illustrations in *Life in Stuart England* (1964), and Stuart culture is also well conveyed in G. Parry, *The Golden Age restor'd: the culture of the Stuart court, 1603–1642* (1981). G. M. Straka and L. O. Straka, *A certainty in the succession* (1973), covers the years from 1640 to 1815. For economic developments, one may turn to C. Wilson, *England's apprenticeship, 1603–1763* (1965), and G. N. Clark, *The wealth of England from 1496 to 1760* (1947), while a wider setting is presented in J. R. Jones, *Britain and Europe in the seventeenth century** (1966), and its sequel, *Britain and the world, 1649–1815** (1980). G. E. Aylmer has written two important studies of politics, society, and bureaucracy: *The king's servants: the civil service of Charles I, 1625–1642* (1961, 1974), and *The state's servants: the civil service of the English republic, 1649–1660* (1973). Books by L. Stone, H. R. Trevor-Roper, and others on the aristocracy and the gentry have been cited in Chapter III, but one should add G. E. Mingay, *The rise and fall of a ruling class* (1976). The English background to settlement in America is ably sketched in W. Notestein, *The English people on the eve of colonization, 1603–1630** (1954), and in C. W. Bridenbaugh, *Vexed and troubled Englishmen, 1590–1642* (1968). An interesting comparative study in social history is R. Thompson, *Women in Stuart England and America* (1974), and an important addition to the social and economic history of the rural lower classes is A. B. Appleby, *Famine in Tudor and Stuart England* (1978).

On the Great Rebellion and subsequent developments, S. R. Gardiner's older history is justly regarded as a classic, and one still reads it with profit. A commendable, recent effort to recount the dramatic story is A. Fletcher, *The outbreak of the English Civil War* (1981). Other good introductions are L. Stone, *The causes of the English Revolution, 1529–1642** (1972), a brief but informative essay; and P. Zagorin, *The court and the country: the beginning of the English Revolution of the mid-seventeenth century* (1970). Some of the most vivid and perceptive writings on these events have been by C. V. Wedgwood, a strong advocate of the theory that analysis (the "why") ought to flow from detailed, accurate, and lively narrative (the "how"); among her works are a trilogy on the mid-century revolution: *The king's peace, 1637–1641** (1955), *The king's war, 1641–1647* (1959), and *A coffin for King Charles: the trial and execution of Charles I* (1964).

Three recent successful studies of the political and religious conflict are R. Ashton, *The English Civil War: conservatism and revolution, 1603–1649* (1978), which shares historians' conflicting interpretations with the reader; two books by C. Russell, *A crisis of Parliaments** (1971) and *Parliaments and English politics, 1621–1629* (1979); and L. Kaplan, *Politics and religion during the English Revolution: the Scots and the Long Parliament, 1643–1645* (1976).

C. Firth, *Oliver Cromwell and the rule of the Puritans in England** (1900, 1925), is still the best biographical account, but there are other studies by S. R. Gardiner, J. Morley, J. Buchan, M. Ashley, and C. V. Wedgwood. A. Fraser, *Cromwell: the Lord Protector* (1973), is an admirable biography, although less lively than her biography of Mary Stuart; and C. Hill, *God's Englishman** (1972), is a provocative account. C. D. Bowen has sketched a vivid portrait in *The lion and the throne: the life and times of Sir Edward Coke, 1552–1634* (1957). Other important studies are H. R. Trevor-Roper's unsympathetic *Archbishop Laud, 1573–1645* (1940); J. H. Hexter, *The reign of King Pym* (1941); D. Underdown, *Pride's purge* (1971); J. M. MacCormack, *Revolutionary politics in the Long Parliament* (1973); and L. G. Schwoerer, *No standing armies! the anti-army ideology in seventeenth century England* (1974). D. Willson has written a biography of the first Stuart, *King James VI and I** (1956), as has A. Fraser (1975); both may be supplemented by M. Lee, Jr., *Government by pen: Scotland under James VI and I* (1980). E. C. Wingfield-Stratford has written a detailed biography of Charles I (3 vols., 1949–1950), and C. Hibbert a briefer one (1969). B. H. Wormald provides an admirable study in *Clarendon: politics, history, and religion, 1640–1660* (1951), as does B. Worden in *The Rump Parliament, 1648–1653* (1974). The effect of the political turmoil on the English imagination is well conveyed in B. Willey, *The seventeenth century background: studies in the thought of the age in relation to poetry and religion* (1934, 1949); D. M. Wolfe, *Milton in the Puritan revolution* (1941); F. E. Hutchinson, *Milton and the English mind** (Teach Yourself History series, 1946); and C. Hill, *Milton and the English Revolution* (1978), a challenging full-length study.

Much of the interest in Stuart and Commonwealth England is directed to the emergence during that period of some recognizably modern political and social problems. One of the earliest of such efforts was G. P. Gooch, *The history of English democratic ideas in the seventeenth century** (1898; ed. H. J. Laski, 1927). The many provocative books of C. Hill in this connection are especially important; among those not already cited are: *Puritanism and revolution** (1958), *Society and Puritanism in pre-revolutionary England** (1964), *Intellectual origins of the English Revolution* (1966), *Anti-Christ in seventeenth-century England* (1971), and *The world turned upside down* (1972). Hill's ideas are ably explored in a series of essays on his writings, D. Pennington and K. Thomas (eds.), *Puritans and revolutionaries: essays in seventeenth-century*

history (1979). B. Manning, *The English people and the English Revolution, 1640–1649* (1976), provides the best evaluation of the Levellers, but see also G. E. Aylmer, *The Levellers in the English Revolution* (1975). Other books include M. Walzer, *The revolution of the saints: a study in the origins of radical politics** (1965); P. G. Rogers, *The Fifth Monarchy men* (1966); J. S. McGee, *The godly man in Stuart England: Anglicans, Puritans, and the two tables, 1620–1670* (1976); W. Schenk, *The concern for social justice in the Puritan revolution* (1948), stressing religious rather than economic compulsions; W. Haller, *The rise of Puritanism** (1938); and M. Ashley, *John Wildman, plotter and postmaster: a study of the English republican movement in the seventeenth century* (1947). An important reassessment of ideology is J. O. Appleby, *Economic thought and ideology in seventeenth century England* (1978), while R. Hamilton, *The liberation of women: a study of patriarchy and capitalism* (1978), explores how preindustrial capitalism redefined the position of women in family and society.

On the Irish question, useful introductions are provided in J. C. Beckett, *The making of modern Ireland* (1966), and L. M. Cullen, *An economic history of Ireland since 1660* (1972); and for the Cromwellian age, there are two important studies: P. B. Ellis, *Ireland, 1652–1660* (1975), and T. C. Barnard, *Cromwellian Ireland: English government and reform in Ireland, 1649–1660* (1975).

Restoration and Revolution of 1688

The background to the Restoration is ably traced in G. Davies, *The restoration of Charles II, 1658–1660* (1955). The best treatment of the Restoration period itself is D. Ogg, *England in the reigns of Charles II, James II, and William III* (3 vols., 1955); a briefer treatment is G. Clark, *The later Stuarts* (rev., 1955). Written from a Tory viewpoint, A. Bryant, *King Charles II* (1932, 1949), makes the best possible case for Charles's relations with Louis XIV. A sympathetic balanced assessment is A. Fraser, *Royal Charles: Charles II and the Restoration** (1979), perhaps the best of her many thoughtful biographies. The nature of monarchy itself is explored in R. Ollard, *The image of the king: Charles I and Charles II* (1980), and a special subject examined in I. M. Green, *The re-establishment of the Church of England, 1660–1663* (1978). F. C. Turner, *James II* (1948), is fair and factual, as is J. Miller, *James II: a study in kingship* (1977), which stresses the monarch's personal integrity but failure as a king.

G. M. Trevelyan, *The English Revolution 1688–1689** (1939, 1946), argues that the revolution strengthened conservatism for the eighteenth century but that the long-run consequences made the revolution a turning point in history; it may be compared with L. Pinkham, *William III and the respectable revolution* (1954); M. Ashley, *The Glorious Revolution of 1688* (1967); J. R. Western, *Monarchy and revolution: the English state in the 1680s* (1972); J. Childs, *The army, James II, and the Glorious Revolution* (1980); S. Prall, *The bloodless revolution: England, 1688* (1972); J. R. Jones, *The Revolution of 1688 in England* (1972); and L. G. Schwoerer, *The Declaration of Rights, 1689* (1981), an admirable study. J. P. Kenyon, *Revolution principles: the politics of party, 1689–1720* (1977), is a subtle study of Lockean and other political theory, and the increased authority of Parliament is discussed in H. Horowitz, *Parliament, policy, and politics in the reign of William III* (1977). Trevelyan's *England under Queen Anne* (3 vols., 1930–1934) vividly portrays the succeeding age, and on the sovereign herself E. Gregg, *Queen Anne* (1980), is excellent. For foreign and military affairs, one may turn to W. S. Churchill, *Marlborough, his life and times* (4 vols., 1933–1938; abr. ed., 1968), and the briefer D. Chandler, *Marlborough as a military commander* (1973). J. H. Clapham, *The Bank of England* (2 vols., 1944), covers the period 1694–1944.

The France of Louis XIV

Many of the general accounts cited at the beginning of this chapter focus on the French predominance in this age. In addition, the following books explore various aspects of Louis XIV and his reign: J. B. Wolf, *Louis XIV** (1968), the most comprehensive biography; D. Ogg, *Louis XIV* (1933), somewhat critical; V. Buranelli, *Louis XIV** (1966), a brief, sympathetic account; M. Ashley, *Louis XIV and the greatness of France** (Teach Yourself History series, 1948); R. M. Hatton, *Louis XIV and absolutism* (1976); and A. Lossky, *Louis XIV and the ascendancy of France* (1977). W. F. Church, *Louis XIV in historical thought: from Voltaire to the Annales school* (1976), offers an historiographical assessment. P. Goubert, *Louis XIV and twenty million Frenchmen** (trans. 1972), and his more

detailed *The ancien regime: French society, 1600–1750** (2 vols., 1969–1973; trans. and abr., 1974), are invaluable as studies of French society and the ordinary people of the time by a historian of the *Annales* school; they may be supplemented by R. E. Mousnier, *The institutions of France under the absolute monarchy, 1598–1789: society and state* (trans. 1979), good on institutional development.

Some special studies are A. L. Moote, *The revolt of the judges: the Parlement of Paris and the Fronde, 1643–1652* (1971); E. E. Reynolds, *Bossuet* (1963); E. I. Perry, *From theology to history: French religious controversy and the revocation of the Edict of Nantes* (1973); L. Rothkrug, *Opposition to Louis XIV: the political and social origins of the Enlightenment* (1965); and A. Sedgwick, *Jansenism in seventeenth-century France: voices from the wilderness* (1977). Other interpretive volumes are W. H. Lewis, *The splendid century: life in the France of Louis XIV** (1953); G. R. R. Treasure, *Seventeenth-century France** (1966); V. L. Tapié, *The age of grandeur* (rev., 1966); and O. Ranum, *Paris in the age of absolutism** (1969).

On the French economy and empire, see C. W. Cole, *Colbert and a century of French mercantilism* (2 vols., 1939), his earlier volume, and a sequel that carries the story to 1700; W. Scoville, *The persecution of the Huguenots and French economic development, 1680–1720* (1960); J. Dent, *Crisis in France: crown, financiers, and society in seventeenth-century France* (1973); and R. Bonney, *The king's debts: finance and politics in France, 1589–1661* (1981). On the empire, see H. I. Priestley, *France overseas through the old regime: a study of European expansion* (1939), and W. J. Eccles, *Canada under Louis XIV, 1663–1701* (1964). P. W. Bamford has written two illuminating books, *Forests and French sea power, 1660–1789* (1956) and *Fighting ships and prisons: the Mediterranean galleys of France in the age of Louis XIV* (1973). C. C. Lougee, *Le paradis des femmes: women, salons, and social stratification in seventeenth century France* (1976), examines the relationship of influential women of the age to seventeenth-century society and culture.

On Louis XIV's wars one may read C. Ekberg, *The failure of Louis XIV's Dutch War* (1979), and H. Kamen, *The War of Succession in Spain, 1700–1715* (1969), along with the same author's impressive *Spain in the later seventeenth century, 1665–1700* (1980), in which he sees revival rather than decline on the eve of the French attack. J. Klaits, *Printed propaganda under Louis XIV: absolute monarchy and public opinion* (1977), demonstrates the monarch's efforts to influence public opinion in favor of his wars.

Problems and Readings*

For the debate over events in England, see P. A. M. Taylor (ed.), *The origins of the English Civil War: conspiracy, crusade, or class conflict?* (1960); L. Stone (ed.), *Social change and revolution in England, 1540–1640* (1965); R. E. Boyer (ed.), *Oliver Cromwell and the Puritan revolution: failure of a man or a faith?* (1966); M. Ashley, *Cromwell* (Great Lives Observed series, 1969); G. M. Straka (ed.), *The Revolution of 1688 and the birth of the English political nation* (rev., 1973); and P. Seaver (ed.), *Seventeenth century England: society in an age of revolution** (1976). For France, one may turn to W. F. Church: *The impact of absolutism in France: national experience under Richelieu, Mazarin, and Louis XIV* (1969), and *The greatness of Louis XIV: myth or reality* (rev., 1972); H. G. Judge (ed.), *Louis XIV* (1965); J. C. Rule (ed.), *Louis XIV and the craft of kingship* (1969); and R. F. Kierstead (ed.), *State and society in seventeenth-century France** (1975).

V: THE TRANSFORMATION OF EASTERN EUROPE, 1648–1740

The following are helpful general introductions to the complexities of eastern and east central Europe: F. Dvornik, *The making of central and eastern Europe* (1949) and *Slavs in European history and civilization* (1962); R. Portal, *The Slavs: a cultural and historical survey of the Slavonic people* (1965, trans. 1970); O. Halecki, *Borderlands of Western civilization: a history of east central Europe* (1952); S. H. Cross, *Slavic civilization through the ages* (1948); and W. H. McNeill, *Europe's steppe frontier, 1500–1800* (1964). Two valuable studies are L. S. Stavrianos, *The Balkans since 1453* (1958), and R. Ristelhueber, *A history of the Balkan peoples* (1950; rev. and trans. 1971); they may be supplemented by the background portions of R. L. Wolff, *The Balkans in our time** (rev., 1978); T. Stoianovich, *A study in Balkan civilization** (1967); and D. Djordjevic and S. Fischer-Galati, *The Balkan revolutionary tradition* (1981). J. S. Bromley (ed.), *The rise of Great Britain and Russia, 1688–1725* (1969), vol. VI of the New Cambridge Modern History, mentioned earlier, has informative but highly specialized chapters. A recent effort at a brief synthesis, not completely successful, is L. C. Tihany, *A history of middle Europe: from the earliest times to the age of the world wars* (1976).

The Ottoman Empire

N. Itzkowitz, *Ottoman Empire and Islamic tradition** (1972), is a useful brief introduction for the years 1300 to the late eighteenth century. P. Balfour [Lord Kinross], *The Ottoman centuries: the rise and fall of the Turkish empire* (1977), is a comprehensive narrative, as are S. Shaw, *History of the Ottoman Empire and modern Turkey*, vol. 1: *Empire of the Gazis: the rise and decline of the Ottoman Empire, 1280–1808** (1976), and H. Inalcik, *The Ottoman Empire: the classical age, 1300–1600* (1973). P. F. Sugar, *Southeastern Europe under Ottoman rule, 1354–1804* (1977), is an outstanding study. A careful account of the Turkish role in European affairs is available in D. M. Vaughan, *Europe and the Turk: a pattern of alliances, 1350–1700* (1954), and P. Coles, *The Ottoman impact on Europe, 1350–1699** (1968). Of interest as a special study is R. Schwoebel, *The shadow of the crescent: the Renaissance image of the Turk, 1453–1517* (1967). A popular but sound account of the empire is F. W. Fernau, *Moslems on the march* (trans. 1954). On the sixteenth century, R. O. Merriman, *Suleiman the Magnificent, 1520–1566* (1944) is the best general introduction. B. H. Sumner, *Peter the Great and the Ottoman Empire* (1949), describes early relations between Turkey and Russia, and C. E. Bosworth, *The Islamic dynasties: a chronological and genealogical handbook* (1967), is a useful reference tool.

Austria and the Habsburgs to 1740

Two basic studies are A. Wandruszka, *The house of Habsburg* (1956, trans. 1964), and R. A. Kann, *A history of the Habsburg empire, 1526–1918* (1974). For the early period, one should read H. G. Koenigsberger, *The Habsburgs and Europe, 1516–1660* (1971); R. J. W. Evans, *The making of the Habsburg monarchy, 1550–1700: an interpretation* (1979); and T. W. Barker, *Army, aristocracy, monarchy: essays on war, society, and government in Austria, 1618–1780* (1982). P. Frischauer, *The imperial crown: the rise and fall of the Holy Roman and the*

Austrian empires (1939), is primarily biographical in nature and treats the house of Habsburg to the death of Leopold II in 1792. J. F. Spielman has written *Leopold I of Austria* (1977), a balanced treatment of the seventeenth-century emperor. For Eugene of Savoy, an outstanding biography is D. McKay, *Prince Eugene of Savoy* (Men in Office series, 1977). Two lively studies of the Turkish siege of 1683 are J. Stoye, *The siege of Vienna* (1964), and T. M. Barker, *Double eagle and crescent: Vienna's second Turkish siege and its historical setting* (1967).

Prussia to 1740

Two convenient introductions are F. L. Carsten, *The origins of Prussia* (1954), and S. B. Fay and K. Epstein, *The rise of Brandenburg-Prussia to 1786** (1937; rev., 1964). H. Holborn in his *History of modern Germany, vol. II, 1648–1840* (1964), covers the fluid situation in the Holy Roman Empire after the Thirty Years' War, and E. Sagarra, *A social history of Germany, 1648–1914* (1977), provides fascinating details on the German states. G. Benecke, *Society and politics in Germany, 1500–1750* (1974), presents the case for the empire as a viable constitutional entity, while two important contributions to understanding the formation of the German political tradition are F. L. Carsten, *Princes and parliaments in Germany* (1959), cited earlier, and M. Walker, *German home towns: community, state, and general estate, 1648–1871* (1971).

On the earlier Hohenzollerns, one may read F. Schevill, *The great elector* (1947); R. Ergang, *The Potsdam Führer: Frederick William I, father of Prussian militarism* (1941); and R. A. Derwart, *The administrative reforms of Frederick William I of Prussia* (1953). An invaluable study going well beyond the scope of this chapter is G. A. Craig, *The politics of the Prussian army, 1640–1945** (1956, 1964); it may be compared with K. Demeter, *The German officer corps in society and state, 1650–1945* (1930, 1962; trans. 1965). Important also, especially for the sociological dimension it adds, is H. Rosenberg, *Bureaucracy, aristocracy, and autocracy: the Prussian experience, 1600–1815** (1958), which may be supplemented by J. A. Armstrong, *The European administrative elite** (1973), a comparative study of European bureaucracies during this period.

Russia to 1725

There are many excellent narrative accounts of Russian history, most of which give good coverage of the early years; among those written or revised in recent years are volumes by B. H. Sumner, B. Pares, M. T. Florinsky, J. D. Clarkson, S. Harcave, A. G. Mazour, N. V. Riasanovsky, G. Vernadsky, W. B. Walsh, M. C. Wren, D. Mackenzie and M. W. Curran, and B. Dmytryshyn. A fascinating impressionistic cultural history is J. H. Billington, *The icon and the axe: an interpretive history of Russian culture** (1966). M. T. Florinsky, *Russia: a history and an interpretation* (2 vols., 1953), is perhaps the best general account for the period to 1917; in briefer form, it is available as *Russia: a short history* (1969). G. Vernadsky, *A history of Russia* (5 vols., 1943–1969), covers Russian history in great detail from earliest times to 1682; the final two volumes, *Tsardom of Moscow, 1547–1682* (2 vols., 1969), are relevant here. There are vivid popular narratives by H. Lamb, *The march of Muscovy: Ivan the Terrible and the growth of the Russian empire, 1400–1648* (1948) and *The city and the tsar: Peter the Great and the move to the West, 1648–1762* (1948). On the early rulers, there are available J. Fennell, *Ivan the Great of Moscow* (1961); H. von Eckhardt, *Ivan the Terrible* (1949); I. Grey, *Ivan III and the unification of Russia* (1965); and the same author's *Ivan the Terrible* (1964). A fascinating large-scale study of all the Romanovs, the fifteen men and four women who ruled Russia between 1613 and 1917, is W. B. Lincoln, *Autocrats of all the Russias* (1981).

On Peter and the reforms of his reign, two masterful brief accounts are B. H. Sumner, *Peter the Great and the emergence of Russia** (Teach Yourself History series, 1950), and M. S. Anderson, *Peter the Great* (Men in Office series, 1978). R. K. Massie, *Peter the Great: his life and world* (1980), is a long, vivid, and colorful popular account, criticized by specialists for scholarly inadequacies. Russian expansion is discussed in R. J. Kerner, *The urge to the sea: the course of Russian history* (1942), which emphasizes the significance of trade routes. An important subject is covered in J. Blum, *Lord and peasant in Russia from the ninth to the nineteenth century** (1961), and in R. E. F. Smith, *The origins of farming in Russia* (1960). A remarkable study in comparative cultural history emphasizing Western influences is D. W. Treadgold, *The West in Rus-*

sia and China: religious and secular thought in modern times* (2 vols., 1973), the first volume covering Russia for the years 1472–1917, the second China for the years 1582–1949. Another important comparative study on a very different subject is R. Mousnier, *Peasant uprisings in seventeenth century France, Russia, and China* (trans. 1970).

For Sweden in this age, Voltaire's *History of Charles XII* (1731) still merits reading, but an outstanding modern biography of the Swedish monarch is R. M. Hatton, *Charles XII of Sweden* (1969). A number of important studies by M. Roberts and others have been cited in Chapter III; for these years Roberts, *The Swedish imperial experience, 1560–1718* (1979), deserves mention.

Poland

For Poland in these years, one may turn to the first volume of an important two-volume synthesis, N. Davies, *A history of Poland: God's playground* (2 vols., 1981), vol. I, *The origins to 1795*; and to O. Halecki, *A history of Poland* (rev., 1961). The quarrel over the succession to the Polish throne is told in J. L. Sutton, *The king's honor and the king's Cardinal* [Fleury]: *the War of the Polish Succession* (1980). On the eighteenth-century partitions, one may consult H. H. Kaplan, *The first partition of Poland* (1962), and the older R. H. Lord, *The second partition of Poland* (1915); and for the years that followed, P. Wandycz, *The lands of partitioned Poland, 1795–1918* * (1974). S. Konovalov, *Russian-Polish relations: an historical survey* (1945), is a brief, well-organized account, while a special subject is treated in B. D. Weinryb, *The Jews of Poland: a social and economic history of the Jewish community in Poland from 1100 to 1800* (1973).

Problems and Readings*

Various volumes of readings in Russian history and Russian civilization from earliest times to the present are available, among them those edited by W. B. Walsh (3 vols., 4th ed., 1963), T. Riha (3 vols.; rev., 1969), and G. Vernadsky and others (3 vols., 1972). On Peter's innovations, there is M. Raeff, *Peter the Great changes Russia* (rev., 1972). L. J. Oliva has edited *Russia and the West from Peter to Khrushchev* (1965), and W. L. Blackwell, *Russian economic development from Peter the Great to Stalin* * (1974). R. V. Burks, *East European history:*

an ethnic approach* (1973), reviews scholarship in this area in the American Historical Association Pamphlets series.

VI: THE STRUGGLE FOR WEALTH AND EMPIRE

For the years covered in this chapter, 1713–1763, the most helpful syntheses are M. S. Anderson, *Europe in the eighteenth century, 1713–1783* * (2nd ed., 1977); R. J. Whyte, *Europe in the eighteenth century* * (1965); D. Ogg, *Europe of the ancien régime, 1715–1783* * (1965); P. Langford, *The eighteenth century, 1688–1815* * (1977); and I. Woloch, *Eighteenth century Europe: tradition and progress, 1715–1789* * (1982). In the Langer series there are available P. Roberts, *The quest for security, 1715–1740* * (1947), and a masterful volume by W. L. Dorn, *Competition for empire, 1740–1763* * (1940), particularly good on the relation of the European state system to the overseas expansion and rivalry of the time. J. O. Lindsay (ed.), *The old regime, 1713–1763* (1957), vol. VII in the New Cambridge Modern History, has informative chapters on domestic and international developments.

Popular Culture

It is for the early modern centuries that the differences between elite and popular cultures have been most closely examined, as in P. Burke, *Popular culture in early modern Europe* (1978), and other books cited in the introductory section. Especially useful is F. Braudel, *The structures of everyday life: the limits of the possible* (trans. 1981), the first volume of his three-volume study mentioned earlier. Popular culture is explored also in many of the works on social history, labor history, and women's history cited in the introduction and elsewhere in this bibliography.

The Colonial Empires and Global Economy

Several of the books on European overseas expansion listed for Chapter IV also discuss the eighteenth century. To these must be added H. Furber's superb synthesis, *Rival empires of trade in the Orient, 1600–1800* (1976), a volume in Europe and the World in the Age of Expansion series; J. H. Parry, *Trade and dominion: the European overseas* *empires in the eighteenth century* (1971); G. Williams, *The expansion of Europe in the eighteenth century: overseas rivalry, discovery, and exploitation* (1960); the relevant chapters of D. K. Fieldhouse, *The colonial empires: a comparative survey from the eighteenth century* (1966); the comprehensive C. E. Carrington, *The British overseas: exploits of a nation of shopkeepers* (1950; rev., 1968); and K. M. Pannikar, *Asia and Western dominance: . . . the Vasco da Gama epoch of Asian history, 1498–1945* * (rev., 1959), by an Indian scholar. The Dutch role in the global economy is ably portrayed in J. C. Riley, *International government finance and the Amsterdam capital market, 1740–1815* (1980), which supplements C. Wilson, *Anglo-Dutch commerce and finance in the eighteenth century* (1941, 1966).

The eighteenth-century impact of India is explored in H. Furber, *John Company at work: a study of European expansion in India in the late eighteenth century* (1948). In addition, the following works on India may be recommended, although they are not confined to the eighteenth century: S. Wolpert, *A new history of India* * (rev., 1982), one of the best introductions; P. Spear, *The Oxford history of modern India, 1740–1975* * (2nd ed., 1979); W. N. Brown, *The United States and India, Pakistan, and Bangladesh* (rev., 1972), with perceptive pages on the historical background; P. Woodruff [Mason], *The men who ruled India* * (2 vols., 1954–1957); and M. Andrewes, *British India* (1964).

Biographical studies include P. Moon, *Warren Hastings and British India* * (Teach Yourself History series, 1947); K. Feiling, *Warren Hastings* (1945); and P. J. Marshall, *The impeachment of Warren Hastings* (1965). An account of these years by Indian scholars is found in R. C. Majumdar (ed.), *The struggle for empire* (1957), the fifth volume in a longer work on Indian history. S. E. Schwartzberg (ed.), *A historical atlas of South Asia* (1978), is a superb collaborative atlas, and J. Nehru, *The discovery of India* * (1946), by the Indian statesman, remains an indispensable introduction to Indian history.

The numerous volumes by F. Parkman on the French regime in Canada are classics of nineteenth-century historiography; a standard twentieth-century account is G. M. Wrong, *The rise and fall of New France* (2 vols., 1928), and his various other writings, but the most useful volume is now W. J. Eccles, *France in America* (1972). On the West Indies, there are available two books by N. M. Crouse, *French pioneers in the West Indies, 1624–1664* (1940) and *The French struggle for the West Indies, 1665–1713* (1944); the importance of the West Indies is examined in R. S. Dunn, *Sugar and slaves* (1972).

The British Empire before the American Revolution

J. R. Seeley, *The expansion of England* (1883, 1895), is a classic essay, while W. B. Willcox, *Star of empire: a study of Britain as a world power, 1485–1945* (1950), is rewarding as narrative and analysis. There are numerous older studies of the old colonial system and of mercantilism by G. L. Beer, C. M. Andrews, and H. L. Osgood. For the mid-eighteenth century from 1748 to 1776, there is L. H. Gipson's monumental work in thirteen volumes, *The British Empire before the American Revolution* (1936–1967); vol. XIII contains in part II a summary of the entire work. Another important large-scale treatment is *The Cambridge history of the British Empire* (9 vols., 1929–1959). C. G. Robertson, *Chatham and the British Empire* * (1948), and J. A. Williamson, *Cook and the opening of the Pacific* * (1948), are two lively studies in the Teach Yourself History series.

British Society and Politics in the Eighteenth Century

Books on eighteenth-century France are listed below in Chapter VIII, but two works should be mentioned here: J. H. Shannon, *Philippe, Duke of Orléans: Regent of France, 1715–1723* (1979), and R. Butler, *Choiseul*, vol. I., *Father and son* (1980), the first volume of a projected three, which vividly portrays the age. Informative recent studies focusing on political parties, political issues, and public opinion in eighteenth-century Britain include W. A. Speck, *Stability and strife: England 1714–1760* * (1977), a volume in the New History of England series, which also gives considerable attention to social and economic developments, and the same author's *Tory and Whig: the struggle in the constituencies, 1701–1715* (1968); C. Holmes, *British politics in the age of Anne* (1967); J. H. Plumb, *The origins of political stability: England, 1675–1725* (1967); and B. W. Hall, *The growth of parliamentary parties, 1689–1742* (1976). Recommended books on personalities and events include R. N. Hatton, *George I, Elector and King* (1979); J. H. Plumb, *Sir Robert Walpole* (2 vols., 1956, 1961); the same author's *The first four Georges** (1956); H. T. Dickinson, *Walpole and the Whig supremacy* (1973); and B. Kemp, *Sir Robert Walpole* (1976). There are three outstanding biographies of the great mid-eighteenth-century statesman: B. Williams, *Life of William Pitt, Earl of Chatham* (2 vols., 1966); S. Ayling, *The elder Pitt, Earl of Chatham* (1976); and P. D. Brown, *William Pitt, Earl of Chatham* (1978). Of special interest is M. Peters, *Pitt and popularity. the patriot minister and London opinion during the Seven Years' War* (1980).

For an institutional approach, one must turn to L. B. Namier's seminal work, *The structure of politics at the accession of George III* (2 vols., 1920; 1 vol., 1957). In progress is a collaborative effort at prosopography, or collective biography, which seeks to reconstruct in minute biographical detail the composition of the modern English parliaments, a project inspired and inaugurated by Namier during his lifetime. An important reassessment of the 1760s is provided in J. Brewer, *Party ideology and popular politics at the accession of George III* (1976).

On social conditions, the following are instructive: L. Kronenberger, *Kings and desperate men: life in eighteenth century England* (1942); G. Rudé, *Hanoverian London, 1714–1808* (1971); B. Malcolmson, *Life and labor in England, 1700–1780* (1981); P. Clark and P. Slack (eds.), *Crisis and order in English towns, 1500–1700* (1972); and D. Marshall's three studies, *The English poor in the eighteenth century* (1926), *Eighteenth-century England* (1962), and *Dr. Johnson's London** (1967). Several additional books relating to social history in this period are cited in the introductory section of this bibliography, notably works by E. P. Thompson, P. Laslett, L. Stone, R. Trumbach, and others, and additional titles appear in Chapter XI in connection with the Industrial Revolution. On justice in these years, one will find illuminating E. P. Thompson, *Whigs and hunters: the origin of the Black Act** (1976), and Thompson and others, *Crime and society in eighteenth century England* (1976).

For economic developments, there are important chapters in R. Floud and D. McCloskey (eds.), *The economic history of Britain since 1700** (2 vols., 1981), of which volume I covers the years 1700 to 1860. On financial subjects a far-reaching book is

P. G. M. Dickson, *The financial revolution in England: a study in the development of public credit, 1688–1756* (1967). Two important studies are J. Thirsk, *Economic policy and projects: the development of a consumer society in early modern England* (1978), focusing on schemes to make money from 1540 on, and P. Mathias, *The transformation of England: essays in the economic and social history of England* (1979). The celebrated speculative ventures of the age are graphically described in J. Carswell, *The South Sea bubble* (1960), and in the relevant chapters of C. P. Kindleberger, *Manias, panics, and crashes: a history of financial crises* (1978), which carries the story into the twentieth century. Kindleberger analyzes the formation of financial centers, among other subjects, in *Economic response: comparative studies in trade, finance, and growth* (1978). A very special subject is treated in two books: R. Carr, *English fox-hunting: a history* (1976), and D. C. Itzkowitz, *Peculiar privilege: a social history of English fox-hunting, 1753–1885* (1977). The Jacobite rebellions are ably discussed in B. Lenman, *The Jacobite risings in Britain, 1689–1746* (1980), and F. J. McLynn, *France and the Jacobite rising of 1745* (1981).

Diplomacy and War in Europe, 1740–1763

[Various titles listed at the beginning of this chapter and Chapter V, and in Chapter VIII for enlightened despotism, should also be consulted.] A. Sorel, *Europe under the old regime** (trans. 1947), the introduction to his study of Europe and the French Revolution (8 vols., 1895 ff.), remains valuable for insights into the European balance of power. C. Petrie, *Diplomatic history, 1713–1933* (1946), provides an overall survey, while C. Duffy, *The army of Maria Theresa: the armed forces of imperial Austria, 1740–1780* (1977), ably explores the nature of the Habsburg army.

On the negotiations ending the Seven Years' War, Z. E. Rashed has written *The Peace of Paris, 1763* (1952). M. Savelle, *The origins of American diplomacy: the international history of Anglo-America, 1492–1763* (1967), covers the diplomacy of these years in a special way.

Problems and Readings*

A sampling of recent scholarship on eighteenth-century English politics and society is provided in D. A. Baugh (ed.), *Aristocratic government and society in eighteenth-century England: the foundations of stability* (1975).

VII: THE SCIENTIFIC VIEW OF THE WORLD

A number of works cited in the introductory section of this bibliography are concerned with various aspects of the history of science, and the reader may wish to consult them. For works in the history of science published in the years 1913–1965, one may consult the *Isis cumulative bibliography* (3 vols., 1971–1976), and for subsequent years the annual bibliographies published in *Isis*.

The Scientific Revolution

The fundamental reorientation of thinking about nature in early modern times has probably had more influence on the later world than any of the specific inventions or technical advances of the period. The best introductions are A. R. Hall, *The scientific revolution, 1500–1800: the formation of the modern scientific attitude** (1954; rev., 1962); H. Butterfield, *The origins of modern science, 1300–1800** (rev., 1965); M. Boas, *The scientific Renaissance, 1450–1630* (1962); W. P. D. Wightman, *Science and the Renaissance* (1963); H. Kearney, *Science and change, 1500–1700** (1971); A. G. R. Smith, *Science and society in the sixteenth and seventeenth centuries* (1972); A. G. Debus, *Man and nature in the Renaissance** (1978); R. S. Westfall, *The construction of modern science** (1978); and R. Mandrou, *From humanism to science, 1480–1700* (1973, trans. 1979). A larger collaborative survey is L. P. Williams and H. J. Steffens (eds.), *The history of science in Western civilization* (3 vols., 1977), from antiquity to the twentieth century. A highly provocative and influential book has been T. S. Kuhn, *The structure of scientific revolutions** (1962), which may be supplemented by the same author's *The essential tension: selected studies in scientific tradition and change* (1977), depicting progress in science as a pull between conservative and innovative forces. Kuhn has also written *The Copernican revolution: planetary astronomy in the development of Western thought* (1956).

   E. A. Burtt, *The metaphysical foundations of modern philosophical science** (1925, 1948), is a searching examination of the ideas of scientists from Copernicus to Newton. Other books exploring the theoretical foundations of science include J. B. Conant, *On understanding science: an historical approach* (1947) and *Science and common sense* (1951); S. E. Toulmin, *The philosophy of science* (1953); R. G. Collingwood, *The idea of nature* (1945); A. N. Whitehead, *Science and the modern world* (1925); C. C. Gillispie, *The edge of objectivity: an essay in the history of scientific ideas* (1960); and two books by G. Holton, *Thematic origins of scientific thought: Kepler to Einstein** (1973) and *The scientific imagination: case studies** (1978). I. B. Cohen has written *The Newtonian revolution: with illustrations of the transformation of scientific ideas* (1980), and a more general account, *Album of science: from Leonardo to Lavoisier, 1450–1800* (1980).

Histories of Science

For individual scientists, one will wish to consult the *Dictionary of scientific biography* (8 vols., 1970–1980) cited in the introductory section; R. Taton, *History of science* (4 vols., trans. 1964–1966), or the briefer T. I. Williams, *A biographical dictionary of scientists* (1969). Two excellent introductions are A. R. Hall and M. B. Hall, *Brief history of science* (1961), and S. F. Mason, *A history of the sciences** (1962). Other studies include C. J. Singer, *A short history of scientific ideas to 1900* (rev., 1949); A. C. Crombie, *Medieval and early modern science** (2 vols., 1959), cited in Chapter I; E. Grant, *Physical science in the Middle Ages** (1978); and F. S. Taylor, *A short history of science and scientific thought* (1949). The older pioneering studies of G. Sarton and L. Thorndike remain important for specialists; some of Sarton's general ideas are presented in *The life of science: essays in the history of civilization* (1948) and in *Six wings: men of science in the Renaissance* (1957). A remarkable achievement is the multivolumed study under way by J. Needham, *Science and civilization in China* (5 vols. to date, many in several parts, 1954–   ); some of his important insights are conveyed in *Science in traditional China: a comparative perspective* (1981).

   On the history of medicine, one may read H. E. Sigerist, *A history of medicine* (1951); L. S. King, *The growth of medical thought* (1963); and E. H. Ackerknecht, *A short history of medicine* (1955; rev., 1982). A revision of the older F. H. Garrison, *An intro-*

duction to the history of medicine (4th ed., 1929), is in progress.

Scientific Organizations in the Seventeenth Century

On the organization of scientific activity and the spread of new ideas, see M. Ornstein, *The role of scientific societies in the seventeenth century* (1928); H. Brown, *Scientific organizations in seventeenth-century France, 1620–1680* (1934); R. Hahn, *The anatomy of a scientific institution: the Paris Academy of Sciences, 1666–1803* (1971); H. Lyons, *The Royal Society, 1660–1940* (1944); D. Stimson, *Scientists and amateurs: a history of the Royal Society* (1948); S. Bethell, *The cultural revolution of the seventeenth century* (1951); and R. F. Jones, *Ancients and moderns: the rise of the scientific movement in seventeenth-century England** (1936, 1961). Of special importance is C. Webster, *The great instauration: science, medicine, and reform, 1616–1660* (1976).

Among the books that explore the technological implications of the new science are: A. Wolf, *A history of science, technology, and philosophy in the sixteenth and seventeenth centuries* (1935) and *. . . in the eighteenth century* (1939); G. N. Clark, *Science and social welfare in the age of Newton* (1937); and the stimulating L. Mumford, *Technics and civilization* (1934).

On technology, one may consult C. Singer and others, *A history of technology* (5 vols., 1954–1958), from prehistory to about 1900, for which T. I. Williams has edited two additional volumes (1978) for the twentieth century; the briefer T. K. Derry and T. I. Williams, *A short history of technology from the earliest times to A.D. 1900* (1961); and W. Beranek, Jr. and G. Ranis, *Science, technology, and human development: a historical and comparative study* (1978).

Biographical Accounts

The contributions of the pioneer astronomers are described in many of the books cited earlier and in A. Armitage, *Copernicus: the founder of modern astronomy* (1938) and *The world of Copernicus* (1947, 1951); J. A. Gade, *The life and times of Tycho Brahe* (1947); M. Caspar, *Kepler* (1948, trans. 1959); and the briefer C. Baumgardt, *Johannes Kepler: life and letters* (1951). F. W. Taylor, *Galileo and the freedom of thought* (1938), is a dispassionate, carefully documented work, and the

opposition that Galileo aroused is well described in G. de Santillana, *The crime of Galileo* (1955, 1959) A brief biographical study is L. Fermi and G. Bernardini, *Galileo and the scientific revolution** (1961), while a technical study with little attention to the scientist's milieu is S. Drake, *Galileo at work: his scientific biography* (1978).

Both F. H. Anderson, *The philosophy of Francis Bacon* (1948), and B. Farrington, *Francis Bacon: philosopher of industrial science** (1949), are concerned with Bacon's ideas and impact, while C. D. Bowen has written a sound, vivid biography, *Francis Bacon: the temper of the man* (1963), which may be supplemented by J. J. Epstein, *Francis Bacon: a political biography* (1977). E. S. Haldane, *Descartes, his life and times* (1905), is primarily biographical, and S. H. Mellone, *The dawn of modern thought: Descartes, Spinoza, Leibniz* (1930), explains the Cartesian system and its influence. For Pascal, see M. Bishop, *Pascal: the life of genius* (1936); and for Pierre Bayle, see H. Robinson, *Bayle the skeptic* (1931). F. L. Baumer, *Religion and the rise of skepticism* (1960), and R. H. Popkin, *The history of skepticism from Erasmus to Spinoza** (rev., 1979), both trace the skeptical tradition. Other seventeenth-century scientists are placed in their intellectual setting in L. T. More, *The life and works of the Honourable Robert Boyle* (1944); M. Boas, *Robert Boyle and seventeenth century chemistry* (1958); and A. E. Bell, *Christian Huygens and the development of science in the seventeenth century* (1947). For Newton, a distinguished large-scale biography is R. S. Westfall, *Never at rest: a biography of Isaac Newton* (1981); there are other biographical accounts by L. T. More (1934), S. Brodetsky (1927), J. Sullivan (1938), E. N. da C. Andrade* (1954), and F. E. Manuel (1968, 1974). The quarrel over the discovery of calculus is portrayed in A. R. Hall, *Philosophers at war: the quarrel between Newton and Leibniz* (1980).

Two provocative studies focusing on the relationship between seventeenth-century science and its political and social context are J. R. Jacob, *Robert Boyle and the English Revolution: a case study in social and intellectual change* (1978), and M. C. Jacob, *The Newtonians and the English Revolution, 1689–1720* (1978); they may be compared with R. K. Merton, *Science, technology, and society in seventeenth century England* (1970), which also stresses the close relationship, and with various essays in

C. Webster (ed.), *The intellectual revolution of the seventeenth century* (1974), which do not.

Law, Political Theory, and Natural Law

[The books on political thought cited in the introductory section of the bibliography and in Chapter VIII on the Enlightenment should also be consulted.] The best introductions are the readings in E. A. Burtt (ed.), *The English philosophers from Bacon to Mill* (1939), and E. Barker (ed.), *Social contract: essays by Locke, Hume, and Rousseau* (1947). W. Seagle, *The quest for law* (1941), treats historically the formulation of law and jurisprudence. J. G. A. Pocock, *The Machiavellian moment: Florentine political thought and the Atlantic republican tradition* (1975), cited in Chapter II, is relevant here. On Locke, one may read M. Cranston, *John Locke: a biography* (1957); M. Seliger, *The liberal politics of John Locke* (1969); and J. Dunn, *The political thought of John Locke* (1969). For Hobbes, there is available D. D. Raphael, *Hobbes: morals and politics* (1978). Especially useful for these years is N. O. Keohane, *Philosophy and the state in France: the Renaissance to the Enlightenment* * (1980). W. S. M. Knight has written *The life and works of Hugo Grotius* (1925).

Problems and Readings*

One pamphlet is relevant: G. Basalla, *The rise of modern science: external or internal factors?* (1968). A useful anthology is M. B. Hall (ed.), *Nature and nature's laws: documents of the scientific revolution* (1969), and two interesting older compilations are F. S. Taylor, *The march of mind* (1939), and F. R. Moulton and J. Schifferes (eds.), *The autobiography of science* (1945).

VIII: THE AGE OF ENLIGHTENMENT

For background, the eighteenth-century accounts listed at the beginning of Chapter VI should be consulted, and to them should be added A. Goodwin (ed.), *The American and French revolutions, 1763–1793* * (1965), vol. VIII of the New Cambridge Modern History; L. Gershoy, *From despotism to revolution, 1763–1789* * (1944), in the Langer series, an illuminating account of Europe in the generation before 1789; and the brief L. Krieger, *Kings and philosophers, 1689–1789* * (1970).

Of special interest here is M. S. Anderson, *Historians and eighteenth-century Europe, 1715–1789* (1979), a provocative historiographical study. Additional general accounts are listed in this chapter and the next.

The Thought of the Enlightenment

Although recent research interests have moved away from intellectual history, some of the most interesting historical writing in the past has focused on the ideas of the European Enlightenment. An ambitious effort to interpret the thought of the era on a European-wide scale is P. Gay, *The Enlightenment: an interpretation* (2 vols., 1966–1969), vol. I, *The rise of paganism*, on the use of the classical past to support the struggle for freedom, and vol. II, *The science of freedom*, on the application of science to all areas of human activity, especially the problems of society. Some of his postulates also are explored in his *The party of humanity: essays on the French Enlightenment* (1964). Another large-scale effort, on the French thinkers and thought of the age, is I. O. Wade, *The structure and form of the French Enlightenment* (2 vols., 1977), focusing on the "philosophical spirit" of the age in the first volume and the "revolutionary spirit" in the second.

The older works by the French scholar P. Hazard may still be read with profit: *The European mind: the critical years, 1680–1715* (1935, trans. 1953), and *European thought in the eighteenth century: from Montesquieu to Lessing* (1946, trans. 1954). Historians tend to reject the provocative thesis of C. Becker, in *The heavenly city of the eighteenth-century philosophers* * (1932), that Enlightenment thought, essentially utopian, represented a secularized version of medieval Christian views. Other important interpretations of the Enlightenment are to be found in E. Cassirer, *The philosophy of the Enlightenment* (1932, trans. 1951); A. Cobban, *In search of humanity: the role of the Enlightenment in modern history* (1960); L. G. Crocker, *An age of crisis; man and world in eighteenth century thought* (1959); and N. Hampson, *A cultural history of the Enlightenment* * (1969).

On the Enlightenment theme of progress, three older accounts, J. B. Bury, *The idea of progress: an inquiry into its origin and growth* (1920, reissued 1955); C. Frankel, *The faith of reason: the idea of progress in the French Enlightenment* (1938); and R. V. Sampson, *Progress in the age of reason: the* seventeenth century to the present day (1956), may be compared with R. Nisbet, *History of the idea of progress* (1980), already cited. On economic thought, M. Beer, *An inquiry into physiocracy* (1939), must be supplemented by E. Fox-Genovese, *The origins of physiocracy: economic revolution and social order in eighteenth-century France* (1976). The volume by L. Rothkrug, *Opposition to Louis XIV: the political and social origins of the Enlightenment*, cited in Chapter IV, also examines economic ideas, as does J. Q. C. Macrell, *The attack on feudalism in eighteenth-century France* (1973). H. G. Payne, *The philosophes and the people* (1971), traces the divergent views of the famous writers toward the lower classes, and may be supplemented by H. Chisick, *The limits of reform in the Enlightenment: attitudes toward the education of the lower classes in eighteenth-century France* (1981). On a lesser known *philosophe* sympathetic to the poorer classes, an excellent account is D. G. Levy, *The ideas and careers of Simon-Nicolas-Henri-Linguet* (1980). A forthcoming study is S. Spencer, *French women and the age of Enlightenment*.

On a special subject, A. Hertzberg, *The French Enlightenment and the Jews* (1968), contends that by stressing universal values the *philosophes* contributed to modern anti-Semitism; also critical of the Enlightenment is J. Katz, *Out of the ghetto: the social background of Jewish emancipation, 1770–1870* (1973). R. Mahler, *A history of modern Jewry, 1780–1815* (1971), examines in a different way the impact of the Enlightenment and Revolution on the existing Jewish communities; on European Jewry in this age and since, see H. M. Sachar, *The course of modern Jewish history* * (rev., 1977).

The Philosophes

There are numerous good books on each of the leading thinkers of the Enlightenment. On Voltaire: P. Gay, *Voltaire's politics: the poet as realist* (1959), reveals Voltaire's pragmatic, nondoctrinaire reactions to the events of his day. Other recent studies of Voltaire include accounts by I. O. Wade (1970); A. D. Aldridge (1975), a good overview; H. Mason (1981); and a comprehensive biography by T. Bestermann (1969), a leading Swiss authority and editor of Voltaire's correspondence. As a writer of history, Voltaire is ably studied in J. H. Brumfitt, *Voltaire historian* (1958). For Montesquieu there is an outstanding study by R. Shackleton, *Montes-*

quieu: a critical biography* (1961). On Diderot, A. M. Wilson's superb biography (2 vols., 1957, 1972) is available, and also L. G. Crocker, *The embattled philosopher: a biography of Denis Diderot* (1954), which may be supplemented by the same author's analytical study, *Diderot's chaotic order: approach to synthesis* (1974). On Rousseau, a good introduction is F. C. Green, *Jean-Jacques Rousseau: a critical study of his life and writings* (1955). In addition to older studies by E. Cassirer (1954) and others, there are available J. Guéhenno, *Jean-Jacques Rousseau* (2 vols., 1948–1962, trans. 1966); W. H. Blanchard, *Rousseau and the spirit of revolt* (1968); R. Grimsley, *Jean-Jacques Rousseau: a study in self-awareness* (1961), and *Rousseau and the religious quest* (1968); J. H. Huizinga, *Rousseau: the self-made man* (1975); and the first volume of M. Cranston's reassessment (1983). On Condorcet, K. M. Baker has written the exhaustive *Condorcet: from natural philosophy to social mathematics* (1975); an older study, J. S. Schapiro, *Condorcet and the rise of liberalism* (1934), is a briefer, general account.

For a sampling of books on other thinkers, see A. L. Lindsay, *Kant* (1934, 1946); D. M. Low, *Edward Gibbon* (1937); N. K. Smith, *The philosophy of David Hume* (1949); and C. Van Doren, *Benjamin Franklin* (1938). On a leading Italian philosopher of the Enlightenment, there are L. Pompa, *Vico: a study of the "new science"* (1975), and G. Tagliocozzo and D. P. Verene (eds.), *Giambattista Vico's science of humanity* (1976). The Enlightenment in general in Italy is studied in F. Venturi, *Italy and the Enlightenment: studies in a cosmopolitan century* (1972).

F. E. Manuel links the eighteenth century to the age that follows in *The prophets of Paris: Turgot, Condorcet, Saint-Simon, Fourier, Comte* * (1962), and with F. P. Manuel masterfully traces an important theme in an even wider setting in *Utopian thought in the Western world* (1979). J. Lough, *The contributors to the Encyclopédie* (1973), is a thoughtful brief study. An outstanding effort to explore the most important collaborative work of the French Enlightenment in a new way is R. Darnton, *The business of Enlightenment: a publishing history of the Encyclopédie, 1775–1800* (1979), while the same author's *Mesmerism and the end of the Enlightenment in France* (1968), has stimulated further research into the popular culture of the age. W. Roberts, *Morality and social class in eighteenth-*

century French literature and painting (1974), links the creative arts to political and social life.

G. R. Cragg has written an excellent study of the Enlightenment in its English setting, *Reason and authority in the eighteenth century* (1964), as has J. Redwood, *Reason, radicals, and religion: the age of Enlightenment in England, 1660–1750* (1976), while T. A. Horne, *The social thought of Bernard de Mandeville: virtue and commerce in early eighteenth-century England* (1978), sets one thinker in the framework of English commercial expansion of the era. A valuable introduction to the important Scottish thinkers of the age is A. C. Chitnis, *The Scottish Enlightenment: a social history* (1976), which may be supplemented by K. Haakonssen, *The science of a legislator: the natural jurisprudence of David Hume and Adam Smith* (1981). B. Semmel, *The Methodist Revolution* (1973), argues that Wesleyan theology was the English counterpart to the democratic stirrings in Europe and America. M. C. Jacob, *The radical Enlightenment: pantheists, freemasons, and republicans* (1981), explores radical ideas of English origin that flourished in Dutch literary and publishing circles.

Other books treating the relationship between religion and Enlightenment include G. R. Cragg, *The church and the age of reason** (1961), a volume in the Pelican History of the Church; J. M. Creed and J. S. Boys Smith, *Religious thought in the eighteenth century* (1934), primarily on English writers; C. E. Elwell, *The influence of the Enlightenment on the Catholic theory of education in France, 1750–1850* (1944); R. R. Palmer, *Catholics and unbelievers in eighteenth century France** (1939); and S. Todsvig, *Emanuel Swedenborg: scientist and mystic* (1948). F. E. Manuel discusses the attitudes of the age in *The eighteenth century confronts the gods** (1959), and in *The changing of the gods* (1983); and J. McManners examines a neglected theme in *Death and Enlightenment: changing attitudes to death among Christians and unbelievers in eighteenth century France* (1982). An important episode is studied in D. D. Bien, *The Calas affair: persecution, toleration, and heresy in eighteenth century Toulouse* (1960).

France under the Old Regime (Political and Economic)

C. B. A. Behrens, *The ancien régime** (1967), and E. N. Williams, *The ancien régime in Europe* (1970), both study the old regime for its own sake and not merely as a prologue to the revolutionary age. J. Lough, *An introduction to eighteenth-century France* (1960), is useful. The continuing financial crisis is explored in depth in J. F. Bosher, *French finances, 1770–1795: from business to bureacracy* (1970), and on Turgot, one may read D. Dakin, *Turgot and the ancien régime in France* (1965). Several good books on modern France begin with developments in the eighteenth century; among them are A. Cobban, *A history of modern France** (3 vols., 1957–1965), of which vol. I is *The old regime and revolution 1715–1799**; G. Wright, *France in modern times: 1760 to the present** (3rd ed., 1981), with outstanding bibliographical chapters throughout the book; and R. Price, *An economic history of modern France 1730–1914* (1981). For France under the old regime, one still reads with profit Alexis de Tocqueville's study (1856), available as *The old regime and the French Revolution** (1947), but the best introduction to French demographic, institutional, and social history is P. Goubert, *The ancien régime: French society, 1600–1750** (trans. and abr., 1974), cited in Chapter IV.

Three impressive special studies published in recent years are J. Kaplow, *The names of kings: Parisian laboring poor in the eighteenth century* (1973); O. Hufton, *The poor of eighteenth-century France, 1750–1789* (1974); and S. L. Kaplan, *Bread, politics and political economy in the reign of Louis XV* (2 vols., 1976). Among many other studies there are: G. T. Matthews, *The royal general farms in eighteenth-century France* (1957); G. P. Gooch, *Louis XV, the monarchy in decline* (1956); and two books on the Parlement of Paris by J. H. Shennan (1968) and B. Stone (1981). Various social classes are examined in F. L. Ford, *Robe and sword: the regrouping of the French aristocracy after Louis XIV** (1953); E. G. Barber, *The bourgeoisie in eighteenth century France** (1955); R. Forster, *The nobility of Toulouse in the eighteenth century* (1960); and the same author's two studies of noble families from the time of Louis XIV through the Revolution, *The house of Saulx-Tavanes* (1971), and *Merchants, landlords, magistrates: the Depont family in eighteenth-century France* (1980). Three other books deserve mention: R. Hahn, *The anatomy of a scientific institution: the Paris Academy of Sciences, 1666–1803* (1971), C. C. Gillispie, *Science and polity in France at the end of* the old régime (1981), and T. Gelfand, *Professionalizing modern medicine: Paris surgeons and medical science and institutions in the eighteenth century* (1980). J. F. Traer, *Marriage and the family in eighteenth century France* (1980), focuses mainly on legal questions.

Enlightened Despotism

An informative introductory synthesis is J. G. Gagliardo, *Enlightened despotism** (1967). L. Krieger, *An essay on the theory of enlightenment and despotism* (1975), is a difficult but rewarding analysis. A. Goodwin (ed.), *The European nobility in the eighteenth century* (1953), brings together an important collection of essays. Among many biographies of Frederick the Great, one may turn to G. P. Gooch, *Frederick the Great: the ruler, the writer, the man* (1947); G. Ritter, *Frederick the Great: a historical profile* (1954, trans. 1968), by the German scholar; and D. B. Horn, *Frederick the Great and the rise of Prussia* (1969). His bureaucracy is effectively examined in H. C. Johnson, *Frederick the Great and his officials* (1975), and in W. Hubatsch, *Frederick the Great of Prussia: absolutism and administration* (Men in Office series, trans. 1977). The best general account of German political fragmentation and cultural stirrings is W. G. Bruford, *Germany in the eighteenth century: the social background of the literary revival** (1935); an important study also is F. Hertz, *The development of the German public mind, a social history of German political sentiments, aspirations and ideas: the age of Enlightenment* (1962), part of a larger work. The nature of the Enlightenment and enlightened despotism in the Spanish framework is portrayed in R. Herr, *The eighteenth-century revolution in Spain* (1958), while the broader framework is presented in W. N. Hargreaves-Mawdsley, *Eighteenth-century Spain, 1700–1788: a political, diplomatic, and institutional history* (1979).

The Habsburg rulers between 1740 and 1792 may be approached through: E. Cruikshank, *Maria Theresa* (1969); P. P. Bernard, *Joseph II** (1968), a brief, balanced account; S. K. Padover, *The revolutionary emperor: Joseph the Second, 1741–90* (1934, 1967); and W. C. Langsam, *Francis the Good: the education of an emperor, 1768–1792* (1949). M. Maestro has written a solid biography of the Italian jurist and reformer who served the Austrian state, *Cesare Beccaria and the origins of penal reform* (1973).

Enlightened despotism in Russia is examined in an outstanding, judicious, large-scale study, I. de Madariaga, *Russia in the age of Catherine the Great** (1981), in which she portrays Catherine as giving her subjects reasonable government and greater personal freedom. There are other biographies of Catherine by I. Grey (1962), Z. Oldenbourg (1965), J. Haslip (1977), and V. Cronin (1978). G. S. Thomson, *Catherine the Great and the expansion of Russia* (Teach Yourself History series, 1947), remains a useful introduction. Other valuable studies of eighteenth-century Russia include M. Raeff, *Origins of the Russian intelligentsia: the eighteenth-century nobility** (1966); H. Rogger, *National consciousness in eighteenth-century Russia* (1960); P. Dukes, *Catherine the Great and the Russian nobility* (1966); D. Ransel, *The politics of Catherinean Russia* (1975); and R. Jones, *The emancipation of the Russian nobility, 1762–1785* (1973). Revolts and social stirrings in Russia may be studied in P. Avrich, *Russian rebels, 1600–1800* (1972), and in two books by J. Alexander on the uprising led by Pugachev, *Autocratic politics in a national crisis* (1969) and *Emperor of the Cossacks* (1973). G. L. Freeze, *The Russian Levites: parish clergy in the eighteenth century* (1977), goes well beyond its title in exploring church-state relations and other subjects.

The American Revolution and the Age of the Democratic Revolution

The attempt by R. R. Palmer, J. Godechot, and others to explore the American and French revolutions in a broader eighteenth-century revolutionary setting is described in more detail at the beginning of the next chapter. H. F. May, *The Enlightenment in America* (1976), ably studies the relationship between Enlightenment thought and such elements as Puritanism; of even broader scope is H. S. Commager, *The empire of reason: how Europe imagined and America realized the Enlightenment** (1977). Other efforts to examine North American civilization in the eighteenth century include L. B. Wright, *The Atlantic frontier: colonial American civilization, 1607–1763* (1947); M. Savelle, *Seeds of liberty: the genesis of the American mind* (1948); M. Kraus, *The Atlantic civilization: eighteenth-century origins* (1949); J. Greene, *The ambiguity of the American Revolution* (1968); and two books by B. Bailyn, *The ideological origins of the American Revolution* (1967) and *The origins of American politics* (1968). M. Beloff (ed.), *The debate on the American Revolution 1761–83* (1949), a collection of source materials, discusses the Revolution within the context of the British Empire, while C. L. Becker, *The Declaration of Independence: a study in the history of political ideas* (1922, 1942), is an engaging essay. There are numerous narrative and analytical accounts of the American Revolution; for discussions of current interpretations, see R. B. Morris, *The American Revolution reconsidered** (1967), and I. R. Christie and B. W. Labaree, *Empire or independence, 1760–1776: a British-American dialogue on the coming of the American Revolution* (1976).

Other important books that relate events in America to British internal politics include L. B. Namier, *England in the age of the American Revolution** (1930); G. H. Guttridge, *English Whiggism and the American Revolution* (1942); H. Butterfield, *George III, Lord North, and the people, 1779–80* (1949) and *George III and the historians* (1957); C. R. Ritcheson, *British politics and the American Revolution* (1954); A. B. Donoughue, *British politics and the American Revolution: the path to war, 1773–1775* (1964); J. R. Pole, *Political representation in England and the origins of the American Revolution* (1967); and H. T. Dickinson, *Liberty and property: political ideology in eighteenth-century Britain* (1978). In addition one may read R. Pares, *King George III and the politicians* (1953); J. S. Watson, *The reign of George III, 1760–1815* (1960); R. J. Whyte, *The age of George III* (1968); and J. Brooke, *King George III* (1972). P. D. G. Thomas, *Lord North* (1976), is a brief biography. J. Carswell, *From revolution to revolution: England, 1688–1776* (1973), may be compared with J. G. A. Pocock (ed.), *Three British revolutions, 1641, 1688, 1776** (1979). On parliamentary reform, see also G. Rudé, *Wilkes and political liberty* (1962); I. R. Christie, *Wilkes, Wyvill, and reform* (1963); C. Cone, *The English Jacobins: reformers in late eighteenth century England* (1968); and C. Bonwick, *English radicals and the American Revolution* (1977). A valuable overall account is I. R. Christie, *Wars and revolutions: Britain, 1760–1815* (1982).

On military and naval subjects, one may read J. Dull, *The French navy and American independence: a study of arms and diplomacy* (1975), and L. Kennett, *The French forces in America, 1780–1783* (1978). On diplomacy and international affairs, one may consult W. C. Stinchcombe, *The American Revolution and the French alliance* (1969); S. R. Bemis, *The diplomacy of the American Revolution* (1935); I. de Madariaga, *Britain, Russia, and the armed neutrality of 1780* (1962); and on the peace negotiations, R. B. Morris, *The peacemakers: the great powers and American independence* (1965). H. G. Nicholas, *The United States and Britain* (1975), is a perceptive essay on Anglo-American relations since 1776.

An excellent study, the sequel to an earlier volume, both cited earlier, is D. B. Davis, *The problem of slavery in the age of revolution, 1770–1823* (1975), and important on a related subject is R. Anstey, *The Atlantic slave trade and British abolition, 1760–1810* (1975).

Relations between France and America are discussed in L. Gottschalk and D. F. Lach, *Toward the French Revolution: Europe and America in the eighteenth-century world** (1973); A. O. Aldridge, *Franklin and his French contemporaries* (1957); D. Echevarria, *Mirage in the West: a history of the French image of American society to 1815** (1957); C. Lopez, *Mon cher papa: Franklin and the ladies of Paris* (1966); and A. Gerbi, *The dispute of the New World, 1750–1900* (1973), an amusing analysis of European arguments over the significance of the Americas for European life and thought. H. Dippel, *Germany and the American Revolution, 1770–1800: a sociohistorical investigation of late eighteenth century thinking* (1977), explores the impact of the events in America in the German states.

Problems and Readings*

Pamphlets relating to this chapter include R. Wines (ed.), *Enlightened despotism: reform or reaction?* (1967); P. Paret (ed.), *Frederick the Great: a profile* (1972); M. Raeff (ed.), *Catherine the Great: a profile* (1972); E. A. Reitan (ed.), *George III: tyrant or constitutional monarch?* (1964); and W. F. Church (ed.), *The influence of the Enlightenment on the French Revolution: creative, disastrous, or non-existent?* (rev., 1972). In the Anvil series, there are L. L. Snyder, *The age of reason* (1955); P. Gay, *Deism: an anthology* (1968); and M. Kraus, *The North Atlantic civilization* (1957). Two useful anthologies are I. Schneider (ed.), *The Enlightenment* (1965), and P. Gay, *The*

Enlightenment: a comprehensive anthology (1976).

IX: THE FRENCH REVOLUTION

The French Revolution and the Revolutionary Age

A. Goodwin (ed.), *The American and French revolutions, 1763–1793*, vol. VIII of the New Cambridge Modern History, has already been cited; its sequel volume, C. W. Crawley (ed.), *War and peace in an age of upheaval, 1793–1830* (1965), also is useful. Some stimulating surveys for the years beginning with the American and French revolutions are G. Rudé, *Revolutionary Europe, 1783–1815* (1964); F. J. Hobsbawm, *The age of revolution: Europe, 1789–1848* (1962); N. Hampson, *The first European revolution, 1776–1850* (1969); and C. Breunig, *The age of revolution and reaction, 1789–1850* (rev., 1977).

On the revolutionary developments in France, important general accounts include C. Brinton, *A decade of revolution, 1789–1799* (1934; rev., 1962) in the Langer series, critical of the Revolution; C. Lefebvre, *The French Revolution* (1951, 2 vols. in trans. 1962–1964), volume I carrying the story to 1793 and volume II to 1799, a balanced account by a distinguished French scholar; L. Gershoy, *The French Revolution and Napoleon* (1932; rev., 1964); J. M. Thompson, *The French Revolution* (1943); N. Hampson, *A social history of the French Revolution* (1963), covering more than its title implies; F. Furet and D. Richet, *The French Revolution* (trans. 1970); and A. Soboul, *The French Revolution, 1789–1799: from the storming of the Bastille to Napoleon* (trans. 1975), by a leading French historian of Marxist persuasion. Three excellent brief accounts are M. J. Sydenham, *The French Revolution* (1965); A. Goodwin, *The French Revolution* (1953); and J. M. Roberts, *The French Revolution* (1978). There are numerous older volumes now more important to historiography than to history by such writers of vastly differing viewpoints as J. Michelet, J. Jaurès, H. Taine, L. Madelin, P. Gaxotte, A. Aulard, and A. Mathiez. In that connection, A. Cobban, *The myth of the French Revolution* (1953) and *The social interpretation of the French Revolution* (1964), may be read and compared with F. Furet, *Interpreting the French Revolution* (trans. 1981). J. H. Stewart has collected many key documents in

A documentary survey of the French Revolution (1951), while R. Cobb has edited *French Revolution documents* (1966). A useful collection of essays is D. Johnson, *French society and the Revolution* (1976), and a unique collection of documents on the role of women in the era is D. G. Levy, H. B. Applewhite, and M. D. Johnson (eds. and translators), *Women in revolutionary Paris, 1789–1815* (1981).

Attention has been given in recent years to the Revolution as part of a European and transatlantic movement. The most extensive treatment of the subject is R. R. Palmer, *The age of the democratic revolution: a political history of Europe and America, 1760–1800* (2 vols., 1959–1964); the first volume, *The challenge*, carries the account to 1792, the second, *The struggle*, to 1800; see also by the same author, *The world of the French Revolution* (1970). Some of the conclusions of a French scholar, J. Godechot [*La grande nation* (2 vols., 1956), and other works], are available in summary form as *France and the Atlantic revolution, 1770–1799* (1965).

Developments within France

An excellent introduction to events beginning in 1789 and ably assessing the literature is W. Doyle, *Origins of the French Revolution* (1980). On the early events, one may read G. Lefebvre, *The coming of the French Revolution* (1939, trans. 1947); the same author's *The great fear of 1789: rural panic in revolutionary France* (1932, trans. 1982); and J. Godechot, *The taking of the Bastille: July 14, 1789* (trans. 1970). On the efforts to cope with the financial crisis, one should consult J. F. Bosher, *French finances, 1770–1793* (1970), cited in the previous chapter, and two books that assess the efforts at reform: R. D. Harris, *Necker: reform statesman of the ancien régime* (1979), and B. Stone, *The Parlement of Paris, 1774–1789* (1981), cited in the last chapter. Two important aspects of the impact of the Revolution are studied in J. McManners, *The French Revolution and the church* (1969), and P. Higonnet, *Class, ideology, and the rights of nobles during the French Revolution* (1981). The counterrevolution may be studied in P. Beik, *The French Revolution seen from the right . . . 1789–1799* (1956) and in J. Godechot, *The counter-revolution: doctrine and action, 1789–1804* (trans. 1971). A special subject is examined in C. L. Donakowski, *A muse for the masses: ritual and music in an age of democratic revolution* (1977).

The Lower Classes, the Reign of Terror, and Related Themes

Considerable attention in recent years has been given to the role of the poorer classes in the social history of the times. Here one may read R. C. Cobb, *The police and the people: French popular protest, 1789–1820* (1970); Cobb has also tried to reconstruct the life of the poor by examining four suicides in *Death in Paris* (1978). A. Forrest, *The French Revolution and the poor* (1981), examines the welfare legislation adopted in the revolutionary decade.

The coming of the war and the radicalization of the Revolution may be studied in two books by M. Sydenham: *The Girondins* (1961), and *The first French republic 1792–1804* (1974); A. Patrick, *The men of the first French republic: political alignments in the National Convention of 1792* (1972); and M. L. Kennedy, *The Jacobin clubs in the French Revolution: the first years* (1981). The Terror and related subjects are studied in R. R. Palmer, *Twelve who ruled: the year of the Terror in the French Revolution** (1941, 1958); A. Soboul, *The Parisian sans-culottes and the French Revolution, 1793–1794* (trans. 1964); G. Rudé, *The crowd in the French Revolution** (1959); and R. B. Rose, *The enragés: socialists of the French Revolution?* (1965). More specialized studies include C. Lucas, *The structure of the Terror* (1973); D. M. Greer, *The incidence of the Terror during the French Revolution: a statistical interpretation* (1935), a revealing study of who was actually executed and by what procedures; its sequel, *The incidence of emigration during the French Revolution* (1951); and R. C. Cobb's impressive *Paris and its provinces, 1792–1802* (1975). Two books focusing on popular unrest in both France and England are G. A. Williams, *Artisans and sans-culottes* (1968), and G. Rudé, *The crowd in history: a study of popular disturbances in France and England, 1730–1848* (1964). J. Talmon, *The origins of totalitarian democracy* (1952), sees the roots of later dictatorships in these years, while C. Brinton, *The anatomy of revolution** (1938), is a comparative study of four revolutions: the English, American, French, and Russian. C. Tilly, *The Vendée* (1964), an important sociological analysis of the counterrevolution of 1793, may be supplemented by G. Lewis, *The second Vendée: the continuity of counter-revolution in the department of the Gard, 1789–1815* (1978). The most useful recent study of the Directory is

M. Lyons, *France under the Directory* (1975), while the best treatment of the socialist extremist crushed by the Directory is R. B. Rose, *Gracchus Babeuf: the first revolutionary communist* (1978), a balanced and sensitive assessment. I. Woloch, *Jacobin legacy: the democratic movement under the Directory* (1970), analyzes the more numerous constitutional democrats.

Biographies

J. M. Thompson, *Leaders of the French Revolution* (1932), gives sketches of the outstanding personalities, which may be filled out with the following biographical accounts: the somewhat sensational A. Vallentin, *Mirabeau* (1948), which does not entirely supersede L. Barthou, *Mirabeau* (1913); G. C. Van Deusen, *Sieyès: his life and his nationalism* (1932); D. L. Dowd, *Pageant-master of the republic: Jacques-Louis David and the French Revolution* (1948), on art and propaganda during the period; L. Gottschalk, *Jean-Paul Marat: a study in radicalism* (1927, 1966); H. Dupré, *Lazare Carnot, republican patriot* (1940), on the "organizer of victory"; and N. Hampson, *Danton* (1978), which depicts him as a pragmatic and somewhat opportunistic political figure. D. F. Hawke, *Paine* (1974), stressing the revolutionist's career in America, England, and France, may be compared with E. Foner, *Tom Paine and the American Revolution* (1976). Mme. Roland is studied in G. May, *Madame Roland and the age of revolution* (1970). The multivolumed, detailed biography of Lafayette by L. Gottschalk and M. Maddox concludes in its ninth volume (1973) by taking the account to July 1790.

The best-rounded biography of the most prominent figure on the Committee of Public Safety is J. M. Thompson, *Robespierre* (2 vols., 1935), on whom the same author has an excellent brief study in the Teach Yourself History series, *Robespierre and the French Revolution** (1953). One also may read N. Hampson, *The life and opinions of Maximilien Robespierre* (1974), and G. Rudé, *Robespierre: portrait of a revolutionary democrat* (1975). Rudé has also edited *Robespierre** in the Great Lives Observed series (1967). A provocative but not convincing psychoanalytical study is M. Gallo, *Robespierre the incorruptible: a psychobiography* (trans. 1971). On Robespierre's associates, E. N. Curtis has written *Saint-Just: colleague of Robespierre* (1935), and L.

Gershoy, *Bertrand Barère: a reluctant terrorist* (1962).

War and Diplomacy

The war and various diplomatic aspects are discussed in S. T. Ross, *European diplomatic history, 1789–1815: France against Europe** (1969); the same author's *Quest for victory: French military strategy, 1792–1799* (1973); P. Mackesy, *Statesmen at war: the strategy of overthrow, 1798–1799* (1974), which studies the Second Coalition; II. Mitchell, *The underground war against revolutionary France, 1794–1800* (1965), which traces British diplomacy and espionage; and J. Ehrman, *The British government and commercial negotiations with Europe, 1783–1793* (1962). H. Ragsdale, *Détente in the Napoleonic era: Bonaparte and the Russians* (1980), focuses on the years 1799–1801. Useful for this and the chapter that follows is T. M. Iiams, *Peacemaking from Vergennes to Napoleon: French foreign relations in the revolutionary era, 1774–1814* (1979). On the emergence of Bonaparte, one may turn to G. Ferrero, *The gamble: Bonaparte in Italy, 1796–1797* (1939); P. G. Elgood, *Bonaparte's adventure in Egypt* (1931); and J. C. Herold's vivid *Bonaparte in Egypt* (1962). Additional books on Napoleon are listed in the following chapter.

Effects of the Revolution outside France

The impact of the Revolution and of subsequent events in France is examined in J. M. Diefendorf, *Businessmen and politics in the Rhineland, 1789–1834* (1980); in K. Epstein, *The genesis of German conservatism* (1966), a rewarding study; and in the older book of G. P. Gooch, *Germany and the French Revolution* (1920), and his subsequent work, *Studies in German history* (1948); other books on the German reactions are cited in the following chapter. Events in the Netherlands are examined in S. Schama, *Patriots and liberators: revolution and government in the Netherlands, 1780–1813* (1977), while the Irish rebellion of 1798 is placed in its European setting in M. Elliott, *Partners in revolution: the United Irishmen in France* (1982), and Ireland in this age in general is ably treated in R. B. McDowell, *Ireland in the age of imperialism and revolution, 1760–1801* (1979). For effects in Haiti and the black world, see C. L. R. James, *The black Jacobins: Toussaint l'Ouverture and the San Domingo Revolution* (1938), which must be supplemented by D. P. Geggus, *Slavery, war, and revolution: the British occupation of Saint Domingue, 1793–1798* (1982). An outstanding study of British reaction to the revolutionary events is A. Goodwin, *The friends of liberty: the English democratic movement in the age of the French Revolution* (1979).

Problems and Readings*

Studies in various problems series that relate to this chapter are R. W. Greenlaw (ed.), *The social origins of the French Revolution* (1975); P. Amann (ed.), *The eighteenth century revolution: French or Western?* (1963); R. Bienvenu (ed.), *The ninth of Thermidor: the fall of Robespierre* (1968); and S. Ross (ed.), *The French Revolution: conflict or continuity?* (1971). For a comprehensive survey examining divergent appraisals of all aspects of the Revolution, see F. A. Kafker and M. Laux (eds.), *The French Revolution: conflicting interpretations* (rev., 1983); and for sociologically oriented analyses of various problems, see J. Kaplow (ed.), *New perspectives on the French Revolution: readings in historical sociology* (1965). In the Anvil series, L. Gershoy provides an essay and documents in *The era of the French Revolution, 1789–1799: ten years that shook the world* (1957). A. Cobban has edited *The debate on the French Revolution, 1789–1799* (1949).

X: NAPOLEONIC EUROPE

Three general surveys of Europe in the age of Napoleon are G. Bruun, *Europe and the French imperium, 1799–1814** (1938; rev., 1957), in the Langer series; J. Godechot, B. Hyslop, and D. Dowd, *The Napoleonic era in Europe* (trans. 1971); and O. Connelly, *The epoch of Napoleon: France and Europe** (1972); but see also many of the books on the Revolution cited in the previous chapter that continue into the Napoleonic age. P. Geyl, *Napoleon: for and against** (1949), is a brilliant interpretation by the Dutch historian of what French historians since 1815 have said about Napoleon. *Napoleon self-revealed in 300 selected letters* (1934), edited by J. M. Thompson, gives Bonaparte's own words, as does I. C. Herold (ed.), *The mind of Napoleon* (1955); the same author has written a colorful account of the period in *The age of Napoleon* (1963).

Napoleon and Napoleonic France

For Napoleonic France, covering political, economic, and social aspects there is now available L. Bergeron, *France under Napoleon** (1972 trans. 1981), by a French scholar; while I. Collins, *Napoleon and his parliaments, 1800–1815* (1979), examines the survival of political activity in these years.

Of the innumerable biographies and biographically oriented studies of Napoleon, the following are recommended: J. M. Thompson, *Napoleon Bonaparte: his rise and fall* (1952); G. Lefebvre, *Napoleon* (2 vols., 1935; trans. 1969), a major work by a distinguished French historian, the first volume carrying the story to Tilsit, the second to Waterloo; and two books by F. M. Markham, *Napoleon** (1964) and *Napoleon and the awakening of Europe** (Teach Yourself History series, 1954). R. Holtman, *The Napoleonic revolution** (1967), is a brief, judicious assessment. E. V. Tarlé, *Bonaparte* (1937), is a Marxist view of unusual interest, emphasizing economic influences.

Napoleon as a military leader may be studied in G. E. Rothenberg, *The art of warfare in the age of Napoleon* (1978), an excellent overview; D. G. Chandler, *The campaigns of Napoleon* (1966); M. Glover, *The Napoleonic wars: an illustrated history, 1792–1815* (1978); C. Duffy, *Austerlitz, 1805* (1977); H. T. Parker, *Three Napoleonic battles* (rev., 1983); and C. Hibbert, *Waterloo: Napoleon's last campaign* (1967). That Napoleon was defeated by British sea power was the theme of A. T. Mahan's *The influence of sea power on the French Revolution and Empire* (1892, many eds.), a subject treated more recently, and carried down to the contemporary era, in P. M. Kennedy, *The rise and fall of British naval mastery* (1976), and in J. Horsfield, *The art of leadership in war: the Royal Navy from the age of Nelson to the end of World War II* (1980). Related topics are covered in B. Mackesy, *War in the Mediterranean, 1803–1810* (1957), and in R. Glover, *Britain at bay: defence against Bonaparte, 1803–1814* (1973).

Other studies of the Napoleonic age include E. Heckscher, *The continental system* (1922); H. C. Deutsch, *The genesis of Napoleonic imperialism* (1938); and H. H. Walsh, *The Concordat of 1801* (1933). Biographical studies of Talleyrand have been written by A. Duff Cooper* (1932), C. Brinton* (1936), E. Dard (1937), L. Madelin (1948), and J. Orieux (1970, trans. 1974);

and S. Zweig has written *Joseph Fouché: the portrait of a politician* (1930).

On the last phase of Napoleon's career, E. Saunders has written a lively account, *The hundred days* (1964), and A. Brett-James has edited an anthology of eyewitness accounts under the same title (1964). Three biographies of notable women of the era are: E. J. Knapton, *Empress Josephine** (1963); the same author's *The lady of the Holy Alliance; the life of Julie de Krüdener* (1939); and J. C. Herold's *Mistress to an age** (1955), on the influential Mme. de Stael. Napoleon's family is studied in O. Connelly, *The gentle Bonaparte: a biography of Joseph, Napoleon's elder brother* (1968), and in F. Markham, *The Bonapartes* (1975). B. Weider and D. Hopgood, *The murder of Napoleon* (1982), tries to unravel the mystery of how Napoleon died.

Britain in the Time of Napoleon

The patriotic British volumes of A. Bryant, *The years of endurance, 1793–1802* (1942), *The years of victory, 1802–1812* (1944), and *The age of elegance, 1812–1822* (1950), treat the period in detail. The war years receive special attention in J. Ehrman, *William Pitt the Younger* (2 vols. to date, 1969, 1983). The impact of the war and other economic changes of the age are explored in C. Ensley, *British society and the French wars, 1793–1815* (1980), and in A. D. Harvey, *Britain in the early nineteenth century* (1978). C. Oman [Lenanton], *Britain against Napoleon* (1944), is useful; the same author also has written a biography of Nelson (1946), as have C. S. Forester (1929), W. James (1948), R. Grenfell (1949), and others. P. Guedalla (1931) and R. Aldington (1943) have each written good popular biographies of Wellington.

Germany in the Time of Napoleon

Especially useful for Prussian and German nationalism during this era are H. Kohn, *Prelude to nation-states: the French and German experience, 1789–1815* (1967); F. Meinecke, *The age of German liberation, 1795–1815* (trans. 1977); J. G. Gagliardo, *Reich and nation: the Holy Roman Empire as idea and reality, 1763–1806* (1980), on the political writings of the period; H. Brunschwig, *Enlightenment and romanticism in eighteenth-century Prussia* (1974), on politics, thought, and feeling during the revolutionary years; and P. Paret, *Clausewitz and the state* (1976).

For the political, diplomatic, and military developments of the age, one may read G. S. Ford, *Stein and the era of reform in Prussia, 1807–1815* (1922); C. de Grunwald, *Napoleon's nemesis: the life of Baron Stein* (1963); H. A. L. Fisher, *Studies in Napoleonic statesmanship: Germany* (1903); W. O. Shanahan, *Prussian military reforms, 1786–1813* (1945); and the acute assessment of W. M. Simon, *The failure of the Prussian reform movement, 1807–1819* (1955). The able and cynical Gentz has been the subject of biographies by C. S. B. Buckland (1933), P. R. Sweet (1941), and G. Mann (1946).

Other Countries in Napoleonic Times

B. Perkins has written a three-volume study of Anglo-American relations in the three decades from 1795 to 1823: *The first rapprochement* (1955), *Prologue to war* (1961), and *Castlereagh and Adams* (1964). The general diplomatic study of H. C. Allen, *Great Britain and the United States . . . 1783–1952* (1955), is valuable. The American domestic scene is presented in M. Smelser, *The democratic republic, 1801–1815* (1968); and a good account of the U.S.-British military conflict is R. Horsman, *The War of 1812* (1969). Other ramifications in the Western Hemisphere during the revolutionary era are examined in W. S. Robertson, *The life of Miranda* (2 vols., 1929) and *France and Latin American independence* (1939). On Napoleonic influences in other countries, the following also may be mentioned: A. Lobanov-Rostovsky, *Russia and Europe 1789–1825* (1947); E. Tarlé, *Napoleon's invasion of Russia, 1812* (1942), by a leading Soviet historian; G. B. McClellan, *Venice and Bonaparte* (1931); O. Connelly, *Napoleon's satellite kingdoms* (1965); and R. J. Rath, *The fall of the Napoleonic kingdom of Italy* (1941). The best account of Spain in the Napoleonic era is G. H. Lovett, *Napoleon and the birth of modern Spain* (2 vols., 1965). M. Glover, *The Peninsular War, 1807–1814* (1974), is illuminating for the military events, and J. K. Severn, *A Wellesley affair: Richard Marquess Wellesley and the conduct of Anglo-Spanish diplomacy, 1809–1812* (1981), for the diplomatic background.

Wartime Diplomacy and the Congress of Vienna

Excellent guides on the diplomacy of these years are C. K. Webster, *The foreign policy of Castlereagh, 1812–1815: Britain and the reconstruction of Europe* (1931); C. S. B. Buckland, *Metternich and the British government from 1809 to 1813* (1932), and his shorter parallel study on Gentz (1933); L. I. Strakhovsky, *Alexander I of Russia: the man who defeated Napoleon* (1947); and A. Palmer, *Alexander I: tsar of war and peace* (1975). E. E. Kraehe, *Metternich's German policy*, vol. I, *The contest with Napoleon, 1799–1814* (1963), and vol. II, *The Congress of Vienna, 1814–1815* (1983), is a highly informative and detailed account.

For the Congress of Vienna, one may read C. K. Webster, *The Congress of Vienna, 1814–1815* (1919), a technical study; G. Ferrero, *The reconstruction of Europe: Talleyrand and the Congress of Vienna, 1814–1815* (1914); and on a special subject, H. A. Straus, *The attitude of the Congress of Vienna toward nationalism in Germany, Italy, and Poland* (1949). Important for this and for the chapter that follows on postwar diplomacy are H. Nicolson, *The Congress of Vienna: a study in allied unity, 1812–1822** (1946), and H. Kissinger, *A world restored: Metternich, Castlereagh and the problem of peace, 1812–1822* (1957), by an astute student of contemporary international affairs.

Problems and Readings*

The best problem study here is the volume by P. Geyl, *Napoleon: for and against* (1949), cited earlier. To it should be added D. H. Pinkney (ed.), *Napoleon: historical enigma* (1969). Some of the problem studies mentioned in the previous chapter relate also to Napoleon's impact on Europe.

XI: REACTION VERSUS PROGRESS, 1815–1848

The resetting of European institutions after the great French outburst in many ways marked the opening of a new historical era. There are numerous general, national, and topical histories, accordingly, that take their starting point in 1815; some that begin in 1789 or slightly earlier are also included here. A number of general works are also listed in the introductory section of this bibliography and should be consulted. For comparative social and economic data for the European countries, B. R. Mitchell, *Euro-*

*pean historical statistics, 1750–1970** (rev. and abr., 1978), cited earlier, is valuable, as is C. Cook and J. Paxton, *European political facts* (3 vols., 1980), covering the years 1789 to the present.

Europe after 1815

The most useful general guides to the era of reconstruction and reorientation after 1815 are two volumes in the Langer series: F. B. Artz, *Reaction and revolution, 1814–1832** (1934), and W. L. Langer, *Political and social upheaval, 1832–1852** (1969); and a volume by G. de Bertier de Sauvigny, *Metternich and his times* (1959, trans. 1967). There are valuable sections in vol. IX of the New Cambridge Modern History, C. W. Crawley (ed.), *War and Peace in an age of upheaval, 1793–1830* (1965), and for this and the following two chapters in vol. X, J. P. T. Bury (ed.), *The zenith of European power, 1830–1870* (1960), with overviews for each volume by the editors. There are informative chapters also in C. Morazé (ed.), *The nineteenth century, 1775 to 1905* (1977), vol. V of the UNESCO History of Mankind. Brief treatments in various historical series include J. Droz, *Europe between revolutions, 1815–1848** (1967); J. Roberts, *Revolution and improvement: the Western world, 1775–1847* (1976); J. L. Talmon, *Romanticism and revolution in Europe, 1815–1848** (1967); H. Hearder, *Europe in the nineteenth century, 1830–1880** (1966); and B. D. Gooch, *Europe in the nineteenth century* (1970). E. J. Hobsbawm has written a provocative Marxist survey, *The age of revolution: Europe, 1789–1848** (1962), and C. Morazé develops an important theme in *The triumph of the middle classes** (trans. 1966). For all aspects of European rural change in the late eighteenth and nineteenth centuries, there is an admirable study by J. Blum, *The end of the old order in rural Europe** (1978). On demographic changes, M. W. Flynn, *The European demographic system, 1500–1820* (1981), already cited for Chapter III, carries his study into these years. For the papacy in the revolutionary ferment of the age, one may read E. E. Y. Hales, *Revolution and papacy, 1769–1846* (1960), and O. Chadwick, *The popes and European revolution* (1981).

For an introduction to selected aspects of the social history of the age, there are two volumes by J. Gillis, *The development of European society, 1770–1870* (1977), and *Youth and history: tradition and change in European age relations, 1770 to the present* (rev., 1981). C. Tilly, L. Tilly, and R. Tilly, *The rebellious century, 1830–1930* (1975), is a sociological analysis of collective action and violence. The growth and development of education may be studied in F. Ringer, *Education and society in modern Europe* (1979); C. E. McClelland, *State, society, and university in Germany, 1700–1914* (1980); and L. Stone (ed.), *The university in society* (2 vols., 1974), cited earlier. For the history of women, there are available P. Branca, *Women in Europe since 1750* (1978); P. Robertson, *An experience of women: patterns and change in nineteenth-century Europe* (1982); and the essays in S. Delamont and L. Duffin (eds.), *The nineteenth-century woman: her cultural and physical world* (1978), focusing in various ways on constraints interfering with full autonomy. The same subject is treated comparatively by a British scholar in R. J. Evans, *The feminists: women's emancipation movements in Europe, America, and Australia, 1840–1920* (1977). On the transformation of values in the various social classes, one may read J. M. Phayer, *Sexual liberation and religion in nineteenth-century Europe* (1977).

National Histories: Britain

The story of how Britain avoided revolution in these years is admirably explored in N. Gash, *Aristocracy and people: Britain, 1815–1865** (New History of England series, 1979). Other accounts focusing on the nineteenth century include A. Wood, *Nineteenth century Britain, 1815–1914* (1960); D. Thomson, *England in the nineteenth century** (Pelican series, 1950, 1964); and R. W. Seton-Watson, *Britain in Europe, 1789–1914; a survey of foreign policy* (1937). P. Gregg, *Modern Britain: a social and economic history since 1760** (1967), and R. K. Webb, *Modern England: from the eighteenth century to the present** (rev., 1980), are especially useful as general accounts. E. Halévy's classic, *History of the English people in the nineteenth century* (6 vols., 1912 ff.), is a work of breadth and imagination by a French scholar, and the older account of G. M. Trevelyan, *British history in the nineteenth century and after* [1782–1919] (1922, reissued 1937), may also be read with profit. Many other books on British economic and social history are listed below. A valuable bibliographical guide for the first half of the century is L. M. Brown and I. R. Christie (eds.), *Bibliography of British history, 1789–1851* (1977); a volume (1976) in the same series, H. J. Hanham (ed.), covers the years 1851 to 1914.

France

A. Cobban, *A history of modern France** (3 vols., 1957–1965), and G. Wright, *France in modern times: 1760 to the present** (3rd ed., 1981), both mentioned in Chapter VIII, are especially useful as general histories, as are the histories by P. A. Gagnon* (1968) and D. J. Harvey* (1968). Two books that take the post-Napoleonic years as their starting points are J. P. T. Bury, *France, 1814–1940: a history* (rev., 1969), a balanced survey, and D. W. Brogan, *The French nation, 1814–1940: from Napoleon to Pétain** (1957), brilliant but often difficult for the general reader. On French society and social developments, there is the somewhat schematic G. Dupeux, *French society, 1789–1970* (trans. 1976), and on education, the informative J. N. Moody, *French education since Napoleon* (1978). A special subject in diplomatic history is explored by a distinguished French historian, J.-B. Duroselle, in *France and the United States: from the beginnings to the present* (1978).

Most recent writings on economic development and policies tend to dispel the traditional picture of French economic retardation; one may turn to F. Caron, *An economic history of modern France* (trans. 1979); two books by R. Price, *The economic modernization of France* (1975), and *An economic history of modern France, 1730–1914* (1981); R. E. Cameron, *France and the economic development of Europe, 1800–1914* (1961, 1968); and P. O. Brien and C. Keyder, *Economic growth in Britain and France, 1780–1914* (1978). Two specialized studies are C. E. Freedeman, *Joint-stock enterprise in France, 1807–1867: from privileged company to modern corporation* (1979), and H. Clout, *Agriculture in France on the eve of the railway age* (1980).

On labor, there is an admirable study, W. H. Sewell, *Work and revolution in France: the language of labor from the old regime to 1848** (1980), which traces working-class ideology to the craft workshops. P. N. Stearns explores class relationships in *Paths to authority: the middle class and the industrial labor force in France, 1820–1848* (1978), while E. Shorter and C. Tilly, *Strikes in France, 1830–1968* (1974),

is a sociological examination of labor unrest in this and later periods.

For France in the years immediately after Napoleon, the best introductions are F. B. Artz, *France under the Bourbon Restoration, 1814–1830* (1931), and G. de Bertier de Sauvigny, *The Bourbon Restoration* (1955, trans. 1966). The somewhat anecdotal J. Lucas-Dubreton, *The Restoration and the July Monarchy* (1929), may be compared with M. R. D. Leys, *Between two Empires* (1955). Rising discontents are studied in A. B. Spitzer, *Old hatreds and young hopes: the French Carbonari against the Bourbon Restoration* (1971), and in D. L. Rader, *The journalists and the July Revolution in France* (1973); and for the July Revolution, an outstanding account is D. H. Pinkney, *The French revolution of 1830* (1972). Subsequent labor stirrings are ably studied in R. J. Bezucha, *The Lyon uprising of 1834: social and political conflict in the early July Monarchy* (1974), and focusing on population growth and other pressures in Paris, there is L. Chevalier, *Laboring classes and dangerous classes in Paris during the first half of the nineteenth century* (trans. 1973).

Of J. M. S. Allison's older studies of nineteenth-century France, the widest in scope is his *Monsieur Thiers* (1932). Centering around Guizot, another historian-statesman, there is an admirable study, D. Johnson, *Guizot: aspects of French history, 1787–1874* (1963); and on Guizot and others, S. Mellon, *The political uses of history: a study of historians in the French Restoration* (1958). For a biography of Charles X, one may read V. D. Beach, *Charles X of France: his life and times* (1971), and for Louis Philippe, one may turn to T. Howarth, *Citizen-King* (1961). Insight into the relationships of science to the economy and to society is provided in M. Crosland, *Gay-Lussac: scientist and bourgeois* (1978). Conservative ideas and activities are examined in P. Spencer, *Politics of belief in nineteenth-century France* (1954); P. N. Stearns, *Priest and revolutionary: Lamennais and the dilemma of French Catholicism* (1967); D. Porch, *Army and revolution: France, 1815–1848* (1974); and R. Rémond, *The right wing in France: from 1815 to de Gaulle* (1954, trans. 1966), useful for this period on into the twentieth century. A. Dansette, *The religious history of modern France* (2 vols., 1948–1951, trans. 1961), is also important in this connection; the first volume covers the years from the Revolution to 1870. G. D.

Painter, *Chateaubriand: a biography* (1978), the first volume of a projected three-volume study, vividly portrays a luminary of the age. Special subjects are examined in I. Collins, *The government and the newspaper press in France, 1814–1881* (1959), and in T. D. Beck, *French legislators, 1880–1834: a study in quantitative history* (1974), analyzing the French lawmakers.

Germany

In addition to H. Holborn, *History of modern Germany* (3 vols., 1959–1968), there are numerous general histories by, among others, V. Valentin, E. J. Passant, K. S. Pinson, A. J. P. Taylor, M. Dill, Jr., W. Carr, G. Mann, E. Vermeil, and H. M. Pachter. Among books that focus on political and economic issues for these years the following are recommended: A. Ramm, *Germany, 1789–1919: a political history* (1967), with considerable attention to political thought; T. Hamerow, *Restoration, revolution, and reaction: economics and politics in Germany, 1815–1871** (1958); R. H. Thomas, *Liberalism, nationalism and the German intellectuals, 1822–1847* (1952); and M. Kitchen, *The political economy of Germany, 1815–1914* (1978). Two outstanding studies on the failure of German liberal democracy to triumph before time ran out in 1914 are J. J. Sheehan, *German liberalism in the nineteenth century* (1978), and J. L. Snell and H. A. Schmitt, *The democratic movement in Germany, 1789–1914* (1976). L. Krieger, *The German idea of freedom* (1957), traces the concept with much insight from the eighteenth century onward. Political manipulation is explored in G. L. Mosse, *The nationalization of the masses: political symbolism and mass movements in Germany from the Napoleonic wars through the Third Reich* (1975).

Austria, Poland, Greece, Spain, Italy, and Other Countries

On the Habsburg monarchy after 1815, the best study is C. A. Macartney, *The Habsburg empire, 1790–1918* (1969), a masterful survey. Recommended also are A. Wandruszka, *The house of Habsburg* (1956, trans. 1964); A. J. P. Taylor, *The Habsburg monarchy, 1809–1918** (1943, 1948 revision changes some conclusions), less paradoxical than his history of Germany; and R. Kann, *The multinational empire: nationalism and national reform in the Habsburg monarchy, 1840–*

1918 (2 vols., 1950–1964), and his shorter *A history of the Habsburg empire, 1526–1918* (1974). An informative brief introduction is B. Jelavich, *The Habsburg empire in European affairs, 1814–1918** (1969). Useful for economic developments are three books written jointly by two Hungarian scholars, I. T. Berend and G. Ranki: *East Central Europe in the nineteenth and twentieth centuries* (1977), *Hungary: a century of economic development* (1974), and *Economic development in East Central Europe in the nineteenth and twentieth centuries* (1974). Additional titles are cited in Chapters XIII and XIV.

Other European countries in the years 1815 to 1848 are treated in numerous books. For Belgium and the Dutch Netherlands in this and subsequent years, a discerning account by an eminent Dutch historian is E. H. Kossman, *The low countries, 1780–1940* (Oxford History of Modern Europe, 1978). For Poland, in addition to the books cited earlier in Chapter V, there are available R. F. Leslie (ed.), *The history of Poland since 1863* (1980), which is a collaborative sequel volume to the older Cambridge History of Poland; R. F. Leslie, *Polish politics and the revolution of November 1830* (1956); and the relevant chapters in P. S. Wandycz, *The United States and Poland* (American Foreign Policy Library series, 1980), covering many political, cultural, and demographic topics. On Greece, the best recent survey is R. Clogg, *A short history of modern Greece** (1979), balanced and authoritative; useful also are C. M. Woodhouse, *A short history of modern Greece* (1968), and J. Campbell and P. Sherrard, *Modern Greece* (1968). For the Balkans and southeastern Europe in general, see, in addition to books cited for Chapter V, C. Jelavich and B. Jelavich, *The establishment of the Balkan national states, 1804–1920* (1977), a comprehensive and informative account, and L. S. Stavrianos, *The Balkans since 1815** (Berkshire series, 1965), a brief survey. A successful study of Serbian history is M. B. Petrovich, *A history of modern Serbia, 1804–1918* (2 vols., 1976).

For Russia, a volume that takes its start in these years is J. N. Westwood, *Endurance and endeavor in Russian history, 1812–1980** (rev., 1982). A major study of the ruler of Russia after 1825 is W. B. Lincoln, *Nicholas I: emperor and autocrat of all the Russias* (1978). Valuable for European attitudes toward the Balkans and the Ottoman Empire is M. S. Anderson, *The Eastern question, 1774–1923* (1966).

For Spain, see especially R. Carr, *Spain, 1808–1939* (1966), a volume in the Oxford History of Modern Europe; R. Herr, *Spain** (1971); and S. G. Payne, *History of Spain and Portugal* (2 vols., 1973), cited earlier. For Italy, one may turn to S. Woolf, *A history of Italy, 1700–1860: the social constraints of political change* (1979), which recounts Italy's reemergence and makes available recent Italian scholarship; D. Mack Smith, *Italy: a modern history* (1969), a vivid and lively account; C. M. Lovett, *The democratic movement in Italy, 1830–1876* (1982); S. B. Clough, *The economic history of modern Italy* (1964); and S. B. Clough and S. Saladino, *A history of modern Italy: documents, readings, and commentary* (1968). [Additional books on the nineteenth-century developments in these countries are cited in connection with international politics at the end of this chapter and in the next three chapters.]

Industrial Revolution

An authoritative treatment is found in the collaborative Cambridge Economic History of Europe, vol. VI, *The industrial revolutions and after* (2 parts, 1965), to which D. S. Landes' important contribution has been published separately, in expanded form, as *The unbound Prometheus: technological change and industrial development in Western Europe from 1750 to the present** (1969). Other informative accounts are C. M. Cipolla (ed.), *The emergence of industrial societies* (2 parts, 1973), vols. III and IV of the Fontana Economic History of Europe; T. Kemp, *Industrialization in nineteenth century Europe* (1969); A. S. Milward and S. B. Saul, *The economic development of continental Europe, 1780–1870* (1973); W. O. Henderson, *The industrialization of Europe* (1973); and S. Pollard, *Peaceful conquest: the industrialization of Europe, 1760–1970** (1981). The social and political implications behind the growth of an industrial civilization are examined with insight in J. McManners, *European history: men, machines, and freedom** (1967).

The complexities of the industrial Revolution and its origins also may be approached through a number of brief, informative books: T. S. Ashton, *The Industrial Revolution, 1760–1830** (1948); P. Deane, *The first Industrial Revolution** (2nd ed., 1979); G. N. Clark, *The idea of the Industrial Revolution* (1953); M. W. Flinn, *Origins of the Industrial Revolution* (1966); and R. M. Hartwell (ed.), *The causes of the Industrial*

Revolution in England (1967). Advanced technical studies investigating rates of industrial growth in Britain include: W. G. Hoffmann, *British industry, 1700–1950* (trans. 1955); W. W. Rostow, *British economy of the nineteenth century* (1948); P. Deane and W. A. Cole, *British economic growth, 1688–1959: trends and structure* (1962); R. M. Hartwell, *The Industrial Revolution and economic growth* (1971); and A. E. Musson, *The growth of British industry* (1978), which does not see a "take-off" or spurt in this period. Deane and B. R. Mitchell also have edited *Abstract of British historical statistics* (1962). Rostow has utilized the British experience as a model for other areas in *The process of economic growth* (1952) and *The stages of economic growth: a non-communist manifesto** (1960).

There are many older studies of the rise of industrialism in Britain that have been superseded, including the classic P. Mantoux, *The Industrial Revolution in the eighteenth century** (1906, reissued 1961, with introduction by T. S. Ashton). British economic history in these years is studied in detail by T. S. Ashton, *The economic history of England: the eighteenth century* (1955); W. H. B. Court, *A concise economic history of Britain** (1954); and J. H. Clapham, *An economic history of modern Britain* (3 vols., 1926–1938). One also may turn to J. D. Chambers, *The workshop of the world: British economic history from 1820 to 1880** (rev., 1969); S. G. Checkland, *The rise of industrial society in England, 1815–1885* (1964); W. O. Henderson, *Britain and industrial Europe, 1750–1870* (1954); and P. Mathias, *The first industrial nation: an economic history of Britain, 1700–1914* (1969). The collaborative history, R. Floud and D. McCloskey (eds.), *The economic history of Britain since 1700** (2 vols., 1981), the first volume to 1860 and the second to the present, cited in Chapter VI, is especially important. S. Pollard and C. Holmes have edited a volume of documents, *The process of industrialization, 1750–1870* (1968).

Changes in British agriculture are analyzed in R. E. Prothero [Lord Ernle], *English farming, past and present* (5th ed., 1936); M. E. Seebohm, *The evolution of the English farm* (rev., 1952); R. Trow-Smith, *English husbandry, from the earliest times to the present day* (1951); and C. S. Orwin and E. H. Whetham, *History of English agriculture, 1846–1914* (rev., 1964). On the changes in the countryside, see also E. C. Wingfield-Stratford, *The squire and his relations* (1956); G. E. Fussell and K. R.

Fussell, *The English countryman: his life and work*, A.D. *1500–1900* (1955); and F. M. L. Thompson, *The English landed gentry in the nineteenth century* (1963). A judicious treatment of earlier and later enclosure movements is J. A. Yelling, *Common field and enclosure in England, 1450–1850* (1977). The crop failure of 1816–1817 is studied in a monograph that goes well beyond its subject, J. D. Post, *The last great subsistence crisis in the Western world* (1977).

Two books by D. B. Grigg may also be mentioned here: *The agricultural systems of the world: an evolutionary approach** (1974), cited in the introductory section, and *Population growth and agrarian change: a historical perspective* (1980); and on population changes in these years in Britain, E. A. Wrigley and R. S. Schofield, *The population history of England, 1541–1871: a reconstruction* (1981), cited in Chapter III, is important.

Social and Political Changes in Britain

There is a large and controversial literature on the effects of industrial change on the well-being of the British working classes. Arnold Toynbee (uncle of the twentieth-century historian) in a series of famous lectures in 1884, in which he coined the term Industrial Revolution, led the way in stressing exploitation; see his *Lectures on the Industrial Revolution in England* (1884, reprinted 1969). J. L. Hammond and B. Hammond in several vehement books such as *The town labourer, 1760–1832: the new civilization** (1919), *The age of the Chartists** (1930), and other works demonstrated indignantly that the common people were exploited. E. P. Thompson, *The making of the English working class** (1963), a remarkable study that has had wide influence, reinforces the picture of exploitation and working-class militancy, as does E. J. Hobsbawm in *Industry and empire: 1750 to the present day* (1968). Hobsbawm also has written *Labouring men: studies in the history of labour** (1964) and other related books. The books by Ashton, Clark, Deane, and others cited above emphasize gradualism in industrial change and provide a less bleak view, as do J. T. Ward, *The factory system, 1830–1855* (1962), M. I. Thomis in *Responses to industrialization: the British experience 1780–1850** (1976), and other writers, but the debate continues. An ex-

tremist viewpoint minimizing the evil effects of early industrialism is set forth in a collection of essays edited by F. A. von Hayek, *Capitalism and the historians** (1954).

For the social and political impact on Britain, the reader may turn to N. Smelser, *Social change in the Industrial Revolution* (1959); P. Laslett, *The world we have lost: England before the industrial age* (1965), cited earlier; D. Marshall, *Industrial England, 1776–1851* (1973); H. Perkin, *The origins of modern English society, 1780–1880** (1969); and W. R. Ward, *Religion and society in England, 1790–1850* (1972). I. Pinchbeck, *Women workers and the Industrial Revolution, 1750–1850* (1930, reissued 1969), remains valuable.

Other recommended books with a balanced viewpoint are A. Briggs, *The age of improvement* (1959); E. L. Woodward, *The age of reform, 1815–1870* (1938), a solid volume in the Oxford History of England; N. Gash, *Politics in the age of Peel, 1830–1850* (1953); and G. S. R. Kitson Clark, *An expanding society: Britain, 1830–1900* (1968). On the Chartists, the many older studies have been superseded by J. T. Ward, *Chartism* (1973), and D. Jones, *Chartism and the Chartists* (1975). R. J. Cruikshank, *Charles Dickens and early Victorian England* (1949), is a colorful study of the novelist and the people he wrote about. Some protest movements of the era are conveyed in R. J. White, *Waterloo to Peterloo* (1957); D. Rend, *Peterloo: the massacre and its background* (1958); E. J. Hobsbawm and G. Rudé, *Captain Swing* (1969), a study of the rural poor and agrarian unrest in the years 1815 to 1830; M. I. Thomis, *The Luddites: machine-breaking in Regency England* (1970); and W. J. Shelton, *English hunger and industrial disorders* (1973), on the riots of the 1760s. Recent informative and provocative studies include E. Gauldie, *Cruel habitations: a history of working class housing, 1790–1918* (1974); K. Williams, *From pauperism to poverty* (1981), on the poor laws and the contemporary definitions of poverty; M. Ignatieff, *A just measure of pain: the penitentiary and the Industrial Revolution, 1750–1850* (1979); and D. Vincent, *Bread, knowledge, and freedom: a study of nineteenth-century working class autobiography* (1981), on the ways in which working men and women saw their lives.

The widening functions of government are analyzed in E. W. Cohen, *The growth of the British civil service, 1780–1939* (1941); M. P. Hall, *The social services* of modern England (rev., 1955); K. B. Smellie, *History of local government* (1946); and D. Owen, *English philanthropy, 1660–1960* (1964). Social policy in general is sketched in D. Fraser, *The evolution of the British welfare state: a history of social policy since the Industrial Revolution* (1973). Reform legislation is discussed in M. W. Thomas, *The early factory legislation* (1948), and in J. T. Ward, *The factory system, 1830–1855* (1962), cited above. On the Corn Laws, there are available D. G. Barnes, *A history of the English Corn Laws, from 1660 to 1846* (1930); N. McCord, *The Anti-Corn-Law League, 1838–1846* (1958); and B. Hilton, *Corn, cash, commerce: the economic policies of the Tory governments, 1815–1830* (1978), informative on the economics and politics of the grain issue. The antislavery movement is treated in two books cited in Chapter VIII, D. B. Davis, *The problem of slavery in the age of revolution, 1770–1823* (1975), and R. Anstey, *The Atlantic slave trade and British abolition, 1760–1810* (1975); in S. Drescher, *Econocide: British slavery in the era of abolition* (1977), which sees humanitarian factors as more important than economic; and in a volume of essays, C. Bolt and S. Drescher (eds.), *Anti-slavery, religion, and reform* (1980). Books on the slave trade are cited in Chapter III. Schools and schooling are examined in E. G. West, *Education and the Industrial Revolution* (1975), and the plight of children, especially of the poorer classes, in the wide-ranging I. Pinchbeck and M. Hewitt, *Children in English society* (2 vols., 1969–1973), cited in the introductory section, covering from the fifteenth to the mid-twentieth century. A different subject is explored in R. W. Malcolmson, *Popular recreations in English society, 1700–1850* (1973); M. Marrus, *The rise of leisure in industrial society* (1974); and H. Cunningham, *Leisure in the Industrial Revolution, 1750–1880* (1980), which explores the interaction of popular culture and agitation for reform. Books on socialism and trade unionism are cited elsewhere in this chapter and in Chapter XIV. On the Reform Bill of 1832, the outstanding study is M. Brock, *The Great Reform Act* * (1973).

There are many biographies of the leading reformers of the age. [Political thinkers are listed below.] Among them are G. M. Trevelyan, *Lord Grey of the Reform Bill* (1920, 1929); N. Gash, *Peel* (1976), a condensation of his outstanding larger work (2 vols., 1968–1972); C. R. Fay, *Huskisson and his age* (1951); G. Wallas, *The life of Francis Place, 1771–1854* (1898, 1925); C. Driver, *Tory radical: the life of Richard Oastler* (1946); G. F. A. Best, *Shaftesbury* (1964); and J. Pollock, *Wilberforce* (1978). Trevelyan's older biography of John Bright (1913) may be compared with K. Robbins, *John Bright* (1979), and G. D. H. Cole's study of William Cobbett (1924) with G. Spater, *William Cobbett: the poor man's friend* (2 vols., 1982). There are biographies by M. Mack on Jeremy Bentham (1963); by G. D. H. Cole on Robert Owen (1930); and studies of Owen by F. Podmore (1924) and M. Cole (1953). On the pioneer feminist of the age, there are biographies of Mary Wollstonecraft by R. M. Wardle (1951), M. George (1970), C. Tomalin (1974), and E. Flexner* (1972); and a broader study of women in the era, J. H. Murray, *Strong-minded women and other lost voices from nineteenth-century England* * (1982).

Studies of the Victorian age, some going beyond the scope of this chapter, are A. Briggs, *Victorian cities* (1965) and *Victorian people* * (1955); O. Chadwick, *The Victorian church, 1829–1860* (1966); W. E. Houghton, *The Victorian frame of mind, 1830–1870* (1957); S. Marcus, *The other Victorians* * (1966); E. Trudgill, *Madonnas and Magdalens: the origins and development of Victorian sexual attitudes* (1976); and E. Longworth, *Eminent Victorian women* (1981). Several others are cited below in Chapter XIV. A monumental multivolumed biographical dictionary of labor figures from 1790 to the present is under way: J. Bellamy and J. Saville (eds.), *The dictionary of labor biography* (5 vols. to date, 1972–1979).

The "Isms" and Social Thought—General

Two overall surveys carrying social and other thought forward to the twentieth century are G. L. Mosse, *The culture of Western Europe: the nineteenth and twentieth centuries* (1961), and R. N. Stromberg, *European intellectual history since 1789* * (3rd ed., 1981); useful anthologies are E. C. Black, *The posture of Europe, 1815–1940: readings in European intellectual history* * (1964), and E. C. Weber (ed.), *Paths to the present: . . . European thought from romanticism to existentialism* * (1960). For the nineteenth century, there are available D. C. Somervell, *English thought in the nineteenth century* * (1929, 1962); C. Brinton, *English political thought in the nineteenth century* * (1933, 1950); and J. Bowle, *Politics and opinion in the nineteenth century* * (1954). For selected English thinkers an interesting study is S. R. Letwin, *The pursuit of certainty: David Hume, Jeremy Bentham, John Stuart Mill, Beatrice Webb* (1963). Political and other meanings of romanticism are examined in J. Barzun, *Classic, romantic, and modern* * (rev., 1961), and in the same author's *Berlioz and the romantic century* * (1950, 1982); D. O. Evans, *Social romanticism in France, 1830–1848* (1951); and in R. F. Gleckner and G. E. Ensco (eds.), *Romanticism* (1962). Other notable studies of the interplay of ideas and politics include H. Marcuse, *Reason and revolution: Hegel and the rise of social theory* (1941); F. Wiedemann, *Hegel* (1968); P. Viereck, *Conservatism revisited: the revolt against revolt, 1815–1949* * (1949, 1965); G. O. Griffith, *Interpreters of man: a review of secular and religious thought from Hegel to Barth* (1943); P. Roubiczek, *The misrepresentation of man: studies in European thought in the nineteenth century* (1947); and M. Peckham, *Beyond the tragic vision: the quest for identity in the nineteenth century* * (1962).

Three good starting places for the study of the revolutionary tradition are F. E. Manuel, *The prophets of Paris: Turgot, Condorcet, Saint-Simon, Fourier, Comte* * (1962), cited in Chapter VIII, which stresses the link between Enlightenment ideas and nineteenth-century social thought; J. L. Talmon, *Political messianism: the romantic phase* (1960); and J. H. Billington, *Fire in the minds of men: origins of the revolutionary faith* (1980), which in colorful detail focuses on the more intense and conspiratorial revolutionaries. J. Plamenatz, *The revolutionary movement in France, 1815–1871* (1932), remains useful.

On historians and their contributions to the view of life in the nineteenth century, among many books one may read T. H. Von Laue, *Leopold von Ranke: the formative years* (1950); L. Krieger, *Ranke: the meaning of history* (1977); G. G. Iggers, *The German conception of history . . . from Herder to the present* (1968); M. Mandelbaum, *History, man and reason: a study of nineteenth-century thought* (1971); B. T. Wilkins, *Hegel's philosophy of history* (1974); H. White, *Metahistory: the historical imagination in nineteenth-century Europe*, a bold but complex book; L. Orr, *Jules Michelet: nature, history, and language* (1976); two books on Macaulay: J. Clive, *Macaulay: the shaping of the historian* (1973), and J. Hamburger, *Macaulay and the Whig tradition* (1976); J. W. Burrow, *A liberal descent: Victorian historians on the English past* (1981); and C. Rearick, *Beyond the Enlightenment: historians and folklore in nineteenth century France* (1974). On the nature of ideology, one may read G. Rudé, *Ideology and popular protest* * (1980); and for political alignments, D. Caute, *The left in Europe since 1789* * (1966), which may be supplemented by H. Rogger and E. Weber (eds.), *The European right: a historical profile* * (1965).

Nationalism

The vast literature on this subject may be approached through the following: C. J. H. Hayes, *The historical evolution of modern nationalism* (1931, 1948); H. Kohn, *The idea of nationalism: a study in its origin and background* (1944), from Hebraic and Hellenic times; L. L. Snyder, *Varieties of nationalism: a comparative study* (1976), a convenient introduction; K. W. Deutsch, *Nationalism and social communication: an inquiry into the foundations of nationality* * (1953); A. D. S. Smith, *Theories of nationalism* (1971); and B. C. Shafer, *Faces of nationalism: new realities and old myths* (1972). Shafer has also contributed *Nationalism: interpretations and interpreters* * (1976) to the American Historical Association Pamphlets series. Also useful are E. Kedourie, *Nationalism* * (1966); K. Deutsch and W. J. Folz (eds.), *Nation-building* * (1963); and K. R. Minogue, *Nationalism* (1967). E. Kamenka (ed.), *Nationalism: the nature and evolution of an idea* (1976), is a collection of provocative essays. R. Bendix, *Kings or people: power and the mandate to rule* (1978), is a bold large-scale effort, drawing on the experiences of England, France, Germany, Russia, and Japan, to examine the transition from traditional to modern conceptions of legitimacy in government. H. Seton-Watson, *Nations and states: an enquiry into the origins of nations and the politics of nationalism* (1977), another large-scale investigation, examines nationalism on a global scale; and an important collaborative study is C. Tilly (ed.), *The formation of national states in Western Europe* (1975). F. M. Barnard, *Herder's social and political thought: from Enlightenment to* *nationalism* (1965), focuses on cultural nationalism.

Liberalism

G. de Ruggiero, *The history of European liberalism* (1927), a comparative analysis of English, French, German, and Italian liberalism, remains a fundamental work, while H. J. Laski, *The rise of European liberalism** (1936), which sees its history as the gradual taming of a revolutionary doctrine, is still provocative. B. Croce, *History of Europe in the nineteenth century* (1933), a philosophical and historical treatment of the idea of liberty, may be compared with H. J. Muller, *Freedom in the modern world** (1966), and with M. Salvadori, *The liberal heresy: origins and historical development* (1977), which sees liberal thought as a "heresy" in a predominantly authoritarian orthodoxy in human history. On German political ideas, one may profitably compare H. Kohn, *The mind of Germany: the education of a nation* (1960), with two books cited earlier: L. Krieger, *The German idea of freedom* (1957), and K. Epstein, *The genesis of German conservatism* (1966). J. S. Schapiro, *Liberalism and the challenge of fascism: social forces in England and France, 1815–1870* (1949), deals with the concurrent growth of liberal and antiliberal ideas; and B. Russell, *Freedom vs. organization, 1814–1914** (1934, 1947), shows the dilemma of liberalism in a period of rapid economic change. There are studies of de Tocqueville by J. P. Mayer (1939), R. Herr (1960), and D. S. Goldstein (1976). Among many books on John Stuart Mill, one may read G. Himmelfarb, *On liberty and liberalism: the case of John Stuart Mill* (1974); M. Packe, *John Stuart Mill* (1954); A. Ryan, *J. S. Mill** (1975); R. J. Halliday, *John Stuart Mill* (1976), a brief introductory account; F. L. Van Holthoon, *The road to utopia: . . . John Stuart Mill's social thought* (1971); B. Mazlish, *James and John Stuart Mill: father and son in the nineteenth century* (1975), an interesting effort at psychohistory; and D. F. Thompson, *John Stuart Mill and representative government* (1976), an important study. In an area where Mill pioneered, A. Rossi has edited John Stuart and Harriet Taylor Mill, *Essays on sex equality* (1970). Two useful anthologies are A. Bullock and M. Shock (eds.), *The liberal tradition** (1957), and D. Sidorsky (ed.), *The liberal tradition in European thought** (1970).

Socialism

Two useful overviews from the late eighteenth century to the present are W. Lorner, *A history of socialism and communism in modern times: theorists, activists, and humanists** (1982), and A. S. Lindemann, *A history of European socialism* (1982); also available are N. I. Mackenzie, *Socialism: a short history* (1949); L. Derfler, *Socialism since Marx: a century of the European left** (1973); and H. W. Laidler, *History of socialism* (rev., 1968). A. Gray, *The socialist tradition: Moses to Lenin** (1946), is a witty, unsympathetic account. G. Lichtheim, *The origins of socialism* (1969), *A short history of socialism** (1970), and other writings are stimulating.

Two large-scale comprehensive studies, stressing the interaction of men, movements, and ideas, are G. D. H. Cole, *A history of socialist thought* (4 vols., 1953–1956), covering the years 1789 to 1939, and C. Landauer, *European socialism: a history of ideas and movements from the Industrial Revolution to Hitler's seizure of power* (2 vols., 1959). E. H. Carr, *Studies in revolution* (1950), is a series of incisive essays on earlier and later socialists. Some useful studies of pre-Marxian socialism are J. Beecher and R. Bienvenu, *The utopian vision of Charles Fourier* (1971); G. G. Iggers, *The cult of authority: the political cult of the Saint-Simonians* (1958); F. E. Manuel, *The new world of Henri Saint-Simon* (1956); D. W. Brogan, *Proudhon* (1934); and H. de Lubac, *The un-Marxian socialist: a study of Proudhon* (1948). On the strengths and weaknesses of the alliance between socialism and feminism, one may read M. J. Boxer and J. H. Quataert (eds.), *Socialist women: European socialist feminism in the nineteenth and early twentieth centuries** (1978). [Additional literature on socialism and Marxism appears in Chapters XII and XIV.] A. Fried and R. Sanders, *Socialist thought: a documentary history** (1964), is a useful anthology.

Economic Thought

For the development of economic ideas, one may turn to the histories of economic doctrine and thought mentioned in the introductory section. J. K. Galbraith, *The age of uncertainty* (1977), is a sprightly series of essays on economic thinkers from Adam Smith to the present, and R. Heilbroner, *The worldly philosophers** (1953), is useful on the economic liberals. E. Whittaker, *Schools and streams of economic thought* (1960), contains an illuminating section on Adam Smith's moral and economic ideas, and may be read along with J. Rae's older biography (1895), but D. A. Riesman, *Adam Smith's sociological economics* (1976), and D. Winch, *Adam Smith's politics: an essay in historiographic revision** (1978), better communicate his unified thought. For Malthus, a biographical account, stronger for his life than for his thought, is P. James, *Population Malthus: his life and times* (1979).

International Politics after the Congress of Vienna

In addition to the books cited at the end of Chapter X, especially H. Nicolson, *The Congress of Vienna: a study in allied unity, 1814–1822** (1946), and at the beginning of this chapter, the reader may turn to W. A. Phillips, *The confederation of Europe: a study of the European alliance 1813–1823* (1914, 1920); E. L. Woodward, *War and peace in Europe, 1815–1870, and other essays* (1931); H. G. Schenk, *The aftermath of the Napoleonic wars: the concert of Europe —an experiment* (1947); and E. V. Gulick, *Europe's classical balance of power** (1955). H. Kissinger, *A world restored: Metternich, Castlereagh and the problems of peace, 1812–1822* (1957), already cited, discusses the balancing of power politics and ideology before the author became a practitioner of the art. I. C. Nichols, Jr., analyzes the congress system in action in *The European pentarchy and the Congress of Verona, 1822* (1971). P. Viereck, *Conservatism revisited: the revolt against revolt, 1815–1949** (1949, 1965), cited above, attempts to rehabilitate the reputations of the post-1815 conservatives, especially Metternich. On the latter, there are sympathetic biographies by A. Herman (1932) and H. du Coudray (1935), and a valuable study by P. W. Schroeder, *Metternich's diplomacy at its zenith, 1820–1823* (1962).

British foreign affairs and diplomatic history in general in the post-Napoleonic era may be followed through the studies already cited and through three outstanding books by C. K. Webster: *The foreign policy of Castlereagh, 1815–1822* (1925), *Palmerston, Metternich, and the European system, 1830–1841* (1934), and *The foreign policy of Palmerston* (2 vols., 1951). Other accounts of men and events include C. J. Bartlett,

Castlereagh (1967); J. Derry, *Castlereagh* (1976); H. Temperley, *The foreign policy of Canning, 1822–1827* (1925); W. Hinde, *George Canning* (1973); P. Dixon, *Canning: politician and statesman* (1976); H. Bell, *Lord Palmerston* (2 vols., 1936); D. Southgate, *'The most English minister' . . . the policies and politics of Palmerston* (1966); and K. Bourne, *Palmerston: The early years* (1982), with a second volume projected.

The situation arising from the interest of the European powers in Latin America is examined in D. Perkins, *A history of the Monroe Doctrine* (1941, 1963); C. K. Webster, *Britain and the independence of Latin America, 1812–1830* (1944); A. P. Whitaker, *The United States and the independence of Latin America, 1800–1830* (1941); D. C. M. Platt, *Latin America and British trade, 1806–1914* (1973); and the detailed study of Anglo-American relations in the years 1775–1823 by B. Perkins, cited earlier (3 vols., 1955–1965). Two biographical introductions to the subject are J. B. Trend, *Bolívar and the independence of Spanish America** (Teach Yourself History series, 1948), and J. Kinsbrunner, *Bernardo O'Higgins** (1968). Accounts of the independence movements are J. Lynch, *The Spanish American revolutions, 1808–1821* (1973), and R. Graham, *Independence in Latin America** (1972). M. Savelle, *Empires to nations* (1974), examines the birth of nations in the late eighteenth and early nineteenth centuries in the Western Hemisphere.

Other important stirrings in the same period are described in C. M. Woodhouse, *The Greek war of independence* (1952); D. Howarth, *The Greek adventure* (1976), a narrative account; two volumes (one of essays, the other of documents) edited by R. Clogg: *The struggle for Greek independence: essays to mark the 150th anniversary . . .* (1973) and *The movement for Greek independence, 1770–1821* (1976); J. H. Brady, *Rome and the Neapolitan revolution of 1820–21* (1937); and G. T. Romani, *The Neapolitan revolution of 1820–1821* (1950). The emerging importance of Belgium in international affairs from these years onward is ably traced in J. E. Helmreich, *Belgium and Europe: a study of small-power diplomacy* (1976). For developments in Russia, one may consult A. G. Mazour, *The first Russian revolution, 1825: the Decembrist movement** (1937); M. Zetlin, *The Decembrists* (1958); and M. Raeff, *The Decembrist movement* (1966), a narrative with documents.

Three interesting books on international affairs transcending this chapter are L. C. B. Seaman, *From Vienna to Versailles** (1956); W. N. Medlicott (ed.), *From Metternich to Hitler: aspects of British and foreign history, 1814–1939** (1963); and C. Howard, *Britain and the casus belli, 1822–1902* (1974), focusing on British foreign ministers in the nineteenth century. A useful reference tool is G. A. Kertesz (ed.), *Documents in the political history of the European continent, 1815–1939* (1969).

Problems and Readings*

P. N. Stearns (ed.), *A century for debate: problems in the interpretation of European history, 1789–1914* (1969), and G. Rudé, *Debate on Europe* (1972), summarize the historiographical debate on selected issues.

Specialized pamphlets include G. A. Cahill (ed.), *The great Reform Bill of 1832: liberal or conservative?* (1969); J. M. Merriman (ed.), *1830 in France* (1976); J. B. Halsted (ed.), *Romanticism: definition, explanation, and evaluation* (1965); H. F. Schwarz (ed.), *Metternich: the "coachman of Europe": statesman or evil genius?* (1962); M. Walker (ed.), *Metternich's Europe, 1815–1848* (1968); and E. E. Kraehe, *The Metternich controversy* (1971). Social and economic themes are explored in P. A. M. Taylor (ed.), *The Industrial Revolution in Britain: triumph or disaster?* (1958); M. L. McDougall (ed.), *The working class in modern Europe* (1975); A. Lees and L. Lees (eds.), *The urbanization of European society in the nineteenth century* (1976); and A. Esler (ed.), *The youth revolution: conflict of generations in modern history* (1974). Many pamphlets of essays and readings in the Anvil series are useful: H. Kohn, *Nationalism: its meaning and history* (1955); P. Viereck, *Conservatism: from John Adams to Churchill* (1956); J. S. Schapiro, *Liberalism: its meaning and history* (1958); the same author's *Movements of social dissent in modern Europe* (1962); J. H. Stewart, *The Restoration era in France, 1814–1830* (1968); and P. Beik, *Louis Philippe and the July Monarchy* (1965). On Latin American subjects, two titles in the same series are useful: R. A. Humphreys and J. Lynch, *The origins of the Latin American revolutions, 1808–1826* (1967), and J. J. Johnson, *Simon Bolívar and Spanish-American independence, 1783–1830* (1968).

XII: REVOLUTION AND THE REIMPOSITION OF ORDER, 1848–1870

The best synthesis for the immediate background, the events of 1848, and their aftermath is W. L. Langer, *Political and social upheaval, 1832–1852** (1969), in the series edited by the author. Other general studies include P. S. Robertson, *Revolutions of 1848: a social history** (1952); P. N. Stearns, *1848: the revolutionary tide in Europe** (1974); J. Sigman, *1848: the romantic and democratic revolutions in Europe* (trans. 1973); and the brief G. Fasel, *Europe in upheaval: the revolutions of 1848** (1970). Also recommended are F. Fejtö, *The opening of an era: 1848, an historical symposium* (1948), and A. Whitridge, *Men in crisis: the revolutions of 1848* (1949), which studies leading personalities in various countries. A. J. Mayer, *The persistence of the old régime: Europe to the Great War* (1981), seeks to demonstrate that even after 1848 a post-feudal nobility continued to dominate European society down to 1914. D. Geary, *European labor protest, 1848–1939* (1981), presents a concise overview of working-class radicalism and political action in Europe in the years following 1848. A special subject is graphically treated in C. B. Woodham-Smith, *The great hunger: Ireland 1845–1849* (1962).

Revolutions in Various Countries

[See also for the various countries books listed in the previous chapter on the years 1815–1848 and in the chapter that follows on the successful unification movements.] In addition to the general accounts described above, the following are important for the ferment of 1815–1850 and for the revolutions of 1848–1849 in the various European countries:

FRANCE. G. Duveau, *The making of a revolution** (trans. 1968); R. Price, *The French Second Republic: a social history* (1972), and the volume of essays edited by him, *Revolution and reaction: 1848 and the Second French Republic* (1976); F. A. De Luna, *The French Republic under Cavaignac* (1969); P. H. Amann, *Revolutions and mass democracy: the Paris club movement in 1848* (1976); and L. Loubère, *Louis Blanc: . . . the rise of French Jacobin socialism* (1961). J. W. Merriman, *The agony of the*

Republic: the repression of the left in revolutionary France, 1848–1851 (1978), is an admirable study of radicalization and repression in the Second Republic, and T. W. Margadant, *French peasants in revolt: the insurrection of 1851* (1979), an excellent study of the provincial response.

ITALY. G. F. H. Berkeley and J. Berkeley, *Italy in the making* (3 vols., 1932–1940), remains a standard account. G. M. Trevelyan, *Garibaldi's defense of the Roman republic, 1848–1849* (1907, reissued 1949), and the same author's *Manin and the Venetian revolution of 1848* (1923), may be compared with the more recent P. Ginsborg, *Daniele Manin and the Venetian revolution of 1848–49* (1979). Also recommended: M. C. Wicks, *The Italian exiles in London, 1816–1848* (1937); R. J. Rath, *The provisional Austrian regime in Lombardy-Venetia, 1814–1815* (1968); K. R. Greenfield, *Economics and liberalism in the Risorgimento: . . . nationalism in Lombardy, 1814–1848* (1934); R. Grew, *A sterner plan for Italian unity: the Italian National Society and the Risorgimento* (1963); A. J. P. Taylor, *The Italian problem in European diplomacy, 1847–1849* (1934); and three books by E. E. Y. Hales: *Pio Nono* [Pius IX], *a study in European politics and religion in the nineteenth century* (1954), *Revolution and papacy, 1769–1846* (1960), and *Mazzini and the secret societies* (1956).

HABSBURG LANDS. J. Redlich, *Emperor Francis Joseph of Austria* (1929), an absorbing biography; J. Blum, *Noble landowners and agriculture in Austria, 1815–1848: . . . the origins of the peasant emancipation of 1848* (1948); A. Schwarzenberg, *Prince Felix zu Schwarzenberg, prime minister of Austria, 1848–1852* (1947); B. K. Király, *Ferenc Deák* (1975), a balanced account of the humanitarian liberal; I. Deák, *The lawful revolution: Louis Kossuth and the Hungarians, 1848–1849* (1979), a vivid account, ably demonstrating Kossuth's shortcomings; R. J. Rath, *The Viennese revolution of 1848* (1957); and S. Z. Pech, *The Czech revolution of 1848* (1969). Metternich's career and fall are recounted in books listed in Chapters X and XI.

GERMANY AND THE FRANKFURT ASSEMBLY. V. Valentin, *1848: chapters of German history* (1940), an abridgment of the author's larger study in German; L. B. Namier, *1848: the revolution of the intellectuals** (1946), sharply critical of the Frankfurt Assembly; and F. Eyck, *The Frankfurt Parliament, 1848–1849* (1968), a detailed account of the assembly itself. An important study (1978) by G. Wollstein stressing the illiberal aspects of the Frankfurt Assembly has not yet been translated.

Marx and Marxism

Two outstanding biographies of Marx written in recent years are: D. McLellan, *Karl Marx: his life and thought** (1973), and J. Seigel, *Marx's fate: the shape of a life* (1978). Other interesting accounts include S. K. Padover, *Karl Marx: an intimate biography* (1978), and older studies by E. H. Carr (1938), F. Mehring (1918, reissued 1972), R. Payne (1968), O. Rühle (1929, 1943), L. Schwarzschild (1947), C. J. Sprigge* (1949), and I. Berlin (rev., 1963). J. H. Jackson, *Marx, Proudhon, and European socialism** (Teach Yourself History series, 1958), explores Marx's break with one rival. Important for understanding Engels' role are D. McLellan, *Friedrich Engels** (1978), an admirable brief introduction; G. Mayer, *Friedrich Engels: a biography* (1920, 1936); and S. Marcus, *Engels, Manchester, and the working class* (1974). The story of Marx's daughter is skillfully told in C. Tsuzuki, *The life of Eleanor Marx* (1967), which is less sympathetic than the detailed, able account by E. Kapp, *Eleanor Marx** (2 vols., 1977).

On the theoretical foundations and concrete manifestations of socialism, there is, of course, an enormous and highly controversial literature, to which the books cited for the beginnings of socialism for Chapter XI and for the years after 1870 for Chapter XIV offer some guidance; much current discussion stresses the relationship between Marx's early writings and his mature thought. Of efforts to rehabilitate the humanistic elements in the younger Marx on the basis of manuscripts now available, one of the most successful is R. N. Hunt, *The political ideas of Marx and Engels*, vol. I, *Marxism and totalitarian democracy, 1818–1850* (1976), the first of two projected volumes, while E. Fromm, *Marx's concept of man* (1969), reprints and comments thoughtfully on the 1844 manuscripts. Informative, interpretive accounts include R. Tucker, *The Marxian revolutionary idea** (1969) and *Philosophy and myth in Karl Marx* (rev., 1972); A. G. Meyer, *Marxism: unity of theory and practice** (1957); G. Lichtheim, *Marxism: an* historical and critical study* (1961); S. Avineri, *The social and political thought of Karl Marx* (1969); B. D. Wolfe, *Marxism: one hundred years in the life of a doctrine* (1965); A. W. Gouldner, *The two Marxisms: contradictions and anomalies in the development of theory* (1979); and A. H. Wood, *Karl Marx* (1981), who is less impressed than others by the importance of the early manuscripts. A large-scale, critical analysis by a distinguished Polish scholar is L. Kolakowski, *Main currents of Marxism: its rise, growth, and dissolution* (3 vols., 1978). E. Wilson, *To the Finland station: a study in the writing and acting of history* (1940), is an imaginative discussion of the way in which early and later socialists, and nonsocialists, interpreted the past to influence the present. Insights into the Marxist interpretations of history are provided in G. A. Cohen, *Karl Marx's theory of history: a defense* (1979), an especially cogent analysis; W. H. Shaw, *Marx's theory of history* (1978); and M. Rader, *Marx's interpretation of history* (1979), all of which supersede older studies by M. M. Bober (1927) and others.

For Comte and positivism, W. M. Simon, *European positivism in the nineteenth century* (1963), may be supplemented by D. G. Charlton, *Positivist thought in France during the Second Empire* (1959). G. Lenzer has edited *Auguste Comte and positivism: the essential writings* (1975).

Napoleon III and Bonapartism

Readable and informative works are J. M. Thompson, *Louis Napoleon and the Second Empire* (1954); three books by R. L. Williams: *The world of Napoleon III* (1957, 1965), *The mortal Napoleon III* (1971), and *Manners and murders in the world of Louis Napoleon* (1975); T. A. B. Corley, *Democratic despot: a life of Napoleon III* (1961); B. D. Gooch, *The Second Empire: the reign of Napoleon III* (1969); and W. H. C. Smith, *Napoleon III* (1973). Other studies include T. Zeldin, *The political system of Napoleon III* (1958); G. P. Gooch, *The Second Empire* (1960), a series of judicious essays; H. C. Payne, *The police state of Louis Napoleon Bonaparte, 1851–1860* (1966); and D. Kulstein, *Napoleon III and the working class* (1969). An important economic aspect is studied in A. L. Dunham, *The Anglo-French treaty of commerce of 1860* (1930). On education and social mobility, there are available R. D. Anderson,

Education in France, 1848–1870 (1975), and P. J. Harrigan, *Mobility, elites, and education in French society of the Second Empire* (1980), which finds more mobility than most traditional accounts. On the rebuilding of Paris, one may turn to D. H. Pinkney, *Napoleon III and the rebuilding of Paris* (1958), and J. M. Chapman and B. Chapman, *The life and times of Baron Haussmann* (1957). A scholarly effort to rehabilitate the empress is H. Kurtz, *The Empress Eugénie, 1826–1920* (1964), which may be supplemented by N. N. Barker, *Distaff diplomacy: the Empress Eugénie and the foreign policy of the Second Empire* (1967). Tendencies in recent years by French historians to praise Napoleon III for political stability and economic planning are carefully explored by S. L. Campbell, *The Second Empire revisited: a study in French historiography* (1978).

Problems and Readings*

Three booklets are useful: M. Kranzberg (ed.), *1848: a turning point?* (1959); S. M. Osgood (ed.), *Napoleon III and the Second Empire* (1973); and B. D. Gooch (ed.), *Napoleon III, man of destiny: enlightened statesman or proto-fascist?* (1963). In the Anvil series, there are G. Bruun, *Revolution and reaction, 1848–1852: a midcentury watershed* (1958), and S. Hook, *Marx and the Marxists: the ambiguous legacy* (1955). R. Tucker has edited an anthology, *The Marx-Engels reader* (2nd ed., 1978), with thoughtful introductions.

XIII: THE CONSOLIDATION OF LARGE NATION-STATES, 1859–1871

R. C. Binkley, *Realism and nationalism, 1852–1871* (1935), in the Langer series, is a valiant effort to clarify the segment of European history that followed the revolutions of 1848; a good synthesis of the era is also provided in N. Rich, *The age of nationalism and reform, 1850–1890* (1970). J. P. T. Bury (ed.), *The zenith of European power, 1830–1871*, already cited, in the New Cambridge Modern History, has many informative chapters. An outstanding attempt to view the period 1848–1918 as a whole, from the point of view of international affairs, is A. J. P. Taylor, *The struggle for mastery in Europe, 1848–1918* (Oxford History of Modern Europe series, 1954). As a sequel to his earlier volume for the years 1789 to 1848,

E. J. Hobsbawm has continued his provocative Marxist analysis in *The age of capital, 1848–1875* (1976), adding a global dimension to his account, and useful for this and the following two chapters. [Books on nationalism and on the earlier phases of national unification have been cited in Chapters XI and XII.]

The Crimean War

Some salient features of the Eastern question and of the Crimean War are treated in detail in M. S. Anderson, *The Eastern question, 1774–1923* (1966), cited in Chapter XI. Other useful books are H. Temperley, *England and the Near East: the Crimea* (1936); V. J. Puryear, *England, Russia, and the Straits question, 1844–1856* (1931); G. B. Henderson, *Crimean War diplomacy, and other historical essays* (1947); and W. Baumgart, *The Peace of Paris, 1856: studies in war, diplomacy, and peacemaking* (1981). An impressive, detailed account rehabilitating Austrian policy is P. W. Schroeder, *Austria, Great Britain, and the Crimean War: the destruction of the European concert* (1972), and J. S. Curtiss, *Russia's Crimean War* (1979), is a detailed, diplomatic and military history that sees the Western powers more responsible than Russia for the outbreak. The military aspects are treated in L. F. V. Blake, *The Crimean War* (1972), and in P. Warner, *The Crimean War: a reappraisal* (1973). The famous "Charge of the Light Brigade" is skillfully recounted in C. B. Woodham-Smith, *The reason why** (1953), and the same author has written a biography of Florence Nightingale (1957), as has F. B. Smith (1982). The impact on England is discussed in O. Anderson, *A liberal state at war: English politics and economics during the Crimean War* (1967). On the changing nature of warfare emerging in this era, see C. B. Falls, *A hundred years of war** (1954).

Unification of Italy

The general history by D. Mack Smith, *Italy: a modern history* (1969), cited for Chapter XI, and other books cited for Italy for Chapters XI and XII should be consulted. A useful introduction is C. Beales, *The Risorgimento and the unification of Italy* (1971). The older studies of Cavour by W. R. Thayer (2 vols., 1911) and A. J. Whyte (1930), and of Garibaldi by G. M. Trevelyan (2 vols., 1920) have largely been superseded; highly recommended now are three volumes by D. Mack Smith: *Cavour and Garibaldi in 1860* (1954), *Garibaldi: a great life in brief* (1956), and *Victor Emmanuel, Cavour, and the Risorgimento* (1971). C. Hibbert, *Garibaldi and his enemies: the clash of arms and personalities in the making of Italy* (1966), is a sound, popular account. G. O. Griffith, *Mazzini: prophet of modern Europe* (1932), remains useful for Mazzini, and J. Ridley, *Garibaldi* (1975), is a detailed, authoritative biography. An informative special study is L. M. Case, *Franco-Italian relations, 1860–1865* (1932).

Bismarck and the Founding of the Second Reich

G. A. Craig, *Germany, 1866–1945** (Oxford History of Modern Europe, 1978), is a magisterial account covering the years from Bismarck to Hitler, with many insights into German society and culture; a companion volume, *The Germans* (1982), equally perceptive, is a series of essays on selected themes in German history. His *Politics of the Prussian army, 1640–1945*, cited in Chapter V, is also useful for the nineteenth and twentieth centuries.

For Bismarck, E. Eyck's extensive indictment (3 vols., 1941–1944) is not translated, but a summary of his conclusions, *Bismarck and the German empire** (1950), is available; also critical is E. Crankshaw, *Bismarck** (1981). A. Palmer, *Bismarck* (1976), is a judicious, well-balanced account; less judicious but provocative is A. J. P. Taylor, *Bismarck: the man and the statesman** (1955), and W. N. Medlicott, *Bismarck and modern Germany** (Teach Yourself History series, 1965), is an excellent brief introduction. G. O. Kent's biography, *Bismarck and his times** (1978), is especially useful for the historiographical debate on questions relating to Bismarck. Two important works are O. Pflanze, *Bismarck and the development of Germany: the period of unification, 1815–71* (vol. I, 1963), with a second volume projected on the period of consolidation, 1871–1890; and T. S. Hamerow, *The social foundations of German unification, 1858–1871* (2 vols., 1969–1972). A remarkable study of Bismarck's Jewish financial advisor, illuminating much of German history during these years, is F. Stern, *Gold and iron: Bismarck, Bleichröder, and the building of the German empire* (1977). L. L. Snyder, *Roots of German nationalism*

(1978), and his other books may also be read for these years.

The outstanding study of the economic basis for unification is W. O. Henderson, *The Zollverein* (1939), supplemented by his larger work, *The rise of German industrial power, 1834–1914** (1976), but see also A. H. Price, *The evolution of the Zollverein* (1949). On the events of 1870, recommended studies include L. D. Steefel, *Bismarck, the Hohenzollern candidacy, and the origins of the Franco-German War of 1870* (1962); H. Oncken, *Napoleon III and the Rhine: the origin of the war of 1870–71* (1928); W. E. Mosse, *The European powers and the German question* (1958); and R. Millman, *British foreign policy and the coming of the Franco-Prussian War* (1965). The relevant documents on the origins of the war of 1870 are available in G. Bonnin (ed.), *Bismarck and the Hohenzollern candidature for the Spanish throne* (1957). M. Howard, *The Franco-Prussian War: the German invasion of France, 1870–1871** (1967, reissued 1981), is a major study of the war and related events.

Austria-Hungary

For Austria-Hungary, the volumes by C. A. Macartney and others, cited for Chapter XI, should be consulted, as well as O. Jászi, *The dissolution of the Habsburg monarchy* (1929); A. J. May, *The Habsburg monarchy, 1867–1914** (1951); and F. R. Bridge, *From Sadowa to Sarajevo: the foreign policy of Austria-Hungary, 1866–1914* (1972). Recommended also are G. E. Rothenberg, *The army of Francis Joseph* (1976), and A. Sked, *The survival of the Habsburg empire* (1980), which also focuses mainly on the army. For Hungary, G. Szabod, *Hungarian political trends between the revolution and the Compromise, 1849–1867* (1977), by a distinguished Hungarian historian, provides many insights into politics and society.

The Russia of Alexander II

An authoritative treatment of nineteenth-century Russia is provided in H. Seton-Watson, *The Russian empire, 1801–1917* (Oxford History of Modern Europe, 1967); in his *Decline of imperial Russia, 1855–1914** (1952); and in R. Pipes, *Russia under the old regime* (1975). On the reign of the five rulers from Alexander I to Nicholas II,

S. Harcave has written *Years of the golden cockerel: the last Romanov tsars, 1814–1917* (1968), which may be compared with W. B. Lincoln, *The Romanovs: autocrats of all the Russias* (1981), a colorful, scholarly account of all the Romanov tsars and tsarinas, cited in Chapter V. On the reforms of Alexander II, one may turn to W. E. Mosse, *Alexander II and the modernization of Russia** (1958), and to S. Graham, *Tsar of freedom: the life and reign of Alexander II* (1935), a sympathetic biography. The place of the peasant emancipation in Russian history may be studied in two books by J. Blum: *Lord and peasant in Russia from the ninth to the nineteenth century** (1961), cited in Chapter V, which carries the story to emancipation, and *The end of the old order in rural Europe** (1978), cited in Chapter XI; and in G. Pavlovsky, *Agricultural Russia on the eve of the Revolution* (1930); G. T. Robinson, *Rural Russia under the old regime** (1930); T. Emmons, *The Russian landed gentry and the peasant emancipation of 1861* (1968); and W. S. Vucinich (ed.), *The peasant in nineteenth-century Russia** (1968).

The following are also useful for these years: M. B. Petrovich, *The emergence of Russian pan-Slavism, 1856–1870* (1956); W. L. Blackwell, *The beginnings of Russian industrialization, 1800–1860* (1968); and J. S. Curtiss, *The Russian army under Nicholas I, 1825–1855* (1965). A special subject is explored in R. F. Leslie, *Reform and insurrection in Russian Poland, 1856–1865* (1963), and for all questions relating to Poland, R. F. Leslie (ed.), *The history of Poland since 1863* (1980), cited in Chapter XI, is valuable. The intellectual world is studied in D. Hecht, *Russian radicals look to America, 1825–1894* (1947); E. H. Carr's books, *The romantic exiles: a nineteenth century portrait gallery** (1933, 1949), and *Michael Bakunin* (1937); A. P. Mendel, *Michael Bakunin: roots of apocalypse* (1982), a detailed psychological study; and V. Broido, *Apostles into terrorists: women and the revolutionary movement in the Russia of Alexander II* (1977). M. E. Malia, *Alexander Herzen and the birth of Russian socialism** (1961), should be read in conjunction with E. Acton, *Alexander Herzen and the role of the intellectual revolutionary* (1979). Two books by N. V. Riasanovsky, *Russia and the West in the teaching of the Slavophiles* (1952), and *A parting of ways: government and the educated public in Russia, 1801–1855* (1976), are also recommended. A special subject is ably treated in J. Frankel, *Prophecy and* *politics: socialism, nationalism, and the Russian Jews, 1862–1917* (1981). Other books on prerevolutionary Russia are described in Chapter XVII.

The United States, Canada

A rich literature has developed on the slave experience in America, of which the following is only a sample of recent writings: E. D. Genovese, *Roll, Jordan, roll: the world the slaves made* (1974); H. G. Gutman, *The black family in slavery and freedom, 1750–1925* (1976); and the controversial R. W. Fogel and S. L. Engerman, *Time on the cross** (2 vols., 1974), on the economic profitability of slavery. The best overall treatment of American black history is J. H. Franklin, *From slavery to freedom: a history of Negro Americans* (rev., 1980), but M. F. Berry and J. Blassingame, *Long memory: the black experience in America* (1982), topically organized, is also useful. A brief survey of the great mid-century conflict is P. J. Parish, *The American Civil War** (1975), and on southern nationalism and the short-lived southern confederacy, E. M. Thomas, *The confederate nation, 1861–1865* (1979), is useful, while the Reconstruction period may be approached through K. M. Stampp, *The era of Reconstruction, 1865–1877* (1965). Standard works on the European implications of the American struggle include E. D. Adams, *Great Britain and the American Civil War* (2 vols., 1925), and D. Jordan and E. J. Pratt, *Europe and the American Civil War* (1931).

A useful introduction to all subjects relating to Canada is G. M. Craig, *The United States and Canada* (American Foreign Policy Library series, 1968). The growth of Canadian self-government within an imperial framework is discussed in J. M. Ward, *Colonial self-government: the British experience, 1759–1856* (1976); and in D. G. Creighton, *Dominion of the North, a history of Canada* (1944). J. B. Brebner, *North Atlantic triangle: the interplay of Canada, the United States and Great Britain* (1945), analyzes external affairs. The Australian story is ably recounted in the collaborative F. K. Crowley (ed.), *A new history of Australia* (1975). The emergence of the commonwealth idea, beginning in these years, is comprehensively treated in W. D. McIntyre, *The Commonwealth of Nations: origins and impact, 1869–1971* (1977).

Japan and the West

G. B. Sansom's two outstanding books, *Japan: a short cultural history* (1931; rev., 1962) and *The Western world and Japan* (1950), describe Japanese civilization before and during the nineteenth century respectively. His detailed multivolumed history carries the narrative to 1867 (3 vols., 1958–1963). Three books by E. O. Reischauer: *Japan: the story of a nation** (rev., 1977), *The United States and Japan** (rev., 1965), and *The Japanese** (1977) are highly recommended. Also recommended are J. W. Hall, *Japan from prehistory to modern times* (1970); H. Borton, *Japan's modern century* (rev., 1970); and W. G. Beasley, *The modern history of Japan** (3rd ed., 1981).

An older standard account, E. H. Norman, *Japan's emergence as a modern state* (1940), which portrayed the pre-1968 era in overly somber tones, has been altered by more recent scholarship. The best account of the Meiji era is W. G. Beasley, *The Meiji restoration* (1972); three other books incorporating newer interpretations are P. Duus, *The rise of modern Japan* (1976); T. Nejita, *Japan* (Modern Nations in Historical Perspective series, 1973); and K. B. Pyle, *The making of modern Japan* (1975). R. Benedict's anthropological study, *The chrysanthemum and the sword* (1946), stimulated many new insights into Japanese culture. On a special subject one may read J. Z. Bowers, *When the twain met: the rise of Western medicine in Japan* (1981).

Problems and Readings*

A number of booklets will be useful for subjects touched on in this chapter. On the Crimean War: B. D. Gooch (ed.), *The origins of the Crimean War* (1969). On Italy: C. F. Delzell (ed.), *The unification of Italy, 1859–1861* (1965); M. Walker (ed.), *Plombières: secret diplomacy and the rebirth of Italy* (1968); D. Mack Smith (ed.), *The making of Italy, 1796–1870* (1968) and *Garibaldi* (Great Lives Observed series, 1969); and M. Salvadori, *Cavour and the unification of Italy* (Anvil series, 1961). On Germany: T. S. Hamerow (ed.), *Otto von Bismarck: a historical assessment* (rev., 1972); O. Pflanze (ed.), *The unification of Germany, 1848–1871* (1979); and F. B. M. Hollyday, *Bismarck* (Great Lives Observed series, 1970). On Austria-Hungary: H. J. Gordon and N. M. Gordon, *The Austrian empire: abor-*

tive federation? (1975). On Japan: A. Tiedemann, *Modern Japan: a brief history* (Anvil series, rev., 1962).

XIV: EUROPEAN CIVILIZATION: 1871–1914

Two volumes in the Langer series provide a good introduction to these years: C. J. H. Hayes, *A generation of materialism, 1871–1900** (1941), which portrays the dual nature of the age as climax of enlightenment and seedtime of future trouble; and O. J. Hale, *The great illusion, 1900–1914** (1971), which explores the many accomplishments of the early twentieth century and the widespread belief in continuing peace and progress. Another thoughtful synthesis is J. K. Munholland, *Origins of contemporary Europe, 1890–1914** (1970). The final two volumes in the New Cambridge Modern History cover these years: F. H. Hinsley (ed.), *Material progress and worldwide problems, 1870–1898* (1962), and C. L. Mowat (ed.), *The shifting balance of world forces, 1898–1945* [1968, a revision of the original vol. XIII edited by D. Thomson under the title *The era of violence, 1898–1945* (1960)]. B. W. Tuchman, *The proud tower: a portrait of the world before the war, 1890–1914* (1966), provides selected vignettes, while E. R. Tannenbaum, *1900: the generation before the Great War* (1976), offers a potpourri of insights into the social history of the times. A. J. Mayer, *The persistence of the old regime: Europe to the Great War* (1981), cited in Chapter XII, argues that Europe was not quite "modern" in 1914. Other syntheses that have their starting point in these years are J. Joll, *Europe since 1870** (1973); F. Gilbert, *The end of the European era, 1890 to the present** (2nd ed., 1979); and J. M. Roberts, *Europe, 1880–1945** (1967), useful on economic and demographic subjects. G. Barraclough, *An introduction to contemporary history** (1964), is a provocative essay, calling for a global approach to contemporary history, a theme developed at length in J. Romein, *The watershed of two eras: Europe in 1900* (trans. 1978), by a Dutch historian. C. F. Ware, K. M. Pannikar, and J. Romein, *The twentieth century* (1966), vol. VI of the UNESCO History of Mankind, stresses cultural subjects but lacks coherent treatment. Special attention is given to intellectual matters in G. Lichtheim, *Europe in the*

twentieth century* (1972), to which one of the best introductions is G. Masur, *Prophets of yesterday: studies in European culture, 1800–1914** (1961). Women's lives and activities are documented in E. O. Hellerstein, L. P. Hume, and K. M. Offen (eds.), *Victorian women: a documentary account of women's lives in nineteenth century England, France, and the United States** (1981), cited in the introductory section of the bibliography.

Basic Demography

An introduction to historical demography is provided in C. M. Cipolla, *The economic history of world populations* (1962), and the sources for demographic studies are described in T. H. Hollingsworth, *Historical demography* (1969). Other important books are listed in the introductory section of the present bibliography, and in earlier chapters. Excellent introductions, all of which have been cited earlier, are: M. W. Flinn, *The European demographic system, 1500–1820* (1981); E. A. Wrigley and R. S. Schofield, *The population history of England, 1541–1870: a reconstruction* (1981); D. Grigg, *Population growth and agrarian change: an historical perspective** (1980), a broad study of world population and resources; and T. McKeown, *The modern rise of population* (1977), which stresses the importance of food availability rather than medical advances for population growth. Other aspects are discussed in: D. V. Glass and D. E. C. Eversley (eds.), *Population in history* (1965); D. V. Glass and R. Revelle (eds.), *Population and social change* (1972); and E. A. Wrigley, *Industrial growth and population change* (1961). C. Tilly (ed.), *Historical studies of changing fertility** (1978), is of major importance.

For population movements, the best starting point is two collections of essays, W. H. McNeill and R. S. Adams (eds.), *Human migration: patterns and politics* (1978), cited in the introductory section, and H. Moller (ed.), *Population movements in modern European history** (1964). Also available are the earlier volumes by W. F. Willcox and others, *International migrations* (2 vols., 1929, 1931); D. R. Taft and R. Robbins, *International migrations: the immigrant in the modern world* (1955); M. L. Hansen, *The Atlantic migration, 1607–1860: a history of the continuing settlement of the United States** (1940); W. D. Forsyth, *The* *myth of open spaces: Australian, British, and world trends of population and migration* (1942); and P. Taylor, *The distant magnet: European migration to the United States* (1971). On the absorption of American immigrants, S. Thernstrom and others (eds.), *Harvard encyclopedia of American ethnic groups* (1980), is valuable. Cities are studied in T. Chandler and G. Fox, *3000 years of urban growth* (1974).

Population statistics for the contemporary era of spectacular expansion must be brought up to date by consulting the United Nations, *Statistical yearbook* (1948 ff.), and *Demographic yearbook* (1948 ff.)

The World Economy

In addition to the economic histories listed in the introductory section and in Chapter XI, one may consult W. Ashworth, *A short history of the international economy since 1850* (rev., 1963); and on European agriculture since the 1800s, M. Tracy, *Agriculture in Western Europe* (1963). Two books by A. S. Milward and S. B. Saul provide an impressive comprehensive synthesis for industrial growth on the continent, with some chronological overlap: *The economic development of Continental Europe, 1780–1870* (1973) and *The development of the economies of Continental Europe, 1850–1914* (1977). An important collaborative history of the world's economies with a focus on Europe is P. Mathias and M. M. Postan (eds.), *The industrial economies: capital, labor, and enterprise,* vol. VII (Cambridge Economic History, 1978). An ambitious effort to study industrial growth from its origins in late-eighteenth-century Britain to its global diffusion in subsequent centuries is W. W. Rostow, *The world economy: history and prospect* (1978). A. J. H. Latham stresses economic developments in the non-Western world in *The international economy and the undeveloped world, 1865–1914* (1978), as does W. Woodruff, *Emergence of an international economy* (1970). A successful collaborative history of modern technology is T. I. Williams (ed.), *A history of technology: the twentieth century* (2 vols., 1978), of which T. P. Hughes, *Networks of power: electrification in Western society, 1880–1930* (1983), examines an important aspect.

Economic studies stressing the role of European capital include L. H. Jenks, *The migration of British capital to 1875* (1927, 1938); H. Feis, *Europe, the world's banker, 1870–1914** (1930); D. C. M. Platt, *Finance, trade, and politics in British foreign policy, 1815–1914* (1968); and R. E. Cameron, *France and the economic development of Europe, 1800–1914* (1961), cited in Chapter XI. Economic growth in two major European countries is studied in C. P. Kindleberger, *Economic growth in France and Britain, 1851–1950* (1963), and A. L. Levine, *Industrial retardation in Britain, 1880–1914* (1967). For Germany, one may read G. Stolper and others, *The German economy, 1870 to the present* (1940, trans. 1967), and W. O. Henderson, *The rise of German industrial power, 1834–1914** (1976), cited in Chapter XIII. American developments in these years may be studied in T. C. Cochran, *American business in the twentieth century* (1972); R. H. Wiebe, *The search for order, 1877–1920* (1967); and J. A. Garraty, *The new commonwealth* (1968).

France, 1870–1914

The general histories of modern France described in Chapter XI should be consulted as well as the bibliographical chapters in G. Wright, *France in modern times** (3rd ed., 1981). For the years since 1870, D. W. Brogan, *France under the Republic, 1870–1939** (1940), although rewarding, is difficult for the general reader. A concise thoughtful synthesis with a positive assessment of the Third Republic is R. D. Anderson, *France, 1870–1914* (1977). Also available are D. Thompson, *Democracy in France since 1870** (rev., 1969), a penetrating analytical study; G. Chapman, *The Third Republic of France: the first phase, 1871–1894* (1962), a detailed narrative; and A. Sedgwick, *The Third French Republic, 1870–1914** (1968), a useful, brief introduction. An unorthodox social history of major importance with many absorbing details and insights is T. Zeldin, *France, 1848–1945: ambition, love, and politics and . . . : intellect, taste, and anxiety* (2 vols., 1973, 1977); it is also available in five paperback volumes with the subtitles, *Politics and anger** (1979), *Ambition and love** (1979), *Intellect and pride** (1980), *Taste and corruption** (1980), and *Anxiety and hypocrisy** (1981). A masterful study arguing that French national unity was accomplished only belatedly by such agencies as the schools and army, with rich detail on rural life in France, is E. Weber, *Peasants into Frenchmen: the modernization of rural France, 1870–1914* (1976). Other recommended studies on France not strictly confined to the years before 1914 are G. Wright, *Rural revolution in France: the peasantry in the twentieth century* * (1964); J. Rothney, *Bonapartism after Sedan* (1969); B. Reardon, *Liberalism and tradition: aspects of Catholic thought in nineteenth century France* (1975); R. Shattuck, *The banquet years: the arts in France, 1885–1918* (1958); and R. J. Smith, *The École Normale Supérieure and the Third Republic* (1982). Religious questions since 1870 are treated comprehensively in A. Dansette's *Religious history of modern France*, vol. II, *Under the Third Republic* (trans. 1961); J. McManners, *Church and state in France, 1870–1914* (1972); M. Larkin, *Church and state after the Dreyfus affair* (1974); and P. A. Bertocci, *Jules Simon: republican anticlericalism and cultural politics in France, 1848–1886* (1978). The military is examined in R. Challener, *The French theory of the nation in arms, 1866–1939* (1952); P. M. de la Gorce, *The French army: a military-political history* (1963); D. G. Ralston, *The army of the republic: the place of the military in the political evolution of France, 1871–1914* (1967); and D. Porch, *The march to the Marne: the French army, 1871–1914* (1981). A special economic question is explored in M. S. Smith, *Tariff reform in France, 1860–1900: the politics of economic interest* (1980).

The tumultuous beginnings of the Third Republic are discussed from various points of view in M. Howard, *The Franco-Prussian War: the German invasion of France, 1870–1871* * (1967), cited in Chapter XIII; A. Horne, *The fall of Paris: the siege and the Commune, 1870–1871* * (1968); R. L. Williams, *The French Revolution of 1870–1871* (1969); M. Kranzberg, *The siege of Paris, 1870–1871* (1950); S. Edwards, *The Paris Commune, 1871* (1971); R. Tombs, *The war against Paris, 1871* (1981); and J. A. Leith (ed.), *Images of the Commune* (1978). On the women active in the Commune, there is E. Thomas, *The women incendiaries* (trans. 1966), and B. Lowry and E. E. Gunter have edited *The red virgin: memoirs of Louise Michel* (1981). Other studies before and beyond the Commune include J. P. T. Bury's three-volume work: *Gambetta and the national defence: a republican dictatorship in France* (1936), *Gambetta and the making of the Third Republic* (1973), and *Gambetta's final years: the era of difficulties, 1877–1882* (1981); J. T. Joughin, *The Paris Commune in French politics, 1871–1880* (2 vols., 1955); P. H. Hutton, *The cult of the revolutionary tradition: the Blanquists in French politics, 1864–1893* (1981); and F. H. Seager, *The Boulanger affair* (1969). S. Elwitt, *The making of the Third Republic: class and politics in France, 1868–1884* (1975), is a Marxist analysis of the early years. A. Mitchell, *The German influence in France after 1870: the formation of the French Republic* * (1979), the first volume of a projected larger study, seeks to demonstrate that anxiety over Germany helped shape the Third Republic.

On the Dreyfus affair, there are detailed and detached accounts by D. Johnson, *France and the Dreyfus affair* (1967); G. Chapman, *The Dreyfus case: a reassessment* (1955); and R. L. Hoffman, *More than a trial: the struggle over Captain Dreyfus* (1980), which reassesses but does not resolve the question of anti-Semitism. R. F. Byrnes presents part of the background in *Antisemitism in modern France: prologue to the Dreyfus affair* (1950). Related studies include M. R. Marrus, *The politics of assimilation: the French Jewish community at the time of the Dreyfus affair* * (1971); N. Wilson, *Bernard Lazare, antisemitism, and the problem of Jewish identity in late nineteenth-century France* (1978); P. Hyman, *From Dreyfus to Vichy: the remaking of French Jewry, 1906–1939* (1979); and S. Wilson, *Ideology and experience: antisemitism in France at the time of the Dreyfus affair* (1982).

On political leaders and movements of the right, there are valuable studies, many reaching beyond 1914, among them: M. Curtis, *Three against the Third Republic: Sorel, Barrès and Maurras* (1959); R. Soucy, *Fascism in France: the case of Maurice Barrès* (1972); C. S. Doty, *From cultural rebellion to counterrevolution: the politics of Maurice Barrès* (1976); E. Weber, *Action Française: royalism and reaction in twentieth-century France* * (1963), a remarkably full account; the same author's *The nationalist revival in France, 1905–1914* (1959); E. R. Tannenbaum, *The Action Française* (1962); M. L. Brown, Jr., *The comte de Chambord: the Third Republic's uncompromising king* (1967); R. R. Locke, *French legitimists and the politics of the moral order in the early Third Republic* (1974); and B. F. Martin, *Count Albert de Mun: paladin of the Third Republic* (1978). Political and intellectual history are brought together in W. R. Keylor, *Jacques Bainville and the renaissance of royalist history in twentieth-century France* (1979). R. Rémond, *The right wing in France: from 1815* to de Gaulle (1954, trans. 1966), has already been cited in Chapter XI, and it may be supplemented by D. Shapiro (ed.), *The right in France, 1890–1914* (St. Antony's Papers, 1962).

Other recommended biographical studies include R. Binion, *Defeated leaders: the political fate of Caillaux, Jouvenel and Tardieu* (1960); D. R. Watson, *Georges Clemenceau: a political biography* (1974); R. Albrecht-Carrié, *Adolphe Thiers, or the triumph of the bourgeoisie* (1977), a brief but vivid account; and H. A. Schmitt, *Charles Péguy: the decline of an idealist* (1967). As a sequel to his study of Louis Blanc, cited earlier, L. A. Loubère has written *Radicalism in Mediterranean France: its rise and decline, 1848–1914* (1974), and on an unrelated subject, *The red and the white: a history of wine in France and Italy in the nineteenth century* (1978), mostly on France. R. L. Williams, *The horror of life* (1980), unforgettably traces the medical history of five nineteenth-century writers and their alienation from society. [Studies of the French left and of labor history are described below in this chapter under Socialist Movement and Socialist Parties.]

The first serious if not completely successful history of women in the Third Republic is J. F. McMillan, *Housewife or harlot: the place of women in French society, 1870–1940* (1981), the title derived from a dictum of Proudhon; it may be supplemented by B. G. Smith, *Ladies of the leisure class: the bourgeoises of northern France in the nineteenth century** (1982), focusing mostly on conservativism in upper-class women. The relationship of women and socialism in France from the late nineteenth century to the present is explored in C. Sowerwine, *Sisters or citizens: women and socialism in France since 1876* (1982). Other examples of social history include M. B. Miller, *The Bon Marché: bourgeois culture and the department store, 1869–1920* (1981); P. O'Brien, *The promise of punishment: prisons in nineteenth century France* (1981); P. N. Stearns, *Old age in European society: the case of France* (1976); S. Barrows, *Distorting mirrors: visions of the crowd in late nineteenth-century France* (1981); and N. Evenson, *Paris: a century of change, 1878–1978* (1980), a study in architecture and urban life. The history of urban planning, which emerged in these years, is ably examined on a comparative basis in A. Sutcliffe, *Towards the planned city: Germany, Britain, the United States, and France, 1780–1914* (1981), focusing on the years after 1890.

Italy and Spain

The best narrative account of Italy since unification is D. Mack Smith, *Italy: a modern history* (rev., 1969), cited in Chapter XI; economic developments are ably presented in S. B. Clough, *The economic history of modern Italy* (1964), also cited in Chapter XI. For the years immediately after unification, the best-balanced account is C. Seton-Watson, *Italy from liberalism to fascism, 1870–1925* (1967), which may be supplemented by J. A. Thayer, *Italy and the Great War: politics and culture, 1870–1915* (1964); S. Saladino, *Italy from unification to 1919: growth and decay of a liberal regime** (1970), a brief, readable introduction; and E. R. Tannenbaum and E. P. Noether (eds.), *Modern Italy: a topical history since 1861* (1974), thematically organized. The background chapters of H. S. Hughes, *The United States and Italy* (rev., 1979), are illuminating. Some specialized studies are A. W. Salomone, *Italian democracy in the making: the political scene in the Giolittian era, 1900–1914* (1949, 1960); F. J. Coppa, *Planning, protectionism and politics in liberal Italy* (1971), sympathetic to Giolitti; and A. C. Jemolo, *Church and state in Italy, 1850–1950* (1960). An important monograph is R. A. Webster, *Industrial imperialism in Italy, 1908–1915* (1976), which argues that Italian foreign policy changed directions because of Italian economic needs. C. F. Delzell, *Italy in the twentieth century** (American Historical Association Pamphlets series, 1981), is a useful bibliographical essay. For Spain, the best account beginning in these years is R. Carr, *Modern Spain, 1875–1980** (1981).

Germany

The several titles for Germany in the nineteenth century cited earlier in Chapters XI, XII, and XIII should also be consulted, especially G. A. Craig's books. Recent writings about imperial Germany, inspired by a new generation of German historians led by Hans-Ulrich Wehler, see authoritarianism outstripping democratization because of the manipulative skills of agrarian and industrial political leaders; Wehler's book for the years 1871–1918 (1973) is not yet translated. Two books cited earlier in Chapter XI are highly recommended: J. J. Sheehan, *German liberalism in the nineteenth century* (1978), and J. A. Snell and H. A. Schmitt, *The democratic movement in Germany, 1789–1914* (1976). Two other useful books are G. Eley, *Reshaping the German right: radical nationalism and political change after Bismarck* (1980), which explores the failure of the National Liberals, and R. J. Evans (ed.), *Society and politics in Wilhelmine Germany* (1978).

Other recommended studies include W. M. Simon (ed.), *Germany in the age of Bismarck* (1968); J. A. Nichols, *Germany after Bismarck** (1959), on the Caprivi era; J. C. G. Röhl, *Germany without Bismarck: the crisis of government in the Second Reich, 1890–1900* (1968); and N. Rich, *Friedrich von Holstein: politics and diplomacy in the era of Bismarck and Wilhelm II* (2 vols., 1965).

Various institutions are examined in M. Kitchen, *The German officer corps, 1890–1914* (1968); H. H. Herwig, *The German naval officer corps, 1890–1918* (1973); and L. Cecil, *The German diplomatic service, 1871–1914* (1976). An important larger study, the last three volumes of which cover the years 1890–1914, is G. Ritter, *The sword and the scepter: the problem of militarism in Germany* (4 vols., trans. 1969–1973). For the universities, there are F. Lilge, *The abuse of learning: the failure of the German university* (1948); F. W. Ringer, *The decline of the German mandarins: the German academic community, 1890–1933* (1969); and K. H. Jarausch, *Students, society, and politics in imperial Germany: the rise of academic illiberalism** (1982). The best biography of William II is M. Balfour, *The Kaiser and his times* (1964), although A. Palmer, *The Kaiser: warlord of the second Reich* (1978), may also be recommended, as may the stimulating essays in J. C. G. Röhl and N. Sombart (eds.), *Kaiser Wilhelm II: new interpretations* (1982).

Books providing background to later developments in Germany include R. Gellately, *The politics of economic despair: shopkeepers and German politics, 1890–1914* (1974); W. Struve, *Elites against democracy: leadership ideals in bourgeois political thought in Germany, 1890–1933* (1973); U. Tal, *Christians and Jews in Germany: religion, politics, and ideology in the Second Reich, 1870–1914* (trans. 1975); R. J. Ross, *Beleaguered towns: the dilemma of political Catholicism in Wilhelmine Germany* (1976); E. L. Evans, *The German Center party, 1870–1933: a study in political Catholicism* (1981); and M. Lamberti, *Jewish activism in imperial Germany: the struggle for civil equality* (1978). Women as a pressure group for political change are ably studied in R. J. Evans, *The feminist*

movement in Germany, 1894–1933* (1976), and in J. H. Quataert, *Reluctant feminists in German social democracy, 1885–1917* (1979). [Other books on German socialism are listed below.]

Austria-Hungary

To the books on Austria cited in Chapter XIII may be added three books by W. A. Jenks: *The Austrian electoral reform of 1907* (1950), *Austria under the iron ring, 1879–1893* (1965), and *Vienna and the young Hitler* (1960); and one by A. C. Whiteside, *The socialism of fools: Georg Ritter von Schönerer and Austrian pan-Germanism* (1975).

A remarkable study, going well beyond its subject in speaking to the contemporary world and exploring political and cultural responses to the failure of bourgeois liberalism in Austria, is C. E. Schorske, *Fin de siècle Vienna: politics and culture** (1980). Important also for the intellectual contributions of the same city to the era is A. Janik and S. Toulmin, *Wittgenstein's Vienna* (1973), and in a broader setting, W. M. Johnston, *The Austrian mind: an intellectual and social history** (1975).

Great Britain, 1871–1914

A valuable bibliographical guide, already mentioned, is H. J. Hanham (ed.), *Bibliography of British history, 1851–1914* (1977). R. C. K. Ensor, *England, 1870–1914* (1936, 1949), remains useful for domestic affairs. G. Dangerfield, *The strange death of liberal England** (1935), is a searching study of tensions in English society between 1910 and 1914, but should be supplemented by S. Hynes, *The Edwardian turn of mind* (1968), and P. Thompson, *The Edwardians: the remaking of British society* (1975). A. P. Thornton, *The habit of authority: paternalism in British history* (1966), is a provocative essay. Syntheses moving into the twentieth century are K. Robbins, *The eclipse of a Great Power: modern Britain, 1870–1975** (1983); A. Havighurst, *Britain in transition: the twentieth century** (rev., 1979); T. Lloyd, *Empire to welfare state: English history, 1906–1976** (rev., 1979); and M. Pugh, *The making of modern British politics, 1867–1939* (1982). Recommended also are the following, in addition to several titles cited in Chapter XI: R. J. Evans, *The Victorian age, 1815–1914* (1950); G. K. Clark, *The making of Victorian England* (1962); W. E. Houghton, *The Victorian frame of mind* (1957); and W. L. Burn, *The age of* *equipoise** (1964). G. M. Young, *Portrait of an age: Victorian England* (2 vols., 1934), is now available in an annotated and enlarged new edition edited by G. K. Clark (1977) and provides an extraordinary range of information. On religion and social issues there are available two impressive studies: E. R. Norman, *Church and society in England, 1770–1970* (1976), and A. D. Gilbert, *Religion and society in industrial England: church, chapel, and social change, 1740–1914** (1976); in addition, there are H. McLeod, *Class and religion in the late Victorian city* (1974); I. Bradley, *The call to seriousness: the evangelical impact on the Victorians* (1976); S. Budd, *Varieties of unbelief: atheists and agnostics in English society, 1850–1960* (1977); and on a special subject, C. Holmes, *Anti-semitism in British society, 1876–1939* (1979).

Economic growth is ably traced in F. Crouzet, *The Victorian economy** (trans. 1982), and in a provocative comparative synthesis, G. M. Holmes, *Britain and America: a comparative economic history, 1850–1939* (1976). The movement to abandon free trade is explored in A. Sykes, *Tariff reform in British politics, 1903–1913* (1979). The patterns of urban and rural life are examined in two outstanding collaborative histories: H. J. Dyos and M. Wolff (eds.), *The Victorian city* (2 vols., 1973), and in G. E. Mingay (ed.), *The Victorian countryside* (2 vols., 1981).

Almost every major figure in this period has been the subject of at least one biography. Among biographical accounts are L. Strachey, *Queen Victoria** (1921), and *Eminent Victorians** (1918, 1933); A. Cecil, *Queen Victoria and her prime ministers* (1952); biographies of Victoria by E. F. Benson (1935), R. Fulford (1951), and E. Longford* (1965). P. Magnus has written *King Edward the Seventh* (1964). On Gladstone: the older work of J. Morley (3 vols., 1903); J. L. Hammond and M. R. D. Foot, *Gladstone and liberalism** (Teach Yourself History series, 1953); P. Magnus, *Gladstone: a biography** (1955); S. G. Checkland, *The Gladstones: a family biography* (1971); E. J. Feuchtwanger, *Gladstone* (1975), an admirable, balanced account; and P. Stansky, *Gladstone** (1979), thoughtful and readable. A detailed political study is M. Barker, *Gladstone and radicalism: the reconstruction of liberal policy, 1885–1894* (1975). On Disraeli: W. F. Monypenny and G. E. Buckle (6 vols., 1913–1920), is superseded by R. Blake, *Disraeli** (1967), and S.

Bradford, *Disraeli* (1983). Blake also has written *The unknown prime minister: the life and times of Andrew Bonar Law* (1955). Joseph Chamberlain is the subject of an exhaustive multivolumed biography, *The life of Joseph Chamberlain*, the first four volumes by J. L. Garvin (1932–1951) and the latter two by J. Amery (1968–1969); a balanced one-volume account is R. Jay, *Joseph Chamberlain: a political study* (1981). An introduction to the lives of Austin and Neville Chamberlain is provided in the somewhat adulatory D. H. Elletson, *The Chamberlains* (1966). Two volumes of a projected four-volume definitive biography of David Lloyd George have been completed: J. Grigg, *The young Lloyd George* (1973) and *Lloyd George: The people's champion, 1902–1911* (1978). S. Koss has written a judicious, well-balanced biography, *Asquith* (1976), which may be compared with that of R. Jenkins (1972). On Balfour, one may read biographical studies by S. Zebel (1973) and M. Egremont (1980). Recommended also are W. Irvine, *The universe of G. B. S.* (1949), on George Bernard Shaw; M. Cole (ed.), *The Webbs and their work* (1949); K. Muggeridge and R. Adam, *Beatrice Webb: a life, 1858–1943* (1968); H. Ausubel, *In hard times: reformers among the late Victorians* (1960); and the same author's *John Bright: Victorian reformer** (1966). R. Kelley, *The transatlantic persuasion: the liberal-democratic mind in the age of Gladstone* (1969), is of special interest.

Political and party issues are examined in depth in M. Cowling, *1867: Disraeli, Gladstone, and revolution: the passing of the Second Reform Bill* (1967); F. B. Smith, *The making of the Second Reform Bill* (1966); and P. Smith, *Disraelian conservatism and social reform* (1967). The vicissitudes of the Liberals in the era after Gladstone and their accomplishments are studied in P. Stansky, *Ambitions and strategies: the struggle for the leadership of the Liberal party in the 1890's* (1964); M. Richter, *The politics of conscience* (1964); and C. Cross, *The Liberals in power, 1905–1914* (1963).

Perhaps the best account explaining the emergence of the "new liberalism" is P. Clarke, *Liberals and social democrats* (1978), focusing on reform ideas and policy; it may be supplemented by D. Roberts, *Origins of the British welfare state* (1960), and M. Freeden, *The new liberalism: an ideology of social reform* (1978). Two books that examine twentieth-century Britain against the pre-1914 background are J. Ramsden,

The age of Balfour and Baldwin, 1902–1940 (1978), and R. R. James, *The British revolution, 1880–1939* (1977). An important detailed account of a critical event is B. K. Murray, *The people's budget, 1909–1910: Lloyd George and liberal politics* (1980). There are useful histories of the Liberal party by J. Vincent (1966, 1976), R. Douglas (1971), and C. Cook* (1976). S. Koss has written, as part of a larger study, an impressive first volume, *The rise and fall of the political press in Britain*, vol. I, *The nineteenth century* (1981).

D. Olsen, *The growth of Victorian London* (1970), relates architectural change to the broader urban context, and R. D. Altick, *The shows of London* (1978), is revealing on popular culture. Other aspects of Victorian culture emerge from B. Haley, *The healthy body and Victorian culture* (1978); M. J. Peterson, *The medical profession in mid-Victorian London* (1978); B. Harrison, *Drink and the Victorians* (1971); and J. Turner, *Reckoning with the beast: animals, pain, and humanity in the Victorian mind* (1980).

On the women's rights movement in this era, see J. Kamm, *Rapiers and battleaxes: the women's movement and its aftermath* (1966); C. Rover, *Women's suffrage and party politics in Britain, 1866–1914* (1967); D. Mitchell's somewhat popular account, *The fighting Pankhursts: a study in tenacity* (1967); D. Morgan, *Suffragists and liberals: the politics of woman suffrage in England* (1975); A. Rosen, *Rise up, women!: . . . the women's Social and Political Union, 1903–1914* (1974); and J. Luddington and J. Norris, *One hand tied behind us: the rise of the women's suffrage movement* (1978). On the restrictions on male voting before 1918, one should read M. Pugh, *Electoral reform in war and peace, 1906–1918* (1978).

Among studies that examine the status and role of women of various backgrounds in this era, one may read: J. N. Burstyn, *Victorian education and the ideal of womanhood* (1980); M. Hewitt, *Wives and mothers in Victorian industry* (2nd ed., 1975); M. Vicinus, *Suffer and be still: women in the Victorian age* (1973), and the volume she has edited, *A widening sphere: changing roles of Victorian women* (1977), with many informative chapters; F. K. Prochaska, *Women and philanthropy in nineteenth century England** (1980); N. C. Solden, *Women in British trade unions, 1874–1976* (1978); P. Branca, *Silent sisterhood: middle class women in the Victorian home* (1975);

and T. McBride, *The domestic revolution: the modernization of household service in England and France, 1820–1920* (1976). The important study by L. A. Tilly and J. W. Scott, *Women, work, and family* (1978), has been cited in the introductory section. A special subject is examined in J. R. Walkowitz, *Prostitution and Victorian society: women, class, and the state* (1980), setting the problem in a broad social context, and in P. McHugh, *Prostitution and Victorian social reform* (1980). An important collection of essays on demography and social and economic developments is T. Barker and M. Drake (eds.), *Population and society in Britain, 1850–1980* (1982), while a related topic is placed in historical perspective in A. Maclaren, *Birth control in nineteenth-century England* (1978).

The Irish question is discussed in J. E. Pomfret, *The struggle for land in Ireland, 1800–1923* (1930); J. C. Beckett, *The making of modern Ireland* (1966), cited in Chapter IV; L. J. McCaffrey, *The Irish question, 1800–1922** (1968); and in a remarkable study focusing on the years 1912 to 1921, G. Dangerfield, *The damnable question: a study of Anglo-Irish relations* (1976).

Socialist Movement and Socialist Parties

[General histories of socialism are listed for Chapter XI, and works on Marx and Marxism for Chapter XII.] On the modern translation of Marxist ideas into institutional form, the books by G. D. H. Cole, *A history of socialist thought*, and by C. Landauer, *European socialism*, both already cited, should be consulted. To them may be added H. Mitchell and P. N. Stearns, *Workers and protest: the European labor movement, the working classes, and the origins of social democracy, 1890–1914** (1971). In addition, there are many specific studies of socialist parties and leaders in each country. For France: A. Noland, *The founding of the French socialist party, 1893–1905* (1956); J. H. Jackson, *Jean Jaurès: his life and work* (1943); H. Goldberg, *A life of Jean Jaurès* (1962), an outstanding biography; and L. Derfler, *Alexandre Millerand: the socialist years* (1977). For Germany: C. E. Schorske, *German social democracy, 1905–1917** (1955), a valuable study; A. J. Berlau, *The German Social Democratic party, 1914–1921* (1949); P. Gay, *The dilemma of democratic socialism: Eduard Bernstein's chal-*

lenge to Marx* (1952), a perceptive examination of Bernstein's revisionism; G. Roth, *The Social Democrats in imperial Germany* (1963); V. L. Lidtke, *The outlawed party: social democracy in Germany, 1878–1890* (1966); and W. H. Maehl, *Auguste Bebel: shadow emperor of the German workers* (1980), a solid study. An important biographical work is J. P. Nettl, *Rosa Luxemburg** (2 vols., 1966; abr. 1 vol., 1969), for whom there is also available N. Geras, *The legacy of Rosa Luxemburg* (1976). A special subject is examined in A. Hussain and K. Tribe, *Marxism and the agrarian question* (2 vols., 1981), focusing on the German and Russian responses.

For Britain: N. MacKenzie and J. MacKenzie, *The Fabians* (1977), successfully combines biography and social and intellectual history, and supersedes older studies by A. H. McBriar (1926) and others. Two volumes by S. Pierson probe the grass-roots origins of British socialism more effectively than earlier studies: *Marxism and the origins of British socialism: the struggle for a new consciousness* (1973), and *British socialists: the journey from fantasy to politics* (1979), which carries the story to 1919. Other recommended books are R. Moore, *The emergence of the Labour party, 1880–1924* (1978), a fine synthesis, and T. Forester, *The British Labour party and the working class* (1976). H. Pelling, *The origins of the Labour party, 1880–1900* (1954, 1965), remains useful. Two thoughtful biographies of William Morris are E. P. Thompson, *William Morris: romantic to revolutionary* (1955; rev., 1977), and P. Meier, *William Morris, the Marxist dreamer* (2 vols., 1972; trans. 1978). Christian socialism is explored in P. d'A. Jones, *The Christian Socialist revival, 1877–1914* (1968).

On the Internationals, there are J. Joll, *The Second International, 1889–1914* (1955; rev., 1974), a concise survey, and J. Braunthal, *History of the International* (3 vols., trans. 1961–1980), more detailed. The breakup of the International is ably described in G. Haupt, *Socialism and the Great War: the collapse of the Second International* (1972). The most comprehensive introduction to anarchism is G. Woodcock, *Anarchism: a history of libertarian ideas and movements* (1962), but also useful is J. Joll, *The anarchists** (2nd ed., 1981).

Labor and Labor Unions

Some recent efforts at writing labor history have attempted to convey the experiences of laboring men and women apart from organized labor movements and to integrate labor protest into a broader cultural context. Here E. P. Thompson, whose works have been cited, has been a pioneer. A successful effort for the English experience in these years is S. Meacham, *A life apart: the English working class, 1890–1914* (1977). A similar orientation, going beyond the English experience, is evident in P. N. Stearns, *Lives of labor: work in a maturing industrial society* (1975). Other examples of sensitivity to rank and file concerns may be found in J. W. Scott, *The glassworkers of Carmaux: French craftsmen and political action in a nineteenth-century city* (1974), portraying the militancy of artisans in the face of mechanization; B. H. Moss, *The origins of the French labor movement: the socialism of skilled workers, 1830–1914* (1977); T. Judt, *Socialism in Provence, 1871–1914: a study in the origins of the modern French left* (1979); and M. P. Hanagan, *The logic of solidarity: artisans and industrial workers in three French towns, 1871–1914** (1981). Other interesting examples, for British labor, are J. Benson, *British coalminers in the nineteenth century* (1980); P. Joyce, *Work, society and politics: the culture of the factory in late Victorian England* (1980); and D. Kynaston, *The British working class, 1850–1914* (1976).

Traditional trade union history in Britain may be studied in H. Pelling, *A history of British trade unionism* (1963), a useful synthesis, and H. A. Clegg, A. Fox, and A. F. Thompson, *A history of British trade unions since 1889*, vol. I, *1889–1910* (1964), the first volume of a detailed history. For French, German, and Italian trade union development, one may turn, among other books, to V. R. Lorwin, *The French labor movement* (1954); E. Anderson, *Hammer or anvil: the story of the German working-class movement* (1945); and M. F. Neufeld, *Italy, school for awakening countries: the Italian labor movement in its political, social, and economic setting from 1860 to 1960* (1961).

The New Movement in Science

A good general history of science in the nineteenth century is W. P. D. Wightman, *The growth of scientific ideas* (1951). On biology, evolution, and Darwinism, one may turn to P. Fothergill, *Historical aspects of organic evolution* (1952); J. C. Greene, *The death of Adam: evolution and its impact on Western thought* (1959); P. B. Sears, *Charles Darwin: the naturalist as a cultural force* (1950); G. Himmelfarb, *Darwin and the*

Darwinian revolution * (1959); L. Eiseley, *Darwin's century* (1961); and G. R. deBeers, *Charles Darwin* (1958). C. C. Gillispie, *The edge of objectivity: an essay in the history of scientific ideas* (1960), cited in Chapter VII, is important for Darwinism and other subjects. On the impact of the scientific developments on religion, the classic account is A. D. White, *A history of the warfare of science and theology* * (1896, many eds.); more recent studies include C. C. Gillispie, *Genesis and geology* (1951); W. Irvine, *Apes, angels, and Victorians* (1955); and J. R. Moore, *The post-Darwinian controversies: a study of the Protestant struggle to come to terms with Darwin in Great Britain and America, 1870–1900* * (1979), a detailed study with an extensive bibliography on the subject. The impact on social thought is studied in J. W. Burrow, *Evolution and society: a study in Victorian social theory* (1966).

On the rise of twentieth-century physics, one may read I. B. Cohen, *The birth of the new physics* (1960); and A. Einstein and L. Infeld, *The evolution of physics* (1938). Einstein may best be approached through L. Infeld, *Albert Einstein: his work and its influence on our world* * (1950); L. Barnett, *The universe and Dr. Einstein* (1952); the brief II. Cuny, *Albert Einstein* * (1962); and R. W. Clark, *Einstein: the life and times* * (1971). For Freud, F. Wittels, *Freud and his time* (1931, 1948); P. Rieff, *Freud: the mind of the moralist* (1959); and R. Clark, *Freud: the man and the cause* (1980), are three of the best interpretive studies of Sigmund Freud; they may be compared with the masterful biography by E. Jones (3 vols., 1953–1957; 1 vol. abr. 1961). On the reception of Freud, one may read H. S. Decker, *Freud in Germany: revolution and reaction in science, 1893–1907* (1977); S. Turkle, *Psychoanalytic politics: Freud's French Revolution* (1978); and B. Bettelheim, *Freud and man's soul* (1983), especially informative on the translation of Freud's writings in the United States. B. P. Babkin has written *Pavlov: a biography* (1949).

Social Thought

Two outstanding contributions are H. S. Hughes, *Consciousness and society: the reorientation of European social thought, 1890–1930* * (1958), and G. Masur, *Prophets of yesterday: studies in European culture, 1890–1914* * (1961), cited earlier in this chapter. Virtually a history of thought from Herbert Spencer to the present is W. W. Wagar, *Good tidings: the belief in progress from Darwin to Marcuse* (1972); on that theme, in addition to R. Nisbet, *History of the idea of progress* (1980), cited in the introductory section, one may read M. Ginsberg, *The idea of progress* (1953), and a thoughtful collaborative volume, G. Almond, M. Chodorow, and R. H. Pierce (eds.), *Progress and its discontents* (1982). A thoughtful study of a dominant thinker of the age is D. Wiltshire, *The social and political thought of Herbert Spencer* (1978). Other recommended works include E. Barker, *Political thought in England* (1915, 1947); E. Wilson, *Axel's castle: a study in the imaginative literature of 1870–1930* (1931); J. Higham and others, *The origins of modern consciousness* (1965); and K. Löwith, *From Hegel to Nietzsche: the revolution in nineteenth-century thought* (1941, trans. 1964). Three books by I. Berlin in this connection are highly recommended: *Russian thinkers* (1978), *Concepts and categories* (1979), and *Against the current* (1980); and two other provocative books are P. Paret, *The Berlin secession: modernism and its enemies in imperial Germany* (1981), and P. Gay, *Freud, Jews, and other Germans: masters and victims in modernist culture* (1978). More specialized studies are W. Irvine, *Walter Bagehot* (1939); H. Alpert, *Emile Durkheim and his sociology* (1939), on a leading French systematizer; J. P. Mayer, *Max Weber and German politics*; and J. Freund, *The sociology of Max Weber* (1966, trans. 1968). The two best studies of Nietzsche are W. A. Kaufmann, *Nietzsche: philosopher, psychologist, antichrist* * (1950), and R. Hayman, *Nietzsche: a critical life* (1980); and on one of Nietzsche's intimates, Lou Andreas Salomé, R. Binion has written a psychoanalytical biography, *Frau Lou: Nietzsche's wayward disciple* * (1968). A useful anthology for these years is R. N. Stromberg (ed.), *Realism, naturalism, and symbolism: modes of thought and expression in Europe, 1848–1914* (1968).

Racism, Integral Nationalism, and the Cult of Violence

The later development of totalitarianism is dealt with in Chapter XIX. In addition to many of the titles cited above, books examining the revolt against rationalism in politics, beginning with the late nineteenth century, are II. Kohn, *The twentieth century* (1957); H. Arendt, *The origins of totalitarianism* * (1951, 1958), a somewhat abstruse work that finds the roots of totalitarianism in late-nineteenth-century imperialism, nationalism, and anti-Semitism; J. Barzun, *Darwin, Marx, Wagner: critique of a heritage** (2nd ed., 1981), which points out resemblances in the assumptions and conclusions of the three men; E. Heller, *The disinherited mind* (1957); J. J. Roth, *The cult of violence: Sorel and the Sorelians* (1980); and J. L. Talmon, *The myth of the nation and the vision of revolution: the origins of ideological polarization in the twentieth century* (1980). Two studies stressing conservative nationalism are A. Dorpalen, *Heinrich von Treitschke* (1957), and K. von Klemperer, *Germany's new conservatism: its history and dilemma in the twentieth century** (1968). Focusing on racism and anti-Semitism are P. W. Massing, *Rehearsal for destruction: a study of political anti-semitism in imperial Germany* (1949); P. G. J. Pulzer, *The rise of political anti-semitism in Germany and Austria* (1964); L. Poliakov, *The Aryan myth: a history of racist and nationalist ideas in Europe* (trans. 1974); J. Katz, *From prejudice to destruction: anti-semitism, 1700–1933* (1980); G. L. Mosse, *Toward the final solution: a history of European racism* (1978); and G. G. Field, *Evangelist of race: the Germanic vision of Houston Stewart Chamberlain* (1981). For nationalism of all kinds, in addition to books listed in Chapter XI, there are A. D. S. Smith, *Nationalism in the twentieth century* (1979), and the collection edited by Smith, *Nationalist movements* (1977).

Religion since 1870

The continuing relationship between secularized European civilization and its Christian origins is ably treated in O. Chadwick, *The secularization of the European mind in the nineteenth century* (1976), and a good brief introduction is H. McLeod, *Religion and the people of Western Europe, 1789–1970** (1981). Two scholarly surveys with considerable attention to contemporary Protestantism are J. H. Nichols, *History of Christianity, 1650–1950* (1956), and E. E. Cairns, *Christianity through the centuries* (1954). The theological contributions of David Friedrich Strauss are examined in books by H. Harris (1976) and R. S. Cromwell (1974).

More specifically on the Catholic church are E. E. Y. Hales's sympathetic study of Pius IX, *Pio Nono* (1954), cited in Chapter XII; L. P. Wallace, *The papacy and European diplomacy, 1869–1878* (1948); C. But-

ler, *The Vatican Council: the story told from inside in Bishop Ullathorne's letters* (2 vols., 1930); R. Fülöp-Miller, *Leo XIII and our times* (1937); and for a detailed inquiry into the Catholic reaction to modernism, one may read T. M. Loome, *Liberal Catholicism, reform Catholicism, and modernism* (1979).

Several valuable books on aspects of Jewish affairs, including Zionism, by J. W. Parkes are *The emergence of the Jewish problem, 1878–1939* (1946), *The Jewish problem in the modern world* (1946), *Anti-Semitism** (1963), and *A history of the Jewish people* (1952). The syntheses of Jewish history by H. M. Sachar, *The course of modern Jewish history** (rev., 1977), cited in Chapter VIII, and *A history of Israel: from the rise of Zionism to our time* (rev., 1979), give attention to nineteenth-century ideology. Also available are B. Halpern, *The idea of the Jewish state* (1961); W. Laqueur, *A history of Zionism* (1976); two impressive books by D. Vital, *The origins of Zionism* (1975) and *Zionism: the formative years* (1982); and S. Avineri, *The making of modern Zionism: the intellectual origins of the Jewish state* (1981). An intriguing if not entirely convincing work is J. M. Cuddihy, *The ordeal of civility: Freud, Marx, Lévi-Strauss and the Jewish struggle with modernity** (1975.)

Problems and Readings*

Pamphlets relating to this chapter are R. L. Williams (ed.), *The Commune of Paris, 1871* (1969); S. Edwards (ed.), *The Communards of Paris* (1973); L. Derfler (ed.), *The Dreyfus affair: tragedy of errors?* (1964); H. R. Kedward (ed.), *The Dreyfus affair: catalyst for tensions in French society* (1965); E. C. Helmreich (ed.), *A free church in a free state: the Catholic church, Italy, Germany, France, 1864–1914* (1964); T. S. Hamerow (ed.), *The age of Bismarck: documents and interpretations* (1974); J. J. Sheehan (ed.), *Imperial Germany* (1976); H. Shultz (ed.), *English liberalism and the state: individualism or collectivism* (1974); E. C. Black (ed.), *Victorian culture and society* (1974); and P. Stansky (ed.), *The Victorian revolution: government and society in Victoria's Britain* (1973). Also useful are H. Vanderpool (ed.), *Darwin and Darwinism* (1974), and N. G. Levin (ed.), *The Zionist movement in Palestine and world politics, 1880–1918* (1973). In the Anvil series, there are H. Ausubel, *The late Victorians: a short history* (1955); R. L. Schuyler and C. Weston, *British constitutional history since 1832* (1957); L. L. Snyder, *The idea of racialism. its meaning and history* (1962); and J. S. Schapiro, *Anticlericalism: conflict between church and state in France, Italy, and Spain* (1967).

XV: EUROPE'S WORLD SUPREMACY

Imperialism in General

Debate in recent years about the roots of imperialism has in large part been stimulated by the seminal study of R. Robinson and J. Gallagher, *Africa and the Victorians: the official mind of imperialism** (1961), and their other writings; they see no sharp break with the past in the 1870s, stress the importance of economic penetration over annexation, and argue that the European powers were drawn into formal empires by internal power vacuums so that imperialism cannot be understood without a study of the indigenous societies involved. An excellent introduction to the debate is W. R. Lewis (ed.), *Imperialism: the Robinson-Gallagher controversy** (1976). Another important writer who stresses national power, prestige, and security over economic motivations is D. Fieldhouse, whose books include *The colonial empires: a comparative survey from the eighteenth century* (1966), cited in Chapter VI; *Economics and empire, 1830–1914* (1973); and *Colonialism, 1870–1945: an introduction* (1981), a concise balanced assessment focusing on the pre-1914 years but setting the stage for the decline of empire as well. The older account by W. L. Langer, *The diplomacy of imperialism, 1890–1902** (2 vols., 1935), remains valuable for its full, balanced discussion of imperialism in all aspects; it may be supplemented by R. Shannon, *The crisis of imperialism, 1865–1915* (1974). Useful introductions include H. Gollwitzer, *Europe in the age of imperialism, 1848–1917* (1974); R. F. Betts, *The false dawn: European imperialism in the nineteenth century* (1979), a volume in the Europe and the World in the Age of Expansion series; and two books by W. Woodruff, *Impact of Western man* (1967), and *The struggle for world power and domination, 1500–1979* (1981). Motives and justifications for imperialist activities are analyzed in E. M. Winslow, *The pattern of imperialism:*

a study in the theories of power (1948); R. Koebner and H. D. Schmidt, *Imperialism: the story and significance of a political word, 1840–1960* (1964); A. P. Thornton, *Doctrines of imperialism* (1965); the same author's *Imperialism in the twentieth century* (1977); and C. Reynolds, *Modes of imperialism* (1981). Other important discussions and studies include R. Maunier, *The sociology of colonies: an introduction to the study of race contact* (2 vols., 1949); D. Mannoni, *Prospero and Caliban: the psychology of colonization** (1956), stressing the psychological impact of colonial rule on both rulers and governed; and T. Geiger, *The conflicted relationship: the West and the transformation of Asia, Africa, and Latin America* (1967). Two classic studies are J. A. Hobson's *Imperialism: a study** (1902), and V. I. Lenin's *Imperialism, the highest stage of capitalism** (1916); a lucid exposition of the Marxist-Leninist interpretation is V. G. Kiernan, *Marxism and imperialism* (1975). An important comparative study is W. Baumgart, *Imperialism: the idea and reality of British and French colonial expansion, 1880–1914* (trans. 1982).

Two good surveys which, like Robinson and Gallagher, downplay directives from London are B. Porter, *The lion's share: a short history of British imperialism, 1850–1970** (1976), an especially lively account, and R. Hyam, *Britain's imperial century, 1815–1914: a study of empire and expansion* (1976). Other recommended books include R. Faber, *The vision and the need: late Victorian imperialist aims* (1966); B. Semmel, *Imperialism and social reform: English social imperial thought, 1895–1914** (1960); B. Porter, *Critics of empire: British radical attitudes to colonialism in Africa, 1895–1914* (1968); A. P. Thornton, *The imperial idea and its enemies: a study in British power** (1959); M. Beloff, *Imperial sunset,* vol. I, *Britain's liberal empire, 1897–1921* (1970); D. C. Gordon, *The moment of power: Britain's imperial epoch* (1970); C. C. Eldridge, *England's mission: the imperial idea in the age of Gladstone and Disraeli, 1868–1880* (1973); D. A. Low, *Lion rampant: essays in the study of British imperialism* (1973); and J. W. Cell, *British colonial administration in the mid-nineteenth century: the policy-making process* (1970). Biographical accounts include V. Halperin, *Lord Milner and the empire: the evolution of British imperialism* (1952); and G. H. Uzoigwe, *Britain and the conquest of Africa:*

the age of Salisbury (1974), focusing on the Conservative statesman.

The imperial activities of the other leading European powers are described in W. O. Henderson, *Studies in German colonial history* (1963); W. D. Smith, *The German colonial empire* (1978); H. Brunschwig, *French colonialism, 1871–1914: myths and realities* (1960, trans, 1966). A. W. Heggoy, *The African policies of Gabriel Hanotaux, 1894–1898* (1972); C. Hollis, *Italy in Africa* (1941); R. A. Webster, *Industrial imperialism in Italy, 1908–1915* (1975), cited earlier; and in other books listed below.

The Americas

For imperialism in the Americas, two important studies are D. C. M. Platt (ed.), *Business imperialism, 1840–1930: an inquiry based on British experience in Latin America* (1977), and S. J. Stein and B. H. Stein, *The colonial heritage of Latin America: essays on economic dependence in perspective* (1970). On the expansion of the United States: A. K. Weinberg, *Manifest destiny** (1935), a standard work, and E. R. May, *Imperial democracy* (1961), and *American imperialism: a speculative essay* (1968), are indispensable on American motivations. C. C. Campbell, *The transformation of American foreign relations, 1865–1900* (1976), and R. L. Beisner, *From the old diplomacy to the new, 1865–1900* (1975), are thoughtful interpretations. Other phases of American foreign policy are treated in U.S. diplomatic histories and in J. W. Pratt, *Expansionists of 1898** (1936), and *America's colonial experiment* (1950); W. Millis, *The martial spirit** (1931), an ironic discussion of the Spanish-American War; and M. Tate, *The United States and the Hawaiian kingdom* (1965). The building of the Panama Canal is graphically narrated in D. McCullough, *The path between the seas: the creation of the Panama Canal, 1870–1914* (1977). D. Dawson, *The Mexican adventure* (1935), is a careful account of Napoleon III's fiasco during the 1860s, and may be supplemented by N. N. Barker, *The French experience in Mexico, 1821–1861: a history of constant misunderstanding* (1979). F. Tannenbaum's *Mexico: the struggle for peace and bread* (1950), provides a thoughtful narrative of Mexican history, and may be read with R. E. Ruíz, *The great rebellion: Mexico, 1905–1924** (1980).

The Ottoman Empire, the Middle East, and the Balkans

Books on Arab history and Islam are cited in Chapter I, on the early Ottoman Empire in Chapter V, and on the Balkans in Chapter XI. S. N. Fisher, *The Middle East: a history* (rev., 1968), is a useful synthesis, and S. J. Shaw and E. K. Shaw, *History of the Ottoman Empire and modern Turkey*, vol. II (1977), a detailed account. B. Lewis, *The emergence of modern Turkey* (1961; rev., 1969), an outstanding work, treats nineteenth-century developments as background. For economic history, there is a major study by R. Owen, *The Middle East and the world economy, 1800–1914* (1981), and two books by C. Issawi: *The economic history of the Middle East, 1800–1914* (1966), and *The economic history of Iran, 1800–1914* (1971). Other studies are J. Haslip, *The Sultan: the life of Abdul Hamid II* (1958), a vivid scholarly account with insight into the empire; S. Mardin, *The genesis of Young Ottoman thought* (1963), on the decade 1867–1878; two books on the Young Turks by E. E. Ramsauer (1957) and F. Ahmad (1969); R. H. Davison, *Reform in the Ottoman Empire, 1856–1876* (1963); and D. Kushner, *The rise of Turkish nationalism, 1876–1908* (1977). For Egypt, there are available H. Dodwell, *The founder of modern Egypt: a study of Muhammad Ali* [Mehemet Ali] (1931); D. S. Landes, *Bankers and pashas: international finance and economic imperialism in Egypt** (1958); P. Grau, *Islamic roots of capitalism: Egypt, 1760–1840* (1979); and R. L. Tignor, *Modernization and British colonial rule in Egypt, 1882–1914* (1966). The diplomacy surrounding the construction of the Suez Canal may be studied in J. Marlowe, *World ditch: the making of the Suez Canal* (1964); J. Pudney, *Suez: de Lesseps' canal* (1969); and P. Balfour [Lord Kinross], *Between two seas* (1969). The French experience in Lebanon is examined in J. F. Spagnolo, *French and Ottoman Lebanon, 1861–1914* (1977), which may be supplemented by A. Williams, *Britain and France in the Middle East and North Africa, 1914–1967* (1969), and C. M. Andrew and A. S. Kanya-Forstner, *The climax of French imperial expansion, 1914–1924* (1981); and the Italian experience in Libya is studied in C. G. Segré, *Fourth shore: the Italian colonization of Libya* (1975).

The best introduction to the diplomatic

status of Turkey in European affairs is M. S. Anderson, *The Eastern question, 1774–1923* (1966), cited in Chapters XI and XIII; other studies include F. E. Bailey, *British policy and Turkish reform: a study in Anglo Turkish relations, 1826–1853* (1942); R. W. Seton-Watson, *Disraeli, Gladstone, and the Eastern question* (1935); W. N. Medlicott, *The Congress of Berlin and after: a diplomatic history of the Near Eastern settlement, 1878–1880* (1938, 1963); E. M. Earle, *Turkey, the Great Powers, and the Bagdad railway* (1923); and M. K. Chapman, *Great Britain and the Bagdad railway* (1948).

On the Balkans, in addition to books cited in Chapter XI by L. Stavrianos, by R. J. Wolff, and by B. and C. Jelavich, one may turn to B. H. Sumner, *Russia and the Balkans, 1870–1880* (1937); C. Sforza, *Fifty years of war and diplomacy in the Balkans* (1941); J. A. Levandis, *The Greek foreign debt and the Great Powers, 1821–1898* (1944); G. J. Bobango, *The emergence of the Romanian national state* (1979); W. C. Vucinich, *Serbia between East and West: the events of 1903–1908* (1954); and C. Jelavich, *Tsarist Russia and Balkan nationalism* (1958).

Africa

Two useful one-volume introductions are R. W. July, *A history of the African people** (3rd ed., 1980), and P. D. Curtin, S. Feierman, L. Thompson, and J. Vansina, *African history** (1978); July has also written *Precolonial Africa: an economic and social history** (1975), and *The origins of modern African thought: its development in West Africa during the nineteenth and twentieth centuries* (1967). How the early kingdoms expanded is explained in L. Mair, *African kingdoms** (1977), and the same author has also written *African societies* (1974). Vivid accounts on a grand scale are R. Hallett, *Africa to 1875* (1970) and *Africa since 1875* (1974); in these books, and in *The penetration of Africa: European exploration in North and West Africa to 1815* (1965), the author seeks to examine the inner workings of African society as well as the European impact. Good also for the presentation of indigenous culture and thought are the essays in P. D. Curtin (ed.), *Africa and the West: intellectual responses to European culture* (1972).

Recommended as detailed studies are R. Oliver and J. A. Atmore, *The African mid-dle ages, 1400–1800** (1981), and *Africa since 1800* (3rd ed., 1981). Other useful introductions and surveys are R. Oliver and J. D. Fage, *A short history of Africa** (rev., 1976); J. D. Fage, *A history of Africa* (1978), in the History of Human Society series; N. R. Bennett, *Africa and Europe from Roman times to the present** (1975), a brief treatment; B. Davidson, *Africa in history: themes and outlines** (rev., 1974); R. I. Rotberg, *A political history of tropical Africa* (1965); and G. P. Murdock, *Africa: its peoples and their culture history* (1959), by an anthropologist. The use of "oral tradition" in the reconstruction of African history is examined in J. Vansina, *Oral tradition: a study of historical methodology* (1961, trans. 1963), and admirably demonstrated by the same author in *Kingdoms of the savanna** (1966). P. Curtin, *The image of Africa: British ideas and action, 1780–1850* (1964), is a study in political and cultural interaction; the same author demonstrates other concerns in *Economic change in precolonial Africa: Senegambia in the era of the slave trade* (2 vols., 1975). In progress is the collaborative *Cambridge History of Africa* (J. E. Flint, ed., 1975–), sound but unimaginative; four volumes of a projected eight have appeared, of which vol. 5 (1977) covers the years 1790 to 1870. W. E. B. Du Bois, *The world and Africa* (1947), presents ideas and historical materials not readily accessible elsewhere. An illuminating survey of African art is F. Willett, *African art: an introduction** (1971).

P. Duignan and L. H. Gann in *Burden of empire: an appraisal of Western colonialism south of the Sahara* (1967), and in their other writings, attempt to demonstrate that the benefits of European expansion outweighed the debits. The same writers are coeditors of a five-volume collaborative history, *Colonialism in Africa, 1870–1960* (1969–1973); they have focused on colonial administration in three books: *The rulers of German Africa, 1884–1914* (1977), *The rulers of British Africa, 1870–1914* (1978), and *The rulers of Belgian Africa, 1884–1914* (1979); and they have coedited *African proconsuls: European governors in Africa* (1978). All their writings emphasize a "benevolent imperialism."

A well-balanced synthesis is H. S. Wilson, *The imperial experience in sub-Saharan Africa since 1870* (1977), vol. 8 in the Europe and the World in the Age of Expansion series. Two books by W. B. Cohen, *Rulers of empire: the French colonial service in Africa* (1971) and *The French encounter with Africans: white response to blacks, 1530–1880* (1981), are recommended; the author sees racism as supportive of imperialism. Resistance to the Europeans is examined in A. J. Isaacman, *The tradition of resistance in Mozambique: the Zambesi Valley, 1850–1921* (1977), and R. Tignor, *The colonial transformation of Kenya: the Kamba, Kikuyu, and Masai from 1900 to 1939* (1976); and on the African leader who defeated the Italians at Adowa, one may read H. G. Marcus, *The life and times of Menelik II: Ethiopia, 1844–1913* (1975). A monumental history of missionary activity in Africa since 1840 is C. P. Groves, *The planting of Christianity in Africa* (4 vols., 1948–1959).

There are biographical studies of Livingstone by J. Simmons (1955), G. Seaver (1957), F. Debenham (1953), and O. Ransford (1978), the latter psychologically oriented. Other leading figures are examined in R. Hall, *Stanley* (1976); R. Oliver, *Sir Harry Johnston and the scramble for Africa* (1957); G. Elton, *Gordon of Khartoum* (1954); J. Marlowe, *Mission to Khartoum* (1969); and M. F. Perham, *Lugard: the years of adventure, 1858–1898* (1936). The best biography of Cecil Rhodes, a brief one, is by J. Flint (1976), although there are others by B. Williams (1921), A. Maurois (1953), and S. G. Millin (1933). B. Williams has written *Botha, Smuts, and South Africa* (Teach Yourself History series, 1948). The best study of the Congo to 1908 is R. Slade, *King Leopold's Congo* (1962), on which subject there also is N. Ascherson, *The king incorporated* (1963), and R. Anstey, *King Leopold's legacy* (1966); Anstey has also written *Britain and the Congo in the nineteenth century* (1962).

On southern Africa and the emergence of South Africa, one may read D. M. Schreuder, *The scramble for southern Africa, 1877–1895* (1981), and two collaborative works, L. Thompson and M. Wilson (eds.), *The Oxford history of South Africa* (2 vols., 1969–1971), and Thompson (ed.), *African societies in southern Africa* (1969). The Boer War is recounted in B. Farwell, *The great Anglo-Boer War* (1976), and T. Pakenham, *The Boer War* (1979).

Other important monographs are R. Coupland, *East Africa and its invaders* (1938), for the years to 1856, and *The exploitation of East Africa, 1856–1890: the slave trade and the scramble* (1939); R. D. Wolff, *The economics of colonialism: Brit-*

ain and Kenya, 1870–1930 (1974); M. M. Knight, *Morocco as a French economic venture: a study of open door imperialism* (1937); H. Rudin, *Germans in the Cameroons, 1884–1914; a case study in modern imperialism* (1938); J. Suret-Canale, *French colonialism in tropical Africa, 1900–1945* (trans. 1971); and S. E. Crowe, *The Berlin West African conference, 1884–1885* (1942). On the slave trade and its abolition, in addition to works cited in Chapter XI and earlier, one may read B. Davidson, *Black mother: the years of the African slave trade* (1961), and on the Brussels conference of 1889, S. Miers, *Britain and the ending of the slave trade* (1975). African integration into the global economy is studied in J. F. Munro, *Africa and the international economy, 1800–1960** (1976).

Asia

[Japan is discussed mainly in Chapter XIII, and Asia in general after 1918 in Chapters XVIII and XXI.] Among informative general surveys of the European impact on the Far East are J. Pratt, *The expansion of Europe in the Far East* (1947); K. M. Pannikar, *Asia and Western dominance: . . . the Vasco da Gama epoch of Asian history, 1498–1945** (rev., 1959), cited in Chapter VI; P. H. Clyde and B. F. Beers, *The Far East: a history of Western impacts and Eastern responses, 1830–1974* (rev., 1975); E. S. Dodge, *Islands and empires: Western impact on the Pacific and East Asia* (1976), vol. 7 of Europe and the World in the Age of Expansion series, somewhat uneven in coverage; and R. Murphey, *The outsiders: Western experience in India and China* (1977), a challenging book which disputes some of Pannikar's conclusions.

The best introduction to East Asia for all phases is J. K. Fairbank, E. O. Reischauer, and A. M. Craig, *East Asia: tradition and transformation* (rev., 1978). Good overviews of Chinese history include J. K. Fairbank, *The United States and China** (rev., 1979), in the American Foreign Policy Library series; C. P. Fitzgerald, *China: a short cultural history* (rev., 1961); L. C. Goodrich, *A short history of the Chinese people* (1943; rev., 1959); C. O. Hucker, *China's imperial past: an introduction to Chinese history and culture** (1975); F. W. Mote, *Intellectual foundations of China** (1971); and J. B. Grieder, *Intellectuals and the state in modern China: a narrative history* (1981). The first volumes to appear of the collaborative Cambridge

History of China, projected in fourteen volumes (D. Twitchett and J. K. Fairbank, gen. eds.), cover the late Ch'ing period, 1800–1911 (1979, 1980).

European relations with China and the Chinese response are taken up in J. K. Fairbank, *Trade and diplomacy on the China coast: the opening of the treaty ports, 1842–1854** (2 vols., 1953); Ssu-yu Teng and J. K. Fairbank, *China's response to the West: a documentary survey, 1839–1923** (1954, 1963); J. Spence, *To change China: Western advisers in China, 1620–1960** (1969); the same author's admirable *The Gate of Heavenly Peace: the Chinese and their revolution, 1895–1980** (1981); and V. Purcell, *The Boxer uprising* (1963). The best studies of the Opium Wars are by J. Beeching (1976), P. W. Fay (1975), and B. Ingles (1976). A massive, authoritative study of the Taiping upheaval is Jen Yu-wen, *The Taiping revolutionary movement* (1973), but one may also read S. Y. Teng, *The Taiping rebellion and the Western powers* (2nd ed., 1977). On the Open Door policy, there is M. H. Hunt, *Frontier defense and the open door: Manchuria in Chinese-American relations, 1895–1911* (1973).

For nineteenth-century developments in India, in addition to books already described in Chapter VI, see P. J. Griffiths, *The British impact on India* (1952); P. Moon, *Strangers in India* (1942); S. Sen, *Eighteen fifty-seven* (1957); and T. R. Metcalf, *The aftermath of revolt: India, 1857–1870* (1964). Especially useful are M. Edwardes, *British India, 1772–1947* (1968); W. Golant, *The long afternoon: British India, 1601–1947* (1975); and M. E. Chamberlain, *Britain and India: the interaction of the peoples* (1974), which shows how little control the British had over forces shaping Indian society. On Indochina: C. Robequain, *The economic development of French Indo-China* (1944), and J. F. Cady, *The roots of French imperialism in eastern Asia* (1954, 1967), may be consulted. On southeastern Asia in general one may read L. E. Williams, *Southeast Asia: a history** (1976), although not completely adequate for the indigenous peoples of the area; D. J. M. Tate, *The making of modern Southeast Asia,* vol. II, *The Western impact: economic and social change* (1979), the second volume of a projected three-volume study; and D. G. E. A. Hall, *A history of Southeast Asia** (4th ed., 1981).

In addition to the works on Russian foreign policy cited in the chapters that follow, there should be added B. H. Sumner, *Tsar-dom and imperialism in the Far East and the Middle East, 1880–1914* (1942). For the story of the Russian fleet that was defeated at Tsushima by the Japanese, one may read A. Nobikov-Privoy, *Tsushima* (trans. 1944); F. Thiess, *The voyage of forgotten men* (1947); and R. Hough, *The fleet that had to die* (1958). The diplomatic history of the war is recounted in J. A. White, *The diplomacy of the Russo-Japanese War* (1964), and an admirable general narrative is D. Walder, *The short victorious war: the Russo-Japanese conflict, 1904–1905* (1975).

Problems and Readings*

Relevant titles include H. M. Wright (ed.), *The "new imperialism": analysis of the late nineteenth century expansion* (rev., 1975); R. W. Winks (ed.), *British imperialism: gold, God, glory* (1963); W. R. Louis (ed.), *Imperialism: the Robinson and Gallagher controversy* (1976), cited earlier in this chapter; R. F. Betts (ed.), *The scramble for Africa: causes and dimensions of empire* (1966); R. I. Rotberg (ed.), *Africa and its explorers* (1970); T. C. Caldwell (ed.), *The Anglo-Boer War* (1965); and R. A. Austen (ed.), *Modern imperialism: Western overseas expansion in the age of industrialism* (1969). On India, there are M. D. Lewis (ed.), *The British in India* (1962); P. J. Marshall (ed.), *Problems of empire: Britain and India, 1757–1813* (1968); and A. T. Embree (ed.), *1857 in India: mutiny or war of independence?* (1963). In the Anvil series, D. N. Rowe has written *Modern China: a brief history* (1959). Studies in the American Historical Association Pamphlets series include P. D. Curtin, *Precolonial African history* (1974); J. C. Miller, *Equatorial Africa* (1976); C. O. Hucker, *Some approaches to China's past* (1973); and R. I. Crane, *A history of South Asia* (1973).

XVI: THE FIRST WORLD WAR

Diplomatic Background

For the diplomatic history of the years 1870–1914, a number of books have already been cited in connection with the general history of these years. A. J. P. Taylor, *The struggle for mastery in Europe, 1848–1918* (1954), cited in Chapter XIII, is invaluable. On diplomacy in the two decades after 1870, there is the important study by W. L. Langer, *European alliances and alignments, 1871–*

1890* (1931, 1950); the same author's *The Franco-Russian alliance, 1880–1894* (1929), and *The diplomacy of imperialism, 1890–1902* (2 vols., 1935), the latter cited in the previous chapter. Two books by W. N. Medlicott, *The Congress of Berlin and after* (1938, 1963), cited in the previous chapter, and *Bismarck, Gladstone, and the concert of Europe* (1956), and W. N. Medlicott and D. K. Coveney, *Bismarck and Europe* (1971), are more critical of Bismarck than is Langer. A detailed account with many valuable insights is G. F. Kennan, *The decline of Bismarck's European order: Franco-Russian relations, 1875–1890* (1979). Two stimulating volumes are G. A. Craig, *From Bismarck to Adenauer* (1958), informative on Bismarck's direction of foreign policy, and A. Hillgruber, *Germany and the two world wars* (trans. 1981), by a leading German scholar.

Analyses for the student and general reader of the background to the First World War are L. C. F. Turner, *Origins of the First World War** (1970), a good brief introduction; L. Lafore, *The long fuse: an interpretation of the origins of World War I** (1965); and J. Remak, *The origins of World War I, 1871–1914** (Berkshire series, 1967). D. E. Lee's careful study, *Europe's crucial years: the diplomatic background of World War I, 1902–1914* (1974), reaffirms the argument that each state acted out of desperation in defense of its own presumed interests. Two successful efforts to study domestic and foreign considerations together, in keeping with the newer emphases of diplomatic historians, are Z. S. Steiner, *Britain and the origins of the First World War* (1978), and V. R. Berghahn, *Germany and the approach of war in 1914* (1973). Among older comprehensive treatments still of great value are S. B. Fay, *The origins of the World War** (1928, 1930); B. E. Schmitt, *The coming of the war, 1914* (2 vols., 1930); P. Renouvin, *The immediate origins of the war* (1928); N. Mansergh, *The coming of the First World War: a study in the European balance, 1878–1914* (1949); and L. Albertini, *The origins of the War of 1914* (3 vols., 1942–1943; trans. 1952–1957), an exhaustive account.

The war-guilt controversy was reopened after 1945 by the West German scholar Fritz Fischer, who on the basis of new archival materials reaffirmed German culpability in *Germany's aims in the First World War** (1961, trans. 1967), the title somewhat modified in translation from the original German *Griff nach der Weltmacht*. Fischer also presents his interpretations in *War of illusions* (1969, trans. 1973) and in the briefer *World power or decline: the controversy over Germany's aims in the First World War* (1965, trans. 1974). His argument that Germany had to grasp for "world power" or decline, and that domestic elite groups pressed for world power to thwart democratization, is reinforced by I. Geiss, *German foreign policy, 1871–1914* (1976). The reopened controversy is ably summarized in J. A. Moses, *The politics of illusion: the Fischer revolution in German historiography* (1976). The question of German insecurity and German ambition, among other topics, is debated in W. Laqueur and G. L. Mosse (eds.), *1914: the coming of the First World War** (1969), published originally as a volume of the *Journal of contemporary history*.

The books cited above will serve as guides to the many specialized accounts, of which the following represent a sampling: A. F. Pribram, *England and the international policy of the European Great Powers, 1871–1914* (1929, 1941); G. Monger, *The end of isolation: British foreign policy, 1900–1907* (1963); C. Andrew, *Théophile Delcassé and the making of the entente cordiale: a reappraisal of French foreign policy, 1898–1905* (1968); S. R. Williamson, *The politics of grand strategy: Britain and France prepare for war, 1904–1914* (1969); F. W. Hinsley (ed.), *British foreign policy under Sir Edward Grey* (1977). The Balkan antecedents of the war are examined in R. W. Seton-Watson, *Sarajevo* (1926); E. C. Helmreich, *The diplomacy of the Balkan wars, 1912–1913* (1938); and V. Dedijer, *The road to Sarajevo* (1966), while the British decision to go to war in 1914 is explored in C. Hazlehurst, *Politicians at war* (1971). A useful survey of French foreign policy for this and the chapters that follow is J. Néré, *The foreign policy of France from 1914 to 1945* (trans. 1975), in the Foreign Policy of the Great Powers series; in the same series is F. R. Bridge, *From Sadowa to Sarajevo: the foreign policy of Austria-Hungary, 1866–1914* (1972), cited in Chapter XIII.

Anglo-German relations are discussed in R. J. Sontag, *Germany and England: background of conflict, 1848–1894** (1938), and in an ambitious study by a British scholar, P. M. Kennedy, *The rise of the Anglo-German antagonism, 1860–1914* (1980). The naval race is studied in the memoirs of Tirpitz, Grey, Fisher, Haldane, and other participants; in J. Steinberg, *Yesterday's deterrent: Tirpitz and the birth of the German* *battleship* (1965); A. J. Marder, *The anatomy of British sea power . . . 1880–1905* (1940), on the predreadnought era, and *From the dreadnought to Scapa Flow: the Royal Navy in the Fisher era, 1904–1919* (5 vols., 1961–1970); and E. L. Woodward, *Great Britain and the German navy* (1935). The Italian role is examined in R. J. B. Bosworth, *Italy, the least of the Great Powers: Italian foreign policy before the First World War* (1980), a comprehensive account focusing on the years 1910–1914, and in the relevant chapters of C. J. Lowe and F. Marzari, *Italian foreign policy, 1870–1940* (1975), in the same series as the Néré volume cited above.

Two books seeking to capture the mood of the summer of 1914 are J. Remak, *Sarajevo: the story of a political murder* (1959), and J. Cameron, *1914* (1959), while an effort to analyze the decision-making process in the crisis by two behavioral scientists is E. V. Nomikos and R. C. North, *International crisis: the outbreak of World War I* (1976). N. Angell, *The great illusion* (1911), was a widely read book whose antiwar message went unheeded.

On the involvement of the United States in the war, one may consult the various general diplomatic histories of the United States, for example, those by S. F. Bemis, T. A. Bailey, R. Ferrell, A. DeConde, and R. Leopold, and the numerous works they cite. Of interest also is B. Perkins, *The great rapprochement: England and the United States, 1895–1914* (1968). An outstanding study is E. F. May, *The World War and American isolation, 1914–1917** (1959), which may be supplemented by A. Link, *Woodrow Wilson and the Progressive era, 1910–1917* (1954); and on a special subject, there is B. W. Tuchman, *The Zimmermann telegram** (1958). T. A. Bailey and P. B. Ryan, *The Lusitania disaster: an episode in modern warfare and diplomacy* (1975), makes a scholarly case for the German legal position.

Military: Strategic and Operational

The available material is staggering. There are general narratives by B. H. Liddell Hart (1934), C. R. M. Cruttwell (1934), H. Baldwin* (1962), C. B. Falls* (1959), and A. J. P. Taylor* (1964). Recommended also is the *American Heritage history of World War I* (1964), superbly illustrated, with the narrative by S. L. A. Marshall. Decisions on strategy are studied in F. Maurice, *Lessons of Allied co-operation: naval, military and air,*

1914–1918 (1942), and in M. Hankey, *The Supreme Command, 1914–1918* (2 vols., 1961). On plans and preparations, see J. Gooch, *The plans of war: the General Staff and British military strategy, 1900 1916* (1974), and P. Kennedy, *The war plans of the Great Powers, 1880–1914* (1979). The most complete history in English is the official *British history of the Great War based on official documents by the historical section of the Committee of Imperial Defence* (32 vols., 1920 ff.). M. Ferro, *The Great War, 1914–1918** (1973), is an admirable effort to communicate the total impact of the war on European society.

On the opening phase of the war: B. W. Tuchman, *The guns of August* (1962), has been praised for its colorful writing and mastery of materials. G. Ritter, *The Schlieffen plan* (trans. 1958), is a valuable analysis, but L. L. Farrar, *The short-war illusion** (1973), also should be consulted. A sampling of literature on episodes of the war would include A. M. Moorehead, *Gallipoli* (1958); J. E. T. Harper, *The truth about Jutland* (1927); A. Horne, *The price of glory: Verdun, 1916** (1963); R. M. Watt, *Dare call it treason* (1963), on the French army mutinies of 1917; and J. Terraine, *To win a war: 1918, the year of victory* (1981). The war in eastern Europe is graphically described in N. Stone, *The eastern front, 1914–1917* (1976). One of the less-known tragedies of the war is recounted in D. H. Boyajian, *Armenia: the case for a forgotten genocide* (1972), and in C. J. Walker, *Armenia: the survival of a nation* (1980), on the ruthless deportation of the Armenian population in Ottoman Turkey. On the human impact of the war as it developed, three moving accounts are P. Fussell, *The Great War and modern memory* (1975); E. J. Leed, *No man's land: combat and identity in World War I* (1979); and T. Ackworth, *Trench warfare, 1914–1918: the live and let-live system* (1980).

Economic and Social Impact of the War

[The Russian Revolution is discussed in Chapter XVII, and additional books on the German revolution and on the long-range effects of the war are also described in Chapter XIX.] For detailed studies of the economic and social aspects of the war, one may turn to the multivolumed Carnegie Endowment series, Economic and Social History of the World War (1921 ff.), under the general editorship of J. T. Shotwell. The best one-volume account of the home front in the various countries is F. P. Chambers, *The war behind the war, 1914–1918* (1939); it can be supplemented by J. Williams, *The other battleground: the home fronts: Britain, France, and Germany, 1914–1918* (1972). Two studies of women workers in the war effort are G. Braybon, *Women workers in the First World War: the British experience* (1981), and M. W. Greenwald, *Women, war, and work: the impact of World War I on women workers in the United States* (1980). The American experience in general is ably recounted in D. M. Kennedy, *Over here: the First World War and American society* (1980). A thoughtful comparative study is A. Marwick, *War and social change in the twentieth century: a comparative study of Britain, France, Germany, Russia, and the United States* (1975). Two admirable studies of the impact of the war on the intellectuals of the era are R. Wohl, *The generation of 1914: France, Germany, England, Spain, and Italy** (1979), and R. N. Stromberg, *Redemption by war: the intellectuals and 1914* (1982).

Wartime internal developments also are treated in E. L. Woodward, *Great Britain and the War of 1914–1918* (1967); P. Guinn, *British strategy and politics, 1914–1918* (1965); J. C. King, *Generals and politicians: conflict between France's high command, parliament, and government, 1914–1918* (1951); G. D. Feldman, *Army, industry, and labor in Germany, 1914–1918* (1966); and R. B. Armeson, *Total warfare and compulsory labor* (1964), also on Germany. Two studies focusing on the end of the Habsburg empire are A. J. May, *The passing of the Hapsburg monarchy, 1914–1918* (2 vols., 1966), and Z. A. B. Zeman, *The breakup of the Habsburg empire, 1914–1918* (1961). The final volume of G. Ritter, *The sword and the scepter: the problem of militarism in Germany*, vol. IV, *The reign of German militarism and the disaster of 1918* (trans. 1973), describes the misuse of the power that the generals had preempted as well as their political ineptitude. The dictatorship of the military leaders is examined with telling detail in M. Kitchen, *The silent dictatorship: the politics of the German High Command under Hindenburg and Ludendorff, 1916–1918* (1976). An illuminating study is J. M. Read, *Atrocity propaganda* (1941). On the human costs of the war, see T. J. Mitchell and G. M. Smith, *Medical services: casualties and medical statistics of the Great War* (1931); and for the devastating world-wide influenza epidemic that doubled the combat toll, A. W. Cosby, *Epidemic and peace, 1918* (1977). A comprehensive study of the economic consequences of the war for each of the major antagonists is G. Hardach, *The First World War, 1914–1918* (1977), which supersedes the older study of E. L. Bogart (1919).

Wartime Diplomacy, Armistice, and Peace

A good introduction to wartime diplomatic maneuvers is Z. A. B. Zeman, *The gentlemen negotiators: a diplomatic history of the First World War* (1971). Among specialized accounts are H. W. Gatzke, *Germany's drive to the West: a study of Germany's Western war aims during the First World War** (1950); J. W. Wheeler-Bennett, *The forgotten peace: Brest-Litovsk, March 1918* (1939); H. C. Meyer, *Mitteleuropa in German thought and action* (1955); L. L. Farrar, Jr., *Divide and conquer: German efforts to conclude a separate peace, 1914–1918* (1978), on overtures to Russia; U. Trumpener, *Germany and the Ottoman Empire, 1914–1918* (1968); V. H. Rothwell, *British war aims and peace diplomacy, 1914–1918* (1971); and D. Stevenson, *French war aims against Germany* (1982). Two provocative studies focusing on the diplomatic duel between the United States and Russia are V. S. Mamatey, *The United States and east central Europe, 1914–1918* (1957), and A. J. Mayer, *Political origins of the new diplomacy, 1917–1918* (1959). The British policy toward the independence movements is explored in K. J. Calder, *Britain and the origins of the new Europe, 1914–1918* (1976). T. E. Lawrence, *Seven pillars of wisdom: a triumph** (1926, 1935), on the revolt of the Arabs against the Turks, is a fascinating account that must be used with caution, and may be supplemented by C. E. Dawn, *From Ottomanism to Arabism* (1973), on the twentieth-century origins of Arab nationalism. Other studies focusing on the Middle East and on developing Arab–Zionist rivalries are E. Kedourie, *England and the Middle East* (1956), on the years 1914–1921; H. M. Sachar, *The emergence of the Middle East, 1914–1924* (1969); E. Monroe, *Britain's moment in the Middle East, 1914–1971* (rev., 1981); P. C. Helmreich, *From Paris to Sèvres: the partition of the Ottoman Empire at the Peace Conference of 1919–1920* (1974); L. Stein, *The Balfour declaration* (1961); and two books by I. Friedman: *The question of Palestine, 1914–1918: British, Jewish, Arab relations* (1973), and *Germany, Turkey, and Zionism, 1897–1918* (1977).

For the armistice, one may turn to H. R. Rudin, *Armistice, 1918* (1944), and F. Maurice, *The Armistice of 1918* (1943).

On the conference, the best brief account is P. Birdsall, *Versailles twenty years after* (1941), sympathetic to Wilson. H. Nicholson, *Peacemaking, 1919* (1933, 1939), and G. B. Noble, *Policies and opinions at Paris, 1919* (1935), describe the intellectual climate in which the momentous decisions were reached. H. W. V. Temperley, *A history of the peace conference of Paris* (6 vols., 1920–1924), is a massive technical study, whereas F. S. Marston, *The peace conference of 1919* (1944), is a brief readable guide dealing mainly with organizational aspects. A brilliant although not entirely convincing study arguing with massive detail that the unconscious preoccupation underlying decisions at Versailles was the threat of Bolshevism and domestic radicalism, is A. J. Mayer, *Politics and diplomacy of peacemaking: containment and counter-revolution at Versailles, 1918–1919* (1967); it may be compared with J. M. Thompson, *Russia, Bolshevism, and the Versailles peace* (1966), which views the revolutionary threat as important but not dominating. A useful balanced account is C. L. Mee, Jr., *The end of order: Versailles, 1919* (1980), and British policy is explored with insight in M. L. Dockrill and J. E. Goold, *Peace without promise: Britain and the peace conferences, 1919–1923* (1981). Other studies examining aspects of the peace conference include M. Hankey, *The Supreme Control at the Paris peace conference, 1919: a commentary* (1963); S. P. Tillman, *Anglo-American relations at the Paris peace conference of 1919* (1961); A. Luckau, *The German delegation at the Paris peace conference* (1941); S. Bonsal, *Suitors and suppliants: the little nations at Versailles* (1946); R. Albrecht-Carrié, *Italy at the Paris peace conference* (1938); I. Morrow, *The peace settlement in the German-Polish borderlands* (1936); and A. Cobban, *National self-determination* (1944).

There are monographs on many of the smaller countries at the conference: F. Deak on Hungary (1942), D. Perman on Czechoslovakia (1962), D. Spector on Rumania (1962), T. Komarnicki on Poland (1957), I. J. Lederer on Yugoslavia (1963), and S. Marks on Belgium (1981). The Polish question is carefully examined by a Danish historian, K. Lundrgreen-Nielsen, *The Polish problem at the Paris Peace Conference: . . . the Great Powers and the Poles, 1918–1919* (trans. 1979). J. C. King explores a special subject in *Foch versus Clemenceau: France and German dismemberment, 1918–1919* (1960), which may be supplemented by W. A. McDougall, *France's Rhineland diplomacy, 1914–1924: the last bid for a balance of power in Europe* (1978).

One of the most hotly disputed issues was reparations, and on this, J. M. Keynes's *The economic consequences of the peace* (1920) has been the most influential single book. Étienne Mantoux, *The Carthaginian peace —or the economic consequences of Mr. Keynes* (1946), is a vigorous reply to Keynes written many years later. C. Bergmann, *The history of reparations* (1927), is a scholarly presentation of a German point of view, and in *The end of reparations* (1931), H. Schacht attempts to vindicate his own policy. A wider point of view is found in A. L. Bowley, *Some economic consequences of the Great War* (1930). [Other books on reparations and related questions are listed in Chapter XVIII.] On the colonial question, see W. R. Louis, *Great Britain and Germany's lost colonies, 1914–1919* (1967). The background to the creation of the League of Nations is explored in H. R. Winkler, *The League of Nations movement in Great Britain, 1914–1919* (1952), and in G. W. Egerton, *Great Britain and the creation of the League of Nations: strategy, politics, and international organization, 1914–1919* (1978).

The revolutionary mood of the early postwar era is described in G. Schulz, *Revolution and peace treaties, 1917–1920* (trans. 1972); F. L. Carsten, *Revolution in central Europe, 1918–1919* (1972); D. Mitchell, *1919: Red mirage* (1970); I. Völgyes (ed.), *Hungary in revolution, 1918–1919: new essays* (1971); and R. Tökés, *Béla Kun* (1967).

Biographies

There are innumerable biographies, which vary widely in quality, of the civilian leaders and military figures of the period. Some of the better biographical studies are G. Wright, *Poincaré and the French presidency* (1943); L. B. Namier, *In the margin of history* (1939); K. Jarausch, *The enigmatic chancellor* (1973), a major study of Bethmann-Hollweg; W. K. Hancock, *Smuts* (2 vols., 1962–1968); R. S. Baker, *Woodrow Wilson: life and letters* (8 vols., 1927–1939); and A. Link's multivolumed biography of

Wilson (1947 ff.) and his other books on Wilson. The attempt to apply techniques of psychoanalysis in S. [Sigmund] Freud and W. Bullitt, *Thomas Woodrow Wilson* (1967), has led to strange and unconvincing results; a more successful psychological approach is achieved in A. L. George and J. L. George, *President Wilson and Colonel House: a personality study** (1956). Biographies of Lloyd George and of Clemenceau have been cited in Chapter XIV.

Problems and Readings*

Pamphlets relating to the war and the peace settlement include D. E. Lee (ed.), *The outbreak of the First World War* (rev., 1976); J. Remak (ed.), *The First World War: causes, conduct, consequences* (1971); H. W. Koch (ed.), *The origins of the First World War* (1972); I. Geiss (ed.), *July 1914* (1969); I. J. Lederer (ed.), *The Versailles settlement: was it foredoomed to failure?* (1960); and T. P. Greene (ed.), *Wilson at Versailles* (1957). Useful also are J. J. Roth (ed.), *World War I: a turning point in modern history* (1967), a brief anthology of essays, and G. Feldman, *German imperialism, 1914–1918* (1972). In the Anvil series, L. L. Snyder has edited *Historic documents of World War I* (1958).

XVII: THE RUSSIAN REVOLUTION AND THE SOVIET UNION

Russia before 1917

[Other books on tsarist Russia are listed for Chapters V, XIII, XV, and XVI.] Two good survey introductions to twentieth-century events are D. W. Treadgold, *Twentieth-century Russia* (5th ed., 1981), and R. V. Daniels, *Russia** (1964).

The situation in late tsarist Russia is best approached through three volumes cited in Chapter XIII: H. Seton-Watson, *The Russian empire, 1801–1917* (1967); the same author's *Decline of imperial Russia, 1855–1914** (1952); and R. Pipes, *Russia under the old regime* (1975). B. H. Sumner, *Russia and the Balkans, 1870–1880* (1947), offers much more than the title suggests.

Economic change is discussed in P. I. Liashchenko, *History of the Russian national economy to the 1917 revolution* (1949); T. H. Von Laue, *Sergei Witte and the industrialization of Russia** (1963); and W. L. Blackwell, *The industrialization of*

Russia: an historical perspective (rev., 1982). The intellectual ferment may be studied in T. G. Masaryk, *The spirit of Russia* (2 vols., 1919; 3rd posthumous vol., 1968), a profound and difficult work of extraordinary value; G. Fedotov, *The Russian religious mind* (1946); E. H. Carr, *Dostoevsky, 1821–1881* (1931); E. J. Simmons, *Leo Tolstoy* (1946); and W. H. Bruford, *Chekhov and his Russia: a sociological study* (1948). Other intellectuals are studied in R. Hare, *Pioneers of Russian social thought** (1951), and A. Vucinich, *Social thought in tsarist Russia: the quest for a general science of society, 1861–1917* (1976).

On the political side, books include G. Fischer, *Russian liberalism: from gentry to intelligentsia* (1958); R. F. Byrnes, *Pobedonostsev: his life and thought* (1968), on an exemplar of tsarist obscurantism; R. Pipes, *Struve* (2 vols., 1970, 1980), a detailed study informative on the sad fate of liberalism; S. H. Baron, *Plekhanov: the father of Russian Marxism** (1963); D. W. Treadgold, *Lenin and his rivals: the struggle for Russia's future, 1898–1906* (1950); L. Haimson, *The Russian Marxists and the origins of Bolshevism* (1955); I. Getzler, *Martov* (1967); F. Venturi, *Roots of revolution** (trans. 1983); A. P. Mendel, *Dilemmas of progress in tsarist Russia* (1961); and A. Ascher, *Pavel Axelrod and the development of Menshevism* (1972). On the anarchists, there is P. Avrich, *The Russian anarchists* (1967), and on a leading exemplar, G. Woodcock and I. Avukamović, *The anarchist prince* (1950), and M. A. Miller, *Kropotkin* (1976).

The events of 1905 are described in W. Sablinsky, *The road to Bloody Sunday: Father Gapon and the St. Petersburg massacre of 1905* (1976); S. Harcave, *First blood: the Russian Revolution of 1905* (1964); and in H. D. Mehlinger and J. M. Thompson, *Count Witte and the tsarist government in the 1905 Revolution* (1972). Other explorations of the ill-fated effort to establish a constitutional monarchy include A. E. Healy, *The Russian autocracy in crisis, 1905–1907* (1976); A. Levin's two studies, *The Second Duma* (1940, 1966) and its sequel, *The Third Duma: election and profile* (1973); and G. A. Hosking, *The Russian constitutional experiment: government and duma, 1907–1914* (1973). Two vivid, popularly written accounts are R. K. Massie, *Nicholas and Alexandra* (1967), on personal relations at the court before and during the war; and E. Crankshaw, *The shadow of the Winter Palace: the drift to revolution, 1825–1917** (1978).

The Revolution of 1917 and the Establishment of the U.S.S.R.

Biographical introductions for the general reader are B. D. Wolfe, *Three who made a revolution: a biographical history* [Lenin, Trotsky, Stalin]* (1948, 1964); C. Hill, *Lenin and the Russian Revolution** (Teach Yourself History series, 1947); and the well-balanced lives of Lenin by D. Shub* (1948), L. F. Fischer* (1964); M. C. Morgan (1971), and R. H. W. Theen (1973). The biographies by R. Payne* (1964) and by R. Conquest (1972) are unsympathetic accounts. Lenin's wife and her fate in the Stalin years are ably studied in R. H. McNeal, *Bride of the revolution: Krupskaya and Lenin* (1972). An intriguing effort to apply Freudian techniques to an important subject is E. V. Wolfenstein, *The revolutionary personality: Lenin, Trotsky, Gandhi* (1967). An outstanding study focusing on Lenin is A. B. Ulam, *The Bolsheviks: the intellectual and political history of the triumph of communism in Russia** (1965), also available as *Lenin and the Bolsheviks** (1969). An important scholarly effort to rehabilitate Lenin as a consistent and coherent Marxist is N. Harding, *Lenin's political thought* (2 vols., 1978–1981), and of special interest is M. Lewin, *Lenin's last struggle** (1978). I. Deutscher has written a remarkably vivid, although overly sympathetic, three-volume life of Trotsky (1954–1963); equally sympathetic is R. Segal, *Leon Trotsky* (1979). Two balanced reappraisals are R. Wistrich, *Trotsky: fate of a revolutionary* (1979), and I. Howe, *Leon Trotsky* (1979), a perceptive analysis. There are biographies also by R. Payne (1977) and J. Carmichael (1973). The best detailed and balanced biography of Stalin is A. B. Ulam, *Stalin: the man and his era** (1973), which may be compared with the sympathetic but rewarding I. Deutscher, *Stalin: a political biography** (1949, 1967). An illuminating effort in psychohistory is R. C. Tucker, *Stalin as revolutionary, 1879–1929: a study in history and personality* (1973), while E. E. Smith has put together the fragmentary evidence on Stalin's early life in *The young Stalin* (1967). T. H. Rigby has edited *Stalin** (1966), in the Great Lives Observed series.

On Russia since 1917, the most comprehensive account in any language—and one of the remarkable achievements of contemporary historical scholarship—is E. H. Carr's massive *A history of Soviet Russia* (14 vols., 1950–1978), carrying the narrative from 1917 to 1929; for the general reader there is a brief one-volume synthesis, *The Russian Revolution from Lenin to Stalin* (1979). There are older accounts of the events of 1917 by W. H. Chamberlin (2 vols., 1935), G. Vernadsky (1932), and B. Pares (1939). The best account of the February revolution is T. Hasegawa, *The February Revolution: Petrograd, 1917* (1981); other studies are G. Katkov, *Russia 1917: the February Revolution* (1967); M. Ferro, *The Russian Revolution of February 1917* (1971); R. V. Daniels, *Red October** (1967); and J. M. Thompson, *Revolutionary Russia, 1917** (1981). Three informative studies focusing on the social dimensions of the vast upheaval are J. L. H. Keep, *The Russian Revolution: a study in mass mobilization* (1977); A. Rabinowitch, *The Bolsheviks come to power: the Revolution of 1917 in Petrograd* (1977); and D. Koenker, *Moscow workers and the 1917 Revolution* (1981). Also focusing on the breadth and depth of the social revolution are two books by M. Ferro, *The fall of tsarism and the origins of Bolshevik power* (trans. 1967) and *October 1917: a social history of the Russian Revolution* (trans. 1980). The dissolution of the army and much else is covered in A. K. Wildman, *The end of the Russian imperial army: the old army and the soldiers' revolt, March–April 1917* (1980), and the peasants' role is ably studied in G. J. Gill, *Peasants and government in the Russian Revolution* (1979).

On the early years, monographs include: L. Schapiro, *The origins of the communist autocracy: political opposition in the Soviet state, 1917–1922* (1955); W. G. Rosenberg, *Liberals in the Russian Revolution: the Constitutional Democratic party, 1917–1921* (1974); R. E. Pipes, *The formation of the Soviet Union: communism and nationalism, 1917–1923** (1954); and P. Avrich, *Kronstadt, 1921* (1970), on the leftist uprising and its suppression. A key institution is studied in O. Anweiler, *The soviets: the Russian workers, peasants, and soldiers councils, 1905–1921* (trans. 1975). Two outstanding scholarly books on the Cheka are L. D. Gerson, *The secret police in Lenin's Russia* (1976), an admirable study, and G. Leggett, *The Cheka: Lenin's political police* (1981).

Soviet Foreign Relations

Foreign relations and the wars of intervention in the crucial early years are discussed in L. I. Strakhovsky, *Intervention at Archangel* (1944); J. A. White, *The Siberian intervention* (1950); R. Luckett, *The White generals: . . . the White movement and the*

Russian civil war (1971); G. A. Brinkley, *The volunteer army and Allied intervention in south Russia, 1917–1921* (1966); P. S. Wandycz, *Soviet-Polish relations, 1917–1921* (1969); R. H. Ullman, *Anglo-Soviet relations, 1917–1921* (3 vols., 1961–1972), a remarkably detailed account; and M. Kettle, *Russia and the Allies, 1917–1920*, vol. I, *The Allies and the Russian collapse, March 1917– March 1918* (1981), part of a projected larger study. The ties with Germany are described in G. Freund, *Unholy alliance* (1957); K. Rosenbaum, *Community of fate: German-Soviet diplomatic relations, 1922– 1928* (1965); and H. L. Dyck, *Weimar Germany and Soviet Russia, 1926–1933* (1966). The most comprehensive study focusing on the American role in the wars of intervention is G. F. Kennan's account: *Russia leaves the war** (1956) and *The decision to intervene** (1958). An interesting biography of an American participant-observer is R. Rosenstone, *Romantic revolutionary: a biography of John Reed** (1975).

Three older provocative books extending to the end of the Second World War are E. H. Carr, *The Soviet impact on the Western world** (1947); G. F. Kennan, *Russia and the West under Lenin and Stalin* (1961); and F. L. Schuman's overly sympathetic narrative and analysis, *Soviet politics at home and abroad* (1946). The best surveys are M. Beloff, *The foreign policy of Soviet Russia, 1929–1941* (2 vols., 1947–1949), a solid and dispassionate narrative; the same author's *Soviet policy in the Far East, 1944–1951* (1953); two books by L. F. Fischer: *The Soviets in world affairs . . . 1917–29* (2 vols., 1930; 1 vol., 1960) and *Russia's road from peace to war: Soviet foreign relations, 1917– 1941* (1969); and R. D. Warth, *Soviet Russia in world politics* (1963). An important volume focusing on the historical background to post-1945 events is A. B. Ulam, *Expansion and coexistence: the history of Soviet foreign policy, 1917–1973** (rev., 1974). An attempt to see continuing elements in foreign policy is B. Jelavich, *St. Petersburg and Moscow: tsarist and Soviet foreign policy, 1814–1974** (1974). [Other books, for the years since 1939, are cited in the chapters that follow.]

U.S.S.R.—Political and Economic Developments

On the structure and functioning of the Soviet government at various stages, the most useful book is J. F. Hough and M. A. Fainsod, *How the Soviet Union is governed* (1979), more than a revision of the original book by Fainsod (1953), and more sympathetic. Two other valuable introductions are P. Sorlin, *The Soviet people and their society from 1917 to the present* (1969), and J. R. Azrael, *The Soviet political system* (1977). There are many older studies of the system in its different stages.

An important monograph is M. Fainsod, *Smolensk under Soviet rule** (1958). On the party itself, there are J. S. Reshetar, *A concise history of the Communist party of the Soviet Union* (1960); L. Schapiro, *The Communist party of the Soviet Union** (1960); J. A. Armstrong, *The politics of totalitarianism: the Communist party of the Soviet Union* (1961); Z. B. Brzezinski, *The permanent purge: politics in Soviet totalitarianism* (1956); and R. H. McNeal, *The Bolshevik tradition* (rev., 1975). R. V. Daniels, *The conscience of the Revolution** (1960), studies the opposition within the party from 1917 to 1969, while A. B. Ulam, *Russia's failed revolutions: from the Decembrists to the dissidents* (1981), and M. S. Shatz, *Soviet dissent in historical perspective* (1980), examine dissent in a broader framework. A stimulating essay is T. H. Von Laue, *Why Lenin? Why Stalin? a reappraisal of the Russian Revolution, 1900–1930** (1964); and a comprehensive analysis of the purges, stressing the enormity of the blood bath, is R. Conquest, *The great terror: Stalin's purges of the thirties* (1968), which may be supplemented by the same author's *Kolyma, the Arctic death camps** (1978); J. Carmichael, *Stalin's masterpiece: the show trials and purges of the thirties* (1976); and A. Antonov-Ovseyenko, *The time of Stalin: portrait of a tyranny* (1982). The life of one Old Bolshevik is recounted in S. F. Cohen, *Bukharin and the Bolshevik Revolution, 1888–1938** (1973), in which Bukharin is presented as a one-time alternative to Stalin, and of another in W. Lerner, *Karl Radek: the last internationalist* (1970). The conditions that led to Stalinism are discussed in R. Pethybridge, *The social prelude to Stalinism* (1974).

The most successful effort to assess economic progress (and the methods used to achieve it) is A. Nove, *An economic history of the U.S.S.R.* (rev., 1975). Two other thoughtful books assessing the accomplishments of the regime are J. P. Nettl, *The Soviet achievement* (1967), and I. Grey, *The first fifty years: Soviet Russia 1917–1967* (1967). Agriculture may be studied in L. Volin, *A century of Russian agriculture:*

from Alexander II to Khrushchev (1970); M. Lewin, *Russian peasants and Soviet power: a study of collectivization* (1968, trans. 1975); and in two books by R. W. Davies, *The socialist offensive: the collectivization of Soviet agriculture, 1929–1930* (1980), and *The Soviet collective farm, 1929–1930* (1980), the first two volumes of a series to study Soviet industrialization. A. C. Sutton examines in detail the role of Western technology during the years 1917 to 1965 in *Western technology and Soviet economic development* (3 vols., 1968–1973).

The role of women, in the pre- and post-revolutionary years, may be studied in R. Stites, *The women's liberation movement in Russia, 1860–1930** (1978), a highly informative synthesis; in B. A. Engel, *Mothers and daughters: women of the intelligentsia in nineteenth-century Russia* (1983); and in two stimulating biographies of Aleksandra Kollontai by B. E. Clements (1979) and B. Farnsworth (1980). The liberation of Soviet women is carefully examined in H. T. Dodge, *Women in the Soviet economy* (1966); D. Atkinson (ed.), *Women in Russia* (1977); and G. W. Lapidus, *Women in Soviet society: equality, development, and social change* (1978).

Other important matters are studied in J. Erikson, *The Soviet high command . . . 1918–1941* (1962); R. Kolkowicz, *The Soviet military and the Communist party* (1967); J. S. Curtiss, *The Russian church and the Soviet state, 1917–1950* (1953); R. Schlesinger, *Soviet legal theory: its social background and development* (1946); J. N. Hazard, *Law and social change in the U.S.S.R.* (1953); I. Deutscher, *Soviet trade unions: their place in Soviet labor policy* (1950); and S. Wolin and R. M. Slusser (eds.), *The Soviet secret police* (1957). The following works also may be suggested: R. Schlesinger, *The spirit of post-war Russia: Soviet ideology, 1917–1946* (1947); J. Somerville, *Soviet philosophy: a study of theory and practice* (1946); C. V. James, *Soviet socialist realism* (1973), on the official government policy for literature and the arts; and L. R. Graham, *Science and philosophy in the Soviet Union* (1972). The historical background to the Jewish question is explored in S. W. Baron, *The Russian Jew under tsars and Soviets* (1964); J. Rothenberg, *The Jewish religion in the Soviet Union* (1971); and L. Kochan (ed.), *The Jews in Soviet Russia since 1917* (1970). There are, in addition, on all subjects relating to the Soviet Union many journalistic accounts and numerous polemical works of uneven quality; works for the years after 1939 are cited in Chapter XXI.

World Communism

On the transformation of earlier socialism and Marxism into communism, a number of studies have been described at the beginning of this chapter and in Chapters XI, XII, and XIV. Two informative books are R. Pethybridge, *The spread of the revolution: essays on 1917* (1972), and P. Dukes, *October and the world: perspectives on the Russian Revolution* (1979). Highly recommended is O. A. Narkiewicz, *Marxism and the reality of power* (1981). Other studies include R. N. C. Hunt, *Theory and practice of communism** (1950) and *Marxism: past and present* (1954); J. Plamenatz, *German Marxism and Russian communism** (1954); R. Schlesinger, *Marx: his time and ours* (1950), written from a Marxian viewpoint; A. B. Ulam, *The unfinished revolution: an essay on the sources of Marxism and communism** (1960); and A. G. Meyer, *Leninism* (1957) and *Communism** (1960). R. T. deGeorge, *Patterns of Soviet thought: the origins and development of dialectical and historical materialism* (1966), is a technical but valuable study.

Personal testimonies about the impact of communism may be found in A. Balabanoff, *My life as a rebel* (1938), and in R. H. Crossman (ed.), *The God that failed** (1950). On the Comintern, one may turn to H. Seton-Watson, *From Lenin to Khrushchev: the history of world communism** (1953, 1960); F. Borkenau, *The Communist International* (1938), as seen by a participant, and *World communism** (1953); and G. Nollan, *International communism and world revolution* (1961). Special studies include J. W. Hulse, *The forming of the Communist International* (1964); R. Fischer, *Stalin and German communism* (1948); K. E. McKenzie, *Comintern and world revolution, 1928–1943* (1964); B. Lazitch and M. M. Drachkovitch, *Lenin and the Comintern* (1972), a detailed account to 1921, with a second volume projected; and E. H. Carr, *Twilight of the Comintern, 1930–1935* (1983). The impact of Bolshevism on French, Italian, and German socialism is ably explored in A. S. Lindemann, *The "red years": European socialism vs. Bolshevism* (1974), while R. Wohl examines the French experience in depth in *French communism in the making, 1919–1924* (1966). Two studies of the Italian Marxist theoretician are C. Boggs, *Gramsci's*

Marxism (1976), and J. Joll, *Antonio Gramsci** (1978).

Problems and Readings*

Pamphlets in various problems series include R. H. McNeal (ed.), *Russia in transition, 1905–1914: evolution or revolution?* (1969); A. E. Adams (ed.), *Imperial Russia after 1861: peaceful modernization or revolution?* (1965); the same author's *The Russian Revolution and Bolshevik victory* (rev., 1973); B. M. Unterberger (ed.), *American intervention in the Russian civil war* (1969); S. W. Page (ed.), *Lenin: dedicated Marxist or pragmatic revolutionary?* (1969); R. V. Daniels (ed.), *The Stalin revolution* (rev., 1973); and R. C. Tucker and S. F. Cohen (eds.), *The great purge trials* (1965). Two booklets in the Anvil series are J. S. Curtiss (ed.), *The Russian Revolutions of 1917* (1957), and A. G. Mazour (ed.), *Soviet economic development: operation outstrip, 1921–1965* (1967). G. B. Carr has contributed *Russia since 1917: the once and future utopia* (1972) to the American Historical Association Pamphlets series, and W. L. Blackwell has edited *Russian economic development from Peter the Great to Stalin* (1974).

XVIII: THE APPARENT VICTORY OF DEMOCRACY

The World since 1919: General

[Other books on internal developments in the European countries and on international relations between the two wars are listed in Chapters XIX and XX respectively.] As a tool for serious study of the forces and events of the twentieth century, one must turn to *Foreign affairs bibliography* (1933 ff.); these volumes are carefully compiled and annotated lists of books on international affairs and domestic affairs. New publications are listed as they appear in the current issues of the quarterly *Foreign affairs* and provide the basis for future cumulative volumes. Recommended also is the bibliographical volume published as *Foreign affairs fifty year bibliography* (1972), an annotated selection of important books published between 1920 and 1970. Another useful compilation is F. Harcourt and F. Robinson, *Twentieth-century world history: a select bibliography* (1979), and a handy reference tool is A. Palmer (ed.), *The Penguin dictionary of twentieth-century history, 1900–1978** (1979).

There are a number of general surveys of twentieth-century history focusing on Europe, among them those by H. S. Hughes (5th ed., 1981), R. O. Paxton (1975), M. D. Richards* (1982), R. B. Jones* (1980), R. N. Stromberg* (1980), and F. Gilbert* (2nd ed., 1979). J. A. S. Grenville has written the first volume of a larger work, *A world history of the twentieth century*, vol. I, *1900–1945: Western dominance* (1980), while P. Johnson has written a stimulating general history, *Modern times: the world from the twenties to the eighties* (1983). G. Barraclough, *Introduction to contemporary history** (1964), a provocative essay focusing on the need to place European events in world perspective, and volume XII of the New Cambridge Modern History, C. L. Mowat (ed.), *The shifting balance of world forces, 1898–1945* (rev., 1968), have already been cited in Chapter XIV.

Problems of the 1920s

A useful synthesis of domestic and international developments for both decades of the interwar years is R. J. Sontag, *A broken world, 1919–1939** (1971), in the Langer series. Historians are now treating the decade of the 1920s as important for its own sake and not merely as a prelude to the 1930s. One such successful effort is C. S. Maier, *Recasting bourgeois Europe: stabilization in France, Germany, and Italy in the decade after World War I** (1975), an analytical study stressing parallel conservative triumphs in these countries. Two outstanding studies of the origins and consequences of the reparations question are M. Trachtenberg, *Reparations in world politics: France and European economic diplomacy, 1916–1923* (1980), and S. A. Schuker, *The end of French predominance in Europe: the financial crisis of 1924 and the adoption of the Dawes plan* (1976), while the American relationship to France is comprehensively examined in M. P. Leffler, *The elusive quest: America's pursuit of European stability and French security* (1979). The general economic problems of the postwar world may be studied in two books by D. N. Aldcroft, *The European economy, 1914–1970* (1978) and *From Versailles to Wall Street, 1919–1929* (1977). I. Svennilson, *Growth and stagnation in the European economy* (1954), remains useful for its statistical information. The best brief introduction to international affairs for the period is S. Marks, *The illusion of peace: international relations in Europe, 1918–1933** (1976), in the Making of the Twentieth Century series. The high point of reconciliation is ably treated in J. Jacobson, *Locarno diplomacy: Germany and the West, 1925–1929* (1972).

On the League of Nations, there are innumerable studies published by the League itself; the following general accounts also may be mentioned: F. P. Walters, *A history of the League of Nations* (2 vols., 1952); J. T. Shotwell and M. Salvin, *Lessons on security and disarmament from the history of the League of Nations* (1949); W. E. Rappard, *The quest for peace since the World War* (1940); and B. Dexter, *The years of opportunity: the League of Nations, 1920–1926* (1967); of special interest is C. M. Kimmich, *Germany and the League of Nations* (1976). Books on disarmament include J. M. Wheeler-Bennett, *Disarmament and security since Locarno, 1925–1931* (1932) and *The pipe dream of peace: the collapse of disarmament* (1935); R. H. Ferrell, *Peace in their time: the origins of the Kellogg-Briand pact* (1952); and R. Dingman, *Power in the Pacific: the origins of naval arms limitation, 1914–1922* (1976). S. R. Smith, *The Manchurian crisis, 1931–1932: a tragedy in international relations* (1948), is a discriminating study.

The Revolt of Asia:
The Middle East and South Asia

[For various peoples of the world in the age of imperialism, see Chapter XV, and in the age of independence, Chapter XXI.] An introduction to the ferment in Asia is provided in J. Romein and J. E. Romein, *The Asian century: a history of modern nationalism in Asia* (1956, trans. 1962).

Various historical surveys of the Middle East with attention to modern developments have been mentioned in Chapter XV. A good introduction is A. Hourani, *The emergence of the modern Middle East* (1981). For Turkey, B. Lewis, *The emergence of modern Turkey* (rev., 1969), cited in Chapter XV, is invaluable; it may be supplemented by H. N. Howard, *The partition of Turkey, 1919–1923* (1931); R. D. Robinson, *The first Turkish republic* (1963); and W. F. Weiker, *The modernization of Turkey: from Ataturk to the present day* (1981), carrying the story forward from 1930 to 1980. An excellent biographical account is P. Balfour (Lord Kinross), *Ataturk: A biography of Mustafa Kemal* (1965). Lord Kinross' *The Ottoman centuries: the rise and fall of the Turkish empire* (1977), has been cited in Chapter V. Stirrings in the Middle East also are discussed in G. Antonius, *The Arab awakening* (1965); Z. B. Zeine, *Struggle for Arab independence* (1960); H. A. R. Gibb, *Modern trends in Islam* (1947); E. Kedouri, *Islam and the modern world* (1980); R. O. Collins and R. L. Tignor, *Egypt and the Sudan* (1967); and T. Little, *Modern Egypt* (1964). For Iran one may read R. W. Cottam, *Nationalism in Iran* (rev., 1979), and N. R. Keddie, *Roots of revolution: an interpretive history of modern Iran* (1981).

For the Indian subcontinent, a number of books have been listed in Chapter VI and Chapter XV. The best introductions to twentieth-century developments are W. N. Brown, *The United States and India, Pakistan, and Bangladesh* (rev., 1972), already cited in Chapter VI, and P. Spear, *India, Pakistan, and the West* (rev., 1967). Other useful books are P. Spear, *India: a modern history* (rev., 1972); S. Wolpert, *A new history of India* (rev., 1982), cited in Chapter VI, which tries to see developments in Indian terms and not as reactions to the West; H. Tinker, *India and Pakistan: a political analysis* (1962, 1968); A. Seal, *The emergence of Indian nationalism* (1968); R. J. Moore, *The crisis of Indian unity, 1917–1940* (1974); A. T. Embree, *India's search for national identity* (1972); and D. J. Mandelbaum, *Society in India* (2 vols., 1970). The tragedy at Amritsar in 1919 is ably examined in H. Fein, *Imperial crime and punishment: the massacre at Jallianwala Bagh and British judgment, 1919–1920* (1977). Nehru's autobiography, *Toward freedom* (1941), his *Glimpses of world history* (1942), and his other writings make absorbing reading, as does Gandhi's *Autobiography: the story of my experiments with truth* (1948). There is a large literature on Gandhi. To an older biography by L. Fischer (1951), one may add G. Ashe, *Gandhi: a study in revolution* (1968); V. Mehta, *Mahatma Gandhi and his disciples* (1977); E. H. Erikson, *Gandhi's truth: on the origins of militant nonviolence* (1969), an account that fruitfully draws upon psychoanalytical insights; and R. N. Iyer, *The moral and political thought of Mahatma Gandhi* (1973), perhaps the best book for grasping the mind of Gandhi. Also valuable are J. M. Brown's two detailed accounts: *Gandhi's rise to power in Indian politics, 1915–1922* (1972), and *Gandhi and civil disobedience: the Mahatma in Indian politics, 1928–1934* (1977). Three recommended biographies of Nehru are by F. Moraes (1957), M. Brecher (1959), and E. N. Pandy (1976), while S. Gopal has published the first two volumes (1976, 1979) of a projected three-volume detailed study.

The Revolt of Asia:
East and Southeast Asia

[Books on the earlier background have been cited in Chapter XV.] For China in the early part of the twentieth century, the best introductions are J. K. Fairbank, *The United States and China** (rev., 1979), cited in Chapter XV; O. E. Clubb, *Twentieth century China** (3rd ed., 1979); C. Hibbert, *The dragon wakes: China and the West, 1793–1911* (1970); F. Wakeman, *The fall of imperial China* (1975); M. C. Wright (ed.), *China in revolution: the first phase, 1900–1913* (1968); M. Gasster, *China's struggle to modernize* (rev., 1983); and J. Chesnaux, F. de Barbier, and M.-C. Bergère, *China from the 1911 Revolution to liberation** (trans. 1979). On the nationalist movement rising out of protests against Versailles in 1919, there are C. Tse-tung, *The May Fourth movement* (1960), and L. Yu-Sheng, *The crises of Chinese consciousness: radical anti-traditionalism in the May Fourth era* (1979). For the post-war era, one may read H. R. Isaacs, *The tragedy of the Chinese revolution** (3rd ed., 1961), and L. Eastman, *The abortive revolution: China under nationalist rule, 1927–1937* (1974). Biographical studies include L. Sharman, *Sun Yat-sen* (1934), still useful; Leng Shao-chuan and N. D. Palmer, *Sun Yat-sen and communism* (1961); C. M. Wilbur, *Sun Yat-sen: frustrated patriot* (1976); and H. Z. Schiffrin, *Sun Yat-sen and the origins of the 1911 revolution* (1969). Sun's immediate successor is studied in E. P. Young, *The presidency of Yuan Shih-kai: liberalism and dictatorship in early republican China* (1978). [Books on Communist China are listed in Chapter XXI.]

On the rise of militarism in Japan in the 1930s, there are J. B. Crowley, *Japan's quest for autonomy: national security and foreign policy, 1930–1938* (1966), the best account; D. M. Brown, *Nationalism in Japan* (1955); R. Storry, *The double patriots* (1957); and G. M. Berger, *Parties out of power in Japan, 1931–1941* (1977). The background is ably presented in two books by A. Iriye, *Pacific estrangement: Japanese and American expansion, 1897–1911* (1972) and *After imperialism: the search for a new order in the Far East, 1921–1931* (1965). [Other books on Japan have been listed in Chapter XIII.]

The Depression: Collapse of the World Economy

A useful background study for twentieth-century economic developments is A. Harri-son, *The framework of economic activity** (1967). On the coming of the depression, J. K. Galbraith has written a vivid history in *The great crash: 1929** (1955). G. Rees, *The great slump: capitalism in crisis, 1929–1933* (1972), is lively and informative, but anecdotal, while C. P. Kindleberger, *The world in depression, 1929–1933** (1973), ably describes economic developments but without giving much political or social detail. C. Bird, *The invisible scar** (1966), is a moving social history of the depression's impact on the United States. Useful economic surveys covering the world economy are H. V. Hodson, *Slump and recovery, 1929–1937* (1938), and W. A. Lewis, *Economic survey, 1919–1939* (1948); and there are valuable contributions in W. Laqueur and G. L. Mosse (eds.), *The great depression** (1970), originally a volume of the *Journal of contemporary history*, and in K. Brunner (ed.), *The great depression revisited* (1981), the latter somewhat technical. A comparative study, with special relevance to the depression, is J. A. Garraty, *Unemployment in history: economic thought and public policy* (1978), and of special interest for international relations is E. W. Bennett, *Germany and the diplomacy of the financial crisis, 1931* (1962). Other studies include M. Palyi, *The twilight of gold, 1914–1936: myths and realities* (1972); H. W. Arndt, *The economic lessons of the nineteen thirties* (1944); G. Haberler, *Prosperity and depression* (3rd ed., 1941); L. C. Robbins, *The great depression* (1934); and A. J. H. Latham, *The depression and the developing world, 1914–1939* (1981). M. Friedman and A. J. Schwartz, *The great contraction, 1929–1933* (1965), an abstraction from the economist's larger *A monetary history of the United States, 1867–1960* (1963), argues the monetary causes of the depression; it should be read with P. Temin, *Did monetary forces cause the great depression?* (1976), and P. Fearon, *The origins and nature of the great slump, 1929–1932* (1979). [For additional books on the impact of the depression on politics and society in various countries, see the following chapter.]

Problems and Readings*

For twentieth-century history in general, a useful anthology is G. Wright and A. Mejia, Jr., *An age of controversy: discussion problems in twentieth century European history* (1963; rev. alternate ed., 1973). In the Anvil series, L. L. Snyder has edited *The world in the twentieth century* (rev., 1964) and *Fifty major documents of the twentieth century*

(1955); and on economic developments, S. B. Clough, T. Moodie, and C. Moodie have edited *Economic history of Europe: twentieth century* (1968). In the Heath Problems series, there are M. D. Lewis (ed.), *Gandhi: maker of modern India?* (1965), and R. F. Himmelberg (ed.), *The great depression and American capitalism* (1968). J. M. Laux, *The great depression in Europe* (1974), is a brief introduction in the Forums in History series.

XIX: DEMOCRACY AND DICTATORSHIP

[Books on international relations for the interwar years as a whole are listed in Chapter XX, and books on the general problems of the interwar years, including the Great Depression, have been listed in Chapter XVIII. The national histories of Britain, France, Germany, and Italy described in Chapters XI and XIV should also be consulted.]

On the general concept of the welfare state, these books may be recommended: J. M. Keynes, *The end of laissez-faire* (1927); J. A. Schumpeter, *Capitalism, socialism, and democracy** (1942); G. Soule, *A planned society* (1934); B. Wooton, *Freedom under planning* (1945); and M. Bruce, *The coming of the welfare state* (rev., 1966). F. A. von Hayek, in *The road to serfdom** (1944) and other writings, which subject the welfare state to an unsympathetic appraisal, may be contrasted with R. Titmuss, *Essays on the welfare state** (rev., 1966), by an advocate. The best introduction to the welfare democracies in the north is F. D. Scott, *Scandinavia* (rev., 1976). A. Sturmthal, *The tragedy of European labor, 1918–1939* (1943, 1951), criticizes labor in the interwar period as too narrow in vision to be politically effective; it may be supplemented for other leaders of the left by the essays in W. Laqueur and G. L. Mosse (eds.), *The left-wing intellectuals between the wars, 1919–1939** (1966), originally a volume of the *Journal of contemporary history.*

The American New Deal

The interwar years and the background and nature of the New Deal can best be approached through two volumes by W. E. Leuchtenburg: *The perils of prosperity** (1958) and *Franklin D. Roosevelt and the New Deal** (1964); D. A. Shannon, *Between the wars: America, 1919–1941** (1965); D. McCoy, *Coming of age during the 1920s and*

*1930s** (1973); and J. J. Hutmacher, *Trial by war and depression, 1919–1941** (1973); other useful introductions are D. W. Brogan, *The era of Franklin D. Roosevelt* (1950), by an astute British writer; B. Mitchell, *Depression decade: from New Era through New Deal, 1929–1941** (1947); D. Wecter, *The age of the Great Depression, 1929–1941* (1948); and the multivolumed study by A. M. Schlesinger, Jr., *The age of Roosevelt** (1957 ff.), of which three lively volumes have appeared to date. Many biographical accounts and memoirs have appeared as well. Two outstanding studies of Roosevelt are J. M. Burns, *Roosevelt: the lion and the fox** (1956), with a sequel volume for the war years, and F. Freidel's multivolumed *Franklin D. Roosevelt* (4 vols., to date, 1952–1973). R. J. Simon has edited *As we saw the thirties* (1967). The impact of the depression on the women of the era is explored in W. D. Wandersee, *Women's work and family values, 1920–1940* (1981).

Britain between the Wars

Thorough and balanced coverage is available in W. N. Medlicott, *Contemporary England, 1914–1964* (1967); C. L. Mowat, *Britain between the wars, 1918–1940* (1955), which remains one of the best accounts; A. J. P. Taylor, *English history, 1914–1945* (1965), written with the author's usual verve; and S. Glynn and J. Oxborrow, *Interwar Britain: a social and economic history** (1976). Briefer surveys are D. Thomson, *England in the twentieth century, 1914–1963** (1964), and B. B. Gilbert, *Britain since 1918* (rev., 1980). These books may be supplemented by the impressionistic R. Graves and A. Hodge, *The long week-end: a social history of Great Britain, 1918–1939** (1940); R. Blythe, *The age of illusion* (1963); J. Symons, *The thirties: a dream revolved* (1960); M. Muggeridge, *The thirties: 1930–1940 in Great Britain* (1940, 1967); W. McElwee, *Britain's locust years, 1918–1940* (1962); and S. Hynes, *The Auden generation: literature and politics in England in the 1930s* (1977). The impact of the war and other aspects of British economic and social change are revealed in A. C. Pigou, *Aspects of British economic history, 1918–1925* (1947); F. W. Hirst, *Consequences of the war to Great Britain* (1934), in the Carnegie series; P. B. Johnson, *Land fit for heroes: the planning of British reconstruction, 1916–1919* (1968); B. B. Gilbert, *British social policy, 1914–1939* (1970); and A. Marwick's two informative books: *The deluge: British* *society and the First World War* (1965) and *Britain in the century of total war: war, peace, and social change, 1900–1967* (1968).

On some specific interwar developments and episodes, one may consult T. Wilson, *The downfall of the Liberal party, 1914–1935* (1966); M. Bentley, *The liberal mind, 1914–1929* (1977); R. McKibbin, *The evolution of the Labour party, 1910–1924* (1974); M. Cowling, *The impact of Labour, 1920–1924: the beginning of modern British politics* (1971); D. E. Moggridge, *The return to gold** (1969); S. Graubard, *British labour and the Russian Revolution, 1919–1924* (1941); R. W. Lyman, *The first Labour government, 1924* (1957); L. Chester, S. Fay, and H. Young, *The Zinoviev letter* (1967); G. Gordetsky, *The precarious truce: Anglo-Soviet relations, 1924–1927* (1977), with attention to domestic developments; and D. Calhoun, *The United Front: the TUC and the Russians, 1923–1928* (1976). Two excellent accounts of the general strike are P. Renshaw, *Nine days that shook Britain: the 1926 general strike** (1976), and G. A. Phillips, *The general strike: the politics of industrial conflict* (1976). The 1931 crisis is explored in R. S. Bassett, *1931: political crisis* (1958); R. Skidelsky, *Politicians and the slump: the Labour government of 1929–1931* (1967); and H. Berkeley, *The myth that will not die: the formation of the National Government, 1931* (1978). For the 1930s in general, there are N. Branson and M. Heinemann, *Britain in the nineteen thirties* (1971), and J. Stevenson and C. Cook, *The slump: society and politics during the depression* (1978), interesting but somewhat journalistic.

There are many biographical studies: the biographies of Ramsay MacDonald by D. Marquand (1977); a detailed and judicious account of Stanley Baldwin by K. Middlemas and J. Barnes (1969); of Lloyd George in the years 1922–1931 by J. Campbell (1977); of Neville Chamberlain by K. Feiling (1946), I. Macleod (1961), and W. R. Rock (1969); and of Halifax by Lord Birkenhead (1965). The multivolumed biography of Winston Churchill by his son R. S. Churchill [to 1914] (2 vols., 1966) and continued for subsequent volumes by M. Gilbert [the fifth volume (1977) covering the years 1922–1939] has been criticized as excessively detailed; there are briefer accounts, among others, by L. Broad (1956) and H. Pelling (1974). H. Nicolson has witten a biography of George V (1953), and J. W. Wheeler-Bennett one of George VI* (1958). A. Bul-

lock, *The life and times of Ernest Bevin* (2 vols., 1960, 1967), is a work of distinction. The best introductions to Keynes are R. F. Harrod, *The life of John Maynard Keynes** (1951), and D. E. Moggridge, *John Maynard Keynes** (1976). R. Lekachman, *The age of Keynes** (1966), is mostly on post-1945 Keynesian influence in the United States. T. Jones, *Diary with letters, 1931–1950* (1954), is valuable on many subjects; and there are other memoirs by H. Dalton (1953), C. Attlee (1954), A. Eden (3 vols., 1960–1965), A. Duff-Cooper (1953), L. S. Amery (3 vols., 1952–1955), S. Hoare (1954), H. Macmillan (2 vols., 1966–1967), and others. R. Skidelsky, *Oswald Mosley* (1976), the study of a Labour leader who became Britain's leading fascist of the era, may be supplemented by G. C. Lebzelter, *Political anti-semitism in England, 1918–1939* (1978). On personalities in the Labour movement, F. Williams, *Fifty years' march: the rise of the Labour party* (1949), is colorful.

Among many useful studies of the Commonwealth of Nations, one may turn to D. Hall, *Commonwealth: history of the British Commonwealth of Nations* (1971), a detailed account, and N. Mansergh, *The Commonwealth experience* (1969). Other titles are cited in Chapter XV. An outstanding study of Ireland in this era is J. M. Curran, *The birth of the Irish Free State, 1921–1923* (1980).

France between the Wars

Histories of the Third Republic as a whole appear under Chapter XIV, and to these may be added three brief syntheses for the interwar years: N. Greene, *From Versailles to Vichy: the Third Republic, 1919–1940** (1970); E. J. Knapton, *France since Versailles** (1952); and H. Tint, *France since 1918** (rev., 1980). S. Hoffman and others, *In search of France: the economy, society, and political system in the twentieth century** (1963), has several incisive essays. The best introduction to French labor is through V. R. Lorwin, *The French labor movement* (1954), cited in Chapter XIV, and H. W. Ehrmann, *French labor: from Popular Front to liberation* (1947). A brief informative inquiry into French economic growth is T. Kemp, *The French economy, 1913–1939: the history of a decline* (1972), and demographic studies are available in C. Dyer, *Population and society in twentieth century France* (1978).

Invaluable for the stormy events of the 1930s, the Popular Front years, and the background to the fall of France is A. Werth, *The twilight of France, 1933–1940* (1942), a condensation of his earlier volumes, all of which may be read with profit. There are some interesting essays in J. Joll (ed.), *The decline of the Third Republic* (St. Antony's papers, 1959). On some specific subjects, there are C. A. Micaud, *The French right and Nazi Germany, 1933–1939* (1943); P. J. Larmour, *The French Radical party in the 1930's* (1964); J. T. Marcus, *French socialism in the crisis years, 1933–36* (1958); N. Greene, *Crisis and decline: the French Socialist party in the Popular Front era* (1969); D. Caute, *Communism and the French intellectuals, 1914–1960* (1964); D. R. Brower, *The new Jacobins: the French Communist party and the Popular Front* (1968); and M. Wolfe, *The French franc between the wars, 1919–39* (1961). For Léon Blum, there is a chapter in J. Joll, *Intellectuals in politics: three biographical essays* [Blum, Rathenau, Marinetti] (1960); a biography by J. Lacouture (trans. 1982); and a political biography, J. Colton, *Léon Blum: humanist in politics** (1966), which attempts to illuminate the Popular Front era as well as the man. A special subject is explored in J. Talbott, *The politics of educational reform in France, 1918–1940* (1969). On an interesting conservative political figure, J. M. Sherwood has written *Georges Mandel and the Third Republic* (1970), and an example of conservative failure is provided in W. D. Irvine, *French conservatism in crisis: the Republic Federation of France in the 1930s* (1979).

Germany, 1919–1945

There are several well-balanced narrative accounts of the Weimar Republic and its fall, among them, D. Abraham, *The collapse of the Weimar Republic: political economy and the crisis** (1981), an outstanding study; S. W. Halperin, *Germany tried democracy: a political history of the Reich from 1918 to 1933** (1946), older but still useful; R. Grunberger, *Germany, 1918–1945** (1964); A. J. Nicholls, *Weimar and the rise of Hitler** (rev., 1980), in The Making of the Twentieth Century series; and D. Childs, *Germany since 1918* (2nd ed., 1980). One should also read the relevant chapters in G. A. Craig, *Germany, 1866–1945** (1978), cited in Chapter XIII. Two excellent annotated guides to the vast litera-

ture are P. D. Stackwin, *The Weimar era and Hitler, 1918–1933: a critical bibliography* (1978), and H. Kehr and J. Langmaid, *The Nazi era, 1919–1945: a selected bibliography of published works from the early roots to 1980* (1982).

E. Eyck, *A history of the Weimar Republic** (2 vols., trans. 1963), is a detailed narrative account by a distinguished liberal German historian. A. Rosenberg, *Imperial Germany: the birth of the German republic, 1871–1918** (1931), provides the background for the same author's *A history of the German republic* (1936). Works on the uneasy early years, many of them raising the question whether a genuine revolution took place, include R. Watts, *The kings depart* (1968); A. J. Ryder, *The German revolution of 1918: a study of German socialism in war and revolt* (1967); S. Haffner, *Failure of a revolution: Germany 1918–1919* (trans. 1973); W. T. Angress, *Stillborn revolution: the communist bid for power in Germany, 1921–1923** (1963); and A. Mitchell, *Revolution in Bavaria* (1965). R. G. L. Waite, *Vanguard of Nazism: the Free Corps movement in postwar Germany, 1918–1923** (1952), may be supplemented by J. M. Riehl, *Paramilitary politics in Weimar Germany* (1977), a comprehensive study. An outstanding study of a special interest group in the war, revolution, and monetary crisis is G. D. Feldman, *Iron and steel in the German inflation, 1916–1923* (1977). Cultural developments are sympathetically treated in P. Gay, *Weimar culture: the outsider as insider* (1968), and many valuable insights are provided in R. Dahrendorf, *Society and democracy in Germany* (1967). Recommended also is O. Friedrich, *Before the deluge: a portrait of Berlin in the 1920s* (1972).

The personalities of the Weimar Republic are discussed in a number of books, among which are J. W. Wheeler-Bennett, *Wooden Titan: Hindenburg in twenty years of German history, 1914–1934* (1936); A. Dorpalen, *Hindenburg and the Weimar Republic* (1964); H. Kessler, *Walter Rathenau* (1929); K. Epstein, *Matthias Erzberger and the dilemma of German democracy* (1959); H. W. Gatzke, *Stresemann and the rearmament of Germany** (1954); and H. A. Turner, *Stresemann and the politics of the Weimar Republic** (1963). The question of army loyalties is studied in G. A. Craig, *The politics of the Prussian army, 1640–1945** (1956, 1964), cited in Chapter V; J. W. Wheeler-Bennett, *The nemesis of power: the German army in politics, 1918–1945**

(1954, 1964); H. J. Gordon, *The Reichswehr and the German republic, 1919–1926* (1957); R. J. O'Neill, *The German army and the Nazi party, 1933–1939* (1968); F. L. Carsten, *The Reichswehr and politics, 1918 to 1933** (1966); G. Post, Jr., *The civil-military fabric and Weimar foreign policy* (1973); M. Cooper, *The German army, 1933–1945: its political and military failure* (1978); and A. Seaton, *The German army, 1933–1945* (1982). The Social Democratic party is examined in R. Breitman, *German socialism and Weimar democracy* (1981), and anti-Semitism before Hitler in two books by D. L. Niewyk, *Socialist, anti-semite, and Jew* (1971), and *The Jews in Weimar Germany* (1980).

D. Orlow, *The history of the Nazi party* (2 vols., 1969, 1973), is a comprehensive account; the first volume covers the years 1919 to 1933; the second to 1945. On the coming to power of the Nazis, one may profit from T. Eschenburg and others, *The path to dictatorship, 1919–1933* (1966); and an intriguing special study, W. S. Allen, *The Nazi seizure of power: the experience of a single German town, 1930–1935** (1965). R. Heberle, *From democracy to Nazism: a regional case study** (trans. 1945), deserves mention as a pioneer study in electoral sociology; a newer study focusing on voting records in a number of cities is R. F. Hamilton, *Who voted for Hitler?** (1982). On the events of 1932–1933, one may read R. Manvell and H. Fraenkel, *The hundred days to Hitler* (1974). On the Nazi era [aspects of Nazism also are discussed below under totalitarianism], there are many studies, but an outstanding comprehensive analysis is K. D. Bracher, *The German dictatorship: the origins, structure, and effects of national socialism** (1969, trans. 1970); equally valuable is M. Broszat, *The Hitler state: the foundation and development of the internal structure of the Third Reich** (trans. 1981). There are good surveys in H. Mau and H. Krausnick, *German history, 1933–1945* (trans. 1958), and H. Vogt, *The burden of guilt: a short history of Germany, 1914–1945** (trans. 1964). Two popular, somewhat oversimplified accounts are W. L. Shirer, *The rise and fall of the Third Reich** (1960), and R. Goldston, *The life and death of Nazi Germany** (1969). Two older analytical and interpretive studies are F. L. Neumann, *Behemoth: the structure and practice of national socialism** (1942), a classic study still valuable, and K. Heiden, *A history of national socialism* (1935). An indispensable newer treatment is D. Schoen-baum, *Hitler's social revolution: class and status in Nazi Germany, 1933–1939** (1966). H. Krausnick and others, *Anatomy of the SS state* (trans. 1965), is the best account of the German police state, while E. N. Peterson corrects some misconceptions in *The limits of Hitler's power* (1969). P. H. Merkl, *Political violence under the swastika: 581 early Nazis** (1975), skillfully analyzes the life histories of a number of Germans who became Nazis and whose accounts were originally gathered by T. Abel, *Why Hitler came to power* (1934); these accounts may be compared also with M. Mayer, *They thought they were free* (1955). Merkl has also written as a sequel to his study, *The making of a stormtrooper* (1980). Youth reactions are explored in P. D. Stachura, *The German youth movement, 1900–1945: an interpretive and documentary history* (1981), and in M. S. Steinberg, *Sabers and Brown Shirts: the German students' path to National Socialism, 1918–1935* (1977).

There has been an avalanche of books on Hitler and the Nazi era, but two biographical accounts stand out and also provide the most informative general introductions to the history of the era: A. Bullock, *Hitler: a study in tyranny** (1952; rev., 1964), and J. C. Fest, *Hitler* (1973, trans. 1975) [the translation and documentation are somewhat condensed from the German original]. J. Toland, *Adolf Hitler* (1976), is a detailed, balanced account written for a general audience, while N. Stone, *Hitler* (1980), is a brief narrative focusing on the war years. R. Binion, *Hitler among the Germans* (1976), uses psychoanalytical methods to explain the inner wellsprings of the man, while R. L. Waite, *The psychopathic god: Adolf Hitler** (1977), combines both psychoanalytical and more conventional techniques to provide some keen insights; additional psychobiographical insights are provided in a brief essay, H. Stierlin, *Adolf Hitler: a family perspective* (1976). W. Maser, *Hitler: legend, myth, and reality* (1971, trans. 1973), corrects some minor legends, but does not present a synthesis. Two analytical interpretive essays that raise some pertinent questions are S. Haffner, *The meaning of Hitler* (1980), and W. Carr, *Hitler: a study in personality and politics* (1979). Hitler's early years are reconstructed in F. Jetzinger, *Hitler's youth* (1956, trans. 1958), and in B. F. Smith, *Adolf Hitler: his family, childhood, and youth** (1967); the same author also has written on the early years of another Nazi, *Heinrich Himmler: a Nazi in the making,*

1900–1926 (1971). J. Fest, The face of the Third Reich* (trans. 1977), provides additional portraits. An important episode is explored in H. J. Gordon, Hitler and the Beer Hall Putsch* (1972), and the end of the leader and his regime is vividly recounted in H. R. Trevor-Roper, The last days of Hitler* (1947; rev., 1966).

Other phases and institutions of the Nazi era are discussed in numerous books, among them, E. Crankshaw, Gestapo: instrument of tyranny* (1956); T. Taylor, Sword and swastika: generals and Nazis in the Third Reich* (1952); P. Seabury, The Wilhelmstrasse: a study of German diplomats under the Nazi regime (1955); G. A. Ziemer, Education for death: the making of the Nazi (1942); O. J. Hale, The captive press in the Third Reich (1964); Z. A. B. Zeman, Nazi propaganda (1964); J. Stephenson, Women in Nazi society (1976); the same author's The Nazi organization of women (1981); A. Schweitzer, Big business in the Third Reich (1964); and G. Reitlinger, SS: alibi of a nation, 1922–1945* (1956). Books on the concentration camps are cited later. Religion and related matters are examined in E. C. Helmreich, The German churches under Hitler: background, struggle and epilogue (1979); J. S. Conway, The Nazi persecution of the churches, 1933–1945 (1968); G. Lewy, The Catholic church and Nazi Germany (1964); and S. Friedländer, Pius XII and the Third Reich: a documentation (1966). A popular overdrawn history of a special subject is W. Manchester, The arms of Krupp, 1587–1968 (1968). G. L. Mosse (ed.) illustrates facets of the Nazi era in Nazi culture (1966), and on a special subject, there are B. M. Lane, Architecture and politics in Germany, 1918–1945 (1968), and B. Hinz, Art in the Third Reich* (trans. 1980). The role of the scientists is examined in A. D. Beyerchen, Scientists under Hitler: politics and the physics community in the Third Reich (1977). Two convenient handbooks on the Nazi regime are L. L. Snyder (ed.), Encyclopedia of the Third Reich (1977), and R. Wistrich, Who's Who in Nazi Germany (1982).

On the opposition to Hitler, the most comprehensive account is P. Hoffman, The history of the German resistance, 1933–1945 (trans. 1977). Among other accounts, the following may be mentioned: H. Rothfels, The German opposition to Hitler (1949); C. FitzGibbon, 20 July [published in England as The shirt of Nessus] (1956); G. Ritter, The German resistance: Carl Goerdeler's struggle against tyranny (1954, trans. 1959);

T. Prittie, Germans against Hitler (1964); R. Manvell and H. Fraenkel, The July plot (1964); the same authors' The Canaris conspiracy (1969); and E. Zeller, The flame of freedom (trans. 1968). H. C. Deutsch has written two authoritative accounts focusing on the military, The German conspiracy against Hitler in the twilight war [1939–1940] (1968) and Hitler and his generals: the hidden crisis, January–June 1938 (1974), while R. Manvell and H. A. Jacobsen have edited a useful collection of essays, July 20, 1944: Germans against Hitler (1969). [Other books on wartime Germany, German dominated Europe, and the Holocaust are listed in the next chapter.]

Totalitarianism, Particularly Nazism

[Communism is discussed mainly in Chapter XVII, and Italian fascism is discussed separately below.]

Various attempts to explore the ideological roots of the German experience, some of which are less than fair to the earlier Germans, have been listed for Chapters XI and XIII. Other thoughtful books are F. Stern, The politics of cultural despair: a study in the use of the Germanic ideology* (1961); the same author's The failure of illiberalism: essays on the political culture of Germany (1972); and G. L. Mosse, The crisis of German ideology: intellectual origins of the Third Reich* (1964) and his other writings. An impressive historiographical study that examines the historical literature on the Nazi experience is P. Ayçoberry, The Nazi question: an essay on the interpretations of National Socialism, 1922–1975* (1979, trans. 1981).

Among efforts to examine totalitarian attitudes and institutions on a comparative basis and to establish definitions are F. L. Carsten, The rise of fascism* (rev., 1980); S. G. Payne, Fascism: comparison and definition (1980), an insightful critique of the debate engendered on the subject; H. R. Kedward, Fascism in Western Europe, 1900–1945 (1969); E. Nolte, Three faces of fascism: Action Française, Italian fascism, national socialism* (1963, trans. 1966), a difficult book for most readers; R. de Felice, Fascism: an informal introduction to its theory and practice (1976); J. Weiss, The fascist tradition: radical right-wing extremism in modern Europe* (1967); A. Cassels, Fascism* (1975); A. J. Gregor, The ideology of fascism: the rationale of totalitarianism (1969); H. Rogger and E. Weber (eds.), The European right: a historical profile* (1965), cited in Chapter XI; W. Laqueur and G. L. Mosse (eds.), *International fascism, 1920–1945** (1966), originally a volume of the *Journal of contemporary history;* and S. J. Woolf and others, *European fascism* (1968) and *The nature of fascism* (1968). To these may be added: C. J. Friedrich and Z. K. Brzezinski, *Totalitarian dictatorship and autocracy** (rev., 1965); K. R. Popper, *The open society and its enemies* (2 vols., rev., 1963); E. Fromm, *Escape from freedom** (1941), a psychological inquiry into the reasons for submission to tyranny; H. Arendt, *The origins of totalitarianism** (1951, 1958), cited in Chapter XIV; G. W. F. Hallgarten, *Why dictators?* (1954); J. L. Talmon, *The origins of totalitarian democracy** (1952), cited in Chapter IX; E. Halévy, *The era of tyrannies** (1938, trans. 1965); and H. Buchheim, *Totalitarian rule: its nature and characteristics* (trans. 1968). The results of a sociological investigation exploring class origins of fascism in twenty-one countries may be examined in S. U. Larsen and others (eds.), *Who were the fascists? social roots of European fascism* (1980). A special subject is explored in A. Hamilton, *The appeal of fascism: . . . the intellectuals and fascism* (1968), and an indispensable comparative study is A. Perlmutter, *Modern authoritarianism: a comparative institutional analysis* (1981).

Italy, 1919–1945

The relevant chapters in C. Seton-Watson, *Italy from liberalism to fascism, 1870–1925* (1967), are valuable, as are those in D. Mack Smith, *Italy: a modern history* (rev., 1969); the same author also has written *Mussolini's Roman empire* (1976). Other useful introductions to the Italian experience include A. Cassels, *Fascist Italy** (1968); E. Wiskemann, *Fascism in Italy: its development and influence** (1969); and F. Chabod, *A history of Italian fascism* (1963). An impressive book on the early years is A. Lyttelton, *The seizure of power: fascism in Italy, 1919–1929* (1973), which for foreign affairs may be supplemented by A. Cassels, *Mussolini's early diplomacy* (1970). On the nature of the fascist state, four important books superseding earlier studies are E. R. Tannenbaum, *The fascist experience: Italian society and culture, 1922–1945* (1972); M. Gallo, *Mussolini's Italy: twenty years of the fascist era* (1973); D. Germino, *The Italian fascist party in power* (1959); and R. Sarti, *Fascism and the industrial leadership in Italy, 1919–1940* (1971). A provocative study is D. D. Roberts, *The syndicalist tradition and Italian fascism* (1979), and a special subject is explored in V. de Grazia, *The culture of consent: mass organization of leisure in fascist Italy* (1981). Three books, not entirely convincing, by A. J. Gregor, *The ideology of fascism* (1969), *Italian fascism and developmental dictatorship** (1979), and *Young Mussolini and the intellectual origins of fascism* (1979), portray Italian fascism as an attempt at forced modernization. Foreign policy is examined in G. Barclay, *The rise and fall of the new Roman Empire: Italy's bid for world power, 1890–1943* (1973), giving emphasis to prefascist dynamism.

On *Il Duce* himself, the best biography is D. Mack Smith, *Mussolini* (1982), straightforward and comprehensive, but there is also a detailed biography by I. Kirkpatrick, *Mussolini: study of a demagogue** (1964); the older G. Megaro, *Mussolini in the making* (1938), remains useful. There are accounts by L. Fermi* (1961); C. Hibbert (1962), mostly on the latter phases of the dictator's career; and R. H. Collier (1971). The multivolumed biography of Mussolini in progress (4 vols. to date, 1965 ff.) by the Italian historian R. de Felice is not available in translation. An outstanding account of the underground struggle from 1924 to 1943 is C. F. Delzell, *Mussolini's enemies: the Italian anti-fascist resistance* (1961). F. W. Deakin, *The brutal friendship: Mussolini, Hitler, and the fall of Italian fascism** (1962; rev., 1966), is a detailed account of the last phase of Mussolini's career from his overthrow to his death, and Mussolini as a failed military leader is ably explored in M. Knox, *Mussolini unleashed, 1939–1941: politics and strategy in Fascist Italy's last war* (1982). On a special subject one may read M. Michaelis, *Mussolini and the Jews: German-Italian relations and the Jewish question in Italy, 1922–1945* (1978), which does not see racism as forced on Mussolini.

Other European Developments

[Spain and the Spanish Civil War are discussed in the following chapter.] The most useful volume on eastern Europe is J. Rothschild, *East Central Europe between the two World Wars** (1975), virtually superseding earlier studies by H. Seton-Watson, *Eastern Europe between the wars, 1918–1941* (1946; rev., 1967), and C. A. Macartney and A. W. Palmer, *Independent eastern*

Europe (1962). The relevant portions of R. L. Wolff, *The Balkans in our time** (rev., 1978), cited in Chapter V; L. S. Stavrianos, *The Balkans since 1815** (1965), cited in Chapter XI; and C. Jelavich and B. Jelavich, *The Balkans** (1965), are also helpful. The best treatment of the economic disruption following the end of the Austro-Hungarian empire is L. Pasvolsky, *Economic nationalism of the Danubian states* (1928), and aspects of the new democracies may be examined in P. F. Sugar (ed.), *Native fascism in the successor states, 1918–1945** (1971), and in K. J. Neuman, *European democracy between the wars* (trans. 1971). Specialized accounts of various countries and selected topics include: For Austria: C. A. Gulick, *Austria from Habsburg to Hitler* (2 vols., 1948), sympathetic to the Austrian socialists; M. MacDonald, *The Republic of Austria, 1918–1934: a study in the failure of democratic government* (1946); C. E. Edmondson, *The Heimwehr and Austrian politics, 1918–1936* (1978); M. Kitchen, *The coming of Austrian fascism* (1980); and two comprehensive accounts: F. L. Carsten, *Fascist movements in Austria: from Schönerer to Hitler** (1977), and B. F. Pauley, *Hitler and the forgotten Nazis: a history of Austrian national socialism* (1981). For Hungary: C. A. Macartney, *October fifteenth: a history of modern Hungary, 1929–1945* (2 vols., 1957) and *Hungary: a short history* (1962); R. L. Tönés, *Béla Kun and the Hungarian Soviet Republic* (1967), on the short-lived Communist regime of 1919; and E. Pambenji (ed.), *A history of Hungary* (1975), a collaborative Marxist work, useful but to be read with caution for the more recent period. For Czechoslovakia: S. H. Thomson, *Czechoslovakia in European history* (1943, 1953); R. W. Seton-Watson, *A history of the Czechs and Slovaks* (1943, 1965); A. H. Hermann, *A history of the Czechs* (1976); E. Wiskemann, *Czechs and Germans* (1938, 1967); Z. Zeman, *The Masaryks: the making of Czechoslovakia* (1976); V. Olivová, *The doomed democracy: Czechoslovakia in a disrupted Europe, 1918–1938* (1972); F. G. Campbell, *Confrontation in Central Europe: Weimar Germany and Czechoslovakia* (1975); and V. S. Mamatey and R. Luza (eds.), *A history of the Czechoslovakian Republic, 1918–1948* (1973), with excellent chapters on important turning points. For Yugoslavia: P. Auty (1965) and S. K. Pavlovitch (1971) have each written useful histories, and H. L. Roberts has written *Rumania: political problems of an agrarian state*

(1951). For Poland: an insightful account is M. K. Dziewanowski, *Poland in the twentieth century* (1977), which may be supplemented by A. Polonsky, *Politics in independent Poland, 1921–1939* (1972). For Finland and the Scandinavian countries: D. G. Kirby, *Finland in the twentieth century* (1979); F. D. Scott, *Sweden: the nation's history* (1977); I. Andersson, *A history of Sweden* (rev., 1970); M. W. Childs, *Sweden: the middle way* (rev., 1947); T. K. Derry, *A history of modern Norway, 1914–1972* (1973); and W. G. Jones, *Denmark* (1970).

Problems and Readings*

On the American New Deal, a selection of conflicting interpretations is conveniently presented in E. C. Rozwenc (ed.), *The New Deal: revolution or evolution?* (rev., 1959), and in M. Keller (ed.), *The New Deal* (1963). For Britain: J. A. Thompson (ed.), *The collapse of the British Liberal party: fate or self-destruction?* (1969). For Italy: S. W. Halperin, *Mussolini and Italian fascism* (1964), in the Anvil series, and R. Sarti (ed.), *The ax within: Italian fascism in action* (1974). For Weimar Germany: R. N. Hunt (ed.), *The creation of the Weimar Republic: stillborn democracy?* (1969), and F. K. Ringer (ed.), *The German inflation of 1923* (1969). For the Nazi era: F. Stern (ed.), *The path to dictatorship* (1967); H. A. Turner (ed.), *Nazism and the Third Reich* (1972); J. L. Snell and A. Mitchell (eds.), *Hitler's dictatorship and the German nation* (1973); R. G. L. Waite (ed.), *Hitler and Nazi Germany* (rev., 1969); J. Noakes and G. Pridham (eds.), *Documents of Nazism, 1919–1945* (1975); and B. M. Lane and L. J. Rupp (eds. and translators), *Nazi ideology before 1933: a documentation with introduction* (1979). G. H. Stein has edited *Hitler* in the Great Lives Observed series, and J. Remak, *The Nazi years* (1969). On fascism and totalitarianism, there are available P. T. Mason, *Totalitarianism: temporary madness or permanent danger?* (1967); E. Weber, *Varieties of fascism: doctrines of revolution in the twentieth century* (Anvil, 1964); N. Greene (ed.), *Fascism: an anthology* (1968); C. F. Delzell (ed.), *Mediterranean fascism* (1970); W. Laqueur (ed.), *Fascism: a reader's guide* (1974); H. A. Turner, Jr. (ed.), *Reappraisals of fascism* (1975); R. de Felice (ed.), *Interpretations of fascism* (1972, trans. 1977); and G. L. Mosse (ed.), *International fascism: new thoughts and new appraisals* (1979).

XX: THE SECOND WORLD WAR

The war is placed in historical perspective in L. Dehio, *The precarious balance: four centuries of the European power struggle* * (1948, trans. 1952), and in H. Holborn, *The political collapse of Europe* (1951), a provocative essay. For the war and its impact, especially for Europe, the final volume in the Langer series is excellent, G. Wright, *The ordeal of total war, 1939–1945* * (1968). One of the best overall treatments of the war, both in its military and domestic developments, is P. Calvocoressi and G. Wint, *Total war: causes and courses of the Second World War* * (1972). A useful collaborative volume, with scholars of many nations contributing, is M. Baudot and others, *The historical encyclopedia of World War II* (trans. 1981).

Spain and the Spanish Civil War

Three outstanding syntheses are G. Jackson, *The Spanish republic and the Civil War, 1931–1939* * (1965) [also available in briefer form as *A concise history of the Spanish Civil War* (1974)]; H. Thomas, *The Spanish Civil War* * (1961; rev., 1977); and P. Broué and E. Témime, *The Revolution and the Civil War in Spain* (1961, trans. 1972). R. Carr, *The Spanish tragedy: the Civil War in perspective* (1977), analytical rather than narrative in form, provides many insights. R. Fraser, *Blood of Spain: an oral history of the Spanish Civil War* * (1979), vividly documents the atrocities on both sides and other matters. An informative book stressing, among other things, the Communist role is B. Bolloten, *The Spanish Revolution: the left and the struggle for power during the Civil War* (published under a different title 1961; rev., 1979). The turbulent background is ably conveyed in G. Brenan, *The Spanish labyrinth* * (1943); the relevant chapters of R. Carr, *Spain, 1808–1939*, cited in Chapter XI; R. A. H. Robinson, *The origins of Franco Spain: the right, the Republic, and the Revolution, 1931–1936* (1971); E. E. Malefakis, *Agrarian reform and peasant revolution in Spain: origins of the Civil War* (1970); R. W. Kern, *Red years, black years: a political history of Spanish anarchism, 1911–1937* * (1978); G. Meaker, *The revolutionary left in Spain, 1914–1923* (1974); and R. Preston, *The coming of the Spanish Civil War: reform, reaction, and revolution in the Second Republic, 1931–1936* (1978). S. G. Payne has written an

informative monograph, *Falange: a history of Spanish fascism* * (1961), and a brief, balanced account of the Civil War in *The Spanish Revolution* * (1969).

On the international aspects of the war, there are P. van der Esch, *Prelude to war: the international repercussions of the Spanish Civil War, 1936–1939* (1951); H. Feis, *The Spanish story: Franco and the nations at war* * (1948); D. A. Puzzo, *Spain and the Great Powers, 1936–1941* (1962); D. T. Cattell's two volumes, *Communism and the Spanish Civil War* (1955) and *Soviet diplomacy and the Spanish Civil War* (1957); J. Edwards, *The British government and the Spanish Civil War, 1936–1939* (1979); and J. F. Coverdale, *Italian intervention in the Spanish Civil War* (1975). The famous bombing is examined in H. R. Southworth, *Guernica! Guernica!: a study of journalism, diplomacy, propaganda in history* (1977). Three studies of the American response to the war are F. J. Taylor, *The United States and the Spanish Civil War* (1956); A. Guttmann, *The wound in the heart: America and the Spanish Civil War* (1962); and R. P. Traina, *American diplomacy and the Spanish Civil War* (1968). Other memorable aspects are touched upon in P. Stansky and W. Abrahams, *Journey to the frontier: Julian Bell and John Cornford: their lives and the 1930's* * (1966); the same authors' *George Orwell* (2 vols., 1972, 1980); Orwell's own *Homage to Catalonia* * (1938), by one who fought and became disillusioned; V. Brome, *The international brigades* (1966); V. B. Johnston, *Legions of Babel* (1967); S. Weintraub, *The last great cause: the intellectuals and the Spanish Civil War* (1968); and R. D. Richardson, *Comintern army: the international brigades and the Spanish Civil War* (1982). A balanced study of Franco is J. W. D. Trythall, *El Caudillo* (1970).

Background to the Second World War

Although there is no one comprehensive treatment taking into account the sources now available for the diplomacy of the interwar years and the background to the Second World War, there has been an enormous outpouring of books on the subject. Two scholarly surveys by French diplomatic historians are: P. Renouvin, *World War II and its origins: international relations 1929–1945* (trans. 1969), and M. Baumont, *The origins of the Second World War* (trans. 1978); an important book by J. B. Duroselle for the years 1932–1939 is not yet translated. Useful introductory accounts include E. Wiskemann, *Europe of the dictators, 1919–1945** (1966); K. Eubank, *The origins of World War II** (1969); L. Lafore, *The end of glory: an interpretation of the origins of World War II** (1970); and J. Remak, *The origins of the Second World War** (1975). The books cited in Chapter XVIII should be consulted, especially S. Marks, *The illusion of peace: international relations in Europe, 1918–1933* (1976).

Of special value for the interwar years are the annual volumes edited for the Royal Institute of International Affairs by A. J. Toynbee and others, *Survey of international affairs* (1920 ff.), and the accompanying *Documents* on international affairs. A *Survey* has been published to cover the years 1939–1946 (1954), and the annual volumes have been resumed for the years since 1946. An excellent series providing bibliographical and archival guidance was inaugurated with C. M. Kimmich (ed.), *German foreign policy, 1918–1945: guide to research and research materials* (1981), with volumes now available for the foreign policy of the other major powers: R. J. Young (ed.), for France; A. Cassels (ed.), for Italy; S. Aster (ed.), for Britain; and G. W. Baer (ed.), for the League and other international organizations. The opening of the British and French archives and the availability of the German archives for these years has made many earlier works obsolete or at least incomplete, among them volumes by A. Wolfers (1940), W. M. Jordan (1943), G. M. Gathorne-Hardy (rev., 1939), W. N. Medlicott (1940), and E. H. Carr (rev., 1946). Highly recommended also for these years, with implications for foreign affairs going beyond their immediate subject, are J. Jacobson, *Locarno diplomacy: Germany and the West, 1925–1929* (1972), cited in Chapter XVIII, and E. W. Bennett, *German rearmament and the West, 1932–1933* (1979). British foreign policy is examined in F. S. Northedge, *The troubled giant: Britain among the Great Powers, 1916–1939* (1966); a collaborative study: D. Dilkes (ed.), *Retreat from power: studies in Britain's foreign policy of the twentieth century*, vol. I, *1906–1939*, and vol. II, *After 1939* (1980); P. Hayes, *The twentieth century, 1880–1933* (1978), in the Modern British Foreign Policy series, with little concession to the case for appeasement; M. Cowling, *The impact of Hitler: British politics and British policy, 1933–1940* (1975), stressing domestic pressures; and

R. P. Shay, Jr., *British rearmament in the thirties: politics and profits* (1977), emphasizing limitations imposed by the Treasury and more critical than the comprehensive official study, N. H. Gibbs, *Rearmament policy* (1976).

Focusing on French foreign policy are: A. Adamthwaite, *France and the coming of the Second World War, 1936–1939* (1977), which may be supplemented by W. E. Scott, *Alliance against Hitler: the origins of the Franco-Soviet pact* (1962); A. H. Furnia, *The diplomacy of appeasement* (1966); and J. E. Dreifort, *Yvon Delbos at the Quai d'Orsay: French foreign policy during the Popular Front, 1936–1938* (1974).

L. B. Namier, *Diplomatic prelude, 1938–1939* (1948) and *Europe in decay: a study in disintegration, 1936–1940* (1950), are highly critical of appeasement, as are A. L. Rowse, *Appeasement: a study in political decline, 1933–1939** (1961); M. Gilbert and R. Gott, *The appeasers* (1963); and M. George, *The warped vision: British foreign policy, 1933–1939* (1965). The opposition to appeasement is examined in W. R. Rock, *Appeasement on trial: British foreign policy and its critics, 1938–1939* (1966); N. Thompson, *The anti-appeasers* (1971); and C. Barnett, *The collapse of British power* (1972). In this connection, one should also read W. S. Churchill, *The gathering storm** (1948), the first volume of his *The Second World War** (6 vols., 1948–1953), covering his years in the opposition. The fifth volume of the massive biography of Churchill deals with these years: M. Gilbert, *Winston S. Churchill*, vol. V, *The prophet of truth, 1922–1939* (1977). Two other biographical studies focusing on British foreign policy are D. Carlton, on Anthony Eden (1981), and J. A. Cross, on Sir Samuel Hoare (1977). An interesting revisionist book that examines economic, and other, restraints on British foreign policy is R. Douglas, *In the year of Munich* (1978).

There are many books on specific episodes and subjects. The Ethiopian conquest is studied in two books by G. W. Baer: *The coming of the Italo-Ethiopian War* (1967) and *Test case: Italy, Ethiopia, and the League of Nations* (1976); E. M. Robertson, *Mussolini as empire-builder: Europe and Africa, 1932–1936* (1977); F. Hardie, *The Abyssinian crisis* (1974); and A. del Boca, *The Ethiopian War, 1935–1941* (1969). The Rhineland episode is examined in J. T. Emmerson, *The Rhineland crisis, 7 March 1936: a study in multilateral diplomacy*

(1977). On the annexation of Austria, one may read G. Brook-Shepherd, *Anschluss: the rape of Austria* (1963) and *Dolfuss* (1961); J. Gehl, *Austria, Germany and the Anschluss, 1931–1938* (1963); and D. Wagner and G. Tomkowitz, *Anschluss: the week Hitler seized Vienna* (1971). For Munich, the best detailed account is T. Taylor, *Munich: the price of peace** (1980); also useful are J. W. Wheeler-Bennett, *Munich: prologue to tragedy** (1948, reissued 1963); K. Eubank, *Munich* (1963); H. Noguères, *Munich: "peace for our time"* (trans. 1963); and K. Robbins, *Munich 1938* (1963). F. Gilbert and G. A. Craig (eds.), *The diplomats, 1919–1939** (1953), include many valuable chapters on the individuals who made foreign policy in the era.

A major study of German foreign policy based on exhaustive use of the documents and strongly emphasizing Hitler's responsibilities and initiatives is G. L. Weinberg, *The foreign policy of Hitler's Germany:* vol. I, *Diplomatic revolution in Europe, 1933–1936* (1970) and vol. II, *Starting World War II, 1937–1939* (1980). A second study with similar conclusions but focusing on objectives rather than events is N. Rich, *Hitler's war aims* (2 vols., 1973–1974). For assessments of German foreign policy, one may also read K. Hildebrand, *The foreign policy of the Third Reich** (1974); D. Calleo, *The German problem reconsidered: Germany and the world order, 1870 to the present* (1978); J. Hiden, *Germany and Europe, 1919–1939* (1978); E. Jäckel, *Hitler's world view* (1981); the essays in V. R. Berghahn and M. Kitchen (eds.), *Germany and the age of total war* (1981); and D. Irving, *The war path: Hitler's Germany, 1933–1945* (1971).

An ambitious study focusing on eastern Europe is D. E. Kaiser, *Economic diplomacy and the origins of the Second World War: Germany, Britain, France, and Eastern Europe, 1930–1939* (1980). Other books dealing with eastern Europe are J. A. Lukacs, *The Great Powers and eastern Europe* (1952); P. Wandycz, *France and her Eastern allies, 1919–1925* (1962); L. Kochan, *The struggle for Germany, 1914–1945* (1963), on the rivalry between the West and Russia; G. Hilger and A. G. Meyer, *The incompatible allies: a memoir history of German-Soviet relations, 1918–1941* (1953); J. Korbel, *Poland between East and West: Soviet-German diplomacy towards Poland, 1919–1933* (1963); A. Cienciala, *Poland and the Western powers, 1938–1939* (1968); and S. Newman, *March 1939: the British guarantee to Poland: a study in the continuity of British foreign policy* (1976). A longer study focusing on eastern Europe, carrying the story to 1941, is J. E. McSherry, *Stalin, Hitler, and Europe* (2 vols., 1968–1972). On the events immediately preceding the outbreak of the war, a Swiss historian, W. Hofer, has written *War premeditated, 1939* (1955); C. Horne, the brief, informative *The approach of war, 1938–1939** (1967); S. Aster, *1939: the making of the Second World War* (1973); N. Fleming, *August 1939: the last days of peace* (1979); and R. Douglas, *The advent of war, 1939–40* (1978); the more recent books use new material from archives opened in 1970. A provocative book based on a wide reading of the sources is D. C. Watt, *Too serious a business: European armed forces and the approach to the Second World War* (1975).

The opening gun in a campaign to "revise" the traditional picture of Nazi war responsibility was launched with A. J. P. Taylor's dazzling but unconvincing performance, *The origins of the Second World War** (1961, 1963), in which he depicted Hitler as one who did not desire war but merely took advantage of the uncertainty of his opponents. Another book in the same category is D. L. Hoggan, *When peaceful revision failed: the origins of World War II* (1964), an English version of a book by an American writer that first appeared in German translation (1961). The revisionists are examined in W. B. Morris, Jr., *The revisionist historians and German war guilt* (1977).

The role of the United States in these years is traced in two comprehensive volumes by W. L. Langer and S. E. Gleason, *The challenge to isolation, 1937–1940* (1952) and *The undeclared war, 1940–1941* (1953); R. Ferrell, *American diplomacy in the Great Depression* (1957); S. Friedländer, *Prelude to downfall: Hitler and the United States, 1939–1941* (trans. 1967); C. A. MacDonald, *The United States, Britain, and appeasement, 1930–1939* (1981); and D. Reynolds, *The creation of the Anglo-American alliance, 1937–1941* (1982). The events in the Far East may be studied through David J. Lu, *From the Marco Polo Bridge to Pearl Harbor: Japan's entry into World War II* (1961); R. Butow, *Tojo and the coming of the war* (1961); J. B. Crowley, *Japan's quest for autonomy: national security and foreign policy, 1930–1938* (1966); P. A. Varg, *The closing of the door: Sino-American relations, 1936–1949* (1973); and B. Lee, *Britain and the Sino-Japanese War, 1937–1939* (1973).

On American involvement, one may turn to P. W. Schroeder, *The Axis alliance and Japanese-American relations, 1941* (1963); R. Wohlstetter, *Pearl Harbor: warning and decision** (1962); and G. W. Prange, *At dawn we slept: the untold story of Pearl Harbor* (1981), the fullest account.

The War: Military and Domestic Developments

G. Wright, *The ordeal of total war,** and P. Calvocoressi and G. Wint, *Total war,** already cited, may be supplemented by A. S. Milward, *War, economy, and society, 1939–1945** (1977). W. S. Churchill, *The Second World War** (6 vols., 1948–1953; authorized 1-vol. condensation, 1959), is a full-dress treatment by a historian with unrivaled opportunities; in some ways, however, the work is as much autobiographical as historical and should be used with caution. For a thoughtful evaluation of Churchill as wartime leader, one may read the essays in A. J. P. Taylor and others, *Churchill revised: a critical assessment* (1969).

Attempts to cover the events of the war in brief compass are L. L. Snyder, *A concise history: the war, 1939–1945** (1960); P. Young, *World war, 1939–1945* (1966); B. Collier, *A short history of the Second World War* (1967); B. H. Liddell Hart, *The history of the Second World War** (1971); and H. Michel, *The Second World War* (trans. 1975). H. Baldwin discusses with verve eleven major battles in *Battles lost and won: great campaigns of World War II* (1966) and also has written a history of the war to 1941 (1977). There are numerous other narrative histories. Many volumes of the detailed official histories of the United Kingdom, Canada, and the United States have appeared. Of special note is the official U.S. Navy history in fifteen volumes prepared by S. E. Morison (1947 ff.) and published in a one-volume abridgement as *The two-ocean war: a short history of the United States navy in the Second World War* (1963). On naval warfare, there also are available S. W. Roskill, *The war at sea, 1939–1945* (1954), and J. Creswell, *Sea warfare, 1939–1945* (1967). The air war, for each of the major powers, is examined in R. J. Overy, *The air war, 1939–1945* (1980), and in M. Hastings, *Bomber command* (1979), which, like earlier studies, find strategic bombing to have been less effective than was thought at the time. The effect on Germany is also examined in C. K. Webster and N. N. Frankland,

Strategic air offensive against Germany, 1939–1945 (1961).

On overall strategy, a valuable discussion of high-level decisions, Allied and Axis, by the Office of the U.S. Chief of Military History is K. R. Greenfield (ed.), *Command decisions* (1959). Also useful on strategy are the following: J. R. M. Butler's volume in the U.K. official history, *Grand strategy* (1957); the succeeding volume on strategy in the same series by J. M. A. Gwyer and J. R. M. Butler (1964), covering the 1941–1942 period; S. E. Morison, *American contributions to the strategy of World War II* (1958); F. H. Hinsley, *Hitler's strategy* (1951); E. Robertson, *Hitler's pre-war policy and military plans* (1963); M. L. Van Creveld, *Hitler's strategy, 1940–1941: the Balkan clue* (1973); and G. H. Liddell Hart, *The other side of the hill** (1951; rev. ed. of *The German generals talk*, 1948), which may be supplemented by H.-A. Jacobsen and J. Rohwer (eds.), *Decisive battles of World War II: the German view* (1965), and D. Downing, *The devil's virtuosos: German generals at war, 1940–1945* (1977). Useful also is H.-A. Jacobsen and A. L. Smith, Jr. (eds.), *World War II: policy and strategy* (1979), a selection of documents and commentary.

For studies of the wartime scene, there are some excellent volumes in the U.K. official history: W. C. Hancock and M. M. Gowing, *British war economy* (1949); R. M. Titmuss, *Problems of social policy* (1950); and M. M. Postan, *British war production* (1950). A graphic documentary and photographic account is A. Marwick, *The home front: the British and the Second World War* (1977). Various phases of the American domestic scene are treated in many books, of which one attempt at a synthesis is A. R. Buchanan, *The United States and World War II** (2 vols., 1964). On the entry of women into the wartime labor force and its impact, K. Anderson has written *Wartime women: sex roles, family relations, and the status of women during World War II* (1981); that the Americans were more successful than the Germans in mobilizing women is clearly demonstrated in L. J. Rupp, *Mobilizing women for war: German and American propaganda, 1939–1945* (1978). B. H. Klein, *Germany's economic preparations for war* (1959), stresses inefficiency and the belatedness of full-scale mobilization, as do A. S. Milward, *The German economy at war* (1965), and B. A. Carroll, *Design for total war: arms and economics in the Third Reich* (1968). The German military effort also is discussed in H. R. Trevor-Roper (ed.), *From Blitzkrieg to defeat* (1965). A special subject is examined in J. W. Baird, *The mythical world of Nazi war propaganda, 1939–1945* (1975), and in R. E. Herzstein, *The war that Hitler won: the most infamous propaganda campaign in history* (1978). For events in Italy, one may read F. W. Deakin, *The brutal friendship: Mussolini, Hitler, and the fall of Italian fascism** (rev., 1966), cited in Chapter XIX, and A. N. Garland and H. M. Smyth, *Sicily and the surrender of Italy* (1965).

For the Russian front, there are some outstanding books. One may read A. Werth, *The year of Stalingrad* (1947) and *Russia at war, 1941–1945** (1964); A. Clark, *Barbarossa: the Russian-German conflict, 1941–1945* (1965); T. Higgins, *Hitler and Russia: the Third Reich in a two-front war, 1937–1943* (1966); A. Seaton, *The Russo-German war* (1971); H. Salisbury, *The 900 days: the siege of Leningrad** (1969); the remarkable J. Erickson, *The road to Stalingrad: Stalin's war with Germany* (1975), the first volume of a projected larger study; and the same author's valuable *The Soviet High Command . . . , 1918–1941* (1962), cited in Chapter XVIII. The Russo-Finnish episode is well treated in R. W. Condon, *The winter war* (1972), and in F. Chew, *The white death* (1971). A. Seaton, *Stalin as military commander* (1976), is a careful study. The war in the Pacific is ably sketched in C. Bateson, *The war with Japan* (1968); S. Ienaga, *The Pacific war: World War II and the Japanese, 1931–1945* (trans. 1978), by a distinguished Japanese historian; and J. H. Boyle, *China and Japan at war* (1972). The Japanese home front is examined in T. R. H. Havens, *Valley of darkness: the Japanese people and World War II* (1978), and some new insights are presented in A. Iriye, *Power and culture: the Japanese-American war, 1941–1945* (1981). A defeat that symbolized the fall of the European supremacy in Asia is recounted in S. L. Folk, *Seventy days to Singapore* (1975), and R. Callahan, *The worst disaster: the fall of Singapore* (1977).

A challenging, personalized interpretation of events to 1941 is provided in J. Lukacs, *The last European war, September 1939–December 1941* (1976). The final phase of the war in Europe is ably recounted in R. F. Weigley, *Eisenhower's lieutenants, the campaign of France and Germany, 1944–1945* (1981). P. E. Schramm, *Hitler: the man and the military leader** (1971), is rewarding.

D. Irving, *Hitler's war* (1977), should be read with extreme caution; the author presents some new materials but strains credulity in trying to exonerate Hitler personally for war responsibility and for Nazi atrocities; he has sketched a more convincing portrait of Rommel in *The trail of the fox* (1977). The war of intelligence, including the Polish-inspired Ultra machine that broke the highest German code, is recounted in P. Calvocoressi, *Top secret Ultra* (1980), which discounts some of the exaggerated claims made for it; in R. Lewin, *Ultra goes to war* (1979); and in a volume in the official British history, F. H. Hinsley and others, *British intelligence in the Second World War: its influence on strategy and operations*, vol. I (1979). A special aspect is examined in R. Jones, *The wizard war: British scientific intelligence, 1939–1945* (1978). German intelligence is examined in D. Kahn, *Hitler's spies: German military intelligence in World War II* (1978).

Informative on the development of the bomb are H. D. Smyth, *Atomic energy for military purposes* (1945), and M. M. Gowing, *Britain and atomic energy, 1939–1945* (1964), with a sequel volume for 1945–1952 (1974).

The Fall of France and the Vichy Regime

[The books dealing with France in the 1930s listed in Chapter XIX and earlier in this chapter also should be consulted.] The political and military background to the fall of France may be approached through A. Horne, *To lose a battle: France, 1940* (1969); G. Chapman, *Why France fell: the defeat of the French army in 1940* (1969); the massive, popularly written W. L. Shirer, *The collapse of the Third Republic: an inquiry into the fall of France in 1940** (1969); P. C. F. Bankwitz, *Maxime Weygand and civil-military relations in modern France* (1967); J. M. Hughes, *To the Maginot Line: the politics of French military preparation in the 1920s* (1971); and R. F. Young, *In command of France: French foreign policy and military planning 1933–1940* (1978). They may be supplemented by A. Goutard, *The fall of France* (trans. 1940); A. Beaufre, *1940: the fall of France* (trans. 1968); L. Thompson, *1940* (1966); and J. A. Gunsberg, *Divided and conquered: the French high command and the defeat of the West, 1940* (1979). The relationship with Britain is explored in E. M. Gates, *End of the affair:*

the collapse of the Anglo-French alliance, 1939–1940 (1981), and P. H. M. Bell, *A certain eventuality: Britain and the fall of France* (1975). A moving memoir is M. Bloch, *Strange defeat* ⃰ (1940), by the eminent medievalist who was executed as a member of the Resistance.

For Vichy the best study is R. O. Paxton, *Vichy France: old guard and new order, 1940–1944* ⃰ (1972); the same author also has written *Parades and politics at Vichy* (1966), and with M. Marrus, *Vichy France and the Jews* (1981), which shows French culpability for many acts during the German occupation. There are older books on Vichy by R. Aron (1958), P. Farmer (1955), D. Pickles (1946), and A. Hytier (1959). A moving personal memoir by an historian who survived the years of Nazi occupation is S. Friedländer, *When memory comes* (trans. 1979). A special subject is explored in W. D. Hall, *The youth of Vichy France* (1981), and economic aspects are covered in A. S. Milward, *The new order and the French economy* (1970). American relations with Vichy are studied in W. L. Langer, *Our Vichy gamble* ⃰ (1947), a somewhat defensive account, and British relations in R. T. Thomas, *Britain and Vichy: the dilemma of Anglo-French relations, 1940–1942* (1979). There is a biography of Laval by H. Cole (1963), and a detailed biographical study focusing on diplomatic events by G. Warner, *Pierre Laval and the eclipse of France, 1931–1945* (1968). The Resistance movement in France [books on the European-wide Resistance are cited below] may be studied in D. Schoenbrun, *Soldiers of the night: the story of the French Resistance* (1980); M. R. D. Foot, *SOE in France* (1966); J. F. Sweets, *The politics of resistance in France, 1940–1944* (1976); H. R. Kedward, *Resistance in Vichy France: a study of ideas and motivation in the southern zone* (1978); and the relevant chapters of A. Werth, *France, 1940–1955* (1957). On collaborationism, one may study B. M. Gordon, *Collaborationism in France during the Second World War* (1980); and for the postwar period, P. Novick, *The Resistance versus Vichy: the purge of collaborators in liberated France* (1969). The liberation is dramatically described in R. Aron, *France reborn . . . the liberation* (trans. 1964). For the years from the 1930s to liberation, the volumes of C. de Gaulle, *War memoirs* ⃰ (3 vols., 1954–1956; trans. 1958–1960), are indispensable; specifically on de Gaulle's unsatisfactory wartime relations with London and Washington, there are three able studies: A. L. Funk, *Charles de Gaulle: the crucial years, 1943–1944* (1959); M. Viorst, *Hostile allies: FDR and Charles de Gaulle* (1965); and F. Kersaudy, *Churchill and de Gaulle* (1982).

Hitler's New Order, the Holocaust, and the Resistance

[See also the many books on the Third Reich listed in Chapter XIX.] The volume of the *Survey of international affairs* covering the years 1939–1946, *Hitler's Europe* (1954), is valuable on all aspects of the German domination. Selected aspects are studied in W. Warmbrunn, *The Dutch under German occupation, 1940–1945* (1963); A. S. Milward, *The fascist economy in Norway* (1972); R. L. Braham, *The Hungarian labor service system, 1939–1945* (1977); J. T. Gross, *Polish society under German occupation: the Generalgouvernement, 1939–1944* (1979); and J. Gillingham, *Belgian business and the Nazi new order* (1977), exploring the collaboration of business circles. A special subject is well treated in A. Dallin, *German rule in Russia, 1941–1945: a study of occupation policies* (rev., 1981), demonstrating the ineptitude of the Germans in exploiting discontent; it may be supplemented by J. A. Armstrong, *Ukrainian nationalism, 1939–1945* (1955).

On the Jewish question, three books serve as a comprehensive introduction to the grim subject of the Holocaust: R. Hilberg, *The destruction of the European Jews* ⃰ (1962; rev. and expanded, 3 vols., 1983), a careful reconstruction; L. S. Dawidowicz, *The war against the Jews, 1933–1945* ⃰ (1976); and G. Reitlinger, *The final solution: the attempt to exterminate the Jews of Europe, 1939–1945* (1953, 1968). Dawidowicz has written other books relating to the subject and has edited *A Holocaust reader* ⃰ (1976). An important synthesis of responses in the occupied countries is H. Fein, *Accounting for genocide: national responses and Jewish victimization during the Holocaust* (1979), and a key episode is superbly recounted in Y. Gutman, *The Jews of Warsaw, 1939–1943: ghetto, underground, revolt* (trans. 1982).

These studies may be supplemented by K. A. Schleunes, *The twisted road to Auschwitz* (1970); K. G. Feig, *Hitler's death camps: the sanity of madness* ⃰ (1981); R. L. Braham, *The politics of genocide: the Holocaust in Hungary* (2 vols., 1980), an outstanding study; and G. M. Kren and L. Rappaport, *The Holocaust and the crisis of human behavior* (1980). E. Kogon, *The theory and practice of hell** (1950), was one of the earliest treatments of the subject. A much discussed essay on the question of responsibility and guilt is H. Arendt, *Eichmann in Jerusalem: a report on the banality of evil** (1963). Y. Bauer, *The Holocaust in historical perspective* (1978), argues the uniqueness of the episode and against later misuses of the word "genocide"; on this, one may also read L. Kuper, *Genocide: its political use in the twentieth century* (1982). Y. Bauer and N. Rotenstreich have edited *The Holocaust as historical experience* (1983), a useful collaborative volume, and Bauer has written *A history of the Holocaust** (1982). There is a large literature on the failure of the authorities in the United States, Britain, and the Vatican to rescue the doomed European Jews; among the more searching inquiries are W. Laqueur, *The terrible secret: an investigation into the suppression of information about Hitler's Final Solution* (1980); B. Wasserstein, *Britain and the Jews of Europe, 1939–1945* (1979); M. Gilbert, *Auschwitz and the Allies* (1981); S. Friedländer, *Pius XII and the Third Reich: a documentation* (1966); and J. F. Morley, *Vatican diplomacy and the Jews during the Holocaust, 1939–1943* (1980). For the United States, A. D. Morse, *While six million died* (1968), may be supplemented with books by D. Wyman (1968), H. L. Feingold (1970), S. S. Friedman (1973), R. W. Ross* (1980), and Y. Bauer (1981). Of special interest is C. R. Browning, *The Final Solution and the German foreign office* (1978).

On other ethnic policies and refugee movements, there are R. L. Koehl, *RKFDV: German resettlement and population policy, 1939–1945* (1957); J. B. Schechtman, *European population transfers, 1939–1945* (1946); E. M. Kulischer, *Europeans on the move: war and population changes, 1917–1947* (1948); and M. J. Proudfoot, *European refugees, 1939–1952* (1957). Two books examining Soviet and Western responsibilities respectively are A. M. Neberich, *The punished peoples: the deportation and fate of Soviet minorities at the end of the Second World War* (1978), and A. M. de Zayas, *Nemesis at Potsdam: the Anglo-Americans and the expulsion of the Germans* (1977), on the population movements resulting from the restoration of pre-Munich boundaries.

For the European-wide Resistance, there is the judicious study by H. Michel, *The shadow war: the European Resistance, 1939–1945* (trans. 1972); the useful though somewhat anecdotal M. R. D. Foot, *Resistance: European resistance to Nazism, 1940–1945* (1977); and J. Haestrup, *Europe ablaze: an analysis of the history of the European Resistance movements, 1939–1945* (1978), massive and detailed. Haestrup has also written a detailed account of the Danish story in *Secret alliance: a study of the Danish Resistance movement, 1940–1945* (3 vols., trans. 1976–1977). The renovative spirit of the Resistance and the emergence from it of the postwar liberal left is ably conveyed in D. Wilkinson, *The intellectual resistance in Europe* (1981). Books on the French Resistance have been cited earlier in this chapter and on the German in Chapter XIX.

The proceedings of the Nuremberg trials have been published as International Military Tribunal, *Trial of the major war criminals before the International Military Tribunal, 1945–1946* (42 vols., 1947–1949), and as *Nazi conspiracy and aggression* (8 vols., 2 supplements, 1946–1958). Two informative books on the nature and origin of the trials by B. F. Smith, *Reaching judgment at Nuremberg* (1977), and *The road to Nuremberg* (1981), argue that they should not be dismissed as merely "victor's justice" and that they prevented an anarchic bloodbath. Other thoughtful discussions are found in P. de Mendelssohn, *Design for aggression* (1946); W. R. Harris, *Tyranny on trial: the evidence of Nuremberg* (1954); J. L. Stipp (ed.), *Devil's diary: the record of Nazi conspiracy and aggression* (1955); P. Calvocoressi, *Nuremberg: the facts, the law, and the consequences* (1948); and E. Davidson, *The trial of the Germans: Nuremberg, 1945–1946* (1966). An outstanding account of the trial is R. E. Conot, *Justice at Nuremberg* (1983). The less-known trials of the Japanese war leaders are critically analyzed in R. Minear, *Victor's justice: the Tokyo war crimes trial* (1979), a study which may be contrasted with P. R. Piccigallo, *The Japanese on trial: Allied war crimes operations in the East, 1945–1951* (1979).

Wartime Diplomacy and Origins of the Cold War

A growing literature has emerged stressing the origins of the Cold War in Soviet-American relations during the Second World War. These books, many critical of the United States, are for the most part listed in the following chapter. Wartime diplomacy and the successes and failures of the Soviet-Western coalition may be approached through the latter volumes of Churchill's history; C. Wilmot, *The struggle for Europe* (1952); W. H. McNeill, *America, Britain, and Russia: their cooperation and conflict, 1941–1946* (1953); W. LaFeber, *America, Russia, and the Cold War* (rev. ed., 1976); G. Smith, *American diplomacy during the Second World War** (1965); and V. Mastny, *Russia's road to the Cold War: diplomacy, warfare, and the politics of communism, 1941–1945* (1979), projecting a case for the logic of Soviet policy-making. A useful book on the overall postwar "settlement" is J. W. Wheeler-Bennett and A. Nicholls, *The semblance of peace: the political settlement after the Second World War** (1972). Invaluable are the volumes of H. Feis, sympathetic to the Western leaders: *Churchill, Roosevelt, Stalin: the war they waged and the peace they sought** (1957), covering the years from 1941 to the collapse of Germany; *Between war and peace: the Potsdam Conference** (1960); and on the last phase, *The atomic bomb and the end of the war in the Pacific** (1961, 1966); a final volume follows, *From trust to terror: the onset of the Cold War, 1945–1950** (1970). On the last phase in the Pacific, see also R. Butow, *Japan's decision to surrender** (1954), and W. Craig, *The fall of Japan* (1968). On the significance of the atomic bomb for relations with the Soviet Union, one may turn to M. J. Sherwin, *A world destroyed: the atomic bomb and the Grand Alliance* (1975), an impressive and balanced study, and the more vehemently critical G. Alperowitz, *Atomic diplomacy: Hiroshima and Potsdam** (1965), which may be supplemented by B. J. Bernstein, *The atomic bomb: the critical issues** (1975). An indispensable collaborative study is A. C. Brown and C. B. MacDonald (eds.), *The secret history of the atomic bomb** (1977). Hitler's relations with his two major allies are discussed in F. W. Deakin's detailed *The brutal friendship,** cited in this chapter and in Chapter XIX, and in J. Menzel, *Hitler and Japan: the hollow alliance* (1966). E. L. Woodward, *British foreign policy in the Second World War* (5 vols., 1962–1977), is based on the Foreign Office archives to which the author was given early access; two special subjects are examined in G. W. Kacewicz, *Great Britain, the Soviet Union, and the Polish government in exile, 1939–1945* (1979), and E. Barker, *British policy in south-east Europe in the Second World War* (1976). F. L. Loewenheim and others have edited *Roosevelt and Churchill: their wartime corre-*

spondence (1976), while J. P. Lash, *Roosevelt and Churchill, 1939–1941: the partnership that saved the West* (1976), is interesting but adulatory. An important, large-scale study is C. Thorne, *Allies of a kind: the United States, Britain, and the war against Japan, 1941–1945* (1978); R. Douglas, *New alliances, 1940–41* (1982), is useful. The best study of Roosevelt's foreign policy, sympathetic yet critical, is R. Dallek, *Franklin D. Roosevelt and American foreign policy, 1932–1945** (1979).

Problems and Readings*

In the various series there are available: H. W. Gatzke (ed.), *European diplomacy between two wars, 1919–1939* (1972); L. F. Schaefer (ed.), *The Ethiopian crisis: touchstone of appeasement?* (1961); G. Jackson (ed.), *The Spanish Civil War: domestic crisis or international conspiracy?* (1967); A. Guttmann (ed.), *American neutrality and the Spanish Civil War* (1963); S. G. Payne (ed.), *Politics and society in twentieth century Spain* (1976); F. L. Loewenheim (ed.), *Peace or appeasement: Hitler, Chamberlain, and the Munich crisis* (1965), an especially full selection of source materials; D. E. Lee (ed.), *Munich: blunder, plot, or tragic necessity?* (1969); S. M. Osgood (ed.), *The fall of France, 1940* (rev., 1972); I. Morris (ed.), *Japan, 1931–1945: militarism, fascism, Japanism?* (1963); and G. O. Totten (ed.), *Democracy and prewar Japan: groundwork or façade?* (1965). W. C. Langsam has edited *Historic documents of World War II,* (Anvil, 1958), and M. Gilbert, *Churchill* (1967), in the Great Lives Observed series. Four useful collections of essays on the origins of the war are H. Gatzke (ed.), *European diplomacy between the wars, 1919–1939* (1972); E. M. Robertson (ed.), *Origins of the Second World War* (1971); W. K. Eubank (ed.), *World War II: roots and causes* (1975); and W. R. Louis, *The origins of the Second World War: A. J. P. Taylor and his critics* (1972). J. C. Cairns has prepared *Consequences of World War II in Europe** (1977) for the Forums in History series.

XXI–XXII: THE CONTEMPORARY AGE

It is difficult to assess the durable value of literature dealing with the events and developments of the recent era. The listings for these chapters therefore have been kept brief. Useful in keeping up with current developments, in addition to many periodical and newspaper sources, are the *Survey of international affairs*, published annually by the Royal Institute of International Affairs; the yearbooks published by the leading encyclopedias; the *Annual register;* and *Keesing's contemporary archives: weekly diary of important world events* (1931 ff.). The bibliographies published quarterly in *Foreign affairs* and in the professional journals should also be used.

The Communist Worlds in Europe and Asia

[The books listed for the Soviet Union in Chapter XVII and for Eastern Europe in Chapter XIX should be consulted.] How communism was imposed on Eastern Europe is explored in H. Seton-Watson, *The East European revolution* (rev., 1956), which may be supplemented by his insightful essay, *The "sick heart" of modern Europe: the problem of the Danubian lands* (1976). The decade after 1953 is comprehensively examined in F. Fejtö, *A history of the people's democracies: Eastern Europe since Stalin* (trans. 1971), while many insights are provided in N. Beloff, *Inside the Soviet empire: the myth and the reality* (1980); D. R. Shanon, *Soviet Europe* (1975), is a useful survey by a journalist. Z. K. Brzezinski, *The Soviet bloc: unity and conflict* (1960; rev., 1967), is a probing analysis, which may be supplemented by S. Fischer-Galati, *Eastern Europe in the 1980s* (1981). Two informative studies of Yugoslavia are D. Rusinow, *The Yugoslav experiment, 1948–1974* (1977), and D. Wilson, *Tito's Yugoslavia* (1979). Czechoslovakia as victim, first of Hitler then of Stalin, is ably examined in E. Taborsky, *President Eduard Beneš: between East and West, 1938–1948* (1981), and the crisis of 1968 in G. Golan, *The Czechoslovak reform movement: communism in crisis, 1962–1968* (1971), and in Z. A. B. Zeman, *Prague spring* (1969). A valuable study of Hungary is B. Kovrig, *Communism in Hungary: from Kun to Kádár* (1979).

The changes in the Soviet Union since 1953 are explored in A. Nove, *Stalinism and after** (1975); R. McNeal, *The Bolshevik tradition: Lenin, Stalin, Khrushchev, Brezhnev** (rev., 1974); S. Bialer, *Stalin's successors: leadership, stability, and change in the Soviet Union* (1980), highly informative; and the same author's *The domestic context of Soviet foreign policy* (1981). L. R. Graham examines Soviet intellectual life in *Science and philosophy in the Soviet Union* (1972), cited earlier, and D. Joravsky a special episode in *The Lysenko affair* (1970). The background to present-day dissidence is explored in one of A. B. Ulam's many books, *Ideologies and illusions: revolutionary thought from Herzen to Solzhenitsyn* (1976).

For the Communist movement as a whole, A. Westoby, *Communism since World War II* (1981), is a valuable survey. G. R. Urban, *Euro-communism* (1978), and C. Boggs, *The impasse of European communism* (1982), are important for the European Communist parties. J. Braunthal examines the years after the dissolution of the Comintern in *History of the International*, vol. III, *World socialism, 1943–1968* (trans. 1980).

On the emergence of communism in China and on the regime since 1949, a number of books have already been cited in Chapter XVIII. Of the growing literature on the subject, only a few titles can be mentioned here. The best overview is to be found in M. Meisner, *Mao's China: a history of the People's Republic* (1977), and in two volumes by an Australian scholar, B. Brugger, *China: liberation and transformation, 1942–1962* and *China: radicalism to revisionism, 1962–1979* (rev., 1981). The Chinese Revolution is explored in its relationship to the outside world in W. Gungwa, *China and the world since 1949: the impact of independence, modernity, and revolution** (1977).

The Communist triumph and the nature of Chinese communism are also explored in C. P. Fitzgerald, *The birth of Communist China** (rev., 1966) and *Mao Tse-tung and China* (1976); B. Schwartz, *Chinese communism and the rise of Mao** (1951); D. Wilson, *The long march, 1935: the epic of Chinese communism's survival* (1972); the older and vivid E. Snow, *Red star over China* (reprinted 1968); the authoritative and balanced J. P. Harrison, *The long march to power: a history of the Chinese Communist party, 1921–1972* (1972); J. Guillermaz, *History of the Chinese Communist party, 1929–1949* (trans. 1972); and R. C. Thornton, *China: the struggle for power, 1917–1972* (1973). For Mao's career, the best biography is S. Schram, *Mao Tse-tung** (rev., 1967); there are others by S. Uhalley (1975), R. Terrill (1980), and H. Suyin (1976), the latter a personalized account. An assessment by leading scholars shortly after Mao's death is provided in D. Wilson (ed.), *Mao Tse-tung on the scales of history** (1977). R. Witke, *Comrade Chiang Ch'ing* (1977), on Mao's wife, is informative but overly sympathetic to its subject. Chiang Kai-shek and the Nationalist defeat are studied in S. Pepper, *Civil war in China: the political struggles, 1945–1948* (1978), and B. Crozier, *The man who lost China* (1976), solid despite the journalistic title. Books focusing on U.S. relations with China include H. Feis, *The China tangle: the American effort in China from Pearl Harbor to the Marshall mission** (1953); W. I. Cohen, *America's response to China: an interpretive history of Sino-American relations** (1971); F. R. Dulles, *American policy toward Communist China, 1949–1969* (1972); M. Schaller, *The U.S. crusade in China, 1938–1945* (1979); and J. K. Fairbank, *China perceived: images and policies in Chinese-American relations* (1977), by one of the most thoughtful students of China. The role of women is examined in M. Wolf and R. Witke (eds.), *Women in Chinese society* (1974); D. Davin, *Womanwork: women and the party in revolutionary China* (1976); and E. Croll, *Feminism and socialism in China* (1978). A challenging book examining "human nature" and government policy is D. J. Munro, *The concept of man in contemporary China** (1977). The best introduction to changes since Mao is R. P. Suttmeier, *Science, technology, and China's drive for modernization* (1980). Two ambitious efforts at comparative studies are W. Rosenberg and M. B. Young, *Transforming Russia and China: revolutionary struggle in the twentieth century* (1982), not completely successful; and T. Skocpol, *Status and social revolutions: a comparative analysis of France, Russia, and China** (1979), by a sociologist. A perceptive study of Western travelers in the past half-century overly exuberant in their observations of the changes brought by revolution is P. Hollander, *Political pilgrims: travels of Western intellectuals to the Soviet Union, China, and Cuba, 1928–1978* (1981).

Developments in southeast Asia are covered in the collaborative volume, D. J. Steinberg (ed.), *In search of southeast Asia: a modern history* (1971); J. F. Cady, *The history of postwar southeast Asia** (1975); and J. M. Van der Kroef, *Communism in southeast Asia* (1980).

The Emergent Nations: Asia and Africa

[The literature here is enormous, and no attempt can be made to cite the many studies of individual countries; the books mentioned in Chapters XV and XVIII also should be consulted.] Works of a general nature that serve as thoughtful introductions are R. Emerson, *From empire to nation: the rise to self-assertion of Asian and African peoples** (1960), a book full of insights; H. Tinker, *Race, conflict, and the international order: from empire to the United Nations* (1977), a concise survey of the transition from colonies to new nations; A. P. Thornton, *Imperialism in the twentieth century* (1977), cited in Chapter XV; M. Perham, *Colonial sequence, 1930–1949* (1967); R. von Albertini, *Decolonization: the administration and future of the colonies, 1919–1960* (1971); E. Kedourie, *Nationalism in Asia and Africa* (1971); and F. Brockway, *The colonial revolution* (1974). Of special interest is W. R. Louis, *Imperialism at bay: the United States and the decolonization of the British Empire, 1941–1945* (1978), focusing on Roosevelt and anti-imperial pressures on Britain during the war. A large-scale, collaborative history of decolonization in Africa is under way, of which the first available volume is P. Gifford and W. R. Louis (eds.), *The transfer of power in Africa: decolonization, 1940–1960* (1982). There are informative volumes on the developing countries in the Modern Nations in Historical Perspective series.

The impact of modernization is examined historically and comparatively in C. E. Black, *The dynamics of modernization: a study in comparative history** (1966); I. R. Sinai's two books, *The challenge of modernization** (1964) and *In search of the modern world* (1968); and D. A. Rustow, *A world of nations: problems of political modernization** (1967). An impressive, and discouraging, study is G. Myrdal, *Asian drama: an inquiry into the poverty of nations** (3 vols., 1968), which may be supplemented by M. Lipton, *Why poor people stay poor* (1977), both emphasizing continuing mass poverty in the poorer countries. A valuable economic analysis is provided in P. Bairoch, *The economic development of the Third World since 1900** (trans. 1975). The status of women in selected parts of the developing world is explored in N. J. Hafkin and E. C. Bay (eds.), *Women in Africa: studies in social and economic change* (1976), and L. Beck and N. R. Keddie (eds.), *Women in the Muslim world* (1978).

For the Middle East and its international implications, see, among many accounts providing a historical perspective, J. J. Malone, *The Arab lands of western Asia** (1973); J. Berque, *Egypt: imperialism and revolution* (1972); A. Marsot, *Egypt's liberal experiment* (1977); A. Williams, *Britain and*

France in the Middle East and North Africa, 1914–1967 (1969), cited in Chapter XV; H. M. Sachar, *Europe leaves the Middle East, 1936–1954* (1976); W. R. Polk, *The United States and the Arab world* (1965); F. J. Khouri, *The Arab-Israeli dilemma* (1968); and N. R. Keddie, *The Middle East and beyond* (1980). The best histories of Israel are N. Lucas, *The modern history of Israel* (1979), and H. M. Sachar, *A history of Israel: from the rise of Zionism to our time* (rev., 1979), cited in Chapter XIV. A detailed study of the founding of the state is M. J. Cohen, *Palestine: retreat from the mandate: the making of British policy, 1936–1945* (1978). Iran may be studied in R. W. Cottam, *Nationalism in Iran* (rev., 1979), the best introduction, and N. R. Keddie, *Roots of revolution: an interpretive history of modern Iran** (1981), both cited in Chapter XVIII; in E. Abrahamian, *Iran between two revolutions** (1983); and in D. Wilber, *Iran: past and present: from monarchy to Islamic republic* (1983).

For contemporary India and south Asia, the best introduction is W. N. Brown, *The United States and India, Pakistan, and Bangladesh* (rev., 1972), cited in Chapter XVIII. One finds a balanced assessment of achievements and shortcomings in K. Batia, *The ordeal of nationhood: a social study of India since independence, 1947–1970* (1971); and the same author also has written *Indira: a biography of Prime Minister Gandhi* (1974), which may be compared with Z. Masani, *Indira Gandhi: a biography* (1976), informative for contemporary India as well as its subject. R. Jahan, *Pakistan: failure in national integration* (1972), is a serious effort to assess the failure to integrate East Bengal which resulted in the emergence of Bangladesh. Developments in Indonesia may be approached through an excellent biographical account, J. D. Legge, *Sukarno: a political biography* (1972).

For Africa, to the general histories cited in Chapter XV, one may add J. Hatch, *A history of postwar Africa** (1965); E. Mortimer, *France and the Africans, 1944–1960* (1969); R. I. Rotberg, *The rise of nationalism in central Africa: the making of Malawi and Zambia, 1873–1964* (1965); G. J. Bender, *Angola under the Portuguese: the myth and the reality* (1978); A. G. Hopkins, *An economic history of West Africa* (1973); and C. Young, *Ideology and development in Africa* (1982).

The stormy beginnings of Zaïre are studied in J. Gérard-Libois, *Katanga secession* (1966), and in C. Young, *Politics in the Congo: decolonization and independence* (1965); and the conflict over the Ibo secession in Nigeria is examined in J. J. Stremlau, *The international politics of the Nigerian civil war, 1967–1970** (1977). For South Africa, the best introduction to the contemporary scene is L. Thompson and A. Prior, *South African politics** (1982); the racial problem is also examined in G. Le May, *Black and white in South Africa** (1971). Two interesting comparative studies are G. M. Frederickson, *White supremacy: a comparative study in American and South African history* (1981), and J. W. Cell, *The highest stage of white supremacy: the origins of segregation in South Africa and the American South* (1982). An excellent historical narrative focusing on the twentieth century is T. R. H. Davenport, *South Africa: a modern history* (1977).

The Western Countries [and Japan] since 1945

WESTERN EUROPE. A thoughtful introduction to Europe as a whole in the postwar era is provided with detail and insight by W. Laqueur, *Europe since Hitler: the rebirth of Europe** (rev., 1982); for the 1970s, the same author has written *A continent astray: Europe, 1970–1978* (1979). Less comprehensive but also useful is M. Crouzet, *The European renaissance since 1945** (1971). Two other informative surveys are N. Luxemburg, *Europe since World War II: the big change* (rev., 1979), and D. W. Urwin, *Western Europe since 1945: a short political history** (rev., 1981). Political parties are examined in R. E. M. Irving, *The Christian Democratic parties of Western Europe* (1979); W. E. Patterson and A. H. Thomas (eds.), *Social Democratic parties in Western Europe* (1977); and N. McInnes, *The Communist parties of Western Europe* (1975). For economic developments in the earlier years, M. M. Postan, *An economic history of Western Europe, 1945–1964** (1967), and C. P. Kindleberger, *Europe's postwar growth* (1967), are important. There are some penetrating observations to be found in R. Aron, *In defense of decadent Europe* (trans. 1979).

The development of the postwar welfare state is carefully examined by the British study group, Political and Economic Planning, in *Economic planning and policies in Britain, France, and Germany* (1968), and in P. Flora and A. J. Heidenheimer (eds.),

Development of welfare states in America and Europe (1981), while A. Shonfield, *Modern capitalism: the changing balance of public and private power** (1969), provides illuminating insights into a key aspect of contemporary economic life as a whole. For social developments, one may turn to S. Rothman, *European society and politics: Britain, France, and Germany** (1976), and for an interesting comparative study, A. Marwick, *Class: image and reality in Britain, France, and America since 1930* (1980).

On postwar European economic cooperation and the movement toward unification, the most important study is W. Lipgens, *A history of European integration*, vol. I, *1945–1947: the formation of the European unity movement* (trans. 1982), with additional volumes projected. Other studies include W. O. Henderson, *The genesis of the Common Market* (1963); F. R. Willis, *France, Germany, and the new Europe, 1945–1967** (1968); R. Pryce, *The politics of the European Community* (1974); R. Vaughan, *Twentieth-century Europe: paths to unity* (1979); and G. N. Minshull, *The new Europe: An economic geography of the EEC* (1978). On progress toward political unity, the best brief guide is D. Marquand, *Parliament for Europe* (1979), which may be supplemented by P. Scalingi, *The European Parliament: the three-decade search for a united Europe* (1980). The historical background to unification may be explored in J. Lukacs, *Decline and rise of Europe** (1965). Special studies include J. Gimbel, *The origins of the Marshall Plan* (1976), an important and controversial study; W. Diebold, Jr., *The Schuman Plan* (1959); H. A. Schmitt, *The path to European union: from the Marshall Plan to the Common Market* (1962); and by the same author, *European union: from Hitler to de Gaulle** (1969).

BRITAIN. [Many of the books cited for Chapter XIX also should be consulted.] Available surveys of postwar Britain are P. Calvocoressi, *The British experience, 1945–1975* (1978); C. J. Bartlett, *A history of postwar Britain, 1945–1974* (1977); D. Childs, *Britain since 1945: a political history* (1979); A. Sked and C. Cook, *Post-war Britain: a political history* (1979); and D. E. Ashford, *Policy and politics in Britain* (1981). Other useful studies are S. H. Beer, *British politics in the collectivist age* (1965); A. Sampson, *The new anatomy of Britain** (rev., 1983); and P. Gregg, *The welfare state: an economic and social history of Great Britain from 1945*

to the present day (1969). Why the nation that launched the industrial era has lagged in the contemporary era is analyzed in different ways in M. J. Wilner, *English culture and the decline of the industrial spirit, 1850–1980* (1981), and in B. Porter, *Britain, Europe, and the world, 1850–1982: illusions of grandeur* (1983). Two other thoughtful analyses are D. Howell, *British social democracy: a study in development and decay* (1976), and A. Marwick, *British society since 1945** (1982).

FRANCE. The early postwar years and history of the Fourth Republic may be approached through G. Wright, *The reshaping of French democracy* (1948); E. M. Earle (ed.), *Modern France: problems of the Third and Fourth Republics* (1951); P. M. Williams, *Crisis and compromise: politics in the Fourth Republic** (1965); and A. Werth, *France, 1940–1955* (1957), cited in Chapter XX. Postwar developments are placed in historical perspective in J. C. Cairns, *France** (1965), and D. Johnson, *France* (1969), and some interesting general observations are available in T. Zeldin, *The French* (1983).

For the Fifth Republic, informative volumes are P. M. Williams and M. Harrison, *Politics and society in de Gaulle's republic** (1972); H. W. Ehrmann, *Politics in France** (rev., 1976); R. C. Macridis, *French politics in transition* (1975); D. L. Hanley and others, *Contemporary France: politics and society since 1945** (1979); and D. Pickles, *Problems of contemporary French politics* (1982). For social changes, J. Ardagh, *The new France: de Gaulle and after* (rev., 1977), is highly informative. Economic developments are traced in J. J. Carré and others, *French economic growth* (trans. 1975), and economic planning in P. Bauchet, *Economic planning: the French experience* (trans. 1964), and R. M. Kuisel, *Capitalism and the state in modern France: renovation and economic management in the twentieth century* (1981), which places governmental direction of the economy in historical perspective. Important political studies are A. Kriegel, *The French Communists: profile of a people* (trans. 1972); R. Tiersky, *French Communism, 1920–1972* (1974); R. E. M. Irving, *Christian democracy in France* (1973); J. Hellman, *Emmanuel Mounier and the new Catholic left, 1930–1950*; and B. E. Brown, *Socialism of a different kind: reshaping the left in France* (1982). J. Lacouture has written a biography of Pierre Mendès-France (trans. 1983). Two valuable sociological studies are J. Marceau, *Class and status in France: economic change and social mobility, 1945–1975* (1977), and E. N. Suleiman, *Elites in French society: the politics of survival* (1979). French and Italian trade unionism are analyzed and compared in P. Lange and others, *Unions, change, and crisis . . . 1945–1980* (1982).

The ill-fated effort to retain Algeria is recounted in A. Horne, *A savage war of peace: Algiers, 1954–1962* (1978), a comprehensive account; J. Talbott, *The war without a name: France in Algeria, 1954–1962* (1980); and T. Smith, *The French stake in Algeria, 1945–1962* (1978). [The war in Indochina is discussed below.] There are biographical accounts of de Gaulle by D. Schoenbrun* (1966), A. Werth* (1966), J. Lacouture (trans. 1966), B. Crozier (1973), and B. Ledwidge (1983). Despite the title, S. Hoffman, *Decline or renewal? France since the 1930s* (1974), focuses on the Fifth Republic and is informative on de Gaulle and his accomplishments. Two insightful analyses of de Gaulle's foreign policy are L. P. de Ménil, *Who speaks for Europe? the vision of Charles de Gaulle* (1977), and P. G. Cerny, *The politics of grandeur: ideological aspects of de Gaulle's foreign policy* (1980). Aspects of French thought are explored in two difficult but rewarding books, H. S. Hughes, *The obstructed path: French social thought, 1930–1960** (1968), and G. Lichtheim, *Marxism in modern France* (1966).

GERMANY, WEST AND EAST. The best introductions are A. Grosser, *Germany in our time** (1971); D. P. Conradt, *The German polity** (1978); F. Cameron, *Contemporary Germany* (1978); and E. Hartrich, *The fourth and richest Reich* (1980); while R. Dahrendorf, *Society and democracy in Germany* (1967), and G. A. Craig, *The Germans* (1982), cited in Chapter XIII, provide important insights. Four other useful introductions are M. Balfour, *West Germany* (1968); L. J. Edinger, *Politics in Germany** (1968); H. W. Gatzke, *Germany and the United States: a "special relationship"?* (American Foreign Policy Library series, 1980); and R. Morgan, *The United States and West Germany, 1945–1973* (1974). On the occupation, the first postwar decade, and economic recovery, there are E. F. Ziemke, *The United States army in the occupation of Germany, 1944–1946* (1977), an outstanding study, one of the final volumes in the 79-volume history of the American army in the Second World War; H. Zink,

The United States and Germany, 1945–1955 (1957); J. Gimbel, *The American occupation of Germany: politics and the military, 1945–1949* (1968); F. Golay, *The founding of the Federal Republic of Germany* (1958); and H. C. Wallich, *Mainsprings of the German revival* (1955). For the Adenauer years, see E. Alexander, *Adenauer and the new Germany* (1957), and R. Hiscocks, *The Adenauer era** (1966). L. J. Edinger offers some psychological interpretations in a biography of the Social Democratic leader, *Kurt Schumacher: a study in personality and political behavior* (1965); and K. P. Tauber studies a special subject in great detail in *Beyond the eagle and swastika: German nationalism since 1945* (2 vols., 1967). For the Eastern zone, J. P. Nettl, *The Eastern zone and Soviet policy in Germany, 1945–1950* (1951), may be supplemented by K. Southeimer and W. Bleek, *The government and politics of East Germany* (1976), and D. Childs, *The GDR: Moscow's German ally** (1983). The conflict over Berlin is ably examined in J. M. Schick, *The Berlin crisis, 1958–1962* (1971), and in R. M. Slusser, *The Berlin crisis of 1961* (1973). Willy Brandt's efforts to improve Soviet-West German relations are studied in A. Stent, *From embargo to Ostpolitik: the political economy of West German-Soviet relations, 1955–1980* (1982).

ITALY. For the Italian republic, the best introduction is H. S. Hughes, *The United States and Italy** (rev., 1979), cited in Chapter XIV; other useful studies are M. Grindrod, *The new Italy: transition from war to peace* (1947) and *The rebuilding of Italy: politics and economics, 1945–1955* (1955); N. Kogan, *A political history of postwar Italy* (2 vols., 1966, 1981); G. Mammarella, *Italy after fascism: a political history, 1943–1965* (rev., 1966); and E. Wiskemann, *Italy since 1945* (1971). Economic developments are studied in K. Allen and A. Stevenson, *An introduction to the Italian economy* (1975).

IBERIAN PENINSULA AND GREECE. S. G. Payne, *A history of Spain and Portugal* (2 vols., 1973), cited in Chapter III, is indispensable as background. On Spain: Payne, *Franco's Spain** (1967) and the essays he has edited, *Politics and society in twentieth-century Spain** (1976), and G. Hills, *Spain* (1970), are informative for the postwar years, as is P. Preston (ed.), *Spain in crisis: the evolution and decline of the Franco regime* (1976); and on the transition to a parliamentary democracy, there is available R. Carr and J. P. Fusi, *Spain: dictatorship to democracy* (1979). On twentieth-century Portugal, one may read D. L. Wheeler, *Republican Portugal: a political history, 1910–1926* (1978); H. Kay, *Salazar and modern Portugal* (1976); A. De Figueiredo, *Portugal: fifty years of dictatorship* (1976); and A. H. De Oliveira Marques, *History of Portugal** (rev., 1976), with an epilogue for the years since 1972. Postwar Greek political and social developments are examined in W. H. McNeill, *The metamorphosis of Greece since World War II* (1978).

JAPAN. E. O. Reischauer, *The United States and Japan** (rev., 1965), *Japan: the story of a nation** (rev., 1977), and *The Japanese** (1977), all cited in Chapter XIII, are invaluable. Two good studies of the occupation are K. Kawai, *Japan's American interlude* (1960), and J. C. Perry, *Beneath the eagle's wings: Americans in occupied Japan* (1980). Two important studies of economic developments are J. B. Cohen, *Japan's post-war economy* (1958), and G. C. Allen, *Japan's economic recovery* (1958), and of special interest is E. F. Vogel, *Japan as number one: lessons for America** (1979).

THE UNITED STATES. Although no listing on domestic developments in the contemporary United States is possible here, an introduction to the depression, war, and postwar years is provided in G. E. Mowry, *The urban nation, 1920–1960** (1965); C. N. Degler, *Affluence and anxiety: the United States since 1945** (1968); and W. E. Leuchtenburg, *A troubled feast: American society since 1945** (rev., 1979). Two volumes providing perspectives on contemporary social and economic problems are J. T. Patterson, *America's struggle against poverty, 1900–1980* (1981), and R. Polenberg, *One nation divisible: class, race, and ethnicity in the United States since 1938* (1980).

The World Economy and International Relations since 1945

Two good introductions to the global economy in the post-1945 years are W. W. Rostow, *The world economy: history and prospect* (1977), and W. M. Scammell, *The international economy since 1945* (1980). One may also read A. Fishlow and others, *Rich and poor nations in the world economy* (1978); P. R. Ehrlich and A. H. Ehrlich,

Population, resources, environment: issues in human ecology (1970); and a brief challenging essay by W. A. Lewis, *The evolution of the international economic order** (1978).

Several books on the wartime origins of the Soviet-Western rift, and "atomic bomb diplomacy" in 1945, have been described at the end of the previous chapter and should be consulted. Among attempts to reconstruct historically the major aspects of the Cold War are the following: P. Calvocoressi, *International politics since 1945** (1968); L. Halle, *The Cold War as history* (1967); W. Knapp, *A history of war and peace, 1939–1965* (1967); J. Lukacs, *A new history of the Cold War** (rev., 1966), and the same author's *1945: year zero* (1978); D. Rees, *The age of containment: the Cold War** (1967); D. Donnelly, *Struggle for the world: the Cold War, 1917–1965* (1965); and A. Fontaine, *History of the Cold War* (2 vols., trans. 1968–1969). Valuable insights are provided in G. F. Kennan, *Russia and the West under Lenin and Stalin** (1961) and *American diplomacy, 1900–1950** (1951); L. F. Fischer, *Russia, America, and the world* (1961); and A. B. Ulam, *The rivals: America and Russia since World War II* (1971), and *Dangerous relations: the Soviet Union in world politics, 1970–1982* (1983).

A large "revisionist" literature has appeared vehemently critical of the United States and generally blaming American foreign policy and American political or economic postwar ambitions for the Cold War. A sampling would include K. Ingram, *History of the Cold War* (1955); D. F. Fleming, *The Cold War and its origins, 1917–1960* (2 vols., 1961); W. A. Williams, *The tragedy of American diplomacy* (1959) and *American-Russian relations, 1781–1947* (1952); G. Kolko, *The politics of war . . . 1943 to 1945** (1969) and, with J. Kolko, *The limits of power . . . 1945 to 1954** (1972); D. Horowitz, *The free world colossus* (rev., 1971); G. Alperowitz, *Atomic diplomacy: Hiroshima and Potsdam** (1965), cited in Chapter XIX; and L. C. Gardner, *Architects of illusion* (1970). Other revisionist accounts, varying in their assessment of blame, would include T. G. Patterson, *Soviet-American confrontation: postwar reconstruction and the origins of the Cold War* (1973); the same author's *On every front: the making of the Cold War** (1979); B. Kuklick, *American policy and the division of Germany: the clash with Russia over reparations* (1972); L. A. Rose, *After Yalta* (1973) and *Dubious victory: the United States and* the end of World War II (1973); G. C. Herring, *Aid to Russia, 1941–1946: strategy, diplomacy, and the origins of the Cold War* (1973); L. E. Davis, *The Cold War begins: Soviet-American conflict over Eastern Europe* (1974); and R. Douglas, *From war to Cold War, 1942–1948* (1981).

A book that does not ignore American errors and miscalculations but rejects conspiratorial interpretations is J. L. Gaddis, *The United States and the origins of the Cold War, 1941–1947** (1972), a judicious study, probably the best on the subject; it may be supplemented by the same author's *Strategies of containment: a critical appraisal of postwar American national security policy* (1982), and by D. Yergin, *Shattered peace: the origins of the Cold War and the national security state* (1977), also a reasonable and persuasive account. Generally sympathetic to the American position are H. Feis, *From trust to terror: the onset of the Cold War, 1945–1950,** cited in Chapter XX, and R. Aron, *The imperial republic: the United States and the world, 1945–1973* (trans. 1974). Many of the revisionists receive harsh treatment in R. J. Maddox, *The new left and the origins of the Cold War* (1973); in J. Siracusa, *New left diplomatic histories and historians* (1973); and in R. W. Tucker, *The radical left and American foreign policy* (1971), the latter, a balanced analysis.

The founding of the United Nations is studied in R. B. Russell, *A history of the United Nations, 1940–1945* (1958), and in F. P. King, *The new internationalism: Allied policy and the European peace, 1939–1945* (1973). Its subsequent history may be traced in C. M. Eichelberger, *The UN: the first twenty years* (1965), and in E. Luard, *A history of the United Nations*, vol. I, *The years of Western domination, 1945–1955* (1982), with other volumes to follow.

On nuclear weapons and international relations, the following interesting, and disturbing, books are recommended: P. M. S. Blackett, *Atomic weapons and East-West relations* (1956); G. Herken, *The winning weapon: the atomic bomb in the Cold War, 1945–1950* (1980); H. A. Kissinger, *Nuclear weapons and foreign policy* (1957); G. F. Kennan, *Russia, the atom, and the West* (1958); the same author's *The nuclear delusion: Soviet-American relations in the atomic age* (1983); H. Kahn, *On thermonuclear war** (1960); D. E. Lilienthal, *Change, hope and the bomb** (1963); M. Lerner, *The age of overkill* (1964); and two books by M. Mandelbaum offering the best

picture of the "balance of terror": *The United States and nuclear weapons, 1946–1976* (1979) and *The nuclear revolution: international politics before and after Hiroshima** (1981). A special subject is examined in R. A. Divine, *Blowing on the wind: the nuclear test ban debate, 1954–1960* (1978).

Two books that admirably examine Western Europe's role in the postwar setting are A. W. DePorte, *Europe between the superpowers: the enduring alliance* (1979), and A. Grosser, *The Western alliance: European-American relations since 1945* (trans. 1980).

An excellent introduction to Asia's role in world politics is D. F. Lach and E. S. Wehrle, *International politics in East Asia since World War II* (1975). The best general account of the Korean War is D. Rees, *Korea: the limited war* (1964), which may be supplemented by G. Henderson, *Korea: the politics of the vortex* (1968); R. R. Simmons, *The strained alliance: Pyongyang, Moscow, and the politics of the Korean civil war* (1975); and for the American role, J. Carridi, *The Korean War and American politics* (1968), and W. W. Stueck, Jr., *The road to confrontation: American policy toward China and Korea, 1917–1950** (1951).

On Vietnam, successful efforts to explore Vietnamese history and to place events in historical perspective are J. T. McAlister, *Vietnam: the origins of revolution* (1969); D. G. Mair, *Vietnamese anticolonialism* (1971); A. B. Woodside, *Community and revolution in modern Vietnam* (1976); W. J. Duiker, *The rise of nationalism in Vietnam, 1900–1941* (1976); and T. Hodgkin, *Vietnam: the revolutionary path* (1981). A widely read book at the time of the war, critical of the American intrusion, was F. Fitzgerald, *Fire in the lake* (1972). The last phase of the French involvement in Indochina is graphically portrayed in B. B. Fall, *Hell in a very small place: the siege of Dien Bien Phu* (1967) and his other writings. The American involvement may be studied in G. Herring, *America's longest war: the United States and Vietnam, 1950–1975** (1979), an outstanding account; two books stressing the military aspects: D. R. Palmer, *Summons of the trumpet: U.S.-Vietnam in perspective* (1977), and H. G. Summers, Jr., *On strategy: a critical analysis of the Vietnam War* (1982); A. L. A. Patti, *Why Vietnam? prelude to America's albatross* (1980); and G. Lewy, *America in Vietnam** (1978), seeking to demonstrate the morality and legality of American conduct. D. Halberstam, *The best* *and the brightest** (1972), demonstrated that American involvement stemmed from the desire to avoid a repetition of the appeasement of the 1930s. Two thoughtful studies are J. Schell, *The time of illusion** (1976), and E. R. May, *Lessons of the past: the use and misuse of history in American foreign policy* (1973). Exceptionally useful for postwar American foreign policy is S. Hoffman, *Primacy or world order: American foreign policy since the Cold War* (1978), and the essays in W. P. Bundy (ed.), *Two hundred years of American foreign policy* (1977). On guerrilla warfare in Vietnam and elsewhere, two outstanding books are W. Laqueur, *Guerrilla: a historical and critical study* (1977), and R. Asprey, *War in the shadows: the guerrilla in history* (1976); on related subjects, see J. B. Bell, *On revolt: strategies of national liberation* (1976), and A. Parry, *Terrorism* (1976).

Science and Thought

[The books described in Chapter XIV should be consulted as well as the histories of science listed in Chapter VII.] An intriguing survey of contemporary intellectual trends is R. N. Stromberg, *After everything: Western intellectual history since 1945** (1975). A successful effort to reassess the idea of progress in the current era is W. W. Wagar, *Good tidings: the belief in progress from Darwin to Marcuse* (1972), cited in Chapter XIV. H. S. Hughes, *An essay for our times* (1950), provides insights into modern cultural perplexities, and in *The sea change: the migration of social thought, 1930–1965* (1975), examines some key social thinkers who fled the Third Reich.

On the new physics, in addition to I. B. Cohen, *The birth of a new physics* (1960), and other titles cited earlier, see B. Schonland, *The atomists 1805–1933* (1968); B. Cline, *The questioners: physicists and the quantum theory** (1965); and L. S. Swenson, Jr., *Genesis of relativity: Einstein in context* (1979). On the biological revolution, one may turn to R. Clowes, *The structure of life* (1967); R. Olby, *The path to the double helix* (1974); P. B. and J. S. Medawar, *The life science: current ideas of biology* (1977); G. Allen, *Life science in the twentieth century* (1975); J. Goodfield, *Playing God: genetic engineering and the manipulation of life* (1977); and H. F. Judson, *The eighth day of creation: the makers of the revolution in biology* (1979). In J. Watson, *The double helix: a personal ac-*

count of the discovery of the structure of DNA (rev., 1979), a scientist describes himself and other biologists at work. A probing and fascinating study is C. Sagan, *The dragons of Eden: speculations on the origins of human intelligence* (1977). Various scientific developments and their implications are discussed in A. E. E. McKenzie, *The major achievements of science* (2 vols., 1960); C. D. Darlington, *The evolution of man and society* (1969); and K. Coutts-Smith, *The dream of Icarus* (1969). On space exploration and its implications, one may turn to V. Cronin, *The view from planet Earth: man looks at the cosmos* (1981). Useful introductions to the activities of the professional philosophers are provided in J. Passmore, *A hundred years of philosophy* (1968); in A. J. Ayer and others, *The revolution in philosophy* (1956); and in M. White (ed.), *The age of analysis** (1955), a convenient anthology. New approaches to literature and other disciplines are explored in E. Kurzweil, *The age of structuralism: Lévi-Strauss to Foucault* (1980). Aspects of modern religious thought are explored in S. P. Schilling, *Contemporary continental theologians* (1966), and a special subject is examined in G. Lewy, *Religion and revolution* (1974). An impressive contemporary effort to reconcile science and traditional religion is S. L. Jaki, *The road of science and the ways to God* (1978). Introductions to the complexities of contemporary art are provided in A. Neumeyer, *The search for meaning in modern art* (trans. 1964); H. Rosenberg, *The anxious object: art today and its audience* (1964); and G. Woods, *Art without boundaries, 1950–1970* (1972). On economic thought, one may read M. Stewart, *Keynes and after* (1968); C. Napoleoni, *Economic thought of the twentieth century* (1971); and R. Skidelsky (ed.), *The end of the Keynesian era: essays on the disintegration of the Keynesian political economy* (1977). Some volumes listed below in the final section of this bibliography also are relevant to science, religion, thought, and society.

Activist Movements

For the events of 1968, one may consult S. M. Lipset, *Rebellion in the university* (1972); R. Aron, *The elusive revolution* (1969); B. E. Brown, *Protest in Paris: anatomy of a revolt** (1974); and A. Touraine, *The May movement: revolt and reform** (trans. 1979). Two documentary collections are A. Schnapp and P. Vidal-Naquest (eds.), *French student uprising, 1967–1968* (1971), and V. Fišera (ed.), *Writing on the wall: France, May 1968, a documentary anthology* (1979). For insight into the emergence of youth as a "social phenomenon," see the study by J. R. Gillis, cited in the introductory section of the bibliography, *Youth and history: tradition and change in European age relations, 1770 to the present* (rev., 1981), and also L. S. Feuer, *The conflict of generations* (1969). For an introduction to the "new left" in the United States, one may turn to I. Unger, *The movement: a history of the American new left, 1959–1972* (1974). On the women's liberation movement, there is no historical account available for Europe or for the non-Western world comparable to M. P. Ryan, *Womanhood in America from colonial times to the present* (rev., 1983), a concise and authoritative study, which may be supplemented by C. R. Berkin and M. B. Norton (eds.), *Women of America: a history* (1979), and W. R. Chafe, *Women and equality: changing patterns in American culture* (1977). To the volumes cited in the introductory section and elsewhere, one may add W. O'Neill, *The woman's movement: feminism in the United States and England* (1969); E. Boserup, *Women's role in economic development* (1970); M. L. Carden, *The new feminist movement* (1974); and O. Banks, *Faces of feminism: a study of feminism as a social movement* (1981). A useful anthology for France is E. Marks and I. de Courtivron (eds.), *New French feminism: an anthology* (1980).

Past, Present, and Future

Although no attempt can be made to list the many assessments of contemporary problems, there may be some point in asking the reader to consider the titles and intents of these books: T. H. Von Laue, *The global city: freedom, power and necessity in the age of world revolutions* (1969); R. A. Nisbet, *Twilight of authority* (1975); B. Ward, *The West at bay** (1948), *Faith and freedom** (1954), *The rich nations and the poor nations** (1962), *Five ideas that changed the world** (1959) [which she identifies as nationalism, industrialism, colonialism, communism, and internationalism], and *The home of man** (1976); E. Fischer, *The passing of the European age: a study of the transfer of Western civilization and its renewal in other continents* (1943, 1948); C. P. Snow, *The two cultures and the scientific revolution* (1959; rev., 1963); L. Graham, *Between science and values* (1981); M. Berman, *The reenchantment of the world** (1981); E. O. Wilson, *On human nature* (1978); and K. Bock, *Human nature and history: a response to sociobiology** (1982).

To these may be added H. Arendt, *The human condition** (1958); K. E. Boulding, *The meaning of the twentieth century* (1964); K. W. Deutsch, *Nationalism and its alternatives* (1969); J. Herz, *The nation-state and the crisis of world politics* (1976); M. Olson, *The rise and decline of nations* (1982); B. Bluestone and B. Harrison, *The deindustrialization of America* (1982); three books by J. K. Galbraith: *The new industrial state* (1967), *Money: whence it came, where it went* (1975), and *The voice of the poor: essays in economic and political persuasion* (1983); W. Leontief, *The future of the world economy* (1978); L. S. Stavrianos, *The promise of the coming dark age** (1976); R. G. Heilbroner, *An inquiry into the human prospect* (1974); G. F. Kennan, *The cloud of danger* (1977); E. P. Thompson, *Beyond the Cold War* (1982); and J. Schell, *The fate of the earth** (1982).

Problems and Readings*

Materials on science and intellectual developments are available in L. P. Williams (ed.), *Relativity theory: its origins and impact on modern thought* (1968), and in W. W. Wagar (ed.), *Science, faith, and man: European thought since 1914* (1968). Events in Asia are examined in T. W. Wallbank (ed.), *The partition of India: causes and responsibilities* (1966), and P. P. Y. Loh, *The Kuomintang debacle of 1949: conquest or collapse?* (1965); and a special subject is explored in J. W. Baird (ed.), *From Nuremberg to My Lai* (1972). Two European countries are studied in H. L. Winkler (ed.), *Twentieth-century Britain: national power and social welfare* (1976), and J. C. Cairns (ed.), *Contemporary France: illusion, conflict, and regeneration* (1978); the movement toward European unity is examined in F. R. Willis (ed.), *European integration* (1975). The background to the Cold War may be examined in N. A. Graebner (ed.), *The Cold War: a conflict of ideology and power* (rev., 1976); T. G. Patterson (ed.), *The origins of the Cold War* (1970); L. C. Gardner (ed.), *Origins of the Cold War* (1970); and C. S. Maier (ed.), *The origins of the Cold War and contemporary Europe* (1978).

Illustration Sources

11 Scala New York/Florence, Vatican Museum; 46 The British Museum; 94 (right) Scala New York/Florence, Biblioteca Estense, Modena; 90 (left) Alinari-Art Reference Bureau; 94–95 Scala New York/Florence, Palazzo Vecchio, Florence; 96 Scala New York/Florence, Palazzo Medici, Riccardi, Florence; 97 Scala New York/Florence, Museo Medici, Florence; 98, 99 Alinari-Art Reference Bureau; 100 (above, below) © G. B. Pineider, Biblioteca Riccardiana, Florence; 101 Scala New York/Florence, Museo San Marco, Florence; 102 Alinari-Art Reference Bureau; 103 Brogi-Art Reference Bureau; 104 Harcourt Brace Jovanovich, Inc., Harbrace Photo, Collection of Mr. and Mrs. David H. H. Felix; 148 (right) Scala New York/Florence, Biblioteca Medicea Laurenziana, Florence; 148 (left) New York Public Library; 149 Patrimonio Nacional, Alcázar, Seville, Foto Mas; 150–151 © Frans Halsmuseum, A. Dingjan; 152 (right, left), 153 (above) New York Public Library; 153 (below) Rijksmuseum, Amsterdam; 154, 155 New York Public Library; 156 The American Numismatic Society; 194 New York Public Library; 195 The British Museum; 196 (above) Collection H. M. the Queen, A. C. Cooper, Ltd.; 196 (below), 197 (right) Musée Versailles, Service Photographic, Musées Nationaux; 197 (left) The Bettmann Archive; 198 (above) Staatsbibliothek Berlin; 198 (below) New York Public Library; 199 Sovfoto; 200 Kunsthistorisches Museum, Vienna; 201 The Mansell Collection; 202 Radio Times Hulton Picture Library; 203 New York Public Library; 204 Novosti Press Agency, The Historical Museum in Moscow; 241 The Chase Manhattan Bank Museum of Moneys of the World, New York; 276 New York Public Library; 302 The Metropolitan Museum of Art, Gift of William H. Huntington; 350 Snark International, Versailles Museum; 391 The British Museum; 425 Kunsthistorisches Museum, Vienna; 470 Historiches Museum, Frankfurt am Main; 502, 503, 504 (above, below) The Mansell Collection; 505 New York Public Library; 506 (above) Staatsbibliothek Berlin; 506 (below) The Mansell Collection; 507 New York Public Library; 508 (above) Radio Times Hulton Picture Library; 508 (below) © René-Jacques; 509 © H. Roger-Viollet; 510 The American Numismatic Society; 550 Snark International, Art Gallery, Birmingham, England; 608 The American Numismatic Society; 650 The Mansell Collection; 651 New York Public Library; 652 (above, below), 653, 654 The Mansell Collection; 655 New York Public Library; 656, 657, 658 Radio Times Hulton Picture Library; 659 Photoworld, Inc.; 660 Popperfoto; 696 Sovfoto from USSR Magazine; 740 The American Numismatic Society; 795 © Fred Ward/Black Star; 830 IBM; 831 © Abbas/Gamma/Liaison Agency; 832 © Camera Tres/Black Star; 833 (top) Alain Nogues/Sygma, (bottom) Gamma/Liaison; 834 © Sanford H. Roth/Rapho/Photo Researchers; 836 © Francois Lochon/Gamma/Liaison Agency; 837 © C. Spengler/Sygma; 838 © Andanson/Sygma; 839 © Marc & Evelyne Bernheim/Woodfin Camp & Associates; 840 © Georg Gerster/Rapho/Photo Researchers; 841 © Sepp Seitz, 1978/Woodfin Camp & Associates; 841 © Richard Nowitz/Black Star; 842 NASA; 884 United Nations

Index

Dates given after names of rulers and popes are the years of reigns or pontificates; those given for all others are the years of birth and death.

Pronunciation is indicated where it is not obvious. With foreign words the purpose is not to show their exact pronunciation in their own language but to suggest how they may be acceptably pronounced in English. Fully Anglicized pronunciations are indicated by the abbreviation *Angl.* Pronunciation is shown by respelling, not by symbols, except that the following symbols are used for vowel sounds not found in English:

ø   Indicates the sound of ö as in Göttingen. To form this sound, purse the lips as if to say *o*, and then say *ay* as in *ate*.

U   indicates the sound of the French *u*, or of German *ü*. To form this sound, purse the lips as if to say *oo*, and then say *ee* as in *eat*.

aN, oN, uN, iN indicate the sounds of the French nasal vowels. Once learned, these are easily pronounced, roughly as follows: For aN, begin to pronounce the English word *on*, but avoid saying the consonant *n* and "nasalize" the *ah* sound instead. For oN do the same with the English *own*; for uN, with the English prefix *un-*; for iN, with the English word *an*.

The sound of *s* as in the word *treasure* is indicated by *zh*. This sound is common in English, though never found at the beginning or end of a word. *igh* always indicates the so-called long *i* as in *high*. The vowel sound of *hoot* is indicated by *oo*, that of *hood* by $\breve{oo}$.

Compared with English, the European languages are highly regular in their spelling, in that the same letters or combinations of letters are generally pronounced in the same way.

About
the Authors

ROBERT ROSWELL PALMER, Professor Emeritus of History at Yale University, was born in Chicago in 1909. After graduating from the University of Chicago, he received his doctorate from Cornell University in 1934. From 1936 to 1963 he taught at Princeton University, and was Dean of the Faculty of Arts and Sciences at Washington University in St. Louis from 1963 to 1966. He was President of the American Historical Association in 1970. Professor Palmer is the author of *Catholics and Unbelievers in Eighteenth Century France* (1939), *Twelve Who Ruled: The Year of the Terror in the French Revolution* (1941, 1958), and the two-volume *Age of the Democratic Revolution* (1959 and 1964), both volumes of which were History Book Club selections and the first of which won the Bancroft Prize in 1960. He has likewise written *The World of the French Revolution* (1970), which was also published in French in 1968, and *The School of the French Revolution* (1975). He edited the *Rand McNally Atlas of World History* (1957) and translated Georges Lefebvre's *Coming of the French Revolution* (1947) and Louis Bergeron's *France under Napoleon* (1981). He has contributed to a variety of journals and collaborative volumes in this country and Europe.

JOEL COLTON, Professor of History at Duke University, was born in New York City. He received his B.A. from the City College of New York and his M.A. and Ph.D. degrees from Columbia University. In 1947 he joined the Department of History at Duke University and chaired the department from 1967 to 1974. From 1974 to 1981, he was Director for Humanities at the Rockefeller Foundation. He has served on the Board of Editors of the *Journal of Modern History*, the advisory board of *Historical Abstracts*, several national committees of the American Historical Association, and as a vice-president of the Society for French Historical Studies and the International Commission on the History of Social Movements and Social Structures. He has been awarded Guggenheim, Rockefeller Foundation, and National Endowment for the Humanities fellowships, and is a Fellow of the American Academy of Arts and Sciences. He is the author of *Compulsory Labor Arbitration in France, 1936–1939* (1951), *Léon Blum: Humanist in Politics* (1966, French translation, 1968), for which he received a Mayflower Award, and *Twentieth Century* (1968, 1980), in the Time-Life Great Ages of Man series, and articles in various journals, encyclopedias, and collaborative volumes. He was appointed to the Phi Beta Kappa Visiting Scholar Program for 1983–1984.

A Note
on the Type

The text of this book is set in CALEDONIA, a Linotype face designed by W. A. Dwiggins, and redesigned for Compugraphic. It belongs to the family of printing types called "modern face" by printers—a term used to mark the change in style of type-letters that occurred about 1800. Caledonia borders on the general design of Scotch Modern, but is more freely drawn than that letter.

This book was composed by Arkotype Inc., New York, N.Y., and printed and bound by Kingsport Press, Kingsport, TN.

The maps were executed by Jean Tremblay.

The text and cover were designed by msl/Levavi & Levavi.

Contemporary Asia

ARCTIC OCEAN

SPITZBERGEN
(Norway)

FRANZ JOSEF LAND

SEVE
Ze

BARENTS SEA

NOVAYA ZEMLYA

KARA SEA

ATLANTIC OCEAN

Igarka

NORWAY

SWEDEN

FINLAND

Archangel

Vorkuta

Leningrad

E U R O P E

Moscow

S O V I E T

MTS. S SI

Yenisei R.

Kiev

Sverdlovsk

Ob R.

Tomsk

Kuibyshev

U R A L

Omsk

Novosibirsk

Istanbul

BLACK SEA

Astrakhan

Karaganda

Ankara

Batum

CASPIAN SEA

ARAL SEA

L. Balkhash

M E D I T E R R A N E A N   S E A

T U R K E Y

Baku

Tashkent

Urumchi

CYPRUS

SINKIANG

Lop Nor

LEBANON

SYRIA

Bukhara

Cairo

Suez Canal

ISRAEL

Teheran

AFGHANISTAN

JAMMU AND KASHMIR

TIBE

JORDAN

IRAQ

Baghdad

Kabul

Indus R.

Lahore

EGYPT

Basra

I R A N

PAKISTAN

SIKKIM

KUWAIT

NEPAL

SAUDI ARABIA

BAHRAIN

PERSIAN GULF

New Delhi

Ganges R.

RED SEA

Mecca

Riyadh

QATAR

SUDAN

UNITED ARAB EMIRATES

Karachi

I N D I A

Calcutta

OMAN

Muscat

BA

YEMEN

SOUTHERN YEMEN

Bombay

DJIBOUTI

Aden

ARABIAN SEA

Hyderabad

BAY OF BENG

SOCOTRA
(Britain)

Goa

ETHIOPIA

A F R I C A

Madras

Pondicherry

SOMALIA

LACCADIVE I.
(India)

Colombo

SRI LANKA

KENYA

MALDIVE ISLANDS

States Recognized as Independent After World War II

TANZANIA

0   500   1000 miles

INDIAN OCEAN